AF688667

Professional Responsibility in Litigation

THIRD EDITION

DOUGLAS R. RICHMOND,
BRIAN S. FAUGHNAN,
AND MICHAEL L. MATULA

AMERICAN BAR ASSOCIATION
Tort Trial and Insurance
Practice Section

Cover design by ABA Design.

The materials contained herein represent the opinions of the authors and/or the editors, and should not be construed to be the views or opinions of the law firms or companies with whom such persons are in partnership with, associated with, or employed by, nor of the American Bar Association or the Tort Trial & Insurance Practice Section unless adopted pursuant to the bylaws of the Association.

Nothing contained in this book is to be considered as the rendering of legal advice for specific cases, and readers are responsible for obtaining such advice from their own legal counsel. This book is intended for educational and informational purposes only.

© 2021 American Bar Association. All rights reserved.

No part of this publication may be reproduced, stored in a retrieval system, or transmitted in any form or by any means, electronic, mechanical, photocopying, recording, or otherwise, without the prior written permission of the publisher. For permission contact the ABA Copyrights & Contracts Department, copyright@americanbar.org, or complete the online form at http://www.americanbar.org/utility/reprint.html.

Printed in the United States of America.

25 24 23 22 21 5 4 3 2 1

A catalog record for this book is available from the Library of Congress.

Discounts are available for books ordered in bulk. Special consideration is given to state bars, CLE programs, and other bar-related organizations. Inquire at Book Publishing, ABA Publishing, American Bar Association, 321 N. Clark Street, Chicago, Illinois 60654-7598.

www.ShopABA.org

Contents

About the Authors ix

Preface to the Third Edition xi

CHAPTER 1

Understanding Conflicts of Interest 1

I. Introduction 1
II. Identifying and Classifying Clients 1
A. Establishing an Attorney-Client Relationship 2
B. Establishing the Attorney-Client Relationship in Insurance Defense Representations 4
C. Terminating the Attorney-Client Relationship 7
III. Concurrent Client Conflicts of Interest 9
A. Direct Adversity Conflicts 10
B. Material Limitation Conflicts 13
C. The Representation of Multiple Parties in Litigation 14
D. Obtaining Client Consent to a Conflict 16
IV. Former Client Conflicts of Interest 25
A. Model Rule 1.9(a) Conflicts 26
B. Former Clients and Lawyers' Lateral Movement 36
C. The Material Adversity Requirement 39
D. The Use and Disclosure of Former Clients' Information under Rule 1.9(c) 41
V. Issue or Positional Conflicts of Interest 45
VI. Conclusion 48

CHAPTER 2

Pre-suit Investigation and the Pursuit of Frivolous Claims 49

I. Introduction and Overview 49
II. The Ethical Prohibition against Pursuing Frivolous Claims and Lawyers' Duty to Investigate 49
A. Lawyers' Duty of Reasonable Inquiry 52
B. Advancing Factually or Legally Unsupportable Positions 62

C. Consequences of Rule 3.1 Violations and Abusive or Persistent Misconduct 69
D. Continued Pursuit of Claims or Contentions That Become Frivolous 72
III. Ethical Restrictions Affecting Lawyers' Ability to Investigate Clients' Claims or Contentions 75
IV. Liability for Malicious Prosecution 85
V. Conclusion 89

CHAPTER 3
Surreptitious Investigations and Discovery 91

I. Introduction 91
II. Applicable Ethics Rules 93
A. Model Rule 4.1(a) 93
B. Model Rule 4.2 95
C. Model Rule 4.3 101
D. Model Rule 4.4(a) 102
E. Model Rule 5.3 103
F. Model Rule 8.4(a) 104
G. Model Rule 8.4(b) 104
H. Model Rule 8.4(c) 105
I. Model Rule 8.4(d) 107
III. Undercover Activities 108
A. Using Undercover Investigators in Civil Litigation 108
B. Lawyers Concealing or Disguising Their Identities in Civil Litigation 115
C. Criminal Cases 117
D. Analyzing the Professional Responsibility Issues 121
E. Advice for Lawyers When Employing Investigators 127
IV. Secret Recording 128
V. Advancing and Developing the Law 133
VI. Conclusion 134

CHAPTER 4
Compensating Fact Witnesses 137

I. Introduction 137
II. Governing Rules and Statutes 140
A. Model Rule of Professional Conduct 3.4(b) 140
B. The Federal Anti-bribery or Anti-gratuity Statute 147
C. Summary and Synthesis 149
III. Illustrative Cases 150
A. Cases Approving Fact Witnesses' Compensation 151
B. Cases Disapproving of Fact Witnesses' Compensation 155
IV. Recommendations for Lawyers 160
V. Conclusion 163

CHAPTER 5

Ex Parte Communications: Critical Concerns for Lawyers 165

I. Introduction 165
II. Applicable Rules of Professional Conduct 165
A. Model Rule 4.2 165
B. Model Rule 4.3 181
C. Model Rule 4.4(a) 182
III. Communications with Organizations' Current and Former Employees 183
A. Precautionary Steps for Lawyers 183
B. Ex Parte Communication Where the Organization Has a Law Department 186
IV. Ex Parte Communications with In-House Counsel 187
V. Ex Parte Communications with Treating Physicians 189
VI. Ex Parte Communications with Expert Witnesses 194
VII. The Special Problem of Class and Collective Actions 198
A. Class Communications by Plaintiffs' Counsel 198
B. Restrictions on Plaintiffs' Counsel and the Issue of Prior Restraint 200
C. Places the First Amendment Does Not Always Reach 205
D. Class Communications by Defendants and Their Counsel 208
VIII. Lawyers' Ex Parte Communications with Government Agencies 214
A. The Model Rule 4.2 "Authorized by Law" Exception 214
B. ABA Formal Opinions 95-396 and 97-408 215
C. Jurisdictions with Express Government Contacts Exceptions 219
D. Special Considerations 220
IX. Conclusion 221

CHAPTER 6

Social Media and Professional Responsibility 223

I. Introduction 223
II. Social Media and Discovery 223
III. Researching Prospective and Sitting Jurors through Social Media 232
A. Ethics Opinions 238
B. The ABA Position 240
C. Summary 242

CHAPTER 7

Accidental and Impromptu Clients 245

I. Introduction 245
II. Accidental Clients 246
A. What Makes a "Client"? 246
B. Ethical Obligations in Dealing with Constituents of an Organizational Client 247

C. Corporate Investigations and *Upjohn* Warnings 250
D. *Office of Disciplinary Counsel v. Baldwin*: An Accidental Client Fiasco 254
E. Summary 262
III. Impromptu Attorney-Client Relationships 262
A. The Duties and Unappreciated Risks of Jointly Representing Non-party Deponents 262
B. Confidentiality in Joint Representation 266
C. Conflicts of Interest in Joint Representation 270
D. Lessons from *Yanez* 274
E. Final Considerations Relating to the Potential Representation of Witness-Deponents 277

CHAPTER 8

Civility and Saber-Rattling 279

I. Introduction 279
II. Civility 280
A. Uncivil Behavior as Unethical Behavior 281
B. Summary 290
III. Saber-Rattling 291
A. Applicable Rules of Professional Conduct 291
B. Threatening Criminal Action 298
C. Summary and Recommendations for Lawyers 303
D. Threatening Professional Discipline 306
IV. Conclusion 313

CHAPTER 9

Candor to the Tribunal 315

I. Introduction 315
II. Candor in Context 316
A. False Statements of Fact or Law 321
B. False Statements and the Duty to Correct 326
C. Silence as Statement: Misrepresentation by Omission 326
D. Materiality 329
E. The Curious Case of Plagiarism 330
F. Ghostwriting and Lawyer Identity 336
G. Conclusion 344
III. Disclosing Directly Adverse Authority 345
IV. Candor in Ex Parte Proceedings 352
A. Illustrative Cases 353
B. Defining Ex Parte Proceedings 354
C. Model Rule 3.3(d) May Not Apply to Prosecutors Presenting Cases to Grand Juries 356

V. Deception and Illusion as Advocacy Techniques 357
A. Court as Theater 358
B. The Critics Speak 363
VI. Conclusion 364

CHAPTER 10
False Testimony by Clients and Witnesses 367

I. Introduction 367
II. Lawyers' Duty of Candor and the Problem of False Testimony 368
A. Applicable Rules of Professional Conduct 369
B. The Duration of the Obligation 373
C. Candor Trumps Confidentiality 375
D. False Testimony and the Knowledge Element 378
E. Knowledge versus Reasonable Belief 388
F. Materiality 390
G. The Model Rule 3.3 Remediation Requirement 392
H. Failing to Remedy False Testimony under Model Rule 3.4(b) 394
III. False Testimony in Criminal Cases 395
A. Lawyers' Options When Confronting Prospective False Testimony 396
B. Illustrative Narrative Cases 399
C. The Problem of Surprise Perjury 403
D. Testimony by Witnesses 406
E. Special Responsibilities of Prosecutors 407
F. Summary 408
IV. Prevention of False Testimony and Reasonable Remedial Measures 408
A. Prospective False Testimony 409
B. False Testimony in Retrospect 411
C. Ex Parte Disclosure of False Testimony 412
D. The Problem of Disclosure in Bench Trials 413
V. Conclusion 415

CHAPTER 11
Lawyers as Witnesses 417

I. Introduction 417
II. An Overview of Lawyers as Fact Witnesses 417
III. Understanding the Advocate-Witness Rule 420
A. The Scope and Reach of Model Rule 3.7(a) 420
B. Excluding the Lawyer's Testimony Rather Than Disqualifying the Lawyer 433
IV. Exceptions to the Advocate-Witness Rule 435
A. The Uncontested Issue Exception to Model Rule 3.7(a) 435
B. The Nature and Value of Legal Services Exception 436
C. The Substantial Hardship Exception to Model Rule 3.7(a) 437

V. Model Rule 3.7(b) and Personal versus Imputed Disqualification 443
VI. Conclusion 446

CHAPTER 12
Professional Responsibility and Liability in Negotiations 447

I. Introduction 447
II. Negotiation and Authority to Settle 448
III. Lawyers' Duty to Communicate with Clients 452
A. The Potential Insurance Defense Trap 456
B. Summary 458
IV. Lawyers' Duty of Confidentiality 459
V. Lawyers' Duty of Honesty to Third Persons 465
A. Applicable Rules of Professional Conduct 465
B. Affirmative Misrepresentation Cases 470
C. The Failure to Disclose and Concealment 472
D. Summary 476
VI. Negotiations Involving Tribunals and Lawyers' Associated Duty of Candor 477
VII. Civil Liability for Fraud or Misrepresentation 484
VIII. Conclusion 491

CHAPTER 13
Ethics on Appeal 493

I. Introduction 493
II. Lawyers' Criticism of Courts 493
A. Limitations on Lawyers' Speech Rights and the First Amendment 495
B. The Problem of Perception and Courts' Willingness to Presume the Worst 509
III. Frivolous Appeals and Other Bad Faith Litigation 519
A. Model Rule 3.1 and Similar Restrictions Apply Equally to Appeals 519
B. Special Issues in Criminal Appeals 524
C. Statutory Prohibitions and Court Rules Regarding Frivolous Appeals 526
IV. Conclusion 529

Table of Cases 531

About the Authors

Douglas R. Richmond is Managing Director in the Professional Services Practice of Aon Risk Solutions. Aon's Professional Services Practice is the world's leading broker of insurance for law firms. Doug consults with Aon's large law firm clients on professional responsibility and liability issues.

Before joining Aon in Chicago, Doug was a partner with Armstrong Teasdale LLP in Kansas City, Missouri (1989–2004), where he had a broad civil trial and appellate practice. In his time at Armstrong Teasdale, he tried numerous major cases as first chair and was often engaged to handle appeals of cases tried by other lawyers. In 1998, he was named the nation's top defense lawyer in an insurance industry poll as reported in the publications *Inside Litigation* and *Of Counsel*. He served on the ABA's Standing Committee on Ethics and Professional Responsibility from 2016 to 2019 and currently is a member of the ABA's Standing Committee on Lawyers' Professional Liability (2020–2023). He is a member of the American Law Institute (ALI), American Board of Trial Advocates (ABOTA), International Association of Defense Counsel (IADC), and Federation of Defense and Corporate Counsel (FDCC). Doug has also been selected to *The Best Lawyers in America* in the areas of legal malpractice, personal injury litigation, and railroad law. In 2003, the Euromoney Legal Media Group named him as one of the nation's top insurance and reinsurance lawyers.

Doug is the co-author of a leading insurance law treatise and an insurance law casebook and has published more than 90 articles in university law reviews. He teaches Legal Ethics at the Northwestern University School of Law, Insurance Law and Legal Malpractice Law at the University of Florida College of Law, and Legal Malpractice Law at the Texas A&M University School of Law. He previously taught Trial Advocacy and Insurance Law at the University of Kansas School of Law, and Insurance Law and a seminar on Damages at the University of Missouri School of Law. In addition, Doug is a regular NITA faculty member, teaching both trial and deposition skills.

Doug earned his J.D. at the University of Kansas, an M. Ed. from the University of Nebraska, and his B.S. from Fort Hays State University.

Brian S. Faughnan is a shareholder in the Memphis, Tennessee, office of Lewis Thomason. In addition to practicing in the areas of legal ethics and lawyers' professional responsibility, Brian maintains a civil litigation practice focused on complex commercial litigation, appellate litigation, and media law. Brian is a Fellow of the American Bar Foundation and a Fellow of the Tennessee Bar Foundation, is listed in *The Best Lawyers in America* (Appellate Law, Ethics and Professional Responsibility Law, and Litigation-First Amendment), and has been recognized as a Super Lawyer by *Mid-South Super Lawyers*. He is President-Elect of the Association of Professional Responsibility Lawyers (APRL).

Brian is a frequent author and speaker on professional responsibility issues. He shares his thoughts on professional responsibility and other aspects of the law of lawyering at www.faughnanonethics.com. He is Chair of the Tennessee Bar Association's Standing Committee on Ethics and Professional Responsibility, and formerly served on the TBA Board of Governors.

Brian completed his undergraduate education at Rhodes College in 1995 and earned his J.D., *magna cum laude,* in 1998 from the University of Memphis School of Law, where he was Comments Editor of the *University of Memphis Law Review.*

Michael L. Matula is a shareholder in the Kansas City, Missouri, office of Ogletree Deakins Nash Smoak & Stewart, P.C., a national labor and employment law firm. Mike previously was an associate and then a partner with Armstrong Teasdale LLP in Kansas City, where he worked closely with Doug Richmond. Mike concentrates his practice in employment litigation and counseling and has represented employers in a wide variety of aggravated and complex litigation. He has significant jury trial experience in employment and civil rights matters. Additionally, Mike has considerable experience in the defense of commercial, tort, and insurance cases, including the representation of lawyers and other professionals, both at trial and on appeal. He continues to handle select matters in these areas. Mike is a member of his firm's Ethics Committee, and he has served as an adjunct professor at the University of Missouri-Kansas City School of Law. He serves as a Disciplinary Hearing Officer for Missouri's Region IV Disciplinary Committee.

Mike's litigation practice includes an emphasis in e-discovery, and he has completed a related certification course. He regularly speaks on employment law subjects to industry and professional audiences and is a frequent author.

Mike earned his J.D. from the University of Kansas School of Law in 1996, where he was selected to the Order of the Coif and was Notes and Comments Editor of the *Kansas Law Review.* He earned his B.A. degree from Claremont McKenna College in 1993.

Preface to the Third Edition

As we noted in the prefaces to the first and second editions of this book, trial and appellate lawyers face numerous professional responsibility challenges. Often the problems they face arise suddenly or in circumstances that are at best difficult. We have long appreciated these facts because of our backgrounds as trial and appellate lawyers. The third edition of this book accordingly remains first and foremost for practicing lawyers. We have again incorporated in the text practical examples and offer practical advice whenever possible.

We have styled the book as an anthology, with the chapters tracing the life of a lawsuit from start to finish. We have attempted to compartmentalize the subjects so that readers do not have to jump back and forth between chapters to understand the principles and rules in play. This results in some small amount of overlap of material in some chapters, but we think the ease of use that comes from compartmentalizing subjects is more important to readers than any minor redundancy. We have added new chapters on conflicts of interest and accidental and impromptu clients, and we have created a separate chapter on social media ethics rather than addressing that subject as a subpart of other chapters. We have substantially updated all other chapters, in most cases attempting to prudently condense them for readers' ease of use. We have also deleted some chapters that appeared in the first and second editions in the belief that their utility had diminished. In discussing the various subjects, we have defined "professional responsibility" broadly to include not only legal ethics but also the related issues of sanctions and professional liability.

We hope this book is authoritative, but we recognize that professional responsibility is a dynamic subject and that answers to seemingly straightforward questions can vary substantially depending on the facts and the law of the jurisdiction. Accordingly, we have attempted to provide ample citations to authority to guide readers in their own research.

We owe special debts of gratitude to Barbara O'Donnell of the ABA/TIPS Publishing Board who first encouraged us to undertake this project, and to our original editor at the ABA, Rick Paszkiet, who provided advice, guidance, and support in developing the first edition of this book. We owe further gratitude to Sarah Orwig, who came on board as the editor for the second edition and thankfully stayed for the third edition. We have, over the years, profited from conversations with many colleagues, and our opinions expressed throughout the book have been influenced and shaped by many thoughtful lawyers with whom we have worked and collaborated. These lawyers are too numerous to mention by name, but we are deeply grateful regardless. Doug Richmond owes a special debt of gratitude to his colleague Matt Corbin. We offer profound thanks to our families, who tolerated our writing when they had other designs on our time.

Finally, we welcome readers' comments, criticisms, and suggestions. Like lawyers everywhere, we continue to learn each day.

1

Understanding Conflicts of Interest

I. Introduction

Conflicts of interest pose recurring professional responsibility and practice management challenges for lawyers and are a persistent source of professional liability exposure. Conflicts of interest may spawn breach of fiduciary duty and professional negligence allegations, require lawyers to decline desirable representations, disqualify lawyers from representations or force their withdrawal from cases, oblige law firms to disgorge fees, and strain lawyers' relationships with clients. In the insurance defense context, a conflict of interest attributed to defense counsel appointed by the insurer may cost the insurer control of the defense and require the appointment of independent counsel to represent the insured at the insurer's expense.

Although conflicts of interest arise in all practice areas, they pervade litigation. Accordingly, this chapter explores conflicts of interest that trial and appellate lawyers are likely to encounter.

II. Identifying and Classifying Clients

The essential first step in any conflict of interest analysis is identifying who the lawyer represents. It is, after all, clients to whom lawyers owe duties of confidentiality and loyalty, which underpin conflict of interest rules.[1] In

1. *See* Dynamic 3D Geosols. LLC v. Schlumberger Ltd., 837 F.3d 1280, 1286 (Fed. Cir. 2016) ("[T]here is an overriding countervailing concern suffusing the ethical rules: a client's entitlement to an attorney's adherence to her duty of loyalty, encompassing a duty of confidentiality."); SWS Fin. Fund A v. Salomon Bros., 790 F. Supp. 1392, 1401 (N.D. Ill. 1992) ("There are basically two purposes behind Rule 1.7. First it serves as a prophylactic to protect confidences that a client may have shared with his or her attorney. In that regard, Rule 1.9 shares the same concern as it prohibits an attorney from representing a client against a former client if the matter is 'substantially related' to the matter(s) of the former representation. The second purpose . . . is to safeguard loyalty as a feature of the lawyer-client relationship."); Antelope Valley-E. Kern Water Agency v. L.A. Cnty. Waterworks Dist. No. 40 (Antelope Valley Groundwater Cases), 241 Cal. Rptr. 3d 692, 702 (Ct. App. 2018) ("The restrictions on an attorney's ability to represent clients with interests that are . . . adverse are designed to protect two distinct values: to assure the attorney represents his or

most cases, client identities are clear. But not all cases are straightforward. Indeed, an attorney-client relationship may arise in the absence of an express contract between the lawyer and the client.[2]

State substantive law, rather than rules of professional conduct, typically governs whether parties have an attorney-client relationship.[3] The existence of an attorney-client relationship, or conversely, the absence of one, is a fact-specific inquiry.[4] That said, some guidelines concerning the creation and termination of an attorney-client relationship are useful to the overall client identity analysis.

A. Establishing an Attorney-Client Relationship

An attorney-client relationship may be expressly created through a written or oral contract. Most attorney-client relationships are created in this fashion. The execution of an engagement agreement or the payment of legal fees is significant when determining whether an attorney-client relationship exists.[5] At the same time, these formalities are not essential because an attorney-client relationship may be implied or inferred from the parties' conduct.[6] Certainly, the payment of fees does not alone determine the existence of an attorney-client relationship.[7]

her client with undivided loyalties, and to assure the attorney will preserve confidential information conveyed by the client to the attorney." (citations omitted)); N.J. Div. of Child Prot. & Permanency v. G.S., 149 A.3d 816, 831 (N.J. Super. Ct. App. Div. 2016) ("The risk in representing clients with conflicting interests is that a lawyer's divided loyalty will result in less vigorous representation of both clients, and that the lawyer will use confidences of one client to benefit the other." (citations omitted)).

2. Bistline v. Parker, 918 F.3d 849, 864 (10th Cir. 2019) (applying Utah law).

3. United States v. Williams, 720 F.3d 674, 686 (8th Cir. 2013); Rozmus v. West, 13 Vet. App. 386, 387 (U.S. App. Vet. Cl. 2000).

4. *In re* Robbins, 192 A.3d 558, 563 (D.C. 2018); Newsome v. Peoples Bancshares, 269 So. 3d 19, 31 (Miss. 2018); *see, e.g.*, Seaman v. Schulte Roth & Zabel LLP, 111 N.Y.S.3d 266, 267 (App. Div. 2019) ("The course of conduct among the parties demonstrated by the documentary evidence, particularly the repeated communications from defendants to plaintiff clearly disclaiming an attorney-client relationship and advising plaintiff and his wife to consult independent counsel, refute plaintiff's general allegations that [the lawyer in question] was his attorney.").

5. Avocent Redmond Corp. v. Rose Elecs., 491 F. Supp. 2d 1000, 1004 (W.D. Wash. 2007); Mays v. Askin, 585 S.E.2d 735, 737 (Ga. Ct. App. 2003); Patel v. Martin, 111 N.E.3d 1082, 1095 (Mass. 2018).

6. *In re* Hodge, 407 P.3d 613, 648 (Kan. 2017); *Patel*, 111 N.E.3d at 1093; State *ex rel.* Couns. for Discipline of the Neb. Sup. Ct. v. Chvala, 935 N.W.2d 446, 471 (Neb. 2019).

7. Edward Wildman Palmer LLP v. Super. Ct., 180 Cal. Rptr. 3d 620, 628 (Ct. App. 2014); Rubin & Norris, LLC v. Panzarella, 51 N.E.3d 879, 891 (Ill. App. Ct. 2016); State *ex rel.* Stovall v. Meneley, 22 P.3d 124, 40 (Kan. 2001); Att'y Grievance Comm'n of Md. v. Brooke, 821 A.2d 414, 424 (Md. 2003); Fuller v. Partee, 540 S.W.3d 864, 869 (Mo. Ct. App. 2018) (quoting Fox v. White, 215 S.W.3d 257, 261 (Mo. Ct. App. 2007)); *In re* Disciplinary Action Against Ward, 881 N.W.2d 226, 230 (N.D. 2016).

In the absence of an express agreement, an implied attorney-client relationship may be found to exist when (1) a person seeks the lawyer's advice or assistance, (2) the requested advice or assistance relates to matters within the lawyer's professional competence, and (3) the lawyer expressly or impliedly agrees to provide or actually furnishes the desired advice or assistance.[8] In some cases, the third element of an implied attorney-client relationship may be established by proof of detrimental reliance, meaning that the person seeking legal services reasonably relied on the lawyer to provide them, and the lawyer, who was aware of the person's reliance, did nothing to negate it.[9]

When deciding whether an implied attorney-client relationship exists, courts focus on the would-be client's expectations and especially the reasonableness of the person's belief "'that he is consulting a lawyer in that capacity and has manifested intention to seek professional legal advice.'"[10] A putative client's unilateral belief that an attorney-client relationship exists, however, is not enough to establish one.[11] Rather, a putative client's subjective expectation that an attorney-client relationship has been formed must be accompanied by facts indicating that the person's belief is objectively reasonable.[12] At base, then, the existence of an attorney-client relationship is measured by an objective standard.[13]

By requiring evidence establishing the reasonableness of the aspiring client's subjective belief that an attorney-client relationship exists, courts ensure that an attorney-client relationship arises only when both the lawyer and client consent to its formation.[14] For example, a person's subjective belief may be deemed reasonable where the surrounding facts and circumstances put the lawyer on notice that the person intended to form an attorney-client relationship, indicate that the lawyer shared the person's subjective intent to create the relationship, or demonstrate that the lawyer acted in a manner that would prompt a reasonable person in the putative client's position to

8. *Chvala*, 935 N.W.2d at 471–72.

9. Cesso v. Todd, 82 N.E.3d 1074, 1078–79 (Mass. App. Ct. 2017) (quoting DeVaux v. Am. Home Assur. Co., 444 N.E.2d 355, 357 (Mass. 1983)); *Chvala*, 935 N.W.2d at 472.

10. Diversified Grp., Inc. v. Daugerdas, 139 F. Supp. 2d 445, 454 (S.D.N.Y. 2001) (quoting Westinghouse Elec. Corp. v. Kerr-McGee Corp., 580 F.2d 1311, 1319 (7th Cir. 1978)).

11. *In re* Rescue Concepts, Inc., 556 S.W.3d 331, 339 (Tex. App. 2017).

12. Hinerman v. Grill on Twenty First, LLC, 112 N.E.3d 1273, 1275–76 (Ohio Ct. App. 2018); O'Kain v. Landress, 450 P.3d 508, 516 (Or. Ct. App. 2019).

13. Barkerding v. Whittaker, 263 So. 3d 1170, 1182 (La. Ct. App. 2018).

14. *See* Cohen v. Jaffe Raitt Heuer & Weiss, P.C., 768 F. App'x 440, 444 (6th Cir. 2019) (recognizing that attorney-client relationships require mutual assent; one party alone cannot create an attorney-client relationship); People v. Shepherd, 99 N.E.3d 513, 518 (Ill. App. Ct. 2018) (explaining that an attorney-client relationship is voluntary and contractual; it requires both parties' consent); Stephens v. Three Finger Black Shale P'ship, 580 S.W.3d 687, 721 (Tex. App. 2019) ("Evidence must exist that both parties intended to create an attorney–client relationship.").

rely on the lawyer's professional advice.[15] Similarly, if a lawyer holds herself out to third parties as representing someone, or acts on that person's behalf, that conduct may evidence an attorney-client relationship.[16]

B. Establishing the Attorney-Client Relationship in Insurance Defense Representations

Conflicts have long been acute in insurance defense practice. Conflicts of interest here trace directly to questions of client identity and, specifically, to the concept of dual representation, commonly described as the dual client doctrine. The dual client doctrine holds that a lawyer appointed by an insurance company to defend its insured represents both the insurer and the insured, meaning that the defense lawyer has an attorney-client relationship with both. As the court in *National Union Fire Insurance Co. v. Stites Professional Law Corp.*[17] once explained, "As long as the interests of the insurer and the insured coincide, they are both clients of the defense attorney and the defense attorney's fiduciary duty runs to both the insurer and the insured."[18] A defense lawyer therefore serves two masters in any given case. The problems created by the dual client doctrine rest on the premise that a defense lawyer cannot loyally represent the insured in a case in which the insured's and the insurer's interests conflict given the defense lawyer's typical ongoing business relationship with the insurer. Forced to choose between a repeat client and the insured, the reasoning goes, defense counsel will side with the insurer.

The dual client doctrine appears to represent the majority rule;[19] however, many jurisdictions hold that the insured is the defense lawyer's sole

15. DG Cogen Partners, LLC v. Lane Powell PC, 917 F. Supp. 2d 1123, 1137 (D. Or. 2013) (quoting *In re* Conduct of Weidner, 801 P.2d 828, 837 (Or. 1990)).

16. *See, e.g.*, *In re* Persaud, 467 B.R. 26, 40 (Bankr. E.D.N.Y. 2012) (explaining that regular communications relating to the subject of the representation as well as activity by the lawyer and the client in furthering the objectives of the representation are pertinent to the analysis); Heine v. Colton, Hartnick, Yamin & Sheresky, 786 F. Supp. 360, 367 (S.D.N.Y. 1992) (noting that a lawyer creates a presumption of an attorney-client relationship by entering an appearance in a proceeding); Davis v. State Bar, 655 P.2d 1276, 1278 (Cal. 1983) (mailing letters to third parties in which the lawyer claimed that he represented the client evidenced an attorney-client relationship).

17. 1 Cal. Rptr. 2d 570 (Ct. App. 1991).

18. *Id.* at 575.

19. *See, e.g.*, Mt. Vernon Fire Ins. Co. v. VisionAid, Inc., 875 F.3d 716 724 (1st Cir. 2017) (interpreting Massachusetts law); Home Indem. Co. v. Lane Powell Moss & Miller, 43 F.3d 1322, 1331 (9th Cir. 1995) (interpreting Alaska law); Lee v. Med. Protective Co., 858 F. Supp. 2d 803, 806 (E.D. Ky. 2012) (interpreting Kentucky law); Mitchum v. Hudgens, 533 So. 2d 194, 198 (Ala. 1988); Bank of Am., N.A. v. Super. Ct., 151 Cal. Rptr. 3d 526, 536 (Ct. App. 2013); Gulf Ins. Co. v. Berger, Kahn, Shafton, Moss, Figler, Simon & Gladstone, 93 Cal. Rptr. 2d 534, 542–44 (Ct. App. 2000); Pa. Ins. Guar. Ass'n v. Sikes, 590 So. 2d 1051, 1052 (Fla. Dist. Ct. App. 1991); Coscia v. Cunningham, 299 S.E.2d 880, 881 (Ga. 1983); Huang v. Brenson, 7 N.E.3d 729, 739 (Ill. App. Ct. 2014); Cincinnati Ins. Co. v. Wills, 717 N.E.2d 151, 161 (Ind. 1999); Teague v. St. Paul Fire & Marine Ins. Co., 10 So. 3d 806, 832 (La. Ct. App. 2009); McCourt Co. v. FPC Props., Inc., 434 N.E.2d 1234, 1235 (Mass. 1982); Moeller v. Am. Guarantee & Liab. Ins. Co., 707 So.

client.[20] At least one state holds that in a case defended under a reservation of rights, the insurer's reservation trumps otherwise acceptable dual representation and transforms the insured into the defense lawyer's sole client.[21]

In fact, the dual client and sole client models are best thought of as default rules. Generally, whether a defense lawyer represents the insurer in addition to the insured—the insured is always a defense lawyer's client—is a matter of contract.[22] Beyond that, the existence of an attorney-client relationship is a question of fact just as in other settings. Consequently, an insurance carrier and the lawyer it hires to defend its insured can share an attorney-client relationship in any given case depending on their conduct and understanding.

Applying an objective standard, defense lawyers likely will be deemed to have an attorney-client relationship with insurers that engage them. Defense lawyers supply insurers with legal advice intended to benefit them in conducting the insured's defense. For instance, defense lawyers advise insurers on verdict value, settlement value, the likelihood that an insured will be found liable, the assessment of comparative fault, whether there are other potential defendants to be joined or against which cross-claims might be asserted, the prospects for winning by dispositive motion, whether the case should be settled or tried, the expected composition of the jury pool, the judge's reputation, the skill of the plaintiff's attorney, prospects on appeal in the event of an unfavorable trial outcome, and more. Insurers expect to receive such advice from defense counsel and incorporate it when making

---

2d 1062, 1070 (Miss. 1996); State Farm Mut. Auto. Ins. Co. v. Hansen, 357 P.3d 338, 343 (Nev. 2015); Lieberman v. Emp'rs Ins., 419 A.2d 417, 423–25 (N.J. 1980); Nationwide Mut. Fire Ins. Co. v. Bourlon, 617 S.E.2d 40, 45–46 (N.C. Ct. App. 2005); United States Fid. & Guar. Co. v. Pietrykowski, No. E99-38, 2000 WL 204475, at *3–4 (Ohio Ct. App. Feb. 11, 2000); Spratley v. State Farm Mut. Auto. Ins. Co., 78 P.3d 603, 607 (Utah 2003); *In re* Illuzzi, 616 A.2d 233, 236 (Vt. 1992); Barry v. USAA, 989 P.2d 1172, 1175 (Wash. Ct. App. 1999); Juneau Cnty. Star-Times v. Juneau Cnty., 824 N.W.2d 457, 467 (Wis. 2013).

20. *See, e.g.*, Cont'l Cas. Co. v. Pullman, Comley, Bradley & Reeves, 929 F.2d 103, 108 (2d Cir. 1991); *In re* A.H. Robins Co., 880 F.2d 694, 751 (4th Cir. 1989); U.S. Underwriters Ins. Co. v. Tauber, 604 F. Supp. 2d 521, 532 (E.D.N.Y. 2009); Gen. Sec. Ins. Co. v. Jordan, Coyne & Savits, LLP, 357 F. Supp. 2d 951, 957 (E.D. Va. 2005) (discussing Virginia law); Essex Ins. Co. v. Tyler, 309 F. Supp. 2d 1270, 1272 (D. Colo. 2004) (discussing Colorado law); Gibbs v. Lappies, 828 F. Supp. 6, 7 (D.N.H. 1993); First Am. Carriers, Inc. v. Kroger Co., 787 S.W.2d 669, 671 (Ark. 1990); Higgins v. Karp, 687 A.2d 539, 543 (Conn. 1997); Finley v. Home Ins. Co., 975 P.2d 1145, 1153 (Haw. 1998); Hackman v. W. Agric. Ins. Co., No. 104,786, 2012 WL 1524060, at *15 (Kan. Ct. App. Apr. 27, 2012); Kirschner v. Process Design Assocs., Inc., 592 NW.2d 707, 711 (Mich. 1999); *In re* Rules of Prof'l Conduct & Insurer Imposed Billing Rules & Procedures, 2 P.3d 806, 814 (Mont. 2000); Feliberty v. Damon, 527 N.E.2d 261, 265 (N.Y. 1988); Sentry Select Ins. Co. v. Maybank Law Firm, LLC, 826 S.E.2d 270, 272 (S.C. 2019); Givens v. Mullikin, 75 S.W.3d 383, 396 (Tenn. 2002); Stewart Title Guar. Co. v. Sterling Sav. Bank, 311 P.3d 1, 3 (Wash. 2013); Barefield v. DPIC Cos., 600 S.E.2d 256, 270 (W. Va. 2004).

21. Mut. of Enumclaw Ins. Co. v. Dan Paulson Constr., Inc., 169 P.3d 1, 8 n.10 (Wash. 2007).

22. Unauthorized Practice of Law Comm. v. Am. Home Assur. Co., 261 S.W.3d 24, 42 (Tex. 2008).

critical decisions, both points being known to the defense lawyers willingly supplying the advice.[23]

Courts increasingly recognize the importance of fact-specific inquiry into the existence of an attorney-client relationship between a liability insurer and the lawyer the carrier appoints to defend its insured.[24] In *Paradigm Insurance Co. v. Langerman Law Offices*,[25] for example, the Arizona Supreme Court embraced the general rule that the existence of an attorney-client relationship turns on whether (1) the would-be client has manifested to the lawyer its intent that the lawyer provide legal services for it and (2) the lawyer manifests her consent to do so.[26]

The Minnesota Supreme Court modified the general rules concerning the creation of attorney-client relationships in *Pine Island Farmers Coop v. Erstad & Riemer, P.A.*,[27] to provide a "bright-line rule to determine whether defense counsel represents the insurer as well as the insured."[28] Under the *Pine Island* approach,

> [I]n the absence of a conflict of interest . . . , the insurer can become a co-client of defense counsel based on contract or tort theory if two conditions are satisfied. First, defense counsel or another attorney must consult with the insured, explaining the implications of dual representation and the advantages and risks involved. . . . Second, after consultation, the insured must give its express consent to the dual representation.[29]

Without this consultation and the insured's express consent, the insured is the defense lawyer's sole client.[30]

The *Pine Island* approach has some flaws. First, it ignores the logical argument that the insured has already agreed to the attorney's dual representation by purchasing an insurance policy that grants the insurer the right to control the defense.[31] Second, it is not clear why the insured alone should

23. On the other hand, a defense lawyer might reasonably argue that in furnishing such information to an insurer, she is simply evaluating the case for the insurer in the justifiable belief that offering the evaluation is compatible with her relationship with the insured, and that no attorney-client relationship results. *See* Model Rules of Prof'l Conduct R. 2.3(a) (2020). The problem with that argument in the absence of an express disclaimer of an attorney-client relationship is that it does not account for the insurer's expectations.

24. *See, e.g.*, CAMICO Mut. Ins. Co. v. Heffler, Radetich & Saitta, LLP, No. 11-4753, 2013 WL 315716, at *2–5 (E.D. Pa. Jan. 28, 2013) (discussing Pennsylvania law); Pa. Nat'l Mut. Cas. Ins. Co. v. Perlberg, 819 F. Supp. 2d 449, 454–55 (D. Md. 2011) (applying Maryland law); Swiss Reinsurance Am. Corp. v. Roetzel & Andress, 837 N.E.2d 1215, 1220–21 (Ohio Ct. App. 2005).

25. 24 P.3d 593 (Ariz. 2001).

26. *Id.* at 595–96 (quoting the Restatement (Third) of the Law Governing Lawyers § 14 (2000)).

27. 649 N.W.2d 444 (Minn. 2002).

28. *Id.* at 451.

29. *Id.* at 452 (citations omitted).

30. *Id.* at 451.

31. Mora v. Lancet Indem. Risk Retention Grp., Inc., 773 F. App'x 113, 117–18 (4th Cir. 2019).

control whether the insurer should have the benefits of an attorney-client relationship with the defense lawyer. In most cases, after all, only the insurer's money is at stake.

Finally, defense lawyers who do not want an attorney-client relationship with an insurance company are free to structure their engagements so that the insured is their sole client. This can be accomplished in an engagement letter sent to the insurer in which the lawyer specifies that the insured is her sole client. The use of such an engagement letter is important given that an attorney-client relationship between the defense lawyer the insurer can generally be implied from their conduct and communications. Even if the lawyer gives the insurer the sort of advice described above, the insurer should not be able to claim an implied attorney-client relationship with the lawyer because the engagement letter's contrary terms render the insurer's expectation of an attorney-client relationship objectively unreasonable. Where the defense lawyer has disclaimed an attorney-client relationship with the insurer, a court should conclude that the defense lawyer is simply evaluating the matter for the insurer in furtherance of the lawyer's representation of the insured.[32]

C. Terminating the Attorney-Client Relationship

Once an attorney-client relationship is established, the lawyer cannot easily end it. Lawyers may withdraw from representations only for good reason and, at least insofar as litigation is concerned, upon reasonable notice. Moreover, in litigation, the court must grant the lawyer's motion to withdraw; unless the court does so, the attorney-client relationship continues to the conclusion of the litigation.[33] In contrast, a client may fire a lawyer at any time and for any reason, or for no reason.[34]

The determination of when an attorney-client relationship ends ordinarily is a question of fact.[35] Only when the evidence presented is sufficiently clear that reasonable minds cannot differ may the issue be decided as a matter of law.[36]

32. *See* Model Rules of Prof'l Conduct R. 2.3(a) (2020) ("A lawyer may provide an evaluation of a matter affecting a client for the use of someone other than the client if the lawyer reasonably believes that making the evaluation is compatible with other aspects of the lawyer's relationship with the client.").

33. Maddox v. State, 407 P.3d 152, 163 (Haw. 2017); State v. Payne, 855 N.W.2d 783, 787 (Neb. 2014).

34. White Pearl Inversiones S.A. (Uruguay) v. Cemusa, Inc., 647 F.3d 684, 689 (7th Cir. 2011); Nabi v. Sells, 892 N.Y.S.2d 41, 43 (App. Div. 2009); Model Rules of Prof'l Conduct R. 1.16 cmt. 4 (2020).

35. *In re* Rossana, 395 B.R. 697, 702 (Bankr. D. Nev. 2008); Lindsley v. Roe, 964 N.E.2d 1063, 1068 (Ohio Ct. App. 2011).

36. *Lindsley*, 964 N.E.2d at 1068.

Courts regularly assess the ways in which an attorney-client relationship may conclude. The relationship clearly may terminate by the explicit statement of either the lawyer or the client.[37] For example, a lawyer might specify in an engagement letter that her representation of the client will cease when she sends a final invoice for services or the lawyer might send a disengagement letter upon completion of the matter. Overt acts inconsistent with the continuation of the attorney-client relationship may also terminate the relationship. Examples of inconsistent conduct include the client filing a professional grievance against the lawyer, a client hiring another lawyer to perform the task for which the first lawyer was retained, or the client refusing to pay the lawyer's bill.[38]

Absent express statements or overt acts by either the lawyer or the client, an attorney-client relationship ends when circumstances imply that it would be objectively unreasonable to continue to bind the parties to each other.[39] When determining the posture of the attorney-client relationship on an implied basis, the parties' reasonable expectations often hinge on the scope of the lawyer's representation.[40] In that regard, the scope of a lawyer's representation loosely falls into one of three categories: (1) the client hires the lawyer as general counsel with the expectation that the lawyer will handle all legal matters that may arise for the client; (2) the client retains the lawyer to handle all matters that arise in a specific practice area, such as employment, litigation, real estate, or tax; or (3) the client engages the lawyer to represent the client in a discrete matter or matters.[41] For all three categories, unless the client fires the lawyer, or the lawyer withdraws from the representation, the attorney-client relationship continues as long as the

37. *See* Artromick Int'l, Inc. v. Drustar Inc., 134 F.R.D. 226, 229 (S.D. Ohio 1991) ("Of course, the simplest way for either attorney or client to end the relationship is by expressly saying so."); *see, e.g.*, NuStar Farms, LLC v. Zylstra, 880 N.W.2d 478, 481 (Iowa 2016) (recounting that the lawyer informed the clients by e-mail that he would not represent them in any future matters and that the clients acknowledged that they understood the e-mail to sever the attorney-client relationship); Rusk v. Harstad, 393 P.3d 341, 344 (Utah Ct. App. 2017) (concluding that a would-be client could not have reasonably believed that the law firm represented him where the lawyer had clearly stated in multiple e-mails that the law firm would not represent him).

38. *See Artromick Int'l, Inc.*, 134 F.R.D. at 230–31 (ruling that the alleged client was a former client because he had refused to pay the attorney's bill and thereafter retained other lawyers to work in areas in which that attorney had previously performed); DeLeo v. Nussbaum, 821 A.2d 744, 750 (Conn. 2003) ("A de facto termination [of the attorney-client relationship] occurs if the client takes a step that unequivocally indicates that he has ceased relying on his attorney's professional judgment in protecting his legal interests, such as hiring a second attorney to consider a possible malpractice claim or filing a grievance against the attorney." (footnotes omitted)); Estate of Mitchell v. Dougherty, 644 N.W.2d 391, 400 (Mich. Ct. App. 2002) (retaining alternate counsel is proof of a client's termination of a lawyer's representation).

39. *Artromick Int'l, Inc.*, 134 F.R.D. at 230.

40. *Id.*

41. Nat'l Med. Care, Inc. v. Home Med. of Am., Inc., No. 00-1225, 2002 WL 31068413, at *4 (Mass. Super. Ct. Sept. 12, 2002).

lawyer remains responsible for a pending matter because the lawyer has accepted responsibility to bring the matter to a successful conclusion.[42] With respect to categories one and two, an attorney-client relationship continues even when the lawyer has no pending matter for the client because the reasonable expectation remains that the lawyer will handle all matters for the client in the future as they arise.[43] In the third category, where a lawyer agrees to undertake a specific matter on the client's behalf, the attorney-client relationship typically ends once the matter is concluded.[44]

III. Concurrent Client Conflicts of Interest

Once clients are identified and classified, it is time to examine potentially applicable rules of professional conduct. Where current clients are concerned, conflicts of interest are governed by Model Rule of Professional Conduct 1.7, which provides as follows:

> (a) Except as provided in paragraph (b), a lawyer shall not represent a client if the representation involves a concurrent conflict of interest. A concurrent conflict of interest exists if:
>
> (1) the representation of one client will be directly adverse to another client; or
>
> (2) there is a significant risk that the representation of one or more clients will be materially limited by the lawyer's responsibilities to another client, a former client or a third person or by a personal interest of the lawyer.
>
> (b) Notwithstanding the existence of a concurrent conflict of interest under paragraph (a), a lawyer may represent a client if:
>
> (1) the lawyer reasonably believes that the lawyer will be able to provide competent and diligent representation to each affected client;
>
> (2) the representation is not prohibited by law;

---

42. *Id.*

43. *See* Berry v. McFarland, 278 P.3d 407, 411 (Idaho 2012) (explaining that if a lawyer agrees to handle any matters a client may have, the attorney-client relationship continues until either the lawyer or client terminates it); Model Rules of Prof'l Conduct R. 1.3 cmt. 4 (2020) ("If a lawyer has served a client over a substantial period in a variety of matters, the client sometimes may assume that the lawyer will continue to serve on a continuing basis unless the lawyer gives notice of withdrawal.").

44. Simpson v. James, 903 F.2d 372, 376 (5th Cir. 1990); DeLeo v. Nussbaum, 821 A.2d 744, 750 (Conn. 2003); *Berry*, 278 P.3d at 411; *Nat'l Med. Care, Inc.*, 2002 WL 31068413, at *4; Model Rules of Prof'l Conduct R. 1.3 cmt. 4 (2020); *see also* Revise Clothing, Inc. v. Joe's Jeans Subsidiary, Inc., 687 F. Supp. 2d 381, 389 (S.D.N.Y. 2010) (noting that an attorney-client relationship is ordinarily terminated by the accomplishment of the purpose for which it was formed); Thayer v. Fuller & Henry Ltd., 503 F. Supp. 2d 887, 892 (N.D. Ohio 2007) (observing that an attorney-client relationship may terminate when the related action has concluded or when the lawyer has exhausted all remedies in the case and declines to perform additional services).

(3) the representation does not involve the assertion of a claim by one client against another client represented by the lawyer in the same litigation or other proceeding before a tribunal; and
(4) each affected client gives informed consent, confirmed in writing.[45]

The restrictions that Model Rule 1.7(a) imposes on individual lawyers generally apply equally to law firms. This is because, with some exceptions, individual lawyers' conflicts of interest are imputed to all other lawyers in the same firm.[46]

A. Direct Adversity Conflicts

As noted above, Model Rule 1.7(a)(1) first establishes that a lawyer has a conflict of interest when the representation of one client will be directly adverse to another current client.[47] The rule does not attempt to define "direct adversity" or to explain when concurrent representations are "directly adverse," although the comments to Model Rule 1.7 offer examples.[48] Some courts have attempted to define "direct adversity," although they have not necessarily achieved clarity in doing so.[49] In any event, Model Rule 1.7(a)(1)'s use of the adverb "directly" to modify "adverse" separates these conflicts from other conflicts premised upon clients' general or indirect adversity.[50]

Celgard, LLC v. LG Chem, Ltd.[51] is an interesting direct adversity conflict case arising out of patent litigation in a North Carolina federal court. Celgard manufactured lithium battery components. It sued LG Chem, which was also in the lithium battery business, for allegedly infringing Celgard's '586 patent in the course of manufacturing and selling LG Chem's lithium batteries. Celgard's lawsuit sought both damages and injunctive relief against LG Chem. Celgard's complaint named only LG Chem and affiliated companies as defendants; the complaint made no mention of LG Chem's customers.[52]

After filing its complaint, Celgard moved to preliminarily enjoin LG Chem from continuing to infringe the '586 patent either directly or by

45. Model Rules of Prof'l Conduct R. 1.7 (2020).
46. *Id.* R. 1.10(a); *see also Ex parte* Osbon, 888 So. 2d 1236, 1238 (Ala. 2004) (asserting that "Rule 1.10(a) requires a law firm to be treated as a single attorney").
47. Model Rules of Prof'l Conduct R. 1.7(a)(1) (2020).
48. *Id.* R. 1.7 cmts. 6 & 7.
49. *See, e.g.*, Bryan Corp. v. Abrano, 52 N.E.3d 95, 103 (Mass. 2016) (stating that direct adversity "involves a conflict between the legal rights and duties of clients").
50. Chapman Eng'rs, Inc. v. Nat. Gas Sales Co., 766 F. Supp. 949, 956 (D. Kan. 1991); Ill. Adv. Op. 95-15, 1996 WL 478489, at *4 (Ill. State Bar Ass'n 1996).
51. 594 F. App'x 669 (Fed. Cir. 2014).
52. *Id.* at 670–71.

inducing others by continuing to sell its batteries to customers, such as the computer and electronics giant Apple. Soon thereafter, Celgard sent Apple a copy of its motion and asked to work with Apple to find a mutually beneficial business arrangement to resolve the issues around LG Chem's alleged infringement of Celgard's intellectual property.[53]

The district court granted Celgard's request to preliminarily enjoin LG Chem and its affiliates but stayed that injunction a few days later. The respected global law firm Jones Day then entered its appearance in the litigation on behalf of Celgard. Jones Day's representation of Celgard against LG Chem was troublesome, however, because (1) Apple was a current client of Jones Day in unrelated commercial litigation matters and (2) Celgard's injunction covered custom lithium batteries manufactured by LG Chem that Apple incorporated in its products.[54]

Apple repeatedly asked Jones Day to withdraw from Celgard's representation, but the firm refused to do so.[55] Jones Day apparently tried to appease Apple by promising that it would not represent Celgard in any matters adverse to Apple, including licensing negotiations.[56] The firm's proposed compromise did not satisfy Apple, which moved to intervene in the case to seek Jones Day's disqualification.

The *Celgard* court agreed with Apple that Jones Day's representation of Celgard compelled the firm's disqualification under North Carolina ethics rules.[57] As the court explained, North Carolina Rule 1.7(a) prohibits representation when the representation will be directly adverse to another client.[58] Here, Jones Day's representation of Celgard was directly adverse to Apple's "interests and legal obligations" and "was not merely adverse in an 'economic sense.'"[59] Consequently, Jones Day's duty of loyalty to Apple prevented the firm from further representing Celgard.[60]

The *Celgard* court noted that where a law firm obtains an injunction on behalf of one client that limits another client's activities, Federal Circuit precedent supported the recognition of a direct adversity conflict.[61] Here, the burden placed on the attorney-client relationship between Apple and

53. *Id.* at 671.
54. *Id.*
55. *Id.*
56. *Id.*
57. *Id.* (explaining that the Federal Circuit applies regional circuit law in disqualification matters, and the Fourth Circuit, which covers North Carolina federal courts, in turn, applies the professional conduct rules of the forum state—here, North Carolina).
58. *Id.* (quoting N.C. Rules of Prof'l Conduct R. 1.7(a) (alteration in the original)).
59. *Id.*
60. *Id.*
61. *Id.* (quoting Freedom Wireless, Inc. v. Boston Commc'ns Grp., Inc., No. 2006-1020, 2006 WL 8071423, at *3 (Fed. Cir. Mar. 20, 2006)).

Jones Day "extend[ed] well beyond the sort of unrelated representation of competing enterprises allowed under Rule 1.7(a)."[62] Apple faced both the possibility of having to find a new battery supplier to replace LG Chem and targeting by Celgard in an effort to exploit the injunction to leverage a business relationship. Thus, in every pertinent sense, Jones Day's representation of Celgard was adverse to Apple.[63]

It was irrelevant to the *Celgard* court that Apple was not named as a defendant in the lawsuit. In the court's view, both ethics rules and case law established that "the total context, and not whether a party is named in a lawsuit," controls the question of whether the adversity between current clients is sufficient to disqualify a law firm.[64]

In conclusion, the *Celgard* court granted Apple's motions to intervene and to disqualify Jones Day. The court allowed Celgard 60 days to secure new counsel.

Although many lawyers probably contemplate direct adversity being an issue in related matters, *Celgard* illustrates the more nuanced point that a lawyer's representation of a client may be directly adverse to another client even if the matters are unrelated.[65] From lawyers' standpoint, the lack of relation between the concurrent matters is no defense to a direct adversity conflict,[66] although it may bear on whether the clients may consent to the conflict, or whether the law firm's disqualification is required. Nor may a lawyer overcome a direct adversity conflict on the basis that the client to whom the lawyer is directly adverse is represented by another lawyer in the matter.[67] In sum, if a lawyer represents one client against another client that the lawyer (or the lawyer's firm) simultaneously represents in an unrelated matter, there is a direct adversity conflict.

---

62. *Id.* at 671–72.

63. *Id.* at 672.

64. *Id.* (citing *Freedom Wireless*, 2006 WL 8071423, at *2; Arrowpac Inc. v. Sea Star Line, LLC, No. 3:12-cv-1180-J-32JBT, 2013 WL 5460027, at *10 (M.D. Fla. Apr. 30, 2013)).

65. El Camino Res., Ltd. v. Huntington Nat'l Bank, 623 F. Supp. 2d 863, 877 (W.D. Mich. 2007) (quoting Fla. Ins. Guar. Ass'n, Inc. v. Carey Canada, Inc., 749 F. Supp. 255, 259 (S.D. Fla. 1990)); Model Rules of Prof'l Conduct R. 1.7 cmt. 6 (2020).

66. *See, e.g.*, GSI Commerce Sols., Inc. v. BabyCenter, L.L.C., 618 F.3d 204, 210 (2d Cir. 2010) ("In this respect, it will not suffice to show that the two matters upon which an attorney represents existing clients are unrelated."); Reed v. Hoosier Health Sys., 825 N.E.2d 408, 412 (Ind. Ct. App. 2005) ("Reed contends IRPC 1.7(a)'s use of 'directly' indicates there must be some relation between the suits before disqualification is proper. . . . However, IRPC 1.7(a)'s use of 'directly' refers to the adverse effect to the client not the attorney-client relationship." (citations to the record omitted)).

67. Quinn v. Anvil Corp., No. C08-0182RSL, 2008 WL 11344647, at *2 (W.D. Wash. Aug. 27, 2008).

B. Material Limitation Conflicts

The second type of concurrent conflict of interest—a material limitation conflict—arises when there is a significant risk that a lawyer's representation of a client will be materially limited by the lawyer's responsibilities to someone else, or by the lawyer's own interests.[68] Material limitation conflicts are more subtle than direct adversity conflicts and require a lawyer to evaluate whether there is a significant risk that her ability to consider, recommend, or carry out an appropriate course of action for the client will be materially limited by her other responsibilities or interests.[69] Normally, there is some pull on the lawyer's judgment or something about the situation that prompts the lawyer to reflect on the propriety of accepting both representations.[70] To use a common example, conflicts of interest attributable to the tripartite relationship of insurance defense are generally classified as material limitation conflicts. Courts that discuss conflicts in the insurance defense context commonly refer to Rule 1.7(a)(2) in doing so.[71]

Material limitation conflicts require careful study of the facts and circumstances of each matter. Indeed, by their very nature, the concepts of materiality and significant risk are case-specific.

The mere suggestion of a potential conflict of interest, or a mere possibility of divergent interests, is insufficient to create a material limitation conflict.[72] The conflict must be clear and specific; it cannot rest on speculation. As the Iowa Supreme Court explained in *Bottoms v. Stapleton*,[73] "only an actual conflict of interest, as defined in [Rule 1.7(a)(2)], will justify [a lawyer's] disqualification."[74] *Bottoms* reflects the majority rule.[75]

---

68. Model Rules of Prof'l Conduct R. 1.7(a)(2) (2020).

69. *Id.* R. 1.7 cmt. 8.

70. *See* Iowa Sup. Ct. Att'y Disciplinary Bd. v. Willey, 889 N.W.2d 647, 653–54 (Iowa 2017) ("The key questions a lawyer must ask are whether it is likely a difference of interests will occur between the clients and, if so, whether that difference in interests will interfere with the lawyer's ability to offer independent, professional judgment to each client." (citation omitted)); Commonwealth v. Cousin, 88 N.E.3d 822, 834–38 (Mass. 2018) (discussing situations that may present Rule 1.7(a)(2) conflicts); State *ex rel.* Union Planters Bank, N.A. v. Kendrick, 142 S.W.3d 729, 736 (Mo. 2004) (noting that this kind of conflict of interest "in effect forecloses alternatives that would otherwise be available to the client").

71. *See, e.g.*, State Farm Mut. Auto. Ins. Co. v. Hansen, 357 P.3d 338, 341–42 & n.6 (Nev. 2015); Arden v. Forsberg & Umlauf, P.S., 402 P.3d 245, 250 (Wash. 2017).

72. *In re* Penning, 930 A.2d 144, 155–56 (D.C. 2007); Frank Settelmeyer & Sons, Inc. v. Smith & Harmer, Ltd., 197 P.3d 1051, 1059 n.33 (Nev. 2008).

73. 706 N.W.2d 411 (Iowa 2005).

74. *Id.* at 417.

75. *See, e.g.*, Shaffer v. Farm Fresh, Inc., 966 F.2d 142, 145 (4th Cir. 1992); P&L Dev. LLC v. Bionpharma Inc., No. 1:17CV1154, 2019 WL 357351, at *4 (M.D.N.C. Jan. 29, 2019) (quoting Plant Genetic Sys., N.V. v. Ciba Seeds, 933 F. Supp. 514, 517 (M.D.N.C. 1996)); Guillen v. City of Chi., 956 F. Supp. 1416, 1422 (N.D. Ill 1997); *Frank Settelmeyer & Sons, Inc.*, 197 P.3d at 1059 n.33.

Although it is true that speculation about a conflict of interest will not trigger Rule 1.7(a)(2), lawyers must not allow the language of the rule to distract them. The reference in Model Rule 1.7(a)(2) to "a significant risk" of a material limitation on a lawyer's ability to represent a client should not be understood to mean that there is a *potential* conflict of interest in such a situation. Rather, when a lawyer recognizes that there is a significant risk that her representation of a client will be materially limited by her responsibilities to another client, a former client, or a third person, or by her personal interests, she has an *actual* conflict of interest.[76] Any disadvantage or harm to the client attributable to the conflict may be only potential or prospective, but the conflict of interest under Model Rule 1.7(a)(2) is real and immediate. As a result, the lawyer must obtain any affected client's informed consent to the conflict if the lawyer wishes to go forward with the representation.

C. The Representation of Multiple Parties in Litigation

The representation of multiple parties in litigation is a regular source of conflicts. Naturally, multiple parties often would like to be represented by a single lawyer to reduce litigation costs. For example, a liability insurer that is obligated to defend multiple insureds would prefer for obvious economic reasons to have a single lawyer represent all the insureds. Representation by a single lawyer can also have other advantages, such as the presentation of a coordinated or unified litigation strategy. And the parties have a common interest: winning the case. But multi-party representations in which the parties' interests appear to be aligned at the outset may not be harmonious, or parties' interests may diverge over time. To offer a few examples, co-plaintiffs may disagree over whether to settle or on what terms. Defendants may have cross-claims or indemnification claims against one another that a disinterested lawyer would conclude should be asserted in the litigation. The representation of both a corporation and its employee may turn out to be impossible if a dispute develops over whether the employee was acting in the course and scope of her employment. The need to assert comparative fault may dislocate defendants' interests. Parties represented by a single lawyer may need to assert inconsistent legal theories.[77]

---

76. *Bottoms*, 706 N.W.2d at 417.

77. In the insurance defense context, a defense lawyer's conflict of interest arising out of the representation of multiple insureds may entitle the insureds to independent counsel at the insurer's expense. *See, e.g.*, Univ. of Miami v. Great Am. Ins. Co., 112 So. 3d 504, 508 (Fla. Dist. Ct. App. 2013) ("[I]n defense of both co-defendants, Great American's counsel would have had to argue conflicting legal positions, that each of its clients was not at fault, and the other was, even to the extent of claiming indemnification and contribution for the other's fault. . . . [T]his legal dilemma clearly created a conflict of interest . . . sufficient to qualify for indemnification for attorney's fees and costs for independent counsel.").

A lawyer who is unable to represent multiple parties because of their inconsistent arguments, claims, or positions is generally deemed to have a material limitation conflict. Indeed, that is an archetypal material limitation conflict: the lawyer's representation of one client is materially limited by the lawyer's responsibilities to another client. In comparison, if a lawyer were to pursue a cross-claim on behalf of one defendant against another defendant that the lawyer also represents, for example, the lawyer would have a direct adversity conflict.

Lawyers who are considering representing multiple parties in litigation need to carefully analyze that approach before agreeing to do so. Lawyers in this situation need to not only identify conflicts of interest but also determine whether any conflicts may be cured by the affected parties' consent. Even where a conflict may be consentable, it may be strategically or tactically preferable to have separate lawyers for each party despite the increased cost.

Once a law firm has carefully considered the situation and decided to undertake a joint representation, some basic precautions at the outset of the representation are generally in order. First, explain in writing the advantages and disadvantages of the joint representation and outline reasonable alternatives. Further explain that if a conflict develops between the clients and they cannot work it out between themselves, the firm will likely need to withdraw from the representation altogether.

Second, if your engagement letter includes a provision stating that you may withdraw from one joint client's representation upon the emergence of a conflict of interest but continue to represent the other joint client, make sure the clients understand the effect of that provision—including your ability to use the dropped client's confidential information in the continuing representation if your engagement letter allows for that possibility. If you can identify circumstances that might trigger that provision, do so in the engagement letter.

Third, explain in writing how you plan to treat confidential client information. The preferred approach in most cases is to state that you intend to share any information material to the representation with all clients in the group. Insofar as information material to the representation is concerned, there will be no secrets between the joint clients.

Fourth, if clients' consent to a conflict of interest is required, be sure to confirm their informed consent in writing. The disclosures required to achieve informed consent will vary with the matter and the client. Firms may prefer that clients sign waiver letters or forms rather than simply confirming the clients' consent in a letter or e-mail message from the responsible lawyer.

Finally, be sensitive to any subsequent changes in the relationship between the clients. If their relationship evolves, it may be necessary to consider the effect of those developments on the firm's representation of them.

D. Obtaining Client Consent to a Conflict

Once it is determined that a concurrent client conflict exists, the next question is whether the conflict may be cured by client consent. In other words, is it possible for the concurrent representations to proceed notwithstanding the lawyer's conflict of interest because the clients will waive the conflict? Again, not all conflicts are consentable or, in common parlance, "waiveable."

A conflict of interest is consentable if three conditions are met. First, the lawyer must reasonably believe that she will be able to competently and diligently represent each affected client.[78] Second, the representation must not be "prohibited by law."[79] Third, the representation cannot "involve the assertion of a claim by one client against another client represented by the lawyer in the same litigation or other proceeding before a tribunal[.]"[80] Unless these three requirements are satisfied, the lawyer should not even attempt to obtain the client's informed consent to the conflict, confirmed in writing, which is the final step necessary for the lawyer to undertake the representation.[81]

1. *A Reasonable Belief of Competent and Diligent Representation*

For a conflict of interest to be consentable, Model Rule 1.7(b)(1) requires the lawyer to reasonably believe that she can competently and diligently represent each affected client.[82] If the lawyer cannot clear this initial hurdle, client consent is impossible; indeed, the lawyer cannot even seek the client's consent.[83] A surprising number of lawyers seem to glide past this requirement, blithely confident in their ability to ably represent their clients notwithstanding the clients' competing interests. This is no time for complacency, however. Model Rule 1.7(b)(1) imposes an objective standard.[84] Accordingly, a lawyer's subjective, good faith belief that she can fulfill her professional obligations to the affected clients despite any competing interests or obligations is immaterial.[85]

---

78. Model Rules of Prof'l Conduct R. 1.7(b)(1) (2020); *see* Johnson v. Clark Gin Serv., Inc., No. 15-3290, 2016 WL 7017267, at *11 (E.D. La. Dec. 1, 2016) (stating that in multiple client representations, "the question of consentability must be resolved as to each client"); State *ex rel.* Horn v. Ray, 325 S.W.3d 500, 507 (Mo. Ct. App. 2010) ("The question of consentability must be resolved as to each client.").

79. Model Rules of Prof'l Conduct R. 1.7(b)(2) (2020).

80. *Id.* R. 1.7(b)(3).

81. *Id.* R. 1.7(b)(4) (requiring "informed consent, confirmed in writing").

82. *Id.* R. 1.7(b)(1).

83. Carnegie Cos. v. Summit Props., Inc., 918 N.E.2d 1052, 1067 (Ohio Ct. App. 2009).

84. People v. Mason, 938 P.2d 133, 136 (Colo. 1997); *In re* Stein, 177 P.3d 513, 519 (N.M. 2008); Ferolito v Vultaggio, 949 N.Y.S.2d 356, 363 (App. Div. 2012); Ill. Adv. Op. 09-02, 2009 WL 8559340, at *3 (Ill. State Bar Ass'n 2009).

85. *In re Stein*, 177 P.3d at 519; *see, e.g.*, So v. Suchanek, 670 F.3d 1304, 1310–11 (D.C. Cir. 2012) (rejecting as irrelevant the lawyer's subjective belief that no conflict existed in a joint

Under the objective standard, the facts and circumstances that the lawyer "knew or should have known at the time of undertaking or continuing a representation" are relevant, as opposed to what became known to the lawyer later or could not have been reasonably anticipated by the lawyer.[86] Thus, a lawyer must familiarize herself with the facts underlying the proposed representation to determine whether she can competently and diligently represent each affected client.

While lawyers must honestly assess the circumstances and make a reasonable judgment that competent and diligent representation is achievable, best practices dictate that they not make that determination in isolation. In short, when deciding whether to accept or continue a representation despite a concurrent conflict of interest, disinterested lawyers in the firm should participate in the analysis.

2. *Representations Prohibited by Law*

Model Rule 1.7(b)(2) bars representations that are prohibited by law.[87] Thus, if a court rule, a rule of professional conduct, a statute, or controlling case law forbids dual representation in the situation at hand, the issue of client consent is irrelevant because the representation may not proceed anyway.[88]

Government agencies are frequent litigants, and they often turn to outside law firms for representation. Unfortunately for lawyers, in some states, government agencies may not be permitted to consent to conflicts of interest. *State ex rel. Morgan Stanley & Co. v. MacQueen*[89] is an illustrative case.

MacQueen involved a lawsuit by the State of West Virginia against three financial institutions to recover a state fund's investment losses.[90] The West Virginia Attorney General appointed the law firm of Wolff Ardis to represent the State.[91] Wolff Ardis also represented seven employees of the State Treasurer's office when they were noticed for deposition as non-party

---

representation; rather, the analysis depended on whether an objective observer with the lawyer's knowledge of the circumstances would have reasonably doubted his ability to undertake the joint representation); Robertson v. Wittenmyer, 736 N.E.2d 804, 807–08 (Ind. Ct. App. 2000) (finding that the lawyer could not have reasonably believed that the representation of one client against another was permissible).

86. Restatement (Third) of the Law Governing Lawyers § 121 cmt. c(iv) (2000).

87. Model Rules of Prof'l Conduct R. 1.7(b)(2) (2020).

88. *See, e.g.*, Brown v. Kelton, 380 S.W.3d 361, 366 (Ark. 2011) (holding that an Arkansas statute prohibited an insurance company from using in-house lawyers to defend its insureds); Baldasarre v. Butler, 625 A.2d 458, 467 (N.J. 1993) (adopting a bright-line rule prohibiting lawyers from representing the buyer and seller in complex commercial real estate transactions even with consent); Iowa Rules of Prof'l Conduct R. 32:1.7(c) (2012) (barring the representation of both parties in a marriage dissolution).

89. 416 S.E.2d 55 (W. Va. 1992).

90. *Id.* at 56–57.

91. *Id.* at 57.

witnesses.[92] The defendants argued that these concurrent representations posed a conflict of interest because the State had alleged that unnamed Treasurer's office staff members had played a role in causing the subject losses.[93]

The court determined that the State's allegations concerning the Treasurer's office created a disqualifying conflict of interest for Wolff Ardis.[94] The State argued that Wolff Ardis should not be disqualified because the seven staff members to be deposed had waived any conflicts.[95] The problem, however, was that the State also had to consent to Wolff Ardis's multiple representations, which was impossible under West Virginia law.[96] The court so concluded based on its statement in an earlier case that "'where the public interest is involved, an attorney may not represent conflicting interests even with the consent of all concerned.'"[97] This rule rests on the rationale that it is "'essential that the public have absolute confidence in the integrity and impartiality of our system of justice.'"[98] In light of the public interest inherent in the State's attempt to recoup its investment losses, the State could not consent to "a dual representation which involve[d] such adversity of interests as to raise even the appearance of such impropriety."[99]

At least three courts have similarly held that governmental entities may not consent to conflicts of interest.[100] New Jersey, which was one of the earliest states to take this position, now enforces its prohibition on public agency conflict waivers through New Jersey Rules of Professional Conduct 1.7(b)(1) and 1.9(d).[101] The better view, however, holds that government clients' ability to consent to conflicts of interest should be evaluated under the customary rules governing conflicts. To the extent the public interest is implicated, citizens have vested their faith in the public officials from whom consent is being sought. Those officials owe a public trust. When government officials believe it is reasonable to consent to conflicts of interest, they are presumably acting in the public interest. Moreover, rules of professional conduct protect government clients against their lawyers' potentially adverse

92. *Id.*
93. *Id.* at 56, 59.
94. *Id.* at 59–60.
95. *Id.* at 60.
96. *Id.*
97. *Id.* at 60 (quoting Graf v. Frame, 352 S.E.2d 31, 38 (W. Va. 1986)).
98. *Id.* (quoting *Graf*, 352 S.E.2d at 38).
99. *Id.*
100. Guthrie Aircraft, Inc. v. Genesee Cnty., N.Y., 597 F. Supp. 1097, 1098 (W.D.N.Y. 1984); *In re* Sup. Ct. Advisory Comm. on Prof'l Ethics Op. No. 697, 911 A.2d 51, 57 (N.J. 2006); City of Little Rock v. Cash, 644 S.W.2d 229, 235 (Ark. 1982), *overruled on other grounds by* T & T Chem., Inc. v. Priest, 95 S.W.3d 750, 753 (Ark. 2003).
101. N.J. Rules of Prof'l Conduct R. 1.7(b)(1) (2018) (providing that a public entity cannot consent to a concurrent client conflict of interest); *id.* R. 1.9(d) (governing public entities and former client conflicts).

interests just as they do private clients. Consistent with this view, several bar ethics committees have reasoned that government agencies or entities may waive conflicts of interest in most instances,[102] as have several courts.[103]

3. *Representing Opposite Sides in the Same Lawsuit*

Model Rule 1.7(b)(3) prohibits any representation that involves the "assertion of a claim by one client against another client represented by the lawyer in the same litigation or other proceeding before a tribunal[.]"[104] Indeed, a lawyer's or law firm's simultaneous representation of opposing parties in the same case is perhaps the most appalling conflict of interest conceivable.[105] Client consent to such a conflict is ineffective.[106]

4. *Obtaining the Clients' Informed Consent, Confirmed in Writing*

Finally, if a lawyer has met the requirements of Model Rules 1.7(b)(1)–(3), she may cure a concurrent client conflict of interest by obtaining the affected clients' informed consent to the conflict and confirming it in writing.[107] A client's mere knowledge of a conflict is not sufficient for informed consent. Rather, informed consent requires a client's agreement "to a proposed course of conduct after the lawyer has communicated adequate information and explanation about the material risks of and reasonably available alternatives to the proposed course of conduct."[108] The disclosures and explanation required to achieve informed consent depend on "the nature of the conflict

102. *See, e.g.*, ABA Comm. on Ethics & Prof'l Responsibility, Formal Op. 97-405, at 4–5 (1997); D.C. Bar, Legal Ethics Comm., Op. 268, at 1 (1996); Ill. Adv. Op. 12-12, 2012 WL 2308109, at *4 (Ill. State Bar Ass'n 2012); N.Y. Ethics Op. 629, 1992 WL 465631, at *4 (N.Y. State Bar Ass'n, Comm. on Prof'l Ethics 1992).

103. *See, e.g.*, City of Cleveland v. Cleveland Elec. Illuminating Co., 440 F. Supp. 193, 205 (N.D. Ohio 1976); Miller v. Norfolk & W. Ry. Co., 538 N.E.2d 1293, 1295–97 (Ill. App. Ct. 1989); State *ex rel.* Nixon v. Am. Tobacco Co., 34 S.W.3d 122, 135–36 (Mo. 2000); Pfizer, Inc. v. Farr, No. M2011-01359-COA-R10-CV, 2012 WL 2370619, at *13 (Tenn. Ct. App. June 22, 2012).

104. Model Rules of Prof'l Conduct R. 1.7(b)(3) (2020).

105. *See* Synergy Tech & Design, Inc. v. Terry, No. C 06-02073 JSW, 2007 WL 1288464, at *7 (N.D. Cal. May 2, 2007) (quoting Flatt v. Super. Ct., 885 P.2d 950, 954 (Cal. 1994)); *see also* Jedwabny v. Phila. Transp. Co., 135 A.2d 252, 254 (Pa. 1957) ("No one could conscionably contend that the same attorney may represent both the plaintiff and defendant in an adversary action."); Vinson v. Vinson, 588 S.E.2d 392, 396, 398–99 (Va. Ct. App. 2003) (noting the trial court's observation that the lawyer's representation of both the husband and wife in a divorce constituted a gross conflict of interest and upholding the trial court's sanctions award).

106. *See* Model Rules of Prof'l Conduct R. 1.7 cmt. 23 (2020) ("Paragraph (b)(3) prohibits representation of opposing parties in litigation, *regardless of the clients' consent.*" (emphasis added)); *see, e.g.*, Nunez v. Lovell, Civ. No. 2005-7, 2008 WL 4525835, at *3–6 (D.V.I. Oct. 3, 2008) (disqualifying a lawyer who represented the plaintiffs and a defendant in the same case despite the clients' consent to the conflict).

107. Model Rules of Prof'l Conduct R. 1.7(b)(4) (2020).

108. *Id.* R. 1.0(e).

and the nature of the risks" involved in the representation.[109] And while a lawyer need not disclose to a client facts or implications about which the client already knows,[110] a lawyer who withholds or glosses over material information pertinent to the client's decision whether to consent to the conflict assumes the risk that the client will in fact be uninformed and that any consent obtained will prove to be invalid.

The amount of information necessary for the client to make an informed decision varies but often pivots on the client's level of sophistication, education, and experience, and whether the client has independent counsel.[111] The more experienced a client is in legal matters generally, and in making decisions of the type involved in the case in which consent is sought in particular, the less information and explanation needed for a client's consent to be informed.

Depending on the complexity or nature of the matter, the lawyer may want to advise the client to seek independent counsel to help evaluate the conflict of interest. Generally, a client who is represented by independent counsel is presumed to have given informed consent to the proposed course of conduct.[112] This is true regardless of whether the other lawyer is the client's in-house counsel or an outside lawyer.[113] When possible, lawyers should give clients adequate time to consider the information bearing on their decisions or to consult independent counsel. Recommending that the client wait a reasonable time before consenting to the conflict will blunt any later argument that the client was unable to reflect on the situation or solicit another lawyer's advice.

As for the writing requirement when obtaining a client's consent to a conflict, it is essential to remember that Model Rule 1.7 does not require a client's written consent to a conflict of interest; it requires that the client's consent be confirmed in writing.[114] Thus, a lawyer may obtain the client's consent in a meeting or over the telephone, for example, and comply with the rule through a confirming letter, e-mail message, or text message.[115] State rules of professional conduct, however, may vary.[116]

---

109. *Id.* R. 1.7 cmt. 18; *see also* MJK Fam. LLC v. Corp. Eagle Mgmt. Servs., Inc., 676 F. Supp. 2d 584, 597 (E.D. Mich. 2009) ("The amount of disclosure required . . . depends on the circumstances.").

110. Galderma Labs., L.P. v. Actavis Mid Atl. LLC, 927 F. Supp. 2d 390, 401–03 (N.D. Tex. 2013).

111. *Id.* at 401.

112. Model Rules of Prof'l Conduct R. 1.0 cmt. 6 (2020).

113. *Galderma Labs.*, 927 F. Supp. 2d at 401.

114. Model Rules of Prof'l Conduct R. 1.7(b)(4) (2020).

115. *See id.* R. 1.0(n) (indicating that e-mail and text messages are "writings" in this context).

116. *See, e.g.*, Cal. Rules of Prof'l Conduct R. 1.7(a) & (b) (2018) (requiring each client's "informed written consent" to concurrent conflicts of interest).

5. *The Enforceability of Advance Conflict Waivers*

While lawyers may seek consent from clients at the time a conflict of interest arises, it is also ethically permissible for lawyers to obtain advance consent to future conflicts of interest.[117] In fact, this practice is common where sophisticated clients are concerned. The overarching test for the enforceability of advance conflict waivers remains the client's informed consent to the conflict.[118] The lawyer bears the burden of proving the client's informed consent.[119]

Whether a court will consider consent to an advance waiver informed ordinarily depends on several factors, including the waiver's specificity and scope, the caliber of the discussion between the lawyer and the client concerning the conflict, the nature of the actual conflict, the client's sophistication, whether independent counsel represented the client in giving consent, and the interests of justice.[120] Like any other agreement between a lawyer and a client, a court will narrowly construe the scope of an advance waiver and resolve any ambiguities against the lawyer.[121]

Galderma Laboratories., L.P. v. Actavis Mid Atlantic LLC[122] is currently the leading case upholding an advance waiver. Beginning in 2003, Vinson & Elkins, LLP (V&E) advised Galderma Laboratories, a global dermatology company, on employment and benefits issues. In its engagement letter, V&E sought Galderma's consent to the following waiver of future conflicts of interest:

> We understand and agree that this is not an exclusive agreement, and you are free to retain any other counsel of your choosing. We recognize that

117. Model Rules of Prof'l Conduct R. 1.7 cmt. 22 (2020); ABA Comm. on Ethics & Prof'l Responsibility, Formal Op. 05-436, at 1, 4–5 (2005); D.C. Bar, Legal Ethics Comm., Op. 309, at 5 (2001) [hereinafter D.C. Op. 309]; N.Y.C. Ethics Op. 2006-1, 2006 WL 1662501, at *1 (Ass'n of the Bar of the City of N.Y., Comm. on Prof'l & Jud. Ethics 2006) [hereinafter N.Y.C. Ethics Op. 2006-1].

118. *Galderma Labs.*, 927 F. Supp. 2d at 396; Visa USA, Inc. v. First Data Corp., 241 F. Supp. 2d 1100, 1106 (N.D. Cal. 2003); N.Y.C. Ethics Op. 2006-1, *supra* note 117, 2006 WL 1662501, at *1.

119. *Galderma Labs.*, 927 F. Supp. 2d at 398.

120. Lennar Mare Island, LLC v. Steadfast Ins. Co., 105 F. Supp. 3d 1100, 1115 (E.D. Cal. 2015) (citing *Visa USA*, 241 F. Supp. 2d at 1106); W. Sugar Coop. v. Archer-Daniels-Midland Co., 98 F. Supp. 3d 1074, 1082–83 (C.D. Cal. 2015) (citing *Visa USA*, 241 F. Supp. 2d at 1106).

121. *See, e.g.*, GSI Commerce Sols., Inc. v. BabyCenter, LLC, 618 F.3d 204, 212–13 (2d Cir. 2010) (concluding that the lawsuit in question did not fall into the category of cases covered by the parties' advance waiver provision); *In re* Rail Freight Fuel Surcharge Antitrust Litig., 965 F. Supp. 2d 104, 118 n.12 (D.D.C. 2013) (rejecting the law firm's argument that the advance waiver covered the client's entire corporate family); Brigham Young Univ. v. Pfizer, Inc., No. 2:06-CV-890 TS BCW, 2010 WL 3855347, at *2–3 (D. Utah Sept. 29, 2010) (construing the advance waiver to apply to the law firm's clients with open intellectual property matters as of the day the consenting client signed the agreement, as opposed to covering all of the law firm's current and future clients with intellectual property matters).

122. 927 F. Supp. 2d 390 (N.D. Tex. 2013).

> we shall be disqualified from representing any other client with interest materially and directly adverse to yours (i) in any matter which is substantially related to our representation of you and (ii) with respect to any matter where there is a reasonable probability that confidential information you furnished to us could be used to your disadvantage. You understand and agree that, with those exceptions, we are free to represent other clients, including clients whose interests may conflict with ours in litigation, business transactions, or other legal matters. You agree that our representing you in this matter will not prevent or disqualify us from representing clients adverse to you in other matters and that you consent in advance to our undertaking such adverse representations.[123]

Quinton Cassady, Galderma's general counsel and a very experienced lawyer, signed the letter and thereby agreed to V&E's engagement terms.

In 2012, while V&E was still advising Galderma on employment issues, Galderma hired another law firm to file patent litigation against Activis Mid Atlantic, LLC. At that time, V&E had represented Activis on intellectual property matters for six years. V&E filed an answer and counterclaims on Activis's behalf. After V&E refused Galderma's requests to withdraw from representing Activis based on the advance waiver, Galderma moved to disqualify V&E. The issue for the court was "whether or not Galderma, a sophisticated client, represented by in house-counsel gave informed consent when it agreed to a general, open-ended waiver of future conflicts of interest in V&E's 2003 engagement letter."[124]

Focusing on the 2003 engagement letter, the court concluded that the information disclosed was reasonably adequate for a client to form informed consent.[125] First, the letter identified a course of conduct regarding concurrent conflicts of interest: V&E could represent clients whose interests conflicted with Galderma's interests unless the adverse representation was substantially related to Galderma's representation or there was a reasonable probability that V&E could use Galderma's confidential information to its disadvantage. Second, the letter explained the material risk in waiving future conflicts: V&E could advocate for another client directly against Galderma. Third, the letter explained an alternative course of conduct for Galderma: it could engage different employment counsel if it did not wish to consent to V&E's terms and conditions.[126]

The *Galderma* court recognized that "[i]n many cases, and for many clients," V&E's general, open-ended advance waiver "would likely not be reasonably adequate to allow a client to make an informed decision."[127]

123. *Id.* at 393.
124. *Id.* at 394.
125. *Id.* at 399.
126. *Id.* at 399–400, 401.
127. *Id.* at 405–06.

The court explained that most clients are not positioned to understand the material risks from the open-ended language of the waiver itself.[128] At the same time, however, V&E's waiver was "reasonably adequate to allow clients in some circumstances to understand the material risk of waiving future conflicts of interest."[129] In the court's view, such circumstances existed here given Galderma's sophistication and representation by independent counsel in the form of its in-house general counsel.[130]

Galderma possessed a high level of business sophistication based on its global operations, worldwide sales of $1.87 billion, and filing of over 5,500 patent applications and patents.[131] Galderma also was a highly experienced consumer of legal services.[132] The company was then involved in over a dozen lawsuits, routinely hired multiple large law firms to advise it on various issues and litigate in courts across the country, and agreed to at least two other advance waivers with another large law firm.[133] Galderma had its own legal department led by Cassady, who had long practice experience.[134] These circumstances, coupled with the advance waiver language itself, established the informed consent necessary to enforce the advance waiver against Galderma.

Based on the fact-intensive nature of the informed consent inquiry, there are few bright line rules guiding lawyers as to the enforceability of advance waiver provisions. For that matter, because of the frequent difficulty of achieving informed consent, advance waiver provisions that might be characterized as open-ended are notoriously unreliable insurance against future disqualifying conflicts despite their ethical permissibility.[135] On the other hand, the closer the actual conflict of interest is to that which the parties contemplated at the time the client agreed to the advance waiver, the more likely it is that a court will enforce the waiver. Furthermore, while a clear link between the prospective and actual conflicts is certainly desirable, a lack of specificity regarding an identifiable future client or matter encompassed by the waiver does not necessarily render an advance conflict waiver

128. *Id.* at 397.
129. *Id.* at 401.
130. *Id.* at 401–04.
131. *Id.* at 402.
132. *Id.*
133. *Id.*
134. *Id.* at 403.
135. *See, e.g.*, S. Visions, LLP v. Red Diamond, Inc., 370 F. Supp. 3d 1314, 1327 (N.D. Ala. 2019) ("[G]iven the advance waivers' lack of specificity, the lack of evidence that Red Diamond was fully counseled regarding their import, and especially the fact that directly adverse litigation between two direct competitors like Red Diamond and Southern Visions is an extremely serious conflict most clients would be unwilling to waive, the court is unable to conclude that the advance waivers, standing alone, provided Red Diamond's effective consent to this conflict."); Mylan, Inc. v. Kirkland & Ellis LLP, No. 15-581, 2015 WL 12733414, at *18–19 (W.D. Pa. June 9, 2015) (rejecting an advance conflicts waiver for lack of informed consent).

unenforceable.[136] An open-ended advance waiver may still be enforceable if its terms outline an approach to determining the firm's obligations should a conflict surface, adequately explain the material risk to the client of waiving future conflicts of interest, and identify for the client reasonably available alternatives to the proposed course of conduct.[137] This is especially true where the client is sophisticated.[138] Indeed, even a more general open-ended advance waiver may be enforceable where the client is sophisticated.[139] Of course, an advance waiver will not excuse a lawyer's failure to disclose a known current conflict of interest.[140]

Although nothing is certain in this area, lawyers increase the likelihood that an advance waiver will be effective if they take the following steps. First, discuss the advance waiver with the client rather than simply inserting the waiver in the engagement letter. There may be times when this is not practicable or necessary, as where, for example, the client has an in-house law department and sends numerous matters to the firm, or the lawyer and client have an understanding regarding matters to which advance waivers will apply or will not be granted. Nonetheless, where feasible, a documented discussion with the client generally reduces the likelihood that the client will later be able to successfully claim that it did not understand the advance waiver or its effect.

Second, if the client does not have an in-house law department, the lawyer should recommend that the client have the advance waiver reviewed by independent counsel.

Third, commit that in any future matter to which the waiver applies, the firm will screen the lawyers and staff handling that matter from the lawyers and staff serving the client, and the respective teams will not share files or information.

Fourth, agree that you will not represent another client with interests materially and directly adverse to the current client's interests (1) in any

136. *See, e.g.*, United States v. Abdelaziz, No. 19-10080-NMG, 2020 WL 618697, at *5 (D. Mass. Feb. 10, 2020) (enforcing an advance waiver against a university); Simpson Strong-Tie Co. v. Oz-Post Int'l, LLC, No. 3:18-cv-01188-WHO, 2018 WL 3956430, at *14–19 (N.D. Cal. Aug. 17, 2018) (commenting on the scope of the advance waiver and ultimately declining to disqualify the law firm).

137. *See, e.g.*, *In re* Fisker Auto. Holdings, Inc. S'holder Litig., C.A. No. 13-2100-DBS-SRF, 2018 WL 3991470, at *4 (D. Del. Aug. 20, 2018) (upholding an advance waiver); Macy's Inc. v. J.C. Penny Corp., 968 N.Y.S.2d 64, 65–66 (App. Div. 2013) (reasoning that the advance waiver was adequate).

138. *In re Fisker*, 2018 WL 3991470, at *4; Galderma Labs., L.P. v. Actavis Mid Atl. LLC, 927 F. Supp. 2d 390, 402–03 (N.D. Tex. 2013).

139. *See, e.g.*, *Abdelaziz*, 2020 WL 618697, at *5 (enforcing an advance waiver against a university).

140. *Galderma Labs.*, 927 F. Supp. 2d at 402–03; Sheppard, Mullin, Richter & Hampton, LLP v. J-M Mfg. Co., 425 P.3d 1, 17–18 (Cal. 2018); D.C. Op. 309, *supra* note 118, at 6.

matter that is substantially related to your representation of the current client and (2) in any matter in which there is a reasonable probability that confidential information the current client furnished to you could be used to the current client's disadvantage. If it is possible to define matters that will be considered substantially related, it is helpful to do so.

Fifth, make the advance waiver as specific as possible. For example, does the firm need an advance waiver only for a certain type of litigated matter, or does the firm want or need an advance waiver to represent a specific client or group of clients regardless of the subject of the litigation? The greater the limitation of the scope of the advance waiver, the greater the likelihood that (1) the client will agree to it and (2) a court will enforce it.

Sixth, if you include an advance waiver in your engagement letter, require the client to countersign the engagement letter.

Seventh, depending on the client and the matter, it may be wise to send the client a separate advance waiver letter rather than incorporating advance waiver language in an engagement letter. If you send a separate letter, require the client to countersign it.

IV. Former Client Conflicts of Interest

As with current client relationships, lawyers' relationships with former clients may create conflicts of interest.[141] Former client conflicts fall under Model Rule 1.9:

> (a) A lawyer who has formerly represented a client in a matter shall not thereafter represent another person in the same or a substantially related matter in which that person's interests are materially adverse to the interests of the former client unless the former client gives informed consent, confirmed in writing.
> (b) A lawyer shall not knowingly represent a person in the same or a substantially related matter in which a firm with which the lawyer formerly was associated had previously represented a client
>> (1) whose interests are materially adverse to that person; and
>> (2) about whom the lawyer had acquired information protected by Rules 1.6 and 1.9(c) that is material to the matter; unless the former client gives informed consent, confirmed in writing.
>
> (c) A lawyer who has formerly represented a client in a matter or whose present or former firm has formerly represented a client in a matter shall not thereafter:

141. If a law firm represents a client in more than one matter, the client is the firm's current client if any of those matters is active or open. ABA Comm. on Ethics & Prof'l Responsibility, Formal Op. 481, at 6 (2018).

(1) use information relating to the representation to the disadvantage of the former client except as these Rules would permit or require with respect to a client, or when the information has become generally known; or
(2) reveal information relating to the representation except as these Rules would permit or require with respect to a client.[142]

Model Rule 1.9 is principally intended to protect a former client's reasonable expectation that confidential information a lawyer or law firm acquires during a representation will not later be used to the former client's detriment when the lawyer or law firm accepts a new representation adverse to the former client.

A. *Model Rule 1.9(a) Conflicts*

For there to be a conflict of interest under Model Rule 1.9(a), the lawyer's current and prior representations must involve either the same matter or substantially related matters. Under the majority rule, the former client bears the burden of establishing that the current and prior matters are either the same or substantially related.[143]

When deciding whether matters are the same or substantially related, a superficial resemblance or incidental similarity between the two matters is insufficient.[144] Rather, two matters should be considered substantially related if (1) they involve the same transaction or legal dispute or (2) there is a substantial risk that confidential factual information as would normally have been obtained in the prior representation of the former client would materially advance the current client's position in the subsequent matter.[145] Accordingly, the "substantial relationship test" can be broken down into two separate inquiries: Does the current representation involve the same work the lawyer performed for the former client? Alternatively, is there a substantial risk that the lawyer acquired confidential information in the former client's representation that would materially advance the new client's representation? The first question asks about matter-specific conflicts, while the second inquires about information-specific conflicts.

142. Model Rules of Prof'l Conduct R. 1.9 (2020).

143. Samnick v. Goodman, 841 S.E.2d 468, 474 (Ga. Ct. App. 2020) (quoting Cardinal Robotics v. Moody, 694 S.E.2d 346, 349 (Ga. 2010)); Robbins v. Gillock, 862 P.2d 1195, 1197 (Nev. 1993); Plein v. USAA Cas. Ins. Co., 463 P.3d 728, 733 (Wash. 2020); State *ex rel.* Ogden Newspapers, Inc. v. Willis, 566 S.E.2d 560, 563 (W. Va. 2002).

144. Nev. Yellow Cab Corp. v. Eighth Jud. Dist. Ct. of Nev., 152 P.3d 737, 742 (Nev. 2007); Foley-Ciccantelli v. Bishop's Grove Condo. Ass'n, 797 N.W.2d 789, 815 (Wis. 2011).

145. Model Rules of Prof'l Conduct R. 1.9 cmt. 3 (2020).

1. *Analyzing Matter-Specific Conflicts of Interest*

For a matter-specific conflict of interest to materialize under Model Rule 1.9(a), "the matters must merely involve the same transaction or legal dispute."[146] Whether current and former matters involve the same transaction or legal dispute is determined by inquiring into whether the two matters are factually related.[147] The matters must turn on the same facts of a particular situation or transaction, as opposed to simply involving the same type of legal issues.[148] The comments to Model Rule 1.9 elaborate on this point:

> When a lawyer has been directly involved in a specific transaction, subsequent representation of other clients with materially adverse interests clearly is prohibited. On the other hand, a lawyer who recurrently handled a type of problem for a former client is not precluded from later representing another client in a factually distinct problem of that type even though the subsequent representation involves a position adverse to the prior client.[149]

A distinction therefore exists between pursuing a claim against a former client on a specific transaction or legal dispute versus adversity centered on a category or type of legal problem that a lawyer handled on a recurring basis.

Regarding the first scenario, the duty of loyalty prohibits a lawyer from depriving a former client of the benefit of the lawyer's work on the former client's behalf. It is thus generally accepted that a current matter is substantially related to a former client's representation if the current matter involves the same work the lawyer performed for the former client.[150] This brand of former client conflict of interest is particularly severe when a lawyer attacks her earlier work or legal advice—a situation sometimes colloquially characterized as fouling one's own nest.[151]

146. *In re* Conduct of Hostetter, 238 P.3d 13, 23 (Or. 2010) (emphasis omitted).

147. Watkins v. Trans Union, LLC, 869 F.3d 514, 520 (7th Cir. 2017); Newton v. Stoneridge Apts., 424 P.3d 1086, 1092–93 (Utah Ct. App. 2018); Model Rules of Prof'l Conduct R. 1.9 cmt. 2 (2020).

148. *Watkins*, 869 F.3d at 521 (quoting Ind. Rules of Prof'l Conduct R. 1.9 cmt. 2).

149. Model Rules of Prof'l Conduct R. 1.9 cmt. 2 (2020).

150. *In re* Conduct of Hostetter, 238 P.3d 13, 23 (Or. 2010); Restatement (Third) of the Law Governing Lawyers § 132(1) (2000).

151. *See, e.g.*, Annie Sloan Interiors, Ltd. v. Kappel, Civ. A. No. 19-807, 2019 WL 2492303, at *1–3 (E.D. La. June 14, 2019) (alleging breach of fiduciary duty and the violation of Rule 1.9(a) where the lawyer helped a client register its trademarks and later represented another client in attacking the trademarks); Acad. of Allergy & Asthma in Primary Care v. La. Health Serv. & Indem. Co., 384 F. Supp. 3d 644, 659–60 (E.D. La. 2018) (concluding that representations "are substantially related where counsel advises its current client on the subject matter it had previously advised its former client, in an effort to help the current client to prevail over the former on a critical issue shared between the two representations; the law firm "placed itself in the position of attacking its own prior advocacy made on behalf of its former client"); Paul v. Jud. Watch, Inc., 571 F. Supp. 2d 17, 21–22 (D.D.C. 2008) (disqualifying a lawyer who supervised the negotiation and drafting of an agreement as Judicial Watch's general counsel and then represented the plaintiff against Judicial Watch in a matter arising from that agreement); Oasis W. Realty, LLC v. Goldman,

In contrast to scenarios where a lawyer attacks her prior work for the client, it is ordinarily permissible for a lawyer who has repeatedly handled a general type of legal problem for a client to later oppose that client in a factually distinct case. Where a lawyer handles recurrent yet factually distinct problems, the factual information that a lawyer acquires in a representation is not necessarily relevant to later matters; hence, there is no substantial risk that the lawyer could use the information to gain an unfair advantage.[152] The upshot is that while a lawyer clearly cannot switch sides in a specific transaction or matter, the lawyer's representation adverse to a former client in the same type of legal matter that she handled for the former client may be a different story.[153] Model Rule 1.9(a) allows for representations opposite former clients to touch upon the particular problem area in which legal advice was previously rendered. When two matters rely on the same legal theories but involve different facts, the two matters are not generally considered to be substantially related.[154]

250 P.3d 1115, 1124–25 (Cal. 2011) (stating tort and contract claims where the lawyer represented the client in obtaining a city council's approval for a redevelopment project, and two years later campaigned to thwart the project); ASI Holding Co. v. Royal Beach & Golf Resorts, LLC, 163 So. 3d 668, 670–71 (Fla. Dist. Ct. App. 2015) (disqualifying a law firm because its representation placed it in a position of "attacking the validity of the very document that it had previously represented to be valid and legally binding"); *In re* Basco, 221 S.W.3d 637, 639 (Tex. 2007) (disqualifying a hospital's defense lawyer and his law firm because the lawsuit required him to challenge the validity of his former law partner's legal advice to the plaintiff doctor).

152. Villas at Highland Park Homeowners Ass'n v. Villas at Highland Park, LLC, 394 P.3d 1144, 1153 (Colo. 2017); *see* ABA Comm. on Ethics & Prof'l Responsibility, Formal Op. 99-415, at 5 n.10 (1999) [hereinafter ABA Formal Op. 99-415] (explaining that "it is not sufficient for the matters merely to be problems of a similar type" for purposes of the substantial relationship test); Restatement (Third) of the Law Governing Lawyers § 132 cmt. h (2000) (observing that "a lawyer may master a particular substantive area of the law while representing a client, but that does not preclude a lawyer from representing another client adversely to the first in a matter involving the same legal issues, if the matters factually are not substantially related").

153. *See* Watkins v. Trans Union, LLC, 869 F.3d 514, 521 (7th Cir. 2017) (stating that where a lawyer defended Trans Union in hundreds of FCRA cases over a two-year period, and almost ten years later represented a FCRA plaintiff against Trans Union, the representations did not turn on the same facts because the plaintiff's FCRA claim was unique to him and not interwoven with any case in which the lawyer had represented Trans Union).

154. United States *ex rel.* Bumbury v. Med-Care Diabetic & Med. Supplies, Inc., 101 F. Supp. 3d 1268, 1275 (S.D. Fla. 2015); *see, e.g.*, Nicholas v. Grapetree Shores, Inc., No. 05-119, 2013 WL 1196960, at *6 (D.V.I. Mar. 21, 2013) (observing that a lawyer is not precluded from representing a client adverse to a former client simply because the cases involve "the same legal issues if the matters *factually* are not substantially related"); Health Care & Ret. Corp. of Am., Inc. v. Bradley, 961 So. 2d 1071, 1072–74 (Fla. Dist. Ct. App. 2007) (finding no substantial relationship where the lawyer defended a nursing home in over 60 cases alleging negligence tied to residents' pressure ulcers and falls and later left his law firm and sued the nursing home alleging neglect and failure to monitor the development of residents' pressure ulcers; the subsequent representation was a "wholly distinct problem" that turned on its own facts).

2. *Analyzing Information-Specific Conflicts*

Even if the prior and current matters do not involve the same transaction or legal dispute, they are still substantially related if there is "a substantial risk that confidential factual information as would normally have been obtained [by the lawyer] in the prior representation would materially advance the [new] client's position in the subsequent matter."[155] This aspect of the substantial relationship test is information-specific and assumes the view of a hypothetical reasonable lawyer.[156] The crux of the issue is "whether a reasonable lawyer would perceive a substantial risk that a competent attorney would normally have learned confidential factual information during the prior representation that could be used against the former client in the new matter."[157]

To prove there is a substantial risk that the lawyer has confidential information that could harm the former client's interests in the subsequent matter, the former client is not required to divulge the confidential information allegedly disclosed to the lawyer.[158] A contrary rule would ironically force former clients to reveal the very information Rule 1.9 is intended to protect. As a result, courts focus on the nature of the legal services that the lawyer provided the former client and the kind of confidential factual information that the lawyer would have typically received during the representation.[159] This may include examining whether "(a) the lawyer and the client ought to have talked about particular facts during the course of the representation; or (b) the information is of such a character that it would not have been unusual for it to have been discussed between lawyer and former client during their relationships."[160]

---

155. Model Rules of Prof'l Conduct R. 1.9 cmt. 3 (2020).

156. N.Y. Ethics Op. 871, 2011 WL 7784081, at *2 (N.Y. State Bar Ass'n, Comm. on Prof'l Ethics 2011).

157. *Id.* at *3.

158. Bowers v. Ophthalmology Grp., 733 F.3d 647, 651 (6th Cir. 2013); Velazquez-Velez v. Molina-Rodriguez, 235 F. Supp. 3d 358, 362 (D.P.R. 2017) (quoting Starlight Sugar Inc. v. Soto, 903 F. Supp. 261, 266 (D.P.R. 1995)); Headfirst Baseball LLC v. Elwood, 999 F. Supp. 2d 199, 211 (D.D.C. 2013) (quoting Derrickson v. Derrickson, 541 A.2d 149, 151 (D.C. 1988)); Persichette v. Owners Ins. Co., 462 P.3d 581, 587 (Colo. 2020); N.Y. Ethics Op. 1008, 2014 WL 11398169, at *4 (N.Y. State Bar Ass'n, Comm. on Prof'l Ethics 2014) [hereinafter N.Y. Ethics Op. 1008]; Pa. Ethics Op. 2012-100, 2012 WL 12314855, at *3 (Pa. Bar Ass'n, Comm. on Legal Ethics & Prof'l Responsibility 2012) [hereinafter Pa. Ethics Op. 2012-100].

159. *Bowers*, 733 F.3d at 652–53; *Headfirst Baseball LLC*, 999 F. Supp. 2d at 210–11; Villas at Highland Park Homeowners Ass'n v. Villas at Highland Park, LLC, 394 P.3d 1144, 1153 (Colo. 2017).

160. Pa. Ethics Op. 2012-100, *supra* note 158, 2012 WL 12314855, at *3; *see also* Atmosphere Hosp. Mgmt. Servs., LLC v. Royal Realties, LLC, 28 F. Supp. 3d 692, 697 (E.D. Mich. 2014) (expressing the same test) (quoting Alpha Capital Mgmt., Inc. v. Rentenbach, 792 N.W.2d 344, 356–57 (Mich. Ct. App. 2010)).

Evidence that a lawyer actually received confidential information relating to the prior representation is unnecessary for Rule 1.9(a) purposes.[161] If it is reasonable to infer that the lawyer received information during the first representation that might be useful in the second representation, thereby creating a substantial risk of exploitation of that information, then the two matters are substantially related.[162] All the same, proof of the lawyer's "*actual* receipt of confidential factual information in the prior matter [is] even more compelling than a mere likelihood of its receipt."[163] A former client's conclusory or unsupported allegations that she shared confidential information during the prior representation, however, ought not be considered.[164]

The existence of a substantial relationship triggers the presumption that the lawyer possesses confidential information that can be used for the current client's benefit and the former client's detriment.[165] In most jurisdictions, the presumption is irrebuttable.[166] In others, it is "rebuttable but difficult to overcome."[167]

Applying this framework has proven to be laborious because of the varying ways in which courts articulate the substantial relationship analysis. One line of authority concentrates on a fact-based comparison of the

161. Analytica, Inc. v. NPD Rsch., Inc., 708 F.2d 1263, 1266 (7th Cir. 1983); Annie Sloan Interiors, Ltd. v. Kappel, No. 19-807, 2019 WL 2492303, at *7 (E.D. La. June 14, 2019); *In re* Conduct of Hostetter, 238 P.3d 13, 23 (Or. 2010).

162. Fernandez v. St. Francis Hosp., Inc., No. 09C-03-008-JRS, 2009 WL 2393713, at *3 (Del. Super. Ct. Aug. 3, 2009).

163. N.Y. Ethics Op. 1008, *supra* note 158, 2014 WL 11398169, at *5;*see* N.Y. Ethics Op. 922, 2012 WL 2058665, at *2 (N.Y. State Bar Ass'n, Comm. on Prof'l Ethics 2012) (recognizing that matters are "substantially related if the lawyer in question actually and knowingly obtained (and now possesses) confidential factual information that would materially advance the prospective client's position in the subsequent matter").

164. Aubrey v. D Mag. Partners, L.P., Civ. A. No. 3:19-CV-0056-B, 2019 WL 2103699, at *2 (N.D. Tex. May 14, 2019); Worley v. Moore, 807 S.E.2d 133, 140 (N.C. 2017).

165. N. Am. Deed Co. v. Joseph, 334 B.R. 443, 455 (Bankr. D. Nev. 2005); Koch v. Koch Indus., Inc., 798 F. Supp. 1525, 1536 (D. Kan. 1992).

166. United States v. Prevezon Holdings Ltd., 839 F.3d 227, 240 (2d Cir. 2016) (quoting DeFazio v. Wallis, 459 F. Supp. 2d 159, 164–65 (E.D.N.Y. 2006)); United States v. Stiger, 413 F.3d 1185, 1196 (10th Cir. 2005) (quoting Smith v. Whatcott, 757 F.2d 1098, 1100 (10th Cir. 1985)), *overruled on other grounds by* United States v. Ellis, 868 F.3d 1155, 1175 (10th Cir. 2017)); Perillo v. Johnson, 205 F.3d 775, 800 (5th Cir. 2000); Mt. Hebron Missionary Baptist Ass'n of AL, Inc. v. Sentinel Ins. Co., No.: 3:16-cv-658-CDL-GMB, 2017 WL 3928269, at *6 (M.D. Ala. Sept. 27, 2017); Audio MPEG, Inc. v. Dell, Inc., 219 F. Supp. 3d 563, 569 (E.D. Va. 2016) (quoting Tessier v. Plastic Surgery Specialists, Inc., 731 F. Supp. 724, 731 (E.D. Va. 1990)); Goff v. Goff, 276 So. 3d 83, (Fla. Dist. Ct. App. 2019) (quoting Galaxy Fireworks, Inc. v. Kozar, 150 So. 3d 256, 257 (Fla. Dist. Ct. App. 2014)); Janczewski v. Janczewski, 94 N.Y.S.3d 142, 145 (App. Div. 2019); *In re* Thetford, 574 S.W.3d 362, 373 (Tex. 2019); Hart v. State, 62 P.3d 566, 573 (Wyo. 2003).

167. *In re* MKC Millennium Ctr. Retail, LLC, 571 B.R. 783, 786 (Bankr. N.D. Ill. 2017); *see, e.g.*, XYZ, D.O. v. Sykes, 20 N.E.3d 582, 588 (Ind. Ct. App. 2014) (applying a rebuttable presumption); Wynveen v. Corsaro, 106 N.E.3d 130, 141 (Ohio Ct. App. 2017) (explaining that when the attorney in the subsequent litigation is not the original attorney but instead another attorney in the same law firm, the presumption of received confidences is rebuttable); Clinard v. Blackwood, 46 S.W.3d 177, 184 (Tenn. 2001) (discussing a rebuttable presumption of shared confidences).

two matters.[168] Another line of authority holds that the current and prior representations must involve common subject matters, issues, or legal problems.[169] A third line of authority requires the relationship between the matters to be "patently clear" or for the matters to sport "identical issues."[170] Finally, a fourth approach focuses on the similarities between the factual circumstances and legal theories of the representations, as well as the degree of the lawyer's involvement.[171]

168. *See, e.g.*, *Whatcott*, 757 F.2d at 1100 (quoting Tr. Corp. of Mont. v. Piper Aircraft Corp., 701 F.2d 85, 87 (9th Cir. 1983)); *Koch*, 798 F. Supp. at 1536 (focusing on "the similarities between the factual bases of the two representations" and noting that "[a] commonality of legal claims or issues is not required"); *In re Thetford*, 574 S.W.3d at 374 (producing specific overlapping facts between the two matters is necessary to show a substantial relationship, but it is not sufficient; those facts must further create a genuine threat of disclosure); Plein v. USAA Cas. Ins. Co., 463 P.3d 728, 736 (Wash. 2020) ("The current RPC 1.9 and its associated comments thus tell us to decide whether the former and current representation are factually related."); ABA Formal Op. 99-415, *supra* note 152, at 5 (stating that the standard "inevitably requires a factual inquiry comparing the two matters").

169. *See, e.g.*, *In re* Am. Airlines, Inc., 972 F.2d 605, 625 (5th Cir. 1992) (explaining that the "two representations need only involve the same 'subject matter'" to be substantially related); Acad. of Allergy & Asthma in Primary Care v. La. Health Serv. & Indem. Co., 384 F. Supp. 3d 644, 657 (E.D. La. 2018) (concluding that representations are substantially related where a lawyer advises a current client on the subject matter she had previously advised a former client about to help the current client prevail over the former client on a critical issue common to both representations); FDIC *ex rel.* AmTrust Bank v. Commonwealth Land Title Ins. Co., No. 1:08CV2390, 2012 WL 3912764, at *7 (N.D. Ohio Sept. 7, 2012) (quoting Campbell v. Indep. Outlook, Inc., No. 04AP-310, 2004 WL 2892884, at *3 (Ohio Ct. App. Dec. 14, 2004)); Estate of Pew, 655 A.2d 521, 545–46 (Pa. Super. Ct. 1994) (stating that the fact that representations involve similar or related facts is not alone sufficient, but "rather the test is whether information acquired by an attorney in his former representation is substantially related to the subject matter of subsequent representation").

170. *See, e.g.*, Gov't of India v. Cook Indus., Inc., 569 F.2d 737, 739–40 (2d Cir. 1978) (Such considerations have [honed] the substantial relationship' test . . . to granting disqualification only upon a showing that the relationship between issues in the prior and present cases is 'patently clear'. . . . [D]isqualification has been granted or approved recently only when the issues involved have been 'identical or essentially the same'." (citations omitted)); Calamar Enters., Inc. v. Blue Forest Land Grp., LLC, 222 F. Supp. 3d 257, 265–66 (W.D.N.Y. 2016) (requiring a patently clear relationship between the matters); Revise Clothing, Inc. v. Joe's Jeans Subsidiary, Inc., 687 F. Supp. 2d 381, 392 (S.D.N.Y. 2010) (quoting *Gov't of India*, 569 F.2d at 739–40); Becker v. Perla, 5 N.Y.S.3d 34, 35 (App. Div. 2015) (requiring the issues in the competing matters to be "identical or essentially the same").

171. *See, e.g.*, Zerger & Mauer LLP v. City of Greenwood, 751 F.3d 928, 933 (8th Cir. 2014) ("To determine if matters are substantially related, we must examine the factual and issue relationship between the two representations."); Leapfrog Enters., Inc. v. Epik Learning, LLC, Case No.16-cv-04269-EDL, 2017 WL 2986604, at *8 (N.D. Cal. Feb. 23, 2017) (stating that "a substantial relationship depends on the similarities between the two factual situations, the legal questions posed, and the nature and extent of the attorney's involvement"); Jessen v. Hartford Cas. Ins. Co., 3 Cal. Rptr. 3d 877, 887–88 (Ct. App. 2003) (deeming two matters substantially related when "[confidential] information material to the evaluation, prosecution, settlement or accomplishment of the former representation given its factual and legal issues is also material to the evaluation, prosecution, settlement or accomplishment of the current representation given its factual and legal issues"); Villas at Highland Park Homeowners Ass'n v. Villas at Highland Park, LLC, 394 P.3d 1144, 1153 (Colo. 2017) (quoting People v. Frisco, 119 P.3d 1093, 1096 (Colo. 2005)); State *ex*

As one might expect, whether prior and current representations are substantially related is a fact-intensive inquiry.[172] Considerations that may guide the analysis include (1) the scope of the representations set forth in the engagement letters; (2) whether the matters share a common subject matter, legal issues, causes of action, or key witnesses or evidence; (3) whether the matters involve the same events or a series of matters or transactions that reveal the former client's pattern of conduct; (4) whether time has rendered all or part of the former client's information obsolete; (5) whether the former client's information has since been disclosed to the public; (6) whether the lawyer' knowledge of the former client's "playbook"—that is, its operations, litigation strategies, business practices, negotiating philosophy, ability to satisfy debts, or decision-making—is relevant to the current matter; (7) the duration of the lawyer's relationship with the clients; and (8) the nature of the lawyer's services.[173]

3. *A Representative Case*

Persichette v. Owners Insurance Co.[174] is an interesting former client conflict case. In *Persichette*, William Persichette, represented by Franklin D. Azar & Associates, P.C. (Azar), sued Owners Insurance Co. (Owners) for its alleged bad faith in connection with his 2018 under-insured motorist (UIM) claim. According to Persichette, Owners failed to (1) reasonably evaluate and investigate his claim, (2) timely pay benefits he was due, (3) timely communicate with his lawyer, and (4) consent to a proposed settlement with the underinsured driver. A few months into the litigation, Persichette engaged Mark R. Levy of Levy Law, P.C. (collectively Levy Law) as co-counsel with Azar. Persichette's retention of Levy Law heralded trouble because the firm had represented Owners in 455 cases between 2004 and 2017 and was one of a handful of law firms that regularly represented Owners in bad faith litigation in Colorado.[175] In the last five years alone, Levy Law had billed Owners for over 1,700 hours of legal work and earned more than $5 million

rel. Swanson v. 3M Co., 845 N.W.2d 808, 816–17 (Minn. 2014) (analyzing the extent to which the factual and legal issues in the two matters overlap); State *ex rel.* Wal-Mart Stores, Inc. v. Kortum, 559 N.W.2d 496, 501 (Neb. 1997) (focusing on the similarity of the factual and legal issues in both cases).

172. *Highland Park Homeowners Ass'n*, 394 P.3d at 1153; Foley-Ciccantelli v. Bishop's Grove Condo. Ass'n, 797 N.W.2d 789, 815 (Wis. 2011); Pa. Ethics Op. 2012-100, *supra* note 158, 2012 WL 12314855, at *3; Utah Ethics Op. 12-01, 2012 WL 740334, at *3 (Utah State Bar, Ethics Advisory Op. Comm. 2012).

173. United States *ex rel.* Bumbury v. Med-Care Diabetic & Med. Supplies, Inc., 101 F. Supp. 3d 1268, 1275–76 (S.D. Fla. 2015); Chrispens v. Coastal Ref. & Mktg., Inc., 897 P.2d 104, 112 (Kan. 1995); *In re* Carey, 89 S.W.3d 477, 494 (Mo. 2002) (quoting *Chrispens*, 897 P.2d at 112); *Kortum*, 559 N.W.2d at 501; Worley v. Moore, 807 S.E.2d 133, 140 (N.C. 2017).

174. 462 P.3d 581 (Colo. 2020).

175. *Id.* at 584.

in attorney's fees.[176] Twenty-three cases in which Levy Law had represented Owners involved claims that mirrored Persichette's allegations.[177]

Owners moved to disqualify Levy Law under Rule 1.9(a). Owners asserted that Levy Law helped institute Owners' claims-handling policies and procedures, including some that Persichette criticized. In addition, Levy Law had advised and trained Owners' claims staff, including Geoffrey Page, the adjuster responsible for Persichette's claim and the principal focus of Persichette's bad faith allegations.[178] Owners asserted that Levy Law had counseled Page and other adjusters on how to minimize Owners' exposure on claims and, in the process, had learned confidential information concerning Owners' general litigation strategy and Page's professional attributes and weaknesses.[179] This information, Owners contended, gave Persichette "a real leg up" in his bad faith case.[180]

The trial court noted that a party moving to disqualify its former lawyer must establish four elements under Rule 1.9(a): (1) the party and the lawyer previously had an attorney-client relationship, (2) the current and the former matters are substantially related, (3) the current and former clients' interests are materially adverse, and (4) the former client declined to consent in writing to the disputed representation.[181] The trial court easily determined that Owners satisfied the first, third, and fourth elements of the analysis but struggled with whether this case was substantially related to any matter in which Levy Law had formerly represented Owners. Finally making what it considered a "close call," the trial court "ruled that, while the present and prior representations [were] 'substantially similar' and involve[d] 'numerous and substantial' similarities, they [were] not 'substantially related.'"[182] The trial court thus denied Owners' motion to disqualify Levy Law. Owners then petitioned the Colorado Supreme Court to intervene in the case, and the court agreed to do so.

The *Persichette* court explained that the trial court had construed Rule 1.9(a) too narrowly.[183] Based on the trial court's findings contained in the record and the trial court's misapplication of a hypothetical example in one of the comments to Rule 1.9, it appeared that the trial court "essentially collapsed 'a substantially related matter' into 'the same' matter."[184] Indeed, the trial court had reasoned that Owners' motion to disqualify hinged on

176. *Id.*
177. *Id.*
178. *Id.* at 584–85.
179. *Id.* at 585.
180. *Id.*
181. *Id.* (relying on Villas at Highland Park Homeowners Ass'n v. Villas at Highland Park, LLC, 394 P.3d 1144, 1152 (Colo. 2017)).
182. *Id.*
183. *Id.* at 589.
184. *Id.*

whether Levy Law's prior representation of Owners included Persichette's claim.[185] But that analysis was plainly wrong under the language of Rule 1.9(a). In effect, the trial court erased "substantially related" from the text of Rule 1.9(a), which it clearly was not permitted to do.[186]

The trial court had also determined that the information about Owners that Levy Law had learned while representing the insurer was not confidential, such that any prior cases in which Levy Law had represented Owners could not be considered substantially related to Persichette's case. That determination did not withstand scrutiny:

> During its prior representation of Owners, Levy Law learned about Owners' general claims-handling policies and procedures, hierarchy of settlement authority, negotiation strategies, settlement pay ranges, and the factors Owners considers in assessing whether to settle a claim. . . . Levy Law provided advice and training to Owners and Owners' employees on the policies and procedures Owners uses to handle claims involving uninsured motorists, unreasonable delay, and bad faith—precisely the types of claims at issue here. Not only did Levy Law defend Owners in many cases against claims like the ones brought by Persichette, it worked closely with Page, the claims adjuster whose actions lie at the core of this case. Levy Law instructed Page on claims-handling and bad-faith-avoidance practices and educated him on being an effective witness. As well, Levy Law is familiar with Page's higher-ups, is keenly aware of their personalities and tendencies, and has inside information on how they come across as witnesses.
>
> This information is not ubiquitous in the insurance industry. Nor is Persichette likely to obtain the bulk of it through discovery. Almost nothing in the record corroborates the district court's outlook on the issue of confidentiality.[187]

In rejecting the trial court's reasoning concerning confidentiality, the *Persichette* court noted that Owners did not have to demonstrate that Levy Law actually possessed its confidential information—only that Levy Law likely did so.[188] Owners successfully carried that burden.

Continuing, the trial court had found that the information Levy Law acquired while representing Owners was "general 'playbook information'" that was not disqualifying.[189] The trial court decided that the information that Levy Law probably possessed about Owners was not likely to impair Owners' defense of Persichette's case. The relevant factual findings, however, sharply undercut the trial court's decision.

185. *Id.*
186. *Id.* (citing two Colorado Supreme Court cases discussing statutory construction principles).
187. *Id.* at 590.
188. *Id.*
189. *Id.*

> In its thorough order, the [trial] court stated that Levy Law's prior representation of Owners and current representation of Persichette involve[d] "the same legal material and theories," including bad faith theories and attacks on claims-handling practices. Along the same lines, the court remarked that the two representations involve[d] substantially similar matters that include[d] numerous and significant similarities. Thus, the court was troubled, as are we, by the prospect that this case will require Levy Law to attack its own work, including the very policies and procedures the firm helped Owners put in place. Indeed, as the court acknowledged, Levy Law ha[d] already come close to doing so.
>
> Not surprisingly, the district court recognized that Persichette may well "derive certain advantages" from Levy Law's prior representation of Owners. We do too.[190]

Persichette argued that any confidential client information Levy Law may have about Owners was immaterial because there was no reason to believe that Owners' current claims-handling policies and procedures were the same as they were when Levy Law represented the company. That argument failed out of the gate because the trial court had "specifically found that, as a result of the prior representation, Levy Law ha[d] knowledge of Owners' current claims-handling policies and procedures."[191] The trial court's finding had ample support in the record.

Arguing against disqualification in the trial court, Persichette had represented to the court that he would not attack Owners' claims-handling policies and procedures to prove its bad faith, "but would instead cabin that claim by arguing only that Owners failed to comply with those policies and procedures."[192] The trial court was apparently persuaded by this argument, but the Colorado Supreme Court was unmoved when Persichette tried it on appeal.

> [I]t makes no meaningful difference whether Persichette attacks Owners for the policies and procedures Levy Law helped put in place or Page for not following them. In either case, confidential client information Levy Law probably possesses about Owners' policies and procedures—including those that are front and center in this litigation—is relevant in this action in a way that likely disadvantages Owners. Certainly[,] Levy Law's intimate familiarity with Page, including as a result of educating and training him as an adjuster and a witness, is likely to give Persichette a head start in alleging that Page failed to follow Owners' policies and procedures.[193]

190. *Id.* at 590–91.
191. *Id.* at 591.
192. *Id.*
193. *Id.*

Regardless, Persichette's offer to reconfigure his case to avoid a Rule 1.9(a) former client conflict was no solution because that tactic would likely create a concurrent client conflict of interest for Levy Law under Rule 1.7(a)(2) by materially limiting the firm's representation of Persichette. In short, "in attempting to stave off Owners' motion for disqualification, Levy Law may be hopping out of the Rule 1.9(a) frying pan and into the Rule 1.7(a)(2) fire."[194]

Although it was apparent that Levy Law's representation of Persichette violated Rule 1.9(a), that alone was not enough to warrant the firm's disqualification.[195] Rather, disqualification is proper only when it is required to preserve the integrity and fairness of the proceedings.[196] Here, allowing Levy Law to continue as Persichette's counsel "would seriously threaten the integrity and fairness of the proceedings" and, unfortunately from Persichette's perspective, there was no viable alternative remedy.[197] At bottom, the trial court erred by not disqualifying Levy Law. Having now signaled the correct outcome, the *Persichette* court remanded the case to the trial court for further proceedings consistent with the opinion.

4. *Summary*

Absent client consent, Model Rule 1.9(a) prohibits a lawyer from representing a client if the proposed matter is the same or substantially related to a former client's matter, and the current and former clients' interests are materially adverse.[198] The centerpiece of this standard, the substantial relationship test, normally requires an analysis of the factual and legal similarities of the two representations, as well as the nature and extent of the lawyer's involvement. The greater the similarities between the facts and the legal issues involved, the greater the chance that the two representations will be deemed to be substantially related.

B. Former Clients and Lawyers' Lateral Movement

Lateral movement by lawyers between law firms is now common. These moves may create former client conflicts of interest for the lawyers and their new firms. Phrased as a question, when a lawyer changes law firms and seeks to represent a client in the same or substantially related matter in which the client's interests are materially adverse to the interests of a client from the

194. *Id.* (footnote omitted).
195. *Id.* at 592.
196. *Id.* (citing *In re* Estate of Myers, 130 P.3d 1023, 1027 (Colo. 2006)).
197. *Id.*
198. Model Rules of Prof'l Conduct R. 1.9(a) (2020).

lawyer's prior firm, does a former client conflict of interest disqualify the lawyer (and the lawyer's new firm) from that representation?

1. *The Model Rule 1.9(b) Framework*

Model Rule 1.9(b) offers specific guidance where a lawyer's previous law firm has represented the former client at issue. Model Rule 1.9(b) states:

> A lawyer shall not knowingly represent a person in the same or substantially related matter in which a firm with which the lawyer formerly was associated had previously represented a client . . . whose interests are materially adverse to that person; and . . . about whom the lawyer had acquired information protected by Rules 1.6 and 1.9(c) that is material to the matter, unless the former client gives informed consent, confirmed in writing.[199]

By its terms, Model Rule 1.9(b) establishes three requirements for disqualifying a lawyer (and her current law firm by imputation) based on work performed for a client at the lawyer's prior law firm: (1) the current client's matter must be the same as, or substantially related to, the former client's matter; (2) the current and former clients' interests must be materially adverse; and (3) the lawyer must have acquired confidential information about the former client's matter that is material to the current client's matter.[200] The third element is pivotal. A violation of Rule 1.9(b) occurs only if a lawyer at her prior law firm acquired confidential information about the former client that is material to the current client's matter.[201] If while working at the prior law firm the lawyer acquired no knowledge or information relating to the client, then neither the lawyer nor the lawyer's new law firm is disqualified from representing another client in the same or substantially related matter even though the two clients' interests conflict.

Recall that under Model Rule 1.9(a), there generally is an irrebuttable presumption that a lawyer received the former client's confidential information in a substantially related matter. Under Rule 1.9(b), it is presumed that a lawyer possesses material, confidential information through her association with her prior firm, but this presumption is rebuttable.[202] The lawyer or her law firm bears the burden of proving the lawyer's lack of actual knowledge

199. *Id.* R 1.9(b).

200. *Id.*

201. Nev. State Bar, Comm. on Ethics & Prof'l Responsibility, Op. 39, at 2–3 (2008); Or. Ethics Op. 2005-120, 2007 WL 2324945, at *2 (Or. State Bar Ass'n 2007); Model Rules of Prof'l Conduct R. 1.9 cmt. 5 (2020).

202. Exterior Sys., Inc. v. Noble Composites, Inc., 210 F. Supp. 2d 1062, 1068 (N.D. Ind. 2002); Park Apts. at Fayetteville, LP v. Plants, 545 S.W.3d 755, 759 (Ark. 2018). *But see* New Horizon Kids Quest III, Inc. v. Eighth Jud. Dist. Ct., 392 P.3d 166, 169 (Nev. 2017) ("The requirement that the attorney actually acquire confidential information about his former firm's client is not a presumption; rather, it is a factual matter for the district court to resolve.").

of the former client's material, confidential information.[203] A lawyer's general access to a former client's protected information will not trigger Rule 1.9(b).[204] If the lawyer does not have actual knowledge of the former client's protected information, disqualification is inappropriate.[205]

2. *Screening to Avoid a Rule 1.9(b) Conflict of Interest*

If a lateral lawyer has actual knowledge of a former client's protected information, she may be able to avoid disqualification by obtaining the former client's consent to her representation of her current client.[206] If the former client will not consent, under Model Rule 1.10(a)(2), the lawyer's new firm may nonetheless avoid imputation of the lawyer's conflict if the firm (1) timely screens the lawyer from participation in the matter; (2) apportions the lawyer no part of the related fee; and (3) promptly notifies the former client in writing, including a description of the firm's screening procedures and a statement of the firm's and the screened lawyer's compliance with the rule.[207] In short, Model Rule 1.10(a)(2) allows the new law firm to unilaterally erect an ethical screen to avoid imputed disqualification. Approximately 30 states have adopted the Model Rule 1.10(a)(2) approach with some variation.

In terms of implementing an effective screen, it is first important to identify the conflict before the lateral lawyer and any colleagues join the firm or as soon as possible thereafter. In any case, the firm should erect a screen as soon as it identifies the conflict. The longer a law firm waits to erect a screen, the less likely it becomes that a court will consider the screen to be timely.

Second, the firm should promptly notify lawyers and staff of the screen. The form of the notice may depend on the firm, but written notice is preferable because (1) it is the easiest way for the firm to demonstrate that it gave such notice; and (2) it best ensures the clarity, consistency, and thoroughness of the notice. Again depending on the firm, notice may go to all lawyers and staff, or it may go to those lawyers and staff members working on the matter from which the lateral lawyer is being screened. A firm may further wish to identify screened matters on its intranet.

---

203. *Park Apts.*, 545 S.W.3d at 758; Model Rules of Prof'l Conduct R. 1.9 cmt. 6 (2020).

204. *Park Apts.*, 545 S.W.3d at 757–59.

205. Baham v. Ass'n of Apt. Owners of Opua Hale Patio Homes, No. 13-00669HG-BMK, 2014 WL 413495, at *2 (D. Haw. Feb. 4, 2014) (quoting Dieter v. Regents of Univ. of Cal., 963 F. Supp. 908, 911 (E.D. Cal. 1997)); *see, e.g.*, Commonwealth v. Cousin, 88 N.E.3d 822, 839–40 (Mass. 2018) (declining to disqualify the lawyer under Rule 1.9(b)).

206. Model Rules of Prof'l Conduct R. 1.9(a) (2020).

207. *Id.* R. 1.10(a)(2).

Third, the firm should implement information technology controls to prevent the screened lawyer from gaining access to electronic files and documents related to the screened matter.

Fourth, a firm should establish physical measures to enforce the screen. For example, the firm should clearly mark paper files related to the screened matter, post notices on relevant file cabinets or shelves, or place screening notices or instructions in individual files so that the screened lawyer knows that materials located there are off-limits. Depending on the facts, the firm may wish to consider other alternatives, such as locating the screened lawyer's office away from those of lawyers and staff members who are working on the screened matter.

Fifth, the firm should periodically remind lawyers and staff of the screen. The firm should also update information related to the screen as necessary, such as when new lawyers or staff join the firm. All reminders and updates should be documented.

Sixth, the firm should reasonably monitor compliance with the screen and document those efforts. More broadly, the firm should periodically analyze its screening procedures to ensure that it is taking proper steps to implement and maintain its screens.

C. The Material Adversity Requirement

Both Model Rules 1.9(a) and (b) include a "material adversity" requirement.[208] In other words, for there to be a conflict of interest under either rule, the current and former client's interests must be materially adverse in addition to the two representations being the same or substantially related. Although Rule 1.9 does not attempt to define material adversity,[209] the issue is seldom contested. This is because most alleged conflicts relating to former clients arise when a lawyer is representing a new client suing a former client (or vice versa), and the alignment of the new and former clients as foes in litigation clearly satisfies the material adversity requirement.[210] A more complicated question arises when a former client is not directly involved in

208. *Id.* R. 1.9(a) & (b)(1).

209. Some courts have attempted to characterize or describe "material adversity," if not define it. *See, e.g.*, Foley-Ciccantelli v. Bishop's Grove Condo. Ass'n, 797 N.W.2d 789, 816 (Wis. 2011) ("The analysis should focus on whether the current representation may cause the former client financial, legal, or some other identifiable harm." (footnote omitted)); Simpson Performance Prods., Inc. v. Horn, 92 P.3d 283, 288 (Wyo. 2004) ("This fact-intensive analysis focuses on whether the current representation may cause legal, financial, or other identifiable detriment to the former client.").

210. *See* N.Y. Ethics Op. 1103, 2016 WL 4414060, at *4 (N.Y. State Bar Ass'n, Comm. on Prof'l Ethics 2016) (stating that "[t]he "materially adverse" prong of Rule 1.9(a) is always met when a former client is on the opposite side of a lawsuit involving the same or a substantially related matter, whether as plaintiff or defendant").

the current matter at issue but may be affected by it in some manner. *Zerger & Mauer LLP v. City of Greenwood*[211] is such a case.

Zerger & Mauer LLP represented the city of Greenwood, Missouri (Greenwood) in a dispute with Martin Marietta Materials (Martin) arising out of a rock quarry located near the city.[212] The dispute centered on Martin truck traffic traveling through town and creating a public nuisance, with Martin finally settling for $7 million.[213] As part of the settlement, Greenwood designated Second Avenue for the truck traffic—the route it deemed most beneficial to the city—and declared that the truck traffic along that route was reasonable and was not a public nuisance.[214]

About one year later, Zerger & Mauer filed a private nuisance action on behalf of multiple plaintiffs with property interests on Second Avenue against Martin and other entitles involved in hauling rock from the quarry.[215] Not long afterward, Greenwood—now a non-party—moved to disqualify Zerger & Mauer from representing the individual plaintiffs.[216] According to Greenwood, the firm was advancing arguments in the private nuisance litigation that directly conflicted with Greenwood's interests.[217] The district court agreed and disqualified Zerger & Mauer.

The Eight Circuit affirmed the district court, first finding that the matters were substantially related.[218] The Eighth Circuit also analyzed whether the plaintiffs' interests were materially adverse to Greenwood's interests.[219] In the court's view, Greenwood's interests in its settlement agreement with Martin would be harmed if the plaintiffs' private nuisance claim disrupted Martin's use of Second Avenue, which would require Greenwood to open other trucking routes.[220] Indeed, Zerger & Mauer's arguments targeting Martin's allegedly tortious use of Second Avenue contradicted a material term in the settlement agreement between Greenwood and Martin because Greenwood wanted to reserve Second Avenue as the exclusive truck route. In short, Greenwood had the right to "demand that its former counsel not advocate positions that pose[d] the serious threat of once again embroiling [it] in protracted litigation."[221]

In conclusion, whether a representation is materially adverse to a former client depends on a case-specific inquiry that evaluates the degree to which

211. 751 F.3d 928 (8th Cir. 2014).
212. *Id.* at 929.
213. *Id.*
214. *Id.* at 929–30.
215. *Id.* at 930.
216. *Id.*
217. *Id.*
218. *Id.* at 933.
219. *Id.* at 934.
220. *Id.*
221. *Id.*

the lawyer's current representation may harm the former client.[222] The key is whether the lawyer's current representation will cause legal, financial, or other identifiable detriment to the former client.[223] The mere fact that the current client and the former client have competing economic interests, however, will not suffice.

D. The Use and Disclosure of Former Clients' Information under Rule 1.9(c)

Although lawyers' duties to clients generally terminate upon conclusion of the representation, the duty of confidentiality does not. Model Rule 1.9(c) prohibits a lawyer who has formerly represented a client in a matter from (1) using information relating to the representation to the former client's disadvantage, except as permitted by the Model Rules or when the information has become generally known; and (2) revealing information relating to the former client's representation, except as permitted by the Model Rules.[224] These restrictions on a lawyer's use and disclosure of a former client's information apply regardless of a substantial relationship determination or other analysis performed under Model Rules 1.9(a) or (b), and regardless of whether a subsequent representation is actually involved.[225]

1. Lawyers' Duty of Confidentiality to Former Clients

Many lawyers have been disqualified or disciplined for overlooking or ignoring their duty of confidentiality to former clients under Rule 1.9.[226] Lawyers should therefore pause before using or revealing information relating to a former client's representation without the former client's informed consent. Remember, lawyers' duty of confidentiality under Model Rule 1.6(a) is quite broad and applies to all information relating to clients' representations.[227] Lawyers may breach their duty of confidentiality by not only

222. Foley-Ciccantelli v. Bishop's Grove Condo. Ass'n, 797 N.W.2d 789, 816 (Wis. 2011); Simpson Performance Prods., Inc. v. Horn, 92 P.3d 283, 288 (Wyo. 2004).

223. *Foley-Ciccantelli*, 797 N.W.2d at 816; *Simpson Performance Prods., Inc.*, 92 P.3d at 288.

224. Model Rules of Prof'l Conduct R. 1.9(c) (2020).

225. ABA Formal Op. 99-415, *supra* note 152, at 3; R.I. Sup. Ct., Ethics Advisory Panel, Op. No. 2007-07, at 2 (2007).

226. *See, e.g.*, United States v. Quest Diagnostics, Inc., 734 F.3d 154, 165 (2d Cir. 2013) (affirming the district court's judgment that a lawyer violated Rule 1.9(c) by participating in a qui tam action against his former client and revealing a former client's information); *In re* Charges of Unprof'l Conduct in Panel File No. 41310, 899 N.W.2d 821, 826 (Minn. 2017) (admonishing a lawyer where, a day after the client terminated the lawyer's representation, the lawyer sent an e-mail to an insurance adjuster explaining the reasons why the client did not want to accept the adjuster's settlement offer); Disciplinary Couns. v. Shimko, 131 N.E.3d 52, 61–65 (Ohio 2019) (suspending a lawyer who, in attempting to establish his claim to legal fees owed by a former client, disclosed more of the former client's confidential information in a court filing than the lawyer could reasonably have believed was necessary to accomplish that purpose).

227. Model Rules of Prof'l Conduct R. 1.6(a) (2020).

disclosing information obtained from clients but also revealing information available from sources other than their clients—including publicly available information. The fact that information about a client is available somewhere in the public domain does not mean that it is known by or readily available to everyone with whom the client deals.[228]

By the same token, and as Model Rule 1.9(c)(1) expressly recognizes, where the former client's information has become generally known, there is no real purpose served by requiring a lawyer to continue to protect it. The generally known exception to former client confidentiality under Model Rule 1.9(c)(1), however, is narrow.

First, the generally known exception applies only to the use of a former client's information and not to the disclosure or revelation of a former client's information.[229] Second, to qualify as generally known, the former client's information must be (1) widely recognized by members of the public in the relevant geographic area or (2) widely recognized in the former client's industry, profession, or trade.[230] For instance, information may

228. *See, e.g.*, *In re* Johnson, 4 Cal. State Bar Ct. Rptr. 179, 189 (Rev. Dep't 2000) (concluding that the lawyer's disclosure of a client's conviction, which was publicly available but not easily discoverable, violated the duty of confidentiality); People v. Braham, No. 15PDJ095, 2017 WL 1046460, at *12 (Colo. Jan. 23, 2017) (stating that Rule 1.6 "contains no exception permitting the disclosure of previously disclosed or publicly available information"); People v. Muhr, 370 P.3d 677, 695 (Colo. 2016) (violating Rule 1.6 by revealing information that had previously been revealed and rejecting the argument that "self-evident" analysis in work product could not be protected against disclosure by Rule 1.6); *In re* Anonymous, 932 N.E.2d 671, 674 (Ind. 2010) (noting there is "no exception allowing revelation of information relating to a representation even if a diligent researcher could unearth it through public sources"); Iowa Sup. Ct. Att'y Disciplinary Bd. v. Marzen, 779 N.W.2d 757, 766 (Iowa 2010) (holding that "confidentiality is breached when an attorney discloses information learned through the attorney-client relationship even if that information is otherwise publicly available"); *In re* Bryan, 61 P.3d 641, 656 (Kan. 2003) (explaining that the fact that a former client's alleged "history of making false claims" had been publicly disclosed in court pleadings did not mean that the lawyer's related disclosure to a store manager and a loss prevention manager was not the disclosure of information protected by Rule 1.6); Turner v. Commonwealth, 726 S.E.2d 325, 333 (Va. 2012) (observing that there "is a significant difference between something being a public record and it also being 'generally known,' that is, within the basic understanding and knowledge of the public"); Lawyer Disciplinary Bd. v. McGraw, 461 S.E.2d 850, 861–62 (W. Va. 1995) (stating that lawyers' duty of confidentiality "is not nullified by the fact that the information is part of a public record or by the fact that someone else is privy to it"). *But see* State v. Mark, 231 P.3d 478, 511 (Haw. 2010) (treating a former client's criminal conviction as "generally known" when discussing a former client conflict); Hunter v. Va. State Bar, 744 S.E.2d 611, 620 (Va. 2013) (holding that the First Amendment protected a lawyer's blog posts discussing public information related to his client's cases); State *ex rel.* Youngblood v. Sanders, 575 S.E.2d 864, 872 (W. Va. 2002) (stating that information in police reports was "generally known" for Rule 1.9 purposes).

229. ABA Comm. on Ethics & Prof'l Responsibility, Formal Op. 479, at 2 (2017) [hereinafter ABA Formal Op. 479].

230. *Id.* at 5; *see also* Ill. Advisory Op. 05-01, 2006 WL 4584283, at *3 (Ill. State Bar Ass'n, Comm. on Prof'l Ethics 2006) (stating that information is generally known within the meaning of Rule 1.9 if it constitutes "common knowledge in the community"); Mich. Eth. Op. RI-377, 2018

become widely recognized and thus generally known as a result of publicity through traditional media sources, such as newspapers, magazines, radio, or television; through publication on Internet websites; or through social media.[231] Likewise, information should be treated as generally known if it is announced, discussed, or identified in what reasonable members of the industry, profession, or trade would consider a leading print or online publication or other resource in the field.[232] At the same time, information that is publicly available is not necessarily generally known.[233]

In summary, a lawyer's duty of confidentiality survives the termination of the attorney-client relationship. Absent the former client's consent, information acquired by the lawyer when representing the client may not subsequently be used by the lawyer to the client's disadvantage. There are a few narrow exceptions to this general rule. First, the limited exceptions to client confidentiality available under Model Rule 1.6(b) also apply in the former client context. Second, a lawyer may use information acquired in connection with the former client's representation if the information has become generally known. Finally, Model Rule 1.9(c)(1) prohibits the use of client information only to the extent it is disadvantageous to the former client. A lawyer is not prohibited from using a former client's information to gain an advantage for herself or a third party (such as another client) if the former client is neither harmed nor placed at risk.

WL 5725274, at *4 (State Bar of Mich., Comm. on Prof'l & Jud. Ethics 2018) ("Information is generally known within the meaning of [Rule] 1.9(c)(1) if it is widely recognized by members of the public in the relevant geographic area, or it is widely recognized in the former client's industry, profession, or trade. Furthermore, information that is publicly available is not necessarily generally known."); N.Y. State Bar Ass'n, Comm. on Prof'l Ethics, Op. 991, at ¶ 20 (2013) (opining that information is generally known only if it is known to a sizeable percentage of people in the local community or in the trade, field, or profession to which the information relates).

231. ABA Formal Op. 479, *supra* note 229, at 5.

232. *Id.*

233. *See, e.g.*, Pallon v. Roggio, Nos. 04-3625(JAP), 06-1068(FLW), 2006 WL 2466854, at *7 (D.N.J. Aug. 24, 2006) ("'Generally known" does not only mean that the information is of public record. . . . The information must be within the basic understanding and knowledge of the public." (citation omitted)); *In re* Gordon Props., LLC, 505 B.R. 703, 707 n.6 (Bankr. E.D. Va. 2013) ("'Generally known' does not mean information that someone can find."); *In re* Tennant, 392 P.3d 143, 148 (Mont. 2017) (explaining that for information to be considered generally known, "the information must be within the basic knowledge and understanding of the public"; it does not suffice that the information is part of the public record, that other available sources for such information exist, or that the lawyer otherwise received the same information from other sources); Dougherty v. Pepper Hamilton LLP, 133 A.3d 792, 800 (Pa. Super. Ct. 2016) (concluding that genuine issues of material fact existed as to whether an erroneously filed FBI Affidavit on PACER that related to the law firm's former client was generally known or whether it required special knowledge to ascertain its existence); ABA Formal Op. 479, *supra* note 229, at 5 (explaining that information is not generally known merely because it "has been discussed in open court, or is available in court records, in libraries, or in other public repositories of information").

2. *Conflicts Arising from a Lawyer's Possession of a Former Client's Information*

A lawyer's possession of a former client's confidential information that might be relevant to a subsequent matter that the lawyer is handing for a current client, but which the lawyer cannot use or disclose, does not alone create a conflict of interest.[234] The critical question is whether the representation of the current client would be materially limited by the lawyer's inability to use or disclose the former client's information.[235]

A material limitation conflict under Model Rule 1.7(a)(2) could arise due to a lawyer's possession of a former client's confidential information that the lawyer is unable to use or disclose in the lawyer's subsequent representation of another client because (1) the lawyer cannot avoid using the former client's confidential information in the subsequent representation or (2) there is a significant risk that possession of the former client's confidential information could impair the lawyer's independent professional judgment in the subsequent representation.[236] One factor in this analysis is whether the former client's information would be uncovered in the ordinary course of the lawyer's subsequent representation of the second client. If so, then the information would be material only if it was important to the second client's representation to have the information earlier than it would be obtained in the ordinary course of affairs. Another factor is the ease with which the lawyer can segregate the former client's confidential information from her work on the current client's matter. In some instances, the former client's confidential information will be the kind that the lawyer is likely to recall, or it will be otherwise impossible for the lawyer to block the information from her mind. In other instances, the information may not have been the focal point of the former client's representation and thus will be unlikely to affect the lawyer's professional judgment absent efforts by the lawyer to review the information from the former client's file.[237]

---

234. Ass'n of the Bar of the City of N.Y., Comm. on Prof'l & Jud. Ethics, Op. 2005-2, at 1 (2005) [hereinafter N.Y.C. Ethics Op. 2005-2].

235. N.Y. Eth. Op. 903, 2012 WL 1514573, at *4 (N.Y. State Bar Ass'n, Comm. on Prof'l Ethics 2012) [hereinafter N.Y. Eth. Op. 903]; N.Y. Eth. Op. 901, 2011 WL 7784115, at *2 (N.Y. State Bar Ass'n, Comm. on Prof'l Ethics 2011) [hereinafter N.Y. Eth. Op. 901]; N.Y.C. Ethics Op. 2005-2, *supra* note 234, at 1.

236. N.Y. Eth. Op. 903, *supra* note 235, 2012 WL 1514573, at *4; N.Y. Eth. Op. 901, *supra* note 235, 2011 WL 7784115, at *2; N.Y.C. Ethics Op. 2005-2, *supra* note 234, at 1–2.

237. A lawyer may, as a practical matter, want to contemplate how easy, or difficult, it may be to ever prove a negative with respect to such information. For example, a lawyer may find it advisable to document either a current lack of awareness of details of the prior representation, a lack of access to file information in the earlier matter, or both. A lawyer may be able to utilize any electronic document management system to password protect the contents of the former client's file and, ultimately, be able to demonstrate that it was not viewed at any point thereafter in working on the new client's matter.

Even if a material limitation conflict exists, the conflict may still be consentable. If a lawyer reasonably believes that she can provide competent and diligent representation to her current client despite her continuing duty of confidentiality to her former client, then the lawyer may obtain the current client's informed consent to that representation.[238] On the other hand, if the lawyer is unable to disclose sufficient information to obtain the current client's informed consent, or if the lawyer believes that her duty of confidentiality to her former client will prevent her from competently and diligently representing her current client, the conflict is not consentable.[239]

A lawyer's duty of confidentiality to a former client does not mean that a lawyer cannot use any information learned in a former client's representation for another client's benefit.[240] But if a former client refuses to consent to the use of its confidential information to its disadvantage in the lawyer's representation of a current client, or if the lawyer is otherwise unable to use or disclose the former client's confidential information where doing so would benefit a client in a subsequent matter, the lawyer must then decide whether possession of the former client's confidential information will create a Rule 1.7(a)(2) material limitation conflict.

V. Issue or Positional Conflicts of Interest

Finally, trial and appellate lawyers must be prepared to navigate issue or positional conflicts of interest. Issue or positional conflicts of interest arise in litigation when a lawyer argues for an interpretation of the law on behalf of one client that is contrary to another client's interests. It is true, of course, that lawyers may advocate any viable interpretation of the law to benefit a client on day one, and on day two represent another client and promote whatever non-frivolous position exists to benefit that client.[241] The ability to advocate different and even competing positions in different matters is lawyers' stock-in-trade. Advocating opposite sides of the same issue on behalf of two current clients in unrelated matters, however, is the archetypal example of an issue or positional conflict of interest.

238. N.Y. Eth. Op. 901, *supra* note 235, 2011 WL 7784115, at *2; N.Y.C. Ethics Op. 2005-2, *supra* note 234, at 2.

239. N.Y. Eth. Op. 901, *supra* note 235, 2011 WL 7784115, at *2; N.Y.C. Ethics Op. 2005-2, *supra* note 234, at 2.

240. *See* N.Y.C. Ethics Op. 2005-2, *supra* note 234, at 6–7 ("Indeed, what a lawyer learns in a representation necessarily becomes part of the storehouse of knowledge and experience that the lawyer may draw on in the lawyer's career and that is part of the value the lawyer brings to each successive representation.").

241. Model Rules of Prof'l Conduct R. 1.7 cmt. 24 (2020).

There is nothing inherently wrong with lawyers concurrently taking inconsistent positions on behalf of different clients in different matters.[242] Were the rule otherwise, lawyers would be compelled to specialize on one side of legal issues. The facts and circumstances of a representation, however, may present a conflict severe enough to undermine a lawyer's credibility and therefore impair the lawyer's ability to represent both clients. Plus, a successful outcome for one client may prejudice the other client, which, in turn, will likely jeopardize the attorney-client relationship, the quality of the representation, or both.

ABA Formal Opinion 93-377[243] is a good starting point for understanding issue and positional conflicts of interest in litigation. In Formal Opinion 93-377, the ABA's Standing Committee on Ethics and Professional Responsibility reasoned that if a law firm litigates two cases on behalf of different clients in the same jurisdiction, and there is a substantial risk that the firm's representation of one client will create a legal precedent, even if not binding, that is likely to materially undercut the firm's legal position on behalf of the other client, there is a material limitation conflict under Model Rule 1.7(a)(2).[244] *Williams v. State*[245] illustrates the archetypal positional conflict of interest where divergent legal positions are presented to the same court.

In that case, Bernard O'Donnell defended Joseph Williams on first-degree murder charges.[246] Following Williams's conviction and death sentence, O'Donnell moved to withdraw and requested the appointment of substitute counsel for Williams's appeal to the Delaware Supreme Court.[247] In so moving, O'Donnell reasoned that Williams could argue on appeal that the trial court erred in affording "'great weight'" to the jury's 10–2 vote in favor the death penalty and that he may have a conflict in presenting this argument.[248] Specifically, O'Donnell explained that he had advocated the contrary position on behalf of another capital murder defendant in a pending appeal before the Delaware Supreme Court; in the second case he asserted that the trial court erred when it failed to confer "'great weight'" to the jury's 10–2 recommendation rejecting the death penalty.[249] Based on these divergent positions, O'Donnell worried that his representation of both

242. Alaska Eth. Op. 96-6, 1996 WL 907642, at *2 (Alaska Bar Ass'n, Ethics Comm. 1996); Model Rules of Prof'l Conduct R. 1.7 cmt. 24 (2020).

243. ABA Comm. on Ethics & Prof'l Responsibility, Formal Op. 93-377 (1993) [hereinafter ABA Formal Op. 93-377].

244. *Id.* at 3.

245. 805 A.2d 880 (Del. 2002).

246. *Id.* at 880–81.

247. *Id.*

248. *Id.* at 881.

249. *Id.*

clients risked creating unfavorable precedent for one client or the other and invited questions as to his credibility and perceived loyalty to each client.[250]

In determining whether a positional conflict required O'Donnell's disqualification, the Delaware Supreme Court articulated the governing standard as follows:

> [T]he question is whether the lawyer can effectively argue both sides of the same legal question without compromising the interests of one client or the other. The lawyer must attempt to strike a balance between the duty to advocate any viable interpretation of the law for one client's benefit versus the other client's right to insist on counsel's fidelity to their legal position.[251]

Against this benchmark, the *Williams* court agreed that O'Donnell had identified a disqualifying positional conflict of interest.[252] Indeed, the court held that O'Donnell would violate Delaware's version of Rule 1.7 if he advocated conflicting legal positions in two capital murder appeals pending simultaneously before the court.[253]

Williams displays positional conflicts in litigation at their extreme: (1) setting legal precedent in favor of one client but adverse to another client and (2) eroding a lawyer's credibility with the court by advocating opposing sides of the same legal issue. Even when the cases are in different jurisdictions, however, a lawyer urging opposite sides of a legal issue must still evaluate whether the representation of either client will materially limit the lawyer's effectiveness in the other matter.[254] In that situation, the risk of an issue or positional conflict is greatest where the arguments involve a new or emerging area of the law and the first-decided case will likely be regarded as persuasive authority by a court in another jurisdiction.[255]

In summary, three questions guide the determination of whether an issue or positional conflict exists in litigation. First, is the issue critically important to both representations? Second, will the determination of the issue in one representation affect its determination in the other representation? Third, will the competing interests materially limit the lawyer's representation of one or both clients? Unfortunately, issue or positional conflicts of interest are difficult to identify because they often elude conflict-checking procedures targeting categories of information such as parties' names. On a positive note, these conflicts generally are consentable under Model Rule 1.7(b).

---

250. *Id.*
251. *Id.* at 881–82.
252. *Id.* at 882.
253. *Id.*
254. ABA Formal Op. 93-377, *supra* note 243, at 3.
255. *Id.*

VI. Conclusion

Conflicts of interest affect all lawyers, regardless of practice area, but they often are an especially difficult challenge in litigation. Trial and appellate lawyers must be sensitive to both concurrent and former client conflicts of interest; recognize them in a timely fashion; evaluate whether they may be cured by client consent; and then, if they wish to go forward with the representation, obtain all affected clients' informed consent to the representation and confirm it in writing. This is often easier said than done. By tackling the core concepts governing concurrent and former client representations under Rules 1.7 and 1.9 of the ABA's Model Rules of Professional Conduct, this chapter attempts to illuminate conflict of interest issues that trial and appellate lawyers regularly confront. Understanding conflicts of interest is unquestionably the first step toward avoiding them and, when necessary, curing them.

2

Pre-suit Investigation and the Pursuit of Frivolous Claims

I. Introduction and Overview

For litigation to occur, someone must of course file a lawsuit, administrative action, or demand for arbitration. Not surprisingly, one of the first professional responsibility issues a lawyer may have to confront is whether the lawsuit or other proceeding is sufficiently well-founded to satisfy relevant ethical standards in the forum. Once a lawsuit is filed, the corresponding first issue of professional responsibility for a lawyer hired to defend the litigation is deciding what defenses can ethically be asserted on the client's behalf and, in a related vein, whether the defendant may have its own claims that can ethically be asserted as counterclaims or third-party claims. Regrettably, lawyers too frequently treat these initial questions blithely. The failure to carefully analyze these issues may expose lawyers to unfortunate consequences, including professional discipline, sanctions under court rules or statutory provisions, and even tort liability in the form of abuse of process or malicious prosecution actions. Moreover, these potential risks persist in the sense that lawyers are prohibited not only from *making* frivolous claims or contentions but also from *maintaining* them. This chapter explores these central ethical obligations that affect both plaintiffs' lawyers and defense attorneys.

II. The Ethical Prohibition against Pursuing Frivolous Claims and Lawyers' Duty to Investigate

Rules of professional conduct in almost every jurisdiction contain a prohibition against the pursuit of fatally deficient claims and contentions patterned after Model Rule of Professional Conduct 3.1. Model Rule 3.1, which is titled "Meritorious Claims and Contentions," provides as follows:

> A lawyer shall not bring or defend a proceeding, or assert or controvert an issue therein, unless there is a basis in law and fact for doing so that is not frivolous, which includes a good faith argument for an extension, modification, or reversal of existing law. A lawyer for the defendant in a criminal proceeding, or the respondent in a proceeding that could result in incarceration, may nevertheless so defend the proceeding as to require that every element of the case be established.[1]

In addition to its obvious application to traditional client representations, Model Rule 3.1 applies to lawyers who represent themselves.[2]

It is worth noting at the outset that although Model Rule 3.1's title speaks of claims and contentions that are "meritorious," the text of the rule does not actually require lawyers to pursue only meritorious claims and contentions. Such a standard would be nearly impossible to enforce given the many factual and legal ambiguities that routinely exist in litigation. Plus, even where the law is clear, there is always the potential for change. Accordingly, Model Rule 3.1 takes the more realistic approach of prohibiting lawyers from pursuing claims and contentions unless they have "a basis for doing so that is not frivolous."[3] In other words, a claim or contention may be meritless without being frivolous.[4] While Model Rule 3.1 does not attempt to define the term "frivolous," it does provide significant guidance on the topic of legal arguments by spelling out a few examples of conduct or practice that satisfy the "not frivolous" standard of the rule, namely, good faith arguments for *extensions* of existing law, good faith arguments for *modifications* of existing law, and good faith arguments for *reversing* existing law.[5]

A reliable definition of what constitutes a frivolous claim or contention with substantial currency across the nation, and that seems to apply

---

1. Model Rules of Prof'l Conduct R. 3.1 (2020).

2. *In re* Shearin, 765 A.2d 930, 936–37 (Del. 2000); *In re* Collie, 765 S.E.2d 835, 838–40 (S.C. 2014).

3. Model Rules of Prof'l Conduct R. 3.1 (2020).

4. *See, e.g.*, Commonwealth v. Chmiel, 30 A.3d 1111, 1190 (Pa. 2011) (distinguishing frivolous claims from meritless ones); *In re* Houston, 675 S.E.2d 721, 723 n.1 (S.C. 2009) (finding that a meritless racial profiling claim did not violate Rule 3.1); Johnson v. Miller, 818 N.W.2d 804, 809 (S.D. 2012) (quoting Stratmeyer v. Engberg, 649 N.W.2d 921, 926 (S.D. 2002)); *In re* S.C., 88 A.3d 1220, 1223–24 (Vt. 2014) (discussing frivolous arguments in the context of appellate practice and appointed counsel's motion to withdraw based on Rule 3.1); *see also* Estate of McLemore v. McLemore, 63 So. 3d 468, 490 (Miss. 2011) (observing that a case may be "weak" or "light-headed" without being "frivolous" for the purpose of awarding sanctions).

5. Model Rules of Prof'l Conduct R. 3.1 (2020). A comment to the Model Rule also explicitly mentions what is otherwise implied by the rule—that "a good faith argument on the merits of the action taken" is also sufficient to be not frivolous. *Id.* cmt. 2. Some jurisdictions with rules patterned after Model Rule 3.1 add to the comment an example, originating from an older version of Model Rule 3.1, indicating that an action will be deemed frivolous when the client wants to pursue it "primarily for the purpose of harassing or maliciously injuring a person." *See, e.g.*, Ariz. Rules of Prof'l Conduct R. 3.1 cmt. 2 (2014); Tenn. Rules of Prof'l Conduct R. 3.1 cmt. 2 (2018); Va. Rules of Prof'l Conduct R. 3.1 cmt. 2 (2018).

as readily to evaluating underlying factual assertions as to legal arguments, is found in the Restatement (Third) of the Law Governing Lawyers.[6] The Restatement describes a claim or contention as being frivolous when it is one "that a lawyer of ordinary competence would recognize as so lacking in merit that there is no substantial possibility that the tribunal will accept it."[7] Courts often describe a contention or claim as being frivolous when it has no basis in fact or law.[8] Applying either standard, and as a general rule, the fact that a lawyer believes that a particular claim or contention is likely to fail still does not render it frivolous.[9] Nor is a claim or contention frivolous merely because it proves to be unsuccessful.[10] This final point holds true even when a claim is defeated by way of a dispositive motion.[11] On the other hand, "the lack of a definitive holding precluding a legal theory does not mean that it cannot be frivolous."[12] Were the rule otherwise, a clearly frivolous but novel legal argument—"novel," perhaps, in the sense that no reputable lawyer would ever consider making it—would not be a basis for discipline.[13]

Lawyers may not defend against alleged Rule 3.1 violations on the basis that they did not know or understand the law or made a "mistake of law."[14] For a lawyer to so argue would be to confess incompetence. Courts and disciplinary authorities rightly expect lawyers to know the law before making claims or contentions, although lawyers are unlikely to be found to have violated Rule 3.1 where the legal issue in question is unsettled.[15]

---

6. Restatement (Third) of the Law Governing Lawyers (2000).

7. *Id.* § 110 cmt. d; *see also Johnson*, 818 N.W.2d at 808–09 (applying a similar standard); *In re* Cottingham, 423 P.3d 818, 824 (Wash. 2018) ("A frivolous position is one that a lawyer of ordinary competence would recognize as being devoid of merit.").

8. *See, e.g.*, People v. Downs, 83 N.E.3d 584, 600 (Ill. App. Ct. 2017) ("A frivolous claim is one with no arguable basis in law or in fact."); *In re* Salomon's Case, 202 A.3d 587, 594 (N.H. 2019) (concluding that the lawyer violated Rule 3.1 when he brought a lawsuit that he knew had no factual or legal basis); *In re* Conduct of McGraw, 414 P.3d 841, 852 (Or. 2018) (using the lack of "a plausible legal basis" for a claim synonymously with a claim having no basis in fact or law); *In re* Conduct of Obert, 282 P.3d 825, 840–41 (Or. 2012); *Chmiel*, 30 A.3d at 1190; Weatherbee v. Va. State Bar, 689 S.E.2d 753, 756 (Va. 2010).

9. *See In re S.C.*, 88 A.3d at 1223 ("[T]he assertion of a claim that an attorney believes to be without merit or lacking any meaningful chance of success does not render an appeal 'frivolous' or unethical.").

10. Iowa Sup. Ct. Att'y Disciplinary Bd. v. Caghan, 927 N.W.2d 591, 601 (Iowa 2019); Att'y Grievance Comm'n of Md. v. Dyer, 162 A.3d 970, 1017 (Md. 2017); Jandrt *ex rel.* Brueggeman v. Jerome Foods, Inc., 597 N.W.2d 744, 755 (Wis. 1999).

11. Vossman v. AirNet Sys., Inc., 113 N.E.3d 987, 994 (Ohio Ct. App. 2018) ("[E]ven where there is not enough evidence to survive a motion for summary judgment, this does not necessarily translate into a frivolous claim."); *Johnson*, 818 N.W.2d at 809 (referring to summary judgment).

12. *In re* Pearson, 228 A.3d 417, 425 (D.C. 2020) (footnote omitted).

13. *Id.* (quoting Ozee v. Am. Council on Gift Annuities, Inc., 143 F.3d 937, 941 (5th Cir. 1998)).

14. Thompson v. Sup. Ct. Comm. on Prof'l Conduct, 252 S.W.3d 125, 128 (Ark. 2007).

15. *Id.*

A. Lawyers' Duty of Reasonable Inquiry

Model Rule 3.1 also requires that the lawyer's conclusion that there is a non-frivolous basis for the claim or contention be formed after reasonable inquiry. Accordingly, lawyers must conduct a reasonable preliminary investigation into clients' intended claims and contentions.[16] Lawyers cannot avoid this obligation by stating in a pleading that allegations are being made upon information and belief. Recognizing a duty to investigate in order to meet the requirements of Model Rule 3.1 is entirely consistent with lawyers' need to satisfy their duty of competence under Model Rule 1.1.[17] The nature and extent of the investigation required will depend on a number of variable factors.[18] These factors include the complexity or nature of the claims or contentions to be investigated or developed, the time in which the investigation must be conducted, the resources available to the lawyer to conduct the investigation, the availability and cooperation of potential fact and expert witnesses, whether expert witnesses must be consulted,[19] the availability of evidence that can be obtained without formal discovery, whether any investigation has been conducted prior to the lawyer undertaking the representation, the existence of parallel proceedings that complicate or expedite matters, and probably more.

16. *See, e.g.*, Jorgensen v. Taco Bell Corp., 58 Cal. Rptr. 2d 178, 181 (Ct. App. 1996) ("Frivolous litigation is frequently avoided by a careful lawyer's investigation of a client's claims before filing suit."); Idaho State Bar v. Hawkley, 92 P.3d 1069, 1074 (Idaho 2002) (calling a lawyer's pre-suit investigation "trivial" in concluding that lawyer violated Rule 3.1); Hunt v. Dresie, 740 P.2d 1046, 1053 (Kan. 1987) ("It is obvious that the client must rely upon his lawyer to make a reasonable investigation of his case. Likewise, the attorney must accept the obligation to conduct a reasonable investigation in an attempt to find what the true facts are before filing a civil action on behalf of his client."); State *ex rel.* Calan v. Kemp Stone, Inc., 418 P.3d 708, 712 (Okla. Civ. App. 2017) ("A plaintiff's attorney has a duty to investigate prior to filing the action. . . . The requirement is to conduct a reasonable inquiry." (citations omitted)); Weatherbee v. Va. State Bar, 689 S.E.2d 753, 756 (Va. 2010) (concluding that the lawyer violated Rule 3.1 where a preliminary investigation would have revealed the falsity of many allegations).

17. Model Rules of Prof'l Conduct R. 1.1 (2020) ("A lawyer shall provide competent representation to a client. Competent representation requires the legal knowledge, skill, thoroughness and preparation reasonably necessary for the representation."); *see, e.g.*, People v. Boyle, 942 P.2d 1199, 1201 (Colo. 1997) (disciplining a lawyer who failed to learn of readily available evidence regarding client's petition for asylum); Attorney Grievance Comm'n of Md. v. Chasnoff, 783 A.2d 224, 231 (Md. 2001) (violating Rule 1.1 by failing to visit an accident scene for two years and not attempting to locate a witness believed to have favorable testimony for the lawyer's client); *In re* Padilla, 456 P.3d 1057, 1063 (N.M. 2019) ("The provision of competent and diligent representation also includes a duty to investigate the factual and legal bases of a client's case or defense.").

18. Mich. Eth. Op. R-9, 1990 WL 504862, at *3 (State Bar of Mich., Standing Comm. on Prof'l & Jud. Ethics 1990); Va. State Bar, Standing Comm. on Legal Ethics, Op. 1445 (1992).

19. *See* Jandrt *ex rel.* Brueggeman v. Jerome Foods, Inc., 597 N.W.2d 744, 759 (Wis. 1999) (discussing frivolous litigation under Wisconsin statutes and stating that while good practice may dictate that an expert be consulted prior to filing a claim upon which expert testimony will be required at trial, a per se rule requiring expert testimony cannot be reconciled with the objective standard by which lawyers' investigations should be judged).

A comment to Model Rule 3.1 addresses to some extent the tensions that can exist between lawyers' obligations under this rule and the practical realities that lawyers may face:

> The filing of an action or defense or similar action taken for a client is not frivolous merely because the facts have not first been fully substantiated or because the lawyer expects to develop vital evidence only by discovery. What is required of lawyers, however, is that they inform themselves about the facts of their clients' cases and determine that they can make good faith arguments in support of their clients' positions. Such action is not frivolous even though the lawyer believes that the client's position ultimately will not prevail.[20]

In time-sensitive matters—as where, for example, a statute of limitations is about to expire—the obligation to investigate the merits of the client's claims or contentions can be deferred until after filing suit.[21] Any deferral must be reasonable under the circumstances; legitimate urgency may temporarily postpone a lawyer's duty to investigate, but it does not eliminate or excuse it. The longer lawyers wait to conduct reasonable post-filing investigations, the greater the risk of discipline or sanctions for pursuing frivolous claims. The question of how long is too long can only be answered on a case-by-case basis.

It is important to remember that Model Rule 3.1 and its analogs not only prohibit lawyers from initiating a proceeding where doing so would be frivolous but also prohibit the pursuit of certain issues within a proceeding if those issues cannot be legitimately supported, even though other claims in the same proceeding are entirely valid. These prohibitions naturally apply with equal force to lawyers who are defending proceedings.[22]

A number of decisions provide helpful insight into the contours of lawyers' ethical duty to satisfy themselves regarding clients' claims and

20. Model Rules of Prof'l Conduct R. 3.1 cmt. 2 (2020).

21. *See, e.g.*, CTC Imps. & Exps. v. Nigerian Petrol. Corp., 951 F.2d 573, 579 (3d Cir. 1991) ("The shorter the time, the more reasonable it is for an attorney to rely on the client or forwarding counsel."); Sanchez v. Liberty Lloyds, 672 So. 2d 268, 273 (La. Ct. App. 1996) (refusing to sanction a lawyer who filed a general denial under time constraints to avoid an entry of default against his client); State Bar of Ga., Formal Advisory Op. 87-1, at 2 (1989) (concluding that an attorney facing the expiration of a statute of limitations acts ethically in filing suit if "a reasonable attorney would conclude that there is a reasonable possibility that facts supporting the cause of action can be established after the filing of the claim"); Or. Eth. Op. 2005-59, 2005 WL 5679648, at *1 (Or. State Bar Ass'n, Bd. of Governors 2005) (concluding that when a statute of limitations would run before an attorney could investigate whether a claim exists sufficient to justify joining additional defendants, the attorney could join the defendants as long as they will not agree to extend the limitation period or an extension is otherwise not feasible, the attorney thereafter investigates diligently, and dismisses the defendants promptly if no claim actually exists).

22. *See, e.g.*, Iowa Sup. Ct. Att'y Disciplinary Bd. v. Barnhill, 885 N.W.2d 408, 420 (Iowa 2016) (concluding that counterclaims and crossclaims were frivolous and that the lawyer accordingly violated Rule 3.1).

contentions, including addressing when, if ever, lawyers can simply take clients at their word without investigating further. Unsurprisingly, the duty is nearly universally measured by an objective standard.[23] The court in *Wisconsin Chiropractic Ass'n v. State*[24] thoroughly described the nature of lawyers' duty to inquire:

> An attorney may rely upon his or her client for the factual basis for a claim when the client's statements are objectively reasonable, but this does not mean that an attorney always acts reasonably in accepting a client's statements. Whether it is reasonable to rely on one's client depends in part upon whether there is another means to verify what the client says without discovery. A party and attorney may not rely on formal discovery after the filing of a suit to establish the factual basis for the cause of action when the required factual basis could be established without formal discovery. In addition, in deciding whether to rely on one's client for the factual foundation of a claim, an attorney must carefully question the client and determine if the client's knowledge is direct or hearsay and is plausible; the attorney may not accept the client's version of the facts on faith alone. Allegations by a client of serious misconduct of another may require a more serious investigation. While the investigation need not be to the point of certainty to be reasonable and need not involve steps that are not cost-justified or are unlikely to produce results, the signer must explore readily available avenues of factual inquiry rather than simply taking a client's word.[25]

Other courts agree that lawyers are entitled to rely upon clients' factual recitations when they are "objectively reasonable" and in some cases even when the client's factual construct is arguably questionable, but only if the lawyer's other pre-suit investigative efforts failed or other sources of information were not available either to verify or to disprove the client's version of events.[26]

23. People v. Bontrager, 407 P.3d 1235, 1247 (Colo. 2017); O'Brien v. Super. Ct., 939 A.2d 1223, 1231 (Conn. App. Ct. 2008); *In re* Yelverton, 105 A.3d 413, 426 (D.C. 2014); *In re* Disciplinary Action Against Butler, 868 N.W.2d 243, 248 (Minn. 2015); *In re* Disciplinary Action Against Hoffman, 670 N.W.2d 500, 506 (N.D. 2003); Lawyer Disciplinary Bd. v. Neely, 528 S.E.2d 468, 473 (W. Va. 1998). *But see In re* Disciplinary Proceedings Against Osicka, 765 N.W.2d 775, 784 (Wis. 2009) (applying a subjective standard to a lawyer's pursuit of a claim).

24. 676 N.W.2d 580 (Wis. Ct. App. 2004).

25. *Id.* at 589 (internal citations omitted).

26. *See, e.g.*, *In re* Taylor, 655 F.3d 274, 284 (3d Cir. 2011) (explaining that it is "usually reasonable for a lawyer to rely on information provided by a client, especially where that information is superficially plausible and the client provides its own records which appear to confirm the information"); Hadges v. Yonkers Racing Corp., 48 F.3d 1320, 1329 (2d Cir. 1995) (discussing attorneys' ability to rely on clients' objectively reasonable assertions); *CTC Imps. & Exps.*, 951 F.2d at 579 (refusing to sanction a lawyer who had no reason to know or suspect underlying documents were forged and who was not in a position, given exigent circumstances, to obtain vital information before acting); Kraemer v. Grant Cnty., 892 F.2d 686, 690 (7th Cir. 1990) (finding that a lawyer who filed a conspiracy claim acted properly where his private investigator was unable to get the defendants to cooperate in providing information addressing his client's allegations); Cont'l

A comparison of two Seventh Circuit cases presents a helpful contrast of circumstances as to when a lawyer's reliance on her client's assertions in pursuing a lawsuit are reasonable.[27] In *Kraemer v. Grant County*,[28] the court agreed that a lawyer who had relied solely upon his client's assertions in deciding to sue Grant County had acted appropriately. The lawyer had advanced a position, consistent with the language in Comment 2 to Model Rule 3.1,[29] that filing the lawsuit alleging a conspiracy would permit him to pursue formal discovery to uncover information to verify the client's contentions. The court explained that, given the secretive nature of a conspiracy, the lawyer did "all he reasonably could have done to investigate his client's account of events" before filing the complaint; after all, it could not impose a standard that would require the lawyer to procure a conspirator's confession before suing.[30] The Seventh Circuit stressed that the lawyer had made other efforts at inquiring about the facts before suing, including hiring a private investigator, but those efforts were fruitless because the defendants did not cooperate in the investigation and stonewalled the lawyer's efforts to obtain information.[31]

In contrast, the conduct of Wisconsin lawyer William J. Nunnery in *Jiminez v. Madison Area Technical College*[32] demonstrates that reliance upon obviously fraudulent documents does not constitute a reasonable investigation. Nunnery's representation of Elvira Jiminez began with a workers' compensation claim brought against her employer, Madison Area Technical College, based on Jiminez's assertion that college administrators had racially and sexually harassed her. To support her claim, Jiminez produced a series of plastic-laminated e-mails containing derogatory racial comments about

Ins. Co. v. Constr. Indus. Servs. Corp., 149 F.R.D. 451, 453 (E.D.N.Y. 1993) (treating counsel's reliance upon information from client's in-house counsel regarding the location of the client's principal place of business as objectively reasonable); Slane v. Rio Grande Water Conservation Dist., 115 F.R.D. 61, 62 (D. Colo. 1987) (explaining that a lawyer who received detailed responses from adverse parties demonstrating that claims were barred by res judicata and without basis before suing could not simply rely on his client's assurances); Coburn Optical Indus. Inc. v. Cilco, Inc., 610 F. Supp. 656, 659 (M.D.N.C. 1985) (involving a defendant that asserted incorrect facts to justify an objection to venue that were well within its control to have confirmed through investigation); *Neely*, 528 S.E.2d at 474 (reversing a finding of a Rule 3.1 violation for allegations in a complaint based on a mother's description of treatment of her child at a facility where the lawyer received no cooperation from the defendants and the child was autistic and unable to assist).

27. Jiminez v. Madison Area Tech. Coll., 321 F.3d 652 (7th Cir. 2003); Kraemer v. Grant Cnty., 892 F.2d 686 (7th Cir. 1990).

28. 892 F.2d 686 (7th Cir. 1990).

29. Model Rules of Prof'l Conduct R. 3.1 cmt. 2 (2020) ("The filing of an action or defense or similar action taken for a client is not frivolous merely because the facts have not first been fully substantiated or because the lawyer expects to develop vital evidence only by discovery.").

30. *Kraemer*, 892 F.2d at 689.

31. *Id.* at 690.

32. 321 F.3d 652 (7th Cir. 2003).

her and discussing sexual harassment visited upon her.[33] As for the odd lamination of the e-mails, Jiminez insisted that the messages were authentic and said that she laminated them after printing to "prevent them from being stolen."[34] In response, the college provided sworn statements from the purported authors of the e-mails denying having written them and characterizing the e-mails as a "complete fabrication" and a "forgery."[35] The college then asked Nunnery to produce the original e-mails. He did not produce the originals and, ultimately, Jiminez's workers' compensation claim was denied and the college fired her.[36]

After the workers' compensation claim was dismissed, Nunnery continued to pursue Jiminez's claims by suing the college in federal court for allegedly discriminating against her. An amended complaint added the purported authors of the e-mails as individual defendants and, after the district court dismissed the amended complaint for failing to state a claim, Nunnery filed a second amended complaint that expanded the factual allegations and specifically referred to the purported e-mails from the unsuccessful workers' compensation action.[37] The lawyers for the college again informed Nunnery that the individual defendants denied authoring the e-mails. When Nunnery would not drop the claims, the college moved for Rule 11 sanctions.[38] After an evidentiary hearing, the district court ordered both monetary sanctions against Nunnery and the most severe sanction possible—the dismissal of Jiminez's case. On appeal, the Seventh Circuit found that the district court had acted within its discretion and further concluded that Jimenez had knowingly manufactured the false e-mails to try to support her claim. The Seventh Circuit reasoned that Jiminez had "exploited the judicial process and subjected her former colleagues and employer to unnecessary embarrassment and mental anguish."[39] Nunnery, a solo practitioner who had never been disciplined, was suspended from practice for two months as a disciplinary sanction imposed, in part, for his conduct in *Jiminez*.[40]

Let's pause to examine Nunnery's conduct. The fact that the college's lawyers insisted that the subject e-mails were fabricated was not enough, standing alone, to compel Nunnery to dismiss Jimenez's lawsuit or withdraw from her representation. Adversaries make baseless or exaggerated

33. *Id.* at 653.
34. *In re* Disciplinary Proc. Against Nunnery, 725 N.W.2d 613, 619 (Wis. 2007).
35. *Jiminez*, 321 F.3d at 654.
36. *Id.*
37. *Id.*
38. *Id.* at 654–55.
39. *Id.* at 657.
40. *In re* Disciplinary Proc. Against Nunnery, 725 N.W.2d 613, 614 (Wis. 2007). The disciplinary case against Nunnery included 14 counts for events spanning a six-year period. Several of the counts involved instances in which Nunnery was accused of pursuing meritless claims, including Jiminez's claims. *Id.* at 619–22.

claims or threats with some regularity. Lawyers are entitled to rely on clients to furnish the factual bases for claims as long as the client's assertions are objectively reasonable, and lawyers are further entitled to give clients the benefit of the doubt in close cases. But the college's insistence on a fraud coupled with Jimenez's implausible claim to have laminated the e-mails to prevent their theft should have alerted Nunnery to the possibility that Jimenez's claims were frivolous. Whatever options Nunnery thought he had, they did not include accepting Jimenez's allegations on faith; some excavation of the foundation for Jimenez's claims was clearly in order. Indeed, reasonable inquiry is generally called for any time a lawyer receives a communication from an adversary asserting that evidence has been falsified.

Board of Professional Responsibility v. Stinson[41] provides another example of a lawyer taking reliance upon a client's side of a story too far and demonstrates that, as circumstances change and new information is obtained, lawyers must reevaluate their clients' positions. In *Stinson*, two surgeons in Cody, Wyoming, found themselves feuding following the acrimonious dissolution of their practice—a feud in which Stinson's client, Dr. Schneider, turned out to be using a third party to fire his shots. Dr. Biles filed a federal lawsuit against an Indiana resident, Lisa Fallon, who allegedly sent a flyer to more than 14,000 Wyoming residents that accused him of having been arrested for DUI, being investigated for being drunk at work, and having lost a dozen lawsuits; only the DUI arrest claim was truthful.[42] Dr. Biles was able to determine that Fallon's only connection to Wyoming was a relationship with Dr. Schneider and his wife. Dr. Biles was also able to uncover a connection between Dr. Schneider and the company that printed the flyer that Fallon mailed.[43]

Dr. Schneider met with Stinson after the lawsuit was filed and told him that Fallon was a close family friend who could not afford to hire an attorney to defend the suit. He asked that Stinson help find Fallon a lawyer and said that he would pay her attorney's fees. Once Fallon had a lawyer, she answered Dr. Biles's lawsuit and admitted that she created and mailed the flyer, and further admitted that she used someone else's money to do so, but denied that she did any of it at anyone's request.[44] Fallon's lawyer soon became highly skeptical of her version of events and told Stinson of his concerns that Fallon was not being truthful and that her version of events was "fanciful and [didn't] make any sense."[45]

Further cause for doubt surfaced when the Park County attorney (Cody is in Park County) mailed three documents that had been printed from a

41. 337 P.3d 401 (Wyo. 2014).
42. *Id.* at 403.
43. *Id.*
44. *Id.*
45. *Id.* at 404.

thumb drive found in the pocket of men's surgical scrubs in the laundry at the West Park County Hospital to Dr. Biles's and Fallon's lawyers. These documents, which came to be known as the "laundry room documents" or "LRDs," included an eight-page document that instructed Fallon on how to testify in her deposition, referred to Dr. Schneider with the word "me," and included many damning passages, perhaps none worse than "'if you are able to withstand the heat of the deposition and "take a bullet", regardless of final economic damages in favor of [Dr.] Biles in any type of judgment, you will be taken care of far in excess of any paycheck. The amount he will get will be negligible and have no impact on your life.'"[46] The second document was a one-page summary of communications between Fallon and Dr. Schneider about the flyer and the lawsuit.[47] The third document set forth draft answers for interrogatories served on Fallon.[48] Fallon's lawyer forwarded the LRDs and the letter from the county attorney to Stinson.[49]

Thereafter, Stinson had a "very heated" meeting with Dr. Schneider in which he sought an explanation for the LRDs and tried to find out whether Dr. Schneider was paying for Fallon's testimony.[50] Dr. Schneider told Stinson "that he was on the telephone with Ms. Fallon as he was typing the document and was merely helping to prepare her and typing the answers as she was providing them."[51] He also denied paying, or attempting to pay, Fallon for her testimony.

After this meeting, Stinson continued to assist Dr. Schneider, which he defended as "resolving the doubt in favor of his client," including representing Dr. Schneider in seeking to quash third-party subpoenas issued by Dr. Biles and representing Dr. Schneider in a lawsuit by Dr. Biles that accused Dr. Schneider of RICO violations and defamation.[52] In answering and counterclaiming on Dr. Schneider's behalf, Stinson asserted that Dr. Biles's allegations were known to be false, credited Fallon's testimony in the federal lawsuit that she was the sole creator of the flyer, and recited a litany of unsavory conduct by Dr. Biles, including serial drunkenness and brandishing a gun in his office.[53] Ultimately, even more damning e-mails between Fallon and Dr. Schneider surfaced that caused Stinson, after conferring with bar counsel, to disclose to the court during a hearing the contents of those messages.

46. *Id.* at 405.
47. *Id.*
48. *Id.*
49. *Id.*
50. *Id.* at 405–06.
51. *Id.* at 406.
52. *Id.*
53. *Id.* at 406–07.

Dr. Schneider confidentially settled Dr. Biles's lawsuit against him very soon thereafter.[54]

Stinson was found to have violated Wyoming Rule 3.1(c), a provision not found in the Model Rules and more akin to Rule 11. Yet, there is little reason to think that his conduct would be viewed differently under Model Rule 3.1. Even ardent advocates for permitting lawyers some latitude when it comes to giving clients the benefit of the doubt on close questions ought to admit that the disclosure of the LRDs should have been a tipping point for Stinson. His willingness to believe Dr. Schneider's strained explanation for the LRDs was objectively unreasonable given both the contents of the LRDs and the other information he had gathered. Remarkably, Stinson received only a public reprimand from the Wyoming Supreme Court.[55]

Suing on behalf of a non-existent plaintiff is a decent indication that a lawyer's pre-suit fact investigation was deficient,[56] as is suing the wrong defendant.[57] A fairly amazing example of a substandard pre-filing inquiry can be seen in the actions of a Virginia lawyer, Michael Weatherbee, who sued a doctor for medical malpractice who was not even in the hospital during the plaintiff's allegedly botched procedure.[58] Weatherbee had included among the defendants in his client's medical malpractice suit a surgeon named Dr. Ward P. Vaughan, who not only was not present at the time of the plaintiff's operation but did not even have privileges to practice at the hospital in question. Weatherbee's only justification for suing Vaughan was his belief that a "Bob Vaughan" who was listed in the medical records was the same person as Dr. Ward P. Vaughan.[59] Making matters worse for Dr. Vaughan, the lawsuit received significant publicity in the form of a local television report and through a local radio station that "repeatedly informed its listeners, approximately once each hour for a full day, that Dr. Vaughan had been sued for medical malpractice."[60] The Virginia Supreme Court faulted Weatherbee for failing to undertake even the most basic research, which would have revealed that his client had no factual or legal basis for suing Dr. Vaughan, and affirmed the imposition of a public reprimand against Weatherbee for violating Rule 3.1.[61] Dr. Vaughn must have thought that sanction awfully light.

54. *Id.* at 407.

55. *Id.* at 426.

56. *See, e.g.*, *In re* Dixon, 435 P.3d 80, 88 (N.M. 2019) (violating Rule 3.1 by suing on behalf of an apparently fictitious person with whom the lawyer never spoke before filing suit).

57. Naming someone who has no colorable claims against the defendant as a member of a group of plaintiffs in a lawsuit can also evidence an inadequate pre-suit investigation. *See, e.g.*, Merritt v. Int'l Ass'n of Machinists & Aerospace Workers, 613 F.3d 609, 626 (6th Cir. 2010).

58. Weatherbee v. Va. State Bar, 689 S.E.2d 753 (Va. 2010).

59. *Id.* at 755.

60. *Id.* at 756.

61. *Id.*

Given the relevant standard, common sense dictates that how much a court will require from a lawyer in terms of pre-filing investigation can also be influenced by the nature of the client's allegations against the adversary. A South Carolina decision concluding that the lawyer's discussions with the client alone could not stand as a reasonable investigation because of the nature of the client's claim provides an example, albeit one open to significant questions. *Ex parte Gregory*[62] arose out of a lawsuit by Annie Melton against her former lawyer, Gerald Malloy, for allegedly misappropriating settlement funds belonging to her. George Gregory represented Melton. Prior to filing suit and after being told by Melton that over two years had passed without her receiving the almost $15,000 in settlement funds she said she was owed, Gregory had communicated with the insurance agency for the party that was liable in the underlying matter and the adjuster who handled the claim, had reviewed the settlement documents, had reviewed telephone records showing how many times Melton had called Malloy, and was able to determine that the settlement check had been presented for payment over two years earlier.[63]

Surprisingly, the South Carolina Supreme Court found that Gregory's pre-filing efforts did not constitute a reasonable investigation because he had not contacted Malloy. This, the court found, hamstrung Gregory's investigation and, in the court's mind, prevented him from learning that the settlement funds were still in Malloy's trust account because of a continuing issue relating to the nature and amount of a Medicaid lien. As the court saw it, "a simple phone call may have led to an explanation by [Malloy] as to why the money was being held."[64] The court discounted Gregory's explanation that he had not contacted Malloy because he did not think that Malloy would respond and that he had not requested Malloy's file because he did not expect it would reveal anything he had not already learned from his communications with the insurance agency and adjuster for the tortfeasor.[65] The court stressed that its opinion should not be treated as establishing a strict rule always requiring a lawyer to go beyond merely discussing a claim with a client before suing, but the court clearly drew a very bright line with its statement that "before alleging conversion against an attorney for misappropriation of client funds or legal malpractice, a reasonable investigation is necessary."[66]

There were, however, some additional facts that might diminish the surprise a detached lawyer might otherwise exhibit upon learning of the court's conclusion that what sounded like a responsible investigation was

62. *Ex parte* Gregory, 663 S.E.2d 46 (S.C. 2008).
63. *Id.* at 48.
64. *Id.* at 51.
65. *Id.* at 50.
66. *Id.* at 51 & n.3.

insufficient. First, Gregory's co-counsel asked him whether they should perhaps communicate with Malloy before filing suit, but Gregory "did not think that it would 'do any good.'"[67] In other words, Gregory had dismissed a reasonable investigatory step raised by a seemingly trusted advisor out-of-hand. Moreover, with the benefit of hindsight, a simple telephone call to Malloy would have avoided the litigation altogether. That conclusion clearly influenced the court's decision,[68] although it should just as clearly be a case- and fact-specific consideration. Second, upon filing and serving the complaint, Gregory had his process server deliver a copy of the complaint to a local newspaper reporter, with whom Gregory then spoke. Gregory stated, in two articles written by the reporter, that Malloy "should have known he couldn't co-mingle funds" and that he "shouldn't have kept it in his pocket and collected all the interest on it."[69] This plainly influenced the court; indeed, the court specifically stated that it was troubled by Gregory's "inflammatory statements" to the media without first performing an appropriate investigation of the conversion claim.[70] Another fact mentioned by the court in its recitation of events that may have colored the result was that Malloy had represented Melton pro bono.[71]

Although the *Gregory* court was entitled to be irked by what it considered "inflammatory statements" to the media and might even have chafed at the notion that a lawyer doing free legal work was unfairly accused of misappropriation, its conclusion that Gregory acted unreasonably in not reaching out to Malloy is suspect. This is especially true given that the court did not, for example, dedicate any of its opinion to Malloy's reputation or otherwise provide a basis for a reader to conclude that members of the legal community might find it hard to believe that he would ever engage in such conduct. Certainly, a lawyer might expect as a matter of professional courtesy that a lawyer in Gregory's position would call or write before suing a fellow attorney, but the *Gregory* decision, in establishing a bright-line requirement that a pre-filing investigation of a claim against a lawyer for misappropriation is not reasonable unless the claimant's lawyer first communicates with the prospective defendant, smacks of favoritism to members of the bar that would not be granted to other professionals. Beyond that, a lawyer contemplating litigation may have good strategic reasons for not first communicating with the target, as where the lawyer reasonably fears that the prospective defendant will somehow put the disputed funds beyond the client's reach or initiate some sort of preemptive action against the client.

67. *Id.* at 48.
68. *Id.* at 49.
69. *Id.*
70. *Id.* at 51.
71. *Id.* at 49.

B. Advancing Factually or Legally Unsupportable Positions

Failing to adequately investigate the circumstances surrounding a claim is, of course, one way that a lawyer can end up pursuing positions that are factually unsupportable. Unfortunately, there are also more pernicious, inexcusable ways, as demonstrated by the two lawyers whose conduct resulted in their suspensions from the practice of law in *In re Rios*.[72]

Lawyers Shane Rios and Daniel Levy were approached by a former client whose mother had allegedly fallen on a "badly cracked sidewalk while exiting a church on Lockwood Avenue, in the Bronx."[73] They accepted the case. The client was unable to remember either the church's name or its precise location. Rios and Levy determined through online searches that there was only one potential church on Lockwood Avenue, but it was in Yonkers—not in the Bronx.[74] They gave notice of the claim to that church and then tried to determine via a Freedom of Information Law (FOIL) request whether the city had received prior notice of sidewalk defects.

They visited the scene without their client, who refused to accompany them, and saw no defects in the church's sidewalk; however, they did notice a "badly cracked" sidewalk across the street.[75] The city's response to their FOIL request indicated that there were no prior notifications of sidewalk defects and thus no viable claim against the church. This led to a fateful meeting with their client, where, instead of explaining that she had no viable claim, "they decided to influence her by first explaining the law, emphasizing that if she fell on the sidewalk abutting the church, she would have no viable claim for her injuries. However, they indicated that if she fell across the street . . . she had a viable case against the owner of the abutting property."[76] After securing their client's assertion that she fell on the homeowner's sidewalk across the street, they sued the homeowner. When it was time to try the case, they retained experienced trial counsel but did not reveal that the client originally said she had fallen elsewhere and "they removed [from the case file] the claim letter they initially sent to the church" and several other documents that showed the full story.[77] For this conduct, which Rios and Levy remorsefully admitted during their disciplinary proceedings, both were suspended from practice for nine months.

A lawyer can be fully cognizant of and forthright about the facts but nonetheless run into trouble by pursuing an unsupportable legal position.

---

72. 965 N.Y.S.2d 418 (App. Div. 2013).
73. *Id.* at 420.
74. *Id.* at 421.
75. *Id.*
76. *Id.*
77. *Id.* at 422.

The Florida Supreme Court considered itself to be dealing with a prime example of such a situation in *Florida Bar v. Richardson.*[78]

Richardson's troubles arose from his representation of the personal representative in a probate proceeding and the probate court's determination that his fee was excessive and had to be reimbursed to the decedent's estate. Richardson appealed that ruling, arguing that the probate court lacked jurisdiction to order reimbursement because his fee had been paid by the personal representative not from the assets of the estate, but out of personal funds. Richardson's appeal was unsuccessful on the merits, but the matter was remanded for a recalculation of the correct amount to be reimbursed.[79] After the recalculation by the probate court, Richardson appealed again, but this appeal was dismissed as untimely. Thereafter, Richardson's excessive fee earned him a 90-day suspension from practice and two years of probation upon reinstatement.[80] He then unsuccessfully petitioned the Florida Supreme Court for two writs of mandamus, one seeking reinstatement of the second appeal that had been dismissed as untimely and another to vacate the probate court judgment and force that court to withdraw jurisdiction. Most lawyers at that point would obey The First Rule of Holes and stop digging. Richardson, however, was undaunted.

Richardson took his legal crusade to federal court, filing a lawsuit claiming that the Florida probate court order requiring reimbursement violated his civil rights because the probate court lacked jurisdiction. He sought both injunctive relief and $1 million in damages, and named as defendants all of the Florida judges involved, his former client, and his former client's new attorneys.[81] This federal suit, which the district court found to be "both manifestly frivolous and malicious," was dismissed, and Richardson was sanctioned under Rule 11.[82] After further disciplinary proceedings were instituted against Richardson and a hearing convened, a disciplinary referee found that "[r]easonable inquiry by a graduate of a law school, a certified member of the Florida Bar, or any lay person would clearly show that the lawsuit as filed by . . . Richardson was clearly unwarranted," and recommended that Richardson be suspended for 90 days.[83] The Florida Supreme Court acknowledged that it was important not "to stifle innovative claims by attorneys" but distinguished Richardson's situation as "an obsessive attempt to relitigate an issue that has failed decisively numerous times."[84]

78. 591 So. 2d 908 (Fla. 1992).
79. *Id.* at 909.
80. *Id.*
81. *Id.* at 909–10.
82. *Id.* at 910.
83. *Id.*
84. *Id.* Because of the other 90-day suspension against Richardson arising out of the same underlying case, the Florida Supreme Court reduced the second 90-day suspension to a 60-day

Lawyers should not read *Richardson* to mean that they can never pursue a case in the face of directly adverse precedent without risking discipline or sanctions. Indeed, *Hunter v. Earthgrains Co. Bakery*[85] furnishes a perfect example of when a lawyer's pursuit of a legal position directly contrary to existing precedent cannot be treated as frivolous. In *Earthgrains*, a federal district court in North Carolina barred lawyer Pamela Hunter from practicing before it for five years as a sanction. Hunter was sanctioned for arguing for an outcome on a question of law that was contrary to clear precedent in the Fourth Circuit, which encompasses North Carolina. Specifically, in 1998, Hunter argued that the district court should rule that arbitration of a federal employment discrimination claim can be required in a collective bargaining agreement only by the use of specific language to that effect. Her argument contradicted a Fourth Circuit decision handed down just two years before.

The Fourth Circuit reversed the sanction order because, as of 1998 when Hunter made the argument, there were six other circuits that had rejected the Fourth Circuit's position and, in fact, the Fourth Circuit was the only circuit to have held as it did. Because the law on the question was in "flux" at the time, the Fourth Circuit held that the district court was "reaching" in trying to characterize the lawyer's conduct as sanctionable.[86] The result in *Earthgrains* makes perfect sense, of course, because the purpose behind Model Rule 3.1 and state equivalents is not to deter lawyers from making novel arguments or pursuing cases of first impression, nor to suppress good faith arguments seeking outright reversal of existing precedent, but only to prohibit lawyers from pursuing truly frivolous positions.[87] While Hunter could expect the district court to rule against her clients because it was bound by the precedent with which she disagreed, she was entitled to contemplate that the Fourth Circuit might be persuaded to retreat from its prior position.[88] Failing that, she might have sought relief in the Supreme Court based on the circuit split. Hunter's only real offense was failing to thoroughly explain to the district court the circuit split and the potential import of a Supreme Court case giving her clients some ammunition for argument, but "that lack of thoroughness [did] not render her position frivolous."[89]

The investigation lawyers must undertake to establish that legal arguments to be made in proposed litigation are not frivolous is relatively easy

suspension. *Id.* at 911.

85. 281 F.3d 144 (4th Cir. 2002).

86. *Id.*

87. *See, e.g.*, Baker v. Alderman, 158 F.3d 516, 524 (11th Cir. 1998) ("[T]he purpose of Rule 11 is to deter frivolous lawsuits and not to deter novel legal arguments or cases of first impression."); Operating Eng'rs Pension Tr. v. A-C Co., 859 F.2d 1336, 1344 (9th Cir. 1988) ("Forceful representation often requires that an attorney attempt to read a case or an agreement in an innovative though sensible way.").

88. *Earthgrains*, 281 F.3d at 156.

89. *Id.* at 156–57.

to determine. Effectively summarized, it is a matter of performing the legal research required to determine whether governing law supports the legal arguments that would need to be advanced for the client to prevail and, if not, whether those arguments can fairly be categorized as good faith arguments for extending, modifying, or reversing that governing law.[90] A good description of the process for determining whether the requisite good faith exists is found in the Restatement (Third) of the Law Governing Lawyers:

> [W]hether good faith exists depends on such factors as whether the lawyer in question or another lawyer established precedent adverse to the position being argued (and, if so, whether the lawyer disclosed that precedent), whether new legal grounds of plausible weight can be advanced, whether new or additional authority supports the lawyer's position, or whether for other reasons, such as a change in the composition of a multi-member court, arguments can be advanced that have a substantially greater chance of success.[91]

Lawyers generally cannot rely upon the possibility of mistakes by the other side to justify pursuing an otherwise unsupportable position, as demonstrated by a review of conduct that led to an Iowa lawyer's indefinite suspension in *Iowa Supreme Court Board of Professional Ethics & Conduct v. Hohnbaum.*[92] *Hohnbaum* started as a simple negligence case. A car driven by Audrey Biere rear-ended Betty Schumann's car. Biere's insurer hired Donald Hohnbaum to defend Biere in a lawsuit by Schumann. Biere had admitted to Hohnbaum and in statements recorded in the accident report that she had rear-ended Schumann's vehicle, and Hohnbaum thus admitted that fact in the answer he filed on her behalf.[93] So far, so good. But Hohnbaum later found another report in which a police officer had stated that it was Schumann who had struck Biere. Hohnbaum then moved for leave to amend the answer to deny that Biere had rear-ended Schumann, and the case proceeded to trial.

At the trial, Schumann testified that it was Biere who struck her vehicle from the rear; Biere did not appear at trial.[94] The jury, which the court had permitted to have access to both the accident report reflecting Biere's original admission and the insurance company's file, returned a verdict for Schumann. The Iowa Supreme Court explained that it was certainly

90. *See, e.g.*, Att'y Grievance Comm'n of Md. v. Worsham, 105 A.3d 515, 528 (Md. 2014) ("A minimal amount of research would have alerted [the lawyer] to the frivolous nature of the arguments he made."); *In re* Richards, 986 P.2d 1117, 1120 (N.M. 1999) ("[W]hen relying upon an exception to a general rule of law, the position the lawyer asserts must either come within the exception, or provide a cogent argument for broadening the exception.").

91. Restatement (Third) of the Law Governing Lawyers § 110 cmt. d (2000).

92. 554 N.W.2d 550 (Iowa 1996).

93. *Id.* at 551.

94. *Id.*

appropriate for a lawyer to make the other side prove her case, but that Hohnbaum had stepped well over that line and persisted in the pursuit of a frivolous position.[95]

Although a lawyer generally cannot hope for an adversary to make a mistake to justify what would otherwise be the pursuit of a meritless position in litigation, it appears to be settled—even if subject to the charge of being intellectually inconsistent with what is normally expected from attorneys when it comes to candor and the duty not to pursue frivolous litigation—that it is not ethically improper for a lawyer to pursue a claim in the hope that the other side will miss a statute of limitations defense. Stated positively, a lawyer may ethically pursue a claim that she knows to be time-barred.[96]

The best-known source for this proposition is ABA Formal Ethics Opinion 94-387.[97] In that opinion, the ABA Standing Committee on Ethics and Professional Responsibility explained that knowingly asserting a time-barred claim did not violate Rule 3.1 because

> The running of the period provided for enforcement of a civil claim creates an affirmative defense which must be asserted by the opposing party, and is not a bar to a court's jurisdiction over the matter. A time-barred claim may still be enforced by a court, and will be if the opposing party raises no objection. And, opposing counsel may fail to raise a limitations defense for any number of reasons, ranging from incompetence to a considered decision to forego the defense in order to have vindication on the merits or to assert some counterclaim.[98]

The committee also explained that its opinion would be different if a jurisdiction were to treat an expired limitations period as a jurisdictional matter or if there were other circumstances surrounding the filing of a lawsuit known to be untimely that could be viewed as indicia of bad faith.[99] One such circumstance noted by the committee was an attorney's act of filing a defamation claim *after* being told by the defendant that the claim was time-barred.[100] Similar conclusions have been reached by state ethics bodies interpreting their own rules.[101] Several courts have echoed these conclusions.[102]

---

95. *Id.* at 552.

96. *But see* Trainor v. Ky. Bar Ass'n, 311 S.W.3d 719, 721 (Ky. 2010) (finding that lawyer violated Rule 3.1 by filing a medical malpractice suit over two years after the statute of limitations had expired).

97. ABA Comm. on Ethics & Prof'l Responsibility, Formal Op. 94-387 (1994).

98. *Id.* at 4.

99. *Id.* at 5.

100. Brubaker v. Richmond, 943 F.2d 1363, 1385 (4th Cir. 1991) (finding that making such a claim is "groundless in law" and violates Rule 11).

101. N.C. State Bar Ethics Comm., Formal Ethics Op. 2003-13, at 1 (2004); Pa. Eth. Op. 96-80, 1996 WL 928177, at *1 (Pa. Bar Ass'n, Comm. on Legal Ethics & Prof'l Responsibility 1996).

102. *See, e.g.*, Hoover v. Armco Inc., 915 F.2d 355, 357 (8th Cir. 1990) ("The statute of limitations is an affirmative defense the defendant must raise . . . and Hoover did not have to anticipate

Not all courts agree with this approach, however, especially where the challenged suit is filed well beyond the applicable limitation period.[103]

The rationale behind the prevailing view is that the expiration of a statute of limitations is merely an affirmative defense and can be waived by the defendant through a failure to raise it, and, moreover, such time restrictions do not divest a court of jurisdiction. On the surface, this approach seems sound, inasmuch as the public policy behind enacting and enforcing statutes of limitations is to provide defendants with certainty as to times in which actions may be pursued and not to protect courts from expending resources on the adjudication of stale claims. Hence the proposition that a plaintiff's lawyer should be free to roll the dice on a claim known to be time-barred based on the hope, however slim, that the defendant will not assert a statute of limitations defense. This might occur because the defendant or its lawyer did not apprehend the untimeliness of the claim, or even because the defendant made a tactical decision to have the matter determined on the merits.

Yet, such logic can be readily extended to justify the pursuit of other meritless claims on the premise that, in the adversary system, the opposing party might not recognize the claim as meritless. In fact, one could imagine a lawyer justifying such conduct on the basis that it is a good faith argument to extend the legal concept that permits pursuit of time-barred claims into other areas in which dispositive arguments are classified as affirmative defenses.[104] For example, a lawyer might sue a defendant even though it is clear that the defendant's conduct was absolutely privileged. Is such a claim frivolous, or does the reasoning of Formal Op. 94-387 permit the lawyer to file the suit? On the one hand, the claim is arguably frivolous because "a lawyer of ordinary competence would recognize [it] as so lacking in merit that there is no substantial possibility that the tribunal will accept it."[105] On the other hand, the defendant must plead its absolute privilege as an affirmative defense, the claim is enforceable by the court, and the privilege is not a bar to the court's exercise of jurisdiction over the matter.

Without extending the debate too far, under Formal Op. 94-387 our hypothetical lawyer could file her client's claim notwithstanding the

---

Armco would raise it."); Ford v. Temple Hosp., 790 F.2d 342, 348–49 (3d Cir. 1986) ("In the real world of litigation, counsel are not expected to be omniscient. No one knows for certain whether a potential affirmative defense will be in fact pled. The law books are replete with decisions where counsel has failed to file an affirmative defense or failed to file it timely.").

103. *See, e.g.*, Trainor v. Ky. Bar Ass'n, 311 S.W.3d 719, 721 (Ky. 2010) (finding that lawyer violated Rule 3.1 by filing medical malpractice suit more than two years after the statute of limitations had run).

104. *Cf.* Or. Eth. Op. 2005-21, 2005 WL 5679607, at *1 (Or. State Bar Ass'n, Bd. of Governors 2005) (opining that a lawyer can file complaint knowing that a valid affirmative defense exists because "it is up to [the] [d]efendant or [the] [d]efendant's own counsel to look after [the] [d]efendant's interests and to discover and assert any available defenses").

105. Restatement (Third) of the Law Governing Lawyers § 110 cmt. d (2000).

defendant's absolute privilege without violating Rule 3.1. The base test in this context seems to be whether the claim would deprive a court of subject matter jurisdiction; because this claim does not, filing it does not violate Rule 3.1 even though it will clearly fail if the defendant asserts its privilege as an affirmative defense.[106] If the defendant is alert and raises its absolute privilege as an affirmative defense, or perhaps responds to the suit by writing to the lawyer to demand that she dismiss the claim, then the lawyer must withdraw the claim to avoid violating Rule 3.1. Furthermore, whether the lawyer's conduct violates Rule 3.1 is a separate and distinct question from whether it violates Federal Rule of Civil Procedure 11, 28 U.S.C. § 1927, or state analogs.[107]

Naturally, a lawyer's ability to ethically pursue a time-barred claim does not mean that she can engage in other misleading conduct in pursuit of that claim. For example, while a lawyer can file a complaint knowing that it is time-barred, the lawyer cannot actively seek to hide that fact by alleging that it is timely filed or by falsely alleging that an event happened on a different date.[108] But how close to the line can lawyers go without violating their duty of candor? May a lawyer set forth in a complaint only the year in which an injury was suffered—for example, describing an automobile collision known to have occurred on December 12, 2007, as having occurred merely in 2007—to help obscure whether the lawsuit was timely filed?

The most straightforward answer is that multiple ethics rules coalesce to send a clear signal that lawyers are expected to understand and comply with high obligations of candor, and that lawyers who wonder whether their conduct treads too close to the line likely are too close to the line. A lawyer pondering whether she can assert only that the collision occurred in 2007 to help obscure whether the lawsuit was timely filed needs to be concerned with the jurisdiction's equivalents of Model Rules 3.3(a), 4.1(a), 8.4(c), and 8.4(d). Model Rule 3.3(a)(1) prohibits a lawyer from making "a false statement of fact" to a tribunal,[109] and Model Rule 4.1(a) prohibits a lawyer from making "a false statement of material fact" to third persons.[110] The commentary to each of those rules notes that there are circumstances

106. In contrast, if the defendant enjoyed absolute *immunity* against the claim instead of an absolute privilege, the lawyer likely would violate Rule 3.1 by filing the claim so long as the defendant's immunity was of a type that would operate to deprive the court of subject matter jurisdiction.

107. *See, e.g.*, Matthews v. Freedman, 128 F.R.D. 194, 206–08 (E.D. Pa. 1989) (sanctioning a lawyer and referring him to Pennsylvania professional authorities for possible discipline where the lawyer filed time-barred claims and did not dismiss them after defense counsel notified him of the defendants' intention to assert a statute of limitations defense).

108. *In re* Shumate, 647 N.E.2d 321, 322 (Ind. 1995).

109. Model Rules of Prof'l Conduct R. 3.3(a)(1) (2020).

110. *Id.* R. 4.1(a).

in which omissions can amount to misrepresentations sufficient to equate to affirmative false statements.[111] Model Rule 8.4(c) broadly declares that it is unethical for a lawyer to "engage in conduct involving dishonesty, fraud, deceit or misrepresentation."[112] Finally, Model Rule 8.4(d) categorizes as professional misconduct any litigation conduct by a lawyer that is "prejudicial to the administration of justice."[113] Even more fundamentally, a lawyer in this situation ought to be concerned that obscuring the date of the accident would ruin her credibility with the court when the truth is exposed, and that any loss of credibility will affect her and her clients in other cases.

C. Consequences of Rule 3.1 Violations and Abusive or Persistent Misconduct

If there is a saving grace for lawyers charged with professional misconduct for pursuing frivolous claims or contentions, it generally resides in the discipline to be imposed. Disciplinary sanctions for Rule 3.1 violations tend to be of a lesser nature[114]—such as an admonition, censure, reprimand, or short suspension[115]—unless the lawyer has engaged in a pattern of such

111. *Id.* R. 3.3 cmt. 3 ("There are circumstances where failure to make a disclosure is the equivalent of an affirmative misrepresentation."); *id.* R. 4.1 cmt. 1 ("Misrepresentations can also occur by partially true but misleading statements or omissions that are the equivalent of affirmative false statements.").

112. *Id.* R. 8.4(c).

113. *Id.* R. 8.4(d).

114. There are notable exceptions. *See, e.g.*, *In re* Caulfield, 683 So. 2d 714, 715–19 (La. 1996) (involving illegal conduct in the form of a staged auto accident to obtain insurance proceeds); *In re* Hess, 406 S.W.3d 37, 41 (Mo. 2013) (involving a lawyer who attempted to further his employment dispute with his former law firm by frivolously claiming to continue to represent clients of the law firm and filing attorney liens on their cases); *In re* Rios, 965 N.Y.S.2d 418, 424 (App. Div. 2013) (involving two lawyers who intentionally induced their client to provide false information about the location of an accident and removed related evidence from the case file before sharing the file with trial counsel); *In re* Yao, 680 N.Y.S.2d 546, 548 (App. Div. 1998) (involving an extortion demand).

115. *See, e.g.*, *In re* Spikes, 881 A.2d 1118, 1119 (D.C. 2005) (suspending a lawyer for 30 days for pursuing a defamation action based on statements made in a disciplinary complaint that were clearly protected by well-settled law applying the litigation privilege to reports of attorney misconduct); Fla. Bar v. Thomas, 582 So. 2d 1177, 1178 (Fla. 1991) (imposing a public reprimand and one-year probation on a lawyer who filed a frivolous suit against other counsel in retaliation for representing clients opposing the lawyer in another action); *In re* Colvin, 336 P.3d 823, 831 (Kan. 2014) (imposing a public censure as discipline); *In re* Hackett, 701 So. 2d 920, 922 (La. 1997) (imposing a public reprimand against lawyers for filing a frivolous motion to dissolve a temporary restraining order); *In re* Panel Case No. 17289, 669 N.W.2d 898, 906–07 (Minn. 2003) (admonishing a lawyer with an extensive prior disciplinary history, including multiple past suspensions, who filed a frivolous defamation claim and who made allegations about damage to a car that could have been proven false by viewing the vehicle); Bd. of Prof'l Responsibility v. Stinson, 337 P.3d 401 (Wyo. 2014) (censuring a lawyer for his assertions in a motion to quash and a separate answer on behalf of a doctor who was known to be funding vindictive litigation by a third party against the doctor's former partner and who had documented efforts to improperly shape the third party's testimony).

behavior.[116] If the lawyer that pursued a frivolous claim or contention is a repeat or serial offender, indefinite or lengthy suspensions or even disbarment may result.[117] One of the more egregious examples of serial misconduct led to a Missouri lawyer being disbarred first by the Missouri Supreme Court and then reciprocally by a Missouri federal court after she had been sanctioned by four federal courts for pursuing frivolous claims.[118]

Not surprisingly, lawyers disciplined for violating Rule 3.1 often are deemed not only to have pursued unfounded allegations but also to have done so for the purpose of harassing or intimidating an opponent.[119] Although Model Rule 3.1 is the most obvious and most direct rule prohibiting a lawyer's pursuit of a frivolous claim or defense, several other ethics rules prohibit types of conduct often present in a lawyer's pursuit of a frivolous claim or defense for some improper purpose. For example, Model Rule 3.4(e) prohibits lawyers from "allud[ing] to any matter [during trial] that the lawyer does not reasonably believe is relevant or that will not be supported by admissible evidence."[120] Model Rule 4.4(a) broadly makes it unethical for a lawyer to "use means that have no substantial purpose other than to

---

116. *See, e.g., In re* Yelverton, 105 A.3d 413, 428–32 (D.C. 2014) (suspending the lawyer for 30 days for violating Rule 3.1 but further requiring that he demonstrate his fitness to practice for reinstatement upon completion of his suspension because of his repeated assertions of objectively meritless positions).

117. *See, e.g., In re* Stern, 11 N.E.3d 917, 921–22 (Ind. 2014) (suspending a lawyer for 18 months without automatic reinstatement); Iowa Sup. Ct. Bd. of Prof'l Ethics & Conduct v. Ronwin, 557 N.W.2d 515, 522–23 (Iowa 1996) (disbarring a lawyer who filed two frivolous lawsuits against the same defendant, a frivolous lawsuit against a judge, and other frivolous lawsuits against attorneys for parties in the litigation); *In re* Benson, 69 P.3d 544, 546–48 (Kan. 2003) (disbarring a lawyer who, as plaintiff and representing himself, filed 14 meritless lawsuits against a number of parties); *In re* Selmer, 568 N.W.2d 702, 703–05 (Minn. 1997) (suspending a lawyer for one year and imposing a five-year probationary period upon reinstatement for involvement in numerous baseless race discrimination claims as defense against lawsuits seeking to require the lawyer to pay creditors); State *ex rel.* Okla. Bar Ass'n v. Godlove, 318 P.3d 1086, 1095 (Okla. 2013) (disbarring a lawyer who "not only overstepped" the "fine line between zealous advocacy and harassing, frivolous litigation" but "trampled it").

118. *In re* Caranchini, 160 F.3d 420, 422–25 (8th Cir. 1998); *In re* Caranchini, 956 S.W.2d 910, 915–20 (Mo. 1997).

119. *See, e.g.*, Thompson v. Sup. Ct. Comm. on Prof'l Conduct, 252 S.W.3d 125, 128 (Ark. 2007) (determining that the lawyer violated Rules 3.1 and 4.4 by filing a frivolous lis pendens action); *In re* Pelkey, 962 A.2d 268, 280 (D.C. 2008) (finding that the lawyer violated Rule 3.1 by filing a frivolous appeal and pursuing frivolous litigation, and violated Rule 4.4 by frivolously attempting to set aside an arbitration award despite having agreed to arbitration, all in connection with a dispute with a former business partner); *In re* Bandaries, 156 So. 3d 1152, 1160 (La. 2014) (finding that the lawyer violated Rule 3.1 by suing the defendant for the purpose of harassing her); Att'y Grievance Comm'n of Md. v. Mixter, 109 A.3d 1, 58 (Md. 2015) (agreeing with the hearing judge's conclusion that the lawyer violated Rule 3.1 by filing numerous frivolous motions to bludgeon parties into complying with his excessive discovery requests); *In re* Hess, 406 S.W.3d 37, 41 (Mo. 2013) (describing a hearing board's finding that the lawyer had filed a frivolous suit "for the purpose of harassing and burdening the [defendants] because of an employment dispute with [his former employer]").

120. Model Rules of Prof'l Conduct R. 3.4(e) (2020).

embarrass, delay, or burden a third person."[121] And when it is determined that the lawyer has engaged in purposeful harassment or intimidation, as opposed to inadequately investigating the merits of the client's allegations, it should also come as little surprise that the disciplinary sanction tends to be more severe.[122]

An Arkansas case, *Dodrill v. Executive Director*,[123] illustrates this principle. The lawyer in that case, Lewis Dodrill, represented Bobby Bratton, a debtor in a bankruptcy proceeding. Dodrill, acting on Bratton's behalf, filed a suit in federal court seeking approximately $15,000 in damages from Bratton's former bankruptcy attorneys and then amended the complaint to add the trustee of Bratton's bankruptcy estate and the trustee's law firm as defendants.[124] The district court referred the case to the bankruptcy court, where the defendants prevailed on dispositive motions. Dodrill did not appeal from any of those rulings. Rather, he moved to have the trustee removed for alleged fraud and waste. The bankruptcy court held a hearing on that motion and, when Dodrill offered no supporting evidence, entered judgment against Bratton. Undaunted, Dodrill then filed another complaint in bankruptcy court against many of the same defendants named in the earlier suit but this time seeking over $150,000 in damages.[125]

The perturbed defendants successfully moved to dismiss the second lawsuit and then sought sanctions against Dodrill under Bankruptcy Rule 9011. The bankruptcy court sustained the sanctions motions. In doing so, the bankruptcy judge stressed that the evidence revealed no misconduct by the defendants and indicated that Dodrill "continuously displayed a complete lack of competence in the practice of bankruptcy law."[126] The bankruptcy judge also referred Dodrill to the Arkansas disciplinary authorities. In the resulting disciplinary case, the bankruptcy judge testified that Dodrill had been "continually insulting, abusive, and disruptive to the court, to

121. *Id.* R. 4.4(a); *see, e.g.*, *In re* Wagner, 744 N.E.2d 418, 421–22 (Ind. 2001) (finding a Rule 4.4(a) violation where, after a homeowner had filed bankruptcy and discharged the obligation created by a judgment lien, the lawyer charged the homeowner $1,000 to agree to release that lien).

122. *See, e.g.*, *In re* Blasi, 660 N.Y.S.2d 151, 152–53 (App. Div. 1997) (suspending the lawyer for five years for pursuing meritless complaints and motions as means of dealing with personal disputes with neighbors); *In re* Sandvoss, 644 N.Y.S.2d 557, 558–59 (App. Div. 1996) (suspending the lawyer for two years for filing a frivolous defamation suit against a client as retaliation for the client's pursuit of disciplinary proceedings against him); *In re* Disciplinary Proc. Against Eisenberg, 778 N.W.2d 645, 661–62 (Wis. 2010) (disbarring a lawyer with a long disciplinary history for pursuing meritless litigation against his client's wife, a victim of domestic violence, to gain leverage in his client's divorce case by intimidating, harassing, and maliciously injuring her).

123. 824 S.W.2d 383 (Ark. 1992).

124. *Id.* at 384.

125. *Id.*

126. *Id.* at 385 (quoting from the letter of referral by the bankruptcy judge reporting that Dodrill had admitted during a hearing that he knew "nothing whatever about bankruptcy," was "thoroughly incompetent in bankruptcy court," and had "no business being there").

witnesses, and to opposing counsel despite repeated warnings."[127] Rather than engaging in routine discovery, Dodrill had "assail[ed] opposing counsel as liars and embezzlers."[128] Dodrill confessed that he was incompetent to handle bankruptcy matters and admitted that the allegations in the second suit were not "founded in fact."[129] He apparently started out wanting only "a clarifying order in bankruptcy court," but instead of pursuing that course, "he sued the attorneys involved for wrongful conduct."[130] All of this bolstered the Arkansas Supreme Court's conclusion that he deserved a one-year suspension for pursuing litigation that "apparently [was] brought for the purposes of harassment and intimidation rather than for legitimate purposes."[131]

D. Continued Pursuit of Claims or Contentions That Become Frivolous

Neither the mere fact that a case is ultimately unsuccessful nor the fact that an attorney narrows the nature of the case or claims ultimately presented to a jury necessarily means that it was somehow unreasonable or improper for the lawyer to continue to pursue the case and obtain a definitive ruling against her client.[132] As Model Rule 3.1 makes clear, however, the obligation to not pursue frivolous litigation continues beyond the initial filing of the action.[133] Thus, even if an attorney can ethically pursue an action at the outset, should events and circumstances change, or should the attorney later learn that continued litigation would require the pursuit of frivolous claims, the lawyer has a duty to drop the case or offending claims.[134] We saw an example of that rule in *Board of Professional Responsibility v. Stinson*,[135] discussed earlier. Another example is found in the conduct of a Connecticut

127. *Id.* at 387.
128. *Id.*
129. *Id.* at 386–87.
130. *Id.* at 387.
131. *Id.*
132. Medtronic Navigation, Inc. v. Brainlab Medizinische Computersysteme Gmbh, 603 F.3d 943, 959 (Fed. Cir. 2010) (reversing a sanction of over $4 million jointly entered against the plaintiff and its counsel in a patent infringement case).
133. *In re* Olsen, 326 P.3d 1004, 1009 (Colo. 2014); *In re* Pearson, 228 A.3d 417, 424 (D.C. 2020); Att'y Grievance Comm'n of Md. v. Mixter, 109 A.3d 1, 59 (Md. 2015).
134. *See, e.g.*, *In re* Caranchini, 956 S.W.2d 910, 916 (Mo. 1997) (stating that "continuing to pursue a claim once it becomes apparent that there is no factual basis to support that claim is clearly contrary to the requirements of the rule"); Jandrt *ex rel.* Brueggeman v. Jerome Foods, Inc., 597 N.W.2d 744, 760 (Wis. 1999) (determining that continued pursuit of action in the absence of any evidence to support causation was frivolous as a matter of law). *But see* Rose v. Tullos, 994 So. 2d 734, 739 (Miss. 2008) ("No continuing duty exists to force an attorney to abandon a claim if it later appears to be without merit." (citing Bean v. Broussard, 587 So. 2d 908, 913 (Miss. 1991)).
135. 337 P.3d 401 (Wyo. 2014).

lawyer who received a reprimand for violating Rule 3.1 through continued efforts to overturn an arbitration ruling against his client.[136]

The lawyer in *Brunswick v. Statewide Grievance Committee*,[137] Max Brunswick, moved to vacate an arbitration award against his client, who had been represented by a different lawyer. Brunswick alleged, among other things, that the award was procured by corruption, fraud, undue means, or the evident partiality of the arbitrators.[138] The court denied the motion and referred Brunswick to state disciplinary authorities for making allegations without reasonable cause. A lower court found that Brunswick had violated Rule 3.1, and Brunswick appealed.

The appellate court acknowledged that the original act of filing the motion to vacate did not violate Rule 3.1 because under the commentary to the Connecticut rule, "'[t]he filing of an action . . . is not frivolous merely because the facts have not first been fully substantiated or because the lawyer expects to develop vital evidence only by discovery.'"[139] Brunswick was not required at the time he filed the motion to have evidence to substantiate all of the allegations in it.[140] In fact, he initially had sufficient grounds to allege the arbitrators' partiality because a time entry in opposing counsel's billing records reflected a lengthy conference with one of the three arbitrators before the arbitration. Likewise, Brunswick was justified in originally making the claims of corruption, fraud, or undue means because "his client had 'claimed to have been told, by a staff person in the office of her former counsel, that the former counsel had received money from' the opposing party."[141] That did not end the inquiry, however, because the court concluded that Rule 3.1 "prohibits an attorney from asserting at any time a claim on which the attorney is reasonably unable to maintain a good faith argument on the merits."[142]

Brunswick's allegations simply did not stand the test of time. He was unable to develop any facts to support the allegations in the motion. His client never delivered a promised affidavit to establish the alleged fraud, corruption, or undue influence. The facts that he did develop were unhelpful. For example, it was clearly established that notwithstanding the troubling time entry in the other lawyer's billing records, the alleged conference with the arbitrator never occurred. More remarkably, Brunswick retreated from that allegation only grudgingly, arguing as a fallback position that he was not actually alleging that the conference really happened but just

136. Brunswick v. Statewide Grievance Comm., 931 A.2d 319 (Conn. App. Ct. 2007).
137. 931 A.2d 319 (Conn. App. Ct. 2007).
138. *Id.* at 332.
139. *Id.* at 330 (quoting the comment to the Connecticut rule).
140. *Id.*
141. *Id.* at 333.
142. *Id.* at 331.

that it was wrong for the opposing counsel to have billed for such a conference and sought to make Brunswick's client pay for a conference that never occurred.[143]

Still retreating and now sensing serious trouble, Brunswick argued that although he had finally come to believe that he lacked a good faith basis for pursuing the motion to vacate, his client refused to allow him to withdraw the offending allegations.[144] The court, however, noted that according to the commentary to Rule 1.2(a),[145] a lawyer is not required to pursue objectives or employ means simply because the client insists. When a lawyer is aware that a good faith basis for a claim or contention is lacking, the lawyer's "duty as a minister of justice every time must trump a client's desire to continue an untenable allegation."[146]

The court in *Brunswick* ultimately determined that Brunswick violated Rule 3.1 by "persisting" in the allegations that the arbitration award was wrongly procured "once he knew that he had no evidence to support those allegations at trial."[147] Brunswick received a reprimand for his misguided tenacity.

It is common for claims or contentions that appeared to be perfectly valid when they were first made to lose their luster. Claims and contentions weaken over time for a variety of reasons. Witnesses who were expected to support allegations turn out to be uncertain or unreliable, and sometimes die or disappear. Clients' beliefs in certain facts, no matter how strongly held, prove to be incorrect or inaccurate in whole or part. Documents cannot be located or are ambiguous. Adverse witnesses have better or more complete knowledge of events. Allegations may be dispelled by scientific testing of some sort. Experts cannot be located who will support a theory for which expert testimony will be required.[148] The list goes on. When these things happen, lawyers on the short end of the stick must be prepared to abandon or withdraw claims or contentions they once considered to be valid. There is no dishonor in justifiable retreat. There potentially is, however, discipline waiting for lawyers who unreasonably persist in pursuing plainly meritless theories in litigation.

---

143. *Id.* at 330.

144. *Id.* at 334.

145. *Id.* ("The commentary to Rule 1.2(a) . . . states in relevant part that 'a lawyer is not required to pursue objectives or employ means simply because a client may wish that the lawyer do so.'").

146. *Id.*

147. *Id.*

148. *See, e.g.*, Jandrt *ex rel.* Brueggeman v. Jerome Foods, Inc., 597 N.W.2d 744, 760–65 (Wis. 1999) (finding that a lawsuit, though not frivolous when filed, was frivolously maintained because the plaintiffs never came forward with competing expert testimony once faced with expert testimony proffered by the defendants that no causal link existed between birth defects and exposure to toxic chemicals).

III. Ethical Restrictions Affecting Lawyers' Ability to Investigate Clients' Claims or Contentions

As discussed previously, the duty to avoid making frivolous claims or contentions means that lawyers must adequately investigate clients' claims and contentions. The need to investigate often creates a need to communicate with third parties, which can raise a host of ethics issues. In a simple example, a lawyer for a plaintiff may first think to confirm the client's factual assertions by interviewing the potential defendant's current or former employees. Unfortunately for the diligent plaintiff's lawyer, her ability to conduct those interviews may be extremely limited by the restrictions in Model Rule 4.2 and state counterparts.

Model Rule 4.2 provides that a lawyer representing a client "shall not communicate about the subject of the representation with a person the lawyer knows to be represented by another lawyer in the matter, unless the lawyer has the consent of the other lawyer or is authorized to do so by law or a court order."[149] Rule 4.2 clearly applies to communications by a lawyer prior to filing a lawsuit if the target person is represented by counsel in the matter encompassed by the contemplated lawsuit.[150] And, of course, a lawyer seeking to make an appropriate pre-filing investigation cannot simply employ the services of another—such as a private investigator or independent insurance claims adjuster—to engage in communications otherwise prohibited by Rule 4.2.[151]

A surprisingly common situation in which an attorney's conduct runs afoul of Rule 4.2 occurs when the attorney is implicated in encouraging the

149. Model Rules of Prof'l Conduct R. 4.2 (2020).

150. *See, e.g.*, Penda Corp. v. STK, LLC, No. Civ. A. 03-5578, Civ. A. 03-6240, 2004 WL 1628907, at *3 (E.D. Pa. July 16, 2004); Stahl v. Wal-Mart Stores, Inc., 47 F. Supp. 2d 783, 789 (S.D. Miss. 1998); *see also* Restatement (Third) of the Law Governing Lawyers § 99 cmt. d (2000) (explaining that the matters encompassed within a representation, as well as their scope and contour, depend upon the particular circumstances).

151. Model Rules of Prof'l Conduct R. 8.4(a) (2020) (making it an ethical violation to violate another ethics rule "through the acts of another"); *see also* ABA Comm. on Ethics & Prof'l Responsibility, Formal Op. 95-396, at 19 (1995) ("Since a lawyer is barred under Rule 4.2 from communicating with a represented party about the subject matter of the representation, she . . . may not circumvent the Rule by sending an investigator to do on her behalf that which she is herself forbidden to do."); *see, e.g.*, United States v. Smallwood, 365 F. Supp. 2d 689, 694–97 (E.D. Va. 2005) (finding that an investigator's communications with a represented person were improper where it would have been unethical for the attorney to have had the communications directly); *In re* Complaint of PMD Enters., Inc., 215 F. Supp. 2d 519, 529 (D.N.J. 2002) (finding a lawyer ethically responsible for an investigator's communication with a represented party where the lawyer knew the investigator would be contacting a represented person); State v. Clark, 738 N.W.2d 316, 338–40 (Minn. 2007) (finding that police contacts with a represented criminal defendant amounted to a Rule 4.2 violation attributable to state prosecutors); Disciplinary Counsel v. Sartini, 871 N.E.2d 543, 544–46 (Ohio 2007) (affirming a public reprimand against two prosecutors for causing a represented criminal defendant's mother to communicate a plea offer to the defendant).

client to obtain an affidavit from someone who is represented by counsel.[152] *In re Pyle*[153] is an interesting case in point. There, Thomas Pyle represented Sallie Moline in a trip-and-fall case against Ricci Gutzman. Moline, who alleged that she hurt her knee tripping over a dog cable in Gutzman's driveway, was romantically involved with Gutzman. Prior to suing on Moline's behalf, and before Gutzman was represented by counsel, Pyle prepared an affidavit for Gutzman's signature that, among other things, contained a statement by Gutzman admitting liability and taking full responsibility for Moline's injuries. Pyle gave the affidavit to Moline to deliver to Gutzman.[154] After suit was filed, Gutzman's insurer hired John Conderman to defend him. Conderman filed an answer denying liability. Pyle went to the well again, creating another affidavit for Moline to take to Gutzman. Pyle provided that affidavit to Moline along with a cover letter stating, "As a party to the case, you have the right to communicate with Mr. Gutzman. Therefore, please talk with him and see if he will sign the enclosed affidavit."[155]

Pyle was ultimately charged with violating Rule 4.2. In rejecting Pyle's argument that Moline could not be considered his agent when he was in fact her agent, the court discussed two similar cases where lawyers had used their clients to deliver documents to a represented party contemplating that a signature would be obtained without that party's lawyer's knowledge[156] and concluded that Pyle violated Rule 4.2 "by encouraging his client to do that which he could not."[157] The Kansas Supreme Court publicly censured Pyle for his misconduct.

Bratcher v. Kentucky Bar Ass'n[158] illustrates how a lawyer can unthinkingly run afoul of ethics rules through communications by an agent. A former employee of R.C. Components, Inc., Dennis Babbs, hired Pamela Bratcher to represent him in a wrongful termination lawsuit. Bratcher, in turn, hired a company in the business of determining what listed references will say about former employees, Document Reference Check (DRC), to contact the owner of R.C. Components to see what he would say about Babbs.[159] A

152. *See, e.g.*, Holdren v. Gen. Motors Corp., 13 F. Supp. 2d 1192, 1195–96 (D. Kan. 1998) (granting a protective order as a result of a violation of Rule 4.2 where the plaintiff's lawyer "facilitated" the plaintiff's efforts in obtaining affidavits from the defendant's employees); *In re* Anonymous, 819 N.E.2d 376, 379 (Ind. 2004) (reprimanding the lawyer for violating Rule 4.2 by giving an affidavit to his client and instigating "a series of contacts calculated to obtain the employee's signature on the affidavit despite [the lawyer's] unsuccessful attempts to obtain the employee's signature through opposing counsel").

153. 91 P.3d 1222 (Kan. 2004).

154. *Id.* at 1225.

155. *Id.* at 1227.

156. Holdren v. Gen. Motors Corp., 13 F. Supp. 2d 1192 (D. Kan. 1998); *In re* Marietta, 569 P.2d 921 (Kan. 1977).

157. *Pyle*, 91 P.3d at 1229.

158. 290 S.W.3d 648 (Ky. 2009).

159. *Id.* at 649.

DRC employee telephoned the owner, said she was an employer considering hiring Babbs, and transcribed the conversation for Bratcher. Bratcher, sensing no wrongdoing, produced the transcript to R.C. Components in discovery.[160] R.C. Components successfully moved to suppress the transcript and to disqualify Bratcher. After losing the disqualification battle in the underlying litigation, Bratcher admitted in her disciplinary case that her conduct constituted an ethical violation and asked that the discipline against her be limited to a public reprimand.[161] The Kentucky Supreme Court accepted her position and publicly reprimanded her for violating Rule 4.2(a).

Rule 4.2 can pose thorny problems for investigating lawyers where potential witnesses are employed by a represented organization. Because organizations can act only through their constituents, lawyers must be able to judge who within a business organization is considered to be represented by the lawyer representing that organization. Different jurisdictions take different approaches to this issue. Comment 7 to Model Rule 4.2 lays out the preferred approach:

> In the case of a represented organization, this Rule prohibits communications with a constituent of the organization who supervises, directs or regularly consults with the organization's lawyer concerning the matter or has authority to obligate the organization with respect to the matter or whose act or omission in connection with the matter may be imputed to the organization for purposes of civil or criminal liability.[162]

Jurisdictions adopting this approach often refer to the individuals within this sphere as the "control group" or the organization's "alter egos." These people are presumptively treated as being represented by counsel for the organization. Under the ABA approach, however, an organization's in-house lawyers are not off-limits under Rule 4.2, and consent from outside counsel for the organization is not required to communicate with in-house lawyers as long as they are not part of the constituent group of the organization described in the comment to Model Rule 4.2 or are not separately represented.[163] This approach to ex parte communications with in-house lawyers makes sense, and going further to even permit ex parte contact with in-house counsel regardless of whether they are acting solely as a lawyer for the

160. *Id.*

161. *Id.*

162. Model Rules of Prof'l Conduct R. 4.2 cmt. 7 (2020).

163. *In re* Grievance Proc., No. 3:01GP6(SRU), 2002 WL 31106389, at *3 (D. Conn. July 19, 2002); *In re* Woodham, 769 S.E.2d 353, 356–57 (Ga. 2015); ABA Comm. on Ethics & Prof'l Responsibility, Formal Op. 06-443, at 2 (2006) [hereinafter ABA Formal Op. 06-443]; *see also* Restatement (Third) of the Law Governing Lawyers § 100 cmt. c (2000) ("Inside legal counsel for a corporation is not generally within [the definition of a represented nonclient] and contact with such counsel is generally not limited by [the general anti-contact rule].").

organization would also make sense, given that "[t]he purpose of Rule 4.2 is to prevent a skilled advocate from taking advantage of a non-lawyer."[164]

Some jurisdictions have deviated from the ABA approach and adopted a "managing-speaking agent test."[165] Under this test, lawyers are prohibited from communicating ex parte with organizational employees who possess "speaking authority" for the organization—those "who 'have managing authority sufficient to give them the right to speak for, and bind the corporation.'"[166] Scholars have criticized the managing-speaking agent test as being confusing and for failing to provide practicing lawyers with a clear standard by which to evaluate a planned course of conduct.[167] Regardless, it is a distinctly minority approach.

Microsoft Corp. v. Alcatel Business Systems[168] demonstrates how lawyers can run afoul of the ethical restriction on ex parte communications with protected employees of a represented organization. In that patent case, the lawyers for Microsoft were not disqualified for their actions but were monetarily sanctioned. Basically, they purchased a piece of equipment that contained components that allegedly infringed the patents at issue and arranged for the equipment to be installed by an employee of the represented defendant.[169] The employee, Po Ching Lin, consistent with his job duties, provided "training on the administration, use and configuration" of the equipment to the Microsoft lawyers.[170] The Microsoft lawyers questioned Lin about those topics. The court determined that Microsoft's lawyers violated Rule 4.2 based on Lin's "position and level of responsibility with respect to the [equipment] and because he was directed (as an employee of a represented party) to engage in conduct directly relevant to the subject matter of this litigation by [Microsoft's lawyers]."[171]

In addition to needing to be aware of differences regarding the language within the comments adopted in relevant jurisdictions, application of Rule 4.2 itself to particular factual situations can be a delicate endeavor and one for which predicting the ultimate outcome is no easy task. The determination by the Third Circuit that an attorney's communications with an

164. ABA Formal Op. 06-443, *supra* note 163, at 2.

165. *See, e.g.*, Messing, Rudavsky & Weliky, P.C. v. President & Fellows of Harvard Coll., 764 N.E.2d 825, 833 (Mass. 2002); Palmer v. Pioneer Inn Assocs., Ltd., 59 P.3d 1237, 1247–48 (Nev. 2002).

166. *Messing*, 764 N.E.2d at 833 (quoting Wright v. Grp. Health Hosp., 691 P.2d 564 (Wash. 1984)).

167. *See, e.g.*, Ernest F. Lidge III, *The Ethics of Communicating with an Organization's Employees: An Analysis of the Unworkable "Hybrid" or "Multifactor" Managing-Speaking Agent, ABA and* Niesig *Tests and a Proposal for a "Supervisor" Standard*, 45 Ark. L. Rev. 801, 834–44 (1993).

168. No. 07-090-SLR, 2007 WL 4480632 (D. Del. Dec. 18, 2007).

169. *Id.* at *1.

170. *Id.*

171. *Id.*

administrative assistant to managerial agents of a represented organization did not violate Pennsylvania's Rule 4.2 readily demonstrates how easily reasonable minds can differ on the scope of Rule 4.2's application.[172]

In *EEOC v. Hora, Inc.*,[173] the district court disqualified Jana Barnett, the intervening plaintiff's counsel, because she communicated with Deborah Richardson, an administrative assistant to the manager and part-owner of the Days Inn where the plaintiff had worked. Apparently motivated by Barnett's communications, Richardson gathered a variety of information that supported the plaintiff's sexual harassment claims.[174] Once defense counsel learned of these communications, they moved to disqualify Barnett. The district court concluded that, given the small number of hotel employees and Richardson's position of intimate business trust as a result of being the only assistant to both the manager and the hotel's part-owner, she could be treated as having managerial responsibilities for purposes of Rule 4.2.[175] The Third Circuit reversed the district court's disqualification order based on the lack of evidence to support a conclusion that Richardson came within the scope of Rule 4.2. There was no evidence that she had regularly consulted with defense counsel in the matter, nor was there evidence that her acts could provide a basis for imputing liability to Days Inn.[176]

Jurisdictions also take differing approaches to ex parte communications with former officers, agents, or employees of a represented organization, but mostly only as to the question of what precautionary measures a lawyer must take to protect against causing a former officer or employee from disclosing confidential or privileged information. Courts generally agree that a lawyer is free to communicate with a former employee of an organization without first obtaining the consent of the organization's lawyer.[177]

172. EEOC v. Hora Inc., 239 F. App'x 728, 731 (3d Cir. 2007).

173. No. 03-cv-01429, 2005 WL 1387982 (E.D. Pa. June 8, 2005), *rev'd*, 239 F. App'x 728 (3d Cir. 2007).

174. *Id.* at *2.

175. *Id.* at *12–13 ("While the standard for determining who has . . . 'authority to bind' a business entity is somewhat imprecise, it includes employees below the level of corporate management because otherwise the third category of employees mentioned in Rule 4.2 would be redundant. . . .'") (quoting Weeks v. Indep. Sch. Dist., 230 F.3d 1201, 1209 (10th Cir. 2000)).

176. *Hora*, 239 F. App'x at 731.

177. *See, e.g.*, Calise v. Brady Sullivan Harris Mills, LLC, No. 18-99WES, 2019 WL 1397245, at *5 (D.R.I. Mar. 28, 2019) (discussing Rhode Island's version of Rule 4.2); Lozama v. Samaritan Daytop Village, Inc., No. 18 CV 4351 (DLI)(RML), 2019 WL 1002954, at *2 (E.D.N.Y. Mar. 1, 2019) (applying New York law); Peterson v. Alaska Commc'ns Sys. Grp. Inc., No. 3:12-cv-00090-TMB, 2019 WL 6331355, at *7 (D. Alaska Nov. 26, 2019) (applying Alaska ethics rules); United States v. Miss., No. 3:16-cv-622-CWR-FKB, 2018 WL 4956658, at *4 (S.D. Miss. Oct. 12, 2018) (discussing Mississippi's version of Rule 4.2); Klorczyk v. Sears, Roebuck & Co., No. 3:13-cv-00257 (JAM), 2017 WL 3272237, at *3 (D. Conn. Aug. 1, 2017) (applying Connecticut ethics rules); Thurston v. Okemo Ltd. Liab. Co., 123 F. Supp. 3d 513, 515 (D. Vt. 2015) (applying Vermont's version of Rule 4.2); EEOC v. SVT, LLC, 297 F.R.D. 336, 345 (N.D. Ind. 2014) (involving a class action); EEOC v. Univ. of Chi. Med. Ctr., No. 11 C 6379, 2012 WL 1329171, at *3–4

As for precautionary measures, courts generally hold that Model Rule 4.2 or Model Rules 4.2 and 4.4(a), read together, prohibit lawyers from asking former employees about documents or information protected by the organization's attorney-client privilege or work product immunity.[178] A lawyer who obtains confidential information from a former employee known to be likely to have had access to it will probably be disqualified from continued participation in the matter.[179]

(N.D. Ill. Apr. 16, 2012); *In re* Digitek Prod. Liab. Litig., 648 F. Supp. 2d 795, 799 (S.D. W. Va. 2009); Davis v. Creditors Interchange Receivable Mgmt., LLC, 585 F. Supp. 2d 968, 979 (N.D. Ohio 2008); Bryant v. Yorktowne Cabinetry, Inc., 538 F. Supp. 2d 948, 949–53 (W.D. Va. 2008); Nuckles v. Wal-Mart Stores, Inc., No. 4:06CV00178 WRW, 2007 WL 1546092, at *2 (E.D. Ark. May 25, 2007); United States v. W.R. Grace, 401 F. Supp. 2d 1065, 1068–69 (D. Mont. 2005); Smith v. Kalamazoo Ophthalmology, 322 F. Supp. 2d 883, 890 (W.D. Mich. 2004); Olson v. Snap Prods., Inc., 183 F.R.D. 539, 545 (D. Minn. 1998); *In re* Prudential Ins. Co., 911 F. Supp. 148, 154 (M.D. Pa. 1995); Browning v. A.T. & T. Paradyne, 838 F. Supp. 1564, 1567 (M.D. Fla. 1993); Lang v. Super. Ct., 826 P.2d 1228, 1233 (Ariz. Ct. App. 1992); DiOssi v. Edison, 583 A.2d 1343, 1345 (Del. Super. Ct. 1990); H.B.A. Mgmt., Inc. v. Estate of Schwartz, 693 So. 2d 541, 544–46 (Fla. 1997); Sanifill of Ga., Inc. v. Roberts, 502 S.E.2d 343, 345 (Ga. 1998); P.T. Barnum's Nightclub v. Duhamell, 766 N.E.2d 729, 737 (Ind. Ct. App. 2002); Humco, Inc. v. Noble, 31 S.W.3d 916, 920 (Ky. 2000); Schmidt v. Gregorio, 705 So. 2d 742, 743–44 (La. Ct. App. 1993); Clark v. Beverly Health & Rehab. Servs., 797 N.E.2d 905, 911–12 (Mass. 2003); Smith v. Kan. City S. Ry., 87 S.W.3d 266, 272–75 (Mo. Ct. App. 2002); Klier v. Sordoni Skanska Constr. Co., 766 A.2d 761, 770 (N.J. Super. Ct. App. Div. 2001); Fulton v. Lane, 829 P.2d 959, 960 (Okla. 1992); State *ex rel.* Charleston Area Med. Ctr. v. Zakaib, 437 S.E.2d 759, 763–64 (W. Va. 1993); Strawser v. Exxon Co., 843 P.2d 613, 622 (Wyo. 1992).

178. *See, e.g.*, Kozowski v. Nelson, No.: 6:18-cv-00275-MK, 2020 WL 1066329, at *3 (D. Or. Mar. 5, 2020) (referring to the attorney-client privilege and citing Oregon Rules 4.2 and 4.4); Harris Davis Rebar, L.L.C. v. Structural Iron Workers Local Union No. 1, Pension Tr. Fund, No. 17 C 6473, 2019 WL 447622, at *6 (N.D. Ill. Feb. 5, 2019) (reading Rules 4.2 and 4.4 together); Martinez v. Cnty. of Antelope, No. 4:15CV3064, 2016 WL 3248241, at *9–10 (D. Neb. June 13, 2016) (disqualifying a lawyer who knowingly obtained privileged information from a former county official); Tomasian v. C.D. Peacock, Inc., No. 09 C 5665, 2012 WL 2590493, at *7 (N.D. Ill. July 3, 2012) (referring to Rule 4.2 and stating that "former employees are barred from discussing privileged information to which they are privy"); Gifford v. Target Corp., 723 F. Supp. 2d 1110, 1118–23 (D. Minn. 2010) (referring to Rule 4.2 cmt. 7 and Rule 4.4(a)); Weber v. Fujifilm Med. Sys., U.S.A., No. 3:10 CV 401(JBA), 2010 WL 2836720, at *4 (D. Conn. July 19, 2010) (quoting Shoreline Computers, Inc. v. Warnaco, Inc., No. CV 990422853S, 2000 WL 371206, at *2 (Conn. Super. Ct. Apr. 3, 2000)); *Kalamazoo Ophthalmology*, 322 F. Supp. 2d at 890–91 (applying Rule 4.2); Zachair, Ltd. v. Driggs, 965 F. Supp. 741, 753–54 (D. Md. 1997) (applying Rule 4.2); Rentclub, Inc. v. Transamerica Rental Fin. Corp., 811 F. Supp. 651, 657 (M.D. Fla. 1992) (discussing Rule 4.2); *Shoreline Computers*, 2000 WL 371206, at *2 (describing former employees who are off-limits under Rule 4.2).

179. *See, e.g.*, Arnold v. Cargill, No. 01-2086, 2004 WL 2203410, at *8, 13 (D. Minn. Sept. 24, 2004) (disqualifying a law firm based on its review, and retention of, privileged and confidential materials obtained from a former high-ranking employee of defendant who the law firm knew "was extensively exposed to confidential and privileged information"). *But see* Forward v. Foschi, No. 9002/08, 2010 WL 1980838, at *17 (N.Y. Sup. Ct. May 18, 2010) (declining to disqualify a law firm where improperly obtained information did not provide a "blueprint" to litigating or defending the case, the opposing party was aware of the other side's acts in obtaining information and delayed seeking a remedy, and the party would be "severely prejudiced" by the disqualification).

With respect to current employees who are not protected under Rule 4.2, lawyers for the organization who are concerned about opponents' ex parte communications with these employees may *ask* the current employees not to voluntarily speak with opposing counsel outside their presence.[180] Such a request can be made only if the lawyer for the organization has a reasonable belief that stiff-arming opposing counsel will not adversely affect the targeted person.[181] Whether the employee chooses to comply is entirely up to her. As to former employees who are unprotected under Rule 4.2, lawyers for the organization cannot make the kind of request they could make of a current employee, but nothing in Rule 3.4(f) restricts the organization's lawyer from telling the former employee that she has the legal right to insist on being subpoenaed before providing information. Nor does Rule 3.4(f) prevent the organization's lawyer from asking the former employee if she is willing to ask that the organization's lawyer be included in any telephone conversations or meetings. But one thing that the lawyer may not do regarding current and former employees alike is *instruct* opposing counsel not to communicate with persons affiliated with, or previously affiliated with, the organization unless the lawyer represents them in the matter.[182]

A topic that is frequently discussed, but that is well-settled and easy to comprehend, is that a lawyer's act of visiting an adversary's public website is not a communication that violates Model Rule 4.2. This is true even if the lawyer goes beyond simply reading information posted on the website as long as the lawyer engages in purely one-way communications through the site, such as ordering products.[183] Even obtaining an archived version of an opponent's public website through a database such as the The Wayback Machine[184] or similar Internet archive websites cannot be said to violate Model Rule 4.4 because it does not constitute obtaining evidence in violation of anyone's legal rights.[185] A Pennsylvania federal court made this

180. Model Rules of Prof'l Conduct R. 3.4(f)(1) (2020). Before making such a request in any criminal matter or a matter involving governmental or regulatory actions, a lawyer should make certain that it would not constitute obstruction of justice.

181. *Id.* R. 3.4(f)(2).

182. Matusick v. Erie Cnty. Water Auth., No. 07CV489A, 2010 WL 681062, at *3 (W.D.N.Y. Feb. 22, 2010); Patriarca v. Ctr. for Living & Working, Inc., 778 N.E.2d 877, 880–81 (Mass. 2002); Utah Eth. Op. 04-06, 2004 WL 2803333, at *1 (Utah State Bar, Ethics Advisory Op. Comm. 2004).

183. Or. Eth. Op. 2001-164, 2001 WL 167177, at *1–2 (Or. State Bar Ass'n, Bd. of Governors 2001).

184. The Wayback Machine is a service provided by the Internet Archive, a nonprofit organization, which was begun in 1996. Web users can input the URL of a website for which they would like to view archived versions and then select from a variety of dates of available archived materials to see the archived screenshot of that website on the selected dates.

185. Model Rules of Prof'l Conduct R. 4.4(a) (2020) ("In representing a client, a lawyer shall not use means that have no substantial purpose other than to embarrass, delay, or burden a third person, or use methods of obtaining evidence that violate the legal rights of such a person.").

point in entering summary judgment against a plaintiff who claimed that by viewing older versions of its website through The Wayback Machine, a law firm violated copyright law and the Computer Fraud and Abuse Act.[186]

Healthcare Advocates, Inc. v. Harding, Earley, Follmer & Frailey[187] involved a lawsuit by a patient advocacy organization, Healthcare Advocates, Inc. (HAI), which had previously lost trademark and trade secret litigation against a competitor. The competitor was represented in that litigation by the Harding firm, and copies of screenshots of older versions of HAI's website that the Harding firm obtained through The Wayback Machine were an important factor in the successful defense of that suit.[188] After summary judgment was entered against HAI in the underlying litigation, HAI filed a multi-count lawsuit against the Harding firm that, at its core, claimed that the Harding firm engaged in unlawful hacking when it used The Wayback Machine to view historical screenshots of HAI's website and that in doing so, the Harding firm must have circumvented HAI's electronic protective measures.[189] Specifically, HAI had implemented an exclusion policy offered by The Wayback Machine to website owners, the robots.txt protocol, whereby a website owner that did not want pages of its website to be archived and viewable could insert a robots.txt file at its website. But, as it turned out, at the time the Harding firm performed its search, The Wayback Machine's servers had malfunctioned. Because of that malfunction, The Wayback Machine's servers did not recognize the robots.txt exclusions, and this allowed the Harding firm to see archived versions of HAI's website that HAI did not want to be archived and viewable.[190] Given that the Harding firm had simply used The Wayback Machine "in the manner it was intended to be used" by any user with a normal web browser, the court rightly concluded that the Harding firm's conduct was lawful.[191]

186. Healthcare Advocates, Inc. v. Harding, Earley, Follmer & Frailey, 497 F. Supp. 2d 627, 649 (E.D. Pa. 2007).

187. 497 F. Supp. 2d 627 (E.D. Pa. 2007).

188. *Id.* at 630.

189. *Id.* at 630–31.

190. *Id.*

191. *Id.* at 648–49.

The Rule 4.2 prohibition on ex parte communications is generally considered to be matter-specific,[192] as demonstrated in *People v. Santiago*.[193] In *Santiago*, the Rule 4.2 question was whether communications by prosecutors investigating potential criminal child endangerment charges against Evelyn Santiago were prohibited by Rule 4.2 because Santiago was represented by appointed counsel in juvenile court proceedings seeking to have her children made wards of the state for their protection. Because it was undisputed that the lawyer representing Santiago in the juvenile court matter had not been engaged to represent her in the criminal investigation, the Illinois court concluded that Rule 4.2 was not violated despite the overlapping case facts.[194] The only "matter" in which Santiago was represented by counsel was the juvenile court case.[195]

When a lawyer knows that a person with whom she wishes to speak is represented in a matter, the lawyer can always seek the other lawyer's consent to the communication. If there is more than one lawyer representing the person, the lawyer need obtain consent from only one of them. The strictures of Rule 4.2 only come into play, however, if the lawyer actually knows that the person is represented by counsel.[196] Because a lawyer's knowledge can be inferred from circumstances,[197] however, a lawyer cannot turn a blind eye

192. *See, e.g.*, United States v. Ford, 176 F.3d 376, 382 (6th Cir. 1999) (interpreting Kentucky's version of Rule 4.2); Miller v. Material Sciences Corp., 986 F. Supp. 1104, 1106–07 (N.D. Ill. 1997) (determining that communication by a plaintiff's attorney in a federal securities class action with a party that was represented in a related SEC investigation but not in the federal class action was permissible); Miano v. AC&R Adver., Inc., 148 F.R.D. 68, 80 (S.D.N.Y. 1993) (finding that corporate employees were not off-limits as a result of ethics rules when the corporation had not retained counsel with respect to the specific matter that was the focus of communications); State *ex rel.* Okla. Bar Ass'n v. Harper, 995 P.2d 1143, 1147 (Okla. 2000) (concluding that a defense lawyer's interview of a driver did not violate Rule 4.2 because it involved the separate claim of a passenger, not other claims involved in same accident in connection with which the driver was represented by counsel).

193. 925 N.E.2d 1122 (Ill. 2010); *see also* Griffin-El v. Beard, No. 06-2719, 2009 WL 2929802, at *7 (E.D. Pa. Sept. 8, 2009) (concluding that there was no violation of Rule 4.2 when defense lawyers communicated with a corrections officer in his role as custodian of records when officer was represented by counsel only in another lawsuit filed by their client and not in the matter in which his status as records custodian made him a potential witness).

194. *Santiago*, 925 N.E.2d at 1128–31.

195. *Id.* at 1129–30.

196. *See, e.g.*, The Turfgrass Grp., Inc. v. Ne. La. Turf Farms, No. 10-1354, 2013 WL 6145294, at *4 (W.D. La. Nov. 20, 2013) (finding that, in the absence of any indication that the lawyer was aware of a person's representation by counsel, the court could not conclude that the lawyer violated ethics rules "by employing an undercover investigator to determine whether [defendant] had violated protected patent and trademark rights"); Humco, Inc. v. Noble, 31 S.W.3d 916, 919 (Ky. 2000) (explaining that the mere fact that in-house counsel was copied on a letter sent by an employee of the defendant company did not constitute actual knowledge on part of the plaintiff's lawyer that the employee was represented by counsel).

197. Model Rules of Prof'l Conduct R. 1.0(f) (2020).

to the obvious with respect to the fact of representation. Although it can be prudent to do so, there is no requirement in the rules mandating that a lawyer ask someone if she is represented by counsel before speaking with her.[198]

If a lawyer does not actually know that a person is represented, or if the person is not represented by counsel in the matter about which the communication is to be made, then the lawyer's communications with the person are governed by a different rule altogether: the jurisdiction's version of Model Rule 4.3. Model Rule 4.3 provides that when acting on behalf of a client, a lawyer who interacts with an unrepresented person:

> [S]hall not state or imply that the lawyer is disinterested. When the lawyer knows or reasonably should know that the unrepresented person misunderstands the lawyer's role in the matter, the lawyer shall make reasonable efforts to correct the misunderstanding. The lawyer shall not give legal advice to an unrepresented person, other than the advice to secure counsel, if the lawyer knows or reasonably should know that the interests of such a person are or have a reasonable possibility of being in conflict with the interests of the client.[199]

Model Rule 4.3 limits the lawyer's ability to exploit the situation by overreaching or otherwise exercising improper influence over the unrepresented person.[200] By requiring the lawyer to disclose the nature of her interest in the matter, the rule seeks to ensure that the unrepresented person will appreciate the risks associated with communicating with the lawyer and be able to rationally decide whether to do so. In evaluating the propriety of communications with unrepresented persons, lawyers may wish to consider any strictures potentially imposed by federal or other state law.[201]

Of course, the general prohibition in Rule 4.1 against making false statements of material fact or law to third parties applies to lawyers' communications with unrepresented persons.[202] And because the Rule 4.4(a) prohibition against using "methods of obtaining evidence that violate the legal rights of

---

198. White Cap Constr. Supply, Inc. v. Tighton Fastener & Supply Corp., No. 8:08CV264, 2010 WL 3259355, at *7 (D. Neb. Aug. 16, 2010) (quoting *In re* User Sys. Servs., Inc., 22 S.W.3d 331, 334–35 (Tex. 1999)); Metrahealth Ins. Co. v. Anclote Psychiatric Hosp., Ltd., 961 F. Supp. 1580, 1583 (M.D. Fla. 1997) (quoting ABA Comm. on Ethics & Prof'l Responsibility, Formal Op. 95-396, at 7 (1995)); Fed. Sav. & Loan Ins. Corp. v. Hildenbrand, Civ. A. No. 89-A-535, 1989 WL 107377, at *4 (D. Colo. Sept. 8, 1989).

199. Model Rules of Prof'l Conduct R. 4.3 (2020).

200. Apple Corps Ltd. v. Int'l Collectors Soc'y, 15 F. Supp. 2d 456, 476 (D.N.J. 1998); People v. Mascarenas, 103 P.3d 339, 345 (Colo. 2003).

201. *See, e.g.*, Arons v. Jutkowitz, 880 N.E.2d 831, 837–43 (N.Y. 2007) (explaining that an attorney can proceed with an interview in private of the treating physician of an adverse party but must be mindful of requirements imposed by federal privacy laws and rules); Tenn. Code Ann. § 29-26-121(f) (2020) (requiring a petition and order from the trial court in a health care liability action before defense counsel can privately interview a plaintiff's treating physician).

202. Model Rules of Prof'l Conduct R. 4.1 (2020).

such a person"[203] applies to lawyers' interactions with unrepresented persons, it is significant to evaluate whether the questions to be asked of the unrepresented person would yield privileged or confidential information. In fact, a number of courts have gone as far as to provide scripts or the equivalent thereof to be followed when a lawyer seeks to speak with unrepresented employees or former employees of a represented organization.[204]

IV. Liability for Malicious Prosecution

Lawyers' concerns related to the pursuit of allegedly frivolous claims are not confined to ethics violations.[205] Tort liability for malicious prosecution may be a legitimate concern.

To be sure, lawyers' efforts in pursuing litigation, including communications at the preparatory stages of a case, are typically protected by a robust litigation privilege.[206] Malicious prosecution actions, however, are universally acknowledged to fall outside the scope of that privilege.[207] A claim for malicious prosecution arising out of the pursuit of civil claims can be established by showing (1) the filing, or continued pursuit, of a civil lawsuit, (2) without probable cause, (3) primarily for a purpose other than that of securing the proper adjudication of the claim on which the proceeding is

---

203. *Id.* R. 4.4(a); *see also* RESTATEMENT (THIRD) OF THE LAW GOVERNING LAWYERS § 102 (2000) ("A lawyer communicating with a nonclient . . . may not seek to obtain information that the lawyer reasonably should know the nonclient may not reveal without violating a duty of confidentiality to another imposed by law.").

204. *See, e.g.*, McCallum v. CSX Transp., Inc., 149 F.R.D. 104, 112 (M.D.N.C. 1993) (mandating that, prior to an interview, a lawyer or investigator must fully disclose her representative capacity, state why the interview is sought, inform the individual of right to refuse, inform the individual of her right to her own counsel, and not seek attorney-client privileged or work product information); Monsanto Co. v. Aetna Cas. & Sur. Co., 593 A.2d 1013, 1021 (Del. Super. Ct. 1990) (ordering that "[n]o interview of any former employee of Monsanto shall be conducted unless the following script is used by the investigator or attorney conducting the interview" and setting forth script as part of order); *In re* Envtl. Ins. Declaratory Judgment Actions, 600 A.2d 165, 173 (N.J. Super. Ct. Law Div. 1991) (declaring that "[n]o interview of any former employee shall be conducted unless the following script is used by the investigator or attorney conducting the interview" and providing detailed script).

205. Lawyers may also be sanctioned under court rules, such as Rule 11 of the Federal Rules of Civil Procedure and state analogs. In federal courts, lawyers must be aware of 28 U.S.C. § 1927 (2018), which states that a lawyer "who so multiplies the proceedings in any case unreasonably and vexatiously may be required by the court to satisfy personally the excess costs, expenses, and attorneys' fees reasonably incurred because of such conduct."

206. RESTATEMENT (SECOND) OF TORTS § 586 (1977).

207. Hagberg v. Cal. Fed. Bank FSB, 81 P.3d 244, 249 (Cal. 2004); Finkelstein, Thompson & Loughran v. Hemispherx Biopharma, Inc., 774 A.2d 332, 346 (D.C. 2001); Debrincat v. Fischer, 217 So. 3d 68, 69–70 (Fla. 2017); Dello Russo v. Nagel, 817 A.2d 426, 433 (N.J. Super. Ct. App. Div. 2003); Hadar v. Pierce, 974 N.Y.S.2d 399, 401 (App. Div. 2013); Mantia v. Hanson, 79 P.3d 404, 408 (Or. Ct. App. 2003); Simpson Strong-Tie Co. v. Stewart, Estes & Donnell, 232 S.W.3d 18, 27 (Tenn. 2007); Clark v. Druckman, 624 S.E.2d 864, 871 (W. Va. 2005).

based, (4) that is terminated in favor of the defendant in the lawsuit.[208] The absence of any of these elements bars a malicious prosecution claim.[209]

In terms of lawyers' exposure, liability for malicious prosecution often distills to whether the lawyer had probable cause for filing, or continuing to pursue, the underlying lawsuit.[210] At bottom, probable cause is evaluated according to an objective standard.[211] "The test is whether, on the basis of facts then known, any reasonable attorney would have believed that instituting or maintaining the prior action was tenable."[212] If probable cause exists, the lawyer cannot be liable for malicious prosecution.[213] Thus, appropriately investigating clients' claims before suing can not only ensure that lawyers satisfy their ethical duties but also erect a helpful shield against liability in any future lawsuit for malicious prosecution.[214]

Given the nature of malicious prosecution claims, lawyers and law firms that are found liable on this theory may well be hit with punitive damages. This point is illustrated by a $9.9 million punitive damage award against a respected law firm for filing a meritless lawsuit.[215] In *Seltzer v. Morton*,[216] Gibson, Dunn & Crutcher, LLP (GDC) was tagged with a punitive damage award that was nine times the already stiff $1.1 million compensatory

208. *See* Restatement (Second) of Torts § 674 (1977).

209. Beaman v. Freesmeyer, 131 N.E.3d 488, 495 (Ill. 2019); *see* Rodenburg Law Firm v. Sira, 931 N.W.2d 687, 691 (N.D. 2019) (stating that for a plaintiff to prevail, "all four of the elements necessary for the claim must be proven").

210. *See* Restatement (Third) of the Law Governing Lawyers § 57(2) (2000); *see also* Zamos v. Stroud, 87 P.3d 802, 808 (Cal. 2004) (listing 12 other states that have concluded, in accord with the Restatement, that continuing to pursue a lawsuit after probable cause no longer exists can amount to malicious prosecution). *But see* Blue Hen Mech., Inc. v. Christian Bros. Risk Pooling Tr., 117 A.3d 549, 557–61 (Del. 2015) (rejecting the argument that Delaware should extend the tort of malicious prosecution to situations in which a party continues to pursue litigation after determining it no longer has a good faith basis to do so).

211. Gruber v. Gruber, 261 Cal. Rptr. 3d 819, 825 (Ct. App. 2020); Rockwell v. Rockwell, 175 A.3d 1249, 1260 (Conn. App. Ct. 2017) (quoting Falls Church Grp., Ltd. v. Tyler, Cooper & Alcorn, LLP, 912 A.2d 1019, 1027 (Conn. 2007)); DeHarrport v. W.E.J., 348 P.3d 1192, 1195 (Or. Ct. App. 2015).

212. Citizens of Humanity, LLC v. Hass, 259 Cal. Rptr. 3d 380, 389 (Ct. App. 2020).

213. Fox v. Fox, 391 P.3d 124, 126 (Okla. Civ. App. 2016) (quoting Lewis v. Crystal Gas. Co., 532 P.2d 431, 433 (Okla. 1975)); Merrill v. A.R.G., 398 P.3d 954, 959 (Or. Ct. App. 2017).

214. *See, e.g.*, Bird v. Rothman, 627 P.2d 1097, 1101 (Ariz. Ct. App. 1981) (crediting the lawyers' pre-filing investigation that involved 25–30 hours of researching and investigating theories, contacting an architect regarding pertinent standard of care, and gathering witness statements regarding the accident); Cent. Fla. Mach. Co. v. Williams, 424 So. 2d 201, 203 (Fla. Dist. Ct. App. 1983) (treating the affidavits of the lawyers regarding their investigative efforts before filing suit as sufficient to show a reasonable investigation "to support a reasonable and honest belief in a tenable claim" in a wrongful death lawsuit); Prewitt v. Sexton, 777 S.W.2d 891, 896 (Ky. 1989) (finding no cause of action against the lawyer with respect to a habeas corpus proceeding where, prior to filing, the lawyer had attempted to check court files to confirm the client's statements regarding events and was denied access to the file based on improper sealing, but was told by the court clerk that no signed order had been entered regarding the removal of the child from the client's custody).

215. Seltzer v. Morton, 154 P.3d 561, 615 (Mont. 2007).

216. 154 P.3d 561 (Mont. 2007).

damages awarded against it for its ruthless pursuit of a lawsuit against an art expert who had unfavorably opined on the authenticity of a painting to GDC's client, Steve Morton.[217] In fact, the punitive award against GDC was originally significantly higher, the jury having entered a punitive verdict of $20 million, but the Montana Supreme Court reduced it based on constitutional factors mandated by Supreme Court precedent.

The *Seltzer* case is a stark reminder that even the largest and most sophisticated law firms can be felled by the poor judgment of just one or two of their lawyers. Morton owned a painting, "Lassoing a Longhorn," which he initially believed was a valuable work by legendary western artist Charles M. Russell. The painting bore a signature that appeared to be Russell's. Morton purchased the piece from New York's Kennedy Galleries in 1972 for $38,000. Morton did so without getting any proof other than oral assurances from the gallery that it was a Russell.[218] In 1998, Morton contacted the director of the Coeur d'Alene Art Auction (CAA), Bob Drummond, about selling the painting at auction. Drummond assumed that the painting was an authentic Russell and thus appraised its market value at $650,000. Prior to the planned auction, Drummond's partner, Stuart Johnson, grew suspicious that the painting was actually by an artist of a similar style and genre, O.C. Seltzer. Johnson thus encouraged Drummond to consult with Steve Seltzer, the world's foremost expert authority on the paintings of O.C. Seltzer, his grandfather, and who also was an expert on the paintings of Russell. Seltzer offered his definitive opinion that the painting was a Seltzer.[219] At Johnson's further recommendation, Drummond also sought an opinion from Ginger Renner, who was the foremost expert on Russell and, to a lesser extent, an expert on O.C. Seltzer. Renner opined that the painting was clearly a Seltzer and that the signature appeared to have been altered to look like Russell had signed the work.[220] Armed with these expert opinions, Drummond informed Morton in January 2001 that CAA could not sell the painting as an authentic Russell because it in fact appeared to be the work of O.C. Seltzer. Unfortunately for Morton, Seltzer's paintings were worth substantially less than paintings by Russell.[221]

After he was told by Drummond that CAA was unwilling to sell "Lassoing a Longhorn" as an authentic Russell, Morton called Seltzer about his opinion. Seltzer explained the reasons for his opinion and followed up with a letter to Morton confirming them. Morton took the painting to Renner at her Arizona home, where she, too, confirmed her opinion that "it was

217. *Id.* at 570, 576.
218. *Id.* at 571.
219. *Id.* at 571–72.
220. *Id.* at 572–73.
221. *Id.* at 571.

unquestionably the work of O.C. Seltzer."[222] Morton then sent a letter to Renner thanking her and advising of his "state of shock" upon learning her opinion regarding the painting being a Seltzer; Morton also asked Renner to provide him with a formal letter expressing that opinion so that he could decide what to do next.[223] Renner complied with Morton's request in February 2001. Morton's then-counsel wrote a letter to the Kennedy Galleries expressing Morton's shock, indicating that "two recognized experts on Western Art have concluded that the painting is obviously a work by" Seltzer, describing the Kennedy Galleries' actions as "fraudulent (or, at the very least, negligent) misrepresentations," and indicating Morton's intent to hold the Kennedy Galleries liable for his damages.[224] Morton subsequently tried to sell the painting as an authentic Russell, but to no avail.

Morton then hired GDC senior counsel Dennis Gladwell to represent him. In April 2002, Gladwell wrote to both Seltzer and Renner to demand that they recant their opinions in a letter drafted to GDC's specifications, agree to pay to Morton the difference between the painting's current market price and what it could have sold for before they issued their opinions, and pay Morton an additional $50,000 for his troubles. The letter ominously concluded that GDC would sue on Morton's behalf if these demands were not met, including a claim for punitive damages. Gladwell sent another similar demand letter in May 2002. In July 2002, GDC sued Seltzer for claims ranging from defamation to intentional interference with prospective economic advantage and sought compensatory and punitive damages.[225] Gladwell appeared on the complaint for GDC, along with William Claster, a partner, and Erin Alexander, an associate.

The problems with this suit obviously were legion. After Seltzer produced ten experts who shared his opinion about the painting and GDC was unable to locate an expert who would support Morton's position, Morton agreed to a stipulation of dismissal.[226] Seltzer then sued GDC for malicious prosecution. In that action, Seltzer learned that, despite having served discovery in the underlying case and having been told by GDC that Morton had produced everything responsive, GDC and Morton had failed to produce copies of Morton's letter to Renner expressing his "state of shock," and his first lawyer's letter to the Kennedy Galleries that accused it of fraud and described Seltzer and Renner as "two recognized experts."[227] Seltzer also secured expert testimony from an experienced trial lawyer who opined that GDC's "failure, before filing the lawsuit, to obtain an expert willing to

222. *Id.* at 573.
223. *Id.*
224. *Id.* at 574.
225. *Id.* at 576–77.
226. *Id.* at 578.
227. *Id.* at 573–74, 580–81.

testify that the painting was a Russell constituted a significant deficiency in their investigation."[228] The Montana Supreme Court, finding that GDC's conduct amounted to "legal thuggery" and was "truly repugnant to Montana's foundational notions of justice" and "highly reprehensible," affirmed the lower court award of both compensatory and punitive damages.[229]

V. Conclusion

A lawsuit can be one of the most important events in a plaintiff's life, bringing with it the risk of sustained stress and unrelenting scrutiny of otherwise private aspects of the plaintiff's personal life. Likewise, being named a defendant in a lawsuit can be a monumental event for an individual and even for some entities, and even as to entities that are so sophisticated or large that being named in litigation can be commonplace, the increasing expense of litigation as a result of the rise of e-discovery means that being sued is not something easily shrugged off. For trial lawyers, however, filing lawsuits is the stuff of everyday life. Nevertheless, lawyers should not forget that filing or defending a lawsuit involves risks for them as well. To protect against those risks, lawyers must appropriately investigate their clients' claims before pulling the trigger in filing a lawsuit or in lodging claims, defenses, or contentions in defense of a lawsuit against a client. The nature of the investigation required will depend on the circumstances of the case.

Further, attorneys must be prepared to reevaluate the merits of their clients' contentions as new and different facts are developed during litigation. Litigation is dynamic, and claims that may have been sufficient at the outset can become unsustainable through no one's fault. Case developments can trigger an attorney's ethical obligation to refrain from continuing to pursue claims or contentions beyond the point at which it becomes clear that the claim or contention is meritless. And, of course, lawyers should never knowingly pursue litigation for the purposes of embarrassing, harassing, or maliciously injuring another.

The consequences of failing to perform sufficient investigation before making assertions in litigation or of using a baseless lawsuit to pursue spiteful ends can resonate well beyond the realm of ethics. Additional risks include potential tort liability for malicious prosecution.

---

228. *Id.* at 584.
229. *Id.* at 609, 615.

3

Surreptitious Investigations and Discovery

I. Introduction

In 2012, Timothy Leysock filed a False Claims Act case against Forest Laboratories, Inc. and Forest Pharmaceuticals, Inc. (collectively Forest), for the allegedly illegal off-label promotion of the Alzheimer's drug Namenda and the resulting submission of False Medicare claims.[1] Weysock's lawyers at Milberg LLP thereafter engaged in an elaborate scheme to obtain information from physicians about their Namenda prescribing practices and in some instances about their patients. In short, Milberg retained a physician and medical researcher, Dr. Mark Godec, to pretextually survey doctors concerning their prescription of Namenda to Medicare patients. Milberg directed the investigation. Godec did not tell Charter Oak, the marketing company he engaged to administer the surveys, that he was working for Milberg or that the information collected from the surveys would be used in litigation rather than for medical research.[2] Charter Oak would not have facilitated the surveys had it known the truth.[3] When communicating with physicians who were surveyed, Godec engaged in similar deception.[4] Among other things, Godec induced the physicians to provide patient medical charts and other confidential medical information, which he then shared with Milberg.[5] The physicians always believed—wrongly, as it turned out—that their patient data would be anonymized and kept confidential and would be used solely for medical research purposes.

Milberg's scheme was ultimately revealed, and Forest moved to dismiss the case as a sanction for the firm's misconduct. The *Leysock* court engaged in an extensive and detailed analysis of Milberg's and Godec's conduct.[6] The

1. Leysock v. Forest Labs., Inc., No. 12-11354-FDS, 2017 WL 1591833, at *1 (D. Mass. Apr. 28, 2017).
2. *Id.* at *3.
3. *Id.* at *4.
4. *Id.* at *4–5.
5. *Id.* at *5.
6. *Id.* at *6–12.

court concluded that the lawyers' conduct violated Massachusetts Rules of Professional Conduct 4.1(a) and 8.4(c).[7] As a sanction, the court struck all the allegations in Leysock's complaint that were derived from Godec's study. With that information excised from the complaint, Leysock's remaining allegations failed, and the *Leysock* court consequently granted Forest's motion to dismiss.[8]

Years earlier and miles to the west in Colorado, William Neal killed several women in gruesome fashion and raped another.[9] He spoke by phone with a sheriff's deputy shortly thereafter, alternating between threats to kill more people and offering to surrender if he could first talk to a lawyer.[10] Deputy District Attorney Mark Pautler, who was present during the telephone negotiations, posed as public defender "Mark Palmer" to obtain Neal's surrender.[11] Neal eventually learned of the deception, and Pautler's tactic allegedly caused Neal to so mistrust the real public defender representing him that he discharged the public defender and forged on pro se.[12] He ultimately pled guilty to three first-degree murder charges, represented himself in the subsequent death penalty proceeding, and was sentenced to death. The Colorado Supreme Court punished Pautler for deceiving Neal by suspending him from practice for three months but stayed the suspension during a probationary year on the condition that he complete 20 hours of ethics CLE and retake the Multistate Professional Responsibility Examination.[13]

These controversies richly illustrate the complex problems that can arise out of lawyers' involvement in, or control of, surreptitious discovery efforts and investigations.[14] Although lawyers' attempts at deception seldom are as extreme as Milberg's or Pautler's ruses, lesser maneuvers can have equally serious consequences. Many courts abhor any conduct by lawyers that embodies or is based on dishonesty or misrepresentation, including even relatively benign acts of deception.

Courts' general frame of reference with respect to honesty and honor in the practice of law is supported by rules of professional conduct that

7. *Id.* at *12; *see* MASS. RULES OF PROF'L CONDUCT R. 4.1(a) (2006) (stating that when representing a client, a lawyer shall not knowingly make a false statement of material fact or law to a third person); *id.* R. 8.4(c) (prohibiting conduct involving dishonesty, fraud, deceit, or misrepresentation).

8. *Leysock*, No. 12-11354-FDS, 2017 WL 1591833, at *14.

9. *In re* Pautler, 47 P.3d 1175, 1176–77 (Colo. 2002) (*In re Pautler II*).

10. People v. Pautler, 35 P.3d 571, 576 (Colo. 2001) (*In re Pautler I*).

11. *Id.*

12. *Id.* at 577.

13. *In re Pautler II*, 47 P.3d at 1178, 1184.

14. *See also, e.g.*, Meyer v. Kalanick, 212 F. Supp. 3d 437 (S.D.N.Y. 2016) (involving the defendants' calamitous employment of a competitive intelligence firm to surreptitiously uncover derogatory personal information about the plaintiff in a putative antitrust class action and one of his lawyers in the hope that such information could be used to intimidate them or to prejudice the court against them).

appear equally rigid. At the same time, surreptitious investigations and discovery have long been a part of the litigation landscape. It is thus fair to ask whether some forms of deception in investigations are justified, so that lawyers should be able to direct or participate in surreptitious information-gathering without fear of professional discipline or judicially imposed sanctions. Practical experience teaches that this question must be affirmatively answered at least some of the time.[15] The difficulty for lawyers is locating the line separating permissible and impermissible investigative tactics. This chapter aims to help lawyers draw that line through a discussion of applicable law and rules of professional conduct, and an examination of illustrative cases.

II. Applicable Ethics Rules

Surreptitious discovery and investigations conducted or directed by lawyers implicate several ethics rules.[16] The application of any rule or combination of rules will naturally depend on the facts of the case.

A. *Model Rule 4.1(a)*

Because concerns about lawyers' honesty permeate their involvement in surreptitious investigations and discovery, any analysis of lawyers' conduct in this context must encompass Model Rule 4.1(a), which states that in the course of representing a client, "a lawyer shall not knowingly . . . make a false statement of material fact or law to a third person."[17]

Model Rule 4.1(a) is generally straightforward. It requires a false "statement," but a lawyer may make a false statement under Rule 4.1(a) by affirming or ratifying another person's false statement,[18] or by failing to correct the other person.[19] The reference to "a third person" clarifies that the rule relates to lawyers' communications with non-clients.[20] "Knowingly" as used here,

15. *See* Leysock v. Forest Labs., Inc., No. 12-11354-FDS, 2017 WL 1591833, at *7 (D. Mass. Apr. 28, 2017) ("[S]ome degree of deception by attorneys, at least under some circumstances, is permissible in order to gather evidence for use in litigation. Such an investigative exception, however, is not set out in the rules [of professional conduct] themselves, but has been created by courts as a judicial gloss on those rules.").

16. They may also implicate numerous federal and state laws—both civil and criminal—as well as employment, tort, and privacy law doctrines.

17. Model Rules of Prof'l Conduct R. 4.1 (2020).

18. *See, e.g., In re* Winkler, 834 N.E.2d 85, 89 (Ind. 2005).

19. *See, e.g., In re* PRB Docket No. 2007-046, 989 A.2d 523, 526 (Vt. 2009).

20. State *ex rel.* Okla. Bar Ass'n v. Bolusky, 23 P.3d 268, 275 (Okla. 2001). *But see In re* Kupka, 458 P.3d 242, 247, 251 (Kan. 2020) (adopting the disciplinary panel's finding that the lawyer violated Rule 4.1(a) when she "provided false information to *many clients* as well as her supervising attorneys" (emphasis added)).

as elsewhere in the Model Rules, "denotes actual knowledge."[21] Although lawyers' knowledge may be inferred from circumstances,[22] the conclusion that a lawyer *should have known* something does not equal knowledge of that fact.[23] Likewise, speculation and suspicion do not equate to knowledge. Furthermore, the term "knowledge" does not describe "evil intent or bad purpose."[24] Innocent misstatements do not implicate Rule 4.1(a),[25] but statements made with reckless disregard for the truth may.[26] A statement of fact or law is "material" if it is significant or essential, if it "could have influenced the hearer,"[27] or if it affected the outcome of the proceedings.[28] Courts understandably evaluate materiality on a case-by-case basis.[29]

Rule 4.1(a) does not include a causation or reliance element. In other words, a lawyer violates the rule merely by making a prohibited statement. The recipient does not have to act or detrimentally rely upon the statement to perfect the violation.[30] Furthermore, Rule 4.1(a) does not require criminal intent by a lawyer, as in cases of perjury or forgery, to justify discipline.[31] Indeed, Rule 4.1(a) does not require any intent to deceive by the lawyer; the lawyer's knowledge that a statement is false when made gives rise to the violation.[32]

---

21. Model Rules of Prof'l Conduct R. 1.0(f) (2020).

22. *In re* Disciplinary Action Against Johnson, 743 N.W.2d 117, 123 (N.D. 2007); Model Rules of Prof'l Conduct R. 1.0(f) (2020).

23. *In re* Tocco, 984 P.2d 539, 543 (Ariz. 1999).

24. *In re* Edison, 724 N.W.2d 579, 584 (N.D. 2006).

25. *See, e.g.*, People v. Dalton, 367 P.3d 126, 132–33 (Colo. 2016) (finding no Rule 4.1(a) violation where the lawyer used arguably interchangeable lien terminology and had a reasonable factual basis for a representation regarding a property); People v. Chambers, 154 P.3d 419, 425–26 (Colo. 2006) (finding no violation for the lawyer's apparently innocent misstatement of the number of claims or suits); Att'y Grievance Comm'n of Md. v. Elmendorf, 946 A.2d 542, 545–46 (Md. 2008) (agreeing that a lawyer's negligence in failing to review files leading to false statements did not violate Rule 4.1(a)).

26. *See In re* Wagner, 744 N.E.2d 418, 421 (Ind. 2001).

27. *In re* Fisher, 202 P.3d 1186, 1202 (Colo. 2009).

28. *In re* Malofiy, 653 F. App'x 148, 153 (3d Cir. 2016); Office of Disciplinary Couns. v. DiAngelus, 907 A.2d 452, 456 (Pa. 2006).

29. Ausherman v. Bank of Am. Corp., 212 F. Supp. 2d 435, 449 (D. Md. 2002).

30. *See, e.g.*, *In re* Winthrop, 848 N.E.2d 961, 980 (Ill. 2006) (finding that the lawyer violated Rule 4.1(a) even though his dishonesty did not impede the actions of the other lawyer to whom the false statement was made).

31. *See, e.g.*, Att'y Grievance Comm'n of Md. v. Pak, 929 A.2d 546, 567–68 (Md. 2007) (rejecting the lawyer's argument that she did not violate Rule 4.1(a) because no perjury charges were filed against her); *In re* Belding, 589 S.E.2d 197, 200 (S.C. 2003) (rejecting the lawyer's argument that he did not violate Rule 4.1 by preparing false documents because he lacked the intent to commit criminal forgery under South Carolina law).

32. *See, e.g.*, *In re* Petition for Disciplinary Action Against Winter, 770 N.W.2d 463, 467 (Minn. 2009) (rejecting the lawyer's argument that he did not violate Rule 4.1(a) because he did not intend a false statement in a motion to deceive the court or the other lawyer involved).

B. Model Rule 4.2

Lawyers' covert investigations and surreptitious discovery activities often target people and organizations represented by counsel in the matter. Model Rule 4.2 addresses lawyers' communications with persons who are represented by counsel. The rule provides:

> In representing a client, a lawyer shall not communicate about the subject of the representation with a person the lawyer knows to be represented by another lawyer in the matter, unless the lawyer has the consent of the other lawyer or is authorized to do so by law or a court order.[33]

Model Rule 4.2 applies only where the person with whom a lawyer communicates is represented in the matter. As for the critical requirement of *knowing* whether a person is represented by a lawyer in a matter, that is easy where the other lawyer has somehow identified herself. Such clarity is not required to find a violation, however, because a lawyer's knowledge can be inferred from circumstances. Lawyers cannot avoid acquiring knowledge by turning a blind eye to circumstances indicating that a person is represented by counsel in the matter.[34] Nonetheless, the Model Rule 4.2 knowledge requirement is clearly one of actual knowledge.[35] The fact that a lawyer *should have known* that a person was represented in a matter will not support a Rule 4.2 violation.[36]

Questions occasionally surface about the existence or scope of a "matter."[37] This is most common where litigation is contemplated but has not been initiated, and lawyers for the putative parties are gathering information in preparation for it, or where a person is involved in several enterprises or projects with legal aspects. Determinations of whether a matter exists, what matters are encompassed within a representation, and the scope and contours of matters all depend on the circumstances.[38] All that said,

33. Model Rules of Prof'l Conduct R. 4.2 (2020).

34. Scanlan v. Eisenberg, 893 F. Supp. 2d 945, 950 (N.D. Ill. 2012); People v. Underhill, 353 P.3d 936, 950 (Colo. 2015).

35. *See, e.g.*, McClellan v. Ready Mixed Concrete Co. of Erie, Inc., Civ. No 13-87 Erie, 2014 WL 4060254, at *1–2 (W.D. Pa. Aug. 14, 2014) (noting and applying the actual knowledge requirement); Mori v. Saito, 785 F. Supp. 2d 427, 433 (S.D.N.Y. 2011) (rejecting the argument that a lawyer violated Rule 4.2 because she "must have known" that an unidentified caller was a represented party); State *ex rel.* Okla. Bar Ass'n v. Harper, 995 P.2d 1143, 1147 (Okla. 2000) (requiring actual knowledge for a Rule 4.2 violation and rejecting a proposed "should have known" standard).

36. *Harper*, 995 P.2d at 1147.

37. *See, e.g.*, Mims v. Chichester, 722 N.Y.S.2d 30, 31 (App. Div. 2001) (noting that while multiple matters may involve the same subjects, they are different matters for purposes of anti-contact rule); Damron v. CSX Transp., Inc., 920 N.E.2d 169, 177–78 (Ohio Ct. App. 2009) (reasoning that extrinsic evidence for impeachment use was outside the scope of the matter).

38. Restatement (Third) of the Law Governing Lawyers § 99 cmt. d (2000).

Rule 4.2 clearly applies to lawyers' ex parte communications with represented persons before a lawsuit is filed.[39]

It is important to understand how Rule 4.2 applies to organizational litigants. This is because organizations speak only through their employees and agents. Crucially, "not every current employee of a represented organization is a 'represented' person for purposes of Rule 4.2."[40] Model Rule 4.2 is not intended to quarantine every employee with knowledge of relevant facts or information concerning a matter and thereby prevent lawyers for other parties from speaking with them ex parte.[41] It is therefore necessary to identify those people affiliated with the organization who hold a position or play a role sufficient to assume its attributes. Such employees are presumptively represented by the organization's lawyers. Employees who are not within this constituent group are open for ex parte communications unless they are separately represented.[42]

Courts typically look to the comments to Rule 4.2 for guidance when deciding which employees are off-limits. Comment 7 to Model Rule 4.2 provides:

> In the case of a represented organization, this Rule prohibits communications with a constituent of the organization who [1] supervises, directs or regularly consults with the organization's lawyer concerning the matter or [2] has authority to obligate the organization with respect to the matter or [3] whose act or omission in connection with the matter may be imputed to the organization for purposes of civil or criminal liability.[43]

A few jurisdictions have departed from the ABA approach and adopted the "managing-speaking agent test."[44] Under this test, ex parte communication is prohibited with employees who have "'speaking authority' for the corporation," meaning those employees "who 'have managing authority

---

39. Stahl v. Wal-Mart Stores, Inc., 47 F. Supp. 2d 783, 789 (S.D. Miss. 1998).

40. Doe v. Super. Ct. of San Diego Cnty., 248 Cal. Rptr. 3d 314, 320 (Ct. App. 2019).

41. *Id.* at 321; *see* Iowa Sup. Ct. Att'y Disciplinary Bd. v. Stowers, 823 N.W.2d 1, 11 (Iowa 2012) (noting that Rule 4.2 does not bar ex parte communication "with all constituents of [a] represented organization"); ABA Comm. on Ethics & Prof'l Responsibility, Formal Op. 95-396, at 14 (1995) [hereinafter ABA Formal Op. 95-396] ("[T]the fact that an entity is represented by counsel does not prevent communication with all current employees of the represented corporation." (footnote omitted)).

42. Davis v. Creditors Interchange Receivable Mgmt., LLC, 585 F. Supp. 2d 968, 978–79 (N.D. Ohio 2008) (discussing Ohio rules); Klier v. Sordoni Skanska Constr. Co., 766 A.2d 761, 770 (N.J. Super. Ct. App. Div. 2001); Hedges v. E. River Plaza, LLC, 981 N.Y.S.2d 894, 897–98 (Sup. Ct. 2013); Newsuan v. Republic Servs., Inc., 213 A.3d 279, 288 (Pa. Super. Ct. 2019).

43. Model Rules of Prof'l Conduct R. 4.2 cmt. 7 (2020).

44. *See, e.g.*, Goodeagle v. United States, No. CIV-09-490-D, 2010 WL 3081520, at *4 (W.D. Okla. Aug. 6, 2010) (quoting Fulton v. Lane, 829 P.2d 959, 960 (Okla. 1992)); Messing, Rudavsky & Weliky, P.C. v. President & Fellows of Harvard Coll., 764 N.E.2d 825, 833 (Mass. 2002); Palmer v. Pioneer Inn Assocs., Ltd., 59 P.3d 1237, 1247–48 (Nev. 2002); Wright v. Grp. Health Hosp., 691 P.2d 564, 569 (Wash. 1984).

sufficient to give them the right to speak for, and bind the corporation.'"[45] This is a distinctly minority approach.

Ex parte communications with current employees of an organization are a regular issue in lawyers' investigations,[46] as *Wal-Mart Stores, Inc. v. Goodman*[47] illustrates. In that case, plaintiff Lashawna Goodman was arrested for allegedly shoplifting a telephone from a Wal-Mart store. She contended that she was exchanging a telephone she had purchased at another store. After beating the criminal charges, she sued Wal-Mart for malicious prosecution and won a sizable verdict. On appeal, Wal-Mart argued that it was entitled to a new trial by virtue of the investigation conducted by Goodman's lawyer.

Goodman's lawyer had gone to the subject Wal-Mart store and attempted to replicate some key events leading to Goodman's arrest in order to cross-examine a Wal-Mart corporate representative at trial.[48] In doing so, he spoke at some length with an assistant store manager. The Alabama Supreme Court determined that the lawyer's interview of the assistant manager was proper because the assistant manager did not act as a corporate agent with authority to bind Wal-Mart, nor did he have the authority to commit Wal-Mart to his statements.[49] Thus, Goodman's counsel was not required to notify Wal-Mart of his intention to speak with its employee, and those communications provided no basis for a new trial.[50]

In many cases, lawyers want to speak with an organization's *former* employees. It is settled that Rule 4.2 generally permits ex parte communications with former employees.[51] This freedom does have limits, however. For

---

45. *Messing*, 764 N.E.2d at 833 (quoting *Wright*, 691 P.2d at 569).

46. *See, e.g.*, Microsoft Corp. v. Alcatel Bus. Sys., No. 07-090-SLR, 2007 WL 4480632 (D. Del. Dec. 18, 2007) (involving lawyers who bought equipment that was the subject of the litigation and then questioned one of the technicians who installed the equipment).

47. 789 So. 2d 166 (Ala. 2000).

48. *Id.* at 176–77.

49. *Id.* at 177.

50. *Id.*

51. *See, e.g.*, Calise v. Brady Sullivan Harris Mills, LLC, No. 18-99WES, 2019 WL 1397245, at *5 (D.R.I. Mar. 28, 2019) (discussing Rhode Island's version of Rule 4.2); Lozama v. Samaritan Daytop Village, Inc., No. 18 CV 4351 (DLI) (RML), 2019 WL 1002954, at *2 (E.D.N.Y. Mar. 1, 2019) (applying New York law); Peterson v. Alaska Commc'ns Sys. Grp. Inc., No. 3:12-cv-00090-TMB, 2019 WL 6331355, at *7 (D. Alaska Nov. 26, 2019) (applying Alaska ethics rules); United States v. Miss., No. 3:16-cv-622-CWR-FKB, 2018 WL 4956658, at *4 (S.D. Miss. Oct. 12, 2018) (discussing Mississippi's version of Rule 4.2); Klorczyk v. Sears, Roebuck & Co., No. 3:13-cv-00257 (JAM), 2017 WL 3272237, at *3 (D. Conn. Aug. 1, 2017) (applying Connecticut ethics rules); Thurston v. Okemo Ltd. Liab. Co., 123 F. Supp. 3d 513, 515 (D. Vt. 2015) (applying Vermont's version of Rule 4.2); EEOC v. SVT, LLC, 297 F.R.D. 336, 345 (N.D. Ind. 2014) (involving a class action); *In re* Digitek Prod. Liab. Litig., 648 F. Supp. 2d 795, 799 (S.D. W. Va. 2009) (involving an MDL case); Bryant v. Yorktowne Cabinetry, Inc., 538 F. Supp. 2d 948, 949–53 (W.D. Va. 2008); Davis v. Creditors Interchange Receivable Mgmt., LLC, 585 F. Supp. 2d 968, 979 (N.D. Ohio 2008) (applying Ohio rules); United States v. W.R. Grace, 401 F. Supp. 2d 1065, 1068–69 (D. Mont. 2005); Smith v. Kalamazoo Ophthalmology, 322 F. Supp. 2d 883, 890 (W.D. Mich. 2004); Lang v. Super. Ct., 826 P.2d 1228, 1233 (Ariz. Ct. App. 1992); DiOssi v. Edison, 583 A.2d 1343,

example, an attorney cannot communicate ex parte with former employees who have their own counsel in a matter, who had managerial responsibility in the matter being litigated,[52] who maintain an ongoing relationship with the organization in relation to the litigation,[53] or whose alleged acts or omissions gave rise to the litigation.[54]

Furthermore, courts generally hold that Model Rule 4.2 or Model Rules 4.2 and 4.4(a), read together, prohibit lawyers from asking former employees about documents or information protected by the organization's attorney-client privilege or work product immunity,[55] as do legal ethics authorities.[56] In fact, Model Rule 4.4(a) is the correct (and certainly the better) source of authority for this proposition. Comment 7 to Model Rule 4.2 clarifies this

1345 (Del. Super. Ct. 1990); H.B.A. Mgmt., Inc. v. Estate of Schwartz, 693 So. 2d 541, 544–46 (Fla. 1997); Sanifill of Ga., Inc. v. Roberts, 502 S.E.2d 343, 345 (Ga. 1998); P.T. Barnum's Nightclub v. Duhamell, 766 N.E.2d 729, 737 (Ind. Ct. App. 2002); Humco, Inc. v. Noble, 31 S.W.3d 916, 920 (Ky. 2000); Schmidt v. Gregorio, 705 So. 2d 742, 743–44 (La. Ct. App. 1993); *Patriarca*, 778 N.E.2d at 881–82; Smith v. Kan. City S. Ry., 87 S.W.3d 266, 272–75 (Mo. Ct. App. 2002); Klier v. Sordoni Skanska Constr. Co., 766 A.2d 761, 770 (N.J. Super. Ct. App. Div. 2001); Fulton v. Lane, 829 P.2d 959, 960 (Okla. 1992); State *ex rel.* Charleston Area Med. Ctr. v. Zakaib, 437 S.E.2d 759, 763–64 (W. Va. 1993); Strawser v. Exxon Co., U.S.A., 843 P.2d 613, 622 (Wyo. 1992); Mich. Eth. Op. RI-360, 2013 WL 9660913, at *1 (State Bar of Mich., Comm. on Prof'l & Jud. Ethics 2013); Pa. Eth. Op. 2004-80, 2004 WL 3323071, at *1 (Pa. Bar Ass'n, Comm. on Legal Ethics & Prof'l Responsibility 2004) [hereinafter Pa. Eth. Op. 2004-80]; Model Rules of Prof'l Conduct R. 4.2 cmt. 7 (2020).

52. *W.R. Grace*, 401 F. Supp. 2d at 1067; *Patriarca*, 778 N.E.2d at 882.

53. *Lang*, 826 P.2d at 1233.

54. Merck v. Swift Transp. Co., No. CV-16-01103-PHX-ROS, 2018 WL 3774007, at *3 (D. Ariz. July 19, 2018); *Lang*, 826 P.2d at 1233.

55. *See, e.g.*, Harris Davis Rebar, L.L.C. v. Structural Iron Workers Local Union No. 1, Pension Tr. Fund, No. 17 C 6473, 2019 WL 447622, at *6 (N.D. Ill. Feb. 5, 2019) (reading rules 4.2 and 4.4 together); Martinez v. Cnty. of Antelope, No. 4:15CV3064, 2016 WL 3248241, at *9–10 (D. Neb. June 13, 2016) (disqualifying a lawyer who knowingly obtained privileged information from a former county official); Tomasian v. C.D. Peacock, Inc., No. 09 C 5665, 2012 WL 2590493, at *7 (N.D. Ill. July 3, 2012) (referring to Rule 4.2 and stating that "former employees are barred from discussing privileged information to which they are privy"); Gifford v. Target Corp., 723 F. Supp. 2d 1110, 1118–23 (D. Minn. 2010) (referring to Rule 4.2 cmt. 7 and Rule 4.4(a)); Weber v. Fujifilm Med. Sys., U.S.A., No. 3:10 CV 401(JBA), 2010 WL 2836720, at *4 (D. Conn. July 19, 2010) (considering whether the defendants' former employees "had 'extensive exposure to privileged communications and sustained access to [defendants'] litigation strategy and the attorney's work product'" before allowing them to be interviewed ex parte (quoting Shoreline Computs., Inc. v. Warnaco, Inc., No. CV 990422853S, 2000 WL 371206, at *2 (Conn. Super. Ct. Apr. 3, 2000))); *Kalamazoo Ophthalmology*, 322 F. Supp. 2d at 890–91 (applying Rule 4.2); Zachair, Ltd. v. Driggs, 965 F. Supp. 741, 753–54 (D. Md. 1997) (applying Rule 4.2); Rentclub, Inc. v. Transamerica Rental Fin. Corp., 811 F. Supp. 651, 657 (M.D. Fla. 1992) (discussing Rule 4.2); *Shoreline Computs.*, 2000 WL 371206, at *2 (describing former employees who are off-limits under Rule 4.2).

56. *See, e.g.*, N.C. State Bar, Formal Ethics Op. 1997-2 (1998) (prohibiting ex parte communication with former employees who "participated substantially in the legal representation of the organization, including participation in and knowledge of privileged communications with legal counsel"); Pa. Eth. Op. 2004-80, *supra* note 51, 2004 WL 3323071, at *1 (referring to Rule 4.2 and the attorney-client privilege).

point by directing lawyers to Model Rule 4.4(a) when they must analyze their communication obligations regarding former employees who possess their former employers' confidential information.[57]

It is common for a represented person or organization to have a public website. Information found there may be relevant to the matter in which the person or organization is represented. May another lawyer conducting informal discovery in the matter visit that website without violating Rule 4.2? Yes, so long as the lawyer simply views or downloads information, or otherwise engages solely in one-way communications, such as providing feedback about the site or ordering products.[58] A lawyer who simply views a website or downloads information from a website cannot reasonably be said to have communicated with the site owner within the meaning of Rule 4.2. Reading information that is available for public consumption does not qualify as communication in this context.[59] Even if such conduct were considered to be a communication, there is no risk that it could result in overreaching by the investigating lawyer, interfere with the represented person's attorney-client relationship, or result in uninformed disclosure of information relating to the person's representation—the dangers against which Rule 4.2 is intended to protect.

If, however, the website is interactive in the sense that it allows visitors to send and receive messages to and from the host or to participate in a chat room, an investigating lawyer may violate Rule 4.2.[60] Obviously, if it is an individual's site, interaction is much more likely to violate Rule 4.2. Where a represented organization is involved, an alleged violation will almost certainly turn on the identity of the person with whom the lawyer communicated via the site. These same principles apply to the review of a represented person's "blog"; mere passive review of a person's publicly available blog posts does not implicate Rule 4.2, but initiating posts with the intent or effect of soliciting a response well might.

Lawyers may have investigators follow, photograph, or otherwise observe represented persons to gather information or evidence. Such observation, without more, is not a communication for Rule 4.2 purposes.[61]

Several remaining points about Rule 4.2 bear mention in the context of surreptitious investigations and discovery. First, a lawyer cannot circumvent

57. *See* Model Rules of Prof'l Conduct R. 4.2 cmt. 7 (2020) ("In communicating with a current or former constituent of an organization, a lawyer must not use methods of obtaining evidence that violate the legal rights of the organization. See Rule 4.4.").

58. Or. Eth. Op. 2001-164, 2001 WL 167177, at *1–2 (Or. State Bar Ass'n, Bd. of Governors 2001) [hereinafter Or. Eth. Op. 2001-164] (interpreting analogous Oregon rule); *see also* Or. Eth. Op. 2005-164, 2005 WL 5679590, at *1–2 (Or. State Bar Ass'n, Bd. of Governors 2005) [hereinafter Or. Eth. Op. 2005-164] (updating Or. Eth. Op. 2001-164).

59. Or. Eth. Op. 2005-164, *supra* note 58, 2005 WL 5679590, at *1.

60. Or. Eth. Op. 2001-164, *supra* note 58, 2001 WL 167177, at *2.

61. 2003 N.C. Eth. Op. 4, 2003 WL 23406943, at *2 (N.C. State Bar 2003).

the rule by directing someone else to communicate with a represented person.[62] This is consistent with the general principle that lawyers may not do through agents that which they cannot ethically do themselves.[63]

Second, Rule 4.2 protects against "contacts that are well meaning but misguided as well as those that are intentionally improper."[64] As a result, lawyers may violate Rule 4.2 through innocent or negligent communications.[65]

Third, a Rule 4.2 violation does not depend on the challenged communication causing harm or damage.[66] Even so, a showing of prejudice may be required where a party invokes the rule as a basis for disqualifying or sanctioning a lawyer.

Finally, courts often decline to preclude evidence obtained in violation of Rule 4.2 on the theory that an exclusionary policy frustrates truth and punishes the party the offending lawyer represents rather than punishing the ethical violation.[67] In other words, a lawyer who violates Rule 4.2 may

62. *See, e.g.*, United States v. Smallwood, 365 F. Supp. 2d 689, 694–97 (E.D. Va. 2005) (involving an investigator); *In re* Complaint of PMD Enters., Inc., 215 F. Supp. 2d 519 (D.N.J. 2002) (attempting to circumvent Rule 4.2 through investigator); Holdren v. Gen. Motors Corp., 13 F. Supp. 2d 1192, 1193–96 (D. Kan. 1998) (having client attempt to obtain affidavits from co-workers); *In re* Anonymous, 819 N.E.2d 376, 377–79 (Ind. 2004) (violating Rules 4.2 and 4.4 through involvement in the client obtaining an affidavit from an employee); *In re* Pyle, 91 P.3d 1222, 1228–29 (Kan. 2004) (having the client deliver an affidavit to the opposing party); Bratcher v. Ky. Bar Ass'n, 290 S.W.3d 648, 649 (Ky. 2009) (hiring a company to contact the client's former employer to determine what the former employer was saying about the client when prospective employers called for references); State v. Clark, 738 N.W.2d 316, 339–40 (Minn. 2007) (finding a Rule 4.2 violation where police officers spoke to a represented person); Awan v. Awan, 906 N.Y.S.2d 70, 72 (App. Div. 2010) (excluding a doctor's testimony in a custody proceeding because the lawyer violated Rule 4.2 by having the doctor examine and question the child without the knowledge of the child's lawyer); Disciplinary Couns. v. Sartini, 871 N.E.2d 543, 544–46 (Ohio 2007) (sanctioning a prosecutor who urged a suspect's mother to speak to him); Bd. of Prof'l Responsibility v. Melchior, 269 P.3d 1088, 1090–91 (Wyo. 2012) (agreeing that the lawyer violated Rule 4.2 when he created and gave to his client a divorce settlement agreement and a financial statement at a time when he knew or reasonably should have known that there was a substantial risk that she would deliver them to the husband, whom the lawyer knew to be represented by counsel).

63. *See* MODEL RULES OF PROF'L CONDUCT R. 8.4(a) (2020) (making it professional misconduct for a lawyer to "violate or attempt to violate the Rules of Professional Conduct, knowingly assist or induce another to do so, or do so through the acts of another").

64. Att'y Grievance Comm'n of Md. v. Kent, 653 A.2d 909, 918 (Md. 1995).

65. Faison v. Thornton, 863 F. Supp. 1204, 1213 (D. Nev. 1993); *see, e.g.*, *In re* Capper, 757 N.E.2d 138, 139–40 (Ind. 2001) (communicating with represented adverse party based on the client's statement that party was no longer represented without confirming truth of that assertion violated Rule 4.2).

66. Runsvold v. Idaho State Bar, 925 P.2d 1118, 1120 (Idaho 1996).

67. *See, e.g.*, *In re* Katrina Canal Breaches Consol. Litig., No. 05-4182 "K" (2), 2008 WL 2066999, at *7 (E.D. La. May 14, 2008) (quoting Weider Sports Equip. Co. v. Fitness First, Inc., 912 F. Supp. 502, 510 (D. Utah 1996)); Fisher v. Town of Boyce, 250 So. 3d 904, 907–11 (La. Ct. App. 2017) (affirming the trial court's exercise of discretion).

rightly be sanctioned or disciplined, but any evidence obtained in violation of the rule will frequently be admissible.[68]

C. Model Rule 4.3

Where a person with whom a lawyer wishes to communicate is unrepresented or is not known to be represented, Model Rule 4.3 governs the lawyer's conduct. The rule provides:

> In dealing on behalf of a client with a person who is not represented by counsel, a lawyer shall not state or imply that the lawyer is disinterested. When the lawyer knows or reasonably should know that the unrepresented person misunderstands the lawyer's role in the matter, the lawyer shall make reasonable efforts to correct the misunderstanding. The lawyer shall not give legal advice to an unrepresented person, other than the advice to secure counsel, if the lawyer knows or reasonably should know that the interests of such person are or have a reasonable possibility of being in conflict with the interests of the client.[69]

Rule 4.3 recognizes that when a person is unrepresented, the danger that a lawyer might overreach or somehow compromise the person's interest is great, and the rule thus restricts the lawyer's ability to exploit the situation.[70] The rule focuses on the lawyer's interest in the matter rather than on the exact nature of the communication because a lawyer's improper influence may be difficult to characterize. By requiring a lawyer to disclose her interest in a matter, the theory goes, the unrepresented person will be warned of the risks attending communication and be able to gauge her need for counsel.

The first sentence of Rule 4.3 makes clear that lawyers cannot misrepresent their interests in matters. Insofar as an unrepresented person may misunderstand a lawyer's role in a matter, however, it is important to recognize that the unrepresented person's confusion does not alone control the analysis.[71] Rather, the lawyer must (1) realize that the person misapprehends the lawyer's role and (2) fail to reasonably attempt to correct that misapprehension before a Rule 4.3 violation will lie.

It is understandable that lawyers' participation in covert investigations and surreptitious discovery might run afoul of Rule 4.3, although that

68. *But see* United States v. Sierra Pac. Indus., 759 F. Supp. 2d 1206, 1214 (E.D. Cal. 2010) (prohibiting the use of evidence obtained through improper ex parte communications); Awan v. Awan, 906 N.Y.S.2d 70, 72 (App. Div. 2010) (excluding a doctor's testimony in a custody proceeding because the lawyer violated Rule 4.2 by having the doctor examine and question the child without the knowledge of the child's lawyer).

69. Model Rules of Prof'l Conduct R. 4.3 (2020).

70. Apple Corps Ltd. v. Int'l Collectors Soc'y, 15 F. Supp. 2d 456, 476 (D.N.J. 1998); People v. Mascarenas, 103 P.3d 339, 345 (Colo. 2003).

71. *In re* Jensen, 191 P.3d 1118, 1129 (Kan. 2008).

conclusion is by no means certain given the different roles of lawyer and investigator. As a New Jersey federal court explained in rejecting a claim that the plaintiff's lawyers and investigators violated Rule 4.3 in surreptitiously checking the defendant's compliance with the terms of a consent decree:

> It is clear from the language of RPC 4.3 that it is limited to circumstances where an attorney is acting in his capacity as a lawyer. . . . Therefore, its prohibitions on allowing the unrepresented person to misunderstand that the lawyer is disinterested only apply to a lawyer who is acting like a lawyer. . . . Like RPC 4.2, RPC 4.3 was intended to prevent a lawyer who fails to disclose his role in a matter from taking advantage of an unrepresented third party. . . .
>
> Plaintiffs' counsel and investigators in testing compliance were not acting in the capacity of lawyers. Therefore, the prohibitions of Rule 4.3 do not apply here.[72]

If Rule 4.3's application to lawyers functioning as investigators is unclear, its application to non-lawyer investigators or testers acting as such seems out of reach. No one is realistically likely to apply her expectations of lawyers to investigators or testers.[73]

D. Model Rule 4.4(a)

Model Rule 4.4(a) provides that in representing a client, a lawyer cannot "use methods of obtaining evidence that violate the legal rights" of a third person.[74] It is impractical to catalog all such rights.[75] Depending on the nature of the case, investigating lawyers potentially risk violating a range of consumer protection and privacy laws—and thus Rule 4.4(a)—unless they are careful.[76] Among other concerns, lawyers who secretly record conversations with witnesses or others must be sure that their conduct does not violate wiretapping or eavesdropping laws.[77]

Importantly, Rule 4.4(a) attributes improper purpose to the action itself rather than to the actor. Thus, lawyers may violate the rule where they are simply carrying out clients' directions. When it comes to evaluating whether

72. *Apple Corps Ltd.*, 15 F. Supp. 2d at 476 (citations omitted).

73. Weider Sports Equip., Inc. v. Fitness First, Inc., 912 F. Supp. 502, 512 (D. Utah 1996).

74. Model Rules of Prof'l Conduct R. 4.4(a) (2015).

75. *Id.* R. 4.4 cmt. 1.

76. *See, e.g.*, Bakker v. McKinnon, 152 F.3d 1007, 1013 (8th Cir. 1998) (observing that lawyers' willful violations of the Fair Credit Reporting Act worked "a clear violation" of Arkansas Rule of Professional Conduct 4.4).

77. ABA Comm. on Ethics & Prof'l Responsibility, Formal Op. 01-422, at 5–6 (2001) [hereinafter ABA Formal Op. 01-422] (stating that surreptitious taping that violates wiretapping laws also violates Rule 4.4).

a lawyer is attempting to obtain evidence in violation of a third person's legal rights, the applicable standard is an objective one.[78]

E. Model Rule 5.3

Lawyers conducting informal discovery, surreptitious discovery, or covert investigations through agents—such as investigators or legal assistants—must recognize their obligations under Model Rule 5.3, which governs lawyers' responsibility for the conduct of non-lawyer assistants. For example, Rule 5.3(b) provides that "a lawyer having direct supervisory authority over [a] nonlawyer shall make reasonable efforts to ensure that the person's conduct is compatible with the professional obligations of the lawyer."[79] Model Rule 5.3(c) specifies when a lawyer is responsible for the conduct of a non-lawyer assistant "that would be a violation of the Rules of Professional Conduct if engaged in by a lawyer."[80]

Lawyers are "completely responsible" for the work of non-lawyers who assist them.[81] This broad expression of accountability does not mean that lawyers are vicariously liable for non-lawyer assistants' actions as a matter of professional responsibility, for they clearly are not;[82] rather, Model Rule 5.3 penalizes supervisory failures,[83] while enforcing and illuminating lawyers' supervisory responsibilities for the non-lawyers who assist them in their practices. This is true regardless of whether the non-lawyers are employees of their law firms or are independent contractors.[84] Furthermore, lawyers must give their assistants and investigators "appropriate instruction and supervision concerning the ethical aspects of their employment," and

78. *In re* Martinez, 462 P.3d 36, 45 (Ariz. 2020); *In re* Comfort, 159 P.3d 1011, 1020 (Kan. 2007).

79. Model Rules of Prof'l Conduct R. 5.3(b) (2020).

80. *Id.* R. 5.3(c).

81. *In re* Comish, 889 So. 2d 236, 245 (La. 2004).

82. *In re* Phillips, 244 P.3d 549, 553 (Ariz. 2010); *see, e.g.*, People v. Peters, 82 P.3d 389, 394–95 (Colo. 2003) (rejecting an alleged Rule 5.3(b) violation where the lawyer reasonably instructed and supervised a process server who submitted false information on service sheets); Iowa Sup. Ct. Att'y Disciplinary Bd. v. Mathahs, 918 N.W.2d 487, 494 (Iowa 2018) ("When a nonlawyer makes a mistake that is not a direct consequence of the attorney's inattentive supervision, the attorney does not violate rule 32:5.3."); Att'y Grievance Comm'n of Md. v. Ficker, 706 A.2d 1045, 1050 (Md. 1998) (finding no Rule 5.3 violation where the lawyer's assistant failed to timely relay a telephone message to the lawyer even though the failure ultimately led to the issuance of a bench warrant against the client); *In re* Galasso, 978 N.E.2d 1254, 1258 (N.Y. 2012) ("To be clear, respondent is not being held responsible for the criminal behavior of his brother [who he employed]. Rather, it is his own breach of his fiduciary duty and failure to properly supervise his employee . . . that warrant this disciplinary action.").

83. *See, e.g.*, *In re* Reger, 421 P.3d 25, 32 (Alaska 2018) ("When Reger delegated duties to his nonlawyer assistant, he remained responsible for ensuring that those duties were performed competently, diligently, and compatibly with his own ethical obligations. Reger violated Rule 5.3(a)(2) by failing to supervise [his nonlawyer assistant] adequately.").

84. Model Rules of Prof'l Conduct R. 5.3 cmt. 1 (2020).

see that they understand these limitations.[85] The amount or level of instruction and supervision required will depend on the matter and on the education, experience, knowledge, skills, and roles of the non-lawyer assistants.

F. Model Rule 8.4(a)

Model Rule 8.4(a) makes it professional misconduct for a lawyer to "violate or attempt to violate the Rules of Professional Conduct, knowingly assist or induce another to do so, or do so through the acts of another."[86] This rule, which prohibits lawyers from using non-lawyer agents to do what the lawyer cannot do directly, is important to ethical litigation practice. Model Rule 8.4(a) applies to lawyers' delegation of assignments to other lawyers, lawyers' employment of consultants and investigators, and lawyers' use of non-lawyer staff to conduct discovery or perform investigative functions.[87] Lawyers may violate Rule 8.4(a) either by directing someone to engage in misconduct or by knowingly ratifying misconduct after the fact.[88] And, as the text of Rule 8.4(a) makes clear, the mere *attempt* to violate another rule violates Rule 8.4(a).

G. Model Rule 8.4(b)

Model Rule 8.4(b) makes it professional misconduct for a lawyer to "commit a criminal act that reflects adversely on the lawyer's honesty, trustworthiness or fitness as a lawyer in other respects."[89] As the language of the rule indicates, not every criminal act by a lawyer violates Rule 8.4(b). Not every criminal act by a lawyer indicates that the lawyer is unfit to practice.[90] Whether a lawyer's criminal act reflects on a lawyer's honesty, trustworthiness, or fitness to practice depends on the facts of the case.[91] A lawyer's criminal conduct while representing a client, however, almost certainly indicates unfitness.[92]

---

85. *In re Comish*, 889 So. 2d at 245.

86. Model Rules of Prof'l Conduct R. 8.4(a) (2020).

87. Ala. State Bar, Eth. Op. RO-2007-05, at 2 (2007) (discussing Rule 8.4(a) and stating that where a lawyer engages a private investigator or other third party who engages in unethical conduct, the private investigator's or other party's misconduct is imputed to the lawyer).

88. *See, e.g.*, *In re* Usher, 987 N.E.2d 1080, 1089 (Ind. 2013) (finding that the lawyer violated Rule 8.4(a) by having his paralegal disseminate a harassing e-mail message).

89. Model Rules of Prof'l Conduct R. 8.4(b) (2020).

90. Iowa Sup. Ct. Att'y Disciplinary Bd. v. Sears, 933 N.W.2d 214, 220 (Iowa 2019); State *ex rel.* Okla. Bar Ass'n v. McMillen, 393 P.3d 219, 223 (Okla. 2017); *In re* Disciplinary Proceedings Against Johns, 847 N.W.2d 179, 185–87 (Wis. 2014).

91. Iowa Sup. Ct. Att'y Disciplinary Bd. v. Templeton, 784 N.W.2d 761, 767 (Iowa 2010) (quoting *In re* Conduct of White, 815 P.2d 1257, 1265 (Or. 1991)).

92. Iowa Sup. Ct. Att'y Disciplinary Bd. v. Engelmann, 840 N.W.2d 156, 163 (Iowa 2013) (quoting Iowa Sup. Ct. Att'y Disciplinary Bd. v. Bieber, 824 N.W.2d 514, 520 (Iowa 2012)).

It is possible for a lawyer's covert investigation or surreptitious discovery tactics to be criminal in some instances. For example, it is easy to imagine a scenario in which a lawyer's surreptitious investigation might violate federal or state electronic privacy laws, computer fraud and abuse acts, or statutes regulating pretexting. Importantly, Model Rule 8.4(b) does not require a criminal charge, complaint, prosecution, guilty plea, *Alford* plea, plea of no contest, or conviction to find a violation,[93] although any of the last four events establishes a violation where the underlying conduct renders the lawyer unfit to practice.[94]

H. Model Rule 8.4(c)

Chief among the rules of professional conduct applicable to lawyers engaged in covert investigations and surreptitious discovery is Model Rule 8.4(c), which states that it is professional misconduct for a lawyer to "engage in conduct involving dishonesty, fraud, deceit or misrepresentation."[95] The standard by which a lawyer's alleged dishonesty is to be judged under Rule 8.4(c) varies.[96] Many courts hold that a lawyer's false statement must be

93. *See, e.g.*, *In re* Ivy, 374 P.3d 374, 379 (Alaska 2016) ("Neither the text of Rule 8.4(b) nor the commentary to it requires an underlying criminal conviction. Rather, . . . Rule 8.4(b) contemplates the criminal *nature* of an attorney's misconduct." (footnote omitted)); Ligon v. Newman, 231 S.W.3d 662, 670 (Ark. 2006) ("Nothing in [Rule 8.4(b)] requires that there be a formal charge or conviction before the rules can be applied to an attorney's conduct."); Iowa Sup. Ct. Att'y Disciplinary Bd. v. Moran, 919 N.W.2d 754, 759 (Iowa 2018) (referring to a criminal conviction); Ky. Bar Ass'n v. Greene, 386 S.W.3d 717, 730 (Ky. 2012) (stating that a lawyer can violate the Kentucky equivalent of Model Rule 8.4(b) absent criminal charges or a conviction); *In re* Williams, 85 So. 3d 583, 591 (La. 2012) (explaining that the lack of a criminal conviction does not bar discipline for violating Rule 8.4(b)); Att'y Grievance Comm'n of Md. v. Bellamy, 162 A.3d 848, 863 (Md. 2017) ("Absence of criminal prosecution does not necessarily mean Rule 8.4(b) has not been violated."); *In re* Treinen, 131 P.3d 1282, 1284 (N.M. 2006) (discussing a New Mexico statute and stating that a criminal conviction is not a prerequisite to discipline for criminal conduct); *In re* Savage, 91 A.3d 356, 357 (R.I. 2014) (discussing criminal convictions); *In re* Disciplinary Proc. Against Kamb, 305 P.3d 1091, 1099 (Wash. 2013) ("[A]n attorney may be sanctioned for committing a crime for which he was never charged."); *In re* Disciplinary Proc. Against Inglimo, 740 N.W.2d 125, 136 n.12 (Wis. 2007) (noting that a lawyer may violate Rule 8.4(b) even without being charged or convicted of a crime).

94. *See, e.g.*, *In re* Najim, 405 P.3d 1223, 1233 (Kan. 2017) (stating that a criminal judgment is conclusive evidence in a disciplinary proceeding that a crime was committed); Att'y Grievance Comm'n of Md. v. Paul, 187 A.3d 625, 634 (Md. 2018) ("Paul's pleading guilty and subsequent conviction is conclusive proof that Paul committed a criminal act."); *In re* Toman, 206 A.3d 345, 345 (N.J. 2019) (basing discipline on the lawyer's no contest plea to corrupting the morals of a minor); Morrissey v. Va. State Bar *ex rel.* Third Dist. Comm., 829 S.E.2d 738, 745 (Va. 2019) (involving an *Alford* plea to contributing to the delinquency of a minor).

95. Model Rules of Prof'l Conduct R. 8.4(c) (2020); *see In re* Ekekwe-Kaufman, 210 A.3d 775, 795–96 (D.C. 2019) (explaining the differences between dishonesty, fraud, deceit, and misrepresentation under Rule 8.4(c)).

96. *See, e.g.*, *In re* Wysolmerski, 237 A.3d 706, 714 (Vt. 2020) (stating that "some scienter is required to support a violation of Rule 8.4(c)").

knowingly made to violate Rule 8.4(c).[97] Other jurisdictions hold that lawyers may violate Rule 8.4(c) through statements made with reckless disregard for their truth or falsity,[98] or through grossly negligent misstatements.[99] A very few courts hold that a lawyer may negligently violate Rule 8.4(c).[100] Whether either of the first two possibilities represents the majority rule is a close call, but the view that a lawyer may violate Rule 8.4(c) through simple negligence is a distinctly minority position, and rightly so.

Model Rule 8.4(c) is very broad; it applies to lawyers' dealings with anyone, including adverse parties, clients, courts and other tribunals, opposing counsel, witnesses, members of the public, and government agencies.[101] The rule attaches to lawyers' conduct outside the practice of law.[102] Model Rule 8.4(c) does not require a statement; deceit and dishonesty can also be based on the concealment or omission of facts or information.[103] Conduct that may not legally be characterized as fraudulent, or that would not constitute a misrepresentation as a matter of criminal or tort law, may still evince dishonesty for purposes of discipline under Rule 8.4(c).[104] Lawyers violate Rule 8.4(c) even if their dishonesty misleads no one or causes no harm.[105] Notably, Model Rule 8.4(c) does not contain an exception for conduct by lawyers engaged in surreptitious discovery or covert investigations. That is an obvious problem given the rule's prohibition of dishonesty, deceit, and misrepresentation by lawyers. As we will see in Part V of this chapter, however, some

---

97. Fla. Bar v. Schwartz, 284 So. 3d 393, 396 (Fla. 2019); Att'y Grievance Comm'n of Md. v. Mungin, 96 A.3d 122, 133–34 (Md. 2014); *In re* Firstenberger, 878 N.E.2d 912, 913–14 (Mass. 2007); *In re* Conduct of Skagen, 149 P.3d 1171, 1184 (Or. 2006). Oklahoma goes even further. To violate Rule 8.4(c) in Oklahoma, "[a]n intent element is required and the complainant must adequately show the attorney had a purpose to deceive." State *ex rel.* Okla. Bar Ass'n v. Siegrist, 461 P.3d 213, 217 (Okla. 2020).

98. People v. Head, 332 P.3d 117, 129 (Colo. 2013); *In re* Ukwu, 926 A.2d 1106, 1113–14 (D.C. 2007); Iowa Sup. Ct. Att'y Disciplinary Bd. v. Kozlik, 943 N.W.2d 589, 595 (Iowa 2020) (quoting Iowa Sup. Ct. Att'y Disciplinary Bd. v. Clarity, 838 N.W.2d 648, 656 (Iowa 2013)); Office of Disciplinary Couns. v. Surrick, 749 A.2d 441, 445 (Pa. 2000).

99. Walker v. Sup. Ct. Comm. on Prof'l Conduct, 246 S.W.3d 418, 424 (Ark. 2007).

100. *See, e.g.*, *In re* Doughty, 832 A.2d 724, 734–35 (Del. 2003).

101. *See, e.g.*, Att'y Grievance Comm'n of Md. v. Maldonado, 203 A.3d 841, 861–62 (Md. 2019) (finding that the lawyer violated Rule 8.4(c) when she referred to herself as a doctor while calling a doctor's office to bypass the doctor's office staff to speak to the doctor about her client; the lawyer testified that she sometimes used the title of "Doctor" to hide the fact that she was a lawyer because she had found that doctors' offices hesitated to speak with lawyers).

102. People v. Pautler, 35 P.3d 571, 581 (Colo. 2001) (*In re Pautler I*); *In re* Mintz, 317 P.3d 756, 761–64 (Kan. 2014); Att'y Grievance Comm'n of Md. v. Johnson, 976 A.2d 245, 261 (Md. 2009); *see, e.g.*, *In re* Savage, 91 A.3d 356, 357–58 (R.I. 2014) (concluding that lawyer violated Rule 8.4(c) by lying on her application for a driver's license).

103. Att'y Grievance Comm'n of Md. v. Floyd, 929 A.2d 61, 70 (Md. 2007); *In re* Disciplinary Proc. Against Knickmeier, 683 N.W.2d 445, 464 (Wis. 2004).

104. *In re* Shorter, 570 A.2d 760, 768 (D.C. 1990).

105. Ansell v. Statewide Grievance Comm., 865 A.2d 1215, 1223 (Conn. App. Ct. 2005).

jurisdictions have modified Rule 8.4 or its commentary to permit lawyers some leeway in this context.

I. Model Rule 8.4(d)

Finally, lawyers' surreptitious discovery and investigations may trigger the Model Rule 8.4(d) prohibition on conduct "prejudicial to the administration of justice."[106] Although such conduct defies precise definition,[107] Model Rule 8.4(d) is sure to apply to lawyers' misconduct in litigation.[108] As one court explained, a lawyer's conduct is "prejudicial to the administration of justice" if it "bears directly on a case in the judicial process with respect to an identifiable case or tribunal" and "taints the judicial process in more than a *de minimis* way."[109] Alternatively, conduct prejudicial to the administration of justice may be described as that which "impedes the efficient operation of the courts and wastes judicial resources,"[110] "harms (or has the potential to harm) either the substantive rights of a party to the proceeding or the procedural functioning of a case or hearing,"[111] or "is likely to impair public confidence in the profession, impact the image of the legal profession and engender disrespect for the court."[112] A lawyer need not intend to impair, impede, or taint the judicial process or harm a party's substantive rights to violate Model Rule 8.4(d);[113] negligent conduct will suffice.[114] With respect to all three descriptions, it is easy to picture investigation and litigation scenarios that implicate the identified concerns.

A lawyer may violate Model Rule 8.4(d) through conduct that merely has the potential to seriously and adversely affect the judicial process; actual impairment or harm is not required.[115] A lawyer's purely private conduct

106. Model Rules of Prof'l Conduct R. 8.4(d) (2020).

107. Iowa Sup. Ct. Att'y Disciplinary Bd. v. Goedken, 939 N.W.2d 97, 107 (Iowa 2020) (quoting Iowa Sup. Ct. Att'y Disciplinary Bd. v. Weiland, 885 N.W.2d 198, 212 (Iowa 2016)).

108. *See, e.g.*, *In re* Anonymous, 896 N.E.2d 916, 917 (Ind. 2008) (determining that lawyer violated Rules 4.4(a) and 8.4(d) through abusive use of subpoenas); *In re* Pyle, 91 P.3d 1222, 1231 (Kan. 2004) (finding that lawyer's conduct that violated Rule 4.4 was "obviously prejudicial to the administration of justice," and therefore violated Rule 8.4(d) as well); *In re* Miniclier, 74 So. 3d 687, 693 (La. 2011) (concluding that a lawyer violated Rule 8.4(d) because his "conduct forced the defendants to expend additional time and money defending his repeated attempts to circumvent the court's rulings and frustrated the legal system by prolonging the underlying legal matter").

109. *In re* Hallmark, 831 A.2d 366, 374 (D.C. 2003).

110. Iowa Sup. Ct. Att'y Disciplinary Bd. v. McGinness, 844 N.W.2d 456, 463 (Iowa 2014).

111. *In re* Conduct of Maurer, 431 P.3d 410, 416 (Or. 2018).

112. Att'y Grievance Comm'n of Md. v. Agbaje, 93 A.3d 262, 274 (Md. 2014).

113. *In re* Disciplinary Action Against Kennedy, 864 N.W.2d 342, 347 (Minn. 2015).

114. *In re* Martinez, 462 P.3d 36, 45 (Ariz. 2020) (quoting *In re* Alexander, 300 P.3d 536, 546 (Ariz. 2013)).

115. *In re* Uchendu, 812 A.2d 933, 941 (D.C. 2002); *see In re Martinez*, 462 P.3d at 45 ("A lawyer's conduct violates [Rule] 8.4(d) if it causes injury or potential injury.").

may be deemed prejudicial to the administration of justice if it is "criminal or so egregious as to make the harm, or potential harm, flowing from it patent."[116]

III. Undercover Activities

The use of undercover operatives, which is widely accepted in criminal investigations by government agencies, is also common in civil cases. For example, members of the American Society of Composers, Authors and Publishers (ASCAP) use undercover operatives to gather evidence for copyright infringement actions. ASCAP operatives visit bars and restaurants to find music being played in violation of copyright protections. Employment and housing applicants who think they were denied opportunities because of illegal discrimination use disguised "discrimination testers" to investigate offending entities. Public interest groups have agents take jobs in industries and then secretly record their activities in efforts to expose inhumane, unsafe, or unlawful practices. Defendants in personal injury and workers' compensation cases employ investigators to detect fraud and malingering by plaintiffs. Employers use undercover investigators to ferret out employee drug use and theft. Lawyers who are seeking to protect their clients' trademarks dispatch investigators posing as customers to distributors' showrooms and warehouses to gather evidence of substitute goods being "palmed off" or "passed off."

In addition to employing undercover investigators, lawyers themselves may conceal or misrepresent their identities to gather information for use in litigation. For example, a lawyer might pose as a customer when calling a company to investigate its sales practices. Lawyers might also direct their secretaries, legal assistants, or associates to do the same thing.

A. Using Undercover Investigators in Civil Litigation

Midwest Motor Sports v. Arctic Cat Sales, Inc.[117] illustrates the risks that accompany lawyers' employment of undercover investigators. This case arose out of a dispute between a snowmobile manufacturer, Arctic Cat, and two Arctic Cat dealers, Elliott and A-Tech. Elliott sued Arctic Cat for unlawfully terminating Elliott's franchise and establishing A-Tech as a new franchisee in the same city. Arctic Cat's lawyers, Roger Damgaard and Timothy Shattuck, hired a private investigator, Timothy Mohr, to visit Elliott's showroom to determine what products Elliott's sales force was promoting, what

116. Att'y Grievance Comm'n v. Link, 844 A.2d 1197, 1211–12 (Md. 2004).
117. 347 F.3d 693 (8th Cir. 2003).

products were on display to determine what brands of snowmobiles were selling best, and whether Elliott was suffering financially from the loss of the Arctic Cat franchise. Mohr wore a hidden recording device to memorialize his conversations with Elliott personnel.[118]

Damgaard and Shattuck did not give Mohr a script of what to ask during his showroom visits, but they did indicate subjects that they wanted him to address. Mohr asked them whether he could legally record conversations with represented parties; they assured him that his conduct was legal but did not discuss with him its ethical implications.[119]

Mohr twice visited the Elliott showroom posing as a customer and recorded his conversations with a salesman. Mohr also visited the A-Tech showroom, where he visited with A-Tech's president, Jon Becker, and recorded that conversation. Mohr did not reveal to Elliott or A-Tech why he was visiting their showrooms or that he was wearing a recording device.[120] At the same time, Arctic Cat's attorneys served Elliott and A-Tech with requests to inspect, photograph, and videotape their dealerships pursuant to Federal Rule of Civil Procedure 34.

Elliott and A-Tech sought sanctions against Arctic Cat for Mohr's clandestine activities. As a sanction, the district court excluded Mohr's audio recordings and any evidence gleaned from those recordings. Arctic Cat appealed.

One of the issues on appeal was Arctic Cat's counsel's alleged violation of Rule 4.2 and, more particularly, whether Mohr spoke with anyone at Elliott or A-Tech who could be said to personify either entity. Of course, Mohr had spoken with A-Tech's president, Becker. Damgaard and Shattuck attempted to deflect responsibility to Mohr, asserting that they directed him to speak only to low-level salespeople, but the Eighth Circuit would have none of it:

> [L]awyers cannot escape responsibility for the wrongdoing they supervise by asserting that it was their agents . . . who committed the wrong. Although Arctic Cat's attorneys did not converse with Becker themselves, the Rules also prohibit contact performed by an investigator acting as counsel's agent. . . . "Since a lawyer is barred under Rule 4.2 from communicating with a represented party about the subject matter of the representation, she may not circumvent the Rule by sending an investigator to do on her behalf that which she herself is forbidden to do." . . . In other words, an attorney is responsible for the misconduct of his nonlawyer employee or associate if the lawyer orders or ratifies the conduct. . . . Accordingly, we conclude that

118. *Id.* at 695.
119. *Id.* at 695–96.
120. *Id.* at 696.

> Arctic Cat's attorneys are ethically responsible for Mohr's conduct in communicating with Becker as if they had made the contact themselves.[121]

The *Midwest Motor Sports* court also was troubled by Mohr's conversations with Elliott's low-level salesman, "Bill," who told him that Elliott had made a business decision to drop the Artic Cat line—a potentially damaging party admission. Because Elliott's counsel clearly would have advised Bill against making such a statement to Mohr, the court had "no doubt" that Rule 4.2 applied to Mohr's conversation with Bill.[122]

Although the Rule 4.2 violations alone justified the trial court's sanctions, the sanctions were further justified by the "false and misleading pretenses" under which Mohr visited Elliott and A-Tech.[123] This justification stood even though South Dakota law permitted one party to a conversation to record that conversation without the other party's consent or knowledge. In brushing aside the South Dakota law on this point, the court observed that "conduct that is legal may not be ethical."[124]

The court reasoned that nonconsensual recordings should be prohibited where they are accompanied by other indicia of unethical behavior.[125] The Rule 4.2 violations tipped the scales against Arctic Cat. Furthermore, the "duty to refrain from conduct that involves deceit or misrepresentation should preclude any attorney from participating in the type of surreptitious conduct that occurred here."[126] Arctic Cat employed Mohr in a ruse to gain an advantage at trial, a tactic falling squarely within the Rule 8.4(c) prohibition on "conduct involving dishonesty, fraud, deceit or misrepresentation."[127] The court also rejected Arctic Cat's defense that it employed Mohr only after traditional means of discovery had failed. If Arctic Cat was frustrated by Elliott's or A-Tech's failure to cooperate in discovery, its remedy was a motion to compel discovery, not self-help.[128]

In the end, the Eighth Circuit affirmed the district court's order excluding Mohr's tapes and any derivative evidence. The *Midwest Motor Sports* court declined to impose monetary sanctions against Arctic Cat or its lawyers, principally reasoning that because South Dakota law concerning the challenged conduct was not then fully developed, the district court's imposition of solely evidentiary sanctions was appropriate and adequate.[129]

121. *Id.* at 698 (citations omitted).
122. *Id.*
123. *Id.* at 698–99.
124. *Id.* at 699.
125. *Id.*
126. *Id.*
127. *Id.* at 700.
128. *Id.*
129. *Id.* at 701.

Midwest Motor Sports certainly is not an aberration.[130] In *In re Nolan*,[131] for example, the South Carolina Supreme Court publicly reprimanded an Arkansas lawyer whose private investigators traveled to South Carolina to pose as customers to obtain evidence to prove that the defendant in the underlying action was violating the plaintiffs' intellectual property rights.[132] The investigators made false statements to the defendant's employees and used tactics designed to induce the employees into making statements about the product at issue. The investigators secretly tape-recorded these conversations. The lawyer was unaware that secret tape-recording, pretexting, and dissembling violated South Carolina's ethics rules.[133] He acknowledged that he was obligated to research South Carolina law before sending his investigators to the state.[134]

The lawyer in *Bratcher v. Kentucky Bar Ass'n*,[135] Pamela Bratcher, represented Dennis Babbs in a wrongful termination case against his former employer, R.C. Components, Inc. Bratcher learned of a company called Document Reference Check (DRC), which was in the business of determining the type of references given by former employers. Bratcher hired DRC to learn what R.C. Components would say about Babbs. A DRC employee called R.C. Components' owner, identified herself as a prospective employer of Babbs, and requested information about him.[136] DRC transcribed the telephone conversation and gave it to Bratcher.

Bratcher sent a copy of the transcript to R.C. Components' defense counsel, who successfully moved to disqualify her from Babbs's representation and to suppress the transcript. In disqualifying Bratcher, the trial court found that she had violated Kentucky Rules of Professional Conduct 4.2 and 8.3(a), the latter of which is analogous to Model Rule 8.4(a) and prohibits lawyers from violating rules of professional conduct through the acts of another.[137] Bratcher's disqualification was affirmed on appeal.[138]

130. *See, e.g.*, *In re* Crossen, 880 N.E.2d 352, 358–68, 382–88 (Mass. 2008) (disbarring a lawyer who had private investigators pose as corporate executives and conduct fake employment interviews with a former judicial clerk to obtain information for use against a trial judge who had ruled against his clients); *In re* Curry, 880 N.E.2d 388, 392–400, 409–11 (Mass. 2008) (involving the same misconduct as *In re Crossen*); *In re* Ositis, 40 P.3d 500, 504–05 (Or. 2002) (reprimanding a lawyer who directed a private investigator to pose as a journalist to interview a party to a potential dispute).

131. 796 S.E.2d 841 (S.C. 2017).

132. *Id.* at 842.

133. *Id.*

134. *Id.*

135. 290 S.W.3d 648 (Ky. 2009).

136. *Id.* at 649.

137. *Id.*

138. Babbs v. Minton, No. 2004-CA-000332-OA, 2004 WL 1367621, at *3–4 (Ky. Ct. App. June 18, 2004).

The Kentucky Bar Association instituted disciplinary proceedings against Bratcher. She admitted to violating Kentucky Rules 4.2 and 8.3(a). The Kentucky Supreme Court publicly reprimanded her for the violations.[139]

Lawyers may land themselves in trouble when they direct non-lawyer staff members in investigative roles, as *Penda Corp. v. STK, LLC*[140] illustrates. There, Penda Corporation sued STK, LLC, Rick's Auto Repair, and CAR-MIC Enterprises, Inc. for patent infringement, unfair trade practices, and Lanham Act violations in the U.S. District Court for the Eastern District of Pennsylvania. STK moved to transfer venue to the Western District of Pennsylvania, where it was headquartered and principally did business, on the basis that it did not sell the allegedly infringing pickup truck bedliners in the Eastern District. Penda resisted the motion on the basis that STK sold the bedliners to a New Jersey distributor, Armor Deck, which in turn sold the product to numerous retailers in the Eastern District of Pennsylvania.

In fact, immediately before filing the first suit, a partner at Woodcock Washburn, Penda's local counsel, directed one of the firm's paralegals to call STK to learn whether STK bedliners were sold in the Philadelphia area.[141] The partner instructed the paralegal to make the call in order to determine whether venue was proper in the Eastern District, but he did not tell the paralegal what to say or how to conduct any conversations.[142] The paralegal made the call and spoke with Daniel Kuritz, an STK customer service manager, who told her that while STK did not sell its bedliners in the Philadelphia area, she should call the company's distributor, Armor Deck, which did. The paralegal then called Armor Deck, where she told the person who answered the phone, "Ray," that her husband wanted to purchase a new bedliner for his pickup truck.[143] She asked Ray whether she could purchase an STK bedliner in Philadelphia.[144] He gave her the name of two local retailers that carried STK bedliners.

When the paralegal's calls came to light, STK sought sanctions from Penda. STK argued that the paralegal's call to Kurtiz violated (1) Rule 4.2 because it concerned matters on which Penda knew STK to be represented and (2) Rule 8.4(c) because the paralegal told neither Kuritz nor Ray that they were speaking to a Woodcock Washburn agent in connection with

139. *Bratcher*, 290 S.W.3d at 649–50.
140. No. Civ. A. 03-5578, 2004 WL 1628907 (E.D. Pa. July 16, 2004).
141. *Id.* at *2.
142. *Id.* at *3.
143. *Id.* at *2.
144. *Id.*

litigation.[145] In response, Penda argued that the rule did not apply because at the time the paralegal made the calls, the first suit had not yet been filed. Even if Rule 4.2 generally applied, Penda continued, it did not apply to the paralegal's call to Kuritz because Kuritz, his title notwithstanding, lacked the requisite managerial capacity and thus was not covered by the rule, and the communication did not concern the subject of the litigation. The court rejected all three arguments.

With respect to the first argument, the court swiftly concluded that Rule 4.2 applied to pre-suit communications.[146] As for the second, the court agreed based on the facts presented that Kuritz did not possess managerial responsibility sufficient to implicate Rule 4.2. Unfortunately for Penda, however, the court went on to find that Kuritz was a person whose statements could constitute admissions on STK's part, thus placing him off-limits for Rule 4.2 purposes. Finally, the court easily determined that the paralegal's call to Kuritz was directly relevant to the subject of the litigation. The court therefore concluded that Woodcock Washburn violated Rule 4.2.[147]

The court determined that the paralegal's conduct in making the calls did not produce a Rule 8.4(c) violation. Although the paralegal may have engaged in misrepresentation by failing to identify herself and posing as a potential customer, the lawyer who directed her to make the calls did not instruct her what to say to anyone with whom she spoke, nor what to do when on the calls. Because the lawyer did not direct the paralegal's misrepresentations or knowingly ratify them, the court reasoned, he could not be responsible for the paralegal's conduct. As a result, there could be no Rule 8.4(c) violation.[148]

The question then became what to do about the Rule 4.2 violation, which, the *Prenda* court noted, "was not egregious."[149] The court decided to preclude Penda from using any information obtained through the ex parte communications, including "the fruit of [the] contact."[150]

---

145. *Id.* at *3.

146. *Id.* at *4 (citing United States v. Grass, 239 F. Supp. 2d 535, 540–41 (M.D. Pa. 2003); Inorganic Coatings, Inc. v. Falberg, 926 F. Supp. 517, 519 n.3 (E.D. Pa. 1995)).

147. *Id.* at *5.

148. *Id.*

149. *Id.*

150. *Id.* at *7 & n.7.

Other courts, however, have accepted litigants' undercover activities as ethical discovery methods,[151] as have state disciplinary authorities.[152] In *Gidatex, S.r.L. v. Campaniello Imports, Ltd.*,[153] for example, the plaintiff's lawyers hired private investigators to visit the defendant's business and secretly tape-record conversations with salespeople. Gidatex, which owned the furniture trademark "Saporiti Italia," correctly suspected that Campaniello was luring customers with signs and advertisements bearing the Saporiti Italia trademark, and then "palming off" or "passing off" other manufacturers' goods.[154] When Campaniello learned of the ruse, it moved to prevent Gidatex from offering its investigators' testimony and reports as evidence at trial, and it sought to exclude tapes made by the investigators. Campaniello asserted that the evidence should be excluded as a sanction for associated ethics violations by Gidatex's counsel.[155]

Campaniello alleged that Gidatex's attorneys had violated New York DR 7-102(A)(4), which prohibited attorneys from circumventing disciplinary rules through the actions of another and banned "conduct involving dishonesty, fraud, deceit or misrepresentation."[156] Campaniello also alleged violations of New York DR 7-104(A)(1), which generally prohibited ex parte communications with represented parties.[157] The court rejected both claims, stating:

151. *See, e.g.*, Turfgrass Grp., Inc. v. Ne. La. Turf Farms, LLC, No. 10-13544, 2013 WL 6145294, at *1–6 (W.D. La. Nov. 20, 2013) (engaging a private investigator to secretly record conversations with an alleged patent infringer's employees during visits to the infringer's business); Cartier v. Symbolix, Inc., 386 F. Supp. 2d 354, 362 (S.D.N.Y. 2005) (approving of the use of an undercover investigator in a trademark infringement case); Design Tex Grp., Inc. v. U.S. Vinyl Mfg. Corp., No. 04 Civ. 5002(JSR), 2005 WL 357125, at *1 (S.D.N.Y. Feb. 14, 2005) (finding no ethics violations where an investigator obtained a sample book by mail through the opponent's normal business routine); A.V. by Versace, Inc. v. Gianni Versace, S.p.A., No. 96 CIV. 972PKLTHK, 2002 WL 2012618, at *9 (S.D.N.Y. Sept. 3, 2002) (approving the actions of an investigator who used a false name to pose as a fashion industry buyer and who did not gain access to non-public portions of the adversary's business); Hill v. Shell Oil Co., 209 F. Supp. 2d 876, 879–80 (N.D. Ill. 2002) (finding no Rule 4.2 violation in a case involving secret videotaping of gas station employees where the plaintiffs alleged that African-American customers had to pre-pay for gas while other customers could pay after fueling); Apple Corps Ltd. v. Int'l Collectors Soc'y, 15 F. Supp. 2d 456, 473–75 (D.N.J. 1998) (finding that a lawyer did not violate New Jersey ethics rules in investigating a marketer's compliance with consent decree; the lawyer's secretary and investigators called the marketer in effort to purchase goods in violation of a consent decree).

152. *See, e.g.*, Ala. State Bar, Eth. Op. RO-2007-05, at 3–5 (2007) (discussing investigators posing as customers in pre-suit investigation into possible trademark infringement); NYCLA Eth. Op. 737, 2007 WL 7281470, at *4–5 (N.Y. Cnty. Lawyers' Ass'n, Comm. on Prof'l Ethics 2007) (permitting "dissemblance" by non-lawyer investigators supervised by lawyers in limited circumstances).

153. 82 F. Supp. 2d 119 (S.D.N.Y. 1999).

154. *Id.* at 120.

155. *Id.* at 119.

156. *Id.* at 121.

157. *Id.*

> These ethical rules should not govern situations where a party is legitimately investigating potential unfair business practices by use of an undercover [investigator] posing as a member of the general public engaging in ordinary business transactions with the target. To prevent this use of investigators might permit targets to freely engage in unfair business practices which are harmful to both trademark owners and consumers in general. Furthermore, excluding evidence obtained by such investigators would not promote . . . preservation of the attorney/client privilege.[158]

Rather than being unprofessional, "hiring investigators to pose as consumers is an accepted investigative technique."[159] This is especially true in trademark cases, where it is often impossible to discover or prove anticompetitive activity by any other means. Moreover, there was no evidence of unfair conduct by the investigators. They did not interview Campaniello's sales clerks or "trick them into making statements that they otherwise would not have made."[160] To the contrary, the investigators merely recorded Campaniello's normal business practices.

Finally, the court noted, Gidatex's attorneys were alleged to have violated disciplinary rules rather than statutes. Courts are free to admit evidence obtained by unethical means; the admissibility of evidence and the means by which it is obtained are separate issues. Because precluding the evidence would not serve the public interest or promote the goals of the New York disciplinary rules, the court denied Campaniello's motion.[161]

B. Lawyers Concealing or Disguising Their Identities in Civil Litigation

Instead of employing undercover investigators, some lawyers conceal or disguise their identities to gather evidence. This type of subterfuge can create a variety of difficult professional responsibility problems for the lawyers involved.[162] *In re Gatti*[163] is a representative case.

Oregon lawyer Daniel Gatti suspected that State Farm Insurance Co. and a medical review company that employed chiropractors to evaluate bodily injury claims, CMR, were scheming to unfairly deny benefits to

158. *Id.* at 122.
159. *Id.*
160. *Id.* at 126.
161. *Id.*
162. *See, e.g.*, Att'y Grievance Comm'n of Md. v. Maldonado, 203 A.3d 841, 861–62 (Md. 2019) (finding that the lawyer violated Rule 8.4(c) when she referred to herself as a doctor while calling a doctor's office to bypass the doctor's office staff to speak to the doctor about her client; the lawyer testified that she sometimes used the title of "Doctor" to hide the fact that she was a lawyer because she had found that doctors' offices hesitated to speak with lawyers); Disciplinary Couns. v. Brockler, 48 N.E.3d 557, 558–62 (Ohio 2016) (suspending but staying with conditions an assistant county prosecutor who created a fictitious Facebook account to contact alibi witnesses of a defendant who had been indicted for murder).
163. 8 P.3d 966 (Or. 2000).

injured claimants. In May 1994, Gatti received a copy of a CMR report concerning one of his clients that was prepared by a chiropractor named Becker. Gatti believed that State Farm had denied his client's claim based on Becker's report. Acting "'more out of stupidity than anything,'"[164] Gatti called Becker, claimed to be a chiropractor, and questioned Becker about his qualifications.[165] Becker soon became uncomfortable with Gatti's questioning and ended the call.

Gatti next called Adams, a CMR vice president who directed the company's operations. Gatti introduced himself as a doctor with experience reviewing insurance claims and performing independent medical examinations (IMEs).[166] Gatti told Adams that he saw patients, conducted IMEs, reviewed cases, and wanted to become involved in CMR's educational programs for insurance adjusters. He also told Adams that he was interested in working for CMR and that Becker and State Farm had referred him to the company.[167] Adams believed Gatti's story and referred him to another CMR executive, Householder, to discuss possible employment. Gatti called Householder, who knew that Gatti was a lawyer with no interest in working for CMR.

In July 1994, Adams filed a disciplinary complaint against Gatti with the Oregon State Bar. The Bar charged Gatti with violating two ethics rules, DR 1-102(A)(3) (prohibiting conduct involving dishonesty, fraud, deceit, or misrepresentation) and DR 7-102(A)(5) (knowingly making false statements of law or fact), as well as violating an Oregon statute, ORS 9.527(4), which prohibited willful deceit or misconduct in the legal profession.[168] The case reached the Oregon Supreme Court.

Gatti clearly violated both DR 1-102(A)(3) and DR 7-102(A)(5).[169] Gatti, however, advocated an "investigatory exception" to the disciplinary rules.[170] He proposed that "as long as misrepresentations are limited only to identity or purpose and [are] made solely for purposes of discovering information, there is no violation of the Code of Professional Responsibility."[171] According to Gatti, this exception was necessary "if lawyers in private practice, like their counterparts in the government, are to be successful in their efforts to 'root out evil.'"[172]

164. *Id.* at 970 (quoting Gatti in characterizing his own conduct).
165. *Id.*
166. *Id.*
167. *Id.*
168. *Id.* at 973–74.
169. *See id.* at 973–74.
170. *Id.* at 974.
171. *Id.*
172. *Id.*

The trial panel Gatti appeared before refused to recognize an exception to the rules or statute either for government lawyers or for private practitioners, reasoning that the disciplinary rules applied to all Oregon lawyers without exception.[173] On appeal, the U.S. Attorney for the District of Oregon and the Oregon Attorney General weighed in as amicus curiae, arguing that government attorneys supervising legitimate law enforcement activities involving deception or covert activities should not be held to violate DR 1-102(A)(3). Oregon consumer groups also appeared as amicus curiae, arguing that private practitioners should also be allowed to ethically engage in covert activities to root out fraud and illegality. Resolving that a clear answer regarding exceptions to the disciplinary rules was in order, the court stated:

> Faithful adherence to the wording of DR 1-102(A)(3), DR 7-102(A)(5), ORS 9.527(4), and this court's case law does not permit an exception for *any* lawyer to engage in dishonesty, fraud, deceit, misrepresentation, or false statements. In our view, this court should not create an exception to the rules by judicial decree. Instead, any exception must await the full debate that is contemplated by the process for adopting and amending the Code of Professional Responsibility. . . . We decline to adopt an exception to DR 1-102(A)(3) and DR 7-102(A)(5), and we are without authority to read into ORS 9.527(4) an exception that the statute does not contain. *Those disciplinary rules and the statute apply to all members of the Bar, without exception.*[174]

The court settled on a public reprimand as appropriate discipline. In doing so, it noted that many lawyers mistakenly believe that they can misrepresent their identities and purposes to obtain information, and it was merely happenstance that Gatti, and not some other Oregon lawyer, was the subject of these proceedings.[175] In response to the *In re Gatti* decision, Oregon adopted a new ethics rule on undercover investigations and surreptitious discovery.[176]

C. Criminal Cases

Although once the subject of considerable controversy and debate, it is now settled that government lawyers, including federal prosecutors, are generally bound to obey Rule 4.2 in the absence of jurisdiction-specific exceptions.[177]

173. *Id.*

174. *Id.* at 976 (latter emphasis added).

175. *Id.* at 979.

176. Or. Rules of Prof'l Conduct R. 8.4(b) (2014).

177. United States v. O'Keefe, 132 F.3d 1252, 1253–57 (8th Cir. 1998) (applying Missouri rule); SEC v. Lines, 669 F. Supp. 2d 460, 463 (S.D.N.Y. 2009) (noting that Rule 4.2 applies to

And, like private attorneys, government lawyers cannot bypass inconvenient ethics rules by directing non-lawyer agents to do for them that which they cannot do directly.[178] Nonetheless, Rule 4.2 does "not prevent non-custodial pre-indictment communications by undercover agents with represented parties which occur in the course of legitimate criminal investigations."[179] Accordingly, government attorneys do not violate these rules by supervising such investigations.

Similarly, government lawyers may supervise lawful covert activities by law enforcement personnel that involve deception and misrepresentation to gather information without violating Rule 8.4(c).[180] Law officers who are licensed attorneys, as many FBI agents are, may engage in lawful covert activities that gather information through dishonesty, deceit, and misrepresentation without violating Rule 8.4(c).[181] In both instances, however, any Rule 8.4(c) exception for government lawyers is a narrow one. Government lawyers who engage in illegal or unlawful conduct may violate Rule 8.4(c) and analogous rules,[182] as well as Rule 8.4(d),[183] and by no means do they have blanket permission to misrepresent themselves or to ignore other legal duties compelling honesty.[184]

As for government lawyers misleading people as to their identities when acting in representational roles, courts' intolerance is evidenced by the decision in *In re Pautler*,[185] where Colorado prosecutor Mark Pautler posed as

SEC lawyers); State v. Buckingham, 772 N.W.2d 64, 70 (Minn. 2009); *In re* Howes, 940 P.2d 159, 165–69 (N.M. 1997) (applying the analogous New Mexico rule).

178. *See Buckingham*, 772 N.W.2d at 70 (explaining that a prosecutor cannot speak with a represented defendant ex parte and that police conduct may be imputed to a prosecutor where the prosecutor orders or ratifies the conduct).

179. United States v. Grass, 239 F. Supp. 2d 535, 541 (M.D. Pa. 2003) (citing cases); *see also* United States v. Carona, 630 F.3d 917, 920–24 (9th Cir. 2011) (applying then-California Rule 2-100); United States v. Balter, 91 F.3d 427, 436 (3d Cir. 1996) (finding no "party" for purposes of New Jersey Rule 4.2 and further applying the "authorized by law" exception to the rule); United States v. Ryans, 903 F.2d 731, 734–40 (10th Cir. 1990) (holding that ethical proscriptions on ex parte communications "do not attach during the investigative process before the initiation of criminal proceedings"; the target had been served with a grand jury subpoena, but "had not been charged, arrested or indicted," or otherwise faced with prosecutorial forces).

180. Utah Eth. Op. 02-05, 2002 WL 459018, at *1 (Utah State Bar 2002) [hereinafter Utah Eth. Op. 02-05].

181. D.C. Bar, Legal Ethics Comm., Op. 323, at 4 (2004) [hereinafter D.C. Op. 323]; Utah Eth. Op. 02-05, *supra* note 180, at *3–4 (discussing Rule 8.4(c)).

182. Utah Eth. Op. 02-05, *supra* note 180, at *4.

183. Model Rules of Prof'l Conduct R. 8.4(d) (2020) (prohibiting conduct prejudicial to the administration of justice); *see, e.g.*, *In re* Neary, 84 N.E.3d 1194, 1196–98 (Ind. 2017) (suspending a prosecutor for four years for violating Rules 4.4(a) and 8.4(d) by eavesdropping on conversations between criminal defendants and their lawyers).

184. D.C. Op. 323, *supra* note 181, at 4; *see, e.g.*, Disciplinary Couns. v. Brockler, 48 N.E.3d 557, 558–60, 562 (Ohio 2016) (finding that a prosecutor who created a fictitious Facebook page to contact a defendant's alibi witnesses violated Rules 8.4(c) and (d)).

185. *In re* Pautler, 47 P.3d 1175 (Colo. 2002) (*In re Pautler II*).

a public defender to secure a murderer's surrender. Responding to Pautler's defense that the circumstances justified his departure from Colorado Rule of Professional Conduct 8.4(c), which prohibits lawyers from engaging "'in conduct involving dishonesty, fraud, deceit or misrepresentation,'"[186] the Colorado Supreme Court explained that "[t]his rule and its commentary are devoid of any exception."[187] Colorado ethics rules generally do not "distinguish lawyers working in law enforcement from other lawyers."[188] Pautler's purposeful deception was "intolerable," regardless of his motives.[189]

In 2009, the Wisconsin Supreme Court expressed tolerance for criminal defense lawyers' surreptitious discovery tactics in an unreported decision.[190] There, Stephen Hurley represented Gordon Sussman in a case involving allegations of sexual assault on a minor, exhibiting harmful material to a child, and possession of child pornography. The sexual assault charges were based on statement made by a 15-year-old boy, S.B., who became acquainted with Sussman through a mentoring program and spent time at Sussman's business. The child pornography charges were based on images found on a computer used by Sussman at his business.

Hurley doubted the boy's credibility and believed that he was lying with respect to the allegations against Sussman—especially his claims that Sussman had forced him to view child pornography. Hurley believed that S.B. had an independent interest in, and access to, child pornography. Because S.B. had access to Sussman's work computer, Hurley considered S.B.'s independent proclivity to view child pornography a critical factor in Sussman's defense. Quite logically, Hurley believed that S.B.'s personal computer would hold exculpatory evidence in the form of illicit images.

Hurley believed that S.B. would destroy any evidence of his wrongdoing if he knew of Hurley's desire to examine his computer. Hurley considered the police detective assigned to the case to be heavily biased toward S.B. and thus of no assistance to the defense. As a result, Hurley considered a private investigation involving deceit to be his only avenue of obtaining the critical evidence he expected to find on S.B.'s computer.[191] Hurley accordingly devised a plan to trick S.B. and his mother into giving S.B.'s computer to Hurley's private investigator.

Hurley's private investigator sent S.B. a letter on letterhead belonging to a company in which the investigator was a part owner.[192] The letter informed S.B. that the company was researching computer usage preferences

186. *Id.* at 1179 (quoting Colo. R. Prof'l Conduct 8.4(c)).
187. *Id.*
188. *Id.*
189. *Id.* at 1176.
190. Office of Lawyer Regul. v. Hurley, No. 2007AP478-D (Wis. Feb. 11, 2009).
191. *Id.* at 2.
192. *Id.*

of students and young adults and that S.B. had been selected to receive a new computer free of charge. The letter further advised S.B. that to receive the new computer, he would have to trade his existing computer for the new model for a 90-day trial period, during which the company would store his old computer. Hurley instructed the investigator not to approach S.B. unless S.B.'s mother was present and to allow S.B. to remove anything he wanted from his computer before making the exchange.[193]

S.B. took the bait, and the investigator met with him and his mother.[194] The boy agreed to exchange his desktop computer for a new laptop model provided by the investigator. After making the deal, the investigator went outside to allow S.B. to remove anything he wanted from his computer. After doing so, the investigator collected S.B.'s desktop and delivered it to a forensic computer specialist. The specialist analyzed the computer and found numerous pornographic images involving adults, animals, and children.[195]

Wisconsin disciplinary authorities charged Hurley with violating Rule 4.1(a) for knowingly making a false statement of material fact or law to a third person and Rule 8.4(c) for conduct involving dishonesty, fraud, deceit, or misrepresentation.[196] A disciplinary referee found that Hurley's conduct was permissible, influenced by the fact that prosecutors routinely employ similar deception in their investigations and by testimony presented at Hurley's disciplinary hearing that made clear that there was a widespread perception among Wisconsin lawyers that Hurley's conduct was acceptable. In finding for Hurley, the referee wrote:

> "Mr. Hurley was faced with a very difficult decision, with concurrent and conflicting obligations: should he zealously defend his client, fulfill his constitutional obligation to provide effective assistance of counsel, and risk breaking a vague ethical rule that, according to the record, had never been enforced in this way? Or should he knowingly fail to represent Mr. Sussman in the manner to which he was entitled and hand him persuasive grounds for appeal, an ethics complaint, and a malpractice claim? The Sixth Amendment seems to have broken the tie for Mr. Hurley. . . . A man's liberty was at stake. Mr. Hurley had to choose, and he chose reasonably, in light of his obligations and the vagueness of the [Wisconsin ethics rules]."[197]

The Wisconsin Supreme Court agreed with the referee and found that the complaint against Hurley should be dismissed. The court reasoned that prosecutors employed the type of dissemblance in which Hurley engaged, and there was no precedent suggesting that defense lawyers should be

193. *Id.*
194. *Id.* at 3.
195. *Id.*
196. *Id.*
197. *Id.* (quoting the referee's report and recommendations).

treated differently in this regard.[198] Moreover, it was clear from the record that there was a widespread belief among Wisconsin lawyers that such tactics were acceptable, that Hurley did not intend to break any ethics rules, and that he may not have known that his conduct would even support disciplinary charges.[199]

D. Analyzing the Professional Responsibility Issues

Before analyzing the various professional responsibility issues that regularly surface in cases involving surreptitious discovery and covert investigations, it must be acknowledged that as a general rule, courts are more likely to tolerate acts of deception by lawyers or their agents if the challenged discovery or investigation uncovered wrongdoing.[200] The result in *Hurley*, for example, arguably illustrates courts' unstated recognition that in the context of investigations, the ends sometimes justify the means. For lawyers, the lesson is simple: choose your targets wisely. Do not employ deceptive investigatory techniques unless you are highly confident that they will reveal suspected misconduct. Investigative success will not guarantee that you escape discipline or sanctions, but as a practical matter, failure increases the likelihood of negative consequences.

Now, looking first at attorneys' employment of undercover investigators in civil cases, the problems that lawyers face are very practical. For example, when a lawyer investigates before suing, it may be difficult for her to know whether the target of her investigation is represented by counsel in the matter.[201] In cases involving organizational litigants, lawyers cannot necessarily avoid problems by instructing investigators to speak only with low-level employees because even low-level employees may be off-limits in some jurisdictions if their acts or omissions can be imputed to the organization, or if they can bind the organization through their admissions. It is also possible that investigators will inadvertently speak to employees with whom ex parte communication clearly is forbidden.

Although it is tempting to say that lawyers "probably can employ persons to play the role of customer seeking services on the same basis as the general public,"[202] cases such as *Midwest Motor Sports* suggest a different

198. *Id.* at 4.

199. *Id.*

200. *See, e.g.*, Apple Corps. Ltd. v. Int'l Collectors Soc'y, 15 F. Supp. 2d 456, 472–76 (D.N.J. 1998) (finding no ethics violations where at least one agent of the lawyer misrepresented her identity while investigating the opponent's compliance with a consent decree).

201. Gidatex, S.r.L. v. Campaniello Imports, Ltd., 82 F. Supp. 2d 119, 125 (S.D.N.Y. 1999) (stating that "[t]ypically, before a complaint is filed, there is uncertainty as to whether a party is represented").

202. Hill v. Shell Oil Co., 209 F. Supp. 2d 876, 880 (N.D. Ill. 2002).

conclusion at least in some jurisdictions.[203] Moreover, many of the cases approving lawyers' use of undercover investigators are district court decisions and therefore are not precedential. If any statement about lawyers' use of undercover investigators can safely be made, it is that, as with other forms of improper ex parte communication, courts should not penalize lawyers' Rule 4.2 violations by excluding any evidence wrongfully obtained.[204] If a lawyer violates Rule 4.2 through the use of undercover investigators, the aggrieved party's remedy is to complain to disciplinary authorities.[205] Alternatively, on the right facts, the court might properly disqualify the offending lawyer or award monetary sanctions. An exclusionary policy, however, often "frustrates truth and does not punish the ethical violation. Instead, it works against the client who may have been wronged by the opposing party as far as the substantive claim is concerned."[206] Thus, evidence obtained in violation of Rule 4.2 should be excluded only where its admission would taint the proceedings.[207] The same rationale applies where a lawyer is alleged to have violated Rule 4.3.[208]

For all the problems that Rules 4.2 and 4.3 pose in surreptitious investigations, it is easy to understand their limits. But what about lawyers' use of undercover investigators in situations potentially involving dishonesty, fraud, deceit, or misrepresentation?[209] This approach may also lead to possible trouble; again, Model Rule 8.4(c) contains no investigatory exceptions.[210]

Lawyers who deploy undercover investigators might argue that *they* do not engage in conduct involving dishonesty, fraud, deceit, or misrepresentation in the process; rather, it is the *investigators* who engage in that conduct. Thus, there is no Rule 8.4(c) violation. This argument is specious for three obvious reasons. First, Rule 8.4(c) prohibits conduct by lawyers "*involving* dishonesty, fraud, deceit or misrepresentation,"[211] which plainly indicates that lawyers may violate the rule through the actions or conduct of their agents. Second, but relatedly, the argument ignores Rule 8.4(a), which makes clear that lawyers may not avoid their professional duties by instructing

---

203. Midwest Motor Sports v. Arctic Cat Sales, Inc., 347 F.3d 693 (8th Cir. 2003).

204. *See, e.g.*, SEC v. Lines, 669 F. Supp. 2d 460, 464–65 (S.D.N.Y. 2009); *Gidatex, S.r.L.*, 82 F. Supp. 2d at 126; Johnson v. Cadillac Plastic Grp., Inc., 930 F. Supp. 1437, 1442 (D. Colo. 1996); Weider Sports Equip. Co. v. Fitness First, Inc., 912 F. Supp. 502, 510–11 (D. Utah 1996); Mena v. Key Food Stores Co-op., Inc., 758 N.Y.S.2d 246, 249 (Sup. Ct. 2003) (quoting cases).

205. *See Johnson*, 930 F. Supp. at 1442; *Weider*, 912 F. Supp. at 511.

206. *Johnson*, 930 F. Supp. at 1442.

207. *Lines*, 669 F. Supp. 2d at 465 (quoting United States v. Dennis, 843 F.2d 652, 657 (2d Cir. 1988)).

208. *See, e.g.*, *In re* Katrina Canal Breaches Consol. Litig., No. 05-4182 "K" (2), 2008 WL 2066999, at *7 (E.D. La. May 14, 2008).

209. *See* Model Rules of Prof'l Conduct R. 8.4(c) (2020).

210. *In re* Pautler, 47 P.3d 1175, 1179 (Colo. 2002) (*In re Pautler II*).

211. Model Rules of Prof'l Conduct R. 8.4(c) (2020) (emphasis added).

non-lawyer agents to do for them that which they cannot do themselves.[212] Third, the argument defies common sense. Undercover investigators do not appear magically in a current or potential adversary's place of business, nor is their secret taping of a current or potential adversary's employees' statements mere fortuity; they do what they do at lawyers' request and direction. Undercover investigators would not be covertly gathering information for use in litigation but for the request of the lawyers employing them. In short, lawyers cannot evade their obligations under Rule 8.4(c) by assigning responsibility to their investigators.[213]

A much better argument is that Model Rule 8.4(c) is not intended to apply to lawyers' use of undercover investigators. Courts analyze conduct allegedly constituting dishonesty, fraud, deceit, and misrepresentation on a case-by-case basis.[214] They generally define these terms to embrace characteristics reflecting negatively on lawyers' fitness to practice law.[215] Thus, it is reasonable to argue that to violate Rule 8.4(c), "the lawyer's conduct must indicate that the lawyer lacks those characteristics of trustworthiness and integrity that are essential to the practice of law."[216] In most cases, nothing about a lawyer's employment of undercover investigators indicates that the lawyer is untrustworthy or lacks integrity. Many legitimate investigations could never be undertaken without deception by investigators, and it is therefore nonsensical to broadly criticize such practices as being dishonest or unethical.[217] Indeed, lawyers employ undercover investigators in cases advancing laudable societal goals or policy objectives,[218] as where they deploy testers to uncover evidence of unlawful discrimination.[219]

This argument, although good, is not sure to succeed. Model Rule 8.4(c) contains no exception for legitimate covert investigations, and some courts hold that noble motives do not justify departures from the rules' clear

212. *Id.* R. 8.4(a) (making it "professional misconduct" for a lawyer to "violate or attempt to violate the Rules of Professional Conduct . . . through the acts of another").

213. *See, e.g.*, *In re* Pajerowski, 721 A.2d 992, 995 (N.J. 1998) (rejecting the lawyer's defense that he did not authorize an investigator to solicit clients to engage in "gross improprieties"); *In re* Ositis, 40 P.3d 500, 503–04 (Or. 2002) (rejecting the lawyer's claim that he did not direct an investigator's actions in posing as reporter to interview an adversary).

214. *In re* Carpenter, 95 P.3d 203, 208 (Or. 2004) (discussing "dishonesty").

215. *Id.* at 209; *In re* PRB Docket No. 2007-046, 989 A.2d 523, 528 (Vt. 2009).

216. *In re Carpenter*, 95 P.3d at 209; *see also In re PRB Docket No. 2007-046*, 989 A.2d at 528 (expressing a similar standard).

217. *See* Chloé v. DesignersImports.com USA, Inc., No. 07-CV-1791 (CS)(GAY), 2009 WL 1227927, at *9 (S.D.N.Y. Apr. 30, 2009).

218. *See, e.g.*, Gidatex, S.r.L. v. Campaniello Imports, Ltd., 82 F. Supp. 2d 119, 124 (S.D.N.Y. 1999) (asserting that "enforcement of the trademark laws to prevent consumer confusion is an important policy objective").

219. *See* Richardson v. Howard, 712 F.2d 319, 321 (7th Cir. 1983) (explaining the important role that testers play in race discrimination cases and observing that the deception they employ, while regrettable, is "a relatively small price to pay to defeat racial discrimination").

language.[220] It is foreseeable that a court weighing the conduct of a lawyer accused of unethically employing undercover investigators may decline to craft any exception to these rules, leaving that task to those bodies in the jurisdiction charged with adopting and amending ethics rules.

On the right facts, a lawyer might be able to argue against sanctions or discipline on the basis that any misrepresentation by an undercover investigator was immaterial, and therefore the lawyer is not guilty of conduct involving "misrepresentation" within the meaning of Rule 8.4(c). The argument goes something like this. Rule 4.1(a) provides that in the course of representing a client, "a lawyer shall not knowingly . . . make a false statement of material fact or law to a third person."[221] It is an established principle of statutory construction that "the drafters of a statute intended no redundancy, so that a statute should be construed, if possible, to give effect to its entire text."[222] Thus, if Rules 8.4(c) and 4.1(a) are to be harmonized, as they must be, a lawyer's "misrepresentation" violates Rule 8.4(c) only if it is "material." Any other reading of Rule 8.4(c) would render Rule 4.1(a) superfluous.[223]

It is easy to see how undercover investigators' misrepresentations could be immaterial. Consider a case in which investigators pose as customers to investigate allegedly unlawful sales practices. The mere fact that the investigators do not reveal their true status or motives to the target's sales staff is not material because it is a salesperson's job to visit with prospective customers.[224] The investigators' inquiries about product availability or features do not constitute material misrepresentations because it is a salesperson's job to answer such questions. As long as the investigators do not try to trick salespeople into doing or saying things that they would not normally do or say, their misrepresentations are immaterial, and the supervising lawyers do not violate Rule 8.4(c).

The problem with this argument is that it may rest on a faulty premise, namely that the failure to read a materiality requirement into the Rule 8.4(c) prohibition on "misrepresentation" renders Rule 4.1(a) superfluous. The comments to Model Rule 4.1 suggest that it is not rendered superfluous by the absence of a materiality requirement in Model Rule 8.4(c). Specifically, the commentary to Model Rule 4.1 states that for "dishonest conduct that

220. *See, e.g.*, *In re* Pautler, 47 P.3d 1175, 1180 (Colo. 2002) (*In re Pautler II*).

221. Model Rules of Prof'l Conduct R. 4.1(a) (2020).

222. Apple Corps Ltd. v. Int'l Collectors Soc'y, 15 F. Supp. 2d 456, 476 (D.N.J. 1998).

223. *Id.*

224. Gidatex, S.r.L. v. Campaniello Imports, Ltd., 82 F. Supp. 2d 119, 122 (S.D.N.Y. 1999) (discussing a plaintiff's use of undercover investigators to visit a defendant's showroom to detect trademark violations, the court observed that having operated a furniture business for two decades, "surely [the defendant] had come to expect that customers would enter the [defendant's] showroom during business hours, engage in conversation with sales clerks, make inquiries regarding various brands of furniture, and leave without making a purchase").

does not amount to a false statement," lawyers should "see Rule 8.4."[225] In other words, while a lawyer's material misrepresentation to a third person necessarily violates both Rule 4.1(a) and Rule 8.4(c), a lawyer may behave deceitfully or dishonestly without ever making a false statement of material fact or law, and thus violate Rule 8.4(c) without implicating Rule 4.1(a). This is consistent with the purpose of Rule 8.4(c), which is written broadly both to cover a wide array of offensive conduct and to prevent attempted manipulation of rules stated more narrowly.[226]

In summary, this is not an area where lines can be confidently drawn; at best, lawyers must evaluate associated risks on a continuum from "clearly impermissible to clearly permissible conduct."[227] In terms of practical guidance, lawyers considering an undercover investigation should first research the law in the relevant jurisdictions relating to Rules 4.1(a) and 8.4(c). If, after conducting the necessary research, the lawyer determines either that there is no law on point or that lawyers may supervise undercover investigations without violating Rules 4.1(a) or 8.4(c), the lawyer may have to conduct more legal research if the target of the investigation is an organization. If an organization is the target, the lawyer must research Rule 4.2 to determine which of the organization's employees the investigators may speak to and which are off limits. After that is done, the lawyer is prepared to plan the investigation. That planning must include careful instructions to investigators about whom they can speak to and what they can say. A target's employees should not be tricked into saying or doing things that they would not say or do in dealing with actual customers.[228]

As for lawyers misrepresenting their identities to gather information in civil cases, the rule is simple: never do it. Never lie. Any notion lawyers may hold about avoiding discipline or sanctions for misrepresenting their identities because they are functioning as investigators rather than as lawyers is misguided. There are several reasons for this. First, lawyers cannot simply switch hats as a matter of ethical convenience.[229] At least in civil cases, lawyers are lawyers even when functioning as investigators. Second, lawyers who misrepresent their identities while functioning as investigators are still involved in judicial proceedings, either because the investigation is

225. Model Rules of Prof'l Conduct R. 4.1 cmt. 1 (2020).

226. For a case reconciling Rules 4.1 and 8.4(c) on grounds different than those stated here, see *In re PRB Docket No. 2007-046*, 989 A.2d 523, 528–29 (Vt. 2009).

227. Hill v. Shell Oil Co., 209 F. Supp. 2d 876, 880 (N.D. Ill. 2002).

228. *See id.* ("Lawyers (and investigators) cannot trick protected employees into doing things or saying things that they otherwise would not do or say."); Gidatex, S.r.L. v. Campaniello Imports, Ltd., 82 F. Supp. 2d 119, 126 (S.D.N.Y. 1999) (finding no ethics violation where Gidatex's investigators did not trick sales clerks into making inadvisable statements).

229. *See, e.g.*, *In re* Malone, 482 N.E.2d 565 (N.Y. 1985) (disciplining the lawyer for violating Rule 8.4(c) analog while investigating allegations of brutality against inmates in his capacity as Inspector General of the State Department of Correctional Services).

a precursor to litigation or because litigation is already under way. The fact that the lawyer may be filling a slightly different role in a judicial proceeding does not change the overall context in which the deception occurs.[230] Third, lawyers may be disciplined for conduct involving dishonesty, fraud, deceit, or misrepresentation even if they are not acting as lawyers at the time because this conduct relates to their ability to practice law. Courts routinely discipline attorneys for dishonest conduct outside their law practices.[231]

In the criminal context, government attorneys enjoy far greater leeway in connection with undercover investigations than do private lawyers.[232] When it comes to misrepresenting their identities while functioning in traditional roles, however, government lawyers are subject to the same absolute prohibition confronting private lawyers.

Regardless of whether they employ investigators or personally engage in subterfuge, lawyers should never attempt to covertly or surreptitiously investigate courts, judges, or their employees.[233] Lawyers may investigate possible judicial bias, corruption, or incompetence for the purpose of taking appropriate action or may employ investigators to do so, but neither lawyers nor their investigators should engage in any sort of deception or

230. *See, e.g.*, NYAT Operating Corp. v. Jackson, Lewis, Schnitzler & Krupman, 741 N.Y.S.2d 385, 386 (App. Div. 2002) (involving a lawyer who allegedly lied in a deposition in her former clients' case and rejecting the lawyer's argument that she was not subject to a claim of deception and collusion because she was not serving as attorney at time of deposition).

231. *See, e.g.*, *In re* Mintz, 317 P.3d 756, 761–64 (Kan. 2014) (concluding that a lawyer violated Rule 8.4(c) by lying to the police about the circumstances of his intoxicated girlfriend's accidental death); Att'y Grievance Comm'n of Md. v. Fraidin, 91 A.3d 1078, 1096–97 (Md. 2014) (disbarring a lawyer who helped his wife commit bankruptcy fraud and observing that professional discipline is not confined to conduct in an attorney-client relationship); Att'y Grievance Comm'n of Md. v. Seltzer, 34 A.3d 498, 511 (Md. 2011) (noting that Rule 8.4(c) applies to lawyers' conduct outside the practice of law and finding that the lawyer violated the rule by acting dishonestly in operating a real estate agency); *In re* Carpenter, 95 P.3d 203, 207, 210 (Or. 2004) (finding that the lawyer violated the analogous Oregon rule by posting an unflattering message intended as a joke in an online forum under a pseudonym; the lawyer's dishonest conduct bore a functional relationship to his ability to practice law because it caused the court to question whether he possessed the trustworthiness and integrity required to handle clients' matters); *In re* Savage, 91 A.3d 356, 357–58 (R.I. 2014) (concluding that the lawyer violated Rule 8.4(c) by lying on her driver's license application); *In re* Disciplinary Proc. Against Michael, 805 N.W.2d 110, 111–12 (Wis. 2011) (disbarring a lawyer for various acts of dishonesty in running a bed and breakfast and apartment complex that she owned).

232. *See* Sequa Corp. v. Lititech, Inc., 807 F. Supp. 653, 663 (D. Colo. 1992) ("Law enforcement authorities are afforded license to engage in . . . deceptive acts to detect and prove criminal violations. Private attorneys are not."). Courts recognize that undercover investigations by law enforcement authorities further important public interests in detecting, preventing, and punishing crime. *See* United States v. Murphy, 768 F.2d 1518, 1529 (7th Cir. 1985) (discussing the role of undercover FBI agents posing as attorneys to investigate judicial corruption, the court observed that "[t]he creation of opportunities for crime is nasty but necessary business").

233. *See In re* Crossen, 880 N.E.2d 352, 370–71 (Mass. 2008) (discussing a lawyer's covert investigation into possible judicial misconduct).

deceit in this delicate process.[234] The safest course for lawyers who reasonably believe that courts or their employees have committed some type of misconduct, however, is to file complaints with the appropriate authorities and entrust any investigation to them.

E. Advice for Lawyers When Employing Investigators

Lawyers often employ private investigators to conduct informal discovery and discreet investigations. Lawyers who hire investigators are responsible for appropriately supervising them in accordance with Model Rule 5.3, just as they are responsible for any other non-lawyer over whom they have supervisory authority. At the same time, Rule 5.3 does not make lawyers strictly liable for the acts of their investigators any more than it does for the actions of other non-lawyer assistants. Depending on the representation, there are several steps that lawyers may wish to consider taking to minimize the chances of private investigators crossing ethical lines.

First, ensure that any investigators you employ are properly licensed and have any necessary business permits.[235] Reputable investigators should be willing to provide their license or permit numbers and any related information, or copies of their licenses or permits. Depending on the jurisdiction, an investigator may need a license or permit from a relevant municipality as well as a state license. Second, ask the investigator for references from other lawyers and check those references. Third, interview the investigator regarding her professional experience. A public law enforcement background is generally a helpful qualification because of the associated education and training, but the lack of such experience is not disqualifying. Fourth, if you are hiring an investigative agency or company, require that the agency or company identify the investigators who will be working on your matter. Check those investigators' licensure and appropriately inquire into their experience. Fifth, check whether the investigator is a member of professional organizations with ethics standards or has obtained certifications or designations reflecting special expertise or professional capability. Sixth, search the investigators online to see what, if anything, is being written or said about them and, for that matter, what they have been saying and writing

234. *Id.* at 370–71 & n.33; *see also, e.g., In re* Order to Show Cause, 741 F. Supp. 1379, 1384–85 (N.D. Cal. 1990) (declining to sanction lawyers where a licensed investigator interviewed a witness in preparation for motion to recuse a judge based on biased statements that the judge was alleged to have made but in fact did not; the investigator did not conceal his identity or misrepresent the purpose for his interviews).

235. *See* Turfgrass Grp., Inc. v. Ne. La. Turf Farms, LLC, No. 10-13544, 2013 WL 6145294, at *4 (W.D. La. Nov. 20, 2013) (finding that a lawyer violated Louisiana law by engaging an unlicensed private investigator but declining to sanction the lawyer because there was no evidence that he acted in bad faith).

online. This may include Lexis or Westlaw searches to see whether the investigator has been involved in litigation. Seventh, where possible, check with the appropriate licensing body to determine whether the investigator has been the subject of any complaints or has been professionally disciplined. Finally, carefully instruct the investigator with respect to ethical or legal limits on the investigator's conduct and document that instruction.

IV. Secret Recording

Investigators working for lawyers often secretly record conversations with witnesses. There are also situations where lawyers surreptitiously record conversations, as when they speak with witnesses whom they reasonably believe may later change their stories. Although some courts and lawyers find surreptitious recording to be distasteful, that does not mean it involves dishonesty, fraud, deceit, or misrepresentation.[236] Indeed, a lawyer's "mere act of secretly but lawfully recording a conversation" is not inherently dishonest or deceitful.[237]

Most ethical complications stem from the manner in which lawyers use surreptitious recordings, not the act of recording itself.[238] Surreptitious recording is often accomplished in circumstances characterized by deceit and deception, and the surrounding circumstances often prejudice courts against the otherwise lawful act of taping.[239] If lawyers engage in surreptitious taping for improper purposes, the fact that the taping itself was legal will not provide much of a defense to professional discipline.

Many states permit surreptitious taping as long as one party to the conversation, including the recording party, consents.[240] In states with permissive eavesdropping or wiretapping laws where only the recording party need

236. *See* Me. Bd. of Overseers of the Bar, Prof'l Conduct Comm'n, Op. No. 168, at 5–6 (1999) (discussing Maine Bar Rule 3.2(f)(3), which is analogous to Model Rule 8.4(c)).

237. ABA Formal Op. 01-422, *supra* note 77, at 2; *see also* Alaska Eth. Op. 2003-1, 2003 WL 255451, at *2 (Alaska Bar Ass'n, Ethics Comm. 2003) [hereinafter Alaska Eth. Op. 2003-1] ("If there is no implied representation that attorneys will not record conversations, there is no basis for a finding of dishonesty, fraud, deceit, or misrepresentation from a failure by an attorney to disclose that the conversation is being recorded."); Ohio Adv. Op. 2012-1, 2012 WL 2307289, at *4 (Sup. Ct. of Ohio Bd. of Comm'rs on Grievances & Discipline 2012) [hereinafter Ohio Adv. Op. 2012-1] (finding that "the general rule should be that legal surreptitious recording by Ohio lawyers is not a violation of [Rule 8.4(c)]").

238. Att'y M v. Miss Bar, 621 So. 2d 220, 224 (Miss. 1992).

239. *See, e.g.*, Midwest Motor Sports v. Arctic Cat Sales, Inc., 347 F.3d 693, 698–99 (8th Cir. 2003) (involving surreptitious taping coupled with Rule 4.2 violations committed under "false and misleading pretenses"); *In re* Crossen, 880 N.E.2d 352, 372 (Mass. 2008) ("[W]e will not detach the legal act of one-party tape recording . . . from the web of knowing and deliberate misstatements and falsehoods in which it was integrally embedded in this case.").

240. Ohio Adv. Op. 2012-1, *supra* note 237, 2012 WL 2307289, at *2 (describing the "one-party consent" approach as the majority rule).

consent, lawyers should be able to secretly record conversations without violating ethics rules prohibiting conduct involving dishonesty, fraud, deceit, or misrepresentation.[241] This is true regardless of whether the attorney is a private practitioner or a prosecutor.[242] Even in one-party consent states, however, a lawyer cannot falsely deny that a conversation is being recorded or attempt to mislead the person into believing that the call is not being recorded.[243]

In some states, recording a conversation without the consent of all parties is prohibited,[244] although legitimate law enforcement activities are usually outside this rule. In these states, attorneys who surreptitiously record conversations in civil matters violate Rule 8.4(c).[245] They may also violate other rules[246] and may face civil and criminal liability. In still other states, surreptitious taping by private attorneys, although "technically legal," may nonetheless be "professionally improper."[247] Courts in these states view surreptitious taping by private lawyers as being inconsistent with general standards of candor and fairness.[248]

In *United States v. Smallwood*,[249] for example, investigators working for two criminal defense lawyers secretly recorded a prosecution witness, a jailhouse informant who had told his cellmates that he hoped to trade his testimony for charging or sentencing considerations or other favors. Although observing that Virginia law permitted surreptitious taping with the consent of one party to the conversation, the court noted that Virginia law also embraced the "sensible conclusion" that such conduct is nonetheless unethical as an underhanded practice designed to ensnare an opponent

241. Turfgrass Grp., Inc. v. Ne. La. Turf Farms, LLC, No. 10-13544, 2013 WL 6145294, at *3–4 (W.D. La. Nov. 20, 2013) (involving a lawyer's private investigator); *Att'y M*, 621 So. 2d at 222–25; ABA Formal Op. 01-422, *supra* note 77, at 7; Alaska Eth. Op. 2003-1, *supra* note 237, 2003 WL 255451, at *3; Neb. Sup. Ct., Lawyers' Advisory Comm., Advisory Op. No. 06-07, at 3–5 (2006).

242. *Att'y M*, 621 So. 2d at 223–24.

243. Miss. State Bar v. Att'y ST, 621 So. 2d 229, 233 (Miss. 1993); *In re* PRB Docket No. 2007-046, 989 A.2d 523, 526–31 (Vt. 2009); ABA Formal Op. 01-422, *supra* note 77, at 8.

244. John Bliss, *The Legal Ethics of Secret Client Recordings*, 33 Geo. J. Legal Ethics 55, 63 & n.37 (2020) (identifying states with "all-party" consent requirements).

245. Sequa Corp. v. Lititech, Inc., 807 F. Supp. 653, 663 (D. Colo. 1992) (discussing Colorado law); Iowa Sup. Ct. Bd. of Prof'l Ethics & Conduct v. Plumb, 546 N.W.2d 215, 217–18 (Iowa 1996); *In re* Nester, 541 S.E.2d 538, 539 (S.C. 2001).

246. *See* Model Rules of Prof'l Conduct R. 4.4(a) (2020) (stating that in representing a client, a lawyer shall not "use methods of obtaining evidence that violate the legal rights of [a third] person"); *id.* R. 8.4(b) (making it professional misconduct for a lawyer to "commit a criminal act that reflects adversely on the lawyer's honesty, trustworthiness or fitness as a lawyer in other respects"); *id.* R. 8.4(d) (making it professional misconduct for a lawyer to "engage in conduct that is prejudicial to the administration of justice").

247. *In re* Ziegler, 637 A.2d 829, 1994 WL 10809, at *1 (Del. Jan. 3, 1994).

248. *Id.* (quoting People v. Selby, 606 P.2d 45, 47 (Colo. 1979); Gunter v. Va. State Bar, 385 S.E.2d 597, 600 (Va. 1989)).

249. 365 F. Supp. 2d 689 (E.D. Va. 2005).

and violates the Rule 8.4(c) prohibition on conduct involving dishonesty, fraud, deceit, or misrepresentation.[250] The court believed that for a lawyer to record or to advise others to record a conversation without the other party's consent offends the standards of candor and fairness that characterize professionalism.[251] This is true regardless of whether lawyers make the recording themselves or encourage or direct others, such as investigators, to do so.[252] Fortunately for the lawyers and the investigators in *Smallwood*, the court recognized that they did not knowingly do anything improper and let them off with a warning.

The view expressed in *Smallwood* is often difficult to understand. In *Smallwood*, the investigators' conduct, and by extension the defense lawyers' conduct, was plainly legal. The investigators were recording the witness's call as part of a well-founded investigation into his intended perjury in a looming criminal trial. Had the defense lawyers advised the witness's lawyer of their intent to record his client, he likely would have prohibited it and alerted his client. No other potential means of impeaching the witness would be as effective as capturing his plans or alternative testimony on tape. Indeed, the *Smallwood* court permitted the defense lawyers to impeach the witness with his statements about selling information to or about other inmates but declined to admit the tape or transcript of the call into evidence when the witness's lawyer and prosecutor objected.[253] The defense lawyers' duties of competence and diligence arguably compelled them to lawfully ensnare the adverse witness who would send their clients to federal prison for decades. Long story short, it is reasonable to argue that lawful surreptitious taping is not the sort of conduct Rule 8.4(c) is intended to prohibit.[254]

In addition to covertly recording conversations with witnesses and other third persons, lawyers sometimes secretly record conversations with judges. This is a uniformly terrible idea.[255] It does not matter whether the lawyer records the conversation herself or whether she has someone else (such as a client) do it; both tactics are equally impermissible and offensive. Nor does it matter that the jurisdiction permits surreptitious recording with the consent of one party to the conversation. A lawyer's duty of candor to a tribunal is

---

250. *Id.* at 698.

251. *Id.* (quoting *Gunter*, 385 S.E.2d at 600).

252. *Id.*

253. *Id.* at 694.

254. *See, e.g.*, Va. Legal Eth. Op. 1802, 2010 WL 3849568, at *6–8 (Va. State Bar, Comm. on Legal Ethics 2010) (discussing situations in which a lawyer could ethically advise a client or another person to secretly record a conversation with a third party).

255. People v. Selby, 606 P.2d 45, 47 (Colo. 1979) ("Particularly reprehensible is the unauthorized recording of the private, informal discussions with a judge in chambers."); Iowa Sup. Ct. Bd. of Prof'l Ethics & Conduct v. Plumb, 546 N.W.2d 215, 217 (Iowa 1996); *In re* Warner, 335 S.E.2d 90, 91 (S.C. 1985) (saying that such conduct brings "discredit upon the legal profession" and calling it "reprehensible").

a very special responsibility that requires forthrightness and frankness in all communications.

Lawyers contemplating surreptitious recording as a means of gathering evidence or documenting information for their clients' benefit should proceed cautiously. First, they must ensure that they understand the relevant law in the jurisdiction in which the recording occurs.[256] Although most states permit surreptitious recording with one party's consent, not all do, and the practice draws keen judicial scrutiny even in jurisdictions where it is lawful. In jurisdictions that forbid recording absent the consent of all parties to the conversation, lawyers' consideration of recording should end with the determination that it is unlawful.

Federal courts have historically applied their own standard to surreptitious recording, regardless of eavesdropping or wiretapping laws in the forum state and separate from state ethics rules.[257] In doing so, unfortunately, they have often followed ABA Formal Ethics Opinion 337,[258] issued in 1974 and superseded in 2001 by ABA Formal Opinion 01-422,[259] which concluded that as a general rule "conduct which involves dishonesty, fraud, deceit or misrepresentation . . . clearly encompasses the making of recordings without the consent of all parties."[260] Courts taking this approach have concluded that the recording lawyer's unethical behavior vitiated any work product immunity that would otherwise have shielded the recording from discovery.[261] Fortunately, federal courts that have considered the issue more recently have declined to follow ABA Formal Ethics Opinion 337 and cases embracing it, sensibly concluding that the burial of Opinion 337 in ABA Formal Opinion 01-422 stripped Opinion 337 and cases applying it of

256. *See* Bliss, *supra* note 244, at 65–66 & nn.58–59 (indicating that secret recording is prohibited in nine states under "all-party" consent laws, is generally forbidden in seven states because it is considered inherently unethical, is generally permitted in 21 states and the District of Columbia, and is an open question in with 13 states that have no opinions on the issue).

257. Anderson v. Hale, 202 F.R.D. 548, 556 (N.D. Ill. 2001); Smith v. WNA Carthage, L.L.C., 200 F.R.D. 576, 578–79 (E.D. Tex. 2001); Northfield Ins. Co. v. George E. Busson Realty Co., No. CIV. A. 99-151, 1999 WL 804076, at *2 (E.D. La. Oct. 7, 1999); Pfeifer v. State Farm Ins. Co., No. CIV. A. 96-1895, 1999 WL 276085, at *3 (E.D. La. May 22, 1997) (involving a plaintiff secretly taping co-workers); Otto v. Box U.S.A. Grp., Inc., 177 F.R.D. 698, 699–701 (N.D. Ga. 1997) (taping by a plaintiff before a lawyer was retained); Sea-Roy Corp. v. Sunbelt Equip. & Rentals, Inc., 172 F.R.D. 179, 184 (M.D.N.C. 1997); Ward v. Maritz, 156 F.R.D. 592, 594–98 (D.N.J. 1994); Bogan v. Nw. Mut. Life Ins. Co., 144 F.R.D. 51, 56 (S.D.N.Y. 1992).

258. *Anderson*, 202 F.R.D. at 555 ("Apparently every federal case to address the surreptitious taping issue presented here has relied on ABA Formal Opinion 337 in some way to find the conduct unethical.").

259. ABA Formal Op. 01-422, *supra* note 77, at 1 (rejecting Formal Op. 337).

260. ABA Comm. on Ethics and Prof'l Responsibility, Formal Op. 337, at 94, 96 (1974).

261. *See, e.g.*, *Anderson*, 202 F.R.D. at 558; *Otto*, 177 F.R.D. at 701; *Sea-Roy Corp.*, 172 F.R.D. at 182–85; *Ward*, 156 F.R.D. at 594.

persuasive force.[262] As a result, these courts uphold work product immunity for clandestine recordings as long all other requirements for work product protection are satisfied and the recordings are not otherwise discoverable.[263]

Second, where surreptitious recording is permitted, lawyers must not construe their right to record as a license to be otherwise deceitful or dishonest in connection with the recording.[264] For example, if a party to a recorded conversation asks the lawyer whether she is recording their discussion, or if a lawyer is asked whether she intends to record a conversation, the lawyer must answer truthfully.[265] If the party objects to being recorded, the lawyer must either agree that she will not record the conversation or tell the party that she intends to record the conversation despite the objection, so that the party can terminate or forgo the conversation. A lawyer who secretly records a conversation with the intent to publish the recording or disseminate a transcript cannot lead the recorded party to believe that the conversation is confidential.

Third, as previously explained, lawyers should never surreptitiously record conversations with judges. In a similar although much less perilous vein, lawyers should generally refrain from secretly recording conversations with opposing counsel.[266] Even if it is legal to secretly record a conversation with another lawyer, professional courtesy counsels against the tactic.[267] Lawyers who believe that their conversations with opponents are being mischaracterized can always confirm communications by e-mail or letter, have another person present during important conversations, or simply decline to speak with opposing counsel and instead communicate in writing.

262. *See, e.g.*, Marceaux v. Lafayette City-Parish Consol. Gov't, 731 F.3d 488, 495 (5th Cir. 2013); Bacote v. Riverbay Corp., No. 16 Civ. 1599 (GHW) (AJP), 2017 WL 945103, at *11 (S.D.N.Y. Mar. 10, 2017); Bahrami v. Price, No. 1:11-CV-4483-SCJ-AJB, 2013 WL 3800093, at *6 (N.D. Ga. July 19, 2013); Turfgrass Grp., Inc. v. Ne. La. Turf Farms, LLC, No. 10-13544, 2013 WL 6145294, at *3 (W.D. La. Nov. 20, 2013).

263. *See, e.g.*, *Bahrami*, 2013 WL 3800093, at *6 (finding "that work product protection of the recordings in question [was] not vitiated because of their clandestine nature").

264. *See, e.g.*, Att'y LS v. Miss. Bar, 649 So. 2d 810, 813 (Miss. 1994) (relying on Rule 4.1 in reprimanding a lawyer who surreptitiously recorded conversations with jurors after telling them that he had the judge's permission to speak with them when he did not).

265. Miss. Bar v. Att'y ST, 621 So. 2d 229, 233 (Miss. 1993); *In re* PRB Docket No. 2007-046, 989 A.2d 523, 526 (Vt. 2009); Conn. Eth. Op. 98-9, 1998 WL 993678, at *1 (Conn. Bar Ass'n, Comm. on Prof'l Ethics 1998); Mo. Sup. Ct. Advisory Comm., Formal Op. 123, at 1 (2006).

266. Nissan Motor Co. v. Nissan Comput. Corp., 180 F. Supp. 2d 1089, 1096 (C.D. Cal. 2002) (branding the practice "inconsistent with the courteous and professional administration of the legal system"); Northfield Ins. Co. v. George E. Busson Realty Co., No. Civ. A. 99-151,1999 WL 804076, at *2 (E.D. La. Oct. 7, 1999) (disapproving of counsel's practice of surreptitiously recording conversations with opposing counsel without notice or consent).

267. N.C. Eth. Op. RPC 171, 1994 WL 899352, at *1 (N.C. State Bar 1994) (opining that it would not be unethical to secretly record a conversation with another lawyer, but, "as a matter of professionalism," encouraging lawyers to disclose to other lawyers that conversations are being recorded).

Fourth, lawyers who surreptitiously record conversations should be certain to preserve the tapes or digital media containing the conversations in addition to having them transcribed. The tapes or digital media may be discoverable in litigation, and the failure to preserve them may, on the right facts, amount to spoliation of evidence. Furthermore, lawyers may need the tapes or other media to prove the accuracy of any challenged transcripts and thus defeat allegations that recordings are incomplete or inaccurate or that they improperly altered transcripts to obtain an unfair advantage. Lawyers certainly should not alter transcripts or offer out of context any transcribed statements.[268]

V. Advancing and Developing the Law

Private lawyers often engage in surreptitious discovery and covert investigations to gather information and evidence for use in litigation. At the same time, many courts and lawyers view these practices through jaundiced eyes, concerned always that such tactics are in some way unfair or dishonorable. In criminal cases, things are different; courts and lawyers accept that some amount of deception is necessary to combat crime. But even government lawyers cannot mislead people as to their identities when they are functioning in representational capacities.

In short, the seemingly rigid principle that lawyers must always be truthful occasionally bends to allow deceptive lawyering. The degree of flexibility depends on the case and court. The problem with a case-by-case approach in the context of lawyers' surreptitious investigations is the lack of support in applicable ethics rules. For example, Model Rule 8.4(c), which prohibits conduct involving "dishonesty, fraud, deceit or misrepresentation," contains no investigative exception. And, if nothing else, undercover investigations embody deceit.

Fortunately, several states have amended their versions of Rule 8.4(c) to provide an investigative exception in at least some circumstances.[269] For example, Florida's version of Rule 8.4(c) now contains exceptions for prosecutors and private lawyers engaged in undercover investigations except where their conduct is "prohibited by law or rule."[270] In 2017, Colorado

268. *See* People v. Selby, 606 P.2d 45, 47 (Colo. 1997) (disbarring a lawyer who secretly recorded a conference with a judge and who "made an improper use of his recording by misrepresenting the nature of the court's remarks and using a partial quotation taken out of context to support his allegations that the court was biased").

269. *See, e.g.*, Mo. Rules of Prof'l Conduct R. 4-8.4(c) (2012) (providing what amounts to a law enforcement exception); Or. Rules of Prof'l Conduct R. 8.4(b) (2014); Va. Rules of Prof'l Conduct R. 8.4(c) (2013) (limiting the proscribed conduct to that "which reflects adversely on the lawyer's fitness to practice law").

270. Fla. Rules of Prof'l Conduct R. 8.4(c) (2014).

amended its version of Rule 8.4(c) to provide that it is professional misconduct for a lawyer to "engage in conduct involving dishonesty, fraud, deceit or misrepresentation, *except that* a lawyer may advise, direct, or supervise others, including clients, law enforcement officers, or investigators, who participate in lawful investigative activities."[271] Other states rely on comments to their version of Rule 8.4 to create investigatory exceptions.[272]

Rather than focusing on Rule 8.4(c), Wisconsin amended its version of Rule 4.1(b) to provide that notwithstanding Rules 5.3(c)(1) and 8.4, "a lawyer may advise or supervise others with respect to lawful investigative activities."[273] Plainly, the rule limits lawyers' involvement in surreptitious discovery and investigations to advisory or supervisory roles. Furthermore, "lawful investigative activities" as used in Rule 4.1(b) "may involve a lawyer as an advisor or supervisor only when the lawyer in good faith believes there is a reasonable possibility that unlawful activity has taken place, is taking place or will take place in the foreseeable future."[274]

VI. Conclusion

In recent years, lawyers have increasingly found themselves the subject of professional discipline because of their involvement in surreptitious discovery and investigations. They are increasingly targeted in criminal investigations and civil litigation arising out of investigatory activities. These trends threaten to continue for several reasons. First, as litigation costs continue to escalate, lawyers will be under more and more pressure to conduct informal discovery both in advance of litigation and once it is underway. Second, much litigation today qualifies as "high stakes," and with those high stakes comes high pressure on the lawyers involved. History unfortunately teaches that lawyers who feel crushing pressure to win sometimes make unwise professional judgments. Third, as in the arena of high-stakes litigation, the competitive pressure of modern litigation practice periodically influences lawyers' strategic and tactical decisions in negative ways. Fourth, and apart from these environmental factors, the law relating to surreptitious discovery and investigations is unclear or undeveloped in many jurisdictions, so that lawyers who are considering such activities may not fully appreciate their duties or potential perils.

271. Colo. Rules of Prof'l Conduct R. 1.7 (2017) (emphasis added). Thus, a Colorado lawyer may counsel or guide others who engage in dishonest, fraudulent, or deceitful conduct during lawful investigative activities, but the lawyer may not engage in such conduct herself. Colo. Bar Ass'n, Ethics Comm., Formal Op. 137, at 1–2 (2019).

272. *See, e.g.*, Iowa Rules of Prof'l Conduct R. 8.4 cmt. 6 (2017); Ohio Rules of Prof'l Conduct R. 8.4 cmt. 2A (2014); Tenn. Rules of Prof'l Conduct R. 8.4 cmts. 5 & 6 (2018).

273. Wis. Rules of Prof'l Conduct R. 4.1(b) (2019).

274. *Id.* R. 4.1 cmt.

For lawyers with litigation practices, then, the ultimate message is simple: recognize that you practice in a challenging environment. Be cautious when planning, directing, and conducting surreptitious investigations. It is possible to conduct professionally responsible investigations and to avoid the misfortune that has befallen many lawyers in this context, and the contours outlined here should provide helpful guidance.

4

Compensating Fact Witnesses

I. Introduction

Testimony by fact witnesses is the backbone of trials. Yet, vital fact witnesses are often beyond parties' control and therefore cannot be compelled to appear at trial as part of their regular paid duties. For example, parties' former employees are often important witnesses. From the former employees' perspectives, however, participating in litigation may take them away from their current jobs, thereby costing them income or vacation time; it may impede their self-employment; or it may interrupt their retirements. It is therefore understandable that former employees may want to be paid for devoting time to litigation in which they have no stake.

Other fact witnesses likewise may be interested in compensation for their time spent on litigation. An inventor who is a fact witness in patent litigation also may be an essential consultant who deserves compensation for time spent in the latter role.[1] Passersby who witness accidents may be critical to the outcome in resulting litigation, and parties may want to compensate them for taking time off from their jobs to testify.

Fact witness compensation was once limited to statutory witness fees or subpoena rates.[2] That is no longer the case. Compensating fact witnesses beyond statutory witness fees and expenses to which they are entitled is now

1. *See, e.g.*, Aristocrat Techs. v. Int'l Game Tech., No. C-06-03717 RMW, 2010 WL 2010 WL 2595151, at *2–3 (N.D. Cal. June 28, 2010) (concluding that a party's $100,000 lump sum payment to an the inventor of the patents-in-suit to consult in litigation would not support a claim that the party had unclean hands; although the inventor was contractually required to cooperate with the party in litigation and to testify as needed, the contracts did not obligate the inventor to consult in litigation).

2. *See, e.g.*, Wright v. Somers, 125 Ill. App. 256, 257 (1906) ("The legislative department of our State has declared that every witness attending in his own county upon trials in the courts of record shall be entitled to receive the sum of one dollar for each day's attendance and five cents per mile each way for necessary travel. . . . This is all the witness is entitled to receive. To demand more is forbidden by the policy and spirit of this statute." (citation omitted)).

a common practice and has been for years.[3] As a general rule, lawyers and litigants may compensate fact witnesses for time spent testifying, preparing to testify, or assisting in the litigation, and they may reimburse witnesses' associated expenses, provided that the amounts paid or reimbursed are reasonable, are not conditioned on the act of testifying or the content or substance of the witnesses' testimony, and are not contingent upon the outcome of the litigation.[4]

At the same time, lawyers and parties may not pay fact witnesses for their testimony even if the testimony is truthful.[5] Lawyers cannot condition fact witnesses' compensation on their agreements not to voluntarily speak with other parties or their counsel.[6] If a fact witness asks that her lawyer attend an interview, meeting, or deposition, it is generally permissible to pay that lawyer's reasonable fees and expenses for attending, again provided that any payment is not tied to the outcome of the case or conditioned on the content or substance of the witness's testimony.[7]

Of course, general rules are subject to exceptions, as where the law of a jurisdiction compels a different result, and the reasonableness of payments to fact witnesses frequently is in the eye of the beholder. Even if payments to a fact witness are reasonable, additional inducements, such as a party's promise to indemnify the witness in connection with the litigation, may go too far.[8] Lawyers' and litigants' failures to disclose fact witnesses' compensation, or their failure to do so timely, as well as fact witnesses' failure to

---

3. *See, e.g.*, Slayton v. Weinberger, 194 S.E.2d 703, 706 (Va. 1973) (calling it a "well known fact" that "agreements to pay witnesses for lost time and expenses incurred, in excess of the statutory fees, are not unusual, extraordinary or improper"). *But see* W. Va. State Bar, Lawyer Disciplinary Bd., Legal Ethics Op. 2017-1, at 2–3 (2017) [hereinafter W. Va. Op. 2017-1] (opining that under § 59-1-16 of the West Virginia Code, fact witnesses are entitled to no compensation beyond the statutory witness fee and mileage reimbursement for attendance in court or for depositions).

4. Restatement (Third) of the Law Governing Lawyers § 117 (2000).

5. Rocheux Int'l of N.J., Inc. v. U.S. Merchs. Fin. Grp., Inc., No. 06-6147, 2009 WL 3246837, at *4 (D.N.J. Oct. 5, 2009); Ward v. Nierlich, No. 99-14227-CIV., 2006 WL 5412626, at *4 (S.D. Fla. Sept. 20, 2006); *In re* Telcar Grp., Inc., 363 B.R. 345, 354 (Bankr. E.D.N.Y. 2007); *In re* Kien, 372 N.E.2d 376, 379 (Ill. 1977).

6. Model Rules of Prof'l Conduct R. 3.4(a) (2020) (prohibiting lawyers from unlawfully obstructing parties' access to evidence); *id.* R. 3.4(f) (providing that lawyers generally cannot "request a person other than a client to refrain from voluntarily giving relevant information to another party").

7. N.Y. Eth. Op. 962, 2013 WL 1781018, at *3 (N.Y. State Bar Ass'n, Comm. on Prof'l Ethics 2013); NYCLA Eth. Op. 729, 2000 WL 684669, at *2–3 (N.Y. Cnty. Lawyers' Ass'n, Comm. on Prof'l Ethics 2000); S.C. Adv. Op. 08-05, 2008 WL 8089789, at *2 (S.C. Bar, Ethics Advisory Comm. 2008).

8. *See, e.g.*, State of N.Y. v. Solvent Chem. Co., 166 F.R.D. 284, 289–90 (W.D.N.Y. 1996) (finding nothing improper in parties paying a fact witness a reasonable hourly fee for his time and reimbursing his expenses but concluding that the parties "went too far" in promising to indemnify the witness in two cases, including the pending case).

reveal their compensation when called upon to do so, can also affect the calculus.[9]

If a lawyer's or a litigant's compensation of a fact witness is held to be improper, there are several possible consequences. The court may order a new trial; the lawyer or litigant or both may be sanctioned; the lawyer may be disqualified from further participation in the litigation;[10] the lawyer may face professional discipline; and the lawyer, party, and witness all may tempt criminal prosecution. Courts generally are reluctant to exclude a witness's testimony on the sole basis that the witness has been paid, preferring to leave it to the jury to weigh the witness's credibility, or, in court-tried cases, to weigh the testimony themselves.[11] Nonetheless, courts have discretion to exclude or strike improperly or unreasonably compensated fact witnesses' testimony as a sanction.[12]

This chapter examines lawyers' and litigants' compensation of fact witnesses, with a primary focus on lawyers' conduct. Although the chapter refers to *fact witnesses*, readers should understand that these are *third-party fact witnesses*—fact witnesses who are not employed by a party to the litigation in which they testify. Most fact witness compensation controversies involve third-party fact witnesses; parties' ordinary compensation of current employees for time spent testifying or preparing to testify is not controversial. Courts and jurors well understand that fact witnesses who are currently employed by parties are being paid for their time devoted to a case and any

9. *See, e.g.*, Thomas v. City of N.Y., 293 F.R.D. 498, 504–07 (S.D.N.Y. 2013) (granting a new trial where the plaintiff did not timely reveal a compensation arrangement with a key fact witness); ESN, LLC v. Cisco Sys., Inc., 685 F. Supp. 2d 631, 651 (E.D. Tex. 2009) (sanctioning the defendants for their "deliberate, willful failure" to disclose an employment agreement with a witness), *aff'd*, 397 F. App'x 630 (Fed. Cir. 2010); United States v. Cinergy Corp., No. 1:99-cv-1693-LJM-JMS, 2008 WL 7679914, at *10–15 (S.D. Ind. Dec. 18, 2008) (ordering a new trial where defense counsel did not reveal fact witness's compensation and allegedly misled jury about witness's compensation, and witness did not reveal employment or compensation when testifying).

10. *See, e.g.*, McIntosh v. State Farm Fire & Cas. Co., No. 1:06CV1080 LTS-RHW, 2008 WL 941640, at *2 (S.D. Miss. Apr. 4, 2008) (disqualifying affiliated law firms for lead law firm's improper witness payments and other improprieties). *But see* Nissan N. Am., Inc. v. Johnson Elec. N. Am., Inc., No. 09-11783, 2011 WL 1812505, at *5–8 (E.D. Mich. May 12, 2011) (declining to disqualify a law firm that compensated a fact witness in alleged violation of Rule 3.4(b)); Dyll v. Adams, No. CIV.A. 3:94-CV-2734-D, 1997 WL 222918, at *3 (N.D. Tex. Apr. 29, 1997) (explaining that disqualification is not an appropriate remedy for a Rule 3.4(b) violation because "[t]he ethical breach is discrete and can be cured, if necessary, by less drastic means").

11. United States v. Davis, 261 F.3d 1, 37–39 & n.31 (1st Cir. 2001) (quoting United States v. Cresta, 825 F.2d 538, 547 (1st Cir. 1987)); *see, e.g.*, Platypus Wear, Inc. v. Horizonte Fabricacao Distribuicao Importacao Exportacao Ltda, No. 08-20738-CV, 2010 WL 625356, at *5 (S.D. Fla. Feb. 17, 2010); TBC Corp. v. Wall, 955 S.W.2d 838, 843 (Tenn. Ct. App. 1997).

12. Golden Door Jewelry Creations, Inc. v. Lloyds Underwriters Non-Marine Ass'n, 865 F. Supp. 1516, 1526–27 (S.D. Fla. 1994) (precluding the defendant from offering the testimony of two witnesses who were improperly compensated); Murray v. Just In Case Bus. Lighthouse, LLC, 374 P.3d 443, 447, 451–53 (Colo. 2016) (explaining that courts have discretion to exclude the testimony of witnesses who have been improperly compensated).

potential bias on the part of such witnesses attributable to their employment is open for evaluation by the fact-finder.

II. Governing Rules and Statutes

Lawyers who are considering compensating third-party fact witnesses for their time spent testifying or preparing to testify must comply with rules of professional conduct in the process. In addition, both lawyers and litigants who compensate fact witnesses must ensure that their conduct is permissible under the federal anti-bribery or anti-gratuity statute,[13] as well as any similar state statutes.[14]

A. Model Rule of Professional Conduct 3.4(b)

The most widely applicable ethics rule is Model Rule of Professional Conduct 3.4(b), which provides that a lawyer shall not "falsify evidence, counsel or assist a witness to testify falsely, *or offer an inducement to a witness that is prohibited by law.*"[15] Although "inducements" to witnesses commonly take the form of monetary payments, the term is not so limited. Various other benefits promised to witnesses, or advantages conferred on them, may qualify as inducements for Model Rule 3.4(b) purposes.[16]

Model Rule 3.4(b) reflects the concern that some financial arrangements with witnesses may encourage them to exaggerate, shade, or even falsify their testimony, thereby undermining the integrity of the judicial process, which depends on truthful testimony.[17] Recognizing that fact witnesses should not have to go out-of-pocket to fulfill their civic responsibilities, however, Comment 3 to Model Rule 3.4 notes that "it is not improper to pay a witness's expenses," while cautioning lawyers that "[t]he common law rule in most jurisdictions is that it is improper to pay an occurrence witness any fee for testifying."[18]

The Model Rule 3.4(b) prohibition on unlawful inducements to witnesses extends beyond bribery. Consistent with the comment to the rule,

---

13. 18 U.S.C. § 201(c)(2) (2018).

14. *See, e.g.*, Ohio Rev. Code Ann. § 2921.02(C) & (D) (2020) (criminalizing under the general heading of bribery the corruption or improper influencing of witnesses); Wash. Rev. Code § 9A.72.090 (2019) (providing that bribing a witness is a felony).

15. Model Rules of Prof'l Conduct R. 3.4(b) (2020) (emphasis added).

16. *See, e.g.*, Biocore Med. Techs., Inc. v. Khosrowshahi, 181 F.R.D. 660, 670 (D. Kan. 1998) ("Counsel can provide an inducement by providing free legal service.").

17. Accrued Fin. Servs., Inc. v. Prime Retail, Inc., No. CIV.JFM-99-2573, 2000 WL 976800, at *3 (D. Md. June 19, 2000) (discussing Maryland law).

18. Model Rules of Prof'l Conduct R. 3.4 cmt. 3 (2020).

lawyers cannot compensate fact witnesses for testifying.[19] Lawyers may not pay fact witnesses for their testimony even if the testimony is truthful.[20] Lawyers cannot condition fact witnesses' compensation on the content, substance, or perceived usefulness of their testimony,[21] nor may lawyers offer to pay fact witnesses fees that are contingent upon the outcome of the matter.[22]

The practical problem when looking at the plain language of Model Rule 3.4(b) and Comment 3 is that neither appears to permit lawyers to pay fact witnesses for time spent testifying at a deposition, hearing, trial, or other proceeding, or preparing to testify. The rule and comment by their terms leave a substantial gap: compensating fact witnesses for their time spent testifying or preparing to testify is not the same as paying them for their testimony, which the common law prohibits, nor is it the same as paying their expenses, which is permissible. At the same time, solid practical and policy reasons support compensating fact witnesses for their time and effort:

> Some witnesses need to reacquaint themselves with voluminous paperwork. Matters that need revisiting may be both complex and far removed in time. Effective, organized testimony (the type useful to the parties and the court) often requires extensive and time-consuming preparation. . . . It would be unrealistic to expect all potential witnesses to be willing (or even able) to devote the tremendous amount of time necessary to make their testimony meaningful without compensating them for their lost time. Thus, payments to fact witnesses may be necessary to provide those witnesses with the proper incentive to prepare for their testimony in a thorough manner.
>
> Payments to fact witnesses are also justifiable on fairness grounds. A conscientious witness may devote a large amount of time preparing to testify. Wholly separate from the question of giving the witness the incentive to prepare properly, there is also the question of what is the fair and equitable

---

19. Golden Door Jewelry Creations, Inc. v. Lloyds Underwriters Non-Marine Ass'n, 865 F. Supp. 1516, 1526 (S.D. Fla. 1994).

20. Rocheux Int'l of N.J., Inc. v. U.S. Merchs. Fin. Grp., Inc., No. 06-6147, 2009 WL 3246837, at *4 (D.N.J. Oct. 5, 2009); Ward v. Nierlich, No. 99-14227-CIV., 2006 WL 5412626, at *4 (S.D. Fla. Sept. 20, 2006); *In re* Telcar Grp., Inc., 363 B.R. 345, 354 (Bankr. E.D.N.Y. 2007); *In re* Kien, 372 N.E.2d 376, 379 (Ill. 1977); *In re* Discipline of Callister, No. 70901, 2017 WL 3160232, at *2 (Nev. July 25, 2017) (quoting HomeDirect, Inc. v. H.E.P. Direct, Inc., No. 10 C 812, 2013 WL 1815979, at *4 (N.D. Ill. Apr. 29, 2013)).

21. Fla. Bar v. Wohl, 842 So. 2d 811, 812, 815–16 (Fla. 2003); *In re Discipline of Callister*, 2017 WL 3160232, at *1.

22. Restatement (Third) of the Law Governing Lawyers § 117(2) (2000); *see, e.g.*, *Accrued Fin. Servs., Inc.*, 2000 WL 976800, at *2–3 & n.3 (discussing California and Maryland law); Wagner v. Lehman Bros. Kuhn Loeb Inc., 646 F. Supp. 643, 656, 659–60 (N.D. Ill. 1986) (disqualifying a lawyer who participated in his client's scheme to offer a witness a contingent fee); Murray v. Just In Case Bus. Lighthouse, LLC, 374 P.3d 443, 450 (Colo. 2016) (explaining that Rule 3.4(b) prohibits paying witnesses contingent fees); Caldwell v. Cablevision Sys. Corp., 984 N.E.2d 909, 912 (N.Y. 2013); Commonwealth v. Miranda, 934 N.E.2d 222, 231–32 (Mass. 2010) (announcing that prosecutors may not offer monetary rewards to witnesses contingent on defendants' convictions); Comm. on Legal Ethics of the W. Va. State Bar v. Sheatsley, 452 S.E.2d 75, 80 (W. Va. 1994) (applying DR 7-109(C), a predecessor to Rule 3.4(b)).

> thing to do. Our court system is an instrument of justice; to compel people to provide testimony that will enable others to be compensated for their wrongs while denying those witnesses compensation seems unjust.[23]

The ABA's Standing Committee on Ethics and Professional Responsibility filled the Model Rule 3.4(b) gap when it issued Formal Opinion 96-402.[24] In Formal Opinion 96-402, the Committee was asked whether, under Model Rule 3.4(b), it was "proper for a lawyer to compensate a non-expert witness for the reasonable value of time expended by the witness while preparing for or giving testimony at a deposition or at a trial."[25] In answering this question affirmatively, the Committee observed that the precursor to Model Rule 3.4, DR 7-109 of the Model Code of Professional Responsibility,[26] expressly permitted the payment of "'[r]easonable compensation to a witness for his loss of time in attending or testifying,'" and there was nothing in the history of Model Rule 3.4(b) that indicated the drafters of the Model Rules intended to eliminate this principle.[27] Plus, the Committee noted, compensating witnesses for time spent attending trials, hearings, and other proceedings was authorized by some statutes and cases.[28] The Committee therefore concluded that Model Rule 3.4(b) does not prohibit lawyers from paying fact witnesses for lost time.[29]

Having determined that it was permissible for lawyers to compensate fact witnesses for time spent attending depositions and trials, the Committee saw no reason to distinguish a lawyer "compensating a witness for time spent in pretrial interviews with the lawyer in preparation for testifying, as long as the lawyer makes it clear to the witness that the payment is not being made for the substance (or efficacy) of the witness's testimony or as an inducement to the witness to 'tell the truth.'"[30] The Committee further concluded that fact witnesses may be compensated for time spent reading and researching records that are germane to their testimony, provided such compensation is not barred by the law of the jurisdiction.[31]

Formal Opinion 96-402 does not, however, limitlessly free lawyers to pay fact witnesses for time spent testifying or preparing to do so. Rather, a

23. Jeffrey S. Kinsler & Gary S. Colton, Jr., *Compensating Fact Witnesses*, 184 F.R.D. 425, 429 (1999).

24. ABA Comm. on Ethics & Prof'l Responsibility, Formal Op. 96-402 (1996) [hereinafter ABA Formal Op. 96-402].

25. *Id.* at 1.

26. Model Code of Prof'l Responsibility DR 7-109 (1969).

27. ABA Formal Op. 96-402, *supra* note 24, at 1–2 (quoting DR 7-109(C)(2)).

28. *Id.* at 2.

29. *Id.*

30. *Id.*

31. *Id.*

witness's compensation "must be reasonable, so as to avoid affecting, even unintentionally, the content of [the] witness's testimony."[32]

> What is a reasonable amount [of compensation] is relatively easy to determine in situations where the witness can demonstrate to the lawyer that he has sustained a direct loss of income because of his time away from work—as, for example, [the] loss of hourly wages or professional fees. In situations, however, where the witness has not sustained any direct loss of income in connection with giving, or preparing to give, testimony—as, for example, where the witness is retired or unemployed—the lawyer must determine the reasonable value of the witness's time based on all relevant circumstances.[33]

Once that determination has been made, however, nothing in the Model Rules prevents lawyers from compensating fact witnesses for their time spent testifying or preparing to testify.[34]

The positions outlined in Formal Opinion 96-402 reflect the majority rule.[35] Some courts and professional authorities, however, have declined to allow lawyers to compensate fact witnesses for preparation time, instead limiting payment for lost time to attendance at a deposition, hearing, or trial.[36]

32. *Id.* at 3.

33. *Id.*

34. *Id.*

35. *See, e.g.*, Chevron Corp. v. Donziger, 11 Civ. 0691 (LAK), 2018 WL 1137119, at *14 (S.D.N.Y. Mar. 21, 2018); Chi. Ins. Co. v. Capwill, No. 1:01cv2588, 2011 WL 6181337, at *1–2 (N.D. Ohio Dec. 13, 2011); Prasad v. MML Inv. Servs., Inc., No. 04 Civ. 380(RWS), 2004 WL 1151735, at *6–7 (S.D.N.Y. May 24, 2004) (citing ABA Formal Op. 96-402, among other authorities); Curley v. N. Am. Man Boy Love Ass'n, No. Civ. A. 00-10956-GAO, 2003 WL 21696550, at *5 (D. Mass. Mar. 31, 2003) (quoting ABA Formal Op. 96-402); Trial Pracs., Inc. v. Hahn, Loeser & Parks, LLP, 260 So. 3d 167, 173 (Fla. 2018) (holding that Florida Rule 4-3.4(b) "permits a party to pay a fact witness for the witness's assistance with case and discovery preparation that is directly related to the witness preparing for, attending, or testifying at proceedings"); Mich. First Credit Union v. Al Long Ford, Inc., No. 291146, 2010 WL 5129890, at *3 (Mich. Ct. App. Dec. 16, 2010); Alaska Eth. Op. 93-2, 1993 WL 849637, at *2 n.2 (Alaska Bar Ass'n, Ethics Comm. 1993) [hereinafter Alaska Eth. Op. 93-2]; Ariz. State Bar, Comm. on the Rules of Prof'l Conduct, Op. 97-07 (1997) [hereinafter Ariz. Op. 97-07]; Cal. Eth. Op. 1997-149, 1997 WL 197243, at *5 (Cal. State Bar, Standing Comm. on Prof'l Responsibility & Conduct 1997) [hereinafter Cal. Eth. Op. 1997-149]; Colo. Bar Ass'n, Ethics Comm., Formal Op. 103 (1998); Conn. Bar Ass'n, Comm. on Prof'l Ethics, Informal Op. 92-30 (1992); Del. State Bar Ass'n, Comm. on Prof'l Ethics, Op. 2003-3, at 9 (2003) [hereinafter Del. Op. 2003-3]; Ill. Adv. Op. 87-5, 1988 WL 525079, at *1 (Ill. State Bar Ass'n 1988); Ky. Bar Ass'n, Eth. Op. KBA E-400 (1997); Mass. Bar Ass'n, Comm. on Prof'l Ethics, Op. 91-3 (1991); Pa. Eth. Op. 2014-2, 2014 WL 2986614, at *2 (Phila. Bar Ass'n, Prof'l Guidance Comm. 2014). *But see* W. Va. Op. 2017-1, *supra* note 3, at 5 (stating that "an attorney in West Virginia can pay reasonable compensation to a fact witness for time spent preparing for testimony and being interviewed, but not for testimony at a deposition or trial").

36. *See, e.g.*, Rocheux Int'l of N.J., Inc. v. U.S. Merchs. Fin. Grp., Inc., No. 06-6147, 2009 WL 3246837, at *3 (D.N.J. Oct. 5, 2009) (describing this approach as the common law rule); McIntosh v. State Farm Fire & Cas. Co., No. 1:06CV1080 LTS-RHW, 2008 WL 941640, at *2 (S.D. Miss. Apr. 4, 2008) (citing Miss. State Bar Ethics Op. No. 145 (1988)); Phila. Eth. Op. 94-27, 1994 WL 711498 (Phila. Bar Ass'n, Prof'l Guidance Comm. 1994).

The Pennsylvania Bar Association has observed that the Pennsylvania version of Rule 3.4(b), which expressly permits a lawyer to pay "[r]easonable compensation to a witness for the witness's loss of time in attending or testifying,"[37] may be read "to disfavor compensation to nonexpert witnesses for the time invested in preparing for testimony" but has neither approved nor disapproved of the practice.[38] In other words, while Formal Opinion 96-402 represents the majority position, that approach is not unanimous.

The challenge for lawyers and courts in most cases is evaluating the reasonableness of witnesses' compensation and expenses. Judging the reasonableness of expenses is easy: what was the actual cost incurred by the witness? The fact that a more frugal witness might have incurred expenses lower than those a particular witness actually incurred does not make the latter's expenses unreasonable. Nor does providing a witness with some level of comfort or convenience in connection with her service necessarily transform an expense reimbursement into an improper inducement. For example, paying for a witness to fly first class rather than coach from Los Angeles to New York should be considered reasonable.[39] Lodging a fact witness in a nice hotel rather than in a budget hotel is similarly reasonable. For that matter, it will be a rare case in which a witness's expense reimbursement will be so generous or unusual that it will constitute an impermissible inducement.

With respect to witness compensation, reasonableness requires a logical relationship between the amount paid to the witness and the time the witness spent in preparing to testify and appearing.[40] The closer a witness's compensation comes to approximating her direct loss of income, the more likely it is to be found reasonable.[41] In contrast, compensation that is disproportionate to the time spent by the witness is potentially troubling, as a New York case, *Caldwell v. Cablevision Systems Corp.*,[42] somewhat awkwardly illustrates.

Plaintiff Bessie Caldwell tripped and injured herself while walking her dog. She sued Communications Specialists, Inc. (CSI), which had been working on the street in the area where she fell. In its defense, CSI subpoenaed the physician who had treated Caldwell in the hospital emergency room and who, when recording her medical history, had noted that she had tripped

37. Pa. Rules of Prof'l Conduct R. 3.4(b)(2) (2019).

38. Pa. Eth. Op. 95-126A, 1995 WL 935696, at *2 (Pa. Bar Ass'n, Comm. on Legal Ethics & Prof'l Responsibility 1995).

39. *But cf. In re* One Infant Child, No. 12 Civ. 7797(PKC), 2014 WL 704037, at *6 (S.D.N.Y. Feb. 20, 2014) (awarding fees and expenses in an international child abduction case and relying on 28 U.S.C. § 1821(c)(1) in declining to reimburse a fact witness's business class airfare and instead reimbursing the witness at a coach class rate).

40. Curley v. N. Am. Man Boy Love Ass'n, No. Civ. A. 00-10956-GAO, 2003 WL 21696550, at *5 (D. Mass. Mar. 31, 2003).

41. ABA Formal Op. 96-402, *supra* note 24, at 3.

42. 984 N.E.2d 909 (N.Y. 2013).

over her dog.[43] The doctor testified consistently with his note on direct examination.[44] On cross-examination by Caldwell's lawyer, the doctor testified that CSI had paid him $10,000 for appearing and testifying.[45] This dwarfed the statutory witness fee of $15 per day and $0.23 per mile to which the doctor was entitled. The doctor denied that the payment influenced his testimony; he testified only to his note in the emergency room record, and he offered no medical opinions.[46] Caldwell asked the court to strike the doctor's testimony or issue a curative instruction or a jury charge regarding monetary influence. CSI argued that there was nothing wrong with paying a fact witness for time missed from work. The court opted to allow the parties to argue the doctor's compensation in their summations as long as they did not specifically refer to the witness fee statute. The court also gave a general bias instruction.

The jury returned a verdict for CSI and Caldwell appealed. The Appellate Division affirmed, holding that the trial court did not err in allowing the doctor's testimony and that while the trial court should have better instructed the jury on bias, that error was harmless.[47] Caldwell then appealed to the New York Court of Appeals.

Although the Court of Appeals ultimately affirmed the Appellate Division on the basis that any trial court error was harmless, the court was disturbed by the fact that CSI paid the doctor $10,000 for *one hour* of testimony.[48] It probably did not help that CSI did not attempt to justify the amount of the payment in the Court of Appeals.

The *Caldwell* court observed that the doctor had received a substantial payment for minimal testimony. This was deeply troubling because payments to fact witnesses that are "exorbitant as compared to the amount of time the witness spends away from work or business, create an unflattering intimation that the testimony is being bought or, at the very least, has been unconsciously influenced by the compensation provided."[49] Although statutory witness fees are merely compensatory minimums, such that Caldwell could not win her argument that the doctor was entitled to nothing more than $15 plus mileage, the doctor's grossly disproportionate witness fee was hard for the court to swallow.[50] The court specifically noted that "the distinction between paying a fact witness for testimony and paying a fact witness for time and reasonable expenses can easily become blurred."[51]

43. *Id.* at 911.
44. *Id.*
45. *Id.*
46. *Id.*
47. *Id.* at 911–12.
48. *Id.* at 913.
49. *Id.* at 912.
50. *Id.* at 912–13.
51. *Id.* at 913.

CSI was almost certainly spared a new trial by the limitation of the doctor's testimony to what he wrote in Caldwell's medical record.[52] There was no opportunity for the doctor to tailor his testimony to benefit CSI.[53] It is a stretch even to think that might have been necessary, since, in a trip-and-fall case, the plaintiff's admission that she stumbled over her own dog is about as good as it gets from a defense perspective.[54]

It appears from the Appellate Division opinion that CSI paid the doctor a fee close to that which he would charge if he appeared as an expert witness.[55] The problem with that approach is that the doctor did not testify as an expert witness; he regurgitated his note in the plaintiff's chart. Furthermore, courts generally view treating physicians as fact witnesses rather than as expert witnesses. CSI might have better argued that it was compensating the doctor for his time away from his practice. This theory at least has legs; the doctor testified on cross-examination that when he testified as an expert in other cases, his fees were a substitute for the fees he would have earned if he was instead seeing patients or performing surgery.[56] By extension, then, although he was a fact witness in Caldwell's case, paying him a fee commensurate with the fee he would have charged as an expert was reasonable because it simply compensated him for his lost time. But even then, the $10,000 witness fee was so disproportionate to the time the doctor spent testifying—testimony that required no preparation—that justifying the amount was effectively impossible.

Finally, for now, there is the question of reasonable compensation for fact witnesses who are retired or unemployed. One ethics body has suggested that compensating a retired former employee of a party for time spent testifying or preparing to testify may be improper because the former employee would not sustain "any direct loss of income" in serving as a fact witness.[57]

52. *Id.* at 912.

53. *Id.*

54. It is easy to craft a hypothetical problem with what would likely be a very different outcome simply by changing a few facts. Assume that the doctor did not record Caldwell's admission about tripping over her dog in the medical history he took from her. Instead, he is called as a witness at trial and testifies that Caldwell admitted stumbling over her dog, but he did not record it in his notes. Caldwell's statement about stumbling over her dog comes into evidence as an admission against interest or as a statement made for medical diagnosis or treatment. *See* FED. R. EVID. 801(d)(2) (specifying statements that are not hearsay); FED. R. EVID. 803(4) (listing exceptions to the rule against hearsay). In our hypothetical case, the $10,000 payment to the doctor arguably takes on the appearance of an improper inducement to a witness, or, to put it slightly differently, the $10,000 at least superficially appears to be payment for the content or substance of the doctor's testimony rather than compensation for his lost time. The question would then become the remedy to be afforded Caldwell, if any, with potential consequences for the defense lawyers and doctor to follow.

55. Caldwell v. Cablevision Sys. Corp., 925 N.Y.S.2d 103, 108 (App. Div. 2011), *aff'd*, 984 N.E.2d 909 (N.Y. 2013).

56. *Id.* at 105.

57. Del. Op. 2003-3, *supra* note 35, at 11.

But a fact witness's retirement or unemployment does not render his or her time valueless.[58] Everyone's time is worth something.[59] For that reason, the better view is that retired and unemployed fact witnesses are entitled to reasonable compensation for time spent testifying or preparing to testify.[60] The amounts to be paid to such witnesses generally do, however, require closer consideration than when a fact witness is being reimbursed for lost wages.[61] Even so, paying a retired or unemployed witness an hourly rate approximating that which they last earned in their most recent employment should generally pass muster.[62]

B. The Federal Anti-bribery or Anti-gratuity Statute

The propriety of fact witness compensation is not solely a professional responsibility issue.[63] The Model Rule 3.4(b) reference to inducements to witnesses that are prohibited by law plainly signals that fact.[64] For example, 18 U.S.C. § 201(c)(2), which is commonly referred to as the federal anti-bribery or anti-gratuity statute, provides that "[w]hoever . . . directly or indirectly gives, offers, or promises anything of value to any person, for or because of the testimony under oath or affirmation given or to be given by such person as a witness upon a trial, hearing, or other proceeding, before any court, any committee or either House or both Houses of Congress, or any agency, commission, or officer authorized by the laws of the United States to hear evidence or take testimony" shall be fined or imprisoned for up to two years, or both.[65] Notably, "whoever" as used in the statute does not include federal prosecutors functioning within the scope of their office who pay cooperating witnesses, even when the payments are solely for the

58. N.Y. Eth. Op. 668, 1994 WL 593255, at *3 (N.Y. State Bar Ass'n, Comm. on Prof'l Ethics 1994) [hereinafter N.Y. Eth. Op. 668].

59. United States v. Davis, 261 F.3d 1, 39 (1st Cir. 2001) (quoting the district court).

60. ABA Formal Op. 96-402, *supra* note 24, at 3; Cal. Eth. Op. 1997-149, *supra* note 35, 1997 WL 197243, at *5; N.Y. Eth. Op. 668, *supra* note 58, 1994 WL 593255, at *2–3; *see, e.g., Davis*, 261 F.3d at 39 (approving the payment of a modest hourly rate to an elderly, unemployed fact witness); Klorczyk v. Sears, Roebuck & Co., No. 3:13-cv-00257 (JAM), 2017 WL 3272237, at *3 (D. Conn. Aug. 21, 2017) (paying a witness $120 per hour was reasonable even though it far exceeded what the witness, who was semi-retired, earned in his part-time job and also exceeded what he earned when he was employed full-time, because that rate accounted for "his many years of relevant professional experience").

61. N.Y. Eth. Op. 668, *supra* note 58, 1994 WL 593255, at *2.

62. Cal. Eth. Op. 1997-149, *supra* note 35, 1997 WL 197243, at *4.

63. Again, states may have bribery or witness-tampering statutes to which lawyers must be sensitive. *See, e.g.*, Ohio Rev. Code Ann. § 2921.02(C) & (D) (West 2020) (criminalizing as bribery the corruption or improper influencing of witnesses); Wash. Rev. Code § 9A.72.090 (2019) (providing that bribing a witness is a felony).

64. *See* Model Rules of Prof'l Conduct R. 3.4(b) (2020) (stating that a lawyer shall not "offer an inducement to a witness that is prohibited by law").

65. 18 U.S.C. § 201(c)(2) (2018).

witnesses' testimony, "so long as the payment is not for or because of any corruption of the truth of testimony."[66] Other lawyers and parties litigating in federal courts, however, are not expressly afforded such leeway.

Section 201(c)(2) by its terms does not prohibit payments to fact witnesses made for purposes other than the fact or content of their testimony.[67] Or, stated positively, the statute permits lawyers and parties to compensate fact witnesses for time lost to testifying.[68] This limit on section 201(c)(2)'s otherwise long reach is made manifest in 18 U.S.C. § 201(d), which states that § 201(c)(2) does not "prohibit the payment . . . of witness fees provided by law, or the payment, by the party upon whose behalf a witness is called . . . of the reasonable cost of travel and subsistence incurred and the reasonable value of time lost in attendance at any such trial, hearing, or proceeding."[69] Furthermore, and consistent with these positions, nothing in § 201(c)(2) establishes that a person violates the law by paying fact witnesses for time spent in legitimate non-testimonial activities, such as meeting with counsel for a party or reviewing documents in preparation for testifying.[70] Payment for such activities is allowable because it is not extended "for or because of [the] testimony" of the witness.[71] Indeed, the weight of authority holds that witnesses' time spent on legitimate non-testimonial activities is permitted under the anti-gratuity statute, provided the amount of compensation is reasonable.[72]

66. United States v. Anty, 203 F.3d 305, 311 (4th Cir. 2000); *see also* United States v. Ihnatenko, 482 F.3d 1097, 1100 (9th Cir. 2007); United States v. Rodriguez-Aguirre, 30 F. App'x 803, 807–08 (10th Cir. 2002); United States v. Albanese, 195 F.3d 389, 395 (8th Cir. 1999); United States v. Barnett, 197 F.3d 138, 144–45 (5th Cir. 1999).

67. *See* 18 U.S.C. § 201(c)(2) (2018) (referring to payments or similar promises "*for or because of* the testimony" of a witness) (emphasis added).

68. Aristocrat Techs. v. Int'l Game Tech., No. C–06–03717 RMW, 2010 WL 2595151, at *2 (N.D. Cal. June 28, 2010).

69. 18 U.S.C. § 201(d) (2018).

70. Centennial Mgmt. Servs., Inc. v. Axa Re Vie, 193 F.R.D. 671, 682 (D. Kan. 2000).

71. Consol. Rail Corp. v. CSX Transp., Inc., No. 09-cv-10179, 2012 WL 511572, at *13 (E.D. Mich. Feb. 16, 2012); *Centennial Mgmt. Servs., Inc.*, 193 F.R.D. at 681.

72. *See, e.g.*, Rajaratnam v. Motley Rice, LLC, No. 18-cv-3234(KAM)(RML), 2020 WL 1476171, at *21 (E.D.N.Y. Mar. 26, 2020) ("A total of $75,000 in payments over the course of nine years, including thousands of miles travelled, equates to less than $8,500 per year. This figure hardly strikes the court as an unreasonable amount of expenses to reimburse, given the importance of [the witness] to Motley Rice's case."); Armenian Assembly of Am., Inc. v. Cafesjian, 924 F. Supp. 2d 183, 194 (D.D.C. 2013) (allowing compensation of fact witness for "countless hours" spent assisting counsel in discovery and trial preparation); *Consol. Rail*, 2012 WL 511572, at *8 (citing ABA Formal Op. 96-402); Chi. Ins. Co. v. Capwill, No. 1:01cv2588, 2011 WL 6181337, at *2 (N.D. Ohio Dec. 13, 2011) ("It was unquestionably proper for plaintiff's counsel to provide payment equivalent to [the witness's] salary for his time spent preparing for his deposition, reviewing his testimony and traveling to and from deposition-related appointments. The payment for [the witness's] time being deposed [was] also proper."); United States v. Kobagaya, No. 09-10005-01, 2011 WL 1466475, at *4 (D. Kan. Apr. 18, 2011) (stating that it is "entirely reasonable to compensate a witness for time and expenses in meeting with a government attorney to prepare for trial as long as the amounts paid are reasonable"); Prasad v. MML Inv. Servs., Inc., No. 04 Civ. 380, 2004

With § 201(d), as with ethics rules, the essential inquiry often is whether a witness's compensation for litigation-related time is reasonable. To make this determination, a court must examine the circumstances of the case. Among the factors a court may consider when evaluating the reasonableness of a witness's compensation are the hourly rate paid to the witness and the number of hours spent by the witness in connection with the litigation.[73] This is always a case-specific inquiry; there is no precise or uniform measure of reasonableness.

Finally, if a court determines that a fact witness's compensation does not violate § 201(c)(2), it necessarily determines in the process that the lawyer who approved, acquiesced in, or orchestrated the payments did not violate the Rule 3.4(b) prohibition on offering an inducement to a witness that is prohibited by law.[74]

C. Summary and Synthesis

In summary, the majority rule holds that lawyers may compensate fact witnesses for time spent testifying, preparing to testify, or otherwise assisting in litigation, and may reimburse witnesses' related expenses, provided the amounts paid are reasonable, are not conditioned on the act of testifying or the content or substance of the witness's testimony, and are not contingent upon the outcome of the litigation.[75] Reasonable compensation for time spent testifying, preparing to testify, or otherwise assisting in litigation is not an inducement to a witness that is prohibited by law within the meaning of Model Rule 3.4(b),[76] nor is it a violation of the federal anti-gratuity statute as interpreted by most courts to have considered the issue.

The reasonableness of a witness's compensation is measured objectively,[77] or at least as objectively as possible on the facts presented. Evaluating reasonableness requires case-specific inquiry.[78] The closer a witness's compensation comes to approximating her direct loss of income, the more likely it is to be found reasonable.[79] Fact witnesses whose agreed compensation cannot

WL 1151735, at *6 (S.D.N.Y. May 24, 2004) ("A witness may be compensated for the time spent preparing to testify or otherwise consulting on a litigation matter in addition to the time spent providing testimony in a deposition or at trial."); *Centennial Mgmt. Servs., Inc.*, 193 F.R.D. at 682 (relying on ABA Formal Op. 96-402); Kocur v. Split Vein Coal Co. (*In re* Split Vein Coal Co.), No. 1:03-BK-02974MDF, 2013 WL 1934669, at *6 (Bankr. M.D. Pa. May 9, 2013) (quoting *Centennial Mgmt. Servs., Inc.*, 193 F.R.D. at 682).

73. *Centennial Mgmt. Servs., Inc.*, 193 F.R.D. at 680.

74. *Id.* at 682.

75. ABA Formal Op. 96-402, *supra* note 24, at 2–3; Cal. Eth. Op. 1997-149, *supra* note 35, 1997 WL 197243, at *5.

76. United States v. Davis, 261 F.3d 1, 38 n.31 (1st Cir. 2001).

77. Alaska Eth. Op. 93-2, *supra* note 35, 1993 WL 849637, at *2 n.2.

78. Ariz. Op. 97-07, *supra* note 35, at 4; W. Va. Op. 2017-1, *supra* note 3, at 6.

79. ABA Formal Op. 96-402, *supra* note 24, at 3.

be shown to be reasonable should not necessarily be denied all payment for their lost time. It may be possible to lower or restructure a witness's compensation to make it reasonable. Alternatively, a court may limit a witness to the recovery of statutory witness fees and expenses.[80]

Courts may consider a number of factors in making reasonableness determinations, including (1) the time spent by the witness in connection with the litigation; (2) the hourly rate paid to the witness by her employer if the witness is currently employed; (3) the witness's regular fees or regular hourly rates if the witness is self-employed; (4) the witness's most recent wages or earnings, or what others earn for comparable activities, if the witness is unemployed or retired; (5) the witness's special qualifications, such as experience, expertise, or specialized knowledge that cannot practicably be supplied by others; (6) the value of opportunities or alternative employment that a witness must forgo to participate in the litigation, whether because of the time commitment required or other factors; (7) the inconvenience or hardship experienced by the witness as a result of her involvement in the litigation, which may or may not overlap with the preceding element; (8) the witness's occupation, trade, or profession, which, again, may or may not intersect with some of the prior factors; and (9) practical constraints, such as whether the witness has unique factual knowledge or is beyond the court's subpoena power. This list is not exhaustive, and other considerations may be relevant in particular cases.

The reasonableness of witnesses' expenses is seldom an issue. The reimbursement of a person's actual expenses is almost uniformly proper.

III. Illustrative Cases

Lawyers who are contemplating paying fact witnesses for time lost to testifying or to preparation for testifying are challenged by several factors when formulating compensation arrangements. For one thing, there is variation among jurisdictions in terms of permissible witness compensation.[81] For another thing, different courts may have significantly different perspectives on the reasonableness of fact witnesses' compensation even when the

80. *See* Kocur v. Split Vein Coal Co. (*In re* Split Vein Coal Co.), No. 1:03-BK-02974MDF, 2013 WL 1934669, at *6–7 (Bankr. M.D. Pa. May 9, 2013) (calculating a witness's administrative claim in a bankruptcy case).

81. *See, e.g.*, *In re* Complaint of PMD Enters. Inc., 215 F. Supp. 2d 519, 530 (D.N.J. 2002) (limiting fact witness compensation to time lost in attending trial or testifying and reasonable expenses incurred in attending trial or testifying); Goldstein v. Exxon Research & Eng'g Co., No. Civ. 95-2410, 1997 WL 580599, at *1–2 (D.N.J. Feb. 28, 1997) (taking the same approach); Trial Pracs., Inc. v. Hahn, Loeser & Parks, LLP, 260 So. 3d 167, 173 (Fla. 2018) (holding that Florida Rule 4-3.4(b) "permits a party to pay a fact witness for the witness's assistance with case and discovery preparation that is directly related to the witness preparing for, attending, or testifying at proceedings").

amounts at issue or the witnesses' status or roles are very similar. Finally, while some compensation arrangements are clearly improper and should have been so recognized before they were entered into, such as where a witness is to be paid for her testimony,[82] in other cases subtle or unappreciated factual differences may lead to very different results. Nonetheless, it is helpful to examine some cases in which courts either approved or disapproved of witnesses' compensation to better understand how related controversies play out.

A. *Cases Approving Fact Witnesses' Compensation*

In *Prasad v. MML Investor Services, Inc.*,[83] the plaintiffs sought to vacate an NASD arbitration award in favor of the defendant, MMLISI. They alleged in the arbitration case that they were defrauded in a Ponzi scheme operated by a former MMLISI representative, Nagajara Thayagarajan. One of the witnesses who testified for MMLISI in the arbitration was Stanley Farr, a former compliance officer with the firm, who, while still employed by MMLISI, had investigated Thayagarajan's alleged misconduct.[84] At the time he testified, Farr was self-employed as a compliance consultant and charged his time to his consulting clients at a rate of $125 per hour.[85] After Farr's third day of testimony in the arbitration, the plaintiffs complained to the arbitrators that Farr was receiving "illegal compensation" as a fact witness and that the time he "spent in 'witness prep' amounted to witness tampering and constituted subornation of perjury."[86] The panel allowed the plaintiffs to recall Farr as a witness and question him regarding his compensation by MMLISI.

Farr testified that MMLISI had reimbursed him for his time spent on the arbitration at an hourly rate of $125, the same rate he charged clients as a self-employed consultant. He explained that he was not paid to testify in any particular manner. He also testified that while he did not prepare any witnesses to testify in the arbitration proceeding, he was present when MMLISI's lawyers prepared other witnesses. Finally, Farr's invoices to MMLISI indicated that he was also reimbursed for his travel expenses, including airfare, car rental, hotels, and meals.

At the close of Farr's testimony, the plaintiffs moved to strike the testimony of all of MMLISI's witnesses on the basis that MMLISI had improperly

82. *See, e.g.*, Golden Door Jewelry Creations, Inc. v. Lloyds Underwriters Non-Marine Ass'n, 865 F. Supp. 1516, 1521–27 (S.D. Fla. 1994) (sanctioning insurer for witness payments that "unquestionably violated the very heart of the integrity of the justice system").

83. No. 04 Civ. 380(RWS), 2004 WL 1151735 (S.D.N.Y. May 24, 2004).

84. *Id.* at *1.

85. *Id.* at *1–2.

86. *Id.* at *2.

paid Farr for his testimony and time. The arbitrators declined to do so and further denied the plaintiffs' claims against MMLISI in their entirety. The plaintiffs then petitioned a New York federal court to vacate the arbitration award.

In the district court, the plaintiffs asserted that the arbitration panel acted in manifest disregard of the law when it declined to strike the witnesses' testimony.[87] The plaintiffs did not challenge the reasonableness of Farr's expenses, nor did they contend that he was paid for anything other than his time and expenses.[88] Rather, they argued it was improper for MMLISI to have paid Farr to participate in witness preparation.[89] The plaintiffs further complained that MMLISI did not reveal Farr's compensation or services before they were exposed on cross-examination, a lapse the plaintiffs characterized as "'troubling.'"[90] Their arguments did not impress the court. As the court explained:

> A witness may be compensated for the time spent preparing to testify or otherwise consulting on a litigation matter in addition to time spent testifying in a deposition or at trial. . . .
>
> That a fact witness has been retained to act as a litigation consultant does not, in and of itself, appear to be improper, absent some indication that the retention was designed as a financial inducement or as a method to secure the cooperation of a hostile witness, or was otherwise improper. . . . Although Farr was retained by MMLISI after he was approached by [the plaintiffs] to testify as a witness . . . that fact alone is insufficient to establish that MMLISI's retention of his services as a consultant was improper as a matter of law, particularly in view of Farr's testimony that he was initially contacted by MMLISI's counsel regarding [the plaintiffs'] claims . . . long before he was approached by [the plaintiffs].[91]

Therefore, the plaintiffs could not show that Farr's compensation by MMLISI violated any governing legal principles.[92]

The amount of Farr's compensation certainly did not concern the court. Indeed, the fact that MMLISI paid Farr the same rate he charged his clients as a self-employed compliance consultant was a compelling display of reasonableness.[93]

Finally, while the court acknowledged that a lawyer's or witness's failure to timely divulge the witness's compensation may sometimes be troubling, not so here. Farr testified during his first day of direct examination that he

87. *Id.* at *3.
88. *Id.*
89. *Id.*
90. *Id.* at *5.
91. *Id.* at *6.
92. *Id.* at *7.
93. *Id.*

had located and interviewed potential witnesses at the request of MMLISI's counsel.[94] At that time he and MMLISI's counsel also clarified that he was being paid for his time spent in connection with the arbitration.[95]

To the extent the plaintiffs were upset by Farr being present when MMLISI's counsel met with other witnesses, they could cite no authority for the proposition that lawyers are prohibited from meeting with multiple witnesses at the same time. The plaintiffs offered no evidence to support their allegations of witness tampering.[96] Accordingly, the *Prasad* court confirmed the arbitration award in favor of MMLISI.

Prasad illustrates at least two key points for lawyers. First, it shows the importance of linking fact witnesses' compensation to their direct losses of income. The tighter the linkage between the two, the greater the probability that the court will hold the witness's compensation to be reasonable. Second, the decision highlights the wisdom of disclosing compensation arrangements with witnesses. In fact, the disclosure in *Prasad* might have been made earlier. Many prudent lawyers disclose fact witnesses' compensation in discovery at a time when an opponent can explore the subject if it wishes, but disclosure on direct examination in a proceeding presents a last clear chance to avoid trouble.[97]

In *Art+Com Innovation Pool Gmbh v. Google Inc.*,[98] the plaintiff, ACI, sued Google for patent infringement. Google retained Stephen Lau, an expert on the technology at issue by virtue of his prior employment, who was then employed at Lawrence Berkeley Labs (LBL). Lau served as a consultant on his own time—not as an LBL employee. In addition to his consulting role, Lau's experience with the technology at issue made him a fact witness. His consulting agreement with Google provided in pertinent part:

> Because your consulting work will take time away from your regular work, you will be reimbursed for your time spent on consulting on [this] matter at your regular hourly rate of $450. This reimbursement is independent of the nature of information that you provide to [Google], does not depend on the ultimate outcome of the [litigation with ACI], and must not influence any testimony that you may provide in the [litigation with ACI]. If you are

94. *Id.*
95. *Id.*
96. *Id.*
97. *See, e.g.*, United States v. Cinergy Corp., No. 1:99-cv-1693-LJM-JMS, 2008 WL 7679914, at *10–15 (S.D. Ind. Dec. 18, 2008) (ordering a new trial where defense counsel did not reveal fact witness's compensation on direct examination and allegedly misled jury about witness's compensation, and witness did not reveal employment or compensation when testifying). *But cf.* Armenian Assembly of Am., Inc. v. Cafesjian, 924 F. Supp. 2d 183, 192–95 (D.D.C. 2013) (finding no basis to hold that witness had to disclose compensation and pointing out that the plaintiff's questioning failed to reveal the compensation not because the witness was dishonest but because the questions were not sufficiently specific).
98. No. 1:14-217-TBD, 2016 WL 10033421 (D. Del. Sept. 9, 2016).

> asked to testify in connection with the [litigation with ACI], you will not be reimbursed for the time spent providing testimony.[99]

The case between ACI and Google went to trial and ACI lost. ACI then moved to set aside the judgment based on Google's purported fraud and misrepresentation.[100] In so moving, ACI focused on Lau's allegedly false and surprising trial testimony.[101] ACI asserted in part that Google's consulting agreement with Lau was an improper inducement to a fact witness.[102] Among other concerns, ACI argued that Lau's $450 hourly consulting rate was unreasonably high given his effective hourly rate based on his $170,000 annual salary at LBL.[103] The *Art+Com* court brushed aside ACI's complaints.

A party can enter into agreements with fact witnesses that compensate them for consulting work and not trial testimony.[104] A fact witness's retention as a litigation consultant is proper unless the arrangement is "'designed as a financial inducement or as a method to secure the cooperation of a hostile witness,'" or is otherwise exposed as illegitimate.[105] That was not the situation here. ACI's argument that Lau's consulting compensation was unreasonably high in relation to his LBL salary was equally unavailing:

> In determining whether a fact witness's compensation is unreasonably high, courts look to the nature of the witness's experience and the nature of the litigation. . . . [P]ast compensation may be relevant to measuring reasonable compensation for consulting work, but it is not necessarily the market value of a witness's . . . time. The mere fact that Mr. Lau's consulting rate is five times his prorated hourly salary is not itself unreasonable. It is not unreasonable for people to command a higher rate for low utilization, a la carte services compared to their effective hourly salary in long-term employment; nor is it unreasonable for people with full-time employment to charge more for consulting work done during limited free time. . . . Here, in light of Mr. Lau's "experience in the . . . industry, his first-hand experience with the [prior art] that are the subject of this lawsuit, and the complex nature of this litigation," he court finds Mr. Lau's rates and total compensation are not unreasonable.[106]

---

99. *Id.* at *1 (alterations in original).

100. *See* Fed. R. Civ. P. 60(b)(3) ("On motion and just terms, the court may relieve a party or its legal representative from a final judgment, order, or proceeding for the following reasons: . . . (3) fraud (whether previously called intrinsic or extrinsic), misrepresentation, or misconduct by an opposing party[.]").

101. *Art+Com*, 2016 WL 10033421, at *3–4.

102. *Id.* at *2.

103. *Id.* at *3.

104. *Id.*

105. *Id.* (quoting Prasad v. MML Inv'rs Servs., Inc., No. 04 CIV. 380 (RWS), 2004 WL 1151735, at *6 (S.D.N.Y. May 24, 2004)).

106. *Id.* (citation omitted) (alteration in the original).

The *Art+Com* court concluded that under the circumstances, there was no basis for relief under Rule 60(b)(3). It therefore denied ACI's motion to set aside the judgment.

Art+Com is an interesting case because the court considered all the circumstances of Lau's retention—including the relative value of work done by a fully employed professional on personal time—when evaluating the reasonableness of his compensation. The case also illustrates the importance of a party clarifying that payments to a fact witness for consulting services bear no relation to the fact or substance of the witness's expected testimony.

B. Cases Disapproving of Fact Witnesses' Compensation

State of New York v. Solvent Chemical Co.[107] is regarded as a leading case opposing fact witness compensation, although that is an ambitious interpretation of the decision. In *Solvent*, the State of New York sued a company named ICC and other defendants for environmental pollution at an industrial chemical facility in the town of Niagara Falls known as the Buffalo Avenue site. The suit was filed in 1983, and in 1986 ICC and Solvent filed a variety of third-party claims. In 1995, discovery finally focused on ICC's potential liability as an operator of the Buffalo Avenue site or as the corporate parent of Solvent Chemical Co., which had run the industrial chemical facility. In turn, a dispute arose over ICC's retention of its former employee Eric Beu, who was an important fact witness, as a litigation consultant.[108]

In the 1970s, Beu was a vice president of both ICC and its wholly owned subsidiary, Dover Chemical Corp. (Dover). He left ICC and Dover in 1979. He later brought an arbitration proceeding against ICC related to his departure, which he lost.[109] Beu had not worked in the chemical industry since. In 1993, Dover filed a CERCLA action in an Ohio federal court against several defendants, including Beu as a former owner or operator of Dover's facility in Dover, Ohio (the *Dover* litigation).[110]

When another defendant, Occidental Chemical Co., or OCC, subpoenaed Beu for a deposition in this case in July 1995, ICC realized that Beu possessed critical knowledge of Solvent's operations at the Buffalo Avenue site and of ICC's relationship with Solvent. ICC's internal documents relevant to Solvent's operations included numerous memoranda to or from Beu, many of which bore his indecipherable handwritten notes. ICC, Solvent, and Dover thus approached Beu through his counsel in the *Dover* litigation and reached several agreements with him. First, Dover settled with

107. 166 F.R.D. 284 (W.D.N.Y. 1996).
108. *Id.* at 286.
109. *Id.*
110. *Id.*

Beu in the *Dover* litigation. Beu paid Dover $4,000, and Dover promised to indemnify him with respect to any claims against him by other parties in that case.[111] Second, ICC and Solvent agreed not to sue Beu in the current action.[112] Third, ICC and Beu entered into a written consulting agreement in the current case. Beu agreed to assist ICC and its lawyers by reviewing and discussing with them documents relevant to the litigation at a rate of $100 per hour plus expenses.[113]

Beu was deposed for three days in November 1995. Before his deposition, neither ICC nor Solvent told any of the other parties about ICC's consulting agreement with Beu, although they did tell them that lawyers from Solvent's law firm would represent Beu at his deposition.[114] On the first day of his deposition, Beu denied any current relationships with ICC, Dover, or Solvent.[115] Neither his lawyers nor the lawyers appearing for ICC and Solvent corrected his testimony.[116] On the third day of the deposition, Beu was asked whether he had consulting relationships with any of the parties. He then explained the terms of his consultancy, testified that he had worked somewhere between 20 and 50 hours on the case, explained that he did all of his work after he had been subpoenaed to give his deposition, and said that he was not being paid for his deposition time.[117] Beu declined to answer questions regarding the details of his consulting work on the advice of his lawyer. He also refused to produce the consulting agreement and the invoices for his time, based on his lawyer's assertion that they constituted work product. A discovery dispute ensued.

The court determined that Beu's consulting agreement and related documents were not immune from discovery as work product.[118] As the court explained, work product immunity must yield to conduct by litigants or their lawyers that "erode[s] the integrity of the adversary process," and here the conduct of ICC and Solvent and their lawyers with respect to Beu had "threatened to undermine the integrity of the adversary process."[119] In particular:

> ICC and Solvent purchased Mr. Beu's cooperation in the instant case, by orchestrating the settlement of Dover's claims against him in the *Dover* litigation, by obtaining Dover's agreement to indemnify him with respect to any claims made against him by other parties in that case, and by

111. *Id.*
112. *Id.*
113. *Id.*
114. *Id.*
115. *Id.* at 286–87.
116. *Id.*
117. *Id.* at 287.
118. *Id.* at 289.
119. *Id.*

undertaking not to sue him in the present action. Those actions were the equivalent of making cash payments to Mr. Beu as a means of making him "sympathetic" and securing his testimony.[120]

There was nothing improper in ICC reimbursing Beu for his travel expenses incurred in consulting with ICC or in ICC's payment of a reasonable hourly fee for his time.[121] But in indemnifying Beu in connection with the *Dover* litigation and this case "as a means of obtaining his cooperation as a fact witness, ICC and Solvent went too far."[122] In addition, the circumstances surrounding ICC's retention of Beu as a consultant were suspicious.

> ICC must have been well aware, prior to OCC's serving of a subpoena on Mr. Beu, that Mr. Beu was an extremely important fact witness in this case. The company has been a defendant since the original complaint was filed in 1983. But it was only after service of the subpoena in July 1995—when it became clear that OCC and other parties were intending to obtain both documents and testimony from Mr. Beu—that ICC moved to acquire Mr. Beu's services as a "litigation consultant." The timing of ICC's actions creates, in and of itself, an appearance of impropriety that serves to further undermine the company's claim of work product protection for the consulting agreement and related materials. And ICC's identification of Mr. Beu as a member of its trial team inevitably raises concerns as to whether he can be counted on to testify fully and impartially on a key issue in this case—the extent to which ICC was involved in the operations of Solvent and the Buffalo Avenue site at the time the site was owned and/or operated by Solvent.[123]

The court was also disturbed by the fact that no one among Beu, his lawyers, ICC's lawyers, and Solvent's lawyers took the initiative to disclose Beu's consulting arrangement.[124] When asked on the first day of his deposition whether he had a current relationship with ICC or Solvent, Beu wrongly denied the existence of his consulting relationship, yet neither his lawyers nor ICC's or Solvent's counsel corrected the record.

Finally, the court shredded ICC for its "perturbing" reliance on the work product doctrine to withhold Beu's consulting agreement.[125]

> The basis for its claim of work product protection is that the agreement "contains and reflects ICC's litigation strategy and the thoughts, mental impressions and opinions of ICC's counsel." . . . The court is at a loss as to why ICC would incorporate such sensitive information in a written contract with an important fact witness. It must have been obvious at the

120. *Id.*
121. *Id.*
122. *Id.* at 289–90.
123. *Id.* at 290.
124. *Id.*
125. *Id.*

> time the contract was drafted that other parties to the litigation would be disturbed by the existence of the agreement, and would be likely to seek production of the document. It may be that the agreement sets forth the contours, and even some details, of Mr. Beu's responsibilities as a "litigation consultant," and that such provisions might in themselves reveal something of ICC's litigation strategy. But the impropriety of ICC's conduct in relation to Mr. Beu dictates that the company must forfeit any protection that it might otherwise claim to such information.[126]

The court ordered ICC to produce to the other parties copies of all documents that Beu reviewed in his consulting, any documents or notes that he prepared as a consultant, and all notes or other documents reflecting communications with or by Beu.[127] The court also ordered ICC to produce Beu for further deposition at its expense, including paying the fees of the moving parties' lawyers.[128]

At base, the *Solvent* court enforced the common law prohibition on paying fact witnesses for their testimony. What the *Solvent* court clearly did *not* do was prohibit lawyers or others from paying fact witnesses for their time spent testifying or preparing to testify, or for otherwise assisting in preparing a case for trial.[129] To the contrary, the court emphasized that "there is nothing improper about the payment of a reasonable hourly fee for the services of a fact witness."[130] Lawyers who rely on *Solvent* in opposing fact witnesses' compensation or seeking remedies for compensation arrangements they consider to be improper should therefore be careful not to overstate the holding.

Rocheux International of New Jersey, Inc. v. U.S. Merchants Financial Group, Inc.[131] was a contract dispute between Rocheux, a distributor of plastic materials, and several plastic product packaging providers. The defendants alleged that a former employee of one of them, Jorge Gutierrez, had approached Rocheux's lawyer, Brian McAlindin, and offered to provide damaging testimony against the defendants for a fee. McAlindin arranged to pay Gutierrez more than $4,000 for his testimony.[132] McAlindin originally identified Gutierrez as a fact witness but, after the deadline for disclosing expert witnesses had passed, he informed defense counsel that he would be eliciting expert testimony from Gutierrez. As part of that expert witness disclosure, McAlindin submitted an affidavit from Gutierrez stating that the

126. *Id.*
127. *Id.* at 292.
128. *Id.*
129. *Id.* at 289 (stating that there was "nothing improper in the reimbursement of expenses incurred by Mr. Beu in travelling to New York to provide ICC with factual information, or in the payment of a reasonable hourly fee for Mr. Beu's time").
130. *Id.* at 290 n.4.
131. Civ. No. 06-6147, 2009 WL 3246837 (D.N.J. Oct. 5, 2009).
132. *Id.* at *1.

defendant for which he once worked had changed data in its accounting system and had engaged in other unethical business practices at its CEO's direction.

The defendants noticed Gutierrez's deposition. McAlindin then informed them that Gutierrez would charge $1,500 for his deposition testimony.[133] The deposition proceeded, and Gutierrez testified that McAlindin had paid him more than $4,000 to date but that he understood that fee to be payment for his consulting work (specifically, his communications with Rocheux's lawyers and reviewing his affidavit) rather than his expert testimony.[134] He said that he had contacted Rocheux's lawyers to tell them he had information he thought might help the lawsuit.[135] He further testified that he first discussed possible compensation with McAlindin when they met for him to sign his affidavit because until then it had been uncertain whether Rocheux would use his testimony.[136] When questioned on the subjects on which he was designated as an expert, Gutierrez gave equivocal and uninformed answers that did not help Rocheux's case.

The defendants moved to exclude Gutierrez as an improperly paid fact witness and contended that Rocheux designated him as an expert witness to deliberately circumvent the prohibition against paying fact witnesses for testifying.[137] They further sought to invalidate Gutierrez's $1,500 deposition fee and requested "appropriate sanctions for the unethical behavior of [the] [p]laintiff's counsel."[138]

After referring to New Jersey Rule of Professional Conduct 3.4(b), the *Rocheux* court asserted that lawyers may (1) reimburse fact witnesses for reasonable expenses incurred in attending trial and (2) reasonably pay witnesses for their time lost in appearing to testify.[139] The court further stated that Congress codified this common law principle in the federal anti-gratuity statute.[140] Here, it was crystal clear that Gutierrez was a fact witness and that McAlindin had improperly paid Gutierrez for his testimony. When asked to identify the expert opinions in Gutierrez's affidavit, McAlindin pointed to "factual evidence based on lay observations" that lacked the reliable methodology required by Federal Rule of Evidence 702 for the admission of expert testimony.[141] McAlindin could not otherwise explain why Gutierrez should be treated as an expert witness. Furthermore, the fee

133. *Id.*
134. *Id.*
135. *Id.* at *2.
136. *Id.*
137. *Id.*
138. *Id.*
139. *Id.* at *3.
140. *Id.*
141. *Id.*

paid to Gutierrez "most certainly did not compensate [him] for his costs of attending trial or time lost during trial."[142] In summary, McAlindin's payment to Gutierrez violated the longstanding ban on paying fact witnesses for their testimony.[143]

The court reasoned that McAlindin's decision to pay Gutierrez for factual testimony had "cast a cloud over the legitimacy of that testimony" and that it was up to it "to prevent this suspect evidence from contaminating future proceedings."[144] The court accordingly excluded Gutierrez's testimony, excused the defendants from paying Gutierrez's expert fee for his deposition, and awarded the defendants their reasonable attorneys' fees and costs incurred as a result of McAlindin's misconduct.

McAlindin's conduct in *Rocheux* was seriously misguided. Gutierrez clearly was a fact witness, and his compensation was objectively unreasonable. McAlindin paid Gutierrez for his testimony rather than for his time. In the end, though, what distinguishes *Rocheux* is the fact that Gutierrez was a former employee of a defendant rather than a former employee of Rocheux. Paying a fact witness who is a former employee of an adversary almost invites accusations of misconduct.[145]

IV. Recommendations for Lawyers

Lawyers handling litigation, arbitrations, or administrative proceedings will, at some point, either want to compensate fact witnesses for assisting them or be asked by fact witnesses about possible compensation for their time or services. How should careful lawyers approach these situations?[146]

First, lawyers should try to ascertain the law of the jurisdiction on compensating fact witnesses. This may require analysis of applicable rules of professional conduct, court rules, case law, and ethics opinions, as well as criminal statutes pertaining to bribery and witness tampering and cases interpreting those statutes. Depending on where a witness lives, a case is pending, or a lawyer practices, there may be choice of law concerns to evaluate.

Second, lawyers should never pay fact witnesses for their testimony, regardless of whether the payment is for the fact of a witness's testimony or its content or substance. A fact witness's compensation may never be

142. *Id.* at *4.

143. *Id.*

144. *Id.*

145. *See, e.g.*, Nissan N. Am., Inc. v. Johnson Elec. N. Am., Inc., No. 09-11783, 2011 WL 1812505, at *3 (E.D. Mich. May 12, 2011) (discussing a magistrate's findings regarding a party's payment of a fact witness who was formerly employed by an opponent).

146. For an excellent article making many of the points discussed below, see John K. Villa, *Paying Fact Witnesses*, ACC Docket, Oct. 2001, at 112; *see also* Marcellus A. McRae & Kim Nortman, *Your Witness*, L.A. Law., Sept. 2012, at 31 (offering related advice).

contingent upon the fact, content, or substance of the witness's testimony or the outcome of the litigation.[147] A requirement that a witness's testimony be truthful will not cure any of these ills.[148]

Third, but consistent with the prior point, lawyers should compensate fact witnesses only for their time lost to testifying, preparing to testify, or otherwise legitimately assisting in the preparation of a case, plus reimbursement of reasonable expenses incurred in connection with those activities. Any compensation should be objectively reasonable. The closer a fact witness's compensation comes to approximating her direct loss of income, the more likely a court will find it to be reasonable.[149] In the absence of direct loss, a lawyer should calculate the reasonable value of the witness's time based on all of the relevant circumstances.[150] At bottom, there must be an explainable and logical connection between the amount of time or effort a fact witness devotes to a matter and the amount of the witness's compensation.[151]

Lawyers should not offer benefits to fact witnesses in addition to reasonable payment for time lost or reimbursement of reasonable expenses that courts or disciplinary authorities may view as influencing, even unintentionally, the witness's testimony. Such benefits might include promises of future employment or business opportunities with the lawyer's client, promises of favorable treatment in business dealings with the lawyer's client, arrangements or extensions of loans or credit, forgiveness of debts owed to the lawyer's client, or indemnity agreements.

Fourth, lawyers should consider waiting for fact witnesses to request compensation for their time before offering it. In some cases, it may be necessary for the lawyer to raise the issue first to obtain the witness's cooperation, but, by waiting for the witness to request payment for her time, a

147. *See, e.g.*, Ward v. Nierlich, No. 99-14227-CIV., 2006 WL 5412626, at *3 (S.D. Fla. Sept. 20, 2006) (recommending sanctions where the plaintiffs and their lawyers "corrupted the judicial process and committed a fraud on this [c]ourt by paying defense witnesses for their testimony," and explaining that the witnesses "were promised a substantial stake in this litigation based on a favorable judgment or settlement"); *In re* Telcar Grp., Inc., 363 B.R. 345, 355 (Bankr. E.D.N.Y. 2007) (refusing to approve a settlement between a bankruptcy trustee and a former principal of the debtor who was a fact witness where "the sums that may become due to [the witness] under the settlement, or the credits to which he may become entitled, have no relation to the amount of time expended by [the witness] or the reasonable cost in attending or testifying at any proceedings, but are entirely contingent upon the outcome of the contemplated litigation").

148. Rocheux Int'l of N.J., Inc. v. U.S. Merchs. Fin. Grp., Inc., No. 06-6147, 2009 WL 3246837, at *4 (D.N.J. Oct. 2009); *Ward*, 2006 WL 5412626, at *4; *In re Telcar Grp., Inc.*, 363 B.R. at 354; *In re* Kien, 372 N.E.2d 376, 379 (Ill. 1977).

149. ABA Formal Op. 96-402, *supra* note 24, at 3.

150. *Id.*

151. In the case of professionals who testify as fact witnesses, for example, it generally is reasonable to compensate them for their lost time at their professional rates. *See* Smith v. Pfizer Inc., 714 F. Supp. 2d 845, 853 (M.D. Tenn. 2010) (discussing payment of a medical doctor who was a fact witness at her professional rate of $500 per hour).

lawyer may help avoid any misperception on the part of the witness or the court about the reason for the compensation.

Fifth, lawyers should avoid paying fact witnesses who were formerly employed by another party in the litigation—especially an opposing party.[152] They should be similarly cautious when considering whether to compensate fact witnesses who, while not formerly employed by an adversary, are expected to be key witnesses for that party.[153] Although cases in which lawyers have been sanctioned or reprimanded for compensating former employees of opposing parties or key witnesses for adversaries have involved obviously impermissible payments for testimony rather than reasonable compensation for time lost, it remains true that certain categories of fact witnesses are more likely to invite misconduct charges, and these are two of them. None of this is to say that fact witnesses falling into these categories can *never* be properly compensated by a party other than a former employer or expected beneficiary of their testimony, but it is to say that lawyers should exercise extreme caution in this area.

Sixth, lawyers should not purport to prohibit fact witnesses from speaking with other parties or their lawyers as part of any compensation arrangement. Rules of professional conduct generally prevent lawyers from attempting to so restrict witnesses.[154]

Seventh, lawyers should put compensation agreements with witnesses in writing. An agreement should clearly state that the witness is being compensated only for the reasonable value of her time and being reimbursed only for reasonable expenses. Accuracy and clarity are important here for two reasons. First, witnesses must understand what is expected of them. Second, compensation agreements with fact witnesses may have to be produced in discovery, and it is critical that they be drafted in ways that will discourage challenges by opposing parties and withstand judicial review. Specifying in writing that witnesses are being compensated solely for the reasonable value of their time and are being reimbursed for reasonable expenses is essential to discouraging and surviving such challenges and scrutiny.

---

152. *See, e.g.*, Nissan N. Am., Inc. v. Johnson Elec. N. Am., Inc., No. 09-11783, 2011 WL 1812505, at *3 (E.D. Mich. May 12, 2011) (discussing a magistrate's findings regarding a party's payment of a fact witness who was formerly employed by an opponent); *Rocheux*, 2009 WL 3246837, at *3–5 (imposing sanctions where the plaintiff's lawyer compensated a disgruntled former employee of a defendant); Rentclub, Inc. v. Transamerica Rental Fin. Corp., 811 F. Supp. 651, 654–57 (M.D. Fla. 1992) (disqualifying lawyer who employed adversary's former employee, who was a fact witness, as a "trial consultant").

153. *See* Ward v. Nierlich, No. 99-14227-CIV., 2006 WL 5412626, at *5 (S.D. Fla. Sept. 20, 2006) (noting that conduct by plaintiffs and their counsel was especially "egregious" because they "did not simply pay their own witnesses, but paid critical witnesses for the defense").

154. Model Rules of Prof'l Conduct R. 3.4(a) & (f) (2020).

Finally, lawyers should inform the other parties in a case of the existence and terms of any agreements to compensate fact witnesses.[155] This should be done sufficiently early in a case to permit other parties to conduct discovery on the issue if they wish. Certainly, lawyers should accurately and timely respond to written discovery regarding fact witnesses' compensation or employment. If witnesses are directly asked about their compensation in depositions and answer inaccurately, the lawyers producing them for their depositions must correct their testimony.[156] If a witness is not asked about her compensation in a deposition and it has not previously been revealed in another context, the lawyer producing the witness may want to consider revealing the compensation arrangement before the deposition is adjourned so that any party who wants to explore the subject is then able to do so.

Paying a fact witness only for the reasonable value of her time and expenses incurred in testifying at a deposition, trial, or other proceeding is rarely controversial. Most battles arise out of consulting arrangements in which witnesses devote significant time to assisting the lawyers for the party paying them. Even so, lawyers may wish to disclose all fact witness compensation agreements, no matter how obviously reasonable or innocuous, simply to avoid accusations of misconduct by aggressive adversaries.

V. Conclusion

It is common for lawyers to compensate fact witnesses for time spent preparing to testify and for time spent testifying. Such payments are generally fair, and they are often necessary to lessen the financial burdens that fact witnesses might otherwise have to shoulder in cases in which they become involved through no choice of their own. But the fact remains that compensating fact witnesses can be a potentially perilous exercise. The general rule that lawyers and the parties they represent may compensate fact witnesses for time spent testifying or preparing to testify, and may reimburse witnesses' associated expenses, so long as the amounts paid to or on behalf of a witness are reasonable, is not uniformly applied or reliably followed. Unfortunately, this general rule, like others, has exceptions, and even in jurisdictions that regularly adhere to it, the reasonableness of fact witnesses' compensation is a recurring point of controversy.

---

155. *See, e.g.*, Rajaratnam v. Motley Rice, LLC, No. 18-cv-3234(KAM)(RML), 2020 WL 1476171, at *21 (E.D.N.Y. Mar. 26, 2020) ("Motley Rice disclosed Rudra's expense reimbursements to Rajaratnam in the NJ Action, producing over 160 pages of expense records in 2016 and 2018. . . . Motley Rice's fulsome disclosure of its expense reimbursements, which exposed in plain sight its payments to Rudra, is not consonant with the often-covert nature of bribes." (footnote omitted)).

156. Model Rules of Prof'l Conduct R. 3.3(a)(3) & 3.4(b) (2020).

5

Ex Parte Communications: Critical Concerns for Lawyers

I. Introduction

Few issues in litigation are as contentious as lawyers' allegedly improper attempts at ex parte communication with parties or people so closely identified with parties that they may be considered off-limits to informal discovery efforts. If a lawyer's ex parte communications are found to be improper, the consequences can be significant. In addition to professional discipline, lawyers may be disqualified from further participation in the cases in which the communications occurred, and they may face sanctions.

There is ample case law on the professional responsibility ramifications of ex parte communications with represented persons. Yet many cases provide little or no guidance to lawyers with respect to the limits of acceptable conduct, and some key areas of the law are incompletely understood or simply unsettled. This chapter examines several ex parte communication issues of recurring importance to trial lawyers.

II. Applicable Rules of Professional Conduct

A. Model Rule 4.2

Any discussion of lawyers' communications with persons represented by counsel must begin with Model Rule of Professional Conduct 4.2,[1] commonly referred to as the "anti-contact rule" or "no-contact rule." Actually, "anti-contact rule" or "no-contact rule" is a misnomer because Model Rule 4.2 does not bar all ex parte communications with a represented person. To use an obvious example, the rule does not prohibit a lawyer from serving process on a person the lawyer knows to be represented by counsel.

1. Model Rules of Prof'l Conduct R. 4.2 (2020).

Nonetheless, the rule places important limits on lawyers who, in representing a client, wish to communicate with people the lawyer knows are represented in the matter. Model Rule 4.2 provides:

> In representing a client, a lawyer shall not communicate about the subject of the representation with a person the lawyer knows to be represented by another lawyer in the matter, unless the lawyer has the consent of the other lawyer or is authorized to do so by law or a court order.[2]

In any dispute concerning the applicability of Rule 4.2, courts, disciplinary authorities, and lawyers must recall the rule's general purposes, which are to "preserve the positions of the parties in an adversarial system and thereby to maintain protections obtained by employing counsel and prevent disruption of the attorney-client relationship,"[3] and to protect a represented person from being taken advantage of by an opposing lawyer.[4] The rule is not designed to inhibit the flow of prejudicial or potentially damaging information.[5]

1. *The Elements of Model Rule 4.2*

At the outset, Model Rule 4.2 requires that a lawyer be representing a client for an ex parte communication to be improper.[6] There is occasional debate over whether a lawyer acting pro se is representing a client for Rule 4.2 purposes or is merely a litigant. The majority view holds that a lawyer appearing pro se is representing a client.[7] This is also the better-reasoned view.

---

2. *Id.*

3. Humco, Inc. v. Noble, 31 S.W.3d 916, 920 (Ky. 2000).

4. Grievance Comm. v. Simels, 48 F.3d 640, 647 (2d Cir. 1995); *In re* Disciplinary Action Against McCormick, 819 N.W.2d 442, 444 (Minn. 2012).

5. Aiken v. Bus. & Indus. Health Grp., Inc., 885 F. Supp. 1474, 1479 (D. Kan. 1995); Hanntz v. Shiley, Inc., 766 F. Supp. 258, 267 (D.N.J. 1991); Messing, Rudavsky & Weliky, P.C. v. President & Fellows of Harvard Coll., 764 N.E.2d 825, 833 (Mass. 2002).

6. United States v. Gonzalez-Lopez, 399 F.3d 924, 931 (8th Cir. 2005); *In re* Benson, 69 P.3d 544, 548 (Kan. 2003); Halverson v. Hardcastle, 163 P.3d 428, 450 n.103 (Nev. 2007).

7. Runsvold v. Idaho State Bar, 925 P.2d 1118, 1120 (Idaho 1996); *In re* Segall, 509 N.E.2d 988, 990 (Ill. 1987); *In re* Hodge, 407 P.3d 613, 654–55 (Kan. 2017); *In re* Discipline of Schaefer, 25 P.3d 191, 199–200 (Nev. 2001); *In re* Disciplinary Action Against Lucas, 789 N.W.2d 73, 76 (N.D. 2010); *In re* Disciplinary Proc. Against Jensen, 430 P.3d 262, 269–70 (Wash. 2018); Sandstrom v. Sandstrom, 880 P.2d 103, 108–09 (Wyo. 1994); Alaska Eth. Op. 2006-01, 2006 WL 339030, at *1 (Alaska Bar Ass'n, Ethics Comm. 2006); S.C. Adv. Op. 11-01, 2011 WL 7657358, at *1 (S.C. Bar, Ethics Advisory Comm. 2011); Va. State Bar, Comm. on Legal Ethics, Op. 1890, at 2, 6 (2020) [hereinafter Va. Op. 1890]. *But see* Duda v. Duda, Nos. 1 CA-CV 09-0146, 1 CA-CV 09-0192, 2010 WL 324452, at *2 n.5 (Ariz. Ct. App. Jan. 28, 2010) (stating that Rule 4.2 "does not diminish the ability of a pro per litigant to communicate with a represented party merely because the litigant holds a license to practice law"); Pinsky v. Statewide Grievance Comm., 578 A.2d 1075, 1079 (Conn. 1990) (reasoning that a lawyer appearing pro se is simply a litigant and not representing a client); State Bar of Tex., Prof'l Ethics Comm., Op. No. 653, at 2 (2016) (concluding that "a lawyer who is a party in a legal matter but who does not represent any other party

After all, Model Rule 4.2 is intended to protect represented persons from overreaching by lawyers and against harm that might result from uncounseled statements, and a lawyer appearing pro se presents these threats. A lawyer appearing pro se is not simply another litigant.

Model Rule 4.2 applies only where the person with whom a lawyer communicates ex parte is represented in the matter. As for the essential requirement of *knowing* whether a person is represented by another lawyer in a matter, that is plain where the other lawyer has entered an appearance, filed a pleading, called to announce her representation, or identified herself in an e-mail message or letter. Such clarity is not required to find a violation, however, because a lawyer's knowledge can be inferred from circumstances. Lawyers cannot avoid acquiring knowledge through willful blindness.[8] Still, the Rule 4.2 knowledge requirement is certainly one of actual knowledge.[9]

Lawyers need not speculate about a person's representation, nor does suspicion about a person's representation determine lawyers' duties.[10] For example, a person's statement that she should speak with someone else—such as a supervisor—before speaking with a lawyer does not support the conclusion that the lawyer knew of the person's representation.[11] The mere fact that a person copies a lawyer on a letter does not establish that the person is represented in a matter,[12] nor does a statement from another lawyer that he or she will be assisting a party without entering a formal appearance necessarily indicate representation for Rule 4.2 purposes.[13] If a lawyer advises a person that she has a right to counsel or may want to retain or consult with counsel and the person fails to mention in response that she is represented, it undermines any claim that the lawyer knew the person was

in the matter may communicate concerning the matter directly with a represented adverse party without the consent of the adverse party's lawyer").

8. Scanlan v. Eisenberg, 893 F. Supp. 2d 945, 950 (N.D. Ill. 2012); People v. Underhill, 353 P.3d 936, 950 (Colo. 2015).

9. *See, e.g.*, McClellan v. Ready Mixed Concrete Co. of Erie, Inc., No. 13-87 Erie, 2014 WL 4060254, at *1–2 (W.D. Pa. Aug. 14, 2014) (noting and applying the actual knowledge requirement); Mori v. Saito, 785 F. Supp. 2d 427, 433 (S.D.N.Y. 2011) (rejecting the argument that a lawyer violated Rule 4.2 because she "must have known" that an unidentified caller was a represented party); State *ex rel.* Okla. Bar Ass'n v. Harper, 995 P.2d 1143, 1147 (Okla. 2000) (requiring actual knowledge and rejecting a proposed "should have known" standard).

10. *See, e.g.*, *Mori*, 785 F. Supp. 2d at 433 (reasoning that where a lawyer eavesdropped on an unidentified caller's conversation with her client, the lawyer's alleged suspicion that the caller was a represented party did not implicate Rule 4.2).

11. Gaylard v. Homemakers of Montgomery, Inc., 675 So. 2d 363, 367 (Ala. 1996).

12. Humco, Inc. v. Noble, 31 S.W.3d 916, 920 (Ky. 2000).

13. *See, e.g.*, McMillan v. Shadow Ridge at Oak Park Homeowner's Ass'n, 81 Cal. Rptr. 3d 550, 554–55 (Ct. App. 2008) (concluding that defense counsel's ex parte contacts with a pro se plaintiff did not violate anti-contact rule even though another attorney had informed defense counsel that he would be assisting the pro se plaintiff on the case, although he would not be substituting as attorney of record and would not be acting as trial counsel).

represented.[14] In sum, the fact that a lawyer *should have known* that a person was represented in a matter will not support a Rule 4.2 violation.[15]

Model Rule 4.2 does not require a lawyer to ask whether someone is represented in a matter before speaking further with the person,[16] although it is often wise to so inquire.[17] A lawyer generally should not attempt ex parte communication where a person's lawyer has moved to withdraw but the court has not yet ruled on the motion; until the court grants the motion, it is best to treat the person as being represented.

As should be apparent, Model Rule 4.2 applies to ex parte communications by lawyers and their agents; it does not prevent parties from communicating with one another outside their lawyers' presence.[18] For example, two businesspeople who are locked in a dispute may decide that they can settle the matter through personal negotiations without their lawyers being present. Alternatively, parties to a marital dissolution proceeding may decide that they can resolve some disputed issues on their own. Lawyers may advise clients concerning communications with represented persons that the client is legally entitled to make.[19] Lawyers may prepare outlines, scripts, or talking points for clients who intend to communicate with a represented person on their own,[20] as long as the lawyer does not encourage or position the client to seek confidential information from the person or otherwise overreach,[21] or encourage or instruct the client to make misrepresentations. To reason otherwise would restrict the client's autonomy and would grant

14. SEC v. Lines, 669 F. Supp. 2d 460, 465 (S.D.N.Y. 2009).

15. State *ex rel.* Okla. Bar Ass'n v. Harper, 995 P.2d 1143, 1147 (Okla. 2000).

16. White Cap Constr. Supply, Inc. v. Tighton Fastener & Supply Corp., No. 8:08CV264, 2010 WL 3259355, at *7 (D. Neb. Aug. 16, 2010) (quoting *In re* User Sys. Servs., Inc., 22 S.W.3d 331, 334–35 (Tex. 1999)); Metrahealth Ins. Co. v. Anclote Psychiatric Hosp. Ltd., 961 F. Supp. 1580, 1583 (M.D. Fla. 1997) (quoting ABA Comm. on Ethics & Prof'l Responsibility, Formal Op. 95-396, at 7 (1995)); Fed. Sav. & Loan Ins. Corp. v. Hildenbrand, No. 89-A-535, 1989 WL 107377, at *4 (D. Colo. Sept. 8, 1989).

17. *See, e.g.*, Ind. State Bar Ass'n, Legal Ethics Comm., Formal Op. 2008-2 (2008), *reprinted as Opinion 2 of 2008*, Res Gestae, Sept. 2008, at 21, 21 (stating that "if the information available to the attorney suggest[s] that the potentially adverse party may have or recently had representation in the matter, he has an affirmative duty to reasonably investigate the possibility of a continuing attorney-client relationship involving the potentially adverse party").

18. Richard v. Caliber Home Loans, Inc., No.: 2:15-cv-2647, 2017 WL 4349082, at *11 (S.D. Ohio Sept. 29, 2017); Coffman v. Indianapolis Fire Dep't, 619 F. Supp. 2d 582, 599 (S.D. Ind. 2008); Jones v. Sci. Colors, Inc., 201 F. Supp. 2d 820, 829 (N.D. Ill. 2001).

19. Model Rules of Prof'l Conduct R. 4.2 cmt. 4 (2020); S.C. Adv. Op. 93-16, 1993 WL 851348, at *2 (S.C. Bar, Ethics Advisory Comm. 1993) [hereinafter S.C. Adv. Op. 93-16].

20. ABA Comm. on Ethics & Prof'l Responsibility, Formal Op. 11-461, at 4 (2011) [hereinafter ABA Formal Op. 11-461]; NYC Eth. Op. 2002-3, 2002 WL 1040177, at *5 (Ass'n of the Bar of the City of N.Y., Comm. on Prof'l & Jud. Ethics 2002) (construing then-New York DR 7-104 in light of Model Rule 4.2 and concluding that a lawyer may advise a client "on the content of communications conceived or initiated by the client").

21. Restatement (Third) of the Law Governing Lawyers § 99(2) & cmt. d (2000); ABA Formal Op. 11-461, *supra* note 20, at 4–5.

an advantage to the represented person, who may have been coached by her lawyer about how to respond in this situation. What lawyers clearly may not do, however, is attempt to circumvent Model Rule 4.2 by directing a client or anyone else to communicate with a represented person as a proxy for the lawyer.[22] Here as elsewhere, Model Rule 8.4(a) prevents lawyers' use of proxies to do that which they cannot do themselves.[23] As long as the lawyer does not initiate or orchestrate the communication, however, Model Rule 4.2 should be immaterial.[24]

2. *The Existence and Scope of a Matter*

Questions occasionally surface about the existence or scope of a "matter" within the meaning of Model Rule 4.2.[25] The determination of the existence or scope of a matter can be crucial because Model Rule 4.2 does not pro-

22. *See, e.g.*, United States v. Smallwood, 365 F. Supp. 2d 689, 694–97 (E.D. Va. 2005) (involving an investigator); *In re* Complaint of PMD Enters., Inc., 215 F. Supp. 2d 519, 526–29 (D.N.J. 2002) (attempting to circumvent Rule 4.2 through an investigator); Holdren v. Gen. Motors Corp., 13 F. Supp. 2d 1192, 1193–96 (D. Kan. 1998) (involving a lawyer who had his client attempt to obtain affidavits from co-workers); *In re* Anonymous, 819 N.E.2d 376, 377–79 (Ind. 2004) (violating Rules 4.2 and 4.4 through involvement in the client obtaining an affidavit from an employee); *In re* Pyle, 91 P.3d 1222, 1228–29 (Kan. 2004) (disciplining a lawyer who had his client deliver an affidavit to the opposing party); Bratcher v. Ky. Bar Ass'n, 290 S.W.3d 648, 649 (Ky. 2009) (finding a violation where the lawyer hired a company to contact her client's former employer to determine what the former employer was saying about the client when prospective employers called for references); State v. Clark, 738 N.W.2d 316, 339–40 (Minn. 2007) (finding a Rule 4.2 violation where police officers spoke to a represented person); Awan v. Awan, 906 N.Y.S.2d 70, 72 (App. Div. 2010) (affirming the exclusion of a doctor's testimony in a custody proceeding because the lawyer violated Rule 4.2 by having the doctor examine and question the child without the knowledge of the child's lawyer); Disciplinary Couns. v. Sartini, 871 N.E.2d 543, 544–46 (Ohio 2007) (sanctioning a prosecutor who urged a suspect's mother to speak to him); Bd. of Prof'l Responsibility v. Melchior, 269 P.3d 1088, 1090–91 (Wyo. 2012) (agreeing that the lawyer violated Rule 4.2 by giving his client a divorce settlement agreement and a financial statement when he knew or reasonably should have known there was a substantial risk that she would deliver them to the husband, whom the lawyer knew to be represented); Bd. of Prof'l Responsibility v. Jenkins, 260 P.3d 264, 265–66 (Wyo. 2011) (involving attempted contacts that were unsuccessful); Or. Eth. Op. 2005-147, 2005 WL 5679571, at *1 (Or. State Bar Ass'n, Bd. of Governors 2005).

23. *See* Model Rules of Prof'l Conduct R. 8.4(a) (2020) ("It is professional misconduct for a lawyer to . . . violate or attempt to violate the Rules of Professional Conduct, knowingly assist or induce another to do so, or do so through the acts of another[.]").

24. *See, e.g.*, United States *ex rel.* Thomas v. Duke Univ., No. 1:17-CV-276, 2018 WL 4211372, at *3–5 (M.D.N.C. Sept. 4, 2018) (involving a relator in a *qui tam* action who spoke with co-workers and took notes while his lawsuit remained under seal; even assuming that the relator's lawyers knew that the defendant was represented by counsel, there was no evidence that they caused, controlled, or directed the relator's conversations with his co-workers); Miano v. AC & R Adver., Inc., 148 F.R.D. 68, 82–90 (S.D.N.Y. 1993) (refusing to exclude secret recordings of the plaintiff's co-employees because the plaintiff's lawyer did not engineer them).

25. *See, e.g.*, Mims v. Chichester, 722 N.Y.S.2d 30, 31 (App. Div. 2001) (noting that while multiple matters may involve the same subjects, they remain different matters for purposes of rule); Damron v. CSX Transp., Inc., 920 N.E.2d 169, 177–78 (Ohio Ct. App. 2009) (reasoning that extrinsic evidence for impeachment use was outside the scope of the matter).

hibit communications with a represented person, or with a represented person's agent or employee, outside the scope of the representation.[26]

Model Rule 4.2 clearly applies to lawyers' ex parte communications with represented persons before a lawsuit is filed,[27] but at what point a matter exists sufficient for the rule to attach can be unclear. In the pre-litigation phase, it has been stated that Rule 4.2 is limited to "those cases in which the attorney and represented parties have an adverse or 'ripening adverse' relationship."[28] Unfortunately, this is not an area that lends itself to uniform rules. Whether a matter exists, what matters are within a lawyer's representation, and the scope and contours of matters are all determinations that depend on the circumstances.[29]

Courts applying versions of Rule 4.2 that closely track or mirror Model Rule 4.2 more often define a matter from a case or representation perspective rather than from a fact perspective,[30] as *People v. Santiago*[31] demonstrates. In *Santiago*, the question was whether ex parte communications by prosecutors investigating potential criminal child endangerment charges against Evelyn Santiago were prohibited by Rule 4.2 because Santiago was

---

26. Model Rules of Prof'l Conduct R. 4.2 cmt. 4 (2020).

27. *See, e.g.*, Penda Corp. v. STK, LLC, Nos. 03-5578, 03-6240, 2004 WL 1628907, at *3 (E.D. Pa. July 16, 2004) (applying Rule 4.2 to pre-suit communications); Stahl v. Wal-Mart Stores, Inc., 47 F. Supp. 2d 783, 789 (S.D. Miss. 1998) (same).

28. SEC v. Lines, 669 F. Supp. 2d 460, 464 (S.D.N.Y. 2009) (quoting a treatise).

29. Restatement (Third) of the Law Governing Lawyers § 99 cmt. d (2000).

30. *See, e.g.*, United States v. Ford, 176 F.3d 376, 382 (6th Cir. 1999) (concluding that because a government informant communicated with the defendant about an offense other than the one for which the defendant was indicted, there was no Rule 4.2 violation); CSX Transp., Inc. v. Gilkison, No. 5:05CV202, 2011 WL 5445114, at *3–6 (N.D. W. Va. Nov. 9, 2011) (relying on the Illinois Supreme Court's decision in *People v. Santiago*); Griffin-El v. Beard, No. 06-2719, 2009 WL 2929802, at *7 (E.D. Pa. Sept. 8, 2009) (finding no Rule 4.2 violation when defense lawyers spoke with a corrections officer in his role as custodian of records when the officer was represented only in another lawsuit filed by their client and not in the matter in which his role as a records custodian made him a potential witness); Miller v. Material Sci. Corp., 986 F. Supp. 1104, 1106–07 (N.D. Ill. 1997) (permitting a communication by the plaintiff's attorney in a securities class action with a party that was represented in a related SEC investigation but not in the class action); Miano v. AC&R Adver., Inc., 148 F.R.D. 68, 80 (S.D.N.Y. 1993) (finding that corporate employees were not off-limits when the corporate entity had not retained counsel in the matter that was the focus of the communications); *In re* Charges of Unprof'l Conduct in Panel File No. 41755, 912 N.W.2d 224, 231 (Minn. 2018) (concluding that, "in litigated matters, the 'matter' is synonymous with the 'case'"); State *ex rel.* Okla. Bar Ass'n v. Harper, 995 P.2d 1143, 1147 (Okla. 2000) (finding that the defense lawyer's interview of the driver did not violate Rule 4.2 because it involved a passenger's separate claim—not other claims arising out of the same accident in connection with which the driver was represented by counsel). *But see* N.C. State Bar v. Weckworth, No. COA18-866, 2019 WL 2353465, at *5 (N.C. Ct. App. June 4, 2019) (concluding that the lawyer violated Rule 4.2 where two cases had overlapping facts and issues); Neb. State Bar Ass'n, Lawyers' Advisory Comm., Eth. Op. 09-03, at 7 (2009) ("Rule 4.2 would prohibit a prosecutor from directly contact a victim/witness for the purpose of obtaining from him a release for his medical records. Although the criminal prosecution and the civil case in which the victim is represented by counsel are different cases, they clearly arise from the same set of facts and involve at least some common issues).

31. 925 N.E.2d 1122 (Ill. 2010).

represented by appointed counsel in parallel juvenile court proceedings seeking to have her children made wards of the state. Because it was undisputed that the lawyer representing Santiago in the juvenile court matter had not been engaged to represent her in the criminal investigation, the court concluded that Rule 4.2 was not violated despite the overlapping case facts.[32] The only "matter" in which Santiago was represented by counsel was the juvenile court case.[33]

3. *Permissible Communications When Representation Is Known*

There are times that a lawyer may communicate ex parte with a person the lawyer knows to be represented in a matter without violating Rule 4.2.[34] Most obviously, Model Rule 4.2 permits ex parte communications with the consent of the lawyer for the represented person. Lawyers' consent to ex parte communications with their clients may be express or implied.[35] The existence of implied consent is always a fact-specific inquiry.

In some circumstances, a person may be represented in a matter by more than one lawyer. For example, a party may have local counsel and lead or national counsel. Employees may have their own counsel and may also be represented by lawyers for their employers. An insured may have personal counsel in addition to defense counsel appointed by the insurer. In such cases, a lawyer wishing to communicate ex parte with a represented person need only obtain the consent of one of the lawyers for the person.[36] The burden is on the person's lawyers to decide among themselves who should be able to consent to ex parte communications with their mutual client, or whether such consent should ever be given.

A person who is represented by a lawyer in a matter may want to obtain a second opinion or additional advice regarding the matter. Under Model Rule 4.2, the second lawyer is free to speak with the person without the first

32. *Id.* at 1128–31.

33. *Id.* at 1129–30.

34. *See, e.g.*, Restatement (Third) of the Law Governing Lawyers § 99 cmt. i (2000) (stating that communication with a represented person "is authorized to protect life or personal safety and to deal with other emergency situations").

35. *In re* Wollrab, 420 P.3d 960, 967 (Colo. 2018) (quoting Restatement (Third) of the Law Governing Lawyers § 99 cmt. j (2000)).

36. *See, e.g.*, Riley v. PK Mgmt., LLC, No. 18-cv-2337-KHV-TJJ, 2019 WL 4256367, at *6–7 (D. Kan. Sept. 9, 2019) (acknowledging that when an employee has personal counsel, that lawyer is better able than the organization's lawyer to decide whether the employee's interests are best served by speaking with another lawyer or by silence; if the employee's personal lawyer decides that the employee's best interests warrant speaking with another lawyer, the agreement of the organization's lawyer is unnecessary); La Jolla Cove Motel & Hotel Apts., Inc. v. Super. Ct., 17 Cal. Rptr. 3d 467, 473–74 (Ct. App. 2004) (discussing and applying California Rule 2-100 and Model Rule 4.2 in a case in which separate counsel for the directors of a corporation consented to the communication but counsel for the corporation did not, and finding that the communication was proper).

lawyer's consent,[37] at least so long as the second lawyer is not otherwise representing a client in the matter.[38] Nothing about such communications implicates the concerns that Model Rule 4.2 is intended to address. Recognizing a contrary position would also preclude clients from hiring additional or different counsel to represent them, which would be antithetical to clients' general right to counsel of their choice. The second lawyer has no duty to inform the first lawyer of the communication; indeed, doing so without the client's consent would, in most instances, violate the second lawyer's duty of confidentiality.[39]

Model Rule 4.2 permits ex parte communications with a represented person where a lawyer is "authorized to do so by law or a court order."[40] Courts often hold that pre-indictment investigative activities by government lawyers and law enforcement agents are exempt from Model Rule 4.2 on the basis that related communications are authorized by law.[41] In contrast, a criminal defense lawyer cannot claim that an ex parte communication is authorized by law on the basis that her client's constitutional rights must be protected and the challenged communication was part of that exercise.[42]

Lawyers cannot exploit the "authorized by law" exception by using subpoenas or notices. For example, a lawyer cannot circumvent Rule 4.2 by issuing a subpoena to a represented person to compel that person to appear

---

37. United States v. Gonzalez-Lopez, 403 F.3d 558, 565–66 (8th Cir. 2005) (interpreting Missouri law); Fla. Eth. Op. 02-5, 2003 WL 22347985, at *2 (Fla. State Bar Ass'n, Comm. on Prof'l Ethics 2003); Ill. Adv. Op. 18-03, 2018 WL 2946495, at *1 (Ill. State Bar Ass'n 2018) [hereinafter Ill. Adv. Op. 18-03]; N.Y. State Bar Ass'n, Comm. on Prof'l Ethics, Op. 1010, at ¶ 4 (2014); State Bar of Mont., Ethics Comm., Ethics Op. 900703 (1990): Or. Eth. Op. 2005-81, 2005 WL 5679671, at *1 (Or. State Bar Ass'n, Bd. of Governors 2005) [hereinafter Or. Eth. Op. 2005-81]; S.C. Adv. Op. 97-07, 1997 WL 582911, at *2 (S.C. Bar, Ethics Advisory Comm. 1997); Utah Eth. Op. 110, 1993 WL 741794, at *1–2 (Utah State Bar, Ethics Advisory Op. Comm. 1993) [hereinafter Utah Eth. Op. 110]; Model Rules of Prof'l Conduct R. 4.2 cmt. 4 (2020) (stating that Rule 4.2 does not "preclude communication with a represented person who is seeking advice from a lawyer who is not otherwise representing a client in the matter").

38. *In re* Charges of Unprof'l Conduct in Panel File No. 41755, 912 N.W.2d 224, 231 (Minn. 2018); Utah Eth. Op. 110, *supra* note 37, 1993 WL 741794, at *1; Model Rules of Prof'l Conduct R. 4.2 cmt. 4 (2020); *see* Ill. Adv. Op. 18-03, *supra* note 37, 2018 WL 2946495, at *1 (noting that the second lawyer was not involved in the matter).

39. Or. Eth. Op. 2005-81, *supra* note 37, 2005 WL 5679671, at *1; Phila. Eth. Op. 04-1, 2004 WL 396814, at *1 (Phila. Bar Ass'n, Prof'l Guidance Comm. 2004).

40. Model Rules of Prof'l Conduct R. 4.2 (2020).

41. *See, e.g.*, United States v. Brown, 595 F.3d 498, 514–16 (3d Cir. 2010) (concluding that a federal prosecutor did not violate Rule 4.2 when he used a confidential informant to contact a represented suspect during a pre-indictment investigation); United States *ex rel.* Fesenmaier v. Cameron-Ehlen Grp., Inc., 442 F. Supp. 3d 1101, 1105–09 (D. Minn. 2020) (involving investigative activities by government lawyers preceding the government's intervention in a qui tam action); United States v. Binday, 908 F. Supp. 2d 485, 493–97 (S.D.N.Y. 2012) (reasoning that federal prosecutors' use of a cooperating co-conspirator to record his telephone conversations with the represented defendants prior to the defendants' indictment for fraud and conspiracy was authorized by law).

42. *In re* Disciplinary Action Against McCormick, 819 N.W.2d 442, 444 (Minn. 2012).

for an ex parte interview or deposition.[43] Likewise, a lawyer cannot circumvent Rule 4.2 by serving a represented person with a deposition notice with the aim of taking an ex parte deposition.[44]

Unlike rules prohibiting ex parte communications with courts, lawyers cannot avoid the Model Rule 4.2 ban on ex parte communications by communicating with a represented person and the person's lawyer simultaneously. For example, a lawyer who copies a represented person on a letter to that person's lawyer, or who sends an e-mail to both the person and her lawyer, violates Rule 4.2 even though the person's lawyer is included in the communication chain.[45] It is no answer to say that this tactic is permissible because the other lawyer's presence in the communication chain eliminates the potential for overreaching by the first lawyer. For one thing, the represented person and her counsel may not receive or read the communication at the same time. For another thing, the potential for overreaching still exists because by sending the communication to the person directly, the lawyer has defeated the other lawyer's important role as a buffer or filter.[46] Finally, it remains possible that the represented person will make an un-counseled response to the communication—especially if the lawyer used e-mail.[47]

4. *Organizational Litigants*

It is important to understand how Model Rule 4.2 applies to organizational litigants. This is because organizations speak only through their employees and agents. Crucially, "not every current employee of a represented

43. Parker v. Pepsi-Cola Gen. Bottlers, Inc., 249 F. Supp. 2d 1006, 1009–11 (N.D. Ill. 2003); *In re* Newell, 234 P.3d 967, 974–76 (Or. 2010); Monceret v. Bd. of Prof'l Responsibility, 29 S.W.3d 455, 461 (Tenn. 2000).

44. *In re Newell*, 234 P.3d at 974–76.

45. *In re* Uttermohlen, 768 N.E.2d 449, 451 (Ind. 2002); *In re* Lung, 122 N.Y.S.3d 364, 366–67, 369 (App. Div. 2020); *In re* Disciplinary Proc. Against Jensen, 430 P.3d 262, 270 (Wash. 2018); NYC Eth. Op. 2009-1, 2009 WL 399764, at *2–3 (Ass'n of the Bar of the City of N.Y., Comm. on Prof'l & Jud. Ethics 2009) [hereinafter NYC Eth. Op. 2009-1]; Ill. Adv. Op. 19-05, 2019 WL 9078543, at *3 (Ill. State Bar Ass'n 2019) (discussing e-mail replies where the first lawyer copied her client on a message); N.C. State Bar, 2012 Formal Ethics Op. 7 (2013) (explaining that this principle may apply even where the first lawyer copies her client on an e-mail message and the second lawyer responds by "reply all"); Pa. Eth. Op. 2020-100, 2020 WL 3960284, at *2 (Pa. Bar Ass'n, Comm. on Legal Ethics & Prof'l Responsibility 2020) (stating that "an opposing counsel who replies to an email chain that includes a represented client may violate the no contact rule by communicating directly with a represented client"); S.C. Adv. Op. 18-04, 2018 WL 4291459, at *1 (S.C. Bar Ethics Advisory Comm. 2018) ("Absent the consent of Lawyer A, Lawyer B may not communicate with Lawyer A's client about the subject of the representation either directly or by copying Lawyer A's client in an email sent in response to Lawyer A's email on which the client was copied."); S.C. Adv. Op. 93-16, *supra* note 19, 1993 WL 851348, at *1.

46. NYC Eth. Op. 2009-1, *supra* note 45, 2009 WL 399764, at *3.

47. *Id.* ("The risk [of an un-counseled response] is magnified with email communications, where a response by a [represented person] can be made with the touch of a button on a keyboard.").

organizational entity is a 'represented' person for purposes of Rule 4.2."[48] Model Rule 4.2 is not intended to quarantine every employee with knowledge of relevant facts or information concerning a matter and thereby prevent lawyers for other parties from speaking with them ex parte.[49] An organization's lawyer may not blanketly prohibit ex parte communications with all the organization's employees.[50] It is therefore necessary to identify those people affiliated with the organization who hold a position or play a role sufficient to assume its attributes. Employees within this group are often referred to as members of the organization's "control group" or are said to be the organization's "alter egos." These shorthand descriptions come from multiple cases applying various standards and are therefore imperfect, but regardless of how they are described for ease of reference, such employees are presumptively represented by the organization's lawyers. Employees who are not within this constituent group are available for ex parte communications unless they are separately represented.[51]

Courts typically look to the comments to Rule 4.2 for guidance when deciding which employees are off-limits. For years, the commentary to the rule provided:

> In the case of an organization, this Rule prohibits communications by a lawyer for another person or entity concerning the matter in representation with persons having a [1] managerial responsibility on behalf of the organization, and [2] with any other person whose act or omission in connection with that matter may be imputed to the organization for purposes of civil or criminal liability or [3] whose statement may constitute an admission on the part of the organization.[52]

Applying this language, there were frequent disputes as to whether an employee's duties equated to "managerial responsibility." To clarify matters, the commentary to Model Rule 4.2 was revised in 2002 as part of the ABA's Ethics 2000 initiative, and Comment 7 to the rule now provides:

---

48. Doe v. Super. Ct. of San Diego Cnty., 248 Cal. Rptr. 3d 314, 320 (Ct. App. 2019).

49. *Id.* at 321; *see* Iowa Sup. Ct. Att'y Disciplinary Bd. v. Stowers, 823 N.W.2d 1, 11 (Iowa 2012) (noting that Rule 4.2 does not bar ex parte communication "with all constituents of [a] represented organization"); ABA Comm. on Ethics & Prof'l Responsibility, Formal Op. 95-396, at 14 (1995) [hereinafter ABA Formal Op. 95-396] ("[T]the fact that an entity is represented by counsel does not prevent communication with all current employees of the represented corporation." (footnote omitted)).

50. ABA Formal Op. 95-396, *supra* note 49, at 15; Ohio Advisory Op. 2016-5, 2016 WL 4268979, at *4 (Sup. Ct. of Ohio, Bd. of Prof'l Conduct 2016).

51. Davis v. Creditors Interchange Receivable Mgmt., LLC, 585 F. Supp. 2d 968, 978–79 (N.D. Ohio 2008) (discussing Ohio rules); Klier v. Sordoni Skanska Constr. Co., 766 A.2d 761, 770 (N.J. Super. Ct. App. Div. 2001); Hedges v. E. River Plaza, LLC, 981 N.Y.S.2d 894, 897–98 (Sup. Ct. 2013); Newsuan v. Republic Servs., Inc., 213 A.3d 279, 288 (Pa. Super. Ct. 2019).

52. MODEL RULES OF PROF'L CONDUCT R. 4.2 cmt. 4 (2001).

> In the case of a represented organization, this Rule prohibits communications with a constituent of the organization who [1] supervises, directs or regularly consults with the organization's lawyer concerning the matter or [2] has authority to obligate the organization with respect to the matter or [3] whose act or omission in connection with the matter may be imputed to the organization for purposes of civil or criminal liability.[53]

The change to Model Rule 4.2's commentary establishes that not every current employee with "managerial responsibility" is off-limits to another lawyer. In jurisdictions that have adopted or otherwise embraced the revised commentary, even current employees whose statements qualify as party admissions under Federal Rule of Evidence 801 are fair game.[54]

A few jurisdictions have departed from the ABA approach and adopted the "managing-speaking agent test."[55] Under this test, ex parte communication is prohibited with employees who have "'speaking authority' for the corporation," meaning those employees "who 'have managing authority sufficient to give them the right to speak for, and bind the corporation.'"[56] Scholars have criticized the managing-speaking agent test as being confusing and for failing to provide practicing lawyers with a clear standard by which to evaluate a planned course of conduct.[57] Regardless, it is a distinctly minority approach.

If lawyers for an organization are concerned about opposing lawyers' ex parte contact with otherwise unprotected employees, they may ask the employees not to voluntarily speak with opposing counsel outside their presence. Although this approach is generally permissible under ethics rules,[58] it

53. Model Rules of Prof'l Conduct R. 4.2 cmt. 7 (2020).

54. *See* Hayes v. Wis. & S. R.R., LLC, No. 18-cv-923, 2019 WL 5595170, at *2 (E.D. Wis. Oct. 30, 2019) (explaining that "the ABA has made clear that [Rule 4.2's] prohibition on ex parte communication is not co-extensive with Rule 801(d)(2)(D)" and finding no Rule 4.2 violation); Mendez v. Hovensa, LLC, No. 02-0169, 2008 WL 906768, at *3–9 (D.V.I. Mar. 31, 2008) (discussing 2002 rule changes and explaining that one of the purposes of modifying Rule 4.2 was to make clear that it did not bar communications with employees just because they could make admissions against the corporation through Rule 801(d)(2)(D)).

55. *See, e.g.*, Goodeagle v. United States, No. CIV-09-490-D, 2010 WL 3081520, at *4 (W.D. Okla. Aug. 6, 2010) (quoting Fulton v. Lane, 829 P.2d 959, 960 (Okla. 1992)); Messing, Rudavsky & Weliky, P.C. v. President & Fellows of Harvard Coll., 764 N.E.2d 825, 833 (Mass. 2002); Palmer v. Pioneer Inn Assocs., Ltd., 59 P.3d 1237, 1247–48 (Nev. 2002); Wright v. Grp. Health Hosp., 691 P.2d 564, 569 (Wash. 1984).

56. *Messing*, 764 N.E.2d at 833 (quoting *Wright*, 691 P.2d at 569).

57. *See, e.g.*, Ernest F. Lidge III, *The Ethics of Communicating with an Organization's Employees: An Analysis of the Unworkable "Hybrid" or "Multifactor" Managing-Speaking Agent, ABA and* Niesig *Tests and a Proposal for a "Supervisor" Standard*, 45 Ark. L. Rev. 801, 834–44 (1993) (focusing on the Washington Supreme Court's decision in *Wright*).

58. *See* Model Rules of Prof'l Conduct R. 3.4(f) (2020) (stating that a lawyer shall not request a person other than a client to refrain from voluntarily giving relevant information to another party unless (1) the person is a relative or an employee or other agent of a client; and (2) the lawyer reasonably believes that the person's interests will not be adversely affected by refraining from giving such information).

may not be available in governmental or regulatory actions, or in criminal cases, where the request might constitute obstruction of justice.

It is common for unrepresented witnesses to ask a lawyer, "What should I do if the lawyer for the other side calls me?," or something to that effect. Assuming there is no reason to believe that doing so would prejudice the witness and possibly implicate Model Rule 4.3,[59] lawyers should be permitted to tell witnesses that they are free to speak with the other side but are not required to do so absent a subpoena or court order. It is wise to stress that the choice of whether to speak with opposing counsel is up to the witness. As to current employee witnesses, a request not to do so is generally permissible under Model Rule 3.4(f) so long as the lawyer does nothing to coerce or improperly influence the witness's decision.[60] Nor is there any ethical problem with lawyers asking witnesses to inform them if they speak with an adversary or even asking to be present should the witness choose to meet with opposing counsel.[61] Lawyers for an organization cannot instruct opposing counsel not to communicate with employees unless they in fact represent the employees in the matter.[62]

In many cases, lawyers want to interview an organization's *former* employees outside the presence of the organization's lawyers. It is now settled that Rule 4.2 generally permits ex parte communications with former employees of an organization.[63] This freedom has limits, however. For

59. *Id.* R. 4.3 (establishing lawyers' duties when dealing with unrepresented persons).

60. *Id.* R. 3.4(f) (prohibiting lawyers from requesting that someone other than a client refrain from providing relevant information to another party unless the person is a relative, employee, or other agent of a client, or the lawyer reasonably believes that the other person's interests will not be adversely affected by refraining from providing such information).

61. Charlap v. Khan, 972 N.Y.S.2d 871, 881–82 (Sup. Ct. 2013) (noting that witnesses may decline such requests).

62. Patriarca v. Ctr. for Living & Working, Inc., 778 N.E.2d 877, 880–81 (Mass. 2002); Utah Eth. Op. 04-06, 2004 WL 2803333, at *1 (Utah State Bar, Ethics Advisory Op. Comm. 2004).

63. Jenkins v. City of Las Vegas, No: 19-656 JAP/JHR, 2020 WL 4347263, at *2–4 (D.N.M. July 29, 2020); Snodgrass v. Esper, No. 18-cv-00450, 2020 WL 5265126, at *2–3 (D. Md. Sept. 3, 2020) (applying Maryland law); Calise v. Brady Sullivan Harris Mills, LLC, No. 18-99WES, 2019 WL 1397245, at *5 (D.R.I. Mar. 28, 2019) (discussing Rhode Island's version of Rule 4.2); Lozama v. Samaritan Daytop Village, Inc., No. 18 CV 4351 (DLI) (RML), 2019 WL 1002954, at *2 (E.D.N.Y. Mar. 1, 2019) (applying New York law); Peterson v. Alaska Commc'ns Sys. Grp. Inc., No. 3:12-cv-00090-TMB, 2019 WL 6331355, at *7 (D. Alaska Nov. 26, 2019) (applying Alaska ethics rules); United States v. Miss., No. 3:16-cv-622-CWR-FKB, 2018 WL 4956658, at *4 (S.D. Miss. Oct. 12, 2018) (discussing Mississippi's version of Rule 4.2); Klorczyk v. Sears, Roebuck & Co., No. 3:13-cv-00257 (JAM), 2017 WL 3272237, at *3 (D. Conn. Aug. 1, 2017) (applying Connecticut ethics rules); Thurston v. Okemo Ltd. Liab. Co., 123 F. Supp. 3d 513, 515 (D. Vt. 2015) (applying Vermont's version of Rule 4.2); EEOC v. SVT, LLC, 297 F.R.D. 336, 345 (N.D. Ind. 2014) (applying Indiana rules in connection with a class action); EEOC v. Univ. of Chi. Med. Ctr., No. 11 C 6379, 2012 WL 1329171, at *3–4 (N.D. Ill. Apr. 16, 2012) (applying Model Rule 4.2); *In re* Digitek Prod. Liab. Litig., 648 F. Supp. 2d 795, 799 (S.D. W. Va. 2009) (applying West Virginia rules); Bryant v. Yorktowne Cabinetry, Inc., 538 F. Supp. 2d 948, 949–53 (W.D. Va. 2008) (employing Virginia's version of Rule 4.2); Nuckles v. Wal-Mart Stores, Inc., No. 4:06CV00178

example, courts have determined that a lawyer cannot communicate ex parte with former employees who have their own counsel in the matter, who had managerial responsibility in the matter being litigated,[64] who have an ongoing relationship with the organization in relation to the litigation,[65] or whose acts or omissions gave rise to the litigation.[66]

Furthermore, courts generally hold that Model Rule 4.2 or Model Rules 4.2 and 4.4(a), read together, prohibit lawyers from asking former employees about documents or information protected by the organization's attorney-client privilege or work product immunity,[67] as do legal ethics authorities.[68]

WRW, 2007 WL 1546092, at *2 (E.D. Ark. May 25, 2007) (applying Model Rule 4.2); United States v. W.R. Grace, 401 F. Supp. 2d 1065, 1068–69 (D. Mont. 2005); Smith v. Kalamazoo Ophthalmology, 322 F. Supp. 2d 883, 890 (W.D. Mich. 2004); Lang v. Super. Ct., 826 P.2d 1228, 1233 (Ariz. Ct. App. 1992); DiOssi v. Edison, 583 A.2d 1343, 1345 (Del. Super. Ct. 1990); H.B.A. Mgmt., Inc. v. Estate of Schwartz, 693 So. 2d 541, 544–46 (Fla. 1997); Sanifill of Ga., Inc. v. Roberts, 502 S.E.2d 343, 345 (Ga. 1998); P.T. Barnum's Nightclub v. Duhamell, 766 N.E.2d 729, 737 (Ind. Ct. App. 2002); Humco, Inc. v. Noble, 31 S.W.3d 916, 920 (Ky. 2000); Schmidt v. Gregorio, 705 So. 2d 742, 743–44 (La. Ct. App. 1993); *Patriarca*, 778 N.E.2d at 881–82; Smith v. Kan. City S. Ry., 87 S.W.3d 266, 272–75 (Mo. Ct. App. 2002); Klier v. Sordoni Skanska Constr. Co., 766 A.2d 761, 770 (N.J. Super. Ct. App. Div. 2001); Fulton v. Lane, 829 P.2d 959, 960 (Okla. 1992); State *ex rel.* Charleston Area Med. Ctr. v. Zakaib, 437 S.E.2d 759, 763–64 (W. Va. 1993); Strawser v. Exxon Co., U.S.A., 843 P.2d 613, 622 (Wyo. 1992); Mich. Eth. Op. RI-360, 2013 WL 9660913, at *1 (State Bar of Mich., Comm. on Prof'l & Jud. Ethics 2013); Pa. Eth. Op. 2004-80, 2004 WL 3323071, at *1 (Pa. Bar Ass'n, Comm. on Legal Ethics & Prof'l Responsibility 2004) [hereinafter Pa. Eth. Op. 2004-80]; Model Rules of Prof'l Conduct R. 4.2 cmt. 7 (2020).

64. *W.R. Grace*, 401 F. Supp. 2d at 1067; *Patriarca*, 778 N.E.2d at 882.

65. *Lang*, 826 P.2d at 1233.

66. Merck v. Swift Transp. Co., No. CV-16-01103-PHX-ROS, 2018 WL 3774007, at *3 (D. Ariz. July 19, 2018); *Lang*, 826 P.3d at 1233.

67. *See, e.g.*, Kozowski v. Nelson, No.: 6:18-cv-00275-MK, 2020 WL 1066329, at *3 (D. Or. Mar. 5, 2020) (referring to the attorney-client privilege and citing Oregon Rules 4.2 and 4.4); *Snodgrass*, 2020 WL 5265126, at *3 (referring to confidential information); Harris Davis Rebar, L.L.C. v. Structural Iron Workers Local Union No. 1, Pension Tr. Fund, No. 17 C 6473, 2019 WL 447622, at *6 (N.D. Ill. Feb. 5, 2019) (reading Rules 4.2 and 4.4 together); Martinez v. Cnty. of Antelope, No. 4:15CV3064, 2016 WL 3248241, at *9–10 (D. Neb. June 13, 2016) (disqualifying a lawyer who knowingly obtained privileged information from a former county official); Tomasian v. C.D. Peacock, Inc., No. 09 C 5665, 2012 WL 2590493, at *7 (N.D. Ill. July 3, 2012) (referring to Rule 4.2 and stating that "former employees are barred from discussing privileged information to which they are privy"); Gifford v. Target Corp., 723 F. Supp. 2d 1110, 1118–23 (D. Minn. 2010) (referring to Rule 4.2 cmt. 7 and Rule 4.4(a)); Weber v. Fujifilm Med. Sys., U.S.A., No. 3:10 CV 401(JBA), 2010 WL 2836720, at *4 (D. Conn. July 19, 2010) (quoting Shoreline Computs., Inc. v. Warnaco, Inc., No. CV 990422853S, 2000 WL 371206, at *2 (Conn. Super. Ct. Apr. 3, 2000)); *Kalamazoo Ophthalmology*, 322 F. Supp. 2d at 890–91 (applying Rule 4.2); Zachair, Ltd. v. Driggs, 965 F. Supp. 741, 753–54 (D. Md. 1997) (applying Rule 4.2); Rentclub, Inc. v. Transamerica Rental Fin. Corp., 811 F. Supp. 651, 657 (M.D. Fla. 1992) (discussing Rule 4.2); *Shoreline Computs.*, 2000 WL 371206, at *2 (describing former employees who are off-limits under Rule 4.2).

68. *See, e.g.*, N.C. State Bar, Formal Ethics Op. 1997-2 (1998) (prohibiting ex parte communication with former employees who "participated substantially in the legal representation of the organization, including participation in and knowledge of privileged communications with legal counsel"); Pa. Eth. Op. 2004-80, *supra* note 63, 2004 WL 3323071, at *1 (referring to Rule 4.2 and the attorney-client privilege).

In fact, Model Rule 4.4(a) is the correct (and certainly the better) source of authority for this proposition. Comment 7 to Model Rule 4.2 clarifies this point by directing lawyers to Model Rule 4.4(a) when they must analyze their communication obligations regarding former employees who possess their former employers' confidential information.[69]

5. *Websites and Weblogs*

A represented person or organization often has a public website. Information found on the website may be relevant to the matter in which the site owner is represented. May another lawyer involved in the matter visit that website without violating Rule 4.2? Yes, provided that the lawyer only views the site or downloads information from it, or otherwise engages solely in one-way interaction, such as giving feedback about the website or ordering products.[70] A lawyer who simply views a website or downloads information from the site cannot reasonably be said to have communicated with the site owner within the meaning of Rule 4.2.[71] Even if such conduct were held to be a communication, it could not result in overreaching by the lawyer, interfere with the represented person's attorney-client relationship, or lead to the uninformed disclosure of information relating to the representation—the dangers against which Rule 4.2 is intended to protect.

If, however, the website is interactive in the sense that it allows visitors to send and receive messages to and from the host or participate in a chat room, a lawyer may violate Rule 4.2 through such interaction.[72] Obviously, if it is an individual's site, any interaction is more likely to violate Rule 4.2. Where a represented organization is involved, an alleged violation will almost certainly turn on the identity of the person with whom the lawyer communicated through the site. These same principles apply to the review of a represented person's weblog, or "blog"; mere passive review of a person's publicly available blog posts does not implicate Rule 4.2, but initiating posts with the intent or effect of soliciting a response from the blogger well might.

---

69. *See* Model Rules of Prof'l Conduct R. 4.2 cmt. 7 (2020) ("In communicating with a current or former constituent of an organization, a lawyer must not use methods of obtaining evidence that violate the legal rights of the organization. See Rule 4.4.").

70. Or. Eth. Op. 2001-164, 2001 WL 167177, at *1–2 (Or. State Bar Ass'n, Bd. of Governors 2001) [hereinafter Or. Eth. Op. 2001-164] (interpreting analogous Oregon rule); *see also* Or. Eth. Op. 2005-164, 2005 WL 5679590, at *1–2 (Or. State Bar Ass'n, Bd. of Governors 2005) [hereinafter Or. Eth. Op. 2005-164] (updating Or. Eth. Op. 2001-164).

71. *See* Or. Eth. Op. 2005-164, *supra* note 70, 2005 WL 5679590, at *1 ("A lawyer who reads information posted for general public consumption simply is not communicating with the represented owner of the Web site." (footnote omitted)).

72. Or. Eth. Op. 2001-164, *supra* note 70, 2001 WL 167177, at *2.

6. *Additional Recurring Issues*

Several remaining points about Model Rule 4.2 bear mention. First, the rule does not protect a person's right to counsel; it protects counsel's right to participate in any communication between her client and opposing counsel.[73] The right to invoke Model Rule 4.2 thus belongs to the lawyer; only the lawyer can consent to ex parte communications or waive the right to be present during them—the client cannot agree to ex parte contact.[74]

Second, Model Rule 4.2 applies even when the represented person initiates the communication.[75] In that situation, the lawyer must either avoid the communication or terminate it as soon as practicable after learning it is improper.[76]

Third, a lawyer's inability to communicate with counsel for a represented person, as where the other lawyer is unavailable or unresponsive, does not permit the lawyer to shortcut Rule 4.2 and communicate with the represented person directly.[77] This is generally not a circumstance in which the other lawyer's consent to ex parte communications can be implied.

---

73. State v. Miller, 600 N.W.2d 457, 464 (Minn. 1999).

74. United States v. Lopez, 4 F.3d 1455, 1462 (9th Cir. 1993) (discussing a Rule 4.2 analog); Nieves v. OPA, Inc., 947 F. Supp. 2d 887, 895 (N.D. Ill. 2013); Scanlan v. Eisenberg, 893 F. Supp. 2d 945, 950 (N.D. Ill. 2012); Faison v. Thornton, 863 F. Supp. 1204, 1213 (D. Nev. 1993) (discussing the Nevada version of Rule 4.2); Iowa Sup. Ct. Att'y Disciplinary Bd. v. Stoller, 879 N.W.2d 199, 211 (Iowa 2016); *In re* Charges of Unprof'l Conduct in Panel File No. 41755, 912 N.W.2d 224, 232 (Minn. 2018).

75. Mullen v. GLV, Inc., 334 F.R.D. 656, 664 (N.D. Ill. 2020); *Scanlan*, 893 F. Supp. 2d at 950; United States v. Smallwood, 365 F. Supp. 2d 689, 696 (E.D. Va. 2005); *Stoller*, 879 N.W.2d at 211; *In re* Charges of Unprof'l Conduct in Panel File No. 41755, 912 N.W.2d 224, 232 (Minn. 2018); Pleasant Mgmt., LLC v. Carrasco, 870 A.2d 443, 446 (R.I. 2005); Engstrom v. Goodman, 271 P.3d 959, 964 (Wash. Ct. App. 2012); ABA Formal Op. 95-396, *supra* note 49, at 16. *But cf.* United States v. Guivas-Soto, 124 F. Supp. 3d 72, 74 (D.P.R. 2015) (concluding that a prosecutor did not violate Rule 4.2 by reading two letters sent to him by a represented defendant because Model Rule 4.2 "prohibits only *communication* by the lawyer, and reading a letter does not communicate anything").

76. *See, e.g.*, Golden v. Brethren Mut. Ins. Co., Civ. No. 3:18-CV-02425, 2019 WL 3216629, at *3 (M.D. Pa. July 17, 2019) ("Once the lawyer learns that the person is one with whom communication is not permitted, the lawyer must immediately terminate the communication."); Merck v. Swift Transp. Co., No. CV-16-01103-PHX-ROS, 2018 WL 3774007, at *3 (D. Ariz. July 19, 2018) (sanctioning a plaintiff's lawyer who, when called by the defendant's former employee who allegedly caused the accident at issue, did not hang up but instead stayed on the line and inquired into events relevant to the plaintiff's claim); Zaug v. Va. State Bar, 737 S.E.2d 914, 917–19 (Va. 2013) (concluding that lawyer did not violate Rule 4.2 when the opposing party called and then launched into an emotional outburst, and the lawyer could not reasonably terminate the conversation for 30 seconds or so; the need to disengage from a communication does not require a lawyer to be discourteous or impolite in the process).

77. *In re* Garcia, 147 P.3d 132, 134–35 (Kan. 2006); *see, e.g.*, *In re* Eddings, 782 S.E.2d 445, 445 (Ga. 2017) (violating Rule 4.2 by communicating with represented individuals on the eve of trial when a critical deadline was imminent and the lawyer had unsuccessfully attempted to communicate with the people's lawyers); *In re* Disciplinary Proc. Against Jensen, 430 P.3d 262, 270 (Wash. 2018) (rejecting the lawyer's "extenuating circumstances" defense to a Rule 4.2 violation).

Fourth, and consistent with the last point, Rule 4.2 protects against "contacts that are well meaning but misguided as well as those that are intentionally improper."[78] As a result, lawyers may violate Rule 4.2 through innocent or negligent communications.[79] The fact that an improper communication was inadvertent rather than intentional bears only on the remedy or sanction selected; it does not negate the violation.[80]

Fifth, a Rule 4.2 violation does not depend on the challenged communication causing harm or damage.[81] Even so, a showing of prejudice may be required where a party invokes the rule as a basis for disqualifying or sanctioning a lawyer or invalidating some agreement obtained through an impermissible communication.[82]

Finally, courts often decline to preclude evidence obtained in violation of Rule 4.2 on the theory that an exclusionary policy frustrates truth and punishes the party the offending lawyer represents rather than punishing the ethical violation.[83] In other words, a lawyer who violates Rule 4.2 may rightly be sanctioned or disciplined, but any evidence obtained in violation of the rule will likely be admissible.

---

78. Att'y Grievance Comm'n of Md. v. Kent, 653 A.2d 909, 918 (Md. 1995).

79. Faison v. Thornton, 863 F. Supp. 1204, 1213 (D. Nev. 1993) (discussing analogous Nevada rule); *see, e.g.*, *In re* Capper, 757 N.E.2d 138, 139–40 (Ind. 2001) (communicating with represented adverse party based on client's statement that adversary was no longer represented by counsel without confirming truth of that assertion violated Rule 4.2).

80. United States v. Franklin, 177 F. Supp. 2d 459, 466 (E.D. Va. 2001); *Faison*, 863 F. Supp. at 1214.

81. Runsvold v. Idaho State Bar, 925 P.2d 1118, 1120 (Idaho 1996).

82. *See, e.g.*, *In re* Estate of Netzorg, 15 P.3d 926, 929–30 (Mont. 2000) (refusing to void a settlement agreement obtained as result of an ex parte communication absent proof of prejudice); Harris v. Erie Cnty. Med. Ctr. Corp., 106 N.Y.S.3d 716, 719 (App. Div. 2019) (declining to disqualify the plaintiff's lawyer for violating Rule 4.2 because any information he obtained through his ex parte communication he likely would have obtained in the ordinary course of discovery). *But see* Sandstrom v. Sandstrom, 884 P.2d 968, 970–71 (Wyo. 1994) (refusing to enforce a settlement agreement obtained in violation of Rule 4.2 without a showing of prejudice; the lawyer was representing himself pro se in a divorce and obtained the agreement from his hospitalized wife, who claimed that her husband unduly influenced her).

83. *See, e.g.*, *In re* Katrina Canal Breaches Consol. Litig., No. 05-4182 "K" (2), 2008 WL 2066999, at *7 (E.D. La. May 14, 2008) (quoting Weider Sports Equip. Co. v. Fitness First, Inc., 912 F. Supp. 502, 510 (D. Utah 1996)); Fisher v. Town of Boyce, 250 So. 3d 904, 907–11 (La. Ct. App. 2017) (affirming the trial court's exercise of discretion). *But see* United States v. Sierra Pac. Indus., 759 F. Supp. 2d 1206, 1214 (E.D. Cal. 2010) (prohibiting the use of evidence obtained through improper ex parte communications); Awan v. Awan, 906 N.Y.S.2d 70, 72 (App. Div. 2010) (excluding a doctor's testimony in a custody proceeding because the lawyer violated Rule 4.2 by having the doctor examine and question the child without the knowledge of the child's lawyer).

B. Model Rule 4.3

Where a person with whom a lawyer wishes to communicate is unrepresented or is not known to be represented, Model Rule 4.3 governs the lawyer's conduct. Model Rule 4.3 provides:

> In dealing on behalf of a client with a person who is not represented by counsel, a lawyer shall not state or imply that the lawyer is disinterested. When the lawyer knows or reasonably should know that the unrepresented person misunderstands the lawyer's role in the matter, the lawyer shall make reasonable efforts to correct the misunderstanding. The lawyer shall not give legal advice to an unrepresented person, other than the advice to secure counsel, if the lawyer knows or reasonably should know that the interests of such a person are or have a reasonable possibility of being in conflict with the interests of the client.[84]

Many communications between lawyers and unrepresented persons are innocent. Yet, Model Rule 4.3 recognizes that when a person is unrepresented, the danger that a lawyer will overreach is great, and the rule thus restricts the lawyer's ability to unfairly exploit the situation. By requiring a lawyer to disclose her interest or position in a matter, an unrepresented person will be warned of the risks attending communication and will know to keep silent until she can consult her own counsel. In the case of written communications, Rule 4.3 requires a lawyer to disclose on the face of any document her interest in the matter.[85]

Model Rule 4.3 distinguishes between situations involving unrepresented persons whose interests may be adverse to the lawyer's client and those in which there is no conflict.[86] In the former instance, the rule assumes that the potential for a lawyer to compromise the unrepresented person's interests is so great that the lawyer must be barred from giving any legal advice other than the advice to obtain counsel.[87] This does not mean, however, that a lawyer has any sort of *Miranda*-type obligation.[88] As long as the lawyer does not mislead the person into believing that she does not need separate counsel or does not have the ability or right to obtain her own counsel, the lawyer has no obligation to advise the person to obtain counsel. Any questions as to whether a lawyer's remarks constitute legal advice should be decided

84. Model Rules of Prof'l Conduct R. 4.3 (2020).

85. *See In re* Air Crash Disaster, 909 F. Supp. 1116, 1123 (N.D. Ill. 1995) (discussing the cover letter from the lawyer accompanying a questionnaire).

86. Model Rules of Prof'l Conduct R. 4.3 cmt. 2 (2020).

87. *Id.*

88. Restatement (Third) of the Law Governing Lawyers § 103 cmt. e (2000).

by focusing on what the person may reasonably have understood, rather than on the lawyer's intent.[89] This determination may be influenced by the unrepresented person's experience and sophistication, as well as the context or setting in which the communication occurs.[90]

C. Model Rule 4.4(a)

Model Rule 4.4(a) also applies to lawyers' ex parte communications.[91] This rule provides that "[i]n representing a client, a lawyer shall not use means that have no substantial purpose other than to embarrass, delay, or burden a third person, or use methods of obtaining evidence that violate the legal rights of such a person."[92] As with Rule 4.2, a lawyer must be representing a client for Rule 4.4(a) to apply to her conduct. When it comes to evaluating whether a lawyer is attempting to obtain evidence in violation of a third person's legal rights, the applicable standard is an objective one.[93]

The Model Rule 4.4(a) ban on using methods of obtaining evidence that violate the "legal rights" of third persons prohibits lawyers from questioning witnesses or opponents about attorney-client privileged information.[94] For example, lawyers may not question adversaries' former employees about privileged matters.[95] Information protected against discovery by the work product doctrine is similarly off-limits.[96] The harder question is whether a third person's "legal rights" under Model Rule 4.4(a) extend to contractual confidentiality claims, such as duties imposed by confidentiality provisions in employment contracts or severance agreements, or other non-disclosure agreements. The black letter of Model Rule 4.4(a) indicates that it covers contractual confidentiality obligations, and the commentary to the rule supports that position.[97] Yet section 102 of the Restatement (Third) of the

89. *See, e.g.*, Att'y Q v. Miss. State Bar, 587 So. 2d 228, 233 (Miss. 1991) (holding that the lawyer's statement, "don't worry about it," constituted legal advice under the circumstances).

90. Model Rules of Prof'l Conduct R. 4.3 cmt. 2 (2020).

91. *See, e.g.*, *In re* Lung, 122 N.Y.S.3d 364, 366–70 (App. Div. 2020) (suspending a lawyer who violated Rules 4.2 and 4.4(a) through repeated disparaging and aggressive e-mail messages to the opposing lawyer on which he copied the opposing party).

92. Model Rules of Prof'l Conduct R. 4.4(a) (2020).

93. *In re* Martinez, 462 P.3d 36, 45 (Ariz. 2020); *In re* Comfort, 159 P.3d 1011, 1020 (Kan. 2007).

94. Vlassis v. Samuelson, 143 F.R.D. 118, 125 (E.D. Mich. 1992).

95. Calise v. Brady Sullivan Harris Mills, LLC, No. 18-99WES, 2019 WL 1397245, at *6 (D.R.I. Mar. 28, 2019); Harris Davis Rebar, LLC v. Structural Ironworkers Local Union No. 1, Pension Tr. Fund, No. 17 C 6473, 2019 WL 447622, at *6 (N.D. Ill. Feb. 5, 2019); Brown v. St. Joseph Cnty., 148 F.R.D. 246, 255 (N.D. Ind. 1993); *Vlassis*, 143 F.R.D. at 125.

96. Restatement (Third) of the Law Governing Lawyers § 102 cmt. b (2000).

97. *See* Model Rules of Prof'l Conduct R. 4.4 cmt. 1 (2020) ("It is impractical to catalogue all such rights, but they include legal restrictions on methods of obtaining evidence from third persons and unwarranted intrusions into privileged relationships, such as the client-lawyer relationship.").

Law Governing Lawyers seemingly implies a narrower construction, since it excludes from "a duty of confidentiality to another imposed by law"[98] those "confidentiality duties based only on contract."[99]

In fact, "legal rights" may be created by contract and, accordingly, the duty imposed under Model Rule 4.4(a) is broader than the Restatement obligation not to violate "a duty of confidentiality to another imposed by law." Given the express language of Model Rule 4.4(a), the safe course for lawyers is to assume that information protected by a confidentiality agreement must be obtained through formal discovery. Lawyers who are concerned about this issue should consult the rules of professional conduct in the jurisdiction and might further consider seeking an advisory opinion from a state or local ethics committee where available. Lawyers also need to tread carefully where some type of confidentiality agreement is in play lest they be accused of tortiously interfering with another party's contract.

III. Communications with Organizations' Current and Former Employees

We have so far briefly examined some aspects of lawyers' ex parte communications with current and former employees of organizational litigants, and it should now be clear that these exchanges are potentially perilous. Even in jurisdictions that specifically exclude former employees from Rule 4.2's reach, such ex parte communications still spawn numerous disputes. Nonetheless, lawyers can take several precautions to avoid or defeat misconduct allegations.

A. Precautionary Steps for Lawyers

Muriel Siebert & Co. v. Intuit Inc.[100] illustrates an appropriate approach to ex parte communication with a former employee of an organizational litigant who was potentially a key witness. In that case, Nicholas Dermigny, Muriel Siebert's chief operating officer, participated in the events giving rise to Intuit's suit against Muriel Siebert. He was also instrumental in formulating Muriel Siebert's defense to the *Intuit* litigation. Two years into the case, Muriel Siebert terminated Dermigny's employment. Thereafter, Intuit's lawyers arranged to secretly interview him. Before beginning the interview, Intuit's lawyers advised Dermigny that he should not reveal any confidential or privileged information, including any conversations with Muriel Siebert's counsel, nor offer any information concerning Muriel Siebert's legal

98. Restatement (Third) of the Law Governing Lawyers § 102 (2000).
99. *Id.* cmt. b.
100. 868 N.E.2d 208 (N.Y. 2007).

strategy.[101] They further cautioned Dermigny that if asked a question that could lead to the disclosure of such information, he should tell them and decline to answer.[102] The Intuit lawyers then questioned Dermigny about the facts of the case but did not elicit any privileged information or inquire about Muriel Siebert's litigation strategy. Muriel Siebert moved to disqualify Intuit's counsel and to enjoin them from using any information provided by Dermigny. The trial court granted Muriel Siebert's motion, but a lower appellate court reversed. The lower appellate court then certified the case to the Court of Appeals, which is New York's highest court.

The Court of Appeals noted that while lawyers may generally communicate ex parte with an adversary's former employees, that right is not a license to elicit confidential or privileged information from them.[103] The disqualification of Intuit's counsel was not warranted, however, merely because Dermigny had been privy to Muriel Siebert's confidential and privileged information.[104] Intuit's lawyers had advised Dermigny of their representation and interest in the litigation, and cautioned him against revealing information to which they were not entitled.[105] Dermigny understood their admonition and disclosed no confidential or privileged information. Accordingly, there was no basis to disqualify Intuit's counsel.[106] The *Muriel Siebert* court therefore affirmed the lower appellate court.

Postorivo v. AG Paintball Holdings, Inc.[107] stands in stark contrast to *Muriel Siebert*. In *Postorivo*, the defendant's lawyers repeatedly communicated ex parte with one of the plaintiffs' former employees. The plaintiffs therefore sought sanctions against the defense lawyers, even though the defense lawyers did not obtain any confidential or privileged information through the communications. The defense lawyers argued that the communications were proper because they had not even inquired into privileged communications or information. Unfortunately, before speaking with the former employees, the defense lawyers had not cautioned them against revealing confidential or privileged information.[108] Nor had they told the former employees of their interest in the case or of the purpose for the interviews.[109] The fact that the lawyers were not seeking confidential or privileged information did not relieve them of their obligation to give these warnings.[110] As

101. *Id.* at 209.
102. *Id.*
103. *Id.* at 210.
104. *Id.*
105. *Id.*
106. *Id.*
107. Nos. 2991-VCP, 3111-VCP, 2008 WL 3876199 (Del. Ch. Aug. 20, 2008).
108. *Id.* at *21.
109. *Id.*
110. *Id.*

a result of their failures, the court disqualified the defense lawyers who conducted the interviews and awarded the plaintiffs monetary sanctions.

Muriel Siebert and *Postorivo* provide lawyers with substantial guidance when attempting ex parte communications with an organization's former employees. Some other precautionary steps are also advisable. First, lawyers should identify themselves, the parties they represent, and the matter at hand. Second, they should ask former employees whether they are represented by counsel in the matter. If the employees are represented in the matter, the lawyers should ask the employees to identify their counsel so that they may communicate with those lawyers in the future. The lawyers should then politely end the communication. Third, assuming the former employees are unrepresented, the lawyers should advise the former employees that they do not have to speak with them if they do not wish to.[111] Although there is authority for the proposition that lawyers have no duty to so caution employees,[112] doing so usually is the safer course. If the former employees decline to speak, the lawyers should politely terminate the communication. Fourth, if the former employees are willing to speak further, the lawyers should instruct them (1) not to reveal confidential or privileged information, or information that might constitute the organization's legal strategy; and (2) if asked a question calling for such information, to decline to answer. If the former employees held high-level positions, it may be prudent to ask whether they are subject to any confidentiality agreements with the organization. Fifth, the lawyers should ask the former employees to affirm (1) that they understand that they need not speak with them and (2) that they understand the warnings they were given. Only then should the interview begin in earnest. If a former employee opts to terminate a communication at any time, a lawyer should honor that request.

The approach is not substantially different where current employees are concerned. The challenge here is for the lawyer to first determine whether the employees to be interviewed ex parte fall within the categories or classes of employees that are off-limits applying either the commentary to Model Rule 4.2 or the managing-speaking agent test. If they are, obviously, there can be no ex parte communications. In making this determination, lawyers must be sensitive to the fact that even low-level current employees may be able to obligate the organization with respect to the matter or have their acts imputed to the organization for liability purposes.[113] As a result, an employee who does not function in an executive capacity may still be protected under Model Rule 4.2. If current employees are not off-limits because

111. Paulson v. Plainfield Trucking, Inc., 210 F.R.D. 654, 659 (D. Minn. 2002).

112. Pa. Eth. Op. 2014-3, 2014 WL 2986615, at *2 (Phila. Bar Ass'n, Prof'l Guidance Comm. 2014).

113. *See, e.g.*, Bynote v. Nat'l Super Mkts., Inc., 891 S.W.2d 117, 123–34 (Mo. 1995) (involving a bagger and checker in a slip-and-fall lawsuit against a grocery store).

of their status or roles, and they are not represented by counsel in the matter, then ex parte communication with them is permitted.[114]

B. Ex Parte Communication Where the Organization Has a Law Department

In many cases, a current employee with whom a lawyer is entitled to speak will work for an organization with a law department. The presence of an in-house law department does not, however, create an automatic or blanket representation of all employees by those lawyers for Model Rule 4.2 purposes.[115] Organizations may impose representation only on employees who are within their constituent groups or are their alter egos under the Model Rule 4.2 commentary or the managing-speaking agent test.[116] Otherwise, an organization "cannot unilaterally create or impose representation of employees by corporate counsel."[117] An otherwise unprotected employee must seek the legal advice or assistance of an in-house lawyer for the employee to be represented within the meaning of Model Rule 4.2.[118] Alternatively, the organization must offer to represent employees, and the employees must accept the offer for Model Rule 4.2 to come into play.[119] This is only logical, given that the attorney-client relationship is a voluntary one, and no lawyer has a right to appear for someone without that person's consent.[120] This position is also consistent with Model Rule 1.13(a)'s mandate that the client of a lawyer employed by an organization is the organization itself rather than any individual constituent.[121] Thus, the fact that an employee copies an in-house lawyer on a letter to a lawyer for an adversary or potential opponent does not give that lawyer knowledge that the employee is represented by in-house counsel in the matter.[122]

---

114. *See, e.g.*, Lee Mem'l Health Sys. v. Smith, 56 So. 3d 808, 812 (Fla. Dist. Ct. App. 2011) (permitting lawyers for a medical malpractice plaintiff to have ex parte communications with treating physicians employed by the defendant hospital).

115. Michaels v. Woodland, 988 F. Supp. 468, 472–74 (D.N.J. 1997); Terra Int'l, Inc. v. Miss. Chem. Corp., 913 F. Supp. 1306, 1316–17 (N.D. Iowa 1996); Carter-Herman v. City of Phila., 897 F. Supp. 899, 903 (E.D. Pa. 1995); *see also* ABA Formal Op. 95-396, *supra* note 49, at 15 (offering an example that supports this view); Banks v. Office of the Senate Sergeant-at-Arms, 222 F.R.D. 1, 5–6 (D.D.C. 2004) (discussing government agencies and their employees).

116. *See* Mendez v. Hovensa, LLC, No. 02-0169, 2008 WL 906768, at *7 (D.V.I. Mar. 31, 2008).

117. *Terra Int'l*, 913 F. Supp. at 1317.

118. *See Carter-Herman*, 897 F. Supp. at 903.

119. *See Michaels*, 988 F. Supp. at 474.

120. Brown v. St. Joseph Cnty., 148 F.R.D. 246, 250 (N.D. Ind. 1993).

121. Model Rules of Prof'l Conduct R. 1.13(a) (2020) ("A lawyer employed or retained by an organization represents the organization acting through its duly authorized constituents.").

122. Humco, Inc. v. Noble, 31 S.W.3d 916, 919 (Ky. 2000).

IV. Ex Parte Communications with In-House Counsel

As noted previously, many organizations have in-house legal departments. If an organization also employs outside counsel to represent it in a matter, lawyers for an opponent may want to bypass outside counsel and communicate directly with the organization's inside lawyers. This approach is generally permissible.[123] Model Rule 4.2 is intended to protect a client against unfair tactics and overreaching by the lawyer making the communication, and against harm arising from ill-advised statements that the client would be unlikely to make if a lawyer was present. These concerns are not implicated where the ex parte communication is aimed at another lawyer. Furthermore, prohibiting lawyers from communicating directly with organizations' inside counsel is inimical to the efficient resolution of disputes. Thus, there is no requirement that the lawyer wishing to speak with inside counsel first obtain the permission of the organization's outside counsel. *In re Grievance Proceeding*[124] is a rare case in point.

In that case, a plaintiff's lawyer twice wrote a defendant's general counsel after outside defense counsel would not respond to discovery or settlement offers. After the first letter, the defense lawyer had asked the plaintiff's lawyer not to communicate with the general counsel.[125] After the second letter, the general counsel reported the plaintiff's lawyer to the local federal court grievance committee for allegedly violating Rule 4.2. The committee concluded that the plaintiff's lawyer had not violated Rule 4.2 and recommended that the district court dismiss the complaint. The district court accepted the committee's recommendation. In doing so, the court observed that ex parte communication with a company's general counsel does not raise the same concerns as an ex parte communication with a lay employee, explaining that a general counsel's "training in the law helps ensure a level playing field of legal expertise in communications with opposing counsel."[126]

123. *In re* Grievance Proc., No. 3:01GP6(SRU), 2002 WL 31106389, at *3 (D. Conn. July 19, 2002); *In re* Woodham, 769 S.E.2d 353, 356–57 (Ga. 2015); State *ex rel.* Okla. Bar Ass'n v. Tweedy, 52 P.3d 1003, 1009 (Okla. 2000); Restatement (Third) of the Law Governing Lawyers § 100 cmt. c (2000); ABA Comm. on Ethics & Prof'l Responsibility, Formal Op. 06-443, at 2 (2006) [hereinafter ABA Formal Op. 06-443]; D.C. Bar, Legal Ethics Comm., Op. 331, at 3 (2005) [hereinafter D.C. Op. 331]; N.Y. Eth. Op. 2007-1, 2007 WL 758153, at *2–3 (Ass'n of the Bar of the City of N.Y., Comm. on Prof'l & Jud. Ethics 2007); Va. Op. 1890, *supra* note 7, at 13; State Bar of Wis., Prof'l Ethics Comm., Formal Op. E-07-01, at 14 (2007); *see* Utah Eth. Op. 15-02, 2015 WL 3513298, at *7 (Utah State Bar, Ethics Advisory Op. Comm. 2015) (permitting ex parte communications with in-house lawyers generally, but outlining possible limits on such communications).

124. No. 3:01GP6(SRU), 2002 WL 31106389, at *3 (D. Conn. July 19, 2002).

125. *Id.* at *1.

126. *Id.* at *3.

It is true that permitting a lawyer to circumvent outside counsel and deal directly with an in-house lawyer creates the potential for mischief. For example, an opposing lawyer might call an in-house lawyer to seek an accommodation that she knows or suspects outside counsel would not grant. But that prospect is not a problem that Model Rule 4.2 is intended to address. Moreover, it is reasonable to put the burden of avoiding associated confusion or inconvenience on the in-house lawyer, who can easily refer the opposing lawyer to outside counsel or decline to make a commitment or state a position until she has conferred with outside counsel.

According to the ABA's Standing Committee on Ethics and Professional Responsibility, there are two possible exceptions to the general rule that ex parte communications with inside counsel are permissible. First, if the inside lawyer is part of the constituent group identified in Comment 7 to Model Rule 4.2 or qualifies as the organization's alter ego under the managing-speaking agent test because of her business advice to the company or participation in events giving rise to the dispute, then Model Rule 4.2 applies.[127] But that hardly seems right because then the exception would almost always swallow the general rule. Indeed, it is precisely because an in-house lawyer directs or supervises outside counsel or can bind the organization that an opposing lawyer wants to communicate with the in-house lawyer, as where outside counsel for the organization is allegedly not communicating settlement offers, refuses to communicate on key issues, is impossible to reach for some reason, or is otherwise acting unreasonably. Second, if the inside lawyer is herself a represented party in the litigation or has independent counsel with respect to the matter and the inquiring lawyer knows of the representation, Model Rule 4.2 prohibits ex parte communication with the inside lawyer.[128] The second exception identified by the Standing Committee makes much more sense.

Another possible exception to the general rule arguably exists where outside counsel asks an adversary not to communicate directly with inside counsel. A communication in disregard of such a directive would not violate Model Rule 4.2, but the ABA's Standing Committee on Ethics and Professional Responsibility has speculated that in this situation ex parte contact with inside counsel might violate Model Rule 4.4(a).[129] Again, Model Rule 4.4(a) states that in representing a client, "a lawyer shall not use means that have no substantial purpose other than to embarrass, delay, or burden a third person, or use methods of obtaining evidence that violate the legal rights of such a person."[130] The ABA position is untenable, however, because

127. ABA Formal Op. 06-443, *supra* note 123, at 3.

128. *See also* D.C. Op. 331, *supra* note 123, at 3 (prohibiting ex parte communication with an in-house lawyer who is separately represented in a matter).

129. ABA Formal Op. 06-443, *supra* note 123, at 2.

130. Model Rules of Prof'l Conduct R. 4.4(a) (2020).

a communication with inside counsel either violates Model Rule 4.4(a) or does not, and if a lawyer's communication with inside counsel has a substantial purpose other than delay, embarrassment, or burden, an outside lawyer's prior request against it does not change that fact. Outside counsel have no legal right to prohibit another lawyer's communications with inside counsel, so ignoring outside counsel's request cannot violate their legal rights. In-house lawyers are not normally included among the group of employees who may be deemed to personify their organizations for Model Rule 4.2 purposes, so communication with them cannot reasonably be characterized as a method of obtaining evidence that violates the organization's legal rights. Consequently, it is difficult to discern how legitimate ex parte communications with an in-house lawyer would ever violate Model Rule 4.4(a).

V. Ex Parte Communications with Treating Physicians

When plaintiffs file lawsuits putting their medical conditions or injuries at issue, they generally waive their physician-patient privilege to the extent of those conditions or injuries. Plaintiffs provide medical authorizations to lawyers for defendants so that they may gather appropriate medical records from health care providers, including treating physicians. But beyond gathering medical records, defense lawyers may wish to speak with plaintiffs' treating physicians outside the presence of plaintiffs' counsel. Treating physicians are not among the categories of people shielded from ex parte communication by Model Rule 4.2. A lawyer's representation of a plaintiff does not equate to concurrent representation of the plaintiff's treating physicians.

Historically, many courts have allowed defense lawyers to have ex parte communications with plaintiffs' treating doctors,[131] although other courts have prohibited such communications as a matter of public policy or in furtherance of physician-patient confidentiality doctrine.[132] The better-reasoned position holds that defense lawyers are permitted to have ex parte communications with treating physicians[133] as long as plaintiffs execute

131. Moreland v. Austin, 670 S.E.2d 68, 71 (Ga. 2008); Morris v. Thomson, 937 P.2d 1212, 1216–17 (Idaho 1997); Butler-Tulio v. Scroggins, 774 A.2d 1209, 1224–25 (Md. Ct. Spec. App. 2001); Holman v. Rasak, 785 N.W.2d 98, 106 (Mich. 2010); Brandt v. Med. Def. Assocs., 856 S.W.2d 667, 674 (Mo. 1993); Arons v. Jutkowitz, 880 N.E.2d 831, 836–39 (N.Y. 2007); *In re* Collins, 224 S.W.3d 798, 805 (Tex. App. 2007).

132. Hampton v. Schimpff, 188 F.R.D. 589, 589 (D. Mont. 1999) (interpreting Montana law); Moss v. Amira, 826 N.E.2d 1001, 1006 (Ill. App. Ct. 2005); Givens v. Mullikin, 75 S.W.3d 383, 409 (Tenn. 2002); Sorensen v. Barbuto, 177 P.3d 614, 619–21 (Utah 2008); Hermanson v. MultiCare Health Sys., Inc., 448 P.3d 153, 157 n.4 (Wash. Ct. App. 2019).

133. *Compare* Pratt v. Petelin, No. 09-2252-CM-GLR, 2010 WL 446474, at *7 (D. Kan. Feb. 4, 2010) (outlining the reasons for permitting ex parte communication), *and* Bryant v. Hilst, 136 F.R.D. 487, 491–92 (D. Kan. 1991) (explaining at length why ex parte communication should be permitted), *with* Sorensen v. Barbuto, 177 P.3d 614, 619–21 (Utah 2008) (reasoning why ex parte communication should be prohibited).

medical authorizations permitting the physicians to disclose relevant patient information.

Today, ex parte communications with treating physicians implicate the Health Insurance Portability and Accountability Act of 1996 (HIPAA). Physicians may not disclose protected health information except as permitted by HHS regulations.[134] HIPAA permits disclosure pursuant to patient authorizations and even permits disclosure without an authorization where "required by law" or "in the course of any judicial or administrative proceeding."[135] HIPAA is silent on the subject of ex parte communications with treating physicians.[136]

HIPAA preempts state law concerning ex parte communications with treating physicians if the HIPAA privacy regulations are more stringent than state law. Thus, even in states that typically permit ex parte communications between lawyers and treating physicians, HIPAA may operate to limit them. HIPAA does not preclude such communications altogether; rather, it merely establishes procedural prerequisites.[137] On the other hand, HIPAA does not preempt contrary provisions of state law if the state law offers more stringent privacy protections. This leads us to the HIPAA regulation governing judicial proceedings, which states:

> (1) Permitted disclosures. A covered entity may disclose protected health information in the course of any judicial or administrative proceeding:
>
> (i) In response to an order of a court or administrative tribunal, provided that the covered entity discloses only the protected health information expressly authorized by such order; or
>
> (ii) In response to a subpoena, discovery request, or other lawful process, that is not accompanied by an order of a court or administrative tribunal, if:
>
> (A) The covered entity receives satisfactory assurance . . . from the party seeking the information that reasonable efforts have been made by such party to ensure that the individual who is the subject of the protected health information that has been requested has been given notice of the request; or
>
> (B) The covered entity receives satisfactory assurance . . . from the party seeking the information that reasonable efforts have been made by such party to secure a qualified protective order. . . .[138]

---

134. Moreland v. Austin, 670 S.E.2d 68, 70 (Ga. 2008).

135. 45 C.F.R. §§ 164.512(a), (e) (2018).

136. Caldwell v. Chauvin, 464 S.W.3d 139, 149 (Ky. 2015); *Holman*, 785 N.W.2d at 105; Smith v. Am. Home Prods. Corp. Wyeth-Ayerst Pharm., 855 A.2d 608, 626 (N.J. Super. Ct. Law Div. 2003).

137. *Caldwell*, 464 S.W.3d at 150–51; *Holman*, 785 N.W.2d at 105–06; Arons v. Jutkowitz, 880 N.E.2d 831, 842 (N.Y. 2007).

138. 45 C.F.R. § 164.512(e) (2018).

Accordingly, under HIPAA, there are four ways to obtain protected health information in litigation. First, have the plaintiff execute a HIPAA-compliant authorization allowing a covered entity to release the information.[139] Such an authorization could be written to permit ex parte communication with the provider. Second, subpoena the information while also providing the covered entity with satisfactory assurances that the plaintiff has been notified of the request and does not object to the disclosure. Third, subpoena the information while providing satisfactory assurances that the requesting party has made reasonable efforts to obtain a qualified protective order. Fourth, obtain a court order authorizing disclosure.[140] Such an order could include a provision permitting certain ex parte communications with a health care provider.[141]

To summarize, where HIPAA controls because it provides greater privacy protection than competing state law, ex parte contact with treating physicians is permitted in conformity with the federal regulations.[142] If state law provides more stringent privacy protection, it controls, and ex parte communications with treating physicians are permitted only to the extent state law allows. In some instances, HIPAA and state law may coexist and thus permit ex parte communications in appropriate instances.[143] For example, if a plaintiff signs a HIPAA-compliant authorization that permits ex parte communication with treating physicians and state law also permits such contact, then ex parte communications are permitted to the extent of the authorization. If a court orders the disclosure of information and both the order and state law permit ex parte communications, then ex parte communications are permitted consistent with the narrower of the two. If state law does not permit ex parte communications with treating physicians, that ends the inquiry. Of course, "contact related to benign topics such as scheduling a

139. 45 C.F.R. § 164.508 (2018).

140. *See Caldwell*, 464 S.W.3d at 152 (holding that this is the only circumstance in which protected health information may be disclosed under HIPAA's litigation exception).

141. *See, e.g.*, Brigham v. Colyer, No. 09-2210-JWL-DJW, 2010 WL 2131967, at *4 (D. Kan. May 27, 2010) (discussing the reasonable scope of the disclosure order and rejecting the plaintiff's request that defendant be required to give advance notice of the date, time, and place of any ex parte interview with a physician); Pratt v. Petelin, No. 09-2252-CM-GLR, 2010 WL 446474, at *7–8 (D. Kan. Feb. 4, 2010) (permitting ex parte communication but noting that good cause for ex parte communications may not exist in all cases). *But see* State *ex rel.* Proctor v. Messina, 320 S.W.3d 145, 153–58 (Mo. 2010) (ruling that HIPAA does not allow courts to enter orders allowing ex parte contacts because such contacts do not occur "in the course of" a "judicial proceeding").

142. *See, e.g.*, Santaniello v. Sweet, No. 3:04CV806 (RNC), 2007 WL 214605, at *3 (D. Conn. Jan. 25, 2007); Hulse v. Suburban Mobile Home Supply Co., No. 06-1168-WEB, 2006 WL 2927519, at *2 (D. Kan. Oct. 12, 2006); Bayne v. Provost, 359 F. Supp. 2d 234, 240–43 (N.D.N.Y. 2005); Law v. Zuckerman, 307 F. Supp. 2d 705, 711 (D. Md. 2004); *Arons*, 880 N.E.2d at 842; Holmes v. Nightingale, 158 P.3d 1039, 1047 (Okla. 2007).

143. *In re* Diet Drug Litig., 895 A.2d 493, 501–06 (N.J. Super. Ct. Law Div. 2005); Caldwell v. Baptist Mem'l Hosp., No. W2015-01076-COA-R10-CV, 2016 WL 3226431, at *5 (Tenn. Ct. App. June 3, 2016).

deposition or trial testimony" is beyond the purview of HIPAA's restrictions on the disclosure of medical records.[144]

In *State ex rel. Proctor v. Messina*,[145] the Missouri Supreme Court ruled that although state law did not prohibit ex parte communications between defense counsel and a plaintiff's physician, such contacts do not occur "in the course of any judicial or administrative proceeding" as required by § 164.512(e)(1).[146] Consequently, the court held that a lower court's order purporting to allow such communications was not valid under HIPAA.[147] In coming to this conclusion, the *Messina* court noted that neither HIPAA nor its regulations define "in the course of" or "judicial proceeding."[148] It found that these terms (at least under Missouri law) should be construed narrowly, so that HIPAA did not authorize courts to enter orders permitting a physician to divulge a patient's protected health information outside a proceeding over which the court "has direct supervision thereof."[149] Since that would not be the case in the context of ex parte discussions, orders allowing such contacts were not permissible.

The rationale and result in *Messina* are highly state-specific, as the court looked primarily to existing Missouri precedent in narrowly construing the phrases "in the course of" and "judicial proceeding." Other courts have rejected the *Messina* court's approach.[150] Moreover, while the *Messina* court's interpretation of what constitutes a "judicial proceeding" is plausible, it is also reasonable to construe "judicial proceeding" as referring to the case as a whole, rather than only those formal discovery methods authorized by rule or statute over which the court has "direct supervision." Although there is no direct judicial oversight during an ex parte communication between a lawyer and a treating physician, the process that generates a court order allowing such contact necessarily entails direct judicial supervision—that is, the filing of a motion and the opposing party's submission of a memorandum in opposition or request for a hearing, and so on. There may be valid reasons for courts not to enter such orders in some cases, but the more reasonable interpretation is that HIPAA gives courts the discretion to allow ex parte contact that would otherwise be allowable under state law.

If defense lawyers are permitted to have ex parte communications with plaintiffs' treating physicians, some essential precautions are always in order. First, they should clearly identify themselves, the parties they represent, and

144. Davidson-Nadwodny v. Wal-Mart Assocs., Inc., No. CCB-07-2595, 2010 WL 1328572, at *10 (D. Md. Mar. 26, 2010).
145. 320 S.W.3d 145 (Mo. 2010).
146. *Id.* at 157–58.
147. *Id.*
148. *Id.* at 156.
149. *Id.* at 156–57.
150. *See, e.g.*, Caldwell v. Chauvin, 464 S.W.3d 139, 150–51 (Ky. 2015).

the matter at hand. Second, they should advise the doctors that they do not have to speak with them. If the doctors decline to speak with them, the lawyers should politely move on. They should never pressure physicians to speak with them. Third, they should accurately outline the injuries that the plaintiff alleges in the case or any conditions the plaintiff claims to suffer as a result of the events at issue. The obvious objective is to appropriately define the boundaries of the discussion. Fourth, if physicians are willing to speak, lawyers should instruct them (1) not to reveal information about a plaintiff beyond that legitimately at issue, and (2) if asked a question calling for information that reasonably ought to be withheld, to decline to answer. If physicians' personal styles are such that lawyers cannot limit communications to only those subjects fairly at issue, they should terminate their communications. These rules apply equally where lawyers are communicating with physicians' staffs rather than the physicians themselves.

Finally, a lawyer who communicates ex parte with a treating physician in violation of HIPAA may violate Model Rules 4.4(a) and 8.4(d).[151] HIPAA itself provides for only a $100 fine for each violation of the Act. A court asked to remedy a HIPAA violation could presumably exercise its discretion to fashion a range of reasonable remedies or sanctions depending on the circumstances of the violation.[152]

A party who seeks to exclude evidence due to allegedly improper contact with her treating physician in violation of HIPAA must establish a record sufficient to establish that protected health information has actually been disclosed during the ex parte communications at issue.[153] Parties relying on a medical authorization to support disclosure of protected health information through ex parte interviews need to ensure that their authorizations are broadly worded to specifically cover them. If an adversary balks at providing such an authorization, HIPAA allows the inquiring party to seek a qualified protective order to this effect. Once satisfied that the requested information is relevant and that applicable state law is not "more stringent" than HIPAA, the majority of courts sensibly agree that orders allowing ex parte physician interviews are permissible and generally appropriate.[154] If

151. Model Rules of Prof'l Conduct R. 4.4(a) (2020) ("Respect for the Rights of Third Persons"); *id.* R. 8.4(d) (prohibiting conduct prejudicial to the administration of justice).

152. *See* Moreland v. Austin, 670 S.E.2d 68, 72 (Ga. 2008) (discussing remedies for HIPAA violations).

153. Beaty v. St. Luke's Hosp. of Kan. City, 298 S.W.3d 554, 588 (Mo. Ct. App. 2009) (rejecting the plaintiff's argument to this effect because record only showed that defense counsel had asked the doctor to "review some data" regarding the plaintiff, but there was no record of what that data was or any additional substance of their communications).

154. *See, e.g.*, Morgan v. Wesley Med. Ctr., No. 18-2158-KHV-KGG, 2018 WL 6696561, at *4–6 (D. Kan. Dec. 20, 2018) (rejecting the plaintiff's attempt to block ex parte interviews by claiming that some treating physicians were off-limits because the plaintiff might name them as retained or consulting experts, and further denying the plaintiff's request that his counsel be

an order is entered, the plaintiff's lawyer need not be specifically notified or consent to an interview, but HIPAA does "require clear and explicit notice to [the] physician both as to the purpose of the interview and to the fact that the interview is not required."[155]

VI. Ex Parte Communications with Expert Witnesses

Model Rule 4.2 generally does not prohibit ex parte communications with expert witnesses. A lawyer for a party who engages an expert witness does not automatically represent the expert as well. As a result, a court may allow ex parte contact with experts[156] as long as the lawyer does not attempt to obstruct another party's access to evidence.[157] *Brown v. Hamid*[158] is an interesting case in point.

Brown was a medical malpractice action. In response to defense counsel's expert witness interrogatories, the plaintiff's attorney summarized the opinion of a non-treating physician. The plaintiff then designated that physician as an expert. The defense lawyer telephoned the expert to confirm that he provided the information used to answer the interrogatories. During this call, the defense lawyer stated that a distinguished retired physician with

permitted to attend the defendant's interviews of his treating physicians); Callahan v. Bledsoe, No. 16-2310-JAR-GLR, 2017 WL 590254, at *2 (D. Kan. Feb. 14, 2017) (granting the defendant's motion seeking ex parte interviews with the plaintiff's treating physicians and explaining that the order was not an advisory opinion to a non-party as the plaintiff's lawyers contended and as some Kansas state court judges were reportedly characterizing similar orders); Carmody v. Mikesell, No. 16-cv-02603-PAB-NYW, 2017 WL 5191802, at *4 (D. Colo. Nov. 9, 2017) (outlining a few conditions governing any interviews); Brigham v. Colyer, No. 09-2210-JWL-DJW, 2010 WL 2131967, at *4 (D. Kan. May 27, 2010) (discussing the reasonable scope of a disclosure order and rejecting the plaintiff's request that the defendant be required to give advance notice of the date, time, and place of any ex parte interview with the physician); Pratt v. Petelin, No. 09-2252-CM-GLR, 2010 WL 446474, at *8 (D. Kan. Feb. 4, 2010) (modifying the defendants' proposed disclosure order); Congress v. Tillman, No. 09-10419, 2009 WL 1738511, at *1–2 (E.D. Mich. June 16, 2009) (citing other cases in that district similarly ruling); Parker v. Upsher-Smith Labs Inc., No 3:06-CV-0518-ECR-VPC, 2009 WL 301938, at *2 (D. Nev. Feb 6, 2009) (collecting cases); Holman v. Rasak, 785 N.W.2d 98, 103–06 (Mich. 2010) (holding that HIPAA was not inconsistent with state law, which permitted ex parte communications).

155. *Tillman*, 2009 WL 1738511, at *2 (quoting Croskey v. BMW of N. Am., No. 02-73747, 2005 WL 4704767, at *5 (E.D. Mich. Nov. 10, 2005)).

156. *See, e.g.*, Jones v. Reichert Jung, Inc., 211 F. Supp. 2d 661, 669 (D. Md. 2002) (concluding that it was proper for the defendant to obtain affidavits from the plaintiff's experts). *But see* Port-A-Pour, Inc. v. Peak Innovations, Inc., No. 13-cv-1511-WYD-NYW, 2016 WL 7868813, at *4 (D. Colo. June 14, 2016) ("The Federal Rules of Civil Procedure are silent as to whether an attorney may make ex parte contact with the opposing side's specially retained expert, but courts have held that ex parte contact by one party of another party's expert while the expert is still employed is a violation of Rule 26(b) arising not from the language of the Rule, but upon the principle of fairness.").

157. *See, e.g.*, Sanderson v. Boddie-Noell Enters., Inc., 227 F.R.D. 448, 452–55 (E.D. Va. 2005) (working through the expert's employer to prevent the expert's testimony).

158. 856 S.W.2d 51 (Mo. 1993).

no interest in the case believed that the defendant did not commit malpractice.[159] The defense attorney further told the expert that he had defended one of his colleagues and that he had once employed another of the doctor's colleagues as an expert witness.[160] The expert believed that the lawyer's comments were not a "'big deal,'" but he also believed "the real reason for the 7- to 10-minute call was to 'dissuade' him from testifying as an expert by exerting 'social pressure.'"[161]

The *Brown* court determined that the portion of the discussion regarding the expert's provision of information to answer interrogatories was proper because no rules prohibit parties from using informal discovery, including ex parte discussions, to learn about matters previously disclosed. The disclosures in the plaintiff's interrogatory answers provided prior to the ex parte conversation were sufficient to waive her claims of work product immunity even though they preceded the physician's deposition.[162] Sounding a cautionary note, the *Brown* court warned that in some instances, attorneys' attempts to pressure experts into not testifying may constitute ethical or criminal violations. The court concluded that the defense lawyer committed no violations because the expert testified at trial without changing his testimony.[163]

As *Brown* cautions, lawyers who communicate with opposing expert witnesses should be alert to the Model Rule 3.4(a) prohibition against "unlawfully obstruct[ing] another party's access to evidence,"[164] as well as the Model Rule 3.4(f) ban on against asking a person other than a client to "refrain from voluntarily giving relevant information to another party."[165] A lawyer may violate Model Rule 3.4(a) by attempting to unlawfully dissuade a witness from testifying.[166] Model Rule 3.4(f) generally prevents attempts to discourage witnesses from testifying for any reason. Nothing in Model Rule 3.4(f) limits its application to fact witnesses. Neither rule requires an explicit instruction or overt threat for a violation.[167] A lawyer may violate either rule by, for example, indicating that a witness's communication with

159. *Id.* at 53.
160. *Id.*
161. *Id.*
162. *Id.* at 54.
163. *Id.* at 54–55.
164. Model Rules of Prof'l Conduct R. 3.4(a) (2020).
165. *Id.* R. 3.4(f). The exceptions to Model Rule 3.4(f) for relatives, employees, or other agents of a client are not relevant here.
166. *See, e.g.*, *In re* Disciplinary Action Against Dvorak, 611 N.W.2d 147, 150–51 (N.D. 2000) (threatening a witness with a defamation action).
167. *See, e.g.*, Davis v. Wieland, 557 S.W.3d 340, 350–51 (Mo. Ct. App. 2018) (affirming sanctions against lawyers who wrote the other side's expert and in that letter "accused her of being 'incorrect' and unfair' and repeatedly emphasized [the lawyers'] connection with [the expert's] colleagues 'in an apparent attempt to pressure [the expert] to change her report and therefore, her testimony,'" which the trial court likened to witness tampering).

or testimony for another party might expose the witness to liability, or that by not testifying or speaking to the other party the witness would avoid potential liability.[168]

There is also an argument that in federal court and in state courts that have adopted rules akin to Federal Rule of Civil Procedure 26(b)(4), a lawyer who communicates with an opposing expert witness other than by deposition violates Model Rule 3.4(c), which states that a lawyer shall not "knowingly disobey an obligation under the rules of a tribunal."[169] This position rests on the reasoning that Rule 26(b)(4)(A), which states that "[a] party may depose any person who has been identified as an expert whose opinions may be presented at trial,"[170] implicitly prevents any communication with an adverse expert except by way of deposition.[171] This is a dubious rationale; Rule 26(b)(4) does not state that a deposition is the *only* manner in which a lawyer may obtain a disclosed expert's opinions or related information—it simply permits expert depositions. Of course, in a jurisdiction that takes this approach, the obvious solution for a lawyer who wants to speak with an opposing expert outside the presence of the opposing lawyer is to file a motion seeking the court's permission to so interview the expert.

Communicating with an expert's employer to prevent an expert from testifying may also violate Model Rules 3.4(a) and (f),[172] as *Sanderson v. Boddie-Noell Enterprises, Inc.*[173] illustrates. *Sanderson* was a slip-and-fall case in which Ronnie Sanderson alleged that Boddie-Noell failed to clear ice and snow from the sidewalk outside its restaurant. Sanderson's lawyer, Joel Bieber, expected that Boddie-Noell would claim that it had no duty to remove the ice and snow because precipitation was falling at the time of Sanderson's accident. Bieber knew that he would need a meteorologist as an expert and called the sales manager at a local television station, Richard DePilla, to see whether the station would permit one of its meteorologists to testify as an expert. Bieber knew DePilla because he was a frequent TV advertiser. DePilla checked with the station's general manager, Robert

168. *See, e.g.*, Harlan v. Lewis, 982 F.2d 1255, 1258–59 (8th Cir. 1993) (affirming sanctions against a defense lawyer who told one of the plaintiffs' treating physicians that he might be called as a witness at the trial of the plaintiffs' medical malpractice case and that the plaintiffs might also sue him in a separate action, but if he did not testify, the plaintiffs' suit would fail; the district court concluded that the lawyer violated Rules 3.4(a) and (f)).

169. Model Rules of Prof'l Conduct R. 3.4(c) (2020).

170. Fed. R. Civ. P. 26(b)(4)(A).

171. *See, e.g.*, Epright v. Liberty Mut. Ins. Co., No. CV166016217S, 2019 WL 3220580, at *3 (Conn. Super. Ct. June 18, 2019) ("These rules do not authorize, and thus implicitly forbid, counsel from making ex parte contact with the opposing party's disclosed expert." (footnote omitted)).

172. *See, e.g.*, WellStar Health Sys., Inc. v. Kemp, 751 S.E.2d 445, 448–53 (Ga. Ct. App. 2013) (disqualifying WellStar's lawyers, who worked through the employer of the plaintiff's medical expert witness to pressure the expert to withdraw).

173. 227 F.R.D. 448 (E.D. Va. 2005).

Peterson, who indicated that station policy forbade outside employment by any of its broadcasters. Bieber thus hired an expert meteorologist elsewhere.

Defense counsel separately retained the station's lead meteorologist, John Bernier, as an expert. Bernier was a popular local television figure. When defense counsel served Bieber with Bernier's expert witness disclosure, Bieber called DePilla to tell him that Bernier was serving as an expert witness contrary to station policy.[174] DePilla ran to Peterson, who promptly instructed a subordinate, Matthew Zelkind, to tell Bernier that he was prohibited from serving as an expert witness. Zelkind told Bernier that he was forbidden to testify, that testifying would breach his employment contract, and that the station could fire him if he testified.[175] Bernier protested that he had served as an expert many times before without complaint, but Zelkind persisted. Bernier accordingly relented and told defense counsel that he could not serve as an expert in Sanderson's case.[176] Defense counsel called Bieber to complain and threatened to seek sanctions. Bieber promptly wrote Peterson to say that he had no objection to Bernier testifying, but to no avail. Boddie-Noell moved for sanctions. The court attempted to undo the damage at a hearing on the sanctions motion by encouraging the station to allow Bernier to testify. The station agreed that it would not fire Bernier if he testified, but it reserved the right to take other disciplinary action, possibly including suspending him.[177] Not wanting to expose Bernier to discipline, Boddie-Noell decided not to insist on his testimony. Boddie-Noell then pressed for sanctions, arguing that Bernier's reputation and local celebrity made him irreplaceable as an expert.[178]

The court found that Bieber had violated Virginia Rule of Professional Conduct 3.4(a), which stated that a lawyer "shall not '[o]bstruct another party's access to evidence.'"[179] While Bieber did not directly prevent Bernier from serving as Boddie-Noell's expert, Bernier's withdrawal was a foreseeable consequence of Bieber's second call to DePilla.[180] Although Bieber disclaimed any improper intent, he "deliberately set into a motion a series of events that had the effect of obstructing the defendant's ability to use the services of its designated expert witness."[181] Bieber was "chargeable with knowledge of the reasonably foreseeable consequences of the acts in which he deliberately engaged."[182] The court sanctioned Bieber by ordering him to

174. *Id.* at 450.
175. *Id.*
176. *Id.*
177. *Id.* at 451.
178. *Id.*
179. *Id.* at 452 (quoting the rule).
180. *Id.*
181. *Id.* at 453–54.
182. *Id.* at 454.

reimburse Boddie-Noell for Bernier's fees, pay all fees associated with the sanctions motion and any related case delay, pay the fees of Boddie-Noell's replacement expert, and pay all of Boddie-Noell's fees associated with retaining and working with a new expert.

Even if lawyers' ex parte communications with experts are permissible under Model Rule 4.2 and are not used to unlawfully obstruct another party's access to evidence, they still may be prohibited. The best illustration of this situation involves rules of civil procedure or other court rules that restrict expert discovery.[183] A lawyer who knowingly violates a court rule also violates Model Rule 3.4(c), which obligates lawyers to obey tribunals' rules, and potentially Model Rule 8.4(d), which prohibits conduct prejudicial to the administration of justice.[184]

In summary, lawyers should never initiate ex parte communications with opposing experts without first checking court rules and existing case law in the jurisdiction. If these rules permit such contact, then the advice given in connection with ex parte interviews of current and former employees and treating physicians is valid here. Lawyers should never try to dissuade experts from testifying or persuade them to change their opinions. Lawyers who do not want their experts to be exposed to ex parte communications are free to request that the experts not reveal information about the case outside of their reports or depositions.

VII. The Special Problem of Class and Collective Actions

Many capable lawyers represent clients in class action litigation. Unfortunately, the subject of ex parte communications with class members is sometimes a murky one. Here rules of civil procedure and professional responsibility uniquely overlap. As a result, lawyers' need for guidance in this area is significant.

A. Class Communications by Plaintiffs' Counsel

A trial court must determine "at an early practicable time" whether a lawsuit can be maintained as a class action.[185] A court's decision to allow a case to be maintained as a class action is referred to as "certifying" the class.

183. *See, e.g.*, Rowe v. Vaagen Bros. Lumber, Inc., 996 P.2d 1103, 1109 (Wash. Ct. App. 2000) (referring to a court rule prohibiting ex parte contact with opposing medical experts).

184. Model Rules of Prof'l Conduct R. 3.4(c) (2020) ("A lawyer shall not . . . knowingly disobey an obligation under the rules of a tribunal, except for an open refusal based on an assertion that no valid obligation exists[.]"); *id.* R. 8.4(d) (stating that lawyers shall not "engage in conduct that is prejudicial to the administration of justice").

185. Fed. R. Civ. P. 23(c)(1)(A).

Although class certification is important for numerous reasons, it has special meaning in the professional responsibility context. This is because courts generally take the position that before certification there is no attorney-client relationship between an attorney and any putative class members other than the plaintiffs who are seeking to be named class representatives.[186] The court's certification of a class is generally deemed to create an attorney-client relationship between class counsel and all class members,[187] although some courts hold that an attorney-client relationship between class counsel and unnamed members of the class does not arise until the time to opt out of the class expires.[188] Regardless, any attorney-client relationship is confined to the class action; a lawyer who represents a class is not automatically imbued with authority to represent class members on separate matters, such as members' individual claims.[189]

Even if there is no formal attorney-client relationship between putative class counsel and putative class members prior to certification, however, they at least share an incipient fiduciary relationship.[190] The existence of this incipient fiduciary relationship gives the plaintiffs' counsel some communication rights with respect to potential class members. For example, they may provide information to putative class members beyond that in notices supervised by the court, respond to inquiries, and seek information necessary to their representation of the class.

186. *See, e.g.*, Jackson v. Bloomberg L.P., No. 13-CV-2001 (JPO), 2015 WL 1822695, at *2 & n.2 (S.D.N.Y. Apr. 22, 2015); EEOC v. Dana Corp., 202 F. Supp. 2d 827, 830 (N.D. Ind. 2002); Parks v. Eastwood Ins. Servs., Inc., 235 F. Supp. 2d 1082, 1083–84 (C.D. Cal. 2002); Hammond v. City of Junction City, Kan., 167 F. Supp. 2d 1271, 1286 (D. Kan. 2001); *In re* McKesson HBOC, Inc. Sec. Litig., 126 F. Supp. 2d 1239, 1245 (N.D. Cal. 2000); Garrett v. Metro. Life Ins. Co., No. 95 CIV. 2406 (PKL), 1996 WL 325725, at *6 (S.D.N.Y. June 12, 1996); Palumbo v. Tele-Commc'ns, Inc., 157 F.R.D. 129, 133 (D.D.C. 1994); Fulco v. Cont'l Cablevision, Inc., 789 F. Supp. 45, 47 (D. Mass. 1992); Tedesco v. Mishkin, 629 F. Supp. 1474, 1483 (S.D.N.Y. 1986); Bower v. Bunker Hill Co., 689 F. Supp. 1032, 1033 (E.D. Wash. 1985); Walker v. Apple, Inc., 209 Cal. Rptr. 3d 319, 325 (Ct. App. 2016); *In re* Chi. Flood Litig., 682 N.E.2d 421, 425–26 (Ill. App. Ct. 1997); Gillespie v. Scherr, 987 S.W.2d 129, 131–32 (Tex. App. 1999). *But see* Dondore v. NGK Metals Corp., 152 F. Supp. 2d 662, 664–66 (E.D. Pa. 2001) (banning ex parte communications between defense counsel and putative class members pre-certification because putative class members are represented by plaintiffs' counsel).

187. *See* Dodona I, LLC v. Goldman, Sachs & Co., 300 F.R.D. 182, 187 (S.D.N.Y. 2014) (describing this position as the majority rule); *see, e.g.*, McKenzie Law Firm, P.A. v. Ruby Receptionists, Inc., No. 3:18-cv-1921-SI, 2020 WL 2789873, at *2 (D. Or. May 29, 2020); Mullen v. GLV, Inc., 334 F.R.D. 656, 664 (N.D. Ill. 2020); Good v. W. Va.-Am. Water Co., No.: 2:14-01374, 2016 WL 6404006, at *2 (S.D. W. Va. Oct. 26, 2016) (quoting Fulco v. Cont'l Cablevision, Inc., 789 F. Supp. 45, 47 (D. Mass. 1992)); McWilliams v. Advanced Recovery Sys., Inc., 176 F. Supp. 3d 635, 642 (S.D. Miss. 2016); *In re Chi. Flood Litig.*, 682 N.E.2d at 425.

188. *See, e.g.*, *In re* Wells Fargo Wage & Hour Emp't Prac. Litig., 18 F. Supp. 3d 844, 851 (S.D. Tex. 2014) (quoting *In re* Katrina Canal Breaches Consol. Litig., No. 05-4182, 2008 WL 4401970, at *3 (E.D. La. Sept. 22, 2008)).

189. Evans v. Prof'l Transp., Inc., No. 1:12-cv-202, 2014 WL 1908808, at *7 (E.D. Tenn. May 13, 2014).

190. *Dondore*, 152 F. Supp. 2d at 665.

Lawyers for a putative class do not have unlimited communication rights regardless of whether their relationship with putative class members is characterized as an attorney-client relationship or something else. If there is no attorney-client relationship, for example, any communication between counsel and putative class members is governed by Model Rule 4.3, which regulates lawyers' communications with unrepresented persons.[191]

It is sometimes necessary for a court to reconsider its decision certifying a class. The discovery of new facts, changes in the parties, or substantive legal developments may compel a court to de-certify a class. Decertification terminates the attorney-client relationship between class counsel and unnamed class members, who revert to being non-party witnesses.[192] Counsel for any party who wishes to communicate with them may then do so, subject to ethics rules governing communications with unrepresented persons and mandating honesty.

B. Restrictions on Plaintiffs' Counsel and the Issue of Prior Restraint

Courts clearly have the authority under Rule 23(d) to enjoin communications between counsel and putative class members, although that authority has limits.[193] *Gulf Oil Co. v. Bernard*[194] is the seminal case on class communications. In *Gulf*, the Equal Employment Opportunity Commission (EEOC) and Gulf Oil Company entered into a conciliation agreement involving Gulf's alleged discrimination against African-American and female employees at one of its Texas refineries. Several plaintiffs soon sued Gulf on behalf of all present and former African-American employees and applicants who were rejected for employment at the refinery. The plaintiffs sought to enforce the alleged rights of many employees and applicants who were receiving settlement offers from Gulf under its conciliation agreement with the EEOC.

Gulf filed a motion in the district court seeking to limit communications by the parties and plaintiffs' counsel with putative class members.[195] Many of the employees who were entitled to back pay under the conciliation agreement had been paid and had signed releases by the time the class action was filed. After being served with the class action, Gulf stopped sending back pay offers and releases to putative class members. Gulf then alleged that one of the plaintiffs' lawyers had attended a meeting of putative class members at which he discussed the case and recommended that the employees return any back pay checks they had received and not sign releases sent under

191. ABA Comm. on Ethics & Prof'l Responsibility, Formal Op. 07-445, at 2 (2007).
192. Daniels v. City of N.Y., 138 F. Supp. 2d 562, 564–65 (S.D.N.Y. 2001).
193. *In re* McKesson HBOC, Inc. Sec. Litig., 126 F. Supp. 2d 1239, 1242 (N.D. Cal. 2000).
194. 452 U.S. 89 (1981).
195. *Id.* at 92.

the conciliation agreement because they would "receive at least double the amounts involved through the class action."[196] The district court entered a temporary order prohibiting all counsel for all parties from having any communications concerning the case with actual or potential class members. The court did not, however, make related findings of fact. Gulf later moved to modify the order to allow it to continue sending mailings to putative class members soliciting releases in exchange for back pay awards fixed under the conciliation agreement. The plaintiffs resisted, arguing that the court's ban on their communications with putative class members violated the First Amendment.[197] The district court heard argument on the motion but took no evidence. Additional briefing, including the submission of affidavits by plaintiffs' counsel, followed.[198]

The district court ultimately issued an order along the lines requested by Gulf with some modifications. More particularly:

> This order imposed a complete ban on all communications concerning the class action between parties or their counsel and any actual or potential class member who was not a formal party, without the prior approval of the court. It gave examples of forbidden communications, including any solicitation of legal representation of potential or actual class members, and any statements "which may tend to misrepresent the status, purposes and effects of the class action" or "create impressions tending without cause, to reflect adversely on any party, any counsel, this Court, or the administration of justice." The order exempted attorney-client communications initiated by the client, and communications in the regular course of business. It further stated that if any party or counsel "assert[ed] a constitutional right to communicate . . . without prior restraint," and did so communicate, he should file with the court a copy or summary of the communication within five days. The order, finally, exempted communications from Gulf involving the conciliation agreement and its settlement process.[199]

In issuing this order, the district court made no findings of fact, nor did it explain its decision.[200]

Plaintiffs' counsel prepared a leaflet to send to putative class members subject to court approval. The leaflet urged them to consult with a lawyer before signing the releases offered by Gulf. The leaflet referred to the class action and identified plaintiffs' counsel.[201] The plaintiffs argued that the notice provided in the leaflet enjoyed constitutional protection and was necessary for continued prosecution of the class action. Gulf opposed the

196. *Id.* at 93.
197. *Id.*
198. *Id.* at 93–94.
199. *Id.* at 94–95.
200. *Id.* at 96.
201. *Id.* at 97.

motion. The district court did not rule on the motion until after a deadline for acceptance of Gulf's offer expired. The court then denied the motion without explanation. As a result, the named plaintiffs and their counsel were prevented from communicating with the putative class before the deadline expired.[202]

Following summary judgment, the plaintiffs appealed to the Fifth Circuit, arguing that the limitations on their communications imposed by the district court exceeded the authority granted to it by Federal Rule of Civil Procedure 23(d) and violated the First Amendment. A divided Fifth Circuit panel affirmed the district court.[203] The Fifth Circuit then granted a rehearing en banc, reversed the panel decision, and held that the district court order was an unconstitutional prior restraint on speech protected by the First Amendment.[204] The full court held that there was "no sufficient particularized showing of need to justify such a restraint, that the restraint was overbroad, and that it was not accompanied by the requisite procedural safeguards."[205] Gulf then successfully petitioned for a writ of certiorari.

The Supreme Court framed the issue as whether the limiting order entered in the district court was "consistent with the general policies embodied in Rule 23."[206] In addressing this issue the *Gulf Oil* Court noted at the outset that because class actions present "opportunities for abuse," district courts have and need broad authority to control them and to enter "appropriate orders governing the conduct of counsel and parties."[207] The Court further observed, however, that district courts do not enjoy unlimited discretion in shepherding class actions and that their exercise of discretion is subject to appellate review.[208]

The Court had no doubt that the district court order created at least potential difficulties for the plaintiffs in their efforts to vindicate the legal rights of the class. As the Court explained:

> The order interfered with their efforts to inform potential class members of the existence of this lawsuit, and may have been particularly injurious—not only to respondents but to the class as a whole—because the employees at that time were being pressed to decide whether to accept a backpay offer from Gulf that required them to sign a full release of all liability for discriminatory acts . . . . In addition, the order made it more difficult for

202. *Id.*
203. *Id.* at 98.
204. *Id.*
205. *Id.*
206. *Id.* at 99.
207. *Id.* at 99–100.
208. *Id.* at 100.

respondents, as the class representatives, to obtain information about the merits of the case from the persons they sought to represent.[209]

Because of these problems, an order limiting communications between parties and potential class members "should be based on a clear record and specific findings that reflect a weighing of the need for a limitation and the potential interference with the rights of the parties."[210] Such a determination is required to ensure that the court is furthering rather than hindering the policies embodied in Rule 23.[211] Any order that results from this weighing should limit speech as little as possible, consistent with the parties' rights under the circumstances.[212]

The Court could find no indication that the district court ever weighed any competing factors.[213] The Court recognized that class action litigation carries with it the possibility for abuse and that such abuses may involve communications with putative class members, but "the mere possibility of abuses does not justify routine adoption of a communications ban that interferes with the formation of a class or the prosecution of a class action" in accordance with Rule 23.[214] The Court thus concluded that the district court abused its discretion and affirmed the Fifth Circuit's en banc judgment.

Courts have scrupulously followed *Gulf Oil*.[215] Courts do, however, limit plaintiffs' communications with putative class members in appropriate circumstances. In *Jackson v. Motel 6 Multipurpose, Inc.*,[216] for example, two race discrimination cases pleaded as class actions were filed against Motel 6 in a Florida federal court. In the first case, known as *Jackson*, five Motel 6 patrons alleged that Motel 6 had a nationwide practice of discriminating against customers based on their race. In the second, known as *Petaccia*, five former Motel 6 employees alleged that Motel 6's racially discriminatory practices created a hostile work environment. The two cases were consolidated. The plaintiffs then sought relief from a local court rule, which provided:

209. *Id.* at 101 (footnote omitted).
210. *Id.*
211. *Id.* at 101–02.
212. *Id.* at 102.
213. *Id.*
214. *Id.* at 104.
215. *See, e.g.*, Williams v. Chartwell Fin. Servs., Inc., 204 F.3d 748, 759 (7th Cir. 2000) (reversing the district court's protective order prohibiting the plaintiffs from communicating with members of the putative class, all of whom were Chartwell customers, because it was not clear what factors the district court considered in holding as it did); Walni v. Swepi LP, No. 13-102 Erie, 2017 WL 319801, at *10–14 (W.D. Pa. Jan. 23, 2017) (noting the continuing control of *Gulf Oil*, rejecting the prior restraint that defense counsel were seeking to impose, and imposing modest limits on class counsel's planned communication with class members).
216. 130 F.3d 999 (11th Cir. 1997).

> In every case sought to be maintained by any party as a class action, all parties thereto and their counsel are hereby forbidden, directly or indirectly, orally or in writing, to communicate concerning such actions with any potential or actual class member, not a formal party to the case, without approval by the Court.[217]

The district court exempted the plaintiffs from the local rule and authorized them to establish an 800 number for potential plaintiffs to call; publish notices about the litigation nationwide and solicit information about putative class members and their experiences with alleged discrimination at Motel 6 properties; respond to requests for information from those who responded to the notices or who called the toll-free number; send mass mailings to Motel 6 employees soliciting information about the plaintiffs' allegations; and communicate with anyone who might know of the alleged discrimination except current Motel 6 managers and supervisors. The district court entered this order even though it had not certified a class in either case.[218]

Motel 6 successfully petitioned the Eleventh Circuit for a writ of mandamus. The *Jackson* court held that the district court's order allowing the plaintiffs to communicate with potential class members was an abuse of discretion.[219] The order was entered months before a class was certified in either case. While the *Jackson* court was unwilling to go so far as to state that plaintiffs should never be allowed to communicate with putative class members prior to certification, it was clear to it that district courts should "strive to avoid authorizing injurious class communications that might later prove unnecessary."[220] As the court further observed:

> An order authorizing class communications prior to class certification is likely to be an abuse of discretion when (1) the communication authorized by the order is widespread and clearly injurious and (2) a certification decision is not imminent or it is unlikely that a class will in fact be certified. In such circumstances, the danger of abuse that always attends class communications—the possibility that plaintiffs might use widespread publication of their claims, disguised as class communications, to coerce defendants into settlement—is not outweighed by any need for immediate communications.[221]

The communications authorized by the district court's order clearly were widespread because they were nationwide in scope. There was also no doubt that they were clearly injurious to Motel 6. The *Petaccia* case was

217. *Id.* at 1002 (quoting M.D. Fla. Local Rule 4.04(e)).
218. *Id.*
219. *Id.* at 1004.
220. *Id.*
221. *Id.*

nowhere near certification at the time the order was issued. The plaintiffs in the *Jackson* case were not suitable class representatives, and that case could not be certified as a class action for other reasons. The two factors suggesting that the district court's order was an abuse of discretion were satisfied. The *Jackson* court thus vacated the district court's order and granted Motel 6 other relief.[222]

In short, pre-certification communications with potential class members by plaintiffs and their counsel present opportunities for abuse.[223] Courts may limit plaintiffs' communications with putative class members even if a communication is not false, misleading, or deceptive.[224] Courts have the "authority and duty" to control class actions to protect all parties' rights and "to prevent abuses which might undermine the proper administration of justice."[225]

Courts should be cautious, however, when placing prior restraints on communications with potential class members.[226] Trial courts should carefully detail the reasons for any restraints they impose so that appellate courts may appropriately study their exercise of discretion.[227] In determining whether to limit class communications prospectively, courts may wish to consider the severity and likelihood of the perceived harm if communications are not limited, the availability of less restrictive alternatives, and the duration of the proposed limitation.[228] Plaintiffs and their counsel should not be allowed to communicate with potential class members before certification when (1) the intended communication is or will be widespread and clearly injurious, and (2) a decision on certification is not imminent, or it is unlikely that a class will be certified.[229]

C. Places the First Amendment Does Not Always Reach

The decision in *Gulf Oil Co. v. Bernard*[230] does not turn the First Amendment into a silver bullet for counsel to communicate with class action plaintiffs. The First Amendment only prohibits certain prior restraints on class

222. *Id.* at 1008–09.

223. Howard Guntz Profit Sharing Plan v. Super. Ct., 105 Cal. Rptr. 2d 896, 902 (Ct. App. 2001).

224. *Id.* at 903.

225. *Id.*

226. *See, e.g.*, Gates v. Cook, 234 F.3d 221, 227 (5th Cir. 2000) (overturning district court's "no contact order" that barred all communications between inmate class members and class counsel without sufficient factual finding justifying the order or its breadth).

227. Williams v. Chartwell Fin. Servs., Ltd., 204 F.3d 748, 759 (7th Cir. 2000).

228. *See* Rankin v. Bd. of Educ. of the Wichita Pub. Schs., U.S.D. 259, 174 F.R.D. 695, 697 (D. Kan. 1997).

229. Jackson v. Motel 6 Multipurpose, Inc., 130 F.3d 999, 1004 (11th Cir. 1997).

230. 452 U.S. 89 (1981).

communications; it does not immunize plaintiffs or their lawyers against sanctions or other corrective measures if they improperly communicate with potential class members.[231] Courts often sanction class action lawyers for misleading class communications.[232]

Plaintiffs' attorneys in class action litigation or wage-and-hour collective actions under the Fair Labor Standards Act (FLSA) sometimes host websites concerning the litigation. FLSA collective actions are different from class actions under Rule 23 in that in collective actions,[233] plaintiffs must affirmatively opt in to the case to be awarded relief,[234] whereas in class actions members will most often be bound by the result of the litigation unless they opt out to pursue their claims individually. Thus, plaintiffs' lawyers in FLSA cases often seek to provide pre-certification notice to potential class members. Courts in FLSA cases generally cannot prohibit all pre-certification contacts by plaintiffs' counsel; any restrictions on pre-certification communications by plaintiffs' counsel should be based on specific evidentiary showings, and, as with any communications with non-clients, plaintiffs' lawyers must adhere to the applicable limits on client solicitation and should never offer inaccurate or misleading information.[235]

In *Jones v. Casey's General Stores*,[236] the court found that the plaintiffs exceeded these limitations. *Jones* was a collective action brought by assistant

231. For example, if parties or their counsel convey misinformation or misrepresent matters to class members, a court may require them to send curative notices at their expense. *See, e.g.*, EEOC v. Mitsubishi Motor Mfg. of Am., Inc., 102 F.3d 869, 871–72 (7th Cir. 1996) (declining to review district court order requiring EEOC to send curative letter to class members because it was not a final order for purposes of appeal).

232. *See, e.g.*, *In re* McKesson HBOC, Inc. Sec. Litig., 126 F. Supp. 2d 1239, 1243–45 (N.D. Cal. 2000) (involving misleading communications by two law firms whose bids to serve as lead class counsel had been rejected); Hernandez v. Vitamin Shoppe Indus. Inc., 95 Cal. Rptr. 3d 737, 750–51 (Ct. App. 2009) (affirming sanctions against attorney who had unilaterally sent letter to class members suggesting they should opt-out of settlement after court-approved settlement notice had been issued); Meeks v. Gem Boat Servs., Inc., 620 N.E.2d 983, 985–87 (Ohio Ct. App. 1993) (sanctioning the lawyer for sending improper notices that also included misleading statements to putative class members).

233. A district court's "certification" of a collective action is a device to facilitate notice to potential class members and does not actually create a class of plaintiffs for an FLSA collective action. Morgan v. Family Dollar Stores, Inc., 551 F.3d 1233, 1259 (11th Cir. 2008). "Thus, 'certification' is neither necessary nor sufficient for the existence of a representative action under FLSA, but may be a useful 'case management' tool for district courts to employ in 'appropriate cases.'" Myers v. Hertz Corp., 624 F.3d 547, 555 n.10 (10th Cir. 2010) (quoting Hoffmann-La Roche Inc. v. Sperling, 493 U.S. 165, 174 (1989)).

234. By opting in, a person creates an attorney-client relationship with class counsel. Scott v. Chipotle Mexican Grill, Inc., No. 12-CV-08333 (ALC) (SN), 2014 WL 4852063, at *3 (S.D.N.Y. Sept. 29, 2014).

235. *See* Maddox v. Knowledge Learning Corp., 499 F. Supp. 2d 1338, 1334–35 (N.D. Ga. 2007) (reviewing these principles).

236. 517 F. Supp. 2d 1080 (S.D. Iowa 2007).

store managers of Casey's, a convenience store chain, claiming that they had not been paid all wages they were due. Before the court had ruled on whether class certification was appropriate, the plaintiffs began calling putative class members and referring them to a website that had been established to provide information about the litigation.[237] Upon learning of the website, the defendant requested that the court order the plaintiffs to remove any information related to the lawsuit from the website and from any other websites that might contain such information.[238]

The court was "dismayed" at the website's content, which contained misleading and inaccurate information.[239] Among other things, the website suggested that Casey's liability had been proven and that the litigation had been established as a "class action" despite there being no ruling yet on whether to conditionally certify the case as a collective action.[240] Noting that the website provided downloadable consent forms that visitors could use to opt in as plaintiffs, the court found the site "to be nothing more than a blatant attempt at solicitation."[241]

The court ordered the plaintiffs' lawyers to immediately strip the website of inappropriate information.[242] The court also suggested that it might invalidate consent/opt-in notices that the site generated and warned that the conduct, if it continued, "could easily have the effect of tainting the entire putative class and jeopardizing this entire litigation."[243]

Jones shows the dangers (and temptations) of over-aggressive pre-certification contacts with putative members of class or collection actions, and it emphasizes the need to show restraint and objectivity when creating and disseminating information about pending litigation through websites or otherwise. If nothing else, *Jones* demonstrates why pre-certification restrictions on plaintiffs' lawyers' communications with putative class members are sometimes justified.[244]

---

237. *Id.* at 1087.

238. *Id.*

239. *Id.*

240. *Id.*

241. *Id.* at 1088.

242. *Id.* at 1089.

243. *Id.*

244. *See also, e.g.*, West v. Mando Am. Corp., No. 3:08-CV-570-WKW [WO], 2008 WL 4493422, at *2–3 (M.D. Ala. Oct. 2, 2008) (denying the employer's motions to stop the plaintiff's counsel from running newspaper ads because the ads were neither misleading nor violated anti-solicitation rules); Maddox v. Knowledge Learning Corp., 499 F. Supp. 2d 1338, 1324–45 (N.D. Ga. 2007) (ordering the plaintiffs to modify a website that was posted prior to conditional certification because it contained unbalanced, misleading, and inaccurate information).

D. Class Communications by Defendants and Their Counsel

Defendants can sometimes anticipate that they will be the target of a class action. Before suit is filed, a prospective defendant is generally free to fairly and honestly communicate with potential class members to try to head off litigation. Even after a suit is filed, if it is not pleaded as a class action, defense counsel may similarly communicate with potential claimants to try to prevent a class action from developing.[245] Once a class action is filed or a lawsuit on file is amended to become a class action, however, the rules change.

1. *Class Communications by Defendants and Their Counsel: An Introduction and Some Fundamentals*

The communication protections afforded by *Gulf Oil* apply equally to plaintiffs and defendants.[246] Before restricting a defendant's communications with prospective class members, a court must make specific findings on the record that reflect an evaluation of the need for limitation and the potential interference with the parties' rights.[247] Just as when plaintiffs or their counsel are sought to be restrained or enjoined, any order restraining defendants' speech must be narrowly drawn, consistent with the parties' rights. Indeed, courts presented with motions to limit defendants' communications with putative class members routinely analyze the issues under the rules established in *Gulf Oil*.[248]

Defendants typically want to communicate with putative class members about settlement. A defendant generally has the right to convey settlement

245. *See* EEOC v. SVT, LLC, 297 F.R.D. 336, 344 (N.D. Ind. 2014) ("Generally, in a class action, either side has the right to communicate with members of the putative class."); Gillespie v. Scherr, 987 S.W.2d 129, 132 & n.6 (Tex. App. 1999) (explaining that until a court certifies a case as a class action, the case proceeds as an ordinary lawsuit brought by the named plaintiffs on their own behalf).

246. Abdallah v. Coca-Cola Co., 186 F.R.D. 672, 675 n.1 (N.D. Ga. 1999).

247. Great Rivers Coop. of Se. Iowa v. Farmland Indus., Inc., 59 F.3d 764, 766 (8th Cir. 1995).

248. *See, e.g.*, EEOC v. Day & Zimmerman NPS, Inc., 265 F. Supp. 3d 179, 196 (D. Conn. 2017) (finding that the defendant's letter was improper); Bobryk v. Durand Glass Mfg. Co., No. 12-cv-5360 (NLH/JS), 2013 WL 5574504, at *4–9 (D.N.J. Oct. 9, 2013) (denying requested restrictions on the defendant's communications with putative class members); Payne v. Goodyear Tire & Rubber Co., 207 F.R.D. 16, 20–22 (D. Mass. 2002) (declining to limit communications); Bublitz v. E.I. du Pont de Nemours & Co., 196 F.R.D. 545, 547–50 (S.D. Iowa 2000) (conditioning the defendant's communications with putative class members); Rankin v. Bd. of Educ. of the Wichita Pub. Schs., U.S.D. 259, 174 F.R.D. 695, 697–98 (D. Kan. 1997) (limiting the defendant's communications); H & R Block, Inc. v. Haese, 82 S.W.3d 331, 336–37 (Tex. App. 2000) (rejecting some limitations imposed by the trial court).

offers to putative class members before a class is certified.[249] Once a class is certified, however, a defendant must negotiate through class counsel.[250]

Defendants also may want to communicate ex parte with potential class members to gain a litigation advantage. For example, a court must give class members the option to withdraw from the litigation. A class member's withdrawal is known as "opting out," and the time that a court gives class members to do that is known as the "opt-out" period. Defendants may want to encourage class members to opt out to defeat class certification by destroying numerosity or to minimize their potential damage exposure. Courts disfavor defendants' attempts to persuade class members to opt out of class litigation.[251] Such communications are believed to reduce the effectiveness of class actions as an economic means of litigation and to otherwise undermine the purposes of Rule 23.[252]

Another pre-certification interest that a defendant in an FLSA case may have in ex parte contacts with its employees is to gather information helpful to its defense, as by trying to secure statements or other evidence from employees who are potential class members. An employer may legitimately speak with, and obtain written statements from, employees and other potential plaintiffs about pending litigation prior to conditional certification as long as it does not coerce or mislead the employees.[253]

249. Christensen v. Kiewit-Murdock Inv. Corp., 815 F.2d 206, 213 (2d Cir. 1987); Kutzman v. Derrel's Mini Storage, Inc., 354 F. Supp. 3d 1149, 1153 (E.D. Cal. 2018); Kay Co., LLC v. Equitable Prod. Co., 246 F.R.D. 260, 263 (S.D. W. Va. 2007); Jenifer v. Del. Solid Waste Auth., No. CIV.A. 98-270 MMS, No. 98-565 MMS, 1999 WL 117762, at *3 (D. Del. Feb. 25, 1999); Cada v. Costa Line, Inc., 93 F.R.D. 95, 98 (N.D. Ill. 1981); *In re* Winchell's Donut Houses, L.P. Sec. Litig., 1988 WL 135503, at *1 (Del. Ch. Dec. 12, 1988); Arriola v. Time Ins. Co., 751 N.E.2d 221, 226 (Ill. App. Ct. 2001); Jankousky v. Jewel Cos., 538 N.E.2d 689, 691 (Ill. App. Ct. 1989); *see also* Parks v. Eastwood Ins. Servs., Inc., 235 F. Supp. 2d 1082, 1084 (C.D. Cal. 2002) ("In a Rule 23 class action, pre-certification communication from the defense to prospective plaintiffs is generally permitted.").

250. *See, e.g.*, Blanchard v. EdgeMark Fin. Corp., 175 F.R.D. 293, 300–05 (N.D. Ill. 1997) (holding that a defense lawyer who negotiated a settlement with the class representative's personal attorney instead of class counsel violated Rule 4.2, disqualifying the defense lawyer, and imposing other sanctions); Larry James Oldsmobile-Pontiac-GMC Truck Co. v. Gen. Motors Corp., 175 F.R.D. 234, 240–46 (N.D. Miss. 1997) (sanctioning a defense lawyer who negotiated a settlement through the class representative's corporate counsel rather than negotiating through class counsel; the court held that lawyer violated Rule 4.2).

251. *See, e.g.*, Kleiner v. First Nat'l Bank of Atlanta, 751 F.2d 1193, 1202–11 (11th Cir. 1985) (affirming district court decision disqualifying and fining defense lawyer who helped formulate scheme to persuade class members to opt out).

252. *Id.* at 1202 & n.19 (discussing Rule 23(b)(3) actions).

253. *See* Longcrier v. HL-A Co., 595 F. Supp. 2d 1218,1226 (S.D. Ala. 2008) ("As a general matter, employers are free to communicate with unrepresented prospective class members about the lawsuit and even to solicit affidavits from them concerning the subject matter of the suit."); Kerce v. W. Telemarketing Corp., 575 F. Supp. 2d 1354, 1366–67 (S.D. Ga. 2008) (declining to

A good example of what an employer cannot do appears in *Longcrier v. HL-A Co.*[254] There, prior to class certification, the employer obtained 245 declarations from employees under the guise of a pay practices survey.[255] The court found that the true purpose of the survey was to secure favorable affidavits for use in the litigation. The employees were not told about the lawsuit, much less that the matters they were being asked to discuss could directly affect their rights. Finding that the declarations were obtained through deception, the court struck them.[256] The court did not bar the employer from thereafter speaking with employees to investigate the case but—based on the improper conduct that had already occurred—ordered that any witness interviews could be conducted only if the witness was given a pre-interview disclosure about the nature of the interview in a form to be agreed upon by both parties.[257]

2. *Pre-certification Settlements and Efforts to Discourage Participation in Litigation*

Although courts routinely hold that defendants may communicate with putative class members about the resolution of their individual claims before a class is certified, they often appear to do so grudgingly. This is because improper communications threaten fair resolution of the litigation.[258] Even so, courts must avoid excessive caution when supervising defendants' conduct. This is especially true where a defendant has an ongoing business relationship with potential class members.[259] Defendants may need to com-

strike employee declarations collected by the defendants at the pre-certification phase of a § 216(b) action because "prior to a decision on the conditional certification question, each side has the right to communicate with potential class members" and "there is nothing improper about [an employer] gathering facts to support its defense"). *But see* Weller v. Dollar Gen. Corp., No. 17-2292, 2019 WL 1045960, at *2–4 (E.D. Pa. Mar. 4, 2019) (sanctioning a lawyer for violating Rule 4.2 through pre-certification communications in a case that was both an FLSA collective action and a Rule 23 class action; the court applied Pennsylvania law, which holds that a plaintiff's lawyer has an attorney-client relationship with putative class members pre-certification).

254. 595 F. Supp. 2d 1218, 1226 (S.D. Ala. 2008).

255. *Id.* at 1228.

256. *Id.* at 1230.

257. *Id.* at 1231.

258. Jennifer v. Del. Solid Waste Auth., No. Civ. A 98-270 MMS, 1999 WL 117762, at *2 (D. Del. Feb. 25, 1999).

259. *See, e.g.*, *In re* Winchell's Donut Houses, L.P. Sec. Litig., 1988 WL 135503, at *1 (Del. Ch. Dec. 12, 1988) ("Particularly where the class is comprised of persons with whom the defendant has an ongoing commercial relationship, it would seem distinctly ill-advised to . . . require the defendant to deal with what may be an important aspect of a commercial relationship only through . . . a self-appointed class action plaintiff. Surely, a defendant may not, in its communications with class members prior to certification, deceive or mislead [them]. But the always present possibility of deception does not itself warrant court supervision of such communication, absent special circumstances; class members do not become wards . . . by reason of the unilateral filing of class action complaints by one of their number.").

municate with class members as part of their regular business activities. Beyond that, putative class members may be interested in receiving settlement offers or in hearing a defendant's perspective on the litigation. Putative class members may have interests or needs that are different from those of the class representatives, and courts are wrong to discount or disregard that possibility, or to assume that putative class members always need protection from defendants.

Courts should, however, limit defendants' pre-certification class communications where they pose a serious potential for harm to class members' interests.[260] A defendant should not be allowed to deceive or mislead class members through otherwise permissible communications. *Weckesser v. Knight Enterprises S.E., LLC*,[261] which was an FLSA class and collective action, illustrates the sort of communications by a defendant that courts will not tolerate.

Patrick Weckesser, a cable installation technician, sued Knight Enterprises on behalf of himself and all others similarly situated. After the court granted conditional class certification, Knight decided to try to settle with the 34 plaintiffs individually. Knight's lawyer sent the plaintiffs' lawyer 34 letters that included a settlement offer specific to each plaintiff. The offer letters asserted that Knight was confident that the court would conclude that the plaintiffs had been correctly classified as independent contractors, and when that happened, Knight would "seek recompense from each contractor who violated their express written agreement with Knight S.E. not to claim employee status."[262] The offer letters further stated that Knight had assessed the plaintiffs' possible recovery if they were successful, represented that the plaintiffs' overtime could not have exceeded a certain number of hours, and opined on the maximum value of each plaintiff's claim.[263] The letters then offered each plaintiff that purported "top dollar" amount, plus 40 percent for attorneys' fees, coupled with a broad release of all claims the parties might have against each other—including potential claims beyond those encompassed by the litigation.[264]

After the plaintiffs' lawyers responded negatively to the offer letters, Knight became concerned that they never delivered the letters to the

260. *See, e.g.*, Hampton Hardware, Inc. v. Cotter & Co., 156 F.R.D. 630, 632–35 (N.D. Tex. 1999); Fraley v. Williams Ford Tractor & Equip. Co., 5 S.W.3d 423, 434–35 (Ark. 1999); H & R Block, Inc. v. Haese, 82 S.W.3d 331, 335–36 (Tex. App. 2000). *But see* Arriola v. Time Ins. Co., 751 N.E.2d 221, 230–31 (Ill. App. Ct. 2001) (finding nothing improper where Time obtained releases from 44 of the 46 Illinois policyholders in an effort to defeat the numerosity required for class certification and thus avoid liability to a larger group of policyholders in other states; there was no evidence of coercion or misrepresentation, and the plaintiffs had not yet moved to certify the class).

261. 392 F. Supp. 3d 631 (D.S.C. 2019).

262. *Id.* at 633.

263. *Id.*

264. *Id.*

plaintiffs. As a result, a Knight executive called multiple plaintiffs, asked whether they had received the letters, told them that Knight had hired an expert to calculate their allegedly unpaid wages, and then e-mailed them a copy of the offer letter to be signed and returned.[265] Three plaintiffs signed the offer letters.

The plaintiffs moved to strike all the settlement offers and sought a protective order limiting future communications with them on the basis that Knight's communications were coercive and misleading.[266] The *Weckesser* court found that Knight's communications were abusive and threatened the proper functioning of the litigation.[267] The FLSA was created in recognition of the unequal bargaining power between employers and employees, and the challenged communications amply illuminated that inequality. The plaintiffs were current or former Knight employees, Knight threatened to sue them if it prevailed in the litigation, Knight's assessment of their maximum potential recovery was possibly inaccurate (the calculation of the plaintiffs' work hours was hotly disputed), and Knight's proposed release language was misleading and unlawfully overbroad.[268] Knight's threat to sue the plaintiffs for indemnification if the plaintiffs did not sign the offer letter and Knight won at trial was particularly offensive.[269] For that matter, Knight's threat of retaliatory litigation if the plaintiffs did not settle their claims was "an independently sufficient ground to find that communication was impermissibly coercive."[270]

Furthermore, after the plaintiffs had moved to strike the settlement offers, Knight had continued to engage in disruptive communications.[271] Notably, Knight had mailed an additional offer letter to the plaintiffs and enclosed an opt-out form and settlement check.[272] This type of repeated communication, even after multiple plaintiffs had recently declined Knight's settlement offers, was an impermissible attempt to circumvent the plaintiffs' lawyers and independently compelled the conclusion that Knight's communications were abusive.[273]

The *Weckesser* court invalidated Knight's settlement offers and documents. The court further instructed the plaintiffs' lawyers to prepare a corrective notice to send to the plaintiffs at Knight's expense. Finally, the court

265. *Id.*
266. *Id.* at 634–35.
267. *Id.* at 635.
268. *Id.*
269. *See id.* at 636 (explaining that defendants' indemnification claims for bringing an FLSA action are impermissible, erode the FLSA's protective purpose, deter plaintiffs from vindicating their rights, and could constitute unlawful retaliation under the FLSA).
270. *Id.*
271. *Id.* at 636–37.
272. *Id.* at 637.
273. *Id.*

entered a protective order that prohibited Knight from communicating with the plaintiffs regarding the litigation, settlement, their decision to participate as plaintiffs, or their representation.[274]

As *Weckesser* illustrates, courts are especially concerned about potential coercion where the defendant has an ongoing business relationship with potential class members[275] or employs the potential class members.[276] At the same time, the mere risk of coercion or speculation that it may occur does not justify courts' prior restraint of defendants' ex parte communications with putative class members.[277] Rather, to justify prior restraint there must be "actual or threatened misconduct of a serious nature."[278] Where actual harm cannot be shown, plaintiffs still must offer evidence that a potential for serious abuse exists.[279] Absent such evidence, a court cannot intervene.[280] This is true even in employment litigation, where the potential for coercion is substantial.[281]

A defendant is free to tell potential class members that it has been sued and even to express its views on the litigation, so long as it does not make explicit or implicit threats, or attempt to mislead potential class members.[282] The mere fact that a defendant chooses to keep its customers or employees informed about litigation affecting the company does not evidence an improper motive.[283] Nor should a defendant's attempts to settle with individual potential class members be considered improper, as long as the

274. *Id.* at 638–39.

275. *See, e.g.*, McKenzie Law Firm, P.A. v. Ruby Receptionists, Inc., No. 3:18-cv-1921-SI, 2020 WL 2789873, at *5–6 (D. Or. May 29, 2020) (noting that the risk of abuse is heightened when the class and the defendant have an ongoing business relationship and concluding that there was a realistic prospect of abuse in this case); Ralph Oldsmobile, Inc. v. Gen. Motors Corp., No. 99 Civ. 4567 (AGS), 2001 WL 1035132, at *4 (S.D.N.Y. Sept. 7, 2001) (finding potential for coercion because GM dealers making up the potential class depended on the defendant for credit, information, and supplies, and were solely dependent upon defendant to supply them with vehicles).

276. *See, e.g.*, Bublitz v. E.I. du Pont de Nemours & Co., 196 F.R.D. 545, 548 (S.D. Iowa 2000) ("Where the defendant is the current employer of putative class members who are at-will employees, the risk of coercion is particularly high; indeed, there may in fact be some inherent coercion in such a situation."); Abdallah v. Coca-Cola Co., 186 F.R.D. 672, 678 (N.D. Ga. 1999) (observing that "simple reality suggests that the danger of coercion is real" when potential class members are employed by the defendant).

277. Burrell v. Crown Cent. Petroleum, Inc., 176 F.R.D. 239, 244 (E.D. Tex. 1997).

278. Great Rivers Coop of Se. Iowa v. Farmland Indus., Inc., 59 F.3d 764, 766 (8th Cir. 1995).

279. Basco v. Wal-Mart Stores, Inc., No. Civ.A. 00-3184, 2002 WL 272384, at *3 (E.D. La. Feb. 25, 2002); *Burrell*, 176 F.R.D. at 244.

280. *Basco*, 2002 WL 272384, at *3; *Burrell*, 176 F.R.D. at 244.

281. *Basco*, 2002 WL 272384, at *3–4; *Burrell*, 176 F.R.D. at 244–45.

282. *Burrell*, 176 F.R.D. at 244–45; *see, e.g.*, Lee v. Am. Airlines, Inc., No. Civ.A. 3:01-CV-1179-P, 2002 WL 226347, at *2 (N.D. Tex. Feb. 12, 2002) (declining to limit defendant's communications with potential class members where plaintiff "failed to allege or prove any instances of targeted letters or announcements designed to threaten or intimidate potential class members if they were to join the litigation").

283. *Burrell*, 176 F.R.D. at 245.

defendant presents no deceptive or misleading information in the process.[284] Similarly, a defendant is free to communicate with putative class members about business transactions that may in some way be related to the subject of the class action as long as the transactions are fair.[285] A defendant's business cannot grind to a halt simply because it is the target of a class action lawsuit. And, of course, defendant is always free to communicate with potential class members about business or employment matters unrelated to the litigation.

VIII. Lawyers' Ex Parte Communications with Government Agencies

Finally, we come to the subject of lawyers' ex parte communications with government agencies.[286] Related controversies are relatively rare, but they raise a variety of issues that can make them challenging to analyze. Indeed, this is an ethical landscape that is in many respects incompletely mapped.

A. The Model Rule 4.2 "Authorized by Law" Exception

Model Rule 4.2 does not expressly permit ex parte communications with government officials; rather, it implies an exception to the general prohibition on ex parte communications with represented persons where a lawyer "is authorized to do so by law."[287] Comment 5 to Model Rule 4.2 offers as an example those communications "by a lawyer on behalf of a client who is exercising a constitutional or other legal right to communicate with the government."[288] Before the 2002 amendments to the Model Rules, comment 1 to Model Rule 4.2 explained that "[c]ommunications authorized by law include, for example, the right of a party to a controversy with a government agency to speak with government officials about the matter."[289] Most states have adopted one of these comments. Yet, the precise scope of the

284. *See* Kay Co., LLC v. Equitable Prod. Co., 246 F.R.D. 260, 263 (S.D. W. Va. 2007) ("Courts have recognized that, generally, a defendant may discuss settlement offers with putative class members prior to class certification." (citing Christensen v. Kiewit-Murdock Inv. Corp., 815 F.2d 206, 213 (2d Cir.1987)).

285. *See, e.g.*, Jenifer v. Del. Solid Waste Auth., No. CIV.A. 98-270 MMS, CIV.A. 98-565 MMS, 1999 WL 117762, at *5 (D. Del. Feb. 25, 1999) (approving communications that related "to a business proposition which potential class members [were] free to reject if they decide[d] the costs outweigh[ed] the benefits").

286. We are grateful to our friend and colleague Matt Corbin, whose thoughtful analysis of this issue and related writings we adapted for this part of the chapter. *See* Matthew K. Corbin, *Restraints on Lawyers' Ex Parte Communications with Government Agencies*, 30 No. 12 ABA/BNA Law. Man. on Prof'l Conduct 392 (June 4, 2014); Matthew K. Corbin, *Restraints on Ex Parte Communications with Government Agencies, Part II*, 30 No. 13 ABA/BNA Law. Man. on Prof'l Conduct 423 (June 18, 2014).

287. Model Rules of Prof'l Conduct R. 4.2 (2020).

288. *Id.* cmt. 5.

289. Model Rules of Prof'l Conduct R. 4.2 cmt. 1 (2001).

authorized by law exception, and, within it, the government contacts exemption, remains uncertain.

B. ABA Formal Opinions 95-396 and 97-408

To start, "a constitutional provision, statute or court rule, having the force and effect of law," that "expressly allows a particular communication to occur in the absence of counsel" will satisfy the Model Rule 4.2 "authorized by law" exception.[290] Government directives seemingly allowing ex parte communications with represented parties fall within the exception only when the directive is "embodied in formal regulations that have been properly promulgated" pursuant to applicable statutory authority.[291] In fact, this interpretation of the exception principally serves to prevent a governmental body from empowering its own lawyers to engage in otherwise unlawful ex parte communications simply by promulgating a regulation or policy.[292]

Open government laws and whistleblower statutes frequently implicate the "authorized by law" exception.[293] Administrative regulations, court rules, and statutes rooted in procedural due process are also a common source of authority for ex parte communications. For example, a lawyer may cause a person to serve a subpoena or other process directly on a represented party because the governing law or court rule requires such service.[294] Finally, but critically, most authorities point to the First Amendment's Petition Clause as the foundation for government contacts exceptions to Rule 4.2.[295] The Petition Clause protects people's rights to appeal to government-established

290. ABA Formal Op. 95-396, *supra* note 49, at 20.

291. *Id.* at 20–21.

292. *Id.* at 21.

293. ABA Comm. on Ethics & Prof'l Responsibility, Formal Op. 97-408, at 10 n.16 (1997) [hereinafter ABA Formal Op. 97-408]; *see, e.g.*, Service v. City of Meriden, No. CV94-0241732, 1995 WL 681537, at *3–5 (Conn. Super. Ct. Nov. 8, 1995) (rejecting the lawyer's argument that the FOIA authorized ex parte contact with a government official and enjoining the lawyer from any contact with the City's managerial employees and employees who were positioned to make admissions or to bind the City); 2011 N.C. Eth. Op. 15, 2011 WL 7574007, at *1–2 (N.C. State Bar 2011) (determining that the North Carolina Public Records Act authorized a lawyer to directly communicate with a government official for the purpose of identifying a custodian of public records and to make a request of the custodian to examine public records, even if the custodian is an adverse party and opposing counsel objects to the communication); Or. Eth. Op. 2005-144, 2007 WL 2324948, at *1–2 (Or. State Bar Ass'n, Bd. of Governors 2007) [hereinafter Or. Eth. Op. 2005-144] (permitting a lawyer to communicate directly with a county employee to obtain a public record).

294. Me. Bd. of Overseers of the Bar, Prof'l Ethics Comm., Op. 181 (2003); *see also* Fernandez v. Bridgeport Janitorial Servs., Inc., No. CV93 03006635, 1993 WL 382510, at *2–3 (Conn. Super. Ct. Sept. 17, 1993) (sending written notice of an action directly to the employer, as opposed to the employer's attorneys, did not violate Rule 4.2 because a state statute authorized the conduct).

295. U.S. Const. amend I ("Congress shall make no law respecting . . . the right of the people peaceably . . . to petition the Government for a redress of grievances.").

forums for the resolution of legal disputes.[296] This right extends to all government agencies and departments.[297]

In Formal Opinion 97-408, the ABA's Standing Committee on Ethics and Professional Responsibility acknowledged that the Petition Clause and the need to ensure people's right of access to government decision makers are important exceptions to the prohibition on ex parte communications.[298] According to ABA Formal Op. 97-408, an ex parte communication with a government official must satisfy three conditions to pass muster under Model Rule 4.2: first, the sole purpose of the communication must be to address a policy issue; second, the government official must have the authority to take or recommend action in the matter; and third, the lawyer representing the private party must give the government's lawyer reasonable advance notice of her intent to communicate with the official.[299] Other authorities have embraced and elaborated on these conditions.[300] ABA Formal Op. 97-408 is now considered the "seminal authority on a lawyer's right to communicate directly with government officials."[301]

1. *The Purpose of the Communication with the Government Official*

Courts and state ethics committees have routinely permitted lawyers to ask government officials about the rationales behind their policy positions, or to lobby government officials for passage of a law, statute, or regulation favorable to their clients.[302] The ability to communicate with government officials

296. Borough of Duryea v. Guarnieri, 131 S. Ct. 2488, 2494 (2011); Johnson v. Cnty. of Hennepin, 915 N.W.2d 889, 893 (Minn. 2018) (quoting *Guarnieri*).

297. City of N.Y. v. Beretta U.S.A. Corp., 524 F.3d 384, 397 (2d Cir. 2008).

298. ABA Formal Op. 97-408, *supra* note 293, at 1.

299. *Id.* at 10.

300. *See, e.g.*, Hammond v. City of Junction City, Kan., No. 00-2146-JWL, 2002 WL 169370, at *6 (D. Kan. Jan. 23, 2002) (relying on ABA Formal Op. 97-408 in rejecting the plaintiffs' "authorized by law" argument); Alaska Eth. Op. 2017-2, 2017 WL 4221171, at *4–5, *7 (Alaska Bar Ass'n, Ethics Comm. 2017) [hereinafter Alaska Eth. Op. 2017-2] (embracing the ABA Formal Ethics Op. 97-408 approach); Conn. Eth. Op. 01-17, 2001 WL 1819217, at *2 (Conn. Bar Ass'n, Comm. on Prof'l Ethics 2001) (adopting ABA Formal Op. 97-408's approach to ex parte communications with government officials).

301. Ill. Adv. Op. 13-09, 2013 WL 5967125, at *3 (Ill. State Bar Ass'n 2013) [hereinafter Ill. Adv. Op. 13-09].

302. *See, e.g.*, United States *ex rel.* Lockyer v. Haw. Pac. Health, 490 F. Supp. 2d 1062, 1089 (D. Haw. 2007) (holding that defense counsel's e-mail conversations with employees at the Centers for Medicare and Medicaid Services, a represented party, about general policies behind certain Medicare Part B rules, as opposed to specific facts concerning the litigation, fell within the government contacts exception); MacArthur v. San Juan Cnty., No. 2:00CV584K, 2001 WL 1806855, at *6 (D. Utah Mar. 6, 2001) (entering a protective order precluding counsel from contacting a county commissioner regarding anything other than policy matters); Ohio Adv. Op. 92-7, 1992 WL 739409, at *3–6 (Sup. Ct. of Ohio, Bd. of Comm'rs on Grievances & Discipline 1992) [hereinafter Ohio Adv. Op. 92-7] (concluding that communications by lawyers at public board or commission meetings on behalf of an individual or group of citizens fell within the "authorized by law" exception,

concerning the wisdom or error of their policy proposals falls squarely within the Petition Clause's scope.[303]

For instance, the Kansas Bar Association's Professional Ethics Advisory Committee held that "communications between a lawyer representing a zoning applicant and an elected or appointed government official regarding the zoning matter fall under the 'authorized by law' exception to Rule 4.2 and are therefore permissible."[304] The State Bar of South Dakota Ethics Committee held that a lawyer representing the board of a municipality could lobby the city council, mayor, and other city entities and officials to pass an ordinance modifying the board's power and authority, without the city attorney's permission.[305] The committee reasoned that efforts to obtain a legislative change favoring a client do not violate Rule 4.2 because they relate "solely to government officials acting on a legislative question rather than in an adjudicative or negotiation capacity."[306] In North Carolina, some lawyers successfully obtained a sign variance for their clients from a town board of adjustment and the town appealed. The North Carolina State Bar advised the lawyers that they could write the elected members of the town council to ask them to place the desirability of the pending appeal on the agenda for the next town council public meeting.[307]

At the opposite end of the spectrum, lawyers violate the policy issue requirement if they interview government employees or officials to develop evidence for use in litigation or to gain admissions against interest.[308] There is, however, room to differ over what constitutes a "policy issue."[309] Some uncertainty in this area stems from the conclusion in ABA Formal Op. 97-408 that "settling a controversy" counts as a "policy issue."[310] In *American Canoe Ass'n, Inc. v. City of St. Albans*,[311] for example, defense counsel moved to prohibit the plaintiff's counsel from discussing settlement with members of the city's governing body. In denying the motion and cit-

but advising the attorney to first identify herself when the communication involved a disputed matter before a represented government party).

303. City of N.Y. v. Beretta U.S.A. Corp., 524 F.3d 384, 397 (2d Cir. 2008).

304. Kan. Bar Ass'n, Prof'l Ethics Advisory Comm., Op. No. 00-06, at 5 (2000).

305. State Bar of S.D., Ethics Comm., Op. 98-9 (1998).

306. *Id.* at 1.

307. N.C. Eth. Op. RPC 202, 1995 WL 853877, at *1–2 (N.C. State Bar 1995).

308. *See, e.g.*, United States v. Sierra Pac. Indus., 759 F. Supp. 2d 1206 (E.D. Cal. 2010) (*Sierra I*); United States v. Sierra Pac. Indus., 759 F. Supp. 2d 1215 (E.D. Cal. 2011) (*Sierra II*); Me. Bd. of Overseers of the Bar, Prof'l Ethics Comm., Op. 181 (2003); State Bar of Mont., Ethics Op. 940430, at 1 (1994); Or. Eth. Op. 2005-144, *supra* note 293, 2007 WL 2324948, at *2.

309. *See, e.g.*, D.C. Bar, Legal Ethics Comm., Op. 340, at 3 (2007) (opining that permissible communications with government officials about "genuine grievances" encompass both "basic policy questions" and discussions about "substantive legal arguments" advanced by government lawyers' court filings).

310. ABA Formal Op. 97-408, *supra* note 293, at 2.

311. 18 F. Supp. 2d 620 (S.D. W. Va. 1998).

ing favorably to ABA Formal Op. 97-408, the court reasoned that "[g]overnment remains the servant of the people even when citizens are litigating against it. Thus, when citizens deal with government agencies, several sorts of direct contact are 'authorized by law' and permissible."[312] Similarly, the Alabama State Bar opined that a lawyer defending the State Board of Education in a lawsuit filed by a County Board of Education could communicate with members of the County Board to discuss settling the lawsuit without obtaining the consent or approval of the County Board's attorney.[313]

In contrast, the Illinois State Bar Association concluded that a lawyer representing a client in a municipal tax assessment proceeding could communicate with a city decision maker as to related tax law policy issues, but that any communications about the possible settlement or resolution of the matter could not "fairly be said to relate to policy issues."[314] This outcome is consistent with several state ethics opinions issued before ABA Formal Op. 97-408.[315] In summary, the formulation of a definitive test as to what constitutes a policy issue remains a work in progress.

2. *The Government Official's Level of Authority*

Even if a planned ex parte communication with a government official will address a policy issue, ABA Formal Op. 97-408 limits the intended recipients of the communication to government officials with the authority to take or recommend action in the matter.[316] In other words, a government official must have the power to redress the client's grievances to excuse lawyers' compliance with Rule 4.2. Government employees who are in no position to resolve any controversies, but whose acts or omissions may be imputed to the government agency, or whose statements may be used as admissions

312. *Id.* at 621.

313. Ala. State Bar, Eth. Op. 2003-03, at 6 (2003).

314. Ill. Adv. Op. 13-09, *supra* note 301, 2013 WL 5967125, at *3.

315. *See, e.g.*, Alaska Eth. Op. 94-1, 1994 WL 924306, at *3–5 (Alaska Bar Ass'n, Ethics Comm. 1994) (reasoning that it would be a Rule 4.2 violation for a litigant's lawyer to present the litigant's settlement position to the government agency's managing board without consent from the agency's counsel, even if the agency's counsel may not have adequately communicated prior settlement offers), *rejected by* Alaska Eth. Op. 2017-2, *supra* note 300, 2017 WL 4221171, at *5–6 (agreeing with ABA Formal Op. 97-408); Ill. State Bar Ass'n, Comm. on Prof'l Ethics, Op. 92-3 (1992) (stating that the defendant's lawyer may not send a city's elected officials copies of his correspondence with the city attorney about the city's litigation with his client); Ill. Adv. Op. 794, 1982 WL 198406, at *1–2 (Ill. State Bar Ass'n 1982) (deciding that a lawyer for a landowner in an eminent domain proceeding could not contact employees of the condemning authority in an attempt to settle the case); State Bar of N.M., Op. 1988-2 (1988) (advising that a lawyer many not initiate settlement discussions with a government agency without the consent of the agency's lawyer); Ohio Adv. Op. 92-7, *supra* note 302, 1992 WL 739409, at *1 (finding it inappropriate for a lawyer to send copies of settlement offers directly to a government agency even if the original is served on the government's attorney).

316. ABA Formal Op. 97-408, *supra* note 293, at 10.

against interest, remain off-limits to opposing counsel.[317] Which camp a government employee falls into is a fact-intensive inquiry.

3. *Notice of the Proposed Communication*

Finally, ABA Formal Op. 97-408 requires the lawyer representing a private party to give the government's lawyer reasonable notice of her intent to communicate with an official.[318] The notice requirement is intended to afford the government lawyer a chance to advise the official about the proposed communication, including whether to entertain it.[319] The notice must provide "sufficient information for opposing counsel to act on it to protect the client's interests," such as the official's identity and the time and place of the intended communication, and allow opposing counsel enough time to act on it and be present if she so chooses.[320]

Not all jurisdictions enforce the notice requirement.[321] Even so, where the intended ex parte communication does not clearly fall within the government contacts exception, notifying opposing counsel may reduce the chances of provoking a court or disciplinary authority if the communication is ultimately challenged.[322]

C. Jurisdictions with Express Government Contacts Exceptions

Currently, the District of Columbia, Maryland, North Carolina, Texas, and Utah have developed specific exceptions that limit the reach of Rule 4.2 in cases involving represented government entities.[323] Lawyers practic-

---

317. *Id.* n.15.

318. *Id.* at 7–8, 10; *see also* Chi. Bar Ass'n, Prof'l Responsibility Comm., Op. No. 00-01 (2000) (concluding that a private attorney may contact a government official with authority to take or recommend action in a controversy to discuss policy matters, including settlement, so long as the private lawyer gives the government lawyer prior notice); N.Y. Eth. Op. 812, 2007 WL 5025457, at *3 (N.Y. State Bar Ass'n, Comm. on Prof'l Ethics 2007) (adopting the ABA Formal Op. 97-408 approach and concluding that a lawyer representing a private party before a town planning board may directly communicate with individual planning board members about pending development applications where the communications solely concern policy issues and the lawyer gives the planning board counsel reasonable advance notice).

319. ABA Formal Op. 97-408, *supra* note 293, at 10.

320. 2005 N.C. Eth. Op. 5, 2006 WL 6135360, at *3 (N.C. State Bar 2006) [hereinafter 2005 N.C. Eth. Op. 5].

321. *See, e.g.*, Ill. Adv. Op. 13-09, *supra* note 301, 2013 WL 5967125, at *4 (rejecting the notice requirement because "it is strictly a creation of the ABA's Opinion and is not mandated by Rule 4.2").

322. *See, e.g.*, United States *ex rel.* Lockyer v. Haw. Pac. Health, 490 F. Supp. 2d 1062, 1089 (D. Haw. 2007) (finding that counsel's communication fell within the Rule 4.2 exception for communications with government officials but suggesting that the "better practice" would have been to notify opposing counsel prior to initiating those communications).

323. D.C. Rules of Prof'l Conduct R. 4.2(d) (2013); Md. Rules of Prof'l Conduct R. 4.2(c) (2016); N.C. Rules of Prof'l Conduct R. 4.2(b) (2013); Tex. Disciplinary Rules of Prof'l Conduct R. 4.02(a) (2019); Utah Rules of Prof'l Conduct R. 4.2(d)(3) (2018).

ing in these jurisdictions obviously should consult these rules and cases and ethics opinions applying or interpreting them when deciding whether to communicate with government officials.

D. Special Considerations

Any lawyer contemplating ex parte communications with a represented government agency must also consider the ramifications of contact with former government employees, communications with government employees who have retained separate counsel, and government lawyers' efforts to prevent ex parte communications with all agency employees.

1. *Communications with Former Government Employees*

As discussed earlier, it is generally settled that Model Rule 4.2 does not prohibit ex parte communications with an organization's former employees. The same principle holds true where a government agency is involved. As in other contexts, however, gaining from a former government employee information that the lawyer knows is legally protected from disclosure may lead to discipline or sanctions even where Rule 4.2 does not apply.[324] In short, even if Rule 4.2 is not an impediment to ex parte communications with a former government official, other rules of professional conduct still restrict the nature, purpose, and substance of those communications.[325]

2. *Communications with Government Officials Sued in Their Personal Capacities*

When government officials are separately represented in a matter—as where they are sued in their personal capacities—the rights guaranteed by the Petition Clause are immaterial and the full protections of Model Rule 4.2 apply.[326] It makes no difference whether the official's lawyer is employed or retained by the government.[327]

324. ABA Formal Op. 97-408, *supra* note 293, at 9 n.14; *see, e.g.*, Camden v. State of Md., 910 F. Supp. 1115, 1117, 1121–24 (D. Md. 1996) (disqualifying the law firm where the plaintiff's lawyer had ex parte communication with the former special assistant to the president of defendant Bowie State University, who consulted with the university's administrative officials and attorneys regarding the case and sent and received confidential communications).

325. *See, e.g.*, Alaska Eth. Op. 2011-2, 2011 WL 497247, at *3 (Alaska Bar Ass'n, Ethics Comm. 2011) (recognizing that investigating counsel may not permit a current or former government employee from disclosing privileged communications).

326. Restatement (Third) of the Law Governing Lawyers § 101 cmt. a (2000); ABA Formal Op. 97-408, *supra* note 293, at 3 n.3.

327. ABA Formal Op. 97-408, *supra* note 293, at 3 n.3.

3. *Government Lawyers' Blanket Bans on Ex Parte Communications*

Courts and state ethics committees dislike directives by government counsel banning all government employees from communicating with opposing counsel without the government counsel's consent.[328] This approach is consistent with the general principle that a lawyer cannot offer to represent a witness purely as a tactic to foreclose potential ex parte communications by opposing counsel.[329]

IX. Conclusion

Lawyers regularly confront thorny issues that revolve around ex parte communications with represented persons. Missteps here can be exceedingly costly, potentially including judicial sanctions, disqualification, and professional discipline. This is true regardless of whether the lawyers involved typically represent plaintiffs, generally represent defendants, have a criminal trial practice, or represent clients across the litigation spectrum. It is therefore incumbent upon lawyers to understand the contours and limits of their related professional responsibilities.

328. *See, e.g.*, Vega v. Bloomsburgh, 427 F. Supp. 593, 595 (D. Mass. 1977) (disapproving of a blanket government policy prohibiting employees from speaking with the plaintiffs' counsel under threat of disciplinary action); Ky. Bar Ass'n, Eth. Op. KBA E-332 (1988) (opining that a lawyer representing a government agency in litigation may not prevent opposing counsel from contacting all agency employees); 2005 N.C. Eth. Op. 5, *supra* note 320, 2006 WL 6135360, at *2 ("Counsel for an organization, be it a corporation or government agency, may not unilaterally claim to represent all of the organization's employees on current or future matters as a strategic maneuver."); Ohio Adv. Op. 92-7, *supra* note 302, 1992 WL 739409, at *7 (opining that a "government department, agency or its counsel should not give blanket instructions to all its employees not to communicate with counsel representing an adverse party without the government's counsel present").

329. *See, e.g.*, Rivera v. Lutheran Med. Ctr., 866 N.Y.S.2d 520, 526–27 (Sup. Ct. 2008) (disqualifying a law firm from representing non-party witnesses where the firm allegedly offered to represent the witnesses to prevent the plaintiff's lawyers' ex parte communications with them), *aff'd*, 899 N.Y.S.2d 859 (App. Div. 2010).

6

Social Media and Professional Responsibility

I. Introduction

People of all ages enjoy online social networking. Indeed, approximately 72 percent of Americans use social media, including Facebook, Instagram, LinkedIn, Snapchat, Twitter, and YouTube. Among other features and uses, having accounts on social networking sites allows people to create pages on which they can post personal information or share information they find interesting. People who enjoy social networking may join groups of other users with similar interests and identify various personal relationships in the process. They may communicate with one another, swap photos, and share videos while enjoying senses of community and intimacy. They are not worried about embarrassing themselves or revealing unflattering or potentially detrimental personal information because they consider themselves to be among friends, or because at the time they post or share an image or thought, they do not consider all the possible ramifications of revealing that information. Understandably, lawyers recognize that social media sites are potentially valuable sources of information on parties, witnesses, and jurors.

II. Social Media and Discovery

Unfortunately, depending on security settings, a person's social media account may be accessible only by invitation or with permission, and a lawyer may not want the person to know that he is viewing her page. Alternatively, a lawyer may reasonably believe that the person will never grant him access to her page or will destroy key information posted there before allowing access. In such a case, may a lawyer ask someone else to engage the person for purposes of obtaining access to the person's page? The idea is that while the third person will not lie to the target in attempting to obtain access or reveal her ties to the lawyer or her true reason for wanting access to the target person's page, she will gain access to information there for tactical use. The Philadelphia Bar Association Professional Guidance Committee answered the question negatively when it was posed by a lawyer seeking information on an unrepresented non-party witness for possible impeachment at trial.[1] The committee reasoned:

> [T]he proposed course of conduct . . . would violate Rule 8.4(c) because the planned communication by the third party with the witness is deceptive. It omits a highly material fact, namely, that the third party who asks to be allowed access to the witness's pages is doing so only because he or she is intent on obtaining information and sharing it with a lawyer for use in a lawsuit. . . . The omission would purposefully conceal that fact from the witness for the purpose of inducing the witness to allow access, when she may not do so if she knew the third person was associated with the [lawyer] and the true purpose of the access was to obtain information for the purpose of impeaching her testimony.[2]

In September 2010, the New York State Bar Association's Committee on Professional Ethics (NYSBA) entered the fray.[3] In Opinion 843, the NYSBA was asked whether a lawyer investigating another party in litigation could view the party's Facebook or MySpace pages so long as the lawyer did not "friend" the party and instead confined her investigation to the party's public pages that were accessible to all members in the network. So long as the lawyer did not "friend" the party being investigated and confined her inquiry to the party's publicly available profile, the NYSBA reasoned, the lawyer's actions were equivalent to obtaining information on a party through searches of publicly available online or print media, or through subscription services such as Nexis or Factiva, all of which are plainly permitted.[4] The NYSBA thus concluded:

> A lawyer who represents a client in pending litigation, and who has access to the Facebook or MySpace network used by another party in litigation, may access and review the public social network pages of that party to search for potential impeachment material. *As long as the lawyer does not "friend" the other party or direct a third person to do so,* accessing the social network pages of the party will not violate Rule 8.4 (prohibiting deceptive or misleading conduct), Rule 4.1 (prohibiting false statements of fact or law), or Rule 5.3(b)(1) (imposing responsibility on lawyers for unethical conduct by nonlawyers acting at their direction.[5]

1. Phila. Eth. Op. 2009-02, 2009 WL 934623, at *2–3 (Phila. Bar Ass'n, Prof'l Guidance Comm. 2009).
2. *Id.* at *2.
3. N.Y. Eth. Op. 843, 2010 WL 3961381 (N.Y. State Bar Ass'n, Comm. on Prof'l Ethics 2010).
4. *Id.* at *2.
5. *Id.* (emphasis added).

More recently, the Massachusetts Bar Association's Committee on Professional Ethics was asked by a lawyer whether she could directly request access to non-public information on a potential defendant's Facebook page when that person was unrepresented without disclosing that the lawyer represented a potential plaintiff.[6] The Massachusetts Bar Committee answered the question "no," reasoning that by doing so the lawyer would be engaging in deceit in violation of Rules 4.1 and 8.4(c).[7] Moreover, this was not only a situation where the potential defendant was likely to misunderstand the lawyer's role but also one where the lawyer enabled the misunderstanding.[8] The committee opined that it was permissible for the lawyer to "friend" the potential defendant in order to access non-public information on her Facebook page only if the lawyer disclosed her identity as the potential plaintiff's lawyer in the process.[9]

In contrast, the Committee on Professional and Judicial Ethics of the New York City Bar Association (formally known as the Association of the Bar of the City of New York) responded differently when asked whether a lawyer, either directly or acting through an agent, could contact an unrepresented person through a social networking website to obtain access to the person's webpage to gather information for use in litigation.[10] The New York City Committee opined "that an attorney or her agent may use her real name and profile to send a 'friend request' to obtain information from an unrepresented person's social networking website without also disclosing the reasons for making the request."[11] Unremarkably, the New York City Committee further concluded that neither a lawyer nor the lawyer's agent could use deception to obtain information from a person's social networking website.[12] For example, it would be improper for the lawyer or her investigator to pose as the person's long-lost classmate, prospective employer, or friend of a friend to gain access to the person's social networking site.[13]

Courts' and disciplinary authorities' positions on lawyers' attempts to view information on social networking sites are difficult to predict. On the one hand, there is no meaningful difference between obtaining access to a person's social networking site and using discrimination testers to expose evidence of unlawful bias or employing a private investigator in a trademark case to visit a business to determine whether it is palming off substitute

6. Mass. Bar Ass'n, Comm. on Prof'l Ethics, Ethics Op. 2014-5 (2014).

7. *Id.* (citing Phila. Eth. Op. 2009-02, 2009 WL 934623 (Phila. Bar Ass'n, Prof'l Guidance Comm. 2009); San Diego Cty. Bar Ass'n, Legal Ethics Comm., Op. 2011-2 (2011)).

8. *Id.* (citing N.H. Bar Ass'n, Ethics Comm., Advisory Op. 2012-13/05 (2013)).

9. *Id.*

10. NYC Eth. Op. 2010-2, 2010 WL 8265845 (Ass'n of the Bar of the City of N.Y., Comm. on Prof'l & Jud. Ethics 2010).

11. *Id.* at *1 (footnote omitted).

12. *Id.* at *3.

13. *Id.* & n.6.

goods. The target of the investigation has knowingly exposed herself to such an inquiry through her social networking. No one who posts anything on a social networking site should expect that her online material will escape detection; neither can she have a reasonable expectation of privacy in the information. Although social media users may prevent widespread access to their pages through heightened security settings and screening those with whom they network, the many gaffes and embarrassing blunders linked to people's social networking are common knowledge. Many employers ask applicants to disclose social networking sites on which the applicants are featured. A substantial majority of employers conduct online searches of prospective employees, and an equal number have rejected prospective employees based on information they learned about candidates online. Even if a person is careful with respect to her privacy, her friends may not be, such that a person must recognize that at least some of her information is likely to be distributed regardless of her preferences. And apart from privacy expectations in the abstract, in this scenario the target is granting someone whom she apparently does not know well access to her page, which itself defeats any claimed expectation of privacy.

On the other hand, analogies to discrimination testers or private investigators visiting a business in a trademark case are inapt because the subjects in those investigations are by their very nature open to such inquiries. Social media users are not inviting outside exploration of their affairs. This is especially true for site users who use privacy controls to reasonably limit access to their pages. As for the publicly reported gaffes and blunders, they reveal nothing about the privacy expectations of most site users; those glaring missteps reflect only the experiences of the ignorant and irresponsible. By way of analogy, just because some people may be too dense or lazy to hang curtains in their homes and thus invite Peeping Toms to watch what should be private aspects of their lives does not mean that someone who has shades on every window in her house should expect her privacy to be invaded. The fact that a reckless or mischievous friend may unilaterally expose one's personal data to strangers is no excuse for intruding into what was meant to be private space. As for the grant of access as defeating the target's reasonable expectation of privacy, the point is that she granted access only because she did not know the motives of the person seeking access—she was not careless; she was *deceived*.

This is an area in which lawyers should exercise caution.[14] In addition to ethics rules, lawyers' conduct may implicate federal and state laws governing

14. *See, e.g.*, Tex. Eth. Op. 671, 2018 WL 1583985, at *3 (Sup. Ct. of Tex., Prof'l Ethics Comm. 2018) (opining "that the failure by attorneys and those acting as their agents to reveal their identities when engaging in online investigations, even for the limited purpose of obtaining identifying or jurisdictional information, can constitute misrepresentation, dishonesty, deceit, or the omission of a material fact").

computer fraud and abuse, data piracy, and the privacy of electronic communications, as well as other statutes. What, then, are lawyers to do? How far can lawyers and their agents safely go in discovering information that may be found on social networking sites?

Certainly, lawyers may conduct online research of parties and witnesses and thereafter use any information that is publicly available.[15] Information on a social networking site should be considered publicly available when it may be viewed without the need for the account holder's permission. A person who makes information publicly available through social media can have no privacy interest in that information. When it comes to social networking sites then, lawyers may view any information that the target person makes freely available. This is true even if the person under investigation is represented in the matter because reviewing the public portions of a person's social network site does not qualify as communicating with the person within the meaning of Rule 4.2.[16] If the person being investigated is represented by counsel in the matter, however, then neither the lawyer nor the lawyer's agent may communicate with the person through the site about the matter in which the person is represented.[17] Indeed, Model Rule 4.2 prevents a lawyer or his agent from even making a "friend" request or otherwise asking the person for access to her page where such requests would qualify as communications about the matter in which the person is represented.[18] In that case, access to the person's page must come through a formal discovery request or through the consent of the person's lawyer.

Lawyers may join a social media network solely to obtain information about a party or witness.[19] Lawyers may ethically attempt to obtain nonpublic information from an unrepresented person's social networking site by sending the person a "friend" request or by way of a similar inquiry.[20] Lawyers must use their own names in the process and cannot otherwise engage in deception, such as by creating false profiles or misrepresenting the

---

15. N.Y. State Bar Ass'n, Social Media Ethics Guidelines 20 (2019) [hereinafter NYSBA Guidelines]; Me. Bd. of Overseers of the Bar, Prof'l Ethics Comm'n, Op. 217, at 2 (2017) [hereinafter Me. Op. No. 217]; 2019 N.C. Eth. Op. 5, 2019 WL 3957896, at *2 (N.C. State Bar 2019) [hereinafter 2019 N.C. Eth. Op. 5]; Or. Eth. Op. 2013-189, 2013 WL 8482075, at *1 (Or. State Bar Ass'n, Bd. of Governors 2013) [hereinafter Or. Eth. Op. 2013-189].

16. Me. Op. No. 217, *supra* note 15, at 2; Or. Eth. Op. 2013-189, *supra* note 15, 2013 WL 8482075, at *1.

17. Model Rules of Prof'l Conduct R. 4.2 (2020).

18. Me. Op. No. 217, *supra* note 15, at 1–2; Or. Eth. Op. 2013-189, *supra* note 15, 2013 WL 8482075, at *2; *see also* San Diego Cty. Bar Ass'n, Legal Ethics Comm., Op. 2011-2 (2011) (analyzing this situation under the then-equivalent California ethics rule).

19. NYSBA Guidelines, *supra* note 15, at 20 (citing N.H. Bar Ass'n, Ethics Comm., Advisory Op. 2012-13/05 (2013)).

20. NYSBA Guidelines, *supra* note 15, at 20; Or. Eth. Op. 2013-189, *supra* note 15, 2013 WL 8482075, at *1–2.

purpose of, or reason for, their requests.[21] If a lawyer uses her own name and does not misrepresent the reason for, or purpose of, her inquiry, there is no basis to argue that the lawyer is being deceitful or dishonest, or is engaging in misrepresentation. Such a request does not violate Model Rule 4.3 governing lawyers' communications with unrepresented persons because:

> [A] [l]awyer's request for access to non-public information does not in and of itself make a representation about the [l]awyer's role. In the context of social networking websites, the holder of the account has full control over who views the information available on his or her pages. The holder of the account may allow access to his or her social network to the general public or may decide to place some, or all, of that information behind "privacy settings," which restrict who has access to that information. The account holder can accept or reject requests for access. Accordingly, the holder's failure to inquire further about the identity or purpose of unknown access requestors is not the equivalent of misunderstanding [the] [l]awyer's role in the matter.[22]

If, however, the holder of the social networking account asks for information to identify the lawyer or the reason for the lawyer's approach, or if the lawyer has some other reason to believe that the person misunderstands her role, the lawyer must provide the information or drop the request.[23] The lawyer cannot misrepresent her identity or motives in making the inquiry.[24] In reality, a person's request for information about the lawyer or the lawyer's interest in the person's on-line presence will probably end the lawyer's informal efforts to gain access to the non-public portions of the person's social networking site.

Similarly, a lawyer should be able to have an investigator send a "friend" request or a similar request to an unrepresented person to obtain access to that person's social networking page, provided the investigator does not misrepresent his identity or the reason for his request. There is nothing dishonest or deceitful about an investigator attempting to "friend" a person in the investigator's own name. Just as where a lawyer inquires in the lawyer's own name, a person who grants an investigator access to her page based on a blind request cannot complain later that her privacy was invaded or that she was otherwise exploited. After all, she could have denied the request or

21. NYSBA Guidelines, *supra* note 15, at 20; *see* Me. Op. No. 217, *supra* note 15, at 2 (stating that lawyers may request access to private portions of unrepresented persons' social media sites so long as they are "truthful and not deceptive" within the meaning of Rules 4.1 and 8.4(c)).

22. Or. Eth. Op. 2013-189, *supra* note 15, 2013 WL 8482075, at *2; *see also* N.C. Eth. Op. 5, *supra* note 15, 2019 WL 3957896, at *2 (explaining why a lawyer who requests access information from the restricted portion of an unrepresented person's social network site in the lawyer's own name does not violate Rule 4.3).

23. NYSBA Guidelines, *supra* note 15, at 20; Or. Eth. Op. 2013-189, *supra* note 15, 2013 WL 8482075, at *2.

24. Or. Eth. Op. 2013-189, *supra* note 15, 2013 WL 8482075, at *3.

questioned the basis for it. If the person responds by asking the investigator to better identify himself or his relationship to her, or to explain his interest or connection, however, the investigator cannot misrepresent his identity or the reason for his inquiry.

To use another example, suppose that you are defending a local company in premises liability litigation in which the plaintiff alleges that he is suffering from serious lingering injuries after an accident on company property. You have heard from a few employees of the company that the plaintiff's sister used to work at the company and that she has told them that the plaintiff has posted photographs on his Facebook page that are worth your attention. You have tried to view those pictures through your own Facebook account but have been unable to do so because of the plaintiff's privacy settings. After you share with one of the employees your frustration at being unable to view the photographs, you get a call from the plaintiff's sister. She tells you that she is a Facebook friend of the plaintiff and would be happy to download the photographs and send them to you. May you take her up on her offer? Would it make a difference if she had not offered to obtain the pictures but instead you had called her and asked her to do so? Should the identity of the person who came up with the idea about how to obtain the pictures make a difference from a professional responsibility standpoint?

The North Carolina State Bar concluded in a 2019 formal ethics opinion that the identity of the person who initiated the social media intrusion should make no difference when analyzing the propriety of the lawyer's conduct, qualified only by the admonition that the lawyer may not direct or encourage a third-party to use deception or misrepresentation in the process.[25] As the North Carolina State Bar explained:

> Nothing in the Rules of Professional Conduct prevents a lawyer from engaging in lawful and ethical informal discovery such as communicating with third party witnesses to collect information and evidence to benefit a client. Witnesses who have obtained information from the restricted portions of a person's (represented or unrepresented) social network presence are no different in this regard than any other witness with information relevant to a client's matter. Therefore, when a lawyer is informed that a third party has access to restricted portions of a person's social network presence and can provide helpful information to the lawyer's client, the lawyer is not prohibited from requesting such information from the third party or accepting information volunteered by the third party.[26]

The North Carolina State Bar further opined that a lawyer may accept information from a client who has access to restricted portions of an

25. N.C. Eth. Op. 5, *supra* note 15, 2019 WL 3957896, at *4.
26. *Id.*

opponent's or a witness's social network sites.[27] As with a third-party, the lawyer may not encourage or instruct the client to engage in deception or misrepresentation when gaining access to or exploring the sites.

For lawyers who are uneasy about the North Carolina State Bar's position, consider a case in which a third-party possesses photographs or e-mail messages from a witness or a represented party that are relevant to the case and makes that fact known to the lawyer. In that situation, everyone should agree that the lawyer may ask the third-party to share the photos or e-mail messages without fear of professional consequences. It also seems clear that the lawyer may ethically accept the photos or e-mails from the third-party if the third-party volunteers to provide them to the lawyer. By sharing the photos with the third-party or sending the third-party the e-mail messages, the witness or opposing party risked their exposure to others. The social media situation perhaps feels different, but as a practical matter it is not.

To be sure, asking a third-party to gain access to restricted portions of a witness's or represented person's website is riskier than accepting information gathered by the third-party without the lawyer's prompting. If the lawyer initiates the request, there is some chance that she ultimately may be accused of violating Model Rule 8.4(a), which prohibits a lawyer from using an agent to do that which the lawyer cannot ethically achieve herself.[28] Still, it is difficult to distinguish this scenario from the analogous and clearly permissible situation in which a third-party possesses photographs or e-mail messages from a witness or represented party that are relevant to the case and the lawyer asks the third-party to share the photos or e-mails. For that matter, consider further a case in which a witness attends an invitation-only party and hears the opposing party discussing the case with other partygoers. Is there any doubt that the lawyer can ethically ask the witness what she heard the opponent say at the party? There should not be. From a professional responsibility standpoint, how is the social media setting different? Again, as a practical matter, it is not.

Regardless of the precise circumstances, the lawyer should strive to ensure that a request for non-public social media information is not construed by the third party as a demand or order to turn over the information. The chances for the witness to construe the request (incorrectly but potentially subjectively) as being coercive are heightened if the witness is an employee of the party the lawyer represents.

As should be clear by now, risks to lawyers planning online investigations increase exponentially if they permit or instruct the person approaching the

---

27. *Id.*

28. *See* Model Rules of Prof'l Conduct R. 8.4(a) (2020) (making it professional misconduct for a lawyer to "violate or attempt to violate the Rules of Professional Conduct, knowingly assist or induce another to do so, or do so through the acts of another").

target to misrepresent his or her identity or reason for wanting access to the target's page, or if they do so themselves. Such deception is never advisable for at least four reasons, depending on the facts. First, it may be criminal under federal or state law. Second, it may be actionable. Although lawyers' litigation privilege should shield them against most claims, it is reasonable to be concerned that some statutory causes of action might not be subject to the litigation privilege depending on the language of the statutes. Third, it may expose the investigating lawyer or the lawyer's client to discovery sanctions. Fourth, lawyers who permit or participate in such subterfuge risk violating numerous ethics rules, including Rules 4.1(a), 4.3, 5.3, 8.4(a), 8.4(b), 8.4(c), and 8.4(d).[29] For the same reasons, lawyers should not knowingly violate a site's terms or conditions of use, or encourage or permit an agent to do so.

Lawyers should never create fictitious social media accounts such as false Facebook identities as a means or method of investigating parties or witnesses,[30] nor should they ever instruct investigators or others to do so on their behalf. If such a ruse ever comes to light, the lawyer's conduct will almost certainly be held to violate the Rule 8.4(c) prohibition on conduct involving dishonesty, fraud, deceit, or misrepresentation.[31] In addition, if the person a lawyer is investigating is represented by counsel in the matter, this tactic may lead to a violation of the Model Rule 4.2 prohibition on ex parte communications with represented persons and perhaps yet other offenses.[32]

When it comes to concerns related to Model Rule 4.2, lawyers should also be mindful of the potential need to know the mechanics involved in any social media platform being accessed. For example, platforms such as LinkedIn, as a default, generate a message to account owners to alert them when someone views their profiles. Revisiting our earlier premises liability litigation hypothetical, if the social media platform involved were LinkedIn instead of Facebook, would the lawyer's unsuccessful efforts at obtaining the photos have put her at risk of violating Model Rule 4.2? Would any automated message by the social media platform to the plaintiff be treated as a communication about the representation made by the lawyer? For

29. *Id.* R. 4.1(a) (prohibiting false statements of material fact or law to third persons); *id.* R. 4.3 (dealing with unrepresented persons); *id.* R. 5.3 (obligating lawyers to supervise non-lawyer assistants); *id.* R. 8.4(a) (making it professional misconduct for a lawyer to attempt to violate rules of professional conduct personally or through another); *id.* R. 8.4(b) (prohibiting criminal acts that reflect adversely on a lawyer's honesty, trustworthiness, or fitness as a lawyer in other respects); *id.* R. 8.4(c) (prohibiting conduct involving dishonesty, fraud, deceit, or misrepresentation); *id.* R. 8.4(d) (banning conduct prejudicial to the administration of justice).

30. *See, e.g.*, Disciplinary Couns. v. Brockler, 48 N.E.3d 557, 558–62 (Ohio 2016) (suspending but staying with conditions an assistant county prosecutor who created a fictitious Facebook account to contact alibi witnesses of a defendant who had been indicted for murder).

31. *Id.* at 560–61.

32. *See, e.g.*, *id.* at 560 (recognizing the lawyer's Rule 8.4(d) violation).

the reasons discussed earlier, we believe that the better view is that such a communication should not be treated as having been made by the lawyer. But lawyers would do well to be aware of the risks. The need for lawyers to understand how social media platforms function is underscored by the recent insertion of language into the Comment of Model Rule 1.1 discussing what is often referred to as a duty of technological competence.[33]

In all cases, of course, whether an activity is ethically permissible and whether it is a good idea from an advocacy or tactical perspective are separate questions. There may be cases in which lawyers decide that online discovery activities might somehow be turned against them by an adversary even though the activities are permissible. Lawyers must be sure to factor such considerations into their discovery plans.

III. Researching Prospective and Sitting Jurors through Social Media

Social media research has potential value beyond pretrial discovery. Indeed, just as lawyers may be obligated as a matter of professional competence to investigate opposing parties and witnesses through appropriate technological means, including social media, attorneys may similarly be obligated to research social media to learn "everything reasonably possible . . . about jurors who will sit in judgment on a case."[34] There are many reasons for this, perhaps most fundamentally the strong public interest in identifying and eliminating potentially biased jurors.[35] Such biases might not be readily discernable from information provided on jury questionnaires or shared during voir dire. Moreover, jurors do not always provide accurate or complete information about themselves or their experiences.[36] They may not reveal relevant information about themselves that is available through a review of social media. Consequently, a lawyer's failure to investigate a juror's online presence could result in a juror being empaneled whose biases,

33. *See* Model Rules of Prof'l Conduct R. 1.1 cmt. 8 (2020) ("To maintain the requisite knowledge and skill, a lawyer should keep abreast of changes in the law and its practice, *including the benefits and risks associated with relevant technology*, engage in continuing study and education, and comply with all continuing legal education requirements to which the lawyer is subject." (emphasis added)).

34. N.Y. Eth. Op. 2012-2, 2012 WL 2304271, at *2 (N.Y. State Bar Ass'n, Comm. on Prof'l Ethics 2012) [hereinafter N.Y. Eth. Op. 2012-2] ("Indeed, the standards of competence and diligence may require doing everything reasonably possible to learn about jurors who will sit in judgment on a case."); *see also* N. H. Bar Ass'n, Op. 2012-13/05 (2013) (stating that lawyers "have a general duty to be aware of social media as a source of potentially useful information in litigation, to be competent to obtain that information directly or through an agent, and to know how to make effective use of that information in litigation").

35. ABA Comm. on Ethics & Prof'l Responsibility, Formal Op. 466, at 2 (2014).

36. *See, e.g.*, United States v. Daugerdas, 867 F. Supp. 2d 445, 452–53 (S.D.N.Y. 2012) (discussing a juror's astounding dishonesty during voir dire), *rev'd sub nom.* United States v. Parse, 789 F.3d 83 (2d Cir. 2015).

prejudices, or misrepresentations have not been revealed but that could have been detected through social media.[37] Courts, reluctant to retry cases, are becoming increasingly demanding with respect to the timing of when such information must be discovered to preserve the right to challenge a verdict based on juror non-disclosure or misrepresentation.[38] Judges expect that dutiful lawyers will use appropriate technology before a jury is empaneled or a verdict rendered.[39] For instance, by rule, Missouri requires lawyers to investigate prospective jurors' litigation history through Internet-based case management resources; the failure to do so before the jury is empaneled may waive the party's ability to obtain post-trial relief for juror non-disclosure.[40] The Missouri rule specifically pertains to disclosure of litigation history, but its rationale—requiring parties to do electronic research before a jury is sworn—arguably applies more broadly.[41]

---

37. *See, e.g.*, Slaybaugh v. State, 44 N.E.3d 111, 118–19 (Ind. Ct. App. 2015) (holding a hearing and allowing the parties to depose a juror who failed to disclose during voir dire that the victim's sibling was among her expansive list of Facebook friends before concluding that the juror had engaged in no misconduct); Sluss v. Commonwealth, 381 S.W.3d 215, 220–24 (Ky. 2012) (ruling that a convicted murderer was entitled to a hearing on the issue of juror non-disclosure; two jurors were Facebook "friends" with the victim's mother but had remained silent when asked during jury selection whether they knew the victim or the victim's family). *But see* McGaha v. Commonwealth, 414 S.W.3d 1, 6 (Ky. 2013) ("It is now common knowledge that merely being friends on Facebook does not, per se, establish a close relationship from which bias or partiality on the part of a juror may reasonably be presumed.").

38. In some jurisdictions, this may also be an ethical obligation. *See, e.g.*, N.Y. Rules of Prof'l Conduct R. 3.5(d) (2018) ("A lawyer shall reveal promptly to the court improper conduct by a member of the venire or a juror, or by another toward a member of the venire or a juror or a member of his or her family of which the lawyer has knowledge.").

39. *See, e.g.*, Burden v. CSX Transp., Inc., No. 08-cv-04-DRH, 2011 WL 3793664, at *10 (S.D. Ill. Aug. 24, 2011) (reasoning that a new trial was not warranted because alleged juror non-disclosures could have been "discovered through the exercise of reasonable diligence" by use of public records databases that were available before verdict); State v. Bailey, No. 1805009348A, 2020 WL 1316838, at *4 (Del. Super. Ct. Mar. 16, 2020) ("[I]t does not appear that the new information in this case would constitute sufficient grounds for a new trial because it is not likely to change the result of the trial, *and* it could have been discovered during the trial by *checking the jurors' Facebook profiles earlier*. No new information was brought to the parties' attention prior to Defense's investigation of the jurors' Facebook profiles. Therefore, it could have been done at any time during the trial."); *McGaha*, 414 S.W.3d at 7 (ruling that a new trial was not warranted following a murder conviction when it was discovered after trial that one of juror's 629 Facebook "friends" was the victim's wife; the juror had not been asked about social media relationships and had not misled court in saying that she knew some of victim's family but was "not close" with them).

40. Mo. Sup. Ct. R. 69.025.

41. In *Khoury v. ConAgra Foods, Inc.*, 368 S.W.3d 189 (Mo. Ct. App. 2012), the court affirmed the trial court's denial of the plaintiffs' motion for a new trial when a stricken alternate juror's non-disclosure was discovered by the defense via Facebook after the jury was selected. The plaintiffs argued that the rule and its rationale applied to all Internet investigation, not just litigation history. The *Khoury* court rejected the notion that "any and all" Internet or other research must be done and raised before a jury is empaneled but acknowledged that "the day may come that technological advances may compel our Supreme Court to rethink the scope of required 'reasonable investigation' into the background of jurors that may impact challenges to the veracity of responses given in voir dire before the jury is empaneled." *Id.* at 202–03.

Of course, juror misconduct is not limited to statements or non-disclosure during jury selection. Sitting jurors may do any number of things after being empaneled that could potentially disqualify them or otherwise show that a party is in danger of not receiving a fair trial, such as disregarding court instructions not to "research" anything outside of evidence presented during trial, communicating with third parties or litigants via social media (even "tweeting" from the courtroom),[42] sharing information about deliberations, or the like. In addition to being an effective investigative tool to spot juror biases and misrepresentations, monitoring social media might be the only practical way for lawyers to discover juror misconduct during trial.

Any competence or diligence-based obligation to investigate jurors' social media, however, must be evaluated in context with restrictions imposed by other rules of professional conduct. Most significantly, Model Rule 3.5(b) states that a lawyer shall not "communicate ex parte with [a juror or prospective juror] during the proceeding unless authorized to do so by law or court order."[43] As conflicting authorities show, in the context of social media, what constitutes an impermissible "communication" is subject to reasonable debate.

Beyond the potential for alleged ethics violations, there are other reasons that lawyers might choose to limit or forgo social media investigations that jurors or prospective jurors might discover. For instance, jurors may feel this is an invasion of their privacy, which may in turn compromise their impartiality. This is not a theoretical concern. A high-profile federal mortgage fraud trial was almost mistried after a sitting juror discovered that one of the defense attorneys had reviewed the juror's LinkedIn profile and informed the court, "I feel intimidated and don't feel I can be objective."[44]

Federal Judicial Center research suggests that many district judges are uncomfortable with attorneys conducting social media research on jurors.[45] Their concerns are significant enough that the issue of what research trial counsel should or should not do is effectively mooted in many cases because courts will not allow it. Over 25 percent of the judges surveyed stated that they prohibited attorneys from using social media during jury selection (the vast majority of responding judges indicated they had not addressed the issue one way or the other).[46] Their reasons included a desire to protect juror privacy,

---

42. Dimas-Martinez v. State, 385 S.W.3d 238, 248–49 (Ark. 2011) (overturning a capital murder conviction because a juror was posting on his Twitter account during trial despite instructions not to do so).

43. Model Rules of Prof'l Conduct R. 3.5(b) (2020).

44. NYSBA Guidelines, *supra* note 15, at 37.

45. Megan Dunn, Jurors' and Attorneys' Use of Social Media during Voir Dire, Trials and Deliberations: A Report to the Judicial Conference Committee on Court Administration Case Management 13 (2014).

46. *Id.*

concerns about prolonged jury selection, and general distraction. Some judges simply believed that it was unnecessary because information otherwise provided during the jury selection process was sufficient for lawyers to evaluate venire members without resorting to social media sources.[47]

In *Oracle America, Inc. v. Google Inc.*,[48] a California federal court articulated "good reasons to restrict, if not forbid," searches of jurors' social media presence by the lawyers, their jury consultants, investigators, and clients in high-profile litigation between two Internet giants.[49]

> The first reason is anchored in the danger that upon learning of counsel's own searches directed at them, our jurors would stray from the Court's admonition to refrain from conducting Internet searches on the lawyers and the case. . . .
>
> * * *
>
> To return to the first concern, the apparent unfairness in allowing the lawyers to do to the venire what the venire cannot do to the lawyers will likely have a corrosive effect on fidelity to the no-research admonition. Once our venire learns of the lawyers' Internet searches (as the venire would via the instruction Oracle requests), a very serious risk will be presented that they will feel justified in doing to the lawyers (and to the case itself) what the lawyers are doing to them, namely, conducting Internet searches—despite the no-research admonition. . . .
>
> A second danger posed by allowing counsel to conduct research about the venire and the jury is that it will facilitate improper personal appeals to particular jurors via jury arguments and witness examinations patterned after preferences of jurors found through such Internet searches. For example, if a search found that a juror's favorite book is *To Kill A Mockingbird*, it wouldn't be hard for counsel to construct a copyright jury argument (or a line of expert questions) based on an analogy to that work and to play upon the recent death of Harper Lee, all in an effort to ingratiate himself or herself into the heartstrings of that juror. The same could be done with a favorite quote or with any number of other juror attitudes on free trade, innovation, politics, or history. Jury arguments may, of course, employ analogies and quotations, but it would be out of bounds to play up to a juror through such a calculated personal appeal, all the more so since the judge, having no access to the dossiers, couldn't see what was really in play. . . .
>
> A third reason is to protect the privacy of the venire. They are not celebrities or public figures. The jury is not a fantasy team composed by consultants, but good citizens commuting from all over our district, willing to serve our country, and willing to bear the burden of deciding a commercial dispute the parties themselves cannot resolve. Their privacy matters.

47. *Id.*
48. 172 F. Supp. 3d 1100 (N.D. Cal. 2016).
49. *Id.* at 1102.

> Their privacy should yield only as necessary to reveal bias or a reluctance to follow the Court's instructions. It is a weak answer that venire persons, through their social media privacy settings, have chosen to expose their profiles to scrutiny, for navigating privacy settings and fully understanding default settings is more a matter of blind faith than conscious choice. (Otherwise, there would be no need for websites explaining the intricacies of privacy settings.)[50]

For these reasons, the *Oracle* court considered exercising its discretion to impose an outright ban preventing the parties and their lawyers from conducting social media and Internet searches on venire persons as well as on the final empaneled jury.[51] The court reasoned that such a ban would be within its discretion to protect the integrity of the judicial process and to restrict unnecessary intrusions into jurors' privacy.[52] As the court recognized, however, "the lawyers would then be precluded from learning information readily available to the press and every member of the public in the gallery. That is, with an outright ban, everyone in the gallery could have more information about the venire persons and the empaneled jurors than the lawyers themselves."[53] Despite that problem, the court called upon the lawyers to voluntarily consent to a ban on Internet research of the venire or jury until the trial was over.[54] If the lawyers agreed, the court proposed to so advise the venire at the start of jury selection and enlarge the lawyers' time to conduct extra voir dire. If the lawyers would not agree to the court's preferred approach, then:

> At the outset of jury selection, each side shall inform the venire of the specific extent to which it (including jury consultants, clients, and other agents) will use Internet searches to investigate and to monitor jurors, including specifically searches on Facebook, LinkedIn, Twitter, and so on, including the extent to which they will log onto their own social media accounts to conduct searches and the extent to which they will perform ongoing searches while the trial is underway. Counsel shall not explain away their searches on the ground that the other side will do it, so they have to do it too. Nor may counsel intimate to the venire that the Court has allowed such searches and thereby leave the false impression that the judge approves of the intrusion. Counsel may simply explain that they feel obliged to their clients to consider all information available to the public about candidates to serve as jurors. Otherwise, counsel must stick to disclosing the full extent to which they will conduct searches on jurors. By this disclosure, the venire

50. *Id.* at 1102–03 (citations omitted).
51. *Id.* at 1103.
52. *Id.*
53. *Id.*
54. *Id.*

> will be informed that the trial teams will soon learn their names and places of residence and will soon discover and review their social media profiles and postings, depending on the social media privacy settings in place. The venire persons will then be given a few minutes to use their mobile devices to adjust their privacy settings, if they wish. The venire persons will also be given the normal admonition that they cannot do any research about the case, the parties, or the lawyers and that they cannot speak to anyone about the case, including by making any social media postings about it. Only the names and places of residence of those called forward to the box shall be provided to counsel (so the identities of venire persons still in the gallery will remain private).[55]

Thereafter, until the trial ended, each side would be allowed to view online only what it told the venire it would review—nothing more.[56] If either party detected seeming misconduct by a juror, the lawyers for that party would be required to immediately report their discovery to the court and the other party regardless of which party's position the juror appeared to favor. Each party would be required to preserve an exact record of every search and all information viewed so that if a motion is later made alleging misconduct by a juror, the court and the other party would be able to see when the objecting side first learned of the problem. In addition, each prospective juror summoned from the gallery for voir dire would be asked if he or she could adhere to the usual prohibitions on research and public statements about the case "despite the one-sidedness (that is, despite the fact that one or both trial teams will be trying to monitor each juror's social media postings)."[57] Any prospective juror who could not do so would be excused on that basis.

As shown above, trial lawyers face difficult decisions in balancing the competing professional obligations and tactical choices associated with investigating jurors through social media. Several bar groups have issued opinions on the issue,[58] although the lack of congruency in those opinions may leave practicing lawyers uncertain of their obligations.

---

55. *Id.* at 1103–04.
56. *Id.* at 1104.
57. *Id.*
58. *See, e.g.*, Colo. Bar Ass'n, Ethics Comm., Formal Op. 127, at 2, 6–7 (2015) [hereinafter Colo. Formal Op. 127] (stating that a lawyer may view the public portions of a juror's social media sites but may not ask a juror to view restricted portions of her website without the court's express authorization); W. Va. State Bar, Lawyer Disciplinary Bd., L.E.O. No. 2015-02, at 18–19 (2015) (opining that lawyers may review the public sections of a juror's social networking websites but are prohibited by Rule 3.5 from attempting to view private sections of a juror's social media pages).

A. Ethics Opinions

The New York County Lawyers' Association Committee on Professional Ethics (NYCLA Committee) was the first ethics body to publish guidance on the professional responsibility boundaries of lawyers' social media investigations of jurors. The NYCLA Committee issued Formal Opinion 743 in 2011,[59] looking at the issue both in the pretrial/jury selection stage and after a jury has been selected.

The NYCLA Committee opined that it was ethically permissible "for a lawyer to undertake a pretrial search of a prospective juror's social networking site, provided that there is no contact or communication with the prospective juror and the lawyer does not seek to 'friend' jurors, subscribe to their Twitter accounts, send jurors tweets or otherwise contact them."[60] Likewise, with respect to sitting jurors, a lawyer may "visit the publicly available Twitter, Facebook or other social networking site of a juror, but must not 'friend' the juror, email, send tweets to the juror or otherwise communicate in any way with the juror *or act in any way by which the juror becomes aware of the monitoring*."[61] In justifying the emphasized language concerning juror awareness, the NYCLA Committee engaged in no analysis. Rather, it stated that "under some circumstances a juror may become aware of a lawyer's visit to the juror's website,"[62] noting that, by way of example, Twitter and LinkedIn have features that allow account holders to learn when a new person starts to follow them (Twitter) or has reviewed their profile (LinkedIn).[63] The opinion summarily concluded that if a juror were to become aware of the lawyer's investigative efforts, "the contact may well consist of an impermissible communication, as it might tend to influence the juror's conduct with respect to the trial."[64]

In 2012, the New York State Bar Association's Committee on Professional Ethics (NYSBA Committee) examined these issues in considerably more detail in Formal Opinion 2012-2.[65] The NYSBA Committee recognized at the outset that "standards of competence and diligence may require doing everything reasonably possible to learn about the jurors who will sit in judgment on a case" but that in the context of social media and Internet investigations, what constitutes an impermissible "communication" is unclear.[66] Framing the identification or definition of a "communication" as

59. NYCLA Eth. Op. 743, 2011 WL 10316182 (N.Y. Cty. Lawyers' Ass'n, Comm. on Prof'l Ethics 2011).

60. *Id.* at *4.

61. *Id.* (emphasis added).

62. *Id.* at *3.

63. *Id.* n.2.

64. *Id.* at *3.

65. N.Y. Eth. Op. 2012-2, *supra* note 34, 2012 WL 2304271, at *2.

66. *Id.* at *2.

the principal issue,[67] the NYSBA Committee concluded that lawyers may use social media services to research jurors but cannot "engage in communication with a juror."[68] A juror's receipt of a "friend" request or other notice "*would* constitute a prohibited communication" if the attorney was aware that he would cause the notice to be sent, and that causing such a notice to be sent to a juror "*might* constitute a prohibited communication even if inadvertent or unintended."[69] The NYSBA Committee also adopted less controversial and common sense positions that (1) under Rule 8.4, third parties working for attorneys must adhere to these same restrictions; and (2) attorneys cannot use deception—"such as pretending to be someone else"—to obtain access to otherwise unavailable information about a juror.[70]

The NYSBA Committee concluded that the term "communication" must be interpreted broadly, with the communicator's intent being irrelevant and the effect on the listener being determinative.[71] Given this understanding, the NYSBA Committee identified the main question that a lawyer must answer before engaging in jury research "is whether her actions will cause the juror to learn of the research."[72] Whether that is the lawyer's intent is irrelevant. Because of how social media services work, lawyers risk violating Rule 3.5 through unintended communications, as where a service automatically sends a notice to the account holder. The problem from the NYSBA Committee's point of view—the reason why even such unintended communications would be prohibited—is that "even such minimal contact raises the specter of the improper influence and/or intimidation that the Rules are intended to prevent."[73] Despite making the case that any communication—whether intentional or not—would violate Rule 3.5, the NYSBA Committee stopped short of that conclusion, ultimately taking no position on whether inadvertent communications constitute an ethical violation.[74] Rather, it warned lawyers to proceed cautiously and to understand the functionality of particular services and websites, lest they cause unintended communications, which *may* violate Rule 3.5.[75]

67. *Compare* Model Rule of Prof'l Conduct R. 3.5(b) (2020) (stating that a lawyer "shall not communicate ex parte with [a juror or prospective juror] unless authorized to do so by law or court order"), *with* N.Y. Rules of Prof'l Conduct R. 3.5(a)(4) (2018) (stating that a lawyer shall not "communicate or cause another to communicate with a member of the jury venire from which the jury will be selected for the trial of a case or, during the trial of a case, with any member of the jury unless authorized to do so by law or court order").

68. N.Y. Eth. Op. 2012-2, *supra* note 34, 2012 WL 2304271, at *4.

69. *Id.* at *2.

70. *Id.*

71. *Id.* at *5.

72. *Id.* at *4.

73. *Id.*at *5.

74. *Id.*at *6

75. *Id.*

B. The ABA Position

In April 2014, the American Bar Association's Standing Committee on Ethics and Professional Responsibility issued Formal Opinion 466, titled "Lawyer Reviewing Juror's Internet Presence."[76] In answering the question of whether a lawyer may review jurors' or potential jurors' Internet presence before and during trial, the committee acknowledged the competing public interests in identifying jurors who may be biased with preventing jurors from ex parte contact by the parties or their agents.[77] "Lawyers need to know where the line should be drawn between properly investigating jurors and improperly communicating with them. In today's Internet-saturated world, the line is increasingly blurred."[78]

Consistent with existing guidance from New York, the committee opined that there is nothing improper about an attorney viewing a juror's publicly available Internet presence before and during trial, assuming that the attorney does not communicate with the juror or prospective juror or there is no court order to the contrary.[79] The committee parsed its analysis into three categories: (1) passive review of a juror's website or social media that is accessible without making an access request and where the juror is unaware that the website or social media is being reviewed, (2) active review where the lawyer requests access to the juror's social media, and (3) passive lawyer review where the juror learns the viewer's identity through a feature of the website or social media platform.[80]

In analyzing these three categories, the committee used the analogy of the attorney driving down a juror's street. Passive review of a website or social media of which the juror is unaware is permissible; it is akin to observantly driving down the street where the juror lives to "glean publicly available information that could inform the lawyer's jury-selection decisions."[81] Merely observing what is open to the public is not a "communicative act" for Model Rule 3.5 purposes.[82] In contrast, actively seeking access to otherwise non-public information inherently involves a "communication" and is analogous to "stopping the car, getting out, and asking the juror for permission to look inside the juror's house."[83] Thus, consistent with other authorities, a lawyer may not personally, or through another, send an access request to a juror.[84]

76. ABA Comm. on Ethics & Prof'l Responsibility, Formal Op. 466 (2014).
77. *Id.* at 1, 2.
78. *Id.* at 2.
79. *Id.* at 1.
80. *Id.* at 2.
81. *Id.* at 4.
82. *Id.*
83. *Id.*
84. *Id.*

The committee, however, diverged sharply from existing authority regarding its analysis of unintended notifications. After recognizing contrary guidance from New York, the committee concluded:

> A lawyer who uses a shared [social media] service platform to passively view juror [social media] under these circumstances does not communicate with the juror. The lawyer is not communicating with the juror; the [social media] service is communicating with the juror based on a technical feature of the [social media]. This is akin to a neighbor recognizing a lawyer's car driving down the juror's street and telling the juror that the lawyer had been seen driving down the street.[85]

The committee encouraged judges to consider informing jurors that lawyers may investigate their backgrounds, including their online presences, which "will dispel any juror misperception that a lawyer is acting improperly merely by viewing what the juror has revealed to all others on the same network."[86] It nevertheless cautioned lawyers who decide to review juror social media to be aware of automatic subscriber-notification features; unlike many people who quickly "click" their consent to the terms of use for a social media platform, attorneys (in accord with comment 8 to Model Rule 1.1) should review those terms and conditions prior to use.[87]

The ABA approach has received mixed reviews. The Pennsylvania Bar Association's Committee on Legal Ethics & Professional Responsibility agreed with Formal Opinion 466 in concluding that passive notification to jurors indicating who has reviewed their profiles is not an impermissible communication.[88] The District of Columbia Bar's Committee on Professional Responsibility reached the same conclusion.[89] The Professional Ethics of the Maine Board of Overseers of the Bar agreed with Formal Op. 466 that passive notification to jurors outside the lawyer's knowledge or control does not violate Rule 3.5(b), but also stated that attorneys "must avoid accessing social media of a juror or potential juror where the attorney knows or reasonably should know that the social media site will alert the juror or potential juror to the fact that the attorney accessed the site."[90]

On the other hand, social media guidelines issued by the Commercial and Federal Litigation Section of the New York Bar Association (NYSBA

85. *Id.*

86. *Id.* at 3.

87. *Id.* at 5–6.

88. Pa. Eth. Op. 2014-300, 2014 WL 10383869, at *15 (Pa. Bar Ass'n, Comm. on Legal Ethics & Prof'l Responsibility 2014).

89. D.C. Bar, Legal Ethics Comm., Op. 371, at 5 (2016) ("[S]ome social media networks automatically provide information to registered users or members about persons who access their information. In the Committee's view, such notification does not constitute a communication between the lawyer and the juror or prospective juror.").

90. Me. Op. No. 217, *supra* note 15, at 3.

Guidelines) disagree.[91] The NYSBA Guidelines reaffirm that lawyers may generally research a prospective or sitting juror's public social media and posts[92] but reject the ABA's position on passive notifications to jurors because of the potential effect on the juror's state of mind, regardless of attorneys' intent.[93] According to critics of the ABA's position, even if the communication was unintended, notice that lawyers have secretly reviewed a juror's social media still might "infect the juror's thought process" and "surely would be disconcerting to most jurors."[94] In critics' views, Formal Opinion 466 only encourages lawyers and their staff to engage in activities that may have this effect. The NYSBA Guidelines thus indicate that "when reviewing social media to perform juror research, a lawyer needs to perform such research in a way that does not leave any 'footprint' or notify the juror that the lawyer or her agent has been viewing the juror's social media profile."[95]

C. Summary

Lawyers may permissibly review jurors' and prospective jurors' social media sites provided they do not alert them to their investigation in the process. In fact, such investigation may be required by attorneys' duty of competence. Unfortunately, other questions are not so easily answered. In many states, lawyers currently lack clear guidance on whether social media research that unintentionally alerts jurors to their investigation, as can be the case with LinkedIn, is acceptable.

Jurisdictions facing the issue for the first time should adopt Formal Opinion 466; the ABA approach reflects the better view that Rule 3.5(b) provides no basis for discipline in the context of derivative, unintentional communications.[96] Undoubtedly, there is risk that some jurors may react adversely to lawyers probing their online lives, including those portions that are publicly available. But that risk is insufficient to justify limiting a vital tool in rooting out potentially biased jurors or sitting jurors who might engage in inappropriate communications or conduct amid trial or during deliberations. More fundamentally, a "communication" initiated by the social media platform, not intended by counsel to be known by the recipient and certainly not done with the intent to influence the juror, simply is not the type of communication contemplated by Rule 3.5(b).

---

91. NYSBA Guidelines, *supra* note 15, at 33–35.

92. *Id.*

93. *Id.*

94. Mark A. Berman et al., *Why ABA Opinion on Jurors and Social Media Falls Short*, N.Y. L.J. (May 4, 2014).

95. NYSBA Guidelines, *supra* note 15, at 35.

96. *See, e.g.*, Colo. Formal Op. 127, *supra* note 58, at 3 (adopting the ABA position).

The best way for lawyers to ensure that social media investigation of jurors or prospective jurors does not create professional responsibility problems is to proactively engage the court. Trial lawyers should strongly consider informing the court of their intentions. Some courts may not allow juror social media investigation. This would be unfortunate considering the strong policy behind weeding out biased jurors, but a court order prohibiting such investigation establishes a clear boundary for lawyers to respect. Alternatively, a disciplinary body will be hard-pressed to punish a lawyer who sought out and obtained court approval in advance of any challenged conduct.

7

Accidental and Impromptu Clients

I. Introduction

The creation of an attorney-client relationship is enormously consequential from a lawyer's perspective for various professional liability and responsibility reasons. Lawyers owe clients fiduciary duties of confidentiality and loyalty. Lawyers owe clients a duty of care when acting within the scope of the representation. Lawyers' ethical obligations include duties that run only to clients, including competence, communication, confidentiality, conflict of interest avoidance or resolution, and diligence. So, when and how does an attorney-client relationship form?

The Model Rules of Professional Conduct recognize this important question but do not answer it, stating that "for purposes of determining the lawyer's authority and responsibility, principles of substantive law external to these Rules determine whether a client-lawyer relationship exists."[1] Ordinarily, there is no confusion. There is an express agreement between the lawyer and the client, which is commonly memorialized in an engagement letter or other writing. An attorney-client relationship, however, can also be implied from circumstances. It is these situations in which "accidental" clients are created.[2] Accidental clients pose professional responsibility risks for several reasons, the most significant one being that when lawyers unknowingly form attorney-client relationships, they may overlook their client-focused ethical obligations. Confidences may be shared, conflicts of interests may be overlooked, informed consent to conflicts may not be obtained, and so on. Indeed, when lawyers unwittingly form attorney-client relationships,

---

1. Model Rules of Prof'l Conduct Pmbl. and Scope cmt. 17 (2020) ("Furthermore, for purposes of determining the lawyer's authority and responsibility, principles of substantive law external to these Rules determine whether a client-lawyer relationship exists.").

2. The description of some clients as "accidental" clients is generally attributed to Prof. Susan R. Martyn, who wrote a seminal article on such relationships. *See* Susan R. Martyn, *Accidental Clients*, 33 Hofstra L. Rev. 913 (2004–2005).

their ignorance of those relationships almost ensures that they will fail to meet at least some professional obligations owed to those clients.[3]

Lawyers may also knowingly and deliberately, but unwisely, agree to represent someone on an impromptu basis without understanding or appreciating the risks they are assuming. This commonly occurs where a lawyer representing a corporate client agrees to jointly represent an employee of the client who is a fact witness for the limited purpose of a deposition or an interview with a government agency. Anytime an attorney jointly represents multiple clients, there are several rules of professional conduct that must be considered but that are often not fully appreciated. When fully considered, the advantages of such limited representations may be outweighed by the associated professional liability and responsibility risks.

II. Accidental Clients

A. What Makes a "Client"?

Usually, an attorney-client relationship is created through an express agreement. But that is not always the case. Courts have long recognized that sometimes, "[w]hat constitutes an attorney client relationship is a rather elusive concept."[4]

Absent an express agreement, an implied attorney-client relationship may be found to exist when (1) a person seeks the lawyer's advice or assistance, (2) the requested advice or assistance relates to matters within the lawyer's professional competence, and (3) the lawyer expressly or impliedly agrees to provide or actually furnishes the desired advice or assistance.[5] In some cases, the third element of an implied attorney-client relationship may be established by proof of detrimental reliance, meaning that the person seeking legal services reasonably relied on the lawyer to provide them, and the lawyer, who was aware of the person's reliance, did nothing to nullify it.[6]

When deciding whether an implied attorney-client relationship exists, courts focus on the would-be client's expectations and especially the reasonableness of the person's belief "'that he is consulting a lawyer in that capacity and has manifested intention to seek professional legal advice.'"[7] A putative

3. Ingrid A. Minott, *The Attorney-Client Relationship: Exploring the Unintended Consequences of Inadvertent Formation*, 86 U. Det. Mercy L. Rev. 269, 293 (2009).

4. Folly Farms I, Inc. v. Trs. of the Clients' Sec. Tr. Fund of the Bar of Md., 387 A.2d 248, 254 (Md. 1978).

5. State *ex rel.* Couns. for Discipline of the Neb. Sup. Ct. v. Chvala, 935 N.W.2d 446, 471–72 (Neb. 2019).

6. Cesso v. Todd, 82 N.E.3d 1074, 1078–79 (Mass. App. Ct. 2017) (quoting DeVaux v. Am. Home Assur. Co., 444 N.E.2d 355, 357 (Mass. 1983)); *Chvala*, 935 N.W.2d at 472.

7. Diversified Grp., Inc. v. Daugerdas, 139 F. Supp. 2d 445, 454 (S.D.N.Y. 2001) (quoting Westinghouse Elec. Corp. v. Kerr-McGee Corp., 580 F.2d 1311, 1319 (7th Cir. 1978)).

client's unilateral belief that an attorney-client relationship exists, however, is not enough to establish one.[8] Rather, a putative client's subjective expectation that an attorney-client relationship has been formed must be accompanied by facts indicating that the person's belief is objectively reasonable.[9] At base, then, the existence of an attorney-client relationship is measured by an objective standard.[10]

It is beyond the scope of this chapter to analyze all facts, circumstances, and legal nuances relevant to determining how an implied attorney-client relationship can be created. There is, however, a recurring scenario that lawyers repeatedly face and that merits special discussion: a lawyer's representation of organizational clients in litigation-related internal investigations and related interactions with its non-party constituents.

B. Ethical Obligations in Dealing with Constituents of an Organizational Client

Because organizations can only act through their constituents, when an organization becomes involved in actual or threatened litigation, or a government investigation, the organization's lawyers must necessarily interact with its constituents—such as executives who run the organization, in-house attorneys or others who oversee litigation, and other employees who may have information needed to provide legal advice to the organization.[11] Some of these constituents may also be potential fact witnesses. Various constituents may have conflicting interests with the organization, or with one another, including conflicts not necessarily linked to the litigation or investigation itself.

Under Model Rule 1.13(a) a lawyer employed or retained by an organization represents the organization.[12] But a lawyer who represents an organization does not, merely because of that engagement, represent any constituent of that organization—such as an officer or director—individually.[13] Still, in

8. *In re* Rescue Concepts, Inc., 556 S.W.3d 331, 339 (Tex. App. 2017).

9. Hinerman v. Grill on Twenty First, LLC, 112 N.E.3d 1273, 1275–76 (Ohio Ct. App. 2018); O'Kain v. Landress, 450 P.3d 508, 516 (Or. Ct. App. 2019).

10. Barkerding v. Whittaker, 263 So. 3d 1170, 1182 (La. Ct. App. 2018).

11. *See* United States v. Graf, 610 F.3d 1148, 1160 (9th Cir. 2010) ("[A]ny time a corporation retains counsel, counsel will have to talk to individual employees to represent the company effectively.").

12. Model Rules of Prof'l Conduct R. 1.13(a) (2020).

13. *Id.* R. 1.7 cmt. 34 ("A lawyer who represents a corporation or other organization does not, by virtue of that representation, necessarily represent any constituent or affiliated organization . . . ."); Restatement (Third) of the Law Governing Lawyers § 96 cmt. b (2000) ("By representing the organization, a lawyer does not thereby also form a client-lawyer relationship with all or any individuals employed by it or who direct its operations or who have an ownership or other beneficial interest in it, such as its shareholders."); *see also* GSI Commerce Sols., Inc. v. BabyCenter, L.L.C., 618 F.3d 204, 210 (2d Cir. 2010) (quoting Model Rule 1.7 cmt. 34); Records v. Geils Unlimited Rsch., LLC, No. CIV.A. 12-11419-FDS, 2013 WL 3967970, at *4 (D. Mass. July 30, 2013) (explaining that it is well-settled that a lawyer retained by a corporation represents the corporation and not its directors, employees, or shareholders).

some situations and with consent, a lawyer representing an organization may also represent its constituents.[14] Absent the constituent having a personal attorney-client relationship jointly with the organization, the organization, not the constituent, holds the right to assert the attorney-client privilege for communications between its attorneys and the constituent. "Any privilege resulting from communications between corporate officers and corporate attorneys concerning matters within the scope of the corporation's affairs and the officer's duties *belongs to the corporation and not the officer.*"[15] An employee or corporate officer "has no power to assert the attorney-client privilege except as to confidential communications with [corporate counsel] in his individual capacity."[16]

To avoid confusion between the attorney and an organizational constituent as to the attorney's role, the constituent's rights, and the privilege implications of communications, the Model Rules require attorneys to clarify who they represent. Model Rule 1.13(f) states: "In dealing with an organization's directors, officers, employees, members, shareholders, or other constituents, a lawyer shall explain the identity of the client when the lawyer knows or reasonably should know that the organization's interests are adverse to those of the constituents with whom the lawyer is dealing."[17] A comment to Rule 1.13 emphasizes that the constituent needs to understand that if there is an adverse interest, the organization's lawyer cannot provide the constituent with legal advice and their discussions may not be privileged.[18]

Model Rule 1.13(f) only applies when the lawyer knows or should reasonably know the organization and an employee have adverse interests. Often such adversity is not apparent before the lawyer hears what the employee has to say or when it is not apparent that the employee is involved in wrongdoing.[19] Even when there is no current conflict, failing to clarify that the lawyer is solely representing the organization could nevertheless cause the employee to believe the lawyer represents her as well, and later contend that the lawyer and the lawyer's firm are disqualified from representing the organization in a subsequent dispute where the organization and the employee are adverse. Regardless of conflict of interest concerns, there is no downside to clarifying whose interests the lawyer is protecting in any interaction with employees or other constituents of an organizational client.

14. Model Rules of Prof'l Conduct R. 1.13(g) (2020) ("A lawyer representing an organization may also represent any of its directors, officers, employees, members, shareholders or other constituents, subject to the provisions of Rule 1.7.").

15. United States v. Merida, 828 F.3d 1203, 1210 (10th Cir. 2016) (quoting Intervenor v. United States, 144 F.3d 653, 658 (10th Cir. 1998)) (internal quotation marks omitted).

16. *Id.* (quoting *Intervenor*, 144 F.3d at 659) (internal quotation marks omitted).

17. Model Rules of Prof'l Conduct R. 1.13(f) (2020).

18. *Id.* R. 1.13 cmt. 10.

19. Gideon Mark, *The Yates Memorandum*, 51 U.C. Davis L. Rev. 1589, 1613 (2018).

Model Rule 1.13(f) should be read in conjunction with Model Rule 4.3, which applies to attorneys' dealings with unrepresented persons.[20] Model Rule 4.3 prohibits attorneys from stating or implying that they are disinterested when dealing with someone not represented by counsel.[21] It also requires attorneys to make reasonable efforts to correct any misunderstanding the unrepresented person might have about the lawyer's role.[22] If attorneys comply with Model Rules 1.13(f) and 4.3, then they should not be accidentally forming attorney-client relationships with organizational clients' constitutes. In contrast, if a lawyer for an organization does not properly clarify the nature of her role, the employee or other constituent may believe the lawyer also represents him. If reasonable, this belief may create an attorney-client relationship.[23] In other words, the person will become an accidental client.

The most widely applied test for determining whether an attorney-client relationship was created between a corporation's attorney and an employee was established in *In re Bevill, Bresler and Schulman Asset Management Corp.*[24] The *Bevill* standard is demanding. To establish an attorney-client relationship with corporate counsel, an employee must prove (1) the employee approached the corporate attorney for legal advice, (2) the employee made clear that the request for advice related to matters that arose in his or her individual capacity, (3) the attorney understood this request and advised on the matter even though there was a potential conflict, (4) the communications were confidential, and (5) the subject matter did not concern a more general corporate matter.[25] The majority of courts apply the *Bevill* standard, albeit in somewhat different forms.[26]

20. Model Rules of Prof'l Conduct R. 4.3 (2020) ("Transactions With Persons Other Than Clients").

21. *Id.* ("In dealing on behalf of a client with a person who is not represented by counsel, a lawyer shall not state or imply that the lawyer is disinterested.").

22. *Id.* ("When the lawyer knows or reasonably should know that the unrepresented person misunderstands the lawyer's role in the matter, the lawyer shall make reasonable efforts to correct the misunderstanding.").

23. *See, e.g.*, Manion v. Nagin, 394 F.3d 1062, 1069 (8th Cir. 2005) (finding that the lawyer had created attorney-client relationship based on prior dealings with shareholder-employee and that stating that if lawyer had been "truly working exclusively" for company in previous interactions with the plaintiff, then he should have made that clear and suggested that the plaintiff seek outside counsel); Home Care Indus., Inc. v. Murray, 154 F. Supp. 2d 861, 869 (D.N.J. 2001) (disqualifying the law firm from representing a company in an action against its former CEO and agreeing with the CEO that, because the lawyers created an environment in which he comfortably confided in them, his "belief that the [law] firm represented him personally was reasonable").

24. 805 F.2d 120 (3d Cir. 1986).

25. *Id.* at 124–25.

26. *See, e.g.*, United States v. Graf, 610 F.3d 1148, 1160 (9th Cir. 2010); *In re* Grand Jury Subpoena (Newparent), 274 F.3d 563, 571–72 (1st Cir. 2001); *In re* Grand Jury Proceedings, 156 F.3d 1038, 1040–41 (10th Cir. 1998); United States v. Int'l Bhd. of Teamsters, 119 F.3d 210, 214–15 (2d Cir. 1997).

C. Corporate Investigations and *Upjohn* Warnings

Corporations and other organizations routinely undertake internal investigations based on information about potential wrongdoing of some kind. There may be numerous business risks and legal issues arising from these investigations. The facts and evidence revealed may expose the organization, its constituents, or both, to potential civil or criminal liability. Consequently, organizations may want to ensure that information obtained during investigations, as well as the ultimate findings, are protected by the attorney-client privilege, thereby preventing unwanted disclosure outside of the organization. For all these reasons, organizations' lawyers frequently manage internal investigations, which inevitably involve interviewing employees and other constituents. Considering potential conflicts of interest and confusion that may arise as to what obligations corporate counsel has and to whom, courts have characterized corporate counsel's involvement in internal investigations as "a potential legal and ethical minefield."[27]

Much of the ethical minefield that lawyers must navigate when conducting an internal investigation relates to privilege; failing to avoid those mines may have disastrous consequences for everyone involved. Ordinarily, "[a]ny privilege resulting from communications between corporate officers and corporate attorneys concerning matters within the scope of the corporation's affairs and the officer's duties belongs to the corporation and not to the officer."[28] A corporate officer "has no power to assert the attorney-client privilege except as to confidential communications with [the corporation's attorneys] in his individual capacity."[29] Often, to avoid prosecution or obtain more favorable disposition in criminal or regulatory enforcement actions, an organization may wish to waive privilege. Doing so, however, may not be in the best interest of individual constituents who are, or who may become, government targets. If an accidental joint attorney-client relationship is created with a constituent, then the constituent will have the right to assert the attorney-client privilege, compromising the organization's ability to cooperate with regulators by waiving the privilege. The attorneys involved will likely have to withdraw from the representation altogether.[30] In the civil

27. *In re* Grand Jury Subpoena Under Seal, 415 F.3d 333, 340 (2d Cir. 2005). For an expansive discussion of the professional responsibility and liability concerns that internal investigations may pose for lawyers, see Douglas R. Richmond, *Navigating the Lawyering Minefield of Internal Investigations*, 63 Vill. L. Rev. 617 (2018).

28. United States v. Merida, 828 F.3d 1203, 1209–10 (10th Cir. 2016) (quoting Intervenor v. United States, 144 F.3d 653, 658 (10th Cir. 1998)) (internal quotation marks omitted).

29. *Id.* (quoting *Intervenor*, 144 F.3d at 659) (internal quotation marks omitted).

30. *See In re Grand Jury Subpoena Under Seal*, 415 F.3d at 340 (ruling that investigating counsel did not create attorney-client relationship with employees despite "watered down" warnings but had that been the case, they could not have waived privilege for either and would have had to withdraw from all representation).

context, aside from the lawyers' potential disqualification, joint representation may turn communications between a former employee and in-house counsel helpful to the corporation into inadmissible evidence.[31] Suffice it to say that there are scenarios in which the accidental creation of an attorney-client relationship with an individual constituent could have potentially career-altering consequences for the lawyer involved. The good news for lawyers having to traverse this minefield is that counsel who are familiar with the relevant Model Rules and case law can readily avoid missteps.

Upjohn warnings, sometimes referred to as "corporate *Miranda* warnings," are the first line of defense to preventing an attorney-client relationship from unintentionally being created between counsel for the organization and an employee or other organizational constituent. In *Upjohn Co. v. United States*,[32] the Supreme Court established a framework for determining when an employee's communications with company counsel are protected under the company's attorney-client privilege. Named after that decision, *Upjohn* warnings are typically given to an organization's employees before being interviewed in connection with an internal investigation to clarify that the corporation's lawyer is not the employees' personal counsel,[33] thereby precluding the formation of any attorney-client relationship between the employee and the company's counsel. A second related but distinct purpose is to ensure that any privilege belongs to the company, and only the company.

There are no magic words required for a proper *Upjohn* warning.[34] Typically, they include the following statements: (1) the lawyer represents only the company and not the witness personally; (2) the lawyer is collecting facts for the purpose of providing legal advice to the company; (3) the communication is protected by the attorney-client privilege, which belongs exclusively to the company, not the witness; (4) the company may choose to waive the privilege and disclose the communication to a third party, including the government; and (5) the communication must be kept confidential, meaning that it cannot be disclosed to any third-party other than the witness's counsel.[35] The American Bar Association has created the following sample *Upjohn* warning, which courts have endorsed and which lawyers can feel comfortable satisfies Model Rules 1.13(f) and 4.3:

31. *See, e.g.*, Wylie v. Marley Co., 891 F.2d 1463, 1471 (10th Cir. 1989) (affirming exclusion of communications between former employee and in-house counsel in former employee's wrongful termination suit because he "could have believed" that he was represented by in-house counsel).

32. 101 S. Ct. 677 (1981).

33. *In re* Grand Jury Investig., No. 19-15 (BAH), 2019 WL 2179116, at *16 (D.D.C. Mar. 4, 2019).

34. *See In re* Kellogg Brown & Root, Inc., 756 F.3d 754, 758 (D.C. Cir. 2014) ("[N]othing in *Upjohn* requires a company to use magic words to its employees in order to gain the benefit of the privilege for an internal investigation.").

35. Mark, *supra* note 19, at 1613–14.

- I am a lawyer for Corporation A. I represent only Corporation A, and I do not represent you personally.
- I am conducting this interview to gather facts in order to provide legal advice for Corporation A. This interview is part of an investigation to determine the facts and circumstances of X in order to advise Corporation A how best to proceed.
- Your communications with me are protected by the attorney-client privilege. But the attorney-client privilege belongs solely to Corporation A, not you. That means Corporation A alone may elect to waive the attorney-client privilege and reveal our discussion to third parties. Corporation A alone may decide to waive the privilege and disclose this discussion to such third parties as federal or state agencies, at its sole discretion, and without notifying you.
- In order for this discussion to be subject to the privilege, it must be kept in confidence. In other words, with the exception of your own attorney, you may not disclose the substance of this interview to any third party, including other employees or anyone outside of the company. You may discuss the facts of what happened but you may not discuss this discussion.
- Do you have any questions?
- Are you willing to proceed?[36]

If they are given proper *Upjohn* warnings, it will be at best difficult for witnesses to satisfy the *Bevill* standard or otherwise to establish they had an attorney-client relationship with corporate counsel, or to convince a court they have standing to assert the attorney-client privilege with respect to communications with corporate counsel. Still, considering the stakes, lawyers must be cautious.

In *In re Grand Jury Subpoena*,[37] the Fourth Circuit emphasized the importance of clear *Upjohn* warnings. As part of an internal investigation at AOL Time Warner, the corporation's lawyers gave employees fairly standard *Upjohn* warnings. But the lawyers also told two or three employees that they could "represent [the employee] too if there is not a conflict."[38] During later grand jury proceedings, the government subpoenaed records relating to these interviews. AOL agreed to waive privilege and produce the requested documents, but the employees objected on the basis that they had individual attorney-client relationships with the investigating attorneys and were

36. Am. Bar Ass'n, White Collar Crime Comm., Upjohn Warnings: Recommended Best Practices When Corporate Counsel Interacts with Corporate Employees (July 17, 2009) [hereinafter Upjohn Report].

37. 415 F.3d 333 (4th Cir. 2005).

38. *Id.* at 336.

not waiving privilege.[39] More specifically, they contended that the lawyers' statements that they "could" represent the employees manifested an intent to represent them personally and asserted that it was "hard to imagine a more straightforward assurance of an attorney client relationship than 'we can represent you.'"[40]

The Fourth Circuit was not persuaded and agreed with the district court that there was insufficient evidence of "an objectively reasonable, mutual understanding" that the employees were seeking legal advice or that the lawyers were rendering personal legal advice.[41] Among other things, the lawyers had stated that they *could* represent the employees, rather than stating that they *did* represent the employees. The AOL lawyers' "hypothetical pronouncements[s]" of attorney-client relationships did not suffice to create actual attorney-client relationships with the employees.[42] Consequently, the privilege belonged only to AOL. Although the court found that the employees did not have an attorney-client relationship with AOL's lawyers, the court added that its opinion "should not be read as an implicit acceptance of the watered-down '*Upjohn* warnings' the investigating attorneys" had given.[43]

Merely telling an employee that a conversation is privileged or confidential, without explaining the scope of the privilege and that the organization may waive it, could also be considered "watered down" and create unnecessary confusion. A layperson could assume that this disclosure means that nothing he says could be revealed to anyone else, or at least that his statements could not be revealed to anyone outside of the corporation.[44]

Lawyers interviewing employees or other constituents of an organization should give clear *Upjohn* warnings before starting interviews. Using a script (such as the ABA's) ensures consistency and completeness. Further, lawyers should contemporaneously memorialize the warnings, preferably by having the witnesses sign written acknowledgments. Also, it is often helpful

39. *Id.* at 337.
40. *Id.* at 340.
41. *Id.* at 338.
42. *Id.*
43. *Id.* at 340.
44. *See* United States v. Merida, 828 F.3d 1203, 1213 (10th Cir. 2016) (stating that " in isolation" an attorney's statement that the conversation "was covered by the attorney-client privilege because you work for Choctaw Nation" could potentially cause a non-attorney to believe that the witness held the privilege) (Lucero, J., concurring); *see also* Office of Disciplinary Couns. v. Baldwin, 225 A.3d 817, 833 (Pa. 2020) (finding that a university general counsel's statements to witnesses that her conversations with them were not privileged did not undermine the argument that she was representing them individually because this admonition was consistent with her representing multiple individuals jointly and she did not tell them their conversations were not privileged vis-à-vis third parties).

to have a second attorney participate in the interviews as a witness, unless doing so would likely have a chilling effect on the interview.[45]

Lawyers may be concerned that reciting the full list of disclosures or asking the witness to acknowledge them in writing could discourage the witness from speaking freely—especially in matters with criminal implications.[46] In the heat of the moment, a lawyer faced with a reluctant witness may feel pressured to cut *Upjohn* corners to lighten the atmosphere and increase the chances the witness will more freely provide information. But providing incomplete or diluted *Upjohn* warnings creates more problems than it solves. Although lawyers must balance the need to extract information from witnesses with how best to satisfy their Rule 1.13(g) and 4.3 obligations and avoid creating accidental clients, it is unquestionably best for all concerned to err on the side of robust disclosure and documentation.

D. Office of Disciplinary Counsel v. Baldwin: *An Accidental Client Fiasco*

A recent Pennsylvania Supreme Court case, *Office of Disciplinary Counsel v. Baldwin*,[47] is filled with lessons in how accidental clients may be created and the ensuing professional responsibility ramifications.

In December 2010, former Pennsylvania Supreme Court justice Cynthia Baldwin was serving as General Counsel for Pennsylvania State University (Penn State) when the Office of Attorney General (OAG) contacted her about a grand jury investigation into multiple claims of child abuse perpetrated by former Penn State assistant football coach Jerry Sandusky. The OAG asked whether Baldwin would accept service of four subpoenas, one directed to the university seeking documents and three others for the testimony of Penn State Athletic Director Tim Curly, former Vice-President of Finance and Business Gary Schultz, and Head Football Coach Joe Paterno. Paterno had his own counsel with respect to the grand jury investigation and thus faded from sight for present purposes.

Baldwin met with Curley and Penn State President Graham Spanier, generally explained the grand jury process, and told Curley that he "could have a personal attorney go with him" to the grand jury but he "shouldn't be nervous, just tell the truth."[48] Spanier instructed her to go with Curley when he appeared before the grand jury. Baldwin would later testify that she told Spanier and Curley she could not be Curley's personal attorney and that

45. The second lawyer can also serve as the notetaker, freeing the first lawyer to concentrate on questioning the witness.

46. Upjohn Report, *supra* note 36, at 6 (noting the potential chilling effect on the constituent's willingness to share information when presented with request to sign a written acknowledgment).

47. 225 A.3d 817 (Pa. 2020)

48. *Id.* at 823–24.

nothing Curley said to her would be confidential, but she unfortunately did not document that advice.[49]

Baldwin then met privately with Curley to review his recollection of events involving Sandusky, particularly including a 2001 incident in which Sandusky allegedly fondled a boy in some showers on the Penn State campus. According to Baldwin, Curley told him that he knew about the incident, but it had been described as "horseplay."[50] Thereafter, in her only private conversation with Schultz before his grand jury appearance, Schulz told her "the same thing"; that is, that he was aware of the 2001 incident; that when it was originally reported it was described as horseplay; and that he, like Curley, did not understand there to have been anything sexual about the situation.[51] Baldwin was unaware of another situation involving allegations against Sandusky and potentially inappropriate conduct with boys in 1998 and thus did not discuss the incident with Curley and Schultz. Both Curley and Schultz told Baldwin that they did not have any documents regarding Sandusky's misconduct.[52]

Baldwin felt that because Curley and Schultz had told her "the same thing" and that their accounts were consistent with Penn State's interests, she could represent them both during their grand jury appearances.[53] On January 12, 2011, the morning that Curley and Schultz were to testify, they provided interviews to the OAG. Baldwin attended the interviews. Later that day, she appeared with them at their respective appearances before the grand jury.

In his appearance before the grand jury, Curley testified that in 2001 Paterno had contacted him and Schultz because graduate assistant Michael McQueary had seen Sandusky in the shower with a child and was "uncomfortable" with it.[54] When Curley and Schultz then spoke with McQueary, he told them it was "horsing around, that they were playful, and that it just did not feel appropriate."[55] Curley insisted that no one suggested that there was any sexual conduct involved. Curley also maintained that he did not know anything about the alleged 1998 incident.

Schultz's testimony, however, materially differed from Curley's in that Schultz said that based on the discussion with McQueary and Paterno, Schultz believed the conduct had been sexual in nature, and that it was Schultz's impression that Sandusky "might have grabbed the young

49. *Id.* at 824.
50. *Id.*
51. *Id.*
52. *Id.*
53. *Id.*
54. *Id.*
55. *Id.*

boy's genitals or something of that sort."[56] He also testified that he did not have any documents in his possession and that any notes or other pertinent documents "probably" would have been destroyed when he retired in 2009.[57] Schultz also testified, unlike Curley, that he was aware of allegations being made in 1998, although he could not remember the details. He believed, however, that in 2001 the three administrators had agreed to contact the same child protection agency that had been contacted regarding the 1998 allegations and that he had told Spanier about both the 1998 and 2001 incidents.[58]

In March 2011, Baldwin accompanied Spanier when he appeared before the grand jury. Baldwin had interviewed Spainer beforehand and considered what he had to say consistent with Curley's and Schultz's testimony (which was odd because their testimony was not consistent with each other's). With respect to the 2001 incident, Spanier testified, like Curley but unlike Schultz, that it was described as "horsing around" but in no way sexual and that he did know anything about the 1998 incident.[59]

In November 2011, the Commonwealth charged Curley and Schultz with one count each of perjury and failure to report suspected child abuse.[60] Baldwin advised them to hire private counsel, which they did. Their new lawyers informed Baldwin that Curley and Schultz had considered her to have been their personal counsel when they appeared before the grand jury and that they never waived the attorney-client privilege with respect to any communications with her.[61] Baldwin, who now had her own lawyer, insisted that she had not been personal counsel to either of the witnesses, that she had acted as counsel only for Penn State, and that she had acted solely in that capacity when appearing with them before the grand jury.[62]

Meanwhile, OAG informed Baldwin that it may seek to hold Penn State in contempt of court because of its failure to provide documents as required by the aforementioned subpoena duces tecum. Baldwin was then served with a subpoena requiring her to testify before the grand jury.[63] Prior to her testimony, the supervising judge held a conference to discuss privilege issues raised by Curley's and Schultz's new attorneys. Based on representations by the OAG's lawyer that he would not ask Baldwin about

56. *Id.* at 825.
57. *Id.*
58. *Id.*
59. *Id.* at 826.
60. *Id.*
61. *Id.*
62. *Id.*
63. *Id.*

confidential communications involving Curley and Schultz, the supervising judge deferred making any privilege rulings.[64]

During Baldwin's subsequent testimony, she proceeded to throw Curley, Schultz, and Spanier under the proverbial bus, claiming she did everything she could on behalf of Penn State to comply with the subpoena but that the three administrators had lied to her about the existence of responsive documents (which had since been located and produced).[65] Despite having told the supervising judge that he would not ask Baldwin about the communications for which Curley and Schultz were asserting privilege, the attorney for OAG did exactly that.[66] In response to specific questions about those interviews, Baldwin "revealed the contents of numerous communications between herself and Curley, Schultz, and Spanier,"[67] including testifying that they had all denied having e-mails,[68] and that Spanier "was not a person of integrity" and had undoubtedly lied to her about his knowledge of the 1998 and 2001 incidents.[69]

Four days after Baldwin provided this testimony, the grand jury recommended criminal charges against Spanier and recommended that additional charges be filed against Curley and Schultz.[70] In the resulting criminal proceedings, Curley, Schultz, and Spanier moved to preclude Baldwin from testifying, arguing that they each had an attorney-client relationship with her and that their communications with her were privileged. They lost their privilege arguments in the trial court but won on appeal. The appellate court concluded that Baldwin had breached the attorney-client privilege; barred her from testifying; and quashed the perjury, obstruction of justice, and related conspiracy charges against the three men.[71] The OAG then reached plea bargains with Curley and Schultz on a child endangerment charge. During the criminal proceedings, the Office of Disciplinary Counsel had initiated disciplinary proceedings against Baldwin, alleging that she had violated Rules 1.1, 1.6(a), 1.7(a), and 8.4(d). After conflicting determinations by a Hearing Committee and the Disciplinary Board, the Pennsylvania Supreme Court addressed the allegations against Baldwin.

---

64. *Id.* at 827.

65. *Id.*

66. For misleading the supervising judge and reneging on his assurances that he would not question Baldwin about her potentially privileged conversations, OAG's lawyer was suspended from practice for a year and one day. Office of Disciplinary Counsel v. Fina, 225 A.3d 568, 573 (Pa. 2020).

67. *Baldwin*, 225 A.3d at 827.

68. *Id.* at 846.

69. *Id.* at 848.

70. *Id.* at 827

71. *Id.* at 828.

The *Baldwin* court first considered whether Baldwin had violated Rule 1.1 (competence) or Rule 1.7 (conflicts of interest). The starting point was whether Baldwin represented Curley, Schultz, and Spanier individually (as they contended) or only in a representative capacity as Penn State employees (as Baldwin contended).

The *Baldwin* court reviewed Baldwin's testimony before the Hearing Committee in which she testified that neither Curley nor Schultz asked to be represented in a personal capacity and that she had told them that if she attended the grand jury with them, "nothing would be confidential" and she would have "to tell the board of trustees."[72] Baldwin also testified that she gave *Upjohn* warnings to the men and advised them that she "was not going in there" if there was a conflict.[73] After all that, Baldwin asserted that each of them had supposedly told her that they understood the 2001 incident to involve "horseplay" and they knew nothing more.[74]

Of special significance to the court, however, was what was said during the grand jury proceedings about Baldwin's role, and, more importantly, what was not said. At the beginning of the proceedings, the judge asked specifically who was representing Curley and Schultz, to which Baldwin responded: "My name is Cynthia Baldwin, general counsel for Pennsylvania State University."[75] When asked if she would be "providing representation for both [ ] witnesses?," Baldwin stated: "[Schultz] is retired but was employed by the university and [Curley] is still an employee."[76] After this non-answer, Baldwin heard the judge advise Curley and Schulz of their rights, including instructions that they could have "your lawyer" be present and "confer with her at that time" and that they each could discuss their testimony with "your lawyer."[77] When Curley's testimony began, OAG's lawyer asked Curley if he had counsel with him, to which Curley said: "My counsel is Cynthia Baldwin."[78] Baldwin did not object or attempt to clarify his statement. Similarly, Schultz's testimony began with him affirming that he was accompanied by counsel, namely "Cynthia Baldwin."[79] Again, Baldwin did

72. *Id.* at 829–30.

73. *Id.*

74. *Id.* at 830. In one of the underlying criminal cases, the appellate court disagreed with Baldwin's perspective on whether she had provided *Upjohn* warnings. Commonwealth v. Schultz, 133 A.3d 294, 325 (Pa. Super. Ct. 2016) ("Ms. Baldwin did not provide anything akin to *Upjohn* warnings."). The *Baldwin* court rejected Baldwin's argument that her administration of *Upjohn* warnings barred any claims she represented the witnesses individually because they were not interviewed as part of an internal investigation, but, instead in an "obvious potentially criminal matter" where they had received subpoenas issued to them personally. *Baldwin*, 225 A.3d at 836 n.11.

75. *Baldwin*, 225 A.3d at 831.

76. *Id.* (alterations in original).

77. *Id.*

78. *Id.* at 832.

79. *Id.*

not dispute this characterization. Essentially the same exchange occurred when Spanier had testified before the grand jury.[80]

Based on these exchanges, the *Baldwin* court found it "impossible to conclude . . . that the [three men] believed anything other than their personal interests were being protected by [Baldwin]."[81] Also, considering that she was the only attorney present when the judge advised the witnesses as to their rights to counsel, "it cannot be fathomed that [Baldwin] did not understand that she was representing them personally."[82] The court also noted that under the Pennsylvania Rules of Criminal Procedure and the Investigating Grand Jury Act, if Baldwin was not personal counsel for the witnesses, she would not have been permitted to be in the grand jury room when they testified.[83]

Having concluded that Baldwin represented the witnesses individually, the *Baldwin* court easily concluded that she had violated all the rules as charged by the ODC. Regarding Rule 1.1, the court agreed with the Disciplinary Board that Baldwin "'failed to exercise the legal knowledge, skill, thoroughness, and preparation reasonably necessary for the representation.'"[84] Supporting this finding was the fact that Baldwin "had no criminal law experience and had never represented a client before a grand jury."[85] It was clear that Baldwin did not understand the magnitude of the challenge she faced, with the OAG investigation clearly expanding beyond Sandusky's conduct. Despite the prospect of significant criminal liability exposure for the individuals and potentially "massive civil liability" on Penn State's part,[86] Baldwin "did very little to advance her clients' appearances before the grand jury."[87] She separately met with Curley and Schultz only once, never discussed what they were likely to be asked or how best to respond to anticipated questioning, and never even informed them of the types of crimes they might be subjecting themselves to by testifying.[88] Simply telling them to "tell the truth" was plainly inadequate.[89] The court was critical of Baldwin's failure to investigate the factual accounts she had been given, particularly since she had access to records from her other client, Penn State, a sophisticated institutional client with document retention capabilities. She never interviewed

80. *Id.*
81. *Id.* at 834.
82. *Id.*
83. *Id.* at 835.
84. *Id.* at 837 (quoting the Disciplinary Board report).
85. *Id.*
86. *Id.* at 837–38.
87. *Id.* at 838.
88. *Id.* at 838.
89. *See id.* ("Despite having three additional months to prepare Spanier for his grand jury testimony, the record does not reflect that she did anything more in this regard than she had done for Curley and Schultz.").

staff or searched e-mails or other electronic records.[90] Such an investigation was not only necessary to do a proper conflict of interest analysis but also to give competent advice to her individual clients on whether to invoke their rights against self-incrimination when they testified before the grand jury.[91]

Turning to Rule 1.7, the *Baldwin* court ruled that Baldwin had "committed multiple violations" in connection with her concurrent representation of Penn State, Curley, Schultz, and Spanier.[92] Again agreeing with the Disciplinary Board, the *Baldwin* court listed many ways in which Baldwin violated Rule 1.7, including (1) failing to recognize potential conflicts between Penn State and the individuals—with the university potentially needing to disassociate itself from anyone engaged in wrongdoing; (2) failing to recognize likely conflicts among the individuals—with Spanier, as president, potentially needing to isolate himself from first-level decisions and Curley and Schultz needing defenses that did not consider the other's defenses or levels of decision-making; (3) failing to act on discrepancies in the individuals' accounts before their grand jury testimony, most notably the clearly conflicting recollections as told to OAG's lawyer the morning prior to Curley and Schultz's testimony, which "cried out" for each witness to have personal counsel;[93] and (4) that it may have been in the best interest of any of the individuals to cooperate with OAG, which would or could have been detrimental to the others.[94] Her concurrent representation of Penn State and the individuals was "patently improper."[95]

With regard to Rule 1.6, the court emphasized that the prohibition on disclosure of client confidences is not limited to privileged communications but applies to all information relating to the representation regardless of the source.[96] Reviewing the substance of Baldwin's testimony to the grand jury, the court concluded that Baldwin had violated Rule 1.6 in many instances while revealing the substance of her communications with Curley, Schultz, and Spanier. The court rejected Baldwin's argument that the men had waived their attorney-client privilege in various court filings and in attacking her conduct as their personal counsel; the court filings had not been made until well after Baldwin had testified to the grand jury,[97] and nothing in Rule 1.6 authorized an attorney to "gratuitously incriminate a client" as she had done.[98]

90. *Id.* at 838–39.
91. *Id.* at 840.
92. *Id.*
93. *Id.* at 842–43.
94. *Id.* at 843.
95. *Id.*
96. *Id.* at 844.
97. *Id.* at 851–52.
98. *Id.* at 854.

Finally, the *Baldwin* court ruled that Baldwin had violated Rule 8.4(d), which prohibits an attorney from engaging "in conduct that is prejudicial to the administration of justice."[99] Baldwin's misconduct resulted in an inability to prosecute Curley, Schultz, and Spanier "on a wide number of criminal charges," which was prejudicial to the administration of justice.[100]

For her violations, Baldwin was publicly remanded and ordered to pay the costs of investigating and prosecuting the proceedings.[101]

The *Baldwin* fiasco provides many lessons:

- To point out the obvious, if you do not consider someone to be your client and a judge asks whether you represent the individual, you should unequivocally clarify that you do not. That is no time for silence, equivocation, or non-answers. Baldwin failed to clarify her claimed role when given multiple opportunities before the grand jury. When asked if she would be providing representation at the grand jury for both Curley and Schulz, Baldwin could and should have said, "I represent only Pennsylvania State University," or otherwise made clear whatever limitation or conditional representation she believed she was providing to the individuals. Her failure to do so caused many problems for many people, not just herself.
- Likewise, regardless of whether a judge or presiding officer raises the subject, if anyone says or implies that you are his attorney when that is not the case, you must promptly correct any such misstatements. For instance, an employee of an organizational defendant may be asked if the attorney appearing at the deposition on behalf of the organization is "your attorney," and it is not unheard of for the deponent to inaccurately respond by saying "yes." If this happens, the attorney should not sit silently by as Cynthia Baldwin did, but must interject and clarify whom she represents. Even without a direct question being put to the deponent about his representation, an examining attorney may make a statement or posit a question using the phrase "your attorney." This inaccuracy needs to be promptly corrected regardless.
- Lawyers for an organization are wise to confirm *Upjohn* warnings in writing, preferably via a document signed and dated by the employee contemporaneously with the interview that contains the exact language of the warnings that were given. This should eliminate disputes about what was said to the employee. In *Baldwin*, Baldwin believed she had given proper *Upjohn* warnings, but the court disagreed.

---

99. Pa. Rules of Prof'l Conduct R. 8.4(d) (2015); Model Rules of Prof'l Conduct R. 8.4(d) (2020).

100. *Baldwin*, 225 A.2d at 856.

101. *Id.* at 859.

- Although providing *Upjohn* warnings will almost always prevent lawyers from inadvertently becoming joint counsel for individuals, subsequent events may render the warnings ineffectual. Although Baldwin "did not provide anything akin to *Upjohn* warnings,"[102] had she done so, she may have negated any prophylactic effect by appearing with the witnesses at their grand jury testimony when they had no other counsel (and the law would not allow someone other than their lawyer to be in the room) and failing to correct the witnesses when they all identified her as being their lawyer.

E. Summary

Attorney-client relationships can be implied in various circumstances, potentially creating accidental clients to whom lawyers owe all the same duties they owe other clients. As *Baldwin* illustrates, accidental client representations can sometimes lead to disastrous consequences. The potential for accidental client relationships regularly surfaces when lawyers for an organization interact with the organization's employees or other constituents during internal investigations or government investigations. To avoid accidentally becoming an attorney for those constituents, attorneys must make clear that they represent the organization alone.

III. Impromptu Attorney-Client Relationships

The preceding portion of this chapter addressed problems stemming from lawyers accidentally creating attorney-client relationships with individual constituents of an existing organizational client. Part III addresses problems stemming from a related situation—that is, purposefully creating such relationships without adequately considering the professional responsibility ramifications.

A. The Duties and Unappreciated Risks of Jointly Representing Non-party Deponents

Employees of organizational litigants often are important fact witnesses in cases even though they are not parties to the litigation. As a result, an adversary may want to depose them. Lawyers representing organizations in litigation routinely produce organizational employees for depositions in cases in which the employees are merely fact witnesses. What should be a routine exercise for the organization's lawyer can, unfortunately, take a wrong turn if the lawyer agrees to also represent the employee in connection with the deposition. The consequences of the wrong turn may be an alleged conflict

102. Commonwealth v. Schultz, 133 A.3d 294, 325 (Pa. Super. Ct. 2016).

of interest on which a disqualification motion or ethics complaint is based or a breach of fiduciary duty or professional negligence claim against the lawyer grounded on an alleged conflict of interest. The basis for the alleged conflict of interest is the lawyer's representation of the employee in addition to the organization in circumstances where their interests were not aligned, with the employee claiming that he or she needed separate counsel.

Regardless of the precise scenario, lawyers in such cases typically failed to appreciate beforehand how the seemingly innocent joint representation of an employee in connection with a deposition could go wrong, let alone the implications of the choice to jointly represent an organization and its employee. A lawyer who represents both an organization and an individual witness owes duties to both clients. Representation of the individual witness forms a fiduciary relationship with the witness and triggers professional responsibility obligations to the witness-client, regardless of whether the witness is a low-level employee or an officer or director of the organization, the organization is paying the lawyer's fees, or the lawyer views the organization as her primary client.

1. *Obtaining the Organization's Consent to the Representation*

A lawyer for an organization who is contemplating representing an employee or other constituent of the organization in connection with a deposition or any other activity must first inform the organization of the possible representation.[103] The lawyer must then obtain the organization's consent to the joint representation.[104] Any such consent must be given by someone other than the prospective individual client.[105] Even if there is no apparent conflict of interest between the individual and the organization, the organization has the right to decide whether it wishes to be part of a joint representation. If the employee or lawyer or both expects the organization to pay for the employee's representation, the organization has the further right to decide whether it wants to incur the related expense.

2. *Scope of Representation*

Assuming the lawyer will represent the employee or other constituent, the next issue to consider is the scope of that person's representation, which

103. *See* Model Rules of Prof'l Conduct R. 1.4(a)(2) (2020) (obligating a lawyer to "reasonably consult with the client about the means by which the client's objectives are to be accomplished").

104. *See id.* R. 1.13(g) ("A lawyer representing an organization may also represent any of its directors, officers, employees, members, shareholders or other constituents, subject to the provisions of Rule 1.7. If the organization's consent to the dual representation is required by Rule 1.7, the consent shall be given by an appropriate official of the organization other than the individual who is to be represented, or by the shareholders.").

105. *Id.*

the lawyer may want to limit. Model Rule 1.2(a) permits limited scope representations, although any limitations must be reasonable under the circumstances and the client must give informed consent to them.[106] A limited scope representation "is one that limits or excludes services that the client would reasonably expect to be included in the representation under the circumstances."[107] The New York State Bar Association's Committee on Professional Ethics has identified several components of such representation for which the witness-client may reasonably expect to be part of the representation or for which the attorney would otherwise be responsible, including:

- Meeting with the witness-client before the deposition to prepare for questioning.
- Reviewing documents and other materials to understand issues and likely topics of questioning.
- Assessing whether potential questioning could expose the witness-client to criminal or civil liability and advising how to avoid or minimize that exposure. If potential liability relates to a practice area outside the attorney's expertise, the attorney may advise the witness-client to retain additional counsel in that area.
- Based on a review of the documents and pre-deposition discussions with the witness-client, assessing if there are potential conflicts of interest that may not have been previously anticipated.
- If the witness has been subpoenaed, helping the witness-client identify, collect, review, and produce documents as appropriate.
- Ensuring the deposition transcript is provided to the witness-client for review, assisting with preparation of an errata sheet if needed, and making sure the signed transcript is returned to the court reporter or opposing counsel.[108]

Again, any limitations on the scope of representation must be "reasonable under the circumstances."[109] There is no bright-line rule as to when limitations on representation of a witness-client are reasonable. Relevant considerations include:

- Whether the witness faces potential liability for her own conduct in connection with underlying events and whether the attorney plans to advise the witness on those risks.
- The sophistication of the witness and her experience with legal matters generally and deposition procedures in particular.

---

106. *Id.* R. 1.2(c).

107. N.Y. Eth. Op. 2016-2, 2016 WL 8997250, at *2 (N.Y. State Bar Ass'n, Comm. on Prof'l Ethics 2016) [hereinafter N.Y. Eth. Op. 2016-2].

108. *Id.* at *2–3.

109. Model Rules of Prof'l Conduct R. 1.2(c) (2020).

- Whether the attorney believes sufficient time has been allocated to prepare the witness's testimony.
- Whether the witness is sophisticated or experienced enough to handle the excluded tasks herself. For example, if document collection is excluded, is the witness capable of searching for and identifying responsive documents to the subpoena without the attorney's assistance?
- Assuming the party-client is paying for the witness's legal fees, whether the party-client has placed any conditions on the payment of those fees and what those conditions are.
- Assuming the party-client is paying the witness's legal fees, whether the party-client has sufficient financial resources to enable the lawyer to devote the necessary time to the representation of the witness.
- Whether there is reason to believe that the witness is being subjected to (or may be vulnerable to) undue pressure from the party-client regarding the witness's testimony.
- Whether the witness has access to separate counsel to advise her on matters that are excluded from the representation.[110]

If the limitations are reasonable, the lawyer must obtain the witness-client's informed consent to proceed with those limitations.[111] "Informed consent" is "the agreement by a person to a proposed course of conduct after the lawyer has communicated adequate information and explanation about the material risks of and reasonably available alternatives to the proposed course of conduct."[112] In assessing whether informed consent has been provided, the lawyer may consider the person's experience in legal matters generally and whether she is represented by other counsel.[113] In limited scope representations, it should be clear what services are to be provided and those that are not.[114] In the context of limited scope representation for a witness-client, attorneys should disclose and explain:

110. N.Y. Eth. Op. 2016-2, *supra* note 107, 2016 WL 8997250, at *4 (footnote omitted).

111. Model Rules of Prof'l Conduct R. 1.2(c) (2020).

112. *Id.* R. 1.0(e).

113. *Id.* R. 1.2(c) cmt. 6.

114. N.Y. Eth. Op. 2016-2, *supra* note 107, 2016 WL 8997250, at *5; *see also* ABA Comm. on Ethics & Prof'l Responsibility, Formal Op. 472, at 3 (2015) ("[A]lthough not required by Rule 1.2(c), the Committee nevertheless recommends that when lawyers provide limited-scope representation to a client, they confirm with the client the scope of the representation—including the tasks the lawyer will perform and not perform—in writing that the client can read, understand, and refer to later."); Colo. Bar Ass'n, Ethics Comm., Formal Op. 101, at 4–6 (Rev. 2006) [hereinafter Colo. Formal Op. 101] (explaining that lawyers providing limited scope services should clearly explain the limitations of the representation, including the types of services that are not being provided and the probable effect of limited representation on the client's rights and interests); D.C. Bar, Legal Ethics Comm., Op. 330 (2005) (stating that "a writing clearly explaining what is and is not encompassed within the agreement to provide services will be helpful in ensuring the parties' mutual understanding").

- What services are included in the representation;
- What services are excluded from the representation;
- The implications of excluding certain services from the representation, such as the possible need to retain separate counsel to advise on those matters and the risk that the witness may face liability or other consequences if she does not secure legal advice with respect to an excluded service;
- Who will be responsible for paying the lawyer's fees;
- The identity of the attorney's other client(s) in the matter;
- Whether there are any conflicts of interest between the witness and the lawyer's other client(s) and the implications of those conflicts of interest;
- What will happen if a conflict of interest arises in the future, including who the attorney will continue to represent;
- How confidential information will be treated in connection with the joint representation; and
- That the witness is not required to accept the limited scope representation and is free to retain separate counsel.[115]

Finally, for now, lawyers must remember that within the confines of a limited scope representation, they still owe the client all the duties they owe clients in other contexts, such as competence, communication, confidentiality, and diligence.[116] The limitation on the scope of the representation is, however, a factor to be considered in gauging the lawyer's fulfillment of those duties.[117]

B. Confidentiality in Joint Representation

A lawyer representing two clients in litigation—even if she represents one of them only for the limited purpose of a deposition—must understand her duty of confidentiality as between her two co-clients with respect to

115. N.Y. Eth. Op. 2016-2, *supra* note 107, 2016 WL 8997250, at *5.

116. *See, e.g.*, *In re* Seare, 493 B.R. 158, 188 (Bankr. D. Nev. 2013) ("[T]he duty of competence both informs and survives any and all limitations on the scope of services. . . . The level of inquiry and investigation required to discharge the duty of competence may be somewhat relaxed, however, under a limited scope agreement." (citations omitted)); Colo. Formal Op. 101, *supra* note 114, at 9 ("Attorneys must be aware that, even in the context of limited scope representation, all of the Colorado Rules of Professional Conduct apply, and the limited scope case should be conducted consistent with the attorney's professional obligations."); Or. Eth. Op. 2011-183, 2011 WL 11741924, at *2 n.3 (Or. State Bar Ass'n Bd. of Gov'rs 2011) ("A limited-scope representation does not absolve the lawyer from any of the duties imposed by the [Rules of Professional Conduct] as to the services undertaken."); Pa. Eth. Op. 2011-100, 2011 WL 7574467, at *5 (Phila. Bar Ass'n, Prof'l Guidance Comm. 2011) (explaining that all rules of professional conduct "which apply to any other engagement apply to a limited scope engagement," and listing several rules as examples).

117. Model Rules of Prof'l Conduct R. 1.2 cmt. 7 (2020).

information relating to the representation that either client shares with her. Under Model Rule 1.6, a lawyer cannot "reveal information relating to the representation of client unless the client gives informed consent, or the disclosures are impliedly authorized in order to carry out the representation" unless an exception applies.[118] Typically, this means that clients can expect that their lawyers will not share their communications with anyone else. But in a joint representation, things are more complicated. In addition to the duty of confidentiality, lawyers also owe clients a duty of loyalty, such that clients have the right to be informed of information relating to the representation that might affect their interests.[119]

Fundamentally, anything that one co-client shares with the lawyer concerning the case is information relating to the representation and is therefore confidential under Model Rule 1.6(a).[120] For the lawyer to share the information with anyone else, the client must consent to the disclosure, the disclosure must be authorized under Rule 1.6(b), or the disclosure must be impliedly authorized to carry out the representation.[121] The obvious complication given the language of Model Rule 1.6(a) is that *the lawyer must keep the information confidential from the other co-client* unless one of the exceptions to Model Rule 1.6(a) applies or the disclosure is impliedly authorized to carry out the representation.[122] Of course, a lawyer's inability to share information between co-clients relating to their joint representation

118. *Id.* R. 1.6(a).

119. *Id.* R. 1.4 & 1.7. cmt. 31.

120. In comparison, the prevailing rule regarding the attorney-client privilege "is that, as between commonly represented clients, the privilege does not attach." D.C. RULES OF PROF'L CONDUCT R. 1.7 cmt. 15 (2019); *see also* Fla. Eth. Op. 95-4, 1997 WL 307142, at *5–6 (Fla. State Bar Ass'n, Comm. on Prof'l Ethics 1997) [hereinafter Fla. Eth. Op. 95-4] ("Communications relevant to a matter of common interest between joint clients generally are not privileged as a matter of law.").

121. MODEL RULES OF PROF'L CONDUCT R. 1.6(a) (2020).

122. *See, e.g.*, An Unnamed Att'y v. Ky Bar Ass'n, 186 S.W.3d 741, 743 (Ky. 2006) ("When the investigation revealed that one of the clients was involved in the homicide, [the lawyer] had a duty with respect to that client to keep that fact confidential."); ABA Comm. on Ethics & Prof'l Responsibility, Formal Op. 480, at 6 (2018) ("Each client is entitled to the benefit of Rule 1.6 with respect to information relating to that client's representation, and a lawyer whose representation of multiple clients is not prohibited by Rule 1.7 is bound to protect the information of each client from disclosure, whether to other clients or otherwise."); D.C. Bar, Legal Ethics Comm., Op. 296, at 1 (2000) ("The mere fact of joint representation, without more, does not provide a basis for implied authorization to disclose one client's confidences to another."); Fla. Eth. Op. 95-4, *supra* note 120, 1997 WL 307142, at *5–6 (rejecting the contrary position); Phila. Eth. Op. 94-8, 1994 WL 187068, at *2 (Phila. Bar Ass'n, Prof'l Guidance Comm. 1994) [hereinafter Phila. Eth. Op. 94-8] (stating that "in undertaking a joint representation counsel are bound by the Rule 1.6 obligation to each client"). *But see* N.Y. Eth. Op. 2016-2, *supra* note 107, 2016 WL 8997250, at *7 ("Among joint clients, there is a presumption that confidential information that is material to the joint representation will be shared among the joint clients, unless some exception applies."); RESTATEMENT (THIRD) OF THE LAW GOVERNING LAWYERS § 60 cmt. l (2000) ("Sharing of information among . . . co-clients with respect to the . . . matter involved in the representation is normal and typically expected.").

has serious implications for the lawyer's Model Rule 1.4 communication duties, and in some instances it may create a conflict of interest that necessitates the lawyer's withdrawal from the joint representation.

Accordingly, a lawyer who agrees to represent two or more clients in the same matter should at the outset of the representation address with the clients the interplay between the lawyer's duty of confidentiality and the clients' joint representation. The lawyer should explain the possibility that her duty of confidentiality could impair her ability to keep both clients reasonably informed about the status of the matter or possibly create a disqualifying conflict of interest, and obtain the clients' informed consent to an arrangement whereby anything either client shares with her regarding the matter will be shared with the other.

In comparison, the prevailing rule regarding the attorney-client privilege "is that, as between commonly represented clients, the privilege does not attach."[123] Consequently, joint clients should also know that the attorney-client privilege will not protect as confidential their separate communications with the lawyer during joint representation in any later litigation between them.

Assuming the clients agree to waive confidentiality as between one another, the lawyer should document their consent in the engagement letter for the matter. Each client should receive a copy of the engagement letter.

Obtaining the co-clients' consent to sharing all material information related to the representation allows the lawyer to fulfill her duty to communicate with both clients and avoid conflicts of interest grounded in the duty of confidentiality otherwise owed to each client. Furthermore, by discussing the situation with the co-clients at the outset of the representation, the lawyer avoids any misunderstanding on the clients' part. Although it may be undesirable for numerous reasons, a client who has material information related to the representation that it does not want the other client to know will be aware that it should not share that information with the lawyer. Better yet, such a client or potential client will forgo joint representation and retain separate counsel.

New York State Bar Association Formal Ethics Opinion 2016-2 posits that, with some limitations and exceptions, there is a presumption that confidential information material to the joint representation will be shared among the joint clients.[124] This view, however, is at best a minority view, and for good reasons.

First, there is no authority for it in Model Rule 1.6 or its comments. Indeed, this claimed presumption is contrary to Model Rule 1.6(a). As a

123. D.C. Rules of Prof'l Conduct R. 1.7 cmt. 15 (2019); *see also* Fla. Eth. Op. 95-4, *supra* note 120, 1997 WL 307142, at *5–6 ("Communications relevant to a matter of common interest between joint clients generally are not privileged as a matter of law.").

124. N.Y. Eth. Op. 2016-2, *supra* note 107, 2016 WL 8997250, at *5.

comment to Model Rule 1.6 explains, "[a] fundamental principle in the client-lawyer relationship is that, in the absence of the client's informed consent, the lawyer must not reveal information relating to the representation."[125] New York Opinion 2016-2 incorrectly concludes that a presumption of shared confidence exists "because the lawyer has an equal duty of loyalty to each client, and each client has the right to be informed of anything on bearing on the representation that might affect that client's interests."[126] But the commentary to Model Rule 1.7 explains that, because of this bilateral duty of loyalty, a lawyer should "advise each client that information will be shared and that the lawyer will have to withdraw if one client decided some matter material to the representation should be kept from the other."[127] Counseling lawyers to expressly advise clients in this regard, and telling them that failing to give consent to the sharing of information related to the representation may result in the lawyer's disqualifications, contradicts—not supports—the notion that lawyers may presume that co-clients' confidences may be shared.

Second, "accurately predicting the expectations of a typical client in a given situation is risky business."[128] There is no reason for a lawyer to take such a risk where it may easily be avoided through the client's agreement in advance regarding whether information will be shared.

Third, even where one client's information is material to the joint representation, it may be detrimental to the communicating client or adverse to the other client, such that the communicating client does not want the lawyer to share it with the other client. To recognize the claimed presumption in that circumstance would gut the communicating client's expectation of confidentiality, destroy the clients' community of interests, place the lawyer squarely in a conflict of interest, and harm the client in the process.[129]

Although in some cases a lawyer's disclosure of one co-client's confidential information to the other co-client may be impliedly authorized to carry out the representation,[130] the mere fact of joint representation does not constitute implied authorization to disclose one co-client's information

125. Model Rules of Prof'l Conduct R. 1.6 cmt. 2 (2020).

126. N.Y. Eth. Op. 2016-2, *supra* note 107, 2016 WL 8997250, at *5 (quoting N.Y. Rules of Prof'l Conduct R. 1.7 cmt. 31 (2016)).

127. Model Rules of Prof'l Conduct R. 1.7 cmt. 31 (2020).

128. Fla. Eth. Op. 95-4, *supra* note 120, 1997 WL 307142, at *5.

129. *Id.* at *4. Of course, as previously noted, a co-client's instruction to the lawyer not to share material information concerning the representation with the other co-client will also create a conflict of interest for the lawyer absent the joint clients' agreement that there will be no confidences between them insofar as information material to the representation is concerned.

130. *See* Phila. Eth. Op. 94-8, *supra* note 122, 1994 WL 187068, at *2 (reasoning that where a co-client does not make a cautionary comment to the lawyer about keeping information confidential, it is more likely that the lawyer is impliedly authorized to share the information with other co-clients).

regarding the representation to the other co-client.[131] Similarly, while there is some authority for the argument that there is a presumption that confidential information material to a joint representation will be shared among the joint clients,[132] that clear minority position is not supportable for the reasons explained here.

C. Conflicts of Interest in Joint Representation

When a lawyer is asked to represent a non-party witness at a deposition, the attorney must assess whether the joint representation will create a conflict of interest with the lawyers' organizational client or other clients, such as other defendants named in the suit that are also being jointly represented. Unfortunately, lawyers for organizational parties too often overlook conflicts of interest when they agree to represent a non-party witness solely for purposes of a deposition. In this situation, there may be no conflict of interest, a consentable conflict, or a non-consentable conflict.[133] In making this determination, the lawyer must (1) identify the client or clients involved, (2) determine whether a conflict of interest exists, (3) decide whether the representation may be undertaken despite the conflict (i.e., decide whether the conflict is consentable), and (4) if so, consult with the affected clients and obtain their informed consent, which must then be confirmed in writing.[134]

The circumstances in which a lawyer establishes an attorney-client relationship with a non-party witness may well come about on short notice or otherwise without the parties having extended prior discussions. Consequently, the lawyer may have limited time and information about the witness to discover or recognize conflicts before the attorney-client relationship is established. Accordingly, the lawyer must be particularly attentive to new information that she learns about her new client—whether learned during pre-deposition preparation meetings, while the witness is testifying, or during conversations over breaks in the deposition.

1. Yanez v. Plummer

Yanez v. Plummer[135] brightly illuminates deposition conflicts and therefore merits discussion, along with an explanation of options available to lawyers

131. *See* Fla. Eth. Op. 95-4, *supra* note 120, 1997 WL 307142, at *5 (discussing confidentiality as between joint clients and stating that "accurately predicting the expectations of a typical client in a given situation is risky business" in rejecting the presumption that information material to the joint clients' representation will be shared between them).

132. *See, e.g.*, Alaska Bar Ass'n, Ethics Comm., Op. 2020-1, at 4 (2020) [hereinafter Alaska Op. 2020-1]; Restatement (Third) of the Law Governing Lawyers § 60 cmt. l (2000).

133. Alaska Op. 2020-1, *supra* note 132, at 4.

134. Model Rules of Prof'l Conduct R. 1.7 cmt. 2 (2020).

135. 164 Cal. Rptr. 3d 309 (Ct. App. 2013).

for avoiding related professional liability risks. The plaintiff in that case, Michael Yanez, worked as a machinist for the Union Pacific Railroad. In September 2008, Yanez and another Union Pacific machinist, Robert Garcia, were replacing locomotive motors. The locomotives were located over a "drop pit."[136] The men were using a "drop table" to raise the motors from the drop pit.[137] Yanez was operating the drop table when Garcia went into the drop pit to retrieve a tool, fell, and was injured. Yanez was the only witness to these events other than Garcia.

Yanez provided Union Pacific with two written statements concerning the accident.[138] He wrote the first statement shortly after the accident at his immediate supervisor's request. In that statement Yanez wrote that he "was watching [the] motor come up while Boby went downstairs & went to retrieve tool *had sliped [sic] & fell on concrete floor, soaked in oil & grease*."[139] Sometime later, a higher-ranking Union Pacific supervisor directed Yanez to write a second statement because his first statement lacked detail. This time Yanez wrote in pertinent part: "I was looking down at [the] motor coming up, but I could see Boby going downstairs & he walked out on [the] concrete floor. *I saw Boby slip & fall down on [the] oil soaked floor*, he was lying on his back when I came downstairs to help him."[140] Compare the italicized portions of the statements and the difference is apparent: in the first statement Yanez reported that he did not see Garcia fall, while in the second statement he wrote that he did see Garcia fall.

Garcia sued the railroad under the Federal Employers Liability Act (FELA), and Union Pacific appointed one of its in-house lawyers, Brian Plummer, to defend the lawsuit. Garcia requested Yanez's deposition. Yanez met with Plummer the morning of the day of his deposition in June 2009. Plummer confirmed that Yanez had not seen Garcia fall and asked Yanez about the conditions at the accident site.[141] Plummer and Yanez did not discuss Yanez's statements.[142] Yanez expressed concern about his job security because his testimony "was likely to be unfavorable to Union Pacific," and

136. *Id.* at 310.
137. *Id.*
138. *Id.* at 310–11.
139. *Id.* at 311.
140. *Id.*
141. *Id.*
142. *Id.* According to the decision in a subsequent attorney disciplinary proceeding, Plummer testified that he did not know about Yanez's first statement when they met to prepare for the deposition; he only had a copy of Yanez's second statement, even though both statements had been in Union Pacific's possession for at least nine months. Yanez did not tell Plummer about the first statement because he had forgotten about it and, in any event, he thought that the only difference between his two statements was that they were "worded differently." Plummer never asked him whether he had given more than one statement. *In re* Plummer, Case No. 13-O-175515-PEM, slip op. at 3 & n.3 (Cal. State Bar Ct. June 4, 2015).

he "asked Plummer who would 'protect' him at the deposition."[143] Plummer responded "that Yanez was a Union Pacific employee and *Plummer was his attorney for the deposition*; as long as Yanez told the truth in the deposition, Yanez's job would not be affected."[144]

In response to questions from Garcia's lawyer at the deposition, Yanez testified that he did not witness the accident but became aware of it shortly after it happened.[145] Garcia's lawyer did not pursue this issue. After eliciting testimony from Yanez about allegedly unsafe conditions at the work site, Garcia's lawyer passed the witness. Plummer then questioned Yanez. Plummer confirmed Yanez's testimony that he did not see Garcia fall and that Garcia was not in Yanez's view when he fell.[146] Plummer then turned to Yanez's statements; however, he only marked as an exhibit the second statement in which Yanez wrote that he had seen Garcia slip and fall.[147] Yanez testified in passing that "he 'had worded [his second statement] wrong,'" but Plummer asked no follow-up questions.[148] As a result, he never gave Yanez the opportunity to explain any discrepancies between the two statements.[149]

The director of the Union Pacific locomotive facility, Dennis Magures, attended Yanez's deposition as a corporate representative.[150] Thinking he heard Yanez testify contrary to his second statement, Magures obtained a copy of the deposition transcript to confirm that Yanez had contradicted his second statement.[151] Union Pacific then initiated disciplinary proceedings against Yanez for lying in his second statement. The railroad acknowledged that the disciplinary charges arose out of Yanez's deposition where, under oath, he had contradicted his second written statement. In an August 2009 disciplinary hearing, Yanez tried to explain that he meant to write in his second statement that he saw that Garcia had slipped and fallen rather than that he actually saw him fall, but in his haste to complete the statement, he effectively misspoke.[152] Union Pacific fired him for dishonesty anyway.[153]

Yanez sued Union Pacific for wrongful discharge. He also sued Plummer for legal malpractice, breach of fiduciary duty, and fraud.[154] The essential issue in Yanez's case against Plummer was whether Plummer's conduct prox-

143. *Yanez*, 164 Cal. Rptr. 3d at 311.
144. *Id.* (emphasis added).
145. *Id.*
146. *Id.*
147. *Id.*
148. *Id.* at 311–12.
149. *In re* Plummer, Case No. 13-O-175515-PEM, slip op. at 4 (Cal. State Bar Ct. June 4, 2015).
150. *Yanez*, 164 Cal. Rptr. 3d at 312.
151. *Id.*
152. *Id.*
153. *Id.*
154. *Id.* at 310.

imately caused Yanez's termination. The trial court agreed with Plummer that it did not and awarded Plummer summary judgment.[155] Yanez appealed the judgment, and the California Court of Appeal reversed the trial court.

After reciting the standard for determining causation, the *Yanez* court observed that Yanez and Union Pacific were adverse to one another in Garcia's case because Yanez was the only witness to the accident and he knew of allegedly unsafe work conditions that may have contributed to Garcia's fall.[156] Relatedly, then-California Rule of Professional Conduct 3-310(C)(1) provided that a lawyer could not accept the representation of more than one client in a matter in which the clients' interests potentially conflict without each client's informed consent.[157] California Rule 3-310(C)(2) similarly stated that a lawyer could not accept or continue the representation of more than one client in a matter in which the clients' interests actually conflict.[158] Nonetheless, Plummer advised Yanez that he would represent him at the deposition while, at the same time, he was representing Union Pacific in Garcia's case.[159] In opposing summary judgment, Yanez offered evidence that Plummer neither told him about the conflict of interest with Union Pacific nor obtained his written consent to represent him despite the conflict.[160] Continuing, the court observed that:

> [P]ursuant to questioning from Garcia's counsel . . . Yanez testified adversely to Union Pacific regarding unsafe work conditions and acknowledged that he did not "witness" Garcia's accident. Then Plummer, without having prepared Yanez for what was coming, had Yanez confirm during the deposition that he did not "see" Garcia slip and fall, only to spring upon Yanez his second statement, in which Yanez stated the opposite. Plummer did not provide Yanez a chance to explain this discrepancy; nor did Plummer mark as a deposition exhibit (as he did the second statement) Yanez's first statement, which effectively acknowledged that Yanez did not see Garcia slip and fall.[161]

As Yanez argued at summary judgment based on this evidence:

> "Plummer's violation of his legal obligations to represent his client, Yanez, was calculated to portray 'in the worst possible light' Yanez's [deposition] testimony in order to benefit Plummer's other client at the deposition, Union Pacific, [which] then relied on that 'worst possible light,' [via facility director Magures and other Union Pacific personnel,] to fire Yanez."[162]

155. *Id.*
156. *Id.* at 313.
157. Cal. Rules of Prof'l Conduct R. 3-310(C)(1) (2005).
158. *Id.* R. 3-310(C)(2).
159. *Yanez*, 164 Cal. Rptr. 3d at 313–14.
160. *Id.* at 314.
161. *Id.*
162. *Id.* (quoting Yanez's brief).

Plummer argued that he played no role in Yanez's termination because (1) he was not involved in Yanez's preparation of his second statement, (2) Yanez admitted to Garcia's lawyer in the deposition that he did not see Garcia fall before Plummer questioned him, (3) the railroad fired Yanez following a disciplinary hearing, (4) Yanez had the chance at the hearing to explain discrepancies in his statements, and (5) he had no role in revealing Yanez's deception or in the disciplinary process.[163] The court disagreed:

> [I]t [was] true Yanez wrote in his second statement that he "saw" Garcia slip and fall, and it is true Yanez first admitted to Garcia's counsel in the deposition that he did not "witness" Garcia's "accident." But it was Plummer who highlighted Yanez's deposition testimony that he did not "see" Garcia slip; it was Plummer who presented the second statement at the deposition; it was Plummer who got Yanez, *under oath at the deposition*, to effectively admit that his deposition testimony conflicted with the second statement; it was Plummer who did not offer Yanez a chance to explain this discrepancy; and it was Plummer who failed to present the first statement as an exhibit at Yanez's deposition.[164]

In short, Yanez had presented a triable issue of material fact as to whether he would have been fired but for Plummer's alleged breach of fiduciary duty, professional negligence, and fraud.[165] Summary judgment for Plummer was therefore inappropriate. The court reversed the trial court's grant of summary judgment to Plummer and awarded Yanez his costs on appeal.[166]

D. Lessons from Yanez

The holding in *Yanez* pivots on the attorney-client relationship between Yanez and Plummer. It is therefore important to understand how this relationship arose.

It appears from the opinion that until Plummer told Yanez he "was his attorney for the deposition," they had no attorney-client relationship.[167] There was no evidence that Plummer had dealt with Yanez in a manner that might have created a de facto or implied attorney-client relationship. Although Yanez was a Union Pacific employee, that status did not derivatively make him Plummer's client.[168] Yanez's communications with Plummer

---

163. *Id.*

164. *Id.* at 315.

165. *Id.*

166. *Id.* at 316.

167. *See also* State *ex rel.* Stivrins v. Flowers, 729 N.W.2d 311, 317 (Neb. 2007) (explaining that a lawyer created an attorney-client relationship with a witness by agreeing to represent him as his lawyer at a deposition).

168. *See* Restatement (Third) of the Law Governing Lawyers § 96 cmt. b (2000) (explaining that "[b]y representing the organization, a lawyer does not thereby also form a client-lawyer

about matters that were relevant to him as well as relevant to Union Pacific could not alone have created an attorney-client relationship between the men.[169] In sum, until Plummer declared himself Yanez's attorney for the deposition, Yanez was simply an unrepresented non-party fact witness who happened to work for Plummer's client.

Plummer might have thought he needed to represent Yanez to be entitled to object to improper questions posed by Garcia's lawyer. If so, Plummer was mistaken. Plummer's role as counsel for Union Pacific gave him standing to object to what he considered improper questions by Garcia's lawyer.[170]

Finally, Plummer might have agreed to represent Yanez because Yanez asked, "who would 'protect' him at the deposition,"[171] and Plummer was trying to be reassuring. But if that was the reason, Plummer misunderstood Yanez's concern. Yanez wanted protection against adverse employment action by Union Pacific—not protection against questioning by Garcia's lawyer.[172] Even assuming that Plummer misunderstood Yanez's apprehension, as noted above, Plummer did not need to represent Yanez to resist objectionable questioning by Garcia's lawyer. Again, Plummer's status as counsel for Union Pacific gave him standing to object to questions by Garcia's lawyer.

If Plummer worried that his joint representation of Yanez and the railroad might pose a conflict of interest, he perhaps thought he could avoid any conflict by limiting his representation of Yanez to the deposition. As noted earlier, however, limiting the scope of a representation does not eliminate lawyers' duties to clients—it merely reduces the likelihood that a problem will arise. Plus, Plummer could not have objectively believed that he could avoid conflicts between Union Pacific and Yanez by limiting Yanez's representation to his deposition in Garcia's case. Yanez's potential deposition testimony was at the core of the conflict.

Assuming Plummer did not want an attorney-client relationship with Yanez, he might have handled the situation differently when Yanez expressed

---

relationship with all or any individuals employed by it"); MODEL RULES OF PROF'L CONDUCT R. 1.13(a) (2020) (explaining that a lawyer employed or retained by an organization represents the organization); *see also* New Destiny Treatment Ctr., Inc. v. Wheeler, 950 N.E.2d 157, 163 (Ohio 2011) ("[A]n attorney employed or retained by a corporation represents the organization acting through its constituents; the attorney does not owe allegiance to a stockholder, director, officer, or other person connected with the corporation.").

169. Hackett v. Feeney, No. 2:09-cv-02075-RLH-LRL, 2010 WL 4102911, at *5 (D. Nev. Oct. 18, 2010).

170. This conclusion flows from the undisputed fact that lawyers representing parties at trial are entitled to object to questions posed by opposing counsel to non-party witnesses, and direct and cross-examination in depositions is conducted as it would be at trial. *See* FED. R. CIV. P. 30(c)(1) ("The examination and cross-examination of a deponent proceed as they would at trial under the Federal Rules of Evidence, except Rules 103 and 615.").

171. *Yanez*, 164 Cal. Rptr. 3d at 311.

172. *Id.*

concern about testifying adversely to Union Pacific and asked who would protect him at his deposition. For example, Plummer could have said:

> Mr. Yanez, I represent the railroad and I will attend your deposition with you as the railroad's lawyer. I will object to any questions Mr. Garcia's lawyer asks you that I believe are improper. I have that right as a lawyer for the railroad. Union Pacific expects you to testify truthfully. Plus, you will be under oath, so you must testify truthfully.

Understandably, Yanez might have responded to such an explanation by asking Plummer whether he needed a lawyer. Plummer could not have given him "legal advice, other than the advice to secure counsel" because he knew or reasonably should have known that Yanez's interests actually or potentially conflicted with Union Pacific's interests.[173] Plummer thus had three reasonable choices. First, he could have said, "Mr. Yanez, you're not my client and I therefore cannot give you legal advice." Second, he could have said, "Mr. Yanez, if you want to get a lawyer, that's up to you." Third, he could have gently but firmly advised Yanez to retain counsel.

Regarding the last point, it is worth asking whether advising Yanez to obtain his separate counsel would have posed a conflict of interest for Plummer because it would have impaired Union Pacific's ability to obtain information important to its defense of Garcia's lawsuit. The short answer to this question is no. Again, Model Rule 4.3 provides that in "dealing on behalf of a client with a person who is not represented by counsel . . . [a] lawyer shall not give legal advice to [the] unrepresented person, other than the advice to secure counsel, if the lawyer knows or reasonably should know that the interests of [the unrepresented] person are or have a reasonable possibility of being in conflict with the interests of the client."[174] Model Rule 4.3 would not be written as it is if by advising an unrepresented person to secure counsel in the face of a possible conflict of interest a lawyer was simultaneously laboring under or creating a conflict of interest. That would be an absurd result. Of course, courts interpret ethics rules according to the same principles that govern statutory interpretation,[175] and courts interpret statutes to avoid absurd results.[176] Courts therefore must interpret ethics rules to avoid

173. Model Rules of Prof'l Conduct R. 4.3 (2020).

174. *Id.*

175. Ferris, Thompson & Zweig, Ltd. v. Esposito, 90 N.E.3d 400, 405 (Ill. 2017); Law Offices of Jeffrey Sherbow, PC v. Fieger & Fieger, PC, 930 N.W.2d 416, 424 (Mich. Ct. App. 2019) (quoting Morris & Doherty, P.C. v. Lockwood, 672 N.W.2d 884, 888 (Mich. Ct. App. 2003)); Comm'n for Lawyer Discipline v. Hanna, 513 S.W.3d 175, 178 (Tex. App. 2016).

176. Cen v. Att'y Gen., 825 F.3d 177, 194 (3d Cir. 2016); Compton Unified Sch. Dist. v. Addison, 598 F.3d 1181, 1184 (9th Cir. 2010); Treadway v. Gateway Chevrolet Oldsmobile, Inc., 362 F.3d 971, 976 (7th Cir. 2004); Bilderback v. McNabb, 474 P.3d 247, 251 (Colo. App. 2020); *In re* Claim of Roberts for Att'y Fees, 949 N.W.2d 299, 319 (Neb. 2020); Brossart v. Janke, 942 N.W.2d 856, 861 (N.D. 2020).

absurd results.[177] As a result, courts must interpret Model Rule 4.3 to hold that a lawyer who advises an unrepresented witness to seek counsel does not create a conflict of interest in the process.

E. Final Considerations Relating to the Potential Representation of Witness-Deponents

Organizations often want their lawyers to represent their employees in litigation in which both the organization and the employee are parties for the simple reason that it is more economical than hiring separate counsel for the employee. There is nothing inherently wrong about an organization trying to achieve such economy. In many cases, there is no conflict of interest when a lawyer represents an organization and its employee. In others, conflicts can be cured through the informed consent of the organization and the employee. Lawyers should nevertheless undertake joint representations carefully. A lawyer generally should not agree to represent an organization and its employee in litigation without reasonably inquiring into whether joint representation is possible. For example, conflicts that are not apparent when the organization's general counsel assigns the matter may be discovered in an initial meeting with the employee or exposed in discovery. Unfortunately, when an organization asks a lawyer to represent its employee too, even meeting with the employee preliminarily may pose challenges because the employee is then a prospective client within the meaning of Model Rule 1.18 and enjoys the rights and protections that status affords.[178] Depending on what the employee tells the lawyer, the lawyer may be disqualified from representing the organization in the litigation.[179] In other cases, employees may be aware of conflicts of interest that cause them to request separate counsel.

If a lawyer chooses to jointly represent an organization and its employee in litigation, it may be possible to structure the engagement so that if a conflict develops, the lawyer may continue to represent the organization and withdraw from the employee's representation.[180] Because this arrangement embodies an advance waiver of conflicts of interest, the uncertainty that generally surrounds judicial enforcement of advance waivers must be taken

177. *See* Chism v. Tri-State Constr., Inc., 374 P.3d 193, 207 (Wash. Ct. App. 2016) (quoting *In re* Marriage of McDermott, 307 P.3d 717, 727 (Wash. Ct. App. 2013)).

178. *See* Model Rules of Prof'l Conduct R. 1.18(a) (2020) ("A person who consults with a lawyer about the possibility of forming a client-lawyer relationship with respect to a matter is a prospective client.").

179. *Id.* R. 1.18(c).

180. *See, e.g., In re* Rite Aid Corp. Sec. Litig., 139 F. Supp. 2d 649, 655–60 (E.D. Pa. 2001) (declining to disqualify law firm); Zador Corp. v. Kwan, 37 Cal. Rptr. 2d 754, 759–63 (Ct. App. 1995) (permitting this approach).

Certainly, some threats are justified. If a client has a valid claim, for instance, a lawyer may ethically threaten the alleged wrongdoer with a lawsuit to enforce that claim.[2] Similarly, a lawyer may ethically assert that unless an adversary fulfills its perceived obligations to the lawyer's client, for example, the client will pursue "all available legal remedies."[3] In some instances, another lawyer's or party's conduct may be unethical or sanctionable. The issue is how or where to draw the line between legitimate and illegitimate threats.

This chapter examines the oft-discussed subject of civility and the opposite side of the same coin, or incivility. It also addresses saber-rattling by lawyers, which includes (1) threats of criminal charges or prosecution intended solely to achieve an advantage in a civil matter and (2) threats of professional disciplinary action against other counsel.

II. Civility

"Civility is basic and fundamental."[4] The other side of the same coin is "incivility." Personal attacks on others, boorish behavior, rudeness, insulting remarks, and obstructionist conduct and unfair litigation tactics all fall under the general rubric of incivility.

There are numerous reported decisions in which lawyers have been penalized in one fashion or another for uncivil behavior.[5] One of the most amazing cases to date involved Los Angeles lawyer Christopher Hook. While representing his clients in a dispute with Allstate Insurance Co., Hook barraged the opposing lawyers with offensive e-mail messages. In e-mails to one of the opposing lawyers, Peter Klee, Hook wrote, among myriad other insults, "Fuck you crooks. Eat a bowl of dicks."; "I am going to let the long

2. Att'y M v. Miss. Bar, 621 So. 2d 220, 225 (Miss. 1992).

3. Cal. Eth. Op. 1991-124, 1991 WL 165018, at *2 (Cal. State Bar, Comm. on Prof'l Responsibility & Conduct 1991).

4. Kohlmayer v. Nat'l R.R. Passenger Corp., 124 F. Supp. 2d 877, 879 (D.N.J. 2000).

5. *See, e.g.*, Golden v. Clear Advantage Mktg., No. 4:16-cv-00529-JAJ-CFB, 2020 WL 2516671, at *8–29 (S.D. Iowa Mar. 30, 2020) (reprimanding an out-of-state lawyer who was admitted pro hac vice for (1) threatening opposing counsel with physical harm and financial ruin; (2) falsely accusing opposing counsel of improprieties; (3) threatening an individual party with financial and personal ruin; (4) repeatedly disparaging Iowa lawyers through slurs, innuendo, and profanity; (5) intimidating and threatening court reporters; and (6) impugning the integrity, competence, and impartiality of the distinguished mediator); LendUS, LLC v. Goede, No. 2018-0233-SG, 2018 WL 6498674, at *4–6, 8–10 (Del. Ch. Dec. 10, 2018) (allowing a lawyer to withdraw his pro hac vice admission after the lawyer insulted and abused a witness during his deposition, was physically menacing during the deposition, accused the witness of using drugs and alcohol, told the witness he was using little words so that the opposing lawyer could understand him, and repeatedly belittled the opposing lawyer—once asking him if he had washed his hands after using the bathroom).

dick of the law fuck Allstate for all of us."; "Hey Klee you Cumstain the demand is now 302 million. Pay up fuckface."; "Peter when you are done felating your copy boy tell Allstate the demand is now 305 million."; and "Hey shit for brains. Allstate owes my clients a lot of money. It's due yesterday. Pay up fucktard or you will be lucky to work as a notary public in El Cajon."[6] Hook also told Klee, "I know where you live," and identified Klee's home address and his wife by name.[7] Hook amazingly defended his writings as "language [that] was used 'for effect,' similar to bluster or 'puffery' and was not intended to actually [be] considered personal insults."[8] The district court was unpersuaded. The court invoked its inherent powers to sanction Hook for his "bad faith" conduct and awarded Allstate just over $17,000 in attorneys' fees.[9]

A. Uncivil Behavior as Unethical Behavior

Uncivil behavior clearly can rise to the level of unethical conduct. Ethics rules amply provide for the discipline of uncivil lawyers in appropriate circumstances. A lawyer may violate multiple rules in any given case.

1. Model Rule 3.2

To start, Model Rule 3.2 provides that a lawyer "shall make reasonable efforts to expedite litigation" consistent with the client's interests.[10] Although Model Rule 3.2 refers to expediting litigation, the rule does not require the delay of litigation for a violation.[11] Conduct by a lawyer that causes other parties to waste time and money or that squanders judicial resources may violate Rule 3.2.[12]

Lawyers' uncivil behavior may rise to a level that violates Rule 3.2.[13] Lawyers who insult or intimidate witnesses, obstruct depositions, or harass other participants in the litigation process are not making reasonable efforts to expedite litigation. Instead, such behavior delays and impedes the resolution of disputes by distracting the parties and their counsel; spawning

6. Staci Zaretsky, *Small-Firm Lawyer Tells Biglaw Team to "Eat Bowl of Dicks" During Settlement Negotiations*, Above the Law (Dec. 5, 2019, 12:45 PM), http://www.abovethelaw.com.

7. Amanda Bronstad, *Judge Demands Resignation of Lawyer Who Wrote Profanity-laced Emails*, Recorder (Jan. 16, 2019, 6:32 PM), https://law.com/therecorder.

8. Zaretsky, *supra* note 6.

9. Baker v. Allstate Ins. Co., No. 2:19-cv-08024-ODW (JCx), 2020 WL 978729, at *2–5 (C.D. Cal. Feb. 28, 2020).

10. Model Rules of Prof'l Conduct R. 3.2 (2020).

11. Att'y Grievance Comm'n of Md. v. Mixter, 109 A.3d 1, 59 (Md. 2015).

12. *Id.* at 59–60 (discussing a lawyer's many frivolous motions).

13. Muster v. Muster, 921 A.2d 756, 766 (Del. Fam. Ct. 2005).

otherwise unnecessary motions and hearings, with accompanying expense; making witnesses reluctant or unwilling to participate in the litigation process; and wasting judicial resources. A lawyer's uncivil behavior is not consistent with a client's interests, either, because it increases the client's costs and may reduce the client's chance of success by motivating an adversary to litigate with a vigor or thoroughness that otherwise would have been lacking.

Uncivil behavior is not limited to verbal abuse, profanity, and the like. This is especially true in depositions, where lawyers can disrupt reasonable inquiry by unreasonably coaching witnesses both on and off the record, interrupting the questioner, making knowingly frivolous objections, or improperly instructing the witness not to answer questions.[14] This kind of behavior potentially violates Model Rule 3.2 and may further violate Model Rule 3.4(a), which provides that a lawyer shall not "unlawfully obstruct another party's access to evidence."[15]

2. *Model Rule 3.5(d)*

Model Rule 3.5(d) states that a lawyer shall not "engage in conduct intended to disrupt a tribunal."[16] As a comment to the rule explains, "[r]efraining from abusive or obstreperous conduct is a corollary of [an] advocate's right to speak on behalf of litigants."[17] An arbitration is a tribunal for Model Rule 3.5(d) purposes.[18] A deposition is also considered to be a proceeding before a tribunal, meaning that a lawyer's uncivil behavior in a deposition

---

14. *See, e.g.*, REC Marine Logistics, LLC v. Richard, No. 19-11149, 2020 WL 1527766, at *4–7 (E.D. La. Mar. 27, 2020) (sanctioning a lawyer for deposition misconduct, including 145 interruptions during questioning; instructing the witness not to answer 16 times; 106 objections, including 52 speaking objections, one of which spanned six pages of the deposition transcript; and 11 instances of the lawyer interrupting questioning to ask his own questions of the witness out of turn); Cadlerock Joint Venture, L.P. v. Sol Greenberg & Sons Int'l, 942 N.Y.S.2d 497, 499 (App. Div. 2012) (finding that the lawyer's "frivolous, outrageous, and unprofessional behavior" warranted sanctions and an award of costs and attorneys' fees).

15. Model Rules of Prof'l Conduct R. 3.4(a) (2020).

16. *Id.* R. 3.5(d).

17. *Id.* R. 3.5 cmt. 4.

18. *See, e.g.*, *In re* Bailey, 96 N.Y.S.3d 583, 584, 586 (App. Div. 2019) (suspending a lawyer for violating Rules 3.5(d) and 8.4(d) by entering an arbitration in a conference room in his law firm's offices in the middle of testimony, taking pictures with his phone, and threatening the witness with bad publicity after his firm won the dispute; although his firm was representing one of the parties, the lawyer was not involved in the arbitration).

may violate the rule.[19] *North Carolina State Bar v. Sutton*[20] is a representative case arising out of a deposition.

In *Sutton*, lawyer David Sutton represented Barbara Pollard in a wrongful death lawsuit against her daughter-in-law. During Pollard's deposition by the opposing lawyer, Kathryn Fagan, Sutton repeatedly interposed his own questions and commentary, made sarcastic remarks, coached Pollard on how to answer Fagan's questions, and answered questions for Pollard.[21] After the deposition was over, and in the presence of Pollard, the court reporter, and an observing law student, Sutton said, "'Fagan, you know what your problem is? Your problem is that you need a boyfriend or a husband or something. . . . I understand your client goes both ways so . . . maybe you could have a little lickety-lick with her.'"[22] The court concluded that Sutton's disruptive and offensive conduct violated North Carolina Rule 3.5(a)(4), which tracks Model Rule 3.5(d), as well as Rule 8.4(d).[23]

There is no bright-line rule for identifying conduct that violates Rule 3.5(d), although uncivil behavior by or between lawyers in court and in depositions certainly implicates the rule.[24] Alleged misconduct should be evaluated in light of the facts and circumstances of the case. Courts apply an objective test to determine whether a lawyer has violated Rule 3.5(d); the lawyer's subjective intent does not control the analysis.[25]

Some courts have held that a lawyer may even violate Rule 3.5(d) through statements in pleadings or other documents submitted to a court

---

19. Model Rules of Prof'l Conduct R. 3.5 cmt. 5 (2020); *see, e.g.*, *In re* McClure, 652 N.E.2d 863, 864 (Ind. 1995) (suspending the lawyer for 60 days for violating Rules 3.5(d), 8.4(b), and 8.4(d) by throwing a soft drink cup at the opposing lawyer and then grabbing him around his neck and restraining him in his chair); Bd. of Prof'l Responsibility v. Richard, 335 P.3d 1036, 1055 (Wyo. 2014) (holding that the lawyer violated Rule 3.5(d) by interrupting the other lawyer's cross-examination of the witness and insisting that she be allowed to finish her questioning so she could leave, thereafter questioning the witness over the other lawyer's objections, and demanding that the other lawyer limit his questioning to a specific time despite the judge's contrary order).

20. 791 N.E.2d 881 (N.C. Ct. App. 2016).

21. *Id.* at 886.

22. *Id.* (quoting Sutton).

23. *Id.* at 897.

24. *See, e.g.*, Fla. Bar v. Ratiner, 238 So. 3d 117, 119–20 (Fla. 2018) (violating the equivalent Florida rule by saying "lie, lie, lie" while opposing counsel examined a witness and repeatedly kicking the leg of opposing counsel's table during a hearing in the same case in an effort to be disruptive); Ky. Bar Ass'n v. Lavit, 351 S.W.3d 210, 213 (Ky. 2011) (reprimanding the lawyer under Kentucky Rule 3.5(c), which tracks Model Rule 3.5(d), for upbraiding and shouting at the opposing lawyer during a hearing); *In re* Spears, 290 So. 3d 645, 647–50 (La. 2020) (reprimanding a lawyer who raised his fists and threatened to "punch the shit out of" opposing counsel during a hearing in open court after the other lawyer called him a liar).

25. *In re* Madison, 282 S.W.3d 350, 353 (Mo. 2009).

or other tribunal.[26] In *In re Abbott*,[27] for example, the Delaware Supreme Court found that the lawyer violated Rules 3.5(d) and 8.4(d) by filing briefs that repeatedly accused opposing counsel of fabricating grounds for the decision under review and otherwise disparaged the opposing lawyer's actions.[28] Whether *In re Abbott* and similar cases are correctly decided with respect to Rule 3.5(d), however, is debatable. The Nevada Supreme Court reached the opposite conclusion in *In re Discipline of Colin*.[29] The lawyer there, James Colin, made several scathing comments about the court and some of the Justices in a petition and motion filed with the court.[30] The Nevada State Bar charged Colin with violating Rule 3.5(d), among other rules. The Nevada Supreme Court rejected the Rule 3.5(d) charge because "Colin's conduct did not occur in a courtroom setting. His statements and conduct all occurred in writing, instead of in-person before a tribunal. Thus, his conduct could not have disrupted the tribunal's proceeding . . . in the sense contemplated by [Rule] 3.5(d)."[31]

3. *Model Rule 4.4(a)*

Next there is Model Rule 4.4(a), which protects litigants and non-parties alike by stating that in representing a client "a lawyer shall not use means that have no substantial purpose other than to embarrass, delay, or burden a third person."[32] As the phrase "no substantial purpose" indicates, the presence of *some* legitimate purpose for a lawyer's offending conduct will not excuse or negate a Rule 4.4(a) violation.[33]

Model Rule 4.4(a) effectively moderates lawyers' zealous representation of their clients, allowing lawyers to legitimately cross-examine witnesses and parties, even if potentially embarrassing or upsetting to the targeted person, while preventing litigation abuses.[34] The rule makes punishable intemperate

26. *See, e.g.*, *In re* O'Dwyer, 221 So. 3d 1, 15–16 (La. 2017) (stating that the lawyer violated Rule 3.5(d) through unprofessional comments in pleadings); *In re* Swan, 656 S.E.2d 374, 374–75 (S.C. 2008) (reprimanding a lawyer who wrote to a Workers' Compensation Commissioner "venting outrage" over a ruling adverse to his client).

27. 925 A.2d 482 (Del. 2007).

28. *Id.* at 484.

29. 448 P.3d 556 (Nev. 2019).

30. *See id.* at 558–59 (reciting Colin's inflammatory comments).

31. *Id.* at 561.

32. Model Rules of Prof'l Conduct R. 4.4(a) (2020).

33. *In re* Member of Bar Hurley, No. 383, 2017, 2018 WL 1319010, at *14 (Del. Mar. 14, 2018); *In re* Conduct of McGraw, 414 P.3d 841, 854 (Or. 2018).

34. *See* Idaho State Bar v. Hawkley, 92 P.3d 1069, 1075 (Idaho 2002) (explaining that Rule 4.4(a) does not prohibit tough deposition questioning).

conduct directed toward witnesses and third parties,[35] opposing counsel,[36] and opposing parties.[37]

In *In re Lung*,[38] for example, the court invoked Rule 4.4(a) in suspending Henry Lung from practice for at least one year after he used e-mail to torment Morghan Richardson, the lawyer for the mother in a family law case in which Lung represented the father. For instance, in a message responding

35. *See, e.g.*, *In re* Blume, 443 P.3d 305, 321 (Kan. 2019) (violating Rule 4.4(a) by calling a videographer of German ancestry a "Nazi"); *In re* Disciplinary Action Against Kurzman, 871 N.W.2d 753, 755–56 (Minn. 2015) (violating Rules 4.4(a) and 8.4(d) by falsely implying in a deposition that the witness had previously been accused of sexual misconduct with minors); *In re* Disciplinary Action Against Torgerson, 870 N.W.2d 602, 610–11 (Minn. 2015) (violating Rules 4.4(a) and 8.4(d) by screaming at court staff); *In re* Vincenti, 704 A.2d 927, 931 (N.J. 1998) (disbarring a lawyer who tried to intimidate witnesses, was abusive and insulting to witnesses, conducted unnecessarily long and confrontational cross-examinations, and belittled an expert's credentials); *In re* Ortiz, 304 P.3d 404, 405–07 (N.M. 2013) (involving remarks directed at the opposing party and counsel); *In re* Hammer, 718 S.E.2d 442, 444–45 (S.C. 2011) (disciplining a lawyer who asked a deponent about his sexual orientation and whether he had HIV, and who further asked whether the witness had Alzheimer's disease when his recollection was incomplete); *In re* Golden, 496 S.E.2d 619, 620–24 (S.C. 1998) (disciplining a lawyer who was sarcastic and rude to witnesses, and who acted in a threatening and demeaning manner).

36. *See, e.g.*, Cruz-Aponte v. Caribbean Petrol. Corp., No. 09-2092 (FAB), 2015 WL 5006213, at *2–3 (D.P.R. Aug. 17, 2015) (finding that a lawyer violated Rule 4.4(a) when his female opponent commented during a deposition that the room was warm and he responded, "You're not getting menopause, I hope"); *In re* Disciplinary Matter of Shea, 273 P.3d 612, 621 (Alaska 2012) (finding that a lawyer whose filings referred to opposing counsel as "a disgrace to the legal profession" and accused the lawyer of perpetuating a fraud on judicial system and of filing "hateful evil litigation," violated Rule 4.4(a)); People v. Piccone, 459 P.3d 136, 158–59 (Colo. 2020) (violating Rule 4.4(a) in a blog post by recirculating an old allegation that a city attorney had an affair with a city client, and by broadcasting the city attorney's former name, current name, and current employment position); *In re* Disciplinary Action Against Williams, 917 N.W.2d 423, 423 (Minn. 2018) (violating Rule 4.4(a) by "intentionally making physical contact with opposing counsel during a deposition which ended the deposition and delayed the litigation"); *In re* Disciplinary Action Against Ulanowski, 800 N.W.2d 785, 794–95 (Minn. 2011) (concluding that a lawyer violated Rule 4.4(a) by repeatedly insulting opposing counsel's intelligence and by threatening her); *In re Vincenti*, 704 A.2d at 931 (disbarring a lawyer who was "invariably abusive, insulting and profoundly vulgar" to opposing counsel); Principe v. Assay Partners, 586 N.Y.S.2d 182, 184–88 (Sup. Ct. 1992) (sanctioning a lawyer for repeated sexist remarks to female opposing counsel, including "I don't have to talk to you little lady," "tell that little mouse over there to pipe down," "what do you know, young girl," "be quiet, little girl," and "go away, little girl").

37. *See, e.g.*, *In re Shea*, 273 P.3d at 621 (finding that a lawyer whose filings described the opposing party's conduct as "satanic," "evil," "terroristic," "POW business torture," "corrupt," "perverted," "predatory," and "deranged," and accused the party and her lawyer of perpetuating a fraud on judicial system and of filing "hateful evil litigation," violated Rule 4.4(a)); *In re* Barker, 993 N.E.2d 1138, 1139 (Ind. 2013) (suspending a lawyer who accused the opposing party of being an illegal alien in a letter to her counsel); *In re* Campiti, 905 N.E.2d 408, 408 (Ind. 2009) (reprimanding a lawyer who ridiculed an opposing party in court based on her citizenship and receipt of free legal services); *In re Blume*, 443 P.3d at 321 (holding that the lawyer violated Rule 4.4(a) "when he flipped off the representative of the opposing party" during a deposition); *In re* Black, 941 P.2d 1380, 1382–86 (Kan. 1997) (suspending a lawyer who insulted and ridiculed the opposing party for wearing his military uniform); *In re Golden*, 496 S.E.2d at 621 (disciplining a lawyer who called the opposing party "a mean-spirited, vicious witch").

38. 122 N.Y.S.3d 364 (App. Div. 2020).

to Richardson's offer to negotiate the parties' visitation schedule for their daughter, Lung wrote, "I know the truth Morghan, and the truth is that you are a liar. You lie and lie and continually pump your client's head with total garbage just so that her parents (the real money train in all of this) continue to pay you. That is the real and only truth that matters in this entire case."[39] Lung impermissibly copied Richardson's client on the e-mail. When Richardson asked Lung to stop communicating with her if he planned to continue "name-calling" and refusing to collaborate, Lung responded, again copying the mother, "Your client is going to lose custody & if you doubt me, keep sending useless emails like this. The 'gravy train' will end for you soon enough. Yes I absolutely do think of you as a liar insofar as you are actively advising your client to continue her current position."[40] Lung sent many more angry messages to Richardson, often in the wee hours of the morning and always impermissibly copying the mother. The common theme in all the messages was that Richardson was an incompetent, greedy liar who was stringing out the case for improper purposes.[41]

In his disciplinary case, Lung explained that he was enraged by delays in the matrimonial case, which he attributed to Richardson's neglect. He considered Richardson to be a liar because he believed that she had violated a court order in the matrimonial case and because of what he considered to be the unnecessary legal fees she charged in connection with her related improper advice to the mother. With respect to at least some of his messages, he claimed that he copied the mother because he did not believe that Richardson was accurately explaining matters to her. In other instances, he copied the mother to ensure that she understood that any delays in concluding the case were attributable to Richardson.[42]

Lung was aware that he should not be communicating with the mother but believed that he was justified in doing so because of his frustration with Richardson.[43] He did not similarly confess to violating Rule 4.4(a) but offered that he had begun a practice of drafting e-mails and then waiting a few hours or overnight before sending them.[44] He also planned "to assess the benefit to a client of a communication with opposing counsel or a judge" before doing so in the future.[45]

39. *Id.* at 366.
40. *Id.*
41. *Id.* at 367–68.
42. *Id.* at 368.
43. *Id.* at 368–69.
44. *Id.* at 369.
45. *Id.*

Rejecting Lung's plea for leniency, the court concluded that his claims of frustration did not justify his conduct.[46]

> [Lung] repeatedly sent emails to a party he knew to be represented, sometimes sending multiple emails on the same day and at inappropriate non-business hours, which emails contained disparaging information in an aggressive tone. We find the respondent did so in an effort to criticize opposing counsel, to accuse her of engaging in professional misconduct, and to try to undermine the relationship between opposing counsel and her client. Even though the respondent knew his actions were improper, and despite being put on notice by opposing counsel that his actions were improper, he continued undeterred and without regard to the Rules of Professional Conduct.[47]

Consequently, and as noted earlier, the court decided that Lung should be suspended from practice for at least one year.

4. *Model Rule 8.4(d)*

Model Rule 8.4(d) provides that it is professional misconduct for a lawyer to "engage in conduct that is prejudicial to the administration of justice."[48] Courts and disciplinary authorities commonly rely on Rule 8.4(d) to sanction lawyers for uncivil behavior.[49] The rule applies to litigation-related misconduct both in court and out.

46. *Id.*

47. *Id.* at 369–70.

48. Model Rules of Prof'l Conduct R. 8.4(d) (2020).

49. *See, e.g.*, Golden v. Clear Advantage Mktg., No. 4:16-cv-00529, 2020 WL 2516671, at *8–29 (S.D. Iowa Mar. 20, 2020) (relying on Rule 8.4(d) to publicly reprimand a lawyer for numerous outrageous acts of abuse in discovery); Fla. Bar v. Norkin, 132 So. 3d 77, 84–87, 90 (Fla. 2013) (involving a lawyer who sent numerous offensive letters and e-mails to opposing counsel, and who further engaged in publicly insulting behavior); *In re* Moore, 665 N.E.2d 40, 41–43 (Ind. 1996) (suspending a lawyer who grabbed opposing counsel by his necktie and then punched him); *In re* Clothier, 344 P.3d 370, 377 (Kan. 2015) (disciplining a lawyer who called a young female lawyer "a histrionic woman" and "a newbie," and jabbed a finger in her face while saying that she "should grow a pair and punch him," threatened to "kick [the] ass" of another lawyer in addition to telling him "to go jump in a lake," and told a pro se litigant, "be quiet kid, I am talking"); *In re* DeJean, 262 So. 3d 424, 426, 429–30 (La. 2019) (suspending a lawyer who "chest-bumped" a prosecutor in chambers); *In re* Disciplinary Action Against Kurzman, 871 N.W.2d 753, 755–56 (Minn. 2015) (violating Rules 4.4(a) and 8.4(d) by falsely implying in a deposition that the witness had been accused of sexual misconduct with minors); *In re* Disciplinary Action Against Torgerson, 870 N.W.2d 602, 610–11 (Minn. 2015) (violating Rules 4.4(a) and 8.4(d) by screaming at court staff); Disciplinary Counsel v. Cox, 862 N.E.2d 514, 517–19 (Ohio 2007) (suspending a lawyer who taunted another lawyer with profanities and racial slurs); *In re* McBurney, 13 A.3d 654, 655 (R.I. 2011) (censuring a lawyer who filed pleadings "replete with false and outrageous libels and accusations" directed at opposing counsel, including falsely accusing the other lawyer of "deceit," falsely alleging that she had engaged in "ambush tactics and trickery," and falsely claiming that she was "dishonest"); *In re* White, 709 S.E.2d 633, 636–37 (S.C. 2011) (sending opposing counsel an e-mail message suggesting that his daughter was a drug user).

In re Pengilly,[50] for example, arose out of Nevada lawyer James Pengilly's deposition antics. During his questioning, Pengilly used vulgarities, insulted the deponent, aggressively interrupted the deponent and the other lawyer, answered questions for the deponent, and made multiple inappropriate comments on the record.[51] At one point, Pengilly asked the deponent if "he was 'ready for it'" while placing his hand near his hip.[52] The deponent briefly left the room, but when he returned, Pengilly displayed a pistol that was holstered on his hip.[53] The Nevada Supreme Court concluded that Pengilly violated Rule 8.4(d) and suspended him from practice for just over six months.

Although it clearly is reasonable to discipline a lawyer for incivility under several rules, a separate question is whether a lawyer can be disciplined or sanctioned for failing to control a disruptive client. The answer to that question is yes.[54]

In *GMAC Bank v. HTFC Corp.*,[55] the plaintiff deposed Aaron Wider, the defendant's owner and CEO. Joseph Ziccardi represented HTFC and defended Wider's deposition. From the start, Wider tried to intimidate GMAC's lawyer through outrageous and profuse vulgarity permeating almost ever answer he gave, by belittling and insulting the lawyer, and by persistently exhibiting unjustified hostility.[56] Wider further impeded the deposition by interposing his own objections to questions posed by GMAC's counsel, providing unnecessarily protracted answers, repeatedly interrupting the questioning, and proudly expressing his intent to frustrate his examination.[57] After particularly odious instances of abuse and obstruction, Wider would pat himself on the back and ask on the record, "'Isn't the law wonderful?'"[58]

Ziccardi did nothing to reign in Wider. Instead, Ziccardi sat idly by as a mere spectator to Wider's insanely abusive, vulgar, and obstructionist antics. When Ziccardi did act, he either incorrectly instructed Wider not to answer a question, dared GMAC's lawyer to file a motion to compel, or laughed at

50. No. 74316, 2018 WL 4297851 (Nev. Sept. 7, 2018).
51. *Id.* at *1.
52. *Id.*
53. *Id.*
54. *See, e.g.*, State v. Mumford, 731 A.2d 831, 833–36 (Del. 1999) (concluding that Rules 3.5(d) and 8.4(d) compelled the lawyer to suppress his client's abominable deposition behavior and revoking his pro hac vice admission for failing to do so).
55. 248 F.R.D. 182 (E.D. Pa. 2008).
56. *Id.* at 186–87.
57. *Id.* at 187–89.
58. *Id.* at 189 (quoting Wider).

Wider's conduct.[59] On other occasions, he meekly asked Wider to answer a question or instructed him not to interrupt opposing counsel.[60]

GMAC sought sanctions against Wider and Ziccardi. The district court was stunned by Wider's misconduct. As for Ziccardi, the court acknowledged that a lawyer "can be blindsided by a recalcitrant client who engages in unexpected sanctionable conduct at a deposition."[61] But here, Ziccardi had ample notice of Wider's intended misconduct and he enabled it through his own behavior. Regardless, a lawyer presented with a disruptive client cannot simply sit back and allow the deposition to proceed.[62] To the contrary, the lawyer must timely intervene to curb the client's misconduct.[63] Because Ziccardi failed to do so and through his own actions contributed to the disruption and frustration of Wider's deposition, the court made him jointly and severally liable with Wider for the roughly $13,000 in fees that GMAC spent on its motion to compel.

Zicardi substantially contributed to his own plight. He made no attempt to control his client, appeared to enjoy his client's repeated disruptions, and exacerbated problems by making improper speaking objections. But lawyers with better sense than Ziccardi exhibited can still find themselves in trouble for a client's misbehavior. This is because Model Rule 3.4(a), which provides that a lawyer shall not "unlawfully obstruct another party's access to evidence," further provides that a lawyer "shall not counsel or assist another person to do any such act."[64] Lawyers who do not counsel clients against obstructionist or abusive behavior, or who do not otherwise attempt to rein in disruptive clients, may be found to "assist" the client's obstruction as that term is used in Model Rule 3.4(a).

Neither *GMAC Bank* nor Model Rule 3.4(a) transform lawyers into guarantors of clients' good behavior. Lawyers must, however, reasonably attempt to prevent or rectify obstructive discovery tactics by clients or witnesses over whom they have control or influence.[65]

59. *Id.* at 194–95.
60. *Id.* at 195.
61. *Id.*
62. *Id.*
63. *Id.*
64. Model Rules of Prof'l Conduct R. 3.4(a) (2020).
65. *See, e.g., In re* Shorenstein Hays-Nederlander Theatres LLC Appeals, 213 A.3d 39, 78 (Del. 2019) ("An attorney representing a client who engages in [flippant, evasive, ridiculous answers and speech-making] during the course of a deposition cannot simply be a spectator and do nothing." (footnote omitted)).

B. Summary

Civility is essential, but not all uncivil behavior is unethical.[66] Although lawyers who are aggrieved by opponents' incivility ought to avoid any sort of tit for tat,[67] and it is true that an opposing lawyer's precipitating misconduct never excuses one's own misconduct,[68] the reality is that some lawyers provoke incivility by their own misbehavior. Deciding whether a lawyer's conduct crosses the line is thus a difficult task. Courts and disciplinary authorities are not the manners police.

In determining whether a lawyer's intemperate or offensive behavior is unethical, courts and disciplinary authorities should consider context. For example, a lawyer who inappropriately expresses anger once is substantially different from a lawyer who is a serial bully. Responding imprudently to an adversary's abusive tactics, while blameworthy, is not the same as initiating or instigating misconduct. When it comes to depositions, some witnesses may rightly be subjected to tough, provocative, or embarrassing questions, especially if their credibility is at issue; the fact that questioning is aggressive or the topic embarrassing to the witness does not necessarily mean that the inquiring lawyer is acting improperly.[69]

In short, although some emotional reactions or overreactions are understandable, and superficially offensive questioning may serve a legitimate purpose, abusive behavior by lawyers is unacceptable. Degrading and disrespectful conduct by lawyers—whether directed at fellow lawyers, judges, or others—does not qualify as zealous advocacy.[70] Even more fundamentally, disparaging an opponent or the court is poor advocacy that does not advance the client's case and may even detract from it.[71]

66. *See In re* Swarts, 30 P.3d 1011, 1031 (Kan. 2001) (noting that boorish conduct is not necessarily an ethics violation); *see, e.g.*, Saldana v. Kmart Corp., 260 F.3d 228, 237 (3d Cir. 2001) (finding that lawyer's use of "fuck" in two telephone conversations with other lawyers and in two asides to other lawyers during depositions, and lawyer's concurrence in post-verdict letter with juror who described an expert witness as a "Nazi," did not merit sanctions).

67. *See In re* Fischer, 684 N.E.2d 197, 199 (Ind. 1997) (stating that lawyers must "adhere to ethical strictures regardless of perceived transgressions of other participants in litigation").

68. Lioce v. Cohen, 174 P.3d 970, 986 (Nev. 2008).

69. *See, e.g.*, Plante v. Stack, 109 A.3d 846, 858–60 (R.I. 2015) (concluding that the trial court erred in revoking a lawyer's pro hac vice admission because the lawyer's deposition questioning, while "somewhat unorthodox, sometimes tedious, and arguably offensive," did not cross the line into sanctionable misconduct).

70. Columbus Bar Ass'n v. Vogel, 881 N.E.2d 1244, 1249 (Ohio 2008).

71. *See* Bearden v. Ballad Health, 967 F.3d 513, 515 (6th Cir. 2020) (explaining why "there are good reasons not to disparage your opponent, especially in court filings").

III. Saber-Rattling

This part examines saber-rattling, which should be understood to include lawyers' (1) threats of criminal prosecution intended to obtain an advantage in a civil matter, whether aimed at parties, witnesses, other lawyers, or other third parties; and (2) threats of professional discipline directed at other lawyers.

A. Applicable Rules of Professional Conduct

With respect first to threats of criminal prosecution, the Model Code of Professional Responsibility stated in DR 7-105(A) that lawyers "shall not present, participate in presenting, or threaten to present criminal charges solely to obtain an advantage in a civil matter."[72] The drafters of the Model Rules omitted the DR 7-105(A) prohibition on the basis that it was overbroad, redundant, or both, although some jurisdictions incorporated the language of DR 7-105(A) or something close in their new rules when they adopted the Model Rules.[73] In most jurisdictions, however, the check on threatening

72. MODEL CODE OF PROF'L RESPONSIBILITY DR 7-105(A) (1969).

73. *See, e.g.*, ALA. RULES OF PROF'L CONDUCT R. 3.10 (1994) ("A lawyer shall not present, participate in presenting, or threaten to present criminal or professional disciplinary charges solely to obtain an advantage in a civil matter."); CAL. RULES OF PROF'L CONDUCT R. 3.10(a) (2018) ("A lawyer shall not threaten to present criminal, administrative, or disciplinary charges to obtain an advantage in a civil dispute."); COLO. RULES OF PROF'L CONDUCT R. 4.5(a) (2018) (providing that lawyers "shall not threaten criminal, administrative or disciplinary charges to obtain an advantage in a civil matter nor shall a lawyer present or participate in presenting criminal, administrative or disciplinary charges solely to obtain an advantage in a civil matter"); CONN. RULES OF PROF'L CONDUCT R. 3.4(7) (2020) (stating that a lawyer shall not "[p]resent, participate in presenting, or threaten to present criminal charges solely to obtain an advantage in a civil matter"); D.C. RULES OF PROF'L CONDUCT R. 8.4(g) (2015) (prohibiting lawyers from seeking or threatening to seek criminal or disciplinary charges solely to obtain an advantage in a civil matter); FLA. RULES OF PROF'L CONDUCT 4-3.4(g) (2019) (stating that lawyers cannot "present, participate in presenting, or threaten to present criminal charges solely to obtain an advantage in a civil matter"); IDAHO RULES OF PROF'L CONDUCT R. 4.4(a)(3) (2014) (stating that a lawyer shall not "present or participate in presenting criminal charges solely to obtain [an] advantage in a civil matter"); *id.* R. 4.4(a)(4) (stating that in representing a client a lawyer shall not "threaten to present criminal charges in order to obtain [an] advantage in a civil matter"); ILL. RULES OF PROF'L CONDUCT R. 8.4(g) (2010) (making it professional misconduct for a lawyer to "present, participate in presenting, or threaten to present criminal or professional disciplinary charges to obtain an advantage in a civil matter"); LA. RULES OF PROF'L CONDUCT R. 8.4(g) (2018) (making it professional misconduct for a lawyer to "[t]hreaten to present criminal or disciplinary charges solely to obtain an advantage in a civil matter"); N.Y. RULES OF PROF'L CONDUCT R. 3.4(e) (2017) (stating that a lawyer shall not "[p]resent, participate in presenting, or threaten to present criminal charges solely to obtain an advantage in a civil matter"); S.C. RULES OF PROF'L CONDUCT R. 4.5 (2017) ("A lawyer shall not present, participate in presenting, or threaten to present criminal or professional disciplinary charges solely to obtain an advantage in a civil matter."); TENN. RULES OF PROF'L CONDUCT R. 4.4(a)(2) (2018) (stating that a lawyer shall not "threaten to present a criminal or

behavior that DR 7-105(A) once provided is now enforced under several rules of professional conduct.

To start, Model Rule 3.1 provides in pertinent part that "[a] lawyer shall not bring or defend a proceeding, or assert or controvert an issue therein, unless there is a basis in fact or law for doing so that is not frivolous."[74] Whether a claim or contention is frivolous under Model Rule 3.1 is generally measured by an objective "reasonable attorney" standard.[75] Thus, lawyers cannot escape discipline, for example, by claiming that they were mistaken as to the applicable law where that law is settled.[76] Still, not every meritless claim or contention is frivolous.[77] For claims or contentions to be frivolous under Model Rule 3.1, there must be such a complete absence of facts or law that reasonable lawyers could not have expected a court to rule for them.[78] Trouble remains, however, because some courts augment Model Rule 3.1's objective test with a subjective standard.[79] If a lawyer in one of these jurisdictions makes a claim or contention with an improper motive or in bad faith, the fact that the position may be objectively non-frivolous will not spare the lawyer from professional discipline.[80]

Model Rule 3.1 provides that a claim or contention is not frivolous if a lawyer can make "a good faith argument for an extension, modification

---

lawyer disciplinary charge for the purpose of obtaining an advantage in a civil matter"); Tex. Disciplinary Rules of Prof'l Conduct R. 4.04(b) (2019) (setting prohibitions on criminal and disciplinary threats); Va. Rules of Prof'l Conduct R. 3.4(i) (2018) (stating that a lawyer shall not "[p]resent or threaten to present criminal or disciplinary charges solely to obtain an advantage in a civil matter").

74. Model Rules of Prof'l Conduct R. 3.1 (2020).

75. People v. Bontrager, 407 P.3d 1235, 1247 (Colo. 2017); O'Brien v. Super. Ct., 939 A.2d 1223, 1231 (Conn. App. Ct. 2008); *In re* Disciplinary Action Against Butler, 868 N.W.2d 243, 248 (Minn. 2015); *In re* Application for Disciplinary Action Against Hoffman, 670 N.W.2d 500, 506 (N.D. 2003); Lawyer Disciplinary Bd. v. Neely, 528 S.E.2d 468, 473 (W. Va. 1998). *But see In re* Disciplinary Proc. Against Bach, 887 N.W.2d 335, 339 (Wis. 2016) (noting that Wisconsin's equivalent rules of professional conduct are enforced using a subjective standard).

76. Thompson v. Sup. Ct. Comm. on Prof'l Conduct, 252 S.W.3d 125, 128 (Ark. 2007).

77. Commonwealth v. Chmiel, 30 A.3d 1111, 1190 (Pa. 2011) (distinguishing frivolous claims from meritless ones); *In re* Houston, 675 S.E.2d 721, 723 n.1 (S.C. 2009) (finding that a meritless racial profiling claim did not violate Rule 3.1); Johnson v. Miller, 818 N.W.2d 804, 809 (S.D. 2012) (quoting Stratmeyer v. Engberg, 649 N.W.2d 921, 926 (S.D. 2002)); *In re* S.C., 88 A.3d 1220, 1223–24 (Vt. 2014) (discussing appellate arguments and appointed counsel's motion to withdraw based on Rule 3.1); *see also* Estate of McLemore v. McLemore, 63 So. 3d 468, 490 (Miss. 2011) (observing that a case may be "weak" or "light-headed" without being "frivolous" for the purpose of awarding sanctions).

78. *In re* Spikes, 881 A.2d 1118, 1125 (D.C. 2005); *In re Application for Disciplinary Action Against Hoffman*, 670 N.W.2d at 506; *see, e.g.*, Weatherbee v. Va. State Bar, 689 S.E.2d 753, 756 (Va. 2010) (finding a Rule 3.1 violation where the underlying suit had "no basis in law or fact" and the lawyer could have discovered this had he conducted a pre-suit investigation).

79. *See, e.g.*, *In re* Levine, 847 P.2d 1093, 1100 (Ariz. 1993) (citing *In re* Mulhall, 822 P.2d 947, 948 (Ariz. 1992)).

80. *Id.*

or reversal of existing law."[81] Although the term "good faith" suggests that lawyers' arguments for extending, modifying, or reversing existing law are measured according to a subjective standard, the test for a violation remains objective.[82] Lawyers cannot defend their conduct on the basis that they were only pushing the envelope, for example, when a reasonable lawyer knowing the facts would conclude that the supposedly novel argument was frivolous.

Lawyers' threats of criminal complaints, disciplinary complaints, sanctions, and lawsuits are often hollow when made; the threatening lawyers have no intention of following through if their targets are not cowed into doing their bidding. Call these threats bluffs or brand them as lies, but they are in any event false statements. Accordingly, if they are deemed to be material—as seems likely to be the case most of the time—they violate Model Rule 4.1(a), which provides that when representing a client, a lawyer cannot "knowingly" make a "false statement of material fact or law to a third person."[83]

The reference to "a third person" in Model Rule 4.1(a) establishes that the rule relates to lawyers' communications with people other than their clients.[84] Lawyers' false statements to clients are punished under other rules.[85] The term "knowingly" when used here, as elsewhere, "denotes actual knowledge";[86] it does not describe "evil intent or bad purpose."[87] Lawyers' knowledge may be inferred from circumstances.[88] Model Rule 4.1(a) applies only to statements of fact or law; lawyers' statements of opinion will not violate the rule.[89] Innocent misstatements do not implicate Rule 4.1(a),[90] although statements made with reckless disregard for the truth may.[91] A statement is "material" for purposes of the rule if it is significant or essential,

81. Model Rules of Prof'l Conduct R. 3.1 (2020).

82. The requirement that courts weigh lawyers' motives when evaluating their alleged misconduct does not preclude application of an objective standard. *But see In re* Disciplinary Proc. Against Bach, 887 N.W.2d 335, 339 (Wis. 2016) (noting that Wisconsin applies a subjective standard).

83. Model Rules of Prof'l Conduct R. 4.1 (2020).

84. State *ex rel.* Okla. Bar Ass'n v. Bolusky, 23 P.3d 268, 275 (Okla. 2001).

85. Model Rules of Prof'l Conduct R. 8.4(c) (2020) (prohibiting conduct involving dishonesty, fraud, deceit, or misrepresentation).

86. *Id.* R. 1.0(f).

87. *In re* Edison, 724 N.W.2d 579, 584 (N.D. 2006).

88. *In re* Disciplinary Action Against Johnson, 743 N.W.2d 117, 123 (N.D. 2007); Model Rules of Prof'l Conduct R 1.0(f) (2020).

89. Office of Disciplinary Couns. v. Wrona, 908 A.2d 1281, 1289 (Pa. 2006).

90. *See, e.g.*, People v. Chambers, 154 P.3d 419, 425–26 (Colo. 2006) (finding no Rule 4.1 violation for an apparently innocent misstatement of the number of claims or suits); Att'y Grievance Comm'n of Md. v. Elmendorf, 946 A.2d 542, 545–46 (Md. 2008) (accepting trial the court's ruling that the lawyer's negligence in failing to review files that led to the false statements did not result in a Rule 4.1(a) violation).

91. *In re* Wagner, 744 N.E.2d 418, 421 (Ind. 2001); Office of Disciplinary Couns. v. Price, 732 A.2d 599, 606 (Pa. 1999).

if it could have influenced the hearer,[92] or if it affected the outcome of the proceeding.[93] Courts evaluate materiality on a case-by-case basis.[94]

Model Rule 4.1(a) does not include a causation or reliance element. A lawyer therefore violates the rule simply by making a prohibited statement. The person to whom the statement is made does not have to act or detrimentally rely on the statement to perfect the violation.[95] The person's reliance on the lawyer's false statement may, however, affect the discipline to be imposed and in some cases support other claims against the lawyer.

Model Rule 4.4(a) is closely related to Model Rule 3.1, and threatening conduct violating the latter likely violates the former.[96] Model Rule 4.4(a) clearly applies to saber-rattling by lawyers.[97] The rule provides, "In representing a client, a lawyer shall not use means that have no substantial purpose other than to embarrass, delay, or burden a third person, or use methods of obtaining evidence that violate the legal rights of such a person."[98] Model Rule 4.4(a) is in essence the successor to DR 7-105(A) insofar as threats of criminal prosecution intended to confer an advantage in a civil matter are concerned. The rule is much broader than DR 7-105(A), however, and it sweeps in a wide range of misconduct.[99] Model Rule 4.4(a) makes clear that lawyers' duty to competently represent clients does not license them to harass others.

---

92. *In re* Fisher, 202 P.3d 1186, 1202 (Colo. 2009); *In re* Smith, 236 P.3d 137, 145 (Or. 2010) (quoting *In re* Kluge, 27 P.3d 102 (Or. 2001)).

93. Office of Disciplinary Couns. v. DiAngelus, 907 A.2d 452, 456–58 (Pa. 2006).

94. Ausherman v. Bank of Am. Corp., 212 F. Supp. 2d 435, 449 (D. Md. 2002).

95. *See, e.g.*, *In re* Winthrop, 848 N.E.2d 961, 980 (Ill. 2006) (finding a Rule 4.1(a) violation even though the lawyer's dishonesty did not impede the other lawyer to whom the false statement was made).

96. *See, e.g.*, *In re* Levine, 847 P.2d 1093, 1101 (Ariz. 1993) (noting that "in almost every count" alleging a violation of Rule 3.1, the lawyer was also charged with violating Rule 4.4, and finding violations of both rules); *In re* Kerr, 640 N.E.2d 1056, 1059 (Ind. 1994) (determining that the lawyer violated Rule 3.1 and Rule 4.4 by filing frivolous petitions); State *ex rel.* Okla. Bar Ass'n v. Chappell, 93 P.3d 25, 29–30 (Okla. 2004) (violating Rules 3.1 and 4.4 through frivolous pleadings and threatening letters).

97. *See, e.g.*, Att'y Grievance Comm'n of Md. v. Rheinstein, 223 A.3d 505, 545 (Md. 2020) (finding that the lawyer violated Rule 4.4(a) when he threatened to report opposing counsel to the Attorney Grievance Commission if they refused to drop their client's appeal or withdraw as counsel); N.Y.C. Eth. Op. 2015-5, 2015 WL 4197679, at *7 (N.Y. City Bar Ass'n, Comm. on Prof'l & Jud. Ethics 2015) [hereinafter N.Y.C. Eth. Op. 2015-5] ("Threatening to file a disciplinary complaint against an adversary in order to gain a strategic advantage violates [Rule 4.4(a)], if the threat serves no substantial purpose other than to embarrass or harm the other lawyer or his client.").

98. Model Rules of Prof'l Conduct R. 4.4(a) (2020).

99. *See, e.g.*, 2005 N.C. Eth. Op. 3, 2005 WL 3964317, at *2 (N.C. State Bar 2005) (relying in part on Rule 4.4(a) in concluding that "a lawyer may not use the threat of reporting an opposing party or a witness to immigration officials in settlement negotiations on behalf of a client in a civil matter").

A lawyer must be representing a client for Model Rule 4.4(a) to apply. A lawyer acting pro se is representing a client for Model Rule 4.4(a) purposes.[100] Prosecutors acting in their official capacity are representing a client, that is, the government, state, or "the people."[101] The rule does not require that a lawyer's misconduct harm anyone to find a violation,[102] nor is the fact that the person who was the target of the lawyer's conduct was upset or offended by it dispositive.[103] Consistent with the rule's plain language, courts evaluating alleged Model Rule 4.4(a) violations focus on the purpose of the lawyers' conduct rather than its effect.[104] This approach is necessary because Model Rule 4.4(a) is commonly applied to lawyers' conduct in litigation, and some amount or degree of embarrassment, delay, and burden is inherent in litigation. The rule's reference to third persons clarifies its application to lawyers' conduct directed at anyone other than the lawyer's client.[105]

Most Rule 4.4(a) controversies pivot on whether the lawyer's actions had "no *substantial* purpose" other than embarrassing, burdening, or delaying a third person.[106] Model Rule 4.4(a) does not penalize legitimate tactics by a lawyer that have the unfortunate effect of embarrassing or inconveniencing someone.[107] The apparent problem with Model Rule 4.4(a) is that a lawyer's actions aimed at harassing a third person are often done with the intent to benefit the lawyer's client, thus suggesting a legitimate alternative purpose. That seeming gap in the rule is inconsequential, however, because incidental or secondary benefit to an accused lawyer's client is no defense

100. *See, e.g., In re* Yarborough, 559 S.E.2d 836, 838–40 (S.C. 2002) (agreeing that the lawyer violated Rule 4.4(a) when he wrote a threatening letter to a witness in his criminal case).

101. *See, e.g., In re* Campbell, 199 P.3d 776, 780 (Kan. 2009) (concluding that a prosecutor who threatened to show pictures of a teenage girl engaging in sex to parents of other teens who attended a party violated Rule 4.4(a)).

102. *See, e.g.,* Idaho State Bar v. Warrick, 44 P.3d 1141, 1145–46 (Idaho 2002) (rejecting a prosecutor's claim that he did not violate Rule 4.4(a) because his characterizations of a jail inmate as a "scumbag" and a "waste of sperm" did not embarrass or injure the inmate).

103. Shepherd v. Am. Broad. Cos., 62 F.3d 1469, 1483–84 (D.C. Cir. 1995) (refusing to sanction a lawyer for discomforting and upsetting a witness during an interview where the lawyer had a legitimate purpose for attempting to talk to the witness); Tex. Eth. Op. 585, 2008 WL 5477781, at *1 (Sup. Ct. of Tex., Prof'l Ethics Comm. 2008).

104. *Warrick*, 44 P.3d at 1145–46; *see, e.g., In re* Krigel, 480 S.W.3d 294, 300 (Mo. 2016) (discussing a lawyer's conduct in connection with an adoption proceeding).

105. *See, e.g.,* Att'y Grievance Comm'n of Md. v. Donnelly, 182 A.3d 743, 791 (Md. 2018) (concluding that a lawyer's clients were not third persons for Rule 4.4(a) purposes); Bd. of Prof'l Responsibility v. Asay, 374 P.3d 295, 306–07 (Wyo. 2016) (finding that the lawyer's threatening letter to his client did not violate Rule 4.4(a)).

106. Model Rules of Prof'l Conduct R. 4.4(a) (2020) (emphasis added); *see also In re* Conduct of McGraw, 414 P.3d 841, 854 (Or. 2018) ("The phrase 'no substantial purpose' [in Rule 4.4(a)] suggests that a lawyer may violate the rule even if he or she had some purpose other than harassing or otherwise burdening another, as long as that other purpose was not 'substantial.'").

107. Chief Disciplinary Couns. v. Rozbicki, No. CV116004519S, 2013 WL 1277298, at *19 (Conn. Super. Ct. Mar. 8, 2013).

to an alleged Model Rule 4.4(a) violation.[108] Were it otherwise, Model Rule 4.4(a) would be ineffective in restraining lawyers' unreasonably aggressive behavior in representing clients.

Determining whether a lawyer's means in representing a client have a substantial purpose other than embarrassing, delaying, or burdening a third person requires a court to examine the lawyer's motives. In doing so, courts apply an objective standard.[109] Lawyers cannot escape responsibility for a Model Rule 4.4(a) violation "based on [their] naked assertion[s] that, in fact, the 'substantial purpose' of conduct was not to 'embarrass, delay or burden' when an objective evaluation of the conduct would lead a reasonable person to conclude otherwise."[110]

Saber-rattling also potentially implicates several parts of Model Rule 8.4. First, Model Rule 8.4(b) makes it professional misconduct for a lawyer to "commit a criminal act that reflects adversely on the lawyer's honesty, trustworthiness or fitness as a lawyer in other respects."[111] Not every criminal act by a lawyer indicates that the lawyer is unfit to practice.[112] Whether a lawyer's criminal act reflects adversely on a lawyer's honesty, trustworthiness, or fitness to practice depends on the facts of the case.[113]

It is possible that a lawyer's threats or efforts at intimidation geared toward achieving an advantage in a matter could in some instances be criminal, as where an alleged threat might constitute extortion. Importantly, Model Rule 8.4(b) does not require a criminal charge, complaint, prosecution, guilty plea, *Alford* plea, plea of no contest, or conviction to find a

108. *In re* White, 707 S.E.2d 411, 414 (S.C. 2011); *see, e.g.*, Fla. Bar v. Charnock, 661 So. 2d 1207, 1208–10 (Fla. 1995) (violating Rule 4.4(a) by securing a tenant to delay transfer of property, which, while benefiting the client, burdened a mechanic's lien claimant); *In re* Royer, 78 P.3d 449, 454–55 (Kan. 2003) (involving facts analogous to those in *Charnock*); Ky. Bar Ass'n v. Reeves, 62 S.W.3d 360, 364–66 (Ky. 2001) (suspending a lawyer who wrote a letter that served both illegitimate and legitimate purposes); *In re* Disciplinary Action Against Mertz, 712 N.W.2d 849, 853–54 (N.D. 2006) (basing a Rule 4.4 violation on an offensive statement in a letter that otherwise served legitimate purposes).

109. *In re* Martinez, 462 P.3d 36, 45 (Ariz. 2020); *In re* Comfort, 159 P.3d 1011, 1020 (Kan. 2007).

110. *In re Comfort*, 159 P.3d at 1020.

111. Model Rules of Prof'l Conduct R. 8.4(b) (2020).

112. Iowa Sup. Ct. Att'y Disciplinary Bd. v. Sears, 933 N.W.2d 214, 220 (Iowa 2019); State *ex rel.* Okla. Bar Ass'n v. McMillen, 393 P.3d 219, 223 (Okla. 2017); *In re* Disciplinary Proceedings Against Johns, 847 N.W.2d 179, 185–87 (Wis. 2014).

113. Iowa Sup. Ct. Att'y Disciplinary Bd. v. Templeton, 784 N.W.2d 761, 767 (Iowa 2010) (quoting *In re* Conduct of White, 815 P.2d 1257, 1265 (Or. 1991)).

violation,[114] although any of the last four events clearly establishes a violation where the underlying conduct renders the lawyer unfit to practice.[115]

Second, Model Rule 8.4(c) prohibits "conduct involving dishonesty, fraud, deceit or misrepresentation."[116] As for the standard to be applied when weighing an alleged Model Rule 8.4(c) violation, many states hold that a lawyer's false statement must be knowingly made to violate Rule 8.4(c).[117] Most other states hold that lawyers violate Rule 8.4(c) through statements made with reckless disregard for their truth or falsity,[118] or through grossly negligent misstatements.[119] A very few courts hold that a lawyer may negligently violate Rule 8.4(c).[120]

---

114. *See, e.g.*, *In re* Ivy, 374 P.3d 374, 379 (Alaska 2016) ("Neither the text of Rule 8.4(b) nor the commentary to it requires an underlying criminal conviction. Rather, . . . Rule 8.4(b) contemplates the criminal nature of an attorney's misconduct." (footnote omitted)); Ligon v. Newman, 231 S.W.3d 662, 670 (Ark. 2006) ("Nothing in [Rule 8.4(b)] requires that there be a formal charge or conviction before the rules can be applied to an attorney's conduct."); Iowa Sup. Ct. Att'y Disciplinary Bd. v. Moran, 919 N.W.2d 754, 759 (Iowa 2018) (referring to a criminal conviction); Ky. Bar Ass'n v. Greene, 386 S.W.3d 717, 730 (Ky. 2012) (stating that a lawyer can violate the Kentucky equivalent of Model Rule 8.4(b) absent criminal charges or a conviction); *In re* Williams, 85 So. 3d 583, 591 (La. 2012) (explaining that the lack of a criminal conviction does not bar discipline for violating Rule 8.4(b)); Att'y Grievance Comm'n of Md. v. Bellamy, 162 A.3d 848, 863 (Md. 2017) ("Absence of criminal prosecution does not necessarily mean Rule 8.4(b) has not been violated."); *In re* Treinen, 131 P.3d 1282, 1284 (N.M. 2006) (involving a New Mexico statute governing conditional discharge of felony convictions and asserting that a criminal conviction is not a prerequisite to discipline for criminal conduct); *In re* Savage, 91 A.3d 356, 357 (R.I. 2014) (discussing criminal convictions); *In re* Disciplinary Proceeding Against Kamb, 305 P.3d 1091, 1099 (Wash. 2013) ("[A]n attorney may be sanctioned for committing a crime for which he was never charged."); *In re* Disciplinary Proc. Against Inglimo, 740 N.W.2d 125, 136 n.12 (Wis. 2007) (noting that a lawyer may violate Rule 8.4(b) even without being charged or convicted of a crime).

115. *See, e.g.*, Iowa Sup. Ct. Att'y Disciplinary Bd. v. Meyer, 944 N.W.2d 61, 68 (Iowa 2020) (referring to an *Alford* plea in connection with fraudulent billing); *In re* Najim, 405 P.3d 1223, 1233 (Kan. 2017) (stating that in a disciplinary matter, a criminal judgment is conclusive evidence of the crime's commission); Att'y Grievance Comm'n of Md. v. Paul, 187 A.3d 625, 634 (Md. 2018) ("Paul's pleading guilty and subsequent conviction is conclusive proof that Paul committed a criminal act."); *In re* Toman, 206 A.3d 345, 345 (N.J. 2019) (basing discipline on the lawyer's no contest plea to corruption of the morals of a minor); Morrissey v. Va. State Bar ex rel. Third Dist. Comm., 829 S.E.2d 738, 745 (Va. 2019) (involving an *Alford* plea to contributing to the delinquency of a minor).

116. Model Rules of Prof'l Conduct R. 8.4(c) (2020).

117. *See, e.g.*, Fla. Bar v. Mogil, 763 So. 2d 303, 309–11 (Fla. 2000); Att'y Grievance Comm'n of Md. v. Smith, 109 A.3d 1184, 1195–96 (Md. 2015); *In re* Firstenberger, 878 N.E.2d 912, 913–14 (Mass. 2007); *In re* Conduct of Skagen, 149 P.3d 1171, 1184 (Or. 2006) (discussing an analogous Oregon rule).

118. *In re* Fisher, 202 P.3d 1186, 1203 (Colo. 2009); *In re* Ukwu, 926 A.2d 1106, 1113–14 (D.C. 2007); Iowa Sup. Ct. Att'y Discipline Bd. v. Gottschalk, 729 N.W.2d 812, 818 (Iowa 2007); Office of Disciplinary Counsel v. Surrick, 749 A.2d 441, 445 (Pa. 2000).

119. Walker v. Sup. Ct. Comm. on Prof'l Conduct, 246 S.W.3d 418, 424 (Ark. 2007).

120. *See, e.g.*, *In re* Doughty, 832 A.2d 724, 734–35 (Del. 2003).

Third, there is Model Rule 8.4(d), which broadly prohibits conduct "prejudicial to the administration of justice."[121] Although such conduct defies precise definition,[122] Model Rule 8.4(d) is guaranteed to apply to misconduct in litigation. As one court explained, a lawyer's conduct is prejudicial to the administration of justice if it "bears directly on a case in the judicial process with respect to an identifiable case or tribunal" and "taints the judicial process in more than a *de minimis* way."[123] Alternatively, conduct prejudicial to the administration of justice may be that which "impedes the efficient operation of the courts and wastes judicial resources";[124] which violates "'the well-understood norms and conventions of the practice of law'" and thereby "hinder[s] the efficiency and operation of [the] court system";[125] or "which is likely to impair public confidence in the profession, impact the image of the legal profession and engender disrespect for the court."[126] For that matter, some courts deem a lawyer's misconduct prejudicial to the administration of justice *only* if it relates to a judicial or similar proceeding.[127] Other courts are willing to enforce Rule 8.4(d) outside of litigation to discipline lawyers for conduct that is in some way an affront to the high professional standards lawyers should be held to in performing their public calling,[128] for conduct unbecoming officers of the court,[129] or for conduct that flagrantly violates professional norms and is plainly serious.[130]

B. Threatening Criminal Action

The Model Code prohibited lawyers from presenting or threatening to present criminal charges "solely to obtain an advantage in a civil matter."[131] The framework around lawyers' conduct is different under the Model Rules. If

121. Model Rules of Prof'l Conduct R. 8.4(d) (2020).
122. Iowa Sup. Ct. Att'y Disciplinary Bd. v. Goedken, 939 N.W.2d 97, 107 (Iowa 2020) (quoting Iowa Sup. Ct. Att'y Disciplinary Bd. v. Weiland, 885 N.W.2d 198, 212 (Iowa 2016)).
123. *In re* Hallmark, 831 A.2d 366, 374 (D.C. 2003).
124. Iowa Sup. Ct. Att'y Disciplinary Bd. v. McGinness, 844 N.W.2d 456, 463 (Iowa 2014).
125. Iowa Sup. Ct. Att'y Disciplinary Bd. v. Capotosto, 927 N.W.2d 585, 588–89 (Iowa 2019) (quoting Iowa Sup. Ct. Att'y Disciplinary Bd. v. Stansberry, 922 N.W.2d 591, 597 (Iowa 2019)).
126. Att'y Grievance Comm'n of Md. v. Agbaje, 93 A.3d 262, 274 (Md. 2014).
127. *See, e.g.*, Rogers v. Miss. Bar, 731 So. 2d 1158, 1171 (Miss. 1999) (finding that the lawyer did not violate Rule 8.4(d) because the misconduct was not related to a judicial proceeding); *In re* Conduct of Lawrence, 98 P.3d 366, 375 (Or. 2004) (listing the elements required to find that conduct is prejudicial to administration of justice).
128. *See* Att'y Grievance Comm'n of Md. v. Mba-Jones, 919 A.2d 669, 676 (Md. 2007) (quoting Rheb v. Bar Ass'n of Baltimore Cnty., 46 A.2d 289, 291 (Md. 1946)).
129. *In re* Pyle, 156 P.3d 1231, 1247 (Kan. 2007).
130. *In re* Discipline of Att'y, 815 N.E.2d 1072, 1077–78 (Mass. 2004) (quoting *In re* Discipline of Two Att'ys, 660 N.E.2d 1093 (Mass. 1996)).
131. Model Code of Prof'l Responsibility DR 7-105(A) (1969).

lawyers threaten criminal action where they know the facts will not support it, they violate Model Rule 4.1. Unfounded threats are also likely to violate Model Rules 3.1, 4.4(a), 8.4(c), and 8.4(d). Lawyers may threaten criminal action, however, if the criminal wrongdoing is related to a client's civil claim, the lawyer reasonably believes the civil claim and possible criminal action are both well founded, and the threat cannot reasonably be construed as exerting or suggesting improper influence over the criminal process.[132] The last element suggests that the lawyer and client must actually intend to press criminal charges if the civil claim is not resolved to their satisfaction.[133]

1. *Two Illustrative Cases*

Committee on Legal Ethics of the West Virginia State Bar v. Printz[134] is the leading case on threatening criminal action in a civil matter. The lawyer there, Charles Printz, Jr. (Printz), was asked by his father, Charles Printz, Sr. (Senior), to help resolve an embezzlement from Senior's business, Kable Oil. Senior had discovered that a valued employee, Larry Kesecker, had embezzled almost $200,000. Senior did not desire Kesecker's criminal prosecution; the men were personally close, and a criminal case would harm Kable Oil's reputation. Thus, Kesecker and the Printzes negotiated for the return of the stolen money. In those negotiations, Printz prepared a written confession for Kesecker to sign, as well as an agreement for Kesecker to sell his home, motorcycle, and all other belongings, and to turn over the proceeds of those sales to Kable Oil. Those events all took place in 1986.

Further investigation revealed that Kesecker had stolen nearly $400,000, not $200,000, as originally believed. This led to additional negotiations in July 1987 concerning repayment of the embezzled funds. In August 1987, Printz sent Kesecker a final demand letter in which he offered him two options: a strict repayment plan or criminal prosecution.[135] Kesecker initially agreed to the repayment plan in September 1987, but negotiations broke down when he hired a lawyer. Printz thereafter reported Kesecker to law enforcement authorities. Kesecker pled guilty to embezzlement and received a sentence of five years of probation plus restitution.[136]

During the Kesecker saga, West Virginia's ethics rules were based on the Model Code. The Legal Ethics Committee of the West Virginia State Bar

132. ABA Comm. on Ethics & Prof'l Responsibility, Formal Op. 92-363, at 1 (1992) [hereinafter ABA Formal Op. 92-363]; Alaska Bar Ass'n, Eth. Op. 97-2, at 3 (1997).

133. State *ex rel.* Okla. Bar Ass'n v. Wortham, 957 P.2d 549, 552 (Okla. 1998) (referring to Rule 4.1 for authority); Del. State Bar Ass'n, Comm. on Prof'l Ethics, Op. 1995-2, at 3 (1995) [hereinafter Del. Eth. Op. 1995-2].

134. 416 S.E.2d 720 (W. Va. 1992).

135. *Id.* at 722.

136. *Id.*

charged Printz with violating DR 7-105(A).[137] By the time Printz's case reached the West Virginia Supreme Court, however, the state had adopted the Model Rules. While West Virginia's new rules did not apply to coynduct occurring before their adoption, the *Printz* court considered the reasons for the omission of a counterpart to DR 7-105(A) in the Model Rules in deciding the case.[138] In doing so, the court was persuaded by the explanation of that reasoning in a leading treatise[139] and thus concluded that ethics rules should not bar lawyers from engaging in "otherwise legitimate negotiations."[140] The court noted, however, that there were limits on how far lawyers could go in negotiations with criminal law implications. Those limits, the court explained, are established by the Rule 4.4 prohibition on conduct having no substantial purpose other than to embarrass, delay, or burden a third person.[141]

Everyone involved probably would have been better served if negotiations had continued and Kesecker had never been prosecuted. Kesecker's prosecution would exonerate Printz, however, "*only* if [Printz's] actions were *otherwise legitimate.*"[142] Here trouble seemingly awaited Printz, because an old West Virginia statute prohibited offers not to prosecute crimes in exchange for the return of funds lost due to those crimes.[143] Fortunately for him, the court concluded that the statute failed under the doctrine of desuetude to the extent it prohibited crime victims or their agents from seeking restitution in lieu of criminal prosecution.[144] No one had been prosecuted under the statute since 1938, nearly 50 years before Printz's alleged misconduct.

Because DR 7-105(A) was shown to be unworkable and because Printz did not have fair notice that he might be prosecuted under the old statute, the court concluded that he did not act wrongly in dealing with Kesecker.[145] The court therefore dismissed the charges against him.

The outcome in *Printz* is easily understandable. The criminal charges were tied closely to the client's civil claims, the criminal charges were clearly well founded, and Kable Oil was sure to win if it sued Kesecker to recover

137. *Id.*

138. *Id.*

139. *Id.* at 722–23 (quoting GEOFFREY C. HAZARD, JR. & W. WILLIAM HODES, THE LAW OF LAWYERING § 4.4:103 (1990)).

140. *Id.* at 723.

141. *Id.* (quoting W. VA. RULES OF PROF'L CONDUCT R. 4.4 (1989)).

142. *Id.*

143. *Id.* at 723–24.

144. *Id.* at 726–27. Like prohibitions on vague statutes, "desuetude" is based on the concept of fairness contained in the due process and equal protection clauses of the constitution. Thus, a law prohibiting an act that has not given rise to a real prosecution in many years is unfair to the one person who is selectively prosecuted under that law. *Id.* at 724.

145. *Id.* at 727.

the embezzled funds. Printz never lied to Kesecker, and he had a valid purpose for threatening Kesecker with criminal prosecution: the assured return of the missing money.

In *State ex rel. Oklahoma Bar Ass'n v. Wortham*,[146] lawyer Diane Wortham represented two women, A.J. and L.F., in actions against a counselor arising out of the counselor's sexual misconduct. The counselor's misconduct was generally well known. The local newspaper had reported the revocation of his counselor's license and the allegations against him, and several other women had sued him. Before engaging Wortham, A.J. discussed her situation with a detective for the local police department. She continued weighing the possibility of criminal charges against the counselor during the civil litigation. Similarly, L.F. had spoken with an investigator with the local district attorney's office but decided not to press criminal charges against the counselor at that time.

Wortham attempted to settle her clients' claims with the counselor's insurance company. When negotiations stalled, Wortham concluded that the insurer was negotiating in bad faith.[147] In early June 1997, Wortham wrote to the counselor's lawyer demanding settlement. The letter stated, "'This offer will remain open until June 20, 1997 at which time it is withdrawn and my client will proceed with trial preparation and will contact the District Attorney concerning the filing of criminal charges.'"[148] Shortly thereafter, Wortham wrote to the counselor's lawyer again, reiterating the settlement deadline and stating, "'If this case cannot be settled by negotiations or during the settlement conference my client has advised she intends to have criminal charges filed against [the counselor].'"[149] Wortham would later testify that she did not intend the letters to extort or gain anything valuable, but rather that she wrote them in an effort to get the litigation "'back on track'" after settlement negotiations stalled.[150] The threats of criminal charges were in fact empty because the district attorney knew of both A.J.'s and L.F.'s claims and could have prosecuted the counselor without the women's permission or request.

The Oklahoma Bar Association (OBA) initiated disciplinary action against Wortham. A Professional Responsibility Tribunal (PRT) found that Wortham was not making threats but was simply stating her clients' positions. The PRT concluded that the Oklahoma Rules of Professional Conduct did not specifically prohibit lawyers from threatening criminal prosecution and that Wortham had committed no crime. The PRT thus recommended that the charges be dismissed. The OBA appealed to the Oklahoma Supreme

146. 957 P.2d 549 (Okla. 1998).
147. *Id.* at 551.
148. *Id.* (quoting Wortham's letter).
149. *Id.* (quoting Wortham's letter).
150. *Id.* (quoting Wortham).

Court, arguing that while Oklahoma ethics rules did not specifically prohibit threats of criminal prosecution, it was "not good practice to allow lawyers to use the threat of prosecution in litigating a civil matter."[151]

The *Wortham* court observed early in its analysis that threats of criminal prosecution did not violate Oklahoma ethics rules unless the threats fell within a range of conduct more broadly prohibited.[152] As the court explained:

> Even though Rules 3.1, 4.1, 4.4, and 8.4 do not specifically address . . . threatening criminal prosecution, these rules limit certain threats. A threat of criminal prosecution without a basis in fact or law is a violation of Rule 3.1, which prohibits the assertion of frivolous claims. Rule 4.1, duty concerning truthfulness, prohibits a lawyer from threatening criminal prosecution unless the lawyer intends to proceed with the criminal charges. Rule 4.4 prohibits a lawyer from making a threat which has "no substantial purpose other than to embarrass, delay or burden a third person. . . ."[153]

The OBA contended that Wortham had violated Rule 8.4(b), which prohibited the commission of a criminal act reflecting adversely on her honesty, trustworthiness, or fitness as a lawyer in other respects.[154] Wortham's underlying crime, the OBA alleged, was blackmail. This argument failed for two reasons. First, there was no evidence that Wortham intended to extort anything of value from the counselor or his lawyer; rather, the threats in her letters were intended to get the underlying litigation back on track and were simply statements of her clients' intent.[155] Second, Oklahoma blackmail law requires that a threat must be intended to degrade or disgrace the targeted person for it to have criminal ramifications.[156] Here, the counselor had his license revoked, the allegations against him had appeared in the media, his conduct had been reported to law enforcement authorities, and the civil suits against him were public records. As a result, there was no evidence that reporting the counselor's misconduct to law enforcement authorities would have subjected him to degradation or disgrace beyond that already apparent. In summary, Wortham's actions did not constitute blackmail as a matter of Oklahoma law.

The court concluded that Wortham's conduct did not violate Rule 8.4(b) and that the complaint against her should therefore be dismissed.[157] In a last-ditch salvage attempt, the OBA expressed concern that lawyers might seize on the lack of an express ban on criminal threats to "threaten

151. *Id.* at 551–52.
152. *Id.* at 552 (quoting and discussing ABA Formal Op. 92-363).
153. *Id.*
154. *Id.* (quoting Okla. Rules of Prof'l Conduct R. 8.4(b) (1988)).
155. *Id.* at 553.
156. *Id.*
157. *Id.* at 553.

charges when none [were] warranted."[158] The *Wortham* court brushed aside this argument, reiterating its position that Rules 3.1, 4.1, 4.4, and 8.4(d) and (e) sufficiently guarded against the abusive use of threats that concerned the OBA.[159]

Wortham offers an interesting contrast to *Printz*. First, Wortham clearly threatened criminal action solely to obtain an advantage in a civil case. The advantage to be gained was settlement; the fact that she hoped simply to rekindle negotiations did not alter the advantage sought. Although that fact alone does not compel the conclusion that she acted unethically, the court should have been frank about her motive. Second, unlike *Printz*, the threatened prosecution in *Wortham* was not a reasonable remedial alternative to civil litigation. In *Printz*, a criminal conviction foreseeably would have carried with it an order of restitution, as Printz's guilty plea ultimately did. In *Wortham*, however, a criminal court could hardly have ordered the counselor to un-molest the plaintiffs. In *Printz*, the lawyer made good his threat of prosecution and never sued the wrongdoer, while in *Wortham*, litigation was well under way and the lawyer never approached law enforcement authorities. Third, the hollowness of Wortham's threats should not have helped her cause. If anything, the fact that her threats were empty arguably suggests that they were frivolous and accordingly violated Rules 3.1 and 8.4(d).

C. Summary and Recommendations for Lawyers

Many threats of criminal charges or prosecution intended to achieve an advantage in a representation are ethically permissible.[160] For example, prosecutors obviously must be able to threaten criminal charges. Even in civil controversies, threats of criminal prosecution may be professionally proper. Many more are not, however, and lawyers must exercise great caution when contemplating such threats.

First, lawyers handling civil matters should never threaten criminal charges without first being satisfied that such threats are not criminal in and of themselves. Some possible crimes that must be ruled out, such as blackmail and extortion, are obvious. Other possible crimes may be less apparent or familiar and may vary considerably among jurisdictions. For example, lawyers must be alert to the offense of "compounding a crime." Compounding a crime is the offense of agreeing not to prosecute a crime that one

158. *Id.*

159. *Id.*

160. *Cf.* J.B.B. Inv. Partners v. Fair, 249 Cal. Rptr. 3d 368, 382 (Ct. App. 2019) (finding no ethical violation where the lawyer threatened to expose the defendant's alleged fraud in civil litigation if the parties did not settle; the lawyer did not thereby either expressly or impliedly threaten the defendant with criminal charges to obtain an advantage in a civil matter).

knows has been committed or agreeing to hamper the prosecution. It is an affirmative defense that the benefit obtained by agreement does not exceed the amount believed to be due as restitution. Threats of criminal action are not punishable as compounding a crime if the benefit or property obtained thereby was honestly claimed as compensation for property or lawful services, or are otherwise based on a claim of right.

Second, a threat of criminal action intended to obtain an advantage in a civil matter is most likely to be judged proper where the criminal wrongdoing is related to the client's civil action or transaction. The closer criminal and civil events are related, the better for professional responsibility purposes.[161] Indeed, in some jurisdictions it may be that the civil and criminal matters *must* be related for such a threat not to violate Rules 4.4 and 8.4(d).[162] In any event, the relatedness requirement helps ensure that lawyers' conduct in threatening criminal charges or prosecution does not compound other crimes.[163] Compounding a crime is a crime in its own right, of course, and threats appropriately classified as compounding are further consequential because they violate the Model Rule 8.4(b) prohibition on criminal conduct reflecting adversely on a lawyer's fitness to practice.[164] The lesson here is that prudent lawyers should not threaten criminal charges or prosecution to obtain any kind of advantage in a civil matter unless the civil matter and criminal conduct are closely related.

Third, a lawyer must satisfy herself that the civil matter in connection with which the threats of criminal consequences are made and the allegations of criminal behavior are both well-founded.[165] Unfounded civil actions may be as problematic as unsubstantiated criminal threats made in connection with them.[166] Lawyers can ethically threaten criminal consequences only if they reasonably believe that such consequences may be warranted as a matter of fact and law.[167] In some instances, this may require lawyers to undertake reasonable investigations and conduct legal research before acting. Regardless, lawyers should never act hastily when weighing the possibility of criminal threats. Furthermore, this is no time for lawyers to make decisions in isolation. To the contrary, lawyers considering the possibility of threatening criminal charges should consult with knowledgeable colleagues or advisors before embarking down this path. In large and sophisticated law

161. *See, e.g.*, Comm. on Legal Ethics of the W. Va. State Bar v. Printz, 416 S.E.2d 720, 727 (W. Va. 1992) (finding no ethics violation where civil and criminal conduct were closely intertwined).

162. Utah Eth. Op. 03-04, 2003 WL 23146204, at *2 (Utah State Bar, Ethics Advisory Op. Comm. 2003) [hereinafter Utah Eth. Op. 03-04].

163. *Id.*

164. ABA Formal Op. 92-363, *supra* note 132, at 2–3.

165. Utah Eth. Op. 03-04, *supra* note 162, 2003 WL 23146204, at *3.

166. *See, e.g.*, La. State Bar Ass'n v. Harrington, 585 So. 2d 514, 520 (La. 1990) (finding Rule 4.4 violation in baseless civil action in which lawyer threatened criminal prosecution).

167. Utah Eth. Op. 03-04, *supra* note 162, 2003 WL 23146204, at *3.

firms, lawyers contemplating criminal threats should first check their judgment with their firms' general counsel or ethics or loss prevention partners.

Fourth, in threatening criminal charges, a lawyer must never state or imply an ability to influence law enforcement authorities other than through legitimate means open to all parties, such as the truthful recitation of facts and persuasive presentation of evidence. To do otherwise risks violating Model Rule 8.4(e), which prohibits lawyers from stating or implying "an ability to influence improperly a government agency or official or to achieve results by means that violate the Rules of Professional Conduct or other law."[168] Lawyers may violate Rule 8.4(e) merely by making inappropriate statements; they need not intend to exercise their claimed influence.[169] Indeed, lawyers may violate the rule through improper statements even if they have no influence or are unable to exercise any influence that they may possess.

Fifth, lawyers must be prepared to follow through on threats if targets of those threats do not respond according to the lawyers' or clients' wishes.[170] Even if the threatened criminal charges were legitimate, the failure to carry through with the threats would potentially expose a lawyer to discipline for violating Rules 4.1, 4.4(a), 8.4(c), and 8.4(d).

Sixth, lawyers must be careful if the target of their threats agrees to resolve the civil matter to avoid criminal charges or prosecution. Lawyers generally may agree, or persuade or allow clients to agree, to refrain from reporting criminal conduct in satisfaction of a claim.[171] Lawyers can also document such agreements. What lawyers cannot do is somehow conceal the criminal behavior at issue. In the case of felonious behavior, the concealment of a felony is itself the offense of misprision of a felony.[172] Conviction for misprision of a felony requires the government to prove (1) the commission and completion of a felony by a third party, (2) the defendant's knowledge of the felony, (3) the defendant's failure to notify authorities of the felony, and (4) that the defendant took an affirmative act to conceal the felony.[173] A defendant must affirmatively act to prevent discovery of an earlier felony; merely failing to report the felony to authorities is insufficient.[174] This conduct does not constitute an affirmative step to conceal

168. Model Rules of Prof'l Conduct R. 8.4(e) (2020).

169. State *ex rel.* Okla. Bar Ass'n v. Erickson, 29 P.3d 550, 554 (Okla. 2001).

170. Del. Eth. Op. 1995-2, *supra* note 133, at 3.

171. Del. Eth. Op. 1995-2, *supra* note 133, at 3; S.C. Adv. Op. 92-32, 1992 WL 810445, at *3 (S.C. Bar Ethics Advisory Comm. 1992).

172. *See* 18 U.S.C. § 4 (2018) (establishing the federal offense of misprision of a felony).

173. United States v. Baumgartner, 581 F. App'x 522, 526 (6th Cir. 2014) (quoting United States v. Goldberg, 862 F.2d 101, 104 (6th Cir. 1988)); United States v. White Eagle, 721 F.3d 1108, 1119 (9th Cir. 2013).

174. *In re* Madden, 423 S.W.3d 39, 45–46 (Ark. 2012).

a related felony because it does not impede authorities' discovery of the crime.[175] Thus, lawyers should never agree, nor allow their clients to agree, to any conduct that might reasonably be perceived as concealing criminal conduct. At the very least, such conduct may be found to violate the Rule 8.4(d) prohibition against conduct that is prejudicial to the administration of justice.[176] Agreeing not to report a crime to law enforcement authorities and otherwise agreeing to keep the matter confidential is probably as far as lawyers reasonably can go.[177]

Finally, while we have focused on criminal charges, lawyers should also generally avoid threatening adversaries or witnesses with similar forms of government action.[178] For example, a lawyer who threatens a witness or opposing party with deportation under immigration laws may violate ethics rules in the process.[179]

D. Threatening Professional Discipline

In addition to threatening criminal action in search of advantage, lawyers sometimes threaten other lawyers with ethics complaints. Although the Model Rules require lawyers to report other lawyers' misconduct in certain circumstances,[180] the rules do not expressly prohibit threats to file disciplinary complaints to gain an advantage in a representation.[181] Such threats do not violate Model Rule 8.3(a).[182] That does not mean, however, that they are proper.[183] Unfounded threats of disciplinary action aimed at achieving an advantage in a representation are offensive and reflect adversely on a

175. Patel v. Mukasey, 526 F.3d 800, 803 (5th Cir. 2008) (quoting United States v. Adams, 961 F.2d 505, 508 (5th Cir. 1992)).

176. *See, e.g.*, Iowa Sup. Ct. Att'y Disciplinary Bd. v. Buchanan, 757 N.W.2d 251, 254–55 (Iowa 2008) (finding that a lawyer who offered to destroy evidence of a forgery and to withhold evidence in a criminal prosecution engaged in conduct that was prejudicial to the administration of justice).

177. *See* United States v. Izarraga-Ponce, No. CR-08-220-E-BLW, 2009 WL 928113, at *1 (D. Idaho Apr. 2, 2009) (explaining what is required for concealment of a crime as an element of misprision of a felony).

178. *See generally* N.Y. Eth. Op. 2017-3, 2017 WL 6614554 (N.Y. State Bar Ass'n, Comm. on Prof'l Ethics 2017) (discussing rules of professional conduct that may apply to lawyers' threats of "ancillary non-criminal proceedings" against adverse parties).

179. *See, e.g.*, 2005 N.C. Eth. Op. 3, 2005 WL 3964317, at *2 (N.C. State Bar 2005) (citing Rules 4.4(a) and 8.4(d) in concluding that "a lawyer may not use the threat of reporting an opposing party or a witness to immigration officials in settlement negotiations on behalf of a client in a civil matter").

180. Model Rules of Prof'l Conduct R. 8.3(a) (2020).

181. ABA Comm. on Ethics & Prof'l Responsibility, Formal Op. 94-383, at 2 (1994) [hereinafter ABA Formal Op. 94-383].

182. *In re* Comfort, 159 P.3d 1011, 1027–28 (Kan. 2007).

183. *See, e.g.*, Iowa State Bar Ass'n, Ethics & Prac. Guidelines Comm., Ethics Op. 14-02, at 1–3 (2014) (discussing threats of disciplinary action, examining warnings to other lawyers that their conduct may have ethical implications, and concluding that "[w]rongfully accusing a fellow lawyer of unethical conduct . . . to gain advantage is the antithesis of professionalism").

lawyer's fitness to practice law.[184] The purposes of the ethics rules are subverted when lawyers invoke them as procedural or tactical weapons.[185] Tactical threats of disciplinary action violate Model Rules 3.1, 4.1, and 4.4(a), or some combination of the three.[186] Lawyers may violate Model Rule 4.4(a) by threatening an ethics violation even if there appear to be legitimate grounds to accuse another lawyer of misconduct if the threat is animated by an improper purpose, or the means by which the threat is conveyed are wrongful. Furthermore, threatening a disciplinary complaint solely to achieve an advantage in a matter constitutes conduct prejudicial to the administration of justice within the meaning of Model Rule 8.4(d) regardless of whether the threatened complaint is valid.[187] If the target lawyer's perceived misconduct is serious enough to warrant reporting under Model Rule 8.3(a), then Model Rule 8.4(a), which prohibits lawyers from violating or attempting to violate ethics rules,[188] necessarily makes it unethical for a lawyer to promise to skip reporting to obtain an advantage in a representation.[189] Beyond the mandatory reporting requirement found in Model Rule 8.3(a) and its overlap with Model Rule 8.4(a), this conclusion is a logical corollary of the general prohibition on lawyers bargaining away disciplinary complaints against themselves or their colleagues.[190]

---

184. *See, e.g.*, *In re* Kenny, 217 P.3d 36, 36–38, 41 (Kan. 2009) (involving a lawyer who wrote two letters to another lawyer saying that his clients would likely file a disciplinary complaint against the second lawyer unless the second lawyer refunded the fees that he had previously charged the clients); Akron Bar Ass'n v. Catanzarite, 893 N.E.2d 835, 841–42 (Ohio 1998) (threatening sham ethics complaints to "exact a toll" on opposing counsel violated Ohio rule prohibiting conduct reflecting adversely on a lawyer's fitness to practice law).

185. Ky. Bar Ass'n v. Blum, 404 S.W.3d 841, 852 (Ky. 2013).

186. *In re* Discipline of Eicher, 661 N.W.2d 354, 367 (S.D. 2003) (referring additionally to Rule 8.4(b)); ABA Formal Op. 94-383, *supra* note 181, at 3; *see, e.g.*, Att'y Grievance Comm'n of Md. v. Rheinstein, 223 A.3d 505, 545 (Md. 2020) (violating Rule 4.4(a) by threatening opposing counsel with a disciplinary complaint if they did not dismiss an appeal or withdraw as counsel for the opposing party).

187. *See, e.g.*, *In re* Dimick, 969 N.E.2d 17, 18 (Ind. 2012) (disciplining a lawyer under Rule 8.4(d) for threatening an opposing lawyer with a disciplinary complaint unless the other lawyer made a settlement proposal).

188. Model Rules of Prof'l Conduct R. 8.4(a) (2020).

189. ABA Formal Op. 94-383, *supra* note 181, at 3; N.Y.C. Eth. Op. 2015-5, *supra* note 97, 2015 WL 4197679, at *3–5.

190. *See* Fla. Bar v. Frederick, 756 So. 2d 79, 86–87 (Fla. 2000) (attempting to bargain away a disciplinary complaint violates Rule 8.4(d)); Iowa Sup. Ct. Bd. of Prof'l Ethics & Conduct v. Furlong, 625 N.W.2d 711, 713–14 (Iowa 2001) (punishing the lawyer for attempting to dissuade a witness from filing a disciplinary complaint); Disciplinary Couns. v. Chambers, 928 N.E.2d 1061, 1065 (Ohio 2010) (attempting to get someone to dismiss a disciplinary complaint violates Ohio Rules 8.4(d) and (h)); *In re Discipline of Eicher*, 661 N.W.2d at 365 ("The duty to report disciplinary violations also embraces a responsibility not to frustrate the reporting by others or dissuading others from cooperating in disciplinary investigations." (footnote omitted)); Ohio Adv. Op. 2010-3, 2010 WL 2522463, at *4 (Sup. Ct. of Ohio, Bd. of Comm'rs on Grievances & Discipline 2010) (asking a current or former client not to file or to withdraw an ethics complaint as part of a legal malpractice settlement is improper).

1. *Two Illustrative Cases*

In re Pyle[191] exemplifies lawyers' use of threatened ethics complaints to obtain leverage in civil litigation.[192] *In re Pyle* stemmed from a personal injury case in which E. Thomas Pyle, III, had represented Sallie Moline against her boyfriend, Ricci Gutzman. Moline had tripped and fallen on Gutzman's driveway. Before suing on Moline's behalf, Pyle helped her prepare an affidavit for Gutzman's signature in which Gutzman purported to admit responsibility for the accident and Moline's injuries. He further stated in the affidavit that he was insured by American Family Insurance, and directed American Family to admit liability and make every possible effort to settle Moline's claim for a fair and reasonable sum.[193]

Pyle then sued Gutzman on Moline's behalf. American Family hired John Conderman to defend Gutzman. Conderman filed an answer denying liability. He also served Pyle with interrogatories and a request for a statement of Moline's alleged damages. Conderman was allegedly aware of the affidavit when he answered and served the discovery. If so, it seems probable that he had sniffed the odor of collusion emanating from the affidavit. Regardless, Pyle went on the offensive. He wrote Conderman and accused him of a conflict of interest:

> "You represent the defendant, not the insurance company. The defendant has admitted liability and taken full responsibility for his actions and omissions. You are his advocate and when you filed the answer, you were not advocating his position, but instead were advocating the insurance company's position and interests. Not only do I find this behavior frivolous, but I also find it unethical."[194]

Pyle offered to settle Moline's claim for $300,000. If that settlement could not be reached in 20 days, Pyle threatened, he would "'[t]urn the facts of the case over to the Disciplinary Administrator'" and recommend to Gutzman "'that he file an ethics complaint against [Conderman] with the Disciplinary Administrator.'"[195] The only way for Conderman to right his wrong, Pyle wrote, was to settle the case as requested or to admit liability and restrict discovery to Moline's alleged damages.[196]

In a second letter to Conderman, Pyle wrote that "any reporting to the Disciplinary Administrator [was] not connected to any settlement offer or negotiation" in the case.[197] Rather than proceeding with a disciplinary

191. 91 P.3d 1222 (Kan. 2004).

192. *See also, e.g.*, *In re* Comfort, 159 P.3d 1011, 1019–22 (Kan. 2007) (concluding that the lawyer violated Rules 4.4(a) and 8.4(d)).

193. *In re Pyle*, 91 P.3d at 1225.

194. *Id.* (quoting Pyle's letter).

195. *Id.* at 1226 (quoting Pyle's letter).

196. *Id.*

197. *Id.* at 1227.

complaint, he asserted, he would prefer that Conderman simply amend the answer to admit liability and amend his discovery requests to focus solely on Moline's damages.[198] Believing his relationship with Gutzman to be irreversibly damaged by Pyle's conduct, Conderman withdrew from the case and sent copies of Pyle's first letter, the petition, and the answer to the Disciplinary Administrator.[199]

A disciplinary hearing panel concluded that Conderman had violated no ethics rules, but the Disciplinary Administrator charged Pyle with several violations. Pyle contended that his first letter to Conderman was not meant as a threat and that he based it on information that Moline provided to him.[200] He admitted that the first letter was "unprofessional" but tried to minimize his misconduct by claiming to have written it in "the 'heat of battle.'"[201] He acknowledged that he should not have sent the letter and that sending it reflected adversely on his fitness to practice law.[202] The hearing panel concluded that Pyle violated several Kansas Rules of Professional Conduct in connection with the letter, including Rules 4.4, 8.3(a), 8.4(d), and 8.4(g) (prohibiting other conduct that adversely reflects on a lawyer's fitness to practice law).

Facing a public censure and additional mandatory continuing education on professional responsibility as a sanction for all of his misconduct in Moline's representation, Pyle admitted that he violated Rule 8.4(g). He resisted the Rule 4.4, 8.3(a), and 8.4(d) violations, however, challenging those in the Kansas Supreme Court.

With respect to Kansas Rule 8.3(a), it is first important to note that unlike the Model Rules version, Kansas Rule 8.3(a) requires lawyers to report "any" misconduct to disciplinary authorities—not just serious misconduct.[203] This is so despite a comment to the rule requiring that a lawyer know of "substantial misconduct" before the duty to report is triggered.[204]

Pyle contended that the "substantial misconduct" requirement in the commentary should be read into the rule, apparently reasoning in hindsight that Conderman's misconduct had been insubstantial.[205] There were three flaws in this argument. First, consistent with basic rules of construction, the court was justifiably unwilling to read the word "substantial" into a clear and unambiguous rule requiring the reporting of "any" misconduct.[206] Second, Pyle had admitted in his brief that he considered Conderman's alleged

198. *See id.* (referring mistakenly to the petition that Pyle filed).
199. *Id.*
200. *Id.*
201. *Id.* (quoting Pyle before the disciplinary hearing panel).
202. *Id.*
203. *Id.* at 1230 (quoting the Kansas rule).
204. *Id.*
205. *Id.*
206. *Id.*

misconduct to be substantial.[207] Third, it was obvious from the record that Pyle thought Conderman's alleged misconduct to be serious.

Retreating, Pyle contended that reporting Conderman's alleged misconduct would have required him to violate his duty of confidentiality and that he *had* reported Conderman when he responded to the Disciplinary Administrator's inquiry into his own misconduct. Neither argument worked. With respect to the first, Conderman's alleged misconduct was embodied in his answer and discovery. Thus, Pyle would not have breached his duty of confidentiality by reporting Conderman to the Disciplinary Administrator.[208] As for Pyle's defense that he had reported Conderman's alleged misconduct as required, his "response to a letter questioning his own misconduct [was] not an independent report of another attorney's misconduct."[209]

With respect to the Rule 4.4 and 8.4(d) violations, Pyle was sunk by his admission to the disciplinary hearing panel that his letter was unprofessional and never should have been sent.[210] Those admissions were "tantamount to acknowledging that the letter was used as a tool to gain a better bargaining position in the lawsuit."[211] There was thus clear and convincing evidence that his conduct violated the Rule 4.4 prohibition on conduct having no substantial purpose other than to embarrass, delay, or burden a third person. Moreover, the court held, Pyle's conduct "was obviously prejudicial to the administration of justice."[212] After weighing several factors, the court publicly censured Pyle.

The decision in *In re Pyle* is clearly correct. If Conderman had a conflict of interest that materially limited his representation of Gutzman, or filed a knowingly false answer, then Pyle should have acted to remedy those problems rather than using Conderman's conduct as a lever to achieve a favorable settlement. On the other hand, the mere fact that Conderman was hired by American Family to defend Gutzman did not necessarily mean that he also represented American Family. Conderman's denial of liability on Gutzman's part and his service of liability-related discovery hardly evidenced a conflict of interest or a lack of candor. It is equally plausible that Gutzman's purported acceptance of responsibility for Moline's injuries was the product of a snap judgment or other influence that he regretted and that he wished to retract his admissions. If Gutzman's first affidavit was not an honest recitation of the facts but was instead a collusive effort to benefit Moline, it was in his interests to begin retreating from any false statements in the affidavit. Conderman was required to file a factually accurate answer.

207. *Id.*
208. *Id.*
209. *Id.*
210. *Id.* at 1231.
211. *Id.*
212. *Id.*

Even if you accept that Gutzman may have borne fault for Moline's alleged injuries, Pyle was in no position to cast ethical stones at Conderman. Pyle almost certainly violated Rule 4.3 by having Gutzman execute his first affidavit.[213]

Barrett v. Virginia State Bar[214] is noteworthy because Virginia Rule of Professional Conduct 3.4(i) prohibits lawyers "from 'present[ing] or threaten[ing] to present criminal or disciplinary charges solely to obtain an advantage in a civil matter.'"[215] The lawyer there, Timothy Barrett, represented himself in his divorce from his wife, Jill Rhudy. In corresponding with Rhudy's lawyer, Lanis Karnes, he repeatedly accused Karnes of unethical behavior.[216] He threatened to seek her disbarment and warned her of his intent to file a complaint against her with the Virginia State Bar.[217] Unsurprisingly, Barrett never filed an ethics complaint against Karnes. When Barrett was faced with professional discipline arising out of a range of alleged misconduct in his divorce case, he defended the Rule 3.4(i) charge on the basis that his threats were not made solely to obtain an advantage in the matter. He pointed out that in one instance he had sought sanctions against Karnes even though he had not filed a disciplinary complaint, thus suggesting that he had honestly thought her behavior to be unethical.[218]

The Virginia Supreme Court concluded that Barrett had violated Rule 3.4(i). It was clear from Barrett's letters that his threats were intended to force Karnes to withdraw from Rhudy's representation because of his dislike for her. He testified in his disciplinary case that he wanted Karnes out "because he 'knew that [she] had it in for [him].'"[219] Barrett had also admitted his improper purpose in a letter to Karnes, telling her in the letter that he had threatened her in the hope that Rhudy would terminate her engagement.[220] In the end, the court remanded the case to the Virginia State Bar Disciplinary Board for consideration of an appropriate sanction.

Barrett perhaps proves only that a lawyer who represents himself has a fool for a client. It is interesting, however, that Barrett apparently thought that his belief that Karnes was acting unethically was a defense to a charge that he had threatened disciplinary charges solely to obtain an advantage in his divorce proceeding. In fact, it is only marginally consequential whether the target lawyer has behaved unethically if the lawyer making the threat is

213. *See* Model Rules of Prof'l Conduct R. 4.3 (2020) (governing lawyers' conduct when dealing with unrepresented persons).

214. 611 S.E.2d 375 (Va. 2007).

215. *Id.* at 381.

216. *Id.*

217. *Id.*

218. *Id.*

219. *Id.*

220. *Id.*

doing so exclusively to obtain some advantage in the matter at hand.[221] The focal point of the ethics rules is the purpose of the threat and not the conduct of the lawyer being threatened.[222]

2. *Guidance for Lawyers*

Lawyers should generally avoid threatening other lawyers with professional discipline. If another lawyer appears to be contemplating or engaging in unethical conduct, however, it may be appropriate to communicate that belief.[223] For example, it may be appropriate to warn another lawyer that a representation will pose a conflict of interest, remind an opponent that an intended ex parte communication would violate Model Rule 4.2, or insist that an adversary correct a false statement to a tribunal. If the other lawyer responds reasonably, as by forgoing the potential misconduct or correcting a previous breach, then the communication had a salutary effect. Regardless, a lawyer should never assert that another lawyer is or will be guilty of professional conduct unless she (1) has a reasonable basis for doing so and (2) has a substantial purpose for doing so other than embarrassing or harassing the second lawyer.

Lawyers who suspect that another lawyer has behaved unethically and who intend to so inform the allegedly offending lawyer are wise to consult with colleagues with expertise in professional responsibility before doing so. It is possible that the first lawyer's belief may be mistaken, or that other good reasons exist for not leveling the accusation. Furthermore, drafting a letter or e-mail message that appropriately raises the lawyer's concerns without reading like a threat can be an art form. Law firms may wish to adopt policies that require such consultation as a precondition for making threats or initiating disciplinary action.

A lawyer must never imply or suggest that a disciplinary complaint is a bargaining chip. Assuming there are no confidentiality issues, lawyers must timely report other lawyers' serious ethical violations to professional authorities. For that matter, there is a good argument that lawyers who accuse another lawyer of misconduct must be prepared to report the second lawyer to professional authorities even if the misconduct would not otherwise require reporting under Model Rule 8.3(a). If they do not make

---

221. Ky. Bar Ass'n v. Blum, 404 S.W.3d 841, 850 (Ky. 2013) (quoting Douglas R. Richmond, *Saber-Rattling and the Sound of Professional Responsibility*, 34 Am. J. Trial Advoc. 27, 61 (2010)).

222. *Id.*

223. *See* N.Y.C. Eth. Op. 2015-5, *supra* note 97, 2015 WL 4197679, at *4 (indicating that a lawyer may confront another lawyer with evidence of the second lawyer's misconduct to confirm an ethics violation, communicate with another lawyer to educate her about a potential ethics violation and allow her the opportunity to change course, or communicate with opposing counsel to induce her to remedy the harm caused by her misconduct).

a report, disciplinary authorities or a court may view their silence as a sign that they had no substantial purpose other than to embarrass or burden the second lawyer.

Lawyers who accuse another lawyer of misconduct should do so in carefully measured tones. Communications concerning another lawyer's alleged breaches of professional duties are no place for insults or intemperance. In addition, such communications should also be confined to that lawyer and, in some cases, to others who truly need to know of the accusations. "Means" count here.

Finally, on the other side of the coin, a lawyer who is accused of professional misconduct must promptly determine whether the allegation is valid. If it is, can the lawyer reasonably cure the lapse or mitigate its effects? Depending on the jurisdiction and the nature of the misconduct alleged, there may be substantial value in reporting oneself to authorities. The lawyer must at least inform her client of the accusation.[224] In some cases, a lawyer accused of misconduct may be required to withdraw from the representation.[225]

IV. Conclusion

Lawyers sometimes lose control of their emotions in litigation and make irresponsible remarks about courts, opposing counsel, and opposing parties. Occasionally lawyers lose all perspective and engage in outrageous personal attacks on others involved in a given matter. In other instances, they may stand idly by while a client engages in abusive or disruptive behavior. Sadly, some lawyers regularly behave this way. In any event, such uncivil behavior is in many instances unethical.

In addition to the sort of abusive behavior that might generally be branded as uncivil, some lawyers baselessly threaten their counterparts, opposing parties, and witnesses with criminal prosecution. Other lawyers threaten one another with meritless disciplinary complaints. Still other lawyers unreasonably threaten a third party with litigation or menace another party with new or aggravating claims or causes of action in existing litigation. All such tactics are ethically impermissible.

At bottom, the behaviors criticized in this chapter represent poor advocacy. They tend to harden opposing parties' positions and frustrate courts. For these reasons, good lawyers—while perhaps guilty of occasional anger that bleeds into a case—practice on a different plane.

---

224. Model Rules of Prof'l Conduct R. 1.4(a)(3) & (b) (2020).

225. *See generally* ABA Comm. on Ethics & Prof'l Responsibility, Formal Op. 94-384 (1994) ("Withdrawal by Lawyer Against Whom Opposing Counsel Has Filed a Disciplinary Complaint").

9

Candor to the Tribunal

I. Introduction

The law places an exceptionally high value on lawyers' honesty. For example, Model Rule of Professional Conduct 4.1(a) mandates lawyers' honesty in communications with others in the course of a representation.[1] Model Rule 8.4(c) and state analogs broadly prohibit conduct "involving dishonesty, fraud, deceit or misrepresentation."[2] Courts discipline lawyers for Rule 8.4(c) violations arising out of lawyers' conduct unrelated to the practice of law.[3] Courts routinely assert that all lawyers must be honest at all times,[4] describe candor and honesty as lawyers' stock-in-trade,[5] proclaim honesty to be "of paramount importance in the practice of law,"[6] and make hortatory statements about truth being "the cornerstone of the judicial system" and a license to practice law requiring "allegiance and fidelity to truth."[7]

Honesty is especially critical in lawyers' dealings with tribunals.[8] Courts necessarily rely on lawyers to present most facts and argument. If lawyers

1. Model Rules of Prof'l Conduct R. 4.1(a) (2020) (stating that in representing a client, a lawyer shall not knowingly "make a false statement of material fact or law to a third person").

2. *Id.* R. 8.4(c).

3. *See, e.g.*, *In re* Mintz, 317 P.3d 756, 761–64 (Kan. 2014) (concluding that the lawyer violated Rule 8.4(c) by lying to the police about circumstances surrounding his intoxicated girlfriend's accidental death); Att'y Grievance Comm'n of Md. v. Seltzer, 34 A.3d 498, 511 (Md. 2011) (noting that Rule 8.4(c) applies to lawyers' conduct outside the practice of law and finding that the lawyer violated the rule by acting dishonestly in operating a real estate agency he owned); *In re* Savage, 91 A.3d 356, 357–58 (R.I. 2014) (concluding that the lawyer violated Rule 8.4(c) by lying on her application for a driver's license).

4. *See, e.g.*, *In re* Baber, 106 A.3d 1072, 1077 (D.C. 2015) (quoting *In re* Guberman, 978 A.2d 200, 209 n.10 (D.C. 2009)); *In re* Kalil's Case, 773 A.2d 647, 648 (N.H. 2001).

5. *In re* Venie, 395 P.3d 516, 523 (N.M. 2017) (quoting *In re* Stein, 177 P.3d 513, 522 (N.M. 2008)).

6. Att'y Grievance Comm'n of Md. v. Agbaje, 93 A.3d 262, 273 (Md. 2014).

7. Office of Disciplinary Couns. v. Kiesewetter, 889 A.2d 47, 56 (Pa. 2005).

8. *See, e.g.*, Hanover Ins. Co. v. United States, 146 Fed. Cl. 447, 450 (Fed. Cl. 2019) ("The duty of candor is paramount, surpassing generalized notions relating to counsel's obligations to other counsel, and in many respects, to the client."); Iowa Sup. Ct. Att'y Disciplinary Bd. v. Barry, 908 N.W.2d 217, 233 (Iowa 2018) (discussing the importance of lawyers' duty of candor to a

do not do so frankly, fully, and honestly, there is a strong possibility that courts will form inaccurate conclusions or reach incorrect results. To that end, the law imposes on lawyers a duty of candor to a tribunal.[9]

This chapter examines several aspects of lawyers' duty of candor. As a practical matter, there should be no need for this chapter. Trial and appellate lawyers ought to recognize the importance of credibility with the judges before whom they appear. Credibility with courts enhances lawyers' effectiveness as advocates, aids clients, and advances lawyers' professional development in the process. Naturally, lawyers' credibility with courts depends heavily on their honesty and trustworthiness. Once lost or diminished, credibility as an advocate is difficult—sometimes impossible—to regain. Despite these obvious truths, experience and abundant case law unfortunately demonstrate that a surprising number of lawyers do not appreciate their duty of candor, the breadth of that duty, or the high standard it imposes.

II. Candor in Context

Model Rule of Professional Conduct 3.3, broadly entitled "Candor Toward the Tribunal," contains several provisions critical to trial and appellate lawyers. The first is Rule 3.3(a)(1), which provides that a lawyer shall not knowingly "make a false statement of fact or law to a tribunal or fail to correct a false statement of material fact or law previously made to the tribunal by the lawyer."[10] Before the 2002 amendments to the Model Rules, this rule provided: "A lawyer shall not knowingly . . . make a false statement of *material* fact or law to a tribunal."[11] The 2002 amendments to Model Rule 3.3(a)(1) reflect the belief that lawyers should never knowingly make false statements to courts and other adjudicatory bodies regardless of whether such statements are material. The addition of the second clause to Model Rule 3.3(a)(1) strengthened lawyers' duty to correct material false statements once made. That duty already existed under Model Rule 3.3(a)(1), as well as Model Rules 8.4(c) and (d), but was not clearly expressed.[12] Some jurisdictions declined to adopt the 2002 amendments to the Model Rules and retain

tribunal); Att'y Grievance Comm'n of Md. v. Fader, 66 A.3d 18, 43 (Md. 2013) ("'[C]andor by a lawyer, in any capacity, is one of the most important character traits of a member of the Bar.' . . . When a lawyer lies to a tribunal, he or she violates a norm that warrants disbarment." (citation omitted)); *In re* McKenna, 110 A.3d 1126, 1148 (R.I. 2015) (calling the duty of candor to a tribunal "the foundation of a lawyer's profession").

9. *See* Att'y Grievance Comm'n of Md. v. Hoerauf, 229 A.3d 802, 821 (Md. 2020) (quoting Att'y Grievance Comm'n of Md. v. Ambe, 218 A.3d 757, 771 (Md. 2019)).

10. Model Rules of Prof'l Conduct R. 3.3(a)(1) (2020).

11. Model Rules of Prof'l Conduct R. 3.3(a)(1) (2001) (emphasis added).

12. Model Rules of Prof'l Conduct R. 8.4(c) (2020) (prohibiting conduct involving dishonesty, fraud, deceit, or misrepresentation); *id.* R. 8.4(d) (prohibiting conduct prejudicial to the administration of justice).

the materiality requirement in all aspects of Rule 3.3(a)(1). Regardless, lawyers' duty of candor continues to the conclusion of a proceeding and applies even if compliance requires the disclosure of client confidences.[13]

It is generally understood that lawyers' duty of candor is not limited to situations in which they are representing clients.[14] Rather, the duty of candor attaches whenever a lawyer communicates with a tribunal. Lawyers who appear pro se owe the same high duty of candor to the tribunal that they would owe if appearing on behalf of a client.[15] Courts' need to rely on the truthfulness of lawyers' statements does not depend on whether a lawyer is appearing pro se or on a client's behalf. Furthermore, lawyers can be disciplined for false statements made to a tribunal as a party or a witness.[16] The requirement that lawyers always be truthful is a simple and unambiguous standard that does not depend on the circumstances and that is not excused by the embarrassment or stress that accompanies being a party or witness in litigation.

There is, however, a competing position. While the text of Model Rule 3.3(a)(1) does not require a lawyer to be representing a client for the duty of candor to attach, a comment to Model Rule 3.3 states that the rule "governs the conduct of a lawyer who is representing a client in the proceedings of a tribunal" or "in an ancillary proceeding conducted pursuant to

13. *Id.* R. 3.3(c).

14. *See, e.g.*, Cohen v. Statewide Grievance Comm., 208 A.3d 676, 690 (Conn. App. Ct. 2019) (concluding that Rule 3.3(a)(1) "is not limited to statements made in the course of attorney-client relationships").

15. *In re* Manning-Wallace, 695 S.E.2d 237, 240 (Ga. 2010); *In re* O'Meara's Case, 834 A.2d 235, 237 (N.H. 2003).

16. *See, e.g.*, People v. Kolbjornsen, 35 P.3d 181, 183–85 (Colo. 1999) (disbarring a lawyer who lied under oath in a bankruptcy proceeding in which he was a party); People v. Small, 962 P.2d 258, 259–60 (Colo. 1998) (censuring a lawyer who falsely testified in small claims court case in which he was a party); *In re* Thomas, 30 N.E.3d 704, 708 (Ind. 2015) (finding that a lawyer who filed for personal bankruptcy violated Rule 3.3(a)(1) by failing to list his trust account in his bankruptcy schedules and statement of financial affairs); *In re* Usher, 987 N.E.2d 1080, 1087 (Ind. 2013) (disciplining the lawyer-litigant in case in which the lawyer-litigant was represented by counsel); *In re* Barratt, 663 N.E.2d 536, 539–40 (Ind. 1996) (suspending a lawyer for false testimony in small claims court); Att'y Grievance Comm'n of Md. v. Kaned, 215 A.3d 242, 271 (Md. 2019) (failing to disclose the existence of an adversary action in the lawyer's personal bankruptcy schedules); Att'y Grievance Comm'n of Md. v. White, 731 A.2d 447, 456–59 (Md. 1999) (disbarring a lawyer who lied in her deposition in her own employment discrimination case and who lied as a witness in her client's post-conviction proceeding); *In re* Balliro, 899 N.E.2d 794, 804 (Mass. 2009) (suspending a lawyer who lied under oath in her boyfriend's trial on domestic violence charges in which the lawyer was the victim); *In re* Disciplinary Action Against Ward, 563 N.W.2d 70, 72 (Minn. 1997) (suspending a lawyer who lied in a deposition); *In re* O'Meara's Case, 834 A.2d 235, 237–38 (N.H. 2003) (censuring a lawyer who lied while appearing pro se in divorce and custody case); *In re* Kornreich, 693 A.2d 877, 879–90 (N.J. 1997) (suspending a lawyer who lied in a municipal court case arising out of a minor traffic accident); Diaz v. Comm'n for Lawyer Discipline, 953 S.W.2d 435, 437–38 (Tex. App. 1997) (suspending a lawyer for false statements in an affidavit in a breach of contract action in which he was a party).

the tribunal's adjudicative authority, such as a deposition."[17] Some courts therefore hold that lawyers owe a duty of candor to tribunals under Rule 3.3(a)(1) only when representing clients—not when they are appearing in a personal capacity.[18] Although the text of the rule should control over the comment and there are good reasons to hold that lawyers owe a duty of candor to tribunals regardless of the capacity in which they appear, whether Rule 3.3(a)(1) is limited to lawyers who are representing clients may be relatively unimportant in the end. After all, lawyers who knowingly make false statements of fact or law to tribunals when appearing as witnesses or when representing themselves tempt serious discipline under other rules of professional conduct.[19]

When addressing a tribunal, a lawyer's statements are essentially made under oath.[20] The duty of candor imposed under Rule 3.3 is exceptionally high.[21] "Candor" in this context describes a duty higher than most people would associate with the term in everyday life. Where lawyers' communications with tribunals are concerned, candor "'means to treat a subject with fairness, impartiality, and to be outspoken, frank, and veracious, and is synonymous with other terms describing morality.'"[22] Lying to a tribunal is never condoned.[23] A lawyer may never knowingly mislead a court or other tribunal.[24] In some instances, a lawyer may be required to disclose relevant information to a court.[25]

---

17. Model Rules of Prof'l Conduct R. 3.3 cmt.1 (2020).

18. *See, e.g.*, *In re* Ivy, 350 P.3d 758, 762–65 (Alaska 2015) (concluding that Rules 3.3 and 3.4 are intended to govern lawyers acting as advocates and not in their personal capacities); People v. Head, 332 P.3d 117, 128 (Colo. 2013) (determining that Rule 3.3(a)(1) did not apply to a lawyer who was representing himself and his firm in a proceeding to collect a judgment); Iowa Sup. Ct. Att'y Disciplinary Bd. v. Rhinehart, 827 N.W.2d 169, 176–77 (Iowa 2013) (concluding that Rule 3.3(a)(1) did not apply to a lawyer who was representing himself in his divorce); *In re* Disciplinary Action Against Albrecht, 845 N.W.2d 184, 191 (Minn. 2014) (deciding that a lawyer representing himself did not violate Rule 3.3(a)(1)); State *ex rel.* Okla. Bar Ass'n v. Dobbs, 94 P.3d 31, 52 (Okla. 2004) (reasoning that Rule 3.3(a)(1) applies only to lawyers functioning as advocates and not to their statements as witnesses).

19. *See, e.g.*, Model Rules of Prof'l Conduct R. 8.4(c) (2020) (prohibiting lawyers from engaging in conduct involving "dishonesty, fraud, deceit or misrepresentation"); *id.* R. 8.4(d) (prohibiting conduct prejudicial to the administration of justice).

20. Kappa Sigma Fraternity v. Price-Williams, 40 So. 3d 683, 693 (Ala. 2009) (quoting Molton v. State, 651 So. 2d 663, 670 n.6 (Ala. Crim. App. 1994)); Fleischer v. Fleischer, 217 A.3d 1028, 1039 n.12 (Conn. App. Ct. 2019) (quoting State v. Webb, 680 A.2d 147, 167 (Conn. 1996)).

21. *See In re* Discipline of Wilka, 638 N.W.2d 245, 249 (S.D. 2001) ("Clearly, the requirement of candor towards the tribunal goes beyond simply telling a portion of the truth. It requires every attorney to be fully honest and forthright.").

22. *In re* Dorothy, 605 N.W.2d 493, 509 (S.D. 2000) (quoting Joiner v. Joiner, 87 S.W.2d 903, 905 (Tex. App. 1935)).

23. Columbus Bar Ass'n v. Vogel, 881 N.E.2d 1244, 1249 (Ohio 2008).

24. Deutscher v. Gabel, 202 P.3d 355, 363 (Wash. Ct. App. 2009).

25. Bruce A. Green, *Resolving Ethics Questions in Good Faith*, Litig., Winter 2020, at 39, 41 (quoting City of Livonia Emps. Ret. Sys. v. Boeing Co., 711 F.3d 754, 758–59 (7th Cir. 2013)).

The Model Rule 3.3(a)(1) prohibitions are not limited to lawyers' statements to courts,[26] as the defined term "tribunal" firmly establishes.[27] Lawyers' duty of candor also attaches in administrative and regulatory proceedings,[28] and private arbitrations.[29] Extending lawyers' duty of candor to arbitrators is necessary, given arbitrators' function as private judges. Arbitrators administer oaths, receive evidence, find facts, apply the law to the facts of the cases they hear, issue binding decisions, and generally assume a judicial or quasi-judicial role in matters over which they preside. Arbitration would be ineffective as a form of dispute resolution if lawyers were not required to be candid with arbitrators. The same rationale holds true with respect to adjudicatory proceedings before administrative and regulatory agencies.

Model Rule 3.3(a)(1) potentially overlaps with Model Rule 4.1(a), which provides that when representing clients, lawyers shall not knowingly make false statements of material fact or law to "a third person."[30] There is ample authority for the proposition that a tribunal is a third person within the meaning of Model Rule 4.1(a).[31] There are, however, competing views on the application of Model Rule 4.1(a) to a lawyer's false statements to a tribunal.[32] On the one hand, Model Rule 4.1(a) refers to "a third person," meaning anyone other than the lawyer's client, and it therefore must apply to lawyers' statements to tribunals. This perspective makes sense given courts' desire to broadly eradicate dishonesty by lawyers, even if the result is apparent overlap or redundancy in ethics rules. On the other hand, if Model Rule 4.1(a) were meant to apply to lawyers' statements to tribunals, the

26. *See, e.g.*, *In re* Montoya, 266 P.3d 11, 16 (N.M. 2011) (holding that a lawyer violated his duty of candor by making false statements of fact and law to a guardian ad litem).

27. Model Rules of Prof'l Conduct R. 1.0(m) (2020) ("'Tribunal' denotes a court, an arbitrator in a binding arbitration proceeding or a legislative body, administrative agency or other body acting in an adjudicative capacity.").

28. *See, e.g.*, *In re* Vohra, 68 A.3d 766, 782 (D.C. 2013) (violating Rule 3.3(a)(1) by submitting forged signatures on visa applications to a government agency); *In re* Ukwu, 926 A.2d 1106, 1120 (D.C. 2007) (suspending the lawyer for dishonesty in an INS administrative proceeding); *In re* Bihlmeyer, 515 N.W.2d 236, 238–39 (S.D. 1994) (censuring a lawyer who lied to the state industrial commission).

29. People v. Bertagnolli, 861 P.2d 717, 720–21 (Colo. 1993); *In re* Forrest, 730 A.2d 340, 343–44 (N.J. 1999).

30. Model Rules of Prof'l Conduct R. 4.1(a) (2020).

31. *See, e.g.*, *In re* Ingersoll, 710 N.E.2d 390, 392–93 (Ill. 1999) (agreeing that the lawyer violated Rule 4.1(a) by filing a false affidavit with the court); *In re* Disciplinary Action Against Adams, 942 N.W.2d 720, 727–28 (Minn. 2020) (involving false statements to a referee); *In re* Disciplinary Action Against Aitken, 787 N.W.2d 152, 159–60 (Minn. 2010) (finding that a lawyer who forged client's signature on a plea petition violated both Rule 4.1 and Rule 8.4(c)); *In re* Discipline of Stubbs, 974 P.2d 296, 299–300 (Utah 1999) (finding that the lawyer violated Rule 4.1(a) by lying to a trial court).

32. *See, e.g.*, *In re* Disbarment of Rogers, No. 2013-0079, 2013 WL 6507168, at *5 (V.I. Dec. 12, 2013) (stating that "a 'third person,' for purposes of Model Rule 4.1(a), is someone other than the parties and the court").

drafters surely would have used the word "tribunal" in the rule, there would have been no need for the prohibition included in Model Rule 3.3(a)(1), and Model Rule 4.1(a) would render Model Rule 3.3(a)(1) redundant. The fact that Model Rule 4.1(a) makes no mention of tribunals while Model Rule 3.3(a)(1) does suggests that only the latter applies to lawyers' communications with courts and other judicial and quasi-judicial bodies. In any event, whether Rule 4.1(a) applies to lawyers' statements to tribunals is in most cases inconsequential because Rule 3.3(a)(1) clearly so applies, and a lawyer who violates Rule 3.3(a)(1) is in substantial trouble on that basis alone.[33]

Model Rule 3.3(a)(1) often overlaps with Model Rule 8.4(c),[34] which broadly prohibits "conduct involving dishonesty, fraud, deceit or misrepresentation."[35] A lawyer who violates Model Rule 3.3(a) generally violates Model Rule 8.4(c) as well,[36] and a lawyer who lies to a tribunal may be disciplined for violating Rule 8.4(c) without any mention by the court of Rule 3.3.[37] Finally, a lawyer's violation of Model Rule 3.3(a) also implicates Model Rule 8.4(d), which prohibits conduct that is prejudicial to the

33. *See, e.g.*, Att'y Grievance Comm'n of Md. v. Fader, 66 A.3d 18, 43 (Md. 2013) (stating that a lawyer who lies to a tribunal has violated a professional norm that warrants disbarment).

34. Att'y Grievance Comm'n of Md. v. Steinhorn, 198 A.3d 821, 829 (Md. 2018).

35. Model Rules of Prof'l Conduct R. 8.4(c) (2020).

36. Att'y Grievance Comm'n of Md. v. Peters-Hamlin, 136 A.3d 374, 385 (Md. 2016); *see, e.g.*, *In re* Tun, 195 A.3d 65, 74 (D.C. 2018) (violating Rules 3.3(a)(1) and 8.4(c) by intentionally making a false statement of fact in a motion); *In re* Magee, 263 So. 3d 845, 858 (La. 2018) (violating Rules 3.3(a)(1) and 8.4(c) by filing forged quitclaim deeds and concealing that fact when seeking declaratory judgments based on the forged deeds); *In re* Dixon, 435 P.3d 80, 86–87 (N.M. 2019) (involving false statements in summary judgment proceedings); N.C. State Bar v. Sutton, 791 S.E.2d 881, 900 (N.C. Ct. App. 2016) (violating Rules 3.3(a)(1), 8.4(c), and 8.4(d) by lying to the trial court about opposing counsel allegedly slipping a provision into a settlement agreement without the lawyer's knowledge); Disciplinary Counsel v. Spinazze, 149 N.E.3d 503, 505–06 (Ohio 2020) (suspending for six months an assistant municipal prosecutor who violated Rules 3.3(a), 8.4(c), and 8.4(d) by lying to the court about the reasons for his reduction of a defendant's criminal charge); State *ex rel.* Okla. Bar Ass'n v. Brooking, 411 P.3d 377, 378–79 (Okla. 2018) (violating both rules by turning back the date on a court clerk's file stamp to make it appear as though documents were filed earlier than they were); Dunlap v. Bd. of Prof'l Responsibility, 595 S.W.3d 593, 607–08 (Tenn. 2020) (concluding that a lawyer's failure to disclose material information violated Rules 3.3(a)(1) and 8.4(c)); Bd. of Prof'l Responsibility v. Custis, 348 P.3d 823, 832–33 (Wyo. 2015) (violating Rules 3.3(a) and 8.4(c) through false statements in an appellate brief). *But see* Iowa Sup. Ct. Att'y Disciplinary Bd. v. Bartley, 860 N.W.2d 331, 337 (Iowa 2015) (stating that when a lawyer's conduct violates a specific rule like Rule 3.3(a)(1), the same conduct cannot be used to support the violation of a general rule like Rule 8.4(c)).

37. *See, e.g.*, *In re* Herron, 441 P.3d 24, 50 (Kan. 2019) (violating Rule 8.4(c) by lying to the court about the reason for the prosecutor's absence from a hearing and the prosecutor's willingness to reschedule the matter); *In re* King, 33 So. 3d 873, 876 (La. 2010) (lying to the judicial commission while testifying under oath violated Rule 8.4(c)); Att'y Grievance Comm'n of Md. v. Rheinstein, 223 A.3d 505, 547 (Md. 2020) (concluding that the lawyer violated Rule 8.4(c) when he falsely told the trial court that the opposing party's principals faced criminal charges in another court); *In re* Disciplinary Action Against Moe, 851 N.W.2d 868, 871 (Minn. 2014) (concluding that a lawyer violated Rules 8.4(c) and (d) by submitting false expense ledgers to the court for his service as a conservator and guardian).

administration of justice.[38] Courts routinely rely on Rule 8.4(d) to discipline lawyers who lie to or mislead tribunals.[39]

In summary, lawyers' duty of candor to tribunals is critical. As the court in *United States v. Shaffer Equipment Co.*[40] explained:

> Our adversary system for the resolution of disputes rests on the unshakable foundation that truth is the object of the system's process which is designed for the purpose of dispensing justice. However, because no one has an exclusive insight into truth, the process depends on the adversarial presentation of evidence, precedent and custom, and argument to reasoned conclusions—all directed with unwavering effort to what, in good faith, is believed to be true on matters material to the disposition. Even the slightest accommodation of deceit or lack of candor in any material respect quickly erodes the validity of the process. As soon as the process falters in that respect, the people are then justified in abandoning support for the system in favor of one where honesty is preeminent.[41]

Indeed, lawyers may owe a duty of candor to tribunals broader than that imposed by any ethics rules and which ethics rules do not supplant.[42] This broader, general duty of candor derives from lawyers' larger duty to protect the integrity of the judicial process. A court may therefore sanction a lawyer for a dishonest act that arguably does not violate Rule 3.3.

A. *False Statements of Fact or Law*

To violate Model Rule 3.3(a)(1), a lawyer's false statement must be knowingly made. In other words, a lawyer must actually know that a statement is or was false to be accountable for it under the rule.[43] The fact that a lawyer

38. Model Rules of Prof'l Conduct R. 8.4(d) (2020).

39. *See, e.g.*, *In re* Balsamo, 780 A.2d 255, 257, 261–62 (D.C. 2001) (invoking Rules 8.4(c) and 8.4(d) to suspend a lawyer who lied about the word count in a brief and offered several false reasons for filing the brief late); *In re* Freeman, 835 N.E.2d 494, 498 (Ind. 2005) (filing of verified petition that, in fact, was not); *In re* Barstow, 817 So. 2d 1123, 1129 (La. 2002) (disciplining lawyer who failed to reveal to court that he had received a fee from the indigent defendant's family); *In re* Petition for Disciplinary Action Against Winter, 770 N.W.2d 463, 467 (Minn. 2009) (involving false statements in a motion).

40. 11 F.3d 450 (4th Cir. 1993).

41. *Id.* at 457.

42. *Id.* at 458; *see also* Va. Innovation Sciences, Inc. v. Samsung Elecs. Co., Ltd., 983 F. Supp. 2d 713, 755 (E.D. Va. 2014) ("In addition to the Rule 3.3 duty of candor, there is also a broader general duty of candor and good faith that encompasses an attorney's duty to advise a district court of any development that may affect the outcome of the litigation."); *In re* McKenna, 110 A.3d 1126, 1148 (R.I. 2015) (explaining that lawyers' duty of candor "is not limited by the dictates of Rule 3.3 . . . rather, courts have held that there is a general duty of candor to the court that is broader than the rule").

43. Iowa Sup. Ct. Att'y Disciplinary Bd. v. Sporer, 897 N.W.2d 69, 86 (Iowa 2017); Att'y Grievance Comm'n of Md. v. Smith, 109 A.3d 1184, 1195–96 (Md. 2015); State *ex rel.* Okla. Bar Ass'n v. Layton, 324 P.3d 1244, 1255–56 (Okla. 2014).

should have known her statements were false will not support a Rule 3.3(a)(1) violation.[44] A lawyer's innocent mistakes or misstatements when communicating with tribunals do not constitute knowingly false statements.[45] Although determining whether a lawyer's statement was knowingly false is sometimes difficult, and lawyers accused of lying generally receive the benefit of the doubt, it is equally the case that a lawyer's knowledge of falsity may be inferred from circumstances.[46] Actual knowledge does not include information that a lawyer could have discovered through reasonable inquiry but did not,[47] but a lawyer may not turn a blind eye to the obvious. Willful blindness will not do. Lawyers must have a reasonable basis for believing statements that they make to tribunals.

What is a false statement for Rule 3.3(a)(1) purposes? Can a lawyer make a *misleading* statement of fact or law without violating the rule? There are differences, after all. "False and untrue mean contrary to fact; 'misleading' suggests something literally correct, but likely to direct the listener away from the truth."[48] Moreover, there is a reasoned argument to be made based on other provisions in the Model Rules that, if Rule 3.3(a)(1) were intended to prohibit misleading statements as well as false ones, it would plainly say as much.[49]

The interpretation favored by courts is that a lawyer who knowingly misleads a tribunal violates Model Rule 3.3(a)(1) even if the statement at

---

44. *See, e.g.*, *In re* Kline, 311 P.3d 321, 345 (Kan. 2013) (rejecting "should have known" as a basis for discipline).

45. *See, e.g.*, *In re* Rogers, 928 N.E.2d 210, 210 (Ind. 2010) (concluding that a lawyer who erroneously cited a vacated opinion and who did not intend to mislead the court did not violate Rule 3.3(a)(1)); *In re* Herron, 441 P.3d 24, 48–49 (Kan. 2019) (concluding that a public defender's misstatement to the court about the number of weeks that his client had provided clean drug tests reflected a miscalculation of the time involved rather than a knowing falsehood); Att'y Grievance Comm'n of Md. v. Ruddy, 981 A.2d 637, 654–55 (Md. 2009) (concluding that the lawyer lacked the requisite knowledge to violate Rule 3.3(a)(1) through misstatements in estate administration affidavit where he did not intend to be misleading or deceitful, but executed affidavits based on his understanding of required language derived from years of practice); State *ex rel.* Okla. Bar Ass'n v. Wilcox, 227 P.3d 642, 661 (Okla. 2009) (stating that "'[s]imple error' is insufficient to constitute knowledge under Rule 3.3(a)(1)"). *But see* Lawyer Disciplinary Bd. v. Busch, 754 S.E.2d 729, 739 (W. Va. 2014) (observing that where the lawyer contended that his false statements were negligently made rather than intentional, that was "an argument best left to the affixation of appropriate sanctions").

46. *In re* Ivy, 350 P.3d 758, 762 (Alaska 2015); Dodge v. Dodge, 108 P.3d 362, 366 (Idaho 2005); Iowa Sup. Ct. Att'y Disciplinary Bd. v. Caghan, 927 N.W.2d 591, 606 (Iowa 2019); *In re* Disciplinary Action Against Hann, 819 N.W.2d 498, 509 (N.D. 2012); Model Rules of Prof'l Conduct R. 1.0(f) (2020).

47. *See In re* Tocco, 984 P.2d 539, 643 (Ariz. 1999) (stating that "knowledge" does not include what a lawyer "reasonably should have known") (emphasis omitted).

48. United States v. Kojayan, 8 F.3d 1315, 1322 (9th Cir. 1993).

49. *See, e.g.*, Model Rules of Prof'l Conduct R. 7.1 (2020) ("A lawyer shall not make a false *or misleading* communication about the lawyer or the lawyer's services." (emphasis added)).

issue is literally true and therefore not false.[50] The prohibition of misleading statements in addition to outright lies inheres in the rule even if it is not expressly stated, and it is consistent with the rule's purpose and spirit.[51] Such a reading of the rule is also required by the use of the term "candor" in Model Rule 3.3's title. Indeed, to hold otherwise—to forbid untruths but permit half-truths—would gut Rule 3.3(a)(1).

Rule 3.3(a)(1) is broadly applied.[52] While lawyers generally are not required to vouch for the accuracy or truthfulness of matters asserted in court documents, they cannot file affidavits, briefs, motions, pleadings, or other court documents that they know to be false.[53] Lawyers cannot misrep-

---

50. Of course, a lawyer who deliberately misleads a tribunal violates Rule 8.4(c), which prohibits dishonesty, fraud, deceit, or misrepresentation. In *In re Zotaley*, 546 N.W.2d 16, 19–20 (Minn. 1996), for example, the court held that a lawyer who submitted evidence to an arbitrator that was "clearly misleading" but "not necessarily false" violated Rules 8.4(c) and (d).

51. *See, e.g.*, *In re* Ravin, 29 Vet. App. 95, 97 (Vet. App. 2017) (observing that a lawyer who misleads a court about relevant facts may violate Rule 3.3(a)(1)): Daniels v. Alander, 818 A.2d 106, 110–11 (Conn. App. Ct. 2003) (faulting a lawyer for a misleading statement that the trial court reasonably could have construed as equivalent to an affirmative misrepresentation), *aff'd*, 844 A.2d 182 (Conn. 2004) (discussing an associate's failure to correct a partner's misstatements); *In re* Discipline of Tornow, 835 N.W.2d 912, 924 (S.D. 2013) ("Candor goes beyond telling a portion of the truth."); *In re* Kalal, 643 N.W.2d 466, 471–75 (Wis. 2002) (giving "knowingly misleading" answers to the court's questions at oral argument).

52. *See* Iowa Sup. Ct. Att'y Disciplinary Bd. v. Weiland, 862 N.W.2d 627, 638 (Iowa 2015) (noting that a lawyer can make a false statement to a court either orally or in writing).

53. *See, e.g.*, People v. Roose, 44 P.3d 266, 271 (Colo. 2002) (holding that a lawyer who misrepresented facts in a notice of appeal violated Rules 3.3(a)(1) and 8.4(c)); Fla. Bar v. Dove, 985 So. 2d 1001, 1006 (Fla. 2008) (suspending a lawyer who made false statements in a pleading); *In re* Morales, 651 S.E.2d 84, 86 (Ga. 2007) (suspending a lawyer who filed a pleading containing statements that he knew lacked factual or legal bases); *In re* Sniadecki, 924 N.E.2d 109, 112–13 (Ind. 2010) (concluding that a lawyer who filed a false affidavit violated Rules 3.3(a), 8.4(b), and 8.4(c)); *In re* Freeman, 835 N.E.2d 494, 498 (Ind. 2005) (filing a petition as a verified pleading when it was not); Iowa Sup. Ct. Att'y Disciplinary Bd. v. Barnhill, 885 N.W.2d 408, 420 (Iowa 2016) (making false statements in pleadings); Iowa Sup. Ct. Att'y Disciplinary Bd. v. McGinness, 844 N.W.2d 456, 462–63 (Iowa 2014) (suspending a lawyer for falsifying certificates of service); *In re* Herron, 441 P.3d 24, 49 (Kan. 2019) (drafting a journal entry for a judge that contained knowingly false information); *In re* Singleton, 111 P.3d 630, 634–35 (Kan. 2005) (suspending a lawyer who misrepresented an order submitted to a judge as having been agreed to by the opponent); Ky. Bar Ass'n v. Devers, 936 S.W.2d 89 (Ky. 1997) (suspending a lawyer who lied about the existence of a bankruptcy stay in an answer and who allowed an answer to be filed in which the client was identified by his alias); Att'y Grievance Comm'n of Md. v. Conwell, 200 A.3d 820, 836–37 (Md. 2019) (violating Rule 3.3(a)(1) by submitting inflated fee invoices to the court); Att'y Grievance Comm'n of Md. v. Barnett, 102 A.3d 310, 317–18 (Md. 2014) (violating Rules 3.3(a)(1), 8.4(c), and 8.4(d) by forging the client's signature on an affidavit of indigency); Att'y Grievance Comm'n of Md. v. Gordon, 991 A.2d 51, 58 (Md. 2010) (violating Rules 3.3(a)(1), 3.3(a)(3), and 8.4(c) by submitting a false signature page of a contract and falsely suggesting that the page was the original in pleadings); Valley Health Sys., LLC v. Estate of Doe, 427 P.3d 1021, 1032 (Nev. 2018) (involving a knowingly false statement of fact in a memorandum opposing summary judgment and rejecting the lawyers' argument that they did not violate Rule 3.3(a)(1) because the false statement was "argument intertwined with opinion"); *In re* Clark's Case, 37 A.3d 327, 329–31 (N.H. 2012) (filing false bankruptcy schedules); *In re* Wolterbeek's Case, 886 A.2d 990, 994 (N.H. 2005)

resent to courts the times or dates on filings, as where, for example, a lawyer misstates the date on which a brief or other court document was filed to make it appear as though the brief was filed timely when in fact it was not.[54] Similarly, a lawyer violates Rule 3.3(a)(1) by failing to serve pleadings or other documents as represented in certificates of service.[55] It is "blatant fraud" for a lawyer to represent to a court that she is offering an entire document when portions have been omitted or redacted.[56] Lawyers cannot sign clients' names to court papers without their authority or consent.[57] It is misconduct for a lawyer to sign another lawyer's name to a court document without the other lawyer's consent.[58] Lawyers may be disciplined for signing a client's name or another lawyer's name to a document without indicating that they are signing in a representative capacity.[59] Lawyers cannot offer documents into evidence that they know are falsified,[60] nor can they knowingly make false statements in discovery responses or responses to requests

(disbarring a lawyer who failed to disclose material facts and made misleading statements in a petition); *In re* Venie, 395 P.3d 516, 522–23 (N.M. 2017) (filing a false affidavit); *In re* Walters, 942 N.Y.S.2d 829, 829 (App. Div. 2012) (submitting an answer and filing two affidavits containing false statements); *In re* Disciplinary Action Against Edwardson, 647 N.W.2d 126, 132 (N.D. 2002) (suspending a lawyer who attempted to excuse her delay by stating that she had been ill when she was not); *In re* Kirchoff, 399 P.3d 453, 454–58 (Or. 2017) (fabricating an e-mail message and submitting it to the court in support of a motion to set aside a default judgment); *In re* Gelfuso, 108 A.3d 208, 211 (R.I. 2015) (filing false affidavits to obtain a default); Cofield v. Va. State Bar *ex rel.* Second Dist. Comm., 827 S.E.2d 602, 603–04 (Va. 2019) (admonishing a lawyer who purported to quote a regulation verbatim in her pleading but included an extra provision that did not exist in the regulation); *In re* Wysolmerski, 237 A.3d 706, 716 (Vt. 2020) (submitting a false affidavit to the court in connection with a motion for a default judgment); Lawyer Disciplinary Bd. v. Grindo, 842 S.E.2d 683, 691 (W. Va. 2020) (submitting knowingly inaccurate fee vouchers to courts for approval in appointed cases violated Rule 3.3(a)(1)); Bd. of Prof'l Responsibility v. Richard, 335 P.3d 1036, 1054 (Wyo. 2014) (violating Rule 3.3(a) through knowingly false statements in an affidavit, pleadings, and memoranda supporting motions).

54. People v. Maynard, 219 P.3d 430, 436 (Colo. 2008).

55. Att'y Grievance Comm'n of Md. v. Byrd, 970 A.2d 870, 886 (Md. 2009).

56. Sierra Glass & Mirror v. Viking Indus., Inc., 808 P.2d 512, 516 (Nev. 1991).

57. Att'y Grievance Comm'n of Md. v. Johnson, 770 A.2d 130, 144–46 (Md. 2001) (finding that a lawyer who signed clients' names to bankruptcy petition without their authority violated Rule 3.3(a)(1)); *In re* Grochowski, 701 A.2d 1013, 1014 (R.I. 1997) ("It is well settled in this jurisdiction that when an attorney forges a client's signature to documents, that lawyer has violated his professional obligation of honesty under Rule 8.4(c).").

58. People v. Wright, 35 P.3d 153, 156–57 (Colo. 1999); Att'y Grievance Comm'n of Md. v. Goodman, 850 A.2d 1157, 1160–67 (Md. 2004).

59. *In re* Howard, 879 A.2d 681, 681–82 & nn.1 & 3 (D.C. 2005); *In re* Disciplinary Action Against Grigsby, 85 N.W.2d 836, 844 (Minn. 2012).

60. *See, e.g.*, *In re* Manning-Wallace, 695 S.E.2d 237, 241 (Ga. 2010) (explaining that a lawyer violates her duty of candor by offering falsified evidence even if she did not have a hand in its fabrication); *In re* Barratt, 663 N.E.2d 536, 539–41 (Ind. 1996) (suspending a lawyer who fabricated a letter); *In re* Watkins, 656 So. 2d 984, 985–87 (La. 1995) (disbarring a lawyer who filed falsified physicians' reports in a Social Security disability case).

for admissions.[61] Lawyers cannot knowingly misrepresent facts or law in appearances before tribunals.[62]

Lawyers who learn that a document submitted on a client's behalf contains a false statement of material fact or law may be required to retract the offending statement.[63] This is true even where the false statement is attributable to carelessness rather than malice. It is no defense that the lawyer's adversary should have objected to the false statement but failed to do so. In the same vein, a lawyer who learns that a falsified document or pleading has been submitted to a court may be required to notify the court. In *Nissenson*

61. *See, e.g.*, Fla. Bar v. Hmielewski, 702 So. 2d 218, 219–21 (Fla. 1997) (suspending a lawyer for serving false interrogatory responses and for submitting an expert report that did not account for information that the lawyer wrongly concealed from the expert and the opposing lawyer); *In re* Usher, 987 N.E.2d 1080, 1088 (Ind. 2013) (concluding that the lawyer violated Rule 3.3(a)(1) by submitting knowingly false responses to requests for admissions); Miss. Bar v. Land, 653 So. 2d 899, 909–10 (Miss. 1994) (suspending a lawyer who lied in interrogatory responses).

62. *See, e.g.*, Davis v. TWC Dealer Grp., Inc., 254 Cal. Rptr. 3d 443, 447 (Ct. App. 2019) (using ellipses to excise 38 lines from a 49-line paragraph of critical text); *In re* Cardwell, 50 P.3d 897, 898–900 (Colo. 2002) (suspending a lawyer who lied about his client's criminal record in a motion and reiterated the false statement at a hearing); Fla. Bar v. Whitney, 132 So. 3d 1095, 1104 (Fla. 2013) (finding that the lawyer violated Rule 3.3(a) where he represented that he could not appear for a deposition because he was seriously ill when, in fact, he had a skin rash and he did not seek medical attention until two days after the deposition); Fla. Bar v. Miller, 863 So. 2d 231, 232–33 (Fla. 2003) (suspending a lawyer who lied about receiving an EEOC notice to avoid the defense that client's suit was untimely); *In re* Johnson, 838 S.E.2d 755, 757 (Ga. 2020) (lying about being ill to avoid a court appearance); Dodge v. Dodge, 108 P.3d 362, 366–67 (Idaho 2005) (lying to a magistrate about the accused's conduct to obtain an arrest warrant); *In re* James, 861 N.E.2d 703, 703 (Ind. 2007) (suspending a lawyer who lied about his client's criminal record); *In re* Blume, 443 P.3d 305, 314, 334 (Kan. 2019) (suspending a lawyer who lied about when he received an e-mail message that should have been produced in discovery); Hubbard v. Ky. Bar Ass'n, 571 S.W.3d 90, 91–92 (Ky. 2019) (suspending the lawyer for lying to the court about sending a picture with an offensive note to the opposing party); Att'y Grievance Comm'n of Md. v. Planta, 225 A.3d 19, 40 (Md. 2020) (stating that the lawyer violated Rule 3.3(a)(1) when he lied to the court by saying that he was late for a hearing because he had been hospitalized, when in fact, he had not); *In re* Entzminger, 831 S.E.2d 642, 646–48 (N.C. 2019) (involving a prosecutor who misrepresented to the court when he learned about a police officer's unavailability as a witness); Disciplinary Couns. v. Spinazze, 149 N.E.3d 503, 505–06 (Ohio 2020) (suspending for six months a prosecutor who lied about why he reduced a defendant's criminal charge); Disciplinary Couns. v. Harmon, 141 N.E.3d 142, 151 (Ohio 2019) (lying to the court about key facts underlying a declaratory judgment action); State *ex rel.* Okla. Bar Ass'n v. Bednar, 441 P.3d 91, 106 (Okla. 2019) (misrepresenting to the court that the lawyer had never received notice of the deposition from opposing counsel, and that based on this lack of notice he was unable to attend); *In re* Kirchoff, 399 P.3d 453, 458 (Or. 2017) (falsifying an e-mail message submitted to the court to vacate a default judgment); *In re* Conduct of Jackson, 223 P.3d 387, 391, 396 (Or. 2009) (finding that the lawyer violated Rule 3.3(a)(1) by lying to the court about why he was unprepared for a settlement conference and why he did not schedule an arbitration); *In re* Disciplinary Proc. Against Kalal, 643 N.W.2d 466, 468–74 (Wis. 2002) (reprimanding a lawyer who misrepresented facts in an appellate oral argument).

63. *See, e.g.*, Sierra Glass & Mirror v. Viking Indus., Inc., 808 P.2d 512, 516–17 (Nev. 1991) (discussing a false statement of material fact in an appellate brief); Beard v. Bd. of Prof'l Responsibility, 288 S.W.3d 838, 842–44, 850 (Tenn. 2009) (failing to correct errors in a proposed final order in a divorce case).

v. Bradley,[64] for example, the court affirmed the sanction of a lawyer who did not withdraw a false medical report submitted by his client's previous counsel. The *Nissenson* court concluded that the attorney had a duty to notify the trial court of the false medical report even though it was prepared before he entered the case, stating that a successor attorney "cannot hide behind his predecessor."[65] The lawyer was required to bring the false medical report to the trial court's attention at the first opportunity even though doing so would have been fatal to his client's case.[66]

B. False Statements and the Duty to Correct

In some circumstances, a lawyer's statements to a tribunal may be false for Model Rule 3.3(a)(1) purposes even if the lawyer is mistaken rather than lying.[67] This application may strike some lawyers as odd because Rule 3.3(a)(1) seems to focus on deliberately false statements rather than innocently mistaken ones. But a statement is false if it is contrary to fact, incorrect, or groundless; falsity does not require dishonesty or intent to mislead. Thus, and as indicated earlier in our general discussion of false statements, if a lawyer makes a statement of fact or law to a tribunal that the lawyer believed to be correct at the time but later discovers was false, the lawyer must correct the misstatement if it was material.[68]

C. Silence as Statement: Misrepresentation by Omission

There are times when a lawyer's failure to make a necessary disclosure to a tribunal is tantamount to an affirmative misrepresentation.[69] The Hawaii Supreme Court's decision in *AIG Hawai'i Insurance Co. v. Bateman*[70] is instructive.

64. 738 N.E.2d 586 (Ill. App. Ct. 2000).

65. *Id.* at 591.

66. *Id.* (quoting Chi. Title & Tr. Co. v. Anderson, 532 N.E.2d 595, 602 (Ill. App. Ct. 1988)).

67. *See, e.g.*, Att'y Grievance Comm'n of Md. v. Bleecker, 994 A.2d 928, 941–42 (Md. 2010) (stating that the lawyer had a duty to correct an inaccurate date of an accident set forth in a pleading even though he did not intentionally misrepresent the date); *Beard*, 288 S.W.3d at 856 (stating that the lawyer had a duty to correct unintentional misrepresentations to a court); Bd. of Prof'l Responsibility v. Dunn, 272 P.3d 941, 942–43 (Wyo. 2012) (finding that the lawyer violated Rule 3.3(a)(1) when she submitted a QDRO and a later affidavit in which she "overlooked" a pivotal letter).

68. Model Rules of Prof'l Conduct R. 3.3(a)(1) (2020).

69. Ndreko v. Ridge, 351 F. Supp. 2d 904, 910–11 (D. Minn. 2004); *In re* Brown, 511 B.R. 843, 852–53 (Bankr. S.D. Tex. 2014); *In re* Alcorn, 41 P.3d 600, 611 (Ariz. 2002); Daniels v. Alander, 844 A.2d 182, 188–89 (Conn. 2004); AIG Haw. Ins. Co. v. Bateman, 923 P.2d 395, 402 (Haw. 1996); *In re* Angwafo, 899 N.E.2d 778, 784 (Mass. 2009); *In re* Discipline of Ortner, 699 N.W.2d 865, 874–81 (S.D. 2005); Dunlap v. Bd. of Prof'l Responsibility, 595 S.W.3d 593, 607–08 (Tenn. 2020); *In re* Wysolmerski, 237 A.3d 706, 716–17 (Vt. 2020).

70. 923 P.2d 395 (Haw. 1996).

Bateman stemmed from an earlier declaratory judgment action, *Vincente*.[71] The parties in *Vincente*, including AIG, settled the declaratory judgment action. They did not reveal the settlement, however, and instead proceeded on appeal because *Vincente* involved insurance coverage issues that AIG wanted resolved.[72] Both AIG's lawyers and Vincente's lawyers briefed the case; neither side revealed the settlement, which had rendered the appeal moot.[73] After the Hawaii Supreme Court in *Vincente* issued an opinion favorable to AIG and remanded the case to the trial court to enter summary judgment in AIG's favor, AIG moved to rescind the parties' settlement. The trial court denied AIG's motion, and the *Bateman* appeal followed.

The *Bateman* court was upset by the lawyers' concealment of the settlement to facilitate the *Vincente* appeal. In discussing their conduct, the court observed that "[t]he failure to make disclosure of a material fact to a tribunal is the equivalent of affirmative misrepresentation."[74] It was clear that the settlement in *Vincente* was a material fact; its disclosure would have rendered the appeal moot. By not revealing the settlement, the lawyers duped the court into entering an opinion. Under the circumstances, the lawyers' secrecy "was tantamount to [an] affirmative misrepresentation."[75] The lawyers' conduct thus appeared to violate Rules 3.3(a)(1) and 8.4(c), and the Hawaii Supreme Court referred the matter to state disciplinary authorities.

The New Jersey Supreme Court once observed that "if an attorney has an obligation to speak in order to comply with his or her duty of candor to the tribunal, then silence may also be a violation" of rules of professional conduct.[76] This is often the situation where a judge asks a question of a lawyer about a material fact that the lawyer does not answer, where a lawyer fails to correct a judge's misimpression or misstatement related to a material aspect of a case involving the lawyer,[77] or where a lawyer hears another lawyer answer a judge's question falsely but remains silent.[78] Similarly, a lawyer's omission or withholding of material facts when communicating with a court either in person or in writing may be held to be the equivalent of an affirmative misrepresentation.[79]

---

71. AIG Haw. Ins. Co. v. Vincente, 891 P.2d 1041 (Haw. 1995).

72. *Bateman*, 923 P.2d at 397–98.

73. *Id.* at 398.

74. *Id.* at 402.

75. *Id.*

76. Brundage v. Estate of Carambio, 951 A.2d 947, 956 (N.J. 2008).

77. *See, e.g.*, *In re* Samad, 51 A.3d 486, 498–99 & n.8 (D.C. 2012) (failing to correct a judge's misimpression regarding the lawyer's obligation to appear before another judge).

78. *See, e.g.*, Daniels v. Alander, 844 A.2d 182, 188–89 (Conn. 2004) (finding that an associate's failure to correct his superior's misstatements violated Rule 3.3(a)(1)); *In re* Bruno, 956 So. 2d 577, 582–83 (La. 2007) (invoking Rule 3.3(a)(1) in suspending a lawyer who did not correct his co-counsel's false statements to a federal judge).

79. *See, e.g.*, Fla. Bar v. Dove, 985 So. 2d 1001, 1006 (Fla. 2008) (withholding facts from court when appearing at an ex parte hearing); *In re* Disciplinary Action Against Houge, 764 N.W.2d 328, 335 (Minn. 2009) (omitting important facts from an affidavit).

A lawyer's duty of candor is also commonly implicated where a lawyer hears another lawyer misstate facts or law to a court but remains silent instead of correcting the other lawyer or at least calling potential discrepancies to the court's attention.[80] A lawyer's duty of candor also comes into play where co-counsel files a brief or pleading that misstates facts or law. Lawyers who know that another lawyer is misstating facts or misrepresenting the law to a court cannot sit or stand silently by—at least where the misstatements or misrepresentations are potentially material. Although a lawyer's silence here may not appear to violate the plain language of Rule 3.3(a)(1), courts regularly conclude that it does.[81] Remaining silent in this situation is certainly inconsistent with lawyers' duties as officers of the court. Moreover, lawyers who remain silent when they should speak almost surely violate Rules 8.4(c) and (d).

Lawyers can also be disciplined for remaining silent when they reasonably should speak because they owe a general duty of candor to tribunals independent of specific ethics rules.[82] A lawyer's silence when disclosure of a material fact is required amounts to a constructive fraud on the court.[83] The defrauded court or another court with jurisdiction over the matter can then invoke its inherent authority to discipline the guilty lawyer.

In re Bruno[84] is an illustrative case. The lawyer there, Joseph Bruno, was the member of the Plaintiffs' Legal Committee (PLC) in a class action. He arranged for the PLC to secretly pay a key witness. When the defendant learned of the payments, it moved to disqualify the firms on the PLC from further participation in the case. At the hearing on the disqualification motion, Bruno sat silently as one of his co-counsel on the PLC lied to the federal district court about the payments.[85] Similarly, Bruno did not reveal the true facts when another one of his co-counsel filed a brief with the district court asserting that the PLC had not paid the witness.[86] Bruno finally revealed the witness payments to the court more than two months later.[87] The Louisiana Supreme Court suspended Bruno from practice for three years for violating his duty of candor to the district court.

There are also times when an attorney's obligation to disclose a fact is so obvious that no one can reasonably dispute such a duty, as where a client or party dies. Lawyers' duty of candor compels them to disclose the death

80. *See, e.g.*, *In re* Wilkinson, 668 S.E.2d 707, 708 (Ga. 2008) (involving a lawyer who stood silent while his partner made a false statement to a bankruptcy court).

81. *See, e.g.*, *Daniels*, 844 A.2d at 188–89; *In re Bruno*, 956 So. 2d at 582–83.

82. Gum v. Dudley, 505 S.E.2d 391, 399–400 (W. Va. 1997).

83. *Id.* at 402.

84. 956 So. 2d 577 (La. 2007).

85. *Id.* at 578.

86. *Id.*

87. *Id.*

of a client or a party even if not specifically asked about it by a court.[88] This makes sense because of the effect that the client's death has on the litigation. A client's death is unquestionably material.[89] Among other effects, the client's death alters the parties—a personal representative or administrator must be appointed, and the estate or another suitable party must be substituted for the decedent. Some causes of action do not survive the client's death. Additionally, the client's death terminates the attorney-client relationship;[90] if the lawyer remains involved in the case, it will be on behalf of a new client, such as the estate or personal administrator. The client's death also terminates the lawyer's agency.[91]

D. *Materiality*

To violate Rule 3.3(a)(1) as it is constituted in some states, a lawyer must knowingly make a false statement of *material* fact or law. Additionally, and again, Model Rule 3.3(a)(1) and identical state rules require lawyers to correct false statements of material fact or law that they previously made to a tribunal.[92] Even in jurisdictions that do not impose a materiality requirement in their ethics rules, the materiality of a lawyer's false statement may affect the sanction or discipline to be imposed, or influence whether professional authorities charge a violation of Rule 3.3(a)(1) in the first place. For all these reasons, the materiality of a lawyer's false statement of fact or law to a tribunal potentially presents a substantial issue.

Materiality is judged according to an objective standard. Whether a lawyer's false statement to a tribunal is material necessarily depends on the facts of the case. Generally speaking, a fact or proposition of law is "material" if it could affect a tribunal's decision-making process, if it is essential or significant, if it could have influenced the hearer,[93] or if it "directly or circumstantially had a reasonable and natural tendency to influence a judge's

88. Kingsdorf v. Kingsdorf, 797 A.2d 206, 212 (N.J. Super. Ct. App. Div. 2002); *In re* Becker, 804 N.Y.S.2d 4, 4–6 (App. Div. 2005).

89. *In re* Disciplinary Action Against Lyons, 780 N.W.2d 629, 636 (Minn. 2010).

90. *In re* Johnson, 402 B.R. 313, 314 (B.A.P. 8th Cir. 2009); People v. Rosen, 199 P.3d 1241, 1249 (Colo. 2007); Mohica v. Cvejin, 990 N.E.2d 720, 729 (Ill. App. Ct. 2013) (quoting cases); Surland v. State, 895 A.2d 1034, 1041 (Md. 2006); Velasquez v. Katz, 840 N.Y.S.2d 410, 412 (App. Div. 2007) (quoting cases); Warehouse Mkt., Inc. v. Layman, 194 P.3d 786, 789 (Okla. Civ. App. 2008) (quoting cases).

91. Beaudry v. TeleCheck Servs., Inc., No. 3:07-0842, 2016 WL 11398115, at *9 (M.D. Tenn. Sept. 9, 2016); Smith v. Shewry, 93 Cal. Rptr. 3d 436, 443 (Ct. App. 2009); *Surland*, 895 A.2d at 1041.

92. Model Rules of Prof'l Conduct R. 3.3(a)(1) (2020) ("A lawyer shall not knowingly . . . fail to correct a false statement of material fact or law previously made to the tribunal by the lawyer[.]").

93. *In re* Fisher, 202 P.3d 1186, 1202 (Colo. 2009); *In re* Smith, 236 P.3d 137, 145 (Or. 2010) (quoting *In re* Kluge, 27 P.3d 102, 105 (Or. 2001)).

determination."[94] Lawyers should assume that courts will deem material any statement about claims, defenses, or other issues being litigated. Lawyers should also assume that statements about key procedural aspects of a case, such as reasons for establishing or extending deadlines, setting hearing or trial dates, or justifications for seeking or opposing continuances, will be considered material. Any knowingly false statements in these contexts tempt fate. Regardless, a lawyer's false statement need not actually influence a tribunal to be material; mere potential to influence a tribunal is sufficient.[95] Rule 3.3(a)(1) does not require harm or reliance to find a violation.[96]

E. The Curious Case of Plagiarism

Lawyers may breach their duty of candor to tribunals in various ways, oddly including plagiarism. Plagiarism involves appropriating another person's words or ideas and attributing them as one's own, or presenting as new or original an idea or material derived from an existing source. Most lawyers probably think of plagiarism as a problem confined to students and scholars, and perhaps as a behavior that complicates or precludes a guilty law student's admission to the bar, but there is more to the issue. There are numerous examples of practicing lawyers engaging in plagiarism. In litigation, lawyers have plagiarized in briefs, pleadings, and other court documents.[97] Outside of litigation, they have plagiarized when writing articles,

94. *In re* Angwafo, 899 N.E.2d 778, 784 (Mass. 2009).

95. People v. Maynard, 219 P.3d 430, 436 (Colo. 2008).

96. *In re Angwafo*, 899 N.E.2d at 784–85.

97. *See, e.g.*, Liberty Towers Realty, LLC v. Richmond Liberty, LLC, 569 B.R. 534, 541 n.6 (E.D.N.Y. 2017) (copying an article without attribution on an appeal to the district court from bankruptcy court; the lawyer cited the article in his bankruptcy court filings); Consol. Paving, Inc. v. Cnty. of Peoria, Ill., No. 10-CV-1045, 2013 WL 916212, at *5–6 (C.D. Ill. Mar. 8, 2013) (declining to award fees for preparing a fee application because the lawyer copied five pages out of a 13-page brief "nearly verbatim" from a Seventh Circuit opinion); Lohan v. Perez, 924 F. Supp. 2d 447, 460 (E.D.N.Y. 2013) (sanctioning a lawyer for plagiarism in a memorandum opposing a motion to dismiss); Venesevich v. Leonard, No. 1:07-CV-2118, 2008 WL 5340162, at *2 n.2 (M.D. Pa. Dec. 19, 2008) (criticizing a lawyer's plagiarism in a brief opposing a motion to dismiss); Kingvision Pay Per View, Ltd. v. Wilson, 83 F. Supp. 2d 914, 916 n.4 (W.D. Tenn. 2000) (involving plagiarism in a summary judgment response; roughly half the response was copied from a treatise); *In re* Burghoff, 374 B.R. 681 (Bankr. N.D. Iowa 2007) (involving plagiarism in a brief supporting a motion; copying an article and string cites); *In re* White, 18 Cal. Rptr. 3d 444, 468 (Ct. App. 2004) (discussing a lawyer's plagiarism of another lawyer's brief in his brief accompanying a petition for a writ as part of basis for sanctions); *In re* Ayeni, 822 A.2d 420, 421 (D.C. 2003) (plagiarizing a co-defendant's brief in an appellate brief); Frith v. State, 325 N.E.2d 186, 188 (Ind. 1975) (noting that the appellant copied ten ALR pages in a brief "without quotation marks, indentation or citation," and without listing ALR in table of citations or in any other identification of authority); Iowa Sup. Ct. Att'y Disciplinary Bd. v. Cannon, 789 N.W.2d 756, 757–59 (Iowa 2010) (violating Rule 8.4(c) through plagiarism in a bankruptcy court brief); Columbus Bar Ass'n v. Farmer, 855 N.E.2d 462, 465, 468–69 (Ohio 2006) (plagiarizing a prior lawyer's appellate brief in second brief filed on the client's behalf).

books, chapters, and continuing legal education materials.[98] Courts condemn all forms of plagiarism by lawyers,[99] and guilty lawyers may face significant discipline or sanctions. Critically, "plagiarism" in this context includes the quotation of judicial opinions and orders without attribution,[100] copying from websites—including government websites—without attribution,[101] and the unattributed quotation of briefs or pleadings prepared by lawyers from other firms or organizations without those lawyers' permission.[102]

Iowa Supreme Court Board of Professional Ethics & Conduct v. Lane[103] is the leading case on plagiarism in litigation. The lawyer there, William Lane, represented a plaintiff in a federal discrimination case. He submitted a post-trial brief to the district court, "in great part" plagiarizing the legal argument from an employment law treatise.[104] Lane later applied for attorney's fees. He asked to be compensated in the amount of $16,000 (representing 80 hours of work charged at $200 per hour) for writing the post-trial brief, which, of course, was "largely copied from an uncredited source."[105]

The magistrate on the case suspected that Lane did not write the legal portion of the post-trial brief. When the magistrate inquired, Lane acknowledged that he had "borrowed liberally" from other sources.[106] The magistrate gave Lane ten days in which to identify the sources on which he relied. Months later, Lane responded by filing a document that "constituted four pages of single-spaced lists of authorities."[107] While he included in those lists the treatise from which he copied, he did not draw it to the magistrate's attention.[108] The magistrate then undertook his own investigation, identified the treatise, and discovered the extent of Lane's plagiarism.

98. *See, e.g.*, *In re* Hinden, 654 A.2d 864, 865–66 (D.C. 1995) (imposing reciprocal public censure on an Illinois lawyer who plagiarized an article in a chapter of a treatise).

99. *See, e.g.*, *Consol. Paving, Inc.*, 2013 WL 916212, at *6 (calling plagiarism by lawyers "a serious issue"); DeWilde v. Guy Gannett Publ'g Co., 797 F. Supp. 55, 56 n.1 (D. Me. 1992) ("Plagiarism is unacceptable in any grammar school, college, or law school, and *even* in politics. It is wholly intolerable in the practice of law.").

100. United States v. Bowen, 194 F. App'x 393, 402 n.3 (6th Cir. 2006); *Consol. Paving, Inc.*, 2013 WL 916212, at *5–6; *Venesevich*, 2008 WL 5340162, at *2 n.2.

101. United States v. La. Crane Co., LLC, OCAHO Case No. 14B00102, at 11–12, 14 (U.S. Dep't of Justice, Exec. Office for Immigration Review Mar. 12, 2015) (reprimanding the respondent's lawyers for intentionally copying verbatim and without attribution text from a government website, which the administrative law judge described as a "blatant act of plagiarism" that "violate[d] counsel's duty to act with integrity and with candor to the court").

102. *See, e.g.*, *In re Ayeni*, 822 A.2d at 421 (plagiarizing a co-defendant's brief in an appellate brief); *Farmer*, 855 N.E.2d at 465, 468–69 (plagiarizing a predecessor lawyer's appellate brief in a second brief filed on the client's behalf).

103. 642 N.W.2d 296 (Iowa 2002).

104. *Id.* at 298.

105. *Id.*

106. *Id.*

107. *Id.*

108. *Id.*

Iowa disciplinary authorities charged Lane with illegal conduct involving moral turpitude; engaging in conduct involving dishonesty, fraud, deceit, or misrepresentation; engaging in conduct prejudicial to the administration of justice; and engaging in other conduct adversely reflecting on his fitness to practice law. They also charged him with charging or collecting a clearly excessive fee. The Grievance Commission recommended that Lane be suspended from practice for three months for these violations. The case then made its way to the Iowa Supreme Court.

The Iowa Supreme Court concluded that Lane's plagiarism was "a misrepresentation to the [federal] court."[109] The court was quite troubled by Lane's attempt to mask his plagiarism "by concealing the treatise among 200 other titles."[110] The court observed that "[p]lagiarism itself is unethical" because it involves deceit and reflects on a lawyer's honesty.[111] The court was equally troubled by Lane's fee application. Lane asserted that despite his plagiarism, he still worked 80 hours writing the brief because he was inefficient.[112] The court rejected this argument because the circumstances demonstrated his attempt to deceive the federal court.

In opposing significant discipline, Lane argued that his actions were the product of ignorance, carelessness, and the like. The court disagreed, stressing the importance of honesty in the law and the fact that Lane's conduct compromised that value.[113] Lane's conduct jeopardized lawyers' integrity and public trust in the legal profession.[114] Thus, the court suspended him for six months, rather than the three months the Grievance Commission had recommended.

Lawyers analyzing plagiarism from a professional responsibility standpoint may discount *Lane* because the lawyer's plagiarism was exacerbated by his billing fraud and lack of candor to the magistrate when the originality of his work was questioned. To be sure, Lane's attempt to charge an unreasonable fee[115] and lack of candor to the magistrate were major errors, but it would be a mistake to suggest that those acts of misconduct somehow lessened the seriousness of the plagiarism charge. Indeed, the Iowa Supreme Court made crystal clear that plagiarism alone amounts to conduct involving dishonesty, fraud, deceit, or misrepresentation. Other courts have

109. *Id.* at 299.
110. *Id.* at 300.
111. *Id.* (quoting cases).
112. *Id.*
113. *Id.* at 302.
114. *Id.*
115. *See also* Liberty Towers Realty, LLC v. Richmond Liberty, LLC, 569 B.R. 534, 541 n.6 (E.D.N.Y. 2017) ("[A]ppellants' counsel is warned that future filings in this court must attribute work that is from another source. He is also cautioned not to commit an additional ethical violation by charging his clients fees that are unreasonable given that half of his brief was copied from another source.").

disciplined lawyers for plagiarism absent harm to clients.[116] In fact, lawyers may be disciplined for plagiarism that affects neither courts nor clients, as *In re Lamberis*[117] demonstrates.

Anthony Lamberis was working on the thesis for his LL.M. at Northwestern University School of Law while practicing law full-time. Half of his LL.M. thesis came from two treatises that he "incorporated, substantially verbatim and without crediting the source."[118] Northwestern expelled him and then filed a disciplinary complaint against him. A disciplinary hearing board found that he had knowingly plagiarized the two treatises. Lamberis disputed that finding before the Illinois Supreme Court.

The Illinois Supreme Court censured Lamberis for his dishonesty and, in doing so, rejected his argument that he should not be disciplined for plagiarism that was unrelated to his law practice.[119] As the court observed:

> In this case, sanctions are appropriate and required because both the extent of the appropriated material and the purpose for which it was used evidence the respondent's complete disregard for values that are most fundamental in the legal profession.
>
> The extent of the respondent's plagiarism displays an extreme cynicism towards the property rights of others. . . . Moreover, this conduct amounted to at least a technical infringement of the publishers' federally protected copyrights. . . .
>
> The purpose for which respondent used the appropriated material also displays a lack of honesty which cannot go undisciplined, especially because honesty is so fundamental to the . . . legal profession. . . . "The public as well as . . . the courts have an interest in [an attorney's] integrity and are entitled to require that he shun even the appearance of any fraudulent design or purpose."[120]

The plagiarism in *Lane* and *Lamberis* was obvious. In practice, however, the line between plagiarism and legitimate borrowing is not always clear. In the interest of providing clarity, courts, disciplinary authorities, and lawyers should agree that copying from a pleading, brief, or other materials prepared by another lawyer in the same firm; copying from one's own pleadings or briefs in a different case (indeed, it is impossible to plagiarize one's own work in any context); signing one's name to a brief or pleading prepared by a colleague working on the same case; or copying parts of a model pleading from a formbook are not acts of plagiarism warranting professional discipline.

116. *See, e.g.*, *In re* Steinberg, 620 N.Y.S.2d 345, 346 (App. Div. 1994) (censuring the lawyer for plagiarizing other lawyers' pleadings in a writing sample required to receive court-appointed cases).

117. 443 N.E.2d 549 (Ill. 1982).

118. *Id.* at 550.

119. *Id.* at 551.

120. *Id.* at 551–52 (citations omitted).

Formbook authors intend their work to be copied, and copying one's own work or the work product of other lawyers in the same firm or organization is a permissible means of achieving efficiency. The lawyer who signs her name to a brief or memorandum prepared by a colleague does so with that lawyer's express or implied permission and, by signing the document, accepts responsibility for its contents, thus avoiding any sort of misrepresentation to the court. The same is true for a lawyer who files a brief or memorandum that includes portions that were cut-and-pasted from documents prepared personally or by another lawyer in the same firm in a different matter.

In contrast, authors of articles and books do not expect their work to be copied—at least not without attribution. Courts consider it unacceptable to copy briefs or pleadings prepared by unaffiliated lawyers in other cases, by lawyers representing a co-defendant or co-plaintiff in the same case, or by an opposing lawyer in a current case.[121] Courts also consider it unacceptable for lawyers to plagiarize court opinions and orders.[122]

There are, however, plausible arguments that lawyers who copy pleadings and briefs prepared by unaffiliated lawyers without attribution, or who copy court orders and opinions without giving credit, should not be

121. *See, e.g.*, DeWilde v. Guy Gannett Publ'g Co., 797 F. Supp. 55, 56 n.1 (D. Me. 1992) ("[Plaintiff's] memorandum plagiarizes Defendants' memorandum in significant part, copying the legal portions of it . . . virtually verbatim. . . . Plaintiff's counsel has inserted his own facts and conclusions . . . but it is clear that he did no legal research and . . . let defense counsel do all the work."); *In re* Ayeni, 822 A.2d 420, 421 (D.C. 2003) (plagiarizing a brief filed by a lawyer for a co-defendant); *In re* Steinberg, 620 N.Y.S.2d 345, 346 (App. Div. 1994) (disciplining a lawyer seeking criminal defense appointments for submitting as writing samples other lawyers' legal memoranda on which he typed new docket numbers and substituted his name); Columbus Bar Ass'n v. Farmer, 855 N.E.2d 462, 465, 468–69 (Ohio 2006) (plagiarizing a predecessor lawyer's appellate brief in a second brief filed on the client's behalf).

122. *See, e.g.*, United States v. Bowen, 194 F. App'x 393, 402 n.2 (6th Cir. 2006) ("While our legal system stands upon the building blocks of precedent, necessitating some amount of quotation or paraphrasing, citation to authority is absolutely required when language is borrowed."); United States v. Lavanture, 74 F. App'x 221, 224 n.2 (3d Cir. 2003) (cutting-and-pasting half of a section of a brief from a Sixth Circuit opinion without attribution); C.L. *ex rel.* K.B. v. Mars Area Sch. Dist., No. 2:14-cv-1666, 2015 WL 3968343, at *6 n.5 (W.D. Pa. June 30, 2015) (calling it "plagiarism" and "unacceptable" where large portions of the defendant's argument on an issue were lifted nearly verbatim or copied identically from two court opinions); Consol. Paving, Inc. v. Cnty. of Peoria, Ill., No. 10-CV-1045, 2013 WL 916212, at *5–6 (C.D. Ill. Mar. 8, 2013) (declining to award otherwise compensable fees for preparing a fee application because the lawyer copied five pages out of a 13-page brief "nearly verbatim" from a Seventh Circuit opinion); State Farm Fire & Cas. Co. v. Harris, No. 3:11-36-DCR, 2012 WL 896253, at *1 & n.3 (E.D. Ky. Mar. 15, 2012) (admonishing a lawyer for copying all but six sentences out of a seven-page brief from a prior opinion by the same court); Venesevich v. Leonard, No. 1:07-CV-2118, 2008 WL 5340162, at *2 n.2 (M.D. Pa. Dec. 19, 2008) (criticizing the lawyer's plagiarism in a brief opposing a motion to dismiss as disappointing and disturbing, and collecting cases); Pagan Velez v. Laboy Alvarado, 145 F. Supp. 2d 146, 160–61 (D.P.R. 2001) (criticizing a lawyer who plagiarized an unpublished opinion for "reprehensible" conduct). *But see* N.Y. Eth. Op. 2018-3, 2018 WL 4608938, at *10 (N.Y. State Bar Ass'n, Comm. on Prof'l Ethics 2018) [hereinafter N.Y. Eth. Op. 2018-3] ("[W]e are not persuaded that copying from a prior judicial opinion without attribution in a brief is always deceptive and therefore a *per se* violation of Rule 8.4(c).").

criticized or sanctioned for plagiarism.[123] First, lawyers intend litigation filings to persuade the court—not to convey an original idea or to express an idea in an original way, as is the case with scholarly publications.[124] Hence, the need for attribution is lessened or eliminated. Second, the lawyer who wrote the original pleading or brief is not harmed by another lawyer using her work without attribution. The first lawyer drafted the original brief or pleading to serve her client's objectives; once it was filed, those objectives were met.[125] The first lawyer's compensation for drafting the brief or pleading is not diminished if another lawyer recycles her work.[126] Certainly, judges are not harmed if lawyers copy their orders or opinions, which, in any event, generally are public documents. Third, lawyers intend court filings to benefit their clients, who typically pay for the lawyer's time in preparing those filings. Cost-conscious clients accordingly have an interest in their lawyers practicing efficiently. If a lawyer can make an effective argument by reusing arguments made by others, the client benefits.[127] For all these reasons, critics contend, courts ought not fault lawyers who copy unaffiliated lawyers' court documents or courts' opinions and orders without attribution.

Furthermore, it might reasonably be argued that courts should focus more on the quality of plagiarized documents rather than their lack of originality. If the subject brief or pleading is unpersuasive because the borrowed arguments are disjointed or are not tailored to the facts of the case, the critical problem maybe the lawyer's inability to fulfill her basic duties of competence and diligence rather than her dishonesty.

Professional responsibility considerations aside, as a matter of style and persuasive writing, it is unquestionably better to paraphrase influential secondary sources and selectively cite them than it is to copy them without attribution. Even lengthy block quotations with due credit are preferable to copying the works of others without attribution. Overall, courts are more likely to be persuaded by the views of legal scholars than they are by the opinions of practicing lawyers, even if they match. It makes yet less sense for lawyers to plagiarize judicial opinions. Even if the opinion the lawyer copies is not precedential, it certainly has greater persuasive value as the analysis or reasoning of another court as compared to the supposition of a single lawyer. Principles of effective advocacy thus ought to overcome the temptation to

123. *See, e.g.*, N.Y. Eth. Op. 2018-3, *supra* note 122, 2018 WL 4608938, at *7 (explaining why copying a brief or pleading prepared by another lawyer or law firm should not be held to violate Rule 8.4(c)); 2008 N.C. Eth. Op. 14, 2009 WL 435074, at *1 (N.C. State Bar 2009) (opining that "it is not an ethical violation when a lawyer fails to attribute or obtain consent when incorporating into his own brief, contract, or pleading excerpts from a legal brief, contract, or pleading written by another lawyer and placed into the public domain").

124. N.Y. Eth. Op. 2018-3, *supra* note 122, 2018 WL 4608938, at *5.

125. *Id.* at *7.

126. *Id.*

127. *Id.* at *5.

copy scholarly works and judicial opinions without attribution every time.[128] Regardless, it is clear that lawyers may not pass off others' work as their own. Courts generally consider such conduct dishonest and deceitful, and as constituting misrepresentation.[129] If the document incorporating the plagiarized text is filed with a court, the lawyer's conduct may further be deemed prejudicial to the administration of justice.[130] Finally, any fees charged for the preparation of plagiarized briefs, pleadings, or other court documents are likely to be deemed unreasonable, thus exposing the lawyer to discipline on that basis.[131] A court may substantially reduce a fee award where the prevailing party seeks fees for its lawyers' plagiarized work or the lawyer submitting the fee request plagiarizes portions of supporting briefs or memoranda.[132]

F. Ghostwriting and Lawyer Identity

"Ghostwriting" occurs when a lawyer anonymously prepares briefs, pleadings or other court documents in whole or substantial part for a pro se litigant with the knowledge that the pro se litigant will present the lawyer's work to the court. This is a potentially risky practice from a professional responsibility perspective. Although lawyers generally violate no ethics rules by assisting family and friends with whom they share their specialized knowledge, lawyers arguably "cross the line" when they "gather and anonymously present legal arguments[ ] with the actual or constructive knowledge that the work will be presented in some similar form" to a court.[133]

Lawyers who ghostwrite pleadings for ostensibly pro se litigants risk breaching their duty of candor to the court in which the pro se litigant's case is pending,[134] potentially engage in conduct prejudicial to the administration

---

128. *See, e.g.*, C.L. *ex rel.* K.B. v. Mars Area Sch. Dist., No. 2:14-cv-1666, 2015 WL 3968343, at *6 n.5 (W.D. Pa. June 30, 2015) ("[A]n attorney does not do his client or the Court any favors by cribbing material from a judicial opinion without adding any additional analysis. Defendants' brief exemplifies why: it is a hard-to-follow mishmash of disjointed paragraphs that do not clearly and specifically address or analyze the unique circumstances of this case. Worse yet, when an attorney resorts to plagiarism, his credibility is diminished in the eyes of the Court.").

129. *See, e.g.*, Iowa Sup. Ct. Att'y Disciplinary Bd. v. Cannon, 789 N.W.2d 756, 759 (Iowa 2010); Iowa Sup. Ct. Bd. of Prof'l Ethics & Conduct v. Lane, 642 N.W.2d 296, 299 (Iowa 2002); *In re* Zbiegien, 433 N.W.2d 871, 875 (Minn. 1988).

130. *See, e.g.*, *Lane*, 642 N.W.2d at 299.

131. *Id.* at 300–01.

132. *See, e.g.*, A.L. v. Chi. Pub. Sch. Dist. No. 299, No. 10 C 494, 2012 WL 3028337, at *6–7 (N.D. Ill. July 24, 2012) (awarding the plaintiffs only 10 percent of their requested fees as a sanction for their lawyers' significant plagiarism in connection with the fee request).

133. Ricotta v. State of Cal., 4 F. Supp. 2d 961, 987 (S.D. Cal. 1998).

134. Snyder v. Daugherty, 899 F. Supp. 2d 391, 414–15 (W.D. Pa. 2012); Delso v. Trs. for the Ret. Plan for the Hourly Emps. of Merck & Co., No. 04-3009, 2007 WL 766349, at *17 (D.N.J. Mar. 6, 2007); United States v. Eleven Vehicles, 966 F. Supp. 361, 367 (E.D. Pa. 1997); Johnson v. Bd. of Cnty. Comm'rs, 868 F. Supp. 1226, 1232 (D. Colo. 1994), *disapproved on other grounds by* 85 F.3d 489 (10th Cir. 1996); *In re* W.A.R. LLP, No. 11-00044, 2012 WL 1576002, at *26 (Bankr. D. Colo. May 4, 2012); *In re* Mungo, 305 B.R. 762, 769–70 (Bankr. D.S.C. 2003).

of justice,[135] may assist a client in committing fraud,[136] and risk engaging in conduct involving dishonesty, fraud, deceit, or misrepresentation.[137] They may also face contempt charges or judicially imposed sanctions. Ghostwriting may be held to violate Federal Rule of Civil Procedure 11, which requires that pleadings, written motions, and other court papers be signed by at least one attorney of record in the attorney's name or by an unrepresented party personally, and imposes certification requirements on the submitting lawyer or unrepresented party.[138] The principal concern expressed in connection with or reference to Rule 11, naturally, is that ghostwriting lawyers may escape accountability and responsibility for their actions.[139] Ghostwriting may also be alleged to work a fraud on the court and to be unfair to the ostensibly pro se litigant's adversary because it allows the ostensibly pro se litigant to reap the advantage of the somewhat relaxed standards often applied to non-lawyers who represent themselves, while actually enjoying the benefit of counsel.[140]

135. *See* Laremont-Lopez v. Se. Tidewater Opportunity Ctr., 968 F. Supp. 1075, 1079 (E.D. Va. 1997); *In re* Young, 849 So. 2d 25, 31 (La. 2003).

136. *See* Wesley v. Don Stein Buick, Inc., 987 F. Supp. 884, 886 (D. Kan. 1997) (quoting ABA Comm. on Ethics and Prof'l Responsibility, Informal Op. 1414 (1978)).

137. *See* Barnett v. LeMaster, 12 F. App'x 774, 778 (10th Cir. 2001) (explaining that a ghostwriting lawyer's failure to identify himself by signing a pleading, written motion, or brief "constitute[d] a misrepresentation to [the] court by both the litigant and attorney"); *In re W.A.R. LLP*, 2012 WL 1576002, at *26 (finding that ghostwriting concealed a conflict of interest from the court and thus violated Rule 8.4(c)); Liguori v. Hansen, No. 2:11-cv-00492-GMN-CWH, 2012 WL 760747, at *5 (D. Nev. Mar. 6, 2012) ("An attorney participating in 'ghost-writing' is engaged in conduct involving misrepresentation to the [c]ourt because another individual is signing pleadings the attorney drafted."); *In re Mungo*, 305 B.R. at 769 (stating that ghostwriting for pro se litigants "is a misrepresentation that violates an attorney's duty and professional responsibility to provide the utmost candor toward the [c]ourt"); *Wesley*, 987 F. Supp. at 886 (quoting Informal Op. 1414). *But see* State *ex rel.* Couns. for Discipline of the Neb. Sup. Ct. v. Hanson, 941 N.W.2d 193, 203 (Neb. 2020) (concluding that the lawyer's failure to disclose that he prepared legal documents for his girlfriend as required by a Nebraska rule did not violate Rule 8.4(c)).

138. *See, e.g.*, Onosko v. Smith, No. 3:14-CV-00004-EJL-CWD, 2015 WL 1003346, at *4 (D. Idaho Mar. 6, 2015) (explaining that ghostwriting circumvents Rule 11 and the court's ability to sanction misconduct); Thigpen v. Banas, No. 08 C 4820, 2010 WL 520189, at *1 (N.D. Ill. Feb. 11, 2010) (explaining that ghostwriting evades the requirements of Rule 11); Ostrovsky v. Monroe (*In re* Ellington), 230 B.R. 426, 435 n.12 (Bankr. D. Mont. 1999) (stating that ghostwriting by lawyers violates Rule 11 as well as ethics rules).

139. *Barnett*, 12 F. App'x at 778; Ellis v. State of Me., 448 F.2d 1325, 1328 (1st Cir. 1971); *Liguori*, 2012 WL 760747, at *5; *Thigpen*, 2010 WL 520189, at *1; *In re Mungo*, 305 B.R. at 768–69.

140. Gordon v. Katri Sales Co., No. 3:17-CV-00320, 2018 WL 2018 WL 1251965, at *2 n.3 (M.D. Pa. Mar. 12, 2018); Chriswell v. Big Score Entm't, LLC, No. 11 C 00861, 2013 WL 315743, at *4–5 (N.D. Ill. Jan. 28, 2013); Snyder v. Daugherty, 899 F. Supp. 2d 391, 414–15 (W.D. Pa. 2012); DeForest v. Johnny Chisholm Global Events, LLC, No. 3:08cv498/MCR/EMT, 2010 WL 1792094, at *5 n.9 (N.D. Fla. May 4, 2010); *Thigpen*, 2010 WL 520189, at *2; CIT Grp./Com. Servs. v. Prsico, 640 F. Supp. 2d 401, 407 (S.D.N.Y. 2009); *Delso*, 2007 WL 766349, at *13–14; United States v. Eleven Vehicles, 966 F. Supp. 361, 367 (E.D. Pa. 1997); *In re Mungo*, 305 B.R. at 769.

Courts generally disapprove of ghostwriting.[141] Indeed, courts often condemn lawyers' ghostwriting as misrepresentation and as an improper means of evading responsibility for their actions. Notwithstanding courts' widespread condemnation of lawyers' ghostwriting, bar groups have generally been more accepting of the practice.[142] In fact, bar groups' general

141. *See, e.g.*, Duran v. Carris, 238 F.3d 1268, 1271–73 (10th Cir. 2001) (criticizing the practice with respect to appeals); *Gordon*, 2018 WL 2018 WL 1251965, at *2 n.3 ("[G]hostwriting by an attorney is generally disfavored by Federal Courts. . . . The practice serves as a means of misrepresentation to the [c]ourt, gives pro se [p]laintiffs an unfair advantage, as they are already entitled to special leniency, and violates an attorney's duty of candor to the [c]ourt." (citation omitted)); Auto Parts Mfg. Miss. Inc. v. King Constr. of Houston, LLC, No. 1:11-CV-00251-GHD-SAA, 2014 WL 1217766, at *7 (N.D. Miss. Mar. 24, 2014) (cautioning that "an attorney who ghostwrites motion briefs and pleadings is acting unethically and is subject to sanctions"); Anderson v. Kohl's Corp., No. 2:12-cv-00822, 2013 WL 1874812, at *2 n.4 (W.D. Pa. May 3, 2013) (stating bluntly that "'ghostwriting' is not permitted"); Falconer v. Leigh Hanson, Inc., No. 4:11–CV–373, 2013 WL 3480382, at *6 n.2 (S.D. Tex. July 9, 2013) (cautioning that ghostwriting is "misconduct" that "exposes both litigants and counsel to the possibility of sanctions, including fines, contempt, and professional discipline"); Makreas v. Moore Law Grp., A.P.C., No. C-11-2406 MMC, 2012 WL 1458191, at *3 (N.D. Cal. Apr. 26, 2012) (criticizing ghostwriting in connection with an attempt to recover attorney's fees); Nationwide Tr. Servs., Inc. v. Rivera, No. 3:11-cv-528-RJC-DSC, 2012 WL 1394916, at *2 n.2 (W.D.N.C. Apr. 23, 2012) (admonishing a lawyer that the court "condemn[ed] the ghostwriting of pleadings for parties purporting to appear pro se"); Davis v. Bacigalupi, 711 F. Supp. 2d 609, 626 (E.D. Va. 2010) (stating that ghostwriting "is strongly disapproved as unethical and as a deliberate evasion of the responsibilities imposed on attorneys"); Gordon v. Dadante, No. 1:05-CV-2726, 2009 WL 1850309, at *27 (N.D. Ohio June 26, 2009) (criticizing ghostwriting, stating that the court would continue to strike ghostwritten pleadings, and threatening parties who submit ghostwritten pleadings with contempt); Bittle v. Elec. Ry. Improvement Co., 576 F. Supp. 2d 744, 755 n.9 (M.D.N.C. 2008) ("This court condemns the ghostwriting of pleadings for parties purporting to appear pro se."); Anderson v. Duke Energy Corp., No. 3:06cv399, 2007 WL 4284904, at *1 n.1 (W.D.N.C. Dec. 4, 2007) (expressing "a dim view" of ghostwriting); Kircher v. Charter Twp. of Ypsilanti, No. 07-13091, 2007 WL 4557714, at *4 (E.D. Mich. Dec. 21, 2007) (branding ghostwriting "improper" even though it may not violate Rule 11); *In re* Dreamplay, Inc., 534 B.R. 106, 120 (Bankr. D. Md. 2015) (stating that ghostwriting "violates an attorney's duty of candor and circumvents Rule 9011 which ensures that submissions of court documents are made in good faith with the responsible party's signature," and that "[a]ttorneys who engage in ghostwriting for pro se litigants may be subject to sanctions, suspension or disbarment" (footnote omitted)); *In re* Smith, Nos. 12-116-3, 12-11857, 2013 WL 1092059, at *14–22 (Bankr. E.D. Tenn. Jan. 20, 2013) (concluding that ghostwriting violated the lawyer's duty of candor and was a misrepresentation within the meaning of Rule 8.4(c)); *In re* Brown, 354 B.R. 535, 541–46 (Bankr. N.D. Okla. 2006) (concluding that ghostwriting was intolerable); *In re Mungo*, 305 B.R. at 767–70 (offering reasons for prohibiting ghostwriting); *In re* Disciplinary Proc. Against Booker, 857 N.W.2d 890, 893–96 (Wis. 2015) (revoking the lawyer's license for ghostwriting state debt relief pleadings, among other violations).

142. *See, e.g.*, Alaska Bar Ass'n, Ethics Comm., Ethics Op. 93-1 (1993) (permitting ghostwriting); Ariz. State Bar, Comm. on the Rules of Prof'l Conduct, Op. 06-03 (2006) (allowing forms of limited scope representation that would include ghostwriting); D.C. Bar, Legal Ethics Comm., Op. 330, at 4 (2005) (declining to require lawyers to reveal assistance to pro se litigants); Mich. Eth. Op. RI-347, 2010 WL 2265461, at *3–4 (State Bar of Mich., Comm. on Prof'l & Jud. Ethics 2010) (allowing ghostwriting); Miss. Bar, Ethics Comm., Op. 261, at 2–3 (2018) [hereinafter Miss. Eth. Op. 261] (permitting ghostwriting); NYCLA Eth. Op. 742, 2010 WL 4260878, at *7 (N.Y. Cnty. Lawyers' Ass'n, Comm. on Prof'l Ethics 2010) (permitting ghostwriting in most situations); 2008 N.C. Eth. Op. 3, 2009 WL 435077, at *3 (N.C. State Bar 2009) (approving of ghostwriting); Pa.

approval of ghostwriting has persuaded at least one federal court that the practice may be permissible.

In re Liu[143] involved a New York immigration lawyer, Fengling Liu, who was accused of various acts of misconduct, including ghostwriting. Liu assisted multiple clients in preparing petitions for review to the Second Circuit after the Board of Immigration Appeals had denied their appeals. Liu's clients could not afford her fees, and Liu testified that "she 'could not see them miss the appeal deadline simply because of financial reasons.'"[144] Liu also hoped that by ghostwriting her clients' petitions she might buy them sufficient time to raise money to pay her fees, which apparently happened on a number of occasions. In any event, Liu ended up being referred to the Second Circuit's Committee on Attorney Admissions and Grievances, which concluded that Liu violated her duty of candor by helping petitioners draft and file petitions for review without disclosing her involvement to the court.[145] The committee grounded Liu's candor violation in then-DR 1-102(A)(4) of the New York Lawyer's Code of Professional responsibility, which prohibited lawyers from engaging in conduct involving dishonesty, fraud, deceit, or misrepresentation.[146] The committee noted, however, Liu's undisclosed assistance was not substantial and did not harm her clients.[147]

Based on her numerous offenses, the committee recommended that the court publicly reprimand Liu. The Second Circuit adopted all the findings in the committee's report—except those pertaining to the ghostwriting charge.

The *In re Liu* court observed that while numerous courts had been harshly critical of ghostwriting, many bar association ethics committees tolerate the practice.[148] The court was especially persuaded by Formal Opinion 07-446 of the ABA's Standing Committee on Ethics & Professional Responsibility, which largely approved of ghostwriting.[149] The court reasoned that

Eth. Op. 2011-100, 2011 WL 7574467, at *7–9 (Pa. Bar Ass'n Comm. on Legal Ethics & Prof'l Responsibility & Phila. Bar Ass'n Prof'l Guidance Comm. 2011) [hereinafter Pa. Eth. Op. 2011-100] (permitting ghostwriting); Utah Eth. Op. 08-01, 2008 WL 2110962, at *5 (Utah State Bar, Ethics Advisory Op. Comm. 2008) (permitting ghostwriting in most circumstances); Va. State Bar, Comm. on Legal Ethics, Op. 1874, at 8 (2014) (opining that it is not dishonest, misleading, or otherwise unethical for a lawyer to provide undisclosed assistance to an unrepresented litigant). *But see* State Bar of Nev., Comm. on Ethics & Prof'l Responsibility, Formal Op. No. 34, at 7–8 (Rev. 2009) (concluding that ghostwriting is unethical "unless both the 'ghost-lawyer's' assistance and identity are disclosed to the court by the signature of the 'ghost-lawyer' under Rule 11 upon every paper filed with the court for which the 'ghost-lawyer' gave substantial assistance to the *pro* se litigant by drafting or otherwise" (footnote omitted)).

143. 664 F.3d 367 (2d Cir. 2011).

144. *Id.* at 381.

145. *Id.* at 386.

146. *Id.*

147. *Id.*

148. *Id.* at 370.

149. *Id.* at 370–71 (quoting and citing ABA Comm. on Ethics & Prof'l Responsibility, Formal Op. 07-446 (2007)).

"[i]n light of the ABA's 2007 ethics opinion, and the other recent ethics opinions permitting various forms of ghostwriting, it is possible that the courts and bars that previously disapproved of attorney ghostwriting of pro se filings will modify their opinion[s] of that practice."[150]

Continuing, the court explained that for Liu to have violated DR 1-102(A)(4), she would have had to have known either of an existing obligation to disclose her role in drafting her clients' petitions for review or of the possibility that nondisclosure in a particular case would materially mislead the court.[151] The court concluded that given its lack of prior holdings on ghostwriting and the many authorities permitting the practice, "Liu could not have been aware of any general obligation to disclose her participation to [the] [c]ourt."[152] Furthermore:

> [T]here [was] no evidence that Liu knew, or should have known, that she was withholding material information from the [c]ourt or that she otherwise acted in bad faith. . . . Additionally, there is no evidence that Liu sought, or was aware that she might obtain, any unfair advantage through ghostwriting. Finally, Liu's motive in preparing the petitions—to preserve the petitioners' right of review by satisfying the thirty-day jurisdictional deadline—demonstrated concern for her clients rather than a desire to mislead [the] [c]ourt or opposing parties.[153]

Under these circumstances, the court determined that Liu's ghostwriting did not constitute misconduct and therefore did not warrant discipline.[154]

Liu's clients were a very sympathetic group, and the documents she prepared were simple. The documents were otherwise inoffensive. On these facts, it is understandable that the court would be reluctant to discipline Liu for ghostwriting. The Second Circuit's uncritical embrace of ABA Formal Opinion 07-446, however, suggests the need to examine that opinion to ascertain whether it is worthy of wider reliance.

As *In re Liu* makes clear, in Formal Opinion 07-446 the ABA's Standing Committee on Ethics and Professional Responsibility determined that the Model Rules do not prohibit lawyers' undisclosed assistance to pro se litigants.[155] In so holding, the committee first reasoned that whether a pro se litigant received undisclosed legal assistance is not material to the merits of the case.[156] Second, the committee discounted the concern that pro se litigants benefit from special treatment by courts and that permitting ghostwriting affords them an undue advantage. As the committee explained,

150. *Id.* at 371 (emphasis omitted).
151. *Id.* at 372.
152. *Id.* (footnote omitted).
153. *Id.* at 372–73 (footnotes omitted).
154. *Id.* at 373 (footnote omitted).
155. ABA Comm. on Ethics & Prof'l Responsibility, Formal Op. 07-446, at 4 (2007).
156. *Id.* at 2.

"if the undisclosed lawyer has provided effective assistance, the fact that a lawyer was involved will be evident to the tribunal. If the assistance has been ineffective, the pro se litigant will not have secured an unfair advantage."[157] Third, concealing the lawyer's assistance is not dishonest because there is no danger that the court will be misled by the nondisclosure. The lawyer's ghostwriting might violate Model Rule 8.4(c) only where the client affirmatively misrepresents to the court that she has not received legal assistance and that misrepresentation may be attributed to the lawyer.[158] Finally, the committee reasoned, ghostwriting does not circumvent court rules requiring lawyers to take responsibility for the content of their pleadings because such rules apply only if a lawyer signs a pleading and "thereby makes an affirmative statement to the tribunal concerning the matter. Where a pro se litigant is assisted, no such duty is assumed."[159]

Regrettably, Formal Op. 07-446 suffers from result-oriented assumptions and incomplete reasoning. First, contrary to the committee's position, whether a pro se litigant received undisclosed assistance can be material to the merits of the litigation. To use but one example, a lawyer may be able to prepare a memorandum in opposition to a motion to dismiss or a summary judgment motion that a pro se litigant would never be able to assemble and thus prolong meritless litigation. Here the lawyer's conduct goes to the merits of the case even if it is as much tactical as it is substantive. Because a case may be meritless without being frivolous,[160] Model Rule 3.1 and state equivalents are no shield against such conduct by lawyers.[161]

Second, there is no assurance that a lawyer's effective assistance of a pro se litigant will be apparent to a court, especially if the pro se litigant is sophisticated. A lawyer's assistance may be ineffective for reasons other than a straight loss, as when frivolous arguments expose the pro se litigant to sanctions. Moreover, allowing lawyers to provide undisclosed assistance to pro se litigants potentially gives those lawyers a free pass to abuse courts without violating Model Rule 8.2(a).[162] Statements that violate Model Rule

157. *Id.* at 3.

158. *Id.* at 3–4.

159. *Id.* at 4.

160. Commonwealth v. Chmiel, 30 A.3d 1111, 1190 (Pa. 2011) (distinguishing frivolous claims from meritless ones); *In re* Houston, 675 S.E.2d 721, 723 n.1 (S.C. 2009); Johnson v. Miller, 818 N.W.2d 804, 809 (S.D. 2012) (quoting Stratmeyer v. Engberg, 649 N.W.2d 921, 926 (S.D. 2002)); *In re* S.C., 88 A.3d 1220, 1223–24 (Vt. 2014); *see also* Estate of McLemore v. McLemore, 63 So. 3d 468, 490 (Miss. 2011) (observing that a case may be "weak" or "light-headed" without being "frivolous" for the purpose of awarding sanctions).

161. Model Rules of Prof'l Conduct R. 3.1 (2020) (providing in pertinent part that a lawyer "shall not bring or defend a proceeding, or assert or controvert an issue therein, unless there is a basis in law and fact for doing so that is not frivolous").

162. *Id.* R. 8.2(a) ("A lawyer shall not make a statement that the lawyer knows to be false or with reckless disregard as to its truth or falsity concerning the qualifications or integrity of a judge. . . .").

8.2(a) are exactly the sort of advocacy that a court might expect from a pro se litigant rather than a lawyer, and there would thus be no reason for a court to suspect a lawyer's undisclosed involvement.

Third, the committee's reasoning that ghostwriting does not circumvent Federal Rule of Civil Procedure 11 and state equivalents, because such rules apply only if a lawyer signs a pleading and thereby makes an affirmative statement to the court concerning the case, is at best circular. Lawyers should not be able to circumvent Rule 11 by not signing pleadings that violate the rule even though they prepared them. The committee's rationale is certainly difficult to reconcile with Model Rule 8.4(a), which prohibits lawyers from violating or attempting to violate the rules of professional conduct through the acts of another, or to knowingly assisting or inducing another person to violate the rules.[163]

At least insofar as Rule 11 is concerned, the committee's reasoning also appears to be incorrect. Rule 11(c)(1) provides that if a document violates Rule 11(b), "the court may impose an appropriate sanction on any attorney, law firm, or party that violated the rule *or is responsible for the violation*."[164] Thus, under Rule 11(c)(1), a lawyer may violate Rule 11(b) without signing the offending document if she can reasonably be described as being responsible for it.[165]

Given the infirmities in Formal Op. 07-446, if the Second Circuit wanted authority for its decision not to discipline Liu for ghostwriting, it might have better considered an opinion from the Board of Professional Responsibility of the Supreme Court of Tennessee.[166] In Opinion 2007-F-153, the board attempted to reconcile courts' concerns about ghostwriting with the practical reality that a pro se litigant might need a lawyer's assistance at the outset of a matter, as where a pro se litigant must act to protect her claim against being time-barred. The board concluded that a lawyer may prepare pleadings for a pro se litigant without identification on the pleadings where doing so allows the pro se litigant to preserve her claim and the lawyer will not provide further assistance.[167]

The Tennessee approach does not fit the *In re Liu* facts perfectly, of course, because Liu hoped her clients would ultimately raise the funds necessary to pay her; that is, she wanted to provide the further assistance that the Board assumed would not come. The Tennessee approach also has a few flaws. For example, a lawyer assisting a pro se litigant still escapes responsibility under Rule 11, and the ostensibly pro se litigant still reaps at least

163. *Id.* R. 8.4(a).

164. FED. R. CIV. P. 11(c)(1) (emphasis added).

165. *See* FED. R. CIV. P. 11 advisory committee's note (1993 amendments).

166. Tenn. Eth. Op. 2007-F-153, 2007 WL 5010859 (Bd. of Prof'l Responsibility of the Sup. Ct. of Tenn. 2007).

167. *Id.* at *2.

briefly the advantage of the relaxed standards often applied to pro se parties while enjoying the benefit of counsel. The threat of the lawyer's unsanctionable violation of Rule 8.2(a) is but a minor risk, however, because lawyers are unlikely to make statements prohibited by Rule 8.2(a) in an initial pleading; such statements are typically the product of experiences with a court over the life of a case. At the same time, allowing a lawyer initial undisclosed involvement in a pro se litigant's case has the salutary effect of protecting the litigant's important rights in circumstances where they might otherwise be lost, and allows the assisting lawyer to avoid the difficulty that may accompany withdrawal once the complaint, petition, or notice of charge has been filed. To the extent the pro se litigant receives an unfair advantage through the lawyer's undisclosed aid, the advantage is fleeting and is unlikely to materially influence the outcome of the litigation. In any event, the Tennessee opinion offers stronger support for ghostwriting than does ABA Formal Op. 07-446.

Nevertheless, ghostwriting is a potentially perilous endeavor for lawyers, and they are well advised to avoid the practice. Lawyers who wish to assist pro se litigants should limit their undisclosed involvement to preparing initial documents necessary for the litigant to commence an action.[168] The less the lawyer is involved in the litigation, the lower the probability of professional discipline or judicially imposed sanctions. To the extent reasonably possible, lawyers must satisfy themselves that all documents they prepare meet the requirements of Rule 11, as well as the requirements of Model Rule 3.1.[169] They must further ensure that the text of any documents could never be characterized as violating Model Rule 8.2(a). This is not a situation in which anonymity should be perceived as liberating.[170] Finally, for the moment, ghostwriting lawyers should accept no compensation of any kind for their limited initial services. If the lawyer's role in the litigation is somehow exposed and her conduct or the party's conduct is challenged, the court may view her receipt of compensation as an aggravating factor if the

168. *See also* Torrens v. Hood (*In re* Hood), 727 F.3d 1360, 1364–65 (11th Cir. 2013) (concluding that lawyers who helped a client file a pro se Chapter 13 bankruptcy petition by completing a preprinted form using answers furnished by the client but who did not identify themselves did not "draft" a document in violation of a Florida ethics rule requiring that documents filed by pro se litigants state that they have been prepared with the assistance of counsel when that is the case, and thus the lawyers should not have been disciplined).

169. Model Rules of Prof'l Conduct R. 3.1 (2020) (providing in pertinent part that a lawyer "shall not bring or defend a proceeding, or assert or controvert an issue therein, unless there is a basis in law and fact for doing so that is not frivolous").

170. *See, e.g.*, Ligon v. Stilley, 371 S.W.3d 615, 663–65 (Ark. 2010) (disciplining a lawyer who, in secretly helping his clients prepare a pro se complaint, either prepared or ratified allegations that were "clearly intemperate, contemptuous, and disrespectful of the Justices of the Arkansas Supreme Court individually and as a [c]ourt").

challenge is well-founded, or at least as a factor weighing against leniency should sanctions be appropriate.

Beyond those mechanical concerns, lawyers must consider at least three other issues. First, what is the nature of the lawyer's relationship with the pro se litigant? If the lawyer is doing anything other than providing temporary assistance to a friend or family member as an accommodation, the lawyer must appropriately define for the client the limited scope of the representation and obtain the client's consent to the limitation.[171] Second, given the many cases in which courts have disapproved of ghostwriting, the lawyer should explain to the client (1) the possible consequences of the lawyer's involvement if it should be revealed and (2) the effects that the lawyer's involvement may have on the client's case in other respects, such as the client's loss of any consideration that a court might otherwise extend to an unrepresented party,[172] or the client's duty to reveal the lawyer's participation if called upon to do so by the court.[173] Third, clients in limited scope representations are still clients to whom lawyers owe the essential duties they owe clients in other representations.[174] Bottom line, ghostwriting lawyers must devote the same attention to their work that they would in any other representation.

G. Conclusion

Questioning the truth of a lawyer's representations is a sensitive matter because, as officers of the court, lawyers are generally presumed to be truthful.[175] Lawyers who lie to tribunals risk substantial discipline. This is true even where a lawyer lies about a seemingly innocuous matter, such as the reason for seeking a continuance or an innocent failure to appear. Lawyers' understandable belief that minor stretches of the truth are rarely tested may lead them into serious misfortune in circumstances where their truthfulness is questioned. Pointedly, some courts hold that suspension from practice is the minimum penalty for a lawyer's breach of candor to a tribunal.[176] It generally does not matter that the lawyer's lie started as a "white lie" or that it is the product of pressures brought on by a difficult case, heavy workload or

171. Model Rules of Prof'l Conduct R. 1.2(c) (2020) (requiring further that any limitation be reasonable).

172. Spira v. J.P. Morgan Chase & Co., 466 F. App'x 20, 22 n.1 (2d Cir. 2012).

173. *See, e.g.*, Evangelist v. Green Tree Servicing, LLC, No. 12-15687, 2013 WL 2393142, at *3–4 (E.D. Mich. May 31, 2013).

174. Miss. Eth. Op. 261, *supra* note 142, at 2–3; Pa. Eth. Op. 2011-100, *supra* note 142, 2011 WL 7574467, at *5.

175. Drost v. Sec'y of Health & Human Servs., No. 01-502V, 2010 WL 3291933, at *2 (Fed. Cl. July 30, 2010).

176. *See, e.g.*, Office of Disciplinary Couns. v. Greene, 655 N.E.2d 1299, 1301–02 (Ohio 1995) (indicating that, at a minimum, suspension is always required).

hectic schedule, or demanding client or superior; courts' dependence on the candor and integrity of the lawyers who appear before them compels serious enforcement of related disciplinary rules. The fact that a lawyer's duty of candor to a tribunal may impair a client's case is unfortunate, but nothing more. Zealous advocacy does not excuse lawyers' dishonesty.[177]

III. Disclosing Directly Adverse Authority

As noted earlier, lawyers are officers of the court.[178] One of a lawyer's basic duties as an officer of the court is to call applicable legal authority to the court's attention,[179] including legal authority in the controlling jurisdiction that is directly adverse to the claim or cause of action being pressed.[180] This duty is enforced under Model Rule 3.3(a)(2), which provides that a lawyer shall not knowingly "fail to disclose to the tribunal legal authority in the controlling jurisdiction known to the lawyer to be directly adverse to the position of the client and not disclosed by opposing counsel."[181] Although critics of the duty to disclose directly adverse legal authority in the controlling jurisdiction argue that it requires lawyers to act contrary to their clients' interests, it is in no one's interest to permit lawyers to potentially facilitate courts' erroneous decisions by knowingly concealing important authority.[182] Moreover, compliance with Rule 3.3(a)(2) only requires a lawyer to reveal authority within its scope; it does not require the lawyer to advance or develop an opponent's related arguments.[183]

As a practical matter, Model Rule 3.3(a)(2) should seldom have to be invoked. After all, credibility with courts is essential for advocates. As with any act of perceived dishonesty by a lawyer, failing to reveal adverse authority destroys judicial trust. It is also possible that a lawyer's failure to reveal directly adverse authority will enhance that authority in the court's eyes, for if it was inapposite or erroneously decided, the lawyer surely would have revealed it. Accordingly, good advocates reveal directly adverse authority in the jurisdiction, accompanied by arguments criticizing or distinguishing

177. *Id.* at 1301.

178. Roche v. Hyde, 265 Cal. Rptr. 3d 301, 348 (Ct. App. 2020); *In re* Venie, 395 P.3d 516, 523 (N.M. 2017); Meisels v. Fox Rothschild LLP, 222 A.3d 649, 657 (N.J. 2020); *In re* M.G., 221 A.3d 774, 775 (R.I. 2019); Lawyer Disciplinary Bd. v. Hassan, 824 S.E.2d 224, 230 (W. Va. 2019).

179. Dike v. People, 30 P.3d 197, 201 (Colo. 2001).

180. *But see In re* Miller, 741 F. App'x 859, 864 (3d Cir. 2018) (finding that the lawyer was not required to reveal directly adverse authority where the related question was no longer at issue in the proceedings).

181. Model Rules of Prof'l Conduct R. 3.3(a)(2) (2020).

182. *See, e.g.*, Ill. Adv. Op. 16-02, 2016 WL 6159375, at *4 (Ill. State Bar Ass'n 2016) (concluding that a criminal defense lawyer could not withhold controlling legal authority from a tribunal as a trial strategy to insure reversible error on appeal).

183. Gibson v. Car Zone, 31 A.3d 76, 2011 WL 5354270, at *2 (Del. Nov. 8, 2011).

it. This diminishes the opponent's argument on the point, builds credibility with the court, and may even favorably influence the court's decision.[184]

"Legal authority" as that term is used in Model Rule 3.3(a)(2) is not limited to case law; it also describes or refers to administrative rulings, codes, ordinances, regulations, rules, and statutes.[185] On the other hand, secondary sources, such as law review and bar journal articles, treatises, texts, legal encyclopedias, hornbooks, and the like, do not qualify as legal authority for Rule 3.3 disclosure purposes. The "controlling jurisdiction" typically means the forum state in state court cases, and the same judicial district or appellate circuit in federal cases.[186] Applicable Supreme Court decisions are always deemed to be from a controlling jurisdiction.[187] This view is consistent with accepted notions of assessing legal precedent.

Lawyers' duty to reveal directly adverse case law is not limited to appellate decisions;[188] lawyers may be required to cite trial court decisions.[189] This obligation is more likely to be imposed in connection with federal district court decisions, which are widely regarded as persuasive authority. State trial court opinions that are deemed to be non-binding should not require disclosure.[190] Lawyers may be required to disclose lower court opinions even if they are on appeal, if the applicable law provides that the decision has precedential value pending appeal.[191] Lawyers also may have to disclose courts'

184. Smith v. Scripto-Tokai Corp., 170 F. Supp. 2d 533, 540 (W.D. Pa. 2001).

185. *See, e.g.*, Dilallo v. Riding Safely, Inc., 687 So. 2d 353, 355 (Fla. Dist. Ct. App. 1997) (holding that a lawyer defending a stable in suit arising out of a horseback-riding accident had a duty to disclose that a statute immunizing the stable from liability did not take effect until after the accident).

186. *See, e.g.*, Pannell v. McBride, 306 F.3d 499, 502 n.1 (7th Cir. 2002) (failing to disclose two cases from the same judicial circuit); Taylor v. Client Servs., Inc., No. 17-CV-05704, 2018 WL 4355819, at *3 (N.D. Ill. Sept. 12, 2018) (failing to cite a Seventh Circuit case); Shelton v. S. Energy Homes, Inc., 420 F. Supp. 2d 579, 583 n.1 (S.D. Miss. 2006) (failing to disclose Supreme Court case and a case from the governing judicial circuit); Chew v. KPMG LLP, 407 F. Supp. 2d 790, 802 n.13 (S.D. Miss. 2006) (failing to cite a case from the governing judicial circuit); United States v. Crumpton, 23 F. Supp. 2d 1218, 1219 (D. Colo. 1998) (failing to disclose a case from the same federal judicial district); Massey v. Prince George's Cnty., 907 F. Supp. 138, 141–43 (D. Md. 1995) (failing to disclose a case from the same federal judicial circuit); Time Warner Entm't Co. v. Does #1-2, 876 F. Supp. 407, 415 (E.D.N.Y. 1994) (failing to disclose an applicable provision of a federal statute and a case from the same federal judicial circuit); *In re* Thonert, 733 N.E.2d 932, 933–34 (Ind. 2000) (reprimanding a lawyer for failing to disclose directly adverse Indiana Supreme Court authority); State v. Cagle, 641 S.E.2d 705, 709 (N.C. Ct. App. 2007) (failing to disclose a directly adverse North Carolina Supreme Court case).

187. Batko v. Sayreville Democratic Org., 860 A.2d 967, 968 (N.J. Super. Ct. App. Div. 2004); State v. Somerlot, 544 S.E.2d 52, 54 n.2 (W. Va. 2000); *see also* Dultra v. US Med. Home, Inc., No. 13 C 07598, 2014 WL 1347107, at *3 (N.D. Ill. Apr. 4, 2014) (describing the failure to cite a controlling Supreme Court decision "inexcusable").

188. Douglass v. Delta Air Lines, Inc., 897 F.2d 1336, 1344 (5th Cir. 1990).

189. *Id.* (discussing U.S. District Court decisions); *Crumpton*, 23 F. Supp. 2d at 1219 (same); Smith v. Scripto-Tokai Corp., 170 F. Supp. 2d 533, 538–40 (W.D. Pa. 2001) (same).

190. *See, e.g.*, Brundage v. Estate of Carambio, 951 A.2d 947, 957 (N.J. 2008).

191. *Douglass*, 897 F.2d at 1344.

unpublished decisions,[192] although they need not do so in jurisdictions in which such opinions are non-binding or non-precedential,[193] nor must they disclose any decisions to which citation is prohibited.[194] For example, some states prohibit citation to intermediate appellate court decisions that are not approved for official publication, such that a lawyer would have no duty to cite one of those decisions that was directly adverse to a client's position. If lawyers do cite unpublished opinions in a jurisdiction that permits the practice, however, they must disclose directly adverse unpublished decisions about which they know to satisfy their duty of candor.[195]

Lawyers occasionally argue that a case is not directly adverse because it is obsolete or stale—that is, it was decided long before the dispute at hand. That is not so. Intervening developments may call into question the vitality of old cases and thus provide a basis for distinguishing them. Changes in legal doctrine or thought may support an argument that a court ought to overrule an old case. The mere passage of time, however, does not transform directly adverse authority into something else and thus excuse its disclosure to the court.[196]

Of course, a lawyer must reveal directly adverse authority in the controlling jurisdiction only if it is not disclosed by opposing counsel.[197] But a lawyer who knows of such authority may not omit the authority from her opening brief or some other initial pleading or document in the hope that an opponent will thereafter find and cite it.[198] A lawyer has "a duty to refrain from affirmatively misleading [a] court as to the state of the law."[199] If a lawyer omits directly adverse authority in the controlling jurisdiction from an initial pleading or brief and her opponent does not assert the authority in a subsequent brief or memorandum, the lawyer must call the omitted authority to the tribunal's attention before the case is submitted for decision.[200]

Lawyers are not required to disclose all adverse authority in the controlling jurisdiction. Rather, lawyers' duty is more limited. A lawyer is required to disclose only *directly adverse* authority in the controlling jurisdiction. In some cases, direct adversity will be obvious. As a general rule, authority should be considered directly adverse if the court would reasonably view it as important or reasonably feel that the lawyer misled it by arguing a

---

192. Piambino v. Bailey, 757 F.2d 1112, 1131 & n.44 (11th Cir. 1985).

193. *Brundage*, 951 A.2d at 956.

194. Restatement (Third) of the Law Governing Lawyers § 111 cmt. d (2000).

195. *Brundage*, 951 A.2d at 956–57.

196. Lieber v. ITT Hartford Ins. Ctr., Inc., 15 P.3d 1030, 1039 n.14 (Utah 2000).

197. Model Rules of Prof'l Conduct R. 3.3(a)(2) (2020); *see, e.g.*, *In re* Stewart, 473 B.R. 612, 639–40 (Bankr. W.D. Pa. 2012); Manokoune v. State Farm Mut. Auto. Ins. Co., 145 P.3d 1081, 1086 n.3 (Okla. 2006).

198. Jorgenson v. Cnty. of Volusia, 846 F.2d 1350, 1352 (11th Cir. 1988).

199. *Id.*

200. Restatement (Third) of the Law Governing Lawyers § 111 cmt. c (2000).

contrary position.[201] Either way, authority may be directly adverse even though the lawyer reasonably believes it to be factually distinguishable or erroneously decided, or understandably thinks that the court will otherwise determine that it does not govern the current case.[202]

Tyler v. State[203] is an illustrative case. David Tyler was convicted of a felony for driving while intoxicated. The issue on appeal was the treatment of two prior DWI offenses, which affected Tyler's status as a repeat offender and, thus, whether he should have been convicted of a felony rather than a misdemeanor. Tyler's attorney, Eugene Cyrus, did not in his briefing reveal as being directly adverse an Alaska Supreme Court case, *McGhee v. State*,[204] which addressed the exact same issue in a slightly different setting. The state's attorney did not cite *McGhee* either; the court located it through its own research. Cyrus could not claim, however, that he was unaware of *McGhee*, for it was he who represented McGhee in the supreme court.[205]

Cyrus explained that he had not cited *McGhee* because he believed that it did not control the outcome of Tyler's case. He contended that *McGhee* was factually distinguishable and that the court was wrong to rely on *McGhee*. Cyrus pointed to a trial court order in another case in which the judge had agreed that *McGhee* did not control the disposition of a case like Tyler's. Thus, because "reasonable attorneys and judges could disagree on . . . whether *McGhee* was controlling authority in Tyler's case," then-Rule 3.3(a)(3) did not require him to reveal it.[206] In short, Cyrus argued that he was required to reveal only "controlling authority."[207]

The court rejected Cyrus's arguments, correctly explaining that a lawyer must disclose directly adverse authority in the controlling jurisdiction, not controlling authority.[208] Because *McGhee* was decided by the Alaska Supreme Court, it clearly constituted authority in the controlling jurisdiction. The question thus became whether *McGhee* could be considered directly adverse. The court determined that it could, stating that a "decision can be 'directly adverse' . . . even though the lawyer reasonably believes that

201. Failing to reveal that a case has been overruled or reversed may expose a lawyer to discipline under Rule 3.3(a)(2) or to sanctions. *See, e.g.*, Kuhnle Bros., Inc. v. City of Geauga, 103 F.3d 516, 520 n.2 (6th Cir. 1997) (sanctioning a lawyer for relying on a case that had been reversed over one year before the lawyer filed his brief); Prizio v. Lincoln Nat'l Life Ins. Co., No. 3:11cv736 (JBA), 2014 WL 1315648, at *1 n.2 (D. Conn. Mar. 31, 2014) (indicating that Rule 3.3(a)(2) obligates lawyers to reveal that cases they cite have been reversed or overruled).

202. Shocklee v. Mass. Mut. Life Ins. Co., 369 F.3d 437, 440 n.3 (5th Cir. 2004); Massey v. Prince George's Cnty., 918 F. Supp. 905, 907–08 (D. Md. 1996); Tyler v. State, 47 P.3d 1095, 1105–06 (Alaska Ct. App. 2001).

203. 47 P.3d 1095 (Alaska Ct. App. 2001).

204. 951 P.2d 1215 (Alaska 1998).

205. *Tyler*, 47 P.3d at 1102.

206. *Id.* at 1104.

207. *Id.*

208. *Id.*

the decision is factually distinguishable . . . or the lawyer reasonably believes that . . . the court will ultimately conclude that the decision does not control the current case."[209]

The court next turned to the issue of whether Cyrus knew that *McGhee* was directly adverse authority, such knowledge being necessary to find a violation. As the court explained:

> We recognize that advocacy invariably includes a process of separating wheat from chaff, of deciding which arguments and legal authorities are important to a case. Moreover . . . an attorney's ethical duties must not be judged in hindsight. When an attorney consciously decides not to cite a court decision or a statute, the attorney's choice should not—and does not—become a violation of Professional Conduct Rule 3.3(a)(3) simply because the court later concludes that the omitted decision or statute is directly adverse to the attorney's position. Rather, an attorney violates Rule 3.3(a)(3) only if the *attorney knew* that the omitted legal authority was directly adverse to the attorney's position.[210]

Cyrus did not claim ignorance of *McGhee*'s potential importance to Tyler's appeal. He contended instead that he was not required to disclose it because he honestly believed that it was factually distinguishable and, thus, should not have controlled the court's decision. The *Tyler* court again rejected this argument. Cyrus was obligated to call *McGhee* to the court's attention even if he reasonably believed that it was inapposite.[211]

The *Tyler* court concluded that Cyrus violated then-Rule 3.3(a)(3).[212] Because Cyrus did not act in bad faith in failing to cite *McGhee*, the court merely fined him $250.

Cyrus oddly petitioned for rehearing. In his petition for rehearing, Cyrus pointed out that he *did* cite *McGhee* in his opening brief; however, he cited it for an unrelated point of law. The court easily dispensed with this argument, stating that Cyrus's citation to *McGhee* on an unrelated point might be an "interesting coincidence," but it was irrelevant to the decision to fine him.[213] Cyrus's late revelation that he had in fact cited *McGhee* perhaps suggested that he always knew that his citation to the case for an unrelated point did not provide a defense to his alleged then-Rule 3.3(a)(3) violation.[214] The *Tyler* court thus denied his petition for rehearing.

From practitioners' perspective, perhaps the most surprising aspect of *Tyler* is the court's conclusion that Cyrus violated then-Rule 3.3(a)(3) even though he cited *McGhee* on an unrelated point of law in his opening brief.

209. *Id.* at 1105–06.
210. *Id.* at 1107.
211. *Id.* at 1108.
212. *Id.* at 1109.
213. *Id.* at 1111.
214. *Id.*

Many lawyers would consider mere citation to the case to be disclosure for purposes of the rule. After all, advocates are only obligated to disclose directly adverse authority; they are not required to engage in disinterested expositions of the law.[215] Thus, a lawyer might reason, mere citation should be treated as sufficient disclosure given that the court ought to be expected to read the case for itself once it is cited.

That line of reasoning, however, takes too crabbed a view of the purpose behind Model Rule 3.3(a)(2). The purpose behind the rule is to require that what is being disclosed to the court is the fact that *directly adverse* authority in the controlling jurisdiction exists. It is precisely such authority that may be important to the court in reaching a correct result. The fact that Cyrus cited *McGhee* for an unrelated point of law demonstrates that the citation did not satisfy the purpose of the rule and that the *Tyler* court therefore reached the correct conclusion.

Had Cyrus simply added a footnote to his argument with a *but see* citation to *McGhee*, he would have avoided discipline. A *but see* signal indicates that cited authority clearly supports a proposition contrary to the writer's main proposition. A lawyer's citation to directly adverse authority on a point other than that on which the authority is directly adverse will not, however, satisfy the lawyer's duty under Model Rule 3.3(a)(2). Courts rely on counsel to supply most legal argument. Conscientious though judges and their law clerks may be, it is unreasonable to rely on them to scour every cited case for issues or points relevant to the dispute at hand. Moreover, requiring courts to read all cases cited to them for discussion of all issues on points mentioned in the brief or document at issue leads to the unnecessary expenditure of judicial resources. Requiring courts to ferret out directly adverse authority delays the resolution of all disputes by increasing their workloads, and it causes other problems. As the *Tyler* court noted:

> When a lawyer practicing before us fails to disclose a decision . . . that is directly adverse to the lawyer's position, the lawyer's conduct will, at the very best, merely result in an unneeded expenditure of judicial resources—the time spent by judges or law clerks in tracking down the adverse authority. At worst, we will not find the adverse authority and we will issue a decision that fails to take account of it, leading to confusion in the law and possibly unfair outcomes for the litigants involved. This potential damage is compounded by the fact that our decision, if published, will be binding in future cases.[216]

Another situation worth considering is that in which the language in a case that appears to render the decision directly adverse is, in the lawyer's good faith view, dicta. If so, must the lawyer disclose the case to the court?

215. Model Rules of Prof'l Conduct R. 3.3 cmt. 4 (2020).
216. *Tyler*, 47 P.3d at 1108 (footnote omitted).

The answer is yes.[217] Whether the unfavorable language is dicta is a question for the court, not the lawyer. The lawyer must therefore reveal the case notwithstanding her belief about its significance. After doing so, the lawyer should explain why the unfavorable language is dicta, and argue that the court should ignore the decision.

What if there is no authority on point in the controlling jurisdiction, but there is directly adverse authority in another jurisdiction? Must a lawyer who knows of such authority cite it even though it is not in the controlling jurisdiction? Model Rule 3.3(a)(2) does not require disclosure in this situation, and disclosure here would seem to undermine advocates' duty to competently represent their clients. If nothing else, it strains credibility to argue that a case from outside a controlling jurisdiction qualifies as directly adverse authority given that the decision has no precedential value.

If, on the other hand, a lawyer cites authority from outside the controlling jurisdiction because there is no authority on-point in the jurisdiction, some courts reason that the lawyer is required to also reveal directly adverse authority from outside the controlling jurisdiction.[218] Courts advocating such an obligation posit that Rule 3.3(a)(2) only establishes a minimum standard of conduct; a lawyer's general duty of candor requires more.[219] Moreover, a lawyer's selective citation of cases from other jurisdictions arguably represents an attempt to deceive the court,[220] thus implicating Rules 8.4(c) and (d).[221] Analogizing to tort law, lawyers may assume a duty to reveal directly adverse authority from outside the controlling jurisdiction if they cite favorable authority from outside the jurisdiction.[222]

Although it is perhaps possible for a lawyer to assume a duty to reveal directly adverse authority from outside the controlling jurisdiction, courts

---

217. *See* Precision Specialty Metals, Inc. v. United States, 315 F.3d 1346, 1358 (Fed. Cir. 2003) (criticizing the defense of a lawyer's dishonest briefing on the basis that the lawyer's misrepresentation of a statement in a Supreme Court opinion concerned an issue that was "not important").

218. *See* Mannheim Video, Inc. v. Cnty. of Cook, 884 F.2d 1043, 1047 (7th Cir. 1989); Plant v. Doe, 19 F. Supp. 2d 1316, 1318–19 (S.D. Fla. 1998); Rural Water Sys. #1 v. City of Sioux Ctr., 967 F. Supp. 1483, 1498 n.2 (N.D. Iowa 1997).

219. *See, e.g.*, *Rural Water*, 967 F. Supp. at 1498 n.2 (stating that "basic notions of professionalism" demand something more than mere compliance with ethics rules regarding the disclosure of directly adverse authority in the controlling jurisdiction in situations such as this).

220. *See Mannheim Video*, 884 F.2d at 1047 (calling the selective citation of such cases "a poor example of an attorney conforming to his duties as an officer of the court"); *Rural Water*, 967 F. Supp. at 1498 n.2 (saying that the selective citation of cases from outside the controlling jurisdiction "smacks of concealment").

221. Model Rules of Prof'l Conduct R. 8.4(c) (2020) (prohibiting conduct involving dishonesty, fraud, deceit, or misrepresentation); *id.* R. 8.4(d) (prohibiting conduct prejudicial to the administration of justice).

222. *See Mannheim Video*, 884 F.2d at 1047 (describing a lawyer's failure to reveal non-dispositive authority from an intermediate state appellate court as "an exercise in gall" when he had cited intermediate appellate court decisions from other states to support his position, in addition to citing federal district court decisions from outside the Seventh Circuit).

inclined to recognize such a duty ought to do so sparingly, as where the lawyer participated in the case not revealed,[223] and in ex parte proceedings.[224] Even lawyers' rigorous duty of candor to the tribunal must have reasonable limits to accommodate their duties to clients as advocates. Furthermore, in the rare case in which such a duty might be imposed, it should be as a corollary of rules other than Model Rule 3.3(a)(2), for the language of that rule in no way supports it. Depending on the facts, Model Rules 8.4(c) and (d) are potentially better authority on which to premise such a duty. Of course, effective advocacy principles should limit opportunities for lawyers to breach assumed duties of disclosure. A lawyer who cites favorable authority from outside a controlling jurisdiction should presume that an adversary will also research outside the jurisdiction and will thus discover the adverse authority that the lawyer would have the court ignore. Beating an adversary to the punch by disclosing and distinguishing or criticizing directly adverse authority from other jurisdictions in this situation is both strategically wise and ethically prudent.

IV. Candor in Ex Parte Proceedings

The law permits ex parte proceedings in a variety of contexts—usually linked to a party's urgent need for judicial relief or intervention—as in requests for temporary restraining orders, or applications for temporary child custody or orders of protection from abuse. The stakes in these proceedings are often substantial, yet there is no opponent to advocate conflicting positions or illuminate contrary facts, and the balance of interests normally found in litigation is therefore lost. At the same time, the court must strive for a just result and, accordingly, must consider the absent party's position to the extent reasonably possible. This leaves a judge hearing an ex parte proceeding wholly dependent on the lawyer who appears to furnish the facts on which any decision will be based. Model Rule 3.3(d) therefore establishes that in an ex parte proceeding, "a lawyer shall inform the tribunal of all material facts known to the lawyer that will enable the tribunal to make an informed decision, whether or not the facts are adverse."[225]

Model Rule 3.3(d) does not require guilty knowledge for a violation. Lawyers may violate Rule 3.3(d) through the inadvertent or negligent omission or misstatement of material facts, as well as through deceit or misrepresentation.[226] For that matter, there is authority for the proposition that

223. *Rural Water*, 967 F. Supp. at 1498 n.2; Ambulatory Infusion Therapy Specialists, Inc. v. N. Am. Adm'rs, Inc., 262 S.W.3d 107, 120 n.10 (Tex. App. 2008).

224. *See, e.g.*, Plant v. Doe, 19 F. Supp. 2d 1316, 1318–19 (S.D. Fla. 1998).

225. Model Rules of Prof'l Conduct R. 3.3(d) (2020).

226. *See, e.g.*, *In re* Lazzo, 150 P.3d 887, 892 (Kan. 2007); Johnson v. Thomas, 982 So. 2d 405, 414 (Miss. 2008).

lawyers may violate the rule by failing to reasonably investigate the bases for assertions before making them.[227] In other words, lawyers may violate Rule 3.3(d) by making statements that they do not know to be false because the test in ex parte proceedings is whether they reasonably believe statements to be true.[228] A lawyer should not simply accept a client's or co-counsel's factual representations as true if the lawyer has knowledge that calls those representations into doubt or that suggests the need for independent investigation.[229] When acting upon the statements of others, prudent lawyers representing clients in ex parte proceedings will remember the maxim that once guided U.S. diplomats in arms control negotiations with representatives of the former Soviet Union—trust, but verify.

A. *Illustrative Cases*

Lawyers have unfortunately failed to honor their Rule 3.3(d) obligations in numerous cases.[230] In *In re Humphrey*,[231] for example, lawyer Bobbie Humphrey obtained a temporary restraining order (TRO) on behalf of her sister based on materially false statements to the court concerning the parties' domicile. In obtaining the TRO, Humphrey knowingly misrepresented that her brother-in-law's office was the family home, thereby causing his eviction from his office and substantially disrupting his business.[232] Had the judge

227. *In re* Brantley, 920 P.2d 433, 446–47 (Kan. 1996).

228. *Id.* at 446–47.

229. *See, e.g.*, *In re Lazzo*, 150 P.3d at 889–92 (reprimanding lawyer who accepted as true another lawyer's and client's statements that client's criminal charges had been resolved).

230. *See, e.g.*, Daniels v. Alander, 844 A.2d 182, 188–91 (Conn. 2004) (disciplining an associate under both Rules 3.3(a)(1) and 3.3(d) where the associate did not correct misstatements by the partner he was second-chairing in an ex parte proceeding); Fla. Bar v. Dove, 985 So. 2d 1001, 1005–10 (Fla. 2008) (suspending a lawyer for three years for misconduct in an adoption case); *In re* Herron, 441 P.3d 24, 49 (Kan. 2019) (involving a lawyer who failed to inform the court that he had not spoken with another party and had not checked to see whether that party would object to the lawyer's attempt to obtain the reversal of an order entered earlier in the day at a hearing in which the other party participated); *In re* Holste, 358 P.3d 850, 852, 854 (Kan. 2015) (obtaining a default judgment by presenting a proposed journal entry reciting that the defendants had not appeared and were in default when they had in fact asked the lawyer for an extension of time in which to answer); Goodsell v. Miss. Bar, 667 So. 2d 7, 10 (Miss. 1996) (suspending a lawyer who forged a client's signature on a motion for a TRO filed in chancery court; a disciplinary tribunal determined that the forgery was material despite the chancellor's testimony that had he known the circumstances surrounding the motion, the fact that the lawyer signed his client's name would have made no difference); Asset Acceptance LLC v. Pham, 415 P.3d 47, 53–54 (Okla. Civ. App. 2016) (setting aside a default judgment where the plaintiff's lawyer failed to inform the trial court of several material facts before the court granted the default judgment); *In re* McAteer, 183 A.3d 1133, 1135 (R.I. 2019) ("The respondent clearly owed a duty of zealous representation to his client. However, he also had a duty to inform the court in an *ex parte* proceeding of all material facts, even those adverse to his clients.").

231. 15 So. 3d 960 (La. 2009).

232. *Id.* at 961.

known of the parties' actual residence, she never would have granted the TRO.[233] The Louisiana Supreme Court found that Humphrey violated Rule 3.3(d) among others and disbarred her for that and unrelated violations.

The lawyer in *In re Holt*,[234] William Holt, represented Melissa Pallini in her divorce from Anthony Pallini. The final judgment for divorce contained a provision concerning the division of Anthony's pension. To achieve that division, it was necessary to prepare a Qualified Domestic Relations Order (QDRO) to be entered by the Family Court; however, the parties could not agree on the QDRO's terms, and they accordingly did not present the court with a QDRO before finalizing the divorce. Years later, when Melissa learned that Anthony had retired, she sought Holt's assistance in obtaining a share of his pension benefits.

Holt prepared a QDRO that was materially different from the terms contained in the final divorce decree and that awarded his client greater rights in Anthony's pension than the court had awarded. Holt made no attempt to contact Anthony or his lawyer to negotiate the QDRO's terms, nor did he tell either of them that he planned to return to court over the QDRO.[235] Rather, he met with the Family Court judge alone and presented the QDRO for her signature.[236] He did not tell the judge that the QDRO varied from the provision in the divorce judgment or that Anthony did not know that the QDRO was being presented to the court.[237]

Unaware of the Holt's deception, the judge signed the QDRO. Holt then sent a copy of the QDRO to Anthony's former employer, which consequently revised Anthony's pension distribution. Anthony learned of the QDRO when his pension benefits changed, and he successfully moved to vacate the order. In a subsequent disciplinary proceeding, the Rhode Island Supreme Court concluded that Holt violated Rule 3.3(d), among others, for his dishonesty in obtaining the QDRO in an ex parte proceeding.[238] For this violation and other offenses in unrelated cases, the court suspended him from practice for three years.

B. Defining Ex Parte Proceedings

Although motions for TROs and similar requests for exigent relief are prototypical examples of ex parte proceedings, there is authority for the proposition that an ex parte proceeding for Model Rule 3.3(d) purposes is any

233. *Id.* at 965.
234. 103 A.3d 147 (R.I. 2014).
235. *Id.* at 150.
236. *Id.*
237. *Id.*
238. *Id.* at 150–51.

activity at which an opponent does not appear.[239] Some courts reason that ex parte proceedings include events and hearings for which one of the parties fails to appear despite proper notice thereof.[240] While it is natural to fault a party for not appearing when it should have and thus allowing it to suffer any negative consequences stemming from its failure to present its views, consider courts' perspective: because the judge hearing the matter must attempt to render a fair decision despite the imbalance in representation, it is arguably just to impose the Rule 3.3(d) disclosure obligations on the lawyer who does appear.[241]

There is ample room for debate on this point. To be sure, any proceeding for which one party does not appear is technically an ex parte proceeding because the fundamental meaning of this Latin phrase is "from or on behalf of only one side to a lawsuit."[242] Yet that is not the only definition of ex parte, and an alternative construction of the term incorporates as an element the lack of notice to the other party.[243] Furthermore, there is a great procedural difference between, say, an application for a TRO, where a lawyer knows that an adversary will not appear, and a hearing or other proceeding in which an adversary is expected to appear but does not.[244] A lawyer's voluntary decision not to appear for a proceeding ought to have consequences—most particularly the inability to have one's arguments heard. If the client is harmed as a result, the client's recourse lies against the lawyer—the client cannot expect to be rescued by opposing counsel. Indeed, there is substantial potential for mischief if a lawyer can voluntarily choose not to participate in a proceeding and, by doing so, force an opponent to argue her client's position. For these reasons, whether a proceeding is ex parte for Model Rule 3.3(d) purposes should pivot on a lawyer's expectation concerning an opponent's appearance.[245] This will, in most cases, focus the inquiry on the issue of notice.[246] If the lawyer has not notified the opponent of the proceeding or

239. *See, e.g.*, Fitzhugh v. Comm. on Prof'l Conduct, 823 S.W.2d 896, 898–99 (Ark. 1992) (involving a lawyer who, following a hearing, prepared an order for the judge's signature with the other parties' consent, but substituted a form more advantageous to his clients than that to which the other parties had agreed).

240. *See, e.g.*, Eagan v. Jackson, 855 F. Supp. 765, 790 (E.D. Pa. 1994); *In re* Malmin, 895 P.2d 1217, 1220 (Idaho 1995).

241. *See Malmin*, 895 P.2d at 1220 (quoting a comment to the Idaho rule).

242. Bryan A. Garner, A Modern Dictionary of Legal Usage 340 (2d ed. 1995).

243. Black's Law Dictionary 597 (7th ed. 1999).

244. *See, e.g.*, Doctor's Assocs., Inc. v. Windham, 81 A.3d 230, 237–39 (Conn. App. Ct. 2013) (declining to apply Rule 3.3(d) to a lawyer's conduct where the opposing party did not appear for an arbitration hearing through no fault of the lawyer).

245. *See* Budny v. Statewide Grievance Comm., No. CV960560637S, 1997 WL 331034, at *7 (Conn. Super. Ct. June 9, 1997) (anticipating that an opposing party will not be represented at a proceeding is "an essential element of an 'ex parte proceeding'" for Rule 3.3(d) purposes).

246. *See, e.g.*, Pa. Eth. Op. 2005-10, 2005 WL 1047078, at *1 (Pa. Bar Ass'n, Comm. on Legal Ethics & Prof'l Responsibility 2005) (opining that Rule 3.3(d) would not govern a lawyer's conduct at a hearing "since the hearing will not be ex parte, even if there is no opponent present,

has given inadequate notice, the proceeding should be considered ex parte. If the lawyer has somehow procured the opponent's absence, the proceeding is clearly ex parte for Rule 3.3(d) purposes.[247] If, on the other hand, the lawyer gives proper notice of the proceeding and the other side simply does not appear, the proceeding should not be considered ex parte and the lawyer's duty of candor should be gauged under Rule 3.3(a) rather than Rule 3.3(d).[248] The same result should follow where the court gives appropriate notice and the other party does not appear. In short, a proceeding should not be considered ex parte for Rule 3.3(d) purposes where the opposing party knowingly chooses not to appear.[249] Similarly, a proceeding should not be considered ex parte where the opposing party appears pro se and is thus able to argue his or her position—even if not through a lawyer.[250]

C. Model Rule 3.3(d) May Not Apply to Prosecutors Presenting Cases to Grand Juries

Ex parte proceedings are not solely a creature of civil litigation; grand jury proceedings are an obvious example of an ex parte proceeding in criminal litigation. Although prosecutors are generally subject to Rule 3.3(d) just as other litigators are, that is not necessarily true when they present cases to grand juries.[251] Although related authority is scarce, there is a strong argument that grand jury proceedings are not considered to be ex parte proceedings within the meaning of Rule 3.3(d).[252] The principal rationale for this position seems to be that requiring prosecutors to present exculpatory as well as incriminating evidence as Rule 3.3(d) contemplates would alter the grand jury's role by "transforming it from an accusatory to an adjudicatory body."[253] To the extent that prosecutors may be required to present exculpatory evidence to grand juries, that obligation arises from sources other than Rule 3.3(d).[254]

---

because all parties in interest have been given notice (on three occasions) and all parties are therefore being offered an opportunity to be heard").

247. Obviously, a lawyer's failure to notify an opponent of a proceeding for improper purposes or procurement of the opponent's absence raises significant ethics issues of its own.

248. N.Y. Eth. Op. 2019-1, 2019 WL 653796, at *5 (N.Y. State Bar Ass'n, Comm. on Prof'l Ethics (2019).

249. *Id.* at *5–6.

250. *Id.* at *5.

251. *See* Restatement (Third) of the Law Governing Lawyers § 112 cmt. c (2000) (asserting that jurisdictions differ on prosecutors' duties of disclosure when presenting matters to grand juries).

252. *See, e.g.*, United States v. Colo. Sup. Ct., 87 F.3d 1161, 1165 (10th Cir. 1996) (applying Rule 3.3(d) to prosecutors appearing before grand juries is "incompatible with the federal grand jury system").

253. United States v. Williams, 504 U.S. 36, 51 (1992).

254. *See* People v. Mitchell, 626 N.E.2d 630, 633 (N.Y. 1993) (explaining that while prosecutors presenting cases to a grand jury need not seek evidence favorable to the defense or present

V. Deception and Illusion as Advocacy Techniques

Trial lawyers routinely use demonstrative evidence. The use of demonstrative evidence sometimes spawns ethics issues. Some issues are clear. For example, lawyers cannot alter demonstrative evidence so that it becomes misleading. Other issues are not so simple. A recurring source of controversy is lawyers' participation in "parlor tricks"—courtroom demonstrations that mislead courts or jurors to make evidentiary points. In a common example, a criminal defense lawyer has someone impersonate her client as a means of challenging a witness's or police officer's identification of the client.[255] This may be as simple as having the impostor sit at counsel table with the lawyer,[256] or it may involve more elaborate techniques, such as altering the client's or stand-in's appearance.

Consistent with Shakespeare's view that all the world's a stage, lawyers also perform parlor tricks in depositions.[257] In *Cincinnati Bar Ass'n v. Statzer*,[258] for example, the lawyer arranged blank cassette tapes in front of the deponent, labeled them as exhibits, and then referred to them during her questioning, thereby implying that she had recorded conversations with the witness. The lawyer also cautioned the witness to testify truthfully under penalty of perjury. The Ohio Supreme Court suspended the lawyer for six months, stayed on the condition of good behavior, for (1) conduct involving dishonesty, fraud, deceit, or misrepresentation and (2) alluding to matters

---

exculpatory evidence, they may need to charge a grand jury with defenses that eliminate needless or unfounded prosecutions).

255. *See, e.g.*, People v. Simac, 641 N.E.2d 416, 422 (Ill. 1994) (affirming a criminal contempt citation against a lawyer who had an employee impersonate his client by sitting at counsel table during trial while the client sat elsewhere in the courtroom); Miskovsky v. State, 586 P.2d 1104, 1108–10 (Okla. Crim. App. 1978) (upholding a criminal contempt citation against a defense lawyer who seated a substitute for the defendant at counsel table without the court's prior knowledge).

256. For example, in 2006, Oregon lawyer Clark Willes appeared at a criminal trial on behalf of the defendant, Brian Shreeve. Willes was joined at the counsel table by a young man roughly fitting Shreeve's description. Willes concealed the imposter's identity until after the State had examined its first witness and after Willes had cross-examined the State's witness. When charged with professional misconduct, Willes admitted that by presenting an imposter as Shreeve at trial, he engaged in or assisted a client in knowingly illegal or fraudulent conduct; violated his duty of candor to the tribunal; engaged in conduct involving dishonesty, fraud, deceit, or misrepresentation; engaged in conduct prejudicial to the administration of justice; and sought to mislead the court by artifice in violation of an Oregon statute. Willes agreed to a 30-day suspension from practice for his misconduct. *In re* Willes, 22 DB Rptr. 82, 83–84, 86 (2008), https://www.osbar.org/_docs/dbreport/dbr22.pdf.

257. *See, e.g.*, Fla. Bar v. Schwartz, 284 So. 3d 393, 395–98 (Fla. 2019) (violating Rule 8.4(c) in connection with a deposition by altering a police photo lineup by replacing his client's image in one exhibit with the image of an alternate suspect whom witnesses other than the victim had identified as the perpetrator and by changing the client's image in the other exhibit by imposing the alternate subject's hairstyle on the client's image, while misleadingly leaving the victim's identifying marks on the original lineup in place).

258. 800 N.E.2d 1117 (Ohio 2003).

unsupported by admissible evidence when appearing before a tribunal.[259] It is noteworthy that the *Statzer* court considered the lawyer's conduct in a deposition to be before a tribunal—a view that courts generally embrace but that seems to elude many lawyers.[260]

A. Court as Theater

United States v. Thoreen[261] is the leading case on lawyers' use of scripted deception as an advocacy technique. Thoreen represented Sibbett, a commercial fisherman, in a bench trial for criminal contempt stemming from alleged violations of a preliminary injunction against salmon fishing. Although there was nothing to suggest that the arresting government agent had picked the wrong man, Thoreen hoped that the agent would be unable to identify Sibbett at trial.[262] He therefore seated at counsel table a fellow by the name of Mason. Mason resembled Sibbett, and Thoreen dressed him in the sort of outdoor clothing a commercial fisherman might be expected to wear. Meanwhile, Sibbett wore a business suit and large round glasses, and sat behind the rail in a row of seats normally reserved for the press. Thoreen did not tell the government's counsel what he was doing, nor did he ask the court's permission to pull the switch.[263]

Thoreen moved at the start of the trial to sequester all witnesses. Mason remained seated at counsel table. Throughout trial Thoreen acted as though Mason were his client; he gave him a pad on which to take notes, and the two of them conferred. Thoreen did not correct the district judge when he referred to Mason as the defendant and caused the record to show Mason's identification as Sibbett by two government witnesses.[264]

When the government rested, Thoreen called Mason as a witness in his case and revealed the switch.[265] The court called a recess and thereafter allowed the government to reopen its case. The government recalled the agent who cited Sibbett for two of the three violations at issue. This time the agent correctly identified Sibbett, who was convicted of all violations.

The district court held Thoreen in criminal contempt for his conduct. The district court condemned the Mason-Sibbett switch because it was done

259. *Id.* at 1123.

260. *Id.* at 1121–22; *see also* N.C. State Bar v. Sutton, 791 S.E.2d 881, 897 (N.C. Ct. App. 2016) (explaining that a deposition is a tribunal); Model Rules of Prof'l Conduct R. 3.5 cmt. 5 (2020) ("The duty to refrain from disruptive conduct applies to any proceeding of a tribunal, including a deposition.").

261. 653 F.2d 1332 (9th Cir. 1981).

262. *Id.* at 1336.

263. *Id.*

264. *Id.*

265. *Id.* at 1336–37.

without the court's or government's knowledge or permission; there was no claimed identification issue before the substitution at trial; it deceived the court and frustrated its responsibility to administer justice; and it violated court custom.[266] Thoreen's conduct also merited contempt because he planned to have Mason testify when he asked the court to exclude witnesses from the courtroom.[267] Finally, the district court found that Thoreen violated three Washington ethics rules: DR 1-102(A)(4), prohibiting conduct involving dishonesty, fraud, deceit, or misrepresentation; DR 7-102(A)(6), prohibiting the creation or presentation of false evidence; and DR 7-106(C)(5), mandating compliance with known local customs of courtesy or practice of the bar or a particular tribunal absent timely notice of intended noncompliance.[268] Thoreen appealed to the Ninth Circuit.

Thoreen's principal defense was that his conduct was a good faith cross-examination tactic and thus fell within "the protected realm of zealous advocacy."[269] He also argued that his conduct did not violate the contempt statute, he did not intend to deceive the court, and the court's order excluding witnesses was not directed at Mason. The Ninth Circuit rejected all his arguments.

Thoreen's conduct crossed the line from zealous advocacy to obstruction of justice because it impeded the court's search for truth, delayed the proceedings, and violated a court custom and rule.[270] Making misrepresentations to the finder of fact "is inherently obstructive because it frustrates the rational search for truth."[271] Thoreen's conduct was also inappropriate because it was done without the court's consent, and it violated court custom to allow only counsel, parties, and others having the court's permission to sit forward of the rail.[272]

Thoreen argued that his decision to keep Mason at counsel table did not violate the court's sequestration order because Mason would not change his testimony based on what he heard in the courtroom and because it was unclear that Mason would be a witness. Thoreen's argument was betrayed by the facts. The sequestration order, which Thoreen requested, did not distinguish between witnesses who might alter their testimony and those who were unlikely to do so. Thoreen also acknowledged that he intended from the start to call Mason as a witness after the expected misidentification.[273]

---

266. *Id.* at 1338.
267. *Id.*
268. *Id.* & nn.4–6.
269. *Id.* at 1338.
270. *Id.* at 1339.
271. *Id.* at 1340–41.
272. *Id.* at 1341.
273. *Id.*

Thoreen's decision to have Mason remain despite the court's order was "an unfortunate error in judgment."[274]

Thoreen also argued that the Mason-Sibbett switch did not obstruct justice because he corrected any misrepresentation before the court ruled on Sibbett's guilt.[275] But Thoreen's argument ignored the disruption that the substitution caused. The substitution delayed the proceedings by virtue of the time spent on the misidentification and by causing the government to recall one witness to correctly identify Sibbett. Furthermore, a court's reliance on a misrepresentation is not necessary to support a finding that deceptive or misleading conduct obstructed justice; mere delay or hindering the court's ability to ascertain the truth suffices.[276]

Finally, Thoreen asserted that he could not be held in contempt because he did not intend to hinder the court's search for truth. This argument also failed. Criminal contempt does not require evil motive or an actual intent to obstruct justice. A lawyer's intent may be inferred if his conduct reflects a reckless disregard for professional duty.[277] That was the case here, primarily because Sibbett's identification was never an issue. Thoreen should have known that his conduct exceeded reasonable limits and hindered the court's search for truth.[278]

Although the Ninth Circuit affirmed the contempt citation, it did so reluctantly. The court noted that certain variations on Thoreen's conduct are acceptable where a defendant's identification is at issue. In such circumstances a lawyer should notify the court and opposing counsel of his intention to test the defendant's identification and seek the court's permission (1) to seat two or more persons at counsel table without identifying the defendant, (2) to have no one at counsel table, or (3) to hold an in-court lineup.[279]

The lawyer in *In re Gross*,[280] Frank Gross, represented a woman charged with drunk driving and leaving the scene of an accident. When arrested, the defendant admitted that she was the driver of the vehicle involved in the accident. Nonetheless, one of her friends approached Gross as an alibi witness, claiming that the defendant had been watching TV with her at the time of the accident. Having done precious little on the case, Gross thus decided to pursue a defense based on alibi and mistaken identification.[281]

On the day of trial, the defendant and her alibi witness went to court. When the case was first called, the defendant answered and requested that

274. *Id.*
275. *Id.*
276. *Id.* at 1342.
277. *See id.* (quoting *In re* Farquhar, 492 F.2d 561, 564 (D.C. Cir. 1973)).
278. *Id.*
279. *Id.* at 1342 n.7.
280. 759 N.E.2d 288 (Mass. 2001).
281. *Id.* at 289.

the case be held for a second call. Gross arrived shortly thereafter and spoke to the accident victim. Based on that conversation, he concluded that the victim probably would not identify his client. He thus told the defendant to remain in the back of the courtroom and had the alibi witness, who resembled the defendant, come forward to the microphone in the courtroom for the second call.[282] The alibi witness complied. The prosecutor then asked for a continuance, and the alibi witness, continuing to impersonate the defendant, signed a form acknowledging the continuance date.[283]

Unfortunately for Gross, the police investigator on the case realized that it was not the defendant who had appeared. He told the prosecutor, and the two of them confronted Gross. Gross initially claimed that the woman who had appeared and who was then signing the continuance form was in fact his client.[284] When the investigator insisted that was not true and pointed out the defendant as she left the courtroom, Gross acknowledged his scheme.[285] The prosecutor then alerted the judge, who issued a warrant for the defendant's arrest for failing to appear.

Gross later lied to the court about his scheme, claiming that he had not realized that the alibi witness had come forward for the defendant, attributing the switch to confusion and his inattention and distraction.[286] The judge then issued an arrest warrant for the alibi witness. Gross continued his efforts to conceal his deceit, only to be done in when the alibi witness turned against him in exchange for the state's agreement not to prosecute her.

Massachusetts disciplinary authorities charged Gross for the impersonation incident and other misconduct. With respect to the impersonation incident, a disciplinary hearing committee found Gross guilty of numerous ethics violations and recommended that he be suspended from practice for one year. The Massachusetts Supreme Judicial Court thought such a sanction too light. The *Gross* court stated:

> A knowing misrepresentation to a court is itself a serious violation, and that serious violation was then compounded by other aggravating factors. [Gross's] orchestration of the impersonation scheme . . . was a form of misrepresentation amounting to criminal contempt and obstruction of justice. . . . When the ruse was uncovered, [Gross] sought to evade responsibility, and asked his client and another witness to make further misrepresentations to the court to assist him in covering up his own wrongdoing. Ensnaring them in the scheme led to the issuance of a default warrant against his client, a capias for the arrest of the witness, and potential criminal charges against the witness. The ruse also operated to undermine the

282. *Id.*
283. *Id.*
284. *Id.* at 289–90.
285. *Id.* at 290.
286. *Id.*

> witness's credibility at the client's trial. Thus, the underlying misconduct is permeated not only by fraud on the court, but by a willingness to jeopardize others (including his own client) in order to perpetrate that fraud and then evade detection.[287]

The court thus suspended Gross for 18 months.

Deception took yet a different form in *In re Swarts*.[288] This time the aspiring magician was John Swarts, a Kansas county prosecutor.

The defendant in the underlying criminal case, James Scott, was accused of ejaculating into a handkerchief in front of a co-worker, which allegedly constituted lewd and lascivious behavior and criminal restraint. The handkerchief was collected as evidence and placed in a brown paper sack. Scott reached a plea agreement with Swarts, and the parties scheduled a sentencing hearing.[289] Sometime before the hearing, the sack containing the handkerchief was lost. Swarts thus located another brown paper sack and placed his own handkerchief inside. He then asked the arresting officer, Sgt. Aubrey Hawpe, to carry the sack into the courtroom as if it were the missing evidence.[290] He also asked Hawpe not to volunteer anything while in court, implying that Hawpe should mislead Scott about the lost evidence.[291] Hawpe angrily refused to participate in the charade. Swarts therefore carried the sack into the courtroom and placed it on the counsel table, where it sat throughout the hearing. He placed the sack on the table to heap embarrassment on Scott. He never told either the judge or Scott that the handkerchief inside the sack was his own rather than the evidence seized in the case.[292]

In his disciplinary case, Swarts admitted that it was improper to have embarrassed Scott, but he argued that he did nothing else wrong because he could have used the substitute sack and handkerchief as demonstrative evidence. A disciplinary hearing panel concluded that Swarts had attempted to falsify evidence in violation of Rule 3.4(b). The panel was influenced by the fact that Hawpe had unflinchingly refused to do that which Swarts did, reasoning that Swarts, as the county's chief law enforcement officer, "should have the same ethical compass."[293] The panel also concluded that Swarts violated Rule 8.4(c) because his conduct involved dishonesty, fraud, deceit, or misrepresentation.[294]

Appearing before the Kansas Supreme Court, Swarts argued that he had not falsified evidence because his handkerchief was never marked as an

287. *Id.* at 293–94 (citations omitted).
288. 30 P.3d 1011 (Kan. 2001).
289. *Id.* at 1016.
290. *Id.*
291. *Id.*
292. *Id.*
293. *Id.* at 1021.
294. *Id.* at 1021–22.

exhibit, and he could have used it as demonstrative evidence. The court considered this argument further evidence of Swarts's bad judgment, especially since he had finally acknowledged at oral argument that he had breached his obligation to disclose essential facts in the case below.[295] The court easily concluded that Swarts violated Rule 8.4(c), although it also found no violation of Rules 3.3 or 3.4.[296]

In reviewing the *Swarts* decision, it is remarkable that the Kansas Supreme Court found no Rule 3.4 violation. While Swarts's violation of Rule 8.4(c) was obvious, his violation of Kansas Rule of Professional Conduct 3.4(b), which made it professional misconduct for a lawyer to "falsify evidence,"[297] was equally obvious. A lawyer need not actually offer or introduce falsified evidence to violate Rule 3.4(b). It is the act of falsification that violates the rule; offering or introducing the falsified evidence simply aggravates the violation, gives rise to a second Rule 3.4(b) violation, or violates other rules, such as Rules 8.4(a), 8.4(c), or 8.4(d).

B. The Critics Speak

Trial lawyers have long looked for ways to align themselves and their clients with jurors, to divert the jury's attention away from evidence or to distract jurors during an adversary's case. This story is attributed to Clarence Darrow:

> Back . . . when people smoked freely in the courtroom, Darrow was sitting at counsel table during the prosecutor's closing argument. He lit a big Havana cigar and started smoking it. As the DA's argument progressed, the cigar ash grew longer and longer. Darrow had placed a straight wire down the center of the cigar, which kept the ash attached. As the prosecutor argued on, the jury paid less and less attention to him and more to whether the cigar ash would fall. The defendant was ultimately acquitted.[298]

Other lawyers remove their wedding bands to flirt with jurors or wheel boxes of paper into the courtroom to signal to jurors that they have more evidence than they could ever hope to present. It is questionable whether these tactics are effective, but they are in any event innocuous. The sorts of parlor tricks discussed in the foregoing cases, however, are serious matters because of their evidentiary aspects.

Some commentators suggest that when it comes to parlor tricks, the ethical litmus test ought to be this: if the trick serves a legitimate purpose, such

295. *Id.* at 1028.

296. *Id.* at 1029.

297. Kan. Rules of Prof'l Conduct R. 3.4(b) (2001).

298. Richard Zitrin & Carol M. Langford, The Moral Compass of the American Lawyer 147 (1999).

as testing a witness's ability to identify a criminal defendant, the lawyer is acting ethically; if the trick serves no legitimate evidentiary purpose, the lawyer's conduct is unethical. That cannot be the correct test, however, because it fails to account for the court. Tactics that deceive or mislead courts are unethical even if they serve legitimate evidentiary purposes.

A truer test is to ask whether the demonstration at issue serves *any* evidentiary purpose. If it does, the sponsoring lawyer should approach the court and ask permission to go forward. Adversaries can then voice objections, and the court can make an appropriate determination. If the answer to this question is no, the demonstration is presumptively unethical.

Lawyers intending to pull parlor tricks may argue that they cannot be required to reveal their intention to the trial court because to do so would somehow improperly influence the court and thus harm their clients. In a criminal case, a defense lawyer intending to substitute a third person for a client might argue that revealing the substitution in advance would compromise the prosecutor by forcing the prosecutor to choose between revealing the trick to the state's identification witness or remaining silent and potentially losing the case. These arguments are infirm. Courts and opposing counsel routinely learn of a lawyer's tactics in advance by way of pretrial motions and arguments and still honor their professional obligations. Courts continue to rule fairly, and opposing counsel do not refer to evidence or matters they know to be off-limits. Seeking a court's permission to perform a demonstration that might be described as a parlor trick is akin to filing a motion in limine.[299] The lawyer is simply seeking a threshold ruling on the use of demonstrative evidence. Requiring a court's permission to attempt a demonstration therefore poses no ethical problems for the parties or the court. A prosecutor who, for example, revealed a defense lawyer's intended act of deception to an identification witness after a court has permitted the tactic would risk a mistrial and perhaps sanctions. In an extraordinary case, a lawyer might seek a court's permission to engage in tactical deception by way of an ex parte application or motion.

VI. Conclusion

Lawyers' duty of candor to tribunals is essential to the fair administration of justice. No matter how diligent they may be, judges and law clerks can never know as much about cases as the lawyers do. As a result, courts rely on lawyers to present most facts and argument. If lawyers do not do so frankly and fully, there is a real chance that courts will form inaccurate conclusions or reach incorrect results. Lawyers' duty of candor takes on increased importance in ex parte proceedings, where the balance of interests normally found

299. People v. Simac, 641 N.E.2d 416, 423 (Ill. 1994).

in adversary matters is lost, but the court still must strive for a just result and must therefore consider the absent party's position to the extent reasonably possible.

Lawyers must appreciate their duty of candor at all times and must understand the broad and stringent obligations the duty imposes on them. Lawyers who lie to tribunals risk significant discipline. It does not matter that the lawyer's lie started as a white lie or that it is the product of pressures brought on by an exceedingly difficult representation. In some cases, lawyers' silence is the equivalent of an affirmative misrepresentation—a principle that lawyers frequently fail to recognize. In short, lawyers must remember that they are officers of the court as well as advocates for clients. Zealous advocacy does not excuse dishonesty.

10

False Testimony by Clients and Witnesses

I. Introduction

Perjury is a perplexing professional responsibility subject. This is especially true where a client testifies falsely. On the one hand, perjury is a crime, and it is therefore wrong for lawyers to suborn or even tolerate it. Lawyers' duty to represent clients competently does not extend to offering false testimony. Perjured testimony threatens the fair administration of justice and seriously undermines the rule of law. False testimony that does not qualify as the crime of perjury may have the same effects. On the other hand, it is not lawyers' role to determine the truth—that is courts' and jurors' role. For that matter, how are lawyers supposed to know what the "truth" is when presented with conflicting testimony? Unless clients admit to lying or state an intention to do so, how do lawyers know whether dubious or inconsistent testimony is the product of dishonesty or a different perception?

Certainly, "even the most inexperienced lawyer knows that he or she should not elicit false testimony,"[1] but seemingly simple rules sometimes become complex in practice. Indeed, the problem of client perjury is often described as creating a professional responsibility "trilemma"[2] for lawyers because of the three competing obligations that lawyers must balance: (1) the requirement that lawyers learn as much as possible about clients' cases to provide competent and diligent representation, and, in the criminal context, effective assistance; (2) the duty of confidentiality, which is intended to encourage clients to trust their lawyers and to be candid with them; and (3) the duty of candor to the tribunal. The perjury trilemma is especially acute in criminal cases because defendants' constitutional rights influence lawyers' professional obligations. For example, criminal defendants have a constitutional right to testify at their trials, yet the same authorities that

1. *In re* Peasley, 90 P.3d 764, 773 (Ariz. 2004).

2. The late Prof. Monroe H. Freedman coined the term "trilemma" in a seminal law review article on client perjury. Monroe H. Freedman, *Professional Responsibility of the Criminal Defense Lawyer: The Three Hardest Questions*, 64 MICH. L. REV. 1469 (1966).

establish defendants' constitutional right to testify indicate that they have no right to testify falsely. This creates severe ethical tensions for criminal defense lawyers who know that their clients intend to testify falsely. Even in civil litigation, it may be difficult for lawyers to fulfill all three duties. For example, a client may reveal information to a lawyer sufficient for the lawyer to know that the client intends to testify falsely or did so. Alternatively, reliable documentary evidence may compel lawyers to firmly conclude that clients intend to lie on the witness stand.[3]

The ethical challenges attending false testimony are not limited to clients. Lawyers cannot allow, assist, or counsel witnesses to testify falsely. Lawyers cannot elicit testimony that, while "technically truthful," is intended to mislead a court.[4] Our professional responsibility regime generally elevates lawyers' duty of candor to tribunals over their duties of competence, diligence, and confidentiality owed to clients.[5] Lawyers' duty of candor accordingly extends to remedying false testimony by clients and witnesses.[6]

This chapter examines the many problems that false testimony poses for trial lawyers in both civil and criminal cases. In doing so, it uses practical examples to illustrate key principles. For lawyers, the ultimate lesson is that it is substantially easier to prevent false testimony than it is to remedy it.

II. Lawyers' Duty of Candor and the Problem of False Testimony

The Model Rules of Professional Conduct address false testimony both prospectively and retrospectively. In other words, what are lawyers' obligations preceding depositions, hearings, or trials when they either know or reasonably believe that clients or witnesses intend to testify falsely, and what are lawyers' duties when confronted by real-time or actual false testimony, as where clients or witnesses unexpectedly lie in depositions or during trial?

3. *See, e.g.*, Webloyalty.com, Inc. v. Consumer Innovations, LLC, 388 F. Supp. 2d 435, 443 n.2 (D. Del. 2005) (concluding that a witness lied based on documentary evidence and stating that nothing about lawyers' duty of zealous advocacy requires them "to advance palpably preposterous testimony").

4. *See, e.g.*, *In re* Krigel, 480 S.W.3d 294, 299 (Mo. 2016) (condemning this tactic as a violation of Missouri's version of Rule 3.3(a)(3)).

5. *See* Hanover Ins. Co. v. United States, 146 Fed. Cl. 447, 450 (Fed. Cl. 2019) ("The duty of candor is paramount, surpassing generalized notions relating to counsel's obligations to other counsel, and in many respects, to the client.").

6. *See, e.g.*, *In re* Page, 774 N.E.2d 49, 50–51 (Ind. 2002) (reprimanding a lawyer who stood silently by while his client testified falsely).

A. Applicable Rules of Professional Conduct

The problem of false testimony is principally governed by Model Rules 3.3 and 3.4. Both rules concern lawyers' roles as advocates.[7] Model Rule 3.3 provides in pertinent part:

> (a) A lawyer shall not knowingly:
>
> * * *
>
> (3) offer evidence that the lawyer knows to be false. If a lawyer, the lawyer's client, or a witness called by the lawyer, has offered material evidence and the lawyer comes to know of its falsity, the lawyer shall take reasonable remedial measures, including, if necessary, disclosure to the tribunal. A lawyer may refuse to offer evidence, other than testimony of a defendant in a criminal matter, that the lawyer reasonably believes is false.
>
> (b) A lawyer who represents a client in an adjudicative proceeding and who knows that a person intends to engage, is engaging or has engaged in criminal or fraudulent conduct related to the proceeding shall take reasonable remedial measures, including, if necessary, disclosure to the tribunal.[8]

A lawyer violates Rule 3.3(a)(3) merely by offering evidence she knows to be false; she need not have encouraged or participated in its fabrication.[9]

Continuing, Model Rule 3.4(b) provides in part that a lawyer shall not "falsify evidence" or "counsel or assist a witness to testify falsely."[10] If lawyers cannot offer unexpected false testimony and must, in fact, disclose clients' and witnesses' perjury in accordance with Rule 3.3, then it follows that they may not falsify testimony themselves or allow or encourage witnesses to testify falsely.[11] This is true even where the witness concocts the false testimony and the lawyer goes along.[12] Moreover, a lawyer violates Model

---

7. These are not the only rules that are implicated when a lawyer knowingly presents false testimony. For example, lawyers' knowing presentation of false testimony also violates the Rule 8.4(c) prohibition against conduct involving dishonesty, fraud, deceit, and misrepresentation, and likewise violates the Rule 8.4(d) ban on conduct prejudicial to the administration of justice. *See* Model Rules of Prof'l Conduct 8.4(c) & (d) (2020). A Rule 8.4(d) violation naturally rests on the principle that the administration of justice depends on parties and witnesses testifying truthfully. Att'y Grievance Comm'n of Md. v. Elmendorf, 946 A.2d 542, 544 (Md. 2006).

8. Model Rules of Prof'l Conduct R. 3.3(a)(3) & (b) (2020).

9. *In re* Manning-Wallace, 695 S.E.2d 237, 241 (Ga. 2010).

10. Model Rules of Prof'l Conduct R. 3.4(b) (2020).

11. There is authority for the proposition that a Rule 3.4(b) violation requires "some action by the lawyer prior to or at the time of the witness's false testimony." *In re* Disciplinary Proc. Against Riley, 882 N.W.2d 820, 837 (Wis. 2016). "[F]ailing to take action in the face of another's decision to give false testimony is different from 'assisting' another person to give false testimony." *Id.* In other words, *allowing* a witness to testify falsely is not the same as *assisting* the witness's false testimony. Following this approach, where a witness testifies falsely without being encouraged or instructed to do so by the lawyer, the lawyer's failure to correct the witness's false testimony would violate Rules 3.3(a)(3) or (b), but not Rule 3.4(b). *See id.* at 837–38 (discussing former Wisconsin Supreme Court Rule 3.3(a)(4)).

12. *In re* Druten, 301 P.3d 319, 321–22, 328–29 (Kan. 2013); *In re* Foley, 787 N.E.2d 561, 569 (Mass. 2003).

Rule 3.4(b) simply by advising or counseling a witness to testify falsely—the witness does not have to actually testify falsely to perfect the violation.[13] Although Model Rule 3.4(b) rule refers only to *witnesses*, it applies equally to cases in which lawyers assist or counsel *clients* to testify falsely.[14] The terms are not exclusive; clients may be witnesses, after all.

Rule 3.4(b) concerns most commonly surface in connection with lawyers' preparation of witnesses to testify, often described as witness "coaching." Although lawyers clearly cannot coerce, induce, or persuade witnesses to testify falsely, there is nothing unethical about lawyers helping witnesses articulate, phrase, rephrase, shape, or polish truthful testimony.[15] Lawyers may work with witnesses to present the facts relevant to the client's case as persuasively as possible. Lawyers may rehearse testimony with witnesses and even suggest word choices.[16] In a criminal case, for example, the Wyoming Supreme Court was unbothered by a defense lawyer instructing his client to describe the client's use of a knife in a fight to "cut" rather than "stab" the victim.[17]

Lawyers are permitted to discuss facts with witnesses, as well as the application of law to facts. Lawyers are not required to passively accept witnesses' characterizations or recollections of events or information. Lawyers may discuss with witnesses other evidence or testimony that has been or will be offered. Indeed, lawyers may attempt to persuade witnesses, "even aggressively," that the witnesses' versions of fact situations are inaccurate or incomplete.[18] Lawyers are therefore entitled to implicitly alter what a witness would have said absent a discussion with the lawyer, as long as the witness's testimony remains truthful. On the other side of the coin, witnesses are entitled to reject lawyers' suggested word choices and urged factual analyses or interpretations. Lawyers must respect witnesses' right to disagree and defer to witnesses who insist that they cannot truthfully testify in the fashion or manner the lawyer advocates.

---

13. *In re Foley*, 787 N.E.2d at 569–70.

14. *See, e.g.*, Harrison v. Miss. Bar, 637 So. 2d 204, 225 (Miss. 1994) (finding that the lawyer violated Rule 3.4(b) when she heard the client testify falsely, but did not reveal the falsity of the client's testimony to the trial court); *In re* Storment, 873 S.W.2d 227, 228–30 (Mo. 1994) (disbarring a lawyer who counseled his client to lie in a custody proceeding); *In re* Feld's Case, 815 A.2d 383, 389 (N.H. 2002) (suspending the lawyer over his client's false testimony).

15. *See* Ibarra v. Baker, 338 F. App'x 457, 465 (5th Cir. 2009) ("An attorney enjoys extensive leeway in preparing a witness to testify truthfully, but the attorney crosses a line when she influences the witness to alter testimony in a false or misleading way.").

16. Smith v. Kelly, No. 7:07CV00536, 2008 WL 345838, at *11 (W.D. Va. Feb. 6, 2008) (stating that "it is not unusual or improper for witnesses to rehearse their direct testimony with counsel"); Restatement (Third) of the Law Governing Lawyers § 116 cmt. b (2000).

17. Haworth v. State, 840 P.2d 912, 914 (Wyo. 1992).

18. Resolution Tr. Corp. v. Bright, 6 F.3d 336, 341 (5th Cir. 1993).

In short, courts acknowledge that lawyers are obligated to prepare witnesses to testify.[19] This obligation is generally expressed as an aspect of lawyers' related duties of competence and diligence.

Courts consider Rule 3.3 and 3.4(b) violations to be extremely serious because knowingly offering false testimony is antithetical to lawyers' oaths and to the legal profession's ideals,[20] and strikes at the very heart of the administration of justice.[21] A lawyer may be found to have violated either rule even where the false testimony did not affect the outcome of the proceedings.[22] The fact that the false testimony was immaterial may mitigate any sanction to be imposed, and perhaps even prevent the imposition of any sanction whatsoever, but it does not erase the violation.

Although it is not apparent from the text of either Model Rule 3.3(a)(3) or Model Rule 3.4(b), both rules sometimes permit lawyers to elicit false testimony from witnesses as long as that testimony is not intended to mislead the trier of fact. This is consistent with the general recognition that lawyers may offer false evidence for the purpose of establishing its falsity.[23] For example, a lawyer might elicit false testimony from an opposing witness for the purpose of later demonstrating its falsity to discredit the witness.[24] Requiring premature disclosure could in some circumstances allow the witness to explain away the false testimony or reframe it to make it seem plausible.[25] Effective cross-examination may pivot on this exact tactic.

Furthermore, the fact that a client or witness may testify falsely on one subject does not preclude a lawyer from offering the client's or witness's testimony altogether. For example, a lawyer who knows that a witness will testify falsely on Subject *A* may nonetheless call the witness to testify truthfully about Subject *B* without violating Rules 3.3(a)(3), 3.3(b), or 3.4(b).[26] Understandably, the lawyer cannot question the witness with respect to Subject *A*.

---

19. Odone v. Croda Int'l PLC., 170 F.R.D. 66, 69 (D.D.C. 1997); State v. McCormick, 259 S.E.2d 880, 882 (N.C. 1979), *superseded by rule as stated in* State v. Squire, 364 S.E.2d 354, 357 (N.C. 1988) (discussing a superseding rule on the introduction of character evidence).

20. *In re* Disciplinary Action Against McDonald, 609 N.W.2d 418, 427 (N.D. 2000).

21. *In re* Disciplinary Action Against Ward, 563 N.W.2d 70, 72 (Minn. 1997) (quoting *In re* Salmen, 484 N.W.2d 253, 254 (Minn. 1992)).

22. *In re Disciplinary Action Against McDonald*, 609 N.W.2d at 427; *In re* Disciplinary Proc. Against Riley, 882 N.W.2d 820, 834 (Wis. 2016) (citing Douglas R. Richmond et al., Professional Responsibility in Litigation 523 (2011)).

23. Model Rules of Prof'l Conduct R. 3.3 cmt. 5 (2020) ("A lawyer does not violate this Rule if the lawyer offers the evidence for the purpose of establishing its falsity.").

24. Restatement (Third) of the Law Governing Lawyers § 120 cmt. e (2000).

25. *Id.*

26. *See, e.g.*, State v. Pendleton, 759 N.W.2d 900, 908–09 (Minn. 2009) (recognizing that prosecution could call a witness to testify on an issue on which he was believed to testify truthfully and narrowly limit questioning to that issue while not questioning the witness on other issues on which he might testify falsely).

Importantly, Model Rules 3.3(a)(3) and 3.4(b) refer to false testimony—not perjury. The crime of perjury typically requires that the subject testimony be (1) willfully false, (2) material to the outcome of the matter, and (3) not earlier discoverable through reasonable diligence. Model Rules 3.3(a)(3) and 3.4(b) plainly incorporate different elements. Thus, and by way of example, a lawyer may be held to violate Rules 3.3(a)(3) or 3.4(b) even when a client's false testimony is not material to the outcome of the matter.[27] A lawyer may be held to have violated these rules even though the witness was never criminally charged or convicted in connection with the false testimony.

Unlike perjured testimony, which must be willfully false, testimony may be false for purposes of Rules 3.3(a)(3) and 3.4(b) even if the witness is mistaken rather than lying.[28] This application may strike some lawyers as odd because both rules—and especially Rule 3.4(b)—seem to focus on deliberately false testimony rather than innocently mistaken testimony. But a statement's falsity under either rule does not depend on whether it is morally objectionable. A statement is false if it is contrary to fact, incorrect, or groundless; falsity does not depend upon or require dishonesty or intent to mislead. And because even innocent misstatements may affect a court's decision or the course of litigation, preventing and correcting mistaken testimony is an important goal. When evaluating falsity under Model Rules 3.3(a)(3) and 3.4(b), then, a witness's state of mind is irrelevant; it is the lawyer's knowledge that counts. Fortunately for lawyers, this broad interpretation of falsity remains reasonably bounded. For witnesses' testimony to be false under Model Rules 3.3(a)(3) and 3.4(b), it must be objectively erroneous or untrue; two witnesses' disagreement on affairs or events, for example, does not render either's testimony false. Additionally, a witness's testimony may change by virtue of new information learned between the first time the witness testified and the second, as where a witness is first deposed and later testifies at trial, or where a witness testifies in multiple proceedings. The fact that the witness testifies differently the second time as a result of the new information does not render either round of testimony false under these rules.[29]

27. *See, e.g.*, *In re* Feld's Case, 815 A.2d 383, 388 (N.H. 2002) (involving Rule 3.4(b)).

28. *See* N.Y. Eth. Op. 837, 2010 WL 2977924, at *3 (N.Y. State Bar Ass'n, Comm. on Prof'l Ethics 2010) (contrasting DR 7-102(B)(1) of the former New York Code of Professional Responsibility, "which required a 'fraud' to have been perpetrated," with Rule 3.3(a)(3) and stating that "Rule 3.3(a)(3) requires a lawyer to remedy false evidence even if it was innocently offered" (footnote omitted)).

29. *See, e.g.*, Shade v. Great Lakes Dredge & Dock Co., 72 F. Supp. 2d 518, 524 (E.D. Pa. 1999) (involving witness who testified to one set of facts in his own case and to another in a co-worker's subsequent trial; the witness learned new information about the injury-causing piece of machinery between the time of his trial and his co-worker's trial).

In obvious contrast, Model Rule 3.3(b) specifically refers to "criminal or fraudulent conduct."[30] As a result, Model Rule 3.3(b) applies only where a witness intends to commit perjury or testify falsely with intent to deceive or does so. While well-meaning but mistaken testimony by a witness may impair a case, and capable lawyers will attempt to prevent or correct inaccurate testimony, such errors do not implicate lawyers' duties under Model Rule 3.3(b).[31]

Finally, it is critical to recognize that Model Rule 3.3 speaks of tribunals and adjudicative proceedings rather than courts, and Rule 3.4 is silent as to the forum. Thus, while reported cases on false testimony typically arise out of court proceedings, lawyers' duties are not so limited. Lawyers must not offer false testimony, cannot counsel or assist witnesses to testify falsely, and must correct material false testimony offered by clients and their witnesses in arbitrations and other types of judicial and quasi-judicial proceedings.[32] Lawyers' duties apply to false testimony given in depositions, just as they do to false testimony presented before a tribunal.[33] This should not surprise, since depositions are conducted pursuant to tribunals' adjudicative authority,[34] and deposition testimony is commonly offered as evidence in support of dispositive motions and at trial.

B. The Duration of the Obligation

Under Model Rule 3.3(c), lawyers' duties under Rules 3.3(a)(3) and (b) "continue to the conclusion of [a] proceeding, and apply even if compliance requires disclosure of information otherwise protected by Rule 1.6."[35]

---

30. Model Rules of Prof'l Conduct R. 3.3(b) (2020).

31. Of course, Rule 3.3(b) reaches lawyers' knowledge of criminal or fraudulent conduct beyond false testimony. For example, the rule requires a lawyer who is representing a client in an adjudicative proceeding to take reasonable remedial measures if the lawyer knows of criminal or fraudulent conduct that undermines the integrity of the adjudicative process, such as someone bribing, intimidating, or otherwise unlawfully communicating with a court employee or official, juror, witness, or other participant in the proceeding. *Id.* R. 3.3 cmt. 12.

32. *See, e.g.*, Ill. Adv. Op. 13-05, 2013 WL 3185023, at *1–2 (Ill. State Bar Ass'n 2013) [hereinafter Ill. Adv. Op. 13-05] (determining that a Social Security Administration hearing is a tribunal for false evidence purposes); Kan. Bar Ass'n, Prof'l Ethics Advisory Comm., Legal Ethics Op. No. 98-1 (1998) (discussing a lawyer's duty to remedy a client's materially false testimony in a workers' compensation proceeding).

33. Comm. on Prof'l Ethics & Conduct of the Iowa State Bar Ass'n v. Crary, 245 N.W.2d 298, 305 (Iowa 1976) (discussing the conduct of a lawyer who permitted his client to perjure herself at her deposition and explaining why lawyers cannot permit false testimony in any context); NYCLA Eth. Op. 741, 2010 WL 4260877, at *3–4 (N.Y. Cnty. Lawyers' Ass'n, Comm. on Prof'l Ethics 2010) [hereinafter NYCLA Eth. Op. 741] (discussing false testimony at depositions and remediation thereof); R.I. Sup. Ct., Ethics Advisory Panel Op. 91-76 (1991) (referring to false deposition testimony by a client's employee).

34. Model Rules of Prof'l Conduct R. 3.3 cmt. 1 (2020).

35. *Id.* R. 3.3(c).

Model Rule 3.3(c) performs the key function of establishing an ending point for lawyers' duty of candor. The rule recognizes that lawyers cannot be forever required to ensure the integrity of their clients and witnesses.[36] Unfortunately, the conclusion of a proceeding is not necessarily self-evident.

A lawyer's discharge by a client or withdrawal from a representation does not conclude a proceeding, regardless of whether the discharge or withdrawal relates to the false testimony at issue.[37] In such a case, disclosing the false testimony to successor counsel may be a reasonable remedial measure.[38] Nor can a proceeding be said to conclude only when the time to move to reopen or vacate the judgment has expired. Although a motion to relieve a party from a final judgment typically must be made within one year of the judgment's date or entry, jurisdictions sometimes impose no deadline for seeking relief from a judgment procured through fraud on a court. As a result, a lawyer would have a perpetual duty to rectify a client fraud, which, as Rule 3.3(c) recognizes, is unworkable.

Generally, a proceeding is concluded either when (1) the judgment has been affirmed on appeal or (2) the time for all parties to appeal has run, including the time for petitioning for a writ of certiorari.[39] In a criminal case, a judgment of acquittal concludes the proceeding because the prohibition against double jeopardy prevents the government from retrying the defendant for substantially the same offense. When criminal defendants are convicted and wish to appeal, the term "appeal" should be confined to direct appeals and not be expanded to include collateral attacks on convictions, such as writs of habeas corpus.[40] To hold otherwise would unreasonably extend lawyers' obligations because defendants who allege that they were wrongfully convicted may pursue extraordinary relief long after any time to appeal has run. In the administrative realm, a proceeding should be deemed to be concluded after the administrative process is exhausted and (1) the time for a permissible judicial challenge to the administrative decision by

---

36. *Id.* R. 3.3 cmt. 13 ("A practical time limit on the obligation to rectify false evidence or false statements . . . has to be established.").

37. RESTATEMENT (THIRD) OF THE LAW GOVERNING LAWYERS § 120 cmt. h (2000).

38. *Id.*

39. Holden v. Blevins, 837 A.2d 1053, 1057 (Md. Ct. Spec. App. 2003); *see also* MODEL RULES OF PROF'L CONDUCT R. 3.3 cmt. 13 (2020) (stating that a proceeding has been concluded when a final judgment has been affirmed on appeal or the time for review has passed).

40. *But cf.* N.Y. Eth. Op. 2013-2, 2013 WL 2997051, at *3 (N.Y. State Bar Ass'n, Comm. on Prof'l Ethics 2013) (stating that a lawyer's duties under Rule 3.3(a)(3) survive the conclusion of a proceeding, but Rule 3.3(a)(3) imposes a duty of disclosure only where "(1) it is still possible to make disclosure of the new evidence either to the tribunal to which the false evidence was presented, or to a tribunal that did or could review the decisions of the tribunal to which the false evidence was submitted, and (2) the tribunal is still in a position to consider the new evidence and provide a basis for reopening the matter and/or amending, modifying or vacating the prior judgment").

any party has expired, or (2) the administrative decision has been judicially upheld.

Unlike Model Rules 3.3(a)(3) and (b), Model Rule 3.4(b) does not specify a duration for a lawyer's duty not to counsel or assist a witness to testify falsely. There is no reason to do so. A lawyer who counsels or assists a witness to testify falsely violates Rule 3.4(b) immediately upon offering the advice or providing the assistance. A lawyer who counsels or assists a witness to testify falsely violates the rule even if the witness never testifies or, despite the lawyer's improper advice or assistance, testifies truthfully. Lawyers who experience a change of heart and attempt to remedy false testimony that they induced or orchestrated may mitigate any associated professional discipline, but there is no curing a Rule 3.4(b) violation.[41] Furthermore, lawyers who counsel or assist witnesses to testify falsely still have a duty to remedy that false testimony under Rules 3.3(a)(3) and (b), which, of course, have durational bounds.

C. Candor Trumps Confidentiality

The law assigns high value both to lawyers' duty of candor to tribunals and to lawyers' duty of confidentiality to clients. This value is clearly reflected in Model Rule 3.3(c), which establishes that lawyers' duty to remedy false testimony by clients and by witnesses they call exists even if compliance with this duty will require them to disclose information otherwise protected by Model Rule 1.6.[42] Rule 1.6 is the general rule on confidentiality and, with a few exceptions, prevents lawyers from revealing information relating to clients' representations.[43] Lawyers' duties with respect to false testimony are consistent with their duty of candor in other contexts. For example, it is generally accepted in jurisdictions adopting the Model Rules approach that lawyers' duty of candor to the tribunal under Rule 3.3(a)(1)[44] and Rule 3.3(b),[45] and their duty of candor as officers of the court, trump their duty of confidentiality to clients.[46]

41. *See, e.g.*, Office of Disciplinary Couns. v. Valentino, 730 A.2d 479, 483 (Pa. 1999).

42. Model Rules of Prof'l Conduct R. 3.3(c) (2020); *see, e.g.*, United States v. Allen, No. 06-40056-01-SAC, 2008 WL 2622872, at *3 (D. Kan. July 1, 2008) (expressing this view in connection with motion to withdraw by criminal defense counsel).

43. Model Rule 1.6(a) expresses lawyers' duty of confidentiality and Model Rule 1.6(b) sets forth the exceptions to lawyers' confidentiality obligation. The exceptions set forth in Rule 1.6(b) may vary substantially between jurisdictions.

44. Model Rules of Prof'l Conduct R. 3.3(a)(1) (2020) (stating that a lawyer shall not knowingly "make a false statement of fact or law to a tribunal or fail to correct a false statement of material fact or law previously made to the tribunal by the lawyer").

45. United States v. Tirado, 890 F.3d 36, 38–39 (1st Cir. 2018).

46. Cleveland Hair Clinic, Inc. v. Puig, 200 F.3d 1063, 1067 (7th Cir. 2000); *In re* Starbrite Props. Corp., No. 11-40758 CEC, 2012 WL 2050745, at *10 (Bankr. E.D.N.Y. June 5, 2012); *In re* Potts, 158 P.3d 418, 424 (Mont. 2007).

It is worth recognizing, however, that not all jurisdictions elevate lawyers' duty of candor to the tribunal over their duty of confidentiality to clients to the extent the Model Rules do. In some jurisdictions, a lawyer who knows that a client intends to testify falsely or has done so and cannot persuade the client to rectify the situation must simply withdraw from the representation without revealing the client's misconduct.[47] The lesson for lawyers is obvious: check case law, ethics opinions, and rules in a jurisdiction before deciding whether and how to reveal false testimony.

Even in jurisdictions adhering tightly to the Model Rules approach, lawyers should, to the extent reasonably possible, attempt to prevent or rectify false testimony without revealing information relating to the client's representation. If lawyers must disclose information otherwise protected by Rule 1.6 to prevent or remedy false testimony, they should be careful to limit those disclosures to only that information necessary to fulfill their duty of candor. Lawyers should preserve as much of their clients' confidentiality as practicable. In some cases, it may be appropriate to seek protective orders or similar safeguards in connection with the disclosure.

In re Mack[48] is an interesting civil case involving false testimony by a client revealed well after the fact and the interplay between a lawyer's duties of candor and confidentiality. In that case, John Mack represented K.G. in a declaratory judgment action against State Farm Mutual Automobile Insurance Co. arising out of an accident in which K.G.'s daughter was injured. State Farm had denied coverage for the accident based on K.G.'s non-payment of her June 15, 1990, premium. Mack attached to the complaint in the declaratory judgment action a copy of a renewal notice bearing a handwritten note indicating that the premium had been paid on June 13, 1990, by check number 8440, and a canceled check bearing the same date made out to State Farm in the amount of the disputed premium. The canceled check indicated that it had been charged to K.G.'s account in late July 1990.

State Farm deposed K.G. in October 1990. She testified that her brother-in-law had mailed the check to State Farm on June 13.[49] She further testified that she made the note on the premium notice and that she and her family did not maintain an accurate check register or even write checks in sequence. In response to a direct question, K.G. denied mailing the check after her daughter's accident.[50] In May or June 1991, however, K.G. confessed to Mack that she had lied in her deposition.[51] K.G. explained to Mack that she had written the check a few days after her daughter's accident and

47. *See, e.g.*, N.D. Rules of Prof'l Conduct R. 3.3(a)(3) (2006); Tenn. Rules of Prof'l Conduct R. 3.3(f) (2018).

48. 519 N.W.2d 900 (Minn. 1994).

49. *Id.* at 901.

50. *Id.*

51. *Id.*

placed the envelope containing the check in an inconspicuous spot in a post office, trusting that someone would eventually find and mail it, and that she could deflect blame for her late payment onto the postal service.

Mack would later contend that he told K.G. that she should reveal her deception should her case go to trial, but until then she could continue her lawsuit and "simply 'rely on her right to remain silent.'"[52] K.G. would eventually testify that Mack never told her to reveal her false testimony, and a disciplinary referee would reach the same conclusion. Mack certainly did not reveal K.G.'s false testimony to the court. In any event, K.G. repeated her false testimony on direct examination at trial but revealed the fraud on cross-examination (Mack did not try the case because he was suspended from practice on unrelated charges in the interim) and State Farm won the case. K.G. was then prosecuted for perjury, but the state dismissed her criminal case during trial when it became clear that K.G. had tried to set the record straight with Mack.[53]

Mack defended his conduct on the basis that the attorney-client privilege prevented him from revealing K.G.'s false testimony.[54] Mack should have invoked his duty of confidentiality under Rule 1.6 instead of the attorney-client privilege—or at least in addition to it—but the Minnesota Supreme Court understood the argument nonetheless. The court acknowledged that while Mack generally had a duty under Minnesota Rule 1.6(a) to protect K.G.'s confidences, Rule 1.6(b) permitted him to reveal her confidences to the extent necessary to rectify her use of his services to further a fraud.[55] Moreover, Minnesota Rule 3.3(a) plainly required Mack to take reasonable remedial action once he learned of K.G.'s false testimony, even if that required him to reveal information otherwise protected by Rule 1.6.[56]

The *In re Mack* court concluded that Mack's silence in the face of K.G.'s perjury violated Rule 3.3(a) and further violated Rules 8.4(c) and (d) because it was deceitful and prejudicial to the administration of justice.[57] Had K.G. not broken down under cross-examination at trial, her lie might well have escaped detection. Finding Mack's failure to take remedial measures or to reveal K.G.'s perjury to be a serious offense, the court suspended him from practice indefinitely.

Pausing for a moment, assume that Mack did tell K.G. that she would have to reveal her lies should her case go to trial, but, until then, she could continue to prosecute her claims and conceal the truth. Would such advice have been reasonable, since neither Rule 3.3(a) nor Rule 3.3(b) establish

52. *Id.* (quoting Mack).
53. *Id.* at 902.
54. *Id.*
55. *Id.*
56. *Id.*
57. *Id.*

time limits for lawyers to remedy clients' false testimony? The short answer to this question is no. First, such advice would have been incompetent because had State Farm discovered K.G.'s dishonesty before she revealed it, she might have been prosecuted for perjury and the court might have imposed sanctions beyond the dismissal of her case. Second, Mack would have been counseling K.G. to engage in fraud in violation of Rule 1.2(d).[58] Third, under both Model Rule 3.3(a) and Rule 3.3(b), a lawyer who knows of a client's wrongdoing must take remedial measures within a reasonable time under the circumstances, or as soon as reasonably practicable. Although Mack would have had some time to decide how best to remedy K.G.'s dishonesty, he could not have waited for trial. The longer he waited, the greater the potential prejudice to State Farm and disruption of the court. Furthermore, by allowing K.G.'s case to proceed for too long after learning of her perjury, Mack risked possible discipline for assisting her in perpetrating a fraud in violation of Rule 1.2(d) and for prosecuting a frivolous action in violation of Rule 3.1.[59]

D. False Testimony and the Knowledge Element

Lawyers are prohibited from offering false testimony, and must remedy perjured or fraudulent testimony, only if they *know* of its falsity.[60] The existence and extent of lawyers' knowledge are frequent points of dispute. For lawyers to know facts or matters in this context, as elsewhere, they must have actual knowledge of them, although knowledge may be inferred from circumstances.[61] The fact that a lawyer *should have known* about something does not equal knowledge of it.[62] Lawyers' belief, speculation, or suspicion that clients or witnesses intend to testify falsely, or in fact have already done so, does not equate to knowledge of false testimony.[63] Not even a lawyer's

58. Model Rules of Prof'l Conduct R. 1.2(d) (2020) (stating that a lawyer shall not counsel a client to engage in conduct that the lawyer knows is fraudulent).

59. *Id.* (providing that a lawyer shall not assist a client in conduct that the lawyer knows is criminal or fraudulent); *id.* R. 3.1 (stating that a lawyer shall not bring a proceeding or assert an issue therein unless there is a basis in fact or law for doing so that is not frivolous).

60. People v. Riel, 998 P.2d 969, 1013–14 (Cal. 2000); *In re* Olsen, 326 P.3d 1004, 1010 (Colo. 2014).

61. Model Rules of Prof'l Conduct R. 1.0(f) (2020) ("A person's knowledge may be inferred from circumstances.").

62. *In re* Tocco, 984 P.2d 539, 543 (Ariz. 1999); *In re Olsen*, 326 P.3d at 1010; *see, e.g.*, Ibarra v. Baker, 338 F. App'x 457, 468 (5th Cir. 2009) (reversing sanctions against lawyers who "should have known" or "should have been aware" of false or inconsistent testimony).

63. United States v. Midgett, 342 F.3d 321, 326 (4th Cir. 2003) (referring to a lawyer's belief); United States v. Stewart, 931 F. Supp. 2d 1199, 1216–17 (S.D. Fla. 2013) (stating that even if the lawyers' suspicion that their client was lying rose to the level of a reasonable belief, that still did not require disclosure); *Riel*, 998 P.2d at 1013–14; People v. Bolton, 82 Cal. Rptr. 3d 671, 681 (Ct. App. 2008) (describing a lawyer's suspicion); State v. Chambers, 994 A.2d 1248, 1260 n.13 (Conn. 2010) (stating that conjecture and speculation do not equal knowledge); Commonwealth v. Brown,

strong suspicion that a client or witness plans to testify falsely or has already done so constitutes knowledge under ethics rules.[64]

Generally speaking, lawyers should not hastily judge clients' or witnesses' truthfulness, nor should they assume that clients or witnesses are liars or are mistaken. Mere inconsistencies in evidence or in a client's or witness's version of events do not equate to knowledge of false testimony.[65] It is permissible for lawyers to give clients and witnesses the benefit of the doubt when weighing evidence and testimony.[66] Indeed, there is authority for the proposition that in criminal cases, anyway, a lawyer generally should resolve any doubt in the client's favor.[67] In both civil and criminal cases, superficially dubious or unsupported accounts of circumstances and events periodically prove to be true. None of this means, however, that lawyers can avoid acquiring knowledge of false testimony through creative rationalization or willful blindness. A lawyer may be considered willfully blind where the facts indicating that evidence is false are "substantial and obvious" or "overwhelmingly clear and unambiguous."[68] If, for example, a credible witness tells a lawyer that the lawyer's client lied while testifying, the lawyer must, at a minimum, reasonably ask the client about the allegation.[69] Furthermore, no matter how stringent a test may be required for knowledge, most courts and disciplinary authorities are unlikely to accept the argument that knowledge requires absolute certainty on a lawyer's part.[70]

Most questions about lawyers' knowledge of false testimony surface in criminal litigation in connection with defendants' intent to commit perjury to avoid conviction.[71] Courts have expressed a range of tests for establishing lawyers' knowledge of false testimony.[72] The Wisconsin Supreme Court

---

226 S.W.3d 74, 84 (Ky. 2007) (referring to conjecture and speculation); Commonwealth v. Mitchell, 781 N.E.2d 1237, 1251 (Mass. 2003) (referring to conjecture and speculation).

64. *In re* Grievance Comm. of the U.S. Dist. Ct., 847 F.2d 57, 63 (2d Cir. 1988).

65. *Chambers*, 994 A.2d at 1260 n.13; *In re* Cross, 327 P.3d 660, 685–86 (Wash. 2014).

66. Model Rules of Prof'l Conduct R. 3.3 cmt. 8 (2020).

67. *In re Cross*, 327 P.3d at 686.

68. *In re* Driscoll, 856 N.E.2d 840, 847 (Mass. 2006).

69. *See* S.C. Adv. Op. 97-14, 1997 WL 861960, at *1 (S.C. Bar, Ethics Advisory Comm. 1997) (discussing a situation in which a client's boyfriend told a lawyer immediately after trial that both he and the lawyer's client committed perjury during trial, and the boyfriend had no reason to lie to the lawyer about the alleged perjury).

70. *See In re Cross*, 327 P.3d at 685 (noting that ethics opinions "suggest that lawyers should have *a high degree of certainty* before acting on client perjury" (emphasis added)).

71. *See* United States v. Williams, 698 F.3d 374, 386 (7th Cir. 2012) (Hamilton, J., concurring in part and dissenting in part) (observing that "[d]efendants facing criminal charges often come up with stupid, even criminal, ideas to try to beat the charges" against them).

72. *See, e.g.*, United States v. Long, 857 F.2d 436, 444–46 (8th Cir. 1988) (requiring a "firm factual basis"); United States *ex rel.* Wilcox v. Johnson, 555 F.2d 115, 122 (3d Cir. 1977) (articulating a "firm factual basis" standard); State v. Chambers, 994 A.2d 1248, 1260 n.13 (Conn. 2010) (expressing a "firm basis in objective fact" standard); Shockley v. State, 565 A.2d 1373, 1379 (Del. 1989) (requiring knowledge "beyond a reasonable doubt"); State v. Abdullah, 348 P.3d 1, 129

articulated the highest standard for knowledge in *State v. McDowell*.[73] The court in *McDowell* was weighing whether a criminal defense lawyer provided ineffective assistance by shifting to narrative testimony when his client was on the stand, as criminal defense lawyers sometimes do when their clients insist on testifying and the lawyer understands that the client intends to lie. The defendant had told his lawyer that if he testified, he would "'say what [he needed] [to] say to help [himself] out and if [he had] to say something untruthful [he'd] say that.'"[74] In determining that this admission did not vest the defense lawyer with knowledge of his client's intent to testify falsely, the *McDowell* court stated that absent "the most extraordinary circumstances, such knowledge must be based on the client's expressed admission of intent to testify untruthfully."[75] The intent to testify falsely "need not be phrased in 'magic words,'" the court explained, but it "must be unambiguous and directly made to the attorney."[76]

Critics of *McDowell* might argue that the defendant *did* expressly admit his intention directly to the lawyer, especially given the court's observation that a person's intent to testify falsely need not be expressed in magic words. Indeed, the defendant could hardly have been clearer about his intent to lie on the witness stand. Whatever the merits of such criticism, it would seem that Wisconsin courts and others that adopt the same approach limit lawyers' knowledge of false testimony to those unusual situations where a client or witness tells a lawyer, "I lied about *X*," or "I intend to testify falsely about *Y*," or something very close.

The favored standard for knowledge requires that a lawyer have a "firm basis in fact," a "firm factual basis," or a "firm basis in objective fact" that a client or witness will testify falsely.[77] A lawyer may determine that such a basis in fact exists from a client's or witness's own statements or from other reliable sources. The firm factual basis standard applies in civil and criminal matters alike. Even this seemingly moderate standard sets a high

(Idaho 2015) (adopting the "firm factual basis" standard); People v. Calhoun, 815 N.E.2d 492, 499 (Ill. App. Ct. 2004) (referring to "a good faith determination" that a defendant intends to commit perjury); Hobson v. State, 675 N.E.2d 1090, 1095 (Ind. 1996) (suggesting "an absolute degree of certainty" standard); State v. Hischke, 639 N.W.2d 6, 10 (Iowa 2002) (requiring "good cause to believe" that testimony would be deliberately false); Commonwealth v. Brown, 226 S.W.3d 74, 84 (Ky. 2007) (requiring that a lawyer "in good faith have a firm basis in objective fact"); Commonwealth v. Mitchell, 781 N.E.2d 1237, 1250–51 (Mass. 2003) (embracing the "firm basis in objective fact" standard); State v. McDowell, 681 N.W.2d 500, 513 (Wis. 2004) (requiring an "expressed admission of intent to testify untruthfully").

73. 681 N.W.2d 500 (Wis. 2004).

74. *Id.* at 509 (quoting the defense lawyer).

75. *Id.* at 513.

76. *Id.*

77. *Long*, 857 F.2d at 444–46; *Johnson*, 555 F.2d at 122; People v. Riel, 998 P.2d 969, 1013 (Cal. 2000) (quoting Lord v. Wood, 184 F.3d 1083, 1095 n.9 (9th Cir. 1999)); *Chambers*, 994 A.2d at 1260 n.13; *Abdullah*, 348 P.3d at 129; *Brown*, 226 S.W.3d at 84; *Mitchell*, 781 N.E.2d at 1247.

bar.[78] Defense lawyers struggling to decide whether they have a firm basis in objective fact "very likely do not."[79]

Lawyers may rely on facts disclosed to them and have no duty to independently investigate the truthfulness of a client's or witness's testimony,[80] although it obviously may be wise to do so from an advocacy perspective. There are multiple cases in which defense lawyers' supposed knowledge of clients' or witnesses' intent to testify falsely was held to be inadequate. *State v. Colson*[81] is illustrative.

The teenage defendant in *Colson*, Kendrick Colson, was arrested for robbery. He was interrogated by police and, after being read his *Miranda* rights, confessed to the crime.[82] The court appointed Robert Leas to represent him. The day before Colson's trial was to begin, Leas moved to withdraw from his representation. Leas reported that Colson wanted to testify on his own behalf and that in Leas's opinion that testimony would be false.[83] The trial judge explained to Colson that Leas could not knowingly present false evidence to the court and that any lawyer appointed to replace him would face the same limitation. The judge informed Colson that if he insisted on testifying on his own behalf, he could discharge Leas and proceed pro se. Colson did just that. Colson then testified at trial that he was at home on the night of the robbery and that the police tricked him into confessing.[84] Unfortunately for Colson, the state's chief witness identified him as the robber and the jury convicted him.

Colson appealed his conviction on constitutional grounds, arguing that the trial court erred by forcing him to choose between testifying on his own behalf and proceeding to trial without the assistance of counsel. The North Carolina Court of Appeals agreed and granted Colson a new trial. In attempting to provide some guidance on remand, the court focused on North Carolina Rule of Professional Conduct 3.3(a)(3) and indicated that while Leas may have reasonably believed that Colson would testify falsely, he did not *know* that he intended to do so.[85] Whether Colson was at home on the night of the robbery and was tricked into confessing by the police or whether he was the robber as indicated by the state's principal witness were credibility questions for the jury to decide.[86]

---

78. Commonwealth v. Leiva, 146 N.E.3d 1093, 1113 (Mass. 2020).
79. *Id.*
80. United States v. Joyce, 311 F. Supp. 3d 398, 405 (D. Mass. 2018) (citing *Mitchell*, 781 N.E.2d at 1247); *Mitchell*, 781 N.E.2d at 1247, 1251.
81. 650 S.E.2d 656 (N.C. Ct. App. 2007).
82. *Id.* at 657.
83. *Id.*
84. *Id.*
85. *See id.* at 659 (discussing a comment to North Carolina Rule 3.3 concerning testimony by criminal defendants).
86. *Id.* (quoting State v. Hyatt, 566 S.E.2d 61, 77 (N.C. 2002)).

United States v. Midgett[87] is another illustrative case. Paul Midgett was charged with three felony counts. Count One stemmed from a robbery in which Midgett allegedly threw gasoline on a stranger, J.W. Shaw, and demanded money from him. After Shaw surrendered his wallet, an assailant set him on fire.[88] Later, Midgett and Theresa Russell allegedly employed a similar technique to rob a bank (Counts Two and Three). Russell agreed to cooperate with the government; Midgett chose to take his chances at trial.

Midgett insisted on mounting a "third person" defense to the Count One crime. Midgett repeatedly told his defense lawyer that a friend of Russell was driving around with the two of them when they encountered Shaw, and it was Russell's friend who cruelly set Shaw ablaze.[89] Midgett asserted that he was asleep in the back of their car when Shaw was attacked. He was prepared to testify to these facts at trial, but his lawyer did not want Midgett to testify because he did not believe Midgett's version of events.[90] Midgett's counsel attempted to withdraw from his representation before trial, but the district court would not permit him to do so.[91]

Midgett's lawyer moved to withdraw again during trial on the basis that Midgett was insisting on offering evidence that the lawyer considered to be improper. The district court gave Midgett the option of proceeding pro se or continuing with counsel's representation.[92] Midgett agreed to his lawyer's continued participation under protest. The next day, Midgett's lawyer again moved to withdraw, stating his belief that Midgett was "'going to offer information when he testifie[d] that [was] not in any way truthful or in existence that [the lawyer could] determine from any source.'"[93] Rather than allowing the lawyer to withdraw, the district court offered Midgett the choice of either not testifying or representing himself without counsel's aid or assistance. Despite desperately wanting to take the witness stand, Midgett believed that he could not testify without counsel's assistance, and he accordingly declined to testify.

A jury convicted Midgett on all three counts. After the trial was concluded, the district court allowed Midgett's defense lawyer to withdraw. New defense counsel was soon appointed and Midgett appealed his conviction to the Fourth Circuit. Midgett argued that the district court erred in conditioning his right to counsel on his waiver of his right to testify.

The Fourth Circuit observed that the question of what lawyers should do when facing potentially perjured testimony "has long caused consternation

87. 342 F.3d 321 (4th Cir. 2003).
88. *Id.* at 322.
89. *Id.*
90. *Id.*
91. *Id.*
92. *Id.* at 323.
93. *Id.* (quoting counsel's statement to the court).

in the legal profession, producing heated debate and little consensus."[94] In criminal cases, a defendant's right to testify on his own behalf is not limitless. A criminal defendant's constitutional right to testify clearly does not include the right to commit perjury,[95] as the Supreme Court recognized in *Nix v. Whiteside*.[96] In this case, however, Midgett never told his lawyer that he intended to lie when he testified, nor did he otherwise indicate an intent to perjure himself. Rather, Midgett consistently maintained that his third-person defense was true and that Russell could corroborate his story.[97] The question was thus whether the information known to Midgett's lawyer was sufficient to show that Midgett's testimony would be perjurious, such that the lawyer's refusal to put Midgett on the witness stand was constitutionally acceptable. The *Midgett* court concluded that it was not.[98]

To be sure, Midgett's third-person defense was shaky. Russell testified that there was no one else in the vehicle at the time of Shaw's assault and robbery, and Shaw identified Midgett in court as his assailant, even though he had earlier been unable to pick him out of a photo lineup. Nonetheless, Mitchell had consistently maintained that someone else attacked Shaw. Midgett never suggested to his lawyer that he might testify falsely in his defense. The defense lawyer's responsibility to Midgett did not pivot on whether he believed him, nor did it depend on the quantum of proof supporting or contradicting Midgett's anticipated testimony.[99] The lawyer therefore had a duty to assist Midgett in testifying to the jury on direct examination.

The defense lawyer's mere belief, although strong and supported by other evidence, was not an adequate basis to refuse to assist Midgett in testifying on direct examination.[100] In other words, the defense lawyer did not know that Midgett's intended testimony would be false. As far-fetched as Midgett's story might have sounded to a jury, it was not his lawyer's place to decide that Midgett was lying and declare this opinion to the district court.[101] Ultimately, the *Midgett* court determined that the district court's act of forcing Midgett to choose between two constitutionally protected rights—the right to testify on his own behalf and the right to effective assistance of counsel—constituted error requiring a new trial.

In *Muff v. Dragovich*,[102] Tricia Muff sought post-conviction relief in federal court on the basis that her former defense lawyer rendered ineffective

94. *Id.* at 324.
95. *Id.* at 325 (quoting United States v. Teague, 953 F.2d 1525, 1530 (11th Cir. 1992)).
96. 475 U.S. 157, 173 (1986).
97. *Midgett*, 342 F.3d at 325.
98. *Id.* at 325–26.
99. *Id.* at 326.
100. *Id.*
101. *Id.*
102. No. 05-5251, 2007 WL 776804 (E.D. Pa. Mar. 12, 2007).

assistance of counsel by failing to dissuade her from testifying falsely in her state criminal trial. Muff was accused of murdering a small child who was in her care. The medical examiner determined that Muff shook and beat the child to death. Muff gave inconsistent versions of events, twice telling investigators that the child died as a result of an accidental fall and once indicating that she once threw the child to the ground in a flash of anger. Leading up to trial, it was apparent that medical evidence was pivotal in the case, and it was equally apparent that Muff's intended testimony would be inconsistent with the medical evidence. Every time that Muff's defense lawyer presented her with factual scenarios that suggested any criminal culpability on her part, however, she adamantly insisted "'that's not what happened.'"[103] Ultimately, he called her as a witness at trial even though he believed that her version of events "had problems."[104]

The district court concluded that the defense lawyer did not know that Muff intended to testify falsely. Although the lawyer acknowledged in the post-conviction proceeding that Muff's intended testimony had problems, the district court reasoned that recognizing that a defendant's testimony "'had problems'" was "a far cry" from knowing that the defendant intended to testify falsely.[105] In a case where it is unclear whether a client is being truthful, a lawyer should resolve doubts about the client's veracity in the client's favor.[106] This was such a case. Because there was no evidence to conclude that the defense lawyer knew that Muff intended to testify falsely, her ineffective assistance of counsel claim failed.

Although most of the cases discussing lawyers' knowledge of clients' or witnesses' false testimony are criminal matters, they are not exclusively so, and it is easy to imagine a civil case in which a lawyer's knowledge of a client's or witness's false testimony might be questioned. Assume, for example, that you are defending a grocery store in a sexual harassment case brought by a female cashier alleging that she was harassed by a male co-worker. The cashier testified in her deposition that the store manager acknowledged the co-worker's inappropriate behavior in a meeting in his office. Another employee who participated in that meeting also testified in his deposition that the manager acknowledged the co-worker's misconduct. The manager denies making any such admission and insists that he will maintain his denial when he testifies at trial. Are you prohibited from calling the manager as a witness at trial based on the Rule 3.3(a)(3) prohibition against knowingly offering evidence that you know to be false?

103. *Id.* at *12 (quoting Muff).
104. *Id.*
105. *Id.* (quoting the defense lawyer).
106. *Id.* (quoting a comment to Pennsylvania Rule 3.3).

In a word, no. You may call the manager as a witness at trial and elicit his denial during his direct examination to refute the plaintiff's and the other employee's testimony, and to blunt any cross-examination on the subject. The fact that two witnesses dispute the manager's version of events does not mean that the manager's expected testimony will be false; all you know is that witnesses have conflicting recollections. It is possible that the manager's recall of events is correct and that the plaintiff and witness are confused, mistaken, or lying. Indeed, testimonial inconsistencies are common in litigation.

Alternatively, assume that in the deposition the plaintiff's lawyer asked the manager if he conducted a "formal investigation" of the plaintiff's harassment allegations, and the manager replied that he did not. Now, at trial, the plaintiff's lawyer calls the manager as a witness in the plaintiff's case in chief and asks whether the manager "investigated" the plaintiff's allegations. Why, yes, the manager responds. He tells the jury how he interviewed the other employees who worked with or near the plaintiff on the day in question, and none of them saw the events described by the plaintiff. Flummoxed by the manager's apparent reversal and thus unable to locate the key passage in the manager's deposition transcript to use to impeach him, the plaintiff's lawyer finishes the manager's direct examination. You decide to forgo any cross-examination, and the court excuses the manager. The court then takes a recess. You meet with the manager privately in an anteroom and ask about the seeming change in his testimony. He responds that his trial testimony was truthful. He never considered his employee interviews to constitute any sort of "formal investigation"; he did only what any good manager would do in light of the plaintiff's allegations. Having recalled your instruction during trial preparation to listen carefully to any question asked, however, he decided that his interviews of the plaintiff's co-workers were indeed an "investigation," and that he should thus tell the plaintiff's lawyer about them. The manager's testimony was certainly material. Must you reveal to the court the seeming discrepancy between the manager's deposition testimony and his trial testimony? Should the plaintiff be allowed to recall the manager to arguably correct the record? Must you call the manager as a witness in your case and have him admit that he in fact conducted no investigation?

The answer to all these questions is no. Model Rule 3.3(a)(3) imposes a corrective duty on a lawyer where the witness who testified falsely was called by the lawyer or was the lawyer's client.[107] You did not call the

107. Model Rules of Prof'l Conduct R. 3.3(a)(3) (2020) ("If a lawyer, the lawyer's client, or a witness called by the lawyer, has offered material evidence and the lawyer comes to know of its falsity, the lawyer shall take reasonable remedial measures, including if necessary, disclosure to the tribunal.").

manager as a witness and, if you reflect for just a minute, you will recognize that the manager is not your client. You represent the store—that organization is your client, not the manager.[108] Even if it could be argued that the manager is your client for Model Rule 3.3(a)(3) purposes on the basis that the store is incorporated and corporations can only act through agents, you do not have a firm basis in fact to conclude that he has testified falsely and you thus have no duty to take remedial measures. At most you have information suggesting that the manager was confused during his deposition, or that he testified differently at trial because the plaintiff's lawyer asked a different question when he inquired about an "investigation" as compared to a "formal investigation." You may suspect that the manager testified falsely, and perhaps you even reasonably believe that he did so, but neither suspicion nor reasonable belief equates to knowledge under Model Rule 3.3(a)(3). Further, because of that lack of knowledge, you can have no remedial duty under Model Rule 3.3(b), which applies when a lawyer knows that a person committed fraud or perjury.[109]

But your opponent might well argue that the manager's testimonial inconsistencies certainly relate to his credibility, and you therefore cannot ignore them. Even if the manager's credibility is in question, however, it is inconsequential from a professional responsibility standpoint. Your possible concern about the manager's credibility does not translate into knowledge that he lied.[110] And, unless the manager's arguably inconsistent deposition testimony somehow comes into evidence—your surprised opponent having failed to impeach the manager with it—you have no concerns as an advocate about the manager's credibility beyond those that attend any witness's testimony.

Next, assume that you are representing a manufacturer in a product liability case. The company's chief engineer tells you that he knew of no similar accidents involving this machine prior to the plaintiff's injury, and as a result he saw no need to design a different guard or alter the product warnings. The chief engineer's deposition is looming, and he intends to so testify there. Unfortunately, you have three company incident reports documenting similar accidents involving the same type of machine that precede the plaintiff's injury, and they all bear the chief engineer's initials, thus indicating that they were routed to him. Do you know that the chief engineer's intended deposition testimony is false?

108. *Id.* R. 1.13(a) (stating that a lawyer employed or retained by an organization represents the organization acting through its duly authorized constituents).

109. *Id.* R. 3.3(b) (establishing a lawyer's duties when the lawyer knows that "a person" has engaged in criminal or fraudulent conduct related to a proceeding).

110. State v. Rivera, 109 P.3d 83, 87–88 (Ariz. 2005).

Here the answer is either yes or maybe. Although the chief engineer denies knowing of the other accidents, you have company reports of them bearing his initials. It is therefore reasonable to argue that you have a firm factual basis for believing that the chief engineer will testify falsely. It is important to recall that testimony may be false for Model Rule 3.3(a)(3) and 3.4(b) purposes even if the witness is merely mistaken; the chief engineer does not have to lie for his testimony to count as false under either rule. For those lawyers who would contend that the answer to our question is yes, the issue becomes what remedial measures are required to prevent the chief engineer from doing so. In all likelihood, all you need to do is refresh his recollection with the three incident reports.

Other lawyers, however, might answer our question "maybe." Lawyers in this camp would argue that you do not know whether the chief engineer intends to testify falsely until you show him the incident reports. Perhaps the chief engineer knows something that you do not, such as that the accidents described in the reports involved machines that had been altered in some way or were otherwise dissimilar. If so, the chief engineer's intended testimony that he knew of no similar accidents preceding the one in your case would be true. Only if the chief engineer reviewed the incident reports you showed to him, acknowledged that he was aware of them, agreed that they accurately described similar accidents, and told you that he still intended to deny knowledge of the other accidents if asked at his deposition would you know that he intended to testify falsely.

Certainly, a good lawyer would show the chief engineer the incident reports before his deposition for strategic reasons. The lawyer would not want the chief engineer to be surprised by the reports or impeached with them. As discussed above, it is possible that the chief engineer does not intend to testify falsely because the incident reports were found to be inaccurate, in which case the lawyer would want to know that as well. These practical considerations, however, should not obscure the lawyer's duty of candor in this situation.

Finally, assume that you recently deposed the plaintiff's expert witness in a medical malpractice case. The expert, an orthopedic surgeon, testified that he had just taken for the first time the examination required to become board-certified and was awaiting the results. After the deposition, your legal assistant checked the doctor's credentials and discovered that he lied; he has taken the examination twice before and failed it both times. It is apparent that the plaintiff's lawyer knows none of this, and it is further apparent that the doctor's false testimony is material. You recognize the obvious: the doctor's examination failures and dishonesty will be explosive cross-examination subjects at trial. Indeed, you relish the opportunity to cross-examine the doctor at trial on his qualifications. But is there any chance that you must reveal the doctor's false testimony before trial—ruining its impeachment value—on the basis that you called him as a witness by deposing him and are therefore required by Model Rule 3.3(a)(3) to take reasonable measures to remedy his false testimony?[111] Alternatively, must you reveal the doctor's false testimony before trial under Model Rule 3.3(b) on the basis that his false statement about his qualifications is material and thus perjurious?[112]

You have no pretrial duty of disclosure for several reasons. First, you did not call the doctor as a witness. The plaintiff is calling the doctor as a witness; you simply deposed the doctor, albeit pursuant to a notice and perhaps a subpoena. As a result, Model Rule 3.3(a)(3) does not impose a duty of disclosure on you. You might choose to reveal the doctor's dishonesty in advance of trial by moving to strike him as a witness or preclude his testimony, but that is a tactical decision rather than an ethical requirement. Second, if the doctor's false testimony is perjurious so as to trigger Model Rule 3.3(b), you will satisfy your duty to take reasonable remedial measures by exposing his dishonesty on cross-examination at trial. Third, even if you were to elicit false testimony from the doctor at trial concerning his board certification status to set him up for impeachment, you would still be permitted to do so as a legitimate advocacy tactic.[113] Model Rule 3.3(a)(3) permits lawyers to offer false testimony for the purpose of establishing its falsity.[114] So does Model Rule 3.3(b). Your cross-examination of the doctor at trial would expose his false testimony, not further it or conceal it.[115]

E. Knowledge versus Reasonable Belief

Model Rule 3.3(a)(3) generally requires that a lawyer know that testimony is false before the rule is implicated.[116] Prospectively, the rule provides that lawyers shall not knowingly offer evidence they know to be false and retrospectively requires lawyers to take reasonable remedial measures where they have offered material evidence and come to know of its falsity.[117] The rule

111. Model Rules of Prof'l Conduct R. 3.3(a)(3) (2020) (requiring a lawyer to take reasonable remedial measures where "a witness called by the lawyer" has offered material evidence and the lawyer comes to know of its falsity).

112. *Id.* R. 3.3(b) (providing that a lawyer representing a client in an adjudicative proceeding who knows that a person has engaged in criminal or fraudulent conduct related to the proceeding must take reasonable remedial measures, including even disclosure to the tribunal).

113. Restatement (Third) of the Law Governing Lawyers § 120 cmt. e (2000).

114. Model Rules of Prof'l Conduct R. 3.3 cmt. 5 (2020).

115. This hypothetical is based on *Flynn v. Edmonds*, 602 N.E.2d 880 (Ill. App. Ct. 1992), in which the plaintiff accused the defense lawyer of violating an Illinois ethics rule that obligated a lawyer who knew that a person other than the lawyer's client had perpetrated a fraud upon a tribunal to reveal the fraud to the tribunal, and another rule roughly equivalent to Model Rule 3.4(b). The court found that the defense lawyer did not violate either rule. *Id.* at 887–90.

116. Model Rules of Prof'l Conduct R. 3.3(a)(3) (2020).

117. *Id.*

further provides, however, that a lawyer may refuse to offer evidence other than the testimony of a criminal defendant that the lawyer "*reasonably believes* is false."[118] The terms "knowledge" and "reasonable belief" express different standards. The latter standard is unquestionably lower; a lawyer may reasonably believe intended testimony to be false without knowing that to be the case.[119]

Although a lawyer may reasonably believe that a witness intends to testify falsely without knowing that to be true, the reasonable belief standard is not lax. Speculation or suspicion that a witness will testify falsely does not constitute a reasonable belief of that fact.[120] To be reasonable, a lawyer's belief must be based upon an independent analysis or investigation of the evidence, or on distinct statements by the client or witness supporting that belief.[121] Mere inconsistencies in the client's or witness's stories are insufficient in and of themselves to conclude that a witness will testify falsely.[122]

Lawyers cannot present testimony they know is false,[123] nor can they present testimony that, while "technically truthful," is intended to mislead the court.[124] This is generally true in both civil and criminal litigation. It is also true regardless of whether the person who would testify falsely is a client or a witness.[125] Many courts take the same approach where criminal defendants are concerned, while other jurisdictions recognize that constitutional considerations override Rule 3.3(a)(3) and accordingly follow a different path, as we will see in the next part of this chapter. If, however, lawyers reasonably believe that testimony is false, they may refuse to offer it without breaching their duties of competence or diligence,[126] again with the exception of criminal defendants testifying on their own behalf. In short,

---

118. *Id.* (emphasis added).

119. *See, e.g.*, State v. Chambers, 994 A.2d 1248, 1259 (Conn. 2010) (quoting Rule 3.3 and contrasting "actual knowledge" with "a 'mere reasonable belief'"); Lucas v. State, 572 S.E.2d 274, 277 n.4 (S.C. 2002) (stating that a lawyer may have a reasonable belief that a witness intends to testify falsely without being able to "say, for certain, that the testimony [would] in fact [be] false").

120. *See* Cal. Eth. Op. 2019-200, 2019 WL 6839934, at *2 (Cal. State Bar, Comm. on Prof'l Responsibility 2019) [hereinafter Cal. Eth. Op. 2019-200] ("A mere suspicion that [a witness'] testimony could be false will not preclude Attorney from using it.").

121. People v. Schultheis, 638 P.2d 8, 11 (Colo. 1981); State v. DeGuzman, 701 P.2d 1287, 1291 (Haw. 1985) (quoting *Schultheis*, 638 P.2d at 11).

122. *Schultheis*, 638 P.2d at 11; *De Guzman*, 701 P.2d at 1291 (quoting *Schultheis*, 638 P.2d at 11); Cal. Eth. Op. 2019-200, *supra* note 120, 2019 WL 6839934, at *2–3.

123. State v. Hagen, 574 N.W.2d 585, 588 (N.D. 1998); Cal. Eth. Op. 2019-200, *supra* note 120, 2019 WL 6839934, at *3.

124. *See, e.g.*, *In re* Krigel, 480 S.W.3d 294, 299 (Mo. 2016) (concluding that this tactic violated Missouri's version of Rule 3.3(a)(3)).

125. Noel v. State, 26 S.W.3d 123, 126–27 (Ark. 2000); State v. Woodard, 9 So. 3d 112, 119 (La. 2009).

126. *See* Frey v. State, 509 N.W.2d 261, 264 (N.D. 1993) (quoting a comment to North Dakota Rule 3.3(b) and referring only to diligence).

Rule 3.3(a)(3) allows a lawyer the discretion to offer questionable testimony when strategy and tactics dictate. At the same time, the rule generally permits the lawyer's judgment to override the client's demands or preferences in the event of a disagreement between the two over offering dubious or unreliable testimony.[127] This approach is consistent with the established principle that decisions concerning trial strategy and tactics ultimately rest with counsel.[128]

F. Materiality

The first sentence of Model Rule 3.3(a)(3) does not contain a materiality requirement.[129] If a lawyer knows that prospective testimony will be false, the lawyer cannot offer the testimony, regardless of whether it is material. The rule is different once false testimony has been offered. If a lawyer's client or a witness called by a lawyer offers material testimony that the lawyer later comes to know was false, the second sentence of Model Rule 3.3(a)(3) provides that the lawyer must take reasonable remedial measures, including, if necessary, disclosure to the tribunal. Lawyers' duty to remedy material false testimony applies equally to false testimony offered during their examinations and to false testimony elicited by an opponent. If false testimony was not material, however, the lawyer has no duty to affect a remedy. What, then, is the standard for determining the materiality of false testimony?

The test for materiality varies between jurisdictions, but most variations are slight. In sum, testimony should be considered material if it is significant or essential; if it could have affected the course or outcome of the proceeding;[130] if it would naturally tend to influence the decision to be made, or is capable of such influence;[131] or if it "could have influenced the hearer."[132] Regardless of how the standard is expressed, materiality is determined from the court's perspective, rather than from counsel's vantage point.[133]

---

127. *See, e.g.*, *Noel*, 26 S.W.3d at 126–27 (refusing to call alibi witnesses in criminal case); *Schultheis*, 638 P.2d at 11–13 (involving alibi witnesses); Lucas v. State, 572 S.E.2d 274, 275–77 (S.C. 2002) (involving prospective false testimony by an alibi witness in a criminal case).

128. *See* State v. Sanborn, 474 So. 2d 309, 312–13 (Fla. Dist Ct. App. 1985) (discussing the problem of false testimony and lawyers' control of tactical decisions).

129. Model Rule of Prof'l Conduct R. 3.3(a)(3) (2020) (providing that a lawyer shall not knowingly "offer evidence that the lawyer knows to be false").

130. State v. Trull, 136 P.3d 551, 555 (Mont. 2006); N.Y. Eth. Op. 1123, 2017 WL 2399749, at *2 (N.Y. State Bar Ass'n, Comm. on Prof'l Ethics 2017).

131. United States v. Leifson, 568 F.3d 1215, 1220 (10th Cir. 2009) (quoting United States v. Durham, 139 F.3d 1325, 1329 (10th Cir. 1998)).

132. *In re* Fisher, 202 P.3d 1186, 1202 (Colo. 2009).

133. Holden v. Blevins, 837 A.2d 1053, 1056–57 (Md. Ct. Spec. App. 2003).

Materiality is often a function of context. Assume, for example, that you are representing the plaintiff in an insurance bad faith case. Your expert witness testified in his deposition that he earned an MBA with a concentration in insurance and risk management. You subsequently learn when reading a deposition from another case that the expert witness does not hold an MBA—the insurance company he was working for at the time of his studies transferred him out of state and he never completed his final semester of course work. Is the expert's false testimony concerning his credentials material evidence, thereby triggering your Rule 3.3(a)(3) retrospective disclosure duty? The answer is yes. The expert's MBA is intended to bolster or enhance his credibility as an expert witness; you were certainly planning on eliciting testimony regarding this credential when you called him as an expert at trial. For that matter, the expert's MBA (or lack thereof) may go to his qualifications to testify as an expert. The issue here is how you should remedy the expert's false testimony, not whether you must do so.

In contrast, assume that you are representing the plaintiff in a motor vehicle accident. You located as a witness a convenience store manager who saw the accident as she was driving to work. You produced her for her deposition, and in preliminary questioning by your opponent, she testified that she earned an associate of arts degree from a local community college. Later, gripped by remorse, the witness calls to tell you that she did not complete her A.A. degree; she left school a few credits short of completion. Must you disclose her false testimony under Rule 3.3(a)(3)? Here the answer is no because the witness's lack of a college degree is immaterial; whether she did or did not earn an A.A. degree has no bearing on her ability to perceive events. Her possession of an A.A. degree will not bolster her credibility as a fact witness. Indeed, it is unlikely that either you or opposing counsel will ask the witness about her education at trial.

Even if you do not have a duty to disclose the assistant manager's false testimony under Rule 3.3(a)(3), however, might you want to correct it anyway? The answer to this question is almost certainly yes because if you do not and her misstatement is exposed at trial, the opposing lawyer may paint her as a liar. If jurors believe that people who lie about little things lie about big ones, they may disregard the assistant manager's testimony altogether and your client may suffer as a result. In contrast, correcting the assistant manager's misstatement, while somewhat embarrassing for her, will be simple and it will be difficult for your opponent to do much with the correction when the assistant manager testifies at trial. This is simply one more example of advocacy considerations and ethics issues overlapping.

Now, turn back time on both examples. Assume that you know before the depositions that your expert intends to falsely testify about his MBA and that the convenience store manager intends to falsely claim an A.A. degree. When it comes to prospective false testimony, Model Rule 3.3(a)(3) imposes no materiality requirement; the rule states simply that a lawyer shall not knowingly "offer testimony that the lawyer knows to be false."[134] Given your knowledge, you clearly cannot allow your expert to falsely testify that he has an MBA, nor can you allow the store manager to misstate her education even though it has absolutely nothing to do with the case. Again, materiality is not a factor when analyzing false testimony prospectively under Model Rule 3.3(a)(3). With further respect to your expert witness, if you cannot persuade him to testify truthfully before the deposition, you must consider whether you can withdraw him as a witness and thus prevent his testimony altogether, or whether you have a prospective disclosure obligation under Model Rule 3.3(b), since his intended false testimony is material, and therefore likely constitutes criminal or fraudulent conduct related to the proceeding.[135]

The last aspect of the foregoing example highlights an interesting point: Model Rule 3.3(b) includes no materiality requirement.[136] There is no need for one. The rule applies only to criminal or fraudulent conduct, meaning that materiality is implied.

G. The Model Rule 3.3 Remediation Requirement

Lawyers' duties under Model Rule 3.3 to take reasonable remedial measures with respect to false testimony attach only if the false testimony was material; the question of which subpart of the rule applies depends on the facts. In some cases, both Model Rule 3.3(a) and Model Rule 3.3(b) may apply.

Model Rule 3.3(a)(3) provides in the second sentence that a lawyer must take reasonable remedial measures if "the lawyer's client, or a witness called by the lawyer, has offered material evidence and the lawyer comes to know of its falsity."[137] The rule thus requires a link between the lawyer and the person who testified falsely on a material issue before the lawyer can have a remedial obligation, and assumes that the lawyer learned that the testimony was false only after it was offered.[138] Although Model Rule 3.3(a)(3) does not specify that a lawyer must be representing the client in the proceeding

---

134. Model Rules of Prof'l Conduct R. 3.3(a)(3) (2020).

135. *Id.* R. 3.3(b).

136. *Id.* ("A lawyer who represents a client in an adjudicative proceeding and who knows that a person intends to engage, is engaging or has engaged in criminal or fraudulent conduct related to the proceeding shall take reasonable remedial measures, including, if necessary, disclosure to the tribunal.").

137. *Id.* R. 3.3(a)(3).

138. *See, e.g.*, *In re* Whitlark, 811 S.E.3d 794, 795–96 (S.C. 2018) (relying on Rule 3.3(a)(3) to suspend a lawyer who failed to disclose to the trial court that he had offered false evidence at and testimony in his client's personal injury trial after learning post-trial that the neurologist whom he had called as an expert witness in his client's case and whose bills he offered into evidence had falsified and inflated some of his charges for treating the lawyer's client).

or an aspect thereof in which the client testified falsely to have a remedial duty, the rule is indeed so limited.[139] Model Rule 3.3(b) requires a lawyer "who represents a client in an adjudicative proceeding" to take reasonable remedial measures if the lawyer "knows that a person intends to engage, is engaging or has engaged in criminal or fraudulent conduct related to the proceeding."[140] Under Model Rule 3.3(b), the materiality required is implied rather than express because a witness's false testimony must be material for it to be criminal or fraudulent. The Model Rule 3.3(b) remediation requirement applies both prospectively and retrospectively, and it applies to testimony by all witnesses regardless of the lawyer's relationship to the person. Under this rule, a lawyer cannot avoid taking reasonable remedial measures on the basis that the witness was not the lawyer's client or was not called by the lawyer. The following example illustrates this point.

Assume that you are representing a party in arbitration and examine several witnesses during the hearing. After the hearing is completed but while briefing is underway, one of the witnesses called by the other party whom you cross-examined calls you to confess that she lied about a material issue during her direct examination. Unfortunately, her recantation will disrupt your client's case in critical respects. Can you avoid taking reasonable remedial measures on the basis that you did not call the witness and have no relationship with her, as Model Rule 3.3(a)(3) would seem to permit? You plainly cannot. Because the witness's false testimony was material, it is probable that she committed either perjury or fraud or both, and you therefore must take reasonable remedial measures under Model Rule 3.3(b) even though she was neither your client nor your witness.

Witnesses may testify falsely outside the confines of a court or hearing room, with the most obvious example being deposition testimony. If a lawyer knows that a witness whom the lawyer called testified falsely in a deposition and the witness's false testimony was material, and the lawyer cannot persuade the witness to correct his testimony, the Model Rules require that the lawyer do more than merely withdraw from the case to satisfy her remedial duty. The lawyer's mere withdrawal from the representation is not a reasonable remedial measure because withdrawal, without more, does not correct the false testimony.[141] Indeed, unless replacement counsel knows of the false testimony, the first lawyer's withdrawal is likely to perpetuate the falsehood. Thus, withdrawal is a reasonable remedy only where the

139. Model Rules of Prof'l Conduct R. 3.3 cmt. 1 (2020) ("This Rule governs the conduct of a lawyer who is representing a client in the proceedings of a tribunal. . . . It also applies when a lawyer is representing a client in an ancillary proceeding conducted pursuant to the tribunal's adjudicative authority, such as a deposition.").

140. *Id.* R. 3.3(b).

141. NYCLA Eth. Op. 741, *supra* note 33, 2010 WL 4260877, at *4.

withdrawing lawyer also communicates the problem to replacement counsel sufficiently to enable the false testimony to be corrected.[142]

Finally, lawyers' efforts to remedy material false testimony, other forms of material false evidence, or fraudulent or criminal conduct related to a proceeding must be timely under the circumstances.[143] Remedial measures that a lawyer knows or should know are or will be untimely are by definition unreasonable, and therefore violate a lawyer's duties under Rules 3.3(a)(3) and 3.3(b).[144] Although there is no set time with which remedial measures must be taken to fulfill a lawyer's duty under either rule, a lawyer should attempt to correct the problem before another party relies on the false testimony or evidence to its detriment.[145] If a witness testifies falsely in a deposition and the lawyer producing the witness knows that the testimony is false, the lawyer should not wait for the opponent to expose the falsity on cross-examination.[146] This approach avoids the possibility of an alleged ethics violation, and it is sound advocacy. After all, if the witness was confused or mistaken, correcting the witness at the time of the error avoids later confusion and either enhances or preserves the witness's credibility. If the witness is being dishonest, immediate correction reinforces the lawyer's expectation that the witness will testify truthfully.

H. Failing to Remedy False Testimony under Model Rule 3.4(b)

Unlike Model Rules 3.3(a)(3) and 3.3(b), which require lawyers to take reasonable remedial measures in specified instances of false testimony, Model Rule 3.4(b) does not expressly impose a similar remediation requirement on lawyers.[147] Yet a lawyer may be held to violate Rule 3.4(b) if a witness testifies falsely, the lawyer knows the witness testified falsely, and the lawyer does not take reasonable remedial measures.[148] This is because a lawyer who does not attempt to correct what she knows is false testimony by a witness

142. *Id.*

143. *See, e.g.*, *In re* Filosa, 976 F. Supp. 2d 460, 466–67 (S.D.N.Y. 2013) (violating Rule 3.3(a)(3) by waiting over three weeks to try to correct client's false deposition testimony and then taking purported remedial measures that would not have corrected the false testimony); *In re* Starbrite Props. Corp., No. 11-40758 CEC, 2012 WL 2050745, at *10–11 (Bankr. E.D.N.Y. June 5, 2012) (criticizing lawyers for revealing client's fraud only after a significant related event had occurred and the disclosure could serve no remedial purpose).

144. *See* Model Rules of Prof'l Conduct R. 3.3(a)(3) & (b) (2020) (requiring lawyers to take "reasonable remedial measures").

145. NYCLA Eth. Op. 741, *supra* note 33, 2010 WL 4260877, at *3.

146. Corbello v. DeVito, No. 2:08-cv-00867-RCJ-PAL, 2011 WL 3859466, at *3 (D. Nev. Aug. 31, 2011).

147. *See* Model Rules of Prof'l Conduct R. 3.4(b) (2020) (providing in pertinent part that a lawyer shall not "counsel or assist a witness to testify falsely").

148. Norelus v. Denny's, Inc., 628 F.3d 1270, 1308 (11th Cir. 2010) (discussing Florida ethics rules).

may be said to have "assisted" the witness in testifying falsely within the meaning of Rule 3.4(b).[149] In other words, a court or disciplinary authorities may read a remediation requirement into Rule 3.4(b) by virtue of the prohibition against "assisting a witness to testify falsely."[150]

Although it would appear to be "piling on" to charge a lawyer with violating Rule 3.4(b) for failing to correct a witness's false testimony when the lawyer's failure would surely violate Rules 3.3(a)(3) or 3.3(b),[151] that is not necessarily so. Rule 3.3(a)(3) applies where the lawyer's client or a witness called by the lawyer testifies falsely on a material issue, while Rule 3.3(b) applies where a witness's false testimony qualifies as criminal or fraudulent. In comparison, Rule 3.4(b) applies where "a witness" "testif[ies] falsely."[152] Thus, there might be a rare case in which a lawyer's failure to reasonably attempt to remedy a witness's false testimony would violate Rule 3.4(b) but not violate Rules 3.3(a)(3) or 3.3(b).

III. False Testimony in Criminal Cases

As noted at the outset, the so-called perjury trilemma is most acute in criminal cases. A lawyer in a civil case presented with potential false testimony by a client can often avoid trouble by not calling the client as a witness. With the possible exception of some civil commitment proceedings, defendants in civil cases have no constitutional right to testify over their lawyers' objections.[153] Clients who want to testify in civil cases and who cannot persuade their lawyers to go along (as should be the case where false testimony is concerned) are left to discharge their lawyers. If a lawyer representing a criminal defendant knows that her client intends to commit perjury when he testifies, however, she may not be able to avoid the problem by refusing to call him as a witness. Although most criminal defendants consult with their lawyers when deciding whether to testify, and generally follow their lawyers' advice, the decision to testify is the defendant's alone to make.[154] Defendants in criminal cases have a constitutional right to testify on their own behalf.[155]

---

149. *Id.*

150. Model Rules of Prof'l Conduct R. 3.4(b) (2020).

151. *See Norelus*, 628 F.3d at 1308 (noting that Rule 3.4(b) works in combination with Rule 3.3).

152. Model Rules of Prof'l Conduct R. 3.4(b) (2020) (providing in pertinent part that a lawyer shall not "counsel or assist a witness to testify falsely").

153. *See, e.g.*, People v. Allen, 187 P.3d 1018, 1037 (Cal. 2008) (holding that defendants in sexually violent predator commitment proceedings have a constitutional right to testify over their lawyers' objections).

154. Sartin v. State, 400 S.W.3d 694, 699 (Ark. 2012); People v. Morris, 16 N.E.3d 269, 283 (Ill. App. Ct. 2014); Savoy v. State, 96 A.3d 842, 852 (Md. Ct. Spec. App. 2014); Commonwealth v. Miranda, 146 N.E.3d 435, 461 (Mass. 2020); Model Rules of Prof'l Conduct R. 1.2(a)(1) (2020).

155. Rock v. Arkansas, 483 U.S. 44, 52 (1987).

Yet this right is not unbridled. Although criminal defendants have a right to testify on their own behalf, there is no constitutional right to commit perjury,[156] nor does the Sixth Amendment right to the assistance of counsel compel a defense lawyer to assist or participate in the presentation of false testimony.[157] As the Supreme Court explained in the seminal case of *Nix v. Whiteside*,[158] whatever the scope of a criminal defendant's constitutional right to testify, "it is elementary that such a right does not extend to testifying falsely."[159]

A. Lawyers' Options When Confronting Prospective False Testimony

Defense lawyers' first option when presented with clients who intend to testify falsely is to attempt to dissuade them from doing so.[160] Common sense compels this approach. Assuming that defense lawyers share relationships of trust and confidence with their clients, it is reasonable to believe that their efforts will succeed. In fact, there is a professional consensus that criminal defense lawyers are frequently successful in dissuading clients from committing perjury.[161] The many negative consequences of false testimony should be sufficient for a client to reject it as a tactic. And, at bottom, perjury usually does not work; the prosecution will have an array of evidence contradicting the false testimony. But if a lawyer is unable to persuade a client to testify truthfully or not at all, what is the lawyer's next step? If the lawyer cannot prevent the defendant from testifying, how can she avoid offering evidence that she knows to be false?

Withdrawal initially seems to be an appealing option for a criminal defense lawyer with a client bent on perjury, but it is often unavailable and is an imperfect solution in any event. First, the lawyer's withdrawal may prejudice the client, especially if it occurs close to trial. Second, withdrawal typically requires leave of court, and a court may not allow a lawyer to withdraw, especially if trial is reasonably near. Courts often deny defense

156. United States v. Norman, 776 F.3d 67, 77 (2d Cir. 2015) (quoting United States v. Dunnigan, 507 U.S. 87, 96 (1993)); United States v. Stenson, 741 F.3d 827, 830–31 (7th Cir. 2014); United States v. Tuma, 738 F.3d 681, 694 (5th Cir. 2013); State v. Abdullah, 348 P.3d 1, 127 (Idaho 2015) (quoting LaChance v. Erickson, 522 U.S. 262, 266 (1998)); Commonwealth v. Leiva, 146 N.E.3d 1093, 1110 (Mass. 2020).

157. People v. DePallo, 754 N.E.2d 751, 753 (N.Y. 2001).

158. 475 U.S. 157 (1986).

159. *Id.* at 173 (emphasis omitted).

160. *Id.* at 169 ("It is universally agreed that at a minimum the attorney's first duty when confronted with a proposal for perjurious testimony is to attempt to dissuade the client from the unlawful course of conduct."); Hernandez v. First Student, Inc., 249 Cal. Rptr. 3d 681, 700 (Ct. App. 2019) ("An attorney has a duty to attempt to dissuade a client from committing perjury."); Miller v. State, 764 S.E.2d 135, 141 (Ga. 2014) (quoting *Nix*, 475 U.S. at 169).

161. Nat'l Ass'n of Crim. Def. Lawyers, Ethics Advisory Comm., Formal Op. 92-2 (1992), *reprinted in* THE CHAMPION, Mar. 1993, at 23, 28.

lawyers' motions to withdraw. If a court denies a lawyer's motion to withdraw, the lawyer must remain in the case even if she has good cause for terminating the attorney-client relationship.[162] Third, allowing lawyers to withdraw to avoid aiding client perjury solves nothing because replacement counsel will confront the identical problem. Once the client reveals his intent to commit perjury to the second lawyer, the cycle will start anew. Alternatively, the client may figure out—especially if the first lawyer was clear in explaining her ethical duties during the course of her remonstrations with him—that he should be less honest with the second lawyer, so that she is unaware of his perjurious intent and puts him on the stand at trial in the mistaken belief that he will testify truthfully. In that case, the trial is tainted by perjury. Finally, it is unfortunately possible that the second lawyer may be willing to assist the client in testifying falsely where the first lawyer was not. Although extraordinarily rare, lawyers sometimes encourage clients to lie on the theory that the client's intended truthful testimony will not be as persuasive as fabricated testimony.[163]

A common solution to the problem of client perjury in cases in which the defense lawyer knows that the client intends to testify falsely, cannot dissuade the client from so testifying, and cannot withdraw, is to allow the lawyer to present the client's testimony in narrative form.[164] The narrative approach allows the lawyer to put the client on the witness stand and ask him what he would like to tell the jury, or what he would like the jury to know, thus launching the client's narrative. The lawyer remains standing while the client testifies as if she were conducting a normal direct examination but asks the client no questions. The lawyer may, both before and after the narrative, conduct a regular direct examination on subjects on which she expects the client to testify truthfully. In closing argument, the lawyer cannot

---

162. Model Rules of Prof'l Conduct R. 1.16(c) (2020).

163. *See, e.g.*, McCombs v. State, 3 So. 3d 950, 952–54 (Ala. Crim. App. 2008) (finding that the lawyer's instruction to his client to lie and deny stabbing a person who was intimidating him constituted ineffective assistance of counsel because it denied the client the ability to claim self-defense).

164. *See, e.g.*, United States v. Omene, 143 F.3d 1167, 1168–72 (9th Cir. 1998); People v. Bolton, 82 Cal. Rptr. 3d 671, 682 (Ct. App. 2008); Shockley v. State, 565 A.2d 1373, 1380 (Del. 1989); Butler v. United States, 414 A.2d 844, 850 (D.C. 1980); Sanborn v. State, 474 So. 2d 309, 313 (Fla. Dist. Ct. App. 1985); *Miller*, 764 S.E.2d at 140–41; State v. Waggoner, 864 P.2d 162, 167–68 (Idaho Ct. App. 1993); People v. DeRosa, No. 5-12-0227, 2013 WL 6221381, at *4 (Ill. App. Ct. Nov. 27, 2013); People v. Bartee, 566 N.E.2d 855, 856–57 (Ill. App. Ct. 1991); Reynolds v. State, 625 N.E.2d 1319, 1321 (Ind. Ct. App. 1993); State v. Fosnight, 679 P.2d 174, 180 (Kan. 1984); Brown v. Commonwealth, 226 S.W.3d 74, 84 (Ky. 2007); Commonwealth v. Mitchell, 781 N.E.2d 1237, 1249–50 (Mass. 2003); Scott v. State, 8 So. 3d 855, 859 (Miss. 2008); People v. Andrades, 828 N.E.2d 599, 603 (N.Y. 2005); Commonwealth v. Jermyn, 620 A.2d 1128, 1131 (Pa. 1993); State v. Layton, 432 S.E.2d 740, 754–55 (W. Va. 1993); State v. McDowell, 681 N.W.2d 500, 513 (Wis. 2004); Conn. Eth. Op. 42, 1993 WL 13152160, at *2 (Conn. Bar Ass'n, Comm. on Prof'l Ethics 1993) [hereinafter Conn. Eth. Op. 42].

rely on or discuss the client's false testimony. The lawyer cannot assist the client in preparing the narrative testimony.[165]

The rationale for the narrative approach is that it preserves the client's constitutional right to testify without implicating defense counsel in the client's perjury. There are glaring flaws in the narrative approach. First, there is no constitutional right to commit perjury. Whether perjury comes in narrative form or in traditional question and answer format is irrelevant—the testimony is false regardless. Second, the defense lawyer remains implicated in the client's false testimony. The client could not testify falsely but for the defense lawyer calling him as a witness. The fact that the lawyer asked one question that elicited false testimony rather than several is immaterial. Third, the narrative approach does not safeguard the client's confidentiality because it clearly alerts the judge and prosecutor that perjury is imminent. As a general rule, the lawyer's shift to narrative questioning is also likely to signal to the jury that something is amiss, either instantly or upon reflection, when jurors realize that the lawyer did not mention the client's exculpatory testimony in closing argument.[166] If the lawyer's shift to narrative questioning does not alert the jury to the defendant's perjury, then the trial is tainted if jurors accept as true any part of the defendant's false testimony. Fourth, and although indisputably the defendant's fault for insisting on testifying falsely, the patent dishonesty of narrative testimony may cause the court to find that the defendant committed perjury and thus enhance any sentence ultimately imposed for the underlying crime.[167]

The ABA's Standing Committee on Ethics & Professional Responsibility rejected the narrative approach in Formal Opinion 87-353.[168] Various jurisdictions agree that defense lawyers may not present false testimony by their clients in any form, so that a defense lawyer's failure to present a client's false testimony does not work a constitutional deprivation.[169] The Model Rules do not permit lawyers to employ the narrative approach. The Model Rules do, however, acknowledge that because of constitutional considerations the narrative approach remains an option for criminal defense lawyers in some jurisdictions. As a comment to Model Rule 3.3 explains:

---

165. Model Rules of Prof'l Conduct R. 3.4(b) (2020).

166. *But see Reynolds*, 625 N.E.2d at 1321 (observing that rather than signaling perjury, a defendant's narrative testimony was consistent "with the jury presuming that [the defendant] wished to offer certain testimony unhampered by the traditional question and answer format").

167. *See, e.g.*, United States v. Garza, 429 F.3d 165, 172 n.4 (5th Cir. 2005); People v. Edgett, 560 N.W.2d 360, 364 (Mich. Ct. App. 1996).

168. ABA Comm. on Ethics & Prof'l Responsibility, Formal Op. 87-353, at 5 (1987).

169. *See, e.g.*, United States v. Henkel, 799 F.2d 369, 370 (7th Cir. 1986); McCombs v. State, 3 So. 3d 950, 953 (Ala. Crim. App. 2008); Noel v. State, 26 S.W.3d 123, 126 (Ark. 2000); State v. Woodard, 9 So. 3d 112, 119 (La. 2009); Utah Eth. Op. 00-06, 2000 WL 1523292, at *5 (Utah State Bar, Ethics Advisory Op. Comm. 2000) [hereinafter Utah Eth. Op. 00-06].

> In some jurisdictions . . . courts have required counsel to present the accused as a witness or to give a narrative statement if the accused so desires, even if counsel knows that the testimony or statement will be false. The obligation of the advocate under the Rules of Professional Conduct is subordinate to such requirements.[170]

Notwithstanding the final sentence of the comment, it is generally acknowledged that the narrative approach does not relieve defense lawyers of the obligation to take reasonable remedial measures following clients' false testimony, including disclosure to the tribunal.[171] But this view of the narrative approach and the lawyer's associated duty is questionable at best given the language of the comment and considering that the narrative approach itself discloses the client's perjury. It is redundant to require the lawyer to disclose the client's perjury to the court after the client's narrative, and it is especially so if the court engaged in a colloquy with the client before the client testified. Any judge who hears narrative testimony by a criminal defendant knows full well why the defendant is testifying in that fashion. If the lawyer moved to withdraw relatively close in time to the defendant's narrative testimony, the motion to withdraw alone was probably enough to inform the court that the defendant intended to testify falsely.[172] That is certainly true where the defense lawyer obliquely stated in the motion that her professional responsibilities or ethical duties required her withdrawal. As for other possible remedies, post-narrative withdrawal by a defense lawyer serves no purpose. At that point the narrative testimony is in evidence. For that matter, the lawyer arguably remedied the client's perjury by not referring to the narrative testimony or not arguing those "facts" in closing argument. Thus, a compelling argument can be made that lawyers who properly employ the narrative approach have fulfilled their responsibilities under Model Rule 3.3(a)(3). Nothing more should be required of them.

B. *Illustrative Narrative Cases*

Commonwealth v. Mitchell[173] is perhaps the leading case on the narrative approach to client perjury.[174] The defendant, Curtis Mitchell, was accused of a double homicide. He allegedly made multiple incriminating statements

170. Model Rules of Prof'l Conduct R. 3.3 cmt. 7 (2020).

171. *See, e.g.*, Restatement (Third) of the Law Governing Lawyers § 120 cmt. i (2000); John Wesley Hall, Jr., Professional Responsibility in Criminal Defense Practice §§ 26:17-26:22, at 904–08 (3d ed. 2005); Ronald D. Rotunda & John S. Dzienkowski, Legal Ethics: The Lawyer's Deskbook on Professional Responsibility § 3.3–5(e), at 807–08 (2018–2019).

172. *Henkel*, 799 F.2d at 370 (citing Lowery v. Cardwell, 575 F.2d 727 (9th Cir. 1978)).

173. 781 N.E.2d 1237 (Mass. 2003).

174. *See also* Brown v. Commonwealth, 226 S.W.3d 74, 81–85 (Ky. 2007) (adopting the *Mitchell* court's approach).

concerning the murders, and his behavior following the murders suggested his culpability. At the same time, he had an alibi witness, and his DNA did not match the DNA taken from hairs found at the crime scene. Mitchell contended that the real murderer was a local drug dealer named Julius Adams, with whom both he and the victims had a relationship.

Mitchell took the stand at trial. His lawyer had him state his name and then asked, "'Mr. Mitchell, what do you wish to tell these jurors?'"[175] Mitchell then testified in narrative fashion, denying the incriminatory statements attributed to him, rationalizing his suspicious behavior, and explaining why Adams was likely the killer. Mitchell's lawyer did not refer to this testimony in closing argument.[176] Rather, he emphasized the state's burden of proof, attacked the credibility of the prosecution witnesses, offered an alternative theory of the crime, pointed to the paucity of physical evidence against Mitchell, and attacked perceived failures in the police investigation. It was a strong closing argument, but Mitchell was nonetheless convicted. Mitchell challenged his conviction on ineffective assistance of counsel grounds based on the following events.

Before putting Mitchell on the stand, defense counsel approached the bench together with the prosecutor. The defense lawyer explained that he was concerned about participating in a fraud on the court but that he could not reveal more without violating the attorney-client privilege.[177] He therefore wanted to put Mitchell on the stand, ask him his name, and instruct him to tell his story to the jury. The judge then took a brief recess to read Massachusetts Rule of Professional Conduct 3.3(e), which provided in pertinent part:

> "In a criminal case, defense counsel who knows that the defendant, the client, intends to testify falsely may not aid the client in constructing false testimony. . . . If a criminal trial has commenced and the lawyer discovers that the client intends to testify falsely at trial, the lawyer need not file a motion to withdraw from the case if the lawyer reasonably believes that seeking to withdraw will prejudice the client. If, during the client's testimony or after the client has testified, the lawyer knows that the client has testified falsely, the lawyer shall call upon the client to rectify the false testimony and, if the client refuses or is unable to do so, the lawyer shall not reveal the false testimony to the tribunal. In no event may the lawyer examine the client in such a manner as to elicit any testimony from the client the lawyer knows to be false, and the lawyer shall not argue the probative value of the false testimony in closing argument. . . ."[178]

175. *Mitchell*, 781 N.E.2d at 1244.
176. *Id.*
177. *Id.*
178. *Id.* at 1241 n.1.

When trial resumed, the defense lawyer indicated that he would remain as counsel so as not to prejudice Mitchell and assured the court that he had attempted to dissuade Mitchell from testifying falsely. The judge instructed the defense lawyer to stand during Mitchell's narrative testimony and to object to the prosecutor's cross-examination questions as appropriate, keeping in mind that he could not assist Mitchell in testifying. Mitchell's narrative testimony proceeded as the court instructed.[179] When Mitchell finished his narrative testimony, the court allowed the defense lawyer a brief recess to confer with his client. Following the recess, the defense lawyer reported to the court that he had fulfilled his responsibilities under Massachusetts Rule 3.3(e).[180] The prosecutor cross-examined Mitchell without incident, and the defense lawyer closed as summarized above.

In a motion for new trial, Mitchell argued that his lawyer did not have an adequate basis to invoke Rule 3.3(e) because he did not know that Mitchell intended to perjure himself, that the judge unconstitutionally applied the rule by failing to conduct a colloquy with him, and that he should have been present at the sidebar conference when his lawyer raised Rule 3.3(e). The trial court rejected these arguments. The trial court found that the defense lawyer had a firm factual basis for believing that Mitchell intended to perjure himself because Mitchell admitted to the murders to the defense lawyer during the course of his representation.[181] In doing so, the court obviously believed the defense lawyer and disbelieved Mitchell's statements in an affidavit denying the admissions.[182] The trial court rejected Mitchell's argument concerning the lack of a colloquy on the basis that Rule 3.3(e) did not require one and, regardless, Mitchell understood his options and the possible consequences of testifying in narrative fashion. The trial judge agreed that Mitchell's exclusion from the sidebar conference was erroneous because the conference represented a critical stage of the proceedings but found that the error was harmless beyond a reasonable doubt. Finally, the trial court rejected Mitchell's contention that requiring his defense lawyer to forego a traditional direct examination and not argue his testimony in closing deprived him of his constitutional rights. On appeal, the Massachusetts Supreme Judicial Court agreed with the trial court across the board.

With respect to Mitchell's narrative testimony, the court thought it "of no consequence" that the prosecutor was present when defense counsel informed the trial judge of his intention to invoke Rule 3.3(e).[183] The defense lawyer did not disclose what expected testimony would be perjurious. Had the defense lawyer omitted the prosecutor from his conversation

179. *Id.* at 1245.
180. *Id.*
181. *Id.* at 1245–46.
182. *Id.* at 1246 n.5.
183. *Id.* at 1249.

with the judge, the court reasoned, the prosecutor almost certainly would have objected when Mitchell began testifying in narrative form, thus drawing the jury's attention to the procedure.[184]

The *Mitchell* court concluded that the narrative testimony was properly directed. The court rejected Mitchell's argument that his defense counsel should have conducted a standard direct examination with respect to the "non-suspect" portions of his testimony and argued the truthful portions of his testimony in closing.[185] Mitchell's position on direct examination was impractical because defense counsel would be unable to control direct examination and could not effectively prepare the client for cross-examination.[186] Mitchell's position on closing argument was also impractical, inasmuch as it would highlight that portion of a defendant's testimony that defense counsel did not mention in closing and would likely produce incoherent closing arguments.[187]

As for the missing colloquy, the court noted that although Rule 3.3(e) did not require one, the record might not always be as clear as it was in this case. Thus, if circumstances warrant, a trial judge has the discretion to conduct a colloquy in which a defendant is informed of (1) his right to testify and to counsel, (2) his lawyer's ethical obligation not to present false testimony, and (3) the consequences of his lawyer's invocation of Rule 3.3 (i.e., that he must testify in narrative form and that defense counsel will not argue his testimony in closing).[188] Any colloquy should be carefully controlled and conducted to elicit simple yes or no answers from the defendant. If the defendant is confused or has doubts about the process, the court should instruct him to consult with his lawyer until he understands the ramifications of testifying.[189]

Having disposed of Mitchell's arguments concerning his narrative testimony, the court summarized its position on prospective false testimony by criminal defendants. First, to invoke Rule 3.3, a defense lawyer must be acting in good faith and have a firm basis in objective fact for believing that the defendant intends to testify falsely.[190] Second, the defense lawyer must raise her concerns about the defendant's intended false testimony with the court.[191] In alerting the court to the issue, the lawyer will have to be cryptic because she is required to maintain client confidentiality to the extent

184. *Id.*
185. *Id.*
186. *Id.* (quoting an ABA Criminal Justice Section report).
187. *Id.*
188. *Id.* at 1249–50.
189. *Id.* at 1250.
190. *Id.* at 1250–51.
191. *See id.* at 1251 (assuming that the defense lawyer calls the problem of expected false testimony to the court's attention but not listing such disclosure as a formal step).

possible and must be prepared to zealously advocate for her client during the remainder of the trial.[192] The lawyer cannot inform the judge of the details that support the invocation of Rule 3.3.[193] Third, once the court is alerted, and recognizing that the judge will have to rely on defense counsel's oblique representations about the nature of the issue, the judge should instruct the lawyer how to proceed.[194] The court may conduct a colloquy with the defendant before instructing the lawyer, but it is not required to do so. The court is certainly not obligated to conduct an evidentiary hearing to determine whether the defense lawyer had an adequate basis to invoke Rule 3.3. Fourth, the defendant may thereafter testify by means of an open narrative.[195] Finally, because each case is unique, a trial court has discretion to vary any of these procedures where required by the interests of justice or effective case management.[196]

The trial court in this case anticipated and followed these principles, with the exception of Mitchell's harmless omission from the sidebar conference that preceded his testimony. As a result, the *Mitchell* court found that the trial court correctly concluded that the defense lawyer's conduct fell within the range of reasonable professional responses to anticipated client perjury and thus satisfied Rule 3.3(e) and constitutional requirements.[197] After considering several additional issues, the court affirmed Mitchell's conviction.[198]

C. The Problem of Surprise Perjury

In contrast to cases in which criminal defense lawyers know that their clients intend to testify falsely, defendants may surprise their lawyers with false testimony at trial. Assume, for example, that you are defending Derek James,

192. *See id.* (discussing this approach from the trial court's perspective); *see, e.g.*, Moore v. Warden, No. CV084002471, 2012 WL 2335283, at *6 (Conn. Super. Ct. May 22, 2012) ("When counseling the petitioner against offering his false testimony failed, defense counsel took the next appropriate step by notifying the court . . . in chambers . . . that he had an 'ethical issue' and then sought to withdraw . . . only providing the trial court with the minimum amount of information necessary to alert the court to the basic nature of the issue, but not revealing . . . attorney-client privileged communications. Under Rule 3.3, the steps counsel took were appropriate, because while meeting his obligation as an officer of the court, he also continued to honor his duty of confidentiality and maintained his role as an advocate. . . .").

193. *Mitchell*, 781 N.E.2d at 1251.

194. *Id.*

195. *Id.*

196. *Id.*

197. *Id.*

198. For two recent Massachusetts Supreme Court cases building on *Mitchell*, see *Commonwealth v. Miranda*, 146 N.E.3d 435 (Mass. 2020), and *Commonwealth v. Leiva*, 146 N.E.3d 1093 (Mass. 2020).

a college fraternity member, in a rape case.[199] The state alleges that Derek slipped a date rape drug into the victim's drink at a party and thereafter sexually assaulted her in his room at the fraternity house. Derek maintains that he did not attend the party because he was ill and, although he was once intimate with the victim, he did not "hook up" with her that night. In fact, one of Derek's fraternity brothers took party pictures using the camera in his smart phone and Derek appears in several of the photographs. When you show the photos to Derek, he tearfully acknowledges that he attended the party but insists that he did not have sex with the victim that evening. You are not pleased by Derek's initial lack of honesty, but nor are you especially bothered by his presence at the party. There are numerous large holes in the victim's story. Because the victim delayed in reporting the alleged rape to the police, there is no forensic evidence and no one can link Derek to a date rape drug. In short, you strongly believe that Derek is innocent and expect to win at trial.

For a variety of good reasons, you and Derek ultimately decide that he should testify in his own defense at trial. You therefore call Derek as your final witness at trial. During his direct examination, Derek astonishingly asserts that he did not attend the fateful party because he was ill. What do you do?

You know that Derek's testimony is false and it is plainly material; thus, you have a duty under Model Rules 3.3(a)(3) and 3.3(b) to "take reasonable remedial measures, including, if necessary, disclosure to the tribunal."[200] It is equally true, however, that you enjoy discretion in how you attempt to remedy Derek's false testimony.[201] Thus, your first step might be to attempt corrective questioning without disrupting the direct examination. For example, without breaking stride, you might lower your voice and in your parental best, ask, "Derek, I know that you are very nervous and that being falsely accused of rape is a terrifying thing, but you *were* at the party that night, weren't you?" Derek will presumably answer truthfully, and you can then continue your direct examination as planned. By leading Derek to correct his false testimony, you have satisfied your remedial obligations under Model Rules 3.3(a)(3) and (b).

Attempting to correct Derek's false testimony during his direct examination is not your only option, and it may not even be your best one. The great weight of authority indicates that you should seek a recess to privately

199. The hypothetical defendant's name is fictitious. Other details have been fictionalized or substantially modified to avoid confusion with actual cases or events. Nothing written here is intended to diminish concerns about campus sexual assaults or about the devastating effects that sexual assaults have on their victims.

200. Model Rules of Prof'l Conduct R. 3.3(a)(3) & 3.3(b) (2020).

201. *See* United States v. Williams, 698 F.3d 374, 382 (7th Cir. 2012) (explaining that lawyers "enjoy a broad discretion in responding to litigation misconduct by their clients").

persuade Derek to correct his testimony.[202] The manner in which you do so is a matter of judgment, but it is clear that in seeking Derek's cooperation, you must be prepared to advise him of your duty to reveal his false testimony to the court.[203]

If Derek will not agree to correct his false testimony, you must move to withdraw.[204] In moving to withdraw, it is sufficient to advise the court of the general nature of the problem without going into specifics or providing details. If the court will not allow you to withdraw, you obviously must remain in the case.[205] If you remain in the case, you may wish to move to strike Derek's false testimony[206] or move for a mistrial. If you are unsuccessful in striking the false testimony or obtaining a mistrial, you must then consider how best to disclose Derek's false testimony to the court. If you took a recess and remonstrated with him privately, it is probable that your motions to withdraw and to strike *have* disclosed Derek's false testimony, but further disclosure may be required. How any such disclosure is accomplished will depend on the situation and the court. In any event, your disclosures should be limited to that information necessary to remedy the situation and, to the extent possible, should be calculated to minimize the harm to Derek's defense. Finally, if you remain in the case and trial continues, you cannot examine Derek in a fashion that endorses or perpetuates his false testimony, and you cannot refer to the false testimony in closing argument.

As much as anything, this example illustrates the importance of avoiding surprise perjury through careful preparation. When you caught Derek lying about not attending the fraternity party—a lie almost certainly fueled by fear—you needed to reassuringly commit him to honesty going forward. You should have expressed your faith in him. You should have explained to him why his defense was quite strong despite his presence at the party. You might have advised him that you could work with any facts presented—even unhelpful ones—as long as you knew of them. On the other side of the coin, you should have told him that his dishonesty would likely be exposed on cross-examination. Testifying falsely will cripple his case. Moreover, the

---

202. Restatement (Third) of the Law Governing Lawyers § 120 cmt. g (2000); Conn. Eth. Op. 42, *supra* note 164, 1993 WL 13152160, at *2; Fla. Eth. Op. 04-1, 2005 WL 3985348, at *3 (Fla. State Bar Ass'n, Comm. on Prof'l Ethics 2005) [hereinafter Fla. Eth. Op. 04-1]; Tenn. Eth. Op. 93-F-133, 1993 WL 814081, at *3 (Bd. of Prof'l Responsibility of the Sup. Ct. of Tenn. 1993) [hereinafter Tenn. Eth. Op. 93-F-133]; Utah Eth. Op. 00-06, *supra* note 169, 2000 WL 1523292, at *4.

203. *See* Model Rules of Prof'l Conduct R. 1.4(b) (2020) ("A lawyer shall explain a matter to the extent reasonably necessary to permit the client to make informed decisions regarding the representation.").

204. *Id.* R. 1.16(a)(1); Conn. Eth. Op. 42, *supra* note 164, 1993 WL 13152160, at *2; Tenn. Eth. Op. 93-F-133, *supra* note 202, 1993 WL 814081, at *3; Utah Eth. Op. 00-06, *supra* note 169, 2000 WL 1523292, at *6.

205. Model Rules of Prof'l Conduct R. 1.16(c) (2020).

206. Restatement (Third) of the Law Governing Lawyers § 120 cmt. g (2000).

court will consider his dishonesty when sentencing him. Finally, you might have informed him of your ethical duties concerning false testimony and again of the potentially serious consequences to him were you forced to uphold your duties. There is no guarantee that Derek would have heeded your advice and testified truthfully at trial, but it is reasonable to assume that he would have. It is well-settled that lawyers are generally successful in dissuading clients from testifying falsely. In short, it is far easier to prevent perjury than it is to fix it.

D. Testimony by Witnesses

The narrative approach is limited to use with criminal defendants; it is not an option when a lawyer knows that a witness in a criminal case intends to testify falsely. Although criminal defendants have a constitutional right to testify on their own behalf, they have no right to require counsel to call particular witnesses to testify when those witnesses will testify falsely,[207] regardless of the perceived importance of the witness to the defense effort.[208] As Model Rule 3.3(a)(3) makes clear, lawyers cannot present testimony by witnesses in criminal cases that they know is false.[209] Short of such testimony, criminal defense lawyers may refuse to call witnesses whom they reasonably believe will testify falsely without violating their duties of competence or diligence. Again, speculation or suspicion that a witness will testify falsely does not constitute a reasonable belief of that fact. To be reasonable, a lawyer's belief must be based upon an independent analysis or investigation of the evidence, or on distinct statements by the client or witness supporting that

207. Although tactical decisions, such as whether to call certain witnesses, generally are the trial lawyer's exclusive province, some courts hold that when a fully informed defendant and defense counsel reach an impasse on those decisions, the defendant's wishes generally must control consistent with the law of agency. *See, e.g.*, State v. Freeman, 690 S.E.2d 17, 21 (N.C. Ct. App. 2010) (quoting State v. Ali, 407 S.E.2d 183, 189 (N.C. 1991)). A lawyer in that situation is left to document her contrary advice to the client as a precaution against a later claim by the client that the lawyer erred by calling the witness. State v. Floyd, 766 S.E.2d 361, 369 (N.C. Ct. App. 2014). The rule that a lawyer, as agent, must obey a client's instruction does not apply, however, where a lawyer knows or reasonably believes that a witness will testify falsely. An agent's duty to comply with a principal's instructions is not absolute. An agent has no duty to obey instructions that may expose the agent to civil, criminal, or administrative liability or sanctions, or that exceed legal limits on the principal's right to direct the agent.

208. *See* Noel v. State, 26 S.W.3d 123, 126–27 (Ark. 2000) ("Given . . . that a lawyer's duty of zealous representation extends only to legitimate, lawful conduct, we conclude that counsel was not ineffective for failing to present . . . false alibi testimony."); People v. Schultheis, 638 P.2d 8, 12 (Colo. 1981) ("A [lawyer's] refusal to call a particular witness because of an obedience to ethical standards which prohibit the presentation of fabricated testimony does not constitute ineffective assistance of counsel.").

209. *Noel*, 26 S.W.3d at 126–27; Tibbs v. United States, 628 A.2d 638, 641 (D.C. 1993); State v. Woodard, 9 So. 3d 112, 118–19 (La. 2009).

belief.[210] In any event, defense lawyers may decline to call even alibi witnesses whom they reasonably believe will testify falsely without breaching duties to their clients or eroding their clients' constitutional rights.[211] Model Rule 3.3(a)(3) expressly grants lawyers this discretion.[212] In addition, courts consider a lawyer's refusal to call witnesses whom the lawyer reasonably believes will testify falsely to be reasonable trial strategy.[213]

E. Special Responsibilities of Prosecutors

Prosecutors are subject to Model Rules 3.3(a)(3) and 3.3(b) just as are defense lawyers, and therefore they are equally bound to take reasonable remedial measures, including disclosure to the tribunal, if government witnesses testify falsely. Prosecutors have a further duty grounded in constitutional law to correct testimony by government witnesses on material issues that they know to be false or misleading.[214] Courts' requirement that prosecutors correct testimony by government witnesses on material issues that they know to be false or misleading for reasons extending beyond ethics rules is consistent with the widespread recognition that prosecutors have special duties commensurate with their unique powers.[215]

For constitutional purposes, it does not matter that jurors may be able to discern the government witness's dishonesty from other sources or that defense counsel may recognize the witness's dishonesty and cross-examine accordingly; if a prosecutor knows that a government witness has lied about a material issue, she has a duty to correct the false impression of the facts.[216] A prosecutor's failure to correct material testimony by a government witness

---

210. *Schultheis*, 638 P.2d at 11; State v. DeGuzman, 701 P.2d 1287, 1291 (Haw. 1985) (quoting *Schultheis*, 638 P.2d at 11).

211. *See, e.g.*, Smith v. State, 931 So. 2d 790, 802 (Fla. 2006); Hill v. State, 658 S.E.2d 863, 871 (Ga. Ct. App. 2008); Grooms v. State, 583 S.E.2d 216, 219 (Ga. Ct. App. 2003); Bennett v. State, 549 S.W.2d 585, 587 (Mo. Ct. App. 1977); Lucas v. State, 572 S.E.2d 274, 275–77 (S.C. 2002).

212. Model Rules of Prof'l Conduct R. 3.3(a)(3) (2020) ("A lawyer may refuse to offer evidence, other than the testimony of a defendant in a criminal matter, that the lawyer reasonably believes is false.").

213. *See, e.g.*, *Hill*, 658 S.E.2d at 871; State v. Woodard, 931 So. 2d 112, 120 (La. 2009).

214. United States v. Leoner-Aguirre, 939 F.3d 310, 320 (1st Cir. 2019) (citing Napue v. Illinois, 360 U.S. 264, 269 (1959)); Ass'n for L.A. Deputy Sheriffs v. Super. Ct., 447 P.3d 234, 241 (Cal. 2019) (quoting *Napue*, 360 U.S. at 269); Woodall v. United States, 842 A.2d 690, 696 (D.C. 2004) (quoting Hawthorne v. United States, 504 A.2d 580, 589 (D.C. 1986)); Birano v. State, 426 P.3d 387, 413–14 (Haw. 2018); Commonwealth v. Ware, 128 N.E.3d 29, 34–40 (Mass. 2019).

215. *See* United States v. LaPage, 231 F.3d 488, 492 (9th Cir. 2000) (quoting Berger v. United States, 295 U.S. 78, 88 (1935)); *Ware*, 128 N.E.3d at 40 (quoting *Berger*, 295 U.S. at 88).

216. *LaPage*, 231 F.3d at 492; *Ware*, 128 N.E.3d at 36 ("[W]here the testimony is blatantly false and pertains to an issue central to the [government's] case, a defendant's ability to discern the statement's falsity does not absolve prosecutors of their duty to correct."). *But see, e.g.*, People v. Spruill, 82 N.Y.S.3d 520, 527 (App. Div. 2018) (refusing to reverse the defendant's conviction where the false testimony that the prosecutor should have corrected was not material).

that the prosecutor knows to be false or misleading violates a defendant's constitutional right to due process and requires reversal of the defendant's conviction unless there is no reasonable possibility that the tainted testimony affected the jury's verdict.[217]

F. Summary

False testimony presents special challenges for criminal defense lawyers. Challenges are perhaps greatest when a criminal defense lawyer knows that a client intends to testify falsely, and the lawyer cannot prevent the client from taking the witness stand. Lawyers seeking guidance in this situation should first examine applicable rules of professional conduct; some jurisdictions specifically address in their rules or comments thereto false testimony by criminal defendants, including narrative testimony.[218] In many jurisdictions there will be no case law on-point, but there may be ethics opinions that will assist lawyers. Alternatively, lawyers may seek advice from knowledgeable colleagues or professional responsibility specialists.[219] Fortunately, exceedingly few criminal defendants insist on testifying falsely. In addition, the standard for a lawyer's knowledge of a defendant's false testimony is sufficiently high that in most cases a lawyer will be able to put a defendant on the stand and conduct a traditional direct examination without fear of violating rules of professional conduct.

IV. Prevention of False Testimony and Reasonable Remedial Measures

Most clients and witnesses testify truthfully. They strive for accuracy in their testimony because they are conscientious and appreciate their oaths. Good lawyers prevent false testimony through prudent investigations that

217. *LaPage*, 231 F.3d at 491; Adams v. Comm'r of Corr., 71 A.3d 512, 520–30 (Conn. 2013); *Woodall*, 842 A.2d at 696; *Ware*, 128 N.E.3d at 34–40.

218. *See, e.g.*, Cal. Rules of Prof'l Conduct R. 3.3 cmt. 4 (2020) (providing that a lawyer may offer a criminal defendant's false testimony in a narrative form if the lawyer reasonably tried to dissuade the client from so testifying and sought permission from the court to withdraw under Rule 1.16); D.C. Rules of Prof'l Conduct R. 3.3(b) (2015) (providing for narrative testimony by criminal defendants and outlining the procedure); Fla. Rules of Prof'l Conduct R. 4-3.3(a)(4) (2019) (guiding lawyers with respect to false testimony by criminal defendants and limiting narrative testimony to cases in which it is ordered by the court); Mass. Rules of Prof'l Conduct R. 3.3(e) (2015) (discussing lawyers' duties in criminal cases); Tenn. Rules of Prof'l Conduct R. 3.3(b) (2018) (permitting a criminal defense lawyer who has been denied permission to withdraw to allow the client to testify by way of an undirected narrative); Tex. Disciplinary Rules of Prof'l Conduct R. 3.03 cmts. 11 & 12 (2019) (rejecting the narrative approach); Va. Rules of Prof'l Conduct R. 3.3 cmts. 13a & 13b (2020) (rejecting the narrative approach).

219. *See* Model Rules of Prof'l Conduct R. 1.6(b)(4) (2020) (permitting lawyers to reveal information relating to a client's representation in order to secure legal advice about the lawyer's obligations under ethics rules).

arm them with necessary facts and frame an accurate picture of what actually transpired. When interviewing clients and witnesses, they reassuringly explain the importance of receiving complete and accurate accounts of events, and they ask open-ended questions to elicit full and frank answers. Capable lawyers also prevent false testimony through normal witness preparation, as where, for example, they refresh witnesses' recollection with documents, statements, and deposition transcripts; conduct mock direct and cross-examinations; and rehearse testimony using expected exhibits. Occasionally, however, lawyers may reasonably believe that clients or their witnesses intend to testify falsely. In rare cases, clients and witnesses surprise lawyers with false testimony.

It is initially important to distinguish between false testimony that is false because it is mistaken and false testimony that is dishonest. Lawyers must take remedial measures in either instance, but false testimony that is simply mistaken is relatively easy to correct. Even in the more difficult situation where the client's or witness's mistaken testimony is a surprise, the lawyer may remedy the problem by eliciting correct testimony through further examination, or refreshing the client's or witness's recollection with a document or prior testimony. If the false testimony occurs in a deposition, the problem can be remedied through further examination or by making changes on an errata sheet, or the lawyer can reopen the deposition. If the mistaken testimony occurs at trial and for whatever reason the witness cannot be immediately refocused, the lawyer may be able to recall the witness or call other witnesses to remove any false impression that the testimony made on the court or jury.

Real trouble lurks where clients or witnesses lie. This is the form of false testimony that gives lawyers fits. What do you do in that situation?

A. Prospective False Testimony

If you either reasonably believe or know that a client intends to testify falsely, you should first caution the client against doing so.[220] The form and content of your remonstration is a matter of judgment; you must attempt to persuade while maintaining the client's trust.[221] In most cases you will be able to dissuade a client from testifying falsely simply by explaining the detrimental effect that the false testimony will have on the matter if it is exposed. Indeed, the revelation of the false testimony will have an effect far more severe than had the client told the truth in the first place. If the client insists on testifying falsely, you must inform the client of your duty not to

220. *See* Hernandez v. First Student, Inc., 249 Cal. Rptr. 3d 681, 700 (Ct. App. 2019) ("An attorney has a duty to attempt to dissuade a client from committing perjury.").

221. Restatement (Third) of the Law Governing Lawyers § 120 cmt. g (2000).

offer false evidence and to take reasonable remedial action if it is offered, including disclosing the intended false testimony to the court.[222] This admonition should be sufficient to abort the client's misguided plan. Assuming you thwart the client's plan, you have no duty to inform the court of the controversy.[223]

The approach is essentially the same where a witness other than a client is concerned. Although Model Rule 4.3 broadly prohibits lawyers from giving legal advice to unrepresented persons,[224] that ban is irrelevant in this context because urging a witness to testify truthfully does not constitute legal advice. Advising a witness about the law and your duties as a lawyer is not the same as giving the witness legal advice.

If the issue surfaces in civil litigation and you cannot dissuade the client or witness from testifying falsely, you have at least two options short of revealing the prospective false testimony to the court. First, you may refuse to present the false testimony.[225] This is true even if you do not know that the client or witness will testify falsely but only reasonably believe that he will do so.[226] Second, you may move to withdraw from the client's representation. Withdrawal is far more likely to be a consideration where it is a client who intends to testify falsely rather than a witness. The challenge in withdrawal is doing so in a fashion that will do the least harm to the client's case. Even assuming the client will experience adverse effects as a result of your withdrawal, however, it is difficult for the client to complain. In *In re Sealed Case*,[227] for example, the court permitted a law firm to withdraw from a case in which it justifiably believed that its client intended to commit perjury.[228] The magistrate assigned to the case had noted that the firm's withdrawal would leave the client unrepresented, while the district judge erroneously conditioned the firm's withdrawal on its willingness to forego unpaid fees owed by the client. As the *In re Sealed Case* court explained, however, "[s]ystemic interests are best served by remitting such litigants to their own devices rather than by forcing lawyers to put both their reputations and their treasury at the disposal of reprobates."[229]

---

222. *Id.*

223. Brown v. Commonwealth, 226 S.W.3d 74, 79 (Ky. 2007).

224. Model Rules of Prof'l Conduct R. 4.3 (2020) ("The lawyer shall not give legal advice to an unrepresented person, other than the advice to secure counsel, if the lawyer knows or reasonably should know that the interests of such a person are or have a reasonable possibility of being in conflict with the interests of the client.").

225. *See* Cal. Eth. Op. 2019-200, *supra* note 120, 2019 WL 6839934, at *3–4 (discussing a civil case and noting that a lawyer may refuse a client's direction to offer false testimony).

226. Model Rules of Prof'l Conduct R. 3.3(a)(3) (2020).

227. 890 F.2d 15 (7th Cir. 1989).

228. *Id.* at 15–16 (explaining the bases for the firm's belief).

229. *Id.* at 18.

If prospective false testimony surfaces in a criminal case, you should try to dissuade the client or witness from testifying falsely as explained before. If you are unsuccessful, the solution is simple regarding witnesses: do not call them. If the client is the problem, your options vary dramatically depending on whether you reasonably believe that the client will testify falsely or whether you know that he will do so. If you *reasonably believe* that the client will testify falsely, you must call him if he insists on testifying. If he testifies truthfully, there is no problem. If he testifies falsely and you know that he did so, you are then put in the position of having to take reasonable remedial measures on the back end. If, on the other hand, you *know* that the client intends to testify falsely, you find yourself on the terrain mapped in Part III. There your options will depend on the jurisdiction. Keep in mind, however, that even jurisdictions that permit knowingly false testimony in the form of a narrative do so only as a last resort—typically after the lawyer has moved to withdraw or has otherwise provided the court with enough information to suspect perjury. You must always do that which you reasonably can to avoid offering false testimony, even in a passive role. You should not offer narrative testimony without revealing to the court your intention to do so and obtaining the court's approval of that approach. That is doubly good advice in any jurisdiction in which there is no case law or reasoned ethics opinion permitting the narrative approach.

B. False Testimony in Retrospect

Clients and witnesses may surprise lawyers with false testimony, as where they testify in a deposition, at a hearing, or at trial in a manner that the lawyer did not expect. Alternatively, a lawyer may learn that a client or witness testified falsely after the fact; for example, subsequent discovery may expose the falsity of a client's or witness's testimony,[230] or a scared or remorseful client may confess an earlier lie.[231] If the false testimony is material and was offered by either the client or a witness the lawyer called, the lawyer must take reasonable remedial measures.[232] The lawyer must also take reasonable remedial measures regardless of who called the witness or the witness's link to the lawyer if the witness's false testimony is material and by extension either criminal or fraudulent.[233] Indeed, in light of some courts' ambitious

230. *See, e.g.*, Mich. Eth. Op. RI-151, 1992 WL 510842, at *1 (State Bar of Mich., Comm. on Prof'l & Jud. Ethics 1992) (involving clients whose dishonesty was exposed when their son, who was to be deposed after they submitted false affidavits, revealed that he would either have to perjure himself or risk sinking his parents' case by testifying truthfully).

231. *See, e.g.*, *In re* Mack, 519 N.W.2d 900, 901 (Minn. 1994) (involving a client who lied in her deposition in a civil case and confessed to her lawyer several months later).

232. Model Rules of Prof'l Conduct R. 3.3(a)(3) (2020).

233. *Id.* R. 3.3(b).

interpretation of the Model Rule 3.4(b) prohibition against assisting witnesses to testify falsely, lawyers may well be required to attempt to remedy any false testimony about which they know by any witness. Fortunately, lawyers have discretion over which remedial measures to adopt, provided that the measures are reasonably calculated to correct the false testimony.[234]

If a witness surprisingly testifies falsely during the sponsoring lawyer's examination, the lawyer might attempt prompt corrective questioning without disrupting the examination. Most authorities, however, instead suggest that lawyer's first and best option is to confer privately with the client or witness and try to persuade the person to correct the false testimony. This exercise will be awkward, especially if the client or witness springs the false testimony on the lawyer in court. The level of difficulty is lowered where, for example, the client or witness testified falsely in a deposition or an affidavit and there is reasonable time between the false testimony and trial.

If the lawyer cannot persuade the client or witness to retract the false testimony, various options remain depending on the timing of the false testimony. The lawyer might move to strike the false testimony, move for a mistrial, or move to withdraw, although withdrawal alone will rarely be sufficient if the false testimony is before the court.[235] Quite simply, the lawyer's withdrawal will not reverse the false testimony's effect. Regardless of how the lawyer discloses the false testimony to the court, she must attempt to limit her disclosure to (1) preserve as much of the client's confidentiality as possible and (2) cause the client minimal adverse effects.[236] Once the lawyer discloses the false testimony to the court, she must leave further steps to the court or opposing party.[237]

C. Ex Parte Disclosure of False Testimony

A recurring concern is whether a lawyer who is required to disclose false testimony to a court may do so outside the presence of the opposing party. Presumably, the likelihood that a client's confidences will be revealed or that a client's case will be seriously impaired by the disclosure of false testimony is diminished if the lawyer can make any necessary disclosure to the tribunal alone. Although there is authority for the proposition that a criminal defense lawyer may disclose a client's false testimony to a tribunal ex parte,[238] and

234. Restatement (Third) of the Law Governing Lawyers § 120 cmt. h (2000).

235. *Id.* (stating that withdrawal is not a reasonable remedial measure once false testimony is before a trier of fact); Ill. Adv. Op. 13-05, *supra* note 32, 2013 WL 3185023, at *6.

236. Restatement (Third) of the Law Governing Lawyers § 120 cmt. h (2000); Ill. Adv. Op. 13-05, *supra* note 32, 2013 WL 3185023, at *5.

237. Restatement (Third) of the Law Governing Lawyers § 120 cmt. h (2000).

238. *See, e.g.*, United States v. Litchfield, 959 F.2d 1514, 1518 (10th Cir. 1992); State v. DeGuzman, 701 P.2d 1287, 1292 (Haw. 1985); Commonwealth v. Brown, 226 S.W.3d 74, 77 (Ky. 2007); Fla. Eth. Op. 04-1, *supra* note 202, 2005 WL 3985348, at *2.

courts conduct colloquies with criminal defendants with only the defendant and defense counsel present to limit sensitive disclosures and otherwise protect defendants' rights,[239] ex parte disclosure requires judicial permission.[240]

A lawyer must inform other parties of her desire to communicate ex parte with the court before attempting to do so. In many cases a request to communicate ex parte with the court will be met either by objection or with questions concerning the reasons for the lawyer's request, although in criminal cases savvy prosecutors may recognize the issue and accede to the request. How the lawyer responds to such objections or inquiries—or to the court's inquiry into the reason for the lawyer's request—requires a measure of judgment on the lawyer's part and will depend on the facts of the case. Even if an opposing party consents to a lawyer's ex parte communications with a court, however, the court retains the discretion to either permit or decline the invitation. A court's refusal to permit ex parte communication does not excuse a lawyer's duty to disclose false testimony.

D. The Problem of Disclosure in Bench Trials

Parties are understandably nervous about their lawyers revealing their false testimony or that of friendly witnesses in cases in which the court sits as the trier of fact out of the fear that any disclosure will prejudice the court against them. Unlike jury trials, where, depending on the circumstances, it is perhaps possible that jurors may never learn of false testimony, a court conducting a bench trial is unavoidably exposed to the issue. This concern is most pronounced in criminal cases, but it exists in civil trials as well. The same concern arises in arbitrations and administrative hearings, where the tribunal to which disclosure must be made is the fact-finder. However valid these concerns may be, what little authority there is on the subject indicates that lawyers' duties concerning false testimony are the same regardless of whether a jury or the tribunal is the fact-finder.[241] After all, the potential for prejudice exists even in jury trials; for example, in a criminal case in which the defendant testifies in narrative form and is convicted, it is the court that will impose any sentence knowing that the defendant committed perjury. In addition, and as a practical matter, appellate courts generally are inclined to presume that trial courts sitting as fact-finders in criminal cases either

239. *See, e.g.*, United States v. Scott, 909 F.2d 488, 494 n.10 (11th Cir. 1990); United States v. Long, 857 F.2d 436, 446 (8th Cir. 1988).

240. Model Rules of Prof'l Conduct R. 3.5(b) (2020) (providing that during a proceeding a lawyer cannot communicate ex parte with the judge "unless authorized to do so by law or court order").

241. *See, e.g.*, People v. Andrades, 828 N.E.2d 599, 604 (N.Y. 2005) (stating that counsel's "ethical obligations do not change simply because a judge rather than a jury is sitting as the factfinder").

are capable of remaining impartial despite hearing evidence of a defendant's culpability[242] or will take appropriate action to ensure fairness to the defendant if they believe the defendant has testified falsely.[243] There is no basis to think that appellate courts would take a different approach in civil matters. Even so, and regardless of the type of litigation, lawyers must recognize that not all courts approach issues the same way. The decision in a criminal case, *Lowery v. Cardwell*,[244] is illustrative.

Jacqueline Lowery was charged with murder and opted for a bench trial in an Arizona state court. A witness testified that Lowery had walked the decedent to his car. The witness then testified that he heard gunshots in that vicinity. The defense lawyer put Lowery on the stand. She testified that she did not accompany the decedent to his car and denied shooting him. The defense lawyer then sharply ended his questioning and requested a recess. In chambers, the defense lawyer moved to withdraw. When the court asked him to state his reason for seeking to withdraw, he responded that he could not.[245] The court denied the motion. In closing argument to the court, the defense lawyer did not mention Lowery's testimony but instead confined his argument to the existence of reasonable doubt.[246] It was later established in a habeas corpus hearing in federal court that the defense lawyer moved to withdraw and argued as he did in closing because he believed Lowery was lying.[247] In the meantime and as the mere mention of a habeas proceeding clearly indicates, the Arizona trial court found Lowery guilty of murder.

On appeal to the Ninth Circuit in the habeas proceeding, Lowery argued that her defense lawyer's motion to withdraw deprived her of a fair trial. The question for the Ninth Circuit was whether the lawyer's motion to withdraw "amounted to such an unequivocal announcement to the fact finder" that it robbed Lowery of due process.[248] The court concluded that it did based on the facts that the trial judge was the fact-finder, the defense lawyer abruptly stopped questioning Lowery and sought a recess when he did, the defense lawyer moved to withdraw immediately after Lowery's testimony, and in so moving told the court that he could not state a reason for his motion.[249] The only conclusion the trial judge could rationally draw was

242. *See, e.g.*, Garrett v. United States, 642 A.2d 1312, 1315–16 (D.C. 1994) (commenting on the trial judge's performance in case in which the defendant argued that the trial judge should have recused herself based on defense counsel's pretrial comments suggesting that the defendant intended to perjure himself).

243. *See, e.g.*, United States v. Elzy, 22 M.J. 640, 641–43 (A.C.M.R. 1986) (discussing military judges sitting as finders of fact).

244. 575 F.2d 727 (9th Cir. 1978).

245. *Id.* at 729.

246. *Id.*

247. *Id.*

248. *Id.* at 730.

249. *Id.*

that the defense lawyer believed that Lowery had perjured herself.[250] The *Lowery* court could not escape the conclusion that Lowery had been denied a fair trial and that a writ of habeas corpus should therefore issue.[251]

V. Conclusion

False testimony by clients and witnesses is an age-old problem. It is also one of the thorniest professional responsibility issues that trial lawyers face. Challenges for lawyers are greatest in criminal cases, where defendants may be entitled to testify on their own behalf even when their lawyers know that they intend to testify falsely. But lawyers' duty of candor creates tensions even in civil litigation. Although lawyers can frequently prevent clients and witnesses in civil matters from testifying falsely simply by keeping them off the witness stand, that is not always a solution, and lawyers' disclosure obligations may seriously impair client relationships in any event. Regardless of the type of case, surprise perjury by a client is a huge advocacy nightmare in addition to posing a substantial ethics challenge. The reality for trial lawyers is that our professional responsibility regime generally enforces their duty of candor to the tribunal over their competing duties of confidentiality and loyalty to clients. As a result, false testimony by clients and witnesses will continue to vex conscientious lawyers well into the future.

250. *Id.*
251. *Id.* at 731.

11
Lawyers as Witnesses

I. Introduction

A lawyer's identification as a fact witness in litigation can be an unfavorable and often complicating development. The possibility that a lawyer may be a witness often suggests that something has gone awry in the lawyer's representation of the client for or against whom she may be testifying. Perhaps the lawyer drafted transactional documents for a client that become the focal point in litigation when the deal unravels. A lawyer may have witnessed events on which a client's liability turns in litigation, making the lawyer a valuable source of proof for the client or an opponent. Lawyers' appearance as witnesses in criminal cases may pose substantial problems, whether because a defense lawyer's status as a necessary witness foreshadows an ineffective assistance of counsel claim, because compelling the defense lawyer's testimony against her client will violate her duty of loyalty, or because a prosecutor's testimony poses a significant risk of prejudice to a defendant. Regardless of the circumstances, lawyers and courts alike are uncomfortable with the dual roles of lawyer and fact witness.

This chapter focuses on the so-called advocate-witness rule or lawyer-witness rule, which generally prohibits lawyers from representing clients at trial in cases in which the lawyer is likely to be a necessary witness. The advocate-witness rule is rooted in evidence law, but it is now a matter of professional responsibility.

II. An Overview of Lawyers as Fact Witnesses

The advocate-witness rule is embodied in Model Rule of Professional Conduct 3.7(a).[1] Model Rule 3.7(a) provides that a lawyer "shall not act as advocate at a trial in which the lawyer is likely to be a necessary witness,"

1. Model Rules of Prof'l Conduct R. 3.7(a) (2020).

except in three instances.[2] The three exceptions to this ban are (1) where the lawyer's testimony relates to an uncontested issue, (2) where the lawyer's testimony relates to the nature and value of legal services rendered in the case, or (3) where the lawyer's disqualification would work substantial hardship on the client.

The prohibition against lawyers testifying as witnesses in trials in which they also serve as advocates is principally intended to protect the fact-finder from confusion.[3] For example, it may not be clear to jurors whether an advocate-witness's testimony is proof of some fact or the lawyer's analysis of the proof. The rule also protects the opposing party from unfair prejudice accompanying the lawyer's dual roles. After all, the act of taking an oath does not change the fact that the lawyer is an advocate and may be less than fully objective when testifying.[4] At the same time, the act of taking the oath may serve to enhance the lawyer's credibility as an advocate in the jury's eyes. Furthermore, a lawyer testifying as a witness may explain evidence rather than offer it, unfairly influencing the jury in the process.

Similarly, permitting a lawyer who is a witness to events at issue in a case to participate as an advocate at trial may create what some courts refer to as the "unsworn witness" problem.[5] In such a case, the lawyer may be able to convey firsthand knowledge of relevant events without having to swear an oath or submit to cross-examination.[6] That places the opposing party at an unfair disadvantage and impairs the fact-finding process.[7]

In criminal cases, the advocate-witnesses are especially pertinent to prosecutors because of the sensitive role they assume as the government's representatives in court.[8] A prosecutor's testimony as a witness plainly poses a heightened risk of prejudice to the defendant.[9] For example, there is sub-

2. *Id.*

3. Walker v. Newman Univ., Inc., No. 19-cv-2005-DDC-TJJ, 2019 WL 2268971, at *3 (D. Kan. May 28, 2019) (referring to jury confusion); Doe v. Yim, 269 Cal. Rptr. 3d 613, 620 (Ct. App. 2020); People v. Ehrnstein, 417 P.3d 813, 817 (Colo. 2018) (referring to jury confusion); Steinert v. Steinert, 897 N.E.2d 603, 606 (Mass. App. Ct. 2008); *In re* Keenan, 501 S.W.3d 74, 77 (Tex. 2016) (quoting Anderson Producing Inc. v. Koch Oil Co., 929 S.W.2d 416, 422 (Tex. 1996)).

4. Along the same general lines, courts' enforcement of the advocate-witness rule "mitigates the potential negative perception by the public that the attorney colored his or her testimony to further the client's case." Smaland Beach Ass'n, Inc. v. Genova, 959 N.E.2d 955, 962 (Mass. 2012).

5. United States v. Evanson, 584 F.3d 904, 909 (10th Cir. 2009); State v. Carlson, 440 P.3d 364, 387 (Alaska Ct. App. 2019).

6. *Evanson*, 584 F.3d at 909 (quoting United States v. Locascio, 6 F.3d 924, 933 (2d Cir. 1993)); *Carlson*, 440 P.3d at 387 (quoting *Locascio*, 6 F.3d at 933–34).

7. *Evanson*, 584 F.3d at 909 (quoting *Locascio*, 6 F.3d at 934); Wyndham Vacation Ownership, Inc. v. Vacation Transfers Unlimited, LLC, No. 3:18-cv-01399, 2020 WL 134132, at *4 (M.D. Tenn. Jan. 10, 2020); *Carlson*, 440 P.3d at 387 (quoting *Locascio*, 6 F.3d at 933–34)).

8. People v. Blue, 724 N.E.2d 920, 940 (Ill. 2000); Walker v. State, 818 A.2d 1078, 1099–1100 (Md. 2003).

9. *See, e.g.*, United States v. Edwards, 154 F.3d 915, 921–22 (9th Cir. 1998) (reversing a defendant's conviction and stating that the policies underlying the advocate-witness rule in a criminal

stantial concern that jurors will be unduly influenced by the prestige and prominence of the prosecutor's office and will base their credibility determinations on improper factors.[10] Accordingly, the principle that a prosecutor should not testify as a witness in a case she is prosecuting is deeply rooted in the law. Prosecutors' assertions of personal knowledge of facts in argument, examinations, or objections at trial may violate the advocate-witness rule even if the prosecutor does not testify.[11]

Finally, Rule 3.7(a) protects a client from conflicts of interest arising from the dual roles of lawyer and witness. For example, if the lawyer must testify adversely or ambivalently with respect to the client's cause, the client may be harmed as a result.[12] Even if the lawyer's testimony assists the client, the lawyer may have a difficult time effectively representing her client while simultaneously trying to protect her own reputation as a truthful witness.[13] Alternatively, a lawyer may not pursue a line of questioning or might abandon a theory of recovery or a defense to avoid disqualification based on the lawyer's status as a necessary witness. The mere possibility of a conflict of

case "are related to the concern that jurors will be unduly influenced by the prestige and prominence of the prosecutor's office and will base their credibility determinations on improper factors," and explaining that in criminal cases the advocate-witness rule was "designed to prevent prosecutors from taking advantage of the natural tendency of jury members to believe in the honesty of lawyers in general, and government attorneys in particular"); State v. Anthony, 266 So. 3d 415, 426–29 (La. Ct. App. 2019) (determining that the defendant did not receive a fair trial where the "screening prosecutor" vouched for the credibility of the State's witnesses and improperly commented on the defendant's guilt, while using the prestige and dignity of his office to bolster the State's case).

10. People v. Linton, 302 P.3d 927, 959–60 (Cal. 2013) (quoting People v. Donaldson, 113 Cal. Rptr. 2d 548, 556 (Ct. App. 2001)).

11. *See, e.g.*, United States v. Rangel-Guzman, 752 F.3d 1222, 1224–25 (9th Cir. 2014) (involving a prosecutor who improperly became "her own rebuttal witness"); *Blue*, 724 N.E.2d at 938–40 (involving prosecutors who essentially testified through speaking objections); *Walker*, 818 A.2d at 1099–1104 (granting a mistrial where prosecutor improperly asserted her personal knowledge of facts while examining a witness); State v. Sierra, 523 S.E.2d 187, 191–92 (S.C. Ct. App. 1999) (finding that the trial court should have sustained objections where the prosecutor injected personal knowledge of facts into her cross-examination and then argued her version of the facts in closing).

12. *See, e.g.*, Sweeney v. Dayton, 416 P.3d 187, 190–91 (Mont. 2018) (barring the trial court from "compelling [the defense lawyer] to take the stand and be examined against her wishes regarding communications with her own client to prove that he committed a new offense").

13. *See, e.g.*, People v. Ortiz, 44 N.E.3d 924, 929 (N.Y. 2015) ("Defendant's counsel was placed in [an] . . . untenable position in this case when the People introduced counsel's statement from arraignment . . . mistakenly stat[ing] that defendant told her Valenzuela came after him with a razor blade instead of a knife. The prosecutor sought to use this statement to attack defendant's credibility, and in doing so, caused defendant's advocate to become his adversary. . . . The situation went from bad to worse when it became clear that the only way for defense counsel to rehabilitate her client's credibility was to impugn her own, moments before she would argue for her client's innocence in summation.").

interest, however, will not support a lawyer's disqualification or withdrawal based on the advocate-witness rule.[14]

III. Understanding the Advocate-Witness Rule

A. The Scope and Reach of Model Rule 3.7(a)

1. An Overview of Model Rule 3.7(a)

Again, Model Rule 3.7(a) provides that "[a] lawyer shall not act as advocate at a trial in which the lawyer is likely to be a necessary witness,"[15] subject to certain exceptions. Model Rule 3.7(a) only disqualifies lawyers in their representational capacity; it does not bar their testimony as witnesses.[16] Thus, the rule does not apply to a lawyer who appears pro se,[17] nor does it apply to a lawyer who is represented by another lawyer in a proceeding. The rule applies regardless of the party the lawyer will testify for.[18] Because the lawyer-witness rule applies where a lawyer representing a client seeks to serve as a witness in that very proceeding, the fact that a client's *former* attorney will likely be a necessary witness at trial provides no basis to object to the testimony.[19]

2. The Model Rule 3.7(a) Limitation to Trials

Breaking down the rule, the first aspect to be addressed is its limitation to trials. The term "trial" encompasses arbitrations and other judicial and quasi-judicial proceedings.[20] The rule generally does not apply to a

---

14. *See, e.g.*, Kenner v. Commonwealth, 835 S.E.2d 107, 116 (Va. Ct. App. 2019) (affirming the trial court's decision not to allow a criminal defense lawyer to withdraw based on a conflict of interest "because an actual conflict had not yet ripened").

15. Model Rules of Prof'l Conduct R. 3.7(a) (2020).

16. First Constitution Bank v. Caldrello, 656 A.2d 1053, 1055 (Conn. App. Ct. 1995).

17. *In re* Waldrop, No. 15-14689-JDL, 2016 WL 6090849, at *4–5 (Bankr. W.D. Okla. Oct. 18, 2016); Succession of Houston, 253 So. 3d 836, 844 (La. Ct. App. 2018) (citing Farrington v. Law Firm of Sessions, Fishman, 687 So. 2d 997, 1000 (La. 1997)); Escobar v. Mazie, 217 A.3d 163, 169 (N.J. Super. Ct. App. Div. 2019); Greenberg v. Grace Plaza Nursing & Rehab. Ctr., 103 N.Y.S.3d 559, 561 (App. Div. 2019); Brooks v. S.C. Comm'n on Indigent Def., 797 S.E.2d 402, 409 (S.C. Ct. App. 2017). The rule certainly does not apply to a non-lawyer who decides to represent herself at trial. *See, e.g.*, United States v. Wilson, 979 F.3d 889, 914 n.13 (11th Cir. 2020) (stating that the advocate-witness rule did not apply to a criminal defendant who represented himself at trial).

18. Weigel v. Farmers Ins. Co., 158 S.W.3d 147, 152–53 (Ark. 2004).

19. *First Constitution Bank*, 656 A.2d at 1055–56 (discussing Rule 3.7); *see also* Ramey v. Dist. 141, Int'l Ass'n of Machinists & Aerospace Workers, 378 F.3d 269, 282–83 (2d Cir. 2004) (mentioning no ethics rules).

20. *See, e.g.*, Demesa v. Adams, 994 N.E.2d 1007, 1019–20 (Ill. App. Ct. 2013) (applying the rule in an administrative proceeding concerning a nurse's licensure before an administrative law judge); *In re* Disciplinary Proceeding Against Pfefer, 344 P.3d 1200, 1203–04 (Wash. 2015) (applying the rule in a lawyer disciplinary proceeding).

lawyer-witness's pretrial involvement in a case,[21] or to a lawyer-witness's representation of a client in other non-advocacy roles.[22] Even in a case in which a lawyer-witness would be disqualified if she were to represent a client at trial, she generally may represent the client in other ways in the litigation, such as preparing documents or pleadings, preparing and responding to written discovery, researching legal issues, handling pretrial negotiations, appearing at mediations and settlement conferences, and so on.[23] A lawyer-witness may represent a client in non-evidentiary pretrial hearings.[24] A lawyer may even testify at a pretrial hearing without being disqualified.[25] In the criminal context, a defense lawyer may testify at a hearing on a client's motion to withdraw a guilty plea without being disqualified.[26] If lawyer-witnesses are disqualified from representing clients at trial, they remain able to consult with substitute counsel and assist with trial preparation.[27] Further-

21. Green v. Am. Fed'n of Teachers/Ill. Fed'n of Teachers Local 604, No. 12 CV 1162, 2015 WL 1509776, at *5 (N.D. Ill. Mar. 30, 2015); Amusement Indus., Inc. v. Stern, 657 F. Supp. 2d 458, 460–63 (S.D.N.Y. 2009); Hill v. Culebra Conservation & Dev. Auth., 599 F. Supp. 2d 88, 95 (D.P.R. 2009); Foster v. JLG Indus., 372 F. Supp. 2d 792, 798–99 (M.D. Pa. 2005); Doe v. Yim, 269 Cal. Rptr. 3d 613, 620 (Ct. App. 2020); People v. Ehrnstein, 471 P.3d 813, 817 (Colo. 2018); KMS Rest. Corp. v. Searcy, Denney, Scarola, Barnhart & Shipley P.A., 107 So. 3d 552, 552 (Fla. Dist. Ct. App. 2013); Smaland Beach Ass'n, Inc. v. Genova, 959 N.E.2d 955, 966–67 (Mass. 2012); Prac. Mgmt. Sols., LLC v. Eighth Jud. Dist. Ct., No. 68901, 2016 WL 2757512, at *4 (Nev. May 10, 2016); Mich. Ethics Op. RI-299, 1997 WL 1108733, at *2 (State Bar of Mich., Comm. on Prof'l & Jud. Ethics 1997); State Bar of Mont., Ethics Comm., Ethics Op. 140519, at 2, 5 (2014) [hereinafter Mont. Ethics Op. 140519]; 2011 N.C. Ethics Op. 1, 2011 WL 1979602, at *1 (N.C. State Bar 2011) [hereinafter 2011 N.C. Ethics Op. 1].

22. *See, e.g.*, Gabayzadeh v. Taylor, 639 F. Supp. 2d 298, 303–04 (E.D.N.Y. 2009) (involving two corporate lawyers who would not advocate for client at trial).

23. Droste v. Julien, 477 F.3d 1030, 1035–36 (8th Cir. 2007); CEF Funding, L.L.C. v. Sher Garner Cahill Richter Klein & Hilbert, L.L.C., No. 09-6623, 2010 WL 2773116, at *2–3 (E.D. La. July 9, 2010); Williams v. Borden Chem., Inc., 501 F. Supp. 2d 1219, 1221–23 (S.D. Iowa 2007) (permitting a lawyer to participate in pretrial activities other than depositions); Merrill Lynch Bus. Fin. Servs., Inc. v. Nudell, 239 F. Supp. 2d 1170, 1174 (D. Colo. 2003) (noting, however, that a lawyer-witness may be disqualified from pretrial activities if the activities include obtaining evidence that, if admitted at trial, would reveal the lawyer's dual role); Main Events Prods., LLC v. Lacy, 220 F. Supp. 2d 353, 356 (D.N.J. 2002); Caplan v. Braverman, 876 F. Supp. 710, 711 (E.D. Pa. 1995); Fognani v. Young, 115 P.3d 1268, 1276–77 (Colo. 2005); Goff v. Goff, 276 So. 3d 83, 88 (Fla. Dist. Ct. App. 2019) (quoting Columbo v. Puig, 745 So. 2d 1106, 1107 (Fla. Dist. Ct. App. 1999)); DiMartino v. Eighth Jud. Dist. Ct., 66 P.3d 945, 946–47 (Nev. 2003); Escobar v. Mazie, 217 A.3d 163, 168 (N.J. Super. Ct. App. Div. 2019); Cunningham v. Sams, 588 S.E.2d 484, 487 (N.C. Ct. App. 2003); *In re* Bahn, 113 S.W.3d 865, 873 (Tex. App. 2000); Mont. Ethics Op. 140519, *supra* note 21, at 5; 2011 N.C. Ethics Op. 1, *supra* note 21, 2011 WL 1979602, at *1. *But see* Giuffra v. Dershowitz, 410 F. Supp. 3d 564, 581 (S.D.N.Y. 2019) (observing that there is no justification for allowing a lawyer who is likely to be a necessary witness at trial to represent a party in pretrial matters).

24. Lowe v. Experian, 328 F. Supp. 2d 1122, 1127 (D. Kan. 2004) (declining, however, to allow the attorney to appear at evidentiary hearings).

25. State v. Van Dyck, 827 A.2d 192, 195 (N.H. 2003).

26. Bridgeman v. Dist. Att'y for the Suffolk Dist., 30 N.E.3d 806, 826 (Mass. 2015).

27. Royal Travel, Inc. v. Shell Mgmt. Haw., Inc., No. 08-00314 JMS-LEK, 2009 WL 649929, at *6 (D. Haw. Mar. 12, 2009).

more, a lawyer who is disqualified from representing a client at trial because the lawyer is a necessary witness may nevertheless represent the client in post-trial proceedings,[28] including appeals.[29]

Given the dominant rationale for the advocate-witness rule, that is, protecting the fact-finder from confusion, a lawyer is more likely to be disqualified where the case will be tried to a jury rather than to the court. In a bench trial, the judge should be able to differentiate between a lawyer's role as advocate or witness.[30] Similarly, there is generally no reason to disqualify a lawyer-witness from representing a client in arbitration, since arbitrators should be able to separate a lawyer-witness's dual roles. The disqualification analysis cannot end at the fact-finder's identity, however, because potential jury confusion is not the only reason for preventing lawyers from functioning as advocates at trial—the unsworn witness problem and conflicts of interest also justify disqualifying lawyer-witnesses in some cases. Certainly, the prejudicial effect that a lawyer-witness's conflict of interest may have on her client's case is a crucial consideration no matter who serves as the finder of fact. As a result, lawyer-witnesses may be disqualified or barred from participating in bench trials and arbitrations on the right facts.[31]

Although the plain language of Model Rule 3.7(a) limits it to trials, and it is generally true that lawyers who are disqualified from serving as advocates at trial may nonetheless represent their clients in pretrial and post-trial activities, some courts hold that disqualification outside of trial is appropriate in other cases at the discretion of the trial court.[32] Such cases should

28. People v. Ehrnstein, 471 P.3d 813, 817 (Colo. 2018); *Goff*, 276 So. 3d at 88 (quoting *Columbo*, 745 So. 2d at 1107); *see, e.g.*, *In re* S.G., 91 P.3d 443, 450 (Colo. App. 2004) (holding that Rule 3.7(a) did not apply to a motion seeking relief from a judgment); Willacy v. State, 967 So. 2d 131, 139 (Fla. 2007) (determining that Rule 3.7(a) did not apply to a hearing on a motion for new trial); State v. Espe, Nos. A10-1569, A11-2066, 2012 WL 4328611, at *5 (Minn. Ct. App. Sept. 24, 2012) (allowing a prosecutor to testify in a post-conviction proceeding).

29. United States v. Berger, 251 F.3d 894, 906 (10th Cir. 2001).

30. *See, e.g.*, *In re* Waldrop, No. 15-14689-JDL, 2016 WL 6090849, at *5 (Bankr. W.D. Okla. Oct. 18, 2016) ("Those considerations are of little concern when a case is tried to the court rather than a jury. This [c]ourt as the trier of fact is not going to be confused, as might a jury, whether [the lawyer's] role of both advocate and witness 'so blurs the line between argument and evidence that the ability to find facts is undermined.'" (quoting Ramey v. Dist. 141, Int'l Ass'n of Machinists & Aerospace Workers, 378 F.3d 269, 282–83 (2d Cir. 2004)); Plymouth Indus., LLC v. Sioux Steel Co., No. 8:05CV196, 2006 WL 3392193, at *3 (D. Neb. Oct. 23, 2006) (declining to a disqualify lawyer in a bench trial); Rayco Mfg., Inc. v. Murphy, Rogers, Sloss & Gambel, 142 N.E.3d 1267, 1292 (Ohio Ct. App. 2019) (reasoning that the judge was not likely to be confused by the lawyers' dual roles in a case tried to the court with an advisory jury).

31. *See, e.g.*, Beary v. Deese, No. 16-15757, 2018 WL 3417878, at *15 (E.D. La. July 13, 2018) (refusing to permit a lawyer-witness to sit at counsel table to assist the lawyer who would be trying the case because the opposing party asked that all witnesses be sequestered; the court could find no reason to treat the lawyer-witness any differently than an ordinary fact witness).

32. *See, e.g.*, Doe v. Yim, 269 Cal. Rptr. 3d 613, 620 (Ct. App. 2020) (stating that Rule 3.7(a) generally prohibits a lawyer from testifying a pretrial evidentiary hearing); Abrishamian v. Wash. Med. Grp., P.C., 86 A.3d 681, 694 (Md. Ct. Spec. App. 2014) (affirming the trial court's

be rare, however, with deviation from the rule most likely to occur where the lawyer's pretrial activity "includes obtaining evidence which, if admitted at trial, would reveal the attorney's dual role."[33] Depositions accordingly pose a special concern.[34] Because depositions often are read into evidence at trial, deposition transcripts may be used at trial to impeach witnesses or refresh their recollections, and videotaped depositions are regularly played for juries, lawyers may be disqualified from representing clients in depositions if the depositions cannot be used at trial without revealing the lawyers' dual roles.[35] In fact, advocate-witness issues should not be a factor where stenographic depositions are used because the jury does not need to be informed of the questioner's identity.[36] Problems are most likely to surface where depositions are recorded on video because the jury may see the lawyer or recognize the lawyer's voice when the video is played at trial. Even then, the lawyer's disqualification may not be required because a court can cure possible jury confusion through less drastic means, such as by issuing a jury instruction[37] or by requiring the parties to edit the video in some reasonable fashion.[38]

Some courts have gone so far as to expand the rule to preclude lawyers' testimony in affidavits at summary judgment.[39] Other courts expressly

disqualification of a lawyer from all participation in the case); Jensen v. Poindexter, 352 P.3d 1201, 1205–08 (Okla. 2015) (concluding that a lawyer in a paternity case who ignored his statutory duty to report suspected child abuse effectively became a forensic interviewer, likely tainted the fact-finding process with improper interviewing techniques, probably unduly influenced the child witness, and submitted affidavits attesting to a fact witness's credibility should be disqualified altogether).

33. World Youth Day, Inc. v. Famous Artists Merch. Exch., Inc., 866 F. Supp. 1297, 1303 (D. Colo. 1994); *see, e.g.*, DP Creations LLC v. Ortiz, No. 2:19-cv-948 HCN DBP, 2020 WL 1249480, at *3 (D. Utah Mar. 16, 2020) (adopting this position); Northbrook Digital, LLC v. Vendio Servs., Inc., 625 F. Supp. 2d 728, 765–66 (D. Minn. 2008) (discussing potential confusion that might result from a lawyer's participation in depositions).

34. *But see, e.g.*, Escobar v. Mazie, 217 A.3d 163, 168 (N.J. Super. Ct. App. Div. 2019) (permitting lawyer-witnesses to represent defendants at depositions).

35. Katica v. Allstate Fire & Cas. Ins. Co., No. CV 16-00150-DLC-RWA, 2018 WL 3475479, at *2 (D. Mont. July 19, 2018) (prohibiting the lawyer from taking depositions and from appearing as trial counsel); Lowe v. Experian, 328 F. Supp. 2d 1122, 1127 (D. Kan. 2004) (prohibiting the lawyer from defending depositions in addition to taking them); Fognani v. Young, 115 P.3d 1268, 1277 (Colo. 2005).

36. Amusement Indus., Inc. v. Stern, 657 F. Supp. 2d 458, 463 (S.D.N.Y. 2009).

37. *Id.*

38. *See, e.g.*, Neelon v. Krueger, No. 12-cv-11198-IT, 2015 WL 874420, at *2 (D. Mass. Mar. 2, 2015) (stating that "should this case proceed to trial, the court will entertain a . . . motion in limine seeking an order excluding particular portions of the relevant depositions or requiring other corrective measures to avoid the potential for jury confusion").

39. *See, e.g.*, Int'l Res. Ventures, Inc. v. Diamond Mining Co. of Am., Inc., 934 S.W.2d 218, 220 (Ark. 1996) ("We have held that Rule 3.7 is applicable to a lawyer's giving evidence by affidavit as well as by testimony in open court."); Franklin Credit Mgmt. Corp. v. Gray, 2 So. 3d 598, 603–05 (La. Ct. App. 2009) (applying the advocate-witness rule to find that a lawyer's affidavit was not competent evidence).

decline to do so,[40] however, and those courts that broadly hold that Rule 3.7(a) does not apply to lawyers' pretrial activities would presumably hold that it therefore does not preclude lawyers from offering affidavits at summary judgment.[41] As a practical and strategic matter, lawyers who offer affidavits in efforts to defeat or support summary judgment must consider the possibility that an affidavit may signal their necessity as witnesses at trial, and thus lead to their future disqualification. In the meantime, the fact that a lawyer offers affidavit testimony should be inconsequential from an evidentiary or procedural standpoint. Although it is generally true that evidence offered to oppose or support summary judgment must be admissible at trial, courts and lawyers alike must remember that Model Rule 3.7(a) disqualifies lawyers from serving in representational capacities at trial—it does not render their testimony inadmissible. Thus, a lawyer's affidavit testimony may properly be used at the summary stage of a case even though the lawyer may be disqualified from representing the client at trial.

In addition to its clear language, there is no policy reason commending the rule's application to lawyers' affidavit testimony at summary judgment. Because it is the judge who reads motions, the lawyer's dual roles should not be confusing.[42] It is equally unlikely that a judge, as compared to a jury, will be unfairly influenced by the lawyer's dual roles.[43] To the extent that the rule

---

40. *See, e.g.*, Carroll v. Town of Univ. Park, 12 F. Supp. 2d 475, 486 (D. Md. 1997) (declining to strike a lawyer's affidavit in apparent acceptance of her argument that Rule 3.7 only applied to her testimony at trial).

41. *See* Jackson v. Adcock, No. Civ. A. 03-3369, 2004 WL 1661199, at *4 (E.D. La. July 22, 2004) (stating that Rule 3.7 plainly does not apply to pretrial activities); Merrill Lynch Bus. Fin. Servs., Inc. v. Nudell, 239 F. Supp. 2d 1170, 1174 (D. Colo. 2003) (explaining that Rule 3.7(a) "does not automatically require that a lawyer be disqualified from pretrial activities, such as . . . motions practice."); Caplan v. Braverman, 876 F. Supp. 710, 711 (E.D. Pa. 1995) (stating that Rule 3.7 "only prevents a lawyer who will be a witness from acting as an 'advocate at trial'"); Columbo v. Puig, 745 So. 2d 1106, 1107 (Fla. Dist. Ct. App. 1999) (noting that Rule 3.7 applies only to a lawyer's performance at trial and does not prohibit a lawyer-witness from serving as an advocate in pretrial and post-trial activities); DiMartino v. Eighth Jud. Dist. Ct., 66 P.3d 945, 946–47 (Nev. 2003) (adopting the view that a lawyer who is likely to be a necessary witness may still represent a client in pretrial matters).

42. *See* State v. Van Dyck, 827 A.2d 192, 195 (N.H. 2003) (discussing a lawyer's testimony at a pretrial hearing, the court observed that "[u]nlike a jury, a judge is unlikely to confuse the roles of advocate and witness or to deem an attorney credible simply because he is an attorney."); *see also* Ramey v. Dist. 141, Int'l Ass'n of Machinists & Aerospace Workers, 378 F.3d 269, 282 (2d Cir. 2004) (explaining that the lawyer-witness rule applies "first and foremost" where the lawyer-witness is representing a client "before a jury"); Roberts v. State, 840 So. 2d 962, 970 (Fla. 2003) (finding no basis for Rule 3.7 disqualification where a prosecutor testified in a post-conviction evidentiary hearing before a judge); *DiMartino*, 66 P.3d at 947 (noting that pretrial disqualification of a lawyer-witness generally is not necessary because there is no danger of the confusion and prejudice that may result from a lawyer appearing as an advocate and a witness before a jury).

43. *See Van Dyck*, 827 A.2d at 195 (asserting that a judge is unlikely to deem an attorney credible as a witness simply because he is an attorney); *see also Roberts*, 840 So. 2d at 970 (noting that lawyer's dual role would not prejudice opponent in hearing before a judge); *DiMartino*, 66 P.3d at

aims at client protection, it is difficult to see how a lawyer's submission of an affidavit could create a conflict of interest. If the lawyer faces a conflict because she has testimony to offer that is harmful to the client's cause, she will not offer that testimony in an affidavit; that sort of conflict is a problem where the opposing party seeks to call the lawyer as a witness, not where the lawyer volunteers testimony. In short, courts are wrong to extend Rule 3.7(a) to lawyers' affidavit testimony at summary judgment.

3. *The Lawyer's Likely Status as a Necessary Witness*

Looking further at the rule, what does it take to establish that a lawyer is "likely to be a necessary witness" at trial? Disqualification cannot be ordered upon an opponent's mere representation that the lawyer identified is a necessary witness,[44] will be called as a witness,[45] or simply *may be* a witness.[46] Conclusory allegations concerning a lawyer's role as a witness will not support the lawyer's disqualification under Model Rule 3.7(a).[47] Rather, a party seeking to disqualify a lawyer under Rule 3.7(a) bears the burden of proving that the lawyer's proposed testimony "is relevant, material, not merely cumulative, and unobtainable elsewhere."[48] Thus, if lawyers'

947 (noting that because the lawyer-witness rule is intended to eliminate confusion and prejudice resulting from the lawyer's dual roles in front of the jury, pretrial disqualification generally is not warranted).

44. Bradford v. State, 734 So. 2d 364, 369 (Ala. Crim. App. 1999) ("The necessity standard requires more than mere speculation that counsel will be required to testify."); Hiatt v. Estate of Hiatt, 837 So. 2d 1132, 1133 (Fla. Dist. Ct. App. 2003); Quality Developers, Inc. v. Thorman, 31 P.3d 296, 306 (Kan. Ct. App. 2001) (noting that the plaintiff could not point to any testimony that the lawyers might give that would be adverse to their client's interests and stating that "[m]ere speculation is not a sufficient basis to disqualify a lawyer as a necessary witness"); Beller v. Crow, 742 N.W.2d 230, 235 (Neb. 2007); *DiMartino*, 66 P.3d at 946–47.

45. Humphrey v. McLaren, 402 N.W.2d 535, 541 (Minn. 1987); *Van Dyck*, 827 A.2d at 194 (quoting *Humphrey*); Thompson v. Goetz, 455 N.W.2d 580, 587 (N.D. 1990) (quoting Sec. Gen. Life Ins. v. Super. Ct., 718 P.2d 986, 988 (Ariz. 1986)); Akron v. Carter, 942 N.E.2d 409, 416 (Ohio Ct. App. 2010); Spence v. Flynt, 816 P.2d 771, 779 (Wyo. 1991).

46. *See, e.g.*, Holbrook v. Benson, 3 N.E.3d 788, 792 (Ohio Ct. App. 2013) (reversing trial court that disqualified a lawyer based on the opponent's "conclusory" representation that the lawyer might be a witness where the trial court "did not make a finding that [the lawyer] was a necessary witness, but found only that [the lawyer] *may* be a material witness in the case").

47. *See, e.g.*, Mills v. Hausmann-McNally, S.C., 992 F. Supp. 2d 885, 895 (S.D. Ind. 2014) (rejecting the defendant's "perfunctory argument" as to why two lawyers for the plaintiff were necessary witnesses); DiNardo Seaside Tower Ltd. v. Sikorsky Aircraft Corp., 100 A.3d 413, 438–39 (Conn. App. Ct. 2014) (rejecting the plaintiff's Rule 3.7(a) disqualification argument where the plaintiff made only bald assertions about the need for disqualification and did not explain why the defense lawyer was a necessary witness); Cathedral Ct. Assocs., L.P. v. Cathedral Props. Corp., 983 N.Y.S.2d 277, 280 (App. Div. 2014) (stating that the appellants' "conclusory assertions" were insufficient for disqualification).

48. Merrill Lynch Bus. Fin. Servs., Inc. v. Nuvell, 239 F. Supp. 2d 1170, 1173 (D. Colo. 2003); *see also* Fognani v. Young, 115 P.3d 1268, 1274 (Colo. 2005) (determining whether a lawyer is likely to be a necessary witness "involves consideration of the nature of the case, with emphasis

intended testimony is irrelevant,[49] immaterial,[50] cumulative,[51] or otherwise inadmissible,[52] or the same evidence can be obtained from other sources,[53]

on the subject of the lawyer's testimony, the weight the testimony might have in resolving disputed issues, and the availability of other witnesses or documentary evidence which might independently establish the relevant issues"); Cohen v. Rogers, 789 S.E.2d 352, 362 (Ga. Ct. App. 2016) (explaining that the party moving to disqualify a lawyer under Rule 3.7 must demonstrate "that the lawyer's testimony is relevant to disputed, material questions of fact and that there is no other evidence available to prove those facts"); Commonwealth v. Delnegro, 75 N.E.3d 73, 80 (Mass. App. Ct. 2017) (quoting Carta v. Lumbermens Mut. Cas. Co., 419 F. Supp. 2d 23, 31 (D. Mass. 2006)); Furstenfeld v. Pepin, 869 N.W.2d 353, 365 (Neb. Ct. App. 2015) ("A party seeking to call opposing counsel can prove that counsel is a necessary witness by showing that (1) the proposed testimony is material and relevant to the determination of the issues being litigated and (2) the evidence is unobtainable elsewhere."); State v. Schmitt, 102 P.3d 856, 859 (Wash. Ct. App. 2004) (stating that a lawyer should be disqualified under Rule 3.7 only upon a showing of "compelling circumstances," which means that the movant "must show that the attorney will provide material evidence unobtainable elsewhere").

49. *See, e.g.*, Satchwell v. Comm'r of Corr., 988 A.2d 907, 913–14 (Conn. App. Ct. 2010) (finding that a subpoena was properly quashed because the subpoenaed lawyer's testimony was not relevant to any issue in the proceeding); Leaseamerica Corp. v. Stewart, 876 P.2d 184, 193 (Kan. Ct. App. 1994) (holding that an attorney should not be disqualified where his potential testimony was unrelated to issues in the lawsuit); *In re* Estate of Susser, 657 N.W.2d 147, 152 (Mich. Ct. App. 2002) (holding that the trial court did not err in refusing to disqualify a lawyer where he would have testified about irrelevant issue); State v. Smith, 749 S.E.2d 507, 510–11 (N.C. Ct. App. 2013) (rejecting the defendant's ineffective assistance of counsel argument where the lawyer's testimony would have been neither relevant nor material).

50. *See, e.g.*, Gateway Fam. Worship Ctrs., Inc. v. H.O.P.E. Found. Ministries, Inc., 535 S.E.2d 286, 289 (Ga. Ct. App. 2000) (holding that an attorney should not have been disqualified because two other witnesses could testify to key facts, thus making the attorney's testimony unnecessary, and because his testimony was immaterial and would amount to hearsay); State v. Cesnik, No. COA 16-590, 2017 WL 490486, at *5–6 (N.C. Ct. App. Feb. 7, 2017) (concluding that the defendant's lawyer was not a necessary witness because his testimony would have been immaterial given the prosecution's theory of the case).

51. *See, e.g.*, Horaist v. Doctor's Hosp. of Opelousas, 255 F.3d 261, 267 (5th Cir. 2001) (deciding issue under Louisiana Rule 3.7(a)); Markham Contracting Co. v. First Am. Title Ins. Co., No. 1 CA-CV 12-0195, 2013 WL 3828690, at *7 (Ariz. Ct. App. July 18, 2013) (concluding that the trial court did not err by excluding testimony by a lawyer that would have been cumulative and superfluous); Martinez v. Hous. Auth. of DeKalb Cnty., 590 S.E.2d 245, 250 (Ga. Ct. App. 2003) ("[The defense attorney] was not needed as a witness because other witnesses testified about the events in which he was involved and were fully available for cross-examination by [the plaintiff]."); State v. Van Dyck, 827 A.2d 192, 194 (N.H. 2003) (reversing disqualification where the attorney's intended testimony was cumulative); Venture v. Preferred Mut. Ins. Co., 118 N.Y.S.3d 583, 586 (App. Div. 2020).

52. *See, e.g.*, Champoir v. Champoir, 138 N.E.3d 530, 534–36 (Ohio Ct. App. 2019).

53. *See, e.g.*, State Farm Mut. Auto. Ins. Co. v. 21st Century Pharm., Inc., No. 17 Civ. 5845 (MKB) (VMS)2020 WL 729775, at *5 (E.D.N.Y. Feb. 12, 2020) (applying New York ethics rules); *In re* Cyr, No. 18-50102-cag, 2020 WL 763253, at *3 (Bankr. W.D. Tex. Feb. 14, 2020) (applying Texas law); Utley v. City of Dover, 101 S.W.3d 191, 202 (Ark. 2003) (rejecting disqualification where the movant did not show that testimony by a lawyer could not be gained from any other source); People v. Rices, 406 P.3d 788, 804–05 (Cal. 2017) (mentioning no ethics rules); Mettler v. Mettler, 928 A.2d 631, 635–36 (Conn. Super. Ct. 2007); Steinberg v. Winn-Dixie Stores, Inc., 121 So. 3d 622, 624 (Fla. Dist. Ct. App. 2013) ("A lawyer is not a necessary witness when there are other witnesses available to testify to the same information."); Schaff v. State, 697 S.E.2d 305, 307–09 (Ga. Ct. App. 2010); State v. Plichta, 172 P.3d 512, 531–32 (Haw. 2007); N. Moraine

they are not necessary witnesses, and Rule 3.7(a) and state analogs do not operate to disqualify them as trial counsel.

Other courts apply a different standard where an opposing party wants to call a lawyer as a witness, holding that disqualification requires a showing that (1) the lawyer will give evidence material to the issues being litigated, (2) the evidence is unobtainable elsewhere, and (3) the testimony is or may be prejudicial to the testifying lawyer's client.[54] The standard for showing prejudice to the testifying lawyer's client is a stringent one to prevent adverse parties from attempting to call opposing counsel as witnesses solely to disqualify them.[55] The moving party must clearly establish the adverse testimony the lawyer-witness will offer; speculation that the lawyer will or

Wastewater Reclamation Dist. v. Ill. Commerce Comm'n, 912 N.E.2d 204, 233 (Ill. App. Ct. 2009) (barring a lawyer's testimony was not appropriate where party did not show that the lawyer was the only person who could testify on subject); Knowledge A-Z, Inc. v. Sentry Ins., 857 N.E.2d 411, 417–19 (Ind. Ct. App. 2006) (declining to disqualify the lawyer when only basis for his designation as a witness was his alleged failure to return the plaintiff's telephone calls, a fact to which the plaintiff could testify); Raster v. Ameristar Casinos, Inc., 280 S.W.3d 120, 133–34 (Mo. Ct. App. 2009) (ruling that the trial court erred in disqualifying the lawyer where the opposing party failed to show that lawyer was the only person who could testify on matters at issue); Chappell v. Cosgrove, 916 P.2d 836, 839–40 (N.M. 1996) (holding that a lawyer who accompanied his client to meeting should not have been disqualified absent showing that similar testimony could not have been obtained from others at the meeting); Ray v. Ray, 995 N.Y.S.2d 567, 568 (App. Div. 2014) (concluding that documentary evidence made the lawyer's testimony unnecessary); GRE Props. Thomasville LLC v. Libertywood Nursing Ctr., Inc., 761 S.E.2d 676, 682 (N.C. Ct. App. 2014) (concluding that the trial court did not err in holding that the plaintiff's lawyer was not a necessary witness whether other witnesses could testify to the competence of the plaintiff's former employee); Reo v. Univ. Hosps. Health Sys., 131 N.E.3d 986, 994 (Ohio Ct. App. 2019) ("A necessary witness under [Rule] 3.7 is one whose testimony is unobtainable through other trial witnesses."); *Smith*, 749 S.E.2d at 510–11 (explaining that the lawyer was not a necessary witness where evidence was obtained from other witnesses on cross-examination); Harter v. Plains Ins. Co., 579 N.W.2d 625, 632 (S.D. 1998) (holding that a lawyer was not a necessary witness where documentary evidence on the subject of his intended testimony was admitted into evidence at trial); State v. Melancon, 339 P.3d 151, 155–56 (Utah Ct. App. 2014) (refusing to disqualify a prosecutor where the same evidence could be obtained from a police investigator and another witness, and a recording of the conversation); Am. States Ins. Co. v. Nammathao, 220 P.3d 1283, 1285 (Wash. Ct. App. 2009) (holding that disqualification was not warranted where other witnesses could testify to relevant events); Smithson v. United States Fid. & Guar. Co., 411 S.E.2d 850, 856 (W. Va. 1991) (finding that disqualification was not warranted where the defendant failed to show that testimony to be offered by the plaintiff's counsel could not be developed by other witnesses).

54. Walker v. Newman Univ., Inc., No. 19-cv-2005-DDC-TJJ, 2019 WL 2268971, at *3 (D. Kan. May 28, 2019); Powers Reinforcing Fabricators, L.L.C. v. Contes *ex rel.* Cnty. of Maricopa, 473 P.3d 714, 721 (Ariz. Ct. Ap. 2020) (quoting Cottonwood Est., Inc. v. Paradise Builders, Inc., 624 P.2d 296, 302 (Ariz. Ct. App. 1981)); Minor v. Barnes, 609 S.W.3d 449, 452 (Ark. Ct. App. 2020); State v. Rivera, 291 P.3d 512, 527 (Kan. Ct. App. 2012); Sargent Cnty. Bank v. Wentworth, 500 N.W.2d 862, 871 (N.D. 1993); State v. O'Neil, 393 P.3d 1238, 1243 (Wash. Ct. App. 2017); *Smithson*, 411 S.E.2d at 856.

55. Zurich Ins. Co. v. Knotts, 52 S.W.3d 555, 560 (Ky. 2001); *Sargent Cnty. Bank*, 500 N.W.2d at 871; *In re* Sanders, 153 S.W.3d 54, 57–58 (Tex. 2004).

must testify adversely to her client will not support disqualification.[56] As where a client may seek to call its own lawyer as a witness, a party seeking to call opposing counsel will be unable to disqualify that lawyer if the lawyer's intended testimony is irrelevant, immaterial, cumulative, or obtainable from other sources.[57]

Schaff v. State[58] is an instructive advocate-witness rule case. Donald Schaff was charged with various crimes related to the alleged sexual molestation of his minor daughter M.S. Kevin Gough was his defense lawyer. After the jury was selected and while the court was hearing pretrial motions, it was revealed that M.S. had recanted her earlier allegations of abuse in a videotaped interview with Gough at which her mother was present. Gough's assistant also heard M.S. recant. The victim's recantation was obviously key evidence. The prosecutor moved to disqualify Gough under the advocate-witness rule. The trial court granted the motion, reasoning that by interviewing M.S., Gough assumed the role of a forensic interviewer and would need to be available for the state to cross-examine.[59] The trial court also was concerned that M.S.'s mother may have exerted undue influence over her out of a desire to reunite the Schaff family, so that Gough's testimony would be necessary to establish the circumstances attending M.S.'s recantation.[60] The trial court certified its disqualification order for immediate review, and the Georgia Court of Appeals accepted Schaff's interlocutory appeal. The appellate court held that the trial court abused its discretion by disqualifying Gough on the basis that his testimony would be necessary at trial and reversed the disqualification order.[61]

The *Schaff* court explained that the trial court's error was rooted in its interpretation of a Georgia child hearsay statute, which required a party offering the statement of a child under the age of 14 in a sex abuse case to demonstrate that the circumstances surrounding the statement provided

---

56. Quality Developers, Inc. v. Thorman, 31 P.3d 296, 306 (Kan. Ct. App. 2001); Steinert v. Steinert, 897 N.E.2d 603, 606 (Mass. App. Ct. 2008); *see, e.g.*, Schaff v. State, 697 S.E.2d 305, 308 (Ga. Ct. App. 2010) (reversing the trial court's disqualification of the defense lawyer on the basis that he was not a necessary witness, in part because of speculative nature of his potential testimony); Zutler v. Drivershield Corp., 790 N.Y.S.2d 485, 486 (App. Div. 2005) (reversing the trial court's disqualification order where the plaintiff's disqualification motion "was supported by affidavits that were speculative and conclusory").

57. *See, e.g.*, *Helena Country Club*, 535 S.W.3d at 275 (concluding that the trial court erred by disqualifying the lawyer where there was no showing that the lawyer's testimony "was material or truly necessary to any of the issues being litigated or that the evidence sought to be admitted through [the lawyer] was unobtainable elsewhere"); *Quality Developers, Inc.*, 31 P.3d at 306 (declining to disqualify counsel under Rule 3.7(a) because the moving party could not show that the lawyer's testimony was material or could not be obtained from other sources).

58. 697 S.E.2d 305 (Ga. Ct. App. 2010).

59. *Id.* at 306.

60. *Id.* at 307.

61. *Id.*

sufficient indicia of reliability. The trial court seemingly believed that Gough was the only witness who could establish the required foundation for the tape of M.S.'s recantation. To the contrary, both M.S.'s mother and Gough's assistant could testify about the circumstances of M.S.'s videotaped interview and thus satisfy the statute. Although Gough's testimony regarding his training and experience, mental impressions of M.S., reasons for asking particular questions, and the mother's actions toward or statements to M.S. would be relevant to the jury when determining the weight and credibility to assign to M.S.'s videotaped recantation, his testimony was not *necessary* to prove any fact related to the videotaped interview or the circumstances surrounding it.[62]

The trial court's decision had also been influenced by its concern that M.S.'s mother might have influenced her decision to recant and that Gough's testimony would therefore be necessary to explain the circumstances surrounding the interview, thus implying that Gough's testimony would be required to impeach the mother's expected testimony that she did not influence her daughter's decision. But such speculation about Gough's possible testimony could not support his disqualification.[63] Indeed, to hold that it could would invite blatant abuse and misuse of Rule 3.7(a), because any party could disqualify opposing counsel simply by averring that the lawyer was a necessary witness because she might possess information damaging to her client's case.[64] The *Schaff* court further observed that the State would have the opportunity at trial to attack M.S.'s recantation by cross-examining her mother to determine whether she cajoled M.S. into recanting and would be able to argue that M.S. was pressured into changing her testimony.

The *Schaff* court clearly reached the correct result. Although Gough might have been the *best* witness regarding M.S.'s recantation and the surrounding circumstances, he was not the *only* witness, and his testimony was therefore unnecessary. The court's further refusal to disqualify Gough based on his speculative value as an impeachment witness was both proper in context and consistent with the general principle that speculation that a lawyer will or must testify adversely to a client will not support disqualification.

Murray v. Metropolitan Life Insurance Co.[65] is another interesting case. The plaintiffs in *Murray* were policyholders in Metropolitan Life Insurance Co. (MetLife) when it was a mutual insurance company. MetLife demutualized in 2000 and was represented in that process by Debevoise & Plimpton LLP (Debevoise). The plaintiffs sued MetLife for allegedly misleading and shortchanging them in the demutualization. Debevoise defended MetLife in

62. *Id.* at 308.
63. *Id.* (quoting Clough v. Richelo, 616 S.E.2d 888, 894 n.7 (Ga. Ct. App. 2005)).
64. *Id.* (quoting *Clough*, 616 S.E.2d at 894 n.7).
65. 583 F.3d 173 (2d Cir. 2009).

the litigation. Nine years after filing suit and just weeks before the trial was to begin, the plaintiffs moved to disqualify Debevoise. In so moving, they invoked the advocate-witness rule, premised on the fact that four Debevoise lawyers were scheduled to testify about disclosures and documents related to the demutualization. Three of the lawyers were transactional lawyers with no advocacy role in the litigation. The fourth lawyer was a member of the trial team but was not going to act as an advocate before the jury. The district court sustained the plaintiffs' motion but stayed its disqualification order to permit MetLife to immediately appeal to the Second Circuit.

The *Murray* court began its analysis by noting that Rule 3.7(a) is open to "opportunistic abuse" and that courts must guard against related claims advanced for tactical reasons.[66] Here, none of the Debevoise lawyers fit within the Rule 3.7(a) framework because none of them would be advocating for MetLife at trial.[67] The plaintiffs contended that Debevoise should nonetheless be disqualified because the lawyers would give testimony so prejudicial to MetLife that the judicial system's integrity would be threatened. After comparing the plaintiffs' hyperbolic characterizations of the lawyers' expected testimony with the lawyers' testimony in the record, however, the court disagreed. In fact, the Debevoise lawyers' testimony appeared to be limited to undisputed facts and to the authentication of documents.[68]

Even if the plaintiffs could demonstrate that allowing Debevoise to continue as MetLife's trial counsel threatened the integrity of the judicial process, the court still had to consider whether the firm's disqualification might harm some vital interest.[69] In this case, disqualifying Debevoise would require MetLife to obtain and educate new counsel after nearly a decade of litigation. Magnifying the potential harm to MetLife, billions of dollars were at stake in the case, the legal issues were complex, and Debevoise's disqualification was raised on the eve of trial.[70]

As to the last point, the court was troubled by the plaintiffs' lengthy and inexcusable delay in moving to disqualify Debevoise, which weighed heavily against disqualification.[71] Despite long knowing of Debevoise's role in the demutualization and its representation of MetLife in the resulting litigation, the plaintiffs did not file their disqualification motion until settlement negotiations broke down. The plaintiffs' delay suggested that their motion was a litigation tactic, thus magnifying the harm to the judicial system and impairing rather than promoting public confidence in the judicial system.[72]

66. *Id.* at 178.
67. *Id.* at 179.
68. *Id.*
69. *Id.* at 180.
70. *Id.*
71. *Id.*
72. *Id.*

Ultimately, the *Murray* court held that the advocate-witness rule did not justify disqualifying Debevoise.The *Murray* court was right. The Debevoise lawyers identified as witnesses were not going to be representing MetLife at trial, such that the case did not even fit within the traditional advocate-witness rule construct.[73]

4. *Additional Important Considerations*

Seven additional points bear mention. First, to the extent reasonably possible, lawyers should attempt to identify and avoid situations that might lead to them becoming necessary witnesses. For example, some lawyers have a "prover" present when interviewing witnesses in cases where there will be no record of the witness's statements. The prover may be another lawyer in the lead attorney's firm, or it may be a non-lawyer assistant, such as a paralegal. The idea is that if the lawyer calls the witness to testify at trial or at a hearing and the witness misrepresents what was said in the interview, the lawyer can have the prover testify and avoid becoming a necessary witness herself. Lawyers also attempt to avoid the advocate-witness rule by not litigating their own work. A lawyer that will defend a company in sexual harassment litigation, for example, generally should not conduct the company's pre-suit investigation into the claimant's allegations out of the reasonable concern that any investigator may be a necessary witness in the litigation that is expected to follow.

Second, a lawyer who recognizes that she is likely to be a necessary witness at trial need not withdraw from her client's representation as soon as the related suit is filed.[74] As explained earlier, the lawyer remains able to participate in a range of pretrial activities even though she cannot serve as a trial advocate.

Third, a lawyer who is likely to be a necessary witness at trial probably cannot avoid disqualification merely by stipulating to the facts on which she would testify, thus rendering her testimony unnecessary.[75] Unless the facts that the lawyer would testify to can be introduced into evidence as a true stipulation by the parties—that is, facts given to the jury truly as stipulated facts and not as testimony by one side or the other—then regardless of whether the lawyer testifies in person or by way of a written stipulation, she is still a necessary witness and remains "in the unseemly position of arguing

73. *See, e.g.*, Waterloo Capital Partners, LLC v. BWX Ltd., No. 18-CV-6542 (RA), 2020 WL 1489813, at *2 (S.D.N.Y. Mar. 27, 2020) (declining to disqualify a law firm under Rule 3.7(a) where the lawyers alleged to be necessary witnesses were corporate lawyers who would have no advocacy role at trial); *In re* Corp. Res. Servs., Inc., 595 B.R. 434, 445 (S.D.N.Y. 2019) (concluding that disqualification was inappropriate where the lawyer was a transactional lawyer who would not serve as counsel in a bankruptcy adversary proceeding).

74. Sheikh v. Wheeler, 790 F. App'x 793, 797 (7th Cir. 2019).

75. *See, e.g.*, Weigel v. Farmers Ins. Co., 158 S.W.3d 147, 155 (Ark. 2004).

his own credibility, [most] notably in opening and closing statements."[76] The lawyer's credibility may further be at issue in cross-examination, as where she must cross-examine witnesses on what she allegedly told them or they told her.[77]

Fourth, a court asked to disqualify a lawyer under Rule 3.7(a) need not rush to judgment. Beyond the fact that lawyers who are likely to be necessary witnesses at trial are generally permitted to participate in pretrial proceedings, circumstances may change between the time a disqualification motion is made and trial. For example, the case may settle, the case may be resolved on a dispositive motion, or the development of new evidence or changes in case theory may eliminate the need for the lawyer's testimony. A court can therefore delay ruling until it can determine whether the lawyer's testimony is, in fact, necessary.[78] To illustrate, a court weighing disqualification before trial might consider establishing a deadline by which a party must declare its intention to call its lawyer or opposing counsel as a witness. The court can then decide the issue at a time calculated to minimize disruption to the parties and to the court itself.[79] Alternatively, a court might deny a premature motion to disqualify a lawyer-witness without prejudice, leaving open the possibility of revisiting the issue at an appropriate time.[80] That said, lawyers must recognize that a court is unlikely to delay ruling if there is no realistic prospect of circumstances changing.[81] Indeed, in a case where there is no reason for delay, the sooner the issue is decided, the better for all concerned.

A court's understandable inclination to proceed cautiously when ruling on a lawyer-witness's potential disqualification does not mean, however, that the moving party must establish with absolute certainty that the lawyer-witness will testify at trial. Rather, the moving party need only show that the lawyer-witness's testimony is likely to be necessary.[82] Determining whether

76. *Id.*

77. *Id.*

78. Std. Quimica de Venez., C.A. v. Cent. Hispano Int'l, Inc., 179 F.R.D. 64, 65–66 (D.P.R. 1998); Chapman Eng'rs, Inc. v. Natural Gas Sales Co., 766 F. Supp. 949, 958 (D. Kan. 1991); Rocky Mountain Helium, LLC v. United States, No. 15-336C, 2019 WL 2246209, at *1–2 (Fed. Cl. May 24, 2019); CVS Caremark Corp. v. Lauriello, 175 So. 3d 596, 610–11 (Ala. 2014); *In re* Est. of Waters, 647 A.2d 1091, 1097 (Del. 1994); Nat'l Bank of Andover, N.A. v. Aero Std. Tooling, Inc., 49 P.3d 547, 553 (Kan. Ct. App. 2002); Am. States Ins. Co. v. Nammathao, 220 P.3d 1283, 1286 (Wash. Ct. App. 2009).

79. Barbee v. Luong Firm, P.L.L.C., 107 P.3d 762, 767–68 (Wash. Ct. App. 2005).

80. *See, e.g.*, Trunzo v. Citi Mortg., No. 2:11-cv-01124, 2014 WL 1317577, at *20 (W.D. Pa. Mar. 31, 2014) (denying without prejudice a motion to disqualify class counsel based on Rule 3.7(a) as premature); Interpharm, Inc. v. Wells Fargo Bank, N.A., No. 08 Civ. 11365(RJH)(HBP), 2010 WL 1141201, at *5–6 (S.D.N.Y. Mar. 25, 2010) (denying without prejudice a motion to disqualify a lawyer under Rule 3.7(a) on the basis that it was premature).

81. *See, e.g.*, Carta *ex rel.* Estate of Carta v. Lumbermens Mut. Cas. Co., 419 F. Supp. 2d 23, 31 n.6 (D. Mass. 2006) (finding no reason to delay ruling on a disqualification motion where the circumstances would not change).

82. Fognani v. Young, 115 P.3d 1268, 1273–74 (Colo. 2005).

a lawyer-witness's testimony is likely to be necessary is a case-specific exercise.[83] A party's statement that it does not intend to call a lawyer as a witness at trial does not mean that the lawyer is not a necessary witness.[84] Circumstances may change, such that a party that did not initially intend to call a lawyer as a witness must recalculate.[85] Similarly, the fact that a party does not ultimately call a lawyer as a witness at trial does not mean retroactively that the lawyer was not likely to be a necessary witness at trial or that a trial court erred by disqualifying the lawyer at the time the moving party sought to enforce the advocate-witness rule.[86]

Fifth, a court weighing a lawyer's possible disqualification based on the advocate-witness rule is not required to hold an evidentiary hearing.[87] The court must, however, give the parties an opportunity to submit evidence supporting their positions before making its decision.

Sixth, courts should carefully weigh motions to disqualify lawyers as witnesses because they hold great potential for tactical abuse.[88] A party can easily use a disqualification motion premised on Rule 3.7(a) as a ploy to cripple its opponent's case.[89]

Seventh, courts' application of the advocate-witness rule is mandatory and generally may not be waived by the client of the offending lawyer.[90] A client generally cannot waive the advocate-witness rule because the interests the rule serves are not personal to the client. Rather, the advocate-witness rule is a prophylactic measure intended to protect the client, the adversary, the fact-finder, and the justice system.[91]

B. Excluding the Lawyer's Testimony Rather Than Disqualifying the Lawyer

The advocate-witness rule is generally understood to restrict only a lawyer's ability to serve as trial counsel. The rule disqualifies lawyers in their

83. *Id.* at 1274 (stating that the likelihood of a lawyer-witness's testimony is based not on the opponent's trial strategy but "on the circumstances of the particular case").

84. Commonwealth v. Delnegro, 75 N.E.3d 73, 81 (Mass. App. Ct. 2017).

85. *Id.*

86. *See, e.g.*, People v. Koen, 6 N.E.3d 354, 364 (Ill. App. Ct. 2014) ("[T]he fact that an attorney does not actually testify at trial is 'irrelevant to the trial court's decision to disqualify' said attorney beforehand." (quoting People v. Rivera, 986 N.E.2d 634, 648 (Ill. 2013)).

87. Befekadu v. Addis Int'l Money Transfer, LLC, 772 S.E.2d 785, 789 (Ga. Ct. App. 2015).

88. Zurich Ins. Co. v. Knotts, 52 S.W.3d 555, 560 (Ky. 2001); Klupt v. Krongard, 728 A.2d 727, 740 (Md. Ct. Spec. App. 1999); Sargent Cnty. Bank v. Wentworth, 500 N.W.2d 862, 871 (N.D. 1993); *In re* Sanders, 153 S.W.3d 54, 57 (Tex. 2004).

89. *See* Weigel v. Farmers Ins. Co., 158 S.W.3d 147, 155 (Ark. 2004) (citing and discussing Purtle v. McAdam, 879 S.W.2d 401, 404 (Ark. 1994)).

90. Premium Prods., Inc. v. Pro Performance Sports, LLC, 997 F. Supp. 2d 433, 436 (E.D. Va. 2014).

91. *Id.* (quoting Est. of Andrews v. United States, 804 F. Supp. 820, 823 (E.D. Va. 1992)).

representational capacity; it does not bar their testimony as witnesses.[92] A lawyer who reasonably anticipates being a necessary witness at trial should withdraw from the representation at a time when withdrawal will cause minimal disruption or harm to the client's case in order to fulfill her critical role as a witness.[93] In some cases, however, courts applying Rule 3.7(a) prohibit a lawyer-witness from testifying while allowing her to represent her client at trial.[94] Courts seem more likely to apply Rule 3.7(a) this way where the lawyer's potential appearance as a witness is first revealed at trial, such that disqualifying the lawyer is a disagreeable option in terms of judicial economy in addition to causing the client substantial hardship.[95]

Although excluding a lawyer's testimony as a witness instead of disqualifying the lawyer as an advocate seems backward, nothing in the rule explicitly prohibits this approach.[96] That does not mean, however, that an exclusionary approach is desirable or workable. Consider the situation in which a client wishes to have its lawyer offer favorable testimony at trial. If the court excludes the testimony instead of disqualifying the lawyer, the opponent cannot complain because the court has prevented the lawyer from mixing the roles of advocate and witness to the opponent's detriment. The risk of confusing the fact-finder is avoided just as surely as if the lawyer-witness was disqualified as an advocate. If the client always intended to call its lawyer as a friendly witness, the exclusion of the lawyer's testimony is a self-inflicted wound because the client should have anticipated the ruling and engaged substitute counsel before trial.[97] But difficulty arises where the client's need for its lawyer's favorable testimony comes as a surprise at trial, perhaps because of another witness's unexpected testimony, the opponent's introduction of new documentary evidence, or the injection of new theories into the case that the judge deems to be tried by consent. Here the client cannot avail itself of the substantial

92. Ramey v. Dist. 141, Int'l Ass'n of Machinists & Aerospace Workers, 378 F.3d 269, 282 (2d Cir. 2004); Graves v. Dudley Maples, L.P., 950 So. 2d 1017, 1023 (Miss. 2007).

93. State v. Vocatura, 922 A.2d 110, 117 (R.I. 2007).

94. *See, e.g.*, Campbell v. State, 432 S.W.3d 673, 679 (Ark. Ct. App. 2014) (affirming the trial court's decision excluding a lawyer's testimony in new trial hearing); *Vocatura*, 922 A.2d at 116–17 (affirming the trial court's decision excluding the lawyer's testimony not on the basis stated below—i.e., a lack of foundation—but on the alternative ground that the lawyer was a necessary witness); Mt. Rushmore Broad., Inc. v. Statewide Collections, 42 P.3d 478, 482 (Wyo. 2002) (involving a lawyer who was the sole shareholder and officer of the defendant corporation and represented it in a bench trial; the court was concerned that if the lawyer were allowed to testify and function as an advocate, he would be challenging the credibility of the plaintiff's witnesses while vouching for his own credibility).

95. *See, e.g.*, *Mt. Rushmore*, 42 P.3d at 479 (involving a defense lawyer who sought to testify after the plaintiff rested its case).

96. Model Rules of Prof'l Conduct R. 3.7(a) (2020) (stating only that "[a] lawyer shall not act as an advocate at a trial in which the lawyer is likely to be a necessary witness").

97. *Vocatura*, 922 A.2d at 116–17.

hardship exception in Model Rule 3.7(a)(3), which expressly deals with a lawyer's disqualification as an advocate.[98] The client is thus left to move for a mistrial or to argue for some sort of relief based on principles of fairness, neither approach being a reliably good option.

Because so few courts invoke Rule 3.7(a) to exclude a lawyer-witness's testimony rather than disqualifying the lawyer as an advocate, those cases should be treated as aberrations or limited to their facts. Disqualification of the lawyer-witness as an advocate is the preferred means of enforcing Model Rule 3.7(a).[99]

IV. Exceptions to the Advocate-Witness Rule

Where Model Rule 3.7(a) applies, it becomes necessary to determine if any of its three exceptions spares the lawyer-witness from disqualification. The lawyer-witness facing potential disqualification bears the burden of establishing the applicability of any exceptions.[100]

A. The Uncontested Issue Exception to Model Rule 3.7(a)

The first exception is contained in Model Rule 3.7(a)(1), which permits a lawyer to act as an advocate at a trial in which the lawyer is likely to be a necessary witness if the lawyer's testimony relates to an "uncontested issue."[101] In such a case, none of the underlying policies against allowing the lawyer to occupy the dual roles of advocate and witness are implicated. Where the lawyer's testimony will be uncontested, the ambiguities in the lawyer's dual roles "are purely theoretical."[102]

For purposes of the rule, an uncontested issue is one that is not opposed or that will not be debated at trial.[103] It is important to understand that for Model Rule 3.7(a)(1) to apply the *issue* must be uncontested, not the *facts* to which the lawyer-witness might testify. If the rule were read as allowing a lawyer to testify concerning undisputed facts to support a contested issue,

98. Smith v. Wharton, 78 S.W.3d 79, 84 (Ark. 2002) (making clear that substantial hardship is linked to lawyer's disqualification as an advocate, not the exclusion of the lawyer's testimony as a witness).

99. *See, e.g.*, First Constitution Bank v. Caldrello, 656 A.2d 1053, 1055–56 (Conn. 1995) (reversing the trial court's exclusion of the lawyer's testimony based on Rule 3.7).

100. *In re* Marriage of Perry, 293 P.3d 170, 178 (Mont. 2013); Rayco Mfg., Inc. v. Murphy, Rogers, Sloss & Gambel, 142 N.E.3d 1267, 1292 (Ohio Ct. App. 2019).

101. Model Rules of Prof'l Conduct R. 3.7(a)(1) (2020).

102. *Id.* R. 3.7 cmt. 3.

103. People v. Pasillas-Sanchez, 214 P.3d 520, 526 (Colo. App. 2009); *see, e.g.*, Branch v. State, 882 So. 2d 36, 63 (Miss. 2004) (concluding that Rule 3.7(a)(1) applied where evidence did not need to be authenticated); Damron v. CSX Transp., Inc., 920 N.E.2d 169, 177 (Ohio Ct. App. 2009) (finding that the trial court erred in disqualifying a lawyer whose potential testimony would relate to an uncontested issue).

the exception would swallow the rule because the lawyer could testify to a range of undisputed facts but still argue the importance of those facts in resolving the contested issue.[104] That approach would defeat the purpose of Model Rule 3.7(a) altogether.

B. The Nature and Value of Legal Services Exception

The second exception to Model Rule 3.7(a) is found in Model Rule 3.7(a)(2), which permits a lawyer who acts as a trial advocate to testify as to "the nature and value of the legal services rendered in the case."[105] In probate matters, for example, a lawyer may be required to testify concerning the fees she has charged to the estate.[106] In many cases, the prevailing party is entitled to recover its fees from the opposing party pursuant to a fee-shifting provision in a contract or under statutory authority. In other cases, a court may award a party its attorneys' fees as a form of sanction. Regardless of the specific bases, awards of attorneys' fees are typically made after the merits of the case are decided or in a proceeding separate from the merits.[107] The party seeking attorneys' fees supports its request with testimony from its lawyers, whether "live" at a hearing or by way of affidavit. It would make no sense to disqualify the lawyers who handled the substantive aspects of the case from representing the client in the attorneys' fees aspect of the litigation. After all, those lawyers know the most about the representation and are best able to explain the reasons for the various actions, activities, circumstances, or decisions that underpin the request for compensation. Such disqualification would likely delay the proceedings and increase the costs.[108] Any fee award will be determined by the court, and there is no danger that the judge will be confused by the lawyers' dual roles. Moreover, because the court is familiar with the case, there is less dependence on the adversary process to test the credibility of the lawyers' testimony.[109]

An adversary might resist a lawyer's testimony as to the nature and value of the lawyer's services or those of others in her firm on the basis that the lawyer's self-interest disqualifies her as a witness. Such challenges

104. *Pasillas-Sanchez*, 214 P.3d at 526.

105. Model Rules of Prof'l Conduct R. 3.7(a)(2) (2020). As should be clear from the rule's plain language, the Rule 3.7(a)(2) exception applies only to legal services "rendered in the case at the bar, not in prior matters." Fine Hous., Inc. v. Sloan, 848 S.E.2d 581, 587 (S.C. Ct. App. 2020).

106. *See, e.g.*, Bernier v. DuPont, 715 N.E.2d 442, 448 (Mass. App. Ct. 1999) (holding that the lawyer for an executrix should have been allowed to testify under Rule 3.7(a)(2)).

107. *See, e.g.*, Rader v. ING Bank, No. 09-340-SLR/LPS, 09-781-SLR/LPS, 2010 WL 1403962, at *8 (D. Del. Apr. 7, 2010) (declining to disqualify lawyers as witnesses where the sole issue left in the case was the defendants' entitlement to attorneys' fees and the amount thereof).

108. *See* Model Rules of Prof'l Conduct R. 3.7 cmt. 3 (2020) (observing that permitting the lawyers to testify avoids the need for a second trial with new counsel).

109. *Id.*

are baseless. The lawyer's interest in the case will be disclosed during direct examination and likely explored on cross-examination, and it is classically left to the fact-finder to weigh the accuracy of the lawyer's testimony and to judge her credibility as a witness.[110]

The "nature and value" of a lawyer's legal services rendered in a case may include non-monetary components or aspects. For example, in *In re Marriage of Perry*,[111] the Montana Supreme Court held that Rule 3.7(a)(2) permitted a lawyer to testify that her disqualification would work a substantial hardship on her client.[112] By way of further example, if an opponent seeks sanctions against a lawyer's client for allegedly asserting frivolous claims and the client raises an advice of counsel defense, the lawyer might be permitted to represent the client at trial and testify as a witness on the basis that the adversary's allegations relate to the nature and value of the lawyer's services to the client.[113] One state ethics committee has concluded that the allegations presented in this scenario "speak directly" to the nature and value of legal services exception in Model Rule 3.7(a)(2).[114] The wisdom of a lawyer serving as both an advocate and a witness in this situation is a separate question, however, and will depend on the facts of the particular case.

C. The Substantial Hardship Exception to Model Rule 3.7(a)

The final exception is found in Model Rule 3.7(a)(3), which allows a lawyer who is likely to be a necessary witness to nonetheless represent the client at trial if "disqualification of the lawyer would work substantial hardship on the client."[115] The term "disqualification" in Model Rule 3.7(a)(3) and state analogs refers to a lawyer's disqualification as an advocate; it does not suggest the exclusion of a lawyer's testimony as a witness.[116] The "client" the substantial hardship exception protects is, of course, the client of the testifying lawyer, not the opponent.[117]

Model Rule 3.7(a)(3) provides an equitable exception to an otherwise strict stance on disqualifying lawyer-witnesses. Basically, Model Rule 3.7(a)(3) allows a lawyer-witness's continued representation of a client any time the detriment to the client caused by the lawyer's disqualification outweighs the prejudice to the opponent caused by the lawyer's dual roles, although courts weighing substantial hardship claims normally dig deeper.

---

110. Fid. Nat'l Title Ins. Co. v. Suburban W. Abstractors, 852 A.2d 318, 322 (Pa. Super. Ct. 2004).
111. 293 P.3d 170 (Mont. 2013).
112. *Id.* at 178.
113. S.C. Adv. Op. 07-07, 2007 WL 7264733, at *1 (S.C. Bar, Ethics Advisory Comm. 2007).
114. *Id.*
115. Model Rules of Prof'l Conduct R. 3.7(a)(3) (2020).
116. Smith v. Wharton, 78 S.W.3d 79, 84 (Ark. 2002).
117. People v. Donaldson, 113 Cal. Rptr. 2d 548, 557 (Ct. App. 2001).

Determining whether a lawyer's disqualification will cause a client substantial hardship is a case-specific exercise. Courts typically consider a variety of factors when weighing related arguments, including (1) the nature of the case; (2) the financial hardship that disqualification will likely visit on the client, focusing on the stage of the proceedings at which disqualification is sought; (3) the time at which the lawyer-witness became aware of the likelihood of his testimony; and (4) whether the client has secured alternative representation or is easily able to do so.[118] A court may factor into this balancing its own interests, although the tribunal's interests often will overlap with the parties' interests, and the fact that a court subordinates its own interests to those of the parties will not invalidate its substantial hardship analysis.[119]

Whether encompassed within one of the foregoing factors or in addition to them, courts should also consider the timing of the disqualification motion,[120] including situations where the timing suggests that the motion is being filed to gain a tactical advantage or where the moving party has unreasonably delayed in acting. In any event, courts must perform the Rule 3.7(a)(3) balancing in all cases in which neither of the other two exceptions applies.[121]

Courts narrowly construe the substantial hardship exception.[122] Indeed, to do otherwise would risk allowing the exception to swallow the rule. Accordingly, to avoid its lawyer's disqualification on undue hardship grounds, a party must demonstrate prejudice beyond the normal delay, expense, and inconvenience associated with changing counsel.[123] A court is unlikely to find substantial hardship where a case is straightforward, such that replacement counsel would not require specialized knowledge or expertise;[124] where the client is easily able to hire substitute counsel;[125] where

118. People v. Pasillas-Sanchez, 214 P.3d 520, 527 (Colo. App. 2009) (citing Fognani v. Young, 115 P.3d 1268, 1275 (Colo. 2005)).

119. DJ Inv. Grp., L.L.C. v. DAE/Westbrook, L.L.C., 147 P.3d 414, 419–20 (Utah 2006).

120. *See, e.g.*, Pulte Home Corp. v. Simerly, 746 S.E.2d 173, 176–77 (Ga. Ct. App. 2013) (holding that the trial court did not err by refusing to disqualify a lawyer where the motion in limine seeking to exclude the lawyer's testimony on spoliation of evidence issue was made three weeks before trial and the lawyer had been litigating the case for more than three years).

121. DiMartino v. Eighth Jud. Dist. Ct., 66 P.3d 945947 (Nev. 2003) (discussing the Nevada equivalent of Model Rule 3.7(a)(3)); Thompson v. Goetz, 455 N.W.2d 580, 588 (N.D. 1990); Mt. Rushmore Broad., Inc. v. Statewide Collections, 42 P.3d 478, 482 (Wyo. 2002).

122. Carta *ex rel.* Estate of Carta v. Lumbermens Mut. Cas. Co., 419 F. Supp. 2d 23, 31 (D. Mass. 2006); Brown v. Daniel, 180 F.R.D. 298, 302 (D.S.C. 1998).

123. Courts may be reluctant to find substantial hardship where the sole basis for invoking the exception is the expense of changing counsel "because, were expense a proper basis for the exception, the exception would soon swallow the rule." Premium Prods., Inc. v. Pro Performance Sports, LLC, 997 F. Supp. 2d 433, 438 (E.D. Va. 2014).

124. *See, e.g.*, *Carta*, 419 F. Supp. 2d at 32 (finding no substantial hardship where the underlying matter was "a relatively straightforward unfair settlement practices case" and a lawyer taking it over "would not need any specialized or unique knowledge").

125. *See, e.g.*, DeBiasi v. Charter Cnty. of Wayne, 284 F. Supp. 2d 760, 772 (E.D. Mich. 2003) (noting that there were "many competent, experienced trial lawyers" in the area who were

another lawyer in the same firm or office is readily available to replace the disqualified lawyer-witness;[126] where existing local counsel is available to step into the lead counsel role;[127] or where the client has substitute counsel in place.[128]

Courts also may consider the time and money the client has invested in the lawyer to be disqualified, as well as proximity to trial.[129] That said, the general expense and delay a party normally would experience with a change in counsel does not constitute substantial hardship.[130] Certainly, the less time or money the client has invested, or the more remote the trial date, the less likely a court is to find substantial hardship. In *Timlick v. Liberty Mutual Insurance Co.*,[131] for example, the court found that the plaintiff would suffer no hardship from his lawyer's disqualification because the case was "still in its earliest stages. The preliminary pretrial conference [was] still three weeks away, and there [was] no pretrial schedule in place yet."[132] Furthermore, his lawyer could still participate in the litigation even though he could not represent the plaintiff at trial.[133]

Additionally, and as noted earlier, courts often evaluate the foreseeability to the lawyer that she is likely to be a necessary witness.[134] If the lawyer

well-versed in the kinds of issues presented in the case).

126. *See, e.g.*, State v. Plichta, 172 P.3d 512, 532–33 (Haw. 2007) (observing that another public defender could have represented the client at trial had the original public defender withdrawn as a necessary witness); Lundy v. Shelter Mut. Ins. Co., No. A-05-034, 2006 WL 2472723, at *7 (Neb. Ct. App. Aug. 29, 2006) (finding that another lawyer from the disqualified lawyer's firm could represent the plaintiff).

127. *See, e.g.*, Beller v. Crow, 742 N.W.2d 230, 236 (Neb. 2007).

128. *See, e.g.*, Katica v. Allstate Fire & Cas. Ins. Co., No. CV 16-00150-DLC-RWA, 2018 WL 3475479, at *2 (D. Mont. July 19, 2018); Std. Quimica de Venez., C.A. v. Cent. Hispano Int'l, Inc., 179 F.R.D. 64, 66 (D.P.R. 1998); USX Corp. v. TIECO, Inc., 929 F. Supp. 1455, 1459 (N.D. Ala. 1996); Int'l Res. Ventures, Inc. v. Diamond Mining Co. of Am., Inc., 934 S.W.2d 218, 222 (Ark. 1996); Fognani v. Young, 115 P.3d 1268, 1275–76 (Colo. 2005); Penna v. Margolis, No. CV030475408S, 2004 WL 377010, at *7 (Conn. Super. Ct. Feb. 9, 2004); Collins Entm't, Inc. v. White, 611 S.E.2d 262, 271 (S.C. Ct. App. 2005).

129. *See, e.g.*, *In re* Cardinal Servs., Inc., No. CIVA 00-1909, CIVA 00-1910, 2006 WL 2089925, at *3 (W.D. La. July 21, 2006) (recognizing undue hardship where the lawyer's disqualification was sought six months prior to trial in a case that had going on for six years); Freeman v. Vicchiarelli, 827 F. Supp. 300, 304–05 (D.N.J. 1993) (finding no hardship where the motion to disqualify was filed one month after the complaint was filed); *Penna*, 2004 WL 377010, at *7 (disqualifying the lawyer in a case in its early stages where no discovery had taken place).

130. Fine Hous., Inc. v. Sloan, 848 S.E.2d 581, 587 (S.C. Ct. App. 2020).

131. CV 19-99-M-DLC-KLD, 2019 WL 4934782 (D. Mont. Oct. 7, 2019).

132. *Id.* at *3.

133. *Id.*

134. *See, e.g.*, Weigel v. Farmers Ins. Co., 158 S.W.3d 147, 156 (Ark. 2004) (discussing the trial court's observations when disqualifying the lawyer and affirming the trial court); Klupt v. Krongard, 728 A.2d 727, 740–41 (Md. Ct. Spec. App. 1999) ("When the attorney in question is so clearly aware before the fact of the potential conflict between his roles as advocate and witness, then the scrutiny usually applied to an opposing party's motion for disqualification is unnecessary, and the burden shifts to the attorney in question."); Senu-Oke v. Modern Moving Sys., Inc., 978 S.W.2d 426, 433 (Mo. Ct. App. 1998) (finding that it was foreseeable that the lawyer would be a necessary witness at trial given his deposition nine months earlier); State v. Vocatura, 922 A.2d

knows early on that she is likely to be a necessary witness, her disqualification as an advocate typically will not be deemed to work a substantial hardship on the client.[135] In *B.B. v. E.E.*,[136] for example, the disqualified lawyer "made the decision to insert himself into the proceeding as a witness to events rather than as a purely legal advocate for his client" at the very outset of the matter.[137] In the lawyer's initial appearance in the case the court raised the concern that the lawyer might have made himself a necessary witness at trial.[138] "As such, from day one," the lawyer's disqualification under Rule 3.7 "should have been foreseeable to everyone involved."[139] While the court recognized the lawyer's arguably unique qualifications to represent his client and appreciated the time and expense of getting replacement counsel up to speed, it concluded that the substantial hardship exception to disqualification did not apply.

Given this interpretation of the substantial hardship exception, it seems clear that in any case in which it is reasonably foreseeable that the lawyer might be a witness, the lawyer should inform the client of that possibility at the outset of the representation or as soon as the lawyer becomes aware of the risk. This advice holds true regardless of whether the lawyer's necessity as a witness is fairly debatable or another lawyer in the same firm or office could assume trial responsibilities. The fact that the lawyer might avoid disqualification in the end does not excuse the lawyer's duty to communicate with the client concerning the possibility of disqualification, the potential expense of a disqualification dispute, the potential effect of such a controversy on the client's case, the identification of substitute counsel, and so on.

110, 116–17 (R.I. 2009) (concluding that the lawyer's early identification of himself as a witness in discovery responses established that his testimony was foreseeable); Mt. Rushmore Broad., Inc. v. Statewide Collections, 42 P.3d 478, 482 (Wyo. 2002) (affirming the trial court's decision not to let a lawyer testify as a witness while serving as an advocate in part because the lawyer's witness role was reasonably foreseeable).

135. *See, e.g.*, *Weigel*, 158 S.W.3d at 156 (discussing the trial court's observations and concluding that the trial court did not abuse its discretion in disqualifying the lawyer); Fognani v. Young, 115 P.3d 1268, 1275–76 (Colo. 2005) (noting that the likelihood that the lawyer would be a necessary witness was apparent before suit was filed and before he entered his appearance); Manero v. Manero, No. FSTFA134024800S, 2015 WL 522249, at *3 (Conn. Super. Ct. Jan. 12, 2015) (disqualifying a lawyer where it was reasonably foreseeable that he would be a necessary witness at the time he entered his appearance); State v. Plichta, 172 P.3d 512, 532–33 (Haw. 2007) (observing that the lawyer's motion to withdraw came too late because she plainly should have foreseen that she would be a necessary witness); *Klupt*, 728 A.2d at 740–41 (noting that the lawyer recognized that he would be a necessary witness when he accepted the engagement); Beller v. Crow, 742 N.W.2d 230, 236 (Neb. 2007) (phrasing the issue as foreseeability to the client rather than the lawyer but applying the same rationale); *Mt. Rushmore*, 42 P.3d at 482 (calling it "obvious from the inception of the case" that the lawyer would be a necessary witness); *see also* Ill. Adv. Op. 93-7, 1994 WL 904179, at *3 (Ill. State Bar Ass'n 1994) (indicating that a lawyer's "knowledge well in advance of the filing of the lawsuit" prevented application of the substantial hardship exception).

136. 133 N.Y.S.3d 186 (Fam. Ct. 2020).

137. *Id.* at 190.

138. *Id.*

139. *Id.*

This obligation is clear from Model Rule 1.4(a)(2), which requires a lawyer to reasonably consult with a client about the means by which the client's objectives are to be accomplished,[140] and Model Rule 1.4(b), which requires a lawyer to explain a matter to the extent reasonably necessary to permit the client to make informed decisions regarding the representation.[141] It is possible that a client who is aware of a lawyer's potential disqualification on Rule 3.7(a) grounds might retain that lawyer anyway. It is also possible, however, that a client might employ a different lawyer to avoid the uncertainty and potential expense and detriment that would accompany the first lawyer's engagement. Either way, the client requires adequate information to make a responsible decision.

On the other side of the coin, a court generally should not disqualify a lawyer who has special knowledge of the case, or in whom the party has unusual confidence and trust.[142] In *Brown v. Daniel*,[143] for example, the court declined to disqualify the plaintiff's lawyers because the case was "quite complex with a remarkable set of facts and an intricate time line" and the firm was intimately familiar with the facts, vesting it with "unique experience and extensive knowledge" particular to the case.[144] In other words, this really was a case where disqualifying the firm would have caused a party substantial hardship.[145] Similarly, in *Cushing v. Greyhound Lines, Inc.*,[146] the court concluded that the trial court erred by disqualifying a plaintiffs' lawyer who had encyclopedic knowledge of the discovery that had taken place throughout the five years of aggressive litigation leading up to trial, including several thousand documents, and whose disqualification would rob the plaintiffs of that knowledge and experience.[147] In short, *Brown* and *Cushing* illustrate the importance that courts attach to lawyers' special knowledge of a case and factual complexities that make engaging new counsel difficult.

The longer a matter is litigated and the greater the client's investment in the litigation, the more likely that a lawyer's disqualification will

---

140. Model Rules of Prof'l Conduct R. 1.4(a)(2) (2020).

141. *Id.* R. 1.4(b).

142. *See, e.g.*, Zurich Ins. Co. v. Knotts, 52 S.W.3d 555, 560 (Ky. 2001) (declining to disqualify a lawyer who "ha[d] in his memory, or at his fingertips, knowledge of the case no one else could duplicate"); State *ex rel.* Wallace v. Munton, 989 S.W.2d 641, 647 (Mo. Ct. App. 1999) (finding that the trial court should have not disqualified a divorce lawyer where the client's husband, a private investigator, had a record of threatening and intimidating people that the lawyer would resist and the client had contacted roughly 100 other lawyers who would not take her case either because they were afraid of her husband or did business with him).

143. 180 F.R.D. 298 (D.S.C. 1998).

144. *Id.* at 302.

145. *Id.*

146. 991 N.E.2d 28 (Ill. App. Ct. 2013).

147. *Id.* at 83.

create substantial hardship sufficient to overcome disqualification.[148] A court should be reluctant to disqualify a lawyer where discovery is complete or nearly so, or where trial is near, unless it is willing to mitigate the related hardship by reopening or extending discovery, or by continuing the trial date to allow substitute counsel time to adequately prepare the case.[149] Certainly a party would experience substantial hardship if its lawyer were disqualified only after trial had begun.[150]

The passage of time or progress of the litigation is not just an expense factor. Critically, disqualification late in a case may strip the party of the knowledge and expertise that its lawyer has acquired throughout the course of the litigation.[151] A lawyer's long involvement in a case may in some instances vest her with expertise in the subject matter or knowledge of events or issues that is deeper or greater than she could effectively convey to replacement counsel. So, as a general rule, as the duration of litigation increases, the likelihood that the disqualification of a lawyer-witness will impose a substantial hardship on the client also increases.[152]

Furthermore, a court weighing substantial hardship must account for the expertise and skill of the lawyer to be disqualified, and the likelihood that available replacement counsel will measure up.[153] It is not enough, however, that the challenged lawyer enjoys a sterling reputation. To invoke the substantial hardship exception to avoid disqualification based on the lawyer's expertise and skill, the client or lawyer must relate these traits to the case at hand.[154] A lawyer is most likely to avoid disqualification if she practices in

148. *See, e.g.*, Nat'l Union Fire Ins. Co. v. L.E. Myers Co. Grp., 937 F. Supp. 276, 280–81 (S.D.N.Y. 1996) (finding substantial hardship where the law firm had represented client in an action spanning 12 years and noting the financial hardship to client if the law firm was disqualified); D.J. Inv. Grp., L.L.C. v. DAE/Westbrook, L.L.C. v. 147 P.3d 414, 422–23 (Utah 2006) (affirming the trial court's finding of substantial hardship where the case had been on file for almost three years, the parties had litigated an extraordinary number of legal issues, almost all key witnesses had been deposed, and the parties had exchanged written discovery).

149. *See* LeRoy v. State, No. 074, 1993, 1994 WL 637310, at *2 (Del. Super. Ct. Jan. 21, 1994) (disqualifying the lawyer but continuing a hearing to allow the client to locate new counsel and thus avoid substantial hardship otherwise caused by disqualification).

150. *See, e.g.*, Ogle v. Ogle, 128 N.E.3d 775, 790–92 (Ohio Ct. App. 2018) (disqualifying the lawyer in the middle of a contested hearing would have worked a substantial hardship); Orangeburg Sausage Co. v. Cincinnati Ins. Co., 450 S.E.2d 66, 75 (S.C. Ct. App. 1994) (affirming the trial court decision that disqualifying plaintiff's lawyer in midst of trial would work a substantial hardship and thus denying disqualification).

151. *See, e.g.*, *Cushing*, 991 N.E.2d at 83 (concluding that the trial court erred in disqualifying a lawyer who had encyclopedic knowledge of the case gained over five years of aggressive litigation).

152. Northbrook Digital, LLC v. Vendio Servs., Inc., 625 F. Supp. 2d 728, 766 (D. Minn. 2008).

153. *See* Religious Tech. Ctr. v. F.A.C.T.Net, Inc., 945 F. Supp. 1470, 1476–78 (D. Colo. 1996) (finding undue hardship where the attorney was one of only a handful of attorneys in the country willing to litigate against the Church of Scientology and was "one of the two most experienced and successful").

154. *See Religious Tech. Ctr.*, 945 F. Supp. at 1476–77 (involving a lawyer with resolve and expertise in litigation against the Church of Scientology).

a specialized area and can demonstrate that the client recognized her special expertise or skill before engaging her.

V. Model Rule 3.7(b) and Personal versus Imputed Disqualification

A lawyer who likely will be a necessary witness in a trial in which she is serving as an advocate, and who cannot find refuge in any of the Rule 3.7(a) exceptions, will be disqualified from representing the client at trial. There may, however, be other lawyers in the same firm who are familiar with the matter and can assume the client's representation at trial. The client would probably prefer such substitution because it minimizes the cost of the representation and avoids delays and other inefficiencies caused by the first lawyer's disqualification. But is it ethically permissible for another lawyer in the disqualified lawyer's firm to try the case? Or, is the first lawyer's disqualification on advocate-witness grounds imputed to all other lawyers in her firm as some conflicts of interest might be?

Imputed disqualification generally is not appropriate in lawyer-witness cases.[155] This is clear from the language of Rule 3.7(b),[156] which states: "A lawyer may act as advocate in a trial in which another lawyer in the lawyer's firm is likely to be called as a witness unless precluded from doing so under Rule 1.7 or Rule 1.9."[157] Thus, where lawyer-witnesses who are expected to testify favorably for their clients cannot escape disqualification by way of Rule 3.7(a)(3), any harm attributable to their disqualification can be lessened by allowing other lawyers in their firms to take over the case.[158] Opposing parties cannot be heard to complain because there is no danger that the lawyer-witness will argue her own credibility to the jury, or that she will enhance her effectiveness as an advocate by taking the oath as a witness. Although a jury may be skeptical of a lawyer's testimony in a case tried by a lawyer from the same firm, that is an insufficient ground for disqualifying the entire firm.[159]

---

155. Iguana, LLC v. Lanham, 628 F. Supp. 2d 1361, 1374 (M.D. Ga. 2008); Fernandez v. Comm'r of Corr., 220 A.3d 216, 227–28 (Conn. App. Ct. 2019); Fleitman v. McPherson, 691 So. 2d 37, 38 (Fla. Dist. Ct. App. 1997); McLaughlin v. Payne, 761 S.E.2d 289, 293 (Ga. 2014); Cunningham v. Sams, 588 S.E.2d 484, 488 (N.C. Ct. App. 2003); Spence v. Flynt, 816 P.2d 771, 778 (Wyo. 1991); Mont. Ethics Op. 140519, *supra* note 21, at 6; *see also* 2010 N.C. Ethics Op. 5, 2010 WL 2020510, at *2 (N.C. State Bar 2010) (opining that under Rule 3.7(b), a lawyer in the North Carolina Attorney General's office could call another lawyer in the same office as an expert witness in a case involving international child support enforcement issues).

156. *Spence*, 816 P.2d at 778 ("One function of Rule 3.7(b) is to make clear that 3.7(a) is personal to the client's trial advocate and will not be imputed to other members of the firm.").

157. Model Rules of Prof'l Conduct R. 3.7(b) (2020).

158. *See, e.g.*, Collins Entm't, Inc. v. White, 611 S.E.2d 262, 271 (S.C. Ct. App. 2005) (finding no substantial hardship where the lawyer-witness's partner could take over the client's representation at trial).

159. Neumann v. Tuccio, No. DBDCCV075002381S, 2009 WL 2506357, at *6 (Conn. Super. Ct. July 17, 2009).

But as Model Rule 3.7(b) further expresses, imputed disqualification is appropriate where the lawyer-witness is also disqualified from representing the client by a conflict of interest under Model Rules 1.7 or 1.9.[160] Under Model Rule 1.10(a), lawyers practicing in a firm generally are disqualified from representing a client "when any one of them practicing alone would be prohibited from doing so by Rules 1.7 or 1.9."[161] Thus, "if the conflict rules alone would preclude the testifying lawyer from acting as both advocate and witness, then no one in the testifying lawyer's firm may serve as an advocate in the case."[162]

This aspect of Rule 3.7(b) is implicated only where the nature of the lawyer-witness's involvement creates a conflict of interest for other lawyers in the firm.[163] It is intended, for example, to protect a client where its current or former lawyer is expected to testify adversely to it at trial, most often where the opponent calls the lawyer as an involuntary witness. As the North Dakota Supreme Court once explained, a conflict contemplated by Rule 3.7(b) arises "when an attorney's testimony would prejudicially contradict or undermine his client's factual assertions."[164] Of course, depending on the facts, a client may waive the conflict of interest. Allowing the client to consent to the representation notwithstanding the conflict of interest prevents "the power of the client to control the progress of his or her case from being placed into the hands of opposing counsel."[165]

That is not the only situation in which Rule 3.7(b) comes into play, however, as *State v. O'Neil*[166] illustrates. The defendant there, James O'Neil, was a repeat criminal offender who was charged with felony harassment. He was represented by Anuradha Zangri of the King County Department of Public Defense (KCDPD). O'Neil pled not guilty at his arraignment. The State later amended the information to replace the harassment charge with an assault charge. Unlike the original harassment charge, the assault charge was a "strike" offense, meaning that O'Neil would face life in prison if he was convicted because the assault conviction would be his "third strike." Then, with a new KCDPD lawyer, Edwin Aralica, O'Neil moved for re-arraignment based on ineffective assistance of counsel. Aralica argued that Zangri should have advised O'Neil to plead guilty to the original harassment charge based on O'Neil's two prior strike convictions.[167]

In response, the State asked to interview Haydee Vargas, a KCDPD lawyer with vast arraignment experience. The State argued that interviewing

160. Model Rules of Prof'l Conduct R. 3.7 cmt. 7 (2020).
161. *Id.* R. 1.10(a).
162. Sargent Cnty. Bank v. Wentworth, 500 N.W.2d 862, 870 (N.D. 1993).
163. Cunningham v. Sams, 588 S.E.2d 484, 488 (N.C. Ct. App. 2003).
164. *Sargent Cnty. Bank*, 500 N.W.2d at 871.
165. Leaseamerica Corp. v. Stewart, 876 P.2d 184, 192 (Kan. Ct. App. 1994).
166. 393 P.3d 1238 (Wash. Ct. App. 2017).
167. *Id.* at 1239.

Vargas would allow it to determine whether Zangri's representation of O'Neil was objectively ineffective. O'Neil objected to the State's request to interview Vargas because Aralica was Vargas's supervisor and they worked in the same office. O'Neil contended that permitting the State to interview Vargas would create a conflict of interest for Aralica under Rule 3.7. Alternatively, O'Neil argued that Aralica should be allowed to withdraw if the court granted the State's request to interview Vargas. The trial court found no conflict of interest and denied all of O'Neil's requested relief, but granted him a stay to pursue a discretionary appeal.[168]

On appeal, O'Neil argued that as Vargas's supervisor, Aralica had a Rule 1.7 personal interest conflict that impaired his ability to be an effective advocate.[169] The Washington Court of Appeals agreed with O'Neil:

> Aralica is a felony supervising attorney in the KCDPD ACA Division. Vargas is a staff attorney for the ACA. . . . Aralica supervises her performance. . . . He is responsible for her professional development, discipline, and work place competence. He is therefore responsible for her doing a competent job. His natural inclinations, if not duty, would be to defend the work of the attorneys he supervises, his work as supervisor, and his employer.
>
> In contrast, Aralica's duty to O'Neil is to show that the previous counsel was ineffective at arraignment by not anticipating that the state would amend the charges to implicate a third strike and life in prison without parole. The State believes Vargas may have information that would help defeat that claim. Aralica has a clear duty to O'Neil to challenge any of Vargas's testimony that is harmful to O'Neil, including arraignment practices performed by her, witnessed by her, supervised by Aralica himself, and/or approved by their employer. He would have a clear duty to attack her credibility if possible. The personal interest at issue is not merely his relationship with Vargas, but how his own supervisory position undermines his advocacy for O'Neil, if Vargas testifies for the State.[170]

The *O'Neil* court concluded that there was a significant risk that Aralica's representation of O'Neil would be materially affected by his personal interests if Vargas was a witness for the State.[171] Building on that conclusion, the court turned to O'Neil's argument that Rule 3.7(b) prevented the State from interviewing Vargas because it was her proposed interview that created Aralica's conflict of interest. The court observed that O'Neil's argument was not typical of Rule 3.7 cases, which usually "involve one side arguing that the other side's attorney should have been disqualified because the attorney is a necessary witness."[172] The unusual posture of the case, however, was

168. *Id.* at 1240.
169. *Id.*
170. *Id.* at 1241 (footnotes omitted).
171. *Id.* at 1241–42.
172. *Id.* at 1242.

not dispositive. Under the "necessary witness" test that Washington courts typically apply in Rule 3.7 cases, a lawyer may be called as a witness only if her testimony is material, is unobtainable elsewhere, and will or may prejudice her client.[173] If the State had sought Aralica's testimony, the necessary witness test unquestionably would control the situation.[174] Thus, although Aralica was but a member of the same firm as Vargas:

> [O]nce the trial court indicated that Vargas was available for interview as a potential witness, the basis for a conflict of interest became apparent. An inquiry into the facts should have led the trial court to conclude that if Vargas was a witness, Aralica would in fact have a personal conflict of interest and would have been required by RPC 1.7 and 3.7 to withdraw. Given our holding that Aralica will face a conflict as a matter of law if Vargas serves as a witness, the consequences are the same as if the State were calling Aralica. The ultimate effect is his obligatory disqualification.[175]

The *O'Neil* court reversed the trial court's order allowing the State to interview Vargas and denying Aralica leave to withdraw, and remanded the case for further proceedings. On remand, the trial court would be required to determine whether Vargas was a necessary witness. If she was a necessary witness, the trial court would have to allow Aralica to withdraw.[176]

VI. Conclusion

Lawyers and courts alike are uncomfortable with the dual roles of lawyer and fact witness. This discomfort probably is exaggerated. A lawyer's disqualification as a trial advocate does not prevent her from representing a client in many other aspects of the same case. Furthermore, a party seeking to disqualify a lawyer under Model Rule 3.7(a) must establish that the lawyer's proposed testimony is relevant, material, not merely cumulative, and unobtainable elsewhere. This is a difficult standard to satisfy, principally because the facts that are the subject of lawyers' intended testimony are so often obtainable from other sources. Finally, a lawyer's disqualification under the advocate-witness rule is generally not imputed to other lawyers in the same firm, so there usually is room for continuity in the client's representation.

173. *Id.* at 1243.
174. *Id.*
175. *Id.*
176. *Id.*

12

Professional Responsibility and Liability in Negotiations

I. Introduction

Lawyers routinely negotiate on clients' behalf. For example, civil litigation is dominated by settlements.[1] Those settlements are typically the product of negotiations between the parties' lawyers, whether conducted directly or facilitated by third-party neutrals. Courts often steer the parties toward settlement and thus their lawyers into negotiations through mandatory mediation and settlement conferences. In other cases, the parties enter negotiations led by their lawyers over the parties' doubts about the strength of their cases, concerns over the cost of continued litigation, or because of business or financial considerations. For that matter, countless civil disputes are resolved through negotiation before suit is ever filed.

Criminal practice is similar when it comes to resolution through negotiation. Most federal and state criminal cases are resolved through guilty pleas. Those pleas derive from negotiations between prosecutors and defense lawyers. In some cases, the threat of the harsh sentence a defendant likely will face if she loses at trial compels plea negotiations.

Although most trial lawyers negotiate in their practices, many overlook their related professional responsibilities, especially with respect to truthfulness. There are several possible reasons for this confusion around honesty, but two stand out. First, negotiation is paradoxical in the sense that lawyers must be honest even as they are attempting to mislead or misdirect their adversaries. Negotiating lawyers often must hope that opponents miscalculate the strength of their positions and, indeed, must facilitate their opponents' inaccurate assessments. Second, but consistent with the first point, most lawyers expect some dissembling in negotiations. This expectation

1. *See* Balducci v. Cige, 223 A.3d 1229, 1245–46 (N.J. 2020) (stating that "most cases are resolved by settlement").

potentially colors their judgment when it comes to evaluating the ethical permissibility of their own statements during negotiations.

Honesty is certainly not the only professional responsibility issue in negotiations. Consider, for example, Model Rule of Professional Conduct 1.2(a), which states that the decision to settle a matter is exclusively the client's call.[2] A lawyer cannot usurp a client's right to control settlement even if the lawyer believes the client's position is unreasonable,[3] or demand that clients relinquish the right to control settlement as a condition of their representations.[4] It is unethical for lawyers to impair clients' right to settle through fee agreements that economically penalize the client for settling on terms that the lawyer deems unsatisfactory.[5] Similarly, in criminal cases, Model Rule 1.2(a) establishes that the decision to plead guilty rests solely with the client.[6] Accordingly, a lawyer cannot refuse a client's request to enter a guilty plea.[7]

In explaining lawyers' professional responsibilities in negotiations, this chapter focuses on some challenging and nuanced problems. Achieving that focus requires an understanding of key ethics rules on a broad level, as well as an appreciation for how those rules play out when applied to the facts of illustrative cases. Additionally, it is important to recognize that lawyers' negotiation conduct may expose them to tort liability as well as to discipline and sanctions.

II. Negotiation and Authority to Settle

Before addressing the professional responsibility aspects of negotiations, it is appropriate to briefly examine the source of lawyers' authority to settle clients' claims. The attorney-client relationship is an agency relationship, with

2. Model Rules of Prof'l Conduct R. 1.2(a) (2020) ("A lawyer shall abide by a client's decision whether to settle a matter.").

3. S.T. v. 1515 Broad St., LLC, 227 A.3d 1190, 1193 (N.J. 2020); *In re* Indeglia, 765 A.2d 444, 447 (R.I. 2001).

4. Compton v. Kittleson, 171 P.3d 172, 176 (Alaska 2007); *In re* Lansky, 678 N.E.2d 1114, 1116–17 (Ind. 1997); Lofton v. Fairmont Specialty Ins. Mgrs., Inc., 367 S.W.3d 593, 597 (Ky. 2012); State Bar of Nev., Comm. on Ethics & Prof'l Responsibility, Formal Op. No. 35, at 2 (2006); *see also In re* Coleman, 295 S.W.3d 857, 865 (Mo. 2009) (invoking Rule 1.7 to discipline a lawyer for such a requirement).

5. *See, e.g., Compton*, 171 P.3d at 176–80 (involving hybrid contingent fee/hourly billing agreement that effectively penalized clients if they declined to settle and fared worse at trial); State v. Bradley, HHDCV166072114S, 2018 WL 3518265, at *3, *6–7 (Conn. Super. Ct. July 3, 2018) (invalidating a contingent fee agreement that used the client's decision to settle as a trigger for converting from a contingent fee to an hourly fee and produced an hourly fee so large that the client received no settlement funds).

6. Model Rules of Prof'l Conduct R. 1.2(a) (2020) (providing that "[i]n a criminal case, the lawyer shall abide by the client's decision, after consultation with the lawyer, as to a plea to be entered").

7. *In re* Garnett, 603 S.E.2d 281, 283 (Ga. 2004).

the client cast as principal and the lawyer as agent.[8] Generally, an agent's acts on behalf of a principal will bind the principal if the acts are expressly authorized or the agent has apparent authority. A person's mere representation by a lawyer, however, does not imply the lawyer's authority to settle the person's claim or suit.[9] Lawyers have no implied or inherent authority to settle clients' claims or suits.[10] Furthermore, a client's authorization of a lawyer to enter into settlement negotiations does not mean that the lawyer is authorized to accept a settlement; there is, after all, a difference between the power to conduct negotiations and the power to conclude a dispute. Lawyers' agency with respect to agreeing to settlement is limited by Model Rule 1.2(a), which requires a lawyer to obtain a client's express authority to settle a matter.[11]

In most cases, however, an opposing party does not know whether a client has expressly authorized her lawyer to settle and cannot ethically inquire of the client concerning the lawyer's actual authority.[12] Certainly, a lawyer's statement that she will "recommend" a settlement to her client rather than accepting an offer should signal to opposing counsel that the lawyer lacks authority to settle on the stated terms, but limitations are not always so plain. This void between what the lawyer knows about the settlement authority the client has expressly granted and what opposing counsel knows about whether a lawyer is truly authorized to settle can result in a common scenario: an opposing party moving to enforce a settlement agreement that the client disclaims on the basis that his lawyer allegedly lacked authority to settle on the specified terms.

---

8. *In re* Kaushas, 616 B.R. 57, 63 (Bankr. M.D. Pa. 2020) (applying Pennsylvania law); Contreras v. Dowling, 208 Cal. Rptr. 3d 707, 725 (Ct. App. 2016); Hoch v. Loren, 273 So. 3d 56, 58 (Fla. Dist. Ct. App. 2019); Primera Beef, LLC v. Ward, 457 P.3d 161, 166 (Idaho 2020) (quoting Caballero v. Wikse, 92 P.3d 1076, 1079 (Idaho 2004)); State v. Parham, 121 N.E.3d 412, 426 (Ohio Ct. App. 2019); Est. of Miller v. Storey, 903 N.W.2d 759, 774–75 (Wis. 2017).

9. *In re* Rosenthal & Watson, P.C., 612 B.R. 507, 540 (Bankr. W.D. Tex. 2020) (applying Texas law); Robertson v. Alling, 351 P.3d 352, 356 (Ariz. 2015); Collado v. Pavlow, 951 So. 2d 69, 71 (Fla. Dist. Ct. App. 2007); Koval v. Simon Telelect, Inc., 693 N.E.2d 1299, 1302 (Ind. 1998); 4900 Park Heights Ave. LLC v. Cromwell Retail 1, LLC, 227 A.3d 757, 768 (Md. Ct. Spec. App. 2020); NC-DSH, Inc. v. Garner, 218 P.3d 853, 860 (Nev. 2009); Bromley v. Seme, 3 N.E.3d 1254, 1258 (Ohio Ct. App. 2013).

10. *See* Teva Pharm. Indus., Ltd. v. United Healthcare Servs., Inc., 341 F. Supp. 3d 475, 504 (E.D. Pa. 2018) (applying Minnesota law); Terra Land Servs., Inc. v. McIntyre, 572 S.W.3d 424, 433 (Ark. Ct. App. 2019) (refusing to enforce a settlement agreement); Marietta Tr. v. J.R. Logging Inc., 225 So. 3d 1144, 1148 (La. Ct. App. 2017) ("[A] party's counsel of record does not have authority to settle a client's claim without his client's clear and express consent. . . . The general authority granted to an attorney in an attorney/client contract of employment to settle the client's case constitutes only authority to negotiate a settlement." (citation omitted)).

11. State *ex rel.* Okla. Bar Ass'n v. Hummel, 89 P.3d 1105, 1111 (Okla. 2004); Model Rules of Prof'l Conduct R. 1.2(a) (2020) ("A lawyer shall abide by a client's decision whether to settle a matter.").

12. *See* Model Rules of Prof'l Conduct R. 4.2 (2020) (prohibiting ex parte communications with represented parties, with limited exceptions).

To fill this knowledge or informational void, some courts indulge the presumption that a lawyer who is representing a client in litigation has apparent authority to settle on the client's behalf.[13] It is the client's burden to rebut this presumption and prove the lawyer's lack of authority.[14] Other courts hold that the lawyer has apparent authority to settle on the client's behalf without mention of a presumption.[15] Where a lawsuit has not been filed at the time of settlement negotiations, however, the result may be different.[16] Outside of litigation, a client's mere engagement of a lawyer does not, in some courts' eyes, cloak the lawyer with apparent authority to settle a dispute.[17] Other courts will not presume a lawyer's authority to settle but will instead require the party moving to enforce the settlement to establish the lawyer's authority,[18] or require the party seeking to set aside a settlement to prove the lawyer's lack of authority.[19] As most lawyers would expect, disputes typically pivot on whether the lawyer had apparent authority to settle on her client's behalf.[20]

Just as in other agency contexts where a principal can communicate her agent's limits of authority to others, clients may limit their lawyers' apparent authority by communicating any limitations to opposing parties. Where the opposing party is represented by counsel, this may not be a practical approach given that, even when the client initiates the communication,

13. United States v. Cox, 743 F. App'x 509, 512 (4th Cir. 2018); Quesada v. Napolitano, 701 F.3d 1080, 1083 (5th Cir. 2012); Anaya v. Coello, 632 S.E.2d 425, 427 (Ga. Ct. App. 2006); 39 Bell, LLC v. K&K, Inc., 584 S.W.3d 823, 831 (Mo. Ct. App. 2019); Messer v. Huntington Anesthesia Grp., Inc., 664 S.E.2d 751, 759–61 (W. Va. 2008).

14. *39 Bell*, 584 S.W.3d at 831; Powell v. City of Newton, 684 S.E.2d 55, 59 (N.C. Ct. App. 2009) (quoting Harris v. Ray Johnston Constr. Co., 534 S.E.2d 653, 654–55 (N.C. Ct. App. 2000)).

15. *See, e.g.*, Nugent v. Myles, 829 S.E.2d 623, 627 (Ga. Ct. App. 2019) (quoting Brumbelow v. N. Propane Gas Co., 308 S.E.2d 544, 546 (Ga. 1983)); Kloian v. Domino's Pizza, L.L.C., 733 N.W.2d 766, 770 (Mich. Ct. App. 2006) ("An attorney has apparent authority to settle a lawsuit on behalf of his or her client.").

16. *Compare Anaya*, 632 S.E.2d at 427 (stating that lawyer has apparent authority regardless of whether an action is pending in court), *with* Koval v. Simon Telelect, Inc., 693 N.E.2d 1299, 1304–07 (Ind. 1998) (differentiating between in- and out-of-court settlements).

17. *Koval*, 693 N.E.2d at 1304.

18. *See, e.g.*, Magallanes v. Ill. Bell Tel. Co., 535 F.3d 582, 584 (7th Cir. 2008) (applying Illinois law); Makins v. D.C., 861 A.2d 590, 593–97 (D.C. 2004) (involving a lawyer's apparent authority to settle); St. Mary's Sch. of Med. Ltd. v. Zabaleta, 252 So. 3d 371, 372 (Fla. Dist. Ct. App. 2018) ("Case law sets a very high standard for a party to meet in order to enforce a settlement agreement."); 4900 Park Heights Ave. LLC v. Cromwell Retail 1, LLC, 227 A.3d 757, 768 (Md. Ct. Spec. App. 2020) (quoting Mitchell Props. v. Real Est. Title Co., 490 A.2d 271, 276 (Md. Ct. Spec. App. 1985)).

19. *See, e.g.*, Yale Univ. v. Out of the Box, LLC, 990 A.2d 869, 873–76 (Conn. App. Ct. 2010) (discussing a lawyer's apparent authority to settle as determined from the totality of the circumstances).

20. *See, e.g.*, Robertson v. Alling, 351 P.3d 352, 356 (Ariz. 2015) (stating that the party seeking to enforce a settlement must establish that its reliance on the opposing lawyer's apparent authority to settle was reasonable, finding that the movants' reliance was reasonable, and thus enforcing the settlement).

the opposing lawyer will still be ethically prohibited from communicating directly with the client. If a client does not communicate alleged limitations to opposing parties and the lawyer allegedly exceeds the scope of her settlement authority, courts often conclude that the client's remedy is against the lawyer rather than against the opposing party.[21]

In conclusion, whether a lawyer had express or apparent authority to settle on a client's behalf, or whether the client ratified an unauthorized settlement, will, as in other agency disputes, depend on the jurisdiction and the facts of the case. Lawyers must always remember that the decision to settle is vested in the client.[22] Lawyers may counsel clients on settlement and explain the desirability or drawbacks of certain approaches or options, and they may even attempt to persuade clients to decide in particular ways, but they may not usurp clients' authority. Lawyers who are negotiating on clients' behalf should seek clear instructions from their clients as to the scope and limits of their authority to compromise. Lawyers may seek those instructions well in advance of any settlement efforts.[23] Lawyers are wise to document those instructions.

On the other side of the coin, lawyers seeking to make certain that opposing counsel has authority to bind the opposing party to a settlement should make reasonable efforts to confirm that opposing counsel have authority to settle, to agree to terms, and the like. When settlement discussions are connected to court-ordered or court-annexed mediation, lawyers can seek to have language included in a court order requiring the opposing party to attend the mediation along with opposing counsel or that the opposing party otherwise represent that its counsel participating in the mediation has full settlement authority. When settlement discussions occur through mediation of any kind, lawyers can insist that prior to adjourning the mediation, the parties come together in the presence of the mediator and their respective counsel to confirm that they have expressly authorized the settlement on the agreed terms.

---

21. *See, e.g.*, Stephens v. Alan V. Mock Constr. Co., 690 S.E.2d 225, 230–31 (Ga. Ct. App. 2010) (enforcing the settlement agreement). *But see* Restatement (Third) of the Law Governing Lawyers § 27 cmt. d (2000) (explaining that "the burden of inconvenience resulting if the client repudiates the settlement is properly left with the opposing party," in part because "[r]efusing to uphold a settlement reached without the client's authority means that the case remains open, while upholding such a settlement deprives the client of the right to have the claim resolved on other terms").

22. Todd v. Coleman, 119 N.E.3d 1137, 1141 (Ind. Ct. App. 2019); Furstenfeld v. Pepin, 869 N.W.2d 353, 366 (Neb. Ct. App. 2015).

23. Model Rules of Prof'l Conduct R. 1.2 cmt. 3 (2020) ("At the outset of a representation, the client may authorize the lawyer to take specific action on the client's behalf without further consultation.").

III. Lawyers' Duty to Communicate with Clients

Returning now to the rules of professional conduct, lawyers' duty to communicate with clients is essential to the attorney-client relationship in negotiations as elsewhere. This duty is primarily enforced through Model Rule 1.4, which provides:

> (a) A lawyer shall:
>
> (1) promptly inform the client of any decision or circumstance with respect to which the client's informed consent . . . is required by these Rules;
>
> (2) reasonably consult with the client about the means by which the client's objectives are to be accomplished;
>
> (3) keep the client reasonably informed about the status of the matter;
>
> (4) promptly comply with reasonable requests for information;
>
> (5) consult with the client about any relevant limitation on the lawyer's conduct when the lawyer knows that the client expects assistance not permitted by the Rules of Professional Conduct or other law.
>
> (b) A lawyer shall explain a matter to the extent reasonably necessary to permit the client to make informed decisions regarding the representation.[24]

Of course, lawyers would have a duty to reasonably communicate with their clients even in the absence of Model Rule 1.4. Again, lawyers are their clients' agents, and agents generally must provide their principals with information related to the subject of the agency. Furthermore, a duty of reasonable communication is implied in every contract between a lawyer and client.

Model Rule 1.4(a) imposes several specific requirements, but some general observations about lawyers' duty to communicate should be made at the outset. First, lawyers' duties under Rule 1.4 are mandatory, not aspirational.[25] Second, lawyers' duty to communicate is an affirmative obligation in the sense that they must initiate communications when necessary;[26] they generally cannot rely on clients to do so. Third, the duty to communicate necessarily requires honest communication. It is impossible for clients who receive untruthful communications from their lawyers to be reasonably informed about the status of their representations.[27] Fourth, the duty to

24. MODEL RULES OF PROF'L CONDUCT R. 1.4 (2020).

25. State *ex rel.* Okla. Bar Ass'n v. Koss, 452 P.3d 427, 432 (Okla. 2019).

26. *In re* Robbins, 192 A.3d 558, 564 (D.C. 2018).

27. *In re* Indeglia, 765 A.2d 444, 447 (R.I. 2001); *see also* Att'y Grievance Comm'n of Md. v. Planta, 225 A.3d 19, 36 (Md. 2020) (discussing Rule 1.2(a) and stating that for a client to make informed decisions regarding the objectives of the representation, the lawyer must give the client honest updates regarding the status of the client's case (quoting Att'y Grievance Comm'n of Md. v. Hamilton, 118 A.3d 958, 968–69 (Md. 2015)).

keep a client informed about the status of a matter is tempered by reason.[28] A lawyer need not apprise a client of all details of a representation. A lawyer has no duty to tell a client that which the client already knows or to convey immaterial information to a client. A lawyer is not required to communicate with a client as often as the client desires, provided that the lawyer's conduct is "reasonable under the circumstances."[29] This rule of reason applies to the lawyer's duty to initiate communications or volunteer information and to the duty to respond to clients' inquiries. Fifth, the quality of the lawyer's communications with the client matters. Thus, frequent attorney-client communications do not guarantee Rule 1.4 compliance.[30] Sixth, in attempting to communicate with clients, lawyers should use means that are reasonably calculated to succeed.[31] If clients do not return telephone calls, for example, lawyers should try letters or e-mail.[32] Seventh, if a lawyer has multiple clients in a matter, the lawyer's duty to communicate extends to each of them. Eighth, whether a lawyer may be said to have reasonably consulted with or informed a client about a matter is always a case-specific inquiry.

Regardless of the specific obligation imposed under Model Rule 1.4(a), and consistent with the reasonableness requirement inherent in the rule, lawyers' duty to communicate with clients is necessarily contextual. A client may agree to limit a lawyer's duty to communicate with her concerning the representation. For example, a client might agree that a lawyer negotiating on her behalf has no duty to convey the opponent's demands or offers unless they are above or below some predetermined threshold. Alternatively, sparse communications between a lawyer and client may be reasonable if they have an established course of dealing, or the client has granted the lawyer broad discretion in carrying out the representation.

---

28. *See, e.g.*, Att'y Grievance Comm'n of Md. v. May, 72 A.3d 174, 177 (Md. 2013) (explaining that "Rule 1.4 does not require repeating the same information each time a client inquires about a matter").

29. *In re* Schoeneman, 777 A.2d 259, 264 (D.C. 2001).

30. *See, e.g.*, Att'y Grievance Comm'n of Md. v. Lang, 191 A.3d 474, 503 (Md. 2018) ("A violation of [Rule] 1.4 turns on the substance, not regularity, of communication; thus, frequent attorney-client communication does not necessarily negate a violation of [Rule] 1.4.").

31. *See, e.g.*, *In re* Askew, 225 A.3d 388, 396 (D.C. 2020) ("[A]n attorney must make more than a pro forma attempt to initiate communications."); Att'y Grievance Comm'n of Md. v. Riely, 242 A.3d 206, 228 (Md. 2020) (holding that the lawyer violated Rule 1.4 by writing to his clients in English when he knew they did not understand English); Att'y Grievance Comm'n of Md. v. Aita, 181 A.3d 774, 784 (Md. 2018) (finding that the lawyer violated Rule 1.4(b) when she sent her Guatemalan client letters written in English—a language he did not read or speak fluently—and included in the letters a statement that it was his responsibility to have them translated if he did not understand them).

32. *See, e.g.*, People v. Podoll, 855 P.2d 1389, 1391–93 (Colo. 1993) (involving client who did not respond to lawyer's faxed letters and did not return telephone calls, and who thus lost favorable settlement opportunity; disciplinary board and court faulted lawyer for attempting to communicate by means that continually failed).

Turning now to Model Rule 1.4(b), explaining matters to clients is an essential aspect of lawyers' work.[33] Clients are entitled to determine the objectives of their representations.[34] They are also entitled to be consulted with respect to the means by which those objectives are to be accomplished.[35] Rule 1.4(b) animates these important principles, recognizing that clients must have sufficient information to "participate intelligently in decisions concerning the objectives of the representation and the means by which they are to be pursued."[36]

The adequacy of a communication for Rule 1.4(b) purposes may depend on a range of factors, including the subject of the representation, the scope of the representation, the nature of the matter or task at hand, time constraints, the lawyer's relationship with the client, the client's unique characteristics, and non-legal considerations. Lawyers generally must discuss "key strategic decisions" with clients.[37] In most cases, a lawyer should be expected to explain to the client the advantages and disadvantages of reasonably available alternatives.[38] In litigation, a lawyer should explain the relative risks of trial versus settlement and, where necessary, the possible effects of either beyond the courtroom.

Although it should be apparent that Rule 1.4 applies to lawyers who are negotiating on clients' behalf, problems attributable to communication lapses are unfortunately common.[39] A recurring source of controversy is

33. *In re* Ukwu, 926 A.2d 1106, 1139 (D.C. 2007).

34. Model Rules of Prof'l Conduct R. 1.2(a) (2020).

35. *Id.*

36. *Id.* R. 1.4 cmt. 5.

37. Bowman v. Gruel Mills Nims & Pylman, LLP, No. 5:06-CV-87, 2007 WL 1203580, at *5 (W.D. Mich. Apr. 24, 2007).

38. *See* Iowa Sup. Ct. Att'y Disciplinary Bd. v. Turner, 918 N.W.2d 130, 146 (Iowa 2018) ("An attorney violates [Rule 1.4(b)] by failing to explain an alternative course of action that is reasonably necessary to permit the client to make an informed decision on the matter.").

39. *See, e.g.*, Att'y Grievance Comm'n of Md. v. Bocchino, 80 A.3d 222, 237 (Md. 2013) (holding that the lawyer violated Rule 1.4(b) by failing to tell his clients about the defendant's request for a settlement demand; even if it was a valid strategy not to tell the defendant the amount for which the clients would have settled, the lawyer was obligated to inform his clients that the defendant wanted to engage in settlement negotiations); *In re* Disciplinary Action Against Eichhorn-Hicks, 916 N.W.2d 32, 35–36, 38 (Minn. 2018) (finding that the lawyer violated Rule 1.4, among others, by failing to convey a plea offer to his criminal defense client).

plaintiffs' lawyers' alleged failure to convey settlement offers to their clients.[40] *First National Bank of LaGrange v. Lowrey*[41] is illustrative.

Lowrey arose out of a medical malpractice action in which John Lowrey represented Mary King, who was the mother and next friend of Jordan King. Jordan had profound birth injuries. Lowrey sued Jordan's doctor and the hospital where Jordan was born. At a pretrial conference, the defendants offered to settle the case for $1 million. Lowrey rejected that offer,[42] apparently believing that it was too low and further speculating that there might be additional insurance available to fund a settlement.[43] Lowrey then proposed a high-low agreement that the defendants rejected. Lowrey did not tell Mary of the $1 million settlement offer, nor did he discuss the proposed high-low agreement with her. A jury ultimately returned a defense verdict.

The guardian of Jordan's estate sued Lowrey for legal malpractice, alleging that Lowrey rejected the defendants' settlement offer in the medical malpractice case without first discussing the offer with Mary. At trial, the guardian's expert witness, Professor Steven Lubet, testified that Lowrey erred by neglecting to inform Mary of the $1 million settlement offer, by failing to tell her that settlement negotiations could be reopened after he rejected that offer, by failing to keep her informed of the status of the case as it headed toward trial, and by not providing her with information necessary to make a settlement decision at a crucial time.[44] Additionally, Professor Lubet testified, Lowrey was obligated to obtain Mary's permission to make the high-low offer, and to explain the potential consequences and ramifications of that offer.[45] A jury returned a $1 million verdict against Lowrey and his law firm. Lowrey and his firm appealed.

40. *See, e.g.*, Burton v. Mottolese, 835 A.2d 998, 1026 & n.42 (Conn. 2003) (finding a Rule 1.4 violation where plaintiffs' counsel failed to transmit the defendants' offer to waive fees and costs to which they would be entitled as prevailing parties and to waive a sanctions award as part of a settlement); *In re* Steele, 868 A.2d 146, 149 (D.C. 2005) (failing to communicate a settlement offer); Att'y Grievance Comm'n of Md. v. Sanderson, 213 A.3d 122, 149–50 (Md. 2019) (finding that the lawyer violated Rule 1.4 by not informing the client that he had received the settlement check, never informing her of the full settlement amount, never giving her a settlement disbursement sheet, and failing to explain the amount she would receive after his fee was accounted for); Att'y Grievance Comm'n of Md. v. Steinberg, 910 A.2d 429, 444–45 (Md. 2006) (violating Rule 1.4 by communicating a settlement offer to one of two clients, but not the other); Stark Cnty. Bar Ass'n v. Russell, 856 N.E.2d 976, 978 (Ohio 2006) (failing to convey a settlement offer until after it had been withdrawn); *In re* Esgar, 642 S.E.2d 563, 564–65 (S.C. 2007) (suspending a lawyer who failed to keep a client informed regarding the status of the lawyer's negotiations with a settlement funding company concerning the client's alleged debt to company).

41. 872 N.E.2d 447 (Ill. App. Ct. 2007).

42. *Id.* at 455.

43. *See id.* at 457–58.

44. *Id.* at 460, 465.

45. *Id.* at 465.

The *Lowrey* court affirmed the judgment against Lowrey. In doing so, the court found that Professor Lubet had established the standard of care applicable to Lowrey's conduct and that he had further established Lowrey's breach of that standard.[46]

A. The Potential Insurance Defense Trap

Again, the most common communication problem in negotiations seems to be lawyers' failure to relay settlement offers to clients. This problem may lurk unnoticed where a lawyer is defending a client at the behest of an insurance company. Although the issue of whether an insurance defense lawyer has one client (the insured) or two (the insured and the insurer) is often debated, it is invariably true that the insured is a client of the defense lawyer. As a client, an insured is owed a duty of communication by the defense lawyer. Unfortunately, because in most cases an insurer controls its insured's defense, has the contractual right to settle as it deems expedient, and pays any settlement, a defense lawyer may keep only the insurer informed during settlement negotiations. Such neglect potentially violates Rule 1.4 and may expose the lawyer to tort liability to the insured. *Teague v. St. Paul Fire & Marine Insurance Co.*[47] is an instructive case.

The plaintiff in *Teague*, Dr. Michael Teague, was sued for medical malpractice. His professional liability insurer, St. Paul, assigned his defense to the law firm of Seale, Smith, Zuber & Barnette. Donald Zuber, a partner, and Catherine Nobile, an associate, were responsible for Dr. Teague's defense. Nobile failed to file a required jury bond, and Teague consequently lost the right to a jury trial. Neither Zuber nor Nobile informed Teague of this error; indeed, they concealed it from him. They promptly informed St. Paul of the mistake, however.[48]

The parties' lawyers eventually mediated the case. Regrettably, the defense lawyers never told Dr. Teague about the mediation.[49] As a result of that mediation, St. Paul agreed to settle the case for $50,000. Notably, Dr. Teague's insurance policy did not contain a consent-to-settle provision, which would have obligated St. Paul to obtain his consent to settle any claim covered by the policy. When the mediation concluded, Nobile left a message for Dr. Teague telling him that the case had been settled, and the doctor confirmed the settlement in a telephone conversation with Nobile later that day.

Dr. Teague called Zuber the next day and complained that the case was settled rather than tried. When St. Paul reported the settlement to the

---

46. *Id.* at 466.
47. 974 So. 2d 1266 (La. 2008).
48. *Id.* at 1269.
49. *Id.*

National Practitioner Data Bank, Dr. Teague became upset and sought other counsel. Nobile's error then came to light, and the doctor sued the law firm, Zuber, and Nobile for malpractice, alleging a litany of wrongdoing. He contended that their mistakes and misconduct harmed his business reputation, caused his malpractice insurance premiums to increase, contributed to a loss of income, and caused him emotional distress and mental anguish.[50] Dr. Teague later amended his complaint to allege that the defendants violated Louisiana Rule of Professional Conduct 1.4 by failing to keep him advised of all pertinent developments in his case and by intentionally concealing the fact that Nobile had forfeited his right to a jury trial by failing to post the jury bond.[51]

The legal malpractice case was tried to a jury, and Teague won a $138,500 verdict. A lower appellate court reversed the trial court judgment on statute of limitations grounds, and Teague sought review by the Louisiana Supreme Court.

The Louisiana Supreme Court resolved the critical statute of limitations issue in the doctor's favor, but, before doing so, analyzed whether the defendants committed malpractice. This required Dr. Teague to prove the existence of an attorney-client relationship, a breach of duty by the lawyers, and resulting damage.

It was undisputed that Dr. Teague shared an attorney-client relationship with Zuber, Nobile, and their law firm. Thus, the defendants unquestionably "owed Dr. Teague a fiduciary duty to legally represent him with integrity, skill and due diligence, which encompassed keeping Dr. Teague reasonably informed about the status of his case."[52]

The defendants conceded their many errors but argued that they were not guilty of malpractice because, under St. Paul's policy, they did not need Dr. Teague's consent to settle the case against him.[53] This argument did not impress the court.

> We fail to see how the ability to settle the case under the policy without Dr. Teague's consent lessens the obligations owed by the attorneys to their client. Indeed, it does not. It is most telling that defendants did keep St. Paul apprised of their omission, but yet decided not to inform Dr. Teague of their course of conduct and strategy in his case. Clearly, defendants breached a fiduciary duty they owed to their client by failing to keep him reasonably informed.[54]

50. *Id.* at 1269–70.
51. *Id.* at 1270.
52. *Id.* at 1272.
53. *Id.*
54. *Id.*

After discussing an analogous Illinois case,[55] the *Teague* court continued its critique of the lawyers. The court was bothered by the lawyers' dishonesty and by the fact that they favored St. Paul over the doctor.

> Here, Dr. Teague was led to believe that his case would not be settled because the claim against him was very defendable. The issue of settling the case was never discussed. We find this a compelling factor in Dr. Teague's claim of legal malpractice.
>
> In the present case, it is apparent that defendants felt more loyalty to St. Paul than they did for Dr. Teague. . . . Here, by failing to inform Dr. Teague of the loss of a jury trial, which in turn led to the mediation and settlement of his case, defendants deprived Dr. Teague of the opportunity of hiring independent counsel to defend him in the malpractice claim against him. This clearly constitutes a claim for legal malpractice. . . .[56]

The court in *Teague* went on to determine that the doctor's legal malpractice claim was not time-barred. It thus reversed the lower appellate court's judgment and remanded the case to that court to consider other alleged errors raised by the defendants.[57] The lower appellate court ultimately cleared the lawyers of malpractice, although it was careful not to condone their failure to communicate with Dr. Teague.[58]

Although the lawyers in *Teague* escaped liability, insurance defense lawyers must remember that the insured is always a client. Even if the insurer controls settlement, a defense lawyer must inform the insured of all settlement offers absent a contrary understanding with the insured. As a prophylactic matter, insurance defense lawyers generally are wise to inform insureds about an insurer's contractual right to settle as it deems expedient early in the representation and certainly before settlement becomes an issue.[59]

B. Summary

Clients require sufficient information to make intelligent decisions concerning their goals and objectives in negotiations. Clients and lawyers may ease the process by agreeing at the start on acceptable and unacceptable settlement offers and plea bargains, reasonable and unreasonable demands, agreeable or objectionable terms and conditions and so on, and thereafter vest suitable discretion in the lawyer with respect to acceptance, rejection,

---

55. *Id.* at 1272–73 (discussing Rogers v. Robson, Master, Ryan, Brummund & Belom, 403 N.E.2d 47 (Ill. 1980)).

56. *Id.* at 1273 (footnote omitted).

57. *Id.* at 1278.

58. Teague v. St. Paul Fire & Marine Ins. Co., 10 So. 3d 806, 847 (La. Ct. App. 2009).

59. *In re* Zuber, 101 So. 3d 29, 34 (La. 2012) (treating insurance defense representations as limited-scope representations and discussing lawyers' related obligations under Rule 1.2).

or compromise.[60] To the extent reasonably possible, lawyers should document such agreements. By thoughtfully discussing settlement alternatives and the boundaries of their authority in advance of expected negotiations, and memorializing those understandings, lawyers both aid their clients and protect themselves. That said, lawyers must always remember that clients' objectives may change and, absent frequent communication during negotiations, those alterations may not become known until after some key event has occurred.

IV. Lawyers' Duty of Confidentiality

Among lawyers' most important duties is the duty to maintain the confidentiality of client information.[61] Maintaining confidentiality is a key aspect of negotiations in terms of shielding clients' goals or strategies from discovery, and, in a worst-case scenario, exposing lawyers to misconduct claims if they wrongly conceal material facts that should have been disclosed to an opponent. Model Rule 1.6 establishes confidentiality as a professional responsibility principle:

> (a) A lawyer shall not reveal information relating to the representation of a client unless the client gives informed consent, the disclosure is impliedly authorized to carry out the representation or the disclosure is permitted by paragraph (b).
>
> (b) A lawyer may reveal information relating to the representation of a client to the extent the lawyer reasonably believes necessary:
>
> (1) to prevent reasonably certain death or substantial bodily harm;
>
> (2) to prevent the client from committing a crime or fraud that is reasonably certain to result in substantial injury to the financial interests or property of another and in furtherance of which the client has used or is using the lawyer's services;
>
> (3) to prevent, mitigate or rectify substantial injury to the financial interests or property of another that is reasonably certain to result or has resulted from the client's commission of a crime or fraud in furtherance of which the client has used the lawyer's services;
>
> (4) to secure legal advice about the lawyer's compliance with these Rules;

60. Absent such agreement, a lawyer cannot, for example, refuse to convey a settlement offer to a client on the basis that the lawyer thinks the offer is too miserly to entertain. *See, e.g.*, Moores v. Greenberg, 834 F.2d 1105, 1107–08 (1st Cir. 1987) (affirming a legal malpractice verdict for the plaintiff based on his lawyer's failure to relay a settlement offer that the lawyer thought was "too niggardly" but that the client allegedly would have accepted).

61. *See* Cal. Eth. Op. 2015-192, 2015 WL 1308145, at *3 (Cal. State Bar, Comm. on Prof'l Responsibility & Conduct 2015) [hereinafter Cal. Eth. Op. 2015-192] ("One of the most important duties of an attorney is to preserve the confidences of her client.").

(5) to establish a claim or defense on behalf of the lawyer in a controversy between the lawyer and the client, to establish a defense to a criminal charge or civil claim against the lawyer based upon conduct in which the client was involved, or to respond to allegations in any proceeding concerning the lawyer's representation of the client;
(6) to comply with other law or a court order; or
(7) to detect and resolve conflicts of interest arising from the lawyer's change of employment or from changes in the composition or ownership of a firm, but only if the revealed information would not compromise the attorney-client privilege or otherwise prejudice the client.

(c) A lawyer shall make reasonable efforts to prevent the inadvertent or unauthorized disclosure of, or unauthorized access to, information relating to the representation of a client.[62]

Model Rule 1.6 is intended to encourage clients to trust their lawyers and to be candid with them.[63] A lawyer's duty of confidentiality exists regardless of a request to that effect by a client.[64] The duty exists even where the client has shared the same information with others.[65] A lawyer may breach the duty of confidentiality through mere inadvertence.[66]

Model Rule 1.6 prevents the disclosure of information that is neither privileged nor work product. "Confidential" is not synonymous with "privileged" or "immune."[67] Thus, a lawyer's duty of confidentiality prevents her from revealing a client's identity or facts that a client communicates to her, even in situations where the attorney-client privilege and work product doctrine do not protect them.

It is apparent that a lawyer's duty of confidentiality is important in negotiations and, in the right situation, that the revelation of confidential client information might impair a client's ability to settle a contested matter, or to settle on terms that the client considers advantageous. Lawyers should therefore tightly guard information relating to a client's representation. But Rule 1.6 does not exist in a vacuum. Lawyers' duty of confidentiality does not necessarily excuse their obligations under other rules. *In re Potts*[68] illustrates this point.

---

62. Model Rules of Prof'l Conduct R. 1.6 (2015).

63. Honolulu Civil Beat Inc. v. Dep't of Att'y Gen., 463 P.3d 942, 955 (Haw. 2020); *In re* Disciplinary Proceeding Against Schafer, 66 P.3d 1036, 1041 (Wash. 2003).

64. Hurley v. Hurley, 923 A.2d 908, 911 (Me. 2007).

65. *In re* Anonymous, 932 N.E.2d 671, 674 (Ind. 2010) (stating that "the fact that a client may choose to confide to others information relating to a representation does not waive or negate the confidentiality protections of the Rules [of Professional Conduct]").

66. *See, e.g.*, *In re* Boyce, 613 S.E.2d 538, 540 (S.C. 2007) (sending client's information to his employer in the mistaken belief that employer was involved in transaction).

67. Doe v. Md. Bd. of Social Workers, 840 A.2d 744, 749 (Md. Ct. Spec. App. 2004).

68. 158 P.3d 418 (Mont. 2007).

In re Potts arose out of a probate dispute. Ernestine Stukey executed a will in 1998 in which she disinherited her daughter, Evon, and Evon's family, and left the bulk of her estate to her niece, Charlene. Unfortunately, Ernestine's mental health soon deteriorated and Evon was appointed as her mother's conservator. Evon filed an initial inventory in the conservatorship proceeding in a Montana district court in which she reported Ernestine's net worth as being approximately $1.2 million. The initial inventory included several accounts worth around $270,000, which Evon held in joint tenancy with her mother.[69]

Evon tried to distribute $160,000 from Ernestine's estate to family members, but the conservatorship court would not allow it. In addition, Ernestine's lawyers sued Evon for otherwise misappropriating and mismanaging her mother's funds. Evon then secretly moved her mother to a nursing home in Washington. There, despite being incapacitated by Alzheimer's disease, Ernestine curiously executed a second will in 2001 purportedly leaving the bulk of her estate to Evon and Evon's family.[70]

Will contests in both Washington and Montana erupted upon Ernestine's death. In the Washington case, Evon filed another inventory reporting the value of Ernestine's estate as being roughly $1.2 million.[71] This matched a third and final inventory that she had filed in the conservatorship case. Both the Washington inventory and the final conservatorship inventory included the joint tenancy accounts as assets of the estate.[72]

Evon hired Steven Potts to represent her and her children, including her son, Tyson, in the disputes. Charlene also had counsel, as did two entities named as beneficiaries in the 1998 will. The law firm of Church Harris Johnson & Williams, which had represented Ernestine in the conservatorship dispute with Evon, continued to represent her estate in the new litigation. The parties agreed to mediate all the pending disputes (i.e., the will contests and Evon's alleged misconduct in the conservatorship proceeding). Ernestine's lawyers submitted a confidential settlement brochure indicating that the parties assumed a total estate value of $1.2 million, consistent with Evon's prior inventories.[73]

The parties reached a settlement during mediation that called for portions of Ernestine's estate to go to specific beneficiaries, and for the remainder to be split 50-50 between Charlene on the one hand and Evon and her family on the other.[74] A related stipulation and memorandum did not

69. *Id.* at 420–21.
70. *Id.* at 421.
71. *Id.*
72. *Id.*
73. *Id.*
74. *Id.* at 422.

mention the estate's total value or Evon's valuation inventories.[75] In agreeing to the settlement, however, Ernestine's lawyers plainly valued the estate at $1.2 million based on Evon's inventories and intended the joint tenancy accounts to count toward that amount.[76]

In the week after the mediation, one of Ernestine's lawyers from the Church law firm, Glenn Tremper, suspected that Evon was attempting to drain the joint tenancy accounts. He called and wrote Potts to confirm that the parties had settled based on the good faith assumption that Ernestine's estate included the joint tenancy accounts. Potts assured Tremper over the phone that the estate included the joint tenancy accounts within its $1.2 million value.[77] Tremper's letter to Potts confirming their telephone conversation asked Potts to inform him immediately if Potts's clients thought differently.[78]

Potts showed Tremper's letter to Evon's son, Tyson, telling him that any questions about estate assets would eventually be resolved but that he would prefer to do it sooner rather than later.[79] Tyson told him not to respond to Tremper's letter because he wanted to deal only with a personal representative appointed by the court.[80] Potts obeyed Tyson's instruction. Naturally, Tremper construed Potts's failure to respond to his letter as confirmation that the settlement was properly based on the $1.2 million value repeatedly established by Evon in her inventories. It would later be revealed that Evon and Tyson had told Potts well in advance of the mediation that they intended to take the joint tenancy accounts outside of any settlement agreement.

After Potts drafted and circulated a settlement stipulation and memorandum stating obliquely that all disputes had been settled, but saying nothing about the value of the estate or the joint tenancy accounts, Evon claimed that the settlement agreement did not include the joint tenancy accounts.[81] Ultimately, the Montana Supreme Court determined that the joint tenancy accounts were part of the $1.2 million estate and that those funds should be distributed along with the rest of the estate as agreed at the mediation.[82]

That might have been the end of things, except someone filed a complaint against Potts with Montana disciplinary authorities for his conduct surrounding the settlement. The Montana authorities alleged that Potts engaged or assisted in a client fraud in violation of Rule 1.2(d), and breached his duty of candor to the tribunal in violation of Rule 3.3(a)(2) by failing

75. *Id.*
76. *Id.* at 423.
77. *Id.*
78. *Id.* at 422.
79. *Id.*
80. *Id.*
81. *Id.*
82. *Id.* at 422–23.

to disclose material information to the district court hearing the will contest.[83] Montana's Commission on Practice concluded that Potts knew that his clients were using his services to perpetrate a fraud in violation of Rule 1.2(d), that he was obligated to inform his clients that he would not assist in their fraud, that his duty of candor to the tribunal superseded his duty of confidentiality to his clients, and that he violated his duty of candor to the tribunal under Rule 3.3(a)(2).[84] The Commission recommended that he be publicly censured and suspended from practice for 30 days. Potts challenged the Commission's recommendation in the Montana Supreme Court.

Potts argued that Montana's version of Rule 1.6 prevented him from revealing his clients' alleged fraud to anyone, including the district court. The Montana rule, like Model Rule 1.6, prohibits a lawyer from revealing "'information relating to a representation of a client unless the client consents after consultation,'" but, at the time, contained no exception for disclosing client fraud.[85] Evon and Tyson never consented to Potts revealing their intentions with respect to the joint tenancy accounts.

The supreme court began its analysis with Montana Rule of Professional Conduct 3.3(a)(2), which prohibits a lawyer from "'failing to disclose a material fact to a tribunal when disclosure is necessary to avoid assisting a criminal or fraudulent act by the client.'"[86] Once Potts made representations to the district court in the stipulation that he drafted and signed, his duty of candor to the tribunal under Rule 3.3(a)(2) "trumped any duty of confidentiality that he owed to his clients."[87]

The court recognized that, standing alone, Rule 1.6 prevented Potts from revealing his clients' alleged fraud to the other parties to the litigation.[88] But Rule 1.6 does not exist in isolation, the court explained, and it must be read in conjunction with Rule 1.2(d), which prohibits a lawyer from counseling or assisting a client to engage in conduct that the lawyer knows to be fraudulent.[89] "Under certain circumstances, a lawyer's nondisclosure can be taken too far even in light of the duty of confidentiality."[90] While maintaining his duty of confidentiality, Potts was also obligated to comply with other ethics rules, including Rule 1.2(d). He should have withdrawn from representing Evon and Tyson as soon as their insistence on his silence "propelled his services into the realm of assisting in [their] fraudulent behavior."[91]

83. *Id.* at 423.
84. *Id.* at 423–24.
85. *Id.* at 424 (quoting Mont. R. Prof'l Conduct 1.6 (2001)).
86. *Id.* (quoting Mont. R. Prof'l Conduct 3.3(a)(2) (2001)).
87. *Id.* (citing State Bar of Mont., Ethics Advisory Op. 870326).
88. *Id.* at 425.
89. *Id.*
90. *Id.*
91. *Id.*

In summary, the *In re Potts* court conceded that Rule 1.6 prevented Potts from revealing his clients' fraud to the other parties.[92] The court would not, however, endorse legitimate non-disclosure under Rule 1.6 as an excuse for violating Rule 1.2(d). As a result, the court held that the Commission did not err by finding that Potts violated Rule 1.2(d). In the end, the court concluded that public censure would be appropriate punishment for Potts's misconduct.[93]

Potts was placed in a terrible position when he learned that Evon intended to drain the joint tenancy accounts, and matters worsened when he made a contrary representation to Tremper and Tyson would not thereafter allow him to respond to Tremper's letter. At that point, Potts had three options: (1) persuade Evon and Tyson to permit him to reveal their intentions with respect to the joint tenancy accounts, (2) persuade them to include the joint tenancy accounts in Ernestine's estate, or (3) withdraw from their representation. Unfortunately, Potts either could not achieve the first or second options or did not attempt those courses of action, and he did not pursue the third option despite what should have been its obvious appeal.

Had Potts chosen to withdraw, he would have had to be careful about the reasons he offered for doing so. A lawyer's request to withdraw from a representation under Rule 1.16 does not relieve her from the duty to protect client confidentiality under Rule 1.6.[94] If Potts had moved to withdraw, it should have been sufficient for him to (1) cite the subparagraphs of Rule 1.16 that required or justified his withdrawal[95] and (2) state that professional or ethical considerations required his withdrawal, or that there had been an irreconcilable breakdown in the attorney-client relationship that prevented his continued representation of Evon and Tyson.[96]

If the same scenario were to arise today, amendments to the Montana Rules of Professional Conduct would permit Potts to reveal Evon's and Tyson's fraud to the other parties claiming a right to distributions from

92. *Id.*

93. *Id.* at 431.

94. ABA Comm. on Ethics & Prof'l Responsibility, Formal Op. 476, at 2 (2016); Sup. Ct. of Ariz., Att'y Ethics Advisory Comm., Op. File No. EO-20-0001, at 4 (2020); N.Y. Eth. Op. 1057, 2015 WL 4592234, at *2 (N.Y. State Bar. Ass'n, Comm. Prof'l Ethics 2015) [hereinafter N.Y. Eth. Op. 1057].

95. *See* Model Rules of Prof'l Conduct R. 1.16(a)(1) (2020) (mandating withdrawal); *id.* R. 1.16(b)(2), (b)(3) & (b)(4) (permitting withdrawal).

96. *See* Cal. Eth. Op. 2015-192, *supra* note 61, 2015 WL 1308145, at *8 ("Ordinarily, for purposes of the motion to withdraw, it will be sufficient to state words to the effect that ethical considerations require withdrawal or that there has been an irreconcilable breakdown in the attorney-client relationship."); N.Y. Eth. Op. 1057, *supra* note 94, 2015 WL4592234, at *3 (indicating that it should be sufficient for the lawyer to advise the court that "professional considerations" require withdrawal).

Ernestine's estate.[97] The mere threat of such disclosure would have given Potts substantial leverage in attempting to persuade Evon and Tyson to abandon their planned fraud.

V. Lawyers' Duty of Honesty to Third Persons

The *In re Potts* story is as much about honesty as it is about confidentiality. Indeed, honesty in negotiations is an exquisitely difficult subject.

A. Applicable Rules of Professional Conduct

Honesty in negotiations may be enforced under several rules of professional conduct.[98] Chief among the applicable rules is Model Rule 4.1(a), which states that when representing a client, "a lawyer shall not knowingly . . . make a false statement of material fact or law to a third person."[99]

Although Model Rule 4.1(a) refers to false statements by a lawyer, it is a bit broader than it appears, in that a lawyer may violate Rule 4.1(a) by knowingly affirming or ratifying another person's false statement,[100] or by failing to correct it.[101] As for the audience, the reference to "a third person" in Model Rule 4.1(a) clarifies that the rule relates to lawyers' communications with people other than their clients.[102] In *State of Nebraska ex rel. Counsel for Discipline of the Nebraska Supreme Court v. Kruger*,[103] for example, the Nebraska Supreme Court relied on Rule 4.1(a) to discipline a lawyer who lied to a Medicaid claims examiner in the course of resolving his

97. *See* Mont. Rules of Prof'l Conduct R. 1.6(b)(2) (2020) (permitting a lawyer to reveal client information "to prevent the client from committing a crime or fraud that is reasonably certain to result in substantial injury to the financial interests or property of another and in furtherance of which the client has used or is using the lawyer's services").

98. *See, e.g.*, Office of Disciplinary Couns. v. DiAngelus, 907 A.2d 452, 454–58 (Pa. 2006) (determining that the lawyer violated Rules 4.1(a), 8.4(c), and 8.4(d) by falsely telling the prosecutor during plea negotiations that the citing officer had agreed to the reduction in charges when he had not).

99. Model Rules of Prof'l Conduct R. 4.1(a) (2020); *see, e.g.*, *In re* Nicholson, 791 S.E.2d 776, 777–79 (Ga. 2016) (disbarring a lawyer for violating Rule 4.1(a) among other rules; in settling a lawsuit with two insurance companies, the lawyer knowingly signed an affidavit falsely stating that all the client's medical bills had been paid).

100. *See, e.g.*, *In re* Winkler, 834 N.E.2d 85, 89 (Ind. 2005).

101. *See, e.g.*, *In re* PRB Docket No. 2007-046, 989 A.2d 523, 526 (Vt. 2009).

102. State *ex rel.* Okla. Bar Ass'n v. Bolusky, 23 P.3d 268, 275 (Okla. 2001); *see, e.g.*, *In re* Dargie, No. 17-BG-1075, 2017 WL 5180719, at *1 (D.C. Nov. 9, 2017) (invoking Rule 4.1(a) in suspending for 60 days a lawyer who knowingly made a false statement to a third party about the amount of a settlement agreement that prompted the third party to take a lesser fee for services provided to the lawyer's client). *But see In re* Kupka, 458 P.3d 242, 247, 251 (Kan. 2020) (adopting a disciplinary panel's finding that the lawyer violated Rule 4.1(a) when she "provided false information to *many clients* as well as her supervising attorneys" (emphasis added)).

103. 839 N.W.2d 262 (Neb. 2013).

client's personal injury claim.[104] In *In re McGrath*,[105] the Alaska Supreme Court determined that a lawyer violated Rule 4.1(a) when, at all times unbeknownst to his client, he negotiated the settlement of the client's personal injury claim with the tortfeasor's insurer premised on the client's approval of the settlement.[106]

Model Rule 4.1(a) certainly applies to lawyers' statements to opposing counsel.[107] In *In re Filosa*,[108] for example, the court relied on New York's version of Rule 4.1 to discipline a plaintiff's lawyer who knowingly served on defense counsel a misleading report by an expert economist and then relied on the incorrect damages calculation in the report when negotiating a settlement.[109] In *In re Hubbard*,[110] a California federal court found that the plaintiff's lawyer, Lynn Hubbard, violated Model Rule 4.1(a) when he sent opposing counsel settlement agreements purportedly signed by his client who had, in fact, died three weeks earlier.[111] The court suspended Hubbard from practice in the judicial district for one year as a sanction for his dishonesty.[112]

A lawyer must knowingly make a false statement to violate Rule 4.1(a). "Knowingly" in this context, as elsewhere in the Model Rules, denotes actual knowledge.[113] Although lawyers' knowledge may be inferred from circumstances,[114] the conclusion that a lawyer *should have known* something does not equal knowledge of that fact.[115] Likewise, speculation and suspicion do not equate to knowledge. Furthermore, "knowledge" does not describe "evil intent or bad purpose" on the lawyer's part.[116] Indeed, Model

104. *Id.* at 264–65 (invoking Rules 8.4(a), 8.4(c), and 8.4(d) in addition to Rule 4.1(a)).

105. 259 P.3d 437 (Alaska 2011).

106. *Id.* at 441.

107. *In re* Corizzi, 803 A.2d 438, 441 & n.5 (D.C. 2002); Iowa Sup. Ct. Att'y Disciplinary Bd. v. Barnhill, 885 N.W.2d 408, 421 (Iowa 2016); *In re* Knox, 432 P.3d 654, 659, 662 (Kan. 2019); Att'y Grievance Comm'n of Md. v. Zhang, 100 A.3d 1112, 1133 (Md. 2014); *In re* Disciplinary Action Against Walsh, 872 N.W.2d 741, 749 (Minn. 2015); *In re* Krigel, 480 S.W.3d 294, 299–300 (Mo. 2016); *In re* Nocella, 79 A.3d 766, 779 (Pa. Ct. Jud. Disc. 2013).

108. 976 F. Supp. 2d 460 (S.D.N.Y. 2013).

109. *Id.* at 465–66. *In re Filosa* arose out of an employment discrimination case. The plaintiff's expert economist calculated her damages based on her current and assumed future unemployment. But by the time the plaintiff's lawyer, Gregory Filosa, served the expert's report on defense counsel, the plaintiff had accepted a new position at a salary higher than she had earned in the position from which she was allegedly fired unlawfully. Thus, the lost income assumptions and damages calculations in her economist's report were fatally flawed. *Id.* at 462.

110. No. 12-cv-1975-L(WMc), 2013 WL 435945 (S.D. Cal. Feb. 4, 2013).

111. *Id.* at *1–2, 5.

112. Hubbard also concealed his client's death from a magistrate judge who conducted a settlement conference in the case. *Id.* at *2–3.

113. Model Rules of Prof'l Conduct R. 1.0(f) (2020).

114. *In re* Disciplinary Action Against Johnson, 743 N.W.2d 117, 123 (N.D. 2007); Model Rules of Prof'l Conduct R. 1.0(f) (2015).

115. *In re* Tocco, 984 P.2d 539, 543 (Ariz. 1999).

116. *In re* Edison, 724 N.W.2d 579, 584 (N.D. 2006).

Rule 4.1(a) does not require any intent to deceive by the lawyer; the lawyer's knowledge that a statement is false when made will support a violation.[117]

Model Rule 4.1(a) applies only to statements of fact or law; lawyers' statements of opinion will not violate the rule.[118] Innocent misstatements do not implicate the rule,[119] although statements made with reckless disregard for the truth may.[120]

In addition, a lawyer's false statement must be material for there to be a violation. A statement of fact or law is "material" if it is significant or essential, if it could have influenced the hearer,[121] if it affected the outcome of the proceedings,[122] or if it "reasonably may be viewed as important to a fair understanding of what is being given up and, in return, gained" in an agreement.[123] Courts evaluate materiality on a case-by-case basis.[124]

Rule 4.1(a) does not include a causation or reliance element. In other words, a lawyer violates the rule simply by making a prohibited statement. The listener does not have to act or detrimentally rely on the statement to perfect the violation.[125]

Most Rule 4.1(a) disputes pivot on whether a statement expresses "fact." A comment to Model Rule 4.1 provides some guidance on this subject related to negotiations:

> Whether a particular statement should be regarded as one of fact can depend on the circumstances. Under generally accepted conventions in negotiation, certain types of statements ordinarily are not taken as statements of material fact. Estimates of price or value placed on the subject of a transaction and a party's intentions as to an acceptable settlement of a claim are ordinarily in this category, and so is the existence of an undisclosed principal except where nondisclosure of the principal would constitute fraud.[126]

117. *See, e.g.*, *In re* Petition for Disciplinary Action Against Winter, 770 N.W.2d 463, 467 (Minn. 2009) (rejecting lawyer's argument that he did not violate Rule 4.1(a) because he did not intend false statement in motion to deceive the court or the other lawyer involved).

118. Office of Disciplinary Couns. v. Wrona, 908 A.2d 1281, 1289 (Pa. 2006).

119. *See, e.g.*, People v. Chambers, 154 P.3d 419, 425–26 (Colo. 2006) (finding no Rule 4.1 violation for apparently innocent misstatement of number of claims or suits); Att'y Grievance Comm'n of Md. v. Elmendorf, 946 A.2d 542, 545–46 (Md. 2008) (agreeing that lawyer's negligence in failing to review files leading to false statements did not violate Rule 4.1(a)).

120. *In re* Wagner, 744 N.E.2d 418, 421 (Ind. 2001); Office of Disciplinary Couns. v. Price, 732 A.2d 599, 606 (Pa. 1999).

121. *In re* Fisher, 202 P.3d 1186, 1202 (Colo. 2009); *In re* Smith, 236 P.3d 137, 145 (Or. 2010) (quoting *In re* Kluge, 27 P.3d 102 (Or. 2001)).

122. Office of Disciplinary Couns. v. DiAngelus, 907 A.2d 452, 456 (Pa. 2006).

123. Ausherman v. Bank of Am. Corp., 212 F. Supp. 2d 435, 449 (D. Md. 2002).

124. *Id.*

125. *See, e.g.*, *In re* Winthrop, 848 N.E.2d 961, 980 (Ill. 2006) (finding that a lawyer violated Rule 4.1(a) even though his dishonesty did not impede the actions of the other lawyer to whom the false statement was made).

126. Model Rules of Prof'l Conduct R. 4.1 cmt. 2 (2020).

Various other forms of disingenuousness are also ethically permissible. For professional responsibility purposes, lawyers' statements about a party's willingness to compromise or resolve a dispute, a party's willingness to compromise or resolve a criminal matter, a party's willingness to concede something or a value placed on a concession, the strength or weakness of a party's factual or legal positions, the strengths or weaknesses of a party's case, the value or worth of the subject of the parties' negotiation, and a party's goals or objectives all qualify as puffery or posturing rather than as statements of fact.[127]

Consider, for example, a situation in which two lawyers are negotiating the settlement of a personal injury claim. The defense lawyer has $100,000 in settlement authority. When the plaintiff's lawyer offers to settle for $85,000, the defense lawyer responds, "I can't do that, but if you'll get your client to take $75,000, I'll make my client accept it." Is the defense lawyer's statement a false statement of fact within the meaning of Rule 4.1(a)? No, it is puffery, posturing, or an invitation to negotiate further. The plaintiff's lawyer understands that and will either counsel her client to accept $75,000, or, more likely, stand on $85,000, or counter-offer.

Model Rule 4.1(b) addresses lawyers' non-disclosures rather than false statements.[128] It states that "[i]n the course of representing a client a lawyer shall not knowingly . . . fail to disclose a material fact when disclosure is necessary to avoid assisting a criminal or fraudulent act by a client, unless disclosure is prohibited by Rule 1.6."[129] A client's act is fraudulent for Rule 4.1(b) purposes if "it is fraudulent under the substantive or procedural law of the applicable jurisdiction and has a purpose to deceive."[130]

Finally, for now, lawyers' duty of honesty may also be enforced under Model Rule 8.4(c), which makes it professional misconduct for a lawyer to "engage in conduct involving dishonesty, fraud, deceit or misrepresentation."[131] The standard by which a lawyer's alleged dishonesty is to be judged varies.[132] Many courts hold that a lawyer's false statement must be knowingly made to violate Rule 8.4(c).[133] Other jurisdictions hold

127. ABA Comm. on Ethics & Prof'l Responsibility, Formal Op. 06-439, at 1–2 (2006) [hereinafter ABA Formal Op. 06-439].

128. Model Rules of Prof'l Conduct R. 4.1(b) (2020) ("In the course of representing a client a lawyer shall not knowingly . . . (b) fail to disclose a material fact when disclosure is necessary to avoid assisting a criminal or fraudulent act by a client, unless disclosure is prohibited by Rule 1.6.").

129. *Id.*

130. *Id.* R. 1.0(d).

131. Model Rules of Prof'l Conduct R. 8.4(c) (2020).

132. *See, e.g.*, *In re* Wysolmerski, 237 A.3d 706, 714 (Vt. 2020) (stating that "some scienter is required to support a violation of Rule 8.4(c)").

133. *See, e.g.*, Fla. Bar v. Schwartz, 284 So. 3d 393, 396 (Fla. 2019); Att'y Grievance Comm'n of Md. v. Levin, 69 A.3d 451, 464–65 (Md. 2013); *In re* Firstenberger, 878 N.E.2d 912, 913–14

that lawyers may violate Rule 8.4(c) through statements made with reckless disregard for their truth or falsity,[134] or, similarly, through grossly negligent misstatements.[135] A very few courts hold that a lawyer may negligently violate Rule 8.4(c).[136] Whether either of the first two possibilities represents the majority rule is a close call, but the view that a lawyer may violate Rule 8.4(c) through simple negligence is a distinctly minority position, as it should be.[137]

Rule 8.4(c) is exceedingly broad; it applies to lawyers' dealings with anyone, including adverse parties, clients, courts and other tribunals, opposing counsel, members of the public, and government agencies. Rule 8.4(c) does not require a statement; deceit and dishonesty can also be based on the concealment or omission of facts or information.[138] Conduct that may not qualify as deceit, fraud, or a misrepresentation as a matter of criminal or tort law may still evince dishonesty for purposes of discipline under Rule 8.4(c).[139]

As with Rule 4.1(a), lawyers violate Rule 8.4(c) even if their dishonesty misleads no one or causes no harm.[140] Unlike Rule 4.1, Rule 8.4(c) has no materiality requirement. Even so, disciplinary authorities fortunately tend to read the rule sensibly, such that lawyers' truly trivial deceptions and representations are often excused. Courts generally confine Rule 8.4(c) to cases in which lawyers' dishonesty reflects negatively on their fitness to practice law.[141]

The cases considering lawyers' duty of honesty in negotiations generally fall into two categories. The first involves lawyers lying in negotiations. The second involves lawyers failing to disclose material facts or failing to correct another party's misimpressions.

(Mass. 2007); *In re* Conduct of Skagen, 149 P.3d 1171, 1184 (Or. 2006) (discussing the analogous Oregon rule). Oklahoma goes even further. To violate Rule 8.4(c) in Oklahoma, "[a]n intent element is required and the complainant must adequately show the attorney had a purpose to deceive." State *ex rel.* Okla. Bar Ass'n v. Siegrist, 461 P.3d 213, 217 (Okla. 2020).

134. *See, e.g.*, People v. Head, 332 P.3d 117, 129 (Colo. 2013); *In re* Ukwu, 926 A.2d 1106, 1113–14 (D.C. 2007); Iowa Sup. Ct. Att'y Disciplinary Bd. v. Kozlik, 943 N.W.2d 589, 595 (Iowa 2020) (quoting Iowa Sup. Ct. Att'y Disciplinary Bd. v. Clarity, 838 N.W.2d 648, 656 (Iowa 2013)); Office of Disciplinary Couns. v. Surrick, 749 A.2d 441, 445 (Pa. 2000).

135. *See, e.g.*, Walker v. Sup. Ct. Comm. on Prof'l Conduct, 246 S.W.3d 418, 424 (Ark. 2007).

136. *See, e.g.*, *In re* Doughty, 832 A.2d 724, 734–35 (Del. 2003).

137. *See* Iowa Sup. Ct. Att'y Disciplinary Bd. v. Stoller, 879 N.W.2d 199, 212 (Iowa 2016) (requiring some level of scienter to find a Rule 8.4(c) violation and stating that "[n]egligent behavior alone does not violate the rule, nor does incompetence").

138. Att'y Grievance Comm'n of Md. v. Floyd, 929 A.2d 61, 70 (Md. 2007); *In re* Disciplinary Proc. Against Knickmeier, 683 N.W.2d 445, 464 (Wis. 2004).

139. *In re* Shorter, 570 A.2d 760, 768 (D.C. 1990).

140. Ansell v. Statewide Grievance Comm., 865 A.2d 1215, 1223 (Conn. App. Ct. 2005).

141. *See, e.g.*, *In re* PRB Docket No. 2007-046, 989 A.2d 523, 528 (Vt. 2009).

B. Affirmative Misrepresentation Cases

The proposition that lawyers must not knowingly misrepresent material facts to gain an advantage in negotiations should be obvious, yet many lawyers seem blind to it. *Ausherman v. Bank of America Corp.*[142] is an interesting case.

Ausherman was a suit against Bank of America (the Bank) for improperly obtaining and disseminating consumer credit reports. The plaintiffs also sued two unidentified defendants, John Doe No. 1, allegedly a Bank employee, and John Doe No. 2, an outside co-conspirator. The Bank attempted to discover the John Doe defendants' identities, but its efforts were obstructed by the plaintiffs' lawyer, Rodney Sweetland. Finally, the Bank was allowed to depose Sweetland to discover the bases for the plaintiffs' factual allegations.[143] In his deposition, Sweetland was questioned about a demand letter that he had sent to defense counsel several months earlier proposing a $1.875 million settlement, as part of which he would reveal the identity of a John Doe No. 3.[144] According to the letter, John Doe No. 3 was the kingpin of the network that obtained and disseminated the plaintiffs' credit reports.[145] Essentially, John Doe. No. 1 sold Bank data to John Doe No. 2 at the instance of John Doe No. 3. Sweetland denied in the letter that he knew John Doe No. 3's identity but claimed that he could obtain it when the litigation concluded.[146] He wrote that he had "'made confidential arrangements . . . to have that information provided to me once any possibility of my own deposition (or answering interrogatories) has passed.'"[147]

During Sweetland's deposition, the Bank's counsel asked him about the "confidential arrangements." Sweetland replied that "[t]here were none. That was language put in there for purposes of settlement bluster."[148] The Bank's counsel pressed Sweetland further, twice getting him to admit that his statement about arranging for John Doe No. 3's identification was a lie. The Bank then pursued sanctions against Sweetland.

The district court imposed monetary sanctions against Sweetland and referred him to the judicial district's disciplinary committee. In doing so, the court noted that "[i]t does not require a rule of professional responsibility for a lawyer to know that, during the process of settlement negotiations, he or she may not lie to opposing counsel about a fact that is material to the resolution of the case."[149] In referring Sweetland to the disciplinary

142. 212 F. Supp. 2d 435 (D. Md. 2002).
143. *Id.* at 438–39.
144. *Id.* at 439.
145. *Id.*
146. *Id.*
147. *Id.* (quoting Sweetland's letter).
148. *Id.* at 440.
149. *Id.* at 443–44.

committee, the *Ausherman* court easily concluded that there was ample cause to believe that he had violated Rule 4.1(a).[150]

Equally wrongful conduct was exposed in *Cleveland Bar Ass'n v. McMahon*.[151] There, McMahon represented a client concerning an accident allegedly caused by another driver, Marrs. The police cited Marrs for an improper lane change in connection with the accident. During negotiations with Marrs's auto liability insurer, State Auto, McMahon naturally insisted that the accident was Marrs's fault. State Auto disputed Marrs's liability. Accordingly, in a letter to State Auto, McMahon fabricated testimony from a fictitious transcript of a municipal court hearing in which Marrs purportedly admitted fault for the accident and was supposedly found guilty of improperly changing lanes.[152] In fact, Marrs had failed to appear in court to answer the charge against her, had never admitted fault for the accident, and had been found guilty of nothing. When State Auto confronted McMahon with these facts, he wrote a second letter in which he acknowledged that Marrs had failed to appear in court, but falsely asserted that a warrant had been issued for her arrest and ominously promised to depose her in her jail cell.[153]

State Auto settled with McMahon's client for $8,500. McMahon wrote the State Auto claims representative and obliquely apologized for the statements in his earlier letters. State Auto did not rely on McMahon's misrepresentations in settling the case.[154]

In his disciplinary case, McMahon offered no good explanation for his misconduct and eventually admitted his dishonesty. Finding that McMahon "flagrantly violated his duty to the legal system" by fabricating evidence, and "breached his duty to the general public by failing to exhibit the highest standards of honesty and integrity,"[155] the Ohio Supreme Court suspended him from practice for six months.

Although McMahon's conduct was offensive, some courts are willing to indulge sharp negotiating practices where the other party is an insurance company or a similarly savvy adversary.[156] In *Statewide Grievance Committee v. Gillis*,[157] for example, Joseph Gillis was representing Nelson Ortiz in connection with injuries allegedly suffered in a series of traffic accidents. In communicating with the insurers involved, Gillis materially inflated the

150. *Id.* at 445–52.
151. 872 N.E.2d 261 (Ohio 2007).
152. *Id.* at 263.
153. *Id.*
154. *Id.* at 264.
155. *Id.*
156. *But see In re* Scanio, 919 A.2d 1137, 1146 (D.C. 2007) (suspending a lawyer for 30 days for violating Rule 8.4(c) in connection with the lawyer's dishonesty in attempting to negotiate a settlement of his bodily injury claim with his auto insurer).
157. No. CV030479677S, 2004 WL 423905 (Conn. Super. Ct. Jan. 28, 2004).

amounts of Ortiz's medical bills.[158] In his demand letters to the insurers, Gillis greatly exaggerated the nature and effects of Ortiz's injuries. As a result, Connecticut disciplinary authorities charged Gillis with violating the state's equivalents of Model Rules 4.1(a) and 8.4(c).

In rejecting the charges against Gillis, the court noted that Gillis's demand letters were rank hyperbole that was unlikely to influence any insurance adjuster receiving them.[159] "Rightly or wrongly," the court observed, "in negotiating the settlement of personal injury cases with insurers, attorneys work in an adversarial setting in which the Rules of Professional Conduct 'do not contemplate paragons of virtue.'"[160] The court concluded that Gillis was guilty only of "imprecision and exaggeration," traits the rules he was charged with violating did not address.[161]

Lawyers would be wise not to rely on the *Gillis* court's reasoning. First, Model Rule 4.1(a) does not permit lawyers to make false statements of material fact to some third parties but not others. Second, the court was more tolerant of Gillis's conduct than other courts might conclude was justified. To take just one example, Gillis represented to one insurer that Ortiz's medical bills were "nearly $1,000," when they were just $193,[162] a misstatement that the court casually dismissed on the basis that Gillis was presenting his client's damages "as approximations and in round numbers."[163] Many courts are likely to mock the view that inflating a client's medical bills by a multiple of five is a rounding error.

C. The Failure to Disclose and Concealment

Although lawyers must be truthful in negotiations, and must be careful to avoid making misrepresentations—especially when they are relying on or incorporating the statements of others in expressing positions—they generally have no duty to inform opponents of relevant facts.[164] They generally

158. *Id.* at *2.
159. *Id.* at *11.
160. *Id.* at *12 (quoting Harduvel v. Gen. Dynamics Corp., 801 F. Supp. 597, 609 (M.D. Fla. 1992)).
161. *Id.* at *13.
162. *Id.* at *2.
163. *Id.* at *6.
164. Model Rules of Prof'l Conduct R. 4.1 cmt. 1 (2020); *see, e.g.*, Cedar Island Improvement Ass'n, Inc. v. Drake Assocs., Inc., No. CV075002871, 2009 WL 415991, at *3 (Conn. Super. Ct. Jan. 28, 2009) (concluding that the defendant-lawyer did not violate Rule 4.1 by failing to reveal a material fact to another lawyer in a telephone conversation because (1) the second lawyer was aware of the fact and the defendant-lawyer could have no duty to remind her of that which she already knew; and (2) the subject never came up in their conversation, so the defendant-lawyer's failure to speak up was not akin to a material misrepresentation).

have no obligation to correct opposing lawyers' mistakes.[165] An opposing lawyer's lack of diligence in identifying facts that will enhance her client's bargaining position should not have professional consequences for counsel for the other party.[166] For that matter, basic freedom of contract principles permit a party to strike what someone else might consider a bad bargain.

Lawyers certainly have no duty to inform opponents about limits on their negotiating or settlement authority, their "top dollar" or "bottom line," or anything of the like. Nor does a lawyer generally have a duty to inform an opponent of perceived weaknesses in a client's case. Information of that sort is confidential and should be revealed only with client consent.

The general rule that a lawyer has no duty to inform an opponent of relevant facts is subject to exceptions. For example, a lawyer unquestionably has a duty to disclose a client's death.[167] Indeed, when a lawyer's client dies amid settlement negotiations, the lawyer has a duty to so inform opposing counsel in the lawyer's first communication with them after the fact.[168] This makes sense because of the significant effects the client's death has on the litigation. The client's death alters the parties; a personal representative or administrator must be appointed, and the estate or another suitable party must be substituted for the decedent.[169] A cause of action may not survive the client's death. Plus, the client's death terminates the attorney-client relationship;[170] if the lawyer remains in the case it will be on behalf of

165. Cal. Eth. Op. 2013-189, 2013 WL 3505630, at *3 (Cal. State Bar Standing Comm. on Prof'l Responsibility & Conduct 2013).

166. *See, e.g.*, Brown v. Cnty. of Genesee, 872 F.2d 169, 175 (6th Cir. 1989) (refusing to void a settlement based on mutual mistake and stating that absent some misrepresentation or fraud, the appellant had no duty to advise the appellee of any factual error on which the appellee premised settlement, whether unknown or suspected).

167. Hubbard v. Plaza Bonita, LP, 630 F. App'x 681, 683 (9th Cir. 2015) (affirming 28 U.S.C. § 1927 and inherent power sanctions against the lawyer); Mok v. 21 Mott St. Rest. Corp., No. 14-cv-8081 (PKC), 2017 WL 3981308, at *4 (S.D.N.Y. Sept. 8, 2017) (citing the New York Rules of Professional Conduct); Virzi v. Grand Trunk Warehouse & Cold Storage Co., 571 F. Supp. 507, 509–12 (E.D. Mich. 1983); *In re* Pagan, No. 14–08824 (ESL), 2017 WL 405611, at *7 (Bankr. D.P.R. Jan. 30, 2017) (sanctioning the lawyer under 28 U.S.C. § 1927); People v. Rosen, 199 P.3d 1241, 1249 (Colo. 2007); *In re* Rosenau, 132 A.3d 1174, 1174 (D.C. 2016); Robison v. Orthotic & Prosthetic Lab, Inc., 27 N.E.3d 182, 184–86 (Ill. App. Ct. 2015); Yoh v. Hoffman, 27 P.3d 927, 931 (Kan. Ct. App. 2001); Harris v. Jackson, 192 S.W.3d 297, 305–07 (Ky. 2006); *In re* Disciplinary Action Against Lyons, 780 N.W.2d 629, 636 (Minn. 2010); Kingsdorf v. Kingsdorf, 797 A.2d 206, 211–15 (N.J. Super. Ct. App. Div. 2002); *In re* Rosner, 3 N.Y.S.3d 132, 136–37 (App. Div. 2015); *In re* Becker, 804 N.Y.S.2d 4, 5–6 (App. Div. 2005); *In re* Edison, 724 N.W.2d 579, 584 (N.D. 2006); ABA Comm. on Ethics & Prof'l Responsibility, Formal Op. 95-397, at 4 (1995) [hereinafter ABA Formal Op. 95-397]; Pa. Eth. Op. 2003-115, 2004 WL 765237, at *2 (Pa. Bar Ass'n, Comm. on Legal Ethics & Prof'l Responsibility 2004).

168. Geisler v. Ky. State Bar Ass'n, 938 S.W.2d 578, 579–80 (Ky. 1997); ABA Formal Op. 95-397, *supra* note 167, at 4.

169. *Robison*, 27 N.E.3d at 185–86; Brass v. State, 306 P.3d 393, 394 (Nev. 2013).

170. *In re* Johnson, 402 B.R. 313, 314 (B.A.P. 8th Cir. 2009); *Rosen*, 199 P.3d at 1249; *Robison*, 27 N.E.3d at 185; Mohica v. Cvejin, 990 N.E.2d 720, 729 (Ill. App. Ct. 2013) (quoting cases); Surland v. State, 895 A.2d 1034, 1041 (Md. 2006); Velasquez v. Katz, 840 N.Y.S.2d 410, 412

a new client, such as the estate or personal administrator. The client's death also terminates the lawyer's agency.[171]

The possibility of misrepresentation through silence exists in other negotiation scenarios. Assume that in a complex business dispute you have completed difficult settlement negotiations with Lawyer *A*. The settlement you negotiated includes a critical term. You and your client did not want to agree to the term, but Lawyer *A* and her client insisted that the settlement could not be achieved without it, so you agreed. You and Lawyer *A* have since been exchanging drafts of the settlement agreement, and you receive from Lawyer *A* what purports to be the final form of the parties' agreement for execution. But the "final" agreement omits the critical term; somehow that provision fell out between drafts. You know that Lawyer *A* did not deliberately delete the term; this is a scrivener's error. Are you ethically obligated to point out the error to Lawyer *A*, or can you have your client execute the document as it is presented and thereafter take advantage of the missing term? Should you seize the advantage? Should you counsel your client to attempt to capitalize on the error in some fashion?

As a practical matter, it is a rare lawyer who would stand mute here. The error will be discovered and, when it is, Lawyer *A* and her client will demand that the agreement be reformed. If your client resists, there will be costly further litigation. You and your client have reputations and relationships that may be affected by an attempt to profit from Lawyer *A*'s error. At the end of the day, it should not be an ethics rule that compels the conclusion that you must alert Lawyer *A* to the error, but good lawyering instinct and common sense. Regardless, there is a substantial risk that remaining silent in this situation would be deemed to be dishonest and deceitful, and thus would violate Rule 8.4(c).[172]

A more difficult question, perhaps, is whether you must inform your client of the dropped provision when you discover it, thus affording the client the opportunity to attempt to capitalize on the error, or whether you can correct the mistake without telling the client and in the process deprive the client of the choice to seek an advantage. As the discussion above clearly indicates, attempting to capitalize on the error will not benefit the client. The client does not have a right to take unfair advantage of the error.[173]

(App. Div. 2007) (quoting cases); Warehouse Mkt., Inc. v. Layman, 194 P.3d 786, 789 (Okla. Civ. App. 2008) (quoting cases).

171. Beaudry v. TeleCheck Servs., Inc., No. 3:07-0842, 2016 WL 11398115, at *9 (M.D. Tenn. Sept. 9, 2016); Smith v. Shewry, 93 Cal. Rptr. 3d 436, 443 (Ct. App. 2009); *Surland*, 895 A.2d at 1041.

172. Model Rules of Prof'l Conduct R. 8.4(c) (2020); *see also* Am. Bar Ass'n, Formal & Informal Ethics Opinions 1983-1998 567–69 (2000) (reprinting Informal Op. 86-1518 (1986), which discusses this scenario in the transactional context and reaches a similar conclusion) [hereinafter ABA Informal Op. 86-1518].

173. ABA Informal Op. 86-1518, *supra* note 172, at 568.

Moreover, the guiding principle behind a lawyer's duty to communicate is that the lawyer "should fulfill reasonable client expectations for information consistent with the duty to act in the client's best interests, and the client's overall requirements as to the character of the representation."[174] The client agreed to the deal with the omitted provision included. The logical conclusion, therefore, is that you do not have a duty to inform the client of the drafting error.[175] Rather, you may correct the error yourself or call it to the other side's attention without telling the client. The fact that some lawyers might choose to inform the client of the error and explain either why they intend to correct it or why the client should not attempt to capitalize on it does not mean that they have a duty to do so.

Now, assume that you are preparing the settlement agreement and rather than the key term simply falling out between drafts, you (1) deliberately omit it from the agreement in the hope of slipping its absence past your adversary and thereby reclaiming your client's desired position or (2) draft the provision in such a way that it is more favorable to your client and less favorable to your adversary, and either way is different from the term to which you and your adversary agreed. Is your conduct in either instance unethical?[176] The answer is yes; in both scenarios your conduct violates the Model Rule 8.4(c) prohibition on conduct involving dishonesty, fraud, deceit, or misrepresentation.[177] Your conduct also potentially implicates Rule 1.2(d), which prohibits lawyers from counseling clients to engage in fraud or assisting them in doing so.[178] Finally, it is possible that your conduct will expose you and your client to civil liability for fraud.[179]

Finally, and in contrast, consider a situation in which you and an injured party's lawyer are attempting to negotiate a settlement pre-suit. The other lawyer tells you on Wednesday that if your client does not agree to pay $100,000 to settle his client's claim by the end of the week, he will file suit on Monday. Apparently unlike him, you know that the statute of limitations will run on Friday. Do you have a duty to inform the other lawyer that if he sues on Monday he will be too late? You do not. There was no agreement as

---

174. Model Rules of Prof'l Conduct R. 1.4 cmt. 5 (2020).

175. ABA Informal Op. 86-1518, *supra* note 172, at 568.

176. *Cf.* Wright v. Pennamped, 664 N.E.2d 394, 395 (Ind. Ct. App. 1996) (stating that a drafting lawyer has a duty to inform opposing counsel of changes to a proposed contract that the opposing party is expected to sign).

177. *See, e.g., In re* Frank, 876 So. 2d 57, 58–59, 66 (La. 2004) (disbarring a lawyer who prepared a judgment that misrepresented the terms of the parties' settlement agreement); *In re* Conduct of Eadie, 36 P.3d 468, 476 (Or. 2001) (suspending a lawyer from practice for three years for misrepresentation by omission in a settlement agreement and for thereafter applying for a default judgment contrary to what he had represented to the opposing party).

178. Model Rules of Prof'l Conduct 1.2(d) (2020).

179. *See* TCS Holdings, Inc. v. Onvoy, Inc., Civ. No. 07-1200 (DWF/AJB), 2008 WL 4151805, at *6–7 (D. Minn. Sept. 4, 2008) (leaving the question of fraud for the fact-finder).

to the terms of a settlement that you are now attempting to avoid or evade by your silence, you did not lead the other lawyer to believe your client would waive its statute of limitations defense if he waited until Monday to sue, you made no misrepresentations, and there is no basis to argue that you had a duty to tell the other lawyer of the applicable limitation period. Your silence will not assist your client in committing a fraud. Thus, there is no basis for a court or disciplinary authority to conclude that you acted unethically by not informing the other lawyer of the consequences of waiting until Monday to sue your client.

D. Summary

Lawyers cannot knowingly make a false statement of material fact or law to a third person. A "third person" is anyone other than the lawyer's client and unquestionably includes opposing counsel.[180] A corollary holds that if lawyers make statements of material fact or law that they believe to be true when they make them, but later learn that the statements were false, they have a duty to correct the prior statements.[181] Lawyers may commit a misrepresentation by affirming or incorporating the statement of another person that the lawyer knows to be false.[182] Moreover, lawyers may not make misleading statements of material fact or law—that is, statements that are literally correct but are intended to divert the listener or recipient from the truth.[183] Luckily, many statements that lawyers must make in negotiations do not qualify as statements of material fact or law and thus permit the gamesmanship often required to successfully negotiate on clients' behalf.

A lawyer's knowing failure to disclose a "non-confidential, material and objective fact" if asked by an opponent is improper.[184] Generally speaking, however, lawyers have no duty to inform opponents of relevant facts.[185] Lawyers need not inform adversaries of weaknesses in the lawyer's case or

180. There is ample authority for the proposition that Rule 4.1(a) applies to statements to opposing counsel. *See, e.g.*, *In re* Corizzi, 803 A.2d 438, 441 & n.5 (D.C. 2002); Iowa Sup. Ct. Att'y Disciplinary Bd. v. Barnhill, 885 N.W.2d 408, 421 (Iowa 2016); *In re* Knox, 432 P.3d 654, 659, 662 (Kan. 2019); Att'y Grievance Comm'n of Md. v. Zhang, 100 A.3d 1112, 1133 (Md. 2014); *In re* Disciplinary Action Against Walsh, 872 N.W.2d 741, 749 (Minn. 2015); *In re* Krigel, 480 S.W.3d 294, 299–300 (Mo. 2016); *In re* Nocella, 79 A.3d 766, 779 (Pa. Ct. Jud. Disc. 2013).

181. *In re* Carpenito's Case, 651 A.2d 1, 4 (N.H. 1994) (relying on Rule 4.1(a)).

182. Model Rules of Prof'l Conduct R. 4.1 cmt. 1 (2020).

183. *See, e.g.*, Fla. Bar v. Joy, 679 So. 2d 1165, 1167–68 (Fla. 1996) (suspending a lawyer who told his opponent that he had disbursed escrowed funds from his trust account, thus suggesting that he no longer controlled them, when he had in fact transferred the funds to an account controlled by his wife); Miss. Bar v. Robb, 684 So. 2d 615, 623 (Miss. 1996) (finding no difference between false and misleading statements for Rule 4.1 purposes).

184. Pendleton v. Cent. N.M. Corr. Facility, 184 F.R.D. 637, 641 (D.N.M. 1999) (citing various provisions of the New Mexico Rules of Professional Conduct).

185. Model Rules of Prof'l Conduct R. 4.1 cmt. 1 (2020).

facts that potentially support the adversary's position. The problem for lawyers is recognizing the three principal exceptions to this general rule related to litigation. First, a lawyer must reveal a client's death. Second, a lawyer must disclose that a document does not reflect the parties' agreement. Third, at least when asked, a lawyer must accurately disclose applicable insurance coverage.[186] This position is consistent with courts' general view that public policy favors settlements, and the fact and amount of liability insurance are essential to purposeful settlement negotiations.[187] Finally, at least one court has recognized that a lawyer has a duty to disclose material facts (other than confidential client information) when she knows that an opponent is laboring under a clearly mistaken belief that, if uncorrected, will substantially deprive the opponent of the benefit of its bargain.[188] Fortunately, this debatable final scenario seldom surfaces.

VI. Negotiations Involving Tribunals and Lawyers' Associated Duty of Candor

Courts often mandate settlement negotiations in the form of court-ordered mediation. Some courts require parties to participate in pretrial settlement conferences facilitated by a judge other than the trial judge. Lawyers negotiating the settlement of litigation in these contexts must mind their duty of candor to the tribunal. This duty is principally enforced under Model Rule 3.3(a)(1), which states that a lawyer shall not knowingly "make a false statement of fact or law to a tribunal."[189] Before the 2002 amendments to the Model Rules, this rule provided that a lawyer was prohibited from making false statements of "material" fact or law.[190] Some states have so far opted to retain the materiality requirement.[191]

186. Statewide Grievance Comm. v. Kennelly, No. CV040833515S, 2005 WL 758055, at *3 (Conn. Super. Ct. Feb. 25, 2005); *see* Cal. Eth. Op. 2015-194, 2015 WL 9702615, at *7 (Cal. State Bar, Comm. on Prof'l Responsibility & Conduct 2015) [hereinafter Cal. Eth. Op. 2015-194] (stating that a lawyer's inaccurate representations regarding a client's insurance policy limits constitute misrepresentations impermissibly calculated to mislead the other party). *But see* NYCLA Eth. Op. 731, 2003 WL 25294953, at *3 (N.Y. Cnty. Lawyers' Ass'n, Comm. on Prof'l Ethics 2003) (opining that "it is not necessary to disclose the existence of insurance coverage in every situation in which there is an issue as to the available assets to satisfy a claim or pay a judgment").

187. Cropp v. Woleslagel, 485 P.2d 1271, 1276 (Kan. 1971).

188. *See, e.g.*, Stare v. Tate, 98 Cal. Rptr. 264, 266–69 (Ct. App. 1971) (allowing reformation of property settlement agreement where wife's lawyer made obvious calculation error that husband's lawyer was alerted to by accountant and took advantage of in negotiations).

189. Model Rules of Prof'l Conduct R. 3.3(a)(1) (2020).

190. Model Rules of Prof'l Conduct R. 3.3(a)(1) (2001).

191. *See, e.g.*, Ala. Rules of Prof'l Conduct R. 3.3(a)(1) (2013); N.C. Rules of Prof'l Conduct R. 3.3(a)(1) (2020).

When addressing a court on a matter before it, a lawyer's statements are essentially made under oath.[192] The duty of candor imposed under Model Rule 3.3(a)(1) is rigorous. "Candor" in this context "'means to treat a subject with fairness, impartiality, and to be outspoken, frank, and veracious, and is synonymous with other terms describing morality.'"[193] The prohibitions of Model Rule 3.3 are not limited to court proceedings, as the term "tribunal" establishes. For example, the rule applies to administrative and regulatory proceedings,[194] and to statements to arbitrators.[195]

To violate Rule 3.3(a)(1), a lawyer's false statement must be knowingly made. Here, as elsewhere, a lawyer's knowledge may be inferred from circumstances.[196] Actual knowledge does not include information that the lawyer could have discovered through reasonable inquiry but did not, although in some jurisdictions a lawyer may breach her duty of candor to a tribunal if she recklessly makes a false statement.[197] Misleading statements also breach a lawyer's duty of candor.[198] A lawyer's failure to reveal information to a tribunal may in some circumstances equate to an affirmative misrepresentation.[199]

Finally, Rule 3.3(a)(1) overlaps with Rule 8.4(c). A lawyer who violates Rule 3.3(a) necessarily violates Rule 8.4(c) as well. A Rule 3.3(a) violation also implicates Rule 8.4(d), which prohibits conduct "prejudicial to the administration of justice."[200]

Assume, for example, that you are defending a client in serious personal injury litigation in a federal court. As is the custom in that judicial district, the district judge slated to try your case refers the case to a magistrate judge to conduct a settlement conference shortly before trial. The magistrate

192. Kappa Sigma Fraternity v. Price-Williams, 40 So. 3d 683, 693 (Ala. 2009) (quoting Molton v. State, 651 So. 2d 663, 670 n.6 (Ala. Crim. App. 1994)); State v. Maskiell, 918 A.2d 293, 300 (Conn. App. Ct. 2007) (quoting State v. Webb, 680 A.2d 147 (Conn. 1996), and citing Rule 3.3).

193. *In re* Dorothy, 605 N.W.2d 493, 509 (S.D. 2000) (quoting Joiner v. Joiner, 87 S.W.2d 903, 905 (Tex. App. 1935)).

194. *See, e.g.*, *In re* Ukwu, 926 A.2d 1106, 1120 (D.C. 2007) (suspending lawyer for dishonesty in federal administrative proceeding); *In re* Bihlmeyer, 515 N.W.2d 236, 238–39 (S.D. 1994) (censuring lawyer who lied in case before state industrial commission).

195. *In re* Forrest, 730 A.2d 340, 343–44 (N.J. 1999); *see also* People v. Bertagnolli, 861 P.2d 717, 720–21 (Colo. 1993) (violating equivalent rule).

196. Dodge v. Dodge, 108 P.3d 362, 366 (Idaho 2005).

197. *In re* Cardwell, 50 P.3d 897, 901 n.5 (Colo. 2002) (noting the recklessness standard).

198. *See, e.g.*, Daniels v. Alander, 818 A.2d 106, 110–11 (Conn. App. Ct. 2003) (faulting lawyer for misleading statement that trial court reasonably could have construed as equivalent to affirmative misrepresentation), *aff'd*, 844 A.2d 182 (Conn. 2004) (discussing associate's failure to correct partner's misstatements); *In re* Discipline of Tornow, 835 N.W.2d 912, 924 (S.D. 2013) ("Candor goes beyond telling a portion of the truth."); *In re* Kalal, 643 N.W.2d 466, 471–75 (Wis. 2002) (giving "knowingly misleading" answers to court's questions at oral argument).

199. *See, e.g.*, Miss. Bar v. Mathis, 620 So. 2d 1213, 1220–21 (Miss. 1993) (failing to reveal autopsy of client's deceased husband in case where cause of death was important).

200. Model Rules of Prof'l Conduct R. 8.4(d) (2020).

functions as a mediator. Either your client must appear at the conference, or someone from the client's insurance company with full settlement authority must attend. Your client has a $1 million liability insurance policy. The claims adjuster responsible for the case attends the settlement conference as required. Before you go to the conference, the adjuster tells you that the insurance company, like you, evaluates this case as having a potential verdict value in excess of the insured's policy limits. He will look to you to handle the negotiations and grants you the full $1 million in authority. That said, he would like to settle the case for less than policy limits if possible.

Negotiations take the entire day, and, near the end of the day, the plaintiff's demand is $1.25 million, and you have offered $750,000. The parties appear to have reached an impasse, which frustrates the conscientious magistrate, because the obvious middle ground is $1 million, and he knows your client has a $1 million insurance policy. The magistrate surmises that the case is not settling because your adjuster is being unreasonable, so he asks to speak with you privately. "Look," he tells you, "we're close to getting this case resolved. You know as well as I do that it ought to settle for $1 million. Why won't your guy pay $1 million?" Reasonably believing that the plaintiff will cave in and settle on your terms if pressed, you respond: "Judge, with all due respect, this case just isn't worth that much. My client will pay $750,000, but no more. That's our top dollar."

Now even more frustrated and absolutely convinced that a reasonable settlement is being held up by a parsimonious insurer, the judge asks the insurance adjuster to join you. He presses the adjuster, asking, "Why won't you pay more than $750,000 to settle this case? You know this case is worth far more than that and it should also be obvious given the plaintiff's last demand that you can get it settled for $1 million. I want to know why you won't pay that. Give me one good reason." The puzzled adjuster responds by telling the magistrate that he extended his full $1 million in authority to you before the settlement conference began and that he and his company have always been willing to settle for $1 million.

Are you in trouble? In a word, yes. Beyond costing yourself and your client vital credibility with the magistrate now and in the future, you have breached your duty of candor under Rule 3.3(a)(1), you have violated Rules 4.1(a) and 8.4(c), and you have also breached Rule 8.4(d). It is impossible for you to defend your dishonesty by claiming that you were merely "posturing" or "puffing." Your expression of a $750,000 "top dollar" in this context was a statement of fact.[201] In states that retain the materiality aspect

201. ABA Comm. on Ethics & Prof'l Responsibility, Formal Op. 93-370, at 5 (1993) [hereinafter ABA Formal Op. 93-370].

of Rule 3.3(a)(1), your "top dollar" representation was a statement of material fact.[202] You lied.

Might you be able to defend against a Rule 3.3(a)(1) violation on the basis that your false statement was not made to a tribunal because the magistrate was not performing an adjudicatory function at the time? Perhaps, but even if you succeed it will be a hollow victory because that conclusion will not spare you from Rule 4.1(a) and 8.4(c) violations.

When pressed by the magistrate about your unwillingness to settle for $1 million, you might have replied that the case did not merit such a settlement value and that you believed that you could settle the case for less than that if only negotiations continued a little longer. This might have irked the magistrate, but it would have been perfectly ethical, and the magistrate surely would have continued his shuttle diplomacy. You might have simply declined to answer, telling him earnestly, "Judge, with all due respect, I don't think I have to tell you my strategy. But, out of respect for you, I will say that I think we can settle this case for less than a million. My client and I would like to get this done now for $750,000. Please reiterate that offer to the plaintiff." Alternatively, you might have said, "Respectfully judge, my client *shouldn't have to* pay more than $750,000."[203] The magistrate should respect this position. In the unlikely event that he does not, you at least have done nothing unethical.

In re Fee[204] illustrates the breadth of a negotiating lawyer's duty of candor under Rule 3.3(a)(1). The lawyers in *In re Fee*, Robert Fee and John Montigo, represented the mother of a brain-damaged baby in a medical malpractice action. Fee and Montigo developed a racketeering theory that drove the defendants into settlement negotiations. After one unproductive settlement conference, a second was scheduled for January 21, 1991—the day before trial. On January 18, the defendants offered a structured settlement

202. Some knowledgeable lawyers contend that statements along the lines of the one in this hypothetical scenario are not false statements of fact "because no sensible lawyer regards them as truthful statements." William J. Wernz & David L. Sasseville, *Negotiation Ethics*, Bench & B. of Minn., Apr. 2009, at 22, 24–25; *see also* Cal. Eth. Op. 2015-194, *supra* note 186, 2015 WL 9702615, at *6 (opining that a lawyer's inaccurate statement of a client's "bottom line" settlement figure is puffery or posturing rather than a misrepresentation of fact). Whether this view is correct is debatable. *See* ABA Formal Op. 93-370, *supra* note 201, at 5 (explaining that while "a certain amount of posturing or puffery in settlement negotiations may be an acceptable convention between opposing counsel, a party's actual bottom line or the settlement authority given to a lawyer is a material fact"). But even if these lawyers are right, it is still important to consider *context*. In our hypothetical case, the statement was made to a judge. That is not to say judges are anything other than sensible. It is to say, however, that even if you believe that one lawyer will not take another lawyer at her word about "top dollar" or "bottom line" values, judges presiding over settlement conferences will assume that the lawyers they are talking to understand the importance of being candid with them.

203. *See* ABA Formal Op. 06-439, *supra* note 127, at 8 (using "wish" in example).

204. 898 P.2d 975 (Ariz. 1995).

consisting of a cash lump sum followed by periodic payments. The settlement proposal designated a separate amount for attorneys' fees. After consulting with an annuities expert, the lawyers and the client decided that the offer would not meet the client's needs.

On January 21, the parties, the attorneys, and their annuities experts met with a settlement judge acting as mediator.[205] Among the subjects discussed was the defendants' divisive tactic of making a separate settlement offer of attorneys' fees. Despite recognizing this tactic and hearing Fee's and Montigo's argument that their fee was an issue for the trial court at the end of the case, the settlement judge told Fee and Montigo that their contingent fee was excessive. The judge soon became very antagonistic. He raised his voice and cursed at them.[206] He threatened that if the case did not settle, he would tell the trial judge that the failure was the result of their greed.[207]

Concerned for the child's interests, the settlement judge finally agreed to press the defendants for more money. Late in the day he called the parties together to discuss a higher settlement offer, which consisted of $175,000 cash, annuities for the plaintiff and her son, $400,000 in attorneys' fees, and $55,000 in costs. Fee and Montigo then met privately with their client and proposed that she pay them an additional $85,000 in fees out of the cash proceeds. Fee penned an agreement concerning the additional attorneys' fees that included a confidentiality provision designed to protect the client and maintain the sanctity of the settlement conference. He also told the client that she should not feel coerced by anyone, and that she could refuse the offer or take extra time to consider it. Fee repeatedly told the client that she had the right to seek independent counsel concerning the fee agreement and received numerous assurances from her that she was comfortable with it. The client then met separately with the annuities expert about the overall settlement and thereafter signed the additional fee agreement.[208]

The plaintiff, Fee, and Montigo then went to the settlement judge's chambers where Fee reported that they agreed "in principle" to the settlement.[209] When the judge repeated the terms previously discussed, however, no one disclosed the new fee agreement. Fee and Montigo did not mention the new agreement because they did not want to upset the settlement judge and they believed it was the trial judge's responsibility to determine the reasonableness of their fees.[210] They intended to reveal the new fee agreement

205. *Id.* at 976.
206. *Id.*
207. *Id.*
208. *Id.* at 977.
209. *Id.*
210. *Id.*

to the trial court in accordance with the standard fee approval procedure in Arizona medical malpractice cases.[211] They never got the chance.

For some reason the client called the settlement judge ten days later, told him of the new fee agreement, and asked whether she had to honor it. The judge obtained a copy of the new agreement and, after a hearing, removed Fee and Montigo from the case, appointed pro bono counsel to complete the settlement, and arranged for the court clerk to distribute the proceeds. He then initiated disciplinary action against Fee and Montigo.[212]

A disciplinary hearing committee found that Fee and Montigo violated Rules 3.3(a)(1) and 8.4(c), and recommended 30-day suspensions. The case then proceeded to Arizona's disciplinary commission, which additionally found a Rule 8.4(d) violation and recommended 60-day suspensions. The state bar appealed to the Arizona Supreme Court and asked that the court disregard both recommendations and instead suspend Fee and Montigo for six months.

The Arizona Supreme Court acknowledged that some commentators had questioned the need for truthfulness in settlement conferences given the negotiation and gamesmanship common there. It nonetheless determined that it was reasonable to expect more than minimal fairness and truthfulness from lawyers engaged in settlement.[213]

The *In re Fee* court observed that "misguided strategies believed to be endemic to the bargaining process and the lack of clearly-defined roles for settlement judges" may create situations in which lawyers do not appreciate their duty of candor or its scope.[214] In addition:

> The hour was late, and trial was scheduled to begin the following morning. The judge . . . became somewhat adversarial on this particular day. . . . Respondents did not want to lose a favorable settlement for their client. At this same time, they neither wished to permit the defense to dictate the amount of their fees, nor felt comfortable with pressure from the judge to reduce them. Moreover, respondents clearly attempted to ensure that their client fully understood and concurred in the separate agreement. . . . The uncontradicted evidence also suggests that respondents thought they were not obligated to disclose the arrangement to the settlement judge.[215]

Despite the many factors influencing the lawyers' decision not to reveal the second fee agreement to the settlement judge, however, the court could not condone their conduct. The lawyers should have disclosed their complete agreement to the settlement judge or should have "politely declined"

211. *Id.*
212. *Id.*
213. *Id.* at 978.
214. *Id.* at 978–79.
215. *Id.* at 979.

to discuss fees at all.[216] Fear that revealing their supplemental fee agreement might have jeopardized the settlement, while understandable, did not excuse their lack of candor. "The system cannot function as intended if attorneys, sworn officers of the court, can lie to or mislead judges in their guise of serving their clients."[217]

The court concluded that the lawyers violated Rules 3.3(a)(1) and 8.4(c), but reasoned that suspension was too severe a punishment under these circumstances. The court settled on censure as the appropriate discipline. In imposing discipline, the court emphasized "that a judge acting as [a] mediator is still a judge to whom the ethical duty of candor is owed."[218]

Fee and Montigo were in a difficult position. They faced a hostile judge functioning as a mediator. With trial set to start the next day, they could not adjourn the conference and seek the appointment of a different neutral. But no matter how unreasonably a settlement judge may behave, lawyers cannot lie or misrepresent matters to that judge.[219] Silence may sometimes be an option for lawyers in this situation, but dishonesty never is.

Finally, insofar as lawyers' duty of candor to a tribunal goes, the application of Rule 3.3(a)(1) to lawyers' statements to mediators bears mention. In *In re Fee*, the mediator was a judge in the court in which the case was pending, making the application of Rule 3.3(a)(1) an easy call. In many cases, however, the mediator is not a judge but rather a lawyer selected by the parties. Such mediators may be drawn from a roster of neutrals registered with a court, or the parties may select them because of their reputations in the relevant legal community. The parties may mediate their case because the court orders them to do so, because a court persuades them that they should, because local court rules mandate mediation, or simply because they believe the process worthwhile. In cases in which the mediator is not an active judge, then, are the lawyers' statements to the mediator in negotiations subject to their duty of candor to the tribunal?

The ABA's Standing Committee on Ethics and Professional Responsibility has answered this question in the negative, reasoning that Model Rule 3.3 does not apply in mediation because a mediator is not a "tribunal" as defined in Model Rule 1.0(m).[220] The committee's analysis was abbreviated, however, and its conclusion is therefore debatable. For example, some courts hold that ethics rules relating to lawyers' conduct before tribunals apply equally in depositions because depositions are subject to judicial intervention and oversight, and thus are within a judicial setting.[221] These courts

216. *Id.*
217. *Id.*
218. *Id.* at 980.
219. ABA Formal Op. 93-370, *supra* note 201, at 4–5.
220. ABA Formal Op. 06-439, *supra* note 127, at 2 n.2.
221. Cincinnati Bar Ass'n v. Statzer, 800 N.E.2d 1117, 1122 (Ohio 2003).

might similarly hold that Rule 3.3(a)(1) applies in mediations conducted pursuant to the court's adjudicatory authority, whether ordered or urged in a particular case or provided for by local rules. Of course, even if Rule 3.3(a)(1) does not apply in such circumstances, lawyers must still mind their duties under Rules 4.1(a) and 8.4(c).

VII. Civil Liability for Fraud or Misrepresentation

We have seen that lawyers who affirmatively misrepresent or conceal material facts in negotiations risk possible professional discipline and judicial sanctions, and agreements achieved through lawyers' dishonesty may be voided. Lawyers' dishonesty in negotiations also exposes them to potential civil liability for fraud and negligent misrepresentation.[222] Indeed, the risk of a lawyer incurring civil liability for misrepresentations in negotiations is well established. Although lawyers may believe that the litigation privilege that normally shields their litigation-related activities from tort liability will protect them against liability arising out of their conduct in negotiations, that is not necessarily true. Lawyers' litigation privilege is generally no defense to fraud.[223]

Slotkin v. Citizens Casualty Co. of New York[224] is the seminal case on lawyers' civil liability for dishonest negotiating tactics.[225] Charlotte Slotkin gave birth to a brain-damaged son, Steven, in Beth-El Hospital in New York City in 1963. She was a diabetic, and Steven's brain damage was attributable to the hospital's failure to properly administer insulin to her shortly before delivery. Steven and his father sued Beth-El for medical malpractice. Beth-El had a $200,000 primary liability insurance policy with Citizens. Beth-El also had a $1 million excess policy issued by Lloyd's of London underwriters.

The case went to trial in February 1971. A Beth-El defense lawyer, Christopher McGrath, who was hired by Citizens, told the plaintiffs' lawyer, Max

222. For a thorough discussion of lawyers' potential liability for fraud and negligent misrepresentation, see Douglas R. Richmond, *Fraud and Misrepresentation Claims Against Lawyers*, 16 Nev. L.J. 57 (2015).

223. Williams v. BASF Catalysts LLC, 765 F.3d 306, 318–20 (3d Cir. 2014) (predicting New Jersey law); Shafer v. Berger, Kahn, Shafton, Moss, Figler, Simon & Gladstone, 131 Cal. Rptr. 2d 777, 799 (Ct. App. 2003); Matsuura v. E.I. du Pont de Nemours & Co., 73 P.3d 687, 700 (Haw. 2003); N.Y. Cooling Towers, Inc. v. Goidel, 805 N.Y.S.2d 779, 783 (Sup. Ct. 2005); Moss v. Parr Waddoups Brown Gee & Loveless, 285 P.3d 1157, 1166 (Utah 2012); Clark v. Druckman, 624 S.E.2d 864, 870 (W. Va. 2005). *But see* Dawley v. NF Energy Corp. of Am., 492 F. App'x 77, 80 (11th Cir. 2012) (applying Florida law); Simms v. Seaman, 69 A.3d 880, 892 (Conn. 2013) (stating that "attorneys are shielded by the litigation privilege from claims of fraud").

224. 614 F.2d 301 (2d Cir. 1979).

225. For another interesting case on lawyers' civil liability for dishonesty in negotiations, see Shafer v. Berger, Kahn, Shafton, Moss, Figler, Simon & Gladstone, 131 Cal. Rptr. 2d 777 (Ct. App. 2003).

Toberoff, that Beth-El had only $200,000 in insurance coverage.[226] McGrath also revealed that he had not told Beth-El's in-house lawyer about the trial, and he refused Toberoff's request that he notify the hospital. Toberoff was concerned about the collectability of any judgment the plaintiffs might receive and he promptly informed the hospital's administrator that Beth-El faced a possible verdict exceeding $1 million. In response, the administrator dispatched George Berkowitz, a lawyer and Beth-El trustee, to the courthouse. Berkowitz also told Toberoff that the hospital had only $200,000 in coverage based on information he obtained from McGrath, another defense lawyer, and Citizens' claims manager, Paul Ratner.[227] Both Toberoff and the trial judge thought it odd that Beth-El had so little insurance.[228]

The trial unfolded nicely for the plaintiffs. Just before they rested, a key medical expert for Beth-El changed his opinion and sided with them. The parties hastily convened a settlement conference before the trial judge. McGrath again stated that the total insurance coverage available was $200,000 and that "he knew that the [h]ospital did not have additional insurance with other companies."[229] Based on that representation the case settled for $185,000. The lawyers drafted a settlement stipulation to read into the record. The stipulation provided that "the attorney for the defendant represents that the total insurance coverage of the defendant is the sum of $200,000, under a policy with Citizens Casualty, and to the best of his knowledge there are no other policies covering this event."[230] McGrath and Berkowitz verbally approved the stipulation on the record.[231]

The obvious problem was that McGrath's and Berkowitz's representations were false. If Berkowitz's statements could be excused because his knowledge was exclusively secondhand, McGrath's could not be. McGrath had "complete access" to documents clearly demonstrating the existence of the excess policy, such as letters from a lawyer for the Lloyd's of London underwriters inquiring about the Slotkin case.[232] The file containing these letters was in the possession of McGrath's firm during the trial.[233]

The existence of the Lloyd's of London excess policy came to light shortly after the settlement.[234] The trial judge had not yet entered an order allocating the settlement funds and thus there was no final judgment, but the parties could not reopen settlement discussions because the Lloyd's

226. *Slotkin*, 614 F.2d at 305.
227. *Id.*
228. *Id.* at 306.
229. *Id.* at 307 (footnote omitted).
230. *Id.*
231. *Id.*
232. *Id.*
233. *Id.* at 307–08.
234. *Id.* at 308.

underwriters refused to participate based on late notice of the Slotkin claim. For a variety of reasons, the plaintiffs could not retry the case. The trial court thus approved the $185,000 settlement, with Toberoff's intention to sue for fraud being well known.[235]

The plaintiffs sued Citizens, its reinsurers, McGrath, Ratner, Berkowitz, and another lawyer for Citizens in federal court. The jury returned a $680,000 verdict for the plaintiffs for fraud, allocating the damages $500,000 to Citizens, $100,000 to Berkowitz, $60,000 to Ratner, and $20,000 to McGrath.[236] The district judge granted the defendants' motion for JNOV. He reasoned that because the plaintiffs learned of the excess policy before the trial court had entered a final judgment, they were bound by the settlement.[237] He further reasoned that the plaintiffs had not significantly changed position to their prejudice before learning the truth.[238] The plaintiffs appealed to the Second Circuit.

The *Slotkin* court concluded that the district judge erred in granting the defendants' motion for JNOV. The court reasoned that the jury could have properly found McGrath liable for fraud.[239] He stipulated that to the best of his knowledge there was only $200,000 in insurance coverage available to Beth-El despite possessing documents indicating that the hospital had $1 million in excess coverage.[240] His insistence that the hospital had only $200,000 in coverage in the face of contrary facts met the New York definition of scienter "as a 'reckless indifference to error,' 'a pretense of exact knowledge,' or '[an] assertion of a false material fact "susceptible of accurate knowledge" but stated to be true on the personal knowledge of the representer.'"[241] Berkowitz, on the other hand, escaped liability. While he was easily negligent or even grossly negligent in making the statements that he did about Beth-El's insurance coverage, he lacked the scienter necessary for fraud liability under New York law. The court ultimately gave the plaintiffs the option of either reinstating the judgment of $680,000 or retrying the case against all defendants except Berkowitz. McGrath petitioned for rehearing to no avail.

It is difficult to understand how McGrath could have made the statements about coverage that he did. The notion that Beth-El had only $200,000 in coverage struck both Toberoff and the trial judge as unusual; it should have similarly impressed McGrath. At the very least, Toberoff's and

235. *Id.* at 310.
236. *Id.* at 310–11.
237. *Id.* at 311.
238. *Id.*
239. *Id.* at 314.
240. *Id.*
241. *Id.*

the judge's reservations should have inspired him to attempt to ascertain the hospital's true coverage before finally committing to $200,000.

It seems much more likely that McGrath knew of the hospital's excess policy and opted to conceal its existence. The existence of excess coverage is something that a defense lawyer hired by a primary insurer should be expected to know.[242] That is especially true where, as here, the defense lawyer had correspondence from a lawyer for the excess carrier inquiring about the status of the case in files in his office.

It is no answer to say that McGrath had nothing to gain and much to lose from concealing the policy.[243] In fact, McGrath arguably *did* have something to gain by concealing the Lloyd's policy. That is, by settling a very difficult case on exceptionally favorable terms, he might have believed that Citizens or the Lloyd's underwriters or both would value his craftiness and reward him with future business. Perhaps McGrath thought that Beth-El administrators would be impressed by his tactical prowess and identify him as their lawyer of choice in future medical malpractice cases. If so, it is reasonable to assume that he failed to appreciate the fraudulent nature of his conduct at least in part because of the context in which it occurred—namely, negotiations.

Slotkin involved discussions between experienced lawyers, who are normally savvy negotiators. But an opponent's sophistication or representation by counsel is not an absolute defense to fraud or negligent misrepresentation claims.[244] Rather, an opponent's sophistication or representation by counsel goes to the element of justifiable or reasonable reliance. This often means that fraud and misrepresentation claims cannot be disposed of at the motion to dismiss stage but instead must wait for summary judgment or resolution at trial. In any event, fraud claims pose potentially serious problems for lawyers, as *Fire Insurance Exchange v. Bell*[245] illustrates.

Bell arose out of a house fire in which a teenage boy, Jason Bell, was severely burned. Phillip Scaletta of the Indiana law firm of Ice Miller was hired by the homeowner's insurer, Farmers, to defend the homeowner in any litigation that might result. Before any suit was ever filed, Scaletta allegedly lied repeatedly to Bell's lawyer, Robert Collins, about the liability limits of the Farmers policy, saying over and over again that its limits were $100,000

242. Today, McGrath would almost certainly have to know about the existence of excess insurance by virtue of routine pretrial discovery and disclosures. *See, e.g.*, Fed. R. Civ. P. 26(a)(1)(A)(iv) (requiring the initial disclosure of "any insurance agreement under which an insurance business may be liable to satisfy all or part of a possible judgment in the action or to indemnify or reimburse for payments made to satisfy the judgment"). Toberoff would know about the presence of excess insurance for the same reason.

243. *Slotkin*, 614 F.2d at 318–19 (Van Graafeiland, J., dissenting).

244. Restatement (Third) of the Law Governing Lawyers § 98 cmt. b (2000).

245. 643 N.E.2d 310 (Ind. 1994).

when he knew them to be $300,000.[246] Based on those representations, Collins advised Bell to settle with the homeowner for $100,000.[247] Collins later sued the manufacturer of the home's water heater on Bell's behalf. During that litigation, Collins learned the true liability limits of the Farmers policy. Bell then sued Scaletta and Ice Miller for fraudulent misrepresentation.

Scaletta and Ice Miller contended that Collins "had, as a matter of law, no right to rely on the alleged misrepresentations because he was a trained professional involved in adversarial settlement negotiation and had access to the relevant facts."[248] This argument disturbed the Indiana Supreme Court, which observed that "[t]he reliability and trustworthiness of attorney representations constitute an important component of the efficient administration of justice. A lawyer's representations have long been accorded a particular expectation of honesty and trustworthiness."[249] Lawyers' commitment to these values is embodied in the oaths that they take when admitted to the bar, various ethics rules, and professional tenets adopted by bar associations. The court then made its position clear a second time:

> We decline to require attorneys to burden unnecessarily the courts and litigation process with discovery to verify the truthfulness of material representations made by opposing counsel. The reliability of lawyers' representations is an integral component of the fair and efficient administration of justice. The law should promote lawyers' care in making statements that are accurate and trustworthy and should foster the reliance upon such statements by others.[250]

The court declined the opportunity to simply vent and leave the issue of reliance as a question of fact for determination by the trial court. The court instead held that Collins's "right to rely upon any material misrepresentations that may have been made by opposing counsel [was] established as a matter of law."[251] As for what representations were made and the extent of Collins's reliance on them, those questions did remain for trial.

Scaletta's and Ice Miller's defense that Collins should not have relied on Scalletta's alleged misrepresentations given the context in which they occurred stood no real chance of success. The amount of available insurance coverage was a material fact. Collins had no reason to doubt the answers he received from Scaletta simply because they were provided during pre-suit negotiations. As the New Jersey Supreme Court once observed, "[i]t

246. *Id.* at 311.
247. *Id.*
248. *Id.* at 312.
249. *Id.*
250. *Id.*
251. *Id.* at 313.

goes without saying that representations in negotiations are made to induce reliance."[252]

Wheatcraft v. Wheatcraft[253] provides a helpful contrast to *Bell*. *Wheatcraft* was a divorce case in which the Wheatcrafts participated in a mediation. One of the issues in the case was the division of the couple's assets, including the value of Mr. Wheatcraft's painting business. Mr. Wheatcraft hired an appraiser to value his interest in the company. The appraiser opined that Mr. Wheatcraft's interest had a value of just over $43,000. That figure was revealed at the mediation. The parties reached a compromise at the mediation, and Mrs. Wheatcraft signed a settlement agreement at the end of the session apparently based in part on her understanding of the value of Mr. Wheatcraft's business interest. She later challenged the settlement agreement based on her husband's alleged fraud in inducing her to sign it.

Mrs. Wheatcraft alleged that her husband had fraudulently misrepresented the value of his interest in his painting company. When pressed on her reliance on the valuation figure offered at the mediation, Mrs. Wheatcraft argued "that she had an absolute right to rely on [Mr. Wheatcraft's] valuation *because his attorney represented that the valuation was accurate*."[254] In making this argument, Mrs. Wheatcraft relied on the Indiana Supreme Court's decision in *Bell*.[255] The *Wheatcraft* court quickly dispatched this argument, explaining that the representation held to be reliable upon in *Bell* "concerned the policy limits of an insurance contract, which is a representation of fact."[256] In contrast, Mr. Wheatcraft's counsel "only represented the valuation of the company based on an appraisal, which is an opinion."[257] Because Mr. Wheatcraft's lawyer simply recited the appraiser's opinion as to the value of his client's business interest, Mrs. Wheatcraft had no right to rely upon the lawyer's representation under the rule announced in *Bell*.[258]

Although *Wheatcraft* was correctly decided, the case is distinguishable from the holding in *Bell* on a more basic ground than the difference between opinion and fact—namely, the absence of a misrepresentation by a lawyer. In *Bell*, Scaletta misrepresented the liability limits of the insurance policy. In *Wheatcraft*, on the other hand, the lawyer did not misrepresent the contents of the appraiser's report; he stated them accurately. Going one step further, there was no evidence that the appraiser's report was fraudulent or somehow fatally flawed, or that the lawyer knew of such facts if they even

252. Banco Popular N. Am. v. Gandi, 876 A.2d 253, 266 (N.J. 2005).
253. 825 N.E.2d 23 (Ind. Ct. App. 2005).
254. *Id.* at 31 (emphasis added).
255. *Id.* (citing Fire Ins. Exch. v. Bell, 643 N.E.2d 310, 313 (Ind. 1994)).
256. *Id.*
257. *Id.*
258. *Id.*

existed. The lawyer in *Wheatcraft* told the truth—the opposing party simply disagreed with the message in hindsight.

It may be difficult in some cases for lawyers to defeat negligent misrepresentation or fraud claims on justifiable or reasonable reliance grounds in light of their Model Rule 4.1(a) duty of truthfulness.[259] The same is true with respect to lawyers' duty of honesty under Model Rule 8.4(c).[260] A jury could well conclude that because lawyers owe a duty of truthfulness even to adversaries and are broadly prohibited from engaging in misrepresentation, an opposing party's reliance on a lawyer's statements in negotiations was reasonable.[261] This assumes, of course, that a party who claims to have relied on a lawyer's statements by virtue of the lawyer's duties under Rules 4.1(a) and 8.4(c) actually knew of lawyers' duty of honesty to third parties at the time of the challenged representation. If the claimant was not then aware of the lawyer's Rule 4.1(a) and Rule 8.4(c) obligations, the rules are irrelevant, and the reasonableness of the claimant's alleged reliance must be judged according to a standard separate from the rules.

Finally, lawyers' duty of truthfulness under Rule 4.1(a) is not perfectly congruent with civil liability for misrepresentation. Many statements that are not treated as statements of material fact as a matter of professional responsibility, but that are instead considered to be "puffery" or "posturing," are not similarly exempted under contract and tort law. As a matter of tort and contract law, the central question with respect to such statements is more commonly one of reasonable reliance. In the civil liability realm, defending misstatements in negotiations on the basis of puffery is of limited utility because whether a statement is or is not actionable depends on its context, the lawyer's actual knowledge, and the person to whom it is made.[262] In the right circumstances, a lawyer's seeming puffery may be actionable fraud.[263] That same statement would be unlikely to expose a lawyer to professional discipline under Rule 4.1(a), although a comment to Rule 4.1 prudently cautions lawyers to "be mindful of their obligations under applicable law to avoid criminal and tortious misrepresentation."[264]

In terms of precautions, lawyers should never knowingly misstate the existence or amount of insurance coverage or fail to disclose the existence of insurance coverage when called upon to do so. Similarly, a lawyer should never knowingly misrepresent a client's financial position. If lawyers are

---

259. *See, e.g.*, Hoyt Props, Inc. v. Prod. Res. Grp., L.L.C., 716 N.W.2d 366, 375 (Minn. Ct. App. 2006), *aff'd*, 736 N.W.2d 313 (Minn. 2007).

260. Model Rules of Prof'l Conduct R. 8.4(c) (2020) (prohibiting conduct involving dishonesty, fraud, deceit, or misrepresentation).

261. *Hoyt Props., Inc.*, 716 N.W.2d at 375.

262. Jeska v. Mulhall, 693 P.2d 1335, 1337 (Or. Ct. App. 1985).

263. *Id.* at 1337–38 (stating that a parcel of land was "a lot of property for the money").

264. Model Rules of Prof'l Conduct R. 4.1 cmt. 2 (2020).

uncertain or unsure about material facts, they should confirm those facts to the extent reasonably practicable before representing them to another party. Lawyers should appropriately qualify their statements when necessary. Finally, where they have no duty to speak, lawyers may more prudently choose to remain silent.

VIII. Conclusion

Negotiating presents lawyers with numerous professional responsibility and liability challenges. Lawyers must reasonably communicate with their clients under penalty of professional discipline and malpractice liability if they do not. Their nearly airtight duty of confidentiality is no shield against professional discipline if a client is dishonest. Lawyers' duty of honesty to third persons has both disciplinary and liability consequences if breached, and it can sometimes be breached through silence. The honesty bar is set especially high when a court is involved in negotiations, as is often the case in litigation.

The overwhelming majority of lawyers are ethical. Even so, the paradoxical nature of negotiation may lead good lawyers astray. The general perception that deception is permissible in negotiations fails to account for the situations in which it is not. Furthermore, because the process of negotiation varies by place and subject, it seems to be governed by shifting rules.

13

Ethics on Appeal

I. Introduction

Appeals follow trial court judgments just as surely as night follows day. Indeed, many lawyers specialize in appellate practice. Lawyers' compliance with rules of professional conduct obviously is as important in appellate litigation as it is in matters before a trial court or any other tribunal. Given the nature of appellate practice and its inherent differences from trial practice or the representation of clients in transactional or other non-litigation contexts, however, there are a variety of ethics rules that simply do not apply to representations of clients before appellate courts. There being no jury, no witness examinations, and no discovery in appellate representations, for example, rules concerning pretrial procedure and conduct in discovery, conduct at trial, and limits on a lawyer's ability to act as advocate at trial when the lawyer is also a witness simply do not apply to an appellate lawyer. Other rules of professional conduct, such as those regarding a lawyer's service as a third-party neutral, limiting lawyers' ability to communicate with jurors after discharge, and establishing lawyers' duties as advocates in non-adjudicative proceedings, are also unlikely to surface in appellate representations.

While some professional responsibility issues will seldom, if ever, confront an appellate lawyer, two professional responsibility issues do tend to either arise more frequently or be of weightier concern in appellate litigation. The first is appellate lawyers' ability to criticize courts and judges. Although lawyers do not necessarily check their First Amendment rights at the courthouse door, those rights are notably scaled back in most jurisdictions. The second involves the pursuit of frivolous appeals and bad faith litigation at the appellate stage.

II. Lawyers' Criticism of Courts

Lawyers generally are deferential to, and respectful of, courts. Nevertheless, litigation is an exceedingly competitive endeavor, and advocates and their clients alike can be very disappointed when decisions go against them. Once a case has reached the appellate stage, opportunities to alter a disappointing outcome often begin to dwindle because of the standard of review or simply because the case is closer to reaching a truly final, non-appealable judgment. Unfortunately, advocates who find themselves on the wrong side of a ruling, and especially those who feel pressured by a disappointed client, may allow personal factors to lead them to improperly criticize the court believed to have wrongly decided a case and, in so doing, potentially violate their ethical obligations.[1]

Appellate lawyers must think very carefully in fashioning their criticisms of lower court decisions to ensure that they are not doing so in ways that are capable of being read as attacks on the judges' integrity or qualifications.[2] Model Rule 8.2(a) provides that "[a] lawyer shall not make a statement that the lawyer knows to be false or with reckless disregard as to its truth or falsity concerning the qualifications or integrity of a judge."[3] Model Rule 8.2(a) also prohibits such statements regarding an "adjudicatory officer or public legal officer," or "a candidate for election or appointment to judicial or legal office."[4]

1. *See, e.g.*, State v. Williams, 225 A.3d 751, 760 (Me. 2020) (cautioning lawyers about including arguments in appellate briefs that might violate Rule 8.2(a) at clients' insistence and sketching an alternative procedure for lawyers in such cases); Disciplinary Couns. v. Shimko, 983 N.E.2d 1300, 1305 (Ohio 2012) (disciplining the lawyer for criticizing a judge in appellate briefs, including "ad hominem attacks and hyperbole," such as "'fabricating allegations,' 'completely fabricating the basis for his decision,' 'deliberately misrepresenting,' 'contriving a reason,' and [being] 'personally invested in the outcome'"); *In re* Disciplinary Proc. Against Isaacson, 860 N.W.2d 490, 494–95 (Wis. 2015) (suspending a lawyer for referring to various judges as a "black-robed bigot," a "dirty Jesuit," and a "dastardly Jesuit," among other slurs, and describing the Minnesota bankruptcy bench as being "composed of a bunch of ignoramus, bigoted Catholic beasts that carry the sword of the church").

2. Lawyers who make disparaging statements about judges in knowing or reckless disregard of the truth run the risk of being disciplined for engaging in conduct prejudicial to the administration of justice in violation of Rule 8.4(d), in addition to violating other rules. *See, e.g.*, Chief Disciplinary Couns. v. Rozbicki, 167 A.3d 351, 363–64 (Conn. 2017) (concluding that the lawyer's relentless and repetitive attacks on the integrity of two judges violated Connecticut's version of Rule 8.4(d)); *In re* Petition for Disciplinary Action Against Michael, 836 N.W.2d 753, 765 (Minn. 2013) (finding that a "flippant rhetorical question at the end of [an] email" alone was a violation of RPC 8.4(d) as "disrespectful conduct directed at a tribunal" that was "prejudicial to the administration of justice"); *In re* Disciplinary Action Against Nathan, 671 N.W.2d 578, 580 (Minn. 2003) (holding that "baseless and derogatory statements about judges" violated Rule 8.4(d)); Office of Disciplinary Couns. v. Surrick, 749 A.2d 441, 445–46 (Pa. 2000) (suspending a lawyer who violated Rule 8.4 by accusing "two judicial officers of violating their oath of office by rendering decisions in official matters on the basis of outside influence"); *In re* Discipline of Colin, 448 P.3d 556, 562 (Nev. 2019) (finding a Rule 8.4(d) violation where the lawyer made repeated efforts to disqualify the four justices who decided an earlier case to either delay the proceedings or obtain another panel of judges to decide the case anew and filed motions to disqualify after the justices had entered a decision on the merits and made serious charges of ethical and criminal violations by the justices without any factual support or legal authority).

3. Model Rules of Prof'l Conduct R. 8.2(a) (2020).

4. *Id.*

In addition to potential exposure to discipline, a lawyer who falsely or recklessly remarks about a court's qualifications or integrity in a brief or motion risks having her brief or motion stricken in whole or part,[5] surely hurting the client's case as a result.

A. *Limitations on Lawyers' Speech Rights and the First Amendment*

The decision to insert the "knowingly or with reckless disregard as to its truth or falsity" standard in Model Rule 8.2(a) was deliberate. The prohibitions in Model Rule 8.2(a) regarding what lawyers can and cannot say about courts and judges obviously have First Amendment implications.[6] The fact that a lawyer's criticism of a court may be in bad taste or reflect poor judgment does not necessarily make the lawyer's statements unethical.[7] That said, "a lawyer's speech may be limited more than that of a lay person."[8] Although lawyers do not surrender their free speech rights upon admission to the bar, they must temper their criticisms of courts in accordance with professional standards.[9] Still, the drafters of the Model Rules expressly acknowledged the influence of groundbreaking Supreme Court precedent

5. *See, e.g.*, Henry v. Eberhard, 832 S.W.2d 467, 474 (Ark. 1992) (striking six pages of the appellants' brief for "inflammatory and disrespectful" remarks about the trial court); McLemore v. Elliot, 614 S.W.2d 226, 227 (Ark. 1981) (striking the appellant's brief in its entirety for "intemperate and distasteful language" directed at the trial court); Peters v. Pine Meadow Ranch Home Ass'n, 151 P.3d 962, 963, 967–68 (Utah 2007) (striking a brief in its entirety, with the result being that the court of appeals decision explicitly acknowledged by the supreme court as in error was summarily affirmed).

6. *See In re* Green, 11 P.3d 1078, 1083–87 (Colo. 2000) (discussing at length the application of the First Amendment to the lawyer's claim that the trial judge was racist, and the standard to be applied to the lawyer's conduct); *In re* Charges of Unprof'l Conduct Involving File No. 17139, 720 N.W.2d 807, 813–15 (Minn. 2006) (discussing First Amendment implications of attorneys' criticism of judges, the appropriate standard to be applied, and Rule 8.2(a)).

7. *See, e.g.*, Iowa Sup. Ct. Att'y Disciplinary Bd. v. Rhinehart, 953 N.W.2d 156, 170–71 (Iowa 2021) (concluding that the lawyer's criticism of the district court "unduly personalized the role of the district court in adjudicating a hard-fought case" but that his "less-than-ideal word choices did not cross the boundary into conduct that violated [Iowa's version of Rule 8.2(a)]").

8. *In re* Gershater, 17 P.3d 929, 936 (Kan. 2001); *see also In re* Zeno, 504 F.3d 64, 66 (1st Cir. 2007) (quoting Gentile v. State Bar of Nev., 501 U.S. 1030, 1071 (1991)); *In re* Shearin, 765 A.2d 930, 938 (Del. 2000) ("[T]here are ethical obligations imposed upon a Delaware lawyer, which qualify the lawyer's constitutional right to freedom of speech.").

9. *In re* Arnold, 56 P.3d 259, 267–68 (Kan. 2002) (quoting *In re* Johnson, 729 P.2d 1175 (Kan. 1986)); *In re* Madison, 282 S.W.3d 350, 353–54 (Mo. 2009) (quoting various sources); Bd. of Prof'l Responsibility v. Slavin, 145 S.W.3d 538, 548–50 (Tenn. 2004) (finding the lawyer's First Amendment defense unavailing and suspending the lawyer for calling an administrative law judge "[p]etty, barbarous and cruel," and a "[d]isgrace [to] his judicial office"); *Anthony*, 621 S.E.2d at 126–27; Lawyer Disciplinary Bd. v. Hall, 765 S.E.2d 187, 198 (W. Va. 2014) (holding that a statement by a lawyer that the lawyer "knows to be false or with reckless disregard as to its truth or falsity concerning the qualifications or integrity of a judge . . . is not protected by the First Amendment . . . where such statement is not supported by an objectively reasonable factual basis"). *But see In re Green*, 11 P.3d at 1083–87 (holding that the lawyer's claim that the trial judge was racist and therefore biased against him was speech protected by the First Amendment).

that determined that a lawyer's speech critical of the judiciary was "speech concerning public affairs" and part of "the essence of self-government."[10] In *Garrison v. Louisiana*,[11] the Supreme Court struck down Louisiana's criminal libel statute as unconstitutional. In so doing, the Court overturned a district attorney's conviction for statements made at a press conference, including speculation about the influence of racketeers on the judiciary and an accusation that the large backlog of criminal cases was caused by "the inefficiency, laziness, and excessive vacations" of certain specifically identified judges.[12] Citing *Garrison*, the drafters of the Model Rules explained in the legal background relevant to Model Rule 8.2(a) that "critical factors in constitutional analysis are the statement's falsity and the individual's knowledge concerning its falsity at the time of the utterance."[13]

Model Rule 8.2(a) might be subject to serious attack on First Amendment grounds if, for example, it were employed to discipline a lawyer for speech about a judicial candidate while campaigning on behalf of a sitting judge during a contested judicial election.[14] It is not as vulnerable when applied to lawyers' speech as advocates in litigation.[15] The First Amendment generally does not exempt a lawyer from discipline for intemperate speech in court,[16] or from inappropriate statements in pleadings or briefs.[17] In most

10. Garrison v. La., 379 U.S. 64, 74 (1964); Am. Bar Ass'n, Model Rules of Prof'l Conduct R. 8.2 Legal Background 206 (Proposed Final Draft, 1981) (explaining that Model Rule 8.2 is consistent with the limitations imposed by the Supreme Court, namely "that false statements about public officials may be punished only if the speaker acts with knowledge that the statement is 'false or with reckless disregard'" of its truth or falsity).

11. 379 U.S. 64 (1964).

12. *Id.* at 65–67.

13. Am. Bar Ass'n, Model Rules of Prof'l Conduct R. 8.2 Legal Background 206 (Proposed Final Draft, 1981).

14. *Cf.* Berry v. Schmitt, 688 F.3d 290, 304–05 (6th Cir. 2012) (holding that Kentucky's Rule 8.2(a) was unconstitutional as applied to a post-proceeding letter written by a lawyer criticizing the Kentucky Legislative Ethics Commission's handling of a fundraising complaint).

15. *See, e.g.*, Iowa Sup. Ct. Att'y Disciplinary Bd. v. Att'y Doe No. 792, 878 N.W.2d 189, 196–99 (Iowa 2016) (concluding that the lawyer's comments about a judge were not entitled to First Amendment protection, but ultimately deciding that because the offending statements were made in a private e-mail message, they did not violate Rule 8.2(a)).

16. *In re* Disciplinary Action against MacDonald, 906 N.W.2d 238, 246–47 (Minn. 2018); *In re* Coe, 903 S.W.2d 916, 917 (Mo. 1995); *In re* Disciplinary Action Against Garaas, 652 N.W.2d 918, 925 (N.D. 2002).

17. *See, e.g.*, Iowa Sup. Ct. Bd. of Prof'l Ethics & Conduct v. Ronwin, 557 N.W.2d 515, 517 (Iowa 1997) (imposing discipline and explaining that "statements and accusations contained in pleadings and briefs do not infringe upon the attorney's constitutional right to freedom of speech"); Ky. Bar Ass'n v. Waller, 929 S.W.2d 181, 182–83 (Ky. 1996) (suspending a lawyer who in a pleading opined that a new judge assigned to a case was "much better than that lying incompetent ass-hole it replaced if you graduated from the eighth grade" and rejecting the lawyer's claim that the First Amendment shielded him from discipline); Peters v. Pine Meadow Ranch Home Ass'n, 151 P.3d 962, 967–68 (Utah 2007) (striking briefs and assessing attorneys' fees as a result of the lawyer's many inflammatory statements regarding the appellate panel, including analogizing its conduct to an alleged slaughter in Haditha of Iraqi civilians).

jurisdictions, lawyers' false statements about courts and judges in such contexts made knowingly or with reckless disregard for the truth simply do not enjoy any significant constitutional protection.[18] Further, despite the historical underpinnings of the adoption of this standard in the rule, "recklessness" as used in Model Rule 8.2(a) is measured by the majority of courts using an objective standard, rather than a subjective one.[19] This principle remains true where the lawyer is a party and appears pro se.[20]

Board of Professional Responsibility v. Parrish[21] offers a prime example of a lawyer finding no solace in the First Amendment as a defense to professional discipline for attacking a court's integrity. In that case, Larry Parrish represented David Morrow and Judy Wright in three cases concerning a trust for their cousin, John Goza. They lost all three cases in the trial courts and on appeal to the Tennessee Court of Appeals. The panel of judges that heard the final appeal—Judges David Farmer, Steven Stafford, and Holly Kirby—concluded that the appeal was frivolous and awarded the appellee its attorney's fees and costs. Parrish unsuccessfully moved for a rehearing and to recuse Judge Farmer; he later moved to recuse Judges Stafford and Kirby. The judges submitted Parrish's recusal motions to the Tennessee Board of Professional Responsibility because the motions contained a litany of inflammatory and often bizarre statements, including:

> Estate's motion is grounded on Estate's contention that Estate has been denied access to indisputable organic law of Tennessee applied to indisputable facts, and that access has been denied because of a prejudicial and

18. *See In re* Palmisano, 70 F.3d 483, 487 (7th Cir. 1995) (explaining this position and the reasoning behind it); *see, e.g.*, Att'y Grievance Comm'n of Md. v. Frost, 85 A.3d 26, 274–78 (Md. 2014) (explaining why the lawyer's statements did not enjoy First Amendment protection and violated Rule 8.2(a)); Miss. Bar v. Lumumba, 912 So. 2d 871, 884–86 (Miss. 2005) (finding a Rule 8.2(a) violation where the lawyer insinuated in court proceedings that the judge could be bribed, accused the judge of unfairness, impugned judge's qualifications, and called the judge a "barbarian" in a press interview); Lawyer Disciplinary Bd. v. Hall, 765 S.E.2d 187, 198 (W. Va. 2014) (holding that "a statement by an attorney that such attorney knows to be false or with reckless disregard as to its truth or falsity concerning the qualifications or integrity of a judge . . . is not protected by the First Amendment as public speech on a matter of public concern where such statement is not supported by an objectively reasonable factual basis"); *In re* Disciplinary Proc. Against Riordan, 824 N.W.2d 441, 448 (Wis. 2012) (rejecting the lawyer's First Amendment religious freedom claims and explaining that "[f]alse statements made knowingly, or with reckless disregard for the truth, are not constitutionally protected").

19. Fla. Bar v. Patterson, 257 So. 3d 56, 62 (Fla. 2018); *In re* Dixon, 994 N.E.2d 1129, 1137 (Ind. 2013); Iowa Sup. Ct. Att'y Disciplinary Bd. v. Att'y Doe No. 792, 878 N.W.2d 189, 194 (Iowa 2016); Ky. Bar Ass'n v. Blum, 404 S.W.3d 841, 856 (Ky. 2013); *In re Disciplinary Action against MacDonald*, 906 N.W.2d at 246–47; State *ex rel.* Couns. for Discipline of the Neb. Sup. Ct. v. Gast, 896 N.W.2d 583, 597 (Neb. 2017); Bd. of Prof'l Responsibility v. Parrish, 556 S.W.3d 153, 166 (Tenn. 2018); *Hall*, 765 S.E.2d at 198; *In re Disciplinary Proceedings Against Riordan*, 824 N.W.2d at 448–49; Bd. of Prof'l Responsibility v. Davidson, 205 P.3d 1008, 1014 (Wyo. 2009) (citing *In re* Cobb, 838 N.E.2d 1197, 1213 (Mass. 2005)).

20. Notopolous v. Statewide Grievance Comm., 890 A.2d 509, 518–20 (Conn. 2006).

21. 556 S.W.3d 153 (Tenn. 2018).

baseless bias, evidently the result of personal sympathies/sensitivities of Judge Farmer.

In contrast, if Estate shows that Judge Farmer (1) ruled the opposite of what he knew undebatable law to be, (2) wrote as fact that which he knew not to be fact to avoid the effect he knew would be required, if he acknowledged what he knew to be fact, (3) ruled as if ipse dixit was a holding and decision, (4) gave obiter dictum preclusive effect, (5) used half-truths to fabricate justification for judicial misconduct, (6) without the slightest justification, demeaned counsel for Estate to create a scapegoat for his judicial misconduct, (7) used the Memorandum Opinion as a vehicle to include unnecessary obiter dictum as a means, practically speaking, to prejudge case-dispositive issues pending in trial courts and, thereby, usurp the role of the trial courts to adjudge the issue independently and, finally, (8) awarded attorney's fees against Estate based on fabrication, Estate will have established that Judge Farmer is serving, in this case, encumbered by a prejudice and bias against Estate to manufacture an outcome against Estate, in the teeth of indisputable organic law and indisputable fact that dictate the opposite.

This is not about miscalling balls and strikes; this is about rigging the game.

Estate's motion further is grounded [sic] how that Judge Farmer adjudicated the appeal in the instant case so as to violate the rights of Estate guaranteed by the Tennessee Constitution, Art. I, Section 17 (open courts). . . .

There is absolutely no way under the sun for Estate to fail to prevail in the instant appeal, except by judges deciding the appeal to turn a deaf ear and blind eye to the clearest possible provisions of § 35-15-203.

Judge Farmer has victimized Estate by saying of a statute . . . even though a person minimally literate in the English language could very easily read the statute and know, without hesitation, that the statute does exactly the opposite.

This is an aberrant misstatement of clear law known to Judge Farmer. . . .

Placing the subject erroneous ipse dixit in Judge Farmer's Memorandum Opinion, in practical effect, is a prejudgment designed to prejudice Estate in cases not before Judge Farmer.

Additionally, the erroneous ipse dixit in Judge Farmer's Memorandum Opinion is a setup, i.e., the point is to forewarn Estate not to exercise its right to an appeal in the case where the erroneous ipse dixit is dispositive and, if Estate exercises Estate's right to appeal, Judge Farmer is poised to punish Estate for not heeding Judge Farmer's forewarnings.

Though it takes slightly more acumen than minimal literacy in the English Language, any person trained in the law and minimally versed in how the law treats ipse dixit and obiter dictum, at once, can see that the court of appeals never before has "held" or "decided" that the putative trust exists.

The repeated statements in Judge Farmer's Memorandum Opinion that the court of appeals, twice before, "held" or "decided" that the putative trust exists, for Judge Farmer, is a convenient and illegitimately purposeful fabrication.

[T]o provide a façade of legitimacy to Judge Farmer's inclusion about the putative trust, Judge Farmer builds a construct on the false presupposition that § 35-15-203 divests circuit court of subject matter jurisdiction, if the putative trust exists.

The illegitimate purpose for Judge Farmer injecting commentary into Judge Farmer's Memorandum Opinion on the subject of the putative trust is to prejudge, erroneously, if (which is certain to occur) the issue is presented to the court of appeals in the future.

By use of a memorandum opinion, Judge Farmer insulates his manipulation/rigging of the legal system from review by the Tennessee Supreme Court. . . . Therefore, a memorandum opinion, which has zero effect on Tennessee law, has zero chance of being reviewed by the Supreme Court. Knowing this, Judge Farmer is confident that Judge Farmer's patent error and abuse of Judge Farmer's judicial power will remain effective to accomplish Judge Farmer's illegitimate objectives.

Judge Farmer has done a masterful job of covering up the fact that Judge Farmer has stepped out of Judge Farmer's role as an even-handed Judge and into the role of adversary of the Estate, willing to abuse the power of his judicial office to deny Estate's access to unexceptional organic law of Tennessee well-known to Judge Farmer.

Many authors, among them Alfred Lord Tennyson, have observed that the half-truth is the most sinister of all deception. . . . Judge Farmer has used the half-truth in constructing [his] Memorandum Opinion. Judge Farmer's Memorandum Opinion is a patchwork of snippets of truth glued together by adhesive design to close to Estate access to controlling organic law.

[T]he Estate of John J. Goza . . . has been and continues to be denied access to the benefit of the organic law of Tennessee by a demonstrated bias and/or appearance of bias, seemingly anchored in Judge Farmer's personal sympathies/sensitivities that dictate an outcome inconsistent with Tennessee's organic law.

Let it be clear that Estate finds no fault with Judge Farmer's personal sympathies/sensitivities. The fault Estate finds is in Judge Farmer permitting his personal sympathies/sensitivities to prejudice him in exercise of his undeviating duty to apply organic law, even if doing so produces a judgment that offends Judge Farmer's personal sympathies/sensitivities.

[T]he personal sympathies/sensitivities are visceral, i.e., based on pure assumptions and presumptions without a scintilla of evidence on which to base a finding of fact consistent with Judge Farmer's personal sympathies/sensitivities. Maybe Judge Farmer's [sic] excuses the lack of evidence with what reasonably would be described as a "Come on now, you know and I know" approach appropriate for common parlance and unknown to the legal system and legal process.

[T]he rights of heirs to receive their inheritance from a predeceased ancestor has been part of the organic law of Tennessee, uninterruptedly, since 1796 and part of Anglo-American jurisprudence since time in memoriam [sic], the personal sympathies/sensitivities of Judge Farmer to the contrary notwithstanding.

[F]or Judge Farmer to be influenced to ignore organic law by his personal sympathies/sensitivities in order to manipulate an outcome to deny the heirs of John J. Goza their inheritance and get the Cash to charities is usurpation of the value judgment of the General Assembly and violates separation of powers guaranteed by [the] Tennessee Constitution. . . .

Judge Farmer knows the ropes as well as anybody. . . . Only the most simpleminded person would conclude that, in this case, Judge Farmer made inadvertent mistakes.

To all of the undebatable propositions of law and fact, Judge Farmer effectively turns a deaf ear fixated on making a result that satiates [his] sympathies. . . .

In a nutshell, . . . Judge Farmer does not feel Estate's case . . . is "right" or "just," and Judge Farmer does not intend, no matter what, ever to render a decision that mandates what Judge Farmer feels is "wrong" or "unjust."

Added to this feeling, what rings true from what is on the lines of Judge Farmer's Memorandum Opinion is that, if Estate can prove the fraud and the conversion by the individuals who are defendants in the instant case, collecting damages from the individuals would deplete neither the fee income to SunTrust or the amount to be dribbled out, presumably, to charity, does not offend the [sic] Judge Farmer's feelings about what is "right" and "just."

What role does a judge's oath, practically speaking, play in the day-to-day functioning of a judge? Are there times when it is permissible for judges to lay aside their oath to render a judgment that, though not what the law dictates, is what the judge feels is the "right" thing to do.

From the outset, Estate makes it clear that Estate has no evidence, has looked for no evidence and makes no accusation that Judge Farmer has taken a bribe; this is completely out of the question. By this, Estate means that there is no evidence that Judge Farmer, in exchange for cash or any other thing of value, has agreed with another person to do what Estate accuses Judge Farmer of having done.

Having said that, Estate takes note of the fact that money received by a bribe-taking judge is not the harm such a bribe wreaks on the legal system, on legal process and on the litigants who are victimized by a bribe.

The harm a bribe wreaks on the legal system and the litigant-victims is what happens when a judge abandons his/her oath of office, surrenders up the impartiality that is essential to a judge functioning in an adjudicative role evenhandedly applying law to facts found from evidence adduced according to rules of evidence.

While Estate has sought no evidence and has no evidence that Judge Farmer sold his oath and surrendered his impartiality in exchange for money, Estate respectfully suggests that Judge Farmer, in order to victimize Estate as a litigant, has abandoned the loyalty to his oath of office, has surrendered his impartiality and has abused the power entrusted to him by the judicial office he holds and has switched from his role as a judge to become an adversary of Estate. . . .

> Otherwise stated, although there is no evidence that Judge Farmer received a bribe to do what he is doing, Judge Farmer is doing what a bribe-taking judge would do to victimize a litigant who was targeted by a bribe. To a litigant who is targeted, it is totally immaterial what caused the judge to victimize the litigant.[22]

A trial court held that Parrish should be suspended from practice for six months for violating Tennessee's version of Rule 8.2(a), among other rules, with five of those months probated. Parrish appealed to the Tennessee Supreme Court.

Parrish contended that his statements in the recusal motions were protected speech under the First Amendment of the U.S. Constitution and Article 1 of the Tennessee Constitution.[23] Both a disciplinary hearing panel and the trial court had concluded that Parrish's statements were not entitled to constitutional protection, and the supreme court agreed.[24]

The court had previously held that lawyers' pejorative statements about judges in motions and pleadings were not entitled to First Amendment protection.[25] The *Parrish* court further noted that "courts in numerous other jurisdictions, as well as the United States Supreme Court, have rejected the proposition that the First Amendment provides absolute protection to attorney speech."[26] Applying an objective standard to Parrish's statements, it was clear that he had made statements in the motions to recuse about the integrity of the appellate judges a reasonable lawyer would believe to be false, and that he had made those statements with reckless disregard for their truth or falsity.[27] Consequently, his statements violated Rule 8.2(a), among others.[28] The *Parrish* court affirmed the trial court's sanction of a six-month suspension, with only one month of actual suspension.

No matter how offensive lawyers' statements about judges may be, Model Rule 8.2(a) is limited to statements of fact as opposed to opinion because only statements of fact can be true or false and Model Rule 8.2(a) is intended to protect the integrity of the judicial system and inspire public confidence in it—not to immunize judges against harsh or undeserved criticism.[29] That said, courts routinely reject lawyers' claims that their criticisms

22. *Id.* at 157–60.
23. *Id.* at 163.
24. *Id.*
25. *Id.* (citing Bd. of Prof'l Responsibility v. Slavin, 145 S.W.3d 538, 549–50 (Tenn. 2004)).
26. *Id.* at 165.
27. *Id.* at 166–67.
28. *Id.* at 167, 170.
29. *In re* Discipline of Colin, 448 P.3d 556, 561 (Nev. 2019) (quoting Att'y Grievance Comm'n of Md. v. Frost, 85 A.3d 264, 274 (Md. 2014)).

of judges were constitutionally protected statements of opinion.[30] In *In re Disciplinary Action Against Nathan*,[31] for example, a lawyer who wrote that the judge whose order he was appealing was "a bad judge" who "won election to the office of judge by appealing to racism" and had "substituted his personal view for the law" was disciplined despite his claim that those statements were expressions of opinion for which he could not be punished.[32] In rejecting the lawyer's argument, the Minnesota Supreme Court explained that "[m]erely cloaking an assertion of fact as an opinion does not give that assertion constitutional protection."[33]

In re Discipline of Colin[34] is an illustrative case testing the line between statements of opinion and statements of fact for Rule 8.2(a) purposes. The case arose out of Nevada lawyer James Colin's representation of a condemned inmate, Charles Lee Randolph, in an appeal from a trial court order denying Randolph's petition for a writ of habeas corpus. Three Nevada Supreme Court justices recused themselves for differing reasons. The remaining four justices ruled against Randolph. Colin filed a petition for rehearing and moved to disqualify the four justices. In doing so, he made numerous baseless and offensive remarks about the court and the justices, some of which were unrelated to Randolph's case.[35] Colin's unfortunate statements included:

> [The Court had] the audacity to affirmatively "alter" the appellate record to conform to the Court's dishonest actions and claims.
>
> [T]he Court took its dishonesty to an unprecedented new level, and . . . the Court affirmatively fabricated a lie, blatantly contrary to the record. . . . Indeed, the Court's own Order proves that the Court is drunk with power, acting like a lawless bully, just lying and cheating to accomplish its evil objective to see Randolph dead.
>
> [T]he four Justices . . . are vindictive, dishonest, and totally biased. . . . They have concocted false and unsupportable legal theories . . . and appear to be willing to do anything to achieve their evil aims.
>
> The Justices are dishonest, and that dishonesty is apparent from the record in this case, and also from their active participation in a lengthy and ongoing unconstitutional judicial scheme and conspiracy to circumvent the Nevada Constitution, steal money from the Nevada taxpayers, and put

30. *In re* Disciplinary Action Against Nathan, 671 N.W.2d 578, 581–84 (Minn. 2003); *see also In re* Palmisano, 70 F.3d 483, 487 (7th Cir. 1996) (explaining that statements like "I think that Judge X is dishonest" imply a factual assertion rather than express an opinion); *In re* Comfort, 159 P.3d 1011, 1025 (Kan. 2007) (explaining that a lawyer cannot avoid discipline merely by characterizing statements as opinions); Pilli v. Va. State Bar, 611 S.E.2d 389, 392 (Va. 2005) (treating a lawyer's accusation that a judge was lying as a false factual assertion and not merely an opinion).

31. 671 N.W.2d 578 (Minn. 2003).

32. *Id.* at 581–82.

33. *Id.* at 584 (citing Milkovich v. Lorain J. Co., 497 U.S. 1 (1990)).

34. 448 P.3d 556 (Nev. 2019).

35. *Id.* at 558.

> $30,000 unconstitutional dollars a year into their own, and/or their judicial friend's pockets.
>
> [T]he Justices are engaged in an ongoing conspiracy to circumvent the Nevada Constitution through bogus "service" on a bogus "Law Library Commission."[36]

The Nevada Supreme Court denied Colin's disqualification motion. He then filed a second motion to disqualify the four justices who had heard Randolph's case and to cement the disqualification of the three justices who had recused themselves in which he wrote:

> This Nevada Supreme Court has no respect for the Nevada Constitution, or the law of the United States of America. The Court's despicable and blatantly lawless actions have repeatedly proven this sad truth.
>
> [F]airness and honesty are anathema [sic] to this Court, which seeks only to use its brute power to make up lies, get paid, and wrongly blame others for its evil objective—the lynching of Charles Lee Randolph.
>
> Just because seven (7) dishonest elected government officials conspire together to disobey the law, and agree that lies are the truth, it sure doesn't mean their lies actually are the truth.
>
> The Nevada Supreme Court works hard to this very day to break the law, make up lies, and complete the judicial lynching of Charles Lee Randolph.[37]

The court denied Colin's motion and referred him to the State Bar of Nevada "'based on the contemptuous tone and unsubstantiated allegations in the pleadings.'"[38] Colin's disciplinary case thereafter reached the Nevada Supreme Court.

The court analyzed Colin's conduct under several rules of professional conduct, including Rule 8.2(a). At the outset, the court observed that Rule 8.2(a) regulates statements of fact by lawyers rather than opinions because only statements of fact can be true or false and Rule 8.2(a) aims to protect the integrity of the judicial system and the public's confidence in it, rather than sparing judges from unkind or unwarranted criticism.[39] A Rule 8.2(a) violation will lie where a lawyer makes (1) a statement of fact that (2) impugns a judge's integrity or qualifications, (3) knowing that the statement is false or with reckless disregard for its truth or falsity.[40] The court addressed each element in turn.

First, while many of Colin's statements were fairly characterized as opinions, some were statements of fact. The clearest examples of factual statements include Colin's claims that the justices "affirmatively 'alter[ed]' the

36. *Id.* (alterations in original).
37. *Id.* at 559.
38. *Id.* (quoting the court's order).
39. *Id.* at 561 (quoting Att'y Grievance Comm'n of Md. v. Frost, 85 A.3d 264, 274 (Md. 2014)).
40. *Id.*

appellate record," "affirmatively fabricated a lie, blatantly contrary to the record," and actively participated "in a lengthy and ongoing unconstitutional judicial scheme and conspiracy to circumvent the Nevada Constitution, steal money from the Nevada taxpayers, and put $30,000 unconstitutional dollars a year into their own, and/or their judicial friend's pockets" through membership on the Law Library Commission.[41]

Second, Colin's statements plainly concerned the justices' qualifications or integrity. He accused them of lying, altering the appellate record in a case, fostering an unconstitutional conspiracy, and stealing taxpayers' money.[42]

Third, there was substantial evidence that Colin either knew the offending statements were false or made them with reckless disregard for their truth or falsity. Indeed, when facing discipline, Colin made several admissions regarding the timing of some of his accusations that indicated that he lied about the justices' conduct in retaliation for their adverse rulings.[43]

Ultimately, the Nevada Supreme Court suspended Colin from practice for six months and one day, thereby requiring him to petition for reinstatement, and further ordered him to take and pass the Multistate Professional Responsibility Examination.

Some courts, however, approach these questions in a manner that seems to acknowledge the context in which the Model Rule 8.2 standard was created, as well as the fact that judges are public officials (and, in many jurisdictions, elected public officials).[44] The Oklahoma Supreme Court, for example, has acknowledged the inappropriateness of allowing attorney speech critical of judges to be subjected to a different level of scrutiny particularly when lawyers are well-situated to know that of which they speak.[45] In *State ex rel. Oklahoma Bar Ass'n v. Porter*,[46] the court declined to punish a lawyer for his post-trial statements to the media that the judge "showed all the signs

41. *Id.*

42. *Id.*

43. *Id.*

44. *See, e.g.*, Hancock v. Bd. of Prof'l Responsibility, 447 S.W.3d 844, 854–55 (Tenn. 2014) (explaining that Rule 8.2 prohibits lawyers from making false statements concerning judges' integrity or qualifications because such statements unfairly undermine public confidence in the justice system; observing that lawyers are among the most credible of witnesses on judges' qualifications of judges, the public routinely relies on their assessments when deciding whether to vote for candidates' seeking judicial office; and that given these purposes and the harm that Rule 8.2 seeks to prevent, "an attorney may be disciplined pursuant to Rule 8.2 only if the false statement is communicated to a third party").

45. State *ex rel.* Okla. Bar Ass'n v. Porter, 766 P.2d 958, 968–69 (Okla. 1988) ("In keeping with the high trust placed in this Court by the people, we cannot shield the judiciary from the critique of that portion of the public most perfectly situated to advance knowledgeable criticism, while at the same time subjecting the balance of government officials to the stringent requirements of *New York Times Co. v. Sullivan* and its progeny.").

46. 766 P.2d 958 (Okla. 1988).

of being a racist," that if the judge "wants to practice his racism that way that's his business," and that the attorney had "never tried a case before [the judge] that [he] felt [he] got an impartial trial out of him."[47] The *Porter* court explained that such statements stood "at the epicenter of those expressive activities protected by the First Amendment."[48] The Colorado Supreme Court, analogizing a disciplinary proceeding against a lawyer for criticizing a judge to a public official pursuing a defamation claim, found that a lawyer's accusation that a judge was "a racist and bigot" was protected by the First Amendment as a statement of opinion and could not be the basis for discipline under Rule 8.2.[49] Likewise, the Ninth Circuit, when studying a lawyer who had blasted a judge as being "ignorant, ill-tempered, [a] buffoon, substandard-human, right-wing fanatic, [and] a bully," concluded that such statements were protected by the First Amendment as statements of opinion.[50]

A Missouri Supreme Court opinion, *Smith v. Pace* (*In re Smith*),[51] reflects both an awareness of the important First Amendment issues in play when lawyers engage in speech critical of courts and the need to examine the lawyer's conduct with respect to the lawyer's own knowledge of whether the statements in question were false, or whether the lawyer acted with reckless disregard as to truth or falsity. Interestingly, however, the *Smith* court did so only with respect to imposition of criminal contempt for such speech and explicitly held open the possibility that discipline could still be imposed upon a lawyer without having to undertake such an examination.[52]

Carl Smith, the lawyer initially convicted of criminal contempt and sentenced to jail for 120 days, had used inflammatory language in two paragraphs of a writ filed with the Missouri Court of Appeals seeking to quash a grand jury subpoena that sought production of documents from his clients.[53] Smith petitioned the Missouri Supreme Court for a writ of habeas corpus. The supreme court issued the writ and stayed the remainder of Smith's jail sentence pending the outcome of the matter. The court then reversed Smith's conviction because "[t]here simply was no evidence from which the jurors could find the requisite state of Smith's mind regarding

47. *Id.* at 960.

48. *Id.* at 966.

49. *In re* Green, 11 P.3d 1078, 1082 (Colo. 2000). *But see* Lawyer Disciplinary Bd. v. Hall, 765 S.E.2d 187, 192 (W. Va. 2014) (affirming a lawyer's three-month suspension for attacks on the integrity of an ALJ that included the allegation that "[c]ounsel can think of no other explanation but that [the ALJ] is engaging in the most heinous of racial bigotry against" the lawyer's clients").

50. Standing Comm. v. Yagman, 55 F.3d 1430, 1440 (9th Cir. 1995).

51. 313 S.W.3d 124 (Mo. 2010).

52. *Id.* at 126 ("The result of this proceeding has no bearing on any disciplinary measures that may result from the attorney's conduct.").

53. *Id.*

the falsity of the statements, nor were they asked to do so."[54] The specific portions of Smith's appellate filing that were at issue involved accusations against both a judge and the prosecutor relating to their role in the grand jury proceedings. Smith had alleged "personal interest, bias, and purported criminal conduct" on the part of the judge and prosecutor and further asserted that the judge's and the prosecutor's participation "in the convening, overseeing, and handling . . . of this grand jury are, in the least, an appearance of impropriety and, at most, a conspiracy by these officers of the court to threaten, instill fear and imprison innocent persons to cover-up and chill public awareness of their own apparent misconduct using the power of their positions to do so."[55] Smith had additionally decried that the grand jury was "being used by those in power in the judicial system as a covert tool to threaten, intimidate and silence any opposition to their personal control—not the laudable common law and statutory purposes for which the grand jury system was created."[56]

The Missouri Supreme Court acknowledged the First Amendment issues in play even though the individual whose speech was being questioned was a lawyer, offered a brief survey of numerous cases examining the question in the disciplinary context, and indirectly acknowledged that one of its own earlier decisions explaining the use of an objective standard for reviewing the lawyer's statements in a disciplinary proceeding[57] might be subjected to much higher scrutiny today in light of more recent First Amendment cases such as *Republican Party of Minnesota v. White*.[58] Because the matter before it involved criminal contempt charges, the *Smith* court concluded that the conviction could not stand because there was no evidence from which a jury could find "that the lawyer's statements were false and that he either knew the statements were false or that he acted with reckless disregard of whether these statements were true or false."[59]

Although it may be difficult to justify limiting the analysis in *Smith* solely to criminal contempt cases, lawyers must remember that most courts employ an objective standard when determining whether such speech will justify discipline. Under that objective standard, a lawyer who impugns the qualifications or integrity of a judge must have an objectively reasonable factual basis for believing the accusations to be true.[60] The prevailing approach

54. *Id.* at 136.
55. *Id.* at 127.
56. *Id.*
57. *In re* Westfall, 808 S.W.2d 829, 937 (Mo. 1991).
58. 536 U.S. 765 (2002).
59. *Smith*, 313 S.W.3d at 136.
60. *In re* Disciplinary Action Against Nathan, 671 N.W.2d 578, 584–85 (Minn. 2003) ("The standard used to determine if a statement is false or made with reckless disregard as to its truth or falsity is 'an objective one dependent on what the reasonable attorney, considered in light of all his

sets the bar so high that even reliance upon information provided by clients, anonymous sources, or the media may not provide a sufficient basis for a lawyer to resist a finding that accusations impugning the integrity or qualifications of a court were made with reckless disregard of the truth.[61] In the flowery language of one court, "sincere personal belief will, in the sweet bye and bye, be an absolute defense when we all stand before the pearly gates on that great day of judgment, but it is not a defense" to disciplinary charges for falsely accusing a court of misconduct.[62]

Strong arguments can be made that the way most courts have read Model Rule 8.2(a)'s restrictions on attorney speech offends public policy.[63] Presumably lawyers are more knowledgeable than the public about judges' qualifications and are better positioned to know when criticism should be leveled against courts. Simultaneously, because ethics rules do not serve in the same manner to chill attorney speech praising judges, the majority interpretation of Model Rule 8.2 further serves to skew the balance of speech about judges heard by the public toward speech lauding the judiciary.

Although the public policy issues and the issue of what the First Amendment rights of a lawyer *should be* are important and intriguing ones, when viewed purely from the standpoint of what clients expect from their lawyers—effective advocacy—such questions should be nothing more than academic. After all, when the lawyer is advocating on behalf of a client, the lawyer's goal should not be to vindicate her own First Amendment rights but to vindicate the client's position. It is difficult to imagine circumstances in which the client's interests on appeal are well served by an advocate's use of rhetoric that can be justified against an ethical challenge only on First Amendment grounds.[64] Courts rarely respond well to personal attacks on

professional functions, would do in the same or similar circumstances.'"); Office of Disciplinary Couns. v. Wrona, 908 A.2d 1281 (Pa. 2006) (determining that although subjective belief in truth was sufficient to defeat a perjury charge, the lawyer had to have objectively reasonable belief to rebut charge of violation of Rule 8.2).

61. Welsh v. Mounger, 912 So. 2d 823, 828 (Miss. 2005) (finding a newspaper editorial to be an insufficient source); Anthony v. Va. State Bar, 621 S.E.2d 121, 125–26 (Va. 2005) (determining that an anonymous letter and telephone calls were not sufficient); Lawyer Disciplinary Bd. v. Turgeon, 557 S.E.2d 235, 242–43 (W. Va. 2000) (concluding that the lawyer's reliance upon the client's word not sufficient to justify accusation of manufacturing evidence against judge).

62. W. Va. Comm. on Legal Ethics v. Farber, 408 S.E.2d 274, 285 (W. Va. 1991).

63. The rule's scope is, of course, not limited to statements made by lawyers in court or in court papers. *See, e.g.*, *In re* Cooper, 78 N.E.3d 1098, 1099 (Ind. 2017) (violating Rule 8.2(a) through a statement to a local newspaper).

64. *See* Bank of Am., N.A. v. Atkin, 305 So. 3d 305, 307 (Fla. Dist. Ct. App. 2018) ("Insults or disparaging comments by lawyers to courts in court filings cannot be justified as zealous advocacy because they risk alienating the very judges the lawyer was hired to persuade. Insults normally reflect—not attempts at persuasion—but the abandonment of any attempt to persuade. A lawyer resorting to insults in court filings is perhaps genuinely expressing his or her frustration at not being able to persuade the court. But this venting can come a high cost to the client's interests.").

any target, including sister courts.[65] Thus, absent a legitimate factual basis capable of overwhelming proof at the time of the allegation, a lawyer should never accuse a judge of bias or prejudice against her client,[66] allege that a judge is biased against her personally,[67] charge a judge with corruption or abuse of office,[68] assert that a judge was bribed,[69] challenge a judge's impartiality,[70] accuse a judge of lying,[71] allege that a judge is guilty of criminal conduct,[72] claim that a judge's decision is politically motivated,[73] suggest that a judge suffers from a mental disability or personality disorder,[74]

65. *See, e.g.*, *In re* Lisse, 921 F.3d 629, 644 (7th Cir. 2019) ("Flippant, unfounded accusations of misconduct and fraud by opposing counsel and court officials demean the profession and impair the orderly operation of the judicial system."); State *ex rel.* C.M., 336 P.3d 1069, 1071 (Utah Ct. App. 2014) ("Assigning Machiavellian motives to errors of judges and lawyers is improper and usually inaccurate. . . . Knowledgeable readers understand that those with persuasive arguments based on law and logic rarely resort to ad hominem attacks.").

66. *See, e.g.*, People v. Thomas, 925 P.2d 1081, 1083 (Colo. 1996) (publicly censuring a lawyer who accused a judge of bias for violating Rule 8.2(a)); Disciplinary Couns. v. Serafinowitz, 123 A.3d 1279, 1283–87 (Conn. App. Ct. 2015) (affirming sanctions against the lawyer); Key Equip. Fin., Inc. v. Hawkins, 985 A.2d 1139, 1146–47 (Me. 2009) (sanctioning the lawyer in the amount of $2,500); Office of Disciplinary Couns. v. West, 706 N.E.2d 760, 761 (Ohio 1999) (suspending the lawyer for accusing a judge of receiving kickbacks from a bankruptcy trustee); Bd. of Prof'l Responsibility v. Parrish, 556 S.W.3d 153, 157–60, 167) (Tenn. 2018) (suspending the lawyer for six months, with five months probated); *In re* Disciplinary Proc. Against Boyd, 767 N.W.2d 226, 231 (Wis. 2009) (suspending the lawyer from practice for six months for this and other violations).

67. *See, e.g.*, *In re* Crenshaw, 815 N.E.2d 1013, 1014–15 (Ind. 2004) (concluding that the lawyer violated Rule 8.2(a) by baselessly accusing the judge of being biased against her because of her race and gender, and for falsely reporting that another judge asked her to sit on his lap); *In re* Eckelman, 144 P.3d 713, 717 (Kan. 2006) (finding a Rule 8.2(a) violation, among others); *In re* Disciplinary Action Against Torgerson, 870 N.W.2d 602, 609–10 (Minn. 2015) (finding that the lawyer violated Rule 8.2(a) by claiming that the trial judge was trying to set her up and to intentionally prejudice her in the eyes of the jury).

68. *See, e.g.*, Ky. Bar Ass'n v. Prewitt, 4 S.W.2d 142, 143–44 (Ky. 1999) (suspending the lawyer for violating Rule 8.2(a)); Att'y Grievance Comm'n of Md. v. Frost, 85 A.3d 264, 274–79 (Md. 2014) (disbarring the lawyer for such statements contained in an e-mail sent to three other members of the bar).

69. *See, e.g.*, Moseley v. Va. State Bar, 694 S.E.2d 586, 588–90 (Va. 2010) (finding that a lawyer violated Rule 8.2 by stating that an order entered against him by a trial court judge "was 'an absurd decision from a whacko judge, whom [he] believe[d] was bribed'") (quoting the lawyer).

70. *See, e.g.*, *In re* Simon, 913 So. 2d 816, 824–27 (La. 2005) (suspending the lawyer for six months); State *ex rel.* Special Couns. for Discipline v. Sivick, 648 N.W.2d 315, 318 (Neb. 2002) (reprimanding the lawyer).

71. *See, e.g.*, Iowa Sup. Ct. Bd. of Prof'l Ethics & Conduct v. Ronwin, 557 N.W.2d 515, 521–23 (Iowa 1997) (disbarring the lawyer).

72. *See, e.g.*, Fla. Bar v. Norkin, 132 So. 3d 77, 90 (Fla. 2013) (suspending the lawyer for two years for numerous offenses, including a Rule 8.2(a) violation); *Ronwin*, 557 N.W.2d at 521–23; *In re* Mordkofsky, 649 N.Y.S.2d 71, 72–73 (App. Div. 1996) (disbarring the lawyer); Comm. on Legal Ethics of the W. Va. State Bar v. Farber, 408 S.E.2d 274, 280–86 (W. Va. 1991) (suspending the lawyer).

73. *See, e.g.*, Idaho State Bar v. Topp, 925 P.2d 1113, 1114–17 (Idaho 1996) (suspending the lawyer for violating Rule 8.2(a)).

74. *See, e.g.*, *In re* Shearin, 765 A.2d 930, 933, 937–38 (Del. 2000) (finding that a lawyer who, among other things, stated that a judge "'suffered a progressive mental disability' which caused him to 'exhibit mood swings and injudicious conduct, including hostility to litigants and court

accuse a judge of being in cahoots with an adversary to shape the outcome of a case,[75] accuse a judge of covering up his relationship with opposing counsel,[76] assert that a judge could have reached a conclusion or made a determination only through ex parte communication with an adversary,[77] allege that a judge is incompetent,[78] accuse a judge of testicular inadequacy,[79] accuse a judge of masturbating during a mediation,[80] suggest that a judge is capable of being unfairly or improperly influenced,[81] or accuse a judge of colluding with opposing counsel.[82] And, although it should go without saying, lawyers cannot escape discipline by phrasing these kinds of accusations against judges in the form of a hypothetical.[83]

B. The Problem of Perception and Courts' Willingness to Presume the Worst

Cases involving obvious false or reckless attacks on a judge's integrity or qualifications to hold office are easy to understand and involve conduct that appellate lawyers can easily avoid. The more difficult issue facing appellate lawyers is that courts sometimes perceive an ambiguous statement as a punishable offense because of its tone rather than adopting an interpretation of the statement as one involving legitimate criticism or mere hyperbole. A

personnel,'" violated Rule 8.2(a)); *Moseley*, 694 S.E.2d at 588–90 (finding that the lawyer violated Rule 8.2 by referring to a trial court judge as a "whacko"); Lawyer Disciplinary Bd. v. Hall, 765 S.E.2d 187, 193 (W. Va. 2014) (affirming a lawyer's 90-day suspension for, among other things, recommending in an appellate filing that the ALJ whose decision was being appealed should "seek professional psychiatric help").

75. *See, e.g.*, Lawyer Disciplinary Bd. v. Turgeon, 557 S.E.2d 235, 242–45 (W. Va. 2000) (suspending the lawyer for two years for violating Rule 8.2(a)).

76. *See, e.g.*, State *ex rel.* Couns. for Discipline of the Neb. Sup. Ct. v. Gast, 896 N.W.2d 583, 597–99 (Neb. 2017) (suspending the lawyer for one year for violating Nebraska's version of Rule 8.2(a)).

77. *See, e.g.*, Att'y Grievance Comm'n of Md. v. Hermina, 842 A.2d 762, 771–72 (Md. 2004) (reprimanding the lawyer); Bd. of Prof'l Responsibility v. Davidson, 205 P.3d 1008, 1012–17 (Wyo. 2009) (finding that the lawyer violated Rule 8.2(a) by making reckless accusations and that he further violated Rule 8.4(d) for the same reason).

78. *See, e.g.*, Key Equip. Fin., Inc. v. Hawkins, 985 A.2d 1139, 1146–47 (Me. 2009) (sanctioning the lawyer in the amount of $2,500).

79. *In re* Lee, 977 So. 2d 852, 854–55 (La. 2008) (suspending a lawyer who reacted angrily and euphemistically characterized a trial judge's lack of courage when the judge indicated that he would recuse himself voluntarily rather than requiring the opposing party to file a motion).

80. *In re* Ireland, 276 P.3d 762, 766, 770–71 (Kan. 2012) (suspending the lawyer for two years).

81. *See, e.g.*, Prudential Ballard Realty Co. v. Weatherly, 769 So. 2d 1045, 1060, 1067–68 (Ala. 2000) (involving elected state supreme court judges and a suggestion by an appellate lawyer that judges who depend on campaign contributions were willing to sell "favorable decisions to the highest bidder"); *In re* Howard, 912 S.W.2d 61, 63–64 (Mo. 1995) (suspending the lawyer for violating Rule 8.2(a), among others).

82. *In re* Clothier, 344 P.3d 370, 377 (Kan. 2015).

83. *See, e.g., In re* Simon, 913 So. 2d 816, 825 (La. 2005) ("We would eviscerate Rule 8.2(a) if we were to shield an attorney from discipline for making knowingly false statements about judges simply because he used the artifice of a 'hypothetical.'").

troubling example of such a case, even though it both involves extrajudicial statements by a lawyer and was decided prior to the Supreme Court's landmark ruling in *Gentile v. State*,[84] is the imposition of discipline against a prosecutor in *In re Westfall*.[85]

After the issuance of an appellate decision holding that the double jeopardy doctrine prohibited his office from prosecuting a defendant, George Westfall, a Missouri prosecutor, criticized the judge by saying that he found the court's reasons to be "somewhat illogical, and I think even a little bit less than honest" and asserted that the court had "distorted the statute" and used "convoluted logic to arrive at a decision that [the judge] personally likes."[86] In defending the statements in his disciplinary proceeding, Westfall indicated that he merely meant that "the court of appeals opinion was 'intellectually dishonest.'"[87]

Instead of evaluating Westfall's actual words, the Missouri Supreme Court, in its opinion imposing discipline, engaged in frequent paraphrasing and restating in its own language what it was Westfall had said. The majority concluded that the imposition of discipline was necessary because Westfall had accused the judge "of deliberate dishonesty," had "purposefully ignore[ed] the law to achieve his personal ends," and asserted that Westfall's statement was not to be read as "an implication of carelessness or negligence but of a deliberate, dishonest, conscious design on the part of the judge to serve his own interests."[88] The majority's decision was subject to serious attack in dissent for having employed "at least six unsupportable paraphrases of [Westfall's] actual words" to support its ruling.[89]

In re Wilkins (*Wilkins I*)[90] is a more recent and troubling example of a court upbraiding a lawyer more for what it claimed he had written about a lower court than what he actually wrote. Wilkins, an Indiana lawyer, represented a Michigan insurance company as its local counsel, working with the insurer's Michigan counsel in appealing from an adverse verdict. The Indiana Court of Appeals affirmed the trial court's verdict and award, but Wilkins believed that in doing so, the court of appeals misstated material facts, and ignored or misapplied controlling precedent, so that a special procedural rule might permit transfer to the Indiana Supreme Court.[91]

---

84. 501 U.S. 1030 (1991).
85. 808 S.W.2d 829 (Mo. 1991).
86. *Id.* at 831.
87. *Id.* at 833.
88. *Id.* at 838.
89. *Id.* at 841 (Blackmar, J., dissenting).
90. 777 N.E.2d 714 (Ind. 2002) (*Wilkins I*).
91. *Id.* at 715. In Indiana, transfer to the supreme court is available under the rules of appellate procedure when an "opinion or memorandum decision of the Court of Appeals erroneously and materially misstates the record." *Id.* at 716 (quoting the rule).

Wilkins's Michigan co-counsel prepared a petition for transfer and accompanying draft brief and forwarded them to Wilkins for review. Wilkins edited the draft provided by Michigan counsel, toning down the tenor of the brief.[92] He then signed and filed the petition and brief. After being toned down from its original version, the revised brief still contained the following statement:

> The Court of Appeals' published Opinion in this case is quite disturbing. It is replete with misstatements of material facts, it misapplies controlling case law, and it does not even bother to discuss relevant cases that are directly on point. Clearly, such a decision should be reviewed by this Court. Not only does it work an injustice on appellant Michigan Mutual Insurance Company, it establishes dangerous precedent in several areas of the law. This will undoubtedly create additional problems in future cases.[93]

This passage was footnoted as follows:

> Indeed, the opinion is so factually and legally inaccurate that one is left to wonder whether the Court of Appeals was determined to find for Appellee Sports, Inc., and then said whatever was necessary to reach that conclusion (regardless of whether the facts or law supported its decision).[94]

The Indiana Supreme Court denied the insurer's petition for transfer and ordered that the supporting brief be stricken as "a 'scurrilous and intemperate attack on the integrity'" of the lower appellate court.[95] Subsequently, Wilkins contacted the chief judge of the Indiana Court of Appeals and the chief justice of the Indiana Supreme Court to schedule meetings with them to personally apologize for the content of the brief. Before he was able to speak personally with either judge, however, the Indiana Supreme Court Disciplinary Commission instituted proceedings against him. Wilkins then wrote to the chief judge and chief justice, respectively, "offering to apologize in person and to acknowledge that the footnote was 'overly-aggressive and inappropriate and never should have made its way into [the] Brief.'"[96]

Indiana disciplinary authorities charged Wilkins with violating Indiana Rule of Professional Conduct 8.2(a), which, like Model Rule 8.2(a), prohibits a lawyer from making statements that he "knows to be false or with reckless disregard as to the truth or falsity concerning the qualifications or

92. *Id.* at 715.

93. *Id.* (footnote omitted). Given the standard established by the rule of appellate procedure being relied upon, these assertions would appear to be required to establish jurisdiction.

94. *Id.* at 716. Although Wilkins did not actually author the quoted text or the footnote, there could be no dispute under Indiana's disciplinary rules that by signing the brief he became jointly responsible for its content.

95. *Id.* at 715 (quoting Mich. Mut. Ins. Co. v. Sports, Inc., 706 N.E.2d 555 (Ind. 1999)).

96. *Id.*

integrity of a judge."[97] In Wilkins's case, the "judge" was the three-judge panel of the court of appeals from whose opinion his client sought transfer.

In his disciplinary hearing, Wilkins contended that a contract that was cited to the court of appeals in the record, as well as the testimony of two trial witnesses, supported the contention that the court of appeals had misstated the record and the facts. He also cited case law alleged to have been ignored by the court of appeals.[98]

The Indiana Supreme Court determined that the language in the body of the brief to which the footnote was anchored, while "heavy-handed," roughly paraphrased the bases for transfer expressed in the Indiana Rules of Appellate Procedure.[99] Thus, the court concluded that language provided no grounds for discipline. The comments about the court of appeals in the footnote, however, the court declared to be "not even colorably appropriate."[100]

The court in *Wilkins I* began its analysis of the footnote by indicating that Rule 8.2(a) is concerned with preserving public confidence in the administration of justice, referring in the process to one of its earlier decisions in which it had observed that "unwarranted public suggestion" by an attorney that a judge "is motivated by criminal purpose and considerations" weakens and erodes public confidence in the judicial system.[101] The court, finding that Wilkins had no evidence to support his contentions in the footnote, determined that the state's interest in preserving public confidence in the judicial system and the administration of justice generally far outweighed Wilkins's need to air his unsubstantiated concerns in an inappropriate forum.[102] Thus, the Indiana Supreme Court determined that the footnote was inappropriate because it suggested that the judges on the court of appeals panel may have been motivated "by something other than the proper administration of justice" in deciding the underlying case.[103] In fact, the supreme court asserted that the language in the footnote suggested that the judges of the court of appeals were driven to decide as they did by "unethical motivations."[104]

Wilkins argued that the statements in the footnote "were merely 'a critique of the Opinion in a format used throughout the bench, bar and journals.'"[105] The supreme court faulted Wilkins for not citing authority to support this argument. Beyond that:

97. *Id.* & n.2.
98. *Id.* at 716.
99. *Id.* at 717.
100. *Id.*
101. *Id.* (citing *In re* Garringer, 626 N.E.2d 809, 813 (Ind. 1994)).
102. *Id.* at 718. "Without evidence, such statements should not be made anywhere. With evidence, they should be made to the Judicial Qualifications Commission." *Id.* at 717.
103. *Id.* at 717.
104. *Id.*
105. *Id.*

> Our current rules of appellate procedure dictate the boundaries of acceptable appellate practice. For example, App.R. 46(A)(8)(a) requires that arguments on appeal must be supported by cogent reasoning, citations to authorities, statutes or the record. A statement used in a document filed before the appellate courts that contains an assertion the lawyer knows to be false or made with reckless disregard as to the truth or falsity concerning the qualifications or integrity of a judge is neither a "format" contemplated by our appellate rules nor allowed by our *Rules of Professional Conduct*.[106]

Having determined that Wilkins violated Rule 8.2(a) by way of the intemperate footnote, the court then discussed an appropriate sanction. The court considered as aggravating factors what can be fairly characterized in the category of lack of remorse. These included Wilkins's continuing belief that the court of appeals had erred (even though he regretted his choice of language in criticizing its opinion) and his decision to defend himself against the charge of misconduct.[107] As the *Wilkins I* court explained:

> [T]he hearing officer found that the respondent's testimony "belied his belief that this disciplinary action stems merely from a poor choice of words." The respondent's stated remorse related only to his feelings of personal embarrassment and public humiliation as the result of this Court's order striking the offending brief. In essence, the respondent averred that, although he might use different language, he believes in the substance of the language contained in the footnote. That he chose to contest this matter through all procedures available under the Admission and Discipline Rules further underscores our conclusion that his remorse only attaches to the fact his statements were not without consequence, notwithstanding his earlier attempts personally to apologize to members of the appellate bench.[108]

The *Wilkins I* court concluded that Wilkins had "alleged deliberately unethical conduct on the part of the Court of Appeals."[109] Accordingly, and because Wilkins was not sufficiently remorseful, the court suspended him for 30 days.[110]

Wilkins I was a 3–2 decision with a vigorous dissent. For the dissenting justices, the footnote was "tasteless" and "poor advocacy,"[111] but it should not have provided a basis for discipline. Nothing about the footnote suggested that the court of appeals harbored criminal motives and, for that matter, it was not all that harsh in its criticism. In the dissent's view:

106. *Id.*
107. *Id.*
108. *Id.* at 719.
109. *Id.*
110. *Id.*
111. *Id.* at 719–20 (Boehm, J., dissenting).

> Although footnote 2 certainly is understood to challenge the intellectual integrity of the opinion, I do not believe it suggests any motive other than deciding the case in favor of the party the court determined should prevail. It certainly does not suggest criminal motives. In this respect, it seems to me no different from the attacks many lawyers and nonprofessionals have launched on many court decisions, including such notable ones as *Bush v. Gore* and *Brown v. Board of Education*. I cannot see how this footnote differs from the charges occasionally leveled by judges at other judges. For example, Justice Scalia recently contended in *Atkins v. Virginia* . . . that "[s]eldom has an opinion of this Court rested so obviously upon nothing but the personal views of its members." *See also Webster v. Reproductive Health Servs.*, 492 U.S. 490, 532, 109 S.Ct. 3040, 106 L.Ed.2d 410 (1989) (Scalia, J., concurring) (stating that assertions by Justice O'Connor were "irrational" and "cannot be taken seriously").[112]

Finally, the dissent warned that the court should be very cautious in imposing discipline for lawyers' acts that implicate judicial actions or processes but do not affect clients' interests. Under the circumstances, and given the supreme court's unique and often conflicting roles when deciding a lawyer discipline case involving criticism of the judiciary, the dissent considered there to have been no basis to discipline Wilkins.[113]

To be sure, the language with which the court took issue was poor advocacy,[114] but it seems clear that *Wilkins I* was wrongly decided. Undoubtedly, the effect of including the allegations in the footnote was to make it much more likely that the court would view the overall effect of the brief as being an attack on the court of appeals than to persuade it to accept transfer. All veteran advocates know that judges often protect their brethren. Wilkins obviously did not go far enough in "toning down" the brief his Michigan co-counsel had drafted. That does not necessarily mean, however, that his decision to spare the red ink when it came time to edit the offending footnote gave rise to a Rule 8.2(a) violation.

Most troubling for appellate lawyers is the supreme court majority's willingness to equate the footnote with a suggestion that the court of appeals was motivated by a criminal purpose[115] and to state that the footnote effectively accused the court of appeals judges of having "unethical motivations."[116] Reasonable people should be able to agree that the footnote is susceptible to several more charitable interpretations. For example, the

112. *Id.* at 720 (Boehm, J., dissenting).

113. *Id.* at 720–21 (Boehm, J., dissenting).

114. *See* Prudential Ballard Realty Co. v. Weatherly, 769 So. 2d 1045, 1060 (Ala. 2000) ("By couching . . . argument in the form of a written temper tantrum, an attorney can detract from the merits of the argument and do his or her client irreparable harm by failing to maintain the required level of professionalism.").

115. *Wilkins I*, 777 N.E.2d at 717.

116. *Id.*

language could be read to indicate that the court of appeals might have been determined to find for the appellee because it thought that would be the just result. Perhaps the court of appeals disregarded the facts and law that Wilkins thought compelled a contrary result because it did not agree with his view of their significance. Of course, by framing the issues the way it wanted to treat the footnote as an attack on the court's integrity, it became significantly easier for the supreme court to find that the statements were made with reckless disregard for their truth or falsity. Although truth would be an absolute defense, it was impossible for Wilkins to prove that the contents of the footnote were true given the supreme court's added gloss. Given that nowhere in the brief had Wilkins actually accused the court of appeals of corrupt or unethical behavior, it would certainly have been surprising if Wilkins had been willing to do so thereafter in trying to defend himself. With the Indiana Supreme Court holding the sole power to characterize Wilkins's claims, and further serving as both judge and jury, any commentator inclined to cynicism might say that the court deprived Wilkins of the ability to defend himself and then declared that he had not met his burden.

The *Wilkins I* court's approach to punishing Wilkins also seems harsh under the circumstances. Although Wilkins tried to apologize to the supreme court and to the court of appeals even before being charged with misconduct, and always expressed remorse, the majority of the supreme court determined that was not sufficient. Rather, it appears that the only remorse that would have been sufficient for the court would have been for Wilkins to declare that the court of appeals had properly applied the facts and law and was right after all.[117] Worse yet, the court opined that by contesting the charges against him, Wilkins supposedly deserved a sanction harsher than his professional record otherwise warranted.[118] That reasoning ought to offend any observer as a gross affront to due process.

It certainly seems ironic that the Indiana Supreme Court majority's ruling is subject to fair criticism as the act of three judges who appear to have been determined to find an ethics violation and then said whatever was necessary to reach that conclusion, regardless of whether the facts or law supported that decision. To be clear, those who would so criticize the court's majority know that the judges did not hold as they did because they were somehow corrupt or unethical, because they were spiteful or vindictive, or because they were motivated by anything other than the proper administration of justice. Those critical of the court in *Wilkins I* would instead stress that the majority lost its way in reaching its decision because it forgot that

117. *See id.* at 719 (faulting Wilkins for believing "in the substance of the language contained in the footnote").

118. *Id.* (criticizing Wilkins for choosing to contest the charges against him "through all procedures available" under Indiana disciplinary rules).

judges "should hesitate to insulate themselves from the slings and arrows that they insist other public officials face."[119]

The Indiana Supreme Court was presented the opportunity to correct its many missteps when Wilkins sought reconsideration of the application of the First Amendment to the offending language in the brief, as well as reconsideration of the sanction imposed.[120] In *In re Wilkins* (*Wilkins II*),[121] the court effectively conceded that it erred in *Wilkins I* by reducing the sanction imposed without really acknowledging error because it stubbornly adhered to its earlier position that Wilkins violated Rule 8.2(a) by way of the troublesome footnote. Noting that "important interests of judicial administration require considerable latitude regarding the content of assertions in judicial pleadings, motions and briefs," the court reasoned that these considerations are tempered by Rule 8.2(a).[122] In this case:

> The language of footnote 2 does not merely argue that the Court of Appeals decision is factually or legally inaccurate. Such would be permissible advocacy. The footnote goes further and ascribes bias and favoritism to the judges authoring and concurring in the majority opinion of the Court of Appeals, and it implies that these judges manufactured a false rationale in an attempt to justify their pre-conceived desired outcome. These aspersions transgress the wide latitude given appellate argument, and they clearly impugn the integrity of a judge in violation of . . . Rule 8.2(a).[123]

The court thus declined to reconsider its holding that Wilkins violated Rule 8.2(a).[124]

Oddly, the court again did not discuss alternative interpretations of the footnote. Rather than explaining why its sinister interpretation of the footnote was correct, it opted to avoid the issue of interpretation altogether. This it presumably did either because Wilkins's attorneys did not raise the possibility of benign interpretations in seeking reconsideration or because to discuss alternative interpretations would be too harmful to its stubborn conclusion that Wilkins had violated Rule 8.2(a).

The *Wilkins II* court did, however, reduce Wilkins's discipline from a suspension to a public reprimand—a public reprimand it said had already been accomplished by the content of the *Wilkins I* opinion.[125] The court based its decision to scold Wilkins rather than suspend him on renewed consideration of his "outstanding and exemplary" professional record and reputation, and on the fact that the offending footnote was actually written not by Wilkins

119. *In re* Palmisano, 70 F.3d 483, 487 (7th Cir. 1995).
120. *In re* Wilkins, 782 N.E.2d 985 (Ind. 2003) (*Wilkins II*).
121. *Id.*
122. *Id.* at 986.
123. *Id.*
124. *Id.*
125. *Id.* at 987.

but by his Michigan co-counsel.[126] Of course, none of these items were new developments or newly discovered information—the court considered these same factors in *Wilkins I* and nonetheless concluded that Wilkins should be suspended.[127] So then, why did the *Wilkins II* court reduce Wilkins's punishment? A likely answer is that by lessening his punishment the court could practically erase the harm caused by its earlier decision without admitting its fundamental error, all the while upholding the perceived honor of the court of appeals.

Although the court in *Wilkins II* moved in the right direction by reducing Wilkins's punishment to a public reprimand, it is difficult to agree that it went far enough. In its opinion denying Wilkins's client's petition for rehearing, the Indiana Supreme Court could have sternly cautioned Wilkins that the offending footnote could be read to imply unethical behavior by the court of appeals in violation of Rule 8.2(a) and warned him against such irresponsible argument in the future;[128] indeed, courts routinely employ such an approach.[129]

Interestingly, and indirectly rubbing salt into Wilkins's wounds a decade later, the Indiana Supreme Court in *In re Dixon*[130] reversed the imposition of discipline against an attorney for similar statements[131] by engaging in what seems like revisionist history to explain where Wilkins went astray. In *Dixon*, Thomas M. Dixon, representing individuals who had been arrested for participating in a pro-life protest on the University of Notre Dame campus, sought to recuse a trial judge who was married to a Notre Dame professor and accused the judge of not "feel[ing] duty bound to apply [a rule of procedure] because she was biased in favor of the abortuary."[132] In concluding that Dixon should not be disciplined, the court distinguished Wilkins's statements in footnote 2 now as "more of a random pot-shot than relevant argument" and as being improper speculation based solely upon the trial

126. *Id.*

127. *In re* Wilkins, 777 N.E.2d 714, 715, 718–19 (Ind. 2002) (*Wilkins I*).

128. Of course, at some level the Indiana Supreme Court had already done so. *See* Mich. Mut. Ins. Co. v. Sports, Inc., 706 N.E.2d 555, 555 (Ind. 1999) ("As a scurrilous and intemperate attack on the integrity of the Court of Appeals, this sentence [in the footnote] is unacceptable, and the Brief in Support of Appellant's Petition to Transfer is hereby stricken.").

129. *See, e.g.*, Cathey v. State, 60 P.3d 192, 197 (Alaska Ct. App. 2002) (discussing an appellate lawyer's obligations under Rule 8.2(a) in connection with allegations of misconduct by a prosecutor and stating that "[w]e urge [appellate counsel] to carefully consider before making similar unfounded charges in the future"); N. Sec. Ins. Co. v. Mitec Elec., Ltd., 965 A.2d 447, 453 n.3 (Vt. 2008) (noting that the advocate's briefs characterizing the lower court's conclusions as "ludicrous" and "inane" lacked "the professional tone the court expected from members of the bar" and pointedly reminding readers that the tenor of one's protestations cannot create error where none exists).

130. 994 N.E.2d 1129 (Ind. 2013).

131. *Id.* at 1140 (Rucker, J., concurring in part and dissenting in part) ("There is little to no daylight between the highlighted portions of Statements C and D and the statements a majority of this Court found sanctionable in *Matter of Wilkins.*").

132. *Id.* at 1139.

court's issuance of the "unfavorable decision itself" rather than criticism of a trial judge, like Dixon's, which was supported "with a lengthy recitation of facts."[133]

Cases such as *Westfall* and *Wilkins I* raise practical questions for appellate lawyers as to how far a lawyer can safely go in criticizing a court with whose decision the lawyer and her client disagree. Returning for a moment to *Wilkins I*,[134] it appears that what Wilkins was really trying to do in the brief and the footnote was to suggest that the court of appeals had engaged in result-oriented reasoning. To critique an opinion as being result-oriented was, Wilkins contended, an approach employed '"throughout the bench, bar, and journals.'"[135] Justice Boehm, coming to Wilkins's defense in his dissent in *Wilkins I*, contended that the offending footnote was no harsher than the criticism that Justice Scalia has directed at other members of the Supreme Court in published opinions.[136] Both of these defenses merit further discussion.

With respect to the first, it is true that commentators and scholars criticize decisions as being result oriented in articles and other media. We have done so in discussing the decision in *Wilkins I*. That does not mean, however, that a lawyer litigating a pending case can similarly chastise the court. Lawyers involved in a pending case operate in a more restrictive environment than do detached lawyers because involved lawyers' criticisms and mischaracterizations are more likely to disrupt the proceedings or impair the fair administration of justice. Comments that might be appropriate in a treatise, or law review or bar journal article, are not necessarily appropriate when made in an appellate brief.

As for the second, judges' criticism of other judges is not an accurate barometer for determining what amounts to appropriate conduct for a lawyer acting as an advocate. The fact that judges may accuse their brethren of "legalized larceny" does not mean that lawyers can do likewise.[137] Lawyers and judges live and work by different rules. Beyond that, and as the *Wilkins II* court recognized, "occasional retorts to uncivil dialogue" are inappropriate no matter who the speaker may be.[138]

Further considering the *Wilkins I* and *Wilkins II* decisions, what might Wilkins have written without violating Rule 8.2(a)? Wilkins surely could have written: "Indeed, the opinion is so factually and legally inaccurate that one is left to wonder how the court of appeals could have found as it did."

133. *Id.*

134. *In re* Wilkins, 777 N.E.2d 714 (Ind. 2002) (*Wilkins I*).

135. *Id.* at 718 (quoting Wilkins's brief in his disciplinary case).

136. *Id.* at 720 (Boehm, J., dissenting).

137. *In re* L.A. Cnty. Pioneer Soc'y, 257 P.2d 1, 14 (Cal. 1953) (Carter, J., dissenting on petition for reh'g) ("The record in this case presents one of the most outrageous examples of legalized larceny which has come under my observation.").

138. *In re* Wilkins, 782 N.E.2d 985, 987 (Ind. 2003) (*Wilkins II*).

Alternatively, he might have tried: "Indeed, one is left to wonder how the court of appeals could find for the appellee given the facts in the record and contrary controlling case law." He could have branded the opinion "incomprehensible" or "incoherent."[139] He could have similarly criticized the decision as being "wrongheaded." Finally, Wilkins might have written: "The court of appeals' apparent determination to find for appellee Sports, Inc., while perhaps justified by reasoning or logic known to the court, is not supported by the facts in the record or law to which the court should have looked."

This is not to say that Wilkins should have filed briefs containing any of those alternative characterizations. Those alternatives still exemplify poor advocacy, even if relegated to a footnote. Like the offending footnote, they add no value to the lawyer's argument, and all run the risk of irritating the court. Even good advocates, however, periodically make mistakes. Pointed criticism of a court's reasoning or harsh comments about the basis for a court's decision, even if tactically unwise, should rarely be declared unethical.

III. Frivolous Appeals and Other Bad Faith Litigation

"It is the obligation of any lawyer—whether privately retained or publicly appointed—not to clog the courts with frivolous motions or appeals."[140] Similarly, lawyers and parties may be sanctioned for pursuing appeals for improper purposes apart from frivolousness.[141] In either regard, many appellate lawyers would be well advised to heed the colorful advice of one federal court of appeals (quoting a Nobel Peace Prize winner) that "[a]bout half the practice of a decent lawyer consists in telling would-be clients that they are damned fools and should stop."[142]

A. *Model Rule 3.1 and Similar Restrictions Apply Equally to Appeals*

Model Rule 3.1, which establishes lawyers' duty to advocate only meritorious claims and contentions, applies equally to litigation at all phases or stages.[143] That rule provides, in pertinent part, that "[a] lawyer shall not bring or defend a proceeding, or assert or controvert an issue therein, unless

---

139. *In re* Green, 11 P.3d 1078, 1083 (Colo. 2000) (stating that "if an attorney criticizes a judge's ruling by saying it was 'incoherent,' he may not be sanctioned").

140. Polk Cnty. v. Dodson, 454 U.S. 312, 323 (1981).

141. Johnson v. Syed, B258701, 2015 WL 4314049, at *5 (Cal. Ct. App. July 15, 2015).

142. Hill v. Norfolk & W. Ry. Co., 814 F.2d 1192, 1202 (7th Cir. 1987) (quoting 1 Jessup, Elihu Root 133 (1938)).

143. *See, e.g.*, Interest of D.C., 573 S.W.3d 860, 863 (Tex. App. 2019) (stating that lawyers are ethically obligated to refuse to prosecute frivolous appeals and citing the Texas equivalent of Model Rule 3.1 in support).

there is a basis in law and fact for doing so that is not frivolous, which includes a good faith argument for an extension, modification, or reversal of existing law."[144] Although Model Rule 3.1's use of terms such as "bring" and "assert" perhaps superficially suggests that the rule applies only at the outset of a proceeding in either a trial or appellate court, that is not the case. Lawyers' duties under Model Rule 3.1 are continuous; they exist throughout the life of a case.[145] Thus, a lawyer must be prepared to abandon claims or issues that initially seemed to be valid but that are later determined to be frivolous. Whether a lawyer has a basis for bringing or continuing a proceeding or an issue therein that is not frivolous under Rule 3.1 is generally measured by an objective "reasonable attorney" standard.[146] Accordingly, a lawyer cannot avoid discipline under this standard by claiming, for example, to have been mistaken about what was actually settled law.[147] Nevertheless, as is clearly indicated by the language of the rule itself regarding arguments for "extension, modification, or reversal of existing law," not every meritless claim or contention is frivolous under this rule.[148] And, although the use of "good faith" suggests that the lawyer's efforts at, for example, reversing existing law could be viewed through a subjective lens, the standard used by courts means that determining whether a violation has occurred remains an objective one.[149] For example, a lawyer cannot defend her conduct as involving a good faith attempt to offer a novel argument when a reasonable lawyer, knowing the facts, would conclude that the argument was frivolous.[150]

144. Model Rules of Prof'l Conduct R. 3.1 (2020).

145. *See In re* Olsen, 326 P.3d 1004, 1009 (Colo. 2014) (recognizing a lawyer's ongoing professional duty to independently assess the factual and legal bases for a client's claims).

146. *Id.* at 1009; O'Brien v. Super. Ct., 939 A.2d 1223, 1231 (Conn. App. Ct. 2008); *In re* Yelverton, 105 A.3d 413, 426 (D.C. 2014); *In re* Disciplinary Action Against Michael, 836 N.W.2d 753, 762 (Minn. 2013); *In re* Disciplinary Action Against Hoffman, 670 N.W.2d 500, 506 (N.D. 2003). *But see In re* Disciplinary Proc. Against Osicka, 765 N.W.2d 775, 784 (Wis. 2009) (applying a subjective standard).

147. Thompson v. Sup. Ct. Comm. on Prof'l Conduct, 252 S.W.3d 125, 128 (Ark. 2007).

148. *See, e.g.*, Vossman v. AirNet Sys., Inc., 113 N.E.3d 987, 994 (Ohio Ct. App. 2018) ("[E]ven where there is not enough evidence to survive a motion for summary judgment, this does not necessarily translate into a frivolous claim."); Commonwealth v. Chmiel, 30 A.3d 1111, 1190 (Pa. 2011) (distinguishing frivolous claims from meritless ones); *In re* Houston, 675 S.E.2d 721, 723 n.1 (S.C. 2009) (finding that a meritless racial profiling claim did not violate Rule 3.1); *In re* S.C., 88 A.3d 1220, 1223 (Vt. 2014) ("[T]he assertion of a claim that an attorney believes to be without merit or lacking any meaningful chance of success does not render an appeal 'frivolous' or unethical.").

149. *See, e.g.*, Att'y Grievance Comm'n of Md. v. Worsham, 105 A.3d 515, 528 (Md. 2014) ("A minimal amount of research would have alerted [the lawyer] to the frivolous nature of the arguments he made.").

150. *See, e.g.*, *In re* Obert, 282 P.3d 825, 841 (Or. 2012) (finding a Rule 3.1 violation in a lawyer's pursuit of an untimely appeal supported only by argument that the statute providing courts with authority to waive time limit clearly limited to criminal cases be "extended" in its application to civil appeals).

The impact of this ethical obligation on appellate litigation means that a lawyer cannot undertake a doubtful appeal as a matter of reflex but must ensure through research and analysis of the record that pursuing an appeal would not be a frivolous act.[151] There are, perhaps, few examples that present a more compelling picture of undertaking a frivolous appeal as a matter of reflex than the appeal pursued by a Wisconsin attorney that resulted in an award of appellate sanctions under Federal Rule of Appellate Procedure 38 and also contributed to the attorney's suspension from the practice of law for two months.[152]

As explained in *Jimenez v. Madison Area Technical College*,[153] William J. Nunnery's representation of Elvira Jimenez began with a workers' compensation claim against her employer, Madison Area Technical College, based on Jimenez's assertion that college administrators had racially and sexually harassed her, causing her severe emotional distress. To support her claim, Jimenez produced a series of e-mails containing derogatory racial comments about her and discussing the sexual harassment visited upon her.[154] In response, the college provided sworn statements from each of the purported authors of the e-mails denying having written them and characterizing them as a "complete fabrication" and a "forgery."[155] The college asked Nunnery to produce the originals of the e-mails. Nunnery did not do so and, ultimately, Jimenez's workers' compensation claim was denied, and she was subsequently fired by the college.[156]

Jimenez, still represented by Nunnery, sued the college for discrimination in federal court. In a subsequent amended complaint, Nunnery added the purported authors of the e-mails as defendants. After that complaint was dismissed for failure to state a claim, Nunnery filed a second amended complaint that specifically referred to the challenged e-mails produced in the unsuccessful workers' compensation action.[157] Jimenez insisted that the e-mails were authentic even though they were "plastic-laminated"; she had the documents laminated, she said, to "prevent them from being stolen."[158] The attorneys for the college again communicated to Nunnery that the individual defendants denied authoring any of the e-mails. When Nunnery

151. *See, e.g.*, Hilmon Co. v. Hyatt Int'l, 899 F.2d 250, 254 (3d Cir. 1990); Hill v. Norfolk & W. Ry. Co., 814 F.2d 1192, 1202 (7th Cir. 1987) ("The filing of an appeal should never be a conditioned reflex."); *In re* Zimmerman, 19 P.3d 160, 162 (Kan. 2001) (finding that a lawyer's filing of notice of appeal of summary judgment ruling violated Rule 3.1 when the lawyer had admitted that he had no good faith basis for opposing summary judgment motion filed by opposing party).

152. Jimenez v. Madison Area Tech. Coll., 321 F.3d 652 (7th Cir. 2003).

153. 321 F.3d 652 (7th Cir. 2003).

154. *Id.* at 653.

155. *Id.* at 654.

156. *Id.*

157. *Id.*

158. *In re* Nunnery, 725 N.W.2d 613, 619 (Wis. 2007).

would not drop the claims against the individuals, the college moved for Rule 11 sanctions.[159]

The district court, after holding an evidentiary hearing, determined that sanctions should be imposed. The district court dismissed Jimenez's case and ordered Nunnery to pay more than $16,000 to the defendants for what the court described as "truly, and without competition, the most blatant case of a Rule 11 violation [it had ever] seen."[160] The district court also found the purported e-mails to be "obviously fraudulent documents" and found incredible Nunnery's claim that whether the e-mails were legitimate "was a judgment call" and that he could wait until taking "depositions to test the credibility of the various letters and e-mails."[161]

On appeal, the Seventh Circuit determined that the district court's ruling was well within its discretion and further concluded that Jimenez had knowingly manufactured the false e-mail evidence to try to support her claim, and "exploited the judicial process and subjected her former colleagues and employer to unnecessary embarrassment and mental anguish."[162] The Seventh Circuit affirmed the district court's dismissal of Jimenez's discrimination claims. The court did not finish there, however, because the college also filed a motion for sanctions for the filing of a frivolous appeal. The Seventh Circuit granted that motion and awarded the college its fees and costs incurred in defending the appeal, with the amount to be determined through further proceedings. In so holding, the Seventh Circuit described the appeal as "a veritable attack on our system of justice."[163] The Seventh Circuit's explanation of why frivolous appeal sanctions were so warranted paints an amazing picture of exactly what Nunnery signed off on in taking the appeal: "The foreordination of Jimenez's failure on appeal could not have been more obvious. Not only did Jimenez cite to the wrong legal standard in her brief before this [c]ourt, she presented only *one page* of legal argument in her favor."[164]

Courts that determine that an attorney cooperated with a client in a frivolous appeal will not only impose statutory damages and penalties, but may also refer the attorney to disciplinary authorities,[165] as the California Court of Appeals demonstrated in *In re Marriage of Gong and Kwong*.[166] In *Gong*,

159. *Jimenez*, 321 F.3d at 654–55.
160. *Id.* at 657.
161. *Id.* at 655.
162. *Id.* at 657.
163. *Id.*
164. *Id.* at 658.
165. *See, e.g., In re* Colvin, 336 P.3d 823, 828 (Kan. 2014) (imposing a public censure in disciplinary proceedings initiated after the court of appeals sent a copy of its decision to disciplinary authorities and awarded $10,000 in attorneys' fees against the lawyer and his client for pursuing a frivolous appeal).
166. 77 Cal. Rptr. 3d 540 (Ct. App. 2008).

the court dismissed Terry Kwong's frivolous appeal, awarded sanctions of over $20,000, remanded to the trial court for a determination of the appropriate amount of reasonable attorneys' fees to award to Monica Gong for having to defend the appeal, and ordered the attorneys involved to forward a copy of the court's opinion to the State Bar of California.[167]

This dispute between former spouses arose after Mr. Kwong failed for several years to make required child support payments pursuant to a marital settlement agreement, and a court order was entered to cause payments to be made to Ms. Gong directly from a partnership interest of Mr. Kwong's. Mr. Kwong, represented by counsel, moved to halt those payments on the alleged basis that he had already paid $30,000 more than he owed.[168] Mr. Kwong's argument in that regard, however, was based entirely upon an effort to take advantage of the fact that some nine months elapsed between when the amount of the arrearages was determined by the trial court after a hearing and the date that the court's written order memorializing its ruling was entered. In short, Mr. Kwong, with his lawyer's assistance, argued that the use of the words "current" and "now" in the written order memorializing the court's ruling from nine months earlier had the effect of freeing him from any child support obligation during that nine-month period.[169] The court found Mr. Kwong's appeal to be "meritless and objectively frivolous" and pursued solely for the purpose of delay, because the reading urged by Mr. Kwong went "against common sense" such that "no reasonable attorney would so interpret" the order.[170] The court, in addition to the disciplinary referral, offered a few choice words for Mr. Kwong's lawyers:

> An inference of willingness to assist Mr. Kwong's harassment of Ms. Gong and to abuse the court's processes could be drawn from his counsels' sophistry and their litigation tactics, which went beyond proper advocacy and common sense. Mr. Kwong's attorneys have taken a phrase or two from [the trial court's] order and fashioned from them an argument that subverts that court's intent. . . . "As a professional, counsel has a professional responsibility not to pursue an appeal that is frivolous or taken for the purposes of delay, just because the client instructs him or her to do so. Under such circumstances, the high ethical and professional standards of a member of the bar and an officer of the court require the attorney to inform the client that the attorney's professional responsibility precludes him or her from pursuing such an appeal, and to withdraw from the representation of the client."[171]

167. *Id.* at 550.

168. *Id.* at 545.

169. *Id.* at 546–47.

170. *Id.* at 548 (citing Zimmerman v. Drexel Burnham Lambert Inc., 252 Cal. Rptr. 115, 121 (Ct. App. 1988)).

171. *Id.* at 549–50 (quoting Cosenza v. Kramer, 200 Cal. Rptr. 18, 20 (Ct. App. 1984)).

With respect to Model Rule 3.1, it is also important to note that the rule not only prohibits the pursuit of an appeal altogether where to do so would be frivolous, but additionally prohibits the pursuit of certain issues on appeal even though it would not be unethical to file an appeal as to one or more other issues. Further, and as noted earlier, the rule not only applies to the commencement of an appeal, but applies equally throughout the life of the appellate proceedings. Thus, a lawyer who acted perfectly ethically in originally undertaking an appeal can violate Rule 3.1 by continuing to pursue the appeal if subsequent events make it apparent that there is no longer a "basis in law and fact for doing so that is not frivolous."[172]

B. Special Issues in Criminal Appeals

Because of the constitutional dimensions implicated in criminal proceedings, Model Rule 3.1 acknowledges that its requirements must be applied differently to lawyers defending criminal cases.[173] The last sentence of Model Rule 3.1 indicates that a lawyer "for the defendant in a criminal proceeding, or the respondent in a proceeding that could result in incarceration, may nevertheless so defend the proceeding as to require that every element of the case be established."[174] As further explained in a comment to Model Rule 3.1, a "lawyer's obligations under this Rule are subordinate to federal or state constitutional law that entitles a defendant in a criminal matter to the assistance of counsel in presenting a claim or contention that would otherwise be prohibited by this Rule."[175] Nevertheless, the constitutional right to counsel that necessitates greater lenience for criminal defense lawyers under Model Rule 3.1 does not create a right to pursue a frivolous appeal. A lawyer must seek to withdraw from an appellate representation when the only grounds for appeal are frivolous.

The procedure for withdrawal varies significantly between jurisdictions as a result of two Supreme Court opinions. The first, *Anders v. California*,[176]

172. Model Rules of Prof'l Conduct R. 3.1 (2020); *see, e.g.*, Brunswick v. Statewide Grievance Comm., 931 A.2d 319, 330–34 (Conn. App. Ct. 2007) (finding that a reasonable lawyer would not have continued to pursue a fraud allegation after client was unwilling to furnish an affidavit in support); *In re* Caranchini, 956 S.W.2d 910, 916–17 (Mo. 1997) (disbarring a lawyer who violated Rule 3.1 on multiple occasions by continuing to pursue claims well after it was clear there was no basis for doing so that was not frivolous, including one case in which the lawyer continued to rely on a forged document after its forgery was clear).

173. *See, e.g.*, Patterson v. N.Y., 432 U.S. 197, 210 (1977) ("[T]he Due Process Clause requires the prosecution to prove beyond a reasonable doubt all of the elements included in the definition of the offense of which the defendant is charged."); D.C. Bar, Legal Ethics Comm., Op. 320, at 2 (2003) ("[L]awyers defending a criminal case are authorized to engage in conduct that, in other contexts, might seem inconsistent with the spirit of the Rules.").

174. Model Rules of Prof'l Conduct R. 3.1 (2020).

175. *Id.* cmt. 3.

176. 386 U.S. 738 (1967).

outlined a procedure for simultaneously submitting a brief along with a motion to withdraw that references "anything in the record that might arguably support the appeal,"[177] a document that has come to be known as an *Anders* brief. The second, *Smith v. Robbins*,[178] indicated that an *Anders* brief is just one of many constitutionally acceptable ways that courts can permit a lawyer to withdraw in the event of a frivolous appeal, making clear that courts could devise their own rules that would prohibit withdrawal.[179]

Consequently, some states have elaborated and expanded upon the requirements for *Anders* briefs. The Pennsylvania Supreme Court, for example, decreed that a lawyer filing such a brief must (1) summarize the procedural history and facts, with citations to the record; (2) refer to anything in the record that arguably supports the appeal; (3) set forth the lawyer's conclusion that the appeal is frivolous; and (4) state the lawyer's reasons for concluding that the appeal is frivolous.[180]

Other states have deviated sharply from the very concept of an *Anders* brief. Indiana prohibits a court-appointed lawyer from filing such a brief and seeking to withdraw altogether and, instead, requires the attorney "to submit an ordinary appellate brief the first time—no matter how frivolous counsel regards the claims to be."[181] In Ohio, a lawyer who believes an appeal is frivolous should try to persuade the defendant to abandon the appeal.[182] If the defendant refuses, the lawyer "must file a merit brief and argue the defendant's appeal as persuasively as possible regardless of any personal belief that the appeal is frivolous."[183] This does not mean, however, that the lawyer must argue every issue that the defendant believes to be meritorious; the lawyer may exercise strategic judgment in briefing the appeal.[184] New Jersey has a special court rule applied to petitions for post-conviction relief prohibiting counsel from withdrawing based on a belief that the petition lacks merit.[185] Other states have confronted these questions in other circumstances where litigants receive court-appointed counsel—such as terminations of parental rights cases—with mixed results.[186]

177. *Id.* at 744.

178. 528 U.S. 259 (2000).

179. *Id.* at 272–73.

180. Commonwealth v. Santiago, 978 A.2d 349, 361 (Pa. 2009).

181. Mosley v. State, 908 N.E.2d 599, 607–08 (Ind. 2009) (describing the *Anders* approach as "cumbersome and inefficient").

182. State v. Wilson, 83 N.E.3d 942, 952 (Ohio Ct. App. 2017).

183. *Id.*

184. *Id.*

185. State v. Rue, 811 A.2d 425, 437 (N.J. 2002) (discussing N.J. Sup. Ct. R. 3:22-6 and explaining that denigrating or dismissing the claims of the client or negatively evaluating those claims is contrary to that rule).

186. *Compare In re* S.C., 88 A.3d 1220, 1222–24 (Vt. 2014) (denying motions to withdraw, rejecting the *Anders* concept, and explaining that the pursuit of even an arguably frivolous claim will not violate Rule 3.1 where the court has refused to permit withdrawal), *with* A.C. v. Cabinet

C. Statutory Prohibitions and Court Rules Regarding Frivolous Appeals

In addition to the ethical prohibition under Model Rule 3.1, appellate litigators in civil matters must be aware of multiple statutes and court rules, both federal and state. In federal cases, at least two statutes and one court rule are worthy of note. Federal Rule of Appellate Procedure 38 provides discretionary authority to a court of appeals that determines an appeal to be frivolous to "award just damages and single or double costs to the appellee," as long as a motion under the rule is separately filed or the court first provides notice and a "reasonable opportunity to respond" before making such an award.[187] The federal statute permitting the imposition of penal sanctions for "multiplying proceedings unreasonably and vexatiously," 28 U.S.C. § 1927, applies to appellate proceedings just as it does to proceedings before the trial court.[188] In addition, 28 U.S.C. § 1912 provides that when a judgment is affirmed on appeal, the court "in its discretion may adjudge to the prevailing party just damages for his delay and single or double costs."[189] While the word "frivolous" does not appear anywhere in § 1912, it is often used by federal courts in tandem with Rule 38 to render awards against lawyers who prosecute frivolous appeals.[190] The term "just damages" has been interpreted both in § 1912 and Rule 38 to include the parties' reasonable attorney's fees incurred in responding to the appeal.[191]

A high-profile example of the confluence of these various federal provisions permitting sanctions, as well as the ability of federal courts to directly impose their own discipline against attorneys, is demonstrated by two related opinions issued by the Ninth Circuit: one in which the court took the highly unusual step of appointing an independent prosecutor to evaluate what sanctions should be imposed against the attorneys involved,[192] and one that adopted the findings of the independent prosecutor as to sanctions and imposed discipline against the attorneys involved ranging from a six-month suspension to a private reprimand.[193] Perhaps even more amazingly, these

for Health & Fam. Servs., 362 S.W.3d 361, 370 (Ky. Ct. App. 2012) (extending *Anders*-style procedure to cases involving the termination of parental rights), *and* Interest of D.C., 573 S.W.3d 860, 862–63 (Tex. App. 2019) ("The procedures set forth in *Anders* apply to an appeal from a case involving the termination of parental rights when court-appointed counsel has determined that the appeal is frivolous.").

187. Fed. R. App. P. 38; *see, e.g.*, Anderson v. Wells Fargo Bank, N.A., 953 F.3d 311, 315–16 (5th Cir. 2020) (finding that the plaintiff's appeal was frivolous under Rule 38 and ordering her to show cause as to why she should not be sanctioned); Jaworski v. Master Hand Contractors, Inc., 882 F.3d 686, 691 (7th Cir. 2018) (explaining what makes an appeal frivolous for Rule 38 purposes and imposing sanctions).

188. 28 U.S.C. § 1927 (2018).

189. 28 U.S.C. § 1912 (2018).

190. *See, e.g.*, Searcy v. Donelson, 204 F.3d 797, 798 (8th Cir. 2000).

191. *See, e.g.*, Lyddon v. Geothermal Props. Inc., 996 F.2d 212, 214–15 (9th Cir. 1993).

192. Girardi v. Dow Chem. Co. (*In re* Girardi), 528 F.3d 1131, 1132 (9th Cir. 2008).

193. Girardi v. Dow Chem. Co. (*In re* Girardi), 611 F.3d 1027, 1067 (9th Cir. 2010).

opinions followed the court's appointment of a district judge as a special master to inquire into the attorneys' conduct

In *Girardi v. Dow Chemical Co.* (*In re Girardi*),[194] four attorneys, including Tom Girardi and Walter Lack, who had collaborated on numerous past matters including what is commonly thought of as the "Erin Brockovich" case, were found to have filed and continued to pursue obviously frivolous litigation, causing the defendants significant expense. After obtaining a Nicaraguan judgment against a nonexistent Dole Foods entity, the attorneys filed an action in California seeking to enforce the foreign judgment that attached a document purporting to be issued by the Nicaraguan court but that had been corrected to name the correct legal entity and, worse yet, was not actually a court document but a notary's affidavit that described and translated the foreign writ.[195] The defendants removed the action to federal court and argued the discrepancy in the documentation. The attorneys for the plaintiffs continued to argue that the documents they provided were the authentic Nicaraguan court documents and repeatedly made those same misstatements in multiple filings. They also supported their submissions with at least one fraudulent affidavit.

The district court dismissed the enforcement action, which it characterized as an "'attempt to enforce a $489.4 million judgment against a nonparty based on an affidavit that purports to be a translation of a writ of execution.'"[196] The attorneys who brought the enforcement action then appealed that ruling. The special master found significant fault with that decision, describing it as being done without first taking appropriate measures to evaluate whether the case had any continued viability. The attorneys delegated the drafting of the appellate brief to a junior associate who had less than two years of experience. The junior associate continued to describe the affidavit/translation in that brief as the actual writ of execution.[197] The attorneys then went further and opposed the defendant's motion to supplement the record on appeal with the actual writ of execution that they had obtained through discovery in another matter. At some point thereafter, the junior associate circulated a memorandum to the other lawyers "expressing his concerns about the viability of their position, noting that the firm risked exposure to a motion under Federal Rule of Appellate Procedure 38."[198] Lack and another one of the target lawyers, Paul Traina, discussed the junior associate's concerns and ultimately persuaded him to draft a further reply brief in support of their appeal.[199] The special master's recom-

194. 611 F.3d 1027 (9th Cir. 2010).
195. *Id.* at 1029–32.
196. *Id.* at 1056 (quoting the district court).
197. *Id.* at 1032–33, 1056.
198. *Id.* at 1033.
199. *Id.* at 1033, 1058.

mendation was that the attorneys be required to pay fees and costs of up to $390,000. Instead of acting on the special master's report itself, the Ninth Circuit appointed a California law professor, Rory Little, as an independent prosecutor to determine what sanctions should be imposed against the lawyers.[200]

Professor Little's report filed with the Ninth Circuit in May 2009 concluded that the special master's findings as to the state of mind of each of the lawyers involved were "'accurate and provable by clear and convincing evidence,'" and indicated that the lawyers involved did not dispute that they had "'acted at least recklessly in failing to detect those falsities and permitting them to appear in their opening appellate brief and to stand uncorrected even through the date of oral argument in July 2005.'"[201] The Ninth Circuit after reviewing all the material before it aptly summarized the situation as follows:

> [T]he history of the enforcement proceedings includes several crucial moments where a reasonable attorney would have, at a minimum, inquired further about the bona fides of the document that was the basis of the action he was prosecuting. At some point, failing to do so becomes willful blindness.[202]

The Ninth Circuit concluded that each of the attorneys involved deserved discipline for their roles in the pursuit of the frivolous litigation but distinguished the appropriate discipline to be imposed pursuant to Federal Rule of Appellate Procedure 46 against the various lawyers. As to Girardi, the Ninth Circuit found that although he took "almost no active part in the actual proceedings to enforce the Nicaraguan Judgment," his practice of permitting lawyers with the Lack firm to sign his name to briefs in this case was reckless conduct and that the "recklessness inhere[d] in his mode of practice."[203] The court opted to formally reprimand Girardi "for his recklessness in determining whether statements or documents central to an action on which his name appears are false."[204] Finding that their efforts before the Ninth Circuit to "attempt to salvage their case became indistinguishable from a knowing submission of false documents," the Ninth Circuit concluded that suspension was an appropriate sanction for Lack and Traina, but limited their suspensions to six months in light of their long and excellent records of

200. Girardi v. Dow Chem. Co. (*In re* Girardi), 528 F.3d 1131, 1132 (9th Cir. 2008) (announcing that a special prosecutor would be appointed by separate order); Girardi v. Dow Chem. Co. (*In re* Girardi), 529 F.3d 1199, 1199–1200 (9th Cir. 2008) (appointing University of California Hastings College of the Law Prof. Rory K. Little as an independent prosecutor).

201. *In re Girardi*, 611 F.3d at 1034.

202. *Id.* at 1036.

203. *Id.* at 1038–39.

204. *Id.* at 1039.

successful practice with no prior disciplinary incidents.[205] As for the junior associate in Lack's firm, whom the Ninth Circuit never named, it treated his inexperience as a mitigating factor and opted to issue a private reprimand against him "for allowing his superiors to overcome his sound instincts and for his role in drafting briefs that contained false statements."[206]

IV. Conclusion

Appellate advocates, like all lawyers, must appreciate their ethical obligations. Zealous advocacy does not excuse lawyers' ignorance of their professional responsibilities in appellate courts any more than it does in trial courts. Appellate lawyers are especially wise to curb their zeal when criticizing courts. While it is true that a party cannot appeal from a lower court decision without criticizing it in some form or fashion, advocates must be careful about how far they go in their criticism. Ethics rules forbid lawyers from knowingly or recklessly making false statements about judges' integrity or qualifications. Appellate lawyers must also remain vigilant about their ethical obligations not to pursue frivolous appeals. The decision to appeal is not one to be made reflexively. Thoughtful consideration and a diligent review of the record are required to ensure a ground for appeal that will satisfy the lawyer's ethical obligations under Rule 3.1, as well as under state or federal court rules and statutes governing frivolous appeals and vexatious litigation.

205. *Id.*
206. *Id.*

Table of Cases

39 Bell, LLC v. K&K, Inc., 584 S.W.3d 823 (Mo. Ct. App. 2019), 450
4900 Park Heights Ave. LLC v. Cromwell Retail 1, LLC, 227 A.3d 757 (Md. Ct. Spec. App. 2020), 450

Abbott, *In re*, 925 A.2d 482 (Del. 2007), 284
Abdallah v. Coca-Cola Co., 186 F.R.D. 672 (N.D. Ga. 1999), 208, 213 n.276
Abdelaziz, United States v., No. 19-10080-NMG, 2020 WL 618697 (D. Mass. Feb. 10, 2020), 24 n.136
Abdullah, State v., 348 P.3d 1 (Idaho 2015), 379 n.72, 396
Abrishamian v. Wash. Med. Grp., P.C., 86 A.3d 681 (Md. Ct. Spec. App. 2014), 422 n.32
Acad. of Allergy & Asthma in Primary Care v. La. Health Serv. & Indem. Co., 384 F. Supp. 3d 644 (E.D. La. 2018), 27 n.151, 31 n.169
Accrued Fin. Servs., Inc. v. Prime Retail, Inc., No. Civ. JFM-99-2573, 2000 WL 976800 (D. Md. June 19, 2000), 140, 141
A.C. v. Cabinet for Health & Family Servs., 362 S.W.3d 361 (Ky. Ct. App. 2012), 525 n.186
Adams v. Comm'r of Corr., 71 A.3d 512 (Conn. 2013), 408
A.H. Robins Co., *In re*, 880 F.2d 694 (4th Cir. 1989), 5
AIG Haw. Ins. Co. v. Bateman, 923 P.2d 395 (Haw. 1996), 326–327
Aiken v. Bus. & Indus. Health Grp., Inc., 885 F. Supp. 1474 (D. Kan. 1995), 166
Air Crash Disaster, *In re*, 909 F. Supp. 1116 (N.D. Ill. 1995), 181 n.85
Akron Bar Ass'n v. Catanzarite, 893 N.E.2d 835 (Ohio 1998), 307 n.184
Akron v. Carter, 942 N.E.2d 409 (Ohio Ct. App. 2010), 425
Albrecht, *In re*, Disciplinary Action Against, 845 N.W.2d 184 (Minn. 2014), 318 n.18
Alcorn, *In re*, 41 P.3d 600 (Ariz. 2002), 326
Alexander, *In re*, 300 P.3d 536 (Ariz. 2013), 107
Allen, People v., 187 P.3d 1018 (Cal. 2008), 395 n.153
Allen, United States v., 06-40056-01-SAC, 2008 WL 2622872 (D. Kan. July 1, 2008), 375
Alpha Capital Mgmt., Inc. v. Rentenbach, 792 N.W.2d 344 (Mich. Ct. App. 2010), 29
A.L. v. Chi. Pub. Sch. Dist. No. 299, No. 10 C 494, 2012 WL 3028337 (N.D. Ill. July 24, 2012), 336 n.132
Am. Airlines, Inc., *In re*, 972 F.2d 605 (5th Cir. 1992), 31 n.168

Ambulatory Infusion Therapy Specialists, Inc. v. N. Am. Adm'rs, Inc., 262 S.W.3d 107 (Tex. App. 2008), 352

American Canoe Ass'n, Inc. v. City of St. Albans, 18 F. Supp. 2d 620 (S.D. W. Va. 1998), 217–218

Am. States Ins. Co. v. Nammathao, 220 P.3d 1283 (Wash. Ct. App. 2009), 427 n.53, 432

AmTrust Bank v. Commonwealth Land Title Ins. Co., No. 1:08CV2390, 2012 WL 3912764 (N.D. Ohio Sept. 7, 2012), 31 n.169

Amusement Indus., Inc. v. Stern, 657 F. Supp. 2d 458 (S.D.N.Y. 2009), 421, 423

Analytica, Inc. v. NPD Rsch., Inc., 708 F.2d 1263 (7th Cir. 1983), 30

Anaya v. Coello, 632 S.E.2d 425 (Ga. Ct. App. 2006), 450

Anderson Producing Inc. v. Koch Oil Co., 929 S.W.2d 416 (Tex. 1996), 418

Anderson v. Duke Energy Corp., No. 3:06cv399, 2007 WL 4284904 (W.D.N.C. Dec. 4, 2007), 338 n.141

Anderson v. Hale, 159 F. Supp. 2d 1116 (N.D. Ill. 2001), 131

Anderson v. Kohl's Corp., Civ. A. No. 2:12-cv-00822, 2013 WL 1874812 (W.D. Pa. May 3, 2013), 338 n.141

Anderson v. Wells Fargo Bank, N.A., 953 F.3d 311 (5th Cir. 2020), 526 n.187

Anders v. California, 386 U.S. 738 (1967), 524–525

Andrades, People v., 828 N.E.2d 599 (N.Y. 2005), 413 n.241

Angwafo, *In re*, 899 N.E.2d 778 (Mass. 2009), 326, 330

Annie Sloan Interiors, Ltd. v. Kappel, Civ. A. No. 19-807, 2019 WL 2492303 (E.D. La. June 14, 2019), 27, 30

Anonymous, *In re*, 819 N.E.2d 376 (Ind. 2004), 76 n.152, 100

Anonymous, *In re*, 896 N.E.2d 916 (Ind. 2008), 107 n.108

Anonymous, *In re*, 932 N.E.2d 671 (Ind. 2010), 42 n.228, 460 n.65

Ansell v. Statewide Grievance Comm., 865 A.2d 1215 (Conn. App. Ct. 2005), 106, 469

Antelope Valley-E. Kern Water Agency v. L.A. Cnty. Waterworks Dist. No. 40 (Antelope Valley Groundwater Cases), 241 Cal. Rptr. 3d 692 (Ct. App. 2018), 1 n.1

Anthony, State v., 266 So. 3d 415 (La. Ct. App. 2019), 419 n.9

Anthony v. Va. State Bar, 621 S.E.2d 121 (Va. 2005), 507 n.61

Anty, United States v., 203 F.3d 305 (4th Cir. 2000), 148

Apple Corps Ltd. v. Int'l Collectors Soc'y, 15 F. Supp. 2d 456 (D.N.J. 1998), 84, 101 n.68, 114 n.151, 121 n.200, 124

Application for Disciplinary Action Against Hoffman, *In re*, 670 N.W.2d 500 (N.D. 2003), 292

Arden v. Forsberg & Umlauf, P.S., 402 P.3d 245 (Wash. 2017), 13

Aristocrat Techs. v. Int'l Game Tech., No. C-06-03717 RMW, 2010 WL 2595151 (N.D. Cal. June 28, 2010), 137 n.1, 148

Armenian Assembly of Am., Inc. v. Cafesjian, 924 F. Supp. 2d 183 (D.D.C. 2013), 148 n.72, 153 n.97

Arnold, *In re*, 56 P.3d 259 (Kan. 2002), 495

Arnold v. Cargill, No. 01-2086, 2004 WL 2203410 (D. Minn. Sept. 24, 2004), 80 n.179

Arons v. Jutkowitz, 880 N.E.2d 831 (N.Y. 2007), 84 n.201, 190, 191 n.141
Arriola v. Time Ins. Co., 751 N.E.2d 221 (Ill. App. Ct. 2001), 209, 211 n.260
Arrowpac Inc. v. Sea Star Line, LLC, No. 3:12-cv-1180-J-32JBT, 2013 WL 5460027 (M.D. Fla. Apr. 30, 2013), 12
Art+Com Innovation Pool Gmbh v. Google Inc., No. 1:14-217-TBD, 2016 WL 10033421 (D. Del. Sept. 9, 2016), 153–155
Artromick Int'l, Inc. v. Drustar Inc., 134 F.R.D. 226 (S.D. Ohio 1991), 8 n.37, 8 n.38
ASI Holding Co. v. Royal Beach & Golf Resorts, LLC, 163 So. 3d 668 (Fla. Dist. Ct. App. 2015), 28 n.151
Askew, *In re*, 225 A.3d 388 (D.C. 2020), 453 n.31
Asset Acceptance LLC v. Pham, 415 P.3d 47 (Okla. Civ. App. 2016), 353 n.230
Ass'n for L.A. Deputy Sheriffs v. Super. Ct., 447 P.3d 234 (Cal. 2019), 407
Atmosphere Hosp. Mgmt. Servs., LLC v. Royal Realties, LLC, 28 F. Supp. 3d 692 (E.D. Mich. 2014), 29
Att'y Grievance Comm'n of Md. v. Agbaje, 93 A.3d 262 (Md. 2014), 107, 298, 315
Att'y Grievance Comm'n of Md. v. Aita, 181 A.3d 774 (Md. 2018), 453 n.31
Att'y Grievance Comm'n of Md. v. Ambe, 218 A.3d 757 (Md. 2019), 316
Att'y Grievance Comm'n of Md. v. Barnett, 102 A.3d 310 (Md. 2014), 323 n.53
Att'y Grievance Comm'n of Md. v. Bellamy, 162 A.3d 848 (Md. 2017), 105 n.93, 297 n.114
Att'y Grievance Comm'n of Md. v. Bleecker, 994 A.2d 928 (Md. 2010), 326 n.67
Att'y Grievance Comm'n of Md. v. Bocchino, 80 A.3d 222 (Md. 2013), 454 n.39
Att'y Grievance Comm'n of Md. v. Brooke, 821 A.2d 414 (Md. 2003), 2
Att'y Grievance Comm'n of Md. v. Byrd, 970 A.2d 870 (Md. 2009), 324
Att'y Grievance Comm'n of Md. v. Chasnoff, 783 A.2d 224 (Md. 2001), 52 n.16
Att'y Grievance Comm'n of Md. v. Conwell, 200 A.3d 820 (Md. 2019), 323 n.53
Att'y Grievance Comm'n of Md. v. Donnelly, 182 A.3d 743 (Md. 2018), 295 n.105
Att'y Grievance Comm'n of Md. v. Dyer, 162 A.3d 970 (Md. 2017), 51
Att'y Grievance Comm'n of Md. v. Elmendorf, 946 A.2d 542 (Md. 2006), 94 n.25, 293 n.90, 369 n.7, 467 n.119
Att'y Grievance Comm'n of Md. v. Fader, 66 A.3d 18 (Md. 2013), 316 n.8, 320 n.33
Att'y Grievance Comm'n of Md. v. Ficker, 706 A.2d 1045 (Md. 1998), 103 n.82
Att'y Grievance Comm'n of Md. v. Floyd, 929 A.2d 61 (Md. 2007), 106, 469
Att'y Grievance Comm'n of Md. v. Fraidin, 91 A.3d 1078 (Md. 2014), 126 n.231
Att'y Grievance Comm'n of Md. v. Frost, 85 A.3d 264 (Md. 2014), 497 n.18, 501, 503, 508 n.68
Att'y Grievance Comm'n of Md. v. Goodman, 850 A.2d 1157 (Md. 2004), 324
Att'y Grievance Comm'n of Md. v. Gordon, 991 A.2d 51 (Md. 2010), 323 n.53
Att'y Grievance Comm'n of Md. v. Hamilton, 118 A.3d 958 (Md. 2015), 452 n.27
Att'y Grievance Comm'n of Md. v. Hermina, 842 A.2d 762 (Md. 2004), 509
Att'y Grievance Comm'n of Md. v. Hoerauf, 229 A.3d 802 (Md. 2020), 316
Att'y Grievance Comm'n of Md. v. Johnson, 770 A.2d 130 (Md. 2001), 324 n.57
Att'y Grievance Comm'n of Md. v. Johnson, 976 A.2d 245 (Md. 2009), 106
Att'y Grievance Comm'n of Md. v. Kaned, 215 A.3d 242 (Md. 2019), 317 n.16

Att'y Grievance Comm'n of Md. v. Kent, 653 A.2d 909 (Md. 1995), 180
Att'y Grievance Comm'n of Md. v. Lang, 191 A.3d 474 (Md. 2018), 453 n.30
Att'y Grievance Comm'n of Md. v. Levin, 69 A.3d 451 (Md. 2013), 468
Att'y Grievance Comm'n of Md. v. Maldonado, 203 A.3d 841 (Md. 2019), 106 n.101, 115 n.162
Att'y Grievance Comm'n of Md. v. May, 72 A.3d 174 (Md. 2013), 453 n.28
Att'y Grievance Comm'n of Md. v. Mba-Jones, 919 A.2d 669 (Md. 2007), 298
Att'y Grievance Comm'n of Md. v. Mixter, 109 A.3d 1 (Md. 2015), 70 n.119, 72, 281
Att'y Grievance Comm'n of Md. v. Pak, 929 A.2d 546 (Md. 2007), 94 n.31
Att'y Grievance Comm'n of Md. v. Paul, 187 A.3d 625 (Md. 2018), 105 n.94, 297 n.115
Att'y Grievance Comm'n of Md. v. Peters-Hamlin, 136 A.3d 374 (Md. 2016), 320 n.36
Att'y Grievance Comm'n of Md. v. Planta, 225 A.3d 19 (Md. 2020), 325 n.62, 452 n.27
Att'y Grievance Comm'n of Md. v. Rheinstein, 223 A.3d 505 (Md. 2020), 294 n.97, 307 n.186, 320 n.37
Att'y Grievance Comm'n of Md. v. Riely, 242 A.3d 206 (Md. 2020), 453 n.31
Att'y Grievance Comm'n of Md. v. Ruddy, 981 A.2d 637 (Md. 2009), 322 n.45
Att'y Grievance Comm'n of Md. v. Sanderson, 213 A.3d 122 (Md. 2019), 455 n.40
Att'y Grievance Comm'n of Md. v. Seltzer, 34 A.3d 498 (Md. 2011), 126 n.231, 315 n.3
Att'y Grievance Comm'n of Md. v. Smith, 109 A.3d 1184 (Md. 2015), 297, 321
Att'y Grievance Comm'n of Md. v. Steinberg, 910 A.2d 429 (Md. 2006), 455 n.40
Att'y Grievance Comm'n of Md. v. Steinhorn, 198 A.3d 821 (Md. 2018), 319
Att'y Grievance Comm'n of Md. v. White, 731 A.2d 447 (Md. 1999), 317 n.16
Att'y Grievance Comm'n of Md. v. Worsham, 105 A.3d 515 (Md. 2014), 65 n.90, 520
Att'y Grievance Comm'n of Md. v. Zhang, 100 A.3d 1112 (Md. 2014), 466, 476
Att'y Grievance Comm'n v. Link, 844 A.2d 1197 (Md. 2004), 108
Att'y LS v. Miss. Bar, 649 So. 2d 810 (Miss. 1994), 132 n.264
Att'y M v. Miss. Bar, 621 So. 2d 220 (Miss. 1992), 280
Att'y Q v. Miss. State Bar, 587 So. 2d 228 (Miss. 1991), 182 n.89
Aubrey v. D Mag. Partners, L.P., Civ. A. No. 3:19-CV-0056-B, 2019 WL 2103699 (N.D. Tex. May 14, 2019), 30
Audio MPEG, Inc. v. Dell, Inc., 219 F. Supp. 3d 563 (E.D. Va. 2016), 30
Ausherman v. Bank of Am. Corp., 212 F. Supp. 2d 435 (D. Md. 2002), 94, 294, 467, 470–471
Auto Parts Mfg. Miss. Inc. v. King Constr. of Houston, LLC, Civ. A. No. 1:11–CV–00251–GHD–SAA, 2014 WL 1217766 (N.D. Miss. Mar. 24, 2014), 338 n.141
A.V. by Versace, Inc. v. Gianni Versace, S.p.A., No. 96 Civ. 972PKLTHK, 98 Civ. 0123PKLTHK, 2002 WL 2012618 (S.D.N.Y. Sept. 3, 2002), 114 n.151
Avocent Redmond Corp. v. Rose Elecs., 491 F. Supp. 2d 1000 (W.D. Wash. 2007), 2

Awan v. Awan, 906 N.Y.S.2d 70 (App. Div. 2010), 100 n.62, 100 n.68, 169 n.22, 180 n.83
Ayeni, *In re*, 822 A.2d 420 (D.C. 2003), 330 n.97, 331 n.102, 334 n.121

Babbs v. Minton, No. 2004-CA-000332-OA, 2004 WL 1367621 (Ky. Ct. App. June 18, 2004), 111
Baber, *In re*, 106 A.3d 1072 (D.C. 2015), 315
Bacote v. Riverbay Corp., No. 16 Civ. 1599 (GHW) (AJP), 2017 WL 945103 (S.D.N.Y. Mar. 10, 2017), 132
Baham v. Ass'n of Apt. Owners of Opua Hale Patio Homes, No. 13-00669HG-BMK, 2014 WL 413495 (D. Haw. Feb. 4, 2014), 38 n.205
Bahn, *In re*, 113 S.W.3d 865 (Tex. App. 2000), 421
Bahrami v. Price, Civ. A. File No. 1:11-CV-4483-SCJ-AJB, 2013 WL 3800093 (N.D. Ga. July 19, 2013), 132
Bailey, *In re*, 96 N.Y.S.3d 583 (App. Div. 2019), 281 n.18, 282 n.18
Bailey, State v., No. 1805009348A, 2020 WL 1316838 (Del. Super. Ct. Mar. 16, 2020), 233 n.39
Baker v. Alderman, 158 F.3d 516 (11th Cir. 1998), 64 n.87
Baker v. Allstate Ins. Co., No. 2:19-cv-08024-ODW (JCx), 2020 WL 978729 (C.D. Cal. Feb. 28, 2020), 281
Bakker v. McKinnon, 152 F.3d 1007 (8th Cir. 1998), 102 n.76
Baldasarre v. Butler, 625 A.2d 458 (N.J. 1993), 17 n.88
Balducci v. Cige, 223 A.3d 1229 (N.J. 2020), 447
Balliro, *In re*, 899 N.E.2d 794 (Mass. 2009), 317 n.16
Balsamo, *In re*, 780 A.2d 255 (D.C. 2001), 321 n.39
Banco Popular N. Am. v. Gandi, 876 A.2d 253 (N.J. 2005), 489
Bandaries, *In re*, 156 So. 3d 1152 (La. 2014), 70 n.119
Bank of Am., N.A. v. Atkin, 305 So. 3d 305 (Fla. Dist. Ct. App. 2018), 507 n.64
Bank of Am., N.A. v. Super. Ct., 151 Cal. Rptr. 3d 526 (Ct. App. 2013), 4
Banks v. Office of the Senate Sergeant-at-Arms, 222 F.R.D. 1 (D.D.C. 2004), 186
Barbee v. Luong Firm, P.L.L.C., 107 P.3d 762 (Wash. Ct. App. 2005), 432
Barefield v. DPIC Cos., 600 S.E.2d 256 (W. Va. 2004), 5
Barkerding v. Whittaker, 263 So. 3d 1170 (La. Ct. App. 2018), 3, 247
Barnett, United States v., 197 F.3d 138 (5th Cir. 1999), 148
Barnett v. LeMaster, 12 F. App'x 774 (10th Cir. 2001), 337
Barratt, *In re*, 663 N.E.2d 536 (Ind. 1996), 317 n.16, 324 n.60
Barrett v. Virginia State Bar, 611 S.E.2d 375 (Va. 2007), 311–312
Barry v. USAA, 989 P.2d 1172 (Wash. Ct. App. 1999), 5
Barstow, *In re*, 817 So. 2d 1123 (La. 2002), 321 n.39
Bartee, People v., 566 N.E.2d 855 (Ill. App. Ct. 1991), 397
Basco, *In re*, 221 S.W.3d 637 (Tex. 2007), 28 n.151
Basco v. Wal-Mart Stores, Inc., No. Civ.A. 00-3184, 2002 WL 272384 (E.D. La. Feb. 25, 2002), 213
Batko v. Sayreville Democratic Org., 860 A.2d 967 (N.J. Super. Ct. App. Div. 2004), 346

Baumgartner, United States v., 581 F. App'x 522 (6th Cir. 2014), 305
Bayne v. Provost, 359 F. Supp. 2d 234 (N.D.N.Y. 2005), 191
B.B. v. E.E., 133 N.Y.S.3d 186 (Fam. Ct. 2020), 440
Bd. of Prof'l Responsibility v. Asay, 374 P.3d 295 (Wyo. 2016), 295 n.105
Bd. of Prof'l Responsibility v. Custis, 348 P.3d 823 (Wyo. 2015), 320 n.36
Bd. of Prof'l Responsibility v. Davidson, 205 P.3d 1008 (Wyo. 2009), 497, 509 n.77
Bd. of Prof'l Responsibility v. Dunn, 272 P.3d 941 (Wyo. 2012), 326 n.67
Bd. of Prof'l Responsibility v. Jenkins, 260 P.3d 264 (Wyo. 2011), 169 n.22
Bd. of Prof'l Responsibility v. Melchior, 269 P.3d 1088 (Wyo. 2012), 100 n.62, 159 n.22
Bd. of Prof'l Responsibility v. Richard, 335 P.3d 1036 (Wyo. 2014), 283 n.19, 324 n.53
Bd. of Prof'l Responsibility v. Stinson, 337 P.3d 401 (Wyo. 2014), 57–59, 69, 72–73
Beaman v. Freesmeyer, 131 N.E.3d 488 (Ill. 2019), 86
Bean v. Broussard, 587 So. 2d 908 (Miss. 1991), 72 n.134
Bearden v. Ballad Health, 967 F.3d 513 (6th Cir. 2020), 290 n.71
Beard v. Bd. of Prof'l Responsibility, 288 S.W.3d 838 (Tenn. 2009), 325 n.63
Beary v. Deese, No. 16-15757, 2018 WL 3417878 (E.D. La. July 13, 2018), 422 n.31
Beaty v. St. Luke's Hosp. of Kan. City, 298 S.W.3d 554 (Mo. Ct. App. 2009), 193 n.153
Beaudry v. TeleCheck Servs., Inc., No. 3:07-0842, 2016 WL 11398115 (M.D. Tenn. Sept. 9, 2016), 329, 474
Becker, *In re*, 804 N.Y.S.2d 4 (App. Div. 2005), 329, 473 n.167
Becker v. Perla, 5 N.Y.S.3d 34 (App. Div. 2015), 31 n.170
Befekadu v. Addis Int'l Money Transfer, LLC, 772 S.E.2d 785 (Ga. Ct. App. 2015), 433
Belding, *In re*, 589 S.E.2d 197 (S.C. 2003), 94
Beller v. Crow, 742 N.W.2d 230 (Neb. 2007), 425, 439, 440 n.135
Bennett v. State, 549 S.W.2d 585 (Mo. Ct. App. 1977), 407
Benson, *In re*, 69 P.3d 544 (Kan. 2003), 70 n.117
Berger, United States v., 251 F.3d 894 (10th Cir. 2001), 422
Berger v. United States, 295 U.S. 78 (1935), 407
Bernier v. DuPont, 715 N.E.2d 442 (Mass. App. Ct. 1999), 436 n.106
Berry v. McFarland, 278 P.3d 407 (Idaho 2012), 9 n.43
Berry v. Schmitt, 688 F.3d 290 (6th Cir. 2012), 496 n.14
Bertagnolli, People v., 861 P.2d 717 (Colo. 1993), 319, 478
Bevill, Bresler and Schulman Asset Management Corp., *In re*, 805 F.2d 120 (3d Cir. 1986), 249
Bihlmeyer, *In re*, 515 N.W.2d 236 (S.D. 1994), 478 n.194
Bilderback v. McNabb, 474 P.3d 247 (Colo. App. 2020), 276
Binday, United States v., 908 F. Supp. 2d 485 (S.D.N.Y. 2012), 172 n.41
Biocore Med. Techs., Inc. v. Khosrowshahi, 181 F.R.D. 660 (D. Kan. 1998), 140
Birano v. State, 426 P.3d 387 (Haw. 2018), 407

Bird v. Rothman, 627 P.2d 1097 (Ariz. Ct. App. 1981), 86 n.214
Bistline v. Parker, 918 F.3d 849 (10th Cir. 2019), 2
Bittle v. Elec. Ry. Improvement Co., 576 F. Supp. 2d 744 (M.D.N.C. 2008), 338 n.141
Black, *In re*, 941 P.2d 1380 (Kan. 1997), 285 n.37
Blanchard v. EdgeMark Fin. Corp., 175 F.R.D. 293 (N.D. Ill. 1997), 209 n.250
Blasi, *In re*, 660 N.Y.S.2d 151 (App. Div. 1997), 71 n.122
Blue, People v., 724 N.E.2d 920 (Ill. 2000), 418, 419 n.11
Blue Hen Mech., Inc. v. Christian Bros. Risk Pooling Tr., 117 A.3d 549 (Del. 2015), 86 n.210
Blume, *In re*, 443 P.3d 305 (Kan. 2019), 285 n.35, 325 n.62
Board of Professional Responsibility v. Parrish, 556 S.W.3d 153 (Tenn. 2018), 497–502, 508 n.66
Bolton, People v., 82 Cal. Rptr. 3d 671 (Ct. App. 2008), 378 n.63, 397
Bontrager, People v., 407 P.3d 1235 (Colo. 2017), 54, 292
Borough of Duryea v. Guarnieri, 131 S. Ct. 2488 (2011), 216
Bottoms v. Stapleton, 706 N.W.2d 411 (Iowa 2005), 13–14
Bowen, United States v., 194 F. App'x 393 (6th Cir. 2006), 331 n.100, 334 n.122
Bowers v. Ophthalmology Grp., 733 F.3d 647 (6th Cir. 2013), 29
Bower v. Bunker Hill Co., 689 F. Supp. 1032 (E.D. Wash. 1985), 199
Bowman v. Gruel Mills Nims & Pylman, LLP, No. 5:06-CV-87, 2007 WL 1203580 (W.D. Mich. Apr. 24, 2007), 454
Boyce, *In re*, 613 S.E.2d 538 (S.C. 2007), 460 n.66
Boyd, *In re*, Disciplinary Proceeding Against, 767 N.W.2d 226 (Wis. 2009), 508 n.66
Boyle, People v., 942 P.2d 1199 (Colo. 1997), 52 n.17
Bradford v. State, 734 So. 2d 364 (Ala. Crim. App. 1999), 425 n.44
Bradley, State v., HHDCV166072114S, 2018 WL 3518265 (Conn. Super. Ct. July 3, 2018), 448 n.5
Braham, People v., No. 15PDJ095, 2017 WL 1046460 (Colo. Jan. 23, 2017), 42 n.228
Branch v. State, 882 So. 2d 36 (Miss. 2004), 435 n.103
Brandt v. Med. Def. Assocs., 856 S.W.2d 667 (Mo. 1993), 189
Bratcher v. Kentucky Bar Ass'n, 290 S.W.3d 648 (Ky. 2009), 76–77, 100 n.62, 111, 169
Bridgeman v. Dist. Att'y for the Suffolk Dist., 30 N.E.3d 806 (Mass. 2015), 421
Brigham v. Colyer, No. 09-2210-JWL-DJW, 2010 WL 2131967 (D. Kan. May 27, 2010), 191 n.141, 194 n.154
Brigham Young Univ. v. Pfizer, Inc., No. 2:06-CV-890 TS BCW, 2010 WL 3855347 (D. Utah Sept. 29, 2010), 21 n.121
Bromley v. Seme, 3 N.E.3d 1254 (Ohio Ct. App. 2013), 449
Brooks v. S.C. Comm'n on Indigent Def., 797 S.E.2d 402 (S.C. Ct. App. 2017), 420 n.17
Brossart v. Janke, 942 N.W.2d 856 (N.D. 2020), 276
Brown, *In re*, 354 B.R. 535 (Bankr. N.D. Okla. 2006), 338 n.141
Brown, *In re*, 511 B.R. 843 (Bankr. S.D. Tex. 2014), 326

Brown, United States v., 595 F.3d 498 (3d Cir. 2010), 172 n.41
Browning v. A.T. & T. Paradyne, 838 F. Supp. 1564 (M.D. Fla. 1993), 80
Brown v. Cnty. of Genesee, 872 F.2d 169 (6th Cir. 1989), 473 n.166
Brown v. Commonwealth, 226 S.W.3d 74 (Ky. 2007), 410
Brown v. Daniel, 180 F.R.D. 298 (D.S.C. 1998), 438, 441
Brown v. Hamid, 856 S.W.2d 51 (Mo. 1993), 194–196
Brown v. Kelton, 380 S.W.3d 361 (Ark. 2011), 17 n.88
Brown v. St. Joseph Cnty., 148 F.R.D. 246 (N.D. Ind. 1993), 186
Brubaker v. Richmond, 943 F.2d 1363 (4th Cir. 1991), 66 n.100
Brumbelow v. N. Propane Gas Co., 308 S.E.2d 544 (Ga. 1983), 450 n.15
Brundage v. Estate of Carambio, 951 A.2d 947 (N.J. 2008), 327, 346, 347
Bruno, *In re*, 956 So. 2d 577 (La. 2007), 327 n.78, 328
Brunswick v. Statewide Grievance Comm., 931 A.2d 319 (Conn. App. Ct. 2007), 73–74, 524 n.172
Bryan, *In re*, 61 P.3d 641 (Kan. 2003), 42 n.228
Bryan Corp. v. Abrano, 52 N.E.3d 95 (Mass. 2016), 10
Bryant v. Hilst, 136 F.R.D. 487 (D. Kan. 1991), 189 n.133
Bryant v. Yorktowne Cabinetry, Inc., 538 F. Supp. 2d 948 (W.D. Va. 2008), 80, 97, 176 n.63
Bublitz v. E.I. du Pont de Nemours & Co., 196 F.R.D. 545 (S.D. Iowa 2000), 208 n.248, 213 n.276
Buckingham, State v., 772 N.W.2d 64 (Minn. 2009), 118
Budny v. Statewide Grievance Comm., No. CV960560637S, 1997 WL 331034 (Conn. Super. Ct. June 9, 1997), 355 n.245
Bumbury v. Med-Care Diabetic & Med. Supplies, Inc., 101 F. Supp. 3d 1268 (S.D. Fla. 2015), 28, 32
Burden v. CSX Transp., Inc., No. 08-cv-04-DRH, 2011 WL 3793664 (S.D. Ill. Aug. 24, 2011), 233 n.38, 233 n.39
Burghoff, *In re*, 374 B.R. 681 (Bankr. N.D. Iowa 2007), 330 n.97
Burrell v. Crown Cent. Petroleum, Inc., 176 F.R.D. 239 (E.D. Tex. 1997), 213
Burton v. Mottolese, 835 A.2d 998 (Conn. 2003), 455 n.40
Butler, *In re*, Disciplinary Action Against, 868 N.W.2d 243 (Minn. 2015), 54
Butler v. United States, 414 A.2d 844 (D.C. 1980), 397
Bynote v. Nat'l Super Mkts., Inc., 891 S.W.2d 117 (Mo. 1995), 185 n.113

Caballero v. Wikse, 92 P.3d 1076 (Idaho 2004), 449
Cada v. Costa Line, Inc., 93 F.R.D. 95 (N.D. Ill. 1981), 209
Cadlerock Joint Venture, L.P. v. Sol Greenberg & Sons Int'l, 942 N.Y.S.2d 497 (App. Div. 2012), 281 n.14, 282 n.14
Cagle, State v., 641 S.E.2d 705 (N.C. Ct. App. 2007), 346 n.186
Calamar Enters., Inc. v. Blue Forest Land Grp., LLC, 222 F. Supp. 3d 257 (W.D.N.Y. 2016), 31 n.170
Calan, State *ex rel.*, v. Kemp Stone, Inc., 418 P.3d 708 (Okla. Civ. App. 2017), 52 n.16
Caldwell v. Baptist Mem'l Hosp., No. W2015-01076-COA-R10-CV, 2016 WL 3226431 (Tenn. Ct. App. June 3, 2016), 191

Caldwell v. Cablevision Sys. Corp., 925 N.Y.S.2d 103 (App. Div. 2011), 146
Caldwell v. Chauvin, 464 S.W.3d 139 (Ky. 2015), 190, 191, 192
Calhoun, People v., 815 N.E.2d 492 (Ill. App. Ct. 2004), 380 n.72
Calise v. Brady Sullivan Harris Mills, LLC, No. 18-99WES, 2019 WL 1397245 (D.R.I. Mar. 28, 2019), 79 n.177, 97, 176, 182
Callahan v. Bledsoe, No. 16-2310-JAR-GLR, 2017 WL 590254 (D. Kan. Feb. 14, 2017), 194 n.154
Callister, *In re*, Discipline of, No. 70901, 2017 WL 3160232 (Nev. July 25, 2017), 141
Camden v. State of Md., 910 F. Supp. 1115 (D. Md. 1996), 220 n.324
CAMICO Mut. Ins. Co. v. Heffler, Radetich & Saitta, LLP, No. 11-4753, 2013 WL 315716 (E.D. Pa. Jan. 28, 2013), 6
Campbell, *In re*, 199 P.3d 776 (Kan. 2009), 295 n.101
Campbell v. Indep. Outlook, Inc., No. 04AP-310, 2004 WL 2892884 (Ohio Ct. App. Dec. 14, 2004), 31 n.169
Campbell v. State, 432 S.W.3d 673 (Ark. Ct. App. 2014), 434 n.94
Campiti, *In re*, 905 N.E.2d 408 (Ind. 2009), 285 n.37
Caplan v. Braverman, 876 F. Supp. 710 (E.D. Pa. 1995), 424 n.41
Capper, *In re*, 757 N.E.2d 138 (Ind. 2001), 100 n.65
Caranchini, *In re*, 956 S.W.2d 910 (Mo. 1997), 70, 72 n.134, 524 n.172
Cardinal Robotics v. Moody, 694 S.E.2d 346 (Ga. 2010), 26
Cardinal Servs., Inc., *In re*, No. CIVA 00-1909, CIVA 00-1910, 2006 WL 2089925 (W.D. La. July 21, 2006), 439 n.129
Cardwell, *In re*, 50 P.3d 897 (Colo. 2002), 325 n.62, 478
Carey, *In re*, 89 S.W.3d 477 (Mo. 2002), 32
Carmody v. Mikesell, No. 16-cv-02603-PAB-NYW, 2017 WL 5191802 (D. Colo. Nov. 9, 2017), 194 n.154
Carnegie Cos. v. Summit Props., Inc., 918 N.E.2d 1052 (Ohio Ct. App. 2009), 16
Carona, United States v., 630 F.3d 917 (9th Cir. 2011), 118 n.179
Carpenter, *In re*, 95 P.3d 203 (Or. 2004), 123
Carpentino's Case, *In re*, 651 A.2d 1 (N.H. 1994), 476
Carroll v. Town of Univ. Park, 12 F. Supp. 2d 475 (D. Md. 1997), 424 n.40
Carta *ex rel.* Estate of Carta v. Lumbermens Mut. Cas. Co., 419 F. Supp. 2d 23 (D. Mass. 2006), 432 n.81, 438
Carta v. Lumbermens Mut. Cas. Co., 419 F. Supp. 2d 23 (D. Mass. 2006), 426 n.48
Carter-Herman v. City of Phila., 897 F. Supp. 899 (E.D. Pa. 1995), 186
Cartier v. Symbolix, Inc., 386 F. Supp. 2d 354 (S.D.N.Y. 2005), 114 n.151
Cathedral Ct. Assocs., L.P. v. Cathedral Props. Corp., 983 N.Y.S.2d 277 (App. Div. 2014), 425 n.47
Cathey v. State, 60 P.3d 192 (Alaska Ct. App. 2002), 517 n.129
Caulfield, *In re*, 683 So. 2d 714 (La. 1996), 69 n.114
Cedar Island Improvement Ass'n, Inc. v. Drake Assocs., Inc., No. CV075002871, 2009 WL 415991 (Conn. Super. Ct. Jan. 28, 2009), 472 n.164
CEF Funding, L.L.C. v. Sher Garner Cahill Richter Klein & Hilbert, L.L.C., Civ. A. No. 09-6623, 2010 WL 2773116 (E.D. La. July 9, 2010), 421
Celgard, LLC v. LG Chem, Ltd., 594 F. App'x 669 (Fed. Cir. 2014), 10–12

Celgene Corp. v. KV Pharm. Co., Civ. Action No. 07-4819 (SDW), 2008 WL 2937415 (D.N.J. July 29, 2008), 278 n.181
Centennial Mgmt. Servs., Inc. v. Axa Re Vie, 193 F.R.D. 671 (D. Kan. 2000), 148, 149 n.72
Cent. Fla. Mach. Co. v. Williams, 424 So. 2d 201 (Fla. Dist. Ct. App. 1983), 86 n.214
Cen v. Att'y Gen., 825 F.3d 177 (3d Cir. 2016), 276
Cesnik, State v., No. COA 16-590, 2017 WL 490486 (N.C. Ct. App. Feb. 7, 2017), 426 n.50
Cesso v. Todd, 82 N.E.3d 1074 (Mass. App. Ct. 2017), 3, 246
Chambers, People v., 154 P.3d 419 (Colo. 2006), 94 n.25, 293 n.90, 467 n.119
Chambers, State v., 994 A.2d 1248 (Conn. 2010), 378 n.63, 379, 379 n.72, 389 n.119
Champoir v. Champoir, 138 N.E.3d 530 (Ohio Ct. App. 2019), 426
Chapman Eng'rs, Inc. v. Natural Gas Sales Co., 766 F. Supp. 949 (D. Kan. 1991), 10, 432
Chappell v. Cosgrove, 916 P.2d 836 (N.M. 1996), 427 n.53
Charges of Unprof'l Conduct in Panel File No. 41310, *In re*, 899 N.W.2d 821 (Minn. 2017), 41 n.226
Charges of Unprof'l Conduct in Panel File No. 41755, 912 N.W.2d 224 (Minn. 2018), 170 n.30, 172, 179
Charges of Unprof'l Conduct Involving File No. 17139, *In re*, 720 N.W.2d 807 (Minn. 2006), 495
Charlap v. Khan, 972 N.Y.S.2d 871 (Sup. Ct. 2013), 176
Charleston Area Med. Ctr., State *ex rel.*, v. Zakaib, 437 S.E.2d 759 (W. Va. 1993), 80, 98, 177
Chevron Corp. v. Donziger, 11 Civ. 0691 (LAK), 2018 WL 1137119 (S.D.N.Y. Mar. 21, 2018), 143
Chew v. KPMG LLP, 407 F. Supp. 2d 790 (S.D. Miss. 2006), 346 n.186
Chicago Flood Litig., *In re*, 682 N.E.2d 421 (Ill. App. Ct. 1997), 199
Chief Disciplinary Counsel v. Rozbicki, No. CV116004519S, 2013 WL 1277298 (Conn. Super. Ct. Mar. 8, 2013), 295, 494 n.1
Chi. Ins. Co. v. Capwill, No. 1:01cv2588, 2011 WL 6181337 (N.D. Ohio Dec. 13, 2011), 143, 148 n.72
Chism v. Tri-State Constr., Inc., 374 P.3d 193 (Wash. Ct. App. 2016), 277
Chi. Title & Tr. Co. v. Anderson, 532 N.E.2d 595 (Ill. App. Ct. 1988), 326
Chloé v. DesignersImports.com USA, Inc., No. 07-CV-1791 (CS) (GAY), 2009 WL 1227927 (S.D.N.Y. Apr. 30, 2009), 123
Chrispens v. Coastal Ref. & Mktg., Inc., 897 P.2d 104 (Kan. 1995), 32
Christensen v. Kiewit-Murdock Inv. Corp., 815 F.2d 206 (2d Cir. 1987), 209, 214 n.284
Chriswell v. Big Score Entm't, LLC, No. 11 C 00861, 2013 WL 315743 (N.D. Ill. Jan. 28, 2013), 337
Cincinnati Bar Ass'n v. Statzer, 800 N.E.2d 1117 (Ohio 2003), 357–358, 483
Cincinnati Ins. Co. v. Wills, 717 N.E.2d 151 (Ind. 1999), 4
Cinergy Corp., United States v., No. 1:99-cv-1693-LJM-JMS, 2008 WL 7679914 (S.D. Ind. Dec. 18, 2008), 139 n.9, 153 n.97
CIT Grp./Commercial Servs. v. Prsico, 640 F. Supp. 2d 401 (S.D.N.Y. 2009), 337
Citizens of Humanity, LLC v. Hass, 259 Cal. Rptr. 3d 380 (Ct. App. 2020), 86

City of Cleveland v. Cleveland Elec. Illuminating Co., 440 F. Supp. 193 (N.D. Ohio 1976), 19
City of Little Rock v. Cash, 644 S.W.2d 229 (Ark. 1982), 18
City of Livonia Emps. Ret. Sys. v. Boeing Co., 711 F.3d 754 (7th Cir. 2013), 318
City of N.Y. v. Beretta U.S.A. Corp., 524 F.3d 384 (2d Cir. 2008), 216, 217
Claim of Roberts for Att'y Fees, 949 N.W.2d 299 (Neb. 2020), 276
Clark, State v., 738 N.W.2d 316 (Minn. 2007), 75 n.151, 100 n.62, 169 n.22
Clark's Case, *In re*, 37 A.3d 327 (N.H. 2012), 323 n.53
Clark v. Beverly Health & Rehab. Servs., 797 N.E.2d 905 (Mass. 2003), 80
Clark v. Druckman, 624 S.E.2d 864 (W. Va. 2005), 85, 484
Cleveland Bar Ass'n v. McMahon, 872 N.E.2d 261 (Ohio 2007), 471
Cleveland Hair Clinic, Inc. v. Puig, 200 F.3d 1063 (7th Cir. 2000), 375
C.L. *ex rel.* K.B. v. Mars Area Sch. Dist., No. 2:14-cv-1666, 2015 WL 3968343 (W.D. Pa. June 30, 2015), 334 n.122, 336 n.128
Clinard v. Blackwood, 46 S.W.3d 177 (Tenn. 2001), 30 n.167
Clothier, *In re*, 344 P.3d 370 (Kan. 2015), 287 n.49, 509
Clough v. Richelo, 616 S.E.2d 888 (Ga. Ct. App. 2005), 429
C.M., State *ex rel.*, 336 P.3d 1069 (Utah Ct. App. 2014), 508 n.65
Coburn Optical Indus. Inc. v. Cilco, Inc., 610 F. Supp. 656 (M.D.N.C. 1985), 55 n.26
Coffman v. Indianapolis Fire Dep't, 619 F. Supp. 2d 582 (S.D. Ind. 2008), 168
Cofield v. Va. State Bar *ex rel.* Second Dist. Comm., 827 S.E.2d 602 (Va. 2019), 324 n.53
Cohen v. Jaffe Raitt Heuer & Weiss, P.C., 768 F. App'x 440 (6th Cir. 2019), 3
Cohen v. Rogers, 789 S.E.2d 352 (Ga. Ct. App. 2016), 426 n.48
Cohen v. Statewide Grievance Comm., 208 A.3d 676 (Conn. App. Ct. 2019), 317
Coleman, *In re*, 295 S.W.3d 857 (Mo. 2009), 448 n.4
Colin, *In re*, Discipline of, 448 P.3d 556 (Nev. 2019), 494 n.1, 501, 502–504
Collado v. Pavlow, 951 So. 2d 69 (Fla. Dist. Ct. App. 2007), 449
Collie, *In re*, 765 S.E.2d 835 (S.C. 2014), 50
Collins, *In re*, 224 S.W.3d 798 (Tex. App. 2007), 189
Collins Entm't, Inc. v. White, 611 S.E.2d 262 (S.C. Ct. App. 2005), 439, 443 n.158
Colo. Sup. Ct., United States v., 87 F.3d 1161 (10th Cir. 1996), 356
Columbo v. Puig, 745 So. 2d 1106 (Fla. Dist. Ct. App. 1999), 424 n.41
Columbus Bar Ass'n v. Farmer, 855 N.E.2d 462 (Ohio 2006), 290, 330 n.97, 334 n.121
Columbus Bar Ass'n v. Vogel, 881 N.E.2d 1244 (Ohio 2008), 318
Colvin, *In re*, 336 P.3d 823 (Kan. 2014), 69 n.115, 522 n.165
Comfort, *In re*, 159 P.3d 1011 (Kan. 2007), 103, 182, 296, 306, 308, 502 n.30
Comish, *In re*, 889 So. 2d 236 (La. 2004), 103, 104
Comm'n for Lawyer Discipline v. Hanna, 513 S.W.3d 175 (Tex. App. 2016), 276
Comm. on Legal Ethics of the W. Va. State Bar v. Farber, 408 S.E.2d 274 (W. Va. 1991), 508 n.72
Comm. on Legal Ethics of the W. Va. State Bar v. Printz, 416 S.E.2d 720 (W. Va. 1992), 299, 301, 303, 304 n.161
Comm. on Legal Ethics of the W. Va. State Bar v. Sheatsley, 452 S.E.2d 75 (W. Va. 1994), 141 n.22

Comm. on Prof'l Ethics & Conduct of the Iowa State Bar Ass'n v. Crary, 245 N.W.2d 298 (Iowa 1976), 372 n.33
Commonwealth v. Brown, 226 S.W.3d 74 (Ky. 2007), 380 n.72, 412
Commonwealth v. Chmiel, 30 A.3d 1111 (Pa. 2011), 50, 292 n.77, 341 n.160, 520 n.148
Commonwealth v. Cousin, 88 N.E.3d 822 (Mass. 2018), 13 n.70, 38 n.205
Commonwealth v. Delnegro, 75 N.E.3d 73 (Mass. App. Ct. 2017), 426 n.48, 433
Commonwealth v. Jermyn, 620 A.2d 1128 (Pa. 1993), 397
Commonwealth v. Leiva, 146 N.E.3d 1093 (Mass. 2020), 381, 396, 403
Commonwealth v. Miranda, 146 N.E.3d 435 (Mass. 2020), 395, 403
Commonwealth v. Miranda, 934 N.E.2d 222 (Mass. 2010), 141 n.22
Commonwealth v. Mitchell, 781 N.E.2d 1237 (Mass. 2003), 379 n.63, 380 n.72, 397, 399–403
Commonwealth v. Santiago, 978 A.2d 349 (Pa. 2009), 525
Commonwealth v. Schultz, 133 A.3d 294 (Pa. Super. Ct. 2016), 258 n.74, 262
Commonwealth v. Ware, 128 N.E.3d 29 (Mass. 2019), 407, 407 n.216
Complaint of PMD Enters., Inc., 215 F. Supp. 2d 519 (D.N.J. 2002), 75 n.151, 100, 150 n.81, 169
Compton v. Kittleson, 171 P.3d 172 (Alaska 2007), 448
Conduct of Hostetter, *In re*, 238 P.3d 13 (Or. 2010), 27, 30
Conduct of Jackson, *In re*, 223 P.3d 387 (Or. 2009), 325 n.62
Conduct of Maurer, *In re*, 431 P.3d 410 (Or. 2018), 107
Conduct of McGraw, *In re*, 414 P.3d 841 (Or. 2018), 51, 284, 295 n.106
Conduct of Obert, *In re*, 282 P.3d 825 (Or. 2012), 51
Conduct of Skagen, *In re*, 149 P.3d 1171 (Or. 2006), 106, 469 n.133
Conduct of Weidner, *In re*, 801 P.2d 828 (Or. 1990), 4
Conduct of White, *In re*, 815 P.2d 1257 (Or. 1991), 104, 296
Congress v. Tillman, No. 09-10419, 2009 WL 1738511 (E.D. Mich. June 16, 2009), 194 n.154
Consol. Paving, Inc. v. Cnty. of Peoria, Ill., No. 10-CV-1045, 2013 WL 916212 (C.D. Ill. Mar. 8, 2013), 330 n.97, 331 n.99, 334 n.122
Consol. Rail Corp. v. CSX Transp., Inc., No. 09-cv-10179, 2012 WL 511572 (E.D. Mich. Feb. 16, 2012), 148
Cont'l Cas. Co. v. Pullman, Comley, Bradley & Reeves, 929 F.2d 103 (2d Cir. 1991), 5
Cooper, *In re*, 78 N.E.3d 1098 (Ind. 2017), 507
Corbello v. DeVito, No. 2:08-cv-00867-RCJ-PAL, 2011 WL 3859466 (D. Nev. Aug. 31, 2011), 394
Corizzi, *In re*, 803 A.2d 438 (D.C. 2002), 466, 476 n.180
Corp. Res. Servs., Inc., *In re*, 595 B.R. 434 (S.D.N.Y. 2019), 431 n.73
Coscia v. Cunningham, 299 S.E.2d 880 (Ga. 1983), 4
Cosenza v. Kramer, 200 Cal. Rptr. 18 (Ct. App. 1984), 523
Cottingham, *In re*, 423 P.3d 818 (Wash. 2018), 51
Cottonwood Est., Inc. v. Paradise Builders, Inc., 624 P.2d 296 (Ariz. Ct. App. 1981), 427

Counsel for Discipline of the Nebraska Supreme Ct. v. Chvala, 935 N.W.2d 446 (Neb. 2019), 2, 3, 246
Couns. for Discipline of the Neb. Sup. Ct., State *ex rel.*, v. Gast, 896 N.W.2d 583 (Neb. 2017), 497, 509 n.76
Couns. for Discipline of the Neb. Sup. Ct., State *ex rel.*, v. Hanson, 941 N.W.2d 193 (Neb. 2020), 337 n.137
Cox, United States v., 743 F. App'x 509 (4th Cir. 2018), 450
Crenshaw, *In re*, 815 N.E.2d 1013 (Ind. 2004), 508 n.67
Cresta, United States v., 825 F.2d 538 (1st Cir. 1987), 139 n.11
Cropp v. Woleslagel, 485 P.2d 1271 (Kan. 1971), 477
Croskey v. BMW of N. Am., No. 02-73747, 2005 WL 4704767 (E.D. Mich. Nov. 10, 2005), 194
Cross, *In re*, 327 P.3d 660 (Wash. 2014), 379, 379 n.70
Crossen, *In re*, 880 N.E.2d 352 (Mass. 2008), 111 n.130, 126 n.233, 128 n.239
Crumpton, United States v., 23 F. Supp. 2d 1218 (D. Colo. 1998), 346
Cruz-Aponte v. Caribbean Petroleum Corp., Civ. No. 09-2092 (FAB), 285 n.36
CSX Transp., Inc. v. Gilkison, Civ. A. No. 5:05CV202, 2011 WL 5445114 (N.D. W. Va. Nov. 9, 2011), 170 n.30
CTC Imps. & Exps. v. Nigerian Petroleum Corp., 951 F.2d 573 (3d Cir. 1991), 53 n.21, 54 n.26
Cunningham v. Sams, 588 S.E.2d 484 (N.C. Ct. App. 2003), 421, 443, 444
Curley v. N. Am. Man Boy Love Ass'n, No. Civ.A. 00-10956-GAO, 2003 WL 21696550 (D. Mass. Mar. 31, 2003), 143 n.35, 144
Curry, *In re*, 880 N.E.2d 388 (Mass. 2008), 111 n.130
Cushing v. Greyhound Lines, Inc., 991 N.E.2d 28 (Ill. App. Ct. 2013), 441
Cuyahoga Cnty. Bar Ass'n v. Gonzales, 733 N.E.2d 587 (Ohio 2000), 279 n.1
CVS Caremark Corp. v. Lauriello, 175 So. 3d 596 (Ala. 2014), 432

Dalton, People v., 367 P.3d 126 (Colo. 2016), 94 n.25
Damron v. CSX Transp., Inc., 920 N.E.2d 169 (Ohio Ct. App. 2009), 95 n.37, 169 n.25, 435 n.103
Daniels v. Alander, 818 A.2d 106 (Conn. App. Ct. 2003), 323 n.51, 326, 327 n.78, 353 n.230, 478 n.198
Daniels v. City of N.Y., 138 F. Supp. 2d 562 (S.D.N.Y. 2001), 200
Dargie, *In re*, No. 17-BG-1075, 2017 WL 5180719 (D.C. Nov. 9, 2017), 465 n.102
Daugerdas, United States v., 867 F. Supp. 2d 445 (S.D.N.Y. 2012), 232 n.36
Davidson-Nadwodny v. Wal-Mart Assocs., Inc., No. CCB-07-2595, 2010 WL 1328572 (D. Md. Mar. 26, 2010), 192
Davis, United States v., 261 F.3d 1 (1st Cir. 2001), 139 n.11, 147, 149
Davis v. Bacigalupi, 711 F. Supp. 2d 609 (E.D. Va. 2010), 338 n.141
Davis v. Creditors Interchange Receivable Mgmt., LLC, 585 F. Supp. 2d 968 (N.D. Ohio 2008), 80, 96, 97, 174
Davis v. State Bar, 655 P.2d 1276 (Cal. 1983), 4
Davis v. TWC Dealer Grp., Inc., 254 Cal. Rptr. 3d 443 (Ct. App. 2019), 325 n.62
Davis v. Wieland, 557 S.W.3d 340 (Mo. Ct. App. 2018), 195 n.167

Dawley v. NF Energy Corp. of Am., 492 F. App'x 77 (11th Cir. 2012), 484
DeBiasi v. Charter Cnty. of Wayne, 284 F. Supp. 2d 760 (E.D. Mich. 2003), 438 n.125
Debrincat v. Fischer, 217 So. 3d 68 (Fla. 2017), 85
DeFazio v. Wallis, 459 F. Supp. 2d 159 (E.D.N.Y. 2006), 30
DeForest v. Johnny Chisholm Global Events, LLC, No. 3:08cv498/MCR/EMT, 2010 WL 1792094 (N.D. Fla. May 4, 2010), 337
DeGuzman, State v., 701 P.2d 1287 (Haw. 1985), 389, 407, 412
DeHarrport v. W.E.J., 348 P.3d 1192 (Or. Ct. App. 2015), 86
DeJean, *In re*, 262 So. 3d 424 (La. 2019), 287 n.49
DeLeo v. Nussbaum, 821 A.2d 744 (Conn. 2003), 8 n.38, 9
Dello Russo v. Nagel, 817 A.2d 426 (N.J. Super. Ct. App. Div. 2003), 85
Delso v. Trustees for the Retirement Plan for the Hourly Emps. of Merck & Co., Civ. A. No. 04-3009, 2007 WL 766349 (D.N.J. Mar. 6, 2007), 336
Demesa v. Adams, 994 N.E.2d 1007 (Ill. App. Ct. 2013), 420 n.20
Dennis, United States v., 843 F.2d 652 (2d Cir. 1988), 122
DePallo, People v., 754 N.E.2d 751 (N.Y. 2001), 396
DeRosa, People v., No. 5-12-0227, 2013 WL 6221381 (Ill. App. Ct. Nov. 27, 2013), 397
Derrickson v. Derrickson, 541 A.2d 149 (D.C. 1988), 29
Design Tex Grp., Inc. v. U.S. Vinyl Mfg. Corp., No. 04 Civ. 5002(JSR), 2005 WL 357125 (S.D.N.Y. Feb. 14, 2005), 114 n.151
Deutscher v. Gabel, 202 P.3d 355 (Wash. Ct. App. 2009), 318
DeVaux v. Am. Home Assur. Co., 444 N.E.2d 355 (Mass. 1983), 3, 246
DeWilde v. Guy Gannett Publ'g Co., 797 F. Supp. 55 (D. Me. 1992), 331 n.99, 334 n.121
DG Cogen Partners, LLC v. Lane Powell PC, 917 F. Supp. 2d 1123 (D. Or. 2013), 4
Diaz v. Comm'n for Lawyer Discipline, 953 S.W.2d 435 (Tex. App. 1997), 317 n.16
Diet Drug Litig., *In re*, 895 A.2d 493 (N.J. Super. Ct. Law Div. 2005), 191
Dieter v. Regents of Univ. of Cal., 963 F. Supp. 908 (E.D. Cal. 1997), 38 n.205
Digitek Prod. Liab. Litig., *In re*, 648 F. Supp. 2d 795 (S.D. W. Va. 2009), 80, 97, 176 n.63
Dike v. People, 30 P.3d 197 (Colo. 2001), 345
Dilallo v. Riding Safely, Inc., 687 So. 2d 353 (Fla. Dist. Ct. App. 1997), 346 n.185
DiMartino v. Eighth Judicial Dist. Ct., 66 P.3d 945 (Nev. 2003), 421 n.23, 424 n.41, 438 n.121
Dimas-Martinez v. State, 385 S.W.3d 238 (Ark. 2011), 234 n.42
Dimick, *In re*, 969 N.E.2d 17 (Ind. 2012), 307 n.187
DiNardo Seaside Tower Ltd. v. Sikorsky Aircraft Corp., 100 A.3d 413 (Conn. App. Ct. 2014), 425 n.47
DiOssi v. Edison, 583 A.2d 1343 (Del. Super. Ct. 1990), 80, 97, 177
Disbarment of Rogers, *In re*, S. Ct. Civ. Nos. 2013-0079, 2013-0044, 2013-0106, 2013-0116, 2013 WL 6507168 (V.I. Dec. 12, 2013), 319 n.32
Disciplinary Action Against Adams, *In re*, 942 N.W.2d 720 (Minn. 2020), 319 n.31
Disciplinary Action Against Butler, 868 N.W.2d 243 (Minn. 2015), 292

Disciplinary Action Against Johnson, 743 N.W.2d 117 (N.D. 2007), 293
Disciplinary Action Against Kennedy, *In re*, 864 N.W.2d 342 (Minn. 2015), 107
Disciplinary Action Against Kurzman, *In re*, 871 N.W.2d 753 (Minn. 2015), 287 n.49
Disciplinary Action Against Mertz, 712 N.W.2d 849 (N.D. 2006), 296 n.108
Disciplinary Action Against Torgerson, *In re*, 870 N.W.2d 602 (Minn. 2015), 285 n.35, 287 n.49
Disciplinary Action Against Ulanowski, *In re*, 800 N.W.2d 785 (Minn. 2011), 285 n.36
Disciplinary Action Against Ward, *In re*, 881 N.W.2d 226 (N.D. 2016), 2
Disciplinary Action Against Williams, *In re*, 917 N.W.2d 423 (Minn. 2018), 285 n.36
Disciplinary Counsel v. Cox, 862 N.E.2d 514 (Ohio 2007), 287 n.49
Disciplinary Counsel v. Sartini, 871 N.E.2d 543 (Ohio 2007), 75 n.151, 100 n.62, 169
Disciplinary Counsel v. Shimko, 983 N.E.2d 1300 (Ohio 2012), 494 n.1
Disciplinary Counsel v. Spinazze, 149 N.E.3d 503 (Ohio 2020), 320 n.36, 325 n.62
Disciplinary Couns. v. Brockler, 48 N.E.3d 557 (Ohio 2016), 115 n.162, 118 n.184, 231 n.30
Disciplinary Couns. v. Chambers, 928 N.E.2d 1061 (Ohio 2010), 307 n.190
Disciplinary Couns. v. Harmon, 141 N.E.3d 142 (Ohio 2019), 325 n.62
Disciplinary Couns. v. Serafinowitz, 123 A.3d 1279 (Conn. App. Ct. 2015), 508 n.66
Disciplinary Couns. v. Shimko, 131 N.E.3d 52 (Ohio 2019), 41 n.226
Disciplinary Couns. v. Valentino, 730 A.2d 479 (Pa. 1999), 375
Disciplinary Matter of Shea, 273 P.3d 612 (Alaska 2012), 285 n.36
Disciplinary Proc. Against Bach, *In re*, 887 N.W.2d 335 (Wis. 2016), 292, 293
Disciplinary Proc. Against Booker, *In re*, 857 N.W.2d 890 (Wis. 2015), 338 n.141
Disciplinary Proc. Against Inglimo, *In re*, 740 N.W.2d 125 (Wis. 2007), 297 n.114
Disciplinary Proceeding Against Kamb, *In re*, 305 P.3d 1091 (Wash. 2013), 297 n.114
Disciplinary Proceedings Against Johns, *In re*, 847 N.W.2d 179 (Wis. 2014), 104, 296
Discipline of Att'y, *In re*, 815 N.E.2d 1072 (Mass. 2004), 298
Discipline of Colin, *In re*, 448 P.3d 556 (Nev. 2019), 284
Discipline of Two Att'ys, 660 N.E.2d 1093 (Mass. 1996), 298
Diversified Grp., Inc. v. Daugerdas, 139 F. Supp. 2d 445 (S.D.N.Y. 2001), 3, 246
Dixon, *In re*, 994 N.E.2d 1129 (Ind. 2013), 59 n.56, 320 n.36, 497, 517–518
D.J. Inv. Grp., L.L.C. v. DAE/Westbrook, L.L.C., 147 P.3d 414 (Utah 2006), 438, 442 n.148
Doctor's Assocs., Inc. v. Windham, 81 A.3d 230 (Conn. App. Ct. 2013), 355 n.244
Dodge v. Dodge, 108 P.3d 362 (Idaho 2005), 322, 325 n.62, 478
Dodona I, LLC v. Goldman, Sachs & Co., 300 F.R.D. 182 (S.D.N.Y. 2014), 199
Dodrill v. Executive Director, 824 S.W.2d 383 (Ark. 1992), 71–72
Doe v. Md. Bd. of Social Workers, 840 A.2d 744 (Md. Ct. Spec. App. 2004), 460

Doe v. Super. Ct. of San Diego Cnty., 248 Cal. Rptr. 3d 314 (Ct. App. 2019), 96, 174
Doe v. Yim, 269 Cal. Rptr. 3d 613 (Ct. App. 2020), 418 n.3, 421, 422 n.32
Donaldson, People v., 113 Cal. Rptr. 2d 548 (Ct. App. 2001), 419, 437
Dondore v. NGK Metals Corp., 152 F. Supp. 2d 662 (E.D. Pa. 2001), 199 n.186
Dorothy, *In re*, 605 N.W.2d 493 (S.D. 2000), 318, 478
Dougherty v. Pepper Hamilton LLP, 133 A.3d 792 (Pa. Super. Ct. 2016), 43 n.233
Doughty, *In re*, 832 A.2d 724 (Del. 2003), 106, 297, 469
Douglass v. Delta Air Lines, Inc., 897 F.2d 1336 (5th Cir. 1990), 346
Downs, People v., 83 N.E.3d 584 (Ill. App. Ct. 2017), 51
Dreamplay, Inc., *In re*, 534 B.R. 106 (Bankr. D. Md. 2015), 338 n.141
Driscoll, *In re*, 856 N.E.2d 840 (Mass. 2006), 379
Droste v. Julien, 477 F.3d 1030 (8th Cir. 2007), 421
Drost v. Sec'y of Health & Human Servs., No. 01-502V, 2010 WL 3291933 (Fed. Cl. July 30, 2010), 344
Druten, *In re*, 301 P.3d 319 (Kan. 2013), 369, 553, 611
Duda v. Duda, Nos. 1 CA-CV 09-0146, 1 CA-CV 09-0192, 2010 WL 324452 (Ariz. Ct. App. Jan. 28, 2010), 166
Dultra v. US Med. Home, Inc., No. 13 C 07598, 2014 WL 1347107 (N.D. Ill. Apr. 4, 2014), 346
Dunlap v. Bd. of Prof'l Responsibility, 595 S.W.3d 593 (Tenn. 2020), 320 n.36, 326
Dunnigan, United States v., 507 U.S. 87 (1993), 396
Duran v. Carris, 238 F.3d 1268 (10th Cir. 2001), 338
Durham, United States v., 139 F.3d 1325 (10th Cir. 1998), 390
Dvorak, *In re*, Disciplinary Action Against, 611 N.W.2d 147 (N.D. 2003), 195 n.166
Dyll v. Adams, No. Civ.A. 3:94-CV-2734-D, 1997 WL 222918 (N.D. Tex. Apr. 29, 1997), 139 n.10
Dynamic 3D Geosols. LLC v. Schlumberger Ltd., 837 F.3d 1280 (Fed. Cir. 2016), 1 n.1

Eagan v. Jackson, 855 F. Supp. 765 (E.D. Pa. 1994), 355
Eckelman, *In re*, 144 P.3d 713 (Kan. 2006), 508 n.67
Edgett, People v., 560 N.W.2d 360 (Mich. Ct. App. 1996), 398
Edison, *In re*, 724 N.W.2d 579 (N.D. 2006), 94, 293, 466, 473 n.167
Edwards, United States v., 154 F.3d 915 (9th Cir. 1998), 418 n.9
Edwardson, *In re*, Disciplinary Action Against, 647 N.W.2d 126 (N.D. 2002), 324 n.53
Edward Wildman Palmer LLP v. Super. Ct., 180 Cal. Rptr. 3d 620 (Ct. App. 2014), 2
EEOC v. Dana Corp., 202 F. Supp. 2d 827 (N.D. Ind. 2002), 199
EEOC v. Day & Zimmerman NPS, Inc., 265 F. Supp. 3d 179 (D. Conn. 2017), 208 n.248
EEOC v. Hora, Inc., No. 03-cv-01429, 2005 WL 1387982 (E.D. Pa. June 8, 2005), 79
EEOC v. Mitsubishi Motor Mfg. of Am., Inc., 102 F.3d 869 (7th Cir. 1996), 206 n.231

EEOC v. SVT, LLC, 297 F.R.D. 336 (N.D. Ind. 2014), 79 n.177, 97, 208 n.245
EEOC v. Univ. of Chi. Med. Ctr., No. 11 C 6379, 2012 WL 1329171 (N.D. Ill. Apr. 16, 2012), 79 n.177, 176 n.63
Ehrnstein, People v., 471 P.3d 813 (Colo. 2018), 421, 422 n.28
Eicher, *In re*, Discipline of, 661 N.W.2d 354 (S.D. 2003), 307, 307 n.190
Eichhorn-Hicks, *In re*, Disciplinary Action Against, 916 N.W.2d 32 (Minn. 2018), 454 n.39
Eisenberg, *In re*, Disciplinary Proceeding Against, 778 N.W.2d 645 (Wis. 2010), 71 n.122
Ekekwe-Kaufman, *In re*, 210 A.3d 775 (D.C. 2019), 105
El Camino Res., Ltd. v. Huntington Nat'l Bank, 623 F. Supp. 2d 863 (W.D. Mich. 2007), 12
Eleven Vehicles, United States v., 966 F. Supp. 361 (E.D. Pa. 1997), 336, 337
Ellis, United States v., 868 F.3d 1155 (10th Cir. 2017), 30
Ellis v. State of Me., 448 F.2d 1325 (1st Cir. 1971), 337 n.138
Elzy, United States v., 22 M.J. 640 (A.C.M.R. 1986), 414
Engstrom v. Goodman, 271 P.3d 959 (Wash. Ct. App. 2012), 179
Entzminger, *In re*, 831 S.E.2d 642 (N.C. 2019), 325 n.62
Envtl. Ins. Declaratory Judgment Actions, *In re*, 600 A.2d 165 (N.J. Super. Ct. Law Div. 1991), 85 n.204
Epright v. Liberty Mut. Ins. Co., No. CV166016217S, 2019 WL 3220580 (Conn. Super. Ct. June 18, 2019), 196 n.171
Escobar v. Mazie, 217 A.3d 163 (N.J. Super. Ct. App. Div. 2019), 421, 423 n.34
Esgar, *In re*, 642 S.E.2d 563 (S.C. 2007), 455 n.40
ESN, LLC v. Cisco Sys., Inc., 685 F. Supp. 2d 631 (E.D. Tex. 2009), 139 n.9
Espe, State v., Nos. A10-1569, A11-2066, 2012 WL 4328611 (Minn. Ct. App. Sept. 24, 2012), 422 n.28
Essex Ins. Co. v. Tyler, 309 F. Supp. 2d 1270 (D. Colo. 2004), 5
Estate of Andrews by Andrews v. United States, 804 F. Supp. 820 (E.D. Va. 1992), 433
Estate of McLemore v. McLemore, 63 So. 3d 468 (Miss. 2011), 50, 292 n.77, 341 n.160
Estate of Miller v. Storey, 903 N.W.2d 759 (Wis. 2017), 449
Estate of Netzorg, *In re*, 15 P.3d 926 (Mont. 2000), 180 n.82
Evangelist v. Green Tree Servicing, LLC, Civ. No. 12-15687, 2013 WL 2393142 (E.D. Mich. May 31, 2013), 344
Evanson, United States v., 584 F.3d 904 (10th Cir. 2009), 418
Evans v. Prof'l Transp., Inc., No. 1:12-cv-202, 2014 WL 1908808 (E.D. Tenn. May 13, 2014), 199
Exterior Sys., Inc. v. Noble Composites, Inc., 210 F. Supp. 2d 1062 (N.D. Ind. 2002), 37

Faison v. Thornton, 863 F. Supp. 1204 (D. Nev. 1993), 100, 179, 180 n.79
Falconer v. Leigh Hanson, Inc., Civ. A. No. 4:11–CV–373, 2013 WL 3480382 (S.D. Tex. July 9, 2013), 338 n.141
Falls Church Grp., Ltd. v. Tyler, Cooper & Alcorn, LLP, 912 A.2d 1019 (Conn. 2007), 86

Farquhar, *In re*, 492 F.2d 561 (D.C. Cir. 1973), 360
Farrington v. Law Firm of Sessions, Fishman, 687 So. 2d 997 (La. 1997), 420
Fed. Sav. & Loan Ins. Corp. v. Hildenbrand, Civ. A. No. 89-A-535, 1989 WL 107377 (D. Colo. Sept. 8, 1989), 84, 168
Fee, *In re*, 898 P.2d 975 (Ariz. 1995), 480–483
Feld's Case, *In re*, 815 A.2d 383 (N.H. 2002), 370 n.14, 372
Feliberty v. Damon, 527 N.E.2d 261 (N.Y. 1988), 5
Fernandez v. Comm'r of Corr., 220 A.3d 216 (Conn. App. Ct. 2019), 443
Fernandez v. St. Francis Hosp., Inc., No. 09C-03-008-JRS, 2009 WL 2393713 (Del. Super. Ct. Aug. 3, 2009), 30
Ferolito v. Vultaggio, 949 N.Y.S.2d 356 (App. Div. 2012), 16
Ferris, Thompson & Zweig, Ltd. v. Esposito, 90 N.E.3d 400 (Ill. 2017), 276
Fesenmaier v. Cameron-Ehlen Grp., Inc., 442 F. Supp. 3d 1101 (D. Minn. 2020), 172 n.41
Fid. Nat'l Title Ins. Co. v. Suburban W. Abstractors, 852 A.2d 318 (Pa. Super. Ct. 2004), 436 n.110
Filosa, *In re*, 976 F. Supp. 2d 460 (S.D.N.Y. 2013), 394 n.143, 466–467, 466 n.109
Fine Hous., Inc. v. Sloan, 848 S.E.2d 581 (S.C. Ct. App. 2020), 436, 439
Finkelstein, Thompson & Loughran v. Hemispherx Biopharma, Inc., 774 A.2d 332 (D.C. 2001), 85
Fire Ins. Exch. v. Bell, 643 N.E.2d 310 (Ind. 1994), 487–489
First Am. Carriers, Inc. v. Kroger Co., 787 S.W.2d 669 (Ark. 1990), 5
First Constitution Bank v. Caldrello, 656 A.2d 1053 (Conn. App. Ct. 1995), 420, 435 n.99
Firstenberger, *In re*, 878 N.E.2d 912 (Mass. 2007), 106, 297 n.117, 468
First National Bank of LaGrange v. Lowrey, 872 N.E.2d 447 (Ill. App. Ct. 2007), 455
Fischer, *In re*, 684 N.E.2d 197 (Ind. 1997), 290 n.67
Fisher, *In re*, 202 P.3d 1186 (Colo. 2009), 94, 294, 297, 329, 467
Fisher v. Town of Boyce, 250 So. 3d 904 (La. Ct. App. 2017), 100, 180 n.83
Fisker Auto. Holdings, Inc. S'holder Litig., *In re*, C.A. No. 13-2100-DBS-SRF, 2018 WL 3991470 (D. Del. Aug. 20, 2018), 24 n.137
Fitzhugh v. Comm. on Prof'l Conduct, 823 S.W.2d 896 (Ark. 1992), 355 n.239
Fla. Bar v. Charnock, 661 So. 2d 1207 (Fla. 1995), 296 n.108
Fla. Bar v. Dove, 985 So. 2d 1001 (Fla. 2008), 323 n.53, 327 n.79, 353 n.230
Fla. Bar v. Frederick, 756 So. 2d 79 (Fla. 2000), 307 n.190
Fla. Bar v. Hmielewski, 702 So. 2d 218 (Fla. 1997), 325 n.61
Fla. Bar v. Joy, 679 So. 2d 1165 (Fla. 1996), 476 n.183
Fla. Bar v. Miller, 863 So. 2d 231 (Fla. 2003), 325 n.62
Fla. Bar v. Mogil, 763 So. 2d 303 (Fla. 2000), 297
Fla. Bar v. Norkin, 132 So. 3d 77 (Fla. 2013), 287 n.49, 508 n.72
Fla. Bar v. Patterson, 257 So. 3d 56 (Fla. 2018), 497 n.19
Fla. Bar v. Ratiner, 238 So. 3d 117 (Fla. 2018), 283 n.24
Fla. Bar v. Richardson, 591 So. 2d 908 (Fla. 1992), 63–64
Fla. Bar v. Schwartz, 284 So. 3d 393 (Fla. 2019), 106, 357 n.257, 468 n.132

Fla. Bar v. Thomas, 582 So. 2d 1177 (Fla. 1991), 69 n.115
Fla. Bar v. Whitney, 132 So. 3d 1095 (Fla. 2013), 325 n.62
Fla. Bar v. Wohl, 842 So. 2d 811 (Fla. 2003), 141
Fla. Ins. Guar. Ass'n, Inc. v. Carey Canada, Inc., 749 F. Supp. 255 (S.D. Fla. 1990), 12
Flatt v. Super. Ct., 885 P.2d 950 (Cal. 1994), 19
Fleischer v. Fleischer, 217 A.3d 1028 (Conn. App. Ct. 2019), 318 n.20
Fleitman v. McPherson, 691 So. 2d 37 (Fla. Dist. Ct. App. 1997), 443
Floyd, State v., 766 S.E.2d 361 (N.C. Ct. App. 2014), 406 n.207
Flynn v. Edmonds, 602 N.E.2d 880 (Ill. App. Ct. 1992), 388 n.115
Fognani v. Young, 115 P.3d 1268 (Colo. 2005), 421 n.23, 423, 425 n.4, 432, 438, 439
Foley, *In re*, 787 N.E.2d 561 (Mass. 2003), 369, 370
Foley-Ciccantelli v. Bishop's Grove Condo. Ass'n, 797 N.W.2d 789 (Wis. 2011), 26, 32, 39 n.209, 41
Folly Farms I, Inc. v. Trs. of the Clients' Sec. Tr. Fund of the Bar of Md., 387 A.2d 248 (Md. 1978), 246 n.4
Ford, United States v., 176 F.3d 376 (6th Cir. 1999), 83 n.192, 170 n.30
Ford v. Temple Hosp., 790 F.2d 342 (3d Cir. 1986), 67 n.102
Forrest, *In re*, 730 A.2d 340 (N.J. 1999), 319, 478
Forward v. Foschi, No. 9002/08, 2010 WL 1980838 (N.Y. Sup. Ct. May 18, 2010), 80 n.179
Fosnight, State v., 679 P.2d 174 (Kan. 1984), 397
Foster v. JLG Indus., 372 F. Supp. 2d 792 (M.D. Pa. 2005), 421
Fox v. Fox, 391 P.3d 124 (Okla. Civ. App. 2016), 86
Fox v. White, 215 S.W.3d 257 (Mo. Ct. App. 2007), 2
Fraley v. Williams Ford Tractor & Equip. Co., 5 S.W.3d 423 (Ark. 1999), 211
Frank, *In re*, 876 So. 2d 57 (La. 2004), 475 n.177
Franklin, United States v., 177 F. Supp. 2d 459 (E.D. Va. 2001), 180
Frank Settelmeyer & Sons, Inc. v. Smith & Harmer, Ltd., 197 P.3d 1051 (Nev. 2008), 13
Freedom Wireless, Inc. v. Boston Commc'ns Grp., Inc., No. 2006-1020, 2006 WL 8071423 (Fed. Cir. Mar. 20, 2006), 11, 12
Freeman, *In re*, 835 N.E.2d 494 (Ind. 2005), 321 n.39, 323 n.53
Freeman, State v., 690 S.E.2d 17 (N.C. Ct. App. 2010), 406 n.207
Freeman v. Vicchiarelli, 827 F. Supp. 300 (D.N.J. 1993), 439 n.129
Frey v. State, 509 N.W.2d 261 (N.D. 1993), 389
Frith v. State, 325 N.E.2d 186 (Ind. 1975), 330 n.97
Fulco v. Cont'l Cablevision, Inc., 789 F. Supp. 45 (D. Mass. 1992), 199
Fuller v. Partee, 540 S.W.3d 864 (Mo. Ct. App. 2018), 2
Fulton v. Lane, 829 P.2d 959 (Okla. 1992), 80, 96, 98, 175, 177
Furstenfeld v. Pepin, 869 N.W.2d 353 (Neb. Ct. App. 2015), 426 n.48, 451

Gabayzadeh v. Taylor, 639 F. Supp. 2d 298 (E.D.N.Y. 2009), 421
Galasso, *In re*, 978 N.E.2d 1254 (N.Y. 2012), 103 n.82
Galaxy Fireworks, Inc. v. Kozar, 150 So. 3d 256 (Fla. Dist. Ct. App. 2014), 30

Galderma Labs., L.P. v. Actavis Mid Atl. LLC, 927 F. Supp. 2d 390 (N.D. Tex. 2013), 20, 21–23, 278 n.181
Garaas, *In re*, Disciplinary Action Against, 652 N.W.2d 918 (N.D. 2002), 496
Garcia, *In re*, 147 P.2d 132 (Kan. 2006), 179 n.77
Garnett, *In re*, 603 S.E.2d 281 (Ga. 2004), 448
Garrett v. Metro. Life Ins. Co., No. 95 Civ. 2406 (PKL), 1996 WL 325725 (S.D.N.Y. June 12, 1996), 199
Garrett v. United States, 642 A.2d 1312 (D.C. 1994), 414 n.242
Garringer, *In re*, 626 N.E.2d 809 (Ind. 1994), 512
Garrison v. Louisiana, 379 U.S. 64 (1964), 496, 496 n.10
Garza, United States v., 429 F.3d 165 (5th Cir. 2005), 398
Gates v. Cook, 234 F.3d 221 (5th Cir. 2000), 205
Gateway Family Worship Ctrs., Inc. v. H.O.P.E. Found. Ministries, Inc., 535 S.E.2d 286 (Ga. Ct. App. 2000), 426 n.50
Gatti, *In re*, 8 P.3d 966 (Or. 2000), 117
Gaylard v. Homemakers of Montgomery, Inc., 675 So. 2d 363 (Ala. 1996), 167
Geisler v. Ky. State Bar Ass'n, 938 S.W.2d 578 (Ky. 1997), 473
Gelfuso, *In re*, 108 A.3d 208 (R.I. 2015), 324 n.53
Gen. Sec. Ins. Co. v. Jordan, Coyne & Savits, LLP, 357 F. Supp. 2d 951 (E.D. Va. 2005), 5
Gentile v. State, 501 U.S. 1030 (1991), 495, 510
Gershater, *In re*, 17 P.3d 929 (Kan. 2001), 495
Gibbs v. Lappies, 828 F. Supp. 6 (D.N.H. 1993), 5
Gibson v. Car Zone, 31 A.3d 76, 2011 WL 5354270 (Del. Nov. 8, 2011), 345
Gidatex, S.r.L. v. Campaniello Imports, Ltd., 82 F. Supp. 2d 119 (S.D.N.Y. 1999), 114, 121 n.201, 122, 123, 124 n.224, 125 n.228
Gifford v. Target Corp., 723 F. Supp. 2d 1110 (D. Minn. 2010), 80, 98, 177 n.67
Gillespie v. Scherr, 987 S.W.2d 129 (Tex. App. 1999), 208 n.245
Girardi v. Dow Chem. Co., 528 F.3d 1131 (9th Cir. 2008), 526, 528 n.200
Girardi v. Dow Chem. Co., 611 F.3d 1027 (9th Cir. 2010), 526–528
Giuffra v. Dershowitz, 410 F. Supp. 3d 564 (S.D.N.Y. 2019), 421 n.23
Givens v. Mullikin, 75 S.W.3d 383 (Tenn. 2002), 5, 189
GMAC Bank v. HTFC Corp., 248 F.R.D. 182 (E.D. Pa. 2008), 288–289
Goff v. Goff, 276 So. 3d 83 (Fla. Dist. Ct. App. 2019), 30, 421 n.23
Goldberg, United States v., 862 F.2d 101 (6th Cir. 1988), 305
Golden, *In re*, 496 S.E.2d 619 (S.C. 1998), 285 n.35, 285 n.37
Golden Door Jewelry Creations, Inc. v. Lloyds Underwriters Non-Marine Ass'n, 865 F. Supp. 1516 (S.D. Fla. 1994), 139 n.12, 141, 151 n.82
Golden v. Brethren Mut. Ins. Co., Civ. No. 3:18-CV-02425, 2019 WL 3216629 (M.D. Pa. July 17, 2019), 179 n.76
Golden v. Clear Advantage Mktg., No. 4:16-cv-00529-JAJ-CFB, 2020 WL 2516671 (S.D. Iowa Mar. 30, 2020), 280 n.5, 287 n.49
Goldstein v. Exxon Research & Eng'g Co., No. Civ. 95-2410, 1997 WL 580599 (D.N.J. Feb. 28, 1997), 150 n.81
Gonzalez-Lopez, United States v., 399 F.3d 924 (8th Cir. 2005), 166, 172 n.37
Goodeagle v. United States, No. CIV-09-490-D, 2010 WL 3081520 (W.D. Okla. Aug. 6, 2010), 96, 175

Goodsell v. Mississippi Bar, 667 So. 2d 7 (Miss. 1996), 353 n.230
Good v. W. Va.-Am. Water Co., No.: 2:14-01374, 2016 WL 6404006 (S.D. W. Va. Oct. 26, 2016), 199
Gordon Props., LLC, *In re*, 505 B.R. 703 (Bankr. E.D. Va. 2013), 43 n.233
Gordon v. Dadante, No. 1:05-CV-2726, 2009 WL 1850309 (N.D. Ohio June 26, 2009), 338 n.141
Gordon v. Katri Sales Co., No. 3:17-CV-00320, 2018 WL 1251965 (M.D. Pa. Mar. 12, 2018), 337 n.140
Gov't of India v. Cook Indus., Inc., 569 F.2d 737 (2d Cir. 1978), 31 n.170
Graf, United States v., 610 F.3d 1148 (9th Cir. 2010), 247 n.11, 249
Graf v. Frame, 352 S.E.2d 31 (W. Va. 1986), 18
Grand Jury Investig., *In re*, No. 19-15 (BAH), 2019 WL 2179116 (D.D.C. Mar. 4, 2019), 251
Grand Jury Proceedings, *In re*, 156 F.3d 1038 (10th Cir. 1998), 249
Grand Jury Subpoena (Newparent), *In re*, 274 F.3d 563 (1st Cir. 2001), 249
Grand Jury Subpoena Under Seal, *In re*, 415 F.3d 333 (2d Cir. 2005), 250 n.27, 250 n.30, 252–253
Grass, United States v., 239 F. Supp. 2d 535 (M.D. Pa. 2003), 113, 118
Great Rivers Coop of Se. Iowa v. Farmland Indus., Inc., 59 F.3d 764 (8th Cir. 1995), 208, 213
Green, *In re*, 11 P.3d 1078 (Colo. 2000), 495 n.5, 495 n.9, 505 n.49, 519 n.139
Greenberg v. Grace Plaza Nursing & Rehab. Ctr., 103 N.Y.S.3d 559 (App. Div. 2019), 420
Green v. Am. Fed'n of Teachers/Ill. Fed'n of Teachers Local 604, No. 12 CV 1162, 2015 WL 1509776 (N.D. Ill. Mar. 30, 2015), 421
Gregory, *Ex parte*, 663 S.E.2d 46 (S.C. 2008), 60–62
GRE Props. Thomasville LLC v. Libertywood Nursing Ctr., Inc., 761 S.E.2d 676 (N.C. Ct. App. 2014), 427 n.53
Grievance Comm. of the U.S. Dist. Ct., *In re*, 847 F.2d 57 (2d Cir. 1988), 379
Grievance Comm. v. Simels, 48 F.3d 640 (2d Cir. 1995), 166
Grievance Proceeding, *In re*, No. 3:01GP6 (SRU), 2002 WL 31106389 (D. Conn. July 19, 2002), 77, 187
Griffin-El v. Beard, No. 06-2719, 2009 WL 2929802 (E.D. Pa. Sept. 8, 2009), 83 n.193, 170 n.30
Grigsby, *In re*, Disciplinary Action Against, 85 N.W.2d 836 (Minn. 2012), 324
Grochowski, *In re*, 701 A.2d 1013 (R.I. 1997), 324 n.57
Grooms v. State, 583 S.E.2d 216 (Ga. Ct. App. 2003), 407
Gross, *In re*, 759 N.E.2d 288 (Mass. 2001), 360–361
Gruber v. Gruber, 261 Cal. Rptr. 3d 819 (Ct. App. 2020), 86
GSI Commerce Sols., Inc. v. BabyCenter, L.L.C., 618 F.3d 204 (2d Cir. 2010), 12 n.66, 21, 247 n.13
Guberman, *In re*, 978 A.2d 200 (D.C. 2009), 315
Guillen v. City of Chi., 956 F. Supp. 1416 (N.D. Ill. 1997), 13
Guivas-Soto, United States v., 124 F. Supp. 3d 72 (D.P.R. 2015), 179 n.75
Gulf Ins. Co. v. Berger, Kahn, Shafton, Moss, Figler, Simon & Gladstone, 93 Cal. Rptr. 2d 534 (Ct. App. 2000), 4
Gulf Oil Co. v. Bernard, 452 U.S. 89 (1981), 200–203, 205–206, 208
Gum v. Dudley, 505 S.E.2d 391 (W. Va. 1997), 328

Gunter v. Va. State Bar, 385 S.E.2d 597 (Va. 1989), 129
Guthrie Aircraft, Inc. v. Genesee Cnty., N.Y., 597 F. Supp. 1097 (W.D.N.Y. 1984), 18

Hackett, *In re*, 701 So. 2d 920 (La. 1997), 69 n.115
Hackett v. Feeney, No. 2:09-cv-02075-RLH-LRL, 2010 WL 4102911 (D. Nev. Oct. 18, 2010), 275
Hackman v. W. Agric. Ins. Co., No. 104,786, 2012 WL 1524060 (Kan. Ct. App. Apr. 27, 2012), 5
Hadar v. Pierce, 974 N.Y.S.2d 399 (App. Div. 2013), 85
Hadges v. Yonkers Racing Corp., 48 F.3d 1320 (2d Cir. 1995), 54 n.26
Hagberg v. Cal. Fed. Bank FSB, 81 P.3d 244 (Cal. 2004), 85 n.207
Hagen, State v., 574 N.W.2d 585 (N.D. 1998), 389
Hallmark, *In re*, 831 A.2d 366 (D.C. 2003), 107, 298
Halverson v. Hardcastle, 163 P.3d 428 (Nev. 2007), 166
Hammer, *In re*, 718 S.E.2d 442 (S.C. 2011), 285 n.35
Hammond v. City of Junction City, Kan., 126 F. App'x 886 (10th Cir. 2005), 199, 216
Hampton Hardware, Inc. v. Cotter & Co., 56 F.R.D. 630 (N.D. Tex. 1994), 211
Hampton v. Schimpff, 188 F.R.D. 589 (D. Mont. 1999), 189
Hancock v. Bd. of Prof'l Responsibility, 447 S.W.3d 844 (Tenn. 2014), 504–505
Hann, *In re*, Disciplinary Action Against, 819 N.W.2d 498 (N.D. 2012), 322
Hanntz v. Shiley, Inc., 766 F. Supp. 258 (D.N.J. 1991), 166
Hanover Ins. Co. v. United States, 146 Fed. Cl. 447 (Fed. Cl. 2019), 315 n.8, 368 n.5
Harduvel v. Gen. Dynamics Corp., 801 F. Supp. 597 (M.D. Fla. 1992), 472 n.160
Harlan v. Lewis, 982 F.2d 1255 (8th Cir. 1993), 196 n.168
Harris Davis Rebar, L.L.C. v. Structural Iron Workers Local Union No. 1, Pension Tr. Fund, No. 17 C 6473, 2019 WL 447622 (N.D. Ill. Feb. 5, 2019), 80, 98, 177, 182
Harrison v. Miss. Bar, 637 So. 2d 204 (Miss. 1994), 370 n.14
Harris v. Jackson, 192 S.W.3d 297 (Ky. 2006), 473 n.167
Harris v. Ray Johnston Constr. Co., 534 S.E.2d 653 (N.C. Ct. App. 2000), 450
Harter v. Plains Ins. Co., 579 N.W.2d 625 (S.D. 1998), 427 n.53
Hart v. State, 62 P.3d 566 (Wyo. 2003), 30
Haworth v. State, 840 P.2d 912 (Wyo. 1992), 370
Hawthorne v. United States, 504 A.2d 580 (D.C. 1986), 407
Hayes v. Wis. & S. R.R., LLC, No. 18-cv-923, 2019 WL 5595170 (E.D. Wis. Oct. 30, 2019), 175 n.54
Haynes, *In re*, No. C 10–4642 PJH, 2013 WL 1195524 (N.D. Cal. Mar. 22, 2013), 279 n.1
H.B.A. Mgmt., Inc. v. Estate of Schwartz, 693 So. 2d 541 (Fla. 1997), 80, 98, 177
Head, People v., 332 P.3d 117 (Colo. 2013), 106, 318 n.18, 469
Headfirst Baseball LLC v. Elwood, 999 F. Supp. 2d 199 (D.D.C. 2013), 29
Healthcare Advocates, Inc. v. Harding, Earley, Follmer & Frailey, 497 F. Supp. 2d 627 (E.D. Pa. 2007), 82

Health Care & Ret. Corp. of Am., Inc. v. Bradley, 961 So. 2d 1071 (Fla. Dist. Ct. App. 2007), 28 n.154
Hedges v. E. River Plaza, LLC, 981 N.Y.S.2d 894 (Sup. Ct. 2013), 96, 174
Heine v. Colton, Hartnick, Yamin & Sheresky, 786 F. Supp. 360 (S.D.N.Y. 1992), 4
Helena Chem. Co. v. Uribe, 281 P.3d 237 (N.M. 2012), 428 n.57
Heller, *In re*, 780 N.Y.S.2d 314 (App. Div. 2004), 279 n.1
Henkel, United States v., 799 F.2d 369 (7th Cir. 1986), 398
Henry v. Eberhard, 832 S.W.2d 467 (Ark. 1992), 495 n.5
Hermanson v. Multi-Care Health Sys., Inc., 448 P.3d 153 (Wash. Ct. App. 2019), 189
Hernandez v. First Student, Inc., 249 Cal. Rptr. 3d 681 (Ct. App. 2019), 409 n.220
Hernandez v. Vitamin Shoppe Indus. Inc., 95 Cal. Rptr. 3d 737 (Ct. App. 2009), 206 n.232
Herron, *In re*, 441 P.3d 24 (Kan. 2019), 320 n.37, 322 n.45, 353 n.230
Hess, *In re*, 406 S.W.3d 37 (Mo. 2013), 69 n.114, 70 n.119
Hiatt v. Estate of Hiatt, 837 So. 2d 1132 (Fla. Dist. Ct. App. 2003), 425 n.44
Higgins v. Karp, 687 A.2d 539 (Conn. 1997), 5
Highland Park Homeowners Ass'n v. Villas at Highland Park, LLC, 394 P.3d 1144 (Colo. 2017), 29, 32, 33
Hill v. Culebra Conservation & Dev. Auth., 599 F. Supp. 2d 88 (D.P.R. 2009), 421
Hill v. Norfolk & W. Ry. Co., 814 F.2d 1192 (7th Cir. 1987), 519, 521 n.151
Hill v. Shell Oil Co., 209 F. Supp. 2d 876 (N.D. Ill. 2002), 114 n.151, 121
Hill v. State, 658 S.E.2d 863 (Ga. Ct. App. 2008), 407
Hilmon Co. v. Hyatt Int'l, 899 F.2d 250 (3d Cir. 1990), 521 n.151
Hinden, *In re*, 654 A.2d 864 (D.C. 1995), 331 n.98
Hinerman v. Grill on Twenty First, LLC, 112 N.E.3d 1273 (Ohio Ct. App. 2018), 3, 247
Hischke, State v., 639 N.W.2d 6 (Iowa 2002), 380 n.72
Hobson v. State, 675 N.E.2d 1090 (Ind. 1996), 380 n.72
Hoch v. Loren, 273 So. 3d 56 (Fla. Dist. Ct. App. 2019), 449
Hodge, *In re*, 407 P.3d 613 (Kan. 2017), 2, 166
Hoffman, *In re*, Disciplinary Action Against, 670 N.W.2d 500 (N.D. 2003), 54
Holbrook v. Benson, 3 N.E.3d 788 (Ohio Ct. App. 2013), 425 n.46
Holden v. Blevins, 837 A.2d 1053 (Md. Ct. Spec. App. 2003), 374 n.39
Holdren v. Gen. Motors Corp., 13 F. Supp. 2d 1192 (D. Kan. 1998), 76 n.152, 100, 169
Holman v. Rasak, 785 N.W.2d 98 (Mich. 2010), 189, 190
Holmes v. Nightingale, 158 P.3d 1039 (Okla. 2007), 191 n.141
Holste, *In re*, 358 P.3d 850 (Kan. 2015), 353 n.230
Holt, *In re*, 103 A.3d 147 (R.I. 2014), 354
Home Care Indus., Inc. v. Murray, 154 F. Supp. 2d 861 (D.N.J. 2001), 249 n.23
HomeDirect, Inc. v. H.E.P. Direct, Inc., No. 10 C 812, 2013 WL 1815979 (N.D. Ill. Apr. 29, 2013), 141
Home Indem. Co. v. Lane Powell Moss & Miller, 43 F.3d 1322 (9th Cir. 1995), 4
Honolulu Civil Beat Inc. v. Dep't of Att'y Gen., 463 P.3d 942 (Haw. 2020), 460
Hoover v. Armco Inc., 915 F.2d 355 (8th Cir. 1990), 66 n.102

Horaist v. Doctor's Hosp. of Opelousas, 255 F.3d 261 (5th Cir. 2001), 426 n.51
Horn v. Ray, 325 S.W.3d 500 (Mo. Ct. App. 2010), 16 n.78
Horton v. Maersk Line, Ltd., 294 F.R.D. 690 (S.D. Ga. 2013), 279 n.1
Houge, *In re*, Disciplinary Action Against, 764 N.W.2d 328 (Minn. 2009), 327 n.79
Houston, *In re*, 675 S.E. 2d 721 (S.C. 2009), 50, 292 n.77, 520 n.148
Howard, *In re*, 879 A.2d 681 (D.C. 2005), 324
Howard, *In re*, 912 S.W.2d 61 (Mo. 1995), 509 n.81
Howard Guntz Profit Sharing Plan v. Super. Ct., 105 Cal. Rptr. 2d 896 (Ct. App. 2001), 205
Howes, *In re*, 940 P.2d 159 (N.M. 1997), 118
Hoyt Props., Inc. v. Prod. Res. Grp., L.L.C., 716 N.W.2d 366 (Minn. Ct. App. 2006), 490
H & R Block, Inc. v. Haese, 82 S.W.3d 331 (Tex. App. 2000), 208 n.248, 211
Huang v. Brenson, 7 N.E.3d 729 (Ill. App. Ct. 2014), 4
Hubbard v. Ky. Bar Ass'n, 571 S.W.3d 90 (Ky. 2019), 325 n.62
Hubbard v. Plaza Bonita, LP, 630 F. App'x 681 (9th Cir. 2015), 473 n.167
Hulse v. Suburban Mobile Home Supply Co., Case No. 06-1168-WEB, 2006 WL 2927519 (D. Kan. Oct. 12, 2006), 191
Humco, Inc. v. Noble, 31 S.W.3d 916 (Ky. 2000), 80, 83 n.196, 98, 166, 167, 186
Humphrey, *In re*, 15 So. 3d 960 (La. 2009), 353
Humphrey v. McLaren, 402 N.W.2d 535 (Minn. 1987), 425
Hunter v. Earthgrains Co. Bakery, 281 F.3d 144 (4th Cir. 2002), 64
Hunter v. Va. State Bar *ex rel.* Third Dist. Comm., 744 S.E.2d 611 (Va. 2013), 42 n.228
Hunt v. Dresie, 740 P.2d 1046 (Kan. 1987), 52 n.16
Hurley v. Hurley, 923 A.2d 908 (Me. 2007), 460
Hyatt, State v., 566 S.E.2d 61 (N.C. 2002), 381

Ibarra v. Baker, 338 F. App'x 457 (5th Cir. 2009), 370 n.15, 378 n.62
Idaho State Bar v. Hawkley, 92 P.3d 1069 (Idaho 2002), 52 n.16, 284 n.34
Idaho State Bar v. Topp, 925 P.2d 1113 (Idaho 1996), 508
Idaho State Bar v. Warrick, 44 P.3d 1141 (Idaho 2002), 295 n.102
Iguana, LLC v. Lanham, 628 F. Supp. 2d 1361 (M.D. Ga. 2008), 443
Ihnatenko, United States v., 482 F.3d 1097 (9th Cir. 2007), 148
Illuzzi, *In re*, 616 A.2d 233 (Vt. 1992), 5
Indeglia, *In re*, 765 A.2d 444 (R.I. 2001), 448, 452
Ingersoll, *In re*, 710 N.E.2d 390 (Ill. 1999), 319 n.31
Inglimo, *In re*, Disciplinary Proceeding Against, 740 N.W.2d 125 (Wis. 2007), 105 n.93
Inorganic Coatings, Inc. v. Falberg, 926 F. Supp. 517 (E.D. Pa. 1995), 113
In re. *See name of party*
Interest of D.C., 573 S.W.3d 860 (Tex. App. 2019), 519 n.143, 526 n.186
Interpharm, Inc. v. Wells Fargo Bank, N.A., No. 08 Civ. 11365(RJH) (HBP), 2010 WL 1141201 (S.D.N.Y. Mar. 25, 2010), 432 n.80
Int'l Bhd. of Teamsters, United States v., 119 F.3d 210 (2d Cir. 1997), 249
Int'l Res. Ventures, Inc. v. Diamond Mining Co. of Am., Inc., 934 S.W.2d 218 (Ark. 1996), 423 n.39, 439

Iowa Sup. Ct. Att'y Disciplinary Bd. v. Att'y Doe No. 792, 878 N.W.2d 189 (Iowa 2016), 496 n.15, 497
Iowa Sup. Ct. Att'y Disciplinary Bd. v. Barnhill, 885 N.W.2d 408 (Iowa 2016), 53 n.22, 96 n.41, 323 n.53, 466, 476
Iowa Sup. Ct. Att'y Disciplinary Bd. v. Barry, 908 N.W.2d 217 (Iowa 2018), 315 n.8
Iowa Sup. Ct. Att'y Disciplinary Bd. v. Bartley, 860 N.W.2d 331 (Iowa 2015), 320 n.36
Iowa Sup. Ct. Att'y Disciplinary Bd. v. Bieber, 824 N.W.2d 514 (Iowa 2012), 104
Iowa Sup. Ct. Att'y Disciplinary Bd. v. Buchanan, 757 N.W.2d 251 (Iowa 2008), 306 n.176
Iowa Sup. Ct. Att'y Disciplinary Bd. v. Caghan, 927 N.W.2d 591 (Iowa 2019), 51, 322
Iowa Sup. Ct. Att'y Disciplinary Bd. v. Cannon, 789 N.W.2d 756 (Iowa 2010), 330 n.97, 336
Iowa Sup. Ct. Att'y Disciplinary Bd. v. Capotosto, 927 N.W.2d 585 (Iowa 2019), 298
Iowa Sup. Ct. Att'y Disciplinary Bd. v. Clarity, 838 N.W.2d 648 (Iowa 2013), 106, 469
Iowa Sup. Ct. Att'y Disciplinary Bd. v. Engelmann, 840 N.W.2d 156 (Iowa 2013), 104
Iowa Sup. Ct. Att'y Disciplinary Bd. v. Goedken, 939 N.W.2d 97 (Iowa 2020), 107, 298 n.122
Iowa Sup. Ct. Att'y Disciplinary Bd. v. Kozlik, 943 N.W.2d 589 (Iowa 2020), 106, 469
Iowa Sup. Ct. Att'y Disciplinary Bd. v. Marzen, 779 N.W.2d 757 (Iowa 2010), 42 n.228
Iowa Sup. Ct. Att'y Disciplinary Bd. v. Mathahs, 918 N.W.2d 487 (Iowa 2018), 103 n.82
Iowa Sup. Ct. Att'y Disciplinary Bd. v. McGinness, 844 N.W.2d 456 (Iowa 2014), 298, 323 n.53
Iowa Sup. Ct. Att'y Disciplinary Bd. v. Meyer, 944 N.W.2d 61 (Iowa 2020), 297 n.115
Iowa Sup. Ct. Att'y Disciplinary Bd. v. Moran, 919 N.W.2d 754 (Iowa 2018), 105 n.93, 297 n.114
Iowa Sup. Ct. Att'y Disciplinary Bd. v. Rhinehart, 827 N.W.2d 169 (Iowa 2013), 318 n.18
Iowa Sup. Ct. Att'y Disciplinary Bd. v. Rhinehart, 953 N.W.2d 156 (Iowa 2021), 495 n.7
Iowa Sup. Ct. Att'y Disciplinary Bd. v. Sears, 933 N.W.2d 214 (Iowa 2019), 104, 296
Iowa Sup. Ct. Att'y Disciplinary Bd. v. Sporer, 897 N.W.2d 69 (Iowa 2017), 321 n.43
Iowa Sup. Ct. Att'y Disciplinary Bd. v. Stansberry, 922 N.W.2d 591 (Iowa 2019), 298
Iowa Sup. Ct. Att'y Disciplinary Bd. v. Stoller, 879 N.W.2d 199 (Iowa 2016), 179, 469

Iowa Sup. Ct. Att'y Disciplinary Bd. v. Stowers, 823 N.W.2d 1 (Iowa 2012), 174 n.49
Iowa Sup. Ct. Att'y Disciplinary Bd. v. Templeton, 784 N.W.2d 761 (Iowa 2010), 104, 296
Iowa Sup. Ct. Att'y Disciplinary Bd. v. Turner, 918 N.W.2d 130 (Iowa 2018), 454 n.38
Iowa Sup. Ct. Att'y Disciplinary Bd. v. Weiland, 862 N.W.2d 627 (Iowa 2015), 323 n.52
Iowa Sup. Ct. Att'y Disciplinary Bd. v. Weiland, 885 N.W.2d 198 (Iowa 2016), 107, 298
Iowa Sup. Ct. Att'y Disciplinary Bd. v. Willey, 889 N.W.2d 647 (Iowa 2017), 13 n.70
Iowa Sup. Ct. Att'y Discipline Bd. v. Gottschalk, 729 N.W.2d 812 (Iowa 2007), 297
Iowa Sup. Ct. Bd. of Prof'l Ethics & Conduct v. Furlong, 625 N.W.2d 711 (Iowa 2001), 307 n.190
Iowa Sup. Ct. Bd. of Prof'l Ethics & Conduct v. Hohnbaum, 554 N.W.2d 550 (Iowa 1996), 65–66
Iowa Sup. Ct. Bd. of Prof'l Ethics & Conduct v. Lane, 642 N.W.2d 296 (Iowa 2002), 331 n.101, 336
Iowa Sup. Ct. Bd. of Prof'l Ethics & Conduct v. Plumb, 546 N.W.2d 215 (Iowa 1996), 129, 130 n.255
Iowa Sup. Ct. Bd. of Prof'l Ethics & Conduct v. Ronwin, 557 N.W.2d 515 (Iowa 1996), 70 n.117, 496, 508 n.68
Ireland, *In re*, 276 P.3d 762 (Kan. 2012), 509 n.80
Isaacson, *In re*, Disciplinary Proceeding Against, 860 N.W.2d 490 (Wis. 2015), 494 n.1
Ivy, *In re*, 350 P.3d 758 (Alaska 2015), 105 n.93, 297 n.114, 318 n.18, 322
Izarraga-Ponce, United States v., No. CR-08-220-E-BLW, 2009 WL 928113 (D. Idaho Apr. 2, 2009), 306 n.177

Jackson v. Adcock, No. Civ. A. 03-3369, 2004 WL 1661199 (E.D. La. July 22, 2004), 424 n.41
Jackson v. Bloomberg L.P., No. 13-CV-2001 (JPO), 2015 WL 1822695 (S.D.N.Y. Apr. 22, 2015), 199
Jackson v. Motel 6 Multipurpose, Inc., 130 F.3d 999 (11th Cir. 1997), 203–204, 205
James, *In re*, 861 N.E.2d 703 (Ind. 2007), 325 n.62
Janczewski v. Janczewski, 94 N.Y.S.3d 142 (App. Div. 2019), 30
Jandrt *ex rel.* Brueggeman v. Jerome Foods, Inc., 597 N.W.2d 744 (Wis. 1999), 51, 52 n.19, 72 n.134, 74 n.148
Jankousky v. Jewel Cos., 538 N.E.2d 689 (Ill. App. Ct. 1989), 209
Jaworski v. Master Hand Contractors, Inc., 882 F.3d 686 (7th Cir. 2018), 526 n.187
J.B.B. Inv. Partners v. Fair, 249 Cal. Rptr. 3d 368 (Ct. App. 2019), 303 n.160
Jedwabny v. Phila. Transp. Co., 135 A.2d 252 (Pa. 1957), 19 n.105
Jenifer v. Del. Solid Waste Auth., No. CIV. A 98-270 MMS, CIV. A 98-565 MMS, 1999 WL 117762 (D. Del. Feb. 25, 1999), 209, 214 n.285

Jenkins v. City of Las Vegas, No: 19-656 JAP/JHR, 2020 WL 4347263 (D.N.M. July 29, 2020), 176
Jennifer v. Del. Solid Waste Auth., No. Civ. A 98-270 MMS, 1999 WL 117762 (D. Del. Feb. 25, 1999), 210
Jensen, *In re*, 191 P.3d 1118 (Kan. 2008), 101
Jensen, *In re*, Disciplinary Proceeding Against, 430 P.3d 262 (Wash. 2018), 166, 173, 179 n.77
Jensen v. Poindexter, 352 P.3d 1201 (Okla. 2015), 423 n.32
Jeska v. Mulhall, 693 P.2d 1335 (Or. Ct. App. 1985), 490
Jessen v. Hartford Cas. Ins. Co., 3 Cal. Rptr. 3d 877 (Ct. App. 2003), 31 n.171
Jimenez v. Madison Area Tech. Coll., 321 F.3d 652 (7th Cir. 2003), 55–57, 521–522
Johnson, *In re*, 4 Cal. State Bar Ct. Rptr. 179 (Rev. Dep't 2000), 42 n.228
Johnson, *In re*, 402 B.R. 313 (B.A.P. 8th Cir. 2009), 329, 473
Johnson, *In re*, 729 P.2d 1175 (Kan. 1986), 495
Johnson, *In re*, 838 S.E.2d 755 (Ga. 2020), 325 n.62
Johnson, *In re*, Disciplinary Action Against, 743 N.W.2d 117 (N.D. 2007), 94, 466
Johnson v. Bd. of Cnty. Comm'rs, 868 F. Supp. 1226 (D. Colo. 1994), 336
Johnson v. Cadillac Plastic Grp., Inc., 930 F. Supp. 1437 (D. Colo. 1996), 122
Johnson v. Clark Gin Serv., Inc., No. 15-3290, 2016 WL 7017267 (E.D. La. Dec. 1, 2016), 16 n.78
Johnson v. Miller, 818 N.W.2d 804 (S.D. 2012), 50, 341 n.160
Johnson v. Syed, B258701, 2015 WL 4314049 (Cal. Ct. App. July 15, 2015), 519
Johnson v. Thomas, 982 So. 2d 405 (Miss. 2008), 352
Joiner v. Joiner, 87 S.W.2d 903 (Tex. App. 1935), 318, 478
Jones v. Casey's Gen. Stores, 517 F. Supp. 2d 1080 (S.D. Iowa 2007), 206–207
Jones v. Reichert Jung, Inc., 211 F. Supp. 2d 661 (D. Md. 2002), 194 n.156
Jones v. Scientific Colors, Inc., 201 F. Supp. 2d 820 (N.D. Ill. 2001), 168
Jorgensen v. Taco Bell Corp., 58 Cal. Rptr. 2d 178 (Ct. App. 1996), 52 n.16, 347
Joyce, United States v., 311 F. Supp. 3d 398 (D. Mass. 2018), 381
Juneau Cnty. Star-Times v. Juneau Cnty., 824 N.W.2d 457 (Wis. 2013), 5

Kalal, *In re*, Disciplinary Proceeding Against, 643 N.W.2d 466 (Wis. 2002), 323 n.51, 325 n.62, 478 n.198
Kamb, *In re*, Disciplinary Proceeding Against, 305 P.3d 1091 (Wash. 2013), 105 n.93
Kappa Sigma Fraternity v. Price-Williams, 40 So. 3d 683 (Ala. 2009), 318 n.20, 478
Katica v. Allstate Fire & Cas. Ins. Co., No. CV 16-00150-DLC-RWA, 2018 WL 3475479 (D. Mont. July 19, 2018), 423 n.35, 439
Katrina Canal Breaches Consol. Litig., *In re*, No. 05-4182 "K" (2), 2008 WL 2066999 (E.D. La. May 14, 2008), 100, 122, 180, 199
Kaushas, *In re*, 616 B.R. 57 (Bankr. M.D. Pa. 2020), 449
Kay Co., LLC v. Equitable Prod. Co., 246 F.R.D. 260 (S.D. W. Va. 2007), 209, 214 n.284
Keenan, *In re*, 501 S.W.3d 74 (Tex. 2016), 418

Kellogg Brown & Root, Inc., *In re*, 756 F.3d 754 (D.C. Cir. 2014), 251 n.34
Kenner v. Commonwealth, 835 S.E.2d 107 (Va. Ct. App. 2019), 420 n.14
Kenny, *In re*, 217 P.3d 36 (Kan. 2009), 307 n.184
Kerce v. W. Telemarketing Corp., 575 F. Supp. 2d 1354 (S.D. Ga. 2008), 209 n.253
Kerr, *In re*, 640 N.E.2d 1056 (Ind. 1994), 294 n.96
Key Equip. Fin., Inc. v. Hawkins, 985 A.2d 1139 (Me. 2009), 509
Khoury v. ConAgra Foods, Inc., 368 S.W.3d 189 (Mo. Ct. App. 2012), 233 n.41
Kien, *In re*, 372 N.E.2d 376 (Ill. 1977), 138, 141
King, *In re*, 33 So. 3d 873 (La. 2010), 320 n.37
Kingsdorf v. Kingsdorf, 797 A.2d 206 (N.J. Super. Ct. App. Div. 2002), 329, 473 n.167
Kingvision Pay Per View, Ltd. v. Wilson, 83 F. Supp. 2d 914 (W.D. Tenn. 2000), 330 n.97
Kircher v. Charter Twp. of Ypsilanti, No. 07-13091, 2007 WL 4557714 (E.D. Mich. Dec. 21, 2007), 338 n.141
Kirchoff, *In re*, 399 P.3d 453 (Or. 2017), 324 n.53, 325 n.62
Kirschner v. Process Design Assocs., Inc., 592 N.W.2d 707 (Mich. 1999), 5
Kleiner v. First Nat'l Bank of Atlanta, 751 F.2d 1193 (11th Cir. 1985), 209, 209 n.251
Klier v. Sordoni Skanska Constr. Co., 766 A.2d 761 (N.J. Super. Ct. App. Div. 2001), 80, 96, 98, 174, 177
Kline, *In re*, 311 P.3d 321 (Kan. 2013), 322 n.44
Kloian v. Domino's Pizza, L.L.C., 733 N.W.2d 766 (Mich. Ct. App. 2006), 450 n.15
Klorczyk v. Sears, Roebuck & Co., No. 3:13-cv-00257 (JAM), 2017 WL 3272237 (D. Conn. Aug. 1, 2017), 79 n.177, 97, 147 n.60, 176 n.63
Kluge, *In re*, 27 P.3d 102 (Or. 2001), 329
Klupt v. Krongard, 728 A.2d 727 (Md. Ct. Spec. App. 1999), 433, 439 n.134, 440 n.135
KMS Rest. Corp. v. Searcy, Denney, Scarola, Barnhart & Shipley P.A., 107 So. 3d 552 (Fla. Dist. Ct. App. 2013), 421
Knickmeier, *In re*, Disciplinary Proceeding Against, 683 N.W.2d 445 (Wis. 2004), 106, 469
Knowledge A-Z, Inc. v. Sentry Ins., 857 N.E.2d 411 (Ind. Ct. App. 2006), 427 n.53
Knox, *In re*, 432 P.3d 654 (Kan. 2019), 476
Kobagaya, United States v., Crim. A. No. 09-10005-01, 2011 WL 1466475 (D. Kan. Apr. 18, 2011), 148 n.72
Koch v. Koch Indus., Inc., 798 F. Supp. 1525 (D. Kan. 1992), 30
Kocur v. Split Vein Coal Co. (*In re* Split Vein Coal Co.), No. 1:03-BK-02974MDF, 2013 WL 1934669 (Bankr. M.D. Pa. May 9, 2013), 149, 150
Koen, People v., 6 N.E.3d 354 (Ill. App. Ct. 2014), 433 n.86
Kohlmayer v. Nat'l R.R. Passenger Corp., 124 F. Supp. 2d 877 (D.N.J. 2000), 280
Kojayan, United States v., 8 F.3d 1315 (9th Cir. 1993), 322
Kolbjornsen, People v., 35 P.3d 181 (Colo. 1999), 317 n.16
Kornreich, *In re*, 693 A.2d 877 (N.J. 1997), 317 n.16
Koval v. Simon Telelect, Inc., 693 N.E.2d 1299 (Ind. 1998), 449, 450 n.16

Kozowski v. Nelson, No.: 6:18-cv-00275-MK, 2020 WL 1066329 (D. Or. Mar. 5, 2020), 80, 177
Kraemer v. Grant Cnty., 892 F.2d 686 (7th Cir. 1990), 54 n.26, 55
Krigel, *In re*, 480 S.W.3d 294 (Mo. 2016), 295 n.104, 368 n.4, 389, 466
Kuhnle Bros., Inc. v. City of Geauga, 103 F.3d 516 (6th Cir. 1997), 348 n.201
Kupka, *In re*, 458 P.3d 242 (Kan. 2020), 93, 465 n.102
Kutzman v. Derrel's Mini Storage, Inc., 354 F. Supp. 3d 1149 (E.D. Cal. 2018), 209
Ky. Bar Ass'n v. Blum, 404 S.W.3d 841 (Ky. 2013), 307, 312, 497
Ky. Bar Ass'n v. Devers, 936 S.W.2d 89 (Ky. 1997), 323
Ky. Bar Ass'n v. Greene, 386 S.W.3d 717 (Ky. 2012), 105 n.93, 297 n.114
Ky. Bar Ass'n v. Lavit, 351 S.W.3d 210 (Ky. 2011), 283 n.24
Ky. Bar Ass'n v. Prewitt, 4 S.W.2d 142 (Ky. 1999), 508 n.68
Ky. Bar Ass'n v. Reeves, 62 S.W.3d 360 (Ky. 2001), 296 n.108
Ky. Bar Ass'n v. Waller, 929 S.W.2d 181 (Ky. 1996), 496 n.17

LaChance v. Erickson, 522 U.S. 262 (1998), 396
L.A. Cnty. Pioneer Soc'y, *In re*, 257 P.2d 1 (Cal. 1953), 518 n.137
La. Crane Co., LLC, United States v., OCAHO Case No. 14B00102 (U.S. Dep't of Justice, Exec. Office for Immigration Review Mar. 12, 2015), 331 n.101
La Jolla Cove Motel & Hotel Apts., Inc. v. Super. Ct., 17 Cal. Rptr. 3d 467 (Ct. App. 2004), 171 n.36
Lang v. Super. Ct., 826 P.2d 1228 (Ariz. Ct. App. 1992), 80, 177
Lansky, *In re*, 678 N.E.2d 1114 (Ind. 1997), 448
LaPage, United States v., 231 F.3d 488 (9th Cir. 2000), 407, 408
Laremont-Lopez v. Se. Tidewater Opportunity Ctr., 968 F. Supp. 1075 (E.D. Va. 1997), 337 n.135
Larry James Oldsmobile-Pontiac-GMC Truck Co. v. Gen. Motors Corp., 175 F.R.D. 234 (N.D. Miss. 1997), 209 n.250
La. State Bar Ass'n v. Harrington, 585 So. 2d 514 (La. 1990), 303 n.166
Lavanture, United States v., 74 F. App'x 221 (3d Cir. 2003), 334 n.122
Law Offices of Jeffrey Sherbow, PC v. Fieger & Fieger, PC, 930 N.W.2d 416 (Mich. Ct. App. 2019), 276
Law v. Zuckerman, 307 F. Supp. 2d 705 (D. Md. 2004), 191
Lawyer Disciplinary Bd. v. Busch, 754 S.E.2d 729 (W. Va. 2014), 322 n.45
Lawyer Disciplinary Bd. v. Grindo, 842 S.E.2d 683 (W. Va. 2020), 324 n.53
Lawyer Disciplinary Bd. v. Hall, 765 S.E.2d 187 (W. Va. 2014), 495 n.9, 497 n.18, 505 n.49, 509 n.74
Lawyer Disciplinary Bd. v. Hassan, 824 S.E.2d 224 (W. Va. 2019), 345
Lawyer Disciplinary Bd. v. McGraw, 461 S.E.2d 850 (W. Va. 1995), 42 n.228
Lawyer Disciplinary Bd. v. Neely, 528 S.E.2d 468 (W. Va. 1998), 54, 292
Lawyer Disciplinary Bd. v. Turgeon, 557 S.E.2d 235 (W. Va. 2000), 507 n.61, 509
Layton, State v., 432 S.E.2d 740 (W. Va. 1993), 397
Lazzo, *In re*, 150 P.3d 887 (Kan. 2007), 352, 353 n.229
Leapfrog Enters., Inc. v. Epik Learning, LLC, Case No.16-cv-04269-EDL, 2017 WL 2986604 (N.D. Cal. Feb. 23, 2017), 31 n.171
Leaseamerica Corp. v. Stewart, 876 P.2d 184 (Kan. Ct. App. 1994), 426 n.49, 444

Lee, *In re*, 977 So. 2d 852 (La. 2008), 509 n.79
Lee Mem'l Health Sys. v. Smith, 56 So. 3d 808 (Fla. Dist. Ct. App. 2011), 186 n.114
Lee v. Am. Airlines, Inc., No. Civ.A. 3:01-CV-1179-P, 2002 WL 226347 (N.D. Tex. Feb. 12, 2002), 213 n.282
Lee v. Med. Protective Co., 858 F. Supp. 2d 803 (E.D. Ky. 2012), 4
Leifson, United States v., 568 F.3d 1215 (10th Cir. 2009), 390
LendUS, LLC v. Goede, No. 2018-0233-SG, 2018 WL 6498674 (Del. Ch. Dec. 10, 2018), 280 n.5
Lennar Mare Island, LLC v. Steadfast Ins. Co., 105 F. Supp. 3d 1100 (E.D. Cal. 2015), 21
Leoner-Aguirre, United States v., 939 F.3d 310 (1st Cir. 2019), 407
LeRoy v. State, No. 074, 1993 WL 637310 (Del. Super. Ct. Jan. 21, 1994), 442 n.149
Levine, *In re*, 847 P.2d 1093 (Ariz. 1993), 292, 294 n.96
Lewis v. Crystal Gas. Co., 532 P.2d 431 (Okla. 1975), 86
Leysock v. Forest Labs., Inc., No. 12-11354-FDS, 2017 WL 1591833 (D. Mass. Apr. 28, 2017), 91–92, 93 n.15
Liberty Towers Realty, LLC v. Richmond Liberty, LLC, 569 B.R. 534 (E.D.N.Y. 2017), 330 n.97, 332 n.115
Lieberman v. Emp'rs Ins., 419 A.2d 417 (N.J. 1980), 5
Lieber v. ITT Hartford Ins. Ctr., Inc., 15 P.3d 1030 (Utah 2000), 347
Ligon v. Newman, 231 S.W.3d 662 (Ark. 2006), 105 n.93, 297 n.114
Ligon v. Stilley, 371 S.W.3d 615 (Ark. 2010), 343 n.170
Liguori v. Hansen, No. 2:11-cv-00492-GMN-CWH, 2012 WL 760747 (D. Nev. Mar. 6, 2012), 337
Lindsley v. Roe, 964 N.E.2d 1063 (Ohio Ct. App. 2011), 7
Linton, People v., 302 P.3d 927 (Cal. 2013), 419
Lioce v. Cohen, 174 P.3d 970 (Nev. 2008), 290
Lisse, *In re*, 921 F.3d 629 (7th Cir. 2019), 508 n.65
Litchfield, United States v., 959 F.2d 1514 (10th Cir. 1992), 412
Liu, *In re*, 664 F.3d 367 (2d Cir. 2011), 339–340, 342–343
Locascio, United States v., 6 F.3d 924 (2d Cir. 1993), 418
Lockyer, United States *ex rel.*, v. Haw. Pac. Health, 490 F. Supp. 2d 1062 (D. Haw. 2007), 216 n.302, 219 n.322
Lofton v. Fairmont Specialty Ins. Mgrs., Inc., 367 S.W.3d 593 (Ky. 2012), 448
Lohan v. Perez, 924 F. Supp. 2d 447 (E.D.N.Y. 2013), 330 n.97
Long, United States v., 857 F.2d 436 (8th Cir. 1988), 379 n.72, 380
Longcrier v. HL-A Co., 595 F. Supp. 2d 1218 (S.D. Ala. 2008), 209 n.253, 210
Lopez, United States v., 4 F.3d 1455 (9th Cir. 1993), 179
Lord v. Wood, 184 F.3d 1083 (9th Cir. 1999), 380
Lowery v. Cardwell, 575 F.2d 727 (9th Cir. 1978), 399
Lowe v. Experian, 328 F. Supp. 2d 1122 (D. Kan. 2004), 421 n.24, 423 n.35
Lozama v. Samaritan Daytop Village, Inc., No. 18 CV 4351 (DLI)(RML), 2019 WL 1002954 (E.D.N.Y. Mar. 1, 2019), 79 n.177, 97, 176
Lucas, *In re*, Disciplinary Action Against, 789 N.W.2d 73 (N.D. 2010), 166

Lucas v. State, 572 S.E.2d 274 (S.C. 2002), 389 n.119, 407
Lundy v. Shelter Mut. Ins. Co., No. A-05-034, 2006 WL 2472723 (Neb. Ct. App. Aug. 29, 2006), 439 n.126
Lung, *In re*, 122 N.Y.S.3d 364 (App. Div. 2020), 173, 182 n.91, 285–286
Lyddon v. Geothermal Props. Inc., 996 F.2d 212 (9th Cir. 1993), 526
Lyons, *In re*, Disciplinary Action Against, 780 N.W.2d 629 (Minn. 2010), 329, 473 n.167

MacArthur v. San Juan Cnty., No. 2:00CV584K, 2001 WL 1806855 (D. Utah Mar. 6, 2001), 216 n.302
MacDonald, *In re*, Disciplinary Action against, 906 N.W.2d 238 (Minn. 2018), 496
Mack, *In re*, 519 N.W.2d 900 (Minn. 1994), 376–378, 411 n.231
Macy's Inc. v. J.C. Penny Corp., 968 N.Y.S.2d 64 (App. Div. 2013), 24 n.137
Madden, *In re*, 423 S.W.3d 39 (Ark. 2012), 305
Maddox v. Knowledge Learning Corp., 499 F. Supp. 2d 1338 (N.D. Ga. 2007), 206, 207 n.244
Maddox v. State, 407 P.3d 152 (Haw. 2017), 7
Madison, *In re*, 282 S.W.3d 350 (Mo. 2009), 283, 495 n.9
Magallanes v. Ill. Bell Tel. Co., 535 F.3d 582 (7th Cir. 2008), 450 n.18
Magee, *In re*, 263 So. 3d 845 (La. 2018), 320 n.36
Main Events Prods., LLC v. Lacy, 220 F. Supp. 2d 353 (D.N.J. 2002), 421 n.23
Makins v. D.C., 861 A.2d 590 (D.C. 2004), 450 n.18
Makreas v. Moore Law Grp., No. C-11-2406 MMC, 2012 WL 1458191 (N.D. Cal. Apr. 26, 2012), 338 n.141
Malmin, *In re*, 895 P.2d 1217 (Idaho 1995), 355
Malofiy, *In re*, 653 F. App'x 148 (3d Cir. 2016), 94
Malone, *In re*, 482 N.E.2d 565 (N.Y. 1985), 125 n.229
Manero v. Manero, No. FSTFA134024800S, 2015 WL 522249 (Conn. Super. Ct. Jan. 12, 2015), 440 n.135
Manion v. Nagin, 394 F.3d 1062 (8th Cir. 2005), 249 n.23
Mannheim Video, Inc. v. Cnty. of Cook, 884 F.2d 1043 (7th Cir. 1989), 351, 351 n.220, 351 n.222
Manning-Wallace, *In re*, 695 S.E.2d 237 (Ga. 2010), 317, 324 n.60, 369
Manokoune v. State Farm Mut. Auto. Ins. Co., 145 P.3d 1081 (Okla. 2006), 347
Mantia v. Hanson, 79 P.3d 404 (Or. Ct. App. 2003), 85
Marceaux v. Lafayette City-Parish Consol. Gov't, 731 F.3d 488 (5th Cir. 2013), 132
Marietta, *In re*, 569 P.2d 921 (Kan. 1977), 76
Marietta Tr. v. J.R. Logging Inc., 225 So. 3d 1144 (La. Ct. App. 2017), 449 n.10
Mark, State v., 231 P.3d 478 (Haw. 2010), 42 n.228
Markham Contracting Co. Inc. v. First Am. Title Ins. Co., No. 1 CA-CV 12-0195, 2013 WL 3828690 (Ariz. Ct. App. July 18, 2013), 426 n.51
Marriage of Gong and Kwong, *In re*, 77 Cal. Rptr. 3d 540 (Ct. App. 2008), 522–523
Marriage of McDermott, *In re*, 307 P.3d 717 (Wash. Ct. App. 2013), 277

Marriage of Perry, *In re*, 293 P.3d 170 (Mont. 2013), 435
Martinez, *In re*, 462 P.3d 36 (Ariz. 2020), 103, 107, 182, 296
Martinez v. Cnty. of Antelope, No. 4:15CV3064, 2016 WL 3248241 (D. Neb. June 13, 2016), 80, 98, 177 n.67
Martinez v. Hous. Auth. of DeKalb Cnty., 590 S.E.2d 245 (Ga. Ct. App. 2003), 426 n.51
Mascarenas, People v., 103 P.3d 339 (Colo. 2003), 84, 101
Maskiell, State v., 918 A.2d 293 (Conn. App. Ct. 2007), 478
Mason, People v., 938 P.2d 133 (Colo. 1997), 16
Massey v. Prince George's Cnty., 907 F. Supp. 138 (D. Md. 1995), 346 n.186, 348
Matsuura v. E.I. du Pont de Nemours & Co., 73 P.3d 687 (Haw. 2003), 484
Matthews v. Freedman, 128 F.R.D. 194 (E.D. Pa. 1989), 68 n.107
Matusick v. Erie Cnty. Water Auth., No. 07CV489A, 2010 WL 681062 (W.D.N.Y. Feb. 22, 2010), 81
Maynard, People v., 219 P.3d 430 (Colo. 2008), 324, 330
Mays v. Askin, 585 S.E.2d 735 (Ga. Ct. App. 2003), 2
McAteer, *In re*, 183 A.3d 1133 (R.I. 2019), 353 n.230
McBurney, *In re*, 13 A.3d 654 (R.I. 2011), 287 n.49
McCallum v. CSX Transp., Inc., 149 F.R.D. 104 (M.D.N.C. 1993), 85 n.204
McClellan v. Ready Mixed Concrete Co. of Erie, Inc., Civ. No 13-87 Erie, 2014 WL 4060254 (W.D. Pa. Aug. 14, 2014), 95 n.35, 167
McClure, *In re*, 652 N.E.2d 863 (Ind. 1995), 283 n.19
McCombs v. State, 3 So. 3d 950 (Ala. Crim. App. 2008), 397, 398
McCormick, *In re*, Disciplinary Action Against, 819 N.W.2d 442 (Minn. 2012), 166, 172
McCormick, State v., 259 S.E.2d 880 (N.C. 1979), 371
McCourt Co. v. FPC Props., Inc., 434 N.E.2d 1234 (Mass. 1982), 4
McDonald, *In re*, Disciplinary Action Against, 609 N.W.2d 418 (N.D. 2000), 371
McDowell, State v., 681 N.W.2d 500 (Wis. 2004), 380–381, 397
McGaha v. Commonwealth, 414 S.W.3d 1 (Ky. 2013), 233 n.37, 233 n.39
McGhee v. State, 951 P.2d 1215 (Alaska 1998), 348, 349
McIntosh Cnty. Bank v. Dorsey & Whitney, LLP, 745 N.W.2d 538 (Minn. 2008), 139 n.10
McIntosh v. State Farm Fire & Cas. Co., Civ. A. No. 1:06CV1080 LTS-RHW, 2008 WL 941640 (S.D. Miss. Apr. 4, 2008), 143 n.36
McKenna, *In re*, 110 A.3d 1126 (R.I. 2015), 316 n.8, 321 n.42
McKenzie Law Firm, P.A. v. Ruby Receptionists, Inc., No. 3:18-cv-1921-SI, 2020 WL 2789873 (D. Or. May 29, 2020), 199, 213 n.275
McKesson HBOC, Inc. Sec. Litig., *In re*, 126 F. Supp. 2d 1239 (N.D. Cal. 2000), 199, 200, 206 n.232
McLaughlin v. Payne, 761 S.E.2d 289 (Ga. 2014), 443
McLemore v. Elliot, 614 S.W.2d 226 (Ark. 1981), 495 n.5
McMillan v. Shadow Ridge at Oak Park Homeowner's Ass'n, 81 Cal. Rptr. 3d 550 (Ct. App. 2008), 167 n.13
Medtronic Navigation, Inc. v. Brainlab Medizinische Computersysteme Gmbh, 603 F.3d 943 (Fed. Cir. 2010), 72 n.132

Meeks v. Gem Boat Services, Inc., 620 N.E.2d 983 (Ohio Ct. App. 1993), 206 n.232
Meisels v. Fox Rothschild LLP, 222 A.3d 649 (N.J. 2020), 345
Member of Bar Hurley, *In re*, No. 383, 2017, 2018 WL 1319010 (Del. Mar. 14, 2018), 284
Mena v. Key Food Stores Co-op., Inc., 758 N.Y.S.2d 246 (Sup. Ct. 2003), 122
Mendez v. Hovensa, LLC, No. 02-0169, 2008 WL 906768 (D.V.I. Mar. 31, 2008), 186
Merck v. Swift Transp. Co., No. CV-16-01103-PHX-ROS, 2018 WL 3774007 (D. Ariz. July 19, 2018), 98, 177, 179 n.76
Merida, United States v., 828 F.3d 1203 (10th Cir. 2016), 248 n.15, 250 n.28, 253 n.44
Merrill Lynch Bus. Fin. Servs., Inc. v. Nudell, 239 F. Supp. 2d 1170 (D. Colo. 2003), 421 n.23, 424 n.41, 425 n.48
Merrill v. A.R.G., 398 P.3d 954 (Or. Ct. App. 2017), 86
Merritt v. Int'l Ass'n of Machinists & Aerospace Workers, 613 F.3d 609 (6th Cir. 2010), 59 n.57
Messer v. Huntington Anesthesia Grp., Inc., 664 S.E.2d 751 (W. Va. 2008), 450
Messing, Rudavsky & Weliky, P.C. v. President & Fellows of Harvard Coll., 764 N.E.2d 825 (Mass. 2002), 78, 96, 166, 175
Metrahealth Ins. Co. v. Anclote Psychiatric Hosp. Ltd., 961 F. Supp. 1580 (M.D. Fla. 1997), 84, 168
Meyer v. Kalanick, 212 F. Supp. 3d 437 (S.D.N.Y. 2016), 92 n.14
M.G., *In re*, 221 A.3d 774 (R.I. 2019), 345
Miano v. AC & R Adver., Inc., 148 F.R.D. 68 (S.D.N.Y. 1993), 83 n.192, 169 n.24, 170 n.30
Michael, *In re*, Disciplinary Action Against, 836 N.W.2d 753 (Minn. 2013), 494 n.1, 520 n.145
Michael, *In re*, Disciplinary Proceeding Against, 805 N.W.2d 110 (Wis. 2011), 126 n.231
Michaels v. Woodland, 988 F. Supp. 468 (D.N.J. 1997), 186
Mich. First Credit Union v. Al Long Ford, Inc., No. 291146, 2010 WL 5129890 (Mich. Ct. App. Dec. 16, 2010), 143
Mich. Mut. Ins. Co. v. Sports, Inc., 706 N.E.2d 555 (Ind. 1999), 511 n.95, 517 n.128
Microsoft Corp. v. Alcatel Bus. Sys., Civ. No. 07-090-SLR, 2007 WL 4480632 (D. Del. Dec. 18, 2007), 78, 97 n.46
Midgett, United States v., 342 F.3d 321 (4th Cir. 2003), 378 n.63, 382–383
Midwest Motor Sports v. Arctic Cat Sales, Inc., 347 F.3d 693 (8th Cir. 2003), 108–110, 121–122, 128 n.239
Milkovich v. Lorain Journal Co., 497 U.S. 1 (1990), 502
Miller, *In re*, 741 F. App'x 859 (3d Cir. 2018), 345 n.180
Miller, State v., 600 N.W.2d 457 (Minn. 1999), 179
Miller v. Material Sciences Corp., 986 F. Supp. 1104 (N.D. Ill. 1997), 83 n.192, 170 n.30
Miller v. Norfolk & W. Ry. Co., 538 N.E.2d 1293 (Ill. App. Ct. 1989), 19
Mills v. Hausmann-McNally, S.C., 992 F. Supp. 2d 885 (S.D. Ind. 2014), 425 n.47

Mims v. Chichester, 722 N.Y.S.2d 30 (App. Div. 2001), 95 n.37, 169 n.25
Miniclier, *In re*, 74 So. 3d 687 (La. 2011), 107 n.108
Minor v. Barnes, 609 S.W.3d 449 (Ark. Ct. App. 2020), 427
Mintz, *In re*, 317 P.3d 756 (Kan. 2014), 126 n.231, 315 n.3
Miskovsky v. State, 586 P.2d 1104 (Okla. Crim. App. 1978), 357 n.255
Miss., United States v., No. 3:16-cv-622-CWR-FKB, 2018 WL 4956658 (S.D. Miss. Oct. 12, 2018), 79 n.177, 97, 176 n.63
Miss. Bar v. Att'y ST, 621 So. 2d 229 (Miss. 1993), 132
Miss. Bar v. Land, 653 So. 2d 899 (Miss. 1994), 325 n.61
Miss. Bar v. Lumumba, 912 So. 2d 871 (Miss. 2005), 497 n.18
Miss. Bar v. Mathis, 620 So. 2d 1213 (Miss. 1993), 478 n.199
Miss. Bar v. Robb, 684 So. 2d 615 (Miss. 1996), 476 n.183
Mitchell, People v., 626 N.E.2d 630 (N.Y. 1993), 356 n.254
Mitchell Props. v. Real Est. Title Co., 490 A.2d 271 (Md. Ct. Spec. App. 1985), 450
Mitchell v. Dougherty, 644 N.W.2d 391 (Mich. Ct. App. 2002), 8 n.38
Mitchum v. Hudgens, 533 So. 2d 194 (Ala. 1988), 4
MJK Fam. LLC v. Corp. Eagle Mgmt. Servs., Inc., 676 F. Supp. 2d 584 (E.D. Mich. 2009), 20 n.109
MKC Millennium Ctr. Retail, LLC, 571 B.R. 783 (Bankr. N.D. Ill. 2017), 30 n.167
Moe, *In re*, Disciplinary Action Against, 851 N.W.2d 868 (Minn. 2014), 320 n.37
Moeller v. Am. Guarantee & Liab. Ins. Co., 707 So. 2d 1062 (Miss. 1996), 4
Mohica v. Cvejin, 990 N.E.2d 720 (Ill. App. Ct. 2013), 329, 473
Mok v. 21 Mott St. Rest. Corp., No. 14-cv-8081 (PKC), 2017 WL 3981308 (S.D.N.Y. Sept. 8, 2017), 473 n.167
Molton v. State, 651 So. 2d 663 (Ala. Crim. App. 1994), 478
Monceret v. Bd. of Prof'l Responsibility, 29 S.W.3d 455 (Tenn. 2000), 173
Monsanto Co. v. Aetna Cas. & Sur. Co., 593 A.2d 1013 (Del. Super. Ct. 1990), 85 n.204
Montoya, *In re*, 266 P.3d 11 (N.M. 2011), 319 n.26
Moore, *In re*, 665 N.E.2d 40 (Ind. 1996), 287 n.49
Moores v. Greenberg, 834 F.2d 1105 (1st Cir. 1987), 459 n.60
Moore v. Warden, No. CV084002471, 2012 WL 2335283 (Conn. Super. Ct. May 22, 2012), 403 n.192
Morales, *In re*, 651 S.E.2d 84 (Ga. 2007), 323 n.53
Mora v. Lancet Indem. Risk Retention Grp., Inc., 773 F. App'x 113 (4th Cir. 2019), 6
Mordkofsky, *In re*, 649 N.Y.S.2d 71 (App. Div. 1996), 508 n.72
Moreland v. Austin, 670 S.E.2d 68 (Ga. 2008), 189, 190, 193
Morgan Stanley & Co. v. MacQueen, 416 S.E.2d 55 (W. Va. 1992), 17–18
Morgan v. Family Dollar Stores, Inc., 551 F.3d 1233 (11th Cir. 2008), 206 n.233
Morgan v. Wesley Med. Ctr., No. 18-2158-KHV-KGG, 2018 WL 6696561 (D. Kan. Dec. 20, 2018), 193 n.154
Mori v. Saito, 785 F. Supp. 2d 427 (S.D.N.Y. 2011), 95 n.35, 167 n.9
Morris, People v., 16 N.E.3d 269 (Ill. App. Ct. 2014), 395
Morris & Doherty, P.C. v. Lockwood, 672 N.W.2d 884 (Mich. Ct. App. 2003), 276
Morrissey v. Va. State Bar *ex rel.* Third Dist. Comm., 829 S.E.2d 738 (Va. 2019), 105 n.94, 297 n.115
Morris v. Thomson, 937 P.2d 1212 (Idaho 1997), 189

Moseley, *In re*, 643 S.E.2d 190 (Va. 2007), 508 n.69
Moseley v. State, 908 N.E.2d 599 (Ind. 2009), 525
Moseley v. Va. State Bar, 694 S.E.2d 586 (Va. 2010), 508 n.69
Moss v. Parr Waddoups Brown Gee & Loveless, 285 P.3d 1157 (Utah 2012), 484
Mt. Hebron Missionary Baptist Ass'n of AL, Inc. v. Sentinel Ins. Co., No.: 3:16-cv-658-CDL-GMB, 2017 WL 3928269 (M.D. Ala. Sept. 27, 2017), 30
Mt. Rushmore Broad., Inc. v. Statewide Collections, 42 P.3d 478 (Wyo. 2002), 434 n.94, 438, 440 n.134
Mt. Vernon Fire Ins. Co. v. VisionAid, Inc., 875 F.3d 716 (1st Cir. 2017), 4
Muff v. Dragovich, Civ. A. No. 05-5251, 2007 WL 776804 (E.D. Pa. Mar. 12, 2007), 383–384
Mulhall, *In re*, 822 P.2d 947 (Ariz. 1992), 292
Mullen v. GLV, Inc., 334 F.R.D. 656 (N.D. Ill. 2020), 179, 199
Mumford, State v., 731 A.2d 831 (Del. 1999), 288 n.54
Mungo, *In re*, 305 B.R. 762 (Bankr. D.S.C. 2003), 336, 337
Muriel Siebert & Co. v. Intuit Inc., 868 N.E.2d 208 (N.Y. 2007), 183–184
Murphy, United States v., 768 F.2d 1518 (7th Cir. 1985), 126 n.232
Murray v. Just In Case Bus. Lighthouse, LLC, 374 P.3d 443 (Colo. 2016), 139 n.12, 141 n.22
Murray v. Metropolitan Life Ins. Co., 583 F.3d 173 (2d Cir. 2009), 429–430
Muster v. Muster, 921 A.2d 756 (Del. Fam. Ct. 2005), 281
Mut. of Enumclaw Ins. Co. v. Dan Paulson Constr., Inc., 169 P.3d 1 (Wash. 2007), 5
Myers, Estate of, *In re*, 130 P.3d 1023 (Colo. 2006), 36
Myers v. Hertz Corp., 624 F.3d 547 (10th Cir. 2010), 206 n.233
Mylan, Inc. v. Kirkland & Ellis LLP, No. 15-581, 2015 WL 12733414 (W.D. Pa. June 9, 2015), 23 n.135

Nabi v. Sells, 892 N.Y.S.2d 41 (App. Div. 2009), 7
Najim, *In re*, 405 P.3d 1223 (Kan. 2017), 105 n.93, 297 n.115
N. Am. Deed Co. v. Joseph, 334 B.R. 443 (Bankr. D. Nev. 2005), 30
Napue v. Ill., 360 U.S. 264 (1959), 407
Nathan, *In re*, Disciplinary Action Against, 671 N.W.2d 578 (Minn. 2003), 494 n.1, 502, 502 n.30, 506 n.60
National Union Fire Insurance Co. v. Stites Professional Law Corp., 1 Cal. Rptr. 2d 570 (Ct. App. 1991), 4
Nationwide Mut. Fire Ins. Co. v. Bourlon, 617 S.E.2d 40 (N.C. Ct. App. 2005), 5
Nationwide Trustee Servs., Inc. v. Rivera, No. 3:11-cv-528-RJC-DSC, 2012 WL 1394916 (W.D.N.C. Apr. 23, 2012), 338 n.141
Nat'l Bank of Andover, N.A. v. Aero Std. Tooling, Inc., 49 P.3d 547 (Kan. Ct. App. 2002), 432
Nat'l Med. Care, Inc. v. Home Med. of Am., Inc., No. 00-1225, 2002 WL 31068413 (Mass. Super. Ct. Sept. 12, 2002), 8, 9
Nat'l Union Fire Ins. Co. v. L.E. Myers Co. Grp., 937 F. Supp. 276 (S.D.N.Y. 1996), 442 n.148
NC-DSH, Inc. v. Garner, 218 P.3d 853 (Nev. 2009), 449
N.C. State Bar v. Weckworth, No. COA18-866, 2019 WL 2353465 (N.C. Ct. App. June 4, 2019), 170 n.30

Ndreko v. Ridge, 351 F. Supp. 2d 904 (D. Minn. 2004), 326
Neary, *In re*, 84 N.E.3d 1194 (Ind. 2017), 118
Neelon v. Krueger, Civ. A. No. 12-cv-11198-IT, 2015 WL 874420 (D. Mass. Mar. 2, 2015), 423 n.38
Nester, *In re*, 541 S.E.2d 538 (S.C. 2001), 129
Neumann v. Tuccio, No. DBDCCV075002381S, 2009 WL 2506357 (Conn. Super. Ct. July 17, 2009), 443
Nev. Yellow Cab Corp. v. Eighth Jud. Dist. Ct. of Nev., 152 P.3d 737 (Nev. 2007), 26
New Destiny Treatment Ctr., Inc. v. Wheeler, 950 N.E.2d 157 (Ohio 2011), 275 n.168
Newell, *In re*, 234 P.3d 967 (Or. 2010), 173
New Horizon Kids Quest III, Inc. v. Eighth Jud. Dist. Ct., 392 P.3d 166 (Nev. 2017), 37 n.202
Newsome v. Peoples Bancshares, 269 So. 3d 19 (Miss. 2018), 2
Newsuan v. Republic Servs., Inc., 213 A.3d 279 (Pa. Super. Ct. 2019), 96, 174
Newton v. Stoneridge Apts., 424 P.3d 1086 (Utah Ct. App. 2018), 27
Nicholas v. Grapetree Shores, Inc., No. 05-119, 2013 WL 1196960 (D.V.I. Mar. 21, 2013), 28 n.154
Nicholson, *In re*, 791 S.E.2d 776 (Ga. 2016), 465 n.98
Nieves v. OPA, Inc., 947 F. Supp. 2d 887 (N.D. Ill. 2013), 179
Nissan Motor Co. v. Nissan Computer Corp., 180 F. Supp. 2d 1089 (C.D. Cal. 2002), 132 n.266
Nissan N. Am., Inc. v. Johnson Elec. N. Am., Inc., No. 09-11783, 2011 WL 1812505 (E.D. Mich. May 12, 2011), 139 n.10, 160 n.145, 162 n.152
Nixon v. Am. Tobacco Co., 34 S.W.3d 122 (Mo. 2000), 19
Nix v. Whiteside, 475 U.S. 157 (1986), 383
N.J. Div. of Child Prot. & Permanency v. G.S., 149 A.3d 816 (N.J. Super. Ct. App. Div. 2016), 2 n.1
N. Moraine Wastewater Reclamation Dist. v. Ill. Commerce Comm'n, 912 N.E.2d 204 (Ill. App. Ct. 2009), 427 n.53
Nocella, *In re*, 79 A.3d 766 (Pa. Ct. Jud. Disc. 2013), 466, 476
Noel v. State, 26 S.W.3d 123 (Ark. 2000), 389, 390 n.127, 406 n.208
Norelus v. Denny's, Inc., 628 F.3d 1270 (11th Cir. 2010), 394 n.148, 395 n.151
Norman, United States v., 776 F.3d 67 (2d Cir. 2015), 396
Northbrook Digital, LLC v. Vendio Servs., Inc., 625 F. Supp. 2d 728 (D. Minn. 2008), 423 n.33, 442
North Carolina State Bar v. Sutton, 791 N.E.2d 881 (N.C. Ct. App. 2016), 283, 320 n.36, 358 n.260
Northfield Ins. Co. v. George E. Busson Realty Co., No. Civ. A. 99-151, 1999 WL 804076 (E.D. La. Oct. 7, 1999), 131, 132 n.266
Notopolous v. Statewide Grievance Comm., 890 A.2d 509 (Conn. 2006), 497
N. Sec. Ins. Co. v. Mitec Elec., Ltd., 965 A.2d 447 (Vt. 2008), 517 n.129
Nuckles v. Wal-Mart Stores, Inc., No. 4:06CV00178 WRW, 2007 WL 1546092 (E.D. Ark. May 25, 2007), 80, 176 n.63
Nugent v. Myles, 829 S.E.2d 623 (Ga. Ct. App. 2019), 450 n.15

Nunez v. Lovell, Civ. No. 2005-7, 2008 WL 4525835 (D.V.I. Oct. 3, 2008), 19
Nunnery, *In re*, Disciplinary Proceeding Against, 725 N.W.2d 613 (Wis. 2007), 56–57, 56 n.40, 521
NuStar Farms, LLC v. Zylstra, 880 N.W.2d 478 (Iowa 2016), 8 n.37
NYAT Operating Corp. v. Jackson, Lewis, Schnitzler & Krupman, 741 N.Y.S.2d 385 (App. Div. 2002), 126 n.230
N.Y. v. Solvent Chem. Co., 166 F.R.D. 284 (W.D.N.Y. 1996), 138 n.8

Oasis W. Realty, LLC v. Goldman, 250 P.3d 1115 (Cal. 2011), 27 n.151
Obert, *In re*, 282 P.3d 825 (Or. 2012), 520 n.150
O'Brien v. Super. Ct., 939 A.2d 1223 (Conn. App. Ct. 2008), 54, 292, 520
Odone v. Croda Int'l PLC, 170 F.R.D. 66 (D.D.C. 1997), 371
O'Dwyer, *In re*, 221 So. 3d 1 (La. 2017), 284 n.26
Office of Disciplinary Counsel v. DiAngelus, 907 A.2d 452 (Pa. 2006), 94, 294, 465 n.98, 467
Office of Disciplinary Counsel v. Fina, 225 A.3d 568 (Pa. 2020), 257
Office of Disciplinary Counsel v. Kiesewetter, 889 A.2d 47 (Pa. 2005), 315
Office of Disciplinary Counsel v. Price, 732 A.2d 599 (Pa. 1999), 293
Office of Disciplinary Counsel v. Surrick, 749 A.2d 441 (Pa. 2000), 106, 297, 469, 494 n.2
Office of Disciplinary Counsel v. West, 706 N.E.2d 760 (Ohio 1999), 508 n.66
Office of Disciplinary Counsel v. Wrona, 908 A.2d 1281 (Pa. 2006), 293, 467, 507 n.60
Office of Disciplinary Couns. v. Baldwin, 225 A.3d 817 (Pa. 2020), 253 n.44, 254–262
Office of Disciplinary Couns. v. Greene, 655 N.E.2d 1299 (Ohio 1995), 344
Office of Disciplinary Couns. v. Price, 732 A.2d 599 (Pa. 1999), 467
Office of Lawyer Regulation v. Hurley, No. 2007AP478-D (Wis. Feb. 11, 2009), 119–121
Ogden Newspapers, Inc. v. Willis, 566 S.E.2d 560 (W. Va. 2002), 26
Ogle v. Ogle, 128 N.E.3d 775 (Ohio Ct. App. 2018), 442 n.150
O'Kain v. Landress, 450 P.3d 508 (Or. Ct. App. 2019), 3, 247
O'Keefe, United States v., 132 F.3d 1252 (8th Cir. 1998), 117
Okla. Bar Ass'n, State *ex rel.*, v. Allder, 48 P.3d 794 (Okla. 2002), 83 n.192, 95 n.35
Okla. Bar Ass'n, United States *ex rel.*, v. Bednar, 441 P.3d 91 (Okla. 2019), 325 n.62
Okla. Bar Ass'n, State *ex rel.*, v. Bolusky, 23 P.3d 268 (Okla. 2001), 93, 293, 465 n.102
Okla. Bar Ass'n v. Brooking, 411 P.3d 377 (Okla. 2018), 320 n.36
Okla. Bar Ass'n, State *ex rel.*, v. Chappell, 93 P.3d 25 (Okla. 2004), 294 n.96
Okla. Bar Ass'n, State *ex rel.*, v. Dobbs, 94 P.3d 31 (Okla. 2004), 318 n.18
Okla. Bar Ass'n, State *ex rel.*, v. Erickson, 29 P.3d 550 (Okla. 2001), 305
Okla. Bar Ass'n, State *ex rel.*, v. Godlove, 318 P.3d 1086 (Okla. 2013), 70 n.117
Okla. Bar Ass'n, State *ex rel.*, v. Harper, 995 P.2d 1143 (Okla. 2000), 167 n.9, 168, 170 n.30

Okla. Bar Ass'n, State *ex rel.*, v. Hummel, 89 P.3d 1105 (Okla. 2004), 449 n.11
Okla. Bar Ass'n, State *ex rel.*, v. Koss, 452 P.3d 427 (Okla. 2019), 452
Okla. Bar Ass'n, State *ex rel.*, v. Layton, 324 P.3d 1244 (Okla. 2014), 321
Okla. Bar Ass'n, State *ex rel.*, v. McMillen, 393 P.3d 219 (Okla. 2017), 104, 296
Okla. Bar Ass'n, State *ex rel.*, v. Porter, 766 P.2d 958 (Okla. 1988), 504–505, 504 n.45
Okla. Bar Ass'n v. Siegrist, 461 P.3d 213 (Okla. 2020), 106
Okla. Bar Ass'n, State *ex rel.*, v. Tweedy, 52 P.3d 1003 (Okla. 2000), 187
Okla. Bar Ass'n, State *ex rel.*, v. Wilcox, 227 P.3d 642 (Okla. 2009), 322 n.45
Okla. Bar Ass'n, State *ex rel.*, v. Wortham, 957 P.2d 549 (Okla. 1998), 299, 301, 302–303
Olsen, *In re*, 326 P.3d 1004 (Colo. 2014), 72, 378, 520 n.145
Olson v. Snap Prods., Inc., 183 F.R.D. 539 (D. Minn. 1998), 80
O'Meara's Case, *In re*, 834 A.2d 235 (N.H. 2003), 317
Omene, United States v., 143 F.3d 1167 (9th Cir. 1998), 397
O'Neil, State v., 393 P.3d 1238 (Wash. Ct. App. 2017), 427, 444–446
One Infant Child, *In re*, No. 12 Civ. 7797 (PKC), 2014 WL 704037 (S.D.N.Y. Feb. 20, 2014), 144 n.39
Onosko v. Smith, No. 3:14-CV-00004-EJL-CWD, 2015 WL 1003346 (D. Idaho Mar. 6, 2015), 337 n.138
Operating Eng'rs Pension Trust v. A-C Co., 859 F.2d 1336 (9th Cir. 1988), 64 n.87
Oracle America, Inc. v. Google Inc., 172 F. Supp. 3d 1100 (N.D. Cal. 2016), 235–237
Orangeburg Sausage Co. v. Cincinnati Ins. Co., 450 S.E.2d 66 (S.C. Ct. App. 1994), 442 n.150
Order to Show Cause, *In re*, 741 F. Supp. 1379 (N.D. Cal. 1990), 127 n.234
Ortiz, *In re*, 304 P.3d 404 (N.M. 2013), 285 n.35
Ortiz, People v., 44 N.E.3d 924 (N.Y. 2015), 419 n.13
Ortner, *In re*, Discipline of, 699 N.W.2d 865 (S.D. 2005), 326
Osbon, *Ex parte*, 888 So. 2d 1236 (Ala. 2004), 10
Osicka, *In re*, Disciplinary Proceeding Against, 765 N.W.2d 775 (Wis. 2009), 54, 520 n.145
Ositis, *In re*, 40 P.3d 500 (Or. 2002), 111 n.130, 123 n.213
Ostrovsky v. Monroe (*In re* Ellington), 230 B.R. 426 (Bankr. D. Mont. 1999), 337 n.138
Otto v. Box U.S.A. Grp., Inc., 177 F.R.D. 698 (N.D. Ga. 1997), 131
Ozee v. Am. Council on Gift Annuities, Inc., 143 F.3d 937 (5th Cir. 1998), 51

Padilla, *In re*, 456 P.3d 1057 (N.M. 2019), 52 n.17
Pagan, *In re*, No. 14–08824 (ESL), 2017 WL 405611 (Bankr. D.P.R. Jan. 30, 2017), 473 n.167
Pagan Velez v. Laboy Alvarado, 145 F. Supp. 2d 146 (D.P.R. 2001), 334 n.122
Page, *In re*, 774 N.E.2d 49 (Ind. 2002), 368 n.6
Pa. Ins. Guar. Ass'n v. Sikes, 590 So. 2d 1051 (Fla. Dist. Ct. App. 1991), 4
Pajerowski, *In re*, 721 A.2d 992 (N.J. 1998), 123 n.213
Pallon v. Roggio, Nos. 04-3625(JAP), 06-1068(FLW), 2006 WL 2466854 (D.N.J. Aug. 24, 2006), 43 n.233
Palmer v. Pioneer Hotel & Casino, 19 F. Supp. 2d 1157 (D. Nev. 1998), 78, 96, 175

Palmisano, *In re*, 70 F.3d 483 (7th Cir. 1995), 497 n.18, 502 n.30, 516 n.119
Palumbo v. Tele-Commc'ns, Inc., 157 F.R.D. 129 (D.D.C. 1994), 199
Pa. Nat'l Mut. Cas. Ins. Co. v. Perlberg, 819 F. Supp. 2d 449 (D. Md. 2011), 6
Panel Case No. 17289, *In re*, 669 N.W.2d 898 (Minn. 2003), 69 n.115
Pannell v. McBride, 306 F.3d 499 (7th Cir. 2002), 346 n.186
Paradigm Insurance Co. v. Langerman Law Offices, 24 P.3d 593 (Ariz. 2001), 6
Parham, State v., 121 N.E.3d 412 (Ohio Ct. App. 2019), 449
Park Apts. at Fayetteville, LP v. Plants, 545 S.W.3d 755 (Ark. 2018), 37
Parker v. Pepsi-Cola Gen. Bottlers, Inc., 249 F. Supp. 2d 1006 (N.D. Ill. 2003), 173
Park Heights Ave. LLC v. Cromwell Retail 1, LLC, 227 A.3d 757 (Md. Ct. Spec. App. 2020), 449
Parks v. Eastwood Ins. Servs., Inc., 235 F. Supp. 2d 1082 (C.D. Cal. 2002), 199, 209, 209 n.249
Parse, United States v., 789 F.3d 83 (2d Cir. 2015), 232 n.36
Pasillas-Sanchez, 214 P.3d 520 (Colo. Ct. App. 2009), 435 n.103, 438
Patel v. Martin, 111 N.E.3d 1082 (Mass. 2018), 2
Patel v. Mukasey, 526 F.3d 800 (5th Cir. 2008), 306
Patriarca v. Ctr. for Living & Working, Inc., 778 N.E.2d 877 (Mass. 2002), 81, 176
Patterson v. N.Y., 432 U.S. 197 (1977), 524 n.173
Paulson v. Plainfield Trucking, Inc., 210 F.R.D. 654 (D. Minn. 2002), 185
Paul v. Jud. Watch, Inc., 571 F. Supp. 2d 17 (D.D.C. 2008), 27 n.151
Pautler, *In re* (*Pautler II*), 47 P.3d 1175 (Colo. 2002), 92, 118, 122, 124
Pautler, People v. (*Pautler I*), 35 P.3d 571 (Colo. 2001), 92, 106
Payne, State v., 855 N.W.2d 783 (Neb. 2014), 7
Payne v. Goodyear Tire & Rubber Co., 207 F.R.D. 16 (D. Mass. 2002), 208 n.248
Pearson, *In re*, 228 A.3d 417 (D.C. 2020), 51, 72
Peasley, *In re*, 90 P.3d 764 (Ariz. 2004), 367
Pelkey, *In re*, 962 A.2d 268 (D.C. 2008), 70 n.119
Penda Corp. v. STK, LLC, No. Civ. A. 03-5578, Civ. A. 03-6240, 2004 WL 1628907 (E.D. Pa. July 16, 2004), 75, 112, 170 n.27
Pendleton, State v., 759 N.W.2d 900 (Minn. 2009), 371 n.26
Pendleton v. Cent. N.M. Corr. Facility, 184 F.R.D. 637 (D.N.M. 1999), 476
Pengilly, *In re*, No. 74316, 2018 WL 4297851 (Nev. Sept. 7, 2018), 288
Penna v. Margolis, No. CV030475408S, 2004 WL 377010 (Conn. Super. Ct. Feb. 9, 2004), 439
Penning, *In re*, 930 A.2d 144 (D.C. 2007), 13
People v. *See name of opposing party*
Perillo v. Johnson, 205 F.3d 775 (5th Cir. 2000), 30
Persaud, *In re*, 467 B.R. 26 (Bankr. E.D.N.Y. 2012), 4
Persichette v. Owners Ins. Co., 462 P.3d 581 (Colo. 2020), 29, 32–33
Peters, People v., 82 P.3d 389 (Colo. 2003), 103 n.82
Peterson v. Alaska Commc'ns Sys. Grp. Inc., No. 3:12-cv-00090-TMB, 2019 WL 6331355 (D. Alaska Nov. 26, 2019), 97, 176
Peters v. Pine Meadow Ranch Home Ass'n, 151 P.3d 962 (Utah 2007), 495 n.5, 496 n.17
Petition for Winter, *In re*, 770 N.W.2d 463 (Minn. 2009), 94 n.32, 321 n.39, 467 n.117

Pew, Estate of, 655 A.2d 521 (Pa. Super. Ct. 1994), 31 n.169
Pfefer, *In re*, Disciplinary Proceeding Against, 344 P.3d 1200 (Wash. 2015), 420 n.20
Pfeifer v. State Farm Ins. Co., No. Civ. A. 96-1895, 1999 WL 276085 (E.D. La. May 22, 1997), 131
Pfizer, Inc. v. Farr, No. M2011-01359-COA-R10-CV, 2012 WL 2370619 (Tenn. Ct. App. June 22, 2012), 19
Phillips, *In re*, 244 P.3d 549 (Ariz. 2010), 103
Piambino v. Bailey, 757 F.2d 1112 (11th Cir. 1985), 347
Piccone, People v., 459 P.3d 136 (Colo. 2020), 285 n.36
Pilli v. Va. State Bar, 611 S.E.2d 389 (Va. 2005), 502 n.30
Pine Island Farmers Coop v. Erstad & Riemer, P.A., 649 N.W.2d 444 (Minn. 2002), 6–7
Pinsky v. Statewide Grievance Comm., 578 A.2d 1075 (Conn. 1990), 166 n.7
Plante v. Stack, 109 A.3d 846 (R.I. 2015), 290 n.69
Plant Genetic Sys., N.V. v. Ciba Seeds, 933 F. Supp. 514 (M.D.N.C. 1996), 13
Plant v. Doe, 19 F. Supp. 2d 1316 (S.D. Fla. 1998), 351, 352
Platypus Wear, Inc. v. Horizonte Fabricacao Distribuicao Importacao Exportacao Ltda, No. 08-20738-CV, 2010 WL 625356 (S.D. Fla. Feb. 17, 2010), 139
P&L Dev. LLC v. Bionpharma Inc., No. 1:17CV1154, 2019 WL 357351 (M.D.N.C. Jan. 29, 2019), 13
Pleasant Mgmt., LLC v. Carrasco, 870 A.2d 443 (R.I. 2005), 179
Plein v. USAA Cas. Ins. Co., 463 P.3d 728 (Wash. 2020), 26, 31 n.168
Plichta, State v., 172 P.3d 512 (Haw. 2007), 426 n.53, 439 n.126, 440 n.135
Plummer, *In re*, Case No. 13-O-175515-PEM (Cal. State Bar Ct. June 4, 2015), 271 n.142, 272
Plymouth Indus., LLC v. Sioux Steel Co., Nos. 8:05CV196, 8:05CV469, 2006 WL 3392193 (D. Neb. Oct. 23, 2006), 422
Podoll, People v., 855 P.2d 1389 (Colo. 1993), 453 n.32
Polk Cnty. v. Dodson, 454 U.S. 312 (1981), 519
Port-A-Pour, Inc. v. Peak Innovations, Inc., No. 13-cv-1511-WYD-NYW, 2016 WL 7868813 (D. Colo. June 14, 2016), 194 n.156
Postorivo v. AG Paintball Holdings, Inc., Civ. A. Nos. 2991-VCP, 3111-VCP, 2008 WL 3876199 (Del. Ch. Aug. 20, 2008), 184
Potts, *In re*, 158 P.3d 418 (Mont. 2007), 375, 461–465
Powell v. City of Newton, 684 S.E.2d 55 (N.C. Ct. App. 2009), 450
Powers Reinforcing Fabricators, L.L.C. v. Contes *ex rel.* Cnty. of Maricopa, 473 P.3d 714 (Ariz. Ct. App. 2020), 427
Prac. Mgmt. Sols., LLC v. Eighth Jud. Dist. Ct., No. 68901, 2016 WL 2757512 (Nev. May 10, 2016), 421
Prasad v. MML Inv. Servs., Inc., No. 04 Civ. 380(RWS), 143 n.35, 148 n.72, 151–153, 154
Pratt v. Petelin, 09-2252-CM-GLR, 2010 WL 446474 (D. Kan. Feb. 4, 2010), 189 n.133, 191 n.141, 194 n.154
PRB Docket No. 2007-046, *In re*, 989 A.2d 523 (Vt. 2009), 93, 123, 129, 132, 465, 469
Precision Specialty Metals, Inc. v. United States, 315 F.3d 1346 (Fed. Cir. 2003), 351 n.217

Premium Prods., Inc. v. Pro Performance Sports, LLC, 997 F. Supp. 2d 433 (E.D. Va. 2014), 433, 438
Prevezon Holdings Ltd., United States v., 839 F.3d 227 (2d Cir. 2016), 30
Prewitt v. Sexton, 777 S.W.2d 891 (Ky. 1989), 86 n.214
Primera Beef, LLC v. Ward, 457 P.3d 161 (Idaho 2020), 449
Prizio v. Lincoln Nat'l Life Ins. Co., Civ. No. 3:11cv736 (JBA), 2014 WL 1315648 (D. Conn. Mar. 31, 2014), 348 n.201
Proctor, State *ex rel.*, v. Messina, 320 S.W.3d 145 (Mo. 2010), 191 n.141, 192
Prudential Ballard Realty Co. v. Weatherly, 769 So. 2d 1045 (Ala. 2000), 509 n.81, 514 n.114
Prudential Ins. Co., *In re*, 911 F. Supp. 148 (M.D. Pa. 1995), 80
P.T. Barnum's Nightclub v. Duhamell, 766 N.E.2d 729 (Ind. Ct. App. 2002), 80, 98, 177
Pulte Home Corp. v. Simerly, 746 S.E.2d 173 (Ga. Ct. App. 2013), 438 n.120
Pyle, *In re*, 91 P.3d 1222 (Kan. 2004), 76, 100 n.62, 308–310

Quality Developers, Inc. v. Thorman, 31 P.3d 296 (Kan. Ct. App. 2001), 425 n.44, 428 n.56
Quesada v. Napolitano, 701 F.3d 1080 (5th Cir. 2012), 450
Quest Diagnostics, Inc., United States v., 734 F.3d 154 (2d Cir. 2013), 41 n.226
Quinn v. Anvil Corp., No. C08-0182RSL, 2008 WL 11344647 (W.D. Wash. Aug. 27, 2008), 12

Rader v. ING Bank, C.A., Nos. 09-340-SLR/LPS, 09-544-SLR/LPS, 09-781-SLR/LPS, 2010 WL 1403962 (D. Del. Apr. 7, 2010), 436 n.107
Rail Freight Fuel Surcharge Antitrust Litig., *In re*, 965 F. Supp. 2d 104 (D.D.C. 2013), 21 n.121
Rajaratnam v. Motley Rice, LLC, No. 18-cv-3234(KAM)(RML), 2020 WL 1476171 (E.D.N.Y. Mar. 26, 2020), 148 n.72, 163 n.155
Ralph Oldsmobile, Inc. v. Gen. Motors Corp., No. 99 Civ. 4567 (AGS), 2001 WL 1035132 (S.D.N.Y. Sept. 7, 2001), 213 n.275
Ramey v. Dist. 141, Int'l Ass'n of Machinists & Aerospace Workers, 378 F.3d 269 (2d Cir. 2004), 420, 422, 424 n.42, 434
Rangel-Guzman, United States v., 752 F.3d 1222 (9th Cir. 2014), 419 n.11
Rankin v. Bd. of Educ. of the Wichita Pub. Schs., U.S.D. 259, 174 F.R.D. 695 (D. Kan. 1997), 205, 208 n.248
Raster v. Ameristar Casinos, Inc., 280 S.W.3d 120 (Mo. Ct. App. 2009), 427 n.53
Ravin, *In re*, 29 Vet. App. 95 (Vet. App. 2017), 323 n.51
Rayco Mfg., Inc. v. Murphy, Rogers, Sloss & Gambel, 142 N.E.3d 1267 (Ohio Ct. App. 2019), 422 n.30, 435
Ray v. Ray, 995 N.Y.S.2d 567 (App. Div. 2014), 427 n.53
REC Marine Logistics, LLC v. Richard, No. 19-11149, 2020 WL 1527766 (E.D. La. Mar. 27, 2020), 281 n.14, 282 n.14
Records v. Geils Unlimited Rsch., LLC, No. CIV.A. 12-11419-FDS, 2013 WL 3967970 (D. Mass. July 30, 2013), 247 n.13
Reed v. Hoosier Health Sys., 825 N.E.2d 408 (Ind. Ct. App. 2005), 12 n.66
Reger, *In re*, 421 P.3d 25 (Alaska 2018), 103 n.83

Religious Tech. Ctr. v. F.A.C.T.Net, Inc., 945 F. Supp. 1470 (D. Colo. 1996), 442 n.153
Rentclub, Inc. v. Transamerica Rental Fin. Corp., 811 F. Supp. 651 (M.D. Fla. 1992), 80, 98, 177 n.67
Reo v. Univ. Hosps. Health Sys., 131 N.E.3d 986 (Ohio Ct. App. 2019), 427 n.53
Reposa, *Ex parte*, No. AP-75965, 2009 WL 3478455 (Tex. Crim. App. Oct. 28, 2009), 279 n.1
Republican Party of Minnesota v. White, 536 U.S. 765 (2002), 506–507
Rescue Concepts, Inc., *In re*, 556 S.W.3d 331 (Tex. App. 2017), 3, 247
Resolution Trust Corp. v. Bright, 6 F.3d 336 (5th Cir. 1993), 370
Revise Clothing, Inc. v. Joe's Jeans Subsidiary, Inc., 687 F. Supp. 2d 381 (S.D.N.Y. 2010), 9 n.44, 31 n.170
Reynolds v. State, 625 N.E.2d 1319 (Ind. Ct. App. 1993), 398 n.166
Rheb v. Bar Ass'n of Baltimore Cnty., 46 A.2d 289 (Md. 1946), 298
Rices, People v., 406 P.3d 788 (Cal. 2017), 426 n.53
Richardson v. Howard, 712 F.2d 319 (7th Cir. 1983), 123 n.219
Richard v. Caliber Home Loans, Inc., No.: 2:15-cv-2647, 2017 WL 4349082 (S.D. Ohio Sept. 29, 2017), 168
Ricotta v. State of Cal., 4 F. Supp. 2d 961 (S.D. Cal. 1998), 336
Riel, People v., 998 P.2d 969 (Cal. 2000), 378, 380
Riley, *In re*, Disciplinary Proceeding Against, 882 N.W.2d 820 (Wis. 2016), 369 n.11
Riley v. PK Mgmt., LLC, No. 18-cv-2337-KHV-TJJ, 2019 WL 4256367 (D. Kan. Sept. 9, 2019), 171 n.36
Riordan, *In re*, Disciplinary Proceeding Against, 824 N.W.2d 441 (Wis. 2012), 497, 497 n.18
Rios, *In re*, 965 N.Y.S.2d 418 (App. Div. 2013), 62, 69 n.114
Rite Aid Corp. Sec. Litig., *In re*, 139 F. Supp. 2d 649 (E.D. Pa. 2001), 277 n.180
Rivera, People v., 986 N.E.2d 634 (Ill. 2013), 433 n.86
Rivera, State v., 109 P.3d 83 (Ariz. 2005), 386
Rivera, State v., 291 P.3d 512 (Kan. Ct. App. 2012), 427
Rivera v. Lutheran Med. Ctr., 866 N.Y.S.2d 520 (Sup. Ct. 2008), 221 n.329
Robbins, *In re*, 192 A.3d 558 (D.C. 2018), 2, 452
Robbins v. Gillock, 862 P.2d 1195 (Nev. 1993), 26
Robertson v. Alling, 351 P.3d 352 (Ariz. 2015), 449, 450 n.20
Robertson v. Wittenmyer, 736 N.E.2d 804 (Ind. Ct. App. 2000), 17 n.85
Roberts v. State, 840 So. 2d 962 (Fla. 2003), 424 n.42
Robison v. Orthotic & Prosthetic Lab, Inc., 27 N.E.3d 182 (Ill. App. Ct. 2015), 473 n.167
Rocheux Int'l of N.J., Inc. v. U.S. Merchants Fin. Grp., Inc., No. 06-6147, 2009 WL 3246837 (D.N.J. Oct. 5, 2009), 138, 141, 143 n.36, 158–160
Roche v. Hyde, 265 Cal. Rptr. 3d 301 (Ct. App. 2020), 345
Rock v. Ark., 483 U.S. 44 (1987), 395
Rockwell v. Rockwell, 175 A.3d 1249 (Conn. App. Ct. 2017), 86

Rocky Mountain Helium, LLC v. United States, No. 15-336C, 2019 WL 2246209 (Fed. Cl. May 24, 2019), 432
Rodenburg Law Firm v. Sira, 931 N.W.2d 687 (N.D. 2019), 86 n.209
Rodriguez-Aguirre, United States v., 30 F. App'x 803 (10th Cir. 2002), 148
Rogers, *In re*, 928 N.E.2d 210 (Ind. 2010), 322 n.45
Rogers v. Miss. Bar, 731 So. 2d 1158 (Miss. 1999), 298 n.127
Rogers v. Robson, Master, Ryan, Brummund & Belom, 403 N.E.2d 47 (Ill. 1980), 458
Roose, People v., 44 P.3d 266 (Colo. 2002), 323 n.53
Rosenau, *In re*, 132 A.3d 1174 (D.C. 2016), 473 n.167
Rosenthal & Watson, P.C., *In re*, 612 B.R. 507 (Bankr. W.D. Tex. 2020), 449
Rose v. Tullos, 994 So. 2d 734 (Miss. 2008), 72 n.134
Rosner, *In re*, 3 N.Y.S.3d 132 (App. Div. 2015), 473 n.167
Rossana, *In re*, 395 B.R. 697 (Bankr. D. Nev. 2008), 7
Rowe v. Vaagen Bros. Lumber, Inc., 996 P.2d 1103 (Wash. Ct. App. 2000), 198 n.183
Royal Travel, Inc. v. Shell Mgmt. Haw., Inc., Civ. No. 08-00314 JMS-LEK, 2009 WL 649929 (D. Haw. Mar. 12, 2009), 421
Royer, *In re*, 78 P.3d 449 (Kan. 2003), 296 n.108
Rozmus v. West, 13 Vet. App. 386 (U.S. App. Vet. Cl. 2000), 2
Rubin & Norris, LLC v. Panzarella, 51 N.E.3d 879 (Ill. App. Ct. 2016), 2
Rue, State v., 811 A.2d 425 (N.J. 2002), 525 n.185
Rules of Prof'l Conduct & Insurer Imposed Billing Rules & Procedures, *In re*, 2 P.3d 806 (Mont. 2000), 5
Runsvold v. Idaho State Bar, 925 P.2d 1118 (Idaho 1996), 100, 166, 180
Rural Water Sys. #1 v. City of Sioux Ctr., 967 F. Supp. 1483 (N.D. Iowa 1997), 351, 351 n.219, 352
Rusk v. Harstad, 393 P.3d 341 (Utah Ct. App. 2017), 8 n.37
Ryans, United States v., 903 F.2d 731 (10th Cir. 1990), 118 n.179

Saldana v. Kmart Corp., 260 F.3d 228 (3d Cir. 2001), 290 n.66
Salomon's Case, *In re*, 202 A.3d 587 (N.H. 2019), 51
Samad, *In re*, 51 A.3d 486 (D.C. 2012), 327 n.77
Samnick v. Goodman, 841 S.E.2d 468 (Ga. Ct. App. 2020), 26
Sanborn v. State, 474 So. 2d 309 (Fla. Dist. Ct. App. 1985), 390 n.128
Sanchez v. Liberty Lloyds, 672 So. 2d 268 (La. Ct. App. 1996), 53 n.21
Sanders, *In re*, 153 S.W.3d 54 (Tex. 2004), 427, 433
Sanderson v. Boddie-Noell Enters., Inc., 227 F.R.D. 448 (E.D. Va. 2005), 194 n.157, 196–197
Sandstrom v. Sandstrom, 880 P.2d 103 (Wyo. 1994), 180 n.82
Sandvoss, *In re*, 644 N.Y.S.2d 557 (App. Div. 1996), 71 n.122
Sanifill of Ga., Inc. v. Roberts, 502 S.E.2d 343 (Ga. 1998), 80, 98, 177
Santaniello v. Sweet, No. 3:04CV806 (RNC), 2007 WL 214605 (D. Conn. Jan. 25, 2007), 191
Santiago, People v., 925 N.E.2d 1122 (Ill. 2010), 83, 170–171
Sargent Cnty. Bank v. Wentworth, 500 N.W.2d 862 (N.D. 1993), 427, 433, 444

Sartin v. State, 400 S.W.3d 694 (Ark. 2012), 395
Satchwell v. Comm'r of Corr., 988 A.2d 907 (Conn. App. Ct. 2010), 426 n.49
Savage, *In re*, 91 A.3d 356 (R.I. 2014), 105 n.93, 106 n.102, 126 n.231, 297 n.114, 315 n.3
Savoy v. State, 96 A.3d 842 (Md. Ct. Spec. App. 2014), 395
S.C., *In re*, 88 A.3d 1220 (Vt. 2014), 50, 51, 525 n.186
Scanio, *In re*, 919 A.2d 1137 (D.C. 2007), 471 n.156
Scanlan v. Eisenberg, 893 F. Supp. 2d 945 (N.D. Ill. 2012), 95, 167, 179
Schaefer, *In re*, Discipline of, 25 P.3d 191 (Nev. 2001), 166
Schafer, *In re*, Disciplinary Proceeding Against, 66 P.3d 1036 (Wash. 2003), 460
Schaff v. State, 697 S.E.2d 305 (Ga. Ct. App. 2010), 426 n.53, 428–429, 428 n.56
Schmidt v. Gregorio, 705 So. 2d 742 (La. Ct. App. 1993), 80, 98, 177
Schmitt, State v., 102 P.3d 856 (Wash. Ct. App. 2004), 426 n.48
Schoeneman, *In re*, 777 A.2d 259 (D.C. 2001), 453
Schultheis, People v., 638 P.2d 8 (Colo. 1981), 389, 407
Scott, United States v., 909 F.2d 488 (11th Cir. 1990), 413
Scott v. Chipotle Mexican Grill, Inc., No. 12–CV–08333 (ALC) (SN), 2014 WL 4852063 (S.D.N.Y. Sept. 29, 2014), 206
Scott v. State, 8 So. 3d 855 (Miss. 2008), 397
Sealed Case, *In re*, 890 F.2d 15 (7th Cir. 1989), 410
Seaman v. Schulte Roth & Zabel LLP, 111 N.Y.S.3d 266 (App. Div. 2019), 2 n.4
Searcy v. Donelson, 204 F.3d 797 (8th Cir. 2000), 526 n.190
Seare, *In re*, 493 B.R. 158 (Bankr. D. Nev. 2013), 266 n.116
Sea-Roy Corp. v. Sunbelt Equip. & Rentals, Inc., 172 F.R.D. 179 (M.D.N.C. 1997), 131
Sec. Gen. Life Ins. v. Super. Ct., 718 P.2d 986 (Ariz. 1986), 425
SEC v. Lines, 669 F. Supp. 2d 460 (S.D.N.Y. 2009), 117, 122
Selby, People v., 606 P.2d 45 (Colo. 1979), 130 n.255, 133 n.268
Selmer, *In re*, 568 N.W.2d 702 (Minn. 1997), 70 n.117
Seltzer v. Morton, 154 P.3d 561 (Mont. 2007), 86–89
Sentry Select Ins. Co. v. Maybank Law Firm, LLC, 826 S.E.2d 270 (S.C. 2019), 5
Senu-Oke v. Modern Moving Sys., Inc., 978 S.W.2d 426 (Mo. Ct. App. 1998), 439 n.134
Sequa Corp. v. Lititech, Inc., 807 F. Supp. 653 (D. Colo. 1992), 126 n.232, 129
Service v. City of Meriden, No. CV94-0241732, 1995 WL 681537 (Conn. Super. Ct. Nov. 8, 1995), 215 n.293
S.G., *In re*, 91 P.3d 443 (Colo. Ct. App. 2004), 422 n.28
Shade v. Great Lakes Dredge & Dock Co., 72 F. Supp. 2d 518 (E.D. Pa. 1999), 372 n.29
Shafer v. Berger, Kahn, Shafton, Moss, Figler, Simon & Gladstone, 131 Cal. Rptr. 2d 777 (Ct. App. 2003), 484
Shaffer Equipment Co., 1 F.3d 450 (4th Cir. 1993), 321
Shaffer v. Farm Fresh, Inc., 966 F.2d 142 (4th Cir. 1992), 13
Shea, *In re*, Disciplinary Matter of, 273 P.3d 612 (Alaska 2012), 285 n.37
Shearin, *In re*, 765 A.2d 930 (Del. 2000), 50, 495, 508 n.74
Sheikh v. Wheeler, 790 F. App'x 793 (7th Cir. 2019), 431
Shelton v. S. Energy Homes, Inc., 420 F. Supp. 2d 579 (S.D. Miss. 2006), 346 n.186

Shepherd, People v., 99 N.E.3d 513 (Ill. App. Ct. 2018), 3
Shepherd v. Am. Broad. Cos., 62 F.3d 1469 (D.C. Cir. 1995), 295 n.103
Sheppard, Mullin, Richter & Hampton, LLP v. J-M Mfg. Co., 425 P.3d 1 (Cal. 2018), 24
Shocklee v. Mass. Mut. Life Ins. Co., 369 F.3d 437 (5th Cir. 2004), 348
Shockley v. State, 565 A.2d 1373 (Del. 1989), 379 n.72, 397
Shoreline Computers, Inc. v. Warnaco, Inc., No. CV 990422853S, 2000 WL 371206 (Conn. Super. Ct. Apr. 3, 2000), 80, 98, 177 n.67
Shorenstein Hays-Nederlander Theatres LLC Appeals, 213 A.3d 39 (Del. 2019), 289 n.65
Shorter, *In re*, 570 A.2d 760 (D.C. 1990), 106, 469
Shumate, *In re*, 647 N.E.2d 321 (Ind. 1995), 68
Sierra, State v., 523 S.E.2d 187 (S.C. Ct. App. 1999), 419 n.11
Sierra Glass & Mirror v. Viking Indus., Inc., 808 P.2d 512 (Nev. 1991), 324, 325 n.63
Sierra Pac. Indus., United States v. (*Sierra I*), 759 F. Supp. 2d 1206 (E.D. Cal. 2010), 217
Sierra Pac. Indus., United States v. (*Sierra II*), 759 F. Supp. 2d 1215 (E.D. Cal. 2011), 217
Simac, People v., 641 N.E.2d 416 (Ill. 1994), 357 n.255, 364
Simms v. Seaman, 69 A.3d 880 (Conn. 2013), 484
Simon, *In re*, 913 So. 2d 816 (La. 2005), 508 n.70, 509 n.83
Simpson Performance Prods., Inc. v. Horn, 92 P.3d 283 (Wyo. 2004), 39 n.209, 41
Simpson Strong-Tie Co. v. Oz-Post Int'l, LLC, No. 3:18-cv-01188-WHO, 2018 WL 3956430 (N.D. Cal. Aug. 17, 2018), 24 n.136, 85
Simpson v. James, 903 F.2d 372 (5th Cir. 1990), 9
Singleton, *In re*, 111 P.3d 630 (Kan. 2005), 323 n.53
Slane v. Rio Grande Water Conserv. Dist., 115 F.R.D. 61 (D. Colo. 1987), 55 n.26
Slavin, *In re*, 145 S.W.3d 538 (Tenn. 2004), 495 n.9, 501
Slaybaugh v. State, 44 N.E.3d 111 (Ind. Ct. App. 2015), 233 n.37
Slayton v. Weinberger, 194 S.E.2d 703 (Va. 1973), 138 n.3
Slotkin v. Citizens Casualty Co. of New York, 614 F.2d 301 (2d Cir. 1979), 484–487
Sluss v. Commonwealth, 381 S.W.3d 215 (Ky. 2012), 233 n.37
Smaland Beach Ass'n, Inc. v. Genova, 959 N.E.2d 955 (Mass. 2012), 418, 421
Small, People v., 962 P.2d 258 (Colo. 1998), 317 n.16
Smallwood, United States v., 65 F. Supp. 2d 689 (E.D. Va. 2005), 75 n.151, 100, 129–130, 169
Smith, *In re*, 236 P.3d 137 (Or. 2010), 294, 329, 467
Smith, *In re*, Nos. 12-116-3, 12-11857, 2013 WL 1092059 (Bankr. E.D. Tenn. Jan. 20, 2013), 338 n.141
Smith, State v., 749 S.E.2d 507 (N.C. Ct. App. 2013), 426 n.49
Smithson v. United States Fid. & Guar. Co., 411 S.E.2d 850 (W. Va. 1991), 427 n.53
Smith v. Am. Home Prods. Corp. Wyeth-Ayerst Pharm., 855 A.2d 608 (N.J. Super. Ct. Law Div. 2003), 190

Smith v. Kalamazoo Ophthalmology, 322 F. Supp. 2d 883 (W.D. Mich. 2004), 80, 97, 177
Smith v. Kan. City S. Ry., 87 S.W.3d 266 (Mo. Ct. App. 2002), 98, 177
Smith v. Kelly, Civ. A. No. 7:07CV00536, 2008 WL 345838 (W.D. Va. Feb. 6, 2008), 370 n.16
Smith v. Pace (*In re* Smith), 313 S.W.3d 124 (Mo. 2010), 505–506
Smith v. Pfizer Inc., 714 F. Supp. 2d 845 (M.D. Tenn. 2010), 161 n.151
Smith v. Robbins, 528 U.S. 259 (2000), 525
Smith v. Scripto-Tokai Corp., 170 F. Supp. 2d 533 (W.D. Pa. 2001), 346
Smith v. Shewry, 93 Cal. Rptr. 3d 436 (Ct. App. 2009), 329, 474
Smith v. State, 931 So. 2d 790 (Fla. 2006), 407
Smith v. Wharton, 78 S.W.3d 79 (Ark. 2002), 435 n.98
Smith v. Whatcott, 757 F.2d 1098 (10th Cir. 1985), 30
Smith v. WNA Carthage, L.L.C., 200 F.R.D. 576 (E.D. Tex. 2001), 131
Sniadecki, *In re*, 924 N.E.2d 109 (Ind. 2010), 323 n.53
Snodgrass v. Esper, No. 18-cv-00450, 2020 WL 5265126 (D. Md. Sept. 3, 2020), 176
Snyder v. Daugherty, 899 F. Supp. 2d 391 (W.D. Pa. 2012), 336, 337
Sorensen v. Barbuto, 177 P.3d 614 (Utah 2008), 189
So v. Suchanek, 670 F.3d 1304 (D.C. Cir. 2012), 16 n.85
Spears, *In re*, 290 So. 3d 645 (La. 2020), 283 n.24
Special Counsel for Discipline, State *ex rel.*, v. Sivick, 648 N.W.2d 315 (Neb. 2002), 508 n.70
Spence v. Flynt, 816 P.2d 771 (Wyo. 1991), 425, 443, 443 n.156
Spikes, *In re*, 881 A.2d 1118 (D.C. 2005), 69 n.115, 292
Spira v. J.P. Morgan Chase & Co., 466 F. App'x 20 (2d Cir. 2012), 344
Spratley v. State Farm Mut. Auto. Ins. Co., 78 P.3d 603 (Utah 2003), 5
Stahl v. Wal-Mart Stores, Inc., 47 F. Supp. 2d 783 (S.D. Miss. 1998), 96, 170 n.27
Standing Comm. v. Yagman, 55 F.3d 1430 (9th Cir. 1995), 505 n.50
Starbrite Props. Corp., *In re*, No. 11-40758 CEC, 2012 WL 2050745 (Bankr. E.D.N.Y. June 5, 2012), 375, 394 n.143
Stare v. Tate, 98 Cal. Rptr. 264 (Ct. App. 1971), 477 n.188
Stark Cnty. Bar Ass'n v. Russell, 856 N.E.2d 976 (Ohio 2006), 455 n.40
Starlight Sugar Inc. v. Soto, 903 F. Supp. 261 (D.P.R. 1995), 29
State *ex rel. See name of relator party*
State v. *See name of opposing party*
State Farm Fire & Cas. Co. v. Harris, No. 3:11-36-DCR, 2012 WL 896253 (E.D. Ky. Mar. 15, 2012), 334 n.122
State Farm Mut. Auto. Ins. Co. v. 21st Century Pharm., Inc., No. 17 Civ. 5845 (MKB) (VMS), 2020 WL 729775 (E.D.N.Y. Feb. 12, 2020), 426 n.53
State Farm Mut. Auto. Ins. Co. v. Hansen, 357 P.3d 338 (Nev. 2015), 5, 13
State of Nebraska *ex rel.* Counsel for Discipline of the Nebraska Supreme Court v. Kruger, 158 P.3d 418 (Mont. 2007), 465–466
State of New York v. Solvent Chemical Co., 166 F.R.D. 284 (W.D.N.Y. 1996), 155–158
Statewide Grievance Comm. v. Gillis, No. CV030479677S, 2004 WL 423905 (Conn. Super. Ct. Jan. 28, 2004), 471–472

Statewide Grievance Comm. v. Kennelly, No. CV040833515S, 2005 WL 758055 (Conn. Super. Ct. Feb. 25, 2005), 477 n.186
Std. Quimica de Venez., C.A. v. Cent. Hispano Int'l, Inc., 179 F.R.D. 64 (D.P.R. 1998), 432, 439
Steele, *In re*, 868 A.2d 146 (D.C. 2005), 455 n.40
Stein, *In re*, 177 P.3d 513 (N.M. 2008), 16, 315
Steinberg, *In re*, 620 N.Y.S.2d 345 (App. Div. 1994), 333 n.116, 334 n.121
Steinberg v. Winn-Dixie Stores, Inc., 121 So. 3d 622 (Fla. Dist. Ct. App. 2013), 426 n.53
Steinert v. Steinert, 897 N.E.2d 603 (Mass. App. Ct. 2008), 418 n.3, 428 n.56
Stenson, United States v., 741 F.3d 827 (7th Cir. 2014), 396
Stephens v. Alan V. Mock Constr. Co., 690 S.E.2d 225 (Ga. Ct. App. 2010), 451 n.21
Stephens v. Three Finger Black Shale P'ship, 580 S.W.3d 687 (Tex. App. 2019), 3
Stern, *In re*, 11 N.E.3d 917 (Ind. 2014), 70 n.117
Stewart, *In re*, 473 B.R. 612 (Bankr. W.D. Pa. 2012), 347
Stewart Title Guar. Co. v. Sterling Sav. Bank, 311 P.3d 1 (Wash. 2013), 5
Stiger, United States v., 413 F.3d 1185 (10th Cir. 2005), 30
Stivrins, State *ex rel.*, v. Flowers, 729 N.W.2d 311 (Neb. 2007), 274 n.167
St. Mary's Sch. of Med. Ltd. v. Zabaleta, 252 So. 3d 371 (Fla. Dist. Ct. App. 2018), 450 n.18
Storment, *In re*, 873 S.W.2d 227 (Mo. 1994), 370 n.14
Stovall v. Meneley, 22 P.3d 124 (Kan. 2001), 2
Stratmeyer v. Engberg, 649 N.W.2d 921 (S.D. 2002), 292 n.77, 341 n.160
Strawser v. Exxon Co., U.S.A., 843 P.2d 613 (Wyo. 1992), 80, 98, 177
Stubbs, *In re*, Discipline of, 974 P.2d 296 (Utah 1999), 319 n.31
S.T. v. 1515 Broad St., LLC, 227 A.3d 1190 (N.J. 2020), 448
Succession of Houston, 253 So. 3d 836 (La. Ct. App. 2018), 420
Susser, *In re*, Estate of, 657 N.W.2d 147 (Mich. Ct. App. 2002), 426 n.49
S. Visions, LLP v. Red Diamond, Inc., 370 F. Supp. 3d 1314 (N.D. Ala. 2019), 23 n.135
Swan, *In re*, 656 S.E.2d 374 (S.C. 2008), 284 n.26
Swanson v. 3M Co., 845 N.W.2d 808 (Minn. 2014), 32 n.171
Swarts, *In re*, 30 P.3d 1011 (Kan. 2001), 290 n.66, 362, 363
Sweeney v. Dayton, 416 P.3d 187 (Mont. 2018), 419 n.12
Swiss Reinsurance Am. Corp. v. Roetzel & Andress, 837 N.E.2d 1215 (Ohio Ct. App. 2005), 6
SWS Fin. Fund A v. Salomon Bros., 790 F. Supp. 1392 (N.D. Ill. 1992), 1 n.1
Synergy Tech & Design, Inc. v. Terry, No. C 06-02073 JSW, 2007 WL 1288464 (N.D. Cal. May 2, 2007), 19

Taylor, *In re*, 655 F.3d 274 (3d Cir. 2011), 54 n.26
Taylor v. Client Servs., Inc., No. 17-CV-05704, 2018 WL 4355819 (N.D. Ill. Sept. 12, 2018), 346 n.186
TBC Corp. v. Wall, 955 S.W.2d 838 (Tenn. Ct. App. 1997), 139
TCS Holdings, Inc. v. Onvoy, Inc., Civ. No. 07-1200 (DWF/AJB), 2008 WL 4151805 (D. Minn. Sept. 4, 2008), 475 n.179

Teague, United States v., 953 F.2d 1525 (11th Cir. 1992), 383
Teague v. St. Paul Fire & Marine Ins. Co., 10 So. 3d 806 (La. Ct. App. 2009), 4, 456–457, 458
Telcar Grp., Inc., *In re*, 363 B.R. 345 (Bankr. E.D.N.Y. 2007), 138, 141, 161 n.147
Tennant, *In re*, 392 P.3d 143 (Mont. 2017), 43 n.233
Terra Int'l, Inc. v. Miss. Chem. Corp., 913 F. Supp. 1306 (N.D. Iowa 1996), 186
Terra Land Servs., Inc. v. McIntyre, 572 S.W.3d 424 (Ark. Ct. App. 2019), 449 n.10
Tessier v. Plastic Surgery Specialists, Inc., 731 F. Supp. 724 (E.D. Va. 1990), 30
Teva Pharm. Indus., Ltd. v. United Healthcare Servs., Inc., 341 F. Supp. 3d 475 (E.D. Pa. 2018), 449 n.10
Thayer v. Fuller & Henry Ltd., 503 F. Supp. 2d 887 (N.D. Ohio 2007), 9 n.44
Thetford, *In re*, 574 S.W.3d 362 (Tex. 2019), 30, 31 n.168
Thigpen v. Banas, No. 08 C 4820, 2010 WL 520189 (N.D. Ill. Feb. 11, 2010), 337 n.138
Thomas, *In re*, 30 N.E.3d 704 (2015), 317 n.16
Thomas, People v., 925 P.2d 1081 (Colo. 1996), 508 n.66
Thomas v. City of N.Y., 293 F.R.D. 498 (S.D.N.Y. 2013), 139 n.9
Thomas, State *ex rel.*, v. Duke Univ., No. 1:17-CV-276, 2018 WL 4211372 (M.D.N.C. Sept. 4, 2018), 169 n.24
Thompson v. Goetz, 455 N.W.2d 580 (N.D. 1990), 425, 438
Thompson v. Sup. Ct. Comm. on Prof'l Conduct, 252 S.W.3d 125 (Ark. 2007), 51, 70 n.119, 292, 520
Thonert, *In re*, 733 N.E.2d 932 (Ind. 2000), 346 n.186
Thoreen, United States v., 653 F.2d 1332 (9th Cir. 1981), 358
Thurston v. Okemo Ltd. Liab. Co., 123 F. Supp. 3d 513 (D. Vt. 2015), 79 n.177, 97, 176 n.63
Tibbs v. United States, 628 A.2d 638 (D.C. 1993), 406
Time Warner Entm't Co. v. Does #1-2, 876 F. Supp. 407 (E.D.N.Y. 1994), 346 n.186
Tirado, United States v., 890 F.3d 36 (1st Cir. 2018), 375
Tocco, *In re*, 984 P.2d 539 (Ariz. 1999), 94, 322 n.47, 378, 466
Todd v. Coleman, 119 N.E.3d 1137 (Ind. Ct. App. 2019), 451
Toman, *In re*, 206 A.3d 345 (N.J. 2019), 105 n.94, 297 n.115
Tomasian v. C.D. Peacock, Inc., No. 09 C 5665, 2012 WL 2590493 (N.D. Ill. July 3, 2012), 80, 98
Torgerson, *In re*, Disciplinary Action Against, 870 N.W.2d 602 (Minn. 2015), 508 n.67
Tornow, *In re*, Discipline of, 835 N.W.2d 912 (S.D. 2013), 323 n.51, 478 n.198
Torrens v. Hood (*In re* Hood), 727 F.3d 1360 (11th Cir. 2013), 343 n.168
Trainor v. Ky. Bar Ass'n, 311 S.W.3d 719 (Ky. 2010), 66 n.96, 67 n.103
Tr. Corp. of Mont. v. Piper Aircraft Corp., 701 F.2d 85 (9th Cir. 1983), 31 n.168
Treadway v. Gateway Chevrolet Oldsmobile, Inc., 362 F.3d 971 (7th Cir. 2004), 276
Treinen, *In re*, 131 P.3d 1282 (N.M. 2006), 105 n.93, 297 n.114
Trial Pracs., Inc. v. Hahn, Loeser & Parks, LLP, 260 So. 3d 167 (Fla. 2018), 143 n.35, 150 n.81

Trull, State v., 136 P.3d 551 (Mont. 2006), 390
Trunzo v. Citi Mortg., No. 2:11-cv-01124, 2014 WL 1317577 (W.D. Pa. Mar. 31, 2014), 432
T & T Chem., Inc. v. Priest, 95 S.W.3d 750 (Ark. 2003), 18
Tuma, United States v., 738 F.3d 681 (5th Cir. 2013), 396
Turfgrass Grp., Inc. v. Ne. La. Turf Farms, LLC, Civ. A. No. 10-13544, 2013 WL 6145294 (W.D. La. Nov. 20, 2013), 83 n.196, 114 n.151, 127 n.235, 129, 132
Turner v. Commonwealth, 726 S.E.2d 325 (Va. 2012), 42 n.228
Tyler v. State, 47 P.3d 1095 (Alaska Ct. App. 2001), 348, 349, 350

Uchendu, *In re*, 812 A.2d 933 (D.C. 2002), 107
Ukwu, *In re*, 926 A.2d 1106 (D.C. 2007), 106, 297, 319 n.28, 454, 469, 478 n.194
Unauthorized Practice of Law Comm. v. Am. Home Assur. Co., 261 S.W.3d 24 (Tex. 2008), 5
Underhill, People v., 353 P.3d 936 (Colo. 2015), 95
Union Planters Bank, N.A. v. Kendrick, 142 S.W.3d 729 (Mo. 2004), 13 n.70
United States *ex rel. See name of relator party*
United States v. *See name of opposing party*
United States Fid. & Guar. Co. v. Pietrykowski, No. E99-38, 2000 WL 204475 (Ohio Ct. App. Feb. 11, 2000), 5
Univ. of Miami v. Great Am. Ins. Co., 112 So. 3d 504 (Fla. Dist. Ct. App. 2013), 14 n.77
Unnamed Att'y v. Ky Bar Ass'n, 186 S.W.3d 741 (Ky. 2006), 267 n.122
Upjohn Co. v. United States, 449 U.S. 383 (1981), 251, 252, 253
User Sys. Servs., Inc., *In re*, 22 S.W.3d 331 (Tex. 1999), 84
Usher, *In re*, 987 N.E.2d 1080 (Ind. 2013), 104 n.88, 317 n.16
U.S. Underwriters Ins. Co. v. Tauber, 604 F. Supp. 2d 521 (E.D.N.Y. 2009), 5
USX Corp. v. TIECO, Inc., 929 F. Supp. 1455 (N.D. Ala. 1996), 439
Utley v. City of Dover, 101 S.W.3d 191 (Ark. 2003), 426 n.53
Uttermohlen, *In re*, 768 N.E.2d 449 (Ind. 2002), 173

Va. Innovation Sciences, Inc. v. Samsung Elecs. Co., Ltd., 983 F. Supp. 2d 713 (E.D. Va. 2014), 321 n.42
Valley Health Sys., LLC v. Estate of Doe, 427 P.3d 1021 (Nev. 2018), 323 n.53
Van Dyck, State v., 827 A.2d 192 (N.H. 2003), 421, 424 n.42, 424 n.43, 426 n.51
Vega v. Bloomsburgh, 427 F. Supp. 593 (D. Mass. 1977), 221 n.328
Velasquez v. Katz, 840 N.Y.S.2d 410 (App. Div. 2007), 329, 473
Velazquez-Velez v. Molina-Rodriguez, 235 F. Supp. 3d 358 (D.P.R. 2017), 29
Venesevich v. Leonard, Civ. A. No. 1:07-CV-2118, 2008 WL 5340162 (M.D. Pa. Dec. 19, 2008), 330 n.97, 331, 334 n.122
Venie, *In re*, 395 P.3d 516 (N.M. 2017), 315, 324 n.53, 345
Venture v. Preferred Mut. Ins. Co., 118 N.Y.S.3d 583 (App. Div. 2020), 426
Villas at Highland Park Homeowners Ass'n v. Villas at Highland Park, LLC, 394 P.3d 1144 (Colo. 2017), 28 n.152, 31 n.171
Vincenti, *In re*, 704 A.2d 927 (N.J. 1998), 285 n.35

Vinson v. Vinson, 588 S.E.2d 392 (Va. Ct. App. 2003), 19 n.105
Virzi v. Grand Trunk Warehouse & Cold Storage Co., 571 F. Supp. 507 (E.D. Mich. 1983), 473 n.167
Visa USA, Inc. v. First Data Corp., 241 F. Supp. 2d 1100 (N.D. Cal. 2003), 21
Vlassis v. Samuelson, 143 F.R.D. 118 (E.D. Mich. 1992), 182
Vocatura, State v., 922 A.2d 110 (R.I. 2009), 434, 434 n.94, 439 n.134
Vohra, *In re*, 68 A.3d 766 (D.C. 2013), 319 n.26
Vossman v. AirNet Sys., Inc., 113 N.E.3d 987 (Ohio Ct. App. 2018), 51 n.11, 520 n.148

Waggoner, State v., 864 P.2d 162 (Idaho Ct. App. 1993), 397
Wagner, *In re*, 744 N.E.2d 418 (Ind. 2001), 71 n.121, 94, 293, 467
Wagner v. Lehman Bros. Kuhn Loeb Inc., 646 F. Supp. 643 (N.D. Ill. 1986), 141 n.22
Waldrop, *In re*, No. 15-14689-JDL, 2016 WL 6090849 (Bankr. W.D. Okla. Oct. 18, 2016), 420, 422 n.30
Walker v. Apple, Inc., 209 Cal. Rptr. 3d 319 (Ct. App. 2016), 199
Walker v. Newman Univ., Inc., No. 19-cv-2005-DDC-TJJ, 2019 WL 2268971 (D. Kan. May 28, 2019), 418, 427
Walker v. State, 818 A.2d 1078 (Md. 2003), 418, 419 n.11
Walker v. Sup. Ct. Comm. on Prof'l Conduct, 246 S.W.3d 418 (Ark. 2007), 106, 297, 469
Wallace, State *ex rel.*, v. Munton, 989 S.W.2d 641 (Mo. Ct. App. 1999), 441 n.142
Wal-Mart Stores, Inc. v. Goodman, 789 So. 2d 166 (Ala. 2000), 97
Wal-Mart Stores, Inc. v. Kortum, 559 N.W.2d 496 (Neb. 1997), 32 n.171
Walni v. Swepi LP, No. 13-102 Erie, 2017 WL 319801 (W.D. Pa. Jan. 23, 2017), 203 n.215
Walsh, *In re*, Disciplinary Action Against, 872 N.W.2d 741 (Minn. 2015), 466, 476
Ward, *In re*, 563 N.W.2d 70 (Minn. 1997), 317 n.16, 336, 371
Ward v. Maritz, 156 F.R.D. 592 (D.N.J. 1994), 131
Ward v. Nierlich, No. 99-14227-Civ., 2006 WL 5412626 (S.D. Fla. Sept. 20, 2006), 138, 141, 161 n.147, 162 n.153
Warehouse Mkt., Inc. v. Layman, 194 P.3d 786 (Okla. Civ. App. 2008), 329, 474
W.A.R. LLP, *In re*, No. 11-00044, 2012 WL 1576002 (Bankr. D. Colo. May 4, 2012), 337
Warner, *In re*, 335 S.E.2d 90 (S.C. 1985), 130 n.255
Waterloo Capital Partners, LLC v. BWX Ltd., No. 18-CV-6542 (RA), 2020 WL 1489813 (S.D.N.Y. Mar. 27, 2020), 431 n.73
Watkins, *In re*, 656 So. 2d 984 (La. 1995), 324 n.60
Watkins v. Trans Union, LLC, 869 F.3d 514 (7th Cir. 2017), 27, 28 n.153
Weatherbee, *In re*, Estate of, 93 A.3d 248 (Me. 2014), 51, 52 n.16, 59, 292 n.78
Webb, State v., 680 A.2d 147 (Conn. 1996), 318, 478
Weber v. Fujifilm Med. Sys., U.S.A., No. 3:10 CV 401(JBA), 2010 WL 2836720 (D. Conn. July 19, 2010), 80, 98

Webloyalty.com, Inc. v. Consumer Innovations, LLC, 388 F. Supp. 2d 435 (D. Del. 2005), 368 n.3
Weckesser v. Knight Enterprises S.E., LLC, 392 F. Supp. 3d 631 (D.S.C. 2019), 211–213
Weider Sports Equip. Co. v. Fitness First, Inc., 912 F. Supp. 502 (D. Utah 1996), 100, 102, 122, 180
Weigel v. Farmers Ins. Co., 158 S.W.3d 147 (Ark. 2004), 420, 431, 433, 439 n.134, 440 n.135
Weller v. Dollar Gen. Corp., No. 17-2292, 2019 WL 1045960 (E.D. Pa. Mar. 4, 2019), 210 n.253
Wells Fargo Wage & Hour Emp't Prac. Litig., 18 F. Supp. 3d 844 (S.D. Tex. 2014), 199
WellStar Health Sys., Inc. v. Kemp, 751 S.E.2d 445 (Ga. Ct. App. 2013), 196 n.172
Welsh v. Mounger, 912 So. 2d 823 (Miss. 2005), 507 n.60
Wesley v. Don Stein Buick, Inc., 987 F. Supp. 884 (D. Kan. 1997), 337
Westfall, *In re*, 808 S.W.2d 829 (Mo. 1991), 506 n.57
Westinghouse Elec. Corp. v. Kerr-McGee Corp., 580 F.2d 1311 (7th Cir. 1978), 3, 246
West v. Mando Am. Corp., No. 3:08-CV-570-WKW [WO], 2008 WL 4493422 (M.D. Ala. Oct. 2, 2008), 207 n.244
Wheatcraft v. Wheatcraft, 825 N.E.2d 23 (Ind. Ct. App. 2005), 489–490
White, *In re*, 18 Cal. Rptr. 3d 444 (Ct. App. 2004), 287 n.49, 330 n.97
White, *In re*, 707 S.E.2d 411 (S.C. 2011), 296 n.108
White Cap Constr. Supply, Inc. v. Tighton Fastener & Supply Corp., No. 8:08CV264, 2010 WL 3259355 (D. Neb. Aug. 16, 2010), 84, 168
White Eagle, United States v., 721 F.3d 1108 (9th Cir. 2013), 305
White Pearl Inversiones S.A. (Uruguay) v. Cemusa, Inc., 647 F.3d 684 (7th Cir. 2011), 7
Whitlark, *In re*, 811 S.E.3d 794 (S.C. 2018), 392 n.138
Wilcox, United States *ex rel.*, v. Johnson, 555 F.2d 115 (3d Cir. 1977), 379 n.72
Wilka, *In re*, Discipline of, 638 N.W.2d 245 (S.D. 2001), 318 n.21
Wilkins, *In re* (*Wilkins I*), 777 N.E.2d 714 (Ind. 2002), 510–516, 510 n.91, 518–519
Wilkins, *In re* (*Wilkins II*), 782 N.E.2d 985 (Ind. 2003), 516–517, 518–519
Wilkinson, *In re*, 668 S.E.2d 707 (Ga. 2008), 328 n.80
Willacy v. State, 967 So. 2d 131 (Fla. 2007), 422 n.28
Willes, *In re*, 22 DB Rptr. 82 (2008), 357 n.256
Williams, *In re*, 85 So. 3d 583 (La. 2012), 105 n.93
Williams, State v., 225 A.3d 751 (Me. 2020), 494 n.1
Williams, United States v., 504 U.S. 36 (1992), 356, 404 n.201
Williams, United States v., 698 F.3d 374 (7th Cir. 2012), 379 n.71
Williams, United States v., 720 F.3d 674 (8th Cir. 2013), 2
Williams v. BASF Catalysts LLC, 765 F.3d 306 (3d Cir. 2014), 484
Williams v. Borden Chem., Inc., 501 F. Supp. 2d 1219 (S.D. Iowa 2007), 421
Williams v. Chartwell Fin. Servs., Ltd., 204 F.3d 748 (7th Cir. 2000), 203 n.215, 205

Wilson, State v., 83 N.E.3d 942 (Ohio Ct. App. 2017), 525
Wilson, United States v., 979 F.3d 889 (11th Cir. 2020), 420 n.17
Winchell's Donut Houses, L.P. Sec. Litig., *In re*, 1988 WL 135503 (Del. Ch. Dec. 12, 1988), 209, 210 n.259
Winkler, *In re*, 834 N.E.2d 85 (Ind. 2005), 93, 465
Winthrop, *In re*, 848 N.E.2d 961 (Ill. 2006), 94, 294 n.95, 467 n.125
Wisconsin Chiropractic Ass'n v. State, 676 N.W.2d 580 (Wis. Ct. App. 2004), 54
Wolterbeek's Case, *In re*, 886 A.2d 990 (N.H. 2005), 323 n.53
Woodall v. United States, 842 A.2d 690 (D.C. 2004), 407
Woodard, State v., 9 So. 3d 112 (La. 2009), 398, 406, 407
Woodham, *In re*, 769 S.E.2d 353 (Ga. 2015), 77, 187
World Youth Day, Inc. v. Famous Artists Merchandising Exch., Inc., 866 F. Supp. 1297 (D. Colo. 1994), 423
Worley v. Moore, 807 S.E.2d 133 (N.C. 2017), 30, 32
W.R. Grace, United States v., 401 F. Supp. 2d 1065 (D. Mont. 2005), 80, 97, 177
Wright, People v., 35 P.3d 153 (Colo. 1999), 324
Wright v. Grp. Health Hosp., 691 P.2d 564 (Wash. 1984), 78, 96
Wright v. Pennamped, 664 N.E.2d 394 (Ind. Ct. App. 1996), 475 n.176
Wright v. Somers, 125 Ill. App. 256 (1906), 137 n.2
W. Sugar Coop. v. Archer-Daniels-Midland Co., 98 F. Supp. 3d 1074 (C.D. Cal. 2015), 21
W. Va. Comm. on Legal Ethics v. Farber, 408 S.E.2d 274 (W. Va. 1991), 507
Wylie v. Marley Co., 891 F.2d 1463 (10th Cir. 1989), 251 n.31
Wyndham Vacation Ownership, Inc. v. Vacation Transfers Unlimited, LLC, No. 3:18-cv-01399, 2020 WL 134132 (M.D. Tenn. Jan. 10, 2020), 418
Wynveen v. Corsaro, 106 N.E.3d 130 (Ohio Ct. App. 2017), 30 n.167
Wysolmerski, *In re*, 237 A.3d 706 (Vt. 2020), 105, 324 n.53, 326, 468 n.132

XYZ, D.O. v. Sykes, 20 N.E.3d 582 (Ind. Ct. App. 2014), 30 n.166

Yale Univ. v. Out of the Box, LLC, 990 A.2d 869 (Conn. App. Ct. 2010), 450 n.19
Yanez v. Plummer, 164 Cal. Rptr. 3d 309 (Ct. App. 2013), 270–277
Yao, *In re*, 680 N.Y.S.2d 546 (App. Div. 1998), 69 n.114
Yarborough, *In re*, 559 S.E.2d 836 (S.C. 2002), 295 n.100
Yelverton, *In re*, 105 A.3d 413 (D.C. 2014), 54, 70 n.116
Yoh v. Hoffman, 27 P.3d 927 (Kan. Ct. App. 2001), 473 n.167
Young, *In re*, 849 So. 2d 25 (La. 2003), 337
Youngblood v. Sanders, 575 S.E.2d 864 (W. Va. 2002), 42 n.228

Zachair, Ltd. v. Driggs, 965 F. Supp. 741 (D. Md. 1997), 80, 98, 177 n.67
Zador Corp. v. Kwan, 37 Cal. Rptr. 2d 754 (Ct. App. 1995), 277 n.180
Zamos v. Stroud, 87 P.3d 802 (Ct. App. 2003), 86 n.210
Zaug v. Va. State Bar, 737 S.E.2d 914 (Va. 2013), 179 n.76

Zbiegien, *In re*, 433 N.W.2d 871 (Minn. 1988), 336
Zeno, *In re*, 504 F.3d 64 (1st Cir. 2007), 495
Zerger & Mauer LLP v. City of Greenwood, 751 F.3d 928 (8th Cir. 2014), 31 n.171, 40
Ziegler, *In re*, 637 A.2d 829, 1994 WL 10809 (Del. Jan. 3, 1994), 129
Zimmerman, *In re*, 19 P.3d 160 (Kan. 2001), 521 n.151
Zimmerman v. Drexel Burnham Lambert Inc., 252 Cal. Rptr. 115 (Ct. App. 1988), 523
Zotaley, *In re*, 546 N.W.2d 16 (Minn. 1996), 323 n.50
Zuber, *In re*, 101 So. 3d 29 (La. 2012), 458 n.59
Zurich Ins. Co. v. Knotts, 52 S.W.3d 555 (Ky. 2001), 427, 433, 441 n.142
Zutler v. Drivershield Corp., 790 N.Y.S.2d 485 (App. Div. 2005), 428 n.56